Boeing Jetliner Databook

William Harms and René J. Francillon

MBI Publishing Company

First published in 2001 by MBI Publishing Company, Galtier Plaza, Suite 200, 380 Jackson Street, St. Paul, MN 55101-3885 USA

MBI Publishing Company books are also available at discounts in bulk quantity for industrial or sales-promotional use. For details write to Special Sales Manager at Motorbooks International Wholesalers & Distributors, Galtier Plaza, Suite 200, 380 Jackson Street, St. Paul, MN 55101-3885 USA.

Library of Congress Cataloging-in-Publication Data Available
ISBN 0-7603-0928-0

On the front cover:
United Airlines B777-222 (ER)
Registration: N782UA
Manufacturer's Serial Number: 26948
Line Number: 57,
Delivery Date: 3/07/97
Engine Type: PW4090

On the back cover:
Virgin Atlantic Airways B747-4Q8
Registration: G-VTOP
Manufacturer's Serial Number: 28194
Line Number: 1100
Delivery Date: 1/28/97
Engine Type: CF6-80C2B1F

Edited by Michael Haenggi
Designed by Katie Sonmor

Printed in the United States of America

CONTENTS

Introduction

The ***Boeing Jetliner Data Book*** ^provides a comprehensive insight into all of the turbine-powered aircraft produced by Boeing for commercial purposes. For completeness, it also includes references to military aircraft that are direct members of the various commercial model families. Because of its ongoing production status following the merger of the McDonnell Douglas Corporation into the Boeing company, the Boeing 717 (known as the MD-95 prior to that merger) is also included.

The book is divided into two sections; a text section, authored by René Francillon, that provides a description of each of the models included and a data section, compiled by Bill Harms, that provides the present status of each aircraft produced of each model. The text section describes, in detail, each aircraft model, its developmental history and the variations of each model.

The data section is primarily geared to the airplane spotter with a main interest in identifying the particular airplane at which he or she is looking. To facilitate this, the list entries within each general Model breakdown are placed in an order prescribed by the registration prefix that is determined by the nationality of the airline involved. Within that general breakdown, there are two features that set the order of the individual aircraft, the basic model gross weight and the registration itself. It will be noted, for instance, that the 737-500 precedes the 737-300 and 737-400— because of its lighter gross weight.

Because of the volume of the data presented, and the need to conserve space, it is necessary that numerous abbreviations be used within the various lists. As these might not be familiar to many of our readers, we have included several abbreviation and code lists. The General Abbreviation list covers many of the abbreviations used in the list headings and in the 'A/C Model' and 'Comments' columns. Separate abbreviation lists are included to identify the various specific Airline (3-letter ICAO), Airport (3-letter IATA) and Lessors (4-letter) that are used in the lists. These are explained further below.

It should be noted that, without exception, every aircraft, whether commercial, military, or privately owned, of each model designation is accounted for in the lists up through the date of publication of this book. There are no missing aircraft. However, certain aircraft appear more than once. This occurs when aircraft are leased from one airline to another. In those instances, the aircraft appears in the fleet listing of both airlines. These aircraft can be easily identified by the "L" in the status (S) column of the entry for the airline to which the airplane is leased.

To identify the players in a leasing arrangement, we use the following process:

If an airplane is leased OUT from one airline (lessor) to another (lessee) airline, that fact is noted in the 'Comments' column for the lessor airline and the 3-letter code of the lessee airline is used. (For example, and by utilizing the General and Airline abbreviation lists, "LST CCL" indicates that the aircraft is leased to Continental Cargo Airlines).

If an airplane is leased IN from a leasing company to an airline, the fact is noted in parenthesis in the 'Last Known Operator (Owner)' column for the lessee and the 4-letter code of the lessor is used. (For example, "LADECO AIRLINES (ILFC)" indicates that Ladeco Airlines is leasing the aircraft from International Lease Finance Corporation.)

In those instances where an abbreviation is not assigned to a leasing company, the full, but possibly truncated, name of the lessor will be used.

The Airport list provides the codes for those airports that are abbreviated in the Comments column in the lists. No attempt has been made to make this list any more comprehensive than is necessary to cover the abbreviations used in the data lists.

The data contained in these lists are compiled from numerous reliable publications as well as the inputs from many readers and several newsgroups. While every attempt has been made to ensure the accuracy and completeness of these data, the authors can accept no responsibility for any errors or omissions that may occur. It should be noted that the publication process itself consumes considerable time and that these data will be less than current by the time the book reaches the reader. The data contained in these pages are effective as of May 21, 2001. The authors would invite all readers to visit Bill Harms' web site at <<http://www.bird.ch/bharms>> for more current data.

Lessor Abbreviations

Code	Institution	Main Location
AARL	AAR Financial Services Corp.	Wood Dale, Illinois, USA
AERO	Aerolease Intl.	Miami, Florida, USA
AFGR	AFG Air Finance Inc.	Boston, Massachusetts, USA
AFIN	Aerospace Finance	Hialeah, Florida, USA
AGES	AGES Aircraft Sales & Leasing	Boca Raton, Florida, USA
AIFS	Airbus Industrie Financial Services	Dublin, Ireland
ALGI	Aviation Leasing Group Inc.	Kansas City, Missouri, USA
ANAU	Aeronautics Leasing Inc.	Golden, Colorado, USA
ARFI	Aerfi Group Plc.	Shannon, Ireland
ARON	Aeron Aviation Corp.	Great Neck, New York, USA
ATAS	Atasco Leasing Inc.	Seattle, Washington, USA
AVII	Aviation Investors Intl.	Montvale, New Jersey, USA
AVIS	Aviation Investor Services, Ltd.	London, England
AWAS	Ansett Worldwide Aviation Services	New South Wales, Australia
BALG	BA Leasing & Capital Corp.	San Francisco, California, USA
BATL	Bell Atlantic Tricon Leasing Inc.	Paramus, New Jersey, USA

Code	Institution	Main Location
BBAM	Babcock & Brown Aircraft Management Inc.	San Francisco, California, USA
BCCI	Boeing Capital Corp. Inc.	Seattle, Washington, USA
BIAL	Bavaria Intl. Aircraft Leasing GmbH	Munich, Germany
BNYT	Bank of New York Trust	New York, New York, USA
BOUL	Boullioun Aviation Services Inc.	Bellevue, Washington, USA
CCAA	China Civil Aeronautics Administration	Taipei, Taiwan
CISA	CIS Air Corp.	Syracuse, New York, USA
CITG	CIT Group - Capital Equipment Financing	New York, New York, USA
CITI	Citibank	New York, New York, USA
CMTC	Chase Manhattan Trust Co.	New York, New York, USA
CSAV	C-S Aviation Services Inc.	New York, New York, USA
DEBI	Debis Airfinance B.V.	Amsterdam, Netherlands
DLLG	Deutsche Lufthansa Leasing	Grunwald, Germany
ELEC	Electra Aviation (EAL)	London, England
EQUA	Equator Leasing Inc.	Glastonbury, Connecticut, USA
FACE	Fivestar Aircraft	Needham Heights, Massachusetts, USA
FINO	Finova Capital Corp.	Phoenix, Arizona, USA
FLIT	Flightlease AG	Zurich, Switzerland
FSBU	First Security Bank of Utah	Salt Lake City, Utah, USA
GATX	GATX Capital Corp.	San Francisco, California, USA
GECA	GE Capital Aviation Services Ltd.	Shannon, Ireland
GECC	GE Capital Corp.	Stamford, Connecticut, USA
GOAL	German Operating Aircraft Leasing	Grunwald, Germany
IALI	International Air Leases Inc.	Hialeah, Florida, USA
IASG	International Airline Support Group Inc.	Atlanta, Georgia, USA
ILFC	International Lease Finance Corp.	Los Angeles, California, USA
INGL	ING Lease Int. Equipment Management B.V.	Amsterdam, Netherlands
INGO	Indigo Aviation AB	Malmo, Sweden
INTL	Interlease Aviation Corp.	Northfield, Illinois, USA
IPID	Intrepid Aviation Partners LLC	Cordova, Tennessee, USA
ITOH	Itochu Airlease Inc.	Seattle, Washington, USA

Code	Institution	Main Location
JETZ	JETZ	Miami, Florida, USA
JFSS	Japan Fleet Service Pte.	Singapore
KAWA	Kawasaki Leasing Intl.	Tokyo, Japan
MSA1	Morgan Stanley Asset Management	New York, New York, USA
NORD	Nordstress (Australia) Pty. Ltd.	New South Wales, Australia
OASI	Oasis Intl. Leasing	Abu Dhabi, United Arab Emirates
OMEG	Omega Air Ltd.	Dublin, Ireland
ORIX	Orix Aviation Systems Ltd.	Dublin, Ireland
PACA	Pacific Aviation Holding Company	San Francisco, California, USA
PACE	Pinnacle Air Cargo Enterprises Inc.	Washington, D.C., USA
PART	Partnairs (NL) N.V.	Hoofddorp, Netherlands
PEGA	Pegasus Capital Corp.	San Francisco, California, USA
PEMB	Pembroke Capital Ltd.	Dublin, Ireland
PLMI	PLM Transportation Equipment Corp.	San Francisco, California, USA
POLA	Polaris Aircraft Leasing Corp.	San Francisco, California, USA
POTO	Potomac Capital Investment Corp.	Washington, D.C., USA
RRAM	Rolls-Royce Capital Ltd.	London, England
SALE	Singapore Aircraft Leasing Enterprise Pte.	Singapore
SNNL	Shannonair Leasing Ltd.	Shannon, Ireland
SSBT	State Street Bank & Trust	Boston, Massachusetts, USA
STAR	Aerostar Leasing Pte.	Singapore
SUNR	Sunrock Aircraft Corp. Ltd.	Dublin, Ireland
TBNY	The Bank of New York	New York, New York, USA
TOMB	Tombo Aviation Inc.	Long Beach, California, USA
TRIT	Triton Aviation Services Inc.	San Francisco, California, USA
UASI	United Aviation Services	Uniondale, New York, USA
USAL	US Airways Leasing & Sales Inc.	Arlington, Virginia, USA
USLI	USL Capital	San Francisco, California, USA
UTFC	United Technologies Finance Corp.	Hartford, Connecticut, USA
WFBN	Wells Fargo Bank Northwest	Salt Lake City, Utah, USA
WTCI	Wilmington Trust Corp. Inc.	Wilmington, Delaware, USA

Airport Codes

This list is a decoding of the various Airport Codes that appear in the Comments column of my Census Lists, mostly those airports at which you will find aircraft being stored or worked on for extensive periods of time. Also included are the various manufacturer's major fabrication sites. Some of the codes listed are unofficial and are used solely for simplification.

Alphabetized by Airport Location

Code	Airport Location
YXX	Abbotsford, British Columbia, Canada
ACY	Atlantic City, New Jersey, USA
AUH	Abu Dhabi, United Arab Emirates
AEX	Alexandria, Louisiana, USA
AFW	Alliance, Fort Worth, Texas, USA
AMA	Amarillo, Texas, USA
AMM	Amman, Jordan
ARD	Ardmore, Oklahoma, USA
BAQ	Barranquilla, Colombia
BED	Bedford (Hanscom), Massachusetts, USA
BOM	Bombay, India
SXF	Berlin, Germany
BQH	Biggin Hill, England
BFI	Boeing Field, Seattle, Washington, USA (Boeing manufacturing)
IAB	Boeing, Wichita, Kansas, USA (Boeing military manufacturing)
BOD	Bordeaux, France
BOH	Bournemouth, England
BQK	Brunswick (Glynco), Georgia, USA
BRU	Brussels, Belgium
EZE	Buenos Aires (Ezeiza), Argentina

Alphabetized by Code

Code	Airport Location
AEP	Buenos Aires (Newbery), Argentina
AEX	Alexandria, Louisiana, USA
AFW	Alliance, Fort Worth, Texas, USA
AMA	Amarillo, Texas, USA
AMM	Amman, Jordan
ARD	Ardmore, Oklahoma, USA
AUH·	Abu Dhabi, United Arab Emirates
BAQ	Barranquilla, Colombia
BED	Bedford (Hanscom), Massachusetts, USA
BFI	Boeing Field, Seattle, Washington, USA (Boeing manufacturing)
BOD	Bordeaux, France
BOH	Bournemouth, England
BQH	Biggin Hill, England
BQK	Brunswick (Glynco), Georgia, USA
BRU	Brussels, Belgium
CDG	Charles DeGaulle, Paris (Roissy), France
CGH	Congohas, Sao Paulo, Brazil
CGK	Jakarta, Indonesia

Alphabetized by Airport Location

Code	Airport Location
AEP	Buenos Aires (Newbery), Argentina
YYC	Calgary, Alberta, Canada
CDG	Charles DeGaulle, Paris (Roissy), France
CHR	Chateauroux, France
CSM	Clinton Sherman, Oklahoma, USA
CGH	Congohas, Sao Paulo, Brazil
DAB	Daytona Beach, Florida, USA
DEN	Denver, Colorado, USA
YUL	Dorval, Montreal, Quebec, Canada
DHN	Dothan, Alabama, USA
EMA	East Midlands, England
FZO	Filton, England
XFW	Finkenwerder, Hamburg, Germany (Airbus manufacturing)
FLL	Ft. Lauderdale, Florida, USA
OZR	Ft. Rucker (Cairns Field), Alabama, USA
LGW	Gatwick, London, England
GYR	Goodyear Aerospace, Tucson, Arizona
YYR	Goose Bay, Newfoundland, Canada
GSO	Greensboro, North Carolina, USA
GWO	Greenwood, Mississippi, USA
GYE	Guayaquil, Ecuador
HGR	Hagerstown, Maryland, USA
HAM	Hamburg, Germany
YHM	Hamilton, Ontario, Canada
HAJ	Hannover, Germany
LHR	Heathrow, London, England
HSV	Huntsville, Alabama, USA
CGK	Jakarta, Indonesia
JNB	Johannesburg, South Africa

Alphabetized by Code

Code	Airport Location
CHR	Chateauroux, France
CSM	Clinton Sherman, Oklahoma, USA
DAB	Daytona Beach, Florida, USA
DAL	Love Field, Dallas, Texas, USA
DHN	Dothan, Alabama, USA
EMA	East Midlands, England
EZE	Buenos Aires (Ezeiza), Argentina
FLL	Ft. Lauderdale, Florida, USA
FZO	Filton, England
GIG	Rio de Janeiro, Brazil
GRU	Sao Paulo, Brazil
GSO	Greensboro, North Carolina, USA
GWO	Greenwood, Mississippi, USA
GYE	Guayaquil, Ecuador
GYR	Goodyear Aerospace, Tucson, Arizona
HAJ	Hannover, Germany
HAM	Hamburg, Germany
HGR	Hagerstown, Maryland, USA
IAB	Boeing, Wichita, Kansas, USA (Boeing military manufacturing)
IGM	Kingman, Arizona, USA
IWA	Williams-Gateway, Arizona, USA
JNB	Johannesburg, South Africa
KHI	Karachi, Pakistan
KUL	Kuala Lumpur, Malaysia
KWI	Kuwait, Kuwait
LAS	Las Vegas, Nevada, USA
LBG	LeBourget, Paris, France

Alphabetized by Airport Location

Code	Airport Location
KHI	Karachi, Pakistan
IGM	Kingman, Arizona, USA
KUL	Kuala Lumpur, Malaysia
KWI	Kuwait, Kuwait
LOS	Lagos, Nigeria
LCQ	Lake City, Florida, USA
LAS	Las Vegas, Nevada, USA
LUX	Luxemborg
QLA	Lasham, England
LBG	LeBourget, Paris, France
XLM	Lemwerder, Germany (Airbus manufacturing)
LIS	Lisbon, Portugal
LGB	Long Beach, California, USA (Douglas manufacturing)
DAL	Love Field, Dallas, Texas, USA
LTN	Luton, England
MAO	Manaus, Brazil
MAN	Manchester, England
MNL	Manila, Philippines
MSE	Manston, England
MZJ	Marana, Arizona, USA
MRS	Marseille, France
MXE	Maxton, North Carolina, USA
MEX	Mexico City, Mexico
MIA	Miami, Florida, USA
MSP	Minneapolis–St. Paul, Minnesota, USA
MHV	Mojave, California, USA
MTY	Monterrey, Mexico
MUC	Munich, Germany

Alphabetized by Code

Code	Airport Location
LCQ	Lake City, Florida, USA
LGB	Long Beach, California, USA (Douglas manufacturing)
LGW	Gatwick, London, England
LHR	Heathrow, London, England
LIS	Lisbon, Portugal
LOS	Lagos, Nigeria
LTN	Luton, England
MAN	Manchester, England
MAO	Manaus, Brazil
MEX	Mexico City, Mexico
MHV	Mojave, California, USA
MIA	Miami, Florida, USA
MNL	Manila, Philippines
MQY	Smyrna, Tennessee, USA
MRS	Marseille, France
MSE	Manston, England
MTY	Monterrey, Mexico
MXE	Maxton, North Carolina, USA
MYR	Myrtle Beach, South Carolina, USA
MZJ	Marana, Arizona, USA
NCL	Newcastle, England
OPF	Opa-Locka, Florida, USA
ORY	Orly Field, Paris, France
OSC	Oscoda, Michigan, USA
OZR	Ft. Rucker (Cairns Field), Alabama, USA

Alphabetized by Airport Location

Code	Airport Location
MYR	Myrtle Beach, South Carolina, USA
NCL	Newcastle, England
OPF	Opa-Locka, Florida, USA
ORY	Orly Field, Paris, France
OSC	Oscoda, Michigan, USA
PMD	Palmdale, California, USA
PAE	Payne Field, Everett, Washington, USA (Boeing manufacturing)
PGF	Perpignan, France
POA	Porto Alegre, Brazil
PSM	Portsmouth, New Hampshire, USA
PIK	Prestwick, Scotland
UIO	Quito, Ecuador
RNO	Reno, Nevada, USA
RNT	Renton, Washington, USA (Boeing manufacturing)
GIG	Rio de Janeiro, Brazil
ROW	Roswell, New Mexico, USA
SAT	San Antonio, Texas, USA
SBD	San Bernardino, California, USA
SDQ	Santo Domingo, Dominican Republic
GRU	Sao Paulo, Brazil
SHJ	Sharjah, United Arab Emirates
MQY	Smyrna, Tennessee, USA
SEN	Southend, England
SNN	Shannon, Ireland
STN	Stansted, England
TNN	Tainan, Taiwan
TPE	Taipei, Taiwan

Alphabetized by Code

Code	Airport Location
PAE	Payne Field, Everett, Washington, USA (Boeing manufacturing)
PGF	Perpignan, France
PIK	Prestwick, Scotland
PMD	Palmdale, California, USA
POA	Porto Alegre, Brazil
PSM	Portsmouth, New Hampshire, USA
QLA	Lasham, England
RNO	Reno, Nevada, USA
RNT	Renton, Washington, USA (Boeing manufacturing)
ROW	Roswell, New Mexico, USA
SAT	San Antonio, Texas, USA
SBD	San Bernardino, California, USA
SDQ	Santo Domingo, Dominican Republic
SEN	Southend, England
SHJ	Sharjah, United Arab Emirates
STN	Stansted, England
SXF	Berlin, Germany
THR	Teheran, Iran
TLS	Toulouse, France (Airbus manufacturing)
TNN	Tainan, Taiwan
TOE	Tozeur, Tunisia
TPE	Taipei, Taiwan
TUS	Tucson, Arizona, USA
UIO	Quito, Ecuador
VCP	Viracopo, Sao Paulo, Brazil
VCV	Victorville, California, USA

Alphabetized by Airport Location

Code	Airport Location
THR	Teheran, Iran
TLV	Tel Aviv, Isreal
YYZ	Toronto, Ontario, Canada
TLS	Toulouse, France (Airbus manufacturing)
TOE	Tozeur, Tunisia
TUS	Tucson, Arizona, USA
YLW	Kelowna, British Columbia, Canada
YVR	Vancouver, British Columbia, Canada
VCV	Victorville, California, USA
VCP	Viracopo, Sao Paulo, Brazil
IWA	Williams-Gateway, Arizona, USA
YIP	Willow Run, Michigan, USA

Alphabetized by Code

Code	Airport Location
XFW	Finkenwerder, Hamburg, Germany (Airbus manufacturing)
XLM	Lemwerder, Germany (Airbus manufacturing)
YHM	Hamilton, Ontario, Canada
YIP	Willow Run, Michigan, USA
YUL	Dorval, Montreal, Quebec, Canada
YVR	Vancouver, British Columbia, Canada
YXX	Abbotsford, British Columbia, Canada
YYC	Calgary, Alberta, Canada
YYR	Goose Bay, Newfoundland, Canada
YYZ	Toronto, Ontario, Canada

Airline Three-Letter Codes

Code	Airline Name	Country Code	Name
AAA	ANSETT AUSTRALIA	VH	Australia
AAF	AIGLE AZUR	F	France
AAH	ALOHA AIRLINES	N	United States of America
AAL	AMERICAN AIRLINES	N	United States of America
AAR	ASIANA AIRLINES	HL	South Korea
ABB	AIR BELGIUM	OO	Belgium
ABD	AIR ATLANTA ICELAND	TF	Iceland
ABH	AEROLINEAS BALEARES	EC	Spain
ABR	AIR CONTRACTORS	EI	Ireland
ABX	ABX AIR	N	United States of America
ABX	AIRBORNE EXPRESS	N	United States of America
ACA	AIR CANADA	C	Canada
ACH	AIR CHARTER SERVICE (ACS)	EL	Liberia
ACI	AIR CALEDONIE INTL. (AIRCALIN)	F	France
ACQ	AERO CONTINENTE	OB	Peru
ADH	AIR ONE	I	Italy
ADK	ADC AIRLINES	5N	Nigeria
ADO	HOKKAIDO INTL. AIRLINES	JA	Japan
ADR	ADRIA AIRWAYS	S5	Slovenia
AEA	AIR EUROPA	EC	Spain
AEF	AERO LLOYD	D	Germany
AEL	AIR EUROPE	I	Italy
AES	ACES COLOMBIA	HK	Colombia
AEW	AEROSVIT AIRLINES (AEROSWEET AIRLINES)	UR	Ukraine
AEY	AEROLYON	F	France
AFB	AMERICAN FALCON	LV	Argentina
AFE	AIRFAST INDONESIA	PK	Indonesia
AFG	ARIANA AFGHAN AIRLINES	YA	Afghanistan

Code	Airline Name	Country Code	Name
AFJ	SA ALLIANCE	5X	Uganda
AFL	AEROFLOT RUSSIAN INTL. AIRLINES (RIA)	RA	Russia
AFR	AIR FRANCE	F	France
AFX	AIRFREIGHT EXPRESS	G	United Kingdom
AGN	AIR GABON	TR	Gabon
AGO	ANGOLA AIR CHARTER (AAC)	D2	Angola
AGX	AVIOGENEX	YU	Yugoslavia
AHK	AIR HONG KONG	B-H	Hong Kong
AHY	AZERBAIJAN AIRLINES (AZAL)	4K	Azerbaijan
AIC	AIR-INDIA	VT	India
AIH	AIRTOURS INTL.	G	United Kingdom
AIK	AFRICAN AIRLINES INTL.	5Y	Kenya
AIN	AFRICAN INTL. AIRWAYS (AIA)	3D	Swaziland
AIS	AERIS	F	France
AIZ	ARKIA ISRAELI AIRLINES	4X	Israel
AJI	AMERISTAR AIR CARGO	N	United States of America
AJK	ALLIED AIR CARGO	5N	Nigeria
AJM	AIR JAMAICA	6Y	Jamaica
AJO	AEROEXO (AEROEJECUTIVO)	XA	Mexico
AJT	AMERIJET INTL.	N	United States of America
ALK	SRILANKAN AIRLINES	4R	Sri Lanka
ALM	AIR ALM	PJ	Netherlands Antilles
ALX	HEWA BORA AIRWAYS	9Q	Congo Kinshasa
AMC	AIR MALTA	9H	Malta
AML	AIR MALAWI	7Q	Malawi
AMM	AIR 2000	G	United Kingdom
AMT	AMERICAN TRANS AIR	N	United States of America
AMU	AIR MACAU	B-M	Macao
AMV	AMC AVIATION	SU	Egypt
AMX	AEROMEXICO	XA	Mexico

Code	Airline Name	Code	Country Name
ANA	ALL NIPPON AIRWAYS	JA	Japan
ANG	AIR NIUGINI	P2	Papua New Guinea
ANI	AIR ATLANTIC CARGO	5N	Nigeria
ANK	AIR NIPPON	JA	Japan
ANL	AIR NACOIA	D2	Angola
ANX	ANEX AIRLINES	TC	Turkey
ANZ	AIR NEW ZEALAND	ZK	New Zealand
AOM	AOM FRENCH AIRLINES	F	France
APW	ARROW AIR	N	United States of America
ARG	AEROLINEAS ARGENTINAS	LV	Argentina
ARP	L'AEROPOSTALE	F	France
ARU	AIR ARUBA	P4	Aruba
ASA	ALASKA AIRLINES	N	United States of America
ASD	AIR SINAI	SU	Egypt
ASG	AFRICAN STAR AIRWAYS	ZS	South Africa
ATC	AIR TANZANIA	5H	Tanzania
ATN	AIR TRANSPORT INTL. (ATI)	N	United States of America
ATT	AER TURAS TEORANTA	EI	Ireland
AUA	AUSTRIAN AIRLINES	OE	Austria
AUH	ABU DHABI AMIRI FLIGHT	A6	United Arab Emirates
AUI	UKRAINE INTL. AIRLINES	UR	Ukraine
AUT	AUSTRAL	LV	Argentina
AVA	AVIANCA COLOMBIA	HK	Colombia
AVE	AVENSA	YV	Venezuela
AVN	AIR VANUATU	YJ	Vanuatu
AWC	TITAN AIRWAYS	G	United Kingdom
AWE	AMERICA WEST AIRLINES	N	United States of America
AWQ	AWAIR INTL. (AIR WAGON)	PK	Indonesia
AXF	ASIAN EXPRESS AIRLINES	VH	Australia
AXM	AIR ASIA	9M	Malaysia
AXO	AXON AIRLINES	SX	Greece

Code	Airline Name	Country Code	Name
AXX	AVIOIMPEX	Z3	Macedonia
AZA	ALITALIA	I	Italy
AZI	AZZURRAAIR	I	Italy
AZW	AIR ZIMBABWE	Z	Zimbabwe
AZZ	AZZA TRANSPORT	ST	Sudan
BAF	BELGIAN AIR FORCE	OO	Belgium
BAG	DEUTSCHE BA	D	Germany
BAH	BAHRAIN AMIRI FLIGHT	A9C	Bahrain
BAL	BRITANNIA AIRWAYS	G	United Kingdom
BAW	BRITISH AIRWAYS	G	United Kingdom
BBB	BALAIR/CTA LEISURE	HB	Switzerland
BBC	BIMAN BANGLADESH AIRLINES	S2	Bangladesh
BBD	BLUEBIRD CARGO	TF	Iceland
BCS	EUROPEAN AIR TRANSPORT - EAT	OO	Belgium
BER	AIR-BERLIN	D	Germany
BGA	AIRBUS TRANSPORT INTL.	F	France
BHS	BAHAMASAIR	C6	Bahamas
BIE	AIR MEDITERRANEE	F	France
BKP	BANGKOK AIRWAYS	HS	Thailand
BLV	BELLVIEW AIRLINES	5N	Nigeria
BLX	BRITANNIA AIRWAYS AB	SE	Sweden
BMA	BRITISH MIDLAND AIRLINES	G	United Kingdom
BOU	BOURAQ INDONESIA AIRLINES	PK	Indonesia
BPA	BLUE PANORAMA AIRLINES	I	Italy
BRA	BRAATHENS	LN	Norway
BSI	BETA CARGO	PP/PR/PT	Brazil
BSK	MIAMI AIR	N	United States of America
BUL	BLUE AIRLINES (BAL)	9Q	Congo Kinshasa
BWA	BWIA INTL.	9Y	Trinidad & Tobago
BWL	BRITISH WORLD AIRLINES	G	United Kingdom
BXI	BRUSSELS INTL. AIRLINES	OO	Belgium

Code	Airline Name	Country Code	Name
CAG	CNAC ZHEJIANG AIRLINES	B	People's Republic of China
CAL	CHINA AIRLINES	B	Taiwan
CAW	COMAIR	ZS	South Africa
CAY	CAYMAN AIRWAYS	VP-C	Cayman Islands
CBB	AIR CARIBBEAN	9Y	Trinidad & Tobago
CBE	AEROCARIBE	XA	Mexico
CBF	CHINA NORTHERN AIRLINES	B	People's Republic of China
CCA	AIR CHINA	B	People's Republic of China
CCI	CAPITOL CARGO INTL. AIRLINES	N	United States of America
CCL	CONTINENTAL CARGO AIRLINES	9G	Ghana
CCP	CHAMPION AIR	N	United States of America
CCU	SEVEN AIR	EC	Spain
CDG	SHANDONG AIRLINES	B	People's Republic of China
CDN	CANADIAN	C	Canada
CES	CHINA EASTERN AIRLINES	B	People's Republic of China
CFG	CONDOR	D	Germany
CFJ	FUJIAN AIRLINES	B	People's Republic of China
CGH	AIR GUIZHOU	B	People's Republic of China
CGW	AIR GREAT WALL	B	People's Republic of China
CHH	HAINAN AIRLINES	B	People's Republic of China
CHP	AVIACSA	XA	Mexico
CIB	CONDOR BERLIN, GMBH	D	Germany
CIC	ICC AIR CARGO CANADA	C	Canada
CJA	CAN JET	C	Canada
CKS	KITTY HAWK INTL.	N	United States of America
CLX	CARGOLUX	LX	Luxembourg
CMI	CONTINENTAL MICRONESIA	N	United States of America
CMM	CANADA 3000 AIRLINES	C	Canada
CMP	COPA PANAMA	HP	Panama
CNW	CHINA NORTHWEST AIRLINES	B	People's Republic of China
CNX	ALL CANADA EXPRESS	C	Canada

Code	Airline Name	Country Code	Name
COA	CONTINENTAL AIRLINES	N	United States of America
CPA	CATHAY PACIFIC	B-H	Hong Kong
CPI	CEBU PACIFIC AIR	RP	Philippines
CRL	CORSAIR	F	France
CRX	CROSSAIR	HB	Switzerland
CSA	CSA CZECH AIRLINES	OK	Czech Republic
CSC	SICHUAN AIRLINES	B	People's Republic of China
CSH	SHANGHAI AIRLINES	B	People's Republic of China
CSN	CHINA SOUTHERN AIRLINES	B	People's Republic of China
CSZ	SHENZHEN AIRLINES	B	People's Republic of China
CTB	CITY BIRD	OO	Belgium
CTN	CROATIA AIRLINES	9A	Croatia
CTT	CUSTOM AIR TRANSPORT	N	United States of America
CUA	CHINA UNITED AIRLINES	B	People's Republic of China
CUB	CUBANA DE AVIACION	CU	Cuba
CUS	CRONUS AIRLINES	SX	Greece
CWC	CHALLENGE AIR CARGO	N	United States of America
CWU	WUHAN AIR LINES	B	People's Republic of China
CXA	XIAMEN AIRLINES	B	People's Republic of China
CXH	CHINA XINHUA AIRLINES	B	People's Republic of China
CXJ	CHINA XINJIANG AIRLINES	B	People's Republic of China
CXN	CHINA SOUTHWEST AIRLINES	B	People's Republic of China
CXP	CASINO EXPRESS	N	United States of America
CYD	IOWAIR	N	United States of America
CYH	CHINA YUNNAN AIRLINES	B	People's Republic of China
CYN	ZHONGYUAN AIRLINES	B	People's Republic of China
CYP	CYPRUS AIRWAYS	5B	Cyprus
DAE	DHL AERO EXPRESO	HP	Panama
DAH	AIR ALGERIE	7T	Algeria
DAL	DELTA AIR LINES	N	United States of America
DAN	MAERSK AIR	OY	Denmark

Code	Airline Name	Country Code	Name
DBR	DUTCHBIRD	PH	Holland
DBY	BRITANNIA AIRWAYS, GMBH	D	Germany
DCS	DAIMLERCHRYSLER AVIATION	D	Germany
DEI	ECOAIR INTL.	7T	Algeria
DHL	DHL AIRWAYS	N	United States of America
DJA	ANTINEA AIRLINES	7T	Algeria
DJU	AIR DJIBOUTI RED SEA AIRLINES	J2	Djibouti
DLH	LUFTHANSA	D	Germany
DSB	AIR SENEGAL	6V	Senegal
DSR	DAS AIR CARGO	5X	Uganda
DTA	TAAG ANGOLA AIRLINES	D2	Angola
DUB	DUBAI AIR WING	A6	United Arab Emirates
EAE	AECA	HC	Ecuador
EAF	EUROPEAN AIRCHARTER (EAC/EAL)	G	United Kingdom
ECA	EUROCYPRIA AIRLINES	5B	Cyprus
EDW	EDELWEISS AIR	HB	Switzerland
EEA	ECUATORIANA	HC	Ecuador
EEZ	EUROFLY	I	Italy
EFA	EURO FIRST AIR	EC	Spain
EIA	EVERGREEN INTL. AIRLINES	N	United States of America
EIN	AER LINGUS	EI	Ireland
EJA	EXECUTIVE JET AVIATION	N	United States of America
EKA	EQUAFLIGHT SERVICE	TN	Congo Brazzaville
ELD	ELECTRA AVIATION	SX	Greece
ELL	ESTONIAN AIR	ES	Estonia
ELV	TANS	OB	Peru
ELY	EL AL ISRAEL AIRLINES	4X	Israel
ESN	EURO SUN	TC	Turkey
ETH	ETHIOPIAN AIRLINES	ET	Ethiopia
EUL	EURALAIR INTL.	F	France
EVA	EVA AIR	B	Taiwan

Code	Airline Name	Country Code	Name
EWG	EUROWINGS	D	Germany
EWW	EMERY WORLDWIDE AIRLINES	N	United States of America
EXD	CIELOS DEL PERU	OB	Peru
EXS	CHANNEL EXPRESS	G	United Kingdom
EZS	EASYJET SWITZERLAND	HB	Switzerland
EZY	EASYJET AIRLINE	G	United Kingdom
FAB	FIRST AIR	C	Canada
FAO	FALCON AIR EXPRESS	N	United States of America
FBF	FINE AIR	N	United States of America
FCN	FALCON AIR	SE	Sweden
FDX	FEDERAL EXPRESS (FEDEX)	N	United States of America
FEA	FAR EASTERN AIR TRANSPORT	B	Taiwan
FFR	FISCHER AIR	OK	Czech Republic
FFT	FRONTIER AIRLINES	N	United States of America
FIN	FINNAIR	OH	Finland
FJI	AIR PACIFIC	DQ	Fiji
FLB	FLY, S.A., LINEAS AEREAS	PP/PR/PT	Brazil
FOB	FORDAIR	G	United Kingdom
FOM	FREEDOM AIR INTL.	ZK	New Zealand
FPR	FUERZA AEREA DEL PERU	OB	Peru
FRD	FORD MOTOR COMPANY	N	United States of America
FRN	TULIP AIR CHARTER	PH	Holland
FTI	FLY FTI	D	Germany
FUA	FUTURA INTL. AIRWAYS	EC	Spain
FWI	AIR GUADELOUPE	F	France
FWL	FLORIDA WEST INTL. AIRWAYS	N	United States of America
GAP	AIR PHILIPPINES	RP	Philippines
GBL	GB AIRWAYS	G	United Kingdom
GCB	LINA CONGO	TN	Congo Brazzaville
GCE	AIR EUROPA CANARIAS	EC	Spain
GCO	GEMINI AIR CARGO	N	United States of America

Code	Airline Name	Country Code	Name
GDI	GRANDAIR	RP	Philippines
GEC	LUFTHANSA CARGO AIRLINES	D	Germany
GFA	GULF AIR COMPANY	A4O	Oman
GHA	GHANA AIRWAYS	9G	Ghana
GHN	AIR GHANA	9G	Ghana
GIA	GARUDA INDONESIA	PK	Indonesia
GIB	AIR GUINEE	3X	Guinea
GLN	GULF FALCON	3D	Swaziland
GLX	GALAXY AIRWAYS	SX	Greece
GMI	GERMANIA	D	Germany
GMT	MAGNICHARTERS	XA	Mexico
GOE	GO FLY	G	United Kingdom
GRL	GREENLANDAIR (GROENLANDSFLY)	OY	Denmark
GRO	ALLEGRO AIR	XA	Mexico
GTI	ATLAS AIR	N	United States of America
GUG	AVIATECA GUATEMALA	TG	Guatemala
GYA	GUYANA AIR 2000	8R	Guyana
HAL	HAWAIIAN AIR	N	United States of America
HCY	HELIOS AIRWAYS	5B	Cyprus
HDA	DRAGONAIR	B-H	Hong Kong
HEP	HELIOPOLIS AIRLINE	SU	Egypt
HHI	HAMBURG INTL.	D	Germany
HLA	HEAVYLIFT CARGO AIRLINES	G	United Kingdom
HLF	HAPAG-LLOYD	D	Germany
HLN	AIR HOLLAND	PH	Holland
HLQ	HARLEQUIN AIR	JA	Japan
HRH	ROYAL TONGAN AIRLINES	A3	Tonga
HUV	HUNAIR HUNGARIAN AIRLINES	HA	Hungary
HVN	VIETNAM AIRLINES	VN	Vietnam
HYC	HYDRO AIR CARGO	ZS	South Africa
IAC	INDIAN AIRLINES	VT	India

Code	Airline Name	Country Code	Name
IAW	IRAQI AIRWAYS	YI	Iraq
IBE	IBERIA	EC	Spain
ICB	ISLANDSFLUG	TF	Iceland
ICE	ICELANDAIR	TF	Iceland
ICL	CARGO AIR LINES (CAL)	4X	Israel
ICT	INTERCONTINENTAL COLOMBIA	HK	Colombia
ILN	INTER AIR	ZS	South Africa
IPU	IMPULSE AIRLINES	VH	Australia
IRA	IRAN AIR	EP	Iran
IRC	IRAN ASEMAN AIRLINES (IAA)	EP	Iran
IRM	MAHAN AIR	EP	Iran
IRZ	SAHA AIRLINES	EP	Iran
ISR	ISRAIR	4X	Israel
ISS	MERIDIANA	I	Italy
IST	ISTANBUL AIRLINES	TC	Turkey
IWD	IBERWORLD	EC	Spain
IYE	YEMENIA YEMEN AIRWAYS	7O	South Yemen
JAA	JAPAN ASIA AIRWAYS	JA	Japan
JAI	JET AIRWAYS	VT	India
JAL	JAPAN AIRLINES	JA	Japan
JAS	JAPAN AIR SYSTEM	JA	Japan
JAT	JAT YUGOSLAV AIRLINES	YU	Yugoslavia
JAZ	JAL WAYS	JA	Japan
JBU	JETBLUE AIRWAYS	N	United States of America
JEX	JAL EXPRESS	JA	Japan
JHM	JHM CARGO EXPRESO	TI	Costa Rica
JKK	SPANAIR	EC	Spain
JLH	JET LINK HOLLAND	PH	Holland
JMC	JMC AIR	G	United Kingdom
JON	JOHNSONS AIR	9G	Ghana
JTA	JAPAN TRANSOCEAN AIR	JA	Japan

Code	Airline Name	Country Code	Name
JUD	JPATS (U.S. DEPARTMENT OF JUSTICE)	N	United States of America
JUS	USA JET AIRLINES	N	United States of America
KAC	KUWAIT AIRWAYS	9K	Kuwait
KAL	KOREAN AIR	HL	South Korea
KFA	KELOWNA FLIGHTCRAFT	C	Canada
KHA	KITTY HAWK AIR CARGO	N	United States of America
KIW	ROYAL NEW ZEALAND AIR FORCE	ZK	New Zealand
KLM	KLM ROYAL DUTCH AIRLINES	PH	Holland
KMP	KAMPUCHEA AIRLINES	XU	Cambodia
KQA	KENYA AIRWAYS	5Y	Kenya
KRE	AEROSUCRE COLOMBIA	HK	Colombia
KYV	KTHY KIBRIS TURKISH AIRLINES	TC	Turkey
KZK	AIR KAZAKSTAN	UN	Kazakhstan
KZW	KHALIFA AIRWAYS	7T	Algeria
LAA	LIBYAN ARAB AIRLINES	5A	Libya
LAJ	BRITISH MEDITERRANEAN AIRWAYS	G	United Kingdom
LAM	LINHAS AEREAS DE MOCAMBIQUE (LAM)	C9	Mozambique
LAN	LAN CHILE	CC	Chile
LAU	LINEAS AEREAS SURAMERICANAS COLOMBIA	HK	Colombia
LAV	AEROPOSTAL LAV	YV	Venezuela
LAZ	BALKAN BULGANIAN AIRLINES	LZ	Bulgaria
LBH	L.B. LIMITED	C6	Bahamas
LBT	NOUVELAIR	TS	Tunisia
LCG	LIGNES AERIENNES CONGOLAISES (LAC)	9Q	Congo Kinshasa
LCO	LADECO AIRLINES	CC	Chile
LDA	LAUDA AIR	OE	Austria
LDA	LAUDA AIR SPA	I	Italy
LDE	LADE	LV	Argentina
LER	LASER	YV	Venezuela
LFA	ALFA AIRLINES	TC	Turkey
LGD	LEGEND AIRLINES	N	United States of America

23

Code	Airline Name	Country Code	Name
LGL	LUXAIR	LX	Luxembourg
LHN	EXPRESS ONE INTL.	N	United States of America
LIB	AIR LIBERTE	F	France
LIL	LITHUANIAN AIRLINES	LY	Lithuania
LLB	LLOYD AEREO BOLIVIANO (LAB) AIRLINES	CP	Bolivia
LLR	ALLIANCE AIR	VT	India
LNT	AEROLINEAS INTERNACIONALES	XA	Mexico
LOT	POLSKIE LINIE LOTNICZE (LOT)	SP	Poland
LPE	LAN PERU	OB	Peru
LPR	LAPA	LV	Argentina
LRC	LACSA COSTA RICA	TI	Costa Rica
LTE	LTE INTL. AIRWAYS	EC	Spain
LTU	LTU INTL. AIRWAYS	D	Germany
LWA	LIBERIA WORLD AIRLINES	EL	Liberia
LXO	LUXOR AIR	SU	Egypt
LXR	AIR LUXOR	CS	Portugal
MAA	MAS AIR CARGO	XA	Mexico
MAH	MALEV HUNGARIAN AIRLINES	HA	Hungary
MAK	MAT MACEDONIAN AIRLINES	Z3	Macedonia
MAL	MORNINGSTAR AIR EXPRESS	C	Canada
MAS	MALAYSIA AIRLINES	9M	Malaysia
MAU	AIR MAURITIUS	3B	Mauritius
MCS	MACEDONIAN AIRLINES	SX	Greece
MDA	MANDARIN AIRLINES	B	Taiwan
MDG	AIR MADAGASCAR	5R	Madagascar
MDI	MD AIRLINES	TF	Iceland
MDJ	JARO INTL.	YR	Romania
MDL	MANDALA AIRLINES	PK	Indonesia
MDW	MIDWAY AIRLINES	N	United States of America
MEA	MIDDLE EAST AIRLINES (MEA)	OD	Lebanon
MEP	MIDWEST EXPRESS	N	United States of America

Code	Airline Name	Country Code	Name
MGL	MIAT MONGOLIAN AIRLINES	JU	Mongolia
MHS	AIR MEMPHIS	SU	Egypt
MKA	MK AIRLINES	9G	Ghana
MKI	MK FLUGFELAGID	TF	Iceland
MNA	MERPATI	PK	Indonesia
MNB	MNG CARGO AIRLINES	TC	Turkey
MON	MONARCH AIRLINES	G	United Kingdom
MPD	AIR PLUS COMET	EC	Spain
MPH	MARTINAIR	PH	Holland
MPX	AEROMEXPRESS	XA	Mexico
MSK	MAERSK AIR U.K.	G	United Kingdom
MSR	EGYPT AIR	SU	Egypt
MWA	MIDWEST AIRLINES	SU	Egypt
MXA	MEXICANA	XA	Mexico
MXC	MEXICARGO	XA	Mexico
MZS	MAHFOOZ AVIATION	C5	Gambia
NAC	NORTHERN AIR CARGO	N	United States of America
NAE	NATIONS AIR	N	United States of America
NAO	NORTH AMERICAN AIRLINES	N	United States of America
NCA	NIPPON CARGO AIRLINES (NCA)	JA	Japan
NCH	CHANCHANGI AIRLINES (CAL)	5N	Nigeria
NDC	NORDIC AIRLINK	SE	Sweden
NES	NORDESTE	PP/PR/PT	Brazil
NGA	NIGERIA AIRWAYS	5N	Nigeria
NGE	ANGEL AIRLINES	HS	Thailand
NHK	FEDERAL AVIATION ADMINISTRATION (FAA)	N	United States of America
NIS	NICA	YN	Nicaragua
NKS	SPIRIT AIRLINES	N	United States of America
NMB	AIR NAMIBIA	V5	Namibia
NRG	ROSS AVIATION	N	United States of America
NRS	ARCO FLIGHT OPERATIONS	N	United States of America

Code	Airline Name	Country Code	Name
NSE	SATENA COLOMBIA	HK	Colombia
NTI	AERO CONTINENTE CHILE	CC	Chile
NTL	ANATOLIA	TC	Turkey
NTW	NATIONWIDE AIRLINES	ZS	South Africa
NVR	NOVAIR	SE	Sweden
NWA	NORTHWEST AIRLINES	N	United States of America
OAE	OMNI AIR INTL. (OAI)	N	United States of America
OAL	OLYMPIC AIRWAYS	SX	Greece
OCA	ASERCA AIRLINES	YV	Venezuela
OEG	ORIENT EAGLE AIRWAYS	UN	Kazakhstan
OHY	ONUR AIR	TC	Turkey
OLY	OLYMPIC AVIATION	SX	Greece
OMA	OMAN AIR	A4O	Oman
ORF	OMAN ROYAL FLIGHT	A4O	Oman
OSC	ORBITAL SCIENCES	N	United States of America
PAA	PAN AM	N	United States of America
PAC	POLAR AIR CARGO	N	United States of America
PAL	PHILIPPINE AIRLINES	RP	Philippines
PAO	POLYNESIAN AIRLINE OF SAMOA	5W	Samoa
PAQ	PACIFIC AIR EXPRESS	H4	Solomon Islands
PFC	PACIFIC INTL. AIRLINES	HP	Panama
PGT	PEGASUS AIRLINES	TC	Turkey
PHR	PHAROAH AIRLINES	SU	Egypt
PIA	PAKISTAN INTL. AIRLINES	AP	Pakistan
PIC	PACIFIC AIRLINES	VN	Vietnam
PLZ	PLANET AIRWAYS	N	United States of America
PNS	PENAS	PK	Indonesia
PNW	PALESTINEAN AIRLINES	SU-Y	Palestine
PRH	PRO AIR	N	United States of America
PTI	PRIVATAIR	HB	Switzerland
PUA	PLUNA	CX	Uruguay

Code	Airline Name	Country Code	Name
PVR	PAN AIR LINEAS AEREAS	EC	Spain
PZR	DISCOVERY AIRLINES	N	United States of America
QFA	QANTAS	VH	Australia
QNK	KABO AIR	5N	Nigeria
QSC	AFRICAN SAFARI AIRWAYS (ASA)	5Y	Kenya
QTR	QATAR AIRWAYS	A7	Qatar
RAM	ROYAL AIR MAROC	CN	Morocco
RBA	ROYAL BRUNEI AIRLINES	V8	Brunei
RDN	DINAR LINEAS AEREAS	LV	Argentina
REU	AIR AUSTRAL	F	France
RGA	REGIONAIR	9V	Singapore
RGN	CYGNUS AIR	EC	Spain
RJA	ROYAL JORDANIAN	JY	Jordan
RKA	AIR AFRIQUE	TU	Ivory Coast
RLT	RELIANT AIRLINES	N	United States of America
RME	ARMENIAN AIRLINES	EK	Armenia
RMV	ROMAVIA	YR	Romania
RNA	ROYAL NEPAL AIRLINES	9N	Nepal
ROK	NATIONAL AIRLINES	N	United States of America
RON	AIR NAURU	C2	Nauru
ROT	TAROM	YR	Romania
ROY	ROYAL AVIATION	C	Canada
RPB	AEROREPUBLICA COLOMBIA	HK	Colombia
RRR	ROYAL AIR FORCE	G	United Kingdom
RSL	RIO-SUL	PP/PR/PT	Brazil
RVV	REEVE ALEUTIAN AIRWAYS	N	United States of America
RYN	RYAN INTL. AIRLINES	N	United States of America
RYR	RYANAIR	EI	Ireland
RZO	SATA INTL	CS	Portugal
SAA	SOUTH AFRICAN AIRWAYS	ZS	South Africa
SAB	SABENA	OO	Belgium

Code	Airline Name
SAM	SAM COLOMBIA
SAN	SAN
SAS	SCANDINAVIAN AIRLINES SYSTEM (SAS)
SBE	SABRE AIRWAYS
SBZ	SCIBE-AIRLIFT CONGO
SCH	SCHREINER AIRWAYS
SCX	SUN COUNTRY AIRLINES
SCY	AIR SCANDIC
SER	AEROCALIFORNIA
SET	SAETA AIR ECUADOR
SEU	STAR AIRLINES
SEY	AIR SEYCHELLES
SFR	SAFAIR
SHJ	SHARJAH RULER'S FLIGHT
SHK	SHOROUK AIR
SHU	SAT AIRLINES (SAKHALINSKIE)
SIA	SINGAPORE AIRLINES
SIC	AIR SICILIA
SJF	SKYJET FRANCE
SKC	SKYMASTER AIRLINES
SKJ	SKYJET
SKY	SKYMARK AIRLINES
SLA	SIERRA NATIONAL AIRLINES
SLK	SILKAIR
SLM	SURINAM AIRWAYS
SLR	SOBELAIR
SMA	SMA AIRLINES
SNB	STERLING EUROPEAN AIRWAYS (SEA)
SNK	SOUTHEAST AIRLINES
SNP	SUN PACIFIC INTL.
SNZ	SANTA CRUZ IMPERIAL AIRLINES (SCI)

Country Code	Name
HK	Colombia
HC	Ecuador
SE	Sweden
G	United Kingdom
9Q	Congo Kinshasa
PH	Holland
N	United States of America
G	United Kingdom
XA	Mexico
HC	Ecuador
F	France
S7	Seychelles
ZS	South Africa
A6	United Arab Emirates
SU	Egypt
RA	Russia
9V	Singapore
I	Italy
F	France
PP/PR/PT	Brazil
V2	Antigua & Barbuda
JA	Japan
9L	Sierra Leone
9V	Singapore
PZ	Suriname
OO	Belgium
5N	Nigeria
OY	Denmark
N	United States of America
N	United States of America
EL	Liberia

Code	Airline Name	Country Code	Name
SOL	SOLOMONS	H4	Solomon Islands
SOO	SOUTHERN AIR	N	United States of America
SPA	SIERRA PACIFIC AIRLINES	N	United States of America
SPZ	AIRWORLD	ZS	South Africa
SRR	STAR AIR	OY	Denmark
SSV	SKYSERVICE	C	Canada
SUD	SUDAN AIRWAYS	ST	Sudan
SVA	SAUDI ARABIAN AIRLINES	HZ	Saudi Arabia
SVI	SETRA	XA	Mexico
SVK	AIR SLOVAKIA	OM	Slovak Republic
SVV	SERVIVENSA	YV	Venezuela
SWA	SOUTHWEST AIRLINES	N	United States of America
SWI	SUNWORLD INTL. AIRLINES	N	United States of America
SWR	SWISSAIR	HB	Switzerland
SWT	SWIFTAIR	EC	Spain
SXS	SUNEXPRESS	TC	Turkey
SYR	SYRIANAIR	YK	Syria
TAE	TAME	HC	Ecuador
TAI	TACA INTL. AIRLINES	YS	El Salvador
TAM	TAM BRASIL	PP/PR/PT	Brazil
TAP	TAP AIR PORTUGAL	CS	Portugal
TAR	TUNISAIR	TS	Tunisia
TAS	LOTUS AIR	SU	Egypt
TAW	SKYAIR CARGO	EL	Liberia
TAY	TNT AIRWAYS	OO	Belgium
TBA	TRANSBRASIL	PP/PR/PT	Brazil
TCG	THAI AIR CARGO	HS	Thailand
TCJ	TRANSPORTES CHARTER DO BRASIL (TCB)	PP/PR/PT	Brazil
TCO	ATC COLOMBIA	HK	Colombia
TCT	TRANSCONTINENTAL SUR	CX	Uruguay
TCV	TACV CABO VERDE AIRLINES	D4	Cape Verde Islands

Code	Airline Name
TDX	TRADEWINDS AIRLINES
TFS	FAST AIRWAYS
TFT	THAI FLYING SERVICE
TGA	AIR TOGO
TGZ	AIRZENA GEORGIAN AIRLINES
THA	THAI AIRWAYS INTL.
THT	AIR TAHITI NUI
THY	TURKISH AIRLINES
TIX	TRIAX AIRLINES
TLA	TRANSAER INTL. AIRLINES
TLX	CARGO LION
TMA	TMA OF LEBANON
TNA	TRANSASIA AIRWAYS
TNI	TRANSAIR INTL.
TOP	TOP AIR
TOW	TOWER AIR
TPA	TAMPA COLOMBIA
TPU	TACA PERU
TRA	TRANSAVIA AIRLINES
TRS	AIRTRAN AIRWAYS
TRT	TRANS ARABIAN AIR TRANSPORT (TAAT)
TRZ	TRANSMERIDIAN AIRLINES
TSC	AIR TRANSAT
TSE	TRANSMILE AIR SERVICES
TSG	TRANS AIR CONGO (TAC)
TSO	TRANSAERO AIRLINES
TSY	TRISTAR AIR
TTL	TOTAL LINHAS AEREAS
TUA	TURKMENISTAN AIRLINES
TUI	TUNINTER
TUS	ABSA CARGO

Country Code	Name
N	United States of America
5Y	Kenya
HS	Thailand
5V	Togo
4L	Georgia
HS	Thailand
F	France
TC	Turkey
5N	Nigeria
EI	Ireland
LX	Luxembourg
OD	Lebanon
B	Taiwan
PP/PR/PT	Brazil
TC	Turkey
N	United States of America
HK	Colombia
OB	Peru
PH	Holland
N	United States of America
ST	Sudan
N	United States of America
C	Canada
9M	Malaysia
TN	Congo Brazzaville
RA	Russia
SU	Egypt
PP/PR/PT	Brazil
EZ	Turkmenistan
TS	Tunisia
PP/PR/PT	Brazil

Code	Airline Name	Country Code	Name
TVS	TRAVEL SERVICE AIRLINES	OK	Czech Republic
TWA	TRANS WORLD AIRLINES (TWA)	N	United States of America
TWJ	TWINJET AIRCRAFT	G	United Kingdom
UAE	EMIRATES	A6	United Arab Emirates
UAL	UNITED AIRLINES	N	United States of America
UBA	MYANMAR AIRWAYS INTL.	XY	Burma
UIA	UNI AIR	B	Taiwan
UKA	KLM UK	G	United Kingdom
UPD	AIRFOYLE PASSENGER AIRLINES	G	United Kingdom
UPS	UNITED PARCEL SERVICE (UPS)	N	United States of America
USA	US AIRWAYS	N	United States of America
UYC	CAMEROON AIRLINES (CAM-AIR)	TJ	Cameroon
UZB	UZBEKISTAN AIRWAYS	UK	Uzbekistan
VAT	AVANT AIRLINES	CC	Chile
VBR	VIABRASIL	PP/PR/PT	Brazil
VEC	VENESCAR INTERNACIONAL	YV	Venezuela
VEI	VIRGIN EXPRESS IRELAND	EI	Ireland
VEX	VIRGIN EXPRESS	OO	Belgium
VGD	VANGUARD AIRLINES	N	United States of America
VIR	VIRGIN ATLANTIC AIRWAYS	G	United Kingdom
VIR	VIRGIN SUN	G	United Kingdom
VKG	PREMIAIR	OY	Denmark
VLE	VOLARE AIRLINES	I	Italy
VND	AVIANDINA	OB	Peru
VOZ	VIRGIN BLUE	VH	Australia
VRG	VARIG BRASIL	PP/PR/PT	Brazil
VSP	VASP	PP/PR/PT	Brazil
WEA	WHITE EAGLE AVIATION	SP	Poland
WGT	VW AIR SERVICES	D	Germany
WJA	WESTJET AIRLINES	C	Canada
WNT	WINNPORT AIR CARGO	C	Canada

Code	Airline Name
WOA	WORLD AIRWAYS
XME	AUSTRALIAN AIR EXPRESS
XNA	EXPRESS.NET AIRLINES
ZAN	ZANTOP INTL. AIRLINES

Code	Country Name
N	United States of America
VH	Australia
N	United States of America
N	United States of America

General Abbreviations

The following is a list of the abbreviations used in the census lists. (Please note that airport codes and lessor codes are contained in separate lists.)

Column Heading Abbreviations

Abbreviation	Explanation
S	Status
L	Leased
M	Military
N	Not yet delivered
O	Out of service
P	Preserved
S	Scrapped
U	Unallocated or unused
W	Written off through accident

Abbreviation	Explanation
Original MSN	Manufacturer's serial number
Line No.	Production line number
A/C Type	Aircraft type
Eng. Type	Engine type
Del. Date	Original delivery date
Reg. No.	Registration number
Fleet No.	Airline fleet number
Prev. Reg.	Previous registrations

General Abbreviations

Abbreviation	Explanation
A/C	Aircraft
AIMS	Airplane Information Management System
A/L	Airline
ALT	Approach and Landing Test
APU	auxilery power unit
ATC	Approved Type Certificate
ATCA	Advanced Tanker Cargo Aircraft
AWACS	Airborne Warning and Control Sytem
BBJ	Boeing Business Jet
BF	Bought from
BOAC	
BU	Broken up
CAD/CAM	computer-aided design/computer aided manufacturing
CATIA	computer-aided three-dimensional interactive application
CONV	Conversion
CVTD	Converted
CX	Cancelled
C/N	Construction number
C/S	Color scheme
DBER	Damaged beyond economical repair
DBF	Destroyed by fire
DD	Delivery date
DEL	Delivered (or delivery)
DMGD	Damaged
DOC	direct operating costs
EFIS	Electronic Flight Instrumentation System
ER	Extended range
EROPS	Extended Range Operations
ET	Extra (fuel) tankage
FAA	Federal Aviation Administration
FAR	Federal Aircraft Regulation
FF	First flight
FRF	First revenue flight
FRTR	Freighter
F/N	Fleet number
HK(x)	Hushkit (stage)
IAE	International Aircraft Engines
ICAO	International Civil Aviation Organization
IGW	Increased Gross Weight
I/S	In service
JAA	Joint Aviation Authorities
JATO	jet-assisted takeoff
JTLY	Jointly
LRF	Last revenue flight
LSF	Leased from
LST	Leased to
L/N	Production line number
MGTOW	maximum gross takeoff weight
MTOW	maximum takeoff weight
MOL	Manned Orbiting Laboratory
MSN	Manufacturer's serial number
MX	Maintenance
NATO	North Atlantic Treaty Organization
NEACP	National Emergency Airborne Command Post
NTU	Not taken up (not used)
OO	On order
OPB	Operated by
OPF	Operated for

General Abbreviations

Abbreviation	Explanation
OPW	Operated with
O/H	Overhaul
O/S	Out of service
PAX	Passengers
PF	Package Freight
QC	quick-change
REG	Registration
RT	Returned to
RTS	Returned to service
R/W	Runway
SCA	Shuttle Carrier Aircraft
SCD	Side cargo door
SF	Special Freighter
SFC	specific fuel consumption
SP	Special Performance
SR	Short Range

General Abbreviations

Abbreviation	Explanation
SST	supersonic transport
ST	Sold to
STD	Stored
SUD	Stretched upper deck (B747)
TBR	To be registered (or re-registered)
UDF	unducted-fan
UHB	ultra-high-bypass
WFU	Withdrawn from use
WL	Winglets
WX	Weather
WO	Written off
XFRD	Transferred
(A)	Advanced
(F)	Converted to freighter
(RE)	Re-engined
(WL)	Winglets

Chapter 1

The Development of Boeing Jetliners

Pan American initiated scheduled service with the Boeing 707 jetliner on October 26, 1958, just 55 years after the Wright Brothers' first controlled flight. Forty-three years later, Boeing jetliners continue to dominate the world's air transport industry as, with one notable exception—Airbus Industrie—all Boeing competitors outside of the former Soviet Union (where Ilyushin, Tupolev, and Yakovlev barely survive as manufacturers of jet transports) have been forced out of the large jetliner business. Over the past five decades, Boeing's tremendous commercial success has resulted from a variety of internal and external factors. At the beginning, however, it came about as the fortuitous result of two military contracts obtained during and immediately after World War II.

During that war, the main military transport aircraft were derivatives of airliners—primarily C-47 and C-54 variants of the Douglas DC-3 and DC-4. Two others—the Curtiss C-46 and Lockheed C-69—had also started as airliners prior to America's entry into the war but had gone into production for the U.S. Army Air Forces (USAAF). The design of four others—the Boeing XC-97, Convair XC-99, and Douglas XC-74 for the USAAF, and the Lockheed XR6O-1 for the U.S. Navy—was funded during the war by the U.S. government, but all had clearly been conceived by their manufacturers for the postwar civil market. As it turned out, the Convair, Douglas, and Lockheed designs proved too big for the

postwar market. Boeing's XC-97, the smallest of the four, did go into production as the Stratocruiser for airline customers.

Boeing's XC-97 made use of the wings, tail surfaces, powerplant installation, and much of the equipment of the B-29 Superfortress. Its all-new double-deck fuselage was optimized for passenger transport but was also fitted with clamshell doors and built-in ramps for loading and unloading military vehicles through the rear fuselage. Production models used the engines and tail surfaces of the B-50, a postwar development of the B-29. Including prototypes, Boeing built 77 military transport C-97s and 56 civil Stratocruisers. The big break for the company, however, was the development of KC-97 tankers, which brought total production of Boeing Models 367 and 377 to 884 aircraft.

In April 1946, Boeing received a letter contract from the War Department for two bomber prototypes. That contract resulted in the B-47 Stratojet. That revolutionary design was fitted with swept wings and was powered by six turbojets in two twin nacelles projecting below and ahead of the wings and two single nacelles attached directly beneath the wings. The innovative configuration of the B-47, the booming tanker business, and the later development by Pratt & Whitney of the J57 (civil designation JTC3) turbojet—all of which were funded by the U.S. government—enabled Boeing to become the first U.S. aircraft manufacturer to build jetliners.

As successful as its KC-97 tankers were, Boeing was well aware that these piston-engined aircraft lacked the performance to refuel jet bombers efficiently at the higher operating altitudes and speeds of the jets. Sooner or later, the U.S. Air Force (USAF; the name was changed when the Air Force was made a service separate from the Army in 1947) would need to procure turbine-powered tankers with performance compatible with those of Boeing B-47 and B-52 jet bombers. To that end, Boeing undertook a number of preliminary design studies for turboprop- and turbojet-powered aircraft capable of meeting both the anticipated USAF tanker requirement and those of the airlines for jetliners. By 1952, the critical criteria for air carriers was for new jetliners to achieve better performance and lower operating costs than those of the pioneering British jetliner, the de Havilland Comet, which had entered service in May 1952. These studies resulted in the Model 367-80, a design that combined features of the proposed Model 473 jetliner and turbine-engined Model 367 designs. Boeing's board of directors approved construction of the Model 367-80 demonstrator in April 1952 (10 days before the British Comet I flew the world's first revenue service by a jetliner).

Fitted with swept wings and powered by four Pratt & Whitney JT3 turbojets in individual nacelles mounted beneath the wings by means of forward-projecting pylons, the 367-80 military-tanker/civilian-jetliner demonstrator first flew on July 15, 1954. Less than one month later, the USAF ordered a first batch of 29 Boeing Model 717 tankers (USAF designation KC-135A) while Pan American ordered an initial batch of 20 Model 707-120 jetliners in October 1955. Boeing was on its way to become the world's foremost manufacturer of jetliners.

Numbers and More Numbers

In the early days of its marketing efforts, Boeing briefly attempted to have the name "Jet Stratoliner" adopted to identify its new jetliner as it would have carried forth the tradition of the "Strato" name of the 1940 Model 307 Stratoliner and that of the 1947 Model 377 Stratocruiser. Despite Boeing's efforts, the name never caught on, so the 707 and later Boeing jetliners have been, and continue to be, known by a bewildering string of numbers. The first three, beginning with 707 for the original Boeing jetliner, identify the basic model (with the latest model committed to production being the 777). Following a dash are what Boeing calls "customer modified series

numbers" (CMSN; two to four digits or digit/letter combinations) identifying series and customers.

Proposals tailored to specific airline requirements were initially given sequential model numbers starting with 707-121, as first given to JT3C-powered aircraft ordered by Pan American. Thus, the 707-122 designation at first identified the version proposed unsuccessfully to United Airlines with JT3C engines. The 707-222 and 707-322 designations then briefly identified aircraft proposed to Scandinavian Airlines System (SAS) respectively with JT3C and JT4A engines. In January 1955, however, Boeing adopted a policy that is still in force nearly five decades later whereby the second and third digits or letters of the dash number identify permanently aircraft proposed or built for a given airline. Thus, ever since, the last two "21" designation digits have identified aircraft for Pan American (such as the 707-121/-321/-321B/-321C, 727-21/-21QC/-221, 747-121/-221F, and 741SP-21), one of the many old Boeing customers no longer in existence. The "22" CMSN has been given to aircraft for United Airlines (such as the 720-022). Similarly, "23" designations have identified aircraft for American Airlines (such as the 767-223), while "24" designations specified aircraft for Continental Airlines (such as the 727-224).

The ink on the first six purchase contracts for 707s was not yet dry when, at the beginning of 1956, Boeing started preliminary design studies for a medium- to short-range jetliner to complement the 707. These studies, which encompassed variants with two, three, or four engines and with a broad range of seating arrangements, were still on the drawing board when Boeing was forced by the competition to come up rapidly with a medium-range aircraft. The resulting Model 720, a derivative of the 707, was first ordered by United Airlines in November 1957 and entered service in July 1960. Work on the all-new medium- to short-range aircraft culminated in the 727 first ordered by Eastern Airlines and

United in December 1960. This "trijet," which entered service in February 1964, soon proved to be a bestseller.

Next came a twin-engine, short-range jetliner, the Model 737. First flown in April 1967, that aircraft succeeded beyond all expectations in spite of intense competition from a number of manufacturers. Extensively revamped in the early 1990s as the Next-Generation 737, this single-aisle winner has become the world's best-selling jetliner (orders as of the end of August, 2001 totaling 4,965 aircraft, of which 4,051 had been delivered).

Supersonic Interlude

In 1952, after Boeing's board of directors had authorized construction of the 367-80 tanker/transport demonstrator, Boeing started contemplating the feasibility of developing a supersonic successor for the yet-to-fly 707. During the mid-1950s, Boeing also worked on the design of a supersonic bomber to meet the requirements of the Weapon System 110A program. After losing that competition to North American (which went on to build two prototypes of the XB-70 Valkyrie) in 1957, Boeing elevated its supersonic transport work to project status.

Although he cancelled plans to have the supersonic XB-70 put into production shortly after taking office in 1961, President Kennedy had a much more favorable attitude toward the development of a supersonic transport (SST). Advised that development of an SST would be beyond the financial capabilities of a single manufacturer, President Kennedy pushed the Federal Aviation Agency (FAA, yet to become the Federal Aviation Administration) to develop plans for a national program and lobbied Congress to finance that project. Following announcement in November 1962 that the British and French governments would fund construction of four prototypes and two structural test airframes of the Sud-Aviation/British Aircraft

Corporation Concorde, the U.S. government, Congress, and American manufacturers felt compelled to take on the European challenge. Boeing was one of the four airframe manufacturers invited to submit an SST proposal by January 1964. Later in that year, the number of competitors was reduced to two, with Boeing and Lockheed being funded by the U.S. government for Phase II of the SST design program.

In May 1963 Air France, BOAC, and Pan American became the first airlines to confirm their interest in supersonic travel by taking options on Concorde deliveries. Although this was merely a paper transaction because the nominal deposit ($100,000, the equivalent of $575,000 in today's dollars) was fully refundable if the airlines chose to cancel their options, the FAA felt compelled to initiate a similar option program for the SST. In August 1963, when the first phase of the U.S. SST program started, American, TWA, and Pan American took delivery options for 27 aircraft. By the time Boeing was announced as the winner of the SST competition on December 31, 1966, options for Concorde totalled 69 delivery positions from 16 airlines while the FAA had 114 options from 28 airlines. The future of the Anglo-French and U.S. SST programs briefly appeared promising.

As detailed in the Model 727 chapter, manufacturers take a look at a great number of configurations during the preliminary design study phase of any aircraft. As the American SST was to be larger, faster, and longer-ranged than the already amazing Concorde, Boeing had to consider the relative merits of a much greater number of configurations before settling on a favored layout. Thus, over the years, the Boeing SST design first evolved from one with variable-sweep wings to one retaining variable-geometry but featuring greatly enlarged horizontal tail surfaces so that at full aft sweep the wings and horizontal surfaces would form a single delta planform for supersonic cruise. For flight at subsonic speeds and on takeoff and landing, the wings were swung forward to achieve a sweep of only 20 degrees at the quarter chord. Later changes saw the addition of canard surfaces and, finally, a change to a fixed delta-wing configuration. Unlike what has been often written, this did not mean that the Boeing SST design was in trouble; it simply reflected traditional approach to preliminary design.

What spelled trouble for the Boeing-designed American SST was not its basic design but the mass of economic, environmental, and operational problems resulting from supersonic flights. Moreover, the U.S. government was running a fast-rising budget deficit as the result of the war in Southeast Asia and of new social programs. With U.S. airlines no longer believing in the future of supersonic travel, President Nixon announced the cancellation of the American SST program on September 23, 1969. Concorde remained a viable alternative until Pan American canceled its six options in February, 1973. The final nail in Concorde's coffin was the sharp rise in fuel prices that occurred in the fall of 1973.

More Girth

Coming after the loss of two equally large government contracts— that for the Manned Orbiting Laboratory (MOL), which went to Douglas in August 1965, and that for the C-5 transport aircraft, which went to Lockheed in October 1965—the cancellation of the SST could have been fatal for Boeing. Fortunately, its subsonic jetliner business was generating good revenues and profits. In addition to its lineup of narrow-body jetliners—the four-engined 707, trijet 727, and twinjet 737, of which it had delivered a combined total of 1,769 by the time of the SST cancellation—Boeing had five Model 747s in flight test and firm orders for 179 of these wide-body aircraft.

Boeing started working on the Model 747's preliminary design studies in 1965 to capitalize on experience gained during the CX-HLS (Experimental Cargo-Heavy Logistics Support) USAF competition, and to make use of the new generation of large-bypass-ratio turbofans developed during that competition. With Boeing and Lockheed then locked in a tough battle for the U.S. SST, it was felt that a large-capacity jetliner such as the proposed Model 747 would only have a short operational life as a passenger transport. Accordingly, Boeing made sure that the 747 would be well suited for use as a freighter. Following the demise of the U.S. SST program and the inability of the Concorde to achieve economic operations and operate on long-range routes without time-consuming intermediate fueling stops, the 747 became the flagship of most of the world's international airlines. As a result, the Model 747 became Boeing's most profitable program, with orders for the advanced version of the 747 still being obtained

35 years after Pan American ordered the first 25 of what became popularly known as "jumbo jets."

The next large-capacity jetliner launched by Boeing was the Model 767 twinjet. It first flew in September 1981 and entered service one year later. Regarded as a "mini wide-body" aircraft on account of its main deck having a width of 15.5 feet (4.72 meters) versus 20 feet (6.10 meters) for that of the 747, the first versions of the twin-aisle 767 were capable of carrying up to 66 more passengers than the largest 707 variants (255 versus 189). Moreover, first conceived primarily for operations on U.S. domestic routes, the 767 soon went on to dominate the transatlantic market. Stretched and given increased range, current 767 versions continue to sell satisfactorily.

With a cabin nearly as wide as that of the 747-400 (19 feet 3 inches [5.87 meters]), the 777 is the world's largest and heaviest twinjet transport. First flown in June 1994, it entered service 12 months later, and soon gained a strong reputation for its reliable ETOPS (Extended-range Twin-engine OPerationS) performance on overwater sectors taking it as much as 207 minutes away from a diversionary field while flying at single-engine speed. Its future, however, may be somewhat clouded by the likely appearance of an advanced Boeing design (the so-called Sonic Cruiser).

More Capacity or More Speed

After apparently bowing out of the competition with Airbus Industrie to develop a larger-capacity replacement for the 747-400, Boeing was at risk of losing its lead in the industry. Confidence in the world's largest jetliner manufacturer was restored when on March 29, 2001, it announced that it was working on a remarkably advanced jetliner. Currently shown in an artist's rendering as a twinjet aircraft with aft-mounted swept wings, canard surfaces, and twin vertical surfaces, this "sonic cruiser" would fly at Mach 0.95 (versus Mach 0.84 for the 777 and Mach 0.85 for the 747-400). Moreover, it has been conceived to operate on very long routes where its high cruising speed would result in substantial time savings. For example, on a flight from New York, New York, to Tokyo, Japan, this "sonic cruiser" would cut 1 hour and 50 minutes from the current schedule. It could even be developed to fly non-stop from London, England, or New York to Sydney, Australia, something no current jetliner can do.

The project is still at the preliminary design study phase and much remains to be done before the first customers will commit to this new aircraft. What is certain is that, with or without the "sonic cruiser," Boeing will continue to play a vital part in the further development of air transportation.

Boeing Jetliner Deliveries
1958–2001 (Annual/Cumulative)

Year	707	720	727	737	747	757	767	777	717	Total
1958	8/8									8/8
1959	77/85									77/85
1960	68/153	23/23								91/176
1961	11/164	69/92								80/256
1962	38/202	30/122								68/324
1963	28/230	6/128	6/6							40/364
1964	32/262	6/134	95/101							133/497
1965	52/314	9/143	111/212							172/669
1966	77/391	6/149	135/347							218/887
1967	113/504	5/154	154/501	4/4						276/1,163
1968	111/615		160/661	105/109						376/1,539
1969	59/674		114/775	114/223	4/4					291/1,830
1970	19/693		55/830	37/260	92/96					203/2,033
1971	10/703		33/863	29/289	69/165					141/2,174
1972	4/707		41/904	22/311	30/195					97/2,271
1973	11/718		92/996	23/334	30/225					156/2,427
1974	21/739		91/1,087	55/389	22/247					189/2,616
1975	7/746		91/1,178	51/440	21/268					170/2,786
1976	9/755		62/1,240	41/481	27/295					139/2,925
1977	8/763		67/1,307	25/506	20/315					120/3,045
1978	13/776		118/1,425	40/546	32/347					203/3,248
1979	6/782		136/1,561	77/623	67/414					286/3,534
1980	3/785		131/1,692	92/715	73/487					299/3,833

(continued, next page)

Boeing Jetliner Deliveries *(continued)*
1958–2001 (Annual/Cumulative)

Year	707	720	727	737	747	757	767	777	717	Total
1981	2/787		94/1,786	108/823	53/540					257/4,090
1982	8/795		26/1,812	95/918	25/565	2/2	20/20			176/4,266
1983	8/803		11/1,823	82/1,000	23/588	25/27	55/75			204/4,470
1984	8/811		8/1,831	67/1,067	16/604	18/45	29/104			146/4,616
1985	3/814			115/1,182	24/628	36/81	25/129			203/4,819
1986	4/818			142/1,324	35/663	35/116	27/156			243/5,062
1987	9/827			161/1,485	23/686	40/156	37/193			270/5,332
1988	0/827			164/1,649	24/710	48/204	53/246			289/5,621
1989	5/832			146/1,795	45/755	51/255	37/283			284/5,905
1990	4/836			174/1,969	70/825	77/332	60/343			385/6,290
1991	14/850			215/2,184	64/889	80/412	62/405			435/6,725
1992	5/855			218/2,402	61/950	99/511	63/468			446/7,171
1993	0/855			152/2,554	56/1,006	71/582	51/519			330/7,501
1994	1/856			121/2,675	40/1,046	69/651	41/560			272/7,773
1995				89/2,764	25/1,071	43/694	37/597	13/13		207/7,980
1996				76/2,840	26/1,097	42/736	43/640	32/45		219/8,199
1997				135/2,975	39/1,136	46/782	42/682	59/104		321/8,520
1998				281/3,256	53/1,189	54/836	47/729	74/178		509/9,029
1999				320/3,576	47/1,236	67/903	44/773	83/261	12/12	573/9,602
2000				281/3,857	25/1,261	45/948	44/817	55/316	32/44	482/10,084
2001				194/4,051	20/1,281	28/976	28/845	42/358	33/77	345/10,429
Total	856	154	1,831	4,051	1,281	976	845	358	77	10,429

Note: The numbers do not include the 367-80 demonstrator for the KC-135/707 program, the second 727, the first 747, the first 757, or the first 767, as these five aircraft were retained by Boeing. Deliveries for 2001 are through August.

Chapter 2

Model 707 and 720

Developed from the Model 367-80, the 707 was initially planned to be slightly heavier and larger than the demonstrator. It also dispensed with the main-deck cargo doors fitted on the left side of the 367-80, one forward and one aft of the wing. Maximum fuselage width, which had been set at 132 inches (3.35 meters) for the 367-80 to provide for the then-prevailing first-class arrangement was increased to 144 inches (3.66 meters) for five-abreast seating in the newly introduced tourist class. After the first 707s had been ordered, however, Boeing had to again increase fuselage width (to 148 inches [3.76 meters]) to accommodate economy-class passengers in six-abreast seating. That fuselage width was retained for all production 707s (and later for 720s, 727s, 737s, and 757s), but over the years, the aircraft grew in size and weight as airlines asked for more capacity and greater range. That growth is best demonstrated by the following comparison of dimensions and weights for the 367-80 demonstrator, the first production version, and the ultimate version of the 707 jetliner.

	367-80	**707-120**	**707-320B**
Span	130 ft (39.62 m)	130 ft 10 in (39.88 m)	145 ft 8.5 in (44.41 m)
Length	127 ft 10 in (38.96 m)	145 ft 1 in (44.22 m)	152 ft 11 in (46.61 m)
Wing area	2,400 sq ft (222.4 m^2)	2,433 sq ft (226 m^2)	2,942 sq ft (273.3 m^2)
Fuselage width	132 in (3.35 m)	144 in (3.66 m)	148 in (3.76 m)
MTOW	190,000 lb (86,182 kg)	246,000 lb (111,584 kg)	335,000 lb (151,953 kg)

707-120

On October 13, 1955, Pan American shook the air transport industry by announcing orders for 45 U.S.-built jetliners. Twenty-five were Douglas DC-8-30 intercontinental jetliners and 20 were shorter-ranged Boeing 707-120s that were to be available earlier. This Pan American contract for Boeing jetliners with 144-inch fuselage width was later amended to cover aircraft with 148-inch fuselage width. Moreover, Pan American subsequently elected in December 1955 to take only six aircraft as JT3C-powered 707-121s while the balance of its original 20-aircraft order was switched to JT4A-powered 707-321s. The first Pan American ordered 707-121 (serial number [s/n] 17586, N708PA) flew on December 20, 1957, and the airline took delivery of its first jetliner (s/n 17588, N709PA) on August 15, 1958. Certification was obtained on September 18, 1958, and scheduled passenger operations—the first by a Boeing jetliner—commenced on October 26, 1958.

In addition to JT3C-powered aircraft with the standard 138 ft 10-inch (42.32-meter) body, Boeing offered a short-body version, with 10 feet (3.05 meters) being removed aft of the wings to reduce fuselage length to 128 feet 10 inches (39.27 meters), tailored for longer flights. This short-body variant was powered by four JT3C-6 engines and fitted with center-section fuel tanks to increase fuel capacity from the basic 13,486 U.S. gallons (51,049 liters) to 17,286 gallons (65,433 liters). Qantas Airlines was the only carrier to order this longer-ranged version as it had to contend with what then were unusually long overwater sectors. These "feet wet" flights included the 2,080-nm (3,853-kilometer) still-air distance San Francisco–Honolulu leg, the 2,269-nm (4,203-kilometer) Honolulu–Pago Pago sector, and the 2,375-nm (4,399-kilometer) Pago Pago–Sydney hop, all of which were then without suitable diversionary jet airfields. The first 707-138 (line number [l/n] 29, s/n 17696, N31239 prior to certification but delivered as VH-EBA) flew on March

20, 1959, and deliveries to Qantas began three months later. The seven 707-138s built for the Australian carrier became the first 707s certificated to carry a spare engine in a pod mounted under the left wing inboard of the number 2 engine.

Known as 707-120s under the Boeing designation system, and briefly publicized as the "Jet Stratoliner," the first Boeing jetliners were designated 707-100s in the FAA Approved Type Certificate (ATC) 4A21 issued on September 18, 1958. Sixty 707-120s were built for six airline customers and the USAF (as VC-137As). They were powered by Pratt & Whitney JT3C-6s or JT3C-6s advanced with dry thrust of 11,200 pounds (49.8 kilonewtons). With water injection, maximum takeoff thrust for these two-engine models was boosted to 13,000 pounds (57.8 kilonewtons) and 13,500 pounds (60 kilonewtons), respectively. Thirty-nine of these aircraft, including the three USAF VIP aircraft and the seven "short-body" -138s, were subsequently re-engined with JT3D turbofans as 707-120Bs. None of the original JT3C-powered 707s remain in service.

707-120B

Boeing and its airline customers soon recognized the merit of incorporating the "glove" wing leading-edge extension and turbofan engines of the Model 720B to improve the performance of 707-120s. Not surprisingly, orders for the resulting 707-120B version rapidly mounted.

The first of these aircraft, a 707-123B for American Airlines, flew on June 22, 1960. The ATC 4A21 was amended on March 1, 1961, to cover the -120B in its "long-body" version and an additional amendment was approved some five months later to cover the "short-body" 707-138B version. Aircraft under these amendments included 75 new-built aircraft for three airlines as well as 39 Model 120s modified and re-engined. Power was provided by Pratt & Whitney JT3D-1 engines with 17,000 pounds (75.6 kilonewtons) of static thrust or JT3D-3 or -3B engines with 18,000 pounds (80.1 kilonewtons) of static thrust.

Deliveries of the original-sized 707 ended on April 22, 1969, when American Airlines accepted N7594A (l/n 801, s/n 19344), the last of its TWA-ordered 707-131Bs. Today, only four of the original 707-120/120Bs remain operational.

707-220

Aimed at airlines operating from high-elevation, high-temperature airports, the 707-220 was initially planned as a straightforward derivative of the JT3C-powered short-body version of the 707-120 with 144-inch fuselage diameter. It progressively evolved with fuselage width being increased to 148 inches, fuselage length increased to the 707-120 long-body standard, addition of 340-gallon (1,287-liter) wing-tip fuel tanks, installation of overseas equipment, and substitution of Pratt & Whitney JT4A-3 engines with 15,800 pounds (70.3 kilonewtons) of static thrust for the initially intended JT3C-6s. It ended up with standard long-body fuselage but without tip tanks or overseas equipment. Wings and high-lift devices were identical to those of the 707-120.

Braniff Airways was the only customer for this "hot-and-high" variant, and only five 707-227s were built. The first flew on May 11, 1959, and certification was obtained six months later in spite of the crash of the first aircraft during an acceptance flight on October 19, 1959. The remaining four -227s were operated by Braniff on its Latin American network until the first quarter of 1971. After services with other operators, the last of the ex-Braniff aircraft were stored in December 1983 and broken up in May 1984.

707-320

In the late 1950s, foreign airlines and U.S. international carriers demanded aircraft with non-stop transatlantic capability without a payload penalty. This range requirement called for operations not just between European capitals relatively close to the eastern shores of the Atlantic (such as London, Madrid, or Paris) and U.S. or Canadian cities near the western shores (such as Boston, Montreal, or New York) but also from major metropolises further inland (such as Chicago, Frankfurt, Rome, and Zurich). To meet this requirement, Boeing developed the 707-320, a more powerful and heavier 707 version powered by Pratt & Whitney JT4A turbojets.

The switch to Pratt & Whitney JT4A turbojets with dry takeoff thrust 17 to 35 percent greater than the wet thrust (i.e., using the cumbersome and noisy water-injection system) of JT3C variants went a long way to keep takeoff field length requirements within reason. Nevertheless, Boeing still needed to redesign the wings to increase area and provide space for additional fuel. This was accomplished by reducing trailing-edge sweep between the wing fillet and the inboard engines and extending the outboard panels to increase span from 130 feet 10 inches to 142 feet 5 inches (39.88 to 43.41 meters) and area from 2,433 to 2,892 square feet (226 to 268.7 m^2). The larger wings, however, retained the 35 degrees of sweep at the quarter chord and two-spar structure adopted for the original 367-80 wings. The larger wings also led to a reduction in cabin noise because the engines were moved further outboard.

To increase lift, the larger wings were fitted with split fillet flaps on the trailing edge between the fuselage and the inboard sections of double-slotted flaps and two additional sections of Krüger-type flaps on the leading edge. This revised configuration enabled approach speed to be reduced from 145 knots (269 km/h) for the 707-120 to 140 knots (260km/h) for the -320, in spite of the greater weight of the latter. Notwithstanding the use of more powerful engines and larger wings, however, the heavier 707-320 with MGTOW (maximum gross takeoff weight) between 18 and 28 percent greater than the 707-120 depending on configuration, still ended up having FAR (Federal Aviation

Regulation) runway-length requirements some 12 percent greater than a fully loaded 707-120.

The 707-320 retained the newly adopted 148-inch fuselage diameter, but cabin length, from the cockpit door to the rear pressure bulkhead, was increased 6 feet 8 inches (2.03 meters) to 111.5 feet (33.99 meters). Standard seating was increased from 96 to 104 first-class passengers with 40-inch (1.02-meter) seat pitch and from 165 to 180 economy-class passengers with 34-inch (0.86-meter) seat pitch. With special seats and inflatable escape hatches, the 707-320 was certificated to carry a maximum of 189 passengers in high-density configuration. Other structural changes included a strengthened undercarriage, stronger skin panels, and larger horizontal tail surfaces (with span increased from 39 feet 8 inches [12.09 meters] to 45 feet 8 inches [13.92 meters]).

Briefly marketed under the "Intercontinental" name, the 707-320 (707-300 for the FAA) was first ordered by Pan American in December 1955 when the original 707 customer amended its contract for 20 aircraft to cover six JT3C-powered 707-121s and 14 JT4A-powered 707-321s.

The first of the larger and heavier models flew on January 11, 1959, and Pan American placed the 707-321 in service on August 26, 1959. Although rapidly supplanted in production by its turbofan-powered derivatives (the 707-420, 707-320B, and 707-320C), the JT4A-powered intercontinental version of the 707 sold better than the original JT3C-powered variant. Altogether 69 were built for six customers. Initial deliveries were with "short" fin and manually operated rudder, but most -320-series aircraft were delivered with the larger surfaces and hydraulically boosted rudder. Aircraft delivered in the early configuration were retrofitted. According to their need, airlines specified different models of the JT4A turbojet with takeoff thrust of 15,800 pounds (70.3 kilonewtons) for the JT4A-3 and -5, 16,800 pounds (74.7 kilonewtons) for the -9, and 17,500 pounds (77.8 kilonewtons) for the -11 and -12 models.

707-320B

The greater thrust and reduced fuel consumption of JT3D turbofans were of greater value to heavy long-range jetliners than to shorter-ranged 707-120Bs and 720Bs. Hence, that led to the development of the 707-320B and -320C. The first JT3D-powered Boeing 707-320Bs were ordered by Pan American in February 1961, and this variant first flew on January 31, 1962. The FAA amended ATC 4A26 on May 31, 1962, to cover the Model 320B, and Pan American began 707-321B operations the following day.

In addition to being powered by JT3Ds turbofans instead of JT4A turbojets, Model 320Bs differed from Model 320s in a number of respects. Their wings had increased span and area as the result of the addition of extended outboard panels with curved wing tips, an extended leading-edge between the fuselage and inboard engines, and revised trailing-edge flaps. Late-production aircraft, referred to as Advanced 707-320Bs, added two segments of Krüger leading edge flaps, further modifications of the trailing-edge flaps, and revised fan cowlings with larger blow-in doors to increase airflow on takeoff. To power their 707-320Bs, customers had a choice of Pratt & Whitney JT3D turbofans with takeoff thrust ranging between 17,000 and 19,000 pounds (75.6 and 84.5 kilonewtons).

Four aircraft built for Northwest Orient Airlines with the 707-351B (SCD) model designation were the first 707s since the 367-80 to be fitted with side cargo doors (hence the SCD in their designation). Located forward of the wing on the port side of the fuselage for loading and unloading cargo on the main deck, the upward-hinging cargo doors measured 91 by 134 inches (2.31 by 3.40 meters). Although the 707-351B (SCD)s were ordered as convertible aircraft and could carry freight, passengers, or mixed passenger/cargo loads, they lacked the reinforced flooring of the more fully modified 707-320Cs. The first 707-351B (SCD) flew on May 15, 1963, nearly three months after the first 707-321C for Pan American.

Including the four hybrid -351B (SCD)s for Northwest, Boeing built a total of 171 Model 320Bs for 15 airlines. One of these aircraft, a 707-336B (l/n 853, s/n 20457, G-AXXZ), became the last passenger-only 707 to be delivered to an airline when it went to BOAC on April 17, 1971. In addition, Boeing built four aircraft for non-airline customers (two 707-353Bs as presidential VC-137Cs for the USAF, a -3F3B for the government of Argentina, and a -3L6B for the Malaysian government).

Most of the fast dwindling number of 707-320Bs remaining in service have received engine "hushkits" to meet FAR Part 36 Stage 2 and ICAO (International Civil Aviation Organization) Annex 16 Chapter 2 noise requirements. Fewer have been brought up to Stage 3/Chapter 3 level.

707-320C

Combining the basic airframe and powerplant installation of the 707-320B with the main-deck cargo door of the 707-351B (SCD) and a reinforced cargo floor with tie-downs, the 707-320C was built both as a convertible passenger/cargo aircraft and as a pure freighter. Pan American became the first customer in April 1962. The last 707 built for an airline was a passenger/convertible 707-3F9C (l/n 929, s/n 21428, 5N-ANO) that was delivered to Nigeria Airways on January 30, 1978, almost 20 years after the first Boeing jetliner had entered service.

The first passenger/cargo convertible 707-320C flew February 19, 1963, and was certificated under an amendment to ATC 4A26 on April 30, 1963. Following the launching of the wide-body 747, most airlines ordered convertible 707-320Cs in preference to all-passenger -320Bs. Production of the convertible and freighter variants thus greatly surpassed that of earlier passenger variants. In the end, Boeing built 304 Model 320Cs for 44 commercial customers. Boeing initially retained another 707-320C and a -385C as development aircraft. In addition, Boeing built 29 Model 320Cs for government and military customers.

The very last 707 was an E-3D Airborne Warning and Control System (AWACS) aircraft delivered to the Royal Air Force on May 28, 1992. Fitted with a pulse Doppler radar in a dorsal rotodome, that aircraft had what was essentially a 707-320C airframe.

Another 707-320C airframe was modified during construction to become the prototype for the proposed 707-700 variant. Powered by four 20,000-pound-class (89-kilonewton) CFM International CFM56 high-bypass-ratio turbofans, it first flew on November 27, 1979. No customers were found for CFM56-powered 707s because, without a costly fuselage stretch, wing redesign, and strengthened and lengthened undercarriage, that version was overpowered. Re-engined with JT3Ds, that aircraft (l/n 941, s/n 21956) became the last 707-320C to be delivered when it was handed over to the government of Morocco as a 707-3W6C in March 1982.

Most airlines ordered their -320Cs in convertible passenger/cargo configuration, but a number of customers ordered their aircraft in all-cargo configuration with provision for all passenger amenities (galleys, lavatories, main-cabin windows, and emergency oxygen equipment) deleted. This enabled operating weight empty of all-cargo configured aircraft to be 12,800 pounds (5,810 kilograms) less than that of a convertible aircraft fitted out for passenger operation and 19,600 pounds (8,890 kilograms) less than that of a convertible aircraft fitted out for cargo operation. Payload weight for all-cargo -320Cs was increased in the corresponding proportion.

Fewer than 200 707-320B/Cs were still in commercial operations as this book was completed in the spring of 2001. Like 707-320Bs, most remaining –320Bs have been fitted with "hushkitss" to meet FAR Part 36 Stage 2 or 3 and ICAO Annex 16 Chapter 2 or 3 noise requirements. A more ambitious proposal to re-engine 707-320Cs with refanned Pratt & Whitney JT8D-219 turbofans rated at 21,000 pounds (93.4 kilonewtons) of static thrust has not proceeded past the prototype stage (l/n 806, s/n 20124, an ex-Lufthansa 707-330C currently registered to Omega Air as N707HE).

707-420

The 707-420 was a derivative of the 707-320 developed to meet BOAC requirements, as the British flag carrier wanted to use UK-built engines to reduce foreign exchange expenditures. Moreover, fitted with a ducted fan ahead of its axial-flow compressor, the Rolls-Royce Conway "bypass" turbojet (a turbofan design) promised to have a lower specific fuel consumption (sfc) than the straight JT4A turbojet powering 707-320s.

Powered by Conway Mark 508 (R.Co.12) bypass engines rated at 17,500 pounds (77.8 kilonewtons) of static thrust, BOAC's first 707-426 flew on May 20, 1959, with a temporary U.S. registration. It was certificated in the United States on February 12, 1960, but service entry was delayed until May 1960 by the need to redesign tail surfaces to meet British certification requirements. With the enlarged surfaces, the 707-420 was granted its British certificate on April 27, 1960.

Thirty-seven 707-420s were built for six airlines. None remain in service.

Boeing 707 Principal Characteristics and Performance

	707-120	707-220	707-320	707-320B	707-320C Freighter	707-420
Span, ft in (m)	130' 10" (39.88)	130' 10" (39.88)	142' 5"(43.41)	145' 8.5" (44.41)	145' 8.5" (44.41)	142' 5" (43.41)
Length, ft in (m)	145' 1" (44.22)	145' 1" (44.22)	152' 11" (46.61)	152' 11" (46.61)	152' 11" (46.61)	152' 11" (46.61)
Height, ft in (m)	38' 8" (11.79)	42' (12.80)	41' 8" (12.70)	42' 5" (12.93)	42' 5" (12.93)	41' 8" (12.70)
Wing area, sq ft (m^2)	2,433 (226)	2,433 (226)	2,892 (268.7)	2,942 (273.3)	2,942 (273.3)	2,892 (268.7)
High-density seating	165/179	181	179/189	179/189	N/A	179/189
Two-class seating	137	142	141	141	N/A	141
Underfloor cargo, cu ft (m^3)	1,668 (47.3)	1,668 (47.3)	1,773 (50.2)	1,770 (50.2)	1,785 (50.6)	1,773 (50.2)
Maximum cargo load, lb (kg)	N/A	N/A	N/A	N/A	94,500 (42,864)	N/A
TO thrust per engine, lb st	13,000/13,500	15,800	15,800/17,500	18,000/19,000	17,000/19,000	17,500
(kN)	(57.8/60.0)	(70.3)	(70.3/77.8)	(80.1/84.5)	(75.6/84.5)	(77.8)
Fuel capacity, U.S. gal	13,486/17,406	17,406	21,262/23,815	23,855	23,855	23,815
(liters)	(51,049/65,887)	(65,887)	(80,484/90,148)	(90,299)	(90,299)	(90,148)
MTOW, lb	246,000/256,000	257,000	301,000/316,000	327,000/335,000	327,000/334,000	316,000
(kg)	(111,584/116,120)	(116,573)	(136,531/143,335)	(148,325/151,953)	(148,325/151,500)	(143,335)
Typical range, nm	3,310	3,400	5,180	5,385	2,800	5,270
(km)	(6,130)	(6,300)	(9,595)	(9,975)	(5,185)	(9,760)

Note: In this and subsequent tables, two values separated by a / indicate the range of values for engine thrust or weights based on customers' options.

Model 720

Barely three months after Pan American had placed its historical order for 707s and Douglas DC-8s, a third competitor entered the U.S. jetliner market. Whereas both Boeing and Douglas had elected to offer initially long-range (by the standard of the day) jetliners with seating capacity significantly greater than that of existing piston liners, Convair chose a more conservative approach. Going after the medium-range U.S. domestic market, the San Diego firm announced in January 1966 its Model 22 Skylark (later redesignated Convair 880). Of generally similar configuration to the Boeing and Douglas jets, the Convair Skylark was proposed with a narrower and shorter cabin with seating for 120 passengers (versus 165 for the 707-120 in a similar high-density configuration). Douglas responded with a DC-9 proposal for a smaller four-engined derivative of the DC-8 (and thus unrelated to the DC-9 twinjet that first flew in February 1965). Boeing also decided to compete.

To minimize development costs, Boeing retained much commonality between the 707-120 and the smaller aircraft aimed primarily at the U.S. domestic market. Thus, the initial configurations called for retaining the wings of the 707-120 but using fuselages shortened from the 138 feet 10 inches (42.32 meters) of the -120 to either 115.5 or 114.5 feet (35.20 or 34.90 meters). Cabin cross-section was to be 144 inches (3.66 meters), the same as then planned for the 707, and engines were to be pylon-mounted, as on the 707. Four-engined configurations with wings of reduced span and area and twin-engined configurations were also briefly considered, with one of the latter being revived eight years later to form the basis for the Model 737 twinjet.

Convair was first off the mark as, in June 1966, TWA and Delta announced orders for 30 and 10 Model 880s, respectively. Sixteen months later, TWA ordered four more 880s. As TWA was already a customer for the 707-120 and -320, its defection to Convair was bad news for Boeing and its proposed 707 derivative (still going by the 707-020 designation). Until November 1957, the news continued to be bad for Boeing as Convair continued to notch orders and add customers for its Model 880 and its faster, turbofan-powered Model 990.

Model 720

While Convair appeared to run away with the medium-range market, Boeing continued refining its proposal for a smaller derivative of its 707-120. With inputs from the airlines, and first redesignated Model 717 (a confusing situation as military C/KC-135 variants already used the 717 designation) but later becoming Model 720, the short- to medium-range, reduced-capacity derivative of the first Boeing jetliner jelled progressively. Finally, in November 1957, United Airlines ordered an initial batch of 11 720-022s. These JT3C-powered Model 720s were to have the then-standard 148-inch-diameter fuselage with internal cabin length reduced from 104 feet 10 inches (31.95 meters) of the 707-120 to 96.5 feet (29.41 meters). The shorter cabin of the 720 provided accommodation for 88 first-class passengers, a maximum of 141 economy-class passengers, or 115 passengers in a 30/70 mixed-class arrangement. The basic wing layout of the 707-120 was retained but the wing leading edge inboard of the inner engines was extended forward to form a "glove," thus increasing the wing chord and reducing the thickness-to-chord ratio. Cruise speed increased slightly, while fuel consumption was reduced.

Direct weight reductions resulting from the shorter fuselage and smaller number of seats, galleys, and lavatories also made possible the use of a lighter undercarriage and the deletion of one of the three turbocompressors for the cabin conditioning system. Thus, operating weight empty was reduced nearly 8 percent from 118,000 pounds (53,524 kilograms) for the 707-120 to 110,800 pounds (50,258 kilograms) for the 720. Power for the lighter Model 720 was provided by either four Pratt & Whitney JT3C-7 engines without water injection or four JT3C-12 engines with water injection, takeoff thrust rating being 12,000 pounds (53.4 kilonewtons) for the former and 13,000 pounds (58.2 kilonewtons) for the latter. Airfield performance was improved due to the lower power and wing loadings but also by the fitting of additional Krüger leading-edge flaps outboard of the engines.

The 720 prototype, s/n 17907, intended for United Airlines, first flew from Renton, Washington, on November 23, 1959. Being sufficiently different from both the 707-100 and 707-300 already FAA-certificated, the 720 was covered by the new ATC 4A28, issued on June 30, 1960. Service was initiated by United on July 5, 1960.

In the end, Boeing sold only 64 turbojet-powered 720s, one less than recorded by Convair for its commercially unsuccessful Model 880, to seven customers. Fortunately for Boeing, as the 720s were built on the same line as the 707s and shared much with that model, they proved financially more successful than the competing Convair model.

Model 720B

Having ordered 707-123s in November 1955 when it became the second customer for Boeing jetliners, American Airlines amended its order in July 1958, canceling orders for five JT3C-powered 707-123s but ordering 25 like-engined 720-023s. Even though it had ordered 720s, American Airlines remained interested in the slightly smaller and faster 990 that Convair was aggressively marketing with General Electric CJ-805-21 engines with a fan mounted behind the turbine. Fearing that American Airlines would reduce or cancel altogether its 720 order if Convair succeeded in promoting its 990 for luxury high-speed service to complement standard but slower 707-120 service, Boeing felt that it

needed to have a turbofan-powered airliner. To achieve this goal, the Seattle manufacturer turned to Pratt & Whitney, which in mid-February 1958 had initiated the self-financed definition phase for the JT3D turbofan engine. Derived from the JT3C turbojet chosen by Boeing to power 707-120s and 720s, the new engine was to be fitted with a two-stage fan and a single-stage stator mounted ahead of the axial-flow compressor.

American Airlines ordered 25 Convair 990s in October 1958. It also forcefully maneuvered Boeing into accelerating its development of turbofan-powered versions of its 707 and 720 and offering these derivatives at "bargain basement" prices. After haggling with Boeing for nearly a year, American finally renegotiated its contracts to have its 707-123s and 720-023s either re-engined with JT3Ds or delivered with these turbofans. Availability of JT3D-powered Boeing jetliners effectively ended Convair's hopes to remain an effective participant in the transport-aircraft business.

The first JT3D-powered 720-023B flew on October 6, 1960, three and one-half months after the first JT3D-powered 707-123B. The ATC for the 720, ATC 4A28, was amended on March 3, 1961, to cover the 720B. American Airlines placed both its 707-123B and 720-023B in service nine days later to start the era of U.S. turbofan-powered airliners.

Boeing went on to build 89 JT3D-powered 720Bs for 10 airlines, comfortably outselling Convair, which produced only 37 of its turbofan-powered Model 990s. Moreover, 10 720-023s were re-engined with JT3D turbofans. While expensive, the development of the 720B to meet American Airlines' demands decisively firmed up Boeing's position as the world's foremost manufacturer of first-generation jetliners.

The last aircraft in the Model 720/720B series—l/n 624, s/n 19523—was delivered to Western Airlines on September 20, 1967. Today, no 720s or 720Bs remain in airline service.

Boeing 720 Principal Characteristics and Performance

	720	720B
Span, ft in (m)	10 (39.88)	10 (39.88)
Length, ft in (m)	9 (41.68)	9 (41.68)
Height, ft in (m)	6.5 (12.66)	6.5 (12.66)
Wing area, sq ft (m^2)	2,510 (233.2)	2,510 (233.2)
High-density seating	141	156
Two-class seating	131	137
Underfloor cargo, cu ft (m^3)	1,380 (39.1)	1,380 (39.1)
TO thrust per engine, lb st (kN)	12,000/13,000 (53.4/58.2)	17,000 (75.6)
Fuel capacity, U.S. gal (liters)	11,850/13,560 (44,856/51,329)	14,830/16,055 (56,136/60,774)
MTOW, lb (kg)	213,000/229,000 (96,615/103,873)	222,000/234,000 (100,698/106,141)
Typical cruise speed, Mach	0.82	0.84
Typical range, nm (km)	2,465 (4,565)	3,300 (7,240)

Boeing 707 and 720 Commercial Jet Aircraft Census

The aircraft in the following tables are listed in order of the following:

1) ICAO country prefixes; 2) operator; 3) aircraft type; and 4) registration.

The total built was 1,010 (154 B720, 138 B707-100, 5 B707-200, 578 B707-300, 37 B707-400, 5 VC-137B/C, 68 E-3A/C, 17 E-6A, and 8 KE-3A) from 1958 to 1992.

Note: Two E-3A aircraft, MSN 20518 (L/N 856) and 20519 (L/N 858), were rebuilt as L/N 898 and 920, respectively.

A/C TYPE	CURRENT REG. NO.	LAST KNOWN OPERATOR (OWNER)	STATUS	ORIGINAL MSN	LINE NO.	DEL. DATE	ENG. TYPE	FLEET NO.	PREV. REG. [COMMENTS]
AP-PAKISTAN									
B707-340C	AP-AXG	PAKISTAN INTL. AIRLINES		20488	849	12/23/70	JT3D-3B (HK2)		AP-AWA, G-AZRO [STD KHI; FOR SALE]
B707-323C	AP-BBK	PAKISTAN INTL. AIRLINES		19576	719	06/17/68	JT3D-3B		N8413 [STD KHI; FOR SALE]
A6-UNITED ARAB EMIRATES									
B707-3J6C	A6-ZYD	FLYING DOLPHIN AIRLINES		20718	872	11/12/73	JT3D-7		B-2410, B-513L
C-CANADA									
B720-023B	C-FETB	PRATT & WHITNEY CANADA		18024	177	02/03/61	JT3D-1		N7538A, OD-AFQ [ENGINE TESTBED. "PRATT 7"]
B720-023 (B)	N720PW	PRATT & WHITNEY CANADA		18021	173	09/14/60	JT3D-1/PW6000		N7535A, OD-AGB, C-FWXI [RTS AS PW6000 ENGINE TESTBED; BASED PLATTSBURG AFB, NY]
CC-CHILE									
B707-321B	CC-PBZ	(PRIVATE)		19374	658	12/19/67	JT3D-3B (HK2)		N453PA, CC-CEK, CC-CYO, FAC904, FAC901 [IN MX SEN]
B707-369C	CC-	PACIFIC AIRLINES		20547	861	02/25/72	JT3D-3B (HK2)		9K-ACN, 70-ACS, EL-ALG, EL-ACP
C5-GAMBIA									
B707-323B	C5-AMM	MAHFOOZ AVIATION		20176	817	07/31/69	JT3D-3B (HK2)		N8437, HR-AMQ, N712PC [OPF DALA AIR SERVICES]
B707-323B	C5-BIN	MAHFOOZ AVIATION		20172	804	04/30/69	JT3D-3B (HK2)		N8433, N161GL, N711PC, HR-AMP
B707-347C	C5-MBM	MAHFOOZ AVIATION		19966	743	09/10/68	JT3D-3B (HK2)		N1504W, OD-AGU [WHITE, NO TITLES]
D2-ANGOLA									
B707-321B	D2-MAN	ANGOLA GOVERNMENT		20025	780	01/24/69	JT3D-3B (HK2)		N886PA, N728Q, N707KS
B707-3J6B	D2-TPR	ANGOLA GOVERNMENT		20715	870	09/17/73	JT3D-7 (HK2)		B-2404
B707-321C	D2-FAV	AIR NACOIA		18717	366	04/03/64	JT3D-3B (HK2)		N793PA, G-BGIS, G-TRAD, HK-3232X
B707-382B	D2-TOP	TAAG ANGOLA AIRLINES		20136	803	04/28/69	JT3D-3B		CS-TBE [STD LAD; NOT AIRWORTHY]
EL-LIBERIA									
B707-323C	EL-ALI	SKYAIR CARGO		18689	354	11/19/63	JT3D-3B (HK2)		N7555A, G-WIND, J6-SLF, N6097C, N902RQ, EL-JNS

A/C TYPE	CURRENT REG. NO.	LAST KNOWN OPERATOR (OWNER)	STATUS	ORIGINAL MSN	LINE NO.	DEL. DATE	ENG. TYPE	FLEET NO.	PREV. REG. [COMMENTS]
EP-IRAN									
B707-321C	EP-IRK	IRAN AIR		19267	541	12/15/66	JT3D-3B		N445PA
B707-386C	EP-IRL	IRAN AIR		20287	832	12/31/69	JT3D-3B		
B707-386C	EP-IRM	IRAN AIR		20288	839	03/17/70	JT3D-3B		
B707-386C	EP-IRN	IRAN AIR		20741	866	05/01/73	JT3D-3B		N1785B
B707-3J9C	EP-SHF	SAHA AIRLINES		21123	908	02/27/76	JT3D-7		5-8307, EP-NHA
B707-3J9C	EP-SHG	SAHA AIRLINES		21125	912	06/18/76	JT3D-3B		5-249, 5-8309
B707-3J9C	EP-SHJ	SAHA AIRLINES		21127	915	09/27/76	JT3D-3B		5-8311
B707-3J9C	EP-SHK	SAHA AIRLINES		21128	917	11/19/76	JT3D-3B		5-8312, EP-SHE
B707-3J9C	EP-SHP	SAHA AIRLINES		20835	895	12/16/74	JT3D-3B		5-246, EP-NHL, 5-8306
G-UNITED KINGDOM									
B707-321C	9G-ADM	GM AIRLINES		19369	648	11/27/67	JT3D-3B (HK2)		N459PA, HL7431, TF-IUB, 9G-ACZ, 5Y-AXG, 9G-ADL [LST/OPB CCL]
HC-ECUADOR									
B707-321C	HC-BGP	AECA		19273	580	05/31/67	JT3D-3B (HK2)		N451PA, N451RN
B707-330C	HC-BTB	AECA (AIR TAXI INTL.)		18937	451	11/10/65	JT3D-3B (HK2)		D-ABUA, VR-HTC, VH-HTC, LZ-PVA
HS-THAILAND									
B707-321C	HS-TFS	THAI FLYING SERVICE		19372	655	12/12/67	JT3D-3B (HK2)		N462PA, HL7427, TF-IUE, 5N-AWO, 9G-ESI, 9G-EBK, 9G-SGF [STD SEN]
HZ-SAUDI ARABIA									
B707-138 (B)	HZ-123	ROYAL EMBASSY OF SAUDI ARABIA		17696	29	07/16/59	JT3D-1 (Q)		N31239, VH-EBA, CF-PWV, N138TA, N220AM, N138MJ [STD SEN]
B720-047B	HZ-KA4	(PRIVATE)-SAUDI ARABIA		18453	314	08/28/62	JT3D-3B (Q)		N93147
B707-368C	HZ-HM2	SAUDI ARABIAN VIP AIRCRAFT		21081	903	09/25/75	JT3D-3B (HK2)		HZ-HM1
B707-368C	HZ-HM3	SAUDI ARABIAN VIP AIRCRAFT		21368	925	06/27/77	JT3D-3B (HK2)		HZ-ACK
JY-JORDAN									
B707-321B	JY-GAA	JORDAN AVIATION (JARO INTL.)		20022	774	12/18/68	JT3D-3B (HK2)		N883PA, N730Q, CC-CYB, YR-JCB
B707-3J6C	JY-AJN	ROYAL JORDANIAN		20720	874	12/13/73	JT3D-7 (HK2)		B-2414
B707-3J6C	JY-AJO	ROYAL JORDANIAN		20723	879	03/19/74	JT3D-7 (HK2)		B-2420
N-UNITED STATES OF AMERICA									
B707-321 (F)	N707GE	GENERAL ELECTRIC COMPANY		17608	122	04/28/60	JT4A/CFM56-5B		N730PA, G-AYXR, N37681 [ENGINE TEST BED; BASED MHV]

A/C TYPE	CURRENT REG. NO.	LAST KNOWN OPERATOR (OWNER)	STATUS	ORIGINAL MSN	LINE NO.	DEL. DATE	ENG. TYPE	FLEET NO.	PREV. REG. [COMMENTS]
B707-330C (RE)	N707HE	OMEGA AIR		20124	806	05/08/69	JT8D-219		D-ABUO [RE-ENGINED; "707RE" TITLES]
B707-138B	N707JT	JET CLIPPER JOHNNY LLC		18740	388	09/10/64	JT3D-1 (Q)		VH-EBM, N108BN, N707XX [JOHN TRAVOLTA'S AIRPLANE]
B707-3J6B (WL)	N717QS	QUIET SKIES INC.		20717	882	05/10/74	JT3D-7 (HK3)		B-2408 [SEEN AT PARIS AIRSHOW 06/99; WL ADDED]
B720-047B	N720JR	J A R AIRCRAFT SERVICES		18451	307	07/27/62	JT3D-3B (Q)		N93145, HZ-NAA, HZ-KA1, N2143J [OPF MALI GOV'T]
B720-051B	N720H	HONEYWELL AVIATION SERVICES		18384	237	09/30/61	JT3D-3B		N795TW, N733US, OY-APZ, OO-TYA, N720GT
B707-330B	N88ZL	LOWA, LTD.		18928	457	12/28/65	JT3D-3B (HK3)		D-ABUF, N5381X

OB-PERU

A/C TYPE	CURRENT REG. NO.	LAST KNOWN OPERATOR (OWNER)	STATUS	ORIGINAL MSN	LINE NO.	DEL. DATE	ENG. TYPE	FLEET NO.	PREV. REG. [COMMENTS]
B707-321C	OB-1716	CIELOS DEL PERU		20017	753	10/25/68	JT3D-3B (HK2)		N871PA, JY-AES, N202DJ, N710FW, N517MA, PT-MTE

OD-LEBANON

A/C TYPE	CURRENT REG. NO.	LAST KNOWN OPERATOR (OWNER)	STATUS	ORIGINAL MSN	LINE NO.	DEL. DATE	ENG. TYPE	FLEET NO.	PREV. REG. [COMMENTS]
B707-323C	OD-AGD	TMA OF LEBANON		18939	437	08/30/65	JT3D-3B (HK2)		N7560A
B707-321C	OD-AGO	TMA OF LEBANON		19269	570	04/30/67	JT3D-3B (HK2)		N447PA
B707-321C	OD-AGP	TMA OF LEBANON		19274	594	06/22/67	JT3D-3B (HK2)		N452PA
B707-331C	OD-AGS	TMA OF LEBANON		19214	626	09/29/67	JT3D-3B (HK2)		N5773T [RTS]
B707-327C	OD-AGX	TMA OF LEBANON		19104	498	05/21/66	JT3D-3B (HK2)		N7095 [ALL WHITE C/S; NO TITLES]
B707-327C	OD-AGY	TMA OF LEBANON		19105	499	05/28/66	JT3D-3B (HK2)		N7096

PP/PT-BRAZIL

A/C TYPE	CURRENT REG. NO.	LAST KNOWN OPERATOR (OWNER)	STATUS	ORIGINAL MSN	LINE NO.	DEL. DATE	ENG. TYPE	FLEET NO.	PREV. REG. [COMMENTS]
B707-323C	PP-BRG	BETA CARGO		19586	670	02/05/68	JT3D-3B (HK2)		N8406, CP-1698
B707-351C	PP-BRI	BETA CARGO (PROMODAL)		19776	732	07/29/68	JT3D-3B (HK2)		N385US, S2-ACE, N8091J [BEING REACTIVATED GRU]
B707-323C	PP-BRR	BETA CARGO (OMEG)		20088	727	07/17/68	JT3D-3B (HK2)		N8416, PT-TCN
B707-330C	PP-BSE	BETA CARGO (OMEG)		19317	557	03/06/67	JT3D-3B		D-ABUI, PT-TCM
B707-369C	PT-MTR	SKYMASTER AIRLINES		20084	758	11/04/68	JT3D-3B (HK2)		9K-ACJ, N525SJ, PP-PHA, N851JB, OB-1699
B707-351C	PT-WSM	SKYMASTER AIRLINES (OMEG)		19773	705	05/03/68	JT3D-3B (HK2)		N382US, CN-RMB, N149DM [RTS]
B707-338C	PT-WSZ	SKYMASTER AIRLINES (CITIZENS)		18808	404	02/09/65	JT3D-3B (HK2)		VH-EBN, 9V-BFW, N707GB, HK-3030X
B707-324C	PT-WUS	SKYMASTER AIRLINES		19352	576	04/21/67	JT3D-3B (HK2)		N17329, 9V-BEX, N707JJ, B-2423, N707PM, HK-3604X

A/C TYPE	CURRENT REG. NO.	LAST KNOWN OPERATOR (OWNER)	STATUS	ORIGINAL MSN	LINE NO.	DEL. DATE	ENG. TYPE	FLEET NO.	PREV. REG. [COMMENTS]
P4-ARUBA									
B707-351B	P4-FDH	COMTRAN INTL.		18586	345	07/30/63	JT3D-3B (HK2)		N353US, VR-HGO, VR-CAO, N651TF, N351SR, EL-SKD, G-BSZA, VR-BMV, VR-BOR, HZ-SAK [STD SEN]
B707-3L6B	P4-TBN	TBN AIRCRAFT ARUBA		21049	896	01/08/75	JT3D-7 (HK3)		N62393, 9M-TDM, A6-HPZ
B707-331C	9G-FIA	FIRST INTL. AIRLINES (ALGI)		20069	815	07/16/69	JT3D-3B (HK2)		N15713, N345FA, CC-CUE, TC-GHA, PP-AJP, N234FA, P4-YYY [LST/OPW JON]
B707-324C	9G-OLD	FIRST INTL. AIRLINES (ALGI)		19350	537	12/02/66	JT3D-3B (HK2)		N17327, PP-VLO, G-HEVY, EL-LAT, YA-PAM [LST/OPW JON]
B707-399C	5Y-BOR	FIRST INTL. AIRLINES (ALGI)		19415	601	07/13/67	JT3D-3B (HK2)		G-AVKA, N319F, CS-TBH, N106BV, 4K-AZ4, 9G-ALD, 9G-OOD [OPF TRANS ATTICO
ST-SUDAN									
B707-330C	ST-AKW	AZZA TRANSPORT (IBIS AV ARUBA)		20123	788	02/27/69	JT3D-3B		D-ABUJ, A6-DPA, P4-AKW
B707-384C	ST-JCC	AZZA TRANSPORT (COMTRAN)		18948	495	05/11/66	JT3D-3B (HK2)		SX-DBA, JY-AEB, JY-AJK, YR-JCC, P4-JCC
B707-3J8C	ST-AFA	SUDAN AIRWAYS		20897	885	06/17/74	JT3D-7		
B707-3J8C	ST-AFB	SUDAN AIRWAYS		20898	887	07/10/74	JT3D-7		
B707-369C	ST-AIX	SUDAN AIRWAYS		20086	764	11/25/68	JT3D-3B		9K-ACL
B707-321C	ST-AMF	TRANS ARABIAN A/T (TRANSASIAN)		19367	637	10/27/67	JT3D-3B (HK2)		N457PA, G-BPAT, 9J-AEQ, ST-ALM, VR-HKL [STD MSE LESS ONE ENGINE]
SU-EGYPT									
B707-366C	SU-AXJ	EGYPT GOVERNMENT		20919	888	08/21/74	JT3D-7 (HK2)		
B707-366C	SU-AVZ	AIR MEMPHIS (TRISTAR)		20762	868	06/29/73	JT3D-7 (HK3)		[ALL WHITE]
B707-328C	SU-PBB	AIR MEMPHIS		19916	762	12/04/68	JT3D-3B (HK2)		F-BLCK, SU-DAA
B707-347C	SU-	AIR MEMPHIS		19967	745	09/19/68	JT3D-3B (HK2)		N1505W, OD-AGV
B707-3B4C	SU-BMV	LUXOR AIR		20260	823	10/28/69	JT3D-3B (HK2)		OD-AFE
TN-CONGO BRAZZAVILLE									
B707-323C	TN-AGO	EQUAFLIGHT SERVICE		19519	619	09/11/67	JT3D-7 (HK2)		N7599A, PT-TCK, N5065T, 9G-OLU, 3D-ASB, 9Q-CKB, EL-RDS, 9G-AYO [FERRIED TO OST FOR MX 11/17/00]
B707-366C	TN-AGO	LINA CONGO		20341	834	01/16/70	JT3D-7 (HK2)		SU-APD, 9Q-CJM

	A/C TYPE	CURRENT REG. NO.	LAST KNOWN OPERATOR (OWNER)	STATUS	ORIGINAL MSN	LINE NO.	DEL. DATE	ENG. TYPE	FLEET NO.	PREV. REG. [COMMENTS]
VT-INDIA										
	B707-337C	K2899	AVIATION RESEARCH CENTRE		19988	736	08/19/68	JT3D-3B/7		VT-DXT [OPB INDIAN AF]
	B707-337C	VT-DVB	AVIATION RESEARCH CENTRE		19248	549	02/12/67	JT3D-3B/7		K2900 [OPB INDIAN AF]
YI-IRAQ										
	B707-370C	YI-AGE	IRAQI AIRWAYS		20889	889	08/27/74	JT3D-7 (HK2)		[STD AMM]
	B707-370C	YI-AGG	IRAQI AIRWAYS		20891	892	10/07/74	JT3D-7		[STD AMM]
YR-ROMANIA										
	B707-3K1C	YR-ABB	ROMAVIA		20804	883	06/03/74	JT3D-3B (HK2)		
	B707-3K1C	YR-ABA	TAROM		20803	878	02/21/74	JT3D-3B (HK2)		[OPF KEY AVIATION BROKER]
	B707-3K1C	YR-ABC	TAROM		20805	884	06/03/74	JT3D-3B (HK2)		[OPF KEY AVIATION BROKER]
ZS-SOUTH AFRICA										
	B707-323C	ZS-IJI	INTER AIR (AV CONSULT)		19517	614	08/28/67	JT3D-3B (HK2)		N7597A, PT-TCL, 4X-AOY, 7P-LAN, CC-CDI, N29AZ
3C-EQUATORIAL GUINEA										
	B707-373C	3C-CSB	TRADEWINDS AIR CARGO		19179	500	05/29/66	JT3D-3B		N372WA, CS-TBJ, 9Q-CSB, 3D-CSB [WFU AFTER HARD LANDING AT JNB]
3D-SWAZILAND										
	B707-3B4C	3D-	GULF FALCON		20259	822	10/01/69	JT3D-3B (HK2)		OD-AFD
	B707-323C	3D-	GULF FALCON		19589	701	04/26/68	JT3D-3B (HK2)		N8410, OD-AHC
	B707-323C	3D-	GULF FALCON		19515	608	08/15/67	JT3D-3B (HK2)		N7595A, OD-AHD
	B707-323C	3D-	GULF FALCON		19516	612	08/23/67	JT3D-3B (HK2)		N7596A, EL-RDS, OD-AHE
	B707-323B	3D-	GULF FALCON		20170	795	04/09/69	JT3D-3B (HK2)		N8431, N708PC, OD-AHF
	B707-307C	ST-AQI	GULF FALCON		19999	756	10/31/68	JT3D-3B (HK2)		68-11073, 10+03, 3D-SGF, 5Y-GFF ["SPIRIT OF AFRICA"]
	B707-336C	5Y-GFG	GULF FALCON		20517	854	05/28/71	JT3D-3B (HK2)		G-AYLT, 9Q-CLY, SU-DAD, VR-HKK, 9G-TWO, 5Y-SIM, 3D-SGG [IN MX SHJ]
	B707-330B	3D-WKU	INFLIGHT AIRLINE MARKETING		18930	464	01/19/66	JT3D-7 (HK)		D-ABUH, VP-WKU, Z-WKU
5A-LIBYA										
	B707-3L5C	5A-DAK	LIBYAN ARAB AIRLINES		21228	911	07/19/76	JT3D-3B		
5N-NIGERIA										
	B707-321C	5N-EEO	AIR ATLANTIC CARGO		19270	572	05/08/67	JT3D-3B (HK2)		N448PA, N448M, G-BGIR, TF-VLL, G-BMAZ, N863BX, N705FW [RTD; PARKED LOS]
	B707-369C	5N-TNO	AIR ATLANTIC CARGO		20085	760	11/14/68	JT3D-3B (HK2)		9K-ACK, N147SP, N720FW, N528SJ, N725FW [DMGD KINSHASA 4/14/00; WO?]

A/C TYPE	CURRENT REG. NO.	LAST KNOWN OPERATOR (OWNER)	STATUS	ORIGINAL MSN	LINE NO.	DEL. DATE	ENG. TYPE	FLEET NO.	PREV. REG. [COMMENTS]
5X-UGANDA									
B707-379C	5X-JEF	DAS AIR CARGO		19821	718	06/27/68	JT3D-3B (HK2)		G-AWHU, 9Q-CKI, VN-B3415, VN-83415, ST-GLD, 9G-OLF, 9G-ONE, 9G-WON
B707-351C	5X-JET	DAS AIR CARGO (JET COM)		19411	540	12/06/66	JT3D-3B (HK2)		N371US, YU-AGJ, N851MA, N740FW
5Y-KENYA									
B707-330B	5Y-AXI	AFRICAN AIRLINES INTL. (AV. CONSULT.)		18927	454	11/24/65	JT3D-7 (HK2)		D-ABUD, VP-WKV, Z-WKV [WFU NBO]
B707-351B	5Y-AXR	AFRICAN AIRLINES INTL. (FRONTIER HOLD.)		19634	695	03/29/68	JT3D-3B		N378US, 5Y-BBI [STD NBO]
9G-GHANA									
B707-323C	9G-ADS	ANALINDA AIRLINES		19587	686	03/15/68	JT3D-3B (HK2)		N8408, N705PC, F-GHFT [IMPOUNDED ATH]
B707-321C	9G-ADM	CONTINENTAL CARGO AIRLINES (GM A/L)	L	19369	648	11/27/67	JT3D-3B (HK2)		N459PA, HL7431, TF-IUB, 9G-ACZ, 5Y-AXG, 9G-ADL [DMGD KINSHASA 4/14/00]
B707-331C	9G-FIA	JOHNSONS AIR (FIRST INTL.)	L	20069	815	07/16/69	JT3D-3B (HK2)		N15713, N345FA, CC-CUE, TC-GHA, PP-AJP, N234FA, P4-YYY
B707-323C	9G-LAD	JOHNSONS AIR (FIRST INTL.)		18940	439	08/27/65	JT3D-3B (HK)		N7561A, PP-VLP, N108BV, 5N-MXX
B707-324C	9G-OLD	JOHNSONS AIR (FIRST INTL.)	L	19350	537	12/02/66	JT3D-3B (HK2)		N17327, PP-VLO, G-HEVY, EL-LAT, YA-PAM
B707-399C	5Y-BDR	JOHNSONS AIR (FIRST INTL.)	L	19415	601	07/13/67	JT3D-3B (HK2)		G-AVKA, N319F, CS-TBH, N106BV, 4K-AZ4, 9G-ALD, 9G-OOD
9Q-CONGO KINSHASA									
B707-138 (B)	9Q-CLK	REPUBLIC OF CONGO GOVERNMENT		17702	64	09/18/59	JT3D-3B (Q)		VH-EBG, G-AWDG, N600JJ, N707KS, N707SK
B707-366C	9Q-CKB	HEWA BORA AIRWAYS		19844	744	09/18/68	JT3D-7 (HK2)		SU-AOU, 9Q-CJM, 9Q-CRA, 9G-CKG [REPAIRED & RTS]
B707-366C	9Q-CKK	HEWA BORA AIRWAYS		20761	867	05/29/73	JT3D-7		N1785B, SU-AVY
MILITARY									
B707-365C	LV-WXL	ARGENTINIAN AIR FORCE	M	19590	654	12/21/67	JT3D-3B (HK2)		G-ATZD, VR-BCP, 5A-DJV, SU-DAI, 5N-AOO, OO-CDE, JY-AJM
B707-387B	T-95	ARGENTINIAN AIR FORCE	M	19241	555	02/24/67	JT3D-3B		LV-ISD, TC-95
B707-387B (SCD)	TC-91	ARGENTINIAN AIR FORCE	M	21070	897	06/11/75	JT3D-3B		T-01, T-91
B707-372C	TC-94	ARGENTINIAN AIR FORCE	M	20076	721	06/14/68	JT3D-3B		N738AL, TC-93, LV-LGO
B707-387C	VR-21	ARGENTINIAN AIR FORCE	M	19962	755	11/04/68	JT3D-3B		LV-JGP, TC-93
E-3C	73-1674	BOEING (USAF)	M	21046	901	07/21/75	JT3D(TF33-100A)		73-1674 [BUILT AS E-3A, MODIFIED TO E-3C BEFORE DEL, NOW JE-3C, E-3 MOD TESTBED]
B707-345C	FAB2401	BRAZILIAN AIR FORCE	M	19840	679	08/20/68	JT3D-3B		N7321S, PP-VJY [BEING REACTIVATED] (KC-137E)

A/C TYPE	CURRENT REG. NO.	LAST KNOWN OPERATOR (OWNER)	STATUS	ORIGINAL MSN	LINE NO.	DEL. DATE	ENG. TYPE	FLEET NO.	PREV. REG. [COMMENTS]
B707-345C (KC-137E)	FAB2402	BRAZILIAN AIR FORCE	M	19842	712	08/06/68	JT3D-3B		N7323S, PP-VJX [STD GIG]
B707-320C (KC-707E)	FAB2403	BRAZILIAN AIR FORCE	M	20008	739	07/14/69	JT3D-3B		N707N, PP-VJH
B707-324C	FAB2404	BRAZILIAN AIR FORCE	M	19870	702	04/24/68	JT3D-3B		N47332, PP-VLK
B707-351C	FAC902	CHILEAN AIR FORCE	M	19443	611	08/12/67	JT3D-3B		N374US, CC-CCK
B707-330B (KC-707)	FAC903	CHILEAN AIR FORCE	M	18926	446	10/05/65	JT3D-3B		D-ABUC, CC-CEA [WFU]
B707-385C	FAC904	CHILEAN AIR FORCE	M	19000	447	12/20/69	JT3D-3B (HK2)		N68657, CC-CEB, 4X-JYI, FAC01, FAC900, FAC905
B707-373C	FAC1201	COLOMBIAN AIR FORCE	M	19716	644	11/13/67	JT3D-3B		N368WA, AP-AWD, HL7425 [ARC-707?]
E-3F	F-ZBCA	FRENCH AIR FORCE	M	24115	1000	05/22/91	CFM56-2A-3		SDA201
E-3F	F-ZBCB	FRENCH AIR FORCE	M	24116	1003	07/23/91	CFM56-2A-3		SDA202
E-3F	F-ZBCC	FRENCH AIR FORCE	M	24117	1006	09/11/91	CFM56-2A-3		SDA203
E-3F	F-ZBCD	FRENCH AIR FORCE	M	24510	1009	02/15/92	CFM56-2A-3		SDA204
B707-355C (EC-8C)	97-0100	GRUMMAN AEROSPACE	M	19986	730	12/12/68	JT3D-3B		F-BJCM, N723GS, EL-AIY, N707MB
B707-347C (CC-137)	97-0124	GRUMMAN AEROSPACE	M	20319	833	05/11/70	JT3D-3B		13705 [TO BE CVTD TO E-8 FOR J-STARS PROGRAM]
B707-347C (CC-137)	97-0200	GRUMMAN AEROSPACE	M	20317	826	03/04/70	JT3D-3B		13703 [TO BE CVTD TO E-8C FOR J-STARS PROGRAM]
B707-347C (CC-137)	97-0201	GRUMMAN AEROSPACE	M	20318	829	03/10/70	JT3D-3B		13704 [TO BE CVTD TO E-8C FOR J-STARS PROGRAM]
B707-3J6C	N719QS	GRUMMAN AEROSPACE	M	20719	873	11/22/73	JT3D-7		B-2412 [BU LAKE CHARLES, LA 01/99]
B707-336C	VR-BZA	GRUMMAN AEROSPACE	M	20375	841	03/25/70	JT3D-3B		G-AXGX, A7-AAC [TO BE CVTD TO E-8 FOR J-STARS PROGRAM]
B707-323C (EC-18B)	81-0898	GRUMMAN AEROSPACE (USAF)	M	19380	525	10/12/66	JT3D-3B		N7565A [BEING CVTD TO TC-18E; TO BE USED AS E-3A TRAINER]
B707-3M1C	A-7002	INDONESIAN AIR FORCE	M	21092	899	04/25/75	JT3D-3B		PK-PJQ, PK-GAU
B707-386C	1001	IRANIAN AIR FORCE	M	21396	928	05/03/78	JT3D-3B		EP-HIM, EP-NHY
B707-370C	1002	IRANIAN AIR FORCE	M	20890	891	09/23/74	JT3D-7		YI-AGF, JY-CAC, 4YB-CAC
B707-3J9C	5-8301	IRANIAN AIR FORCE	M	20830	876	05/29/74	JT3D-3B		N1790B, 5-241
B707-3J9C	5-8302	IRANIAN AIR FORCE	M	20831	881	05/10/74	JT3D-3B		5-242 [IN STORAGE]
B707-3J9C	5-8303	IRANIAN AIR FORCE	M	20832	886	07/26/74	JT3D-3B		5-243
B707-3J9C	5-8304	IRANIAN AIR FORCE	M	20833	890	09/30/74	JT3D-3B		5-244
B707-3J9C	5-8305	IRANIAN AIR FORCE	M	20834	894	11/17/74	JT3D-3B		5-245, EP-NHB, EP-NHW
B707-3J9C	5-8308	IRANIAN	M	21124	910	06/14/76	JT3D-3B		5-248
B707-3J9C	5-8310	IRANIAN AIR FORCE	M	21126	914	08/31/76	JT3D-3B		5-250
B707-3J9C	5-8313	IRANIAN AIR FORCE	M	21129	918	12/14/76	JT3D-3B		5-213
B707-3J9C	5-8314	IRANIAN AIR FORCE	M	21475	936	12/20/78	JT3D-3B		
B707-3P1C		ISRAELI AIR FORCE	M	21334	923	07/28/77	JT3D-3B (HK2)	275	A7-AAA
B707-3W6C	4X-980	ISRAELI AIR FORCE	M	21956	941	03/10/82	JT3D-3B (HK2)	290	N707QT, CN-ANR, CN-CCC, N707JU [CVTD -700C]
B707-3H7C (EC-707)	4X-JYB	ISRAELI AIR FORCE	M	20629	863	11/20/72	JT3D-3B	255	TJ-CAA, 4X-BYR

A/C TYPE	CURRENT REG. NO.	LAST KNOWN OPERATOR (OWNER)	STATUS	ORIGINAL MSN	LINE NO.	DEL. DATE	ENG. TYPE	FLEET NO.	PREV. REG. [COMMENTS]
B707-328B (EC-707)	4X-JYC	ISRAELI AIR FORCE	M	19291	536	03/07/67	JT3D-3B	258	F-BLCE, TU-TXL, TU-TXN, 3X-GCC, OO-TYC, N2090B, 4X-BYC
B707-3J6C	4X-JYH	ISRAELI AIR FORCE	M	20721	875	01/14/74	JT3D-7 (HK2)	264	2416, B-2416, 4X-BYH [ISRAELI PRIME MINISTERÆS A/C]
B707-329 (EC-707)	4X-JYL	ISRAELI AIR FORCE	M	18374	283	04/16/62	JT4A	128	OO-SJF, OE-LBA, 4X-BYL [SEEN TLV MINUS TWO ENGINES AND OTHER PARTS]
B707-329 (RC-707)	4X-JYM	ISRAELI AIR FORCE	M	18460	328	01/19/63	JT4A	137	OO-SJG, 4X-BYM [SEEN TLV WITHOUT ENGINES]
B707-3J6B (EC-707)	4X-JYN	ISRAELI AIR FORCE	M	20716	880	04/15/74	JT3D-7 (HK2)	260	2406, B-2406, 4X-BYN [GREY C/S; NO TITLES OR LOGO; REFUELING BOOM]
B707-328 (EC-707)	4X-JYP	ISRAELI AIR FORCE	M	17921	160	09/18/60	JT4A-	120	F-BHSN, OO-SBR, N90287 [RTD?]
B707-344C (EC-707)	4X-JYQ	ISRAELI AIR FORCE	M	20110	800	04/17/69	JT3D-7	242	(ZS-FKT), ZS-SAG, VP-WGA, 4X-BYQ
B707-344C	4X-JYS	ISRAELI AIR FORCE	M	20230	819	08/28/69	JT3D-7	246	(ZS-FKG), ZS-SAH, 4X-BYS [STD TLV SINCE 1995]
B707-329 (KC-707)	4X-JYT	ISRAELI AIR FORCE	M	17625	99	02/13/60	JT4A	140	OO-SJC, 4X-BYT [SEEN TLV WITHOUT ENGINES AND OTHER PARTS]
B707-331C (KC-707)	4X-JYU	ISRAELI AIR FORCE	M	20429	846	08/25/70	JT3D-3B	248	N794TW, 4X-BYB
B707-3L6C	4X-JYV	ISRAELI AIR FORCE	M	21096	900	06/09/75	JT3D-7 (HK2)	272	9M-TMS, N48055, G-CDHW, A6-HRM, P4-MDJ [VIP 001]
B707-328	4X-JYV	ISRAELI AIR FORCE	M	17615	82	12/12/59	JT4A-	115	N74615, F-BHSC, 4X-BYV [WFU TLV]
B707-328	4X-JYX	ISRAELI AIR FORCE	M	17922	161	09/16/60	JT4A	117	F-BHSO, TU-TBY, 4X-BYX [WFU TLV]
B707-331C (KC-707)	4X-JYY	ISRAELI AIR FORCE	M	20428	845	07/23/70	JT3D-3B	250	N1793T, 4X-BYY [CVTD TO ELINT A/C]
B707-382B	MM62148	ITALIAN AIR FORCE	M	19740	676	02/19/68	JT3D-3B	14-01	CS-TBC
B707-382B	MM62149	ITALIAN AIR FORCE	M	20298	840	03/25/70	JT3D-3B	14-02	CS-TBG
B707-3F5C	MM62150	ITALIAN AIR FORCE	M	20514	857	09/23/71	JT3D-3B	14-03	CS-DGI, 8801, CS-TBT
B707-3F5C	MM62151	ITALIAN AIR FORCE	M	20515	859	12/14/71	JT3D-3B	14-04	CS-DGJ, 8802, CS-TBU
B707-307C (C-137)	LX-N19997	NATO	M	19997	747	09/30/68	JT3D-3B (HK2)		68-11071, 10+01 [STD HAM]
B707-307C (C-137)	LX-N20000	NATO	M	20000	759	11/18/68	JT3D-3B (HK2)		68-11074, 10+04 [STD HAM]
B707-329C	LX-N20198	NATO	M	20198	813	06/17/69	JT3D-7		OO-SJM, PH-TVK [E-3A TRAINER; TO BE BU NAPLES]
B707-329C	LX-N20199	NATO	M	20199	816	07/22/69	JT3D-7		OO-SJN, N3238S [E-3A TRAINER]
E-3B	LX-N90442	NATO	M	22855	945	01/22/82	JT3D(TF33-100A)		79-0442
E-3B	LX-N90443	NATO	M	22838	947	05/19/82	JT3D(TF33-100A)		79-0443
E-3B	LX-N90444	NATO	M	22839	949	08/19/82	JT3D(TF33-100A)		79-0444
E-3B	LX-N90445	NATO	M	22840	951	11/12/82	JT3D(TF33-100A)		79-0445
E-3B	LX-N90446	NATO	M	22841	953	03/10/83	JT3D(TF33-100A)		79-0446
E-3B	LX-N90447	NATO	M	22842	954	06/05/83	JT3D(TF33-100A)		79-0447
E-3B	LX-N90448	NATO	M	22843	956	06/27/83	JT3D(TF33-100A)		79-0448
E-3B	LX-N90449	NATO	M	22844	957	08/19/83	JT3D(TF33-100A)		79-0449
E-3B	LX-N90450	NATO	M	22845	959	10/12/83	JT3D(TF33-100A)		79-0450
E-3B	LX-N90451	NATO	M	22846	961	01/20/84	JT3D(TF33-100A)		79-0451
E-3B	LX-N90452	NATO	M	22847	963	04/27/84	JT3D(TF33-100A)		79-0452
E-3B	LX-N90453	NATO	M	22848	964	05/18/84	JT3D(TF33-100A)		79-0453

A/C TYPE	CURRENT REG. NO.	LAST KNOWN OPERATOR (OWNER)	STATUS	ORIGINAL MSN	LINE NO.	DEL. DATE	ENG. TYPE	FLEET NO.	PREV. REG. [COMMENTS]
E-3B	LX-N90454	NATO	M	22849	966	11/02/84	JT3D(TF33-100A)		79-0454
E-3B	LX-N90455	NATO	M	22850	967	02/11/85	JT3D(TF33-100A)		79-0455
E-3B	LX-N90456	NATO	M	22851	968	11/07/84	JT3D(TF33-100A)		79-0456
E-3B	LX-N90458	NATO	M	22853	970	03/18/85	JT3D(TF33-100A)		79-0458
E-3B	LX-N90459	NATO	M	22854	971	04/30/85	JT3D(TF33-100A)		79-0459
B707-351B	68-19635	PAKISTANIAN AIR FORCE	M	19635	706	05/10/68	JT3D-3B		N379US, AP-BAA
B707-340C	68-19866	PAKISTANIAN AIR FORCE	M	19866	738	08/26/68	JT3D-3B		AP-AVL, YU-AGD, AP-AWY
B707-321B	FAP-01	PARAGUAYAN AIR FORCE	M	18957	472	02/15/66	JT3D-3B (HK2)		N415PA, ZP-CCF
B707-323C	FAP319	PERUVIAN AIR FORCE	M	19575	714	06/04/68	JT3D-3B		N8412, HK-2842X, HP-1028, OB-1371
E-3D	ZH101	ROYAL AIR FORCE	M	24109	993	05/22/91	CFM56-2A-3		
E-3D	ZH102	ROYAL AIR FORCE	M	24110	996	03/25/91	CFM56-2A-3		
E-3D	ZH103	ROYAL AIR FORCE	M	24111	1004	07/08/91	CFM56-2A-3		
E-3D	ZH104	ROYAL AIR FORCE	M	24112	1007	09/19/91	CFM56-2A-3		
E-3D	ZH105	ROYAL AIR FORCE	M	24113	1010	11/21/91	CFM56-2A-3		
E-3D	ZH106	ROYAL AIR FORCE	M	24114	1011	03/09/92	CFM56-2A-3		
E-3D	ZH107	ROYAL AIR FORCE	M	24499	1012	05/12/92	CFM56-2A-3		
B707-368C	A20-261	ROYAL AUSTRALIAN AIR FORCE	M	21261	919	12/23/76	JT3D-3B		HZ-ACI, N7486B
B707-338C	A20-623	ROYAL AUSTRALIAN AIR FORCE	M	19623	671	02/05/68	JT3D-3B		VH-EAC, G-BDKE, C-GRYN
B707-338C	A20-624	ROYAL AUSTRALIAN AIR FORCE	M	19624	689	03/27/68	JT3D-3B		VH-EAD
B707-338C	A20-627	ROYAL AUSTRALIAN AIR FORCE	M	19627	707	05/16/68	JT3D-3B		VH-EAG
B707-338C	A20-629	ROYAL AUSTRALIAN AIR FORCE	M	19629	737	08/22/68	JT3D-3B		VH-EAI, G-BDLM, C-GGAB
B707-138B	CNA-NS	ROYAL MOROCCAN AIR FORCE	M	18334	229	08/29/61	JT3D-1		VH-EBK, 9Y-TDB, N58937, CN-ANS
E-6A/YE8B	1902	ROYAL SAUDI AIR FORCE	M	24503	1001	10/03/91	CFM56-2A-2		88-0322, N707UM
E-3A	1801	ROYAL SAUDI AIR FORCE (FMS)	M	23419	974	06/29/86	CFM56-2A-2		82-0068
E-3A	1802	ROYAL SAUDI AIR FORCE (FMS)	M	23418	973	08/29/86	CFM56-2A-2		82-0067
E-3A	1803	ROYAL SAUDI AIR FORCE (FMS)	M	23417	972	10/31/86	CFM56-2A-2		82-0066
E-3A	1804	ROYAL SAUDI AIR FORCE (FMS)	M	23420	976	12/23/86	CFM56-2A-2		82-0069
E-3A	1805	ROYAL SAUDI AIR FORCE (FMS)	M	23421	980	04/02/87	CFM56-2A-2		82-0070
KE-3A	1811	ROYAL SAUDI AIR FORCE (FMS)	M	23422	975	06/24/87	CFM56-2A-2		82-0071
KE-3A	1812	ROYAL SAUDI AIR FORCE (FMS)	M	23423	977	03/02/87	CFM56-2A-2		82-0072
KE-3A	1813	ROYAL SAUDI AIR FORCE (FMS)	M	23424	978	06/16/87	CFM56-2A-2		82-0073
KE-3A	1814	ROYAL SAUDI AIR FORCE (FMS)	M	23425	979	02/12/87	CFM56-2A-2		82-0074
KE-3A	1815	ROYAL SAUDI AIR FORCE (FMS)	M	23426	981	07/08/87	CFM56-2A-2		82-0075
KE-3A	1816	ROYAL SAUDI AIR FORCE (FMS)	M	23427	982	06/11/87	CFM56-2A-2		82-0076
KE-3A	1818	ROYAL SAUDI AIR FORCE (FMS)	M	23429	985	08/13/87	CFM56-2A-2		83-0511
KE-3A	1901	ROYAL SAUDI AIR FORCE (FMS)	M	23428	984	09/16/87	CFM56-2A-2		83-0510, 1817
B707-328C	1415	SOUTH AFRICAN AIR FORCE	M	19522	596	06/29/67	JT3D-7		F-BLCH, ZS-LSI, AF-615
B707-328C	1417	SOUTH AFRICAN AIR FORCE	M	19723	665	01/17/68	JT3D-7		F-BLCI, ZS-LSJ, AF-617
B707-328C	1419	SOUTH AFRICAN AIR FORCE	M	19917	763	12/10/68	JT3D-7		F-BLCL, ZS-LSK, AF-619
B707-344C	1421	SOUTH AFRICAN AIR FORCE	M	20283	831	12/18/69	JT3D-7		ZS-SAI, LX-LGS, JY-AFQ, ZS-LSF, EL-TBA, AF-621

A/C TYPE	CURRENT REG. NO.	LAST KNOWN OPERATOR (OWNER)	STATUS	ORIGINAL MSN	LINE NO.	DEL. DATE	ENG. TYPE	FLEET NO.	PREV. REG. [COMMENTS]
B707-344C	1423	SOUTH AFRICAN AIR FORCE	M	19706	691	04/02/68	JT3D-7		ZS-EUX, ZS-SAF, LX-LGT, OO-SJR, JY-AFR, ZS-LSL, 3D-ASC, AF-623
B707-331B (KC-137E)	T17-1	SPANISH AIR FORCE	M	20060	773	03/03/69	JT3D-3		BN8731, N708A, N256B [SEEN AT HELSINKI 12/11/99; RTS?]
B707-331C (KC-137E)	T17-2	SPANISH AIR FORCE	M	18757	387	08/29/64	JT3D-3BN792TW		
B707-368C (KC-137E)	T17-3	SPANISH AIR FORCE	M	21367	922	04/04/77	JT3D-3BHZ-ACJ, N7667B		
B707-355C (EC-137E)	67-19417	USAF	M	19417	582	05/19/67	JT3D-3B		N525EJ, G-AYEX, N707HL
E-3B	71-1407	USAF	M	20518	898	10/23/78	JT3D(TF33-100A)		[REBUILT FROM EC-137 L/N 856]
E-3B	71-1408	USAF	M	20519	920	12/15/78	JT3D(TF33-100A)		[REBUILT FROM EC-137 L/N 858]
VC-137C	72-7000	USAF	M	20630	862	08/09/72	JT3D-3B		N8459 [PRESIDENTIAL AIRCRAFT; STILL IN SERVICE; FOR MUSEUM OF FLIGHT BFI
(B707-353B)									
E-3B	73-1675	USAF	M	21185	904	08/18/78	JT3D(TF33-100A)		
E-3B	75-0556	USAF	M	21047	902	05/05/78	JT3D(TF33-100A)		
E-3B	75-0557	USAF	M	21207	907	03/23/77	JT3D(TF33-100A)		
E-3B	75-0558	USAF	M	21208	909	05/29/77	JT3D(TF33-100A)		
E-3B	75-0559	USAF	M	21209	913	10/21/77	JT3D(TF33-100A)		
E-3B	75-0560	USAF	M	21250	916	11/22/77	JT3D(TF33-100A)		
E-3B	76-1604	USAF	M	21434	921	01/19/78	JT3D(TF33-100A)		
E-3B	76-1605	USAF	M	21435	924	05/25/78	JT3D(TF33-100A)		
E-3B	76-1606	USAF	M	21436	926	06/22/78	JT3D(TF33-100A)		
E-3B	76-1607	USAF	M	21437	927	09/29/78	JT3D(TF33-100A)		
E-3B	77-0351	USAF	M	21551	930	09/29/78	JT3D(TF33-100A)		
E-3B	77-0352	USAF	M	21552	931	11/20/78	JT3D(TF33-100A)		
E-3B	77-0353	USAF	M	21553	932	12/19/78	JT3D(TF33-100A)		
E-3B	77-0355	USAF	M	21555	934	03/16/79	JT3D(TF33-100A)		
E-3B	77-0356	USAF	M	21556	935	05/22/79	JT3D(TF33-100A)		
E-3B	78-0576	USAF	M	21752	937	09/14/79	JT3D(TF33-100A)		
E-3B	78-0577	USAF	M	21753	939	12/20/79	JT3D(TF33-100A)		
E-3B	78-0578	USAF	M	21754	940	06/03/80	JT3D(TF33-100A)		
E-3B	79-0001	USAF	M	21755	942	09/18/80	JT3D(TF33-100A)		
E-3B	79-0002	USAF	M	21756	943	12/19/80	JT3D(TF33-100A)		
E-3B	79-0003	USAF	M	21757	944	03/19/81	JT3D(TF33-100A)		
E-3C	80-0137	USAF	M	22829	946	12/04/80	JT3D(TF33-100A)		
E-3C	80-0138	USAF	M	22830	948	04/06/82	JT3D(TF33-100A)		
E-3C	80-0139	USAF	M	22831	950	07/23/82	JT3D(TF33-100A)		

A/C TYPE	CURRENT REG. NO.	LAST KNOWN OPERATOR (OWNER)	STATUS	ORIGINAL MSN	LINE NO.	DEL. DATE	ENG. TYPE	FLEET NO.	PREV. REG. [COMMENTS]
E-3C	81-0004	USAF	M	22832	952	10/19/82	JT3D(TF33-100A)		
E-3C	81-0005	USAF	M	22833	955	04/20/83	JT3D(TF33-100A)		
B707-323C (EC-18B)	81-0891	USAF	M	19518	616	08/31/67	JT3D-3B		N7598A
B707-323C (EC-18E)	81-0892	USAF	M	19382	627	10/02/67	JT3D-3B		N7567A
B707-323C (TC-18E)	81-0893	USAF	M	19384	647	11/21/67	JT3D-3B		N7569A [TO BE USED AS E-3A TRAINER]
B707-323C (EC-18B)	81-0894	USAF	M	19583	650	11/28/67	JT3D-3B		N8403
B707-323C (EC-18D)	81-0895	USAF	M	19381	610	08/10/67	JT3D-3B		N7566A
B707-323C (EC-18B)	81-0896	USAF	M	19581	638	10/31/67	JT3D-3B		N8401
E-3C	82-0006	USAF	M	22834	958	07/29/83	JT3D(TF33-100A)		
E-3C	82-0007	USAF	M	22835	960	11/01/83	JT3D(TF33-100A)		
E-3C	83-0008	USAF	M	22836	962	04/18/84	JT3D(TF33-100A)		
E-3C	83-0009	USAF	M	22837	965	06/19/84	JT3D(TF33-100A)		
B707-396C (C-137C)	85-6973	USAF	M	20043	786	03/14/69	JT3D-3B		N1786B, CF-ZYP, OE-IDA [BEING CVTD TO E-8 01/00]
B707-382B (C-137C)	85-6974	USAF	M	20297	836	02/13/70	JT3D-3B		CS-TBF, N105BV
B707-338C (E-8C)	90-0175	USAF	M	19621	652	12/08/67	JT3D-3B		VH-EAA, OO-YCK, P2-ANB, TF-AEB, 5Y-AXA, N733Q, N526SJ
B707-338C (E-8C)	92-3289	USAF	M	19622	660	01/10/68	JT3D-3B		VH-EAB, OO-YCL, P2-ANA, TF-AEC, SU-DAE, ST-ALL, 5B-DAY, N4131G
B707-338C (E-8C)	92-3290	USAF	M	19295	617	09/06/67	JT3D-3B		VH-EBV, 9J-AEL, ST-ALP, N4115J
B707-384C (E-8C)	93-0011	USAF	M	18949	497	05/21/66	JT3D-3B		SX-DBB, JY-AEC, 66-30052
B707-338C (E-8C)	93-0597	USAF	M	19294	550	03/08/67	JT3D-3B		VH-EBU, P2-ANH, N707MB, 9Q-CDA, N707HW, OB-T-1264, B-2426, G-EOCO, 67-30053
B707-338C (E-8C)	93-1097	USAF	M	19296	630	10/10/67	JT3D-3B		VH-EBW, G-BDEA, EL-AKH, PT-TCT, N6546L, 98-0598
B707-338C (E-8C)	94-0284	USAF	M	19293	546	01/28/67	JT3D-3B		VH-EBT, G-BFLE, N861BX, N2178F
B707-373C (E-8C)	94-0285	USAF	M	19442	609	08/03/67	JT3D-7		N370WA, OO-SBU, N760FW, 67-30054
B707-321C (E-8C)	95-0121	USAF	M	20016	752	12/12/68	JT3D-3B		N870PA, 9K-ACS, N146SP, N527SJ, N770FW, 68-11174
B707-3D3C (E-8C)	95-0122	USAF	M	20495	852	03/12/71	JT3D-7		JY-ADP, 71-1841
B707-347C	95-0123	USAF	M	20316	825	02/28/70	JT3D-3B		N1785B, 13702(CC-137), HR-AMF, EL-AKT [TO BE CVTD TO E-8 FOR J-STARS PROGRAM]
B707-307C (C-137)	99-0006	USAF	M	19998	750	10/15/68	JT3D-3B		68-11072, 10+02 [TO GRUMMAN FOR J-STARS]
B707-338C (E-8A)	86-0416	USAF (GRUMMAN)	M	19626	703	05/04/68	JT3D-3B		VH-EAF, HL7432, N770JS
B707-323C (E-8A)	86-0417	USAF (GRUMMAN)	M	19574	710	05/21/68	JT3D-3B		N8411, N707MR, N8411
E-6A	162782	U.S. NAVY	M	23430	983	03/18/92	CFM56-2A-2		[PROTOTYPE]
E-6A	162783	U.S. NAVY	M	23889	986	09/07/89	CFM56-2A-2		
E-6A	162784	U.S. NAVY	M	23890	987	08/02/89	CFM56-2A-2		
E-6A	163918	U.S. NAVY	M	23891	988	08/02/89	CFM56-2A-2		
E-6A	163919	U.S. NAVY	M	23892	989	10/01/89	CFM56-2A-2		
E-6A	163920	U.S. NAVY	M	23893	990	12/18/89	CFM56-2A-2		

A/C TYPE	CURRENT REG. NO.	LAST KNOWN OPERATOR (OWNER)	STATUS	ORIGINAL MSN	LINE NO.	DEL. DATE	ENG. TYPE	FLEET NO.	PREV. REG. [COMMENTS]
E-6A	164386	U.S. NAVY	M	23894	991	07/13/90	CFM56-2A-2		
E-6A	164387	U.S. NAVY	M	24500	992	04/12/90	CFM56-2A-2		
E-6A	164388	U.S. NAVY	M	24501	994	08/29/90	CFM56-2A-2		
E-6A	164404	U.S. NAVY	M	24502	995	05/28/92	CFM56-2A-2		
E-6A	164405	U.S. NAVY	M	24504	997	12/20/90	CFM56-2A-2		[TO BE CVTD TO E-6B]
E-6B	164406	U.S. NAVY	M	24505	998	04/25/91	CFM56-2A-2		
E-6A	164407	U.S. NAVY	M	24506	999	08/02/91	CFM56-2A-2		[TO BE CVTD TO E-6B]
E-6A	164408	U.S. NAVY	M	24507	1002	08/01/91	CFM56-2A-2		[TO BE CVTD TO E-6B]
E-6A	164409	U.S. NAVY	M	24508	1005	12/21/91	CFM56-2A-2		[TO BE CVTD TO E-6B]
E-6A	164410	U.S. NAVY	M	24509	1008	09/30/91	CFM56-2A-2		[TO BE CVTD TO E-6B]
B707-384C (KC-137E)	6944	VENEZUELAN AIR FORCE	M	19760	715	06/05/68	JT3D-3B		SX-DBD
B707-384C	8747	VENEZUELAN AIR FORCE	M	18950	504	06/18/66	JT3D-3B		SX-DBC

OUT OF SERVICE (STORED BUT INTACT)

A/C TYPE	CURRENT REG. NO.	LAST KNOWN OPERATOR (OWNER)	STATUS	ORIGINAL MSN	LINE NO.	DEL. DATE	ENG. TYPE	FLEET NO.	PREV. REG. [COMMENTS]
B707-328	F-BHSD	AIR FRANCE TRAINING SCHOOL	O	17616	93	01/29/60	JT4A-		[GROUND TRAINER]
B707-328	4X-JYW	ISRAELI AIR FORCE	O	17617	110	03/20/60	JT4A	116	F-BHSE, 4X-BYW [WFU; STD HATZERIM 1996]
B707-123 (B)	5B-DAK	CYPRUS AIRWAYS	O	17632	11	01/31/59	JT3D-1-MC6		N7505A, G-BFMI [WFU AND STD CYPRUS]
B707-131	4X-JYE	ISRAELI AIR FORCE	O	17672	55	08/01/59	JT3C-		N745TW, N197CA [STD TLV 1986; TO BE USED FOR SPARE PARTS]
B707-124	4X-BYA	ISRAELI AIRPORT AUTHORITY	O	18012	57	03/17/60	JT3C-		N74612, 4X-JYA [WFU AND USED FOR GROUND TRAINING 09/83]
B720-023 (B)	60-SAW	SOMALI AIRLINES	O	18015	149	08/13/60	JT3D-1-MC7		N7529A [CVTD -023; DERELICT MOGADISHU SINCE 10/81]
B720-023 (B)	N18KM	TEN MILES HIGH LTD.	O	18019	158	09/19/60	JT3D-1-MC7		N7533A, OD-AFS [CVTD -023; WFU AND STD LONG BEACH, CA 07/86]
B720-023B	70-ABQ	ALYEMDA YEMEN	O	18032	199	04/19/61	JT3D-1-MC7		N7546A [DERELICT ADEN]
B720-048	9Q-CFT	FONTSHI AVIATION SERVICE	O	18043	188	04/07/61	JT3C-7		EI-ALC, N7082, 9Y-TCS, N8790R, LN-TUV, OO-TEB [STD MBUJI-MAYI]
B720-022	HI-401	HISPANIOLA AIRWAYS	O	18049	186	02/13/61	JT3C-7		N7217U, N304AS, N421MA [DERELICT AT PUERTO PLATA SINCE 01/84]
B707-138B	VR-CAN	OMNI AIR INTL.	O	18067	201	07/29/61	JT3D-1		N93134, VH-EBH, 9Y-TDC [STD MZJ 10/81]
B707-138B	SU-FAA	MISR OVERSEAS AIRWAYS	O	18069	228	08/24/61	JT3D-1		N93135, VH-EBJ, N106BN, OE-INA, OE-UNA [DERELICT AT CAIRO SINCE 1988]
B720-022	XA-SDL	LAMBDA AIR	O	18072	252	12/01/61	JT3C-7		N7219U, HI-415 [STD MIA SINCE 09/84]
B720-022	N64696	GEORGE T. BAKER AVIATION SCHOOL	O	18073	253	12/14/61	JT3C-7		N7220U, OO-VGM [STATIC TRAINING, MIAMI]
B720-022	N62215	CALEDONIAN AIRLINES	O	18080	284	05/15/62	JT3C-7		N7227U [WFU AND STD KILIMANJARO, KENYA 1984]
B720-022	B-2101	CAAC	O	18081	297	06/01/62	JT3C-7		N7228U [STATIC TRAINING BEIJING 01/85]
B720-025	VT-ERS	CONTINENTAL AVIATION	O	18159	235	09/27/61	JT3C-7		N8705E, OY-DSL, N7229L [STD NAGPUR 03/91]
B720-025	HL7402	KOREAN AIR	O	18160	236	10/06/61	JT3C-7		N8706E [DERELICT AT SEOUL SINCE 1996]

A/C TYPE	CURRENT REG. NO.	LAST KNOWN OPERATOR (OWNER)	STATUS	ORIGINAL MSN	LINE NO.	DEL. DATE	ENG. TYPE	FLEET NO.	PREV. REG. [COMMENTS]
B707-331C (TC-18E)	84-1398	USAF	0	18713	378	06/12/64	JT3D-3B		N788TW, N131EA [ST STEWART INDUSTRIES; PARKED OKC; NO ENGINES; TO BE BU]
B707-321C	HR-AMX	(ATLANTIC A/C LSG)	0	18716	365	03/27/64	JT3D-3B		N792PA, JY-AED, JY-CAB, 4YB-CAB, J6-SLR, TF-AYE, CX-BPQ, HI-596CA, N66651 [STD 1996]
B707-351C	N21AZ	GRECO AIR	0	18747	369	04/18/64	JT3D-3B (HK2)		N357US, VR-HHB, 5X-UAC, CC-CDN, Z-WST [STD JNB]
B707-351C	N80AZ	GRECO AIR (AVN CONSULT.)	0	18748	379	06/18/64	JT3D-3B (HK2)		N358US, VR-HHD, VR-CAR, 3X-GAZ, N18AZ, CC-CCE, D2-TOR, N18AZ [DERELICT ADDIS ABABA]
B707-321C	5A-DHL	LIBYAN ARAB AIR CARGO	0	18765	371	04/30/64	JT3D-3B		N795PA, N795RN, G-BEZT, SU-BAG, 5X-UAL [ADDIS ABABA]
B707-338C	5N-ARQ	ALLIED AIR CARGO	0	18809	407	03/05/65	JT3D-3B (HK2)		VH-EBO, 9V-BFN, N4225J [STD MSE; RTD]
B707-321B	N404PA	USAF MATERIEL COMMAND	0	18835	408	03/05/65	JT3D-3B[STD BED]		
B707-321B	N454PC	OMEGA AIR	0	18839	417	04/16/65	JT3D-3B (HK)		N408PA, N4408F, N470PC, C5-GOC, HR-AMV, OM-UFB, EL-AKF [STD MHV LESS ENGINES]
B707-321B	ZP-CCE	LINEAS AEREAS PARAGUAYAS	0	18841	419	04/27/65	JT3D-3B (HK)		N410PA [STD ASU SINCE 04/92]
B707-348C	5A-DIX	NATIONAL OVERSEAS AIRLINE	0	18880	413	04/13/65	JT3D-3B		EI-ANO, N318F, SU-BLJ [STD CAI SINCE 11/93]
B707-351C	5A-DJU	LIBYAN ARAB AIRLINES	0	18889	428	06/12/65	JT3D-3B		N360US, VR-HHJ [STD TRIPOLI SINCE 01/92]
B707-351C	OB-1401	OMEGA AIR	0	18921	440	08/13/65	JT3D-3B (HK)		N361US, VR-HGR, S2-ACF, N8090P, HR-AMB [STD LIM SINCE 10/94]
B707-351C	EL-AKL	OMEGA AIR	0	18922	444	09/15/65	JT3D-3B (HK)		N362US, VR-HGP, N82TF, 5N-ASY, 5N-JIL, HR-AME, EL-AKF [STD SNN SINCE 06/96]
B707-330B	Z-WKS	AIR ZIMBABWE	0	18923	435	08/04/65	JT3D-7		D-ABUB, VP-WKS [STD HARARE 11/17/97]
B707-321B	EP-IRJ	IRAN AIR	0	18958	475	02/25/66	JT3D-3B		N416PA
B707-382B (TC-18F)	165343	U.S. NAVY	0	18962	501	06/08/66	JT3D-3B		CS-TBB, TF-VLV, N46RT [E-6A TRAINER; WFU; CRACKED WING SPARS; ST STEWART INDUSTRIES; PARKED OKC]
B707-348C	5A-DIY	NATIONAL OVERSEAS AIRLINE	0	19001	488	04/21/66	JT3D-3B		EI-ANV, 9G-ACR, SU-BLI [STD CAI SINCE 04/96]
B707-351C (KC-137E)	TM17-4	SPANISH AIR FORCE	0	19164	505	06/24/66	JT3D-3B		N366US, SX-DBO, 4X-JYF
B707-324C	YA-GAF	BALKH AIRLINES	0	19177	513	07/29/66	JT3D-3B (HK)		N17325, PP-VLN, N110BV, 5X-UCM, 73-601 [STD OST 01/97]
B707-351C	EL-AJB	MATERIEL	0	19210	515	08/12/66	JT3D-3B (HK)		N369US, YU-AGI, CX-BPZ, N152LM, HR-ANG, HP-1235CTH, N777FB [STD LIEGE 08/97]
B707-321B	ZP-CCG	LINEAS AEREAS PARAGUAYAS	0	19264	527	11/06/66	JT3D-3B (HK)		N419PA [STD ASU SINCE 12/91]
B707-321C	N707HT	(FLIGHT DIRECTOR INC.)	0	19271	574	05/15/67	JT3D-3B (HK)		N449PA, G-BEVN, TC-JCF [RT IAL 01/96; STD ROW SINCE 04/96]
B707-341C	4K-AZ3	(ALG INC.)	0	19321	532	12/28/66	JT3D-3B (HK)		PP-VJS, N107BV, N8190U [STD SEN MINUS THREE ENGINES]
B707-123B	3D-ADK	TRANSAIR CARGO (NEW ACS TANZANIA)	0	19335	593	06/20/67	JT3D-1-MC6		N7585A, N703PC, EL-AKA, YN-CDE, C5-GOB, HR-AMG, OM-WFA, 9Q-CJT, EL-WAM [GONE FROM JNB]

A/C TYPE	CURRENT REG. NO.	LAST KNOWN OPERATOR (OWNER)	STATUS	ORIGINAL MSN	LINE NO.	DEL. DATE	ENG. TYPE	FLEET NO.	PREV. REG. [COMMENTS]
B707-324C	9G-JNR	JASON AIR	O	19353	587	05/27/67	JT3D-3B (HK)		N47330, 9V-BEY, N707SH, B-2422, N707HG, N750FW, JY-AJL, 5N-ONE [SUSP. OPS 1997; WFU LOS]
B707-321C	N722GS	MILLON AIR (AIR TRADE)	O	19373	656	12/11/67	JT3D-3B (HK)		N463PA, F-BYCO [DERELICT MIA]
B707-321C	N2NF	OMEGA AIR	O	19375	662	01/09/68	JT3D-3B (HK)		N473RN, N473RN, HK-2473, OB-R1243, N864BX, 5N-TAS, 9Q-CSW, PP-BRR, EL-AKJ [STD SEN; NOT DERELICT]
B707-321B	5A-DJM	NATIONAL OVERSEAS AIRLINE	O	19378	672	02/06/68	JT3D-3B		N455PA, OO-PSI, OO-PST, SU-BLK [STD CAI SINCE 06/96]
B707-351C	OB-1400	AERONAVES DEL PERU	O	19434	566	03/20/67	JT3D-3B (HK)		N373US, C-GTAI, S2-ACA, N8090Q [STD LIM SINCE 02/95]
B707-336C	5Y-BNJ	GRECO AIR	O	19498	645	11/30/67	JT3D-3B (HK2)		G-ATWV, 9G-ACX, N14AZ [PARKED JNB; NO TITLES; AERO ZAMBIA C/S]
B707-327C	N707AD	ASNET INC.	O	19529	632	10/10/67	JT3D-3B (HK)		N7102, 9M-AQB, 9V-BFC, PT-TCJ [AKA 80065 AND/OR 86005?]
B707-327C	YR-JCA	JARO INTL. (COMTRAN)	O	19530	635	10/18/67	JT3D-3B (HK)		N7103, 9V-BDC, N707ME, B-2424, CC-CYA
B707-331C (TC-18E)	84-1399	USAF	O	19566	717	06/26/68	JT3D-3B		N15710, N132EA [ST STEWART INDUSTRIES; PARKED OKC; TO BE BU]
B707-323C	XA-ABU	ALLEGRO AIR	O	19585	668	01/26/68	JT3D-3B (HK2)		N8405, P4-CCC, XA-MAS [PARKED TUS BY 11/00]
B707-338C	5A-DTF	LIBYAN ARAB AIR CARGO	O	19628	716	06/12/68	JT3D-3B		VH-EAH, HL7433, TF-IUD [STD TIP]
B707-351C	ST-ANP	TRANS ARABIAN A/T (TAAT UGANDA)	O	19632	649	11/21/67	JT3D-3B (HK2)		N376US, 9Y-TEK, 8P-CAD, N707KV, 5X-ARJ [DMGD JUBA, SUDAN 08/14/99; REPAIRABLE?]
B707-351B	5Y-BBJ	BOTSWANA GOVERNMENT	O	19633	690	03/26/68	JT3D-3B		N377US [GROUND TRAINER FOR BOTSWANA POLICE FORCE]
B707-321B	N808ZS	JET CARGO LIBERIA	O	19695	684	03/14/68	JT3D-3B		N493PA, N498GA [STD MONROVIA SINCE 1996]
B707-399C	HI-442CT	DOMINICANA DE AVIACION	O	19767	659	12/29/67	JT3D-3B (HK)		G-AVTW, CS-TBI, HI-442 [STD SDQ]
B707-351C	N677R	OMEGA AIR	O	19774	708	05/14/68	JT3D-3B (HK2)		N383US, CN-RMC, XA-TDZ, PT-WSY [HANGARED MIA; DMGD NOSE CONE]
B707-351C	SU-EAA	MISR OVERSEAS AIRWAYS	O	19775	729	07/18/68	JT3D-3B		N384US, SU-BAO [DERELICT AT CAIRO]
B707-324C	D2-TOK	ANGOLA AIR CHARTER (EQUA)	O	19869	700	04/18/68	JT3D-3B (HK2)		N47331, PP-VLM, N112HM, S7-2HM, N707EL [STD LUANDA; FLYABLE?]
B707-324C	D2-TON	ANGOLA AIR CHARTER (EQUA)	O	19871	711	05/16/68	JT3D-3B (HK2)		N67333, PP-VLL, N114HM, S7-4HM, TC-GHB [STD LUANDA; PARTS MISSING]
B707-347C	D2-TOL	ANGOLA AIR CHARTER	O	19963	723	06/22/68	JT3D-3B		N1501W [STD LUANDA; NOT AIRWORTHY]
B707-382B	9T-MSS	CONGO KINSHASA GOVERNMENT	O	19969	751	10/14/68	JT3D-3B		CS-TBD [STD LIS; NOT DERELICT]
B707-321B	N707AR	OMEGA AIR	O	20029	790	03/04/69	JT3D-3B		N892PA, N729Q ["OMEGA AIR TANKER-TRANSPORT"; SEEN STN 03/24/01]
B707-321B	N893PA	CAAC	O	20030	791	03/11/69	JT3D-3B		[WFU AND USED AS GROUND TRAINER TIANJIN, CHINA]

A/C TYPE	CURRENT REG. NO.	LAST KNOWN OPERATOR (OWNER)	STATUS	ORIGINAL MSN	LINE NO.	DEL. DATE	ENG. TYPE	FLEET NO.	PREV. REG. [COMMENTS]
B707-323C	SU-FAC	MISR OVERSEAS AIRWAYS	O	20087	724	07/05/68	JT3D-3B		N8415 [DERELICT CAIRO SINCE 08/89]
B707-358C	9Q-CVG	CONGO AIRLINES	O	20122	807	05/15/69	JT3D-3B (HK)		4X-ATX [WFU FOR SPARES USE 02/98]
B707-323B	N145SP	(AVIATION CONSULTANTS)	O	20174	808	05/23/69	JT3D-3B (HK)		N8435, 4X-ATG [STD ELP SINCE 1996; ON TRESTLES, NO ENGINES]
B707-323B	N706PC	OMEGA AIR	O	20177	818	08/19/69	JT3D-3B (HK2)		N8438, EL-AKC, C5-GOA, HR-AMW, EL-AKK [STD MHV LESS ENGINES; STILL AS EL-AKK]
B707-329C	9Q-CBW	SCIBE-AIRLIFT CONGO	O	20200	828	12/03/69	JT3D-7 (HK2)		OO-SJO, 9Q-CBS [STD SEN]
B707-309C	EL-ZGS	JET CARGO LIBERIA	O	20261	827	11/07/69	JT3D-3B		B-1824, N707ZS [SERVICE SUSPENDED; STD DUBAI 1996]
B707-358C COLOMBIANA	ARC-707	ARMADA REPUBLICA	O	20301	835	01/26/70	JT3D-3B (HK)		4X-ATY, N707WJ, OB-1592 [PARKED BOG 11/00]
B707-347C	XA-ABG	ALLEGRO AIR	O	20315	824	02/25/70	JT3D-3B		13701(CC-137), N803CK, HR-AMN, N108RA, CX-BSI [PARKED TUS 11/00]
B707-3J6C	5X-TRA	TRIANGLE AIRLINE	O	20722	877	02/26/74	JT3D-7		B-2418, B606L [STD TLV SINCE 03/96]

PRESERVED

A/C TYPE	CURRENT REG. NO.	LAST KNOWN OPERATOR (OWNER)	STATUS	ORIGINAL MSN	LINE NO.	DEL. DATE	ENG. TYPE	FLEET NO.	PREV. REG. [COMMENTS]
B367-80	N70700	BOEING	P	17158	-	07/15/54	JT3D-1		[B707 DEVELOPMENT TESTBED; WFU AND STD MUSEUM OF FLIGHT BFI]
B707-321	RP-C911	CLUB 707	P	17606	107	03/06/60	JT4A-		N728PA, N11RV, N99WT [PRESERVED AS NIGHTCLUB IN MANILA 10/82]
B707-124	4X-JYD	HATZERIM MUSEUM	P	17612	56	08/10/59	JT3C-		N70785 [PRESERVED, TEL AVIV]
B707-131 (F)	4X-BYD	HATZERIM MUSEUM	P	17667	34	05/24/59	JT3C-		N740TW, 4X-JYD [PRESERVED HATZERIM MUSEUM 06/83 AS CINEMA]
B707-436	G-APFJ	COSFORD AEROSPACE MUSEUM	P	17711	163	09/22/60	CONWAY 508		[PRESERVED COSFORD]
B707-430	D-AFHG	HAM	P	17720	115	04/24/60	CONWAY 508		D-ABOD [ON STATIC DISPLAY HAM]
B707-328	F-BHSL	AIR FRANCE TECHNICAL SCHOOL	P	17919	153	08/20/60	JT4A-		[USED FOR INSTRUCTION AFR MECHANICS TRAINING SCHOOL "VILGENIS"]
VC-137B (B707-153(B))	58-6970	USAF	P	17925	33	05/04/59	JT3D-3B		[B707-153(B); TO MUSEUM OF FLIGHT BFI 06/17/96]
VC-137B (B707-153(B))	58-6971	USAF	P	17926	40	05/31/59	JT3D-3B		[ON DISPLAY AT PIMA AIR MUSEUM]
B707-344	VN-A304	HANG KHONG VIETNAM	P	17929	154	08/22/60	JT4A-12		ZS-CKD, ZS-SAB, EI-BFU [PRESERVED IN PARK AT HO CHI MINH CITY SINCE 1985]
B707-458	D-ABOC	MUSEUM FUR VERKEHR UND TECHNIK	P	18071	216	06/07/61	CONWAY 508		4X-ATB, N32824, N130KR [PRESERVED, BERLIN-TEGEL 11/86]
B720-030B	HK-749	MUSEO DEL LOS NINOS	P	18248	258	01/05/62	JT3D-1		D-ABON, N786PA [FUSELAGE ON DISPLAY AT BOGOTA; CVTD TO RESTAURANT]

A/C TYPE	CURRENT REG. NO.	LAST KNOWN OPERATOR (OWNER)	STATUS	ORIGINAL MSN	LINE NO.	DEL. DATE	ENG. TYPE	FLEET NO.	PREV. REG. [COMMENTS]
B720-030B	AP-AZP	PAKISTAN INTL.	P	18250	263	03/23/62	JT3D-3B		N93137, D-ABOQ, N787PA, JY-ADS [PRESERVED AT KHI AS A FUN FAIR]
B720-051B	18351	ROCAF MUSEUM	P	18351	211	06/22/61	JT3D-3B		N721US [TO ROCAF MUSEUM, GANGSHAN]
B707-131B	N751TW	PIMA COUNTY MUSEUM	P	18390	296	05/31/62	JT3D-		[PRESERVED, ON DISPLAY]
VC-137C	62-6000	USAF	P	18461	303	09/10/62	JT3D-3B		[PRESIDENTIAL AIRCRAFT; BEING RTD TO USAF MUSEUM AT WPAFB]
(B707-353B) B707-330B	CC-CCG	MUSEO NACIONAL DE AERONAUTICA	P	18462	333	02/28/63	JT3D-3B		D-ABOS, D-ABOV [AT MUSEO NACIONAL DE AERONAUTICA, SANTIAGO, CHILE]
B720-047B	AP-AXM	KARACHI PLANETARIUM	P	18749	374	05/21/64	JT3D-3B		N93151 [ON DISPLAY KARACHI PLANETARIUM]
B720-047B	AP-AXL	PAKISTAN INTL.	P	18818	390	09/25/64	JT3D-3B		N93152 [FUSELAGE TO MUSEUM AT LAHORE]
B707-328B	F-BLCD	MUSEE DE L'AIR, LE BOURGET	P	18941	471	02/09/66	JT3D-3B		[PRESERVED]

SCRAPPED

A/C TYPE	CURRENT REG. NO.	LAST KNOWN OPERATOR (OWNER)	STATUS	ORIGINAL MSN	LINE NO.	DEL. DATE	ENG. TYPE	FLEET NO.	PREV. REG. [COMMENTS]
B707-121 (B)	N707PA	(IALI)	S	17587	2	12/19/58	JT3D-3B		TC-JBA, HP-551, HP-780 [BU MIA 05/88]
B707-121 (B)	N4594A	E-SYSTEMS INC.	S	17589	4	09/29/58	JT3D-3B		N710PA, TC-JBB, HP-760, HP-793 [BU TPE 08/84]
B707-121 (B)	N4593U	E-SYSTEMS INC.	S	17590	5	10/17/58	JT3D-3B		N711PA, TC-JBC, HP-807 [BU TPE 08/84]
B707-121 (B)	N4591Y	E-SYSTEMS INC.	S	17591	6	10/30/58	JT3D-3B		N712PA, TC-JBD, HP-756, HP-794 [BU TPE 08/84]
B707-321	N714FC	AEROAMERICA	S	17592	13	08/28/58	JT4A-		N714PA, 9M-AQD, N714PT [BU BFI 08/81]
B707-321	C9-ARF	DAN AIR	S	17593	20	07/19/59	JT4A-		N715PA, TC-JAH, G-41-174, 9G-ACB [BU BRU 1983]
B707-321	N716HH	CAA FIRE SCHOOL	S	17594	58	08/22/59	JT4A-		N716PA, TC-JAN, YU-AGH [BU STANSTED 1981]
B707-321	4X-JYZ	ISRAELI AIRCRAFT INDUSTRIES	S	17595	61	09/01/59	JT4A-		N717PA, 4X-BYZ [BU; FUSELAGE DERELICT AT TLV 1995]
B707-321	4X-JYZ	ISRAELI AIR FORCE	S	17596	62	09/22/59	JT4A-		N718PA, 4X-BYZ [BU TLV 1984]
B707-321	N431MA	JET POWER INC.	S	17597	68	10/03/59	JT4A-		N719PA, G-AYBJ [BU SHARJAH 1998]
B707-321	N3791G	JET POWER INC.	S	17598	70	10/06/59	JT4A-		N720PA, G-AYVG [BU MIA 10/83]
B707-321	N80703	KIVU CARGO	S	17599	71	10/19/59	JT4A-		N721PA, G-AYSL [BU LASHAM 02/83]
B707-321 (F)	G-AZTG	DAN-AIR	S	17600	75	10/15/59	JT4A-12		N722PA [BU LASHAM 04/82]
B707-321	9Q-CRY	TURKISH GOVERNMENT	S	17601	76	10/27/59	JT4A-		N723PA, YU-AGA, N711UT, TC-JCF [BU ANKARA 1985]
B707-321 (F)	9Q-CJW	NEW ACS	S	17602	83	08/12/59	JT4A-12		N724PA, G-BAEL, HK-2477X, N2276X, 9Q-CZK, 9Q-CGO [DERELICT AT KISANGANI SINCE 1992]
B707-321	N725CA	GENERAL AIR SERVICE	S	17603	84	12/12/59	JT4A-		N725PA, TC-JAJ, G-41-274, G-BCRS, 9G-ACD [BU MIA 01/84]
B707-321	RP-C7074	AIR MANILA INTL.	S	17604	91	01/13/60	JT4A-12		N726PA [BU MIA 12/85]
B707-321	N427MA	JET POWER INC.	S	17607	121	04/26/60	JT4A-		N729PA, TC-JAM, N729JP, N731BA, N731JP [BU MIA 07/83]

A/C TYPE	CURRENT REG. NO.	LAST KNOWN OPERATOR (OWNER)	STATUS	ORIGINAL MSN	LINE NO.	DEL. DATE	ENG. TYPE	FLEET NO.	PREV. REG. [COMMENTS]
B707-328	F-BHSB	AIR FRANCE	S	17614	81	12/12/59	JT4A-		[BU PARIS 1977]
B707-328	F-BHSF	INST. AERO. AMAURY DE LA GRANGE	S	17618	111	03/24/60	JT4A-		[SCR 1997]
B707-328	4X-BYN	ISRAELI AIRCRAFT INDUSTRIES	S	17619	126	05/13/60	JT4A	119	N5093K, F-BHSG, CN-RMD, 4X-JYN [PARTIALLY SCR TLV 11/93]
B707-328	F-BHSI	AIR FRANCE	S	17621	139	07/11/60	JT4A-		[BU PARIS 09/77]
B707-328	F-BHSJ	AIR FRANCE	S	17622	151	08/01/60	JT4A-		[BU PARIS 1978]
B707-329	OO-SJD	SABENA	S	17626	118	04/10/60	JT4A-		[BU ZAVENTEM 07/82]
B707-123 (B)	N7503A	AMERICAN AIRLINES	S	17630	9	12/31/58	JT3D-1-MC6		[BU 10/77]
B707-123 (B)	N2235W	BOEING	S	17631	10	01/28/59	JT3D-1-MC6		N7504A, 5B-DAL, EL-AJW [HULK EXTANT AT DMAFB SINCE 05/90 (CZ176)]
B707-123 (B)	N960CC	SKYWAYS INTL.	S	17634	14	02/27/59	JT3D-3B (HK)		N7507A, N707AR [BU AMA 02/98]
B707-123 (B)	EL-AJV	BOEING	S	17635	15	03/27/59	JT3D-1-MC6		N7508A, 5B-DAP [HULK EXTANT AT DMAFB SINCE 08/90 (CZ180)]
B707-123 (B)	N7509A	BOEING	S	17636	16	04/03/59	JT3D-1-MC6		[HULK EXTANT AT DMAFB SINCE 05/83 (CZ072)]
B707-123 (B) (F)	HK-1818	AEROCONDOR COLOMBIA	S	17637	17	04/23/59	JT3D-1-MC6		N7510A, D-ALAM, N8418 [BU BOGOTA 1990]
B707-123 (B)	HK-1802X	AEROCONDOR COLOMBIA	S	17638	26	05/12/59	JT3D-1-MC6		N7511A, D-ALAL, N8420 [BU BARRANQUILLA 1990]
B707-123 (B)	N701PC	BOEING	S	17639	30	05/21/59	JT3D-1-MC6		N7512A [HULK EXTANT AT DMAFB SINCE 08/87 (CZ161)]
B707-123 (B)	N62TA	BOEING	S	17640	31	05/28/59	JT3D-1-MC6		N7513A, 9G-ACN, G-TJAB, G-BHOX [HULK EXTANT AT DMAFB SINCE 05/83 (CZ073)]
B707-123 (B)	N7515A	OBERSCHLEISSHEIM MUSEUM	S	17642	41	06/24/59	JT3D-1-MC6		[BU IGM 1986; NOSE ON DISPLAY AT MUC]
B707-123 (B)	HK-1942	AEROCONDOR COLOMBIA	S	17643	42	06/29/59	JT3D-1-MC6		N7516A [BU BARRANQUILLA 1990]
B707-123 (B)	N2143H	ESS JAY AR INC.	S	17644	50	07/27/59	JT3D-1-MC6		N7517A, HZ-DAT [BU SAT 04/96]
B707-123 (B)	N702PC	BOEING	S	17645	51	07/31/59	JT3D-1-MC6		N7518A [BU DMAFB 01/91]
B707-123 (B)	N519GA	BOEING	S	17646	52	08/24/59	JT3D-1-MC6		N7519A, PH-TVA [HULK EXTANT AT DMAFB SINCE 04/83 (CZ063)]
B707-123 (B)	N3951A	TECHNIK MUSEUM	S	17647	53	08/12/59	JT3D-1-MC6		N7520A, C-GQBG, 5A-DHO, 5A-DHM [BU BRU 08/84; NOSE ON DISPLAY AT SINSHEIM, GERMANY]
B707-123 (B)	N752TA	MRH LSG & FIN.	S	17648	63	09/14/59	JT3D-1-MC6		N7521A [BU MARANA 09/84]
B707-123 (B)	N751TA	MONARCH AIRLINES	S	17649	66	10/03/59	JT3D-1-MC6		N7522A [BU LUTON 03/82; PART OF FUSELAGE USED FOR GROUND TRAINING]
B707-123 (B)	N61TA	BOEING	S	17651	72	10/28/59	JT3D-1-MC6		N7524A, ST-AHG, 9G-ACO, G-TJAC, G-BHOY [HULK EXTANT AT DMAFB SINCE 10/83 (CZ080)]
B707-123 (B)	N5038	BOEING	S	17652	77	11/21/59	JT3D-1-MC6		N7525A [HULK EXTANT AT DMAFB SINCE 07/83 (CZ078)]
B707-131 (F)	9Q-CKP	OMEGA AIR	S	17658	18	01/29/59	JT3C-6		N731TW, F-BUZJ, 9Q-CBD [BU SNN 11/86]
B707-131	OO-TEC	TRANS EUROPEAN AIRWAYS	S	17659	19	03/17/59	JT3C-		N732TW [BU; HULK EXTANT AT BRU FOR FIRE TRAINING]

A/C TYPE	CURRENT REG. NO.	LAST KNOWN OPERATOR (OWNER)	STATUS	ORIGINAL MSN	LINE NO.	DEL. DATE	ENG. TYPE	FLEET NO.	PREV. REG. [COMMENTS]
B707-131	N733TW	RAMACOR AG	S	17660	21	03/30/59	JT3C-		[BU TLV 06/77; AIRFRAME USED FOR GROUND TRAINING]
B707-131	N198CA	WORLD AIR FREIGHT	S	17661	22	04/03/59	JT3C-		N734TW, PI-C7071, N16648, 4X-AGT, 4X-JYI, N6232G [DERELICT MHV; USED IN MOVIE "SPEED"]
B707-131	N735T	AEROAMERICA	S	17662	23	04/18/59	JT3C-		N735TW [BU SEATTLE 05/81]
B707-131	N194CA	RODMAR AVIATION	S	17663	24	04/29/59	JT3C-		N736TW, HS-VGC [DERELICT AT MHV]
B707-131	I-SAVA	ISRAELI AIRCRAFT INDUSTRIES	S	17664	27	05/10/59	JT3C-		N737TW [BU TLV 05/77; TAIL SECTION REMAINS]
B707-131	OO-TED	TRANS EUROPEAN AIRWAYS	S	17665	28	05/13/59	JT3C-6		N738TW, 4X-ACN [BU BRU 09/87]
B707-131	OO-TEE	TRANS EUROPEAN AIRWAYS	S	17666	32	05/28/59	JT3C-		N739TW, HS-VGA, 4X-ACU, 4X-JYC [BU; HULK EXTANT AT MXE]
B707-131	N195CA	FEDERAL AVIATION ADMINISTRATION	S	17668	38	06/13/59	JT3C-		N741TW, PI-C7072, N16649, 4X-AGU, 4X-JYH, 4X-BYH [BU ACY 06/82]
B707-331	N701PA	FIELD A/C SERVICE	S	17674	73	11/05/59	JT4A-12		[BU EAST MIDLANDS 06/76]
B707-331	YN-BWL	AERO NICA	S	17675	74	11/10/59	JT4A-12		N762TW [DERELICT DAR-ES-SALAAM SINCE 06/84]
B707-331	N763AB	AVIATION TRADERS	S	17676	79	11/25/59	JT4A-12		N763TW [BU STANSTED 07/81 FOR SPARES]
B707-331	N702PT	MONARCH AVIATION	S	17677	80	12/15/59	JT4A-12		N702PA, N702TA [BU STANSTED 03/80]
B707-331	N764TW	TRANS WORLD AIRLINES	S	17678	86	12/23/59	JT4A-12		[BU KANSAS CITY 06/80]
B707-331	N765TW	TRANS WORLD AIRLINES	S	17679	88	01/18/60	JT4A-12		[BU KANSAS CITY 06/80]
B707-331	RP-C7073	AIR MANILA INTL.	S	17680	89	12/30/59	JT4A-12		N703PA, PI-C7073, S2-ABM [BU MANILA 02/84]
B707-331	N766TW	TRANS WORLD AIRLINES	S	17681	103	04/01/60	JT4A-12		[BU KANSAS CITY 08/80]
B707-331	N767AB	AVIATION TRADERS	S	17682	104	04/05/60	JT4A-12		N767TW [BU STANSTED 05/81]
B707-331	N9230Z	AEROTRON AIRCRAFT RADIO	S	17683	116	03/23/60	JT4A-12		N704PA, XV-NJD [BU CARSON, CA 06/77]
B707-331	N768TW	CONTINENTAL AIRLINES	S	17684	117	04/15/60	JT4A-12		[BU KANSAS CITY 05/82; FWD FUSELAGE USED AS CABIN CREW TRAINER]
B707-331	N705PA	MALAYSIAN CIVIL AVIATION	S	17686	124	04/29/60	JT4A-12		OO-SJP, 9Q-CMA [WAS ON DISPLAY AT KELAUA JAYA PARK, KUALA LUMPUR 1984; NOW BU]
B707-331	N770TW	TRANS WORLD AIRLINES	S	17687	125	05/26/60	JT4A-12		[BU KANSAS CITY 06/80]
B707-331	N771TW	TRANS WORLD AIRLINES	S	17688	135	07/01/60	JT4A-12		[BU KANSAS CITY 05/80]
B707-331(F)	N425MA	JET POWER INC.	S	17689	136	06/09/60	JT4A-12		N706PA, N706TA [BU MIAMI 10/83]
B707-331	N772TW	ALLEN AIRCRAFT CORP	S	17690	137	07/01/60	JT4A-12		[BU KANSAS CITY 05/82]
B707-227	N3842X	MONARCH AVIATION	S	17692	87	12/03/59	JT4A-3		N7072, 9Y-TDO, N64757, N811UT [BU MIA 1987]
B707-227	9Y-TDR	ISRAELII AIRCRAFT SERVICES	S	17693	96	01/15/60	JT4A-3		N7073 [BU TLV 09/77]
B707-227	N64740	AIR BOREALIS	S	17694	97	01/21/60	JT4A-3		N7074, 9Y-TDP [BU MOSES LAKE 09/81]
B707-227	9Y-TDQ	BRITISH WEST INDIAN AIRWAYS	S	17695	102	02/10/60	JT4A-3		N7075 [BU FOR SPARES 1977]
B707-138 (B)	N500JJ	TRAFALGAR LSG	S	17699	54	08/01/59	JT3D-		VH-EBD, G-AVZZ [BU LBG 07/83]
B707-138 (B)	N793NA	NATIONAL AIRCRAFT	S	17700	59	08/24/59	JT3D-		VH-EBE, N793SA, CF-PWW, VP-BDE [BU 1996; HULK EXTANT]

A/C TYPE	CURRENT REG. NO.	LAST KNOWN OPERATOR (OWNER)	STATUS	ORIGINAL MSN	LINE NO.	DEL. DATE	ENG. TYPE	FLEET NO.	PREV. REG. [COMMENTS]
B707-138 (B)	N792FA	FB AYER & ASSOCIATES	S	17701	60	09/04/59	JT3D-		VH-EBF, N792SA, D-ADAQ, TC-JBP [BU MZJ 10/93]
B707-436	G-APFB	BOEING	S	17703	35	05/09/60	CONWAY 508		N31241 [BU IGM 07/88; FORWARD FUSELAGE USED FOR E-3A TESTS AT RNT]
B707-436	G-APFC	BOEING	S	17704	101	05/16/60	CONWAY 508		N5088K [TESTED TO DESTRUCTION IGM 1976]
B707-436	N888NW	D & L AVIATION	S	17705	112	04/28/60	CONWAY 508		N5091K, G-APFD [BU FT. LAUDERDALE 08/86]
B707-436	G-APFF	BOEING	S	17707	127	05/13/60	CONWAY 508		[BU IGM 07/88]
B707-436	G-APFG	UK CIVIL AVIATION AUTHORITY	S	17708	128	06/23/60	CONWAY 508		N5094K [USED FOR FIRE SUPPRESSION TESTS, CARDINGTON 04/89; BU 1991]
B707-436	G-APFH	BOEING	S	17709	144	07/15/60	CONWAY 508		[BU MARANA 05/77]
B707-436	G-APFI	BOEING	S	17710	145	07/23/60	CONWAY 508		[BU IGM 1980]
B707-436	5X-CAU	UGANDA GOVERNMENT	S	17713	169	10/14/60	CONWAY 508		G-APFL, 9Q-CRW, N9194M [WFU 1/83; DERELICT AT ENTEBBE 01/95]
B707-436	G-APFM	BOEING	S	17714	170	11/05/60	CONWAY 508		[BU IGM 1980]
B707-436	G-APFN	BOEING	S	17715	171	11/16/60	CONWAY 508		[BU IGM 07/88]
B707-436 (ECX/E-6A)	G-APFO	BOEING	S	17716	175	12/09/60	CONWAY 508		[BU IGM 08/88]
B707-436	G-APFP	FRANKLIN INSTITUTE	S	17717	176	12/22/60	CONWAY 508		[PRESERVED 01/76, PHILADELPHIA; BU 10/88 DUE TO LACK OF SPACE]
B707-430 (F)	5A-CVA	UNITED AFRICAN AIRLINES	S	17719	106	03/10/60	CONWAY 508		D-ABOC, N64739, EI-BFN [DERELICT TRIPOLI 12/82]
B707-430	EL-AJC	BOURNEMOUTH FIRE SERVICE	S	17721	162	10/01/60	CONWAY 508		D-ABOF, 9G-ACK, N90498, 3C-ABI [WINGS REMOVED; USED FOR FIRE TRAINING]
B707-437	VT-DJK	AIR INDIA	S	17724	105	03/07/60	CONWAY 508		[BU BOMBAY 11/81]
B707-139 (B)	N778PA	BOEING	S	17903	108	05/13/60	JT3D-		N74613, TC-JBE, S2-AAL, 9G-ACJ, G-TJAA [BU DMAFB 10/92]
B707-441	N59RD	BLUE AIR	S	17905	114	06/07/60	CONWAY 508		N5090K, PP-VJA [BU HOUSTON 07/90]
B720-022	N7201U	AEROAMERICA	S	17907	85	10/01/60	JT3C-7		[BU LUTON 07/82]
B720-022	N7202U	AVIATION SALES CO.	S	17908	95	07/29/60	JT3C-7		[BU MSP 12/76]
B720-022	N7203U	AVIATION SALES CO.	S	17909	109	04/30/60	JT3C-7		[BU MSP 12/76]
B720-022	N7204U	AVIATION SALES CO.	S	17910	130	05/21/60	JT3C-7		[BU MSP 12/76]
B720-022	N7205U	AVIATION SALES CO.	S	17911	131	05/25/60	JT3C-7		[BU MSP 12/76]
B720-022	N7206U	AVIATION SALES CO.	S	17912	132	06/09/60	JT3C-7		[BU MSP 12/76]
B720-022	N7207U	MARSHALL M. LUNDY	S	17913	141	06/29/60	JT3C-7		[BU MIA 06/83]
B720-022	N7208U	AVIATION SALES CO.	S	17914	142	06/26/60	JT3C-7		[BU DEN 12/76]
B720-022	HI-372	AEROMAR AIRLINES	S	17915	146	07/27/60	JT3C-7		N7209U, N720CC [BU MIA 06/87]
B720-022	N7210U	AVIATION SALES CO.	S	17916	147	08/05/60	JT3C-7		[BU MSP 12/76]
B720-022	VP-HCP	BELIZE AIRWAYS	S	17917	148	08/13/60	JT3C-7		N7211U [BU MIA 02/83]
B707-328	F-BHSK	AIR FRANCE	S	17918	152	08/20/60	JT4A-		N5095K, N35674 [BU PARIS 09/77]
B707-328	F-BHSP	CHARLOTTE AIRCRAFT	S	17923	167	11/07/60	JT4A-		[BU MAXTON 1997; HULK STILL EXTANT]
B707-328	F-BHSQ	AIR FRANCE	S	17924	168	10/22/60	JT4A-		TU-TDC [BU PARIS 10/77]

A/C TYPE	CURRENT REG. NO.	LAST KNOWN OPERATOR (OWNER)	STATUS	ORIGINAL MSN	LINE NO.	DEL. DATE	ENG. TYPE	FLEET NO.	PREV. REG. [COMMENTS]
VC-137B	)58-6972	USAF	S	17927	47	06/30/59	JT3D-3B		[BU IAB 1996] (B707-153[B])
B707-344	N90651	COLUMBIA PICTURES	S	17928	134	07/01/60	JT4A-12		ZS-CKC, ZS-SAA, CC-CGM [DESTROYED IN MOVIE 1985]
B707-344	9Q-CZF	AIR REGION	S	17930	155	08/22/60	JT4A-12		ZS-CKE, ZS-SAC, LX-LGW, OO-SBW [BU KISANGANI 1987]
B720-023 (B)	4X-JYG	ISRAELI AIRCRAFT INDUSTRIES	S	18013	120	07/30/60	JT3D-1-MC7		N7527A, G-BCBB, 60-SAU, C9-ARG, 4R-ACS [CVTD -023; BU TLV 06/86; FUSELAGE ON DISPLAY AT HATZERIM]
B720-023 (B)	N341A	NATIONAL AIRCRAFT	S	18014	143	07/24/60	JT3D-1-MC7		N7528A, G-BCBA, P2-ANG, 4X-BMA [CVTD -023; BU TUS 11/91]
B720-023 (B)	N720AC	NATIONAL AIRCRAFT	S	18016	150	09/22/60	JT3D-1-MC7		N7530A, A6-HHR, 70-ACP [CVTD -023; BU ARIZONA 01/91]
B720-023 (B)	N1R	BOEING	S	18022	174	12/03/60	JT3D-1-MC7		N7536A [CVTD -023; HULK EXTANT AT DMAFB SINCE 04/83 (CZ067)]
B720-023B	HK-1973	MED-AIR INTL. SALES	S	18023	166	04/27/61	JT3D-1-MC7		N7537A [BU MIA 03/81]
B720-023B	OD-AFZ	MIDDLE EAST AIRLINES	S	18025	180	03/17/61	JT3D-1-MC7		N7539A [CVTD TO RESTAURANT NEAR BEIRUT]
B720-023B	C-FWXL	PRATT & WHITNEY CANADA	S	18027	189	02/27/61	JT3D-1-MC7		N7541A, OD-AFM [STD MHV; BEING BU FOR SPARES FOR MSN 18024]
B720-023B	HK-1974	BARRANQUILLA AIRPORT	S	18028	193	03/29/61	JT3D-1-MC7		N7542A [DERELICT AT BARRANQUILLA SINCE 06/80]
B720-023B	EL-AKD	AER RIANTA FIRE DEPT.	S	18030	195	04/10/61	JT3D-1-MC7		N7544A, OD-AFN [BU 9/96, SHANNON (FIN USED AS MONUMENT AT AIRPORT)]
B720-023B	60-SAX	SOMALI AIRLINES	S	18031	198	04/16/61	JT3D-1-MC7		N7545A [BU MOGADISHU 1985]
B720-023B (F)	N720BG	NATIONAL AIRCRAFT	S	18033	206	05/23/61	JT3D-1-MC7		N7547A, N780PA, N780EC, HC-AZO, HC-BDP [CVTD 023B; BU ARIZONA 08/91]
B720-023B	HC-AZP	COMMUNITY TRANSPORT INC.	S	18036	215	07/02/61	JT3D-1-MC7		N7550A, N781PA [BU MZJ 05/88]
B720-023B	N782PA	NATIONAL AIRCRAFT	S	18037	220	06/28/61	JT3D-1-MC7		N7551A, HC-AZQ [BU ARIZONA 1996]
B720-048	N1776Q	AEROAMERICA	S	18041	172	10/25/60	JT3C-7		EI-ALA, N7083, LN-TUU, N734T [BU BFI 11/83]
B720-048	N303AS	AEROAMERICA	S	18042	182	01/24/61	JT3C-7		EI-ALB, N7081 [BU BFI 09/80]
B720-022	VP-HCO	BELIZE AIRWAYS	S	18045	179	12/19/60	JT3C-7		N7213U [BU MIA 01/83]
B720-022	VP-HCM	BELIZE AIRWAYS	S	18046	183	01/14/61	JT3C-7		N7214U [BU MIA 03/83]
B720-022	N7215U	AVIATION SALES CO.	S	18047	184	01/27/61	JT3C-7		[BU DENVER 12/76]
B720-022	N7216U	HONG KONG GOVERNMENT	S	18048	185	02/02/61	JT3C-7		[DERELICT AT HONG KONG SINCE 09/80]
B720-022	N7218U	ONYX AVIATION	S	18050	191	03/06/61	JT3C-7		[BU MIA 12/83]
B707-123B	5B-DAO	OMEGA AIR	S	18054	140	05/25/61	JT3D-1-MC6		N7526A, G-BGCT, YN-CCN [DERELICT AT SNN SINCE 09/96]
B707-430	3C-ABH	ISRAELI AIRCRAFT INDUSTRIES	S	18056	192	03/17/61	CONWAY 508		D-ABOG, N9985F [GROUND TRAINER; TLV]
B720-030B	HK-677	AVIATION SALES CO.	S	18057	190	03/08/61	JT3D-1		D-ABOH, N783PA [BU ST PETERSBURG 04/81]

A/C TYPE	CURRENT REG. NO.	LAST KNOWN OPERATOR (OWNER)	STATUS	ORIGINAL MSN	LINE NO.	DEL. DATE	ENG. TYPE	FLEET NO.	PREV. REG. [COMMENTS]
B720-030B	N3831X	NATIONAL AIRCRAFT	S	18059	203	05/02/61	JT3D-1		D-ABOL, N784PA, HK-676 [BU ARIZONA 04/92; HULK EXTANT]
B720-030B	HK-2558	AEROTAL COLOMBIA	S	18060	210	06/03/61	JT3D-1		D-ABOM, N785PA, YA-HBA, N3746E [BU MIA 06/84]
B720-047B	AP-AXQ	PAKISTAN INTL.	S	18062	204	05/10/61	JT3D-3B		N93142 [DERELICT AT KHI SINCE 1974]
B720-047B	N110DS	BOEING	S	18063	213	06/07/61	JT3D-3B		N93143, 9H-AAK [HULK EXTANT AT DMAFB SINCE 08/89 (CZ165)]
B720-027	N736T	PACIFIC ALASKA AIRLINES	S	18064	187	02/11/61	JT3C-		N7076 [BU BFI 03/83]
B720-027	N734T	FIREHOUSE SIX	S	18065	196	03/22/61	JT3C-		N7077 [BU BFI 1984]
B720-027	N833NA	NASA	S	18066	208	05/12/61	JT3C-		N113, N23, N2697V [DESTROYED IN CONTROLLED CRASH AT EDWARDS AFB 12/01/84]
B707-138B	N245AC	NATIONAL AIRCRAFT	S	18068	227	08/16/61	JT3D-1		VH-EBI, N105BN, OE-IRA, OE-URA, SU-FAB [BU TUS 1991]
B707-458	4X-ATA	EL AL	S	18070	205	04/22/61	CONWAY 508		[BU 07/84; FUSELAGE AT TLV; COCKPIT ON DISPLAY IN USS INTREPID MUSEUM]
B720-022	VP-HCN	BELIZE AIRWAYS	S	18074	259	12/21/61	JT3C-7		N7221U [BU MIA 03/83]
B720-022	TF-VVB	KEFLAVIK FIRE DEPT.	S	18075	260	01/10/62	JT3C-7		N7222U [HULK USED FOR FIRE TRAINING AT KEFLAVIK SINCE 1982]
B720-022	VP-HCQ	BELIZE AIRWAYS	S	18076	261	01/17/62	JT3C-7		N7223U [BU MIA 04/83]
B720-022	N7224U	BOEING	S	18077	265	04/10/62	JT3C-7		[BU DMAFB 02/87]
B720-022	9Q-CTM	AIR CHARTER SERVICE	S	18078	267	04/24/62	JT3C-7		N7225U [BU FOR SPARES AT KINSHASA 12/89]
B720-022	N7226U	AVIATION SALES CO.	S	18079	278	05/08/62	JT3C-7		[BU MSP 12/76]
B720-022 (F)	N419MA	INDIAN GOVERNMENT	S	18082	298	06/12/62	JT3C-7		N7229U, TF-VVA [BU BOM 08/96]
B707-321	N432MA	JET POWER INC.	S	18083	209	05/16/61	JT4A-		N757PA, G-AYVE [BU MIA 07/83]
B707-321	TY-BBW	MR. W. GOVAERT	S	18084	212	05/23/61	JT4A-		N758PA, G-AYRZ, VP-BDG, C6-BDG, N433MA, N707HD, TY-AAM [BU 07/96 OSTEND; RESTAURANT AT WETTEREN, BELGIUM]
B707-321	VP-BDF	SOUTHEAST AVIATION ENTHUSIASTS	S	18085	217	06/13/61	JT4A-		N759PA, G-AYAG, G-41-372, N435MA [BU DUBLIN 07/84; NOSE TO WATERFORD]
B720-059B	N4451B	LEASEWAY INTL.	S	18086	245	11/08/61	JT3D-		HK-724 [BU MIAMI BY BMI 1989]
B720-027	N730T	AEROAMERICA	S	18154	226	08/09/61	JT3C-		N7078 [BU BFI 1988]
B720-025	OO-TEA	TRANS EUROPEAN AIRWAYS	S	18155	225	08/14/61	JT3C-7		N8701E [BU SNN 08/80]
B720-025	N10VG	AMBASSADOR	S	18156	232	08/25/61	JT3C-7		N8702E [BU MIA 01/80]
B720-025	N3124Z	PACIFIC AERO SUPPORT	S	18157	233	02/02/62	JT3C-7		N8703E, OY-DSK [BU LUTON 1987]
B720-025	N40102	BOEING	S	18158	234	09/20/61	JT3C-7		N8704E, LN-TUW, N3183B [BU IGM 07/88]
B720-025	OY-DSM	CONAIR OF SCANDINAVIA	S	18161	239	10/17/61	JT3C-7		N8707E [BU COPENHAGEN 07/84]
B720-025	9Q-CTD	NEW ACS	S	18162	240	11/08/61	JT3C-7		N8708E, D-ACIP, VP-YNL, Z-YNL [BEING BU KINSHASA]

A/C TYPE	CURRENT REG. NO.	LAST KNOWN OPERATOR (OWNER)	STATUS	ORIGINAL MSN	LINE NO.	DEL. DATE	ENG. TYPE	FLEET NO.	PREV. REG. [COMMENTS]
B720-025	TF-VLA	EAGLE AIR	S	18163	241	10/23/61	JT3C-7		N8709E, D-ACIQ, N15VG, TF-VVE [BU KEFLAVIK 01/79; FUSELAGE EXTANT]
B720-025	HL7403	BOEING	S	18164	242	10/23/61	JT3C-7		N8710E [BU KINGMAN 1982]
B720-068B	N2628Y	SONICO INC.	S	18165	250	12/20/61	JT3D-		N93136, HZ-ACA [BU MOSES LAKE 10/82]
B720-068B	HZ-ACB	BOEING	S	18166	251	12/20/61	JT3D-		[BU VAN NUYS 06/83]
B720-047B	N210DS	AAR ALLEN AIRCRAFT CORP.	S	18167	221	07/11/61	JT3D-3B		N93144, 9H-AAL [BU MZJ 07/88]
B720-025	N8711E	AEROTOURS DOMINICANA	S	18240	246	01/09/62	JT3C-7		D-ACIR [BU PORT-AU-PRINCE 03/99]
B720-025	OY-DSP	DANISH AVIATION MUSEUM	S	18241	247	11/13/61	JT3C-7		N8712E [BU CPH]
B720-025	Z-YNM	AIR ZIMBABWE	S	18242	248	11/22/61	JT3C-7		N8713E, D-ACIS, VP-YNM [WFU; FUSELAGE USED AS CABIN TRAINER HARARE 06/84]
B720-025	Z-YNN	AIR CHARTER SERVICE	S	18244	255	12/16/61	JT3C-7		N8715E, D-ACIT, VP-YNN [BU HARARE; FUSELAGE USED FOR CABIN STAFF TRAINING]
B707-328	F-BHSR	AIR FRANCE	S	18245	264	02/01/62	JT4A-		N93138, TU-TDB [BU ORY 04/77; FORWARD FUSELAGE ON DISPLAY]
B707-328	4X-JYK	ISRAELI AIR FORCE	S	18246	269	02/16/62	JT4A-	118	F-BHSS, 4X-BYK [TO BECOME A RESTAURANT ELIFELET; SOLD BY IAI 1993]
B720-030B	N720BC	NATIONAL AIRCRAFT	S	18251	273	02/26/62	JT3D-3B		D-ABOR, N788PA, JY-ADT, 9L-LAZ [BU ARIZONA 1991]
B707-321B	N4605D	E-SYSTEMS INC.	S	18335	268	06/15/62	JT3D-3B		N760PA, RP-C7076 [BU TPE 08/85]
B707-321B	N944JW	BOEING	S	18336	270	06/13/62	JT3D-3B		N761PA, RP-C7075 [HULK EXTANT DMAFB SINCE 05/86 (CZ149)]
B707-321B	N762TB	AVIATION SYSTEMS INTL.	S	18337	276	04/12/62	JT3D-3B		N762PA, HL7430 [BU MZJ 10/85]
B707-321B	HZ-TAS	OMEGA AIR	S	18338	287	06/01/62	JT3D-3B		N763PA, N763W, N111MF, N98WS [BU MSE 05/94]
B707-321B	N897WA	BOEING	S	18339	292	06/01/62	JT3D-3B		N764PA, N764SE, OE-IEB [HULK EXTANT AT DMAFB SINCE 09/89 (CZ172)]
B720-051B	SX-DBG	CLUB 720	S	18352	218	06/22/61	JT3D-3B		N722US [WFU AND STD ATHENS 01/80; LATER BU AND USED AS BAR/RESTAURANT AT THRAKOMAKEDONES]
B720-051B	SX-DBH	OMEGA AIR	S	18353	219	07/11/61	JT3D-3B		N723US [BU ATH 1985]
B720-051B	SX-DBI	OMEGA AIR	S	18355	231	08/31/61	JT3D-3B		N725US [BU SNN 07/85]
B720-051B	SX-DBK	OMEGA AIR	S	18356	238	10/05/61	JT3D-3B		N726US [WFU AND STD ATHENS 01/80; LATER BU AND USED AS BAR/RESTAURANT AT ARCAIA]
B707-465	G-ARWD	BOEING	S	18372	271	02/27/62	CONWAY 508		VR-BBW [BU IGM 1983]
B707-328	N707RZ	DELTA INTL. SALES	S	18375	293	05/11/62	JT4A-		F-BHSU, CN-RMA [BU FLL 04/85]
B720-062	N301AS	AVIATION SALES	S	18376	279	03/23/62	JT3C-		N720V [BU MIA 01/84]
B720-062	N302AS	AEROAMERICA	S	18377	285	04/18/62	JT3C-		N720W [BU TEMPELHOF 11/76]
B720-040B	9H-AAM	MALTA FIRE DEPT.	S	18378	257	12/21/61	JT3D-3B		AP-AMG [USED FOR FIRE PRACTICE, THEN BU AT MALTA 1997]

A/C TYPE	CURRENT REG. NO.	LAST KNOWN OPERATOR (OWNER)	STATUS	ORIGINAL MSN	LINE NO.	DEL. DATE	ENG. TYPE	FLEET NO.	PREV. REG. [COMMENTS]
B720-040B	N5487N	BOEING	S	18380	324	11/29/62	JT3D-3B		AP-AMJ, 9H-AAN [BU ARIZONA 1991]
B720-051B	N2464C	BOEING	S	18381	222	07/23/61	JT3D-3B		N791TW, N730US, G-AZFB [BU ARIZONA 10/90]
B720-051B	N2464K	NATIONAL AIRCRAFT	S	18382	223	08/02/61	JT3D-3B		N792TW, N731US, G-AZKM [BU TUS 06/91]
B720-051B	N24666	NATIONAL AIRCRAFT	S	18383	230	08/27/61	JT3D-3B		N793TW, N732US, G-AZNX [BU ARIZONA 10/90]
B707-131B	N746TW	NATIONAL AIRCRAFT	S	18385	277	03/29/62	JT3D-		[BU ARIZONA 05/82]
B707-131B	N747TW	NATIONAL AIRCRAFT	S	18386	280	04/10/62	JT3D-		[BU ARIZONA 05/92]
B707-131B	N748TW	NATIONAL AIRCRAFT	S	18387	286	04/30/62	JT3D-		[BU ARIZONA 04/92]
B707-131B	N749TW	NATIONAL AIRCRAFT	S	18388	291	05/18/62	JT3D-		[BU ARIZONA 1988]
B707-131B	N750TW	NATIONAL AIRCRAFT	S	18389	294	05/23/62	JT3D-		[BU TUS 05/91]
B707-131B	N752TW	BOEING	S	18391	299	06/16/62	JT3D-		[HULK EXTANT AT DMAFB SINCE 04/82 (CZ025)]
B707-131B	N754TW	BOEING	S	18392	301	06/28/62	JT3D-		[BU DMAFB 04/93]
B707-131B	N755TW	NATIONAL AIRCRAFT	S	18393	306	07/23/62	JT3D-		[BU ARIZONA 04/92]
B707-131B	N756TW	BOEING	S	18394	308	08/02/62	JT3D-		[HULK EXTANT AT DMAFB SINCE 04/82 (CZ018)]
B707-131B	N758TW	BOEING	S	18396	311	08/21/62	JT3D-		[HULK EXTANT AT DMAFB SINCE 04/82 (CZ019)]
B707-131B	N759TW	NATIONAL AIRCRAFT	S	18397	312	08/29/62	JT3D-		[BU ARIZONA 12/90]
B707-131B	N781TW	NATIONAL AIRCRAFT	S	18400	313	08/31/62	JT3D-		[BU TUS 02/92]
B707-131B	N782TW	NATIONAL AIRCRAFT	S	18401	315	09/21/62	JT3D-		[BU ARIZONA 1989]
B707-131B	N783TW	NATIONAL AIRCRAFT	S	18402	316	09/26/62	JT3D-		[BU ARIZONA 12/90]
B707-131B	N784TW	BOEING	S	18403	317	09/28/62	JT3D-		[HULK EXTANT AT DMAFB SINCE 04/82 (CZ022)]
B707-131B	N785TW	BOEING	S	18404	318	10/12/62	JT3D-		[BU TUS 1990]
B707-331B	N773TW	BOEING	S	18405	305	03/11/63	JT3D-3B		[HULK EXTANT AT DMAFB SINCE 10/83 (CZ083)]
B707-331B	N774TW	BOEING	S	18406	320	11/01/62	JT3D-3B		[HULK EXTANT AT DMAFB SINCE 12/83 (CZ090)]
B707-331B	52-6314	USAF	S	18407	323	12/03/62	JT3D-3B		N775TW [HULK EXTANT AT DMAFB SINCE 05/84 (CZ109); FORWARD FUSELAGE USED FOR SECURITY POLICE DOG TRAINING]
B707-331B	N28714	BOEING	S	18408	326	01/23/63	JT3D-3B		N776TW [REBUILT AFTER 1969 BOMB EXPLOSION; HULK EXTANT AT DMAFB SINCE 12/83 (CZ089)]
B707-331B	N778TW	BOEING	S	18409	331	02/21/63	JT3D-3B		[HULK EXTANT AT DMAFB SINCE 04/84 (CZ102)]
B707-436	G-ARRB	BOEING	S	18412	330	02/12/63	CONWAY 508		[BU KINGMAN 09/80]
B707-436	9Q-CTK	NEW ACS	S	18413	334	03/15/63	CONWAY 508		G-ARRC, N4465C [BU KINSHASA 04/95; SOME PIECES EXTANT]
B707-437	VT-DNY	AIR INDIA	S	18414	275	03/07/62	CONWAY 508		[BU BOMBAY 1982]
B707-437	VT-DNZ	AIR INDIA	S	18415	282	04/12/62	CONWAY 508		[BU BOMBAY 1987]
B720-024B	N57201	AAR ALLEN AIRCRAFT	S	18416	288	04/30/62	JT3D-3B		[BU MIA 1977]
B720-024B	N550DS	BOEING	S	18417	295	05/27/62	JT3D-3B		N57202, ET-AFK [HULK EXTANT AT DMAFB SINCE 08/89 (CZ164)]
B720-024B	N769BE	NATIONAL AIRCRAFT	S	18418	300	06/20/62	JT3D-3B		N57203, ET-AFA [BU ARIZONA 10/90]
B720-024B	N770BE	NATIONAL AIRCRAFT	S	18419	304	07/09/62	JT3D-3B		N57204, ET-AFB [BU ARIZONA 01/91]

A/C TYPE	CURRENT REG. NO.	LAST KNOWN OPERATOR (OWNER)	STATUS	ORIGINAL MSN	LINE NO.	DEL. DATE	ENG. TYPE	FLEET NO.	PREV. REG. [COMMENTS]
B720-051B	SX-DBL	OMEGA AIR	S	18420	243	10/25/61	JT3D-3B		N727US [BU ATH 1985]
B720-051B	TF-AYC	BOEING	S	18421	244	11/15/61	JT3D-3B		N728US, OY-APY, G-BHGE [HULK EXTANT AT DMAFB SINCE 07/87 (CZ159)]
B720-051B	TF-AYB	NATIONAL AIRCRAFT	S	18422	256	12/13/61	JT3D-3B		N729US, OY-APW [BU ARIZONA 12/90]
B720-027	N321E	REEMER AVIATION	S	18423	289	05/10/62	JT3C-		N7079M, N731T [BU BOU 04/82]
B720-058B (F)	N8498S	USAF	S	18424	281	06/23/62	JT3D-3B		4X-ABA [CVTD -058B; BU DMAFB 1985]
B720-058B	N4228G	NATIONAL AIRCRAFT	S	18425	290	04/30/62	JT3D-3B		4X-ABB, N8498T [BU ARIZONA 07/91]
B720-047B	N92GS	BLUE METALS INC.	S	18452	310	08/08/62	JT3D-3B		N93146 [BU MIA 09/98]
B720-060B	N330DS	TUCSON IRON & METAL	S	18455	322	11/30/62	JT3D-3B		ET-AAH [BU ARIZONA 05/96]
B707-328B	4X-ATE	TEAMCO	S	18456	325	12/15/62	JT3D-3B		F-BHSV [BU BRU 11/89]
B707-328B	F-BHSX	CARGOLUX	S	18457	327	01/17/63	JT3D-3B		TU-TXA, TU-TXB [BU LUX 06/84]
B707-328B	F-BHSY	CARGOLUX	S	18458	329	02/17/63	JT3D-3B		TU-TXF, TU-TXJ [BU LUX 11/83]
B720-027	N733T	AEROAMERICA	S	18581	347	08/22/63	JT3C-		N7080 [BU BFI 01/82]
B707-373C	D2-TOG	NASCO LEASING	S	18583	346	08/20/63	JT3D-3B		N374WA, HZ-ACF, D2-TAG [BU MSE 02/93]
B707-351B	G-BFBZ	TRADAN ASSOCIATION	S	18585	343	06/19/63	JT3D-3B		N352US, VR-HGI [BU LASHAM 11/88]
B720-024B	N57205	AAR ALLEN AIRCRAFT	S	18587	340	05/11/63	JT3D-3B		[BU FOR SPARES 1977]
B720-047B	5Y-BBX	KENYA AIRWAYS	S	18588	337	04/03/63	JT3D-3B		N93148 [GROUND TRAINER NAIROBI; LESS WINGS AND TAIL]
B720-047B	AP-BAF	PAKISTAN INTL.	S	18589	338	04/24/63	JT3D-3B		N93149 [BU KHI 1983]
B707-321C	LV-MSG	TRANSPORTES AEREO RIOPLATENSE	S	18591	341	06/07/63	JT3D-3B		N767PA, G-BEAF [BU BUE 10/96]
B707-328B	F-BLCA	TRATCO	S	18685	359	01/13/64	JT3D-3B		3X-GCC, 3X-GCA [BU LUX 11/83]
B707-328B	N83658	NATIONAL AIRCRAFT	S	18686	360	01/30/64	JT3D-3B		F-BLCB, TU-TXI, TU-TXM, 5R-MFK, F-BLLB, 5A-DLT, SU-DAJ [BU ARIZONA 04/91]
B720-051B	SX-DBM	OMEGA AIR	S	18687	351	10/22/63	JT3D-3B		N734US [BU ATH 1985]
B720-051B	N8215Q	BOEING	S	18688	361	01/23/64	JT3D-3B		N735US, SX-DBN, YN-BYI, G-BRDR [HULK EXTANT AT DMAFB SINCE 11/89 (CZ174)]
B707-323C	G-SAIL	BOEING	S	18690	356	12/13/63	JT3D-3B		N7556A [HULK EXTANT AT DMAFB SINCE 04/86 (CZ147)]
B707-323C	G-BFEO	BOEING	S	18691	357	12/20/63	JT3D-3B		N7557A, 5X-UWM [HULK EXTANT AT DMAFB SINCE 04/86 (CZ146)]
B707-351B	G-BFBS	MIDAIR	S	18693	348	09/09/63	JT3D-3B		N354US, VR-HGN [BU LASHAM 1987]
B707-441	9Q-CMD	BLUE AIRLINES	S	18694	353	11/12/63	CONWAY 508		PP-VJJ, N58RD [WFU GOMA 05/93 FOR SPARES-VERY DERELICT]
B707-337B	N8880A	BOEING	S	18708	375	05/25/64	JT3D-3B/7		VT-DPM, TF-IUE [HULK EXTANT AT DMAFB SINCE 10/89 (CZ173)]
B707-373C	HC-BLY	SAETA	S	18709	350	11/18/63	JT3D-3B (HK)		N789TW, HK-2606, HP-1027 [BU UIO 04/95; COCKPIT REMAINS EXTANT 08/95]
B707-351B	B-1828	AAR ALLEN AIRCRAFT	S	18710	352	10/13/63	JT3D-3B		N355US, G-BCLZ [BU TPE 06/85]
B707-321C	HK-3333X	TAMPA COLOMBIA (COMTRAN)	S	18714	362	02/27/64	JT3D-3B (HK2)		N790PA, HK-1718X, TF-AEA, N228VV [BU BY TAMPA 12/00]

A/C TYPE	CURRENT REG. NO.	LAST KNOWN OPERATOR (OWNER)	STATUS	ORIGINAL MSN	LINE NO.	DEL. DATE	ENG. TYPE	FLEET NO.	PREV. REG. [COMMENTS]
B707-138B	N46D	OMEGA AIR	S	18739	385	08/19/64	JT3D-		VH-EBL, N107BN, PK-MBA [BU SNN 1993]
B720-040B	AP-ATQ	ATASCO LEASING	S	18745	380	04/28/65	JT3D-3B		N68646 [BU TLV 04/86]
B707-331C	N5791	BOEING	S	18756	383	08/06/64	JT3D-3B		N791TW [BU DMAFB 1985]
B707-131B	N795TW	BOEING	S	18758	391	10/29/64	JT3D-		[HULK EXTANT AT DMAFB SINCE 02/83 (CZ054)]
B707-131B	N796TW	NATIONAL AIRCRAFT	S	18759	392	11/13/64	JT3D-		[BU ARIZONA 05/91]
B707-131B	N798TW	NATIONAL AIRCRAFT	S	18761	395	12/31/64	JT3D-		[BU ARIZONA 04/92]
B707-131B	N799TW	BOB'S AIR PARK	S	18762	396	12/23/64	JT3D-		[BU ARIZONA 1990]
B720-024B	N57206	AAR ALLEN AIRCRAFT	S	18763	382	07/23/64	JT3D-3B		[BU 1976]
B707-331B	N779TW	BOEING	S	18764	399	01/15/65	JT3D-3B		[HULK EXTANT AT DMAFB SINCE 12/83 (CZ085)]
B707-321C	CX-BSB	TRANSCONTINENTAL SUR (RACE)	S	18766	372	05/09/64	JT3D-3B (HK2)		N796PA, HK-1849, N865BX, HR-AMZ, P4-CCG [BU FOR PARTS MVD]
B720-051B	N92038	BOEING	S	18792	381	06/26/64	JT3D-3B		N736US, OY-APU, G-BBZG, TF-AYA [HULK EXTANT AT DMAFB SINCE 05/87 (CZ155)]
B720-051B	N771BE	BOEING	S	18793	384	04/27/64	JT3D-3B		N737US, OY-APV, TF-AYD [BU PAE 02/92]
B707-338C	SU-BBA	KAMAL EL GOHARY	S	18810	438	08/11/65	JT3D-3B		VH-EBP, N14791 [USED AS "THE PLANE" RESTAURANT AT CAIRO AIRPORT SINCE 1993]
B707-330B	5Y-AXM	AFRICAN AIRLINES INTL.	S	18819	398	01/10/65	JT3D-7 (HK)		D-ABOX, VP-WKR, Z-WKR [DERELICT AT NAIROBI LESS ENGINE SINCE 1996]
B720-047B	TF-VLC	AER LINGUS	S	18820	401	01/21/65	JT3D-3B		N93153 [BU STANSTED 05/81]
B720-047B	TF-VLB	(ILFC)	S	18827	410	03/10/65	JT3D-3B		N3154 [BU SNN; HULK EXTANT SINCE 08/83]
B720-047B	CX-BQG	BOEING	S	18829	427	06/02/65	JT3D-3B		N3156, 9H-AAO [HULK EXTANT AT DMAFB SINCE 08/90 (CZ181)]
B720-047B	OD-AGF	MIDDLE EAST AIRLINES	S	18830	429	06/17/65	JT3D-3B		N3157 [SOLD LESS ENGINES; TO BE CVTD TO RESTAURANT AT BEIRUT BUT DBF]
B720-059B	N4450Z	NATIONAL AIRCRAFT	S	18831	414	04/08/65	JT3D-		HK-726 [BU ARIZONA 03/91]
B707-321B	5X-JCR	BOEING	S	18832	403	02/05/65	JT3D-3B		N401PA, EI-BKO, VN-A305, VN-B1416, VN-81416 [HULK EXTANT AT DMAFB SINCE 12/89 (CZ175)]
B707-321B	N402PA	BOEING	S	18833	405	02/17/65	JT3D-3B		[HULK EXTANT AT DMAFB SINCE 05/86 (CZ148)]
B707-321B	N5519V	BOEING	S	18834	406	02/24/65	JT3D-3B		N403PA, TC-JBS [HULK EXTANT AT DMAFB SINCE 01/86 (CZ140)]
B707-321B	N5519U	BOEING	S	18836	409	03/10/65	JT3D-3B		N405PA, TC-JBT [HULK EXTANT AT DMAFB SINCE 12/85 (CZ139)]
B707-321B	XT-BBH	BOEING	S	18837	411	03/17/65	JT3D-3B		N406PA, F-OGIV, F-BSGT, XT-ABZ [HULK EXTANT AT DMAFB SINCE 10/90 (CZ185)]
B707-321B	N707GE	BOEING	S	18840	418	04/21/65	JT3D-3B		N409PA, F-OGIW [HULK EXTANT AT DMAFB SINCE 04/84 (CZ107)]
B707-321B	N5517Z	BOEING	S	18842	421	05/21/65	JT3D-3B		N412PA, TC-JBU [BU ARIZONA; HULK MOVED TO HSV 06/87]
B707-337B	N8870A	BOEING	S	18873	402	03/12/65	JT3D-3B/7		N68655, VT-DSI, EL-AJS [HULK EXTANT AT DMAFB SINCE 09/89 (CZ170)]

A/C TYPE	CURRENT REG. NO.	LAST KNOWN OPERATOR (OWNER)	STATUS	ORIGINAL MSN	LINE NO.	DEL. DATE	ENG. TYPE	FLEET NO.	PREV. REG. [COMMENTS]
B707-123B	N7550A	BOEING	S	18882	420	05/27/65	JT3D-1-MC6		[HULK EXTANT AT DMAFB SINCE 09/81 (CZ011)]
B707-123B	N7551A	NATIONAL AIRCRAFT	S	18883	422	05/26/65	JT3D-1-MC6		[BU ARIZONA 1990]
B707-123B	N7552A	NATIONAL AIRCRAFT	S	18884	426	06/15/65	JT3D-1-MC6		[BU ARIZONA 1994]
B707-123B	N7553A	PIMA COMMUNITY COLLEGE	S	18885	432	07/23/65	JT3D-1-MC6		[HULK USED FOR TRAINING SINCE 05/91]
B707-344B	EL-AJT	OMEGA AIR	S	18891	441	08/27/65	JT3D-7 (HK)		ZS-DYL, ZS-SAD, LX-LGR, VP-WKW, 3B-NAE [BU AT MSE 02/97]
B707-331B	N760TW	BOEING	S	18913	400	01/29/65	JT3D-3B		[HULK EXTANT AT DMAFB SINCE 12/83 (CZ091)]
B707-331B	N780TW	BOEING	S	18914	415	04/09/65	JT3D-3B		[HULK EXTANT AT DMAFB SINCE 05/84 (CZ110); FORWARD FUSELAGE USED FOR SECURITY POLICE DOG TRAINING]
B707-331B	N793TW	BOEING	S	18915	424	05/25/65	JT3D-3B		[HULK EXTANT AT DMAFB SINCE 05/84 (CZ111); FORWARD FUSELAGE USED FOR SECURITY POLICE DOG TRAINING]
B707-331B	N8705T	BOEING	S	18916	455	12/10/65	JT3D-3B		[HULK EXTANT AT DMAFB SINCE 12/83 (CZ087)]
B707-331B	N8725T	BOEING	S	18918	462	01/12/66	JT3D-3B		[HULK EXTANT AT DMAFB SINCE 12/83 (CZ093)]
B707-336C	PP-BRB	BRAZILIAN AIR FORCE	S	18925	452	12/19/66	JT3D-3B (HK)		G-ASZG, LX-FCV, XT-ABX, EL-AKI [BU GIG]
B707-330B	ST-NSR	SUDAN AIRWAYS	S	18931	482	03/27/66	JT3D-3B		D-ABUK, A6-UAE [BU KHARTOUM 03/95]
B707-338C	N342A	BOEING	S	18953	443	09/14/65	JT3D-3B		VH-EBQ, 9M-ASQ, 9M-MCQ, 60-SBM [HULK EXTANT AT DMAFB SINCE 04/86 (CZ145)]
B707-338C	N449J	NATIONAL AIRCRAFT	S	18954	458	12/28/65	JT3D-3B		VH-EBR, 9M-ATR, 9M-MCR, 60-SBN, G-BMJE [BU ARIZONA 02/92; HULK EXTANT AT NATIONAL]
B707-321B	N414PA	AIR CARRIER SUPPLY	S	18956	466	01/29/66	JT3D-3B		[BU MIAMI 03/81; COCKPIT USED AS SIMULATOR]
B707-321B	N418PA	ISRAELI AIRCRAFT INDUSTRIES	S	18960	484	04/07/66	JT3D-3B		[ON FIRE DUMP TLV; NOSE SECTION AT WEEKS MUSEUM, TAMIAMI, FL]
B707-382B (TC-18F)	165342	U.S. NAVY	S	18961	456	12/16/65	JT3D-3B		CS-TBA, N45RT [E-6A TRAINER; BU]
B707-351C	D2-TOU	NASCO LEASING	S	18964	453	11/15/65	JT3D-3B		N363US, VR-HGQ, TF-VLP, 5A-DJS, 5Y-BFB [ON FIRE DUMP AT MSE 4/97]
B720-060B	N7381	RAYTHEON COMPANY	S	18977	442	09/20/65	JT3D-3B		ET-ABP, N440DS [BU MHV]
B707-331B	N18702	BOEING	S	18979	468	02/03/66	JT3D-3B		[BU ARIZONA; HULK MOVED TO HSV FOR TESTS]
B707-331B	N18703	BOEING	S	18980	469	02/05/66	JT3D-3B		[HULK EXTANT AT DMAFB SINCE 10/83 (CZ081)]
B707-331B	N18704	BOEING	S	18981	476	03/05/66	JT3D-3B		[HULK EXTANT AT DMAFB SINCE 12/83 (CZ092)]
B707-331B	N18706	BOEING	S	18982	483	04/04/66	JT3D-3B		[HULK EXTANT AT DMAFB SINCE 10/83 (CZ082)]
B707-331B	N18707	BOEING	S	18983	485	04/15/66	JT3D-3B		[HULK EXTANT AT DMAFB SINCE 02/84 (CZ094)]
B707-331B	N18708	BOEING	S	18984	487	04/20/66	JT3D-3B		[HULK EXTANT AT DMAFB SINCE 12/83 (CZ086)]
B707-331B	N707HP	BOEING	S	18985	496	05/21/66	JT3D-3B		N18709, 4X-ATD [HULK EXTANT AT DMAFB SINCE 08/89 (CZ166)]
B707-131B	N6720	NATIONAL AIRCRAFT	S	18986	479	03/25/66	JT3D-		[BU ARIZONA 1989]
B707-131B	N6721	NATIONAL AIRCRAFT	S	18987	486	04/16/66	JT3D-		[BU ARIZONA 06/91]
B707-131B	N6722	NATIONAL AIRCRAFT	S	18988	489	04/28/66	JT3D-		[BU ARIZONA 04/92]
B707-131B	N6723	NATIONAL AIRCRAFT	S	18989	492	05/06/66	JT3D-		[BU ARIZONA 04/92]
B707-373C	AP-AWU	PAKISTAN INTL.	S	18991	450	10/22/65	JT3D-3B (HK)		N376WA [BU FOR SPARES KHI 12/93]

A/C TYPE	CURRENT REG. NO.	LAST KNOWN OPERATOR (OWNER)	STATUS	ORIGINAL MSN	LINE NO.	DEL. DATE	ENG. TYPE	FLEET NO.	PREV. REG. [COMMENTS]
B720-024B	N17207	AAR ALLEN AIRCRAFT	S	19002	473	02/16/66	JT3D-3B		[BU 03/76]
B720-024B	N17208	AAR ALLEN AIRCRAFT	S	19003	474	02/19/66	JT3D-3B		[BU BFI 1984]
B707-358B	N53302	BOEING	S	19004	459	01/07/66	JT3D-3B		4X-ATR, N317F [STD DMAFB SINCE 09/89 (CZ171)]
B707-351C	RP-C1886	BOEING	S	19034	463	01/08/66	JT3D-3B		N364US, VR-HGU [HULK EXTANT AT DMAFB SINCE 12/85 (CZ138)]
B707-344B	N6598W	BOEING	S	19133	538	01/09/67	JT3D-7		ZS-EKV, ZS-SAE, LX-LGU, 3B-NAF, N237G, TF-IUC, 5Y-AXS, 5Y-LKL [HULK EXTANT AT DMAFB SINCE 10/90 (CZ183)]
B707-351C	N65010	BOEING	S	19163	494	05/17/66	JT3D-3B		N365US, SX-DBP [STD DMAFB SINCE 08/90 (CZ179)]
B707-324C	B-1830	AAR ALLEN AIRCRAFT	S	19178	517	08/23/66	JT3D-3B		N17326 [BU TPE 06/85]
B707-123B	N7554A	NATIONAL AIRCRAFT	S	19185	490	04/30/66	JT3D-1-MC6		[BU ARIZONA 1990]
B707-123B	N7570A	NATIONAL AIRCRAFT	S	19186	491	05/04/66	JT3D-1-MC6		[BU ARIZONA 05/92]
B707-123B	N7571A	BOEING	S	19187	493	05/12/66	JT3D-1-MC6		[HULK EXTANT AT DMAFB SINCE 09/81 (CZ010)]
B707-123B	N7572A	NATIONAL AIRCRAFT	S	19188	506	06/30/66	JT3D-1-MC6		[BU TUCSON 1990]
B720-047B	N3161	NATIONAL AIRCRAFT	S	19207	512	07/29/66	JT3D-3B		[BU TUCSON 07/91; HULK EXTANT AT NATIONAL]
B720-047B	N3162	BOEING	S	19208	514	07/29/66	JT3D-3B		[HULK EXTANT AT DMAFB SINCE 04/83 (CZ062)]
B707-331C	N730FW	(JETLEASE)	S	19212	588	06/18/67	JT3D-3B (HK)		N5771T, EI-BER, LX-FCV, CX-BJV, LX-BJV, 5A-DKA, 9G-ACY, 9G-MAN, N227VV, N851MA [BU MIA BY BMI 11/95]
B707-131B	N6724	BOB'S AIR PARK	S	19215	530	11/12/66	JT3D-		[BU ARIZONA 1991]
B707-131B	N6726	NATIONAL AIRCRAFT	S	19216	558	03/08/67	JT3D-		[BU ARIZONA 10/90]
B707-131B	N6727	NATIONAL AIRCRAFT	S	19217	564	04/02/67	JT3D-		[BU ARIZONA 06/91; NOSE SECTION IN MEXICAN MUSEUM SINCE 1986(?)]
B707-131B	N6728	BOEING	S	19218	567	03/29/67	JT3D-		[HULK EXTANT AT DMAFB SINCE 09/82 (CZ043)]
B707-131B	N6729	NATIONAL AIRCRAFT	S	19219	569	04/14/67	JT3D-		[BU ARIZONA 02/92]
B707-131B	N6763T	NATIONAL AIRCRAFT	S	19220	573	04/22/67	JT3D-		[BU ARIZONA 04/91]
B707-131B	N6764T	NATIONAL AIRCRAFT	S	19221	577	05/13/67	JT3D-		[BU ARIZONA 05/91]
B707-131B	N6771T	NATIONAL AIRCRAFT	S	19222	583	05/27/67	JT3D-		[BU ARIZONA 06/91]
B707-131B	N6789T	BOEING	S	19223	598	07/13/67	JT3D-		[HULK EXTANT AT DMAFB SINCE 05/82 (CZ027)]
B707-331B	52-6317	USAF	S	19224	559	03/15/67	JT3D-3B		N18710 [HULK EXTANT AT DMAFB SINCE 04/84 (CZ104); FORWARD FUSELAGE USED FOR SECURITY POLICE DOG TRAINING]
B707-331B	N18711	BOEING	S	19225	568	04/04/67	JT3D-3B		[HULK EXTANT AT DMAFB SINCE 06/84 (CZ112)]
B707-331B	N18712	USAF	S	19226	585	05/31/67	JT3D-3B		[HULK EXTANT AT DMAFB SINCE 04/84 (CZ108); REMAINS USED FOR AIRCRAFT BATTLE DAMAGE REPAIR TRAINING]
B707-331B	N18713	BOEING	S	19227	607	08/06/67	JT3D-3B		[HULK EXTANT AT DMAFB SINCE 04/84 (CZ105)]
B707-323C (C-18A)	81-0897	USAF	S	19236	521	09/28/66	JT3D-3B		N7563A [BU FOR SPARES GREENVILLE, TX 1986; FUSELAGE EXTANT]
B707-323C	N7564A	NATIONAL AIRCRAFT	S	19237	523	09/30/66	JT3D-3B		[BU 1997; FORWARD FUSELAGE HULK EXTANT AT NATIONAL]

A/C TYPE	CURRENT REG. NO.	LAST KNOWN OPERATOR (OWNER)	STATUS	ORIGINAL MSN	LINE NO.	DEL. DATE	ENG. TYPE	FLEET NO.	PREV. REG. [COMMENTS]
B707-387B	CX-BNU	BRAZILIAN AIR FORCE	S	19239	542	12/16/66	JT3D-3B (HK)		LV-ISB [HULK EXTANT AT RIO DE JANEIRO SINCE 09/96]
B707-387B	LV-ISC	AEROLINEAS ARGENTINAS	S	19240	543	12/22/66	JT3D-3B		CX-BOH [BU FOR SPARES EZE 02/93]
B707-337B	N8840A	BOEING	S	19247	520	10/12/66	JT3D-3B/7		VT-DVA, EL-AJR [HULK EXTANT AT DMAFB SINCE 09/89 (CZ169)]
B707-351C	N720FW	LONSDALE JET	S	19263	516	08/19/66	JT3D-3B (HK)		N370US, 9J-AEB, EI-ASM, 5N-AOO [PARTIALLY BU MIA BY BMI 03/08/98]
B707-321B	HC-BCT	AECA	S	19265	529	11/09/66	JT3D-3B		N420PA [BU GYE 1997]
B707-321B	9Q-CBL	BOEING	S	19266	531	11/29/66	JT3D-3B		N421PA, HK-2070X [HULK EXTANT AT DMAFB SINCE 10/90 (CZ184)]
B707-321B	N422PA	(IALI)	S	19275	590	06/28/67	JT3D-3B		[BU MIAMI 07/84]
B707-321B	4X-ATF	ATASCO	S	19277	603	07/23/67	JT3D-3B (HK)		N424PA, HC-BFC [PARTLY DISMANTLED TLV 94]
B707-321B	N425PA	AVIATION TRADERS LTD.	S	19278	605	07/29/67	JT3D-3B		[BU STANSTED 1984]
B707-340C	YU-AGE	JAT YUGOSLAV AIRLINES	S	19284	509	07/23/66	JT3D-3B		AP-AUN [PROBABLY BU 1989]
B707-340C	YU-AGG	JAT YUGOSLAV AIRLINES	S	19285	524	10/22/66	JT3D-3B		AP-AUO [BU BELGRADE 1990]
B707-340C	AP-AXA	PAKISTAN INTL.	S	19286	625	09/21/67	JT3D-3B		AP-AUP, YU-AGF [BU FOR SPARES KHI 1995]
B707-328C	P4-ESP	OCCIDENTAL AIRLINES (MERLIN)	S	19292	560	03/15/67	JT3D-3B (HK)		F-BLCF, 9XR-JA, 9XR-VO, EL-WTZ [BEING BU MSE]
B707-338C	LV-MZE	TRANSPORTES AEREO RIOPLATENSE	S	19297	636	10/23/67	JT3D-3B		VH-EBX, G-BCAL [BU BY BMI MIA 10/94]
B707-330B	EL-AJU	BOEING	S	19315	545	12/31/66	JT3D-3B		D-ABUL, 60-SBS [HULK EXTANT AT DMAFB SINCE 11/90 (CZ186)]
B707-123B	N7573A	NATIONAL AIRCRAFT	S	19323	526	11/11/66	JT3D-1-MC6		[BU ARIZONA 06/92]
B707-123B	N7574A	NATIONAL AIRCRAFT	S	19324	533	12/19/66	JT3D-1-MC6		[BU ARIZONA 02/91]
B707-123B	N7575A	BOEING	S	19325	535	01/05/67	JT3D-1-MC6		[HULK EXTANT AT DMAFB SINCE 09/81 (CZ008)]
B707-123B	N7576A	BOEING	S	19326	539	01/24/67	JT3D-1-MC6		[HULK EXTANT AT DMAFB SINCE 09/81 (CZ004)]
B707-123B	N7577A	BOEING	S	19327	562	04/04/67	JT3D-1-MC6		[HULK EXTANT AT DMAFB SINCE 09/81 (CZ016)]
B707-123B	N7578A	BOEING	S	19328	565	03/23/67	JT3D-1-MC6		[HULK EXTANT AT DMAFB SINCE 09/81 (CZ005)]
B707-123B	N7579A	BOEING	S	19329	571	04/14/67	JT3D-1-MC6		[HULK EXTANT AT DMAFB SINCE 09/81 (CZ015)]
B707-123B	N7580A	BOEING	S	19330	575	04/28/67	JT3D-1-MC6		[HULK EXTANT AT DMAFB SINCE 09/81 (CZ002)]
B707-123B	N7581A	BOEING	S	19331	579	05/08/67	JT3D-1-MC6		[HULK EXTANT AT DMAFB SINCE 09/81 (CZ003)]
B707-123B	N7582A	BOEING	S	19332	586	05/26/67	JT3D-1-MC6		[HULK EXTANT AT DMAFB SINCE 09/81 (CZ004)]
B707-123B	N7583A	BOEING	S	19333	589	06/06/67	JT3D-1-MC6		[HULK EXTANT AT DMAFB SINCE 04/83 (CZ064)]
B707-123B	N7584A	BOEING	S	19334	591	06/16/67	JT3D-1-MC6		[HULK EXTANT AT DMAFB SINCE 09/81 (CZ012)]
B707-123B	N7586A	NATIONAL AIRCRAFT	S	19336	595	06/27/67	JT3D-1-MC6		[BU ARIZONA 1990]
B707-123B	N7587A	BOEING	S	19337	600	07/07/67	JT3D-1-MC6		[STD IAB SINCE 09/81]
B707-123B	N7588A	BOEING	S	19338	602	07/14/67	JT3D-1-MC6		[HULK EXTANT AT DMAFB SINCE 05/83 (CZ071)]
B707-123B	N7589A	NATIONAL AIRCRAFT	S	19339	604	07/20/67	JT3D-1-MC6		[BU ARIZONA 1991]
B707-123B	N7590A	NATIONAL AIRCRAFT	S	19340	622	09/15/67	JT3D-1-MC6		[BU ARIZONA 06/92]
B707-123B	N7591A	NATIONAL AIRCRAFT	S	19341	682	03/02/68	JT3D-1-MC6		[BU ARIZONA 05/92]
B707-123B	N7592A	BOEING	S	19342	787	03/12/69	JT3D-1-MC6		[HULK EXTANT AT DMAFB SINCE 09/81 (CZ013)]

A/C TYPE	CURRENT REG. NO.	LAST KNOWN OPERATOR (OWNER)	STATUS	ORIGINAL MSN	LINE NO.	DEL. DATE	ENG. TYPE	FLEET NO.	PREV. REG. [COMMENTS]
B707-123B	N7593A	BOB'S AIR PARK	S	19343	794	03/28/69	JT3D-1-MC6		[BU ARIZONA 1990]
B707-123B	N7594A	BOEING	S	19344	801	04/22/69	JT3D-1-MC6		[HULK EXTANT AT DMAFB SINCE 09/81 (CZ007)]
B707-324C	N419B	BOEING	S	19351	552	02/01/67	JT3D-3B		N17328, 9V-BEW, TF-VLJ [BU ARIZONA 06/87]
B707-351B	N707LE	MILLON AIR	S	19361	618	09/08/67	JT3D-3B (HK)		N426PA, HK-2015 [BU MIA 03/96]
B707-321B	N427PA	AVIATION TRADERS	S	19362	620	09/14/67	JT3D-3B		[BU STANSTED 11/81]
B707-321B	N433PA	AVIATION TRADERS	S	19364	628	09/29/67	JT3D-3B		[BU STANSTED AFTER 1984]
B707-321B	N434PA	AVIATION TRADERS	S	19365	631	10/12/67	JT3D-3B		[BU STANSTED 11/81]
B707-321B	5Y-AXW	AFRICAN AIRLINES INTL. (CONT'L C&T)	S	19366	633	10/13/67	JT3D-3B		N435PA, HL7435 [DERELICT WITHOUT ENGINES AT NAIROBI]
B707-321C	N720GS	PAN AVIATION	S	19370	651	11/30/67	JT3D-3B		N460PA, F-BYCN [BU MIA BY BMI 1992]
B707-323C	N7568A	BOEING	S	19383	641	11/02/67	JT3D-3B		[HULK EXTANT AT DMAFB SINCE 06/84 (CZ113)]
B720-047B	N3163	NATIONAL AIRCRAFT	S	19413	581	05/13/67	JT3D-3B		[BU TUCSON 01/91]
B720-047B	N3164	SOUTHWEST ALLOYS	S	19414	597	06/28/67	JT3D-3B		[BU TUCSON 07/91]
B707-131B	N6790T	BOEING	S	19436	606	08/01/67	JT3D-		[BU ARIZONA 04/91]
B720-047B	N3165	NATIONAL AIRCRAFT	S	19438	615	08/18/67	JT3D-3B		[BU TUCSON 1990]
B707-358B	N898WA	BOEING	S	19502	551	02/02/67	JT3D-3B		4X-ATS [HULK EXTANT AT DMAFB SINCE 08/89 (CZ167)]
B720-047B	N3833L	NATIONAL AIRCRAFT	S	19523	624	09/20/67	JT3D-3B		N3167, 5V-TAD [BU ARIZONA 07/91]
B707-331C	N15711	NATIONAL AIRCRAFT	S	19567	720	06/27/68	JT3D-3B		[BU TUCSON 1992]
B707-131B	N16738	NATIONAL AIRCRAFT	S	19568	669	03/11/68	JT3D-		[BU ARIZONA 1988]
B707-131B	N16739	SOUTHWEST ALLOYS	S	19569	680	03/08/68	JT3D-		[BU ARIZONA 1988]
B707-331B (H)	N7232X	R.A. MEDRANO CORP.	S	19570	674	02/16/68	JT3D-3B (HK)		N28724, OK-XFJ, LZ-PVB [BU BY HAMILTON AVN TUS; SOME PARTS STILL EXTANT]
B707-331B	N28726	BOEING	S	19571	685	03/27/68	JT3D-3B		[BU 1985]
B707-331B	N28728	BOEING	S	19573	704	05/07/68	JT3D-3B		[BU 1985]
B707-338C	5N-BBD	ADC AIRLINES	S	19625	693	04/04/68	JT3D-3B (HK2)		VH-EAE, G-BFLD, N862BX [STD MSE; ENGINELESS; BEING SCR]
B707-351C	N2215Y	(ALGI)	S	19631	634	10/14/67	JT3D-3B (HK)		N375US, 9Y-TEJ, 5N-OCL [HULK DERELICT AT SMYRNA SINCE 09/97]
B707-351B	AP-AZW	PAKISTAN INTL.	S	19636	731	07/24/68	JT3D-3B		N380US [BU KHI 12/93]
B707-321B	N1181Z	BOEING	S	19693	673	02/08/68	JT3D-3B		N491PA, CC-CEJ [HULK EXTANT AT DMAFB SINCE 02/86 (CZ143)]
B707-321B	N492PA	BAROCAS AIRCRAFT PARTS	S	19694	678	02/22/68	JT3D-3B		[BU JFK 11/84]
B707-321B	N495PA	BOEING	S	19697	694	04/09/68	JT3D-3B		[HULK EXTANT AT DMAFB SINCE 02/84 (CZ097)]
B707-321B	N496PA	BOEING	S	19698	697	04/17/68	JT3D-3B		[HULK EXTANT AT DMAFB SINCE 03/84 (LE001)]
B707-321B	N497PA	BOEING	S	19699	699	04/24/68	JT3D-3B		[HULK EXTANT AT DMAFB SINCE 03/84 (CZ101)]
B707-312B	4R-ALB	SHANNON AIRPORT	S	19737	713	05/28/68	JT3D-		9V-BBA [BU SNN 03/82; SOME PARTS EXTANT]
B707-312B	4R-ALA	GUINESS PEAT AVIATION	S	19738	725	07/03/68	JT3D-		9M-AOT, 9V-BFB [BU SNN 08/83]
B707-359B	HK-1402	AVIANCA	S	19741	681	03/07/68	JT3D-3B (HK)		[BU MIA 06/93]
B707-351C	7O-ABY	MID AIR	S	19777	740	08/28/68	JT3D-3B		N386US [BU ADEN 1987]

A/C TYPE	CURRENT REG. NO.	LAST KNOWN OPERATOR (OWNER)	STATUS	ORIGINAL MSN	LINE NO.	DEL. DATE	ENG. TYPE	FLEET NO.	PREV. REG. [COMMENTS]
B707-311C	N715FW	AIR ATLANTIC CARGO	S	19789	698	04/17/68	JT3D-3B (HK)		CF-FAN, 9K-ACX, N524SJ [BU MIA BY BMI 11/96; COCKPIT EXTANT]
B707-368C	A20-809	ROYAL AUSTRALIAN AIR FORCE	S	19809	657	01/08/68	JT3D-3B		HZ-ACC, N1486B [HULK EXTANT FOR APPRENTICE TRAINING AT RICHMOND, AUSTRALIA]
B707-368C	N1673B	BOEING	S	19810	664	01/19/68	JT3D-3B		HZ-ACD [HULK EXTANT AT DMAFB SINCE 06/87 (CZ158)]
B707-347C	EL-AKU	OCCIDENTAL AIRLINES (INTEREVIAIR)	S	19964	733	07/25/68	JT3D-3B (HK)		N1502W, TF-VLG, EI-BLC, N707PD, B-2425, TT-WAB, TT-EAP, HR-AMA, 9J-AFT, ZS-NLJ [STD MSE; BEIN
B707-329C	LX-N19996	NATO	S	19996	748	09/30/68	JT3D-7		OO-SJL, N3238N [E-3A TRAINER; DISMANTLED 12/98]
B707-321C	PT-TCR	BOEING	S	20018	761	11/22/68	JT3D-3B		N872PA, 9K-ACU, S2-ACK [HULK EXTANT AT DMAFB SINCE 08/87 (CZ162)]]
B707-321B	N880PA	BOEING	S	20019	767	12/10/68	JT3D-3B		[HULK EXTANT AT DMAFB SINCE 02/84 (CZ098)]
B707-321B	N881PA	USAF	S	20020	768	12/13/68	JT3D-3B		[HULK EXTANT AT DMAFB SINCE 04/84 (CZ182)]
B707-321B	N884PA	AVIATION TRADERS LTD.	S	20023	775	01/08/69	JT3D-3B		[BU STANSTED 07/86]
B707-321B	N885PA	FRITZ ENTERPRISES	S	20024	776	01/10/69	JT3D-3B		[HULK MOVED BY LAND TO TAYLOR, MI 06/12/97]
B707-321B	52-6318	USAF	S	20026	781	01/31/69	JT3D-3B		N887PA, N160GL [HULK EXTANT AT DMAFB SINCE 09/85 (CZ128); USED FOR SECURITY POLICE DOG TRAINING]
B707-321B	N2213E	BOEING	S	20027	782	02/06/69	JT3D-3B		N890PA, 9Y-TEX [BU TUCSON]
B707-321B	N731Q	JETRAN INC.	S	20031	792	03/14/69	JT3D-3B		N894PA [BU PHL 10/88]
B707-321B	N895SY	(WTCI)	S	20032	793	03/14/69	JT3D-3B		N895PA [BU SAT 07/96]
B707-321B	HC-BHY	AECA	S	20033	797	06/23/69	JT3D-3B (HK)		N896PA [PARTIALLY BU GYE 08/ 96]
B707-321B	N732Q	RESOLUTION TRUST	S	20034	798	03/31/69	JT3D-3B (HK)		N897PA [BU SNN 1997]
B707-384B	EL-AKB	BOEING	S	20035	770	12/19/68	JT3D-3B		SX-DBE, N6504K [HULK EXTANT AT DMAFB SINCE 11/90 (CZ187)]
B707-384B	N7158T	BOEING	S	20036	778	01/23/69	JT3D-3B		SX-DBF [HULK EXTANT AT DMAFB SINCE 07/90 (CZ177)]
B707-131B	N86740	NATIONAL AIRCRAFT	S	20056	771	01/08/69	JT3D-		[BU ARIZONA 04/91]
B707-131B	N86741	NATIONAL AIRCRAFT	S	20057	777	01/23/69	JT3D-		[BU ARIZONA 06/82; HULK EXTANT AT NATIONAL]
B707-331B	N8729	BOEING	S	20058	766	12/12/68	JT3D-3B		[HULK EXTANT AT DMAFB SINCE 02/84 (CZ095)]
B707-331B	N8730	BOEING	S	20059	772	01/15/69	JT3D-3B		[HULK EXTANT AT DMAFB SINCE 04/84 (CZ103)]
B707-331B	N8732	BOEING	S	20061	784	03/07/69	JT3D-3B		[HULK EXTANT AT DMAFB SINCE 12/83 (CZ088)]
B707-331B	N8733	BOEING	S	20062	785	04/02/69	JT3D-3B		[HULK EXTANT AT DMAFB SINCE 05/86 (CZ150)]
B707-331B	N8735	BOEING	S	20064	799	05/01/69	JT3D-3B		[HULK EXTANT AT DMAFB SINCE 06/84 (CZ115)]
B707-331B	N8736	BOEING	S	20065	802	05/07/69	JT3D-3B		[HULK EXTANT AT DMAFB SINCE 11/85 (CZ133)]
B707-331B	N8737	BOEING	S	20066	810	06/12/69	JT3D-3B		[HULK EXTANT AT DMAFB SINCE 10/85 (CZ131)]
B707-331B	N8738	BOEING	S	20067	812	06/17/69	JT3D-3B		[HULK EXTANT AT DMAFB SINCE 07/84 (CZ116)]
B707-323C	N162GL	BOEING	S	20089	741	08/30/68	JT3D-3B		G-AYZZ, N8417 [HULK EXTANT AT DMAFB SINCE 11/85 (CZ135)]

A/C TYPE	CURRENT REG. NO.	LAST KNOWN OPERATOR (OWNER)	STATUS	ORIGINAL MSN	LINE NO.	DEL. DATE	ENG. TYPE	FLEET NO.	PREV. REG. [COMMENTS]
B707-358B	TF-AYF	BOEING	S	20097	779	01/22/69	JT3D-3B		4X-ATT [HULK EXTANT AT DMAFB SINCE 09/89 (CZ168)]
B707-323B	N910PC	PORTS OF CALL	S	20171	796	04/16/69	JT3D-3B		N8432 [BU WACO 09/86]
B707-323B	N709PC	OMEGA AIR	S	20175	811	06/13/69	JT3D-3B (HK)		N8436 [RT OMEGA AIR 11/93; BEING BU SNN]
B707-323B	N457PC	FLORIDA WEST AIRLINES (JETLEASE)	S	20178	820	09/09/69	JT3D-3B		N8439 [BU MIA BY BMI 05/94]
B707-323B	N7158Z	BOEING	S	20179	821	09/22/69	JT3D-3B		N8440, N165GL, S7-LAS, 5Y-BFF [HULK EXTANT AT DMAFB SINCE 07/90 (CZ178)]
B707-359B	N22055	ENTERPRISE AIR	S	20340	842	04/24/70	JT3D-3B (HK)		HK-1410 [BU FOR SPARES BOG 08/94; FUSELAGE EXTANT]
B707-336C	7O-ACO	YEMENIA	S	20374	838	03/06/70	JT3D-3B		G-AXGW [BU ADEN 05/96]
B707-336B	PT-TCQ	NATIONAL AIRCRAFT	S	20456	851	02/18/71	JT3D-3B		G-AXXY, 4X-BMC, VR-HKC, N343A [BU ARIZONA 06/91]
B707-3F9C	5N-ABJ	EQUATOR LEASING	S	20474	843	05/11/71	JT3D-3B (HK)		[BU SNN 01/98]
B707-366C	SU-AXK	EGYPT AIR	S	20920	893	11/15/74	JT3D-7		[BU CAIRO 10/93]
B707-368C	P4-DRS	COMTRAN INTL.	S	21104	906	12/18/75	JT3D-3B		HZ-ACH, ST-DRS, N707MJ [BU SAT 03/01]
B707-3F9C	5N-ANO	NIGERIA AIRWAYS	S	21428	929	01/30/78	JT3D-3B		[BU DUB]

WRITTEN OFF

A/C TYPE	CURRENT REG. NO.	LAST KNOWN OPERATOR (OWNER)	STATUS	ORIGINAL MSN	LINE NO.	DEL. DATE	ENG. TYPE	FLEET NO.	PREV. REG. [COMMENTS]
B707-121 (B)	N708PA	PAN AMERICAN	W	17586	1	11/30/58	JT3D-3B		[WO 09/17/65 MONTSERRAT, W.I.]
B707-121	N709PA	PAN AMERICAN	W	17588	3	08/15/58	JT3C-		[WO 12/08/63 ELKTON, MD]
B707-321 (F)	HK2410	AEROTAL COLOMBIA	W	17605	98	01/28/60	JT4A-12		N727PA, G-AZWA, N70798 [WO 12/20/80 EL DORADO, COLOMBIA]
B707-124	N70773	CONTINENTAL AIRLINES	W	17609	25	04/19/59	JT3C-		[WO 07/01/65 KANSAS CITY]
B707-124	HI-384HA	HISPANIOLA AIRWAYS	W	17610	37	05/27/59	JT3C-		N70774, 4X-JYA, 4X-JYB, N196CA [WO 12/12/81 MIA; BU MIA BY BMI 1987]
B707-124	N70775	CONTINENTAL AIRLINES	W	17611	49	07/16/59	JT3C-		[WO 05/22/62 UNIONVILLE, MO]
B707-328	F-BHSA	AIR FRANCE	W	17613	65	10/21/59	JT4A		[WO 07/27/61 HAM]
B707-328	F-BHSH	AIR FRANCE	W	17620	138	06/23/60	JT4A		[WO 09/07/76 AJACCIO, CORSICA]
B707-329	OO-SJA	SABENA	W	17623	78	12/04/59	JT4A-		[WO 03/29/81 BRU; NOSE PRESERVED; BRUSSELS AIR MUSEUM 4/82]
B707-329	OO-SJB	SABENA	W	17624	92	01/15/60	JT4A		[WO 02/15/61 BRU]
B707-329	OO-SJE	SABENA	W	17627	133	06/08/60	JT4A		[WO 02/15/78 TENERIFE, CANARY IS.]
B707-123 (B)	5B-DAM	CYPRUS AIRWAYS	W	17628	7	10/23/58	JT3D-1-MC6		N7501A [WO 08/19/79 BAHRAIN]
B707-123	N7502A	AMERICAN AIRLINES	W	17629	8	01/23/59	JT3C-		[WO 01/28/61 MONTAUK, NY]
B707-123 (B)	N7506A	AMERICAN AIRLINES	W	17633	12	02/12/59	JT3D-1-MC6		[WO 03/01/62 JAMAICA BAY, NY]
B707-123	N7514A	AMERICAN AIRLINES	W	17641	36	06/05/59	JT3C-		[WO 08/15/59 CALVERTON, NY]
B707-123 (B)	N311AS	QUEBECAIR	W	17650	67	10/14/59	JT3D-1-MC6		N7523A, C-GQBH [WO 02/19/79 ST. LUCIA, W.I.]
B707-131	N742TW	TRANS WORLD AIRLINES	W	17669	43	07/01/59	JT3C-		[WO 11/06/67 CINCINNATI]
B707-131	N743TW	TRANS WORLD AIRLINES	W	17670	46	07/10/59	JT3C-		[WO 04/22/70 INDIANAPOLIS]
B707-131 (F)	N730JP	LLOYD AERO BOLIVIANA	W	17671	48	07/14/59	JT3C-		N744TW, HB-IEG, HK-1773 [WO 10/14/76 SANTA CRUZ, BOLIVIA]

A/C TYPE	CURRENT REG. NO.	LAST KNOWN OPERATOR (OWNER)	STATUS	ORIGINAL MSN	LINE NO.	DEL. DATE	ENG. TYPE	FLEET NO.	PREV. REG. [COMMENTS]
B707-331	N761TW	TRANS WORLD AIRLINES	W	17673	69	11/10/59	JT4A-12		[WO 03/08/72 LAS]
B707-331	N769TW	TRANS WORLD AIRLINES	W	17685	123	05/09/60	JT4A-12		[WO 11/23/64 ROME, ITALY]
B707-227	N7071	BOEING/BRANIFF	W	17691	45	10/19/59	JT4A-3		[WO 10/19/59 PAE; BEFORE DEL ON ACCEPTANCE/TRAINING FLIGHT]
B707-138 (B)	N138SR	COMTRAN INTL.	W	17697	39	06/26/59	JT3D-1 (HK)		VH-EBB, N790SA, D-ADAP, TC-JBP, N790FA [WO 01/99 PORT HARCOURT, NIGERIA]
B707-138 (B)	N791SA	CANADIAN PACIFIC AIRLINES	W	17698	44	07/07/59	JT3D-		VH-EBC [WO 02/07/68 YVR]
B707-436	G-APFE	B.O.A.C.	W	17706	113	04/29/60	CONWAY 508		N5092K [WO 03/05/66 MT. FUJI, JAPAN]
B707-436	G-APFK	BRITISH AIR TOURS	W	17712	164	09/29/60	CONWAY 508		[WO 03/17/77 PIK]
B707-430	9Q-CRT	PEARL AIR	W	17718	90	02/03/60	CONWAY 508		N31240, D-ABOB [WO 08/09/77 SANAA, YEMEN]
B707-437	VT-DJI	AIR INDIA	W	17722	94	02/18/60	CONWAY 508		N5089K [WO 01/23/71 BOMBAY]
B707-437	VT-DJJ	AIR INDIA	W	17723	100	02/19/60	CONWAY 508		[WO 06/22/82 BOMBAY]
B707-139 (B)	N779PA	PAN AMERICAN	W	17904	119	05/04/60	JT3D-		N74614 [WO 04/07/64 JAMAICA BAY, NY]
B707-441	PP-VJB	VARIG	W	17906	129	06/16/60	CONWAY 508		[WO 11/27/62 LIMA, PERU]
B707-328	F-BHSM	AIR FRANCE	W	17920	159	09/21/60	JT4A-		[WO 06/03/62 PARIS]
B720-023 (B)	OD-AFP	MIDDLE EAST AIRLINES	W	18017	156	09/01/60	JT3D-1-MC7		N7531A [CVTD -023; WO 06/12/82 BEIRUT]
B720-023 (B)	OD-AFR	MIDDLE EAST AIRLINES	W	18018	157	09/08/60	JT3D-1-MC7		N7532A [CVTD -023; WO 08/31/81 BEIRUT]
B720-023 (B)	OD-AFT	MIDDLE EAST AIRLINES	W	18020	165	10/10/60	JT3D-1-MC7		N7534A [CVTD -023; WO 01/01/76 AL QAYSUMAH, SAUDI ARABIA]
B720-023B	OD-AFW	MIDDLE EAST AIRLINES	W	18026	181	02/17/61	JT3D-1-MC7		N7540A [WO 06/16/82 BEIRUT]
B720-023B	OD-AFU	MIDDLE EAST AIRLINES	W	18029	194	03/28/61	JT3D-1-MC7		N7543A [WO 06/16/82 BEIRUT]
B720-023B	OD-AFL	MIDDLE EAST AIRLINES	W	18034	207	06/22/61	JT3D-1-MC7		N7548A [WO 08/21/85 BEIRUT]
B720-023B	OD-AFO	MIDDLE EAST AIRLINES	W	18035	214	06/09/61	JT3D-1-MC7		N7549A [WO 06/01/82 BEIRUT]
B720-022	N37777	U.S. GLOBAL	W	18044	178	12/22/60	JT3C-7		N7212U, HP-685, N28JS [WO 04/22/76 BARRANQUILLA, COLOMBIA]
B707-437	VT-DMN	AIR INDIA	W	18055	200	04/17/61	CONWAY 508		[WO 01/24/66 MONT BLANC, SWITZERLAND]
B720-030B	D-ABOK	LUFTHANSA	W	18058	202	04/28/61	JT3D-1		[WO 12/04/61 EBERSHEIM, GERMANY]
B720-047B	HK-723	AVIANCA	W	18061	197	04/07/61	JT3D-3B		N93141 [WO 08/16/76 MEX]
B720-059B	HK-725	AVIANCA	W	18087	249	11/16/61	JT3D-		[WO 01/27/80 UIO]
B720-025	OY-DSR	CONAIR OF SCANDINAVIA	W	18243	254	12/08/61	JT3C-7		N8714E [WO 09/13/74 COPENHAGEN]
B707-328	F-BHST	AIR FRANCE	W	18247	274	03/09/62	JT4A-		[WO 06/22/62 GUADALOUPE, W.I.]
B720-030B	D-ABOP	LUFTHANSA	W	18249	262	01/12/62	JT3D-1		[WO 07/15/64 PETERSDORF, GERMANY]
B720-051B	N724US	NORTHWEST AIRLINES	W	18354	224	07/26/61	JT3D-3B		[WO 02/13/63 EVERGLADES, FL]
B707-458	9Q-CWR	WOLF AVIATION	W	18357	272	02/13/62	CONWAY 508		4X-ATC, 9Q-CPM [WO 10/01/84]
B707-465	G-ARWE	B.O.A.C.	W	18373	302	07/07/62	CONWAY 508		[WO 04/08/68 LONDON]
B720-040B	AP-AMH	PAKISTAN INTL.	W	18379	321	11/07/62	JT3D-3B		[WO 05/20/65 CAIRO]
B707-131B	N757TW	TRANS WORLD AIRLINES	W	18395	309	08/01/62	JT3D-		[WO 01/16/74 LOS ANGELES]
B707-436	N4465D	COASTAL AIRWAYS	W	18411	266	02/16/62	CONWAY 508		G-ARRA [WO 10/14/83 PERPIGNAN, FRANCE]
B720-060B	ET-AAG	MIDDLE EAST AIRLINES	W	18454	319	11/02/62	JT3D-3B		[WO 01/09/68 BEIRUT]
B707-328B	F-BHSZ	AIR FRANCE	W	18459	335	03/30/63	JT3D-3B		[WO 12/03/69 CARACAS]
B707-330B	D-ABOT	LUFTHANSA	W	18463	363	03/05/64	JT3D-3B		[WO 12/20/73 NEW DELHI]

A/C TYPE	CURRENT REG. NO.	LAST KNOWN OPERATOR (OWNER)	STATUS	ORIGINAL MSN	LINE NO.	DEL. DATE	ENG. TYPE	FLEET NO.	PREV. REG. [COMMENTS]
B707-321C	G-BEBP	DAN AIR	W	18579	332	06/07/63	JT3D-3B		N765PA [WO 05/14/77 LUSAKA, ZAMBIA]
B707-321C	5X-UAL	UGANDA AIRLINES	W	18580	336	05/02/63	JT3D-3B		N766PA [WO 04/01/79 KAMPALA, UGANDA]
B707-373C	HZ-ACE	SAUDIA	W	18582	344	07/16/63	JT3D-3B		N373WA [WO 11/15/79 JEDDAH]
B707-351B	CC-CCX	LAN CHILE	W	18584	342	06/05/63	JT3D-3B		N351US, VR-HGH [WO 08/03/78 AEP]
B720-047B	AP-AXK	PAKISTAN INTL.	W	18590	339	05/02/63	JT3D-3B		N93150 [WO 01/08/81 QUETTA, PAKISTAN]
B707-323C	CP-1365	LAB AIRLINES	W	18692	358	12/31/63	JT3D-3B (HK)		N7558A, N309EL [WO 08/31/91 DHN]
B707-373C	HK2401	TAMPA COLOMBIA	W	18707	349	09/26/63	JT3D-3B		N375WA, G-AYSI, N3751Y [WO 12/15/83 MEDELLIN, COLOMBIA]
B707-331C	PT-MST	SKYMASTER AIRLINES	W	18711	370	04/25/64	JT3D-3B (HK2)		N786TW, CC-CER, N700FW, PP-PHB, N777FB, OB-1696 [WO 03/07/01 GRU]
B707-331C	N787TW	TRANS WORLD AIRLINES	W	18712	373	05/20/64	JT3D-3B		[WO 07/26/69 POMONA, NJ]
B707-321C	ST-ALX	GOLDEN STAR AIR CARGO	W	18715	364	03/20/64	JT3D-3B		N791PA, TC-JCC [WO 03/24/92 ATHENS]
B707-321C	5N-MAS	TRANS-AIR SERVICES (SOVEREIGN)	W	18718	368	04/30/64	JT3D-3B (HK)		N794PA, N794EP, N794RN, G-BFZF, G-BNGH [WO 03/31/92 ISTRES, FRANCE]
B707-348C	70-ACJ	ALYEMDA	W	18737	377	06/10/64	JT3D-3B		EI-AMW, LX-LGV [WO 01/26/82; "THE PLANE" RESTAURANT]
B707-373C	N790TW	TRANS WORLD AIRLINES	W	18738	355	12/23/63	JT3D-3B		[WO 11/30/70 TEL AVIV]
B707-351C	9G-RBO	G.A.S. AIR	W	18746	367	04/09/64	JT3D-3B (HK)		N356US, CF-PWJ, OO-ABA, C-GRYO, 5A-DIZ, 5Y-AXC, N8163G, TF-ANC, 9G-RCA [WO 03/29/92 LOS]
B707-131B	N797TW	TRANS WORLD AIRLINES	W	18760	393	11/20/64	JT3D-		[WO 11/30/80 SAN FRANCISCO]
B707-321C	JY-AEE	JORDAN WORLD AIRWAYS	W	18767	376	05/21/64	JT3D-3B		N797PA [WO 08/03/75 AGADIR, MOROCCO]
B707-321C	N798PA	PAN AMERICAN	W	18790	394	12/03/64	JT3D-3B		[WO 06/13/68 CALCUTTA]
B707-321C	N799PA	PAN AMERICAN	W	18824	397	12/31/64	JT3D-3B		[WO 12/26/68 ELMENDORF, AK]
B707-321C	5X-DAR	DAS AIR CARGO (EQUA)	W	18825	386	08/21/64	JT3D-3B (HK)		N17321, B-1832, N987AA [WO 11/25/92 KANO, NIGERIA]
B707-321C	CF-PWZ	PACIFIC WESTERN AIRLINES	W	18826	389	09/17/64	JT3D-3B		N17322 [WO 01/02/73 EDMONTON]
B720-047B	OD-AGG	MIDDLE EAST AIRLINES	W	18828	423	05/19/65	JT3D-3B		N3155 [WO 08/01/82 BEIRUT]
B707-321B	N407PA	PAN AMERICAN	W	18838	412	03/26/65	JT3D-3B		[WO 12/17/73 ROME]
B707-328C	D2-TOV	TAAG ANGOLA AIRLINES	W	18881	436	08/05/65	JT3D-3B		F-BLCC, TF-VLR, 5A-DIK, 5Y-BFC [WO 07/21/88 LOS]
B707-324C	HK-3355X	TAMPA COLOMBIA (COMTRAN)	W	18886	430	06/17/65	JT3D-3B (HK)		N17323, G-AZJM, HK-2600X [WO 10/09/94 GRU]
B707-324C	B-1834	CHINA AIRLINES	W	18887	431	06/21/65	JT3D-3B		N17324 [WO 09/11/79 CHUWEI, TAIWAN]
B707-351C	5A-DJT	LIBYAN ARAB AIRLINES	W	18888	425	05/22/65	JT3D-3B		N359US, VR-HHE [WO 12/07/91 TRIPOLI]
B707-329C	OO-SJH	ZAIRE INTL. CARGO (SABENA)	W	18890	416	04/17/65	JT3D-7		[WO 05/11/80 DOUALA, CAMEROON]
B707-331B	N8715T	TRANS WORLD AIRLINES	W	18917	460	12/21/65	JT3D-3B		[WO 09/13/70 AMMAN, JORDAN]
B707-336C	5N-ARO	RN AIR CARGO	W	18924	448	12/19/65	JT3D-3B		N2978G, G-ASZF [WO 09/25/83 ACCRA, GHANA]
B707-330B	Z-WKT	AIR ZIMBABWE	W	18929	461	01/07/66	JT3D-7		D-ABUG, VP-WKT [WO 11/15/88 HARARE, ZIMBABWE; TO BE USED AS RESTAURANT]
B707-330C	PT-TCO	TRANSBRASIL	W	18932	477	03/11/66	JT3D-3B		D-ABUE [WO 04/11/87 MANAUS, BRAZIL]
B707-323C	OD-AGN	TRANS MEDITERRANEAN AIRWAYS	W	18938	434	07/30/65	JT3D-3B		N7559A [WO 06/16/82 BEIRUT]

A/C TYPE	CURRENT REG. NO.	LAST KNOWN OPERATOR (OWNER)	STATUS	ORIGINAL MSN	LINE NO.	DEL. DATE	ENG. TYPE	FLEET NO.	PREV. REG. [COMMENTS]
B707-338C	5A-DJO	JAMAHIRIYAN AIR TRANSPORT	W	18955	467	02/03/66	JT3D-3B		VH-EBS, 9M-ASO, 9M-MCS [WO 04/14/83 SEBAH, LIBYA]
B707-321B	N417PA	PAN AMERICAN	W	18959	478	05/21/66	JT3D-3B		[WO 07/22/73 PAPETTE, TAHITI]
B720-047B	OD-AGE	MIDDLE EAST AIRLINES	W	18963	433	07/21/65	JT3D-3B		N3158 [WO 06/27/76 BEIRUT]
B707-349C	D2-TOI	TAAG ANGOLA AIRLINES	W	18975	445	09/27/65	JT3D-3B		N322F, G-AWTK, G-BDCN, D2-TAC, D2-TOB [WO 02/15/88 LUANDA]
B707-349C	ST-ALK	TRANS ARABIAN A/T	W	18976	449	10/13/65	JT3D-3B		N323F, EI-ASN, 9J-ADY [WO 07/14/90, KHARTOUM, SUDAN]
B707-331B	N18701	TRANS WORLD AIRLINES	W	18978	465	01/25/66	JT3D-3B		[WO 12/22/75 MILAN, ITALY]
B707-327C	PP-VLJ	VARIG	W	19106	502	06/18/66	JT3D-3B		N7097 [WO 06/09/73 RIO DE JANEIRO]
B707-327C	OD-AFX	TRANS MEDITERRANEAN AIRWAYS	W	19107	507	06/29/66	JT3D-3B		N7098, PH-TRV [WO 07/23/79 BEIRUT]
B707-327C	OD-AFY	TMA OF LEBANON	W	19108	511	07/27/66	JT3D-3B (HK)		N7099 [WO 07/26/93 AMSTERDAM; COCKPIT IS STD AT OUDE TONGE, NETHERLANDS]
B720-047B	OD-AGQ	MIDDLE EAST AIRLINES	W	19160	470	01/26/66	JT3D-3B		N3159 [WO 08/21/85 BEIRUT]
B720-047B	OD-AGR	MIDDLE EAST AIRLINES	W	19161	481	03/12/66	JT3D-3B		N3160 [WO 06/16/82 BEIRUT]
B707-329C	9Q-CVG	KATALE AERO TRANSPORT	W	19162	480	03/23/66	JT3D-7		OO-SJJ [WO 03/01/90 GOMA, ZAIRE]
B707-351C	5N-AYJ	GAS AIR NIGERIA	W	19168	508	07/12/66	JT3D-3B		N367US, S2-ABN [WO 12/14/88 LUXOR, EGYPT]
B707-351C	N144SP	BURLINGTON AIR TRANSPORT	W	19209	510	07/20/66	JT3D-3B		N368US, 9Y-TED, N29796 [WO 04/13/87 KANSAS CITY]
B707-329C	OO-SJK	SABENA	W	19211	518	08/30/66	JT3D-7		[WO 07/13/68 LOS]
B707-331C	OD-AGT	TRANS MEDITERRANEAN AIRWAYS	W	19213	613	08/29/67	JT3D-3B		N5772T [WO 10/22/81 TOKYO]
B707-323C	PP-VLU	VARIG	W	19235	519	08/31/66	JT3D-3B		N7562A [WO 01/30/79 TOKYO]
B707-387B	T-96	LADE	W	19238	528	11/23/66	JT3D-3B		LV-ISA [WO 01/31/93 RECIFE, BRAZIL]
B707-321C	N446PA	PAN AMERICAN	W	19268	544	12/21/66	JT3D-3B		[WO 04/22/74 BALI, INDONESIA]
B707-321C	YR-ABM	AIR AFRIQUE (TAROM)	W	19272	578	05/23/67	JT3D-3B (HK)		N450PA [WO 01/15/93 ABIDJAN, IVORY COAST]
B707-321B	HK2016	AVIANCA	W	19276	592	06/30/67	JT3D-3B		N423PA [WO 01/25/90 COVE NECK, NY]
B707-330B	6O-SBT	SOMALI AIRLINES	W	19316	547	01/30/67	JT3D-3B		D-ABUM [WO 05/17/89 NAIROBI; TAIL SECTION AT EMBAKASI HEADQUARTERS AT KQA]
B707-341C	PP-VJR	VARIG	W	19320	522	12/28/66	JT3D-3B		[WO 09/07/68 RIO DE JANEIRO]
B707-341C	PP-VJT	VARIG	W	19322	561	03/22/67	JT3D-3B		[WO 06/11/81 MANAUS, BRAZIL]
B707-349C	PT-TCS	TRANSBRASIL	W	19354	503	06/21/66	JT3D-3B		N324F, EI-ASO, VH-EBZ, G-BAWP, 9J-AEC, S2-ACG, [WO 03/21/89 GRU]
B707-349C	D2-TOJ	TAAG ANGOLA AIRLINES	W	19355	553	02/06/67	JT3D-3B		N325F, G-AWWD, D2-TAD, D2-TOC [WO 02/20/92 LUANDA, ANGOLA]
B707-321B	HL7429	KOREAN AIRLINES	W	19363	623	09/21/67	JT3D-3B		N428PA [WO 04/20/78 MURMANSK, RUSSIA]
B707-321C	N458PA	PAN AMERICAN	W	19368	640	11/07/67	JT3D-3B		[WO 11/03/73 BOSTON]
B707-321C	N461PA	PAN AMERICAN	W	19371	653	11/30/67	JT3D-3B		[WO 07/25/71 MANILA]
B707-321B	N454PA	PAN AMERICAN	W	19376	661	12/20/67	JT3D-3B		[WO 01/30/74 PAGO PAGO, AM. SAMOA]
B707-321C	ST-SAC	TRANS ARABIAN A/T	W	19377	666	01/17/68	JT3D-3B		N474PA, F-BYCP, EL-AJA, N5366Y, N721GS [WO 12/04/90 NAIROBI]

A/C TYPE	CURRENT REG. NO.	LAST KNOWN OPERATOR (OWNER)	STATUS	ORIGINAL MSN	LINE NO.	DEL. DATE	ENG. TYPE	FLEET NO.	PREV. REG. [COMMENTS]
B707-321C	YR-ABN	TAROM	W	19379	677	02/21/68	JT3D-3B (HK)		N475PA [WO 08/17/95 N'DJAMENA, TCHAD; ON LEASE TO RKA]
B707-348C	ST-AIM	SUDAN AIRWAYS	W	19410	599	07/01/67	JT3D-3B		EI-APG, N8789R, CF-TAI [WO 09/10/82 NILE RIVER, SUDAN]
B707-351C	ST-APY	TRANS ARABIAN A/T	W	19412	563	03/18/67	JT3D-3B (HK2)		N372US, 9Y-TEE, 8P-CAC, N707DY [WO 02/02/00 MWANZA, TANZANIA]
B707-365C	PT-TCP	AEROBRASIL CARGO	W	19416	556	04/14/67	JT3D-3B (HK)		N737AL, PH-TRW, G-ATZC, C-GFLG [WO 11/26/92 MANAUS]
B707-385C	ET-AJZ	ETHIOPIAN AIRWAYS	W	19433	534	12/06/66	JT3D-3B (HK)		N8400, PP-VLI, N109BV [WO 03/25/91 ASMARA, ETHIOPIA]
B707-331C (H)	P4-OOO	FIRST INTL. AIRLINES	W	19435	629	10/12/67	JT3D-3B (HK)		N5774T, CC-CAF, CX-BPL, YV-671C [WO 01/16/97 KINSHASA]
B720-047B	N3166	WESTERN AIRLINES	W	19439	621	09/07/67	JT3D-3B		[WO 03/31/71 ONTARIO, CA]
B707-327C	OD-AGW	TRANS MEDITERRANEAN AIRWAYS	W	19440	554	02/17/67	JT3D-3B		N7100 [WO 07/05/81 BEIRUT]
B707-373C	S2-ABQ	BANGLADESH BIMAN	W	19441	548	12/22/66	JT3D-3B		N371WA, AP-AWV [WO 04/03/80 SINGAPORE]
B707-328C	9G-ROX	CLIPPER INTL. (AVISTAR)	W	19521	584	06/03/67	JT3D-3B (HK)		F-BLCG, SU-DAB, ST-AKR, XT-BBF, HB-IEI, P4-BEK, 5B-DAZ [WO 02/07/99 BRATISLAV, SLOVAKIA]
B707-327C	9Q-CGC	REPUBLIC OF CONGO GOVERNMENT	W	19531	646	11/20/67	JT3D-3B		N7104, OD-AGZ, ET-AIV [WO 02/14/00 KINSHASA, CONGO]
B707-331B	N7231T	INDEPENDENT AIR	W	19572	687	03/22/68	JT3D-3B (HK)		N28727 [WO 02/08/89 SANTA MARIA, AZORES]
B707-323C	9Q-CKK	CONGO AIRLINES	W	19577	722	06/26/68	JT3D-7 (HK)		N8414, ZS-LSH, 9Q-CSZ [WO 11/01/97 KINSHASA, CONGO]
B707-323C	N751MA	MILLON AIR (WTC TRUST)	W	19582	639	10/27/67	JT3D-3B (HK)		N8402, EL-GNU [WO 10/23/96 MANTA, ECUADOR]
B707-323C	4K-401	AZERBAIJAN AIRWAYS (PHOENIX)	W	19584	663	01/11/68	JT3D-3B (HK)		N8404, LZ-FEB [WO 11/30/95 BAKU, AZERBAIJAN]
B707-323C	OD-AHB	MIDDLE EAST AIRLINES	W	19588	692	04/04/68	JT3D-3B		N8409 [WO 01/07/87 BEIRUT]
B707-338C	5X-UBC	UGANDA AIRLINES	W	19630	746	09/25/68	JT3D-3B		VH-EAJ, G-BDSJ [WO 10/17/88 ROME]
B707-355C	5N-VRG	IAT CARGO AIRLINES	W	19664	643	11/09/67	JT3D-3B (HK)		N526EJ, PH-TRF, G-AXRS, TF-VLX, 5N-AOQ [WO 11/14/98 OSTEND, BELGIUM]
B707-321B	N494PA	PAN AMERICAN	W	19696	688	03/28/68	JT3D-3B		N494PA [WO 12/12/68 CARACAS]
B707-344C	ZS-EUW	SOUTH AFRICAN AIRWAYS	W	19705	675	02/22/68	JT3D-7		[WO 04/20/68 WINDHOEK]
B707-373C	HL7412	KOREAN AIRLINES	W	19715	642	11/07/67	JT3D-3B		N369WA, AP-AWE [WO 08/02/76 TEHRAN, IRAN]
B707-328C	F-BLCJ	AIR FRANCE	W	19724	667	01/24/68	JT3D-3B		[WO 03/05/68 GUADALOUPE, W.I.]
B707-360C	ET-ACD	ETHIOPIAN AIRLINES	W	19736	696	04/08/68	JT3D-		[WO 11/19/77 ROME]
B707-312B	5V-TAG	TOGO GOVERNMENT	W	19739	765	12/09/68	JT3D-3B (HK2)		9V-BBB, N600CS [WO 09/21/00 NIAMEY, NIGER]
B707-379C	ET-ACQ	ETHIOPIAN AIRLINES	W	19820	709	05/20/68	JT3D-3B		[WO 07/25/90 ADDIS ABABA]
B707-379C	PP-VJK	VARIG	W	19822	726	11/04/68	JT3D-3B		N763U(NTU) [WO 01/03/87 ABIJAN, IVORY COAST]
B707-345C	PP-VJZ	VARIG	W	19841	683	08/20/68	JT3D-3B		N7322S [WO 07/11/73 PARIS]
B707-336C	SU-PBA	AIR MEMPHIS	W	19843	735	08/13/68	JT3D-3B (HK)		G-AVPB, SU-DAC [WO 03/10/98 MOMBASA, KENYA]

A/C TYPE	CURRENT REG. NO.	LAST KNOWN OPERATOR (OWNER)	STATUS	ORIGINAL MSN	LINE NO.	DEL. DATE	ENG. TYPE	FLEET NO.	PREV. REG. [COMMENTS]
B707-366C	SU-AOW	EGYPT AIR	W	19845	809	05/26/69	JT3D-7		[WO 12/05/72 BENI SUEIF, EGYPT]
B707-351B	5Y-BBK	KENYA AIRWAYS	W	19872	742	08/28/68	JT3D-3B		N381US [WO 07/11/89 ADDIS ABABA]
B707-387C	LV-JGR	AEROLINEAS ARGENTINAS	W	19961	754	11/04/68	JT3D-3B		[WO 01/27/86 AEP]
B707-347C	D2-TOM	TAAG ANGOLA AIRLINES	W	19965	734	07/29/68	JT3D-3B		N1503W [WO 10/10/88 LUANDA, ANGOLA; FUSELAGE STD LUANDA]
B707-321B	CC-CEI	LAN CHILE	W	20021	769	12/17/68	JT3D-3B		N882PA [WO 06/23/90 SANTIAGO, CHILE]
B707-321B	N320MJ	OMEGA AIR	W	20028	783	02/06/69	JT3D-3B		N891PA, 9Y-TEZ, N3127K, VR-CBN [WO 09/20/90 MARANA, AZ]
B707-331B	N8734	TRANS WORLD AIRLINES	W	20063	789	04/07/69	JT3D-3B		[WO 09/08/74 IONIAN SEA, GREECE]
B707-331C	N15712	TRANS WORLD AIRLINES	W	20068	814	07/02/69	JT3D-3B		[WO 09/14/72 SAN FRANCISCO]
B707-372C	LV-LGP	ARGENTINIAN AIR FORCE	W	20077	728	07/11/68	JT3D-3B		N739AL, TC-92 [WO 10/25/96 AEP]
B707-323B	N8434	GLOBAL INTL.	W	20173	805	05/09/69	JT3D-3B		[WO 12/04/82 BRASILIA, BRAZIL]
B707-3B4C	OD-AFB	MIDDLE EAST AIRLINES	W	20224	749	11/18/68	JT3D-3B		[WO 06/16/82 BEIRUT]
B707-3B4C	OD-AFC	MIDDLE EAST AIRLINES	W	20225	757	11/18/68	JT3D-3B		[WO 12/28/68 BEIRUT]
B707-309C	B-1826	CHINA AIRLINES	W	20262	830	12/11/69	JT3D-3B		[WO 02/27/80 MANILA]
B707-340C	AP-AWZ	PAKISTAN INTL.	W	20275	844	08/10/70	JT3D-3B		AP-AWB, G-AZPW [WO 11/26/79 JEDDAH]
B707-366C	SU-APE	EGYPT AIR	W	20342	837	03/24/70	JT3D-7		N4094B [WO 10/17/82 GENEVA]
B707-330C	D-ABUY	LUFTHANSA	W	20395	848	10/16/70	JT3D-3B		[WO 07/26/79 RIO DE JANEIRO]
B707-336B	TY-BBR	BENIN GOVERNMENT	W	20457	853	04/17/71	JT3D-3B		G-AXXZ, 9G-ADB [WO 06/13/85 SEBHA, LIBYA]
B707-340C	AP-AVZ	PAKISTAN INTL.	W	20487	847	10/15/70	JT3D-3B		[WO 12/15/71 SIN KIANG, CHINA]
B707-3D3C	JY-ADO	ALIA-ROYAL JORDANIAN	W	20494	850	01/26/71	JT3D-		[WO 01/22/73 KANO, NIGERIA]
B707-3B5C	HL7406	KOREAN AIRLINES	W	20522	855	08/06/71	JT3D-3B		[WO 11/29/87 BURMA/THAILAND]
B707-369C	5X-JON	DAS AIR CARGO (OP FOR AIR AFRIQUE)	W	20546	860	01/15/72	JT3D-3B (HK)		9K-ACM, N523SJ [WO 06/30/96 NBAMAKO, MALI]
B707-3F9C	5N-ABK	NIGERIA AIRWAYS	W	20669	864	01/16/73	JT3D-3B (HK)		[WO 12/19/94 KANO, NIGERIA]
B707-3J6B	B-2402	CHINA SOUTHWEST AIRLINES	W	20714	869	08/23/73	JT3D-7		[WO 10/02/90 CANTON, CHINA; REMAINS STD GUANGZHOU]
B707-366C	SU-AVX	EGYPT AIR	W	20760	865	03/30/73	JT3D-7		[WO 08/21/96 ISTANBUL]
B707-366C	SU-AXA	EGYPT AIR	W	20763	871	09/20/73	JT3D-7		[WO 12/25/76 BANGKOK]
B707-368C	A20-103	ROYAL AUSTRALIAN AIR FORCE	W	21103	905	10/14/75	JT3D-3B		HZ-ACG, N1987B [WO 10/29/91 VICTORIA, AUSTRALIA]
E-3A	77-0354	USAF	W	21554	933	01/19/79	JT3D(TF33-100A)		[WO 09/22/95 ELMENDORF AFB, AK]
B707-3K1C	YR-ABD	TAROM	W	21651	938	03/30/79	JT3D-3B		[WO 01/10/91 BUCHAREST]
E-3A	LX-N90457	NATO	W	22852	969	12/19/84	JT3D(TF33-100A)		79-0457 [WO 07/14/96 AKTION, GREECE]

Model 717

The Model 717 is the odd member of the Boeing jetliner family. It is only a Boeing in name as, in reality, it is the ultimate development of the Douglas DC-9, long the leading competitor of the Model 737. Developed in Long Beach, California, as the MD-95, this aircraft is the only McDonnell Douglas jetliner retained by Boeing for continued production after the merger with McDonnell Douglas Corporation. (Production of the MD-80, MD-90, and MD-11 was allowed to continue after the merger only to fill existing orders and satisfy requests from long-established customers.)

As the only McDonnell Douglas jetliner retained for long-term production, the MD-95 had to be given a Boeing model number in the 7X7 jetliner series. By then, Boeing jetliner designations had reached 777. Logically, the "adopted child" ought to have been designated Model 787. Apparently, however, that designation did not sit well with older Boeing managers as its use could have been seen as implying that the "Douglas" design was more modern than the 777. Some are said to have favored giving it a 7D7 designation, making it sound as being part of the seven-something-seven family while the "D" would have preserved a tie with the DC designations of yore. In the end, the MD-95 became the Model 717, an infelicitous choice as that model number was, and remains, that of the KC-135 and its transport and electronic-reconnaissance derivatives. Moreover, Model 717 had also been, briefly, the designation of the jetliner that became the Model 720 to satisfy the wish of its launch customer, United Airlines, for a newer-sounding designation.

The New Model 717-200

The latest member of the Boeing family, the Model 717 is the only California native in this prestigious family. It traces its roots to studies undertaken by Douglas Aircraft Company in 1963 after that southern California firm concluded that its marketing arrangement with Sud-Aviation of France would not result in the sale of many of the French Caravelle twinjets in the face of stiff competition from the Boeing 727. The resulting DC-9, was announced in April 1963. Its configuration was remarkably like that of the aircraft that Boeing chose to keep in production after merging with McDonnell Douglas 34 years later.

Planned from the onset with provision for substantial growth, the DC-9 entered service in December 1965 in the original Series 10 with maximum seating for 90 passengers. That number grew to 115 for the DC-9-30 of 1967, to 125 for the DC-9-40 of 1968, and to 139 for the DC-9-50 of 1975. Further growth in seating capacity occurred after the aircraft was given new MD-80 and MD-90 designations by McDonnell Douglas (which had acquired Douglas in April 1967), maximum seating for both versions being 172. The exception to that growth was the MD-87, which with a shortened fuselage providing accommodation for up to 139 passengers in high-density configuration, was intended as a successor to the DC-9-30.

By the mid-1990s, however, the MD-87 and other MD-80 models powered by refanned Pratt & Whitney JT8D-200 series turbofans and even the IAE V2500-powered MD90, were faced with increasing competitive pressure from the Airbus A320 family. Furthermore, after taking the lead in the twinjet market away from McDonnell Douglas with its CFM56-powered 737-300/400/500s, Boeing was in the process of launching the Next-Generation 737. The only promising alternative available to McDonnell Douglas was to "go under" the larger-capacity

Airbus and Boeing single-aisle twins by capitalizing on the five-abreast configuration of its twinjet (the 737 and A320 having both being designed for six-abreast economy accommodation). The result was the MD-95 launched in October 1995. Less than two months later, on December 1, the first contract for 50 aircraft was finalized with ValuJet.

Stemming from 30 years of progressive development, the MD-95 was expected to look much like its DC-9 forebear. However, it was designed to incorporate a new skin (composite materials having been introduced with the MD-80 development), revised tail surfaces (as developed for the MD-87), all-new engines (18,500 pounds [82.2 kilonewtons] of static thrust BMW Rolls-Royce BR715 high-bypass turbofans), and a state-of-the-art cockpit (with six advanced liquid-crystal displays and provision for Future Air Navigation System).

Other significant changes, announced when the McDonnell Douglas MD-95 was launched and incorporated when the aircraft was built as the Boeing 717-200, included a new cabin interior with large-capacity overhead racks, vacuum-evacuation lavatories, and a modern air-conditioning system.

The newly labeled 717 first flew at Long Beach on September 2, 1998, and the 717-200 received joint certification from the FAA and Europe's Joint Aviation Authorities (JAA) one day short of the first anniversary of its maiden flight. It was placed into service by AirTran Airways (the former ValuJet) shortly afterward.

Comparing their basic characteristics highlights the size and performance similarities between the Douglas DC-9 Series 30 and the Boeing 717-200.

	DC-9-32	717-200/717-200 High Gross Weight
Span	93 ft 5 in (28.47 m)	93 ft 3 in (28.42 m)
Length	119 ft 5 in (36.39 m)	124 ft (37.80 m)
Height	27ft 6in (8.38m)	29ft 1in (8.86m)
Wing area	1,000.7 sq ft (93 m^2)	1,000 sq ft (92.9 m^2)
High-density seating	115	117
Two-class seating	85	106
Underfloor cargo	610 cu ft (17.3 m^3)	935/730 cu ft (26.5/20.7 m^3)
TO thrust per engine	14,000 lb (62.3 kN)	18,500 lb (82.2 kN)
Fuel capacity	3,680 gal (13,930 l)	3,785/4,540 gal (14,327/17,185 l)
Operating weight, empty	56,850lb (25,787kg)	67,124/68,124 lb (30,447/31,059 kg)
MTOW	108,000lb (48,498kg)	110,000/121,000 lb (49,895/54,885 kg)
Typical cruise speed	0.77 Mach	0.77 Mach
Typical range	1,350 nm (2,500 km)	1,430/2,060 nm (2,650/3815 km)

Plans for a version with a shortened fuselage, the 717-100, and one for a version with a longer fuselage and increased seating capacity, the 717-300, have been discussed with prospective customers. However, by the time this was written neither had been ordered. For customers requiring greater range, the 717-200 is available with additional fuel tanks in the lower fuselage.

Boeing 717 (MD-95) Commercial Jet Aircraft Census

The aircraft in the following tables are listed in order of the following: 1) ICAO country prefixes; 2) operator; 3) aircraft type; and 4) registration.

The total built was 60-plus from 1998 to present, but the Model 717 was still in production at the time of publication.

A/C TYPE	CURRENT REG. NO.	LAST KNOWN OPERATOR (OWNER)	STATUS	ORIGINAL MSN	LINE NO.	DEL. DATE	ENG. TYPE	FLEET NO.	PREV. REG. [COMMENTS]
EC-SPAIN									
B717-2CM	EC-HNY	AEROLINEAS BALEARES		55059	5023	06/22/00	BR715		N6203U
B717-2CM	EC-HNZ	AEROLINEAS BALEARES		55060	5026	06/29/00	BR715		N9010L
B717-2CM	EC-HOA	AEROLINEAS BALEARES		55061	5029	07/30/00	BR715		
B717-23S	EC-HUZ	AEROLINEAS BALEARES (PEMB)		55066	5054	05/15/01	BR715		
EZ-TURKMENISTAN									
B717-22K	EZ-	TURKMENISTAN AIRLINES	N	55153	5072		BR715		
HS-THAILAND									
B717-23S	HS-PGO	BANGKOK AIRWAYS (PEMB)		55067	5059	04/30/01	BR715		
B717-23S	HS-PGP	BANGKOK AIRWAYS (PEMB)		55064	5037	11/07/00	BR715		N9014S
N-UNITED STATES OF AMERICA									
B717-2BD	N940AT	AIRTRAN AIRWAYS		55004	5005	11/26/99	BR715	702	N717XE [P2]
B717-2BD	N942AT	AIRTRAN AIRWAYS		55005	5006	09/23/99	BR715	703	
B717-2BD	N943AT	AIRTRAN AIRWAYS		55006	5007	09/24/99	BR715	704	
B717-2BD	N944AT	AIRTRAN AIRWAYS		55007	5008	10/26/99	BR715	705	
B717-2BD	N945AT	AIRTRAN AIRWAYS		55008	5009	10/27/99	BR715	706	
B717-2BD	N946AT	AIRTRAN AIRWAYS		55009	5010	11/29/99	BR715	707	
B717-2BD	N947AT	AIRTRAN AIRWAYS		55010	5011	12/22/99	BR715	708	
B717-2BD	N948AT	AIRTRAN AIRWAYS		55011	5012	12/22/99	BR715	709	
B717-2BD	N949AT	AIRTRAN AIRWAYS (FSBU)		55003	5004	01/27/00	BR715	701	N717XD [P1]
B717-2BD	N950AT	AIRTRAN AIRWAYS (FSBU)		55012	5018	03/28/00	BR715	710	
B717-2BD	N951AT	AIRTRAN AIRWAYS (FSBU)		55013	5021	05/31/00	BR715	711	
B717-2BD	N952AT	AIRTRAN AIRWAYS (FSBU)		55014	5027	07/19/00	BR715	712	
B717-2BD	N953AT	AIRTRAN AIRWAYS (FSBU)		55015	5033	09/28/00	BR715	713	
B717-2BD	N954AT	AIRTRAN AIRWAYS (FSBU)		55016	5036	10/26/00	BR715	714	
B717-2BD	N955AT	AIRTRAN AIRWAYS (FSBU)		55017	5040	11/28/00	BR715	715	
B717-2BD	N956AT	AIRTRAN AIRWAYS (FSBU)		55018	5044	12/21/00	BR715	716	
B717-2BD	N957AT	AIRTRAN AIRWAYS (FSBU)		55019	5047	01/17/01	BR715		
B717-2BD	N958AT	AIRTRAN AIRWAYS (FSBU)		55020	5051	02/28/01	BR715		
B717-2BD	N959AT	AIRTRAN AIRWAYS		55021	5057	03/29/01	BR715		
B717-2BD	N960AT	AIRTRAN AIRWAYS		55022	5058	04/30/01	BR715		
B717-2BD	N961AT	AIRTRAN AIRWAYS	N	55023	5062		BR715		

A/C TYPE	CURRENT REG. NO.	LAST KNOWN OPERATOR (OWNER)	STATUS	ORIGINAL MSN	LINE NO.	DEL. DATE	ENG. TYPE	FLEET NO.	PREV. REG. [COMMENTS]
B717-200	N717XA	BOEING	N	55000	5001		BR715		FF 09/02/98 [1ST PROTOTYPE -T1]
B717-22A	N475HA	HAWAIIAN AIR (FSBU)		55121	5050	02/28/01	BR715		
B717-22A	N476HA	HAWAIIAN AIR (FSBU)		55118	5053	03/14/01	BR715		
B717-22A	N477HA	HAWAIIAN AIR		55122	5061	04/30/01	BR715		
B717-22A	N478HA	HAWAIIAN AIR	N	55123	5064		BR715		
B717-231	N401TW	TRANS WORLD AIRLINES (FSBU)		55058	5017	02/18/00	BR715	2401	
B717-231	N402TW	TRANS WORLD AIRLINES (FSBU)		55069	5019	04/11/00	BR715	2402	
B717-231	N403TW	TRANS WORLD AIRLINES (FSBU)		55070	5022	05/15/00	BR715	2403	
B717-231	N2404A	TRANS WORLD AIRLINES (FSBU)		55071	5024	06/08/00	BR715	2404	
B717-231	N405TW	TRANS WORLD AIRLINES (FSBU)		55072	5025	06/15/00	BR715	2405	
B717-231	N406TW	TRANS WORLD AIRLINES (FSBU)		55073	5028	07/12/00	BR715	2406	
B717-231	N407TW	TRANS WORLD AIRLINES (FSBU)		55074	5030	08/01/00	BR715	2407	
B717-231	N408TW	TRANS WORLD AIRLINES (FSBU)		55075	5032	09/26/00	BR715	2408	
B717-231	N409TW	TRANS WORLD AIRLINES (FSBU)		55076	5035	09/28/00	BR715	2409	
B717-231	N2410W	TRANS WORLD AIRLINES		55077	5038	10/24/00	BR715	2410	
B717-231	N411TW	TRANS WORLD AIRLINES (FSBU)		55078	5039	10/26/00	BR715	2411	
B717-231	N412TW	TRANS WORLD AIRLINES (MDFC)		55079	5042	11/29/00	BR715	2412	
B717-231	N413TW	TRANS WORLD AIRLINES (MDFC)		55080	5043	12/15/00	BR715	2413	
B717-231	N2414E	TRANS WORLD AIRLINES (MDFC)		55081	5045	12/28/00	BR715	2414	
B717-231	N415TW	TRANS WORLD AIRLINES (MDFC)		55082	5046	12/28/00	BR715	2415	

A/C TYPE	CURRENT REG. NO.	LAST KNOWN OPERATOR (OWNER)	STATUS	ORIGINAL MSN	LINE NO.	DEL. DATE	ENG. TYPE	FLEET NO.	PREV. REG. [COMMENTS]
B717-231	N416TW	TRANS WORLD AIRLINES (MDFC)		55083	5049	04/12/01	BR715	2416	
B717-231	N2417F	TRANS WORLD AIRLINES (MDFC)		55084	5052	04/12/01	BR715	2417	
B717-231	N418TW	TRANS WORLD AIRLINES (MDFC)		55085	5055	04/12/01	BR715	2418	
B717-231	N2419C	TRANS WORLD AIRLINES (MDFC)		55086	5056	04/12/01	BR715	2419	
B717-231	N420TW	TRANS WORLD AIRLINES		55087	5060	04/26/01	BR715	2420	
B717-231	N2421A	TRANS WORLD AIRLINES	N	55088	5063		BR715	2421	

SX-GREECE

A/C TYPE	CURRENT REG. NO.	LAST KNOWN OPERATOR (OWNER)	STATUS	ORIGINAL MSN	LINE NO.	DEL. DATE	ENG. TYPE	FLEET NO.	PREV. REG. [COMMENTS]
B717-2K9	SX-BOA	OLYMPIC AVIATION (BAVA)		55056	5015	12/29/99	BR715		
B717-2K9	SX-BOB	OLYMPIC AVIATION (BAVA)		55053	5016	12/29/99	BR715		
B717-23S	SX-BOC	OLYMPIC AVIATION (PEMB)		55065	5048	01/26/01	BR715		

VH-AUSTRALIA

A/C TYPE	CURRENT REG. NO.	LAST KNOWN OPERATOR (OWNER)	STATUS	ORIGINAL MSN	LINE NO.	DEL. DATE	ENG. TYPE	FLEET NO.	PREV. REG. [COMMENTS]
B717-2K9	VH-IMD	IMPULSE AIRLINES (BAVA)		55055	5014	12/29/99	BR715		N9012S
B717-2K9	VH-IMP	IMPULSE AIRLINES (BAVA)		55054	5013	12/29/99	BR715		N9012J
B717-2K9	VH-LAX	IMPULSE AIRLINES (BAVA)		55057	5020	04/28/00	BR715		N6202S
B717-23S	VH-AFR	IMPULSE AIRLINES (PEMB)		55062	5031	08/17/00	BR715		
B717-23S	VH-SMH	IMPULSE AIRLINES (PEMB)		55063	5034	09/05/00	BR715		
B717-2BD	VH-VQA	IMPULSE AIRLINES		55001	5002	02/07/01	BR715		N717XB
B717-2BD	VH-VQB	IMPULSE AIRLINES		55002	5003	12/29/00	BR715		N717XC
B717-2CM	VH-VQC	IMPULSE AIRLINES (PEMB)		55151	5041	12/29/00	BR715		N6202S

Chapter 4

Model 727

The second type of all-new jetliners developed by Boeing—the trijet Model 727—was built in larger numbers than the combined 707/720 series. In fact, with 1,832 Model 727s built between 1963 and 1984, the Boeing trijet transport aircraft remained for many years the most successful jetliner produced anywhere in the world. In terms of deliveries, however, the 727 was overtaken by the 737 in March 1990 and by the DC-9/MD-80 in April 1991, and will next be topped by the Airbus family of single-aisle twinjets.

The 727 saga began in 1956 when Boeing, having just obtained 70 orders from six airlines for its first jetliner, initiated preliminary design studies for a smaller jetliner. The new jetliner was intended mainly as a replacement for twin-engine propliners such as the Convair 240/340/440 series. As such it was to be optimized for short- to medium-range operations from airports with runways not suited for the larger and heavier four-engined jetliners.

How Many Engines and Where?

The first concept drawings in February 1956 were for a 70-seat aircraft with a maximum takeoff weight (MTOW) of 120,000 pounds (54,430 kilograms) and wing area of 1,800 square feet (167.2 m^2). One design called for the use of two Rolls-Royce Conway turbofans rated at 14,450 pounds (64.3 kilonewtons) of static thrust, while another was planned around four Pratt & Whitney JT8A-1 turbojets (civilian derivatives of the military J52) rated at 7,600 pounds of static thrust (33.8 kilonewtons). These two concepts quickly led to parallel studies of aircraft to be

powered by two, three, or four turbojets or turbofans. In most instances two- and four-engine designs called for wing-mounted engine pods, while finding a suitable powerplant arrangement proved more challenging in the case of three-engine studies. This led to proposals for mounting two of the engines either under the wings or on the sides of the fuselage, with the third engine to be tail-mounted.

In addition, Boeing studied several more unusual powerplant arrangements. Notably, a May 1956 conceptual study called for a 46-seat design to be powered by eight General Electric J85 turbojets rated at 2,450 pounds (10.9 kilonewtons) of static thrust mounted in four underwing pods. An aircraft with greater seating was considered in October 1960 with two Pratt & Whitney JT3D-3 turbofans rated at 18,000 pounds (80.1 kilonewtons) of static thrust in wing pods and a 6,000-pound-static (26.7-kilonewton) booster engine in the tail. Conversely, in July 1957 Boeing had also looked at a more conservative turboprop-powered alternative, not unlike the four-turboprop Lockheed Electra.

Number and location of engines were not the only variables because for more than four years neither Boeing nor the airlines could decide what size of aircraft would best fit the market. Thus, in the case of two-engine designs, seating capacity ranged between 42 and 93, wing area between 1,035 and 1,800 square feet (96.2 and 167.2 m^2), and MTOW between 64,000 and 120,000 pounds (29,030 and 54,430 kilograms). Corresponding values varied just as much for three- and four-engine designs.

Three-engine studies had initially centered on using Pratt & Whitney JT8A turbojets. By 1959, however, the favored engine was the Allison ARB 163 or 963 (the Rolls-Royce Spey built under license in the United States) with static thrust of between 10,000 and 12,000 pounds (44.5 and 53.4 kilonewtons). Then, after Pratt & Whitney specially developed the JT8D by fitting a two-stage JT3D fan in front of the gas generator of the JT8A turbojet, this new turbofan got the nod. Briefly, consideration was still given to having two engines in wing pods and one in the rear fuselage before it was decided to cluster the three JT8Ds in the rear of the aircraft. At that time, two- and four-engine studies were terminated. In October 1960, before the 727 was officially announced, Boeing ordered JT8D-1s rated at 14,000 pounds (62.2 kilonewtons) of static thrust to power its trijet prototype.

Time would prove that the selection of the more powerful Pratt & Whitney JT8D in preference to the Allison-built Rolls-Royce Spey would give a clear performance advantage to the 727 over the rival Spey-powered de Havilland Trident. In addition, the decision to retain the upper-fuselage cross-section of the 707/720 for the 727 resulted in greater comfort for passengers traveling in the Boeing trijet than for those flying in the slightly slimmer Trident. Beneath the floor, the 727 fuselage was made narrower than that of the 707/720 because passengers on short-range flights were expected to carry less baggage than passengers on longer flights.

While questions pertaining to the powerplant installation had long been the main focus of design activities, work proceeded on optimizing the 727 for operations from regional airports with shorter runways and less developed terminal facilities. For optimum airfield performance, the wings were to have 32 degrees of sweep at the quarter-chord and were to be fitted with triple-slotted trailing-edge flaps and, on their leading edge, with Kruger flaps inboard and slats outboard. For ease of operations at these airports, the 727 was to be provided with self-contained airstairs (aft of the cockpit on the left side of the fuselage and centrally under the rear fuselage) and with an auxiliary power unit (APU) housed in the right landing-gear wheel-well.

By the early fall of 1960, the design of wings, powerplant installation, and passenger accommodation had reached satisfactory levels, thus allowing formal sale proposals to be made to U.S. and foreign carriers.

The first airlines to firm up their interest by ordering the new trijet were Eastern Air Lines and United Airlines, which both contracted for 40 aircraft on December 5, 1960. Unfortunately, the trijet was committed to production just as the air transportation industry entered one of its most troubled periods. Consequently, orders for 727s were rare for three years (37 aircraft and two new customers in 1961, 10 aircraft and only one customer in 1962, and 20 aircraft for three new and one prior customer in 1963). Thereafter, however, business improved rapidly, and sales of the 727 overtook combined 707/720 sales in 1970 and passed the 1,000 mark—a first for a jetliner—in September 1972.

727-100

The first 727 trijet layout in the fall of 1956 had called for an aircraft with a wing area of 1,245 square feet (115.7 m^2), a takeoff gross weight of 90,000 pounds (40,823 kilograms), and accommodation for only 52 passengers. By the time the 727 was committed to production at the end of 1960, these figures had increased to 1,650 square feet (153.3 m^2), 152,000 pounds (68,946 kilograms), and 129 passengers in six-abreast configuration. During this long gestation several tail configurations were evaluated before Boeing settled on a T-tail design with a dual-powered, variable-incidence tailplane mounted near the top of the fin. Unlike what they had done for the 707 and 720, Boeing engineers also chose to have all other control surfaces hydraulically powered, with automatic reversion to manual controls.

Built in the Renton plant, the Boeing-owned prototype of the 727-100 (l/n 1, s/n 18293, N7001U) first flew on February 9, 1963. Retained by Boeing, this historic aircraft was donated to the Museum of Flight in Seattle in January 1991, more than six years after the 1,832nd and last Boeing trijet had been delivered. The 727 was awarded its ATC on December 24, 1963—the first time a new-type jetliner was certified in less than one year—with customer deliveries starting on October 29, 1963, when United Airlines accepted l/n 5, s/n 18296. It was Eastern Air Lines, however, that initiated Boeing trijet service, doing so on February 1, 1964, between Miami, Florida; Washington, D.C.; and Philadelphia, Pennsylvania. Four months later, the 727-100 became the first jetliner allowed to operate from the noise-sensitive La Guardia Airport in New York because its nacelle design, which mixed fan and main jet exhausts, made it significantly quieter than other types.

During the course of production, MTOW was increased to a maximum of 160,000 pounds (72,575 kilograms) and airlines were given a choice of JT8D variants, with static thrust increasing slightly to 14,500 pounds (64.5 kilonewtons).

Deliveries of 727-100s continued until October 1972, when Dominicana obtained the 408th and last of these passenger-configured jetliners. That aircraft, a 727-1J1, was l/n 829, s/n 20426, which was registered HI-212 in the Dominican Republic. Before closing the entry on the Series 100, mention must be made of an ex-Faucett 727-63 (l/n 555, s/n 19846), which was modified in 1986 as a test bed for the General Electric unducted-fan (UDF) engine. The UDF, which was under consideration to power the proposed 7J7 advanced-technology twin propeller-turbine transport, replaced the JT8D on the starboard side of the 727 and drove contra-rotating pusher propellers.

Most of the more than 200 Model 727-100s remaining in service in 2001 have been either re-engined and/or modified as freighters, as described separately.

727-100QC and Freighter Conversions

Preliminary design studies for a cargo version of the 727 were initiated in July 1960, before the design of the passenger-configured 727 was finalized. However, no customer for cargo 727s was found until July 1964, when Northwest Airlines ordered two passenger/cargo convertible aircraft and amended its initial contract for 11 trijets to have one delivered as a 727-100C.

Ordered by Northwest as a 727-51C but retained by Boeing and subsequently leased to various airlines, the first passenger/cargo convertible trijet (l/n 211, s/n 18897) flew on December 30, 1965. Deliveries to Northwest commenced in April 1966. Altogether, 164 Series 100C passenger/cargo 727s were delivered to 24 airlines and a leasing company. The last was l/n 857, s/n 20476, which went to South African Airways in March 1971.

All 727-100Cs had a 86- by 134-in (2.18- by 3.40-meter) upward-opening main-deck cargo door on the left side of the forward fuselage, reinforced flooring with tie-downs, and quickly removable cabin equipment for conversion between passenger, cargo, or passenger/cargo configurations. In addition, beginning in April 1965 with orders from United and Pan American, Boeing conversion kits were acquired by several airlines to speed up configuration changes by mounting all passenger amenities (seats, galleys, and additional lavatories) on pallets secured directly onto the cargo floor. When using the modification kits, the quick-change aircraft were designated 727-100QCs. Later, the designation 727-100F was given to 727-100s retrofitted with a main-deck cargo door and reinforced flooring and to 727-100Cs and QCs permanently modified as freighters.

Cargo-modified 727-100s and 100C/QCs account for the majority of the more than 300 Series 100 trijets still in service in the spring of 2001. To comply with current FAA and ICAO noise regulations these aircraft have been re-engined, fitted with hushkitts, and/or fitted with winglets.

The most extensive of these modifications aimed at reducing noise emission was undertaken by The Dee Howard Company in San Antonio, Texas, for United Parcel Service (UPS). It entailed substituting three Rolls-Royce Tay 651-54 turbofans rated at 15,100 pounds (67.2 kilonewtons) of static thrust for the JT8Ds powering 61 previously owned 727-100C/QCs and to another 727 belonging to a corporate operator. In addition, the re-engined aircraft had their cockpit upgraded with Collins Electronic Flight Instrumentation System (EFIS). A Tay-engined aircraft first flew in April 1992, and FAA approval was obtained in November of that year.

A less drastic upgrade was developed by Federal Express (FedEx), which designed lightweight hushkitss for 727-100s and 727-200s. Furthermore, Winglets Systems Inc. in White Plains, New York, and Kelowna Flightcraft in British Columbia, Canada, have developed winglets, which not only bring 727-100s in compliance with noise regulations but also improve takeoff performance and increase payload range.

727-200

Design of a larger-capacity version of the 727 was initiated in July 1965 and announced one month later when the news of a six-aircraft order from Northeast Airlines was released. Except for the insertion of two 10-foot (3.05-meter) plugs, one fore and one aft of the wings, the resulting 727-200 was to be nearly identical to the -100. Ten rows of seats could be added to bring high-density seating accommodation up to 189.

Line number 433, s/n 19536, first flew on July 27, 1967, and FAA certification was received four months later. Aircraft were initially delivered with a MTOW of 169,000 pounds (76,675 kilograms), but that was later increased to 175,000 pounds (79,379 kilograms). Power was usually provided by JT8D-9s or -9As rated at 14,500 pounds (64.5 kilonewtons) of static thrust or JT8D-11s rated at 15,000 pounds (66.7 kilonewtons).

Further weight and thrust increases came with the development of the Advanced 727-200. Deliveries of that version started in June 1972 when All Nippon Airways received l/n 881, s/n 20572. The MTOW for this variant started at 191,000 pounds (86,636 kilograms) and rose to 210,000 pounds (37,119 kilograms) with power being provided by JT8D-15 engines rated at 15,500 pounds (68.9 kilonewtons) of static thrust or JT8D-17s rated at 16,000 pounds (71.2 kilonewtons). Some aircraft were powered by JT8D-17Rs with automatic thrust reverse and a reserve setting boosting takeoff power to 17,400 pounds (77.4 kilonewtons) of static thrust. In addition, aircraft for Mexicana Airlines were fitted with jet-assisted take-off (JATO) bottles for use on takeoff on hot days from the "hot-and-high" airport in Mexico City. However, JATOs were exceedingly noisy and saw little use. Other changes during the course of production included a "wide-body-look" interior as introduced by Lufthansa and Air Algerie in April 1971.

A total of 1,245 passenger-configured 727-200s and Advanced 727-200s were built, with the last (l/n 1817, s/n 23052) being delivered to US Air in April 1983. They were followed by 15 cargo-configured 727-200Fs for FedEx that were fitted with a main-deck cargo door and reinforced flooring similar to those of the 727-100Cs. The -200Fs, however, had no cabin windows or provision for conversion to passenger configuration. Maximum cargo payload for that version was 58,000 pounds (26,310 kilograms) in 11 main-deck pallets and in underfloor bulk holds. The last of these aircraft (s/n 22938, N217FE), which was the 1,832nd and final Boeing trijet, was delivered on September 18, 1984.

In addition to the 15 purpose-built 727-2S2Fs for FedEx, the world's airlines are now operating a large number of passenger-configured -200s modified as freighters by FedEx, Hamilton Aviation, and Pemco.

At the instigation of American Airlines, Boeing studied in 1981–1982 the feasibility of re-engining 727-200s with a pair of advanced-technology Pratt & Whitney PW2037 turbofans. The cost of re-engining was estimated at half the price of an all-new 757. Nevertheless, American Airlines and other carriers lost interest. Less drastic noise reduction modifications have been developed to enable passenger- and cargo-configured 727-200s to operate within current noise standards with hushkitss being developed by FedEx while Winglets Systems Inc. came up with winglets. A more extensive conversion has been undertaken under the aegis of Boeing, with the center engine being fitted with acoustic treatment and having its thrust reverser removed, while the outer engines were replaced by refanned JT8D-217C engines rated at 20,000 pounds (89 kilonewtons) of static thrust.

In the spring of 2001, there were still some 870 Series 200 aircraft in service. Most had been fitted with hushkitss and other noise reduction devices, and many had been converted as freighters.

Boeing 727 Principal Characteristics and Performance

	727-100	727-100QC	Advanced 727-200
Span, ft in (m)	108' (32.92)	108' (32.92)	108' (32.92)
Length, ft in (m)	133' 2" (40.59)	133' 2" (40.59)	153' 2" (40.59)
Height, ft in (m)	34' (10.36)	34' (10.36)	34' (10.36)
Wing area, sq ft (m^2)	1,650 (153.3)	1,650 (153.3)	1,650 (153.3)
High-density seating	129	129	189
Two-class seating	94	94	118
Underfloor cargo, cu ft (m^3)	900 (25.5)	890 (25.2)	1,485 (42.1)
Maximum cargo load, lb (kg)	N/A	40,900 (18,550)	N/A
TO thrust per engine, lb st (kN)	14,000/14,500 (62.3/64.5)	14,000/14,500 (62.3/64.5)	14,500/17,400 (64.5/77.4)
Fuel capacity, U.S. gal (liters)	7,174/10,586 (27,156/40,072)	8,186 (30,987)	8,186/9,806 (30,987/37,119)
MTOW, lb (kg)	152,000/160,000 (68,946/72,575)	169,000 (76,675)	191,000/210,000 (86,636/95,254)
Typical cruise speed, mph (km/h)	495 (917)	495 (917)	495 (917)
Typical range, nm (km)	2,100/3,100 (3,890/5,740)	1,300/2,300 (cargo/pax: 2,410/4,260)	2,175/2,500 (4,030/4,630)

Boeing 727 Commercial Jet Aircraft Census

The aircraft in the following tables are listed in order of the following: 1) ICAO country prefixes; 2) operator; 3) aircraft type; and 4) registration.

The total built was 1,832 (572 B727-100 and 1,260 B727-200) from 1963 to 1984.

A/C TYPE	CURRENT REG. NO.	LAST KNOWN OPERATOR (OWNER)	STATUS	ORIGINAL MSN	LINE NO.	DEL. DATE	ENG. TYPE	FLEET NO.	PREV. REG. [COMMENTS]
A40-OMAN									
B727-086	EP-IRB	OMAN AIR (IRA)	L	19172	323	10/13/66	JT8D-7B		
A6-UNITED ARAB EMIRATES									
B727-294(A)	A6-SAA	NOVA GULF (ETA AIR SERVICES)		22043	1559	12/10/79	JT8D-17 (HK3)		YV-74C, N921TS, A7-ABG [LST SIERRA NATIONAL]
A7-QATAR									
B727-2M7(A)	A7-ABC	QATAR AIRWAYS		21951	1680	11/07/80	JT8D-17R		N741RW, A6-HRR, A6-EMA [STD DOH; FOR SALE]
B727-264(A)	A7-ABD	QATAR AIRWAYS		22982	1802	07/17/82	JT8D-17R		N4554N, A6-HHM, A6-EMB [STD DOH; FOR SALE]
A9C-BAHRAIN									
B727-2M7(A) (RE) (WL)	A9C-BA	BAHRAIN AMIRI FLIGHT		21824	1595	03/24/80	JT8D-217C/-17R N740RW		
C-CANADA									
B727-027 (F)	C-FACX	ALL CANADA EXPRESS		19500	448	08/14/67	JT8D-7B		N7290, PT-TYM, N727EV
B727-243 (A) (F)	C-FACA	ALL CANADA EXPRESS (PAC COAST)		22052	1568	01/17/80	JT8D-15		I-DIRM, N581PE, N12411, VT-LCA, N179PC
B727-260 (A) (F)	C-FACJ	ALL CANADA EXPRESS		21979	1534	10/17/79	JT8D-17R (HK3)		ET-AHM, N979AL
B727-217 (A) (F)	C-FACK	ALL CANADA EXPRESS		21056	1122	04/08/75	JT8D-17 (HK3)		C-GCPB, G-BKNG, G-NROA, C-GRYR
B727-260 (A) (F)	C-FACM	ALL CANADA EXPRESS		22759	1789	12/21/81	JT8D-17R (HK3)		ET-AHK, HK-3834, N980AL
B727-221 (A) (F)	C-FACN	ALL CANADA EXPRESS		22540	1796	05/26/82	JT8D-17 (HK3)		N368PA
B727-217 (A) (F)	C-FACR	ALL CANADA EXPRESS		21055	1117	03/20/75	JT8D-15 (HK3)		C-GCPA, G-BKAG, C-GRYC
B727-227 (A) (F)	C-FACW	ALL CANADA EXPRESS (FINO)		21366	1274	07/07/77	JT8D-9A		N452BN, N70755
B727-223 (A) (F)	C-FUAC	ALL CANADA EXPRESS (AIRCORP)		22012	1655	09/04/80	JT8D-15 (HK3)		N896AA
B727-277 (A) (F)	C-GACC	ALL CANADA EXPRESS		20550	1030	04/05/74	JT8D-15 (HK3)		VH-RMW, N276WC, G-BPNS, C-GRYZ
B727-223 (A) (F)	C-GACG	ALL CANADA EXPRESS (AIRCRAFT 22011 INC)		22011	1653	08/28/80	JT8D-15 (HK3)		N895AA
B727-171C	C-FPXD	CORP AIR		19859	559	04/16/68	JT8D-7A		N1727T
B727-027C	C-GFRB	FIRST AIR		19120	396	04/17/67	JT8D-7B (HK3)		N7281, 3X-GCA, 3X-GCH, 5N-AWH
B727-044C	C-GVFA	FIRST AIR		20475	854	02/09/71	JT8D-7B (HK3)		ZS-SBH, N26879 [OPF CAY FROM 03/00]
B727-225 (F)	C-FIFA	FIRST AIR		20381	823	07/14/70	JT8D-7B (HK3)		N8838E, EI-BVO [LST ABR 09/00]
B727-233 (A) (F)	C-FUFA	FIRST AIR		20941	1128	05/08/75	JT8D-15 (HK3)		C-GAAJ, N727LS
B727-233 (A) (F)	C-GXFA	FIRST AIR		20938	1105	03/13/75	JT8D-15		N727GC, C-GAAG
B727-2H3 (A) (F)	C-GYFA	FIRST AIR		21234	1209	06/18/76	JT8D-9A		TS-JHS, N724SK [LST ABR 10/15/00]
B727-025 (F)	C-FKFO	KELOWNA FLIGHTCRAFT		18971	230	02/15/66	JT8D-7B (HK3)	700	N8147N, N280NE [LST WINNPORT AC]

A/C TYPE	CURRENT REG. NO.	LAST KNOWN OPERATOR (OWNER)	STATUS	ORIGINAL MSN	LINE NO.	DEL. DATE	ENG. TYPE	FLEET NO.	PREV. REG. [COMMENTS]
B727-022C	C-FKFP	KELOWNA FLIGHTCRAFT		19205	438	08/03/67	JT8D-7B (HK3)	703	N7430U, N109FE [OPF PUROLATOR COURIER]
B727-022C	C-GKFA	KELOWNA FLIGHTCRAFT		19806	547	03/25/68	JT8D-7B (HK3)	704	N7432U, N110FE [OPF PUROLATOR COURIER]
B727-025C	C-GKFB	KELOWNA FLIGHTCRAFT		19358	367	03/18/67	JT8D-7B (HK3)	705	N8158G, N122FE [OPF PUROLATOR COURIER]
B727-051C (WL)	C-GKFC	KELOWNA FLIGHTCRAFT		18897	211	04/06/67	JT8D-7B (HK3)	701	N7270C, N303BN, N15512, OB-R-1115 [OPF PUROLATOR COURIER]
B727-025C (WL)	C-GKFN	KELOWNA FLIGHTCRAFT		19359	368	02/24/67	JT8D-7B (HK3)	707	N8159G, N123FE [OPF PUROLATOR COURIER]
B727-172C (WL)	C-GKFT	KELOWNA FLIGHTCRAFT		19807	575	05/31/68	JT8D-7B (HK3)	702	N727AL, N722JE [OPF PUROLATOR COURIER]
B727-092C	C-GKFV	KELOWNA FLIGHTCRAFT		19173	308	10/03/66	JT8D-9	708	N5055, N18476 [STD YLW; BEING STRIPPED FOR PARTS]
B727-022C	C-GKFW	KELOWNA FLIGHTCRAFT		19805	543	03/14/68	JT8D-7B (HK3)	709	N7431U, N111FE [OPF PUROLATOR COURIER]
B727-022C	C-GKFZ	KELOWNA FLIGHTCRAFT		19204	436	07/25/67	JT8D-7B (HK3)	706	N7429U, N108FE [OPF PUROLATOR COURIER]
B727-225 (F) (WL)	C-GACU	KELOWNA FLIGHTCRAFT		20152	775	11/26/69	JT8D-7B (HK3)	710	N8833E [OPF PUROLATOR COURIER]
B727-227 (A) (F)	C-GIKF	KELOWNA FLIGHTCRAFT		20772	982	10/23/73	JT8D-7B (HK3)	721	N426BN, N551PE, N99763 [OPF PUROLATOR COURIER]
B727-227 (A) (F)	C-GJKF	KELOWNA FLIGHTCRAFT		21042	1106	02/20/75	JT8D-9A (HK3)	722	N435BN, N560PE, N10756 [OPF PUROLATOR COURIER]
B727-225 (F) (WL)	C-GKFH	KELOWNA FLIGHTCRAFT		20153	779	12/12/69	JT8D-7B (HK3)	711	XA-SJP, N8834E [OPF PUROLATOR COURIER]
B727-227 (A) (F)	C-GKKF	KELOWNA FLIGHTCRAFT		21043	1113	03/13/75	JT8D-9A (HK3)	723	N436BN, N561PE, N16758 [OPF PUROLATOR COURIER]
B727-227 (A) (F)	C-GLKF	KELOWNA FLIGHTCRAFT		21118	1167	10/01/75	JT8D-9A (HK3)	724	N439BN, N564PE, N14760 [OPF PUROLATOR COURIER]
B727-227 (A) (F)	C-GMKF	KELOWNA FLIGHTCRAFT		21119	1175	12/02/75	JT8D-9A (HK3)	725	N440BN, N565PE, N16761 [OPF PUROLATOR COURIER; BEING CVTD TO FRTR]
B727-227 (A) (F)	C-GNKF	KELOWNA FLIGHTCRAFT		20839	1031	04/19/74	JT8D-9A (HK3)	726	N432BN, N557PE, N88770
B727-214	C-GOKF	KELOWNA FLIGHTCRAFT		20162	715	04/24/69	JT8D-9A (HK3)	729	N7279F, XA-SJM, N409BN [LST SSV]
B727-243 (A)	C-	KELOWNA FLIGHTCRAFT		21265	1226	10/18/76	JT8D-9A		N17402 [TO BE CVTD TO FRTR]
B727-227 (A)	N17773	MONFORT AVIATION LLC		21045	1133	05/15/75	JT8D-9A		N438BN, N563PE
B727-025 (F)	C-FBWX	MORNINGSTAR AIR EXPRESS (FDX)	L	18286	182	09/24/65	JT8D-7B (HK3)		N8135N, N153FE [OPF FDX]
B727-022 (F)	C-FBWY	MORNINGSTAR AIR EXPRESS (FDX)	L	19085	349	12/22/66	JT8D-7B (HK3)		N7072U, N192FE [OPF FDX]
B727-116C	C-GBWH	MORNINGSTAR AIR EXPRESS (FDX)	L	19814	600	07/11/68	JT8D-7B (HK3)		CC-CFE, N115FE [OPF FDX]
B727-022 (F)	C-GBWS	MORNINGSTAR AIR EXPRESS (FDX)	L	18867	247	03/30/66	JT8D-7B (HK3)		N7060U, N180FE [OPF FDX]
B727-214	C-GOKF	SKYSERVICE (KFA)	L	20162	715	04/24/69	JT8D-9A (HK3)		N7279F, XA-SJM, N409BN [OPF ROOTS AIR]
B727-231	C-GSHI	SKYSERVICE (SPORT HAWK)	L	20055	719	05/28/69	JT8D-9A		N64322
B727-231	C-GSHI	SPORT HAWK INTL. AIRLINES		20055	719	05/28/69	JT8D-9A		N64322 [LST/OPB SSV]

A/C TYPE	CURRENT REG. NO.	LAST KNOWN OPERATOR (OWNER)	STATUS	ORIGINAL MSN	LINE NO.	DEL. DATE	ENG. TYPE	FLEET NO.	PREV. REG. [COMMENTS]
B727-243 (A)	N521DB	SPORT HAWK INTL. AIRLINES (RIVERHORSE)		21266	1227	10/18/76	JT8D-9A (HK3)		N40115, I-DIRO, N573PE, N17403 [LST/OPB RYN]
B727-231	N64320	SPORT HAWK INTL. AIRLINES		20053	713	04/28/69	JT8D-9A (HK3)		[STD TUS]
B727-025 (F)	C-FKFO	WINNPORT AIR CARGO (KFA)	L	18971	230	02/15/66	JT8D-7B (HK3)	700	N8147N, N280NE

CP-BOLIVIA

A/C TYPE	CURRENT REG. NO.	LAST KNOWN OPERATOR (OWNER)	STATUS	ORIGINAL MSN	LINE NO.	DEL. DATE	ENG. TYPE	FLEET NO.	PREV. REG. [COMMENTS]
B727-023	CP-2377	AEROSUR (JIS A/C)		20044	592	06/24/68	JT8D-7B		N1969 [PARKED SCL; NO ENGINES]
B727-171C	CP-1070	LAB AIRLINES		19860	599	07/05/68	JT8D-9A		N1728T
B727-078	CP-1223	LAB AIRLINES		18795	104	01/13/65	JT8D-9A		9Y-TCP, N306BN
B727-1A0	CP-861	LAB AIRLINES		20279	748	02/17/70	JT8D-9A		
B727-2K3 (A)	CP-1276	LAB AIRLINES		21082	1124	10/08/75	JT8D-17R		N48054
B727-2K3 (A) (WL)	CP-1366	LAB AIRLINES		21494	1373	08/04/78	JT8D-17R (HK3)		[TO BE CVTD TO QWS]
B727-2K3 (A)	CP-1367	LAB AIRLINES		21495	1403	10/25/78	JT8D-17R		
B727-287 (A)	CP-2323	LAB AIRLINES (PACA)		22605	1787	01/08/82	JT8D-17		N1782B, LV-OLP, OK-MGS, N917PG [DMGD EZE 01/09/01; L/H LANDING GEAR COLLAPSED ON TAXIOUT; WO?]
B727-2M7 (A)	CP-2324	LAB AIRLINES (PACA)		21823	1591	03/21/80	JT8D-17		N730RW, LV-ODY, YV-131C, N918PG

C5-GAMBIA

A/C TYPE	CURRENT REG. NO.	LAST KNOWN OPERATOR (OWNER)	STATUS	ORIGINAL MSN	LINE NO.	DEL. DATE	ENG. TYPE	FLEET NO.	PREV. REG. [COMMENTS]
B727-228	C5-DMB	MAHFOOZ AVIATION		20411	847	12/22/70	JT8D-7B		F-BPJP, J2-KBH, TT-DMB
B727-228	C5-DSZ	MAHFOOZ AVIATION		20470	853	03/12/71	JT8D-7B		F-BPJQ, J2-KBG, TT-DSZ [LST LAA]
B727-251	C5-SMM	MAHFOOZ AVIATION		19973	665	11/27/68	JT8D-7B/-9A		N254US, N386PA, YV-466C, HK-3871X

C6-BAHAMAS

A/C TYPE	CURRENT REG. NO.	LAST KNOWN OPERATOR (OWNER)	STATUS	ORIGINAL MSN	LINE NO.	DEL. DATE	ENG. TYPE	FLEET NO.	PREV. REG. [COMMENTS]
B727-2J7 (A)	N553NA	L.B. LIMITED (IALI)		20707	953	06/21/73	JT8D-15 (HK3)		N553PS, OY-SBB
B727-247 (A)	N580CR	L.B. LIMITED (IALI)		20580	889	06/13/72	JT8D-15		N2808W, EI-BRD, XA-TCW, PP-AIU, N502AV

D2-ANGOLA

A/C TYPE	CURRENT REG. NO.	LAST KNOWN OPERATOR (OWNER)	STATUS	ORIGINAL MSN	LINE NO.	DEL. DATE	ENG. TYPE	FLEET NO.	PREV. REG. [COMMENTS]
B727-227 (A)	D2-FAS	AIR NACOIA		20773	983	10/25/73	JT8D-9A		N427BN, N552PE
B727-023 (F)	D2-FCI	ANGOLA AIR CHARTER		18429	26	03/27/64	JT8D-7B		N1973, N517FE, HP-1229PFC
B727-023 (F)	D2-FCJ	ANGOLA AIR CHARTER		18435	51	06/29/64	JT8D-7B		N1979, N518FE, N518PM, HP-1299PFC [PARKED MIA LESS ENGINES]
B727-044 (F)	D2-FCK	ANGOLA AIR CHARTER		18892	148	06/03/65	JT8D-7B		ZS-DYM, ZS-SBA, EL-AIY, N92GS, N94GS
B727-023 (F)	D2-ESU	SONAIR		19431	372	02/12/67	JT8D-7A		N1955, N942FT, N516FE
B727-029C	D2-EVD	SONAIR		19403	435	07/22/67	JT8D-7A		OO-STD, CB-02
B727-029C	D2-EVG	SONAIR		19402	415	06/06/67	JT8D-7A		OO-STB, CB-01, N70PA

A/C TYPE	CURRENT REG. NO.	LAST KNOWN OPERATOR (OWNER)	STATUS	ORIGINAL MSN	LINE NO.	DEL. DATE	ENG. TYPE	FLEET NO.	PREV. REG. [COMMENTS]
EC-SPAIN									
B727-256 (A)	EC-CBF	IBERIA		20600	912	03/15/73	JT8D-9		N1789B [STD MAD]
B727-256 (A)	EC-CBG	IBERIA		20601	913	03/01/73	JT8D-9		N1790B [RTD 07/00; PARKED MAD]
B727-256 (A)	EC-CFA	IBERIA		20811	1003	01/15/74	JT8D-9		[FOR REPUBLIC FINANCIAL(USA)]
B727-256 (A)	EC-CFB	IBERIA		20812	1004	01/22/74	JT8D-9		[RTD 07/00; PARKED MAD]
B727-256 (A)	EC-CFD	IBERIA		20814	1006	02/06/74	JT8D-9		[RTD 07/00; PARKED MAD]
B727-256 (A)	EC-CFE	IBERIA		20815	1007	02/15/74	JT8D-9		[RTD 07/00; PARKED MAD]
B727-256 (A)	EC-CFF	IBERIA		20816	1008	02/25/74	JT8D-9		[RTD 09/00; PARKED MAD]
B727-256 (A)	EC-CFG	IBERIA		20817	1009	03/07/74	JT8D-9		
B727-256 (A)	EC-CFI	IBERIA		20819	1018	04/02/74	JT8D-9		
B727-256 (A)	EC-CID	IBERIA		20974	1077	10/24/74	JT8D-9		[STD MAD]
B727-256 (A)	EC-CIE	IBERIA		20975	1080	10/30/74	JT8D-9		[RTD 07/00; PARKED MAD]
B727-256 (A)	EC-DCE	IBERIA		21611	1382	09/05/78	JT8D-9		[FOR REPUBLIC FINANCIAL (USA)]
B727-256 (A)	EC-DDX	IBERIA		21779	1498	06/28/79	JT8D-9		[FOR REPUBLIC FINANCIAL (USA)]
B727-256 (A)	EC-GCJ	IBERIA		20602	914	01/06/73	JT8D-9		EC-CBH, N8281B [FOR REPUBLIC FINANCIAL (USA); STD MAD]
B727-256 (A)	EC-GCK	IBERIA		20603	915	02/02/73	JT8D-9		N1788B, EC-CBI
B727-256 (A)	EC-GCL	IBERIA		20604	916	01/17/73	JT8D-9		EC-CBJ [STD MAD]
B727-256 (A)	EC-GCM	IBERIA		20606	937	04/20/73	JT8D-9		EC-CBL, LV-VFL, EC-327 [FOR REPUBLIC FINANCIAL (USA); STD MAD]
B727-223 (A) (F)	EC-HAH	SWIFTAIR (BCS)	L	21084	1199	04/27/75	JT8D-9A (HK3)		N857AA, OO-DHV [OP IN DHL C/S]
B727-224 (A) (F)	EC-HBH	SWIFTAIR (FINO)		20661	1064	09/05/74	JT8D-9A (HK3)		N66732, N695CA [OP IN DHL C/S]
B727-224 (A) (F)	EC-HBR	SWIFTAIR (FINO)		20662	1072	10/07/74	JT8D-9A (HK3)		N66733, N707CA [OP IN DHL C/S]
B727-277 (A) (F)	EC-HHU	SWIFTAIR (IPID)		22644	1768	07/24/81	JT8D-15 (HK3)		VH-ANF, N72381, N626DH [OP IN DHL C/S]
B727-277 (A) (F)	EC-HIG	SWIFTAIR (IPID)		22641	1753	06/11/81	JT8D-15 (HK3)		N8278V, VH-ANA, N6393X, N627DH [OP IN DHL C/S]
B727-264 (A) (F)	EC-HJV	SWIFTAIR		20895	1049	06/25/74	JT8D-17R (HK3)		XA-DUJ, N623DH [OP IN DHL C/S]
B727-264 (A) (F)	EC-HLP	SWIFTAIR		20896	1051	06/25/74	JT8D-17R (HK3)		XA-DUK, N622DH [OP IN DHL C/S]
EI-IRELAND									
B727-225 (F)	EI-HCA	AIR CONTRACTORS (TTC HUNT II)		20382	825	07/21/70	JT8D-7B (HK3)		N8839E
B727-223 (F)	EI-HCB	AIR CONTRACTORS (TTC HUNT II)		19492	652	11/01/68	JT8D-7B (HK3)		N6817
B727-223 (F)	EI-HCC	AIR CONTRACTORS (TTC HUNT II)		19480	545	03/25/68	JT8D-7B (HK3)		N6805
B727-223 (F)	EI-HCD	AIR CONTRACTORS (TTC HUNT II)		20185	710	04/18/69	JT8D-7B (HK3)		N6832
B727-223 (F)	EI-HCI	AIR CONTRACTORS (TTC HUNT II)		20183	705	04/07/69	JT8D-7B (HK3)		N6830

A/C TYPE	CURRENT REG. NO.	LAST KNOWN OPERATOR (OWNER)	STATUS	ORIGINAL MSN	LINE NO.	DEL. DATE	ENG. TYPE	FLEET NO.	PREV. REG. [COMMENTS]
B727-281 (F)	EI-LCH	AIR CONTRACTORS (TTC HUNT II)		20466	865	01/15/71	JT8D-7B (HK3)		JA8332, HL7355, N903PG, N528MD
B727-225 (F)	C-FIFA	AIR CONTRACTORS (FAB)	L	20381	823	07/14/70	JT8D-7B (HK3)		N8838E, EI-BVO
B727-2H3 (A) (F)	C-GYFA	AIR CONTRACTORS (FAB)	L	21234	1209	06/18/76	JT8D-9A		TS-JHS, N724SK
EP-IRAN									
B727-081	EP-GDS	IRAN GOVERNMENT		19557	405	05/04/67	JT8D-7		JA8321, N329K, EP-MRP, 1002 [STD THR]
B727-030	EP-PLN	IRAN GOVERNMENT		18363	35	04/07/64	JT8D-7		D-ABIF, N16768, N44CR, EP-SHP [STD THR]
B727-086	EP-IRB	IRAN AIR		19172	323	10/13/66	JT8D-7B		[LST OMA]
B727-086	EP-IRC	IRAN AIR		19816	505	12/19/67	JT8D-7B		
B727-286 (A)	EP-IRP	IRAN AIR		20945	1048	07/29/74	JT8D-15		
B727-286 (A)	EP-IRR	IRAN AIR		20946	1052	07/09/74	JT8D-15		
B727-286 (A)	EP-IRS	IRAN AIR		20947	1070	09/25/74	JT8D-15		
B727-286 (A)	EP-IRT	IRAN AIR		21078	1114	07/02/75	JT8D-15		
B727-228 (A)	EP-ASA	IRAN ASEMAN AIRLINES		22081	1594	03/26/80	JT8D-15A		N8288V, F-GCDA, LX-IRA
B727-228 (A)	EP-ASB	IRAN ASEMAN AIRLINES		22082	1603	04/11/80	JT8D-15A		F-GCDB, LX-IRB
B727-228 (A)	EP-ASC	IRAN ASEMAN AIRLINES		22084	1638	07/09/80	JT8D-15A		N5711E, F-GCDD, LX-IRC
B727-228 (A)	EP-ASD	IRAN ASEMAN AIRLINES		22085	1665	09/30/80	JT8D-15A		F-GCDE, LX-IRD
G-UNITED KINGDOM									
B727-276 (A)	G-BNNI	EXCEL AIRWAYS		20950	1081	10/31/74	JT8D-15 (HK3)		VH-TBK [FERRIED TO SEN 11/01/00; TO BE CVTD TO FRTR; WAS SABRE AIRWAYS]
B727-2D3 (A)	G-BPND	EXCEL AIRWAYS (COUGAR)		21021	1082	11/05/74	JT8D-17A		JY-ADV, HI-452, N500AV, PH-AHZ, OK-EGK
B727-225 (A)	G-OKJN	EXCEL AIRWAYS (COUGAR)		21453	1314	02/02/78	JT8D-217C/-15		N8880Z [DEL TO SBE DELAYED FOR C OF A; SEEN AT INT 10/29/00]
B727-225 (A) (RE)	G-OPMN	EXCEL AIRWAYS (COUGAR)		21578	1409	11/10/78	JT8D-217C/-15		N8881Z [LST SCX]
B727-230 (A)	N359PA	GM AIRLINES		20789	1015	02/25/74	JT8D-15		D-ABSI [OPF GMH-GEN MED HOLDING/OPB CCL; PARKED PGF; NO ENGINES]
B727-212 (A) (RE)	P4-SKI	TWINJET AIRCRAFT (PRECISION AIR)		21460	1340	05/04/78	JT8D-217C/17		9V-SGF, HZ-DA5, VR-CBQ, VP-CBQ [BASED BOH]
HC-ECUADOR									
B727-251 (A)	HC-BVY	AEROGAL (AIRLEASE FIN.)		21505	1391	09/26/78	JT8D-15/-15A		N294US
B727-287 (A)	HC-BVT	ECUATORIANA (PACA)		22603	1732	04/09/81	JT8D-17		LV-OLN, N914PG [PARKED TUS]
B727-095	HC-BJL	SAETA		19596	479	10/23/67	JT8D-9A		N1638, PP-VLR [PARTLY LST/JOINTL.Y OPW SAN]

A/C TYPE	CURRENT REG. NO.	LAST KNOWN OPERATOR (OWNER)	STATUS	ORIGINAL MSN	LINE NO.	DEL. DATE	ENG. TYPE	FLEET NO.	PREV. REG. [COMMENTS]
B727-095	HC-BJL	SAN (SET)	L	19596	479	10/23/67	JT8D-9A		N1638, PP-VLR [PARTLY LSF/JOINTLY OPW SET]
B727-134	HC-BLE	TAME		19691	487	11/13/67	JT8D-7A		SE-DDA, RP-C1240, FAE691
B727-134	HC-BLF	TAME		19692	498	11/30/67	JT8D-9A		SE-DDB, RP-C1241, FAE692
B727-017	HC-BLV	TAME		20328	806	04/20/70	JT8D-9A		CF-CPK, N116TA, XA-GUU, HC-BIC, G-BKCG, FAE328
B727-2T3 (A)	HC-BHM	TAME		22078	1644	09/30/80	JT8D-17		N1293E, FAE078
B727-230 (A)	HC-BRI	TAME		20560	887	05/23/72	JT8D-15		D-ABHI, FAE560
B727-230 (A)	HC-BSC	TAME		20788	1011	02/11/74	JT8D-15		D-ABRI, FAE788
B727-230 (A)	HC-BZR	TAME		21618	1404	10/30/78	JT8D-15		D-ABKN, TC-AFT
B727-230 (A)	HC-BZS	TAME		21620	1419	12/07/78	JT8D-15 (HK3)		D-ABKQ, TC-AFO

HK-COLOMBIA

A/C TYPE	CURRENT REG. NO.	LAST KNOWN OPERATOR (OWNER)	STATUS	ORIGINAL MSN	LINE NO.	DEL. DATE	ENG. TYPE	FLEET NO.	PREV. REG. [COMMENTS]
B727-095 (F)	FAC-1146	COLOMBIAN AIR FORCE		19595	467	09/27/67	JT8D-7B		N1637, PP-VLQ, HK-3771X
B727-227 (A)	HK-3738X	ACES COLOMBIA (BANKERS TRUST)		21997	1573	01/29/80	JT8D-17R		N474BN, N306AS
B727-277 (A)	HK-3977X	ACES COLOMBIA (ARON)		20548	907	11/20/72	JT8D-17		VH-RMU, N274WC
B727-225 (A)	HK-3998X	ACES COLOMBIA (KELLSTROM)		20620	903	10/24/72	JT8D-15		N8858E, N407PA
B727-243 (A)	HK-4010X	ACES COLOMBIA (KELLSTROM)		21267	1228	12/20/76	JT8D-9A		I-DIRU, N574PE
B727-046	HK-3840X	AEROREPUBLICA COLOMBIA		18879	254	04/16/66	JT8D-7B/-9A		JA8312, G-BAEF, 9N-ABV, HK-3384X, HK-3599X, HR-ALZ [PARKED ENGINELESS AND LESS TITLES AT BOG]
B727-023 (F)	HK-3667X	AEROSUCRE COLOMBIA		19430	366	02/03/67	JT8D-7B		N1935, N934FT
B727-059 (F)	HK-727	AEROSUCRE COLOMBIA		19127	243	03/26/66	JT8D-7		
B727-224 (F)	HK-3985X	AEROSUCRE COLOMBIA		20465	814	08/01/71	JT8D-9A		N1781B, N1355B, N32723 [CVTD -2F2; CVTD TO FRTR 06/25/99]
B727-2H3 (A)	HK-3480X	AVIANCA COLOMBIA (LATIN AM.)		20739	952	06/25/73	JT8D-9A		TS-JHO, N189CB, PH-AHB, G-BOKV, OY-SCA, N726VA [STD BOG LESS ENGINES]
B727-024C	HK-1271	L.A. SURAMERICANAS COLOMBIA		19524	428	06/30/67	JT8D-7B (HK3)		N2471, N5475
B727-024C	HK-1273	L.A. SURAMERICANAS COLOMBIA		19526	442	08/01/67	JT8D-7B (HK3)		N2473, N5473, N1781B, N8320
B727-0C3 (F)	HK-3745	L.A. SURAMERICANAS COLOMBIA		20420	819	01/29/71	JT8D-9A		PP-CJG, HK-3745X [CVTD TO FRTR; TO BE HK3]
B727-025 (F)	HK-3814X	L.A. SURAMERICANAS COLOMBIA		18270	79	10/07/64	JT8D-7B (HK3)		N8119N, VH-LAP, YV-728C, YV-448, YV-480C, N5111Y
B727-051 (F)	HK-4154X	L.A. SURAMERICANAS COLOMBIA (FLYING CARGO)		18804	162	07/23/65	JT8D-7B (HK3)		N468US, N5607
B727-2B7	FAC1147	SATENA COLOMBIA		20303	793	04/21/70	JT8D-7B		N751VJ, N405BN, N208US, N384PA, YV-462C, HK-3872X

	A/C TYPE	CURRENT REG. NO.	LAST KNOWN OPERATOR (OWNER)	STATUS	ORIGINAL MSN	LINE NO.	DEL. DATE	ENG. TYPE	FLEET NO.	PREV. REG. [COMMENTS]
HP-PANAMA										
	B727-264 (A) (F)	HP-1310DAE	DHL AERO EXPRESO		20894	1047	06/25/74	JT8D-17R (HK3)		XA-DUI, N9184X
	B727-264 (A) (F)	HP-1510DAE	DHL AERO EXPRESO		20709	950	06/18/73	JT8D-17R (HK3)		XA-CUB, N624DH
	B727-264 (A) (F)	HP-1610DAE	DHL AERO EXPRESO		20780	986	11/02/73	JT8D-17R (HK3)		XA-CUN, N625DH
	B727-025 (F)	HP-1261PVI	PANAVIA PANAMA (AERO INVERSIONES)		18965	205	12/15/65	JT8D-7B		N8141N
HZ-SAUDI ARABIA										
	B727-2U5 (A) (RE) (WL)	HZ-AB3	AL-ANWA ESTABLISHMENT		22362	1657	09/16/80	JT8D-217C/-17		JY-HNH, V8-HM1, V8-HM2, V8-BG1
	B727-051	HZ-DG1	DALLAH ALBARAKA		19124	347	12/16/66	JT8D-7B (HK3)		N478US, N604NA
	B727-029C	HZ-HE4	(PRIVATE) SAUDI		19987	634	10/01/68	JT8D-7		OO-STE, N696WA, N444SA [BEING CVTD TO FRTR AT QLA; OO TO ANGOLA]
	B727-2K5 (A)	HZ-HR1	MATRIX GROUP (JET FIN.)		21853	1640	07/18/80	JT8D-17		N8290V, D-AHLV, LX-MJM, LX-MMM
	B727-2Y4 (A) (RE) (WL)	HZ-HR3	SHEIK RAFIQ HARIRI		22968	1815	01/28/83	JT8D-217C/-15		HZ-RH3
	B727-021	VP-BNA	MID EAST JET (SKYJET)		19262	426	06/28/67	JT8D-7B (HK3)		N360PA, N727WE, N199AM, VR-BNA
	B727-021	HZ-OCV	SAUDI ARABIAN VIP AIRCRAFT		19006	262	05/05/66	JT8D-7B (HK3)		N324PA, N324AS, N2CC, HZ-TFA
JU-MONGOLIA										
	B727-281 (A)	JU-1036	MIAT-MONGOLIAN AIRLINES		20572	881	06/30/72	JT8D-9A		N1790B, JA8343, HL7351, MT-1036
	B727-281 (A)	JU-1037	MIAT-MONGOLIAN AIRLINES		20573	888	06/23/72	JT8D-9A		JA8344, HL7352, MT-1037
JY-JORDAN										
	B727-076 (WL)	JY-HS1	HMS AIRWAYS		20228	766	10/27/69	JT8D-7B		VH-TJE, HZ-GP2, HZ-GRP, N727RE, VR-CCB, VR-CHS
	B727-2L4 (A) (WL)	JY-HS2	HMS AIRWAYS		21010	1100	01/25/75	JT8D-17		N111AK, V8-HB1, VR-CCA [STD FTW]
N-UNITED STATES OF AMERICA										
	B727-017 (RE) (WL)	N624VA	ENTERPRISE AVIATION		20327	797	03/11/70	JT8D-217C/-7B		CF-CPN, N115TA, N4002M, N529AC
	B727-017 (RE) (WL)	N311AG	EXECUTIVE AIR FLEET/BAKER CORP.		20512	858	03/10/71	JT8D-217C/-7B		CF-CUR, N99548, CP-1339, N99548, N767RV
	B727-281 (A)	N724YS	HORTA LLC (T.C.I. LTD.)		21474	1378	08/18/78	JT8D-17		JA8355, HL7357, N240RC

A/C TYPE	CURRENT REG. NO.	LAST KNOWN OPERATOR (OWNER)	STATUS	ORIGINAL MSN	LINE NO.	DEL. DATE	ENG. TYPE	FLEET NO.	PREV. REG. [COMMENTS]
B727-051	N727AK	MARBYIA INVESTMENTS INC.		19123	334	11/13/66	JT8D-7B (HK3)		N477US, TP-01, XC-UJA [RTS]
B727-027	N766JS	AIRCRAFT GUARANTY LLC		19535	456	08/31/67	JT8D-7 (HK3)		N7294, N60FM
B727-223 (A)	N706AA	AMERICAN AIRLINES		22463	1755	06/12/81	JT8D-15 (HK3)	706	
B727-223 (A)	N707AA	AMERICAN AIRLINES		22464	1758	06/18/81	JT8D-15 (HK3)	707	
B727-223 (A)	N709AA	AMERICAN AIRLINES		22466	1763	07/09/81	JT8D-15 (HK3)	709	
B727-223 (A)	N712AA	AMERICAN AIRLINES		22468	1766	07/21/81	JT8D-15 (HK3)	712	[LRF 02/16/01; RTD TUL]
B727-227 (A)	N716AA	AMERICAN AIRLINES		20608	891	07/03/72	JT8D-9A (HK3)	716	N1780B, N410BN
B727-227 (A)	N717AA	AMERICAN AIRLINES		20610	893	07/19/72	JT8D-9A (HK3)	717	N412BN
B727-227 (A)	N718AA	AMERICAN AIRLINES		20611	894	08/01/72	JT8D-9A (HK3)	718	N413BN
B727-227 (A)	N719AA	AMERICAN AIRLINES		20612	928	03/13/73	JT8D-9A (HK3)	719	N414BN
B727-227 (A)	N720AA	AMERICAN AIRLINES		20613	929	03/14/73	JT8D-9A (HK3)	720	N415BN
B727-227 (A)	N721AA	AMERICAN AIRLINES		20729	955	07/10/73	JT8D-9A (HK3)	721	N416BN
B727-227 (A)	N722AA	AMERICAN AIRLINES		20730	956	07/12/73	JT8D-9A (HK3)	722	N417BN
B727-227 (A)	N723AA	AMERICAN AIRLINES		20731	957	07/16/73	JT8D-9A (HK3)	723	N418BN
B727-227 (A)	N725AA	AMERICAN AIRLINES		20732	963	08/10/73	JT8D-9A (HK3)	725	N419BN
B727-227 (A)	N726AA	AMERICAN AIRLINES		20733	964	08/16/73	JT8D-9A (HK3)	726	N420BN
B727-227 (A)	N727AA	AMERICAN AIRLINES		20734	965	08/21/73	JT8D-9A (HK3)	727	N421BN
B727-227 (A)	N728AA	AMERICAN AIRLINES		20735	973	09/18/73	JT8D-9A (HK3)	728	N422BN
B727-227 (A)	N729AA	AMERICAN AIRLINES		20736	974	09/24/73	JT8D-9A (HK3)	729	N423BN
B727-227 (A)	N730AA	AMERICAN AIRLINES		20737	976	09/28/73	JT8D-9A (HK3)	730	N424BN
B727-227 (A)	N731AA	AMERICAN AIRLINES		20738	977	10/05/73	JT8D-9A (HK3)	731	N425BN
B727-223 (A)	N843AA	AMERICAN AIRLINES		20984	1121	05/09/75	JT8D-9A (HK3)	843	
B727-223 (A)	N844AA	AMERICAN AIRLINES		20985	1123	05/13/75	JT8D-9A (HK3)	844	
B727-223 (A)	N846AA	AMERICAN AIRLINES		20987	1126	05/20/75	JT8D-9A (HK3)	846	
B727-223 (A)	N848AA	AMERICAN AIRLINES		20989	1144	06/25/75	JT8D-9A (HK3)	848	
B727-223 (A)	N849AA	AMERICAN AIRLINES		20990	1184	05/26/76	JT8D-9A (HK3)	849	
B727-223 (A)	N859AA	AMERICAN AIRLINES		21086	1248	03/07/77	JT8D-9A (HK3)	859	
B727-223 (A)	N860AA	AMERICAN AIRLINES		21087	1250	03/07/77	JT8D-9A (HK3)	860	
B727-223 (A)	N861AA	AMERICAN AIRLINES		21088	1255	04/07/77	JT8D-9A (HK3)	861	
B727-223 (A)	N862AA	AMERICAN AIRLINES		21089	1263	05/13/77	JT8D-9A (HK3)	862	
B727-223 (A)	N863AA	AMERICAN AIRLINES		21090	1267	06/01/77	JT8D-9A (HK3)	863	
B727-223 (A)	N864AA	AMERICAN AIRLINES		21369	1275	06/28/77	JT8D-9A (HK3)	864	
B727-223 (A)	N865AA	AMERICAN AIRLINES		21370	1276	07/12/77	JT8D-9A (HK3)	865	
B727-223 (A)	N866AA	AMERICAN AIRLINES		21371	1277	07/15/77	JT8D-9A (HK3)	866	
B727-223 (A)	N867AA	AMERICAN AIRLINES		21372	1278	07/20/77	JT8D-9A (HK3)	867	
B727-223 (A)	N868AA	AMERICAN AIRLINES		21373	1279	07/22/77	JT8D-9A (HK3)	868	
B727-223 (A)	N869AA	AMERICAN AIRLINES		21374	1280	08/02/77	JT8D-9A (HK3)	869	
B727-223 (A)	N870AA	AMERICAN AIRLINES		21382	1304	11/17/77	JT8D-9A (HK3)	870	
B727-223 (A)	N871AA	AMERICAN AIRLINES		21383	1324	03/10/78	JT8D-9A (HK3)	871	

A/C TYPE	CURRENT REG. NO.	LAST KNOWN OPERATOR (OWNER)	STATUS	ORIGINAL MSN	LINE NO.	DEL. DATE	ENG. TYPE	FLEET NO.	PREV. REG. [COMMENTS]
B727-223 (A)	N872AA	AMERICAN AIRLINES		21384	1328	03/23/78	JT8D-9A (HK3)	872	
B727-223 (A)	N873AA	AMERICAN AIRLINES		21385	1331	04/04/78	JT8D-9A (HK3)	873	
B727-223 (A)	N874AA	AMERICAN AIRLINES		21386	1333	04/13/78	JT8D-9A (HK3)	874	
B727-223 (A)	N875AA	AMERICAN AIRLINES		21387	1335	04/18/78	JT8D-9A (HK3)	875	
B727-223 (A)	N876AA	AMERICAN AIRLINES		21388	1345	05/17/78	JT8D-9A (HK3)	876	
B727-223 (A)	N877AA	AMERICAN AIRLINES		21389	1349	05/31/78	JT8D-9A (HK3)	877	[STD MHV]
B727-223 (A)	N878AA	AMERICAN AIRLINES		21390	1361	07/07/78	JT8D-9A (HK3)	878	
B727-223 (A)	N879AA	AMERICAN AIRLINES		21391	1367	07/25/78	JT8D-9A (HK3)	879	
B727-223 (A)	N880AA	AMERICAN AIRLINES		21519	1459	03/23/79	JT8D-9A (HK3)	880	
B727-223 (A)	N881AA	AMERICAN AIRLINES		21520	1461	03/29/79	JT8D-9A (HK3)	881	
B727-223 (A)	N882AA	AMERICAN AIRLINES		21521	1463	04/03/79	JT8D-9A (HK3)	882	
B727-223 (A)	N883AA	AMERICAN AIRLINES		21522	1465	04/10/79	JT8D-9A (HK3)	883	
B727-223 (A)	N884AA	AMERICAN AIRLINES		21523	1467	04/12/79	JT8D-9A (HK3)	884	
B727-223 (A)	N885AA	AMERICAN AIRLINES		21524	1473	04/27/79	JT8D-9A (HK3)	885	
B727-223 (A)	N886AA	AMERICAN AIRLINES		21525	1475	05/02/79	JT8D-9A (HK3)	886	
B727-223 (A)	N887AA	AMERICAN AIRLINES		21526	1476	05/04/79	JT8D-9A (HK3)	887	
B727-223 (A)	N889AA	AMERICAN AIRLINES		21527	1477	05/08/79	JT8D-9A (HK3)	889	
B727-223 (A)	N890AA	AMERICAN AIRLINES (AV. CAP.)		22006	1636	07/16/80	JT8D-15 (HK3)	890	
B727-223 (A)	N891AA	AMERICAN AIRLINES (AV. CAP.)		22007	1643	07/22/80	JT8D-15 (HK3)	891	
B727-223 (A)	N892AA	AMERICAN AIRLINES (AV. CAP.)		22008	1646	07/31/80	JT8D-15 (HK3)	892	
B727-223 (A)	N893AA	AMERICAN AIRLINES		22009	1649	08/07/80	JT8D-15 (HK3)	893	
B727-223 (A)	N894AA	AMERICAN AIRLINES		22010	1650	08/22/80	JT8D-15 (HK3)	894	[PARKED TUS]
B727-2B7 (A)	N760AT	AMERICAN TRANS AIR		21954	1525	09/27/79	JT8D-17 (HK3)	760	N762AL, N760US
B727-2B7 (A)	N762AT	AMERICAN TRANS AIR		22162	1717	12/02/81	JT8D-17 (HK3)	762	N762US
B727-264 (A)	N763AT	AMERICAN TRANS AIR		22983	1806	12/03/82	JT8D-17A (HK3)	763	N4555E, N773AL, N763US
B727-264 (A)	N764AT	AMERICAN TRANS AIR		22984	1813	12/13/82	JT8D-17 (HK3)	764	N774AL, N764US
B727-264 (A)	N765AT	AMERICAN TRANS AIR		23014	1816	02/15/83	JT8D-17 (HK3)	765	N775AL, N765US
B727-227 (A)	N766AT	AMERICAN TRANS AIR		21999	1581	02/24/80	JT8D-17 (HK3)	766	N476BN, N780AL, N766US
B727-227 (A)	N767AT	AMERICAN TRANS AIR		22001	1585	02/28/80	JT8D-17 (HK3)	767	N478BN, N781AL, N767US
B727-227 (A)	N768AT	AMERICAN TRANS AIR		21996	1571	01/22/80	JT8D-17 (HK3)	768	N473BN, N782AL, N768US
B727-227 (A)	N769AT	AMERICAN TRANS AIR		21998	1577	02/07/80	JT8D-17A (HK3)	769	N475BN, N783AL, N769US
B727-2B7 (A)	N770AT	AMERICAN TRANS AIR (FINO)		21953	1516	08/30/79	JT8D-17 (HK3)	770	N760AL, N755US
B727-227 (A)	N772AT	AMERICAN TRANS AIR (TEXAS NATIONALEASE)		22003	1629	09/10/81	JT8D-17 (HK3)	772	N271AF, N288AS
B727-227 (A)	N773AT	AMERICAN TRANS AIR (TEXAS NATIONALEASE)		22004	1631	09/18/81	JT8D-17 (HK3)	773	N272AF, N289AS
B727-290 (A)	N774AT	AMERICAN TRANS AIR		21510	1359	06/28/78	JT8D-17 (HK3)	774	N290AS
B727-290 (A)	N775AT	AMERICAN TRANS AIR (HANCOCK)	21511	1439	03/02/79	JT8D-17 (HK3)	775	N291AS	
B727-2Q8 (A)	N776AT	AMERICAN TRANS AIR		21608	1426	12/20/78	JT8D-17A (HK3)	776	N791L, N297AS
B727-227 (A)	N778AT	AMERICAN TRANS AIR		22005	1651	11/01/81	JT8D-17A (HK3)	778	N273AF, N304AS

A/C TYPE	CURRENT REG. NO.	LAST KNOWN OPERATOR (OWNER)	STATUS	ORIGINAL MSN	LINE NO.	DEL. DATE	ENG. TYPE	FLEET NO.	PREV. REG. [COMMENTS]
B727-227 (A)	N779AT	AMERICAN TRANS AIR		22091	1706	11/02/81	JT8D-17 (HK3)	779	N274AF, N305AS
B727-208 (A)	N780AT	AMERICAN TRANS AIR		22295	1622	05/30/80	JT8D-17A (HK3)	780	TF-FLI, N329AS
B727-2Q6 (A)	N782AT	AMERICAN TRANS AIR		21972	1637	07/10/80	JT8D-17 (HK3)	782	N1280E
B727-227 (A)	N783AT	AMERICAN TRANS AIR (BTM CAP)		22000	1583	02/21/80	JT8D-17 (HK3)	783	N477BN, N307AS
B727-247 (A)	N784AT	AMERICAN TRANS AIR (NAT. CITY LSG)		21393	1307	12/21/77	JT8D-17 (HK3)	784	N2828W, N749US
B727-214 (A)	N785AT	AMERICAN TRANS AIR (COMERICA LEASE)		21691	1480	05/15/79	JT8D-17A (HK3)	785	N557PS, N752US
B727-214 (A)	N786AT	AMERICAN TRANS AIR (SUNTRUST)		21692	1482	05/21/79	JT8D-17 (HK3)	786	N558PS, N753US
B727-214 (A)	N788AT	AMERICAN TRANS AIR (FSBU)		21958	1533	10/10/79	JT8D-17A (HK3)	788	N559PS, N754US
B727-227 (A) (F)	N196AJ	AMERIJET INTL.		20838	1017	03/06/74	JT8D-9A (HK3)		N431BN, N556PE
B727-2F9 (A) (F) (WL)	N199AJ	AMERIJET INTL.		21426	1285	08/19/77	JT8D-17		5N-ANP, N528D, N298AS, N83428
B727-251 (A) (F)	N296AJ	AMERIJET INTL.		21156	1170	10/31/75	JT8D-15 (HK3)		N277US
B727-2F9 (A) (F)	N299AJ	AMERIJET INTL.		21427	1291	09/23/77	JT8D-17		5N-ANQ, N528E, N299AS, N75429
B727-233 (A) (F)	N395AJ	AMERIJET INTL.		21100	1148	08/21/75	JT8D-15		C-GAAL, N727SN
B727-2X3 (A) (F)	N397AJ	AMERIJET INTL. (IPID)		22608	1727	03/20/81	JT8D-15 (HK3)		F-GCMV, F-WQCK, OO-LLS
B727-233 (A) (F)	N495AJ	AMERIJET INTL.		20937	1103	03/06/75	JT8D-15 (HK3)		C-GAAF, N7152J, C-GAAD
B727-212 (A) (F) (WL)	N598AJ	AMERIJET INTL.		21947	1506	07/20/79	JT8D-17 (HK3)		9V-SGI, N309AS, N86430
B727-227 (A) (F) (WL)	N794AJ	AMERIJET INTL.		21243	1197	04/23/76	JT8D-15 (HK3)		N442BN, N567PE
B727-2X3 (A) (F)	N797AJ	AMERIJET INTL. (IPID)		22609	1731	03/31/81	JT8D-15 (HK3)		F-GCMX, OO-CAH
B727-224 (A) (F)	N895AJ	AMERIJET INTL.		20660	985	10/31/73	JT8D-9A (HK3)		N66731
B727-233 (A) (F) (WL)	N994AJ	AMERIJET INTL.		20942	1130	05/15/75	JT8D-15		C-GAAK, N727JH
B727-212 (A) (F) (WL)	N319NE	ASIA PACIFIC AIRLINES (AERO MICRONESIA)		21349	1289	10/21/77	JT8D-17		(HK3) 9V-SGC, G-BHVT, TI-LRR, C-FRYS, N591DB
B727-030 (WL)	N727EC	ATLANTIC AIRCRAFT		18365	52	06/19/64	JT8D-9A (HK3)		D-ABIH, N16767, HZ-TA1, G-BMZU, N96B, N700TE [OPF EMCOM]
B727-223 (F)	N6816	BAX GLOBAL (KHA)	L	19491	611	07/31/68	JT8D-9 (HK3)		
B727-223 (F)	N6831	BAX GLOBAL (KHA)	L	20184	707	04/15/69	JT8D-9		
B727-223 (A) (F)	N858AA	BAX GLOBAL (KHA)	L	21085	1200	04/27/76	JT8D-9A (HK3)		
B727-2Q6 (A) (F)	N1279E	CAPITAL CARGO INTL. AIRLINES (PEGA)		21971	1540	11/01/79	JT8D-17		
B727-2J7 (A) (F)	N128NA	CAPITAL CARGO INTL. AIRLINES (PEGA)		20879	1033	05/04/74	JT8D-15 (HK3)		
B727-214 (A) (F)	N227JL	CAPITAL CARGO INTL. AIRLINES (PACA)		20875	1020	03/15/74	JT8D-15 (HK3)		N554PS, N375PA
B727-2A1 (A) (F)	N286SC	CAPITAL CARGO INTL. AIRLINES (ACG ACQ.)		21601	1694	12/12/80	JT8D-17		PP-SNJ, N328AS

A/C TYPE	CCURRENT REG. NO.	LAST KNOWN OPERATOR (OWNER)	STATUS	ORIGINAL MSN	LINE NO.	DEL. DATE	ENG. TYPE	FLEET NO.	PREV. REG. [COMMENTS]
B727-2A1 (A) (F)	N287SC	CAPITAL CARGO INTL. AIRLINES (ACG ACQ.)		21345	1673	10/16/80	JT8D-17		PP-SNG, N327AS
B727-227 (A) (F)	N308AS	CAPITAL CARGO INTL. AIRLINES		22002	1627	06/06/80	JT8D-17R (HK3)		N479BN
B727-230 (A) (F)	N357KP	CAPITAL CARGO INTL. AIRLINES (PEGA)		20675	924	03/04/73	JT8D-15 (HK3)		D-ABMI, N727VA, G-BPNY
B727-223 (A)	N708AA	CAPITAL CARGO INTL. AIRLINES (ACG ACQ.)		22465	1761	06/24/81	JT8D-15 (HK3)		
B727-223 (A) (F)	N713AA	CAPITAL CARGO INTL. AIRLINES (ACG ACQ.)		22469	1769	08/05/81	JT8D-15 (HK3)		[CVTD TO FRTR]
B727-223 (A) (F)	N715AA	CAPITAL CARGO INTL. AIRLINES (ACG ACQ.)		22470	1771	09/04/81	JT8D-15 (HK3)		[CVTD TO FRTR]
B727-225 (A) (F)	N808EA	CAPITAL CARGO INTL. AIRLINES		22439	1689	12/02/80	JT8D-15A (HK3)		C-GCWW, TC-DEL
B727-231 (A) (F)	N84357	CAPITAL CARGO INTL. AIRLINES (FINO)		21989	1590	04/03/80	JT8D-15		
B727-227 (A) (F)	N89427	CAPITAL CARGO INTL. AIRLINES		21365	1273	07/08/77	JT8D-17R		N451BN, N323AS [TO SJO 04/01/00 FOR FRTR CONV]
B727-223 (A) (F)	N898AA	CAPITAL CARGO INTL. AIRLINES (ACGA)		22014	1663	09/23/80	JT8D-15 (HK3)		
B727-223 (A) (F)	N899AA	CAPITAL CARGO INTL. AIRLINES (ACG ACQ.)		22015	1666	10/01/80	JT8D-15 (HK3)		
B727-212 (A)	N292AS	CHAMPION AIR (CITG)		21458	1327	03/22/78	JT8D-17 (HK3)		9V-SGD, HK-4047X
B727-212 (A)	N293AS	CHAMPION AIR (CITG)		21348	1287	09/26/77	JT8D-17 (HK3)		9V-SGB, PP-SMK, N26729
B727-290 (A)	N294AS	CHAMPION AIR (CITG)		22146	1621	05/30/80	JT8D-17 (HK3)		XA-SPH, PP-OPR
B727-290 (A)	N295AS	CHAMPION AIR (CITG)		22147	1623	05/29/80	JT8D-17 (HK3)		
B727-2S7 (A)	N681CA	CHAMPION AIR (PEGA)		22020	1592	03/14/80	JT8D-17 (HK3)		N712RC
B727-2S7 (A)	N682CA	CHAMPION AIR (PEGA)		22019	1584	02/28/80	JT8D-17 (HK3)		N715RC
B727-2S7 (A)	N683CA	CHAMPION AIR (NWA)	L	22490	1721	02/26/81	JT8D-17 (HK3)		N719RC
B727-2S7 (A)	N684CA	CHAMPION AIR (NWA)	L	22491	1726	03/17/81	JT8D-17 (HK3)		N720RC
B727-2S7 (A)	N685CA	CHAMPION AIR (NWA)	L	22492	1729	03/26/81	JT8D-17 (HK3)		N721RC
B727-2S7 (A)	N686CA	CHAMPION AIR (NWA)	L	22021	1617	06/02/80	JT8D-17 (HK3)		N716RC
B727-2J4 (A)	N696CA	CHAMPION AIR (FINO)		22574	1733	04/03/81	JT8D-17 (HK3)		OY-SBG, C-GRYQ
B727-270 (A)	N697CA	CHAMPION AIR (FINO)		23052	1817	04/06/83	JT8D-17A (HK3)		N779AL, OY-SBI
B727-051	N724CL	CLAY LACY AVIATION		19121	264	05/05/66	JT8D-7B (HK)		N475US, TP-02, XC-UJB, N299LA
B727-035	N727HC	CLAY LACY AVIATION		19835	501	12/28/67	JT8D-7B (HK3)		N1959, N900CH
B727-031 (F)	N220NE	CUSTOM AIR TRANSPORT (CHARTER AMERICA)		18905	160	07/12/65	JT8D-7B		N840TW [OPF CHARTER AMERICA IN CHARTER AMERICA C/S; STD OPF]
B727-044C	N2688Z	CUSTOM AIR TRANSPORT (NEW QUICK)		20476	857	03/09/71	JT8D-7B (HK3)		ZS-SBI [OPF CHARTER AMERICA IN CHARTER AMERICA C/S]

A/C TYPE	CURRENT REG. NO.	LAST KNOWN OPERATOR (OWNER) STATUS	ORIGINAL MSN	LINE NO.	DEL. DATE	ENG. TYPE	FLEET NO.	PREV. REG. [COMMENTS]
B727-022C	N753AS	CUSTOM AIR TRANSPORT(NEW QUICK)	19203	434	07/30/67	JT8D-7B (HK3)		N7428U, N753AL [OPF CHARTER AMERICA IN CHARTER AMERICA C/S]
B727-291 (F)	N406BN	CUSTOM AIR TRANSPORT (ARRIVA AIR)	19991	521	02/08/68	JT8D-7B (HK3)		N7276F, HI-630CA [OPF CHARTER AMERICA IN CHARTER AMERICA C/S]
B727-2H3 (F)	N723SK	CUSTOM AIR TRANSPORT (KALITTA LSG)	20545	877	02/14/72	JT8D-9A		TS-JHN [CVTD TO FRTR 09/30/99; OPF CHARTER AMERICA IN CHARTER AMERICA C/S; PARKED YIP, NO ENGINES]
B727-225 (A) (F)	N8887Z	CUSTOM AIR TRANSPORT (PEGA)	21856	1537	11/01/79	JT8D-15		[ALL WHITE, NO TITLES; RTS]
B727-225 (A) (F)	N8892Z	CUSTOM AIR TRANSPORT (NEW QUICK)	21861	1554	12/07/79	JT8D-9A (HK3)		[OPF CHARTER AMERICA IN CHARTER AMERICA C/S]
B727-030	N25AZ	DAVID TOKOPH	18370	134	04/17/65	JT8D-7		D-ABIP, N26565, VR-BHN, Z-WYY
B727-044(WL)	N44MD	DAVIS OIL	19318	348	01/06/67	JT8D-7 (HK3)		ZS-EKW, ZS-SBF, N2689E, N727MB, N727EC
B727-247 (A)	N2812W	DELTA AIRLINES	20868	1024	03/29/74	JT8D-15 (HK3)	562	
B727-247 (A)	N2815W	DELTA AIRLINES	20871	1039	05/29/74	JT8D-15 (HK3)	565	
B727-247 (A)	N2816W	DELTA AIRLINES	20872	1040	05/25/74	JT8D-15 (HK3)	566	
B727-247 (A)	N2817W	DELTA AIRLINES	20873	1043	06/05/74	JT8D-15 (HK3)	567	
B727-247 (A)	N2819W	DELTA AIRLINES	21057	1135	05/23/75	JT8D-15 (HK3)	568	
B727-247 (A)	N2820W	DELTA AIRLINES	21058	1136	07/29/75	JT8D-15	569	
B727-247 (A)	N2821W	DELTA AIRLINES	21059	1137	06/03/75	JT8D-15 (HK3)	570	
B727-247 (A)	N2829W	DELTA AIRLINES	21481	1338	06/20/78	JT8D-15 (HK3)	576	
B727-247 (A)	N282WA	DELTA AIRLINES	21484	1362	07/12/78	JT8D-15 (HK3)	579	
B727-247 (A)	N283WA	DELTA AIRLINES	21485	1364	07/13/78	JT8D-15 (HK3)	580	
B727-247 (A)	N290WA	DELTA AIRLINES	22108	1587	03/05/80	JT8D-15 (HK3)	582	
B727-247 (A)	N291WA	DELTA AIRLINES	22109	1589	03/11/80	JT8D-15 (HK3)	583	
B727-247 (A)	N292WA	DELTA AIRLINES	22110	1613	05/06/80	JT8D-15 (HK3)	584	
B727-247 (A)	N293WA	DELTA AIRLINES	22111	1615	05/09/80	JT8D-15 (HK3)	585	
B727-247 (A)	N294WA	DELTA AIRLINES	22112	1618	05/19/80	JT8D-15 (HK3)	586	
B727-247 (A)	N295WA	DELTA AIRLINES	22532	1730	05/29/81	JT8D-15 (HK3)	587	
B727-247 (A)	N296WA	DELTA AIRLINES	22533	1736	06/05/81	JT8D-15 (HK3)	588	
B727-247 (A)	N297WA	DELTA AIRLINES	22534	1738	05/22/81	JT8D-15 (HK3)	589	
B727-232 (A)	N410DA	DELTA AIRLINES	21222	1205	07/08/76	JT8D-15	410	
B727-232 (A)	N501DA	DELTA AIRLINES	21303	1262	05/03/77	JT8D-15 (HK3)	501	
B727-232 (A)	N502DA	DELTA AIRLINES	21304	1264	05/10/77	JT8D-15 (HK3)	502	
B727-232 (A)	N503DA	DELTA AIRLINES	21305	1268	06/03/77	JT8D-15	503	
B727-232 (A)	N504DA	DELTA AIRLINES	21306	1270	06/15/77	JT8D-15 (HK3)	504	
B727-232 (A)	N505DA	DELTA AIRLINES	21307	1272	06/22/77	JT8D-15 (HK3)	505	

A/C TYPE	CURRENT REG. NO.	LAST KNOWN OPERATOR (OWNER)	STATUS	ORIGINAL MSN	LINE NO.	DEL. DATE	ENG. TYPE	FLEET NO.	PREV. REG. [COMMENTS]
B727-232 (A)	N506DA	DELTA AIRLINES		21308	1292	09/16/77	JT8D-15 (HK3)	506	
B727-232 (A)	N507DA	DELTA AIRLINES		21309	1294	10/24/77	JT8D-15 (HK3)	507	
B727-232 (A)	N508DA	DELTA AIRLINES		21310	1298	10/26/77	JT8D-15 (HK3)	508	
B727-232 (A)	N509DA	DELTA AIRLINES		21311	1300	10/21/77	JT8D-15 (HK3)	509	
B727-232 (A)	N510DA	DELTA AIRLINES		21312	1330	03/31/78	JT8D-15 (HK3)	510	[WINGLETS REMOVED]
B727-232 (A)	N511DA	DELTA AIRLINES		21313	1347	06/24/78	JT8D-15 (HK3)	511	[WINGLETS REMOVED]
B727-232 (A)	N512DA	DELTA AIRLINES		21314	1358	06/28/78	JT8D-15 (HK3)	512	
B727-232 (A)	N513DA	DELTA AIRLINES		21315	1360	06/30/78	JT8D-15 (HK3)	513	
B727-232 (A)	N514DA	DELTA AIRLINES		21430	1374	08/12/78	JT8D-15 (HK3)	514	
B727-232 (A)	N515DA	DELTA AIRLINES		21431	1376	08/18/78	JT8D-15 (HK3)	515	
B727-232 (A)	N516DA	DELTA AIRLINES		21432	1381	08/31/78	JT8D-15 (HK3)	516	
B727-232 (A)	N517DA	DELTA AIRLINES		21433	1384	09/08/78	JT8D-15 (HK3)	517	
B727-232 (A)	N518DA	DELTA AIRLINES		21469	1398	10/24/78	JT8D-15 (HK3)	518	
B727-232 (A)	N519DA	DELTA AIRLINES		21470	1400	10/18/78	JT8D-15 (HK3)	519	
B727-232 (A)	N520DA	DELTA AIRLINES		21471	1411	11/10/78	JT8D-15 (HK3)	520	
B727-232 (A)	N521DA	DELTA AIRLINES		21472	1413	11/17/78	JT8D-15 (HK3)	521	["SHUTTLE"]
B727-232 (A)	N522DA	DELTA AIRLINES		21582	1422	12/13/78	JT8D-15 (HK3)	522	
B727-232 (A)	N523DA	DELTA AIRLINES		21583	1423	12/15/78	JT8D-15 (HK3)	523	["SHUTTLE"]
B727-232 (A)	N524DA	DELTA AIRLINES		21584	1478	05/10/79	JT8D-15 (HK3)	524	["SHUTTLE"]
B727-232 (A)	N525DA	DELTA AIRLINES		21585	1479	05/11/79	JT8D-15 (HK3)	525	["SHUTTLE"]
B727-232 (A)	N526DA	DELTA AIRLINES		21586	1488	06/06/79	JT8D-15 (HK3)	526	["SHUTTLE"]
B727-232 (A)	N527DA	DELTA AIRLINES		21587	1492	06/14/79	JT8D-15 (HK3)	527	
B727-232 (A)	N528DA	DELTA AIRLINES		21702	1522	10/25/79	JT8D-15 (HK3)	528	
B727-232 (A)	N529DA	DELTA AIRLINES		21703	1550	11/21/79	JT8D-15 (HK3)	529	["SHUTTLE"]
B727-232 (A)	N531DA	DELTA AIRLINES		21814	1556	12/07/79	JT8D-15 (HK3)	531	
B727-232 (A)	N532DA	DELTA AIRLINES		22045	1602	04/09/80	JT8D-15 (HK3)	532	
B727-232 (A)	N533DA	DELTA AIRLINES		22046	1604	04/16/80	JT8D-15 (HK3)	533	
B727-232 (A)	N534DA	DELTA AIRLINES		22047	1606	04/23/80	JT8D-15 (HK3)	534	
B727-232 (A)	N535DA	DELTA AIRLINES		22048	1608	05/07/80	JT8D-15 (HK3)	535	
B727-232 (A)	N536DA	DELTA AIRLINES		22049	1610	05/09/80	JT8D-15 (HK3)	536	
B727-232 (A)	N537DA	DELTA AIRLINES		22073	1624	05/30/80	JT8D-15 (HK3)	537	
B727-232 (A)	N538DA	DELTA AIRLINES		22076	1656	10/01/80	JT8D-15 (HK3)	538	
B727-232 (A)	N539DA	DELTA AIRLINES		22385	1667	10/08/80	JT8D-15 (HK3)	539	N1786B
B727-232 (A)	N540DA	DELTA AIRLINES		22386	1669	10/15/80	JT8D-15 (HK3)	540	
B727-232 (A)	N541DA	DELTA AIRLINES		22387	1672	10/22/80	JT8D-15 (HK3)	541	
B727-232 (A)	N542DA	DELTA AIRLINES		22391	1705	01/21/81	JT8D-15 (HK3)	542	
B727-232 (A)	N543DA	DELTA AIRLINES		22392	1707	01/28/81	JT8D-15 (HK3)	543	
B727-232 (A)	N544DA	DELTA AIRLINES		22493	1741	05/01/81	JT8D-15 (HK3)	544	
B727-232 (A)	N545DA	DELTA AIRLINES		22494	1749	05/20/81	JT8D-15 (HK3)	545	
B727-232 (A)	N546DA	DELTA AIRLINES		22677	1785	11/12/81	JT8D-15 (HK3)	546	
B727-225 (A)	N805EA	DELTA AIRLINES		22436	1677	11/12/80	JT8D-15 (HK3)	590	

A/C TYPE	CURRENT REG. NO.	LAST KNOWN OPERATOR (OWNER)	STATUS	ORIGINAL MSN	LINE NO.	DEL. DATE	ENG. TYPE	FLEET NO.	PREV. REG. [COMMENTS]
B727-247 (A)	N830WA	DELTA AIRLINES		21482	1341	05/09/78	JT8D-15 (HK3)	577	
B727-2Q8 (A)	N831L	DELTA AIRLINES (INTL. AC INVEST)		21826	1509	07/26/79	JT8D-15 (HK3)	581	
B727-247 (A)	N831WA	DELTA AIRLINES		21483	1350	05/31/78	JT8D-15 (HK3)	578	
B727-225 (A)	N8873Z	DELTA AIRLINES (FINO)		21291	1239	12/20/76	JT8D-15	445	
B727-225 (A)	N8875Z	DELTA AIRLINES (FINO)		21293	1241	12/23/76	JT8D-15 (HK3)	441	
B727-225 (A)	N8882Z	DELTA AIRLINES		21579	1412	11/17/78	JT8D-15 (HK3)	591	
B727-225 (A)	N8889Z	DELTA AIRLINES		21858	1542	12/04/79	JT8D-15 (HK3)	440	
B727-225 (A)	N8890Z	DELTA AIRLINES		21859	1544	11/30/79	JT8D-15 (HK3)	438	
B727-225 (A)	N8891Z	DELTA AIRLINES		21860	1546	11/27/79	JT8D-15 (HK3)	439	
B727-030C (WL)	N701DH	DHL AIRWAYS		19011	387	03/31/67	JT8D-7 (HK3)		D-ABIA, EP-AMU, OO-TJN, 4X-AGJ, OO-ATJ, N727JE
B727-030C	N702DH	DHL AIRWAYS		19793	519	01/20/68	JT8D-7 (HK3)		D-ABBI, CX-BKA, N4555W, N725JE, N748EV
B727-030C	N703DH	DHL AIRWAYS		19010	382	03/17/67	JT8D-7B (HK3)		D-ABIZ, CX-BKB, N4585L, N724JE, N750EV
B727-022C	N705DH	DHL AIRWAYS		19191	386	03/31/67	JT8D-7B (HK3)		N7416U, C-GAGX, N725PL
B727-022 (F)	N707DH	DHL AIRWAYS		18321	122	03/25/65	JT8D-7B (HK3)		N7029U, HL7336, HK-2833X, N8700R
B727-025 (F) (WL)	N708DH	DHL AIRWAYS		18275	101	12/18/64	JT8D-7		N8124N, N238DH
B727-082C (WL)	N709DH	DHL AIRWAYS		19968	660	11/21/68	JT8D-7		CS-TBO, N251DH
B727-029 (F)	N712DH	DHL AIRWAYS		19401	419	06/09/67	JT8D-7		OO-STC, D-AHLO, N577JB, N711GN
B727-155C	N715DH	DHL AIRWAYS		19618	461	09/29/67	JT8D-7B (HK3)		N530EJ, CS-TBV, N3254D, N720JE
B727-023 (F)	N717DH	DHL AIRWAYS		19389	343	12/13/66	JT8D-7B (HK3)		N1931, N514FE
B727-228 (F)	N720DH	DHL AIRWAYS		19544	562	04/23/68	JT8D-7B (HK3)		F-BOJB, N606AR
B727-228 (F)	N721DH	DHL AIRWAYS		19545	564	05/02/68	JT8D-7 (HK3)		F-BOJC, N605AR
B727-228 (F)	N724DH	DHL AIRWAYS		19862	685	02/06/69	JT8D-7B (HK3)		F-BOJF, N603AR
B727-228 (F)	N726DH	DHL AIRWAYS		20409	845	12/07/70	JT8D-7B (HK3)		F-BPJN, N604AR
B727-228 (F)	N727DH	DHL AIRWAYS		20204	778	12/16/69	JT8D-7B (HK3)		F-BPJM
B727-2Q9 (A) (F)	N740DH	DHL AIRWAYS		21930	1508	12/21/79	JT8D-17R (HK3)		N1273E, N200AV
B727-2Q9 (A) (F)	N741DH	DHL AIRWAYS		21931	1531	12/21/79	JT8D-17R (HK3)		N202AV
B727-225 (A) (F)	N742DH	DHL AIRWAYS		21290	1238	12/16/76	JT8D-15 (HK3)		N8872Z
B727-225 (A) (F)	N743DH	DHL AIRWAYS (PEGA)		22438	1685	11/21/80	JT8D-15A (HK3)		N807EA, F-GKDY, N928PG
B727-224 (A) (F)	N745DH	DHL AIRWAYS (PEGA)		20665	1149	08/26/75	JT8D-9A		YV-880C, N69736
B727-224 (A)	N746DH	DHL AIRWAYS (PEGA)		22252	1697	02/04/81	JT8D-15		N79743
B727-224 (A)	N747DH	DHL AIRWAYS (PEGA)		22253	1702	02/04/81	JT8D-15 (HK3)		N79744
B727-021 (F)	N329QS	EMERY WORLDWIDE AIRLINES		19038	285	06/29/66	JT8D-7B (HK3)		N329PA [LST/OPB RYN IN EWW C/S]
B727-021 (F)	N355QS	EMERY WORLDWIDE AIRLINES		19257	385	03/17/67	JT8D-7B (HK3)		N355PA [LST/OPB RYN IN EWW C/S]
B727-021 (F)	N356QS	EMERY WORLDWIDE AIRLINES		19258	397	04/13/67	JT8D-7B		N356PA [LST/OPB RYN IN EWW C/S]
B727-021 (F)	N357QS	EMERY WORLDWIDE AIRLINES		19259	408	05/10/67	JT8D-7B (HK3)		N357PA [LST/OPB RYN IN EWW C/S]
B727-021 (F)	N359QS	EMERY WORLDWIDE AIRLINES		19007	269	05/18/66	JT8D-7B (HK3)		N325PA, HK-2846X [LST/OPB RYN IN EWW C/S]
B727-051C	N413EX	EMERY WORLDWIDE AIRLINES		19206	294	08/24/66	JT8D-7B (HK3)		N495US [LST RYN/USPS C/S]

A/C TYPE	CURRENT REG. NO.	LAST KNOWN OPERATOR (OWNER)	STATUS	ORIGINAL MSN	LINE NO.	DEL. DATE	ENG. TYPE	FLEET NO.	PREV. REG. [COMMENTS]
B727-051C	N416EX	EMERY WORLDWIDE AIRLINES		19287	383	03/12/67	JT8D-7B (HK3)		N496US [LST RYN/USPS C/S]
B727-051C	N417EX	EMERY WORLDWIDE AIRLINES		19290	417	05/27/67	JT8D-7B (HK3)		N499US [LST RYN/USPS C/S]
B727-022C	N421EX	EMERY WORLDWIDE AIRLINES		19099	322	10/27/66	JT8D-7B (HK3)		N7411U, HK-2474 [LST RYN/USPS C/S]
B727-134C	N424EX	EMERY WORLDWIDE AIRLINES		20042	626	09/05/68	JT8D-7B (HK3)		SE-DDC [LST RYN/USPS C/S]
B727-022C	N426EX	EMERY WORLDWIDE AIRLINES		19089	250	05/14/66	JT8D-7B (HK3)		N7401U [LST RYN/USPS C/S]
B727-022C	N427EX	EMERY WORLDWIDE AIRLINES		19090	277	06/29/66	JT8D-7B (HK3)		N7402U [LST RYN/USPS C/S]
B727-022C	N428EX	EMERY WORLDWIDE AIRLINES		19097	307	09/01/66	JT8D-7B (HK3)		N7409U [LST RYN/USPS C/S]
B727-022C	N429EX	EMERY WORLDWIDE AIRLINES		19100	324	10/31/66	JT8D-7B (HK3)		N7412U [LST RYN/USPS C/S]
B727-151C	N432EX	EMERY WORLDWIDE AIRLINES		19867	514	01/11/68	JT8D-7B (HK3)		N488US [LST RYN/USPS C/S]
B727-151C	N433EX	EMERY WORLDWIDE AIRLINES		19868	529	01/29/68	JT8D-7B (HK3)		N489US [LST RYN/USPS C/S]
B727-051C	N435EX	EMERY WORLDWIDE AIRLINES		19288	389	03/28/67	JT8D-7B (HK3)		N497US [LST RYN/USPS C/S]
B727-051C	N436EX	EMERY WORLDWIDE AIRLINES		19289	403	04/22/67	JT8D-7B (HK3)		N498US [LST RYN/USPS C/S]
B727-077C	N526PC	EMERY WORLDWIDE AIRLINES		20370	821	07/08/70	JT8D-7B (HK3)		VH-RMT, C2-RN4, N555BN [LST RYN/USPS C/S]
B727-172C	N527PC	EMERY WORLDWIDE AIRLINES		19665	476	10/23/67	JT8D-7B (HK3)		N725AL, CS-TBQ, N444GM, N45498 [LST RYN/USPS C/S]
B727-082C	N528PC	EMERY WORLDWIDE AIRLINES		19597	524	02/08/68	JT8D-7B (HK3)		CS-TBN, N4564U [LST RYN/USPS C/S]
B727-076 (F)	N721JE	EMERY WORLDWIDE AIRLINES		18843	170	08/20/65	JT8D-7B (HK3)		VH-TJC, AN-BSQ, YN-BSQ, N4602D [LST RYN/USPS C/S]
B727-223 (F)	N311NE	EMERY WORLDWIDE AIRLINES		19703	684	01/30/69	JT8D-9A (HK3)		N6825 [LST LHN/USPS C/S]
B727-223 (F)	N312NE	EMERY WORLDWIDE AIRLINES		20193	755	09/26/69	JT8D-9A (HK3)		N6841 [LST LHN/USPS C/S]
B727-223 (F)	N313NE	EMERY WORLDWIDE AIRLINES		19702	680	01/17/69	JT8D-9A (HK3)		N6824 [LST LHN/USPS C/S]
B727-222 (F)	N7635U	EMERY WORLDWIDE AIRLINES		19908	653	12/05/68	JT8D-7B (HK3)		[LST/OPB RYN IN EWW C/S]
B727-222 (F)	N7638U	EMERY WORLDWIDE AIRLINES		19911	668	12/27/68	JT8D-7B (HK3)		[LST/OPB RYN IN EWW C/S]
B727-222 (F)	N7639U	EMERY WORLDWIDE AIRLINES		19912	670	01/06/69	JT8D-7B (HK3)		[LST/OPB RYN IN EWW C/S]
B727-222 (F)	N7640U	EMERY WORLDWIDE AIRLINES		19913	672	02/10/69	JT8D-7B (HK3)		[LST/OPB RYN IN EWW C/S]
B727-222 (F)	N7642U	EMERY WORLDWIDE AIRLINES		19915	681	03/03/69	JT8D-7B (HK3)		[LST/OPB RYN IN EWW C/S]
B727-222 (F)	N7643U	EMERY WORLDWIDE AIRLINES		20037	701	03/19/69	JT8D-7B (HK3)		[LST/OPB RYN IN EWW C/S; DMGD 06/27/00 AT CAE; WINGTIP SCRAPED ON LDG]
B727-222 (F)	N7644U	EMERY WORLDWIDE AIRLINES		20038	716	05/14/69	JT8D-7B (HK3)		[LST/OPB RYN IN EWW C/S]
B727-222 (F)	N7645U	EMERY WORLDWIDE AIRLINES		20039	720	05/26/69	JT8D-7B (HK3)		[LST/OPB RYN IN EWW C/S]
B727-225 (A) (F)	N801EA	EMERY WORLDWIDE AIRLINES (FSBU)		22432	1658	10/06/80	JT8D-15/-15A		[LST/OPB RYN IN EWW C/S]
B727-225 (A) (F)	N815EA	EMERY WORLDWIDE AIRLINES (FSBU)		22552	1773	10/02/81	JT8D-15/-15A		[LST/OPB RYN IN EWW C/S]
B727-225 (A) (F)	N8878Z	EMERY WORLDWIDE AIRLINES (FSBU)		21451	1310	01/20/78	JT8D-15/-15A		[LST/OPB RYN IN EWW C/S]
B727-173C	N704A	EXPRESS.NET AIRLINES (CLARK)		19504	427	07/12/67	JT8D-7B (HK3)		N690WA
B727-022C	N792A	EXPRESS.NET AIRLINES (CLARK)		19195	406	05/11/67	JT8D-7B		N7420U, C-GAGZ, N727PL, N727CK
B727-227 (A)	N793A	EXPRESS.NET AIRLINES (CLARK)		20774	997	12/14/73	JT8D-9A (HK3)		N428BN, N553PE, N926TS
B727-025 (F)	N290NE	EXPRESS ONE INTL.		18972	242	03/18/66	JT8D-7B (HK3)		N8148N [OPF DHL IN EUROPE]
B727-082 (F)	N357NE	EXPRESS ONE INTL.		19405	398	04/24/67	JT8D-7B (HK3)		CS-TBL, C-GWGT, C-FACW
B727-231 (F)	N12305	EXPRESS ONE INTL. (PREWITT)		19562	576	05/25/68	JT8D-9A (HK3)		

111

A/C TYPE	CURRENT REG. NO.	LAST KNOWN OPERATOR (OWNER)	STATUS	ORIGINAL MSN	LINE NO.	DEL. DATE	ENG. TYPE	FLEET NO.	PREV. REG. [COMMENTS]
B727-264 (A) (F)	N15DF	EXPRESS ONE INTL. (PREWITT)		20710	975	09/25/73	JT8D-17R (HK3)		XA-CUE, N788BR, EI-BRF, N728ZV, G-BMLP, C-GRYO [OP IN DHL C/S]
B727-243 (A) (F)	N17410	EXPRESS ONE INTL. (PREWITT)		21663	1438	07/01/79	JT8D-9A		I-DIRG, N580PE
B727-277 (A) (F)	N275WC	EXPRESS ONE INTL. (AV. ENT.)		20549	989	11/07/73	JT8D-15 (HK3)		VH-RMV, YU-AKR [OPF USPS IN USPS C/S]
B727-2A7 (F)	N310NE	EXPRESS ONE INTL.		20241	726	05/27/69	JT8D-9A (HK3)		N8791R, N6842 [OPF USPS/USPS C/S]
B727-223 (F)	N311NE	EXPRESS ONE INTL. (EWW)	L	19703	684	01/30/69	JT8D-9A (HK3)		N6825 [OPF USPS/USPS C/S]
B727-223 (F)	N312NE	EXPRESS ONE INTL. (EWW)	L	20193	755	09/26/69	JT8D-9A (HK3)		N6841 [OPF USPS/USPS C/S]
B727-223 (F)	N313NE	EXPRESS ONE INTL. (EWW)	L	19702	680	01/17/69	JT8D-9A (HK3)		N6824 [OPF USPS/USPS C/S]
B727-223 (F)	N314NE	EXPRESS ONE INTL.		19495	664	12/03/68	JT8D-9A (HK3)		N6820 [OPF USPS/USPS C/S]
B727-223 (F)	N315NE	EXPRESS ONE INTL.		20190	738	07/22/69	JT8D-9A (HK3)		N6837 [OPF USPS/USPS C/S]
B727-223 (F)	N316NE	EXPRESS ONE INTL.		19475	511	02/01/68	JT8D-9A (HK3)		N6800 [OPF USPS/USPS C/S]
B727-225 (A) (F)	N352PA	EXPRESS ONE INTL. (AIRCORP)		20616	899	10/06/72	JT8D-15 (HK3)		N8853E [ALL WHITE; NO TITLES]
B727-225 (A) (F)	N353PA	EXPRESS ONE INTL. (AIRCORP)		20622	933	04/06/73	JT8D-15 (HK3)		N8860E [ALL WHITE; NO TITLES]
B727-225 (A) (F)	N354PA	EXPRESS ONE INTL. (AIRCORP)		20624	940	05/04/73	JT8D-15 (HK3)		N8862E
B727-225 (A) (F)	N356PA	EXPRESS ONE INTL. (AIRCORP)		20626	946	05/30/73	JT8D-15 (HK3)		N8864E [ALL WHITE; NO TITLES]
B727-225 (A) (F)	N361KP	EXPRESS ONE INTL. (AIRCORP)		20627	947	06/05/73	JT8D-15 (HK3)		N8865E, N357PA
B727-223 (A) (F)	N6813	EXPRESS ONE INTL. (PREWITT)		19488	588	06/12/68	JT8D-9A (HK3)		
B727-223 (F)	N6815	EXPRESS ONE INTL. (AIRCORP)		19490	602	07/15/68	JT8D-9A (HK3)		
B727-223 (A) (F)	N6819	EXPRESS ONE INTL. (PREWITT)		19494	661	11/22/68	JT8D-9A (HK3)		[OP IN DHL C/S]
B727-223 (F)	N6826	EXPRESS ONE INTL. (PREWITT)		19704	689	02/13/69	JT8D-9A (HK3)		[PARKED CLT; ALL WHITE; NO TITLES]
B727-223 (F)	N6839	EXPRESS ONE INTL. (AIRCORP)		20192	752	09/22/69	JT8D-7B (HK3)		
B727-223 (A) (F) (WL)	N701NE	EXPRESS ONE INTL. (JRW A/C)		22459	1742	04/30/81	JT8D-15A (HK3)		N701AA [LANDED SHORT AT POHNPEI, CAROLINE IS. 03/12/01; WO?]
B727-223 (A) (WL)	N702NE	EXPRESS ONE INTL. (JRW A/C)		22460	1746	05/11/81	JT8D-15A (HK3)		N702AA [CVTD TO FRTR?]
B727-2M7 (A) (F)	N721RW	EXPRESS ONE INTL.		21200	1206	08/19/76	JT8D-17R (HK3)		[ALL WHITE; NO TITLES]
B727-2M7 (A) (F)	N725RW	EXPRESS ONE INTL. (PEGA)		21502	1339	05/02/78	JT8D-17R		HC-BVM
B727-2M7 (A) (F)	N742RW	EXPRESS ONE INTL.		21952	1693	12/18/80	JT8D-17R (HK3)		
B727-231 (F)	N74318	EXPRESS ONE INTL. (PREWITT)		20051	708	04/16/69	JT8D-9A (HK3)		
B727-259 (A)	N203AV	FALCON AIR EXPRESS (PEGA)		22474	1688	12/04/80	JT8D-17R (HK3)		
B727-231 (A) (F) (RE)	N24343	FALCON AIR EXPRESS (PACA)		21630	1458	03/22/79	JT8D-217C/-9A		[PARKED MIA]
B727-251	N266US	FALCON AIR EXPRESS (FSBU)		19985	745	08/08/69	JT8D-9A		
B727-224	N32719	FALCON AIR EXPRESS (PEGA)		20388	805	04/15/70	JT8D-9A (HK3)		
B727-224 (A)	N79749	FALCON AIR EXPRESS (PEGA)		22451	1767	07/21/81	JT8D-15 (HK3)		[LST LAV]
B727-224 (A)	N79750	FALCON AIR EXPRESS (PEGA)		22452	1772	09/01/81	JT8D-15 (HK3)		[LST LAV]
B727-276 (A)	N908PG	FALCON AIR EXPRESS (PEGA)		20951	1101	04/24/75	JT8D-15		VH-TBL, TF-FLK, YU-AKO, TF-AIA
B727-025C	N40	FEDERAL AVIATION ADMINISTRATION		19854	628	09/10/68	JT8D-7 (HK3)		N8171G [R&D]
B727-022C	N101FE	FEDERAL EXPRESS (GECA)		19197	410	05/23/67	JT8D-7B (HK3)		N7422U

A/C TYPE	CURRENT REG. NO.	LAST KNOWN OPERATOR (OWNER)	STATUS	ORIGINAL MSN	LINE NO.	DEL. DATE	ENG. TYPE	FLEET NO.	PREV. REG. [COMMENTS]
B727-022C	N102FE	FEDERAL EXPRESS		19193	392	04/17/67	JT8D-7B (HK3)		N7418U
B727-022C	N103FE	FEDERAL EXPRESS		19199	414	06/12/67	JT8D-7B (HK3)		N7424U
B727-022C	N104FE	FEDERAL EXPRESS		19198	413	06/05/67	JT8D-7B (HK3)		N7423U
B727-022C	N105FE	FEDERAL EXPRESS		19194	394	04/25/67	JT8D-7B (HK3)		N7419U
B727-022C	N107FE	FEDERAL EXPRESS		19202	424	06/30/67	JT8D-7B (HK3)		N7427U
B727-022C	N112FE	FEDERAL EXPRESS		19890	630	09/19/68	JT8D-7B (HK3)		N7433U
B727-022C	N113FE	FEDERAL EXPRESS		19894	647	10/25/68	JT8D-7B (HK3)		N7437U
B727-024C	N114FE	FEDERAL EXPRESS		19527	460	09/16/67	JT8D-7B (HK3)		N2474, N5474, N1781B, N1335B, CC-CAN
B727-025C	N116FE	FEDERAL EXPRESS (RFC A/C)		19298	335	12/08/66	JT8D-7B (HK3)		N8151G
B727-025C	N117FE	FEDERAL EXPRESS		19299	344	12/18/66	JT8D-7B (HK3)		N8152G
B727-025C	N118FE	FEDERAL EXPRESS		19300	346	12/21/66	JT8D-7B (HK3)		N8153G
B727-025C	N119FE	FEDERAL EXPRESS		19301	352	01/27/67	JT8D-7 (HK3)		N8154G
B727-025C	N120FE	FEDERAL EXPRESS (RFC A/C)		19356	356	02/10/67	JT8D-7B (HK3)		N8156G
B727-025C	N124FE	FEDERAL EXPRESS		19360	371	03/09/67	JT8D-7B (HK3)		N8160G
B727-025C	N127FE	FEDERAL EXPRESS		19719	478	10/27/67	JT8D-7B (HK3)		N8163G
B727-025C	N128FE	FEDERAL EXPRESS		19720	482	11/09/67	JT8D-7B (HK3)		N8164G [WFU MEM; TO BE DONATED TO TECH SCHOOL]
B727-025C	N133FE	FEDERAL EXPRESS		19851	510	01/09/68	JT8D-7 (HK3)		N8168G
B727-025C	N134FE	FEDERAL EXPRESS		19852	517	01/23/68	JT8D-7 (HK3)		N8169G [STD MHV]
B727-025C	N135FE	FEDERAL EXPRESS		19853	522	01/31/68	JT8D-7B (HK3)		N8170G
B727-025C	N136FE	FEDERAL EXPRESS		19855	632	09/20/68	JT8D-7B (HK3)		N8172G
B727-021C	N143FE	FEDERAL EXPRESS (RFC A/C)		19136	314	09/27/66	JT8D-7B (HK3)		N341PA, PT-TCA, PT-TCG, N727GB, N727BB, N722EV
B727-021C	N144FE	FEDERAL EXPRESS		19137	316	10/07/66	JT8D-7B (HK3)		N342PA, PT-TCB, N2969V, N727LJ, N723EV
B727-027C	N145FE	FEDERAL EXPRESS		19109	271	05/27/66	JT8D-7 (HK3)		N7270, PT-TYU, N724EV
B727-027C	N146FE	FEDERAL EXPRESS		19110	283	06/24/66	JT8D-7 (HK3)		N7271, PT-TYQ, N730EV, HP-1063
B727-022 (F)	N147FE	FEDERAL EXPRESS		19080	270	05/18/66	JT8D-7B (HK3)		N7067U
B727-022 (F)	N148FE	FEDERAL EXPRESS		19086	353	01/23/67	JT8D-7B (HK3)		N7073U
B727-022 (F)	N149FE	FEDERAL EXPRESS		19087	359	01/27/67	JT8D-7B (HK3)		N7074U
B727-022 (F)	N150FE	FEDERAL EXPRESS		19141	370	02/18/67	JT8D-7B (HK3)		N7077U
B727-022 (F)	N151FE	FEDERAL EXPRESS		19147	472	10/11/67	JT8D-7B (HK3)		N7083U
B727-025 (F)	N152FE	FEDERAL EXPRESS		18285	172	08/25/65	JT8D-7B (HK3)		N8134N
B727-025 (F)	N154FE	FEDERAL EXPRESS		18287	190	10/13/65	JT8D-7B (HK3)		N8136N, HK-2604, N4753B
B727-025 (F)	N155FE	FEDERAL EXPRESS		18288	192	09/27/65	JT8D-7B (HK3)		N8137N
B727-025 (F)	N156FE	FEDERAL EXPRESS		18289	194	11/10/65	JT8D-7B (HK3)		N8138N [STD MHV]
B727-022 (F)	N166FE	FEDERAL EXPRESS		18863	227	02/03/66	JT8D-7B (HK3)		N7056U
B727-022 (F)	N167FE	FEDERAL EXPRESS		18864	231	02/22/66	JT8D-7B (HK3)		N7057U
B727-022 (F)	N168FE	FEDERAL EXPRESS		18865	232	02/18/66	JT8D-7B (HK3)		N7058U
B727-022 (F)	N169FE	FEDERAL EXPRESS		18866	241	03/13/66	JT8D-7B (HK3)		N7059U
B727-022 (F)	N181FE	FEDERAL EXPRESS		18868	248	04/01/66	JT8D-7B (HK3)		N7061U
B727-022 (F)	N184FE	FEDERAL EXPRESS		18870	258	04/27/66	JT8D-7B (HK3)		N7063U [STD MHV]

A/C TYPE	CURRENT REG. NO.	LAST KNOWN OPERATOR (OWNER)	STATUS	ORIGINAL MSN	LINE NO.	DEL. DATE	ENG. TYPE	FLEET NO.	PREV. REG. [COMMENTS]
B727-022 (F)	N185FE	FEDERAL EXPRESS		18871	259	04/29/66	JT8D-7B (HK3)		N7064U
B727-022 (F)	N186FE	FEDERAL EXPRESS		18872	261	04/30/66	JT8D-7B (HK3)		N7065U
B727-022 (F)	N187FE	FEDERAL EXPRESS		19079	268	05/17/66	JT8D-7B (HK3)		N7066U
B727-022 (F)	N188FE	FEDERAL EXPRESS		19081	275	06/06/66	JT8D-7B (HK3)		N7068U
B727-022 (F)	N189FE	FEDERAL EXPRESS		19082	279	06/09/66	JT8D-7B (HK3)		N7069U
B727-022 (F)	N190FE	FEDERAL EXPRESS		19083	281	06/21/66	JT8D-7B (HK3)		N7070U
B727-022 (F)	N191FE	FEDERAL EXPRESS		19084	337	12/21/66	JT8D-7B (HK3)		N7071U
B727-022 (F)	N193FE	FEDERAL EXPRESS		19142	440	07/30/67	JT8D-7B (HK3)		N7078U
B727-022 (F)	N194FE	FEDERAL EXPRESS		19143	446	08/17/67	JT8D-7B (HK3)		N7079U
B727-022 (F)	N195FE	FEDERAL EXPRESS		19144	450	08/29/67	JT8D-7B (HK3)		N7080U
B727-022 (F)	N196FE	FEDERAL EXPRESS		19145	451	08/31/67	JT8D-7B (HK3)		N7081U
B727-022 (F)	N198FE	FEDERAL EXPRESS		19154	512	12/29/67	JT8D-7B		N7090U
B727-173C	N199FE	FEDERAL EXPRESS		19509	459	09/14/67	JT8D-7B (HK3)		N695WA, TZ-ADR
B727-025 (F)	N502FE	FEDERAL EXPRESS		18271	82	10/19/64	JT8D-7B		[STD MHV]
B727-025 (F)	N503FE	FEDERAL EXPRESS		18273	91	11/13/64	JT8D-7B (HK3)		N8122N [STD MHV]
B727-025 (F)	N504FE	FEDERAL EXPRESS		18274	96	12/04/64	JT8D-7B (HK3)		N8123N [STD MHV]
B727-025 (F)	N505FE	FEDERAL EXPRESS		18276	103	01/06/65	JT8D-7B (HK3)		N8125N
B727-025 (F)	N506FE	FEDERAL EXPRESS		18277	107	01/22/65	JT8D-7B (HK3)		N8126N
B727-025 (F)	N507FE	FEDERAL EXPRESS		18278	113	02/12/65	JT8D-7B (HK3)		N8127N [STD MHV]
B727-025 (F)	N508FE	FEDERAL EXPRESS		18279	121	03/10/65	JT8D-7B (HK3)		N8128N [STD MHV]
B727-025 (F)	N509FE	FEDERAL EXPRESS		18280	129	04/07/65	JT8D-7B (HK3)		N8129N
B727-025 (F)	N510FE	FEDERAL EXPRESS		18282	149	06/09/65	JT8D-7B (HK3)		N8131N, HK-2705X, N4556W
B727-025 (F)	C-FBWX	FEDERAL EXPRESS		18286	182	09/24/65	JT8D-7B (HK3)		N8135N, N153FE [LST/OPB MEI]
B727-022 (F)	C-FBWY	FEDERAL EXPRESS		19085	349	12/22/66	JT8D-7B		N7072U, N192FE [LST/OPB MEI]
B727-116C	C-GBWH	FEDERAL EXPRESS		19814	600	07/11/68	JT8D-7B (HK3)		CC-CFE, N115FE [LST/OPB MEI]
B727-022 (F)	C-GBWS	FEDERAL EXPRESS		18867	247	03/30/66	JT8D-7B (HK3)		N7060U, N180FE [LST/OPB MEI]
B727-2S2F (A) (RE)	N201FE	FEDERAL EXPRESS		22924	1818	06/27/83	JT8D-217C/17A		
B727-2S2F (A)	N203FE	FEDERAL EXPRESS		22925	1819	08/01/83	JT8D-17A (HK3)		
B727-2S2F (A)	N204FE	FEDERAL EXPRESS		22926	1820	08/01/83	JT8D-17A (HK3)		
B727-2S2F (A) (RE)	N205FE	FEDERAL EXPRESS		22927	1821	09/01/83	JT8D-217C/17A		
B727-2S2F (A) (RE)	N206FE	FEDERAL EXPRESS		22928	1822	09/20/83	JT8D-217C/17A		
B727-2S2F (A) (RE)	N207FE	FEDERAL EXPRESS		22929	1823	10/17/83	JT8D-217C/17A		
B727-2S2F (A) (RE)	N208FE	FEDERAL EXPRESS		22930	1824	11/17/83	JT8D-217C/17A		
B727-2S2F (A) (RE)	N209FE	FEDERAL EXPRESS		22931	1825	01/11/84	JT8D-217C/17A		
B727-2S2F (A) (RE)	N210FE	FEDERAL EXPRESS		22932	1826	02/17/84	JT8D-217C/17A		
B727-2S2F (A)	N211FE	FEDERAL EXPRESS		22933	1827	03/23/84	JT8D-17A (HK3)		
B727-2S2F (A) (RE)	N212FE	FEDERAL EXPRESS		22934	1828	04/20/84	JT8D-217C/17A		
B727-2S2F (A)	N213FE	FEDERAL EXPRESS		22935	1829	05/24/84	JT8D-17A (HK3)		
B727-2S2F (A) (RE)	N215FE	FEDERAL EXPRESS		22936	1830	06/29/84	JT8D-217C/17A		
B727-2S2F (A) (RE)	N216FE	FEDERAL EXPRESS		22937	1831	08/14/84	JT8D-217C/17A		
B727-2S2F (A) (RE)	N217FE	FEDERAL EXPRESS		22938	1832	09/18/84	JT8D-217C/17A		[LAST B727 BUILT]

A/C TYPE	CURRENT REG. NO.	LAST KNOWN OPERATOR (OWNER)	STATUS	ORIGINAL MSN	LINE NO.	DEL. DATE	ENG. TYPE	FLEET NO.	PREV. REG. [COMMENTS]
B727-233 (A) (F)	N218FE	FEDERAL EXPRESS		21101	1150	08/28/75	JT8D-15 (HK3)		C-GAAM
B727-233 (A) (F)	N219FE	FEDERAL EXPRESS		21102	1152	09/05/75	JT8D-15 (HK3)		C-GAAN
B727-233 (A) (F)	N220FE	FEDERAL EXPRESS		20934	1074	10/17/74	JT8D-15 (HK3)		C-GAAC
B727-233 (A) (F)	N221FE	FEDERAL EXPRESS		20932	1069	09/30/74	JT8D-15 (HK3)		C-GAAA
B727-233 (A) (F)	N222FE	FEDERAL EXPRESS		20933	1071	10/13/74	JT8D-15 (HK3)		C-GAAB
B727-233 (A) (F)	N223FE	FEDERAL EXPRESS		20935	1076	10/22/74	JT8D-15 (HK3)		C-GAAD, 6Y-JMP
B727-247 (A) (F)	N233FE	FEDERAL EXPRESS		21327	1249	03/09/77	JT8D-15 (HK3)		N2822W
B727-247 (A) (F)	N234FE	FEDERAL EXPRESS		21328	1251	03/09/77	JT8D-15 (HK3)		N2823W
B727-247 (A) (F)	N235FE	FEDERAL EXPRESS		21329	1254	03/29/77	JT8D-15 (HK3)		N2824W
B727-247 (A) (F)	N236FE	FEDERAL EXPRESS		21330	1260	05/03/77	JT8D-15 (HK3)		N2825W
B727-247 (A) (F)	N237FE	FEDERAL EXPRESS		21331	1266	05/24/77	JT8D-15 (HK3)		N2826W
B727-277 (A) (F)	N240FE	FEDERAL EXPRESS		20978	1083	11/07/74	JT8D-15 (HK3)		VH-RMY, 6Y-JML
B727-277 (A) (F)	N241FE	FEDERAL EXPRESS		20979	1098	04/30/75	JT8D-15 (HK3)		VH-RMZ
B727-277 (A) (F)	N242FE	FEDERAL EXPRESS		21178	1237	12/10/76	JT8D-15 (HK3)		VH-RMK
B727-277 (A) (F)	N243FE	FEDERAL EXPRESS		21480	1352	06/08/78	JT8D-15 (HK3)		VH-RML
B727-277 (A) (F)	N244FE	FEDERAL EXPRESS		21647	1436	01/29/79	JT8D-15 (HK3)		VH-RMM
B727-277 (A) (F)	N245FE	FEDERAL EXPRESS		22016	1566	01/15/80	JT8D-15 (HK3)		VH-RMO [OO TO CCI]
B727-277 (A) (F)	N246FE	FEDERAL EXPRESS		22068	1660	09/10/80	JT8D-15 (HK3)		VH-RMP
B727-233 (A) (F)	N254FE	FEDERAL EXPRESS		20936	1078	10/23/74	JT8D-15 (HK3)		C-GAAE, 6Y-JMH
B727-233 (A) (F)	N257FE	FEDERAL EXPRESS		20939	1112	04/04/75	JT8D-15 (HK3)		C-GAAH
B727-233 (A) (F)	N258FE	FEDERAL EXPRESS		20940	1120	04/10/75	JT8D-15 (HK3)		C-GAAI
B727-233 (A) (F)	N262FE	FEDERAL EXPRESS		21624	1468	04/17/79	JT8D-15 (HK3)		C-GAAO
B727-233 (A) (F)	N263FE	FEDERAL EXPRESS		21625	1470	04/24/79	JT8D-15 (HK3)		C-GAAP
B727-233 (A) (F)	N264FE	FEDERAL EXPRESS		21626	1472	04/26/79	JT8D-15 (HK3)		C-GAAQ
B727-233 (A) (F)	N265FE	FEDERAL EXPRESS		21671	1523	09/27/79	JT8D-15 (HK3)		C-GAAR
B727-233 (A) (F)	N266FE	FEDERAL EXPRESS		21672	1538	11/01/79	JT8D-15 (HK3)		C-GAAS
B727-233 (A) (F)	N267FE	FEDERAL EXPRESS		21673	1541	11/02/79	JT8D-15 (HK3)		C-GAAT
B727-233 (A) (F)	N268FE	FEDERAL EXPRESS		21674	1543	11/30/79	JT8D-15 (HK3)		C-GAAU
B727-233 (A) (F)	N269FE	FEDERAL EXPRESS		21675	1555	12/06/79	JT8D-15 (HK3)		C-GAAV
B727-233 (A) (F)	N270FE	FEDERAL EXPRESS		22035	1578	02/14/80	JT8D-15 (HK3)		C-GAAW
B727-233 (A) (F)	N271FE	FEDERAL EXPRESS		22036	1596	03/27/80	JT8D-15 (HK3)		N57002, C-GAAX, 6Y-JMC
B727-233 (A) (F)	N272FE	FEDERAL EXPRESS		22037	1600	04/10/80	JT8D-15 (HK3)		C-GAAY
B727-233 (A) (F)	N273FE	FEDERAL EXPRESS		22038	1612	05/09/80	JT8D-15 (HK3)		N57000, C-GAAZ
B727-233 (A) (F)	N274FE	FEDERAL EXPRESS		22039	1614	05/15/80	JT8D-15 (HK3)		N57002, C-GYNA
B727-233 (A) (F)	N275FE	FEDERAL EXPRESS		22040	1626	06/11/80	JT8D-15 (HK3)		N57008, C-GYNB
B727-233 (A) (F)	N276FE	FEDERAL EXPRESS		22041	1628	06/13/80	JT8D-17 (HK3)		C-GYNC
B727-233 (A) (F)	N277FE	FEDERAL EXPRESS		22042	1630	06/19/80	JT8D-15 (HK3)		C-GYND
B727-233 (A) (F)	N278FE	FEDERAL EXPRESS		22345	1699	12/19/80	JT8D-17 (HK3)		C-GYNE
B727-233 (A) (F)	N279FE	FEDERAL EXPRESS		22346	1704	01/22/81	JT8D-17 (HK3)		C-GYNF
B727-233 (A) (F)	N280FE	FEDERAL EXPRESS		22347	1708	01/29/81	JT8D-17 (HK3)		C-GYNG, 6Y-JMQ
B727-233 (A) (F)	N281FE	FEDERAL EXPRESS		22348	1714	02/13/81	JT8D-17 (HK3)		C-GYNH

A/C TYPE	CURRENT REG. NO.	LAST KNOWN OPERATOR (OWNER)	STATUS	ORIGINAL MSN	LINE NO.	DEL. DATE	ENG. TYPE	FLEET NO.	PREV. REG. [COMMENTS]
B727-233 (A) (F)	N282FE	FEDERAL EXPRESS		22349	1722	03/16/81	JT8D-17 (HK3)		N8278V, C-GYNI
B727-233 (A) (F)	N283FE	FEDERAL EXPRESS		22350	1745	05/14/81	JT8D-17 (HK3)		C-GYNJ
B727-233 (A) (F)	N284FE	FEDERAL EXPRESS		22621	1791	02/04/82	JT8D-17 (HK3)		N5573E, C-GYNK
B727-233 (A) (F)	N285FE	FEDERAL EXPRESS		22622	1792	03/09/82	JT8D-17 (HK3)		C-GYNL
B727-233 (A) (F)	N286FE	FEDERAL EXPRESS		22623	1803	06/17/82	JT8D-15 (HK3)		C-GYNM
B727-2D4 (A) (F)	N287FE	FEDERAL EXPRESS (BALG)		21849	1527	10/11/79	JT8D-15 (HK3)		N720ZK, N361PA
B727-2D4 (A) (F)	N288FE	FEDERAL EXPRESS		21850	1536	10/25/79	JT8D-15 (HK3)		N721ZK, N362PA
B727-225 (A) (F)	N461FE	FEDERAL EXPRESS		22548	1734	04/09/81	JT8D-15 (HK3)		N811EA
B727-225 (A) (F)	N462FE	FEDERAL EXPRESS		22550	1739	04/27/81	JT8D-15 (HK3)		N813EA
B727-225 (A) (F)	N463FE	FEDERAL EXPRESS		22551	1744	05/07/81	JT8D-15 (HK3)		N814EA
B727-225 (A) (F)	N464FE	FEDERAL EXPRESS		21288	1234	11/23/76	JT8D-15 (HK3)		N8870Z
B727-225 (A) (F)	N465FE	FEDERAL EXPRESS		21289	1235	12/03/76	JT8D-15 (HK3)		N8871Z
B727-225 (A) (F)	N466FE	FEDERAL EXPRESS		21292	1240	12/21/76	JT8D-15 (HK3)		N8874Z
B727-225 (A) (F)	N467FE	FEDERAL EXPRESS		21449	1306	11/18/77	JT8D-15 (HK3)		N8876Z
B727-225 (A) (F)	N468FE	FEDERAL EXPRESS		21452	1312	01/27/78	JT8D-15 (HK3)		N8879Z
B727-225 (A) (F)	N469FE	FEDERAL EXPRESS		21581	1437	01/31/79	JT8D-15 (HK3)		N8884Z, TF-RMR
B727-227 (A) (F)	N477FE	FEDERAL EXPRESS		21394	1281	07/27/77	JT8D-9A (HK3)		N453BN
B727-227 (A) (F)	N478FE	FEDERAL EXPRESS		21395	1283	08/01/77	JT8D-9A (HK3)		N454BN
B727-227 (A) (F)	N479FE	FEDERAL EXPRESS		21461	1337	04/27/78	JT8D-17 (HK3)		N455BN
B727-227 (A) (F)	N480FE	FEDERAL EXPRESS		21462	1342	05/10/78	JT8D-17 (HK3)		N456BN
B727-227 (A) (F)	N481FE	FEDERAL EXPRESS		21463	1353	06/13/78	JT8D-17 (HK3)		N457BN
B727-227 (A) (F)	N482FE	FEDERAL EXPRESS		21464	1355	06/15/78	JT8D-17 (HK3)		N458BN
B727-227 (A) (F)	N483FE	FEDERAL EXPRESS		21465	1363	07/17/78	JT8D-15 (HK3)		N459BN
B727-227 (A) (F)	N484FE	FEDERAL EXPRESS		21466	1372	08/09/78	JT8D-9A (HK3)		N460BN
B727-227 (A) (F)	N485FE	FEDERAL EXPRESS		21488	1388	09/21/78	JT8D-9A (HK3)		N461BN
B727-227 (A) (F)	N486FE	FEDERAL EXPRESS		21489	1390	09/27/78	JT8D-9A (HK3)		N462BN
B727-227 (A) (F)	N487FE	FEDERAL EXPRESS		21490	1396	10/11/78	JT8D-15 (HK3)		N463BN
B727-227 (A) (F)	N488FE	FEDERAL EXPRESS		21491	1402	10/26/78	JT8D-15 (HK3)		N464BN
B727-227 (A) (F)	N489FE	FEDERAL EXPRESS		21492	1440	02/07/79	JT8D-15 (HK3)		N465BN
B727-227 (A) (F)	N490FE	FEDERAL EXPRESS		21493	1442	02/09/79	JT8D-15 (HK3)		N466BN
B727-227 (A) (F)	N491FE	FEDERAL EXPRESS		21529	1444	02/17/79	JT8D-9A (HK3)		N467BN
B727-227 (A) (F)	N492FE	FEDERAL EXPRESS		21530	1446	02/22/79	JT8D-15 (HK3)		N468BN
B727-227 (A) (F)	N493FE	FEDERAL EXPRESS		21531	1450	03/02/79	JT8D-15 (HK3)		N469BN
B727-227 (A) (F)	N494FE	FEDERAL EXPRESS		21532	1453	03/10/79	JT8D-15 (HK3)		N470BN
B727-227 (A) (F)	N495FE	FEDERAL EXPRESS		21669	1484	05/25/79	JT8D-15 (HK3)		N471BN
B727-227 (A) (F)	N496FE	FEDERAL EXPRESS		21670	1486	05/31/79	JT8D-15 (HK3)		N472BN
B727-232 (A) (F)	N497FE	FEDERAL EXPRESS		20866	1067	09/13/74	JT8D-15 (HK3)		N486DA, CS-TCH
B727-232 (A) (F)	N498FE	FEDERAL EXPRESS		20867	1068	09/19/74	JT8D-15 (HK3)		N487DA, CS-TCI
B727-232 (A) (F)	N499FE	FEDERAL EXPRESS		21018	1095	02/21/75	JT8D-15 (HK3)		N488DA, CS-TCJ

A/C TYPE	CURRENT REG. NO.	LAST KNOWN OPERATOR (OWNER)	STATUS	ORIGINAL MSN	LINE NO.	DEL. DATE	ENG. TYPE	FLEET NO.	PREV. REG. [COMMENTS]
B727-021	N727LA	FUN AIR CORP.		19260	412	05/21/67	JT8D-7B (HK3)		N358PA, N727SG
B727-212 (A) (WL)	N727NK	FUN AIR CORP. (F.B.A. AIRPLANE)		21945	1502	07/10/79	JT8D-17A (HK3)		9V-SGG, TI-LRQ, N200LR, OY-SCC, N317NE [OPF FOR MIAMI HEAT]
B727-030(RE)	N18HH	GENI AIRCRAFT CORP		18936	249	04/07/66	JT8D-217C/9A		D-ABIV, N16764, N33UT, N5073L
B727-021	N30MP	ICN PHARMACEUTICALS INC. (PLUEGER)		18998	239	03/13/66	JT8D-7		N320PA, N320AS, N1CC, N727S, N300DK, N109HT, N7271P, N111JL
B727-030(WL)	N7271P	IMPERIAL PALACE AIR		18933	185	09/29/65	JT8D-7 (HK3)		D-ABIR, N727CH, VR-BHK, VR-BGW, N129JK, N727BE
B727-282 (A) (RE) (WL)	N727RE	IMPERIAL PALACE AIR		22430	1715	03/02/81	JT8D-217C/17		N8285V, CS-TBY, 6O-SCG, N6167D
B727-030	N113	JPATS-U.S. DEPARTMENT OF JUSTICE		18935	234	02/24/66	JT8D-7		D-ABIT, N90557, N833N, VR-CBA, N18G
B727-061	N530KF	JPATS-U.S. DEPARTMENT OF JUSTICE		19176	290	07/13/66	JT8D-7		N127, N27, N2777
B727-251 (A)	N109KM	JPATS-U.S. DEPARTMENT OF JUSTICE		21155	1169	10/27/75	JT8D-15/-15A		N276US
B727-281	N7128T	JPATS-U.S. DEPARTMENT OF JUSTICE		20286	875	05/10/72	JT8D-9A		N1780B, JA8336, N864N, N744US
B727-243 (A) (F)	N1269Y	KITTY HAWK AIR CARGO (WFBN)		21269	1230	11/19/76	JT8D-7B (HK3)		N40133, I-DIRC, N576PE, N17406, EI-EWW, OY-SEU
B727-222 (F)	N180AX	KITTY HAWK AIR CARGO		20041	732	06/30/69	JT8D-7B (HK3)		N7647U
B727-251 (F)	N252US	KITTY HAWK AIR CARGO (ACFT LSG)		19971	655	11/21/68	JT8D-7B (HK3)		
B727-251 (F)	N255US	KITTY HAWK AIR CARGO		19974	667	12/07/68	JT8D-7B (HK3)		
B727-251 (F)	N264US	KITTY HAWK AIR CARGO (PEGA)		19983	741	08/01/69	JT8D-7B (HK3)		
B727-251 (A) (F)	N278US	KITTY HAWK AIR CARGO (ACFT LSG)		21157	1173	11/18/75	JT8D-15 (HK3)		
B727-251 (F)	N279US	KITTY HAWK AIR CARGO (ACFT LSG)		21158	1177	12/11/75	JT8D-15 (HK3)		
B727-2J0 (A) (F)	N281KH	KITTY HAWK AIR CARGO		21105	1158	08/29/75	JT8D-15 (HK3)		6Y-JMA, VR-CMA, 6Y-JMM
B727-2J0 (A) (F)	N284KH	KITTY HAWK AIR CARGO		21108	1174	11/19/75	JT8D-15 (HK3)		6Y-JMD, VR-CMD, 6Y-JMP
B727-232 (A)	N511PE	KITTY HAWK AIR CARGO (PEGA)		20634	917	01/23/73	JT8D-15		N452DA [BEING CVTD TO FRTR AT MIA]
B727-243 (A) (F)	N579PE	KITTY HAWK AIR CARGO (FSBU)		21662	1421	12/12/78	JT8D-9A (HK3)		I-DIRF
B727-223 (F)	N6806	KITTY HAWK AIR CARGO		19481	548	04/02/68	JT8D-9 (HK3)		N719CK [BAX C/S]
B727-223 (F)	N6807	KITTY HAWK AIR CARGO		19482	557	04/17/68	JT8D-9 (HK3)		N729CK
B727-223 (F)	N6808	KITTY HAWK AIR CARGO		19483	558	04/11/68	JT8D-9 (HK3)		
B727-223 (F)	N6809	KITTY HAWK AIR CARGO (ACFT LSG)		19484	560	04/23/68	JT8D-9 (HK3)		
B727-223 (F)	N6810	KITTY HAWK AIR CARGO		19485	571	05/11/68	JT8D-9 (HK3)		N722CK [OP IN USPS C/S]
B727-223 (F)	N6811	KITTY HAWK AIR CARGO		19486	578	05/27/68	JT8D-9 (HK3)		
B727-223 (F)	N6812	KITTY HAWK AIR CARGO		19487	579	05/29/68	JT8D-9 (HK3)		N720CK
B727-223 (F)	N6816	KITTY HAWK AIR CARGO		19491	611	07/31/68	JT8D-9 (HK3)		[LST/OPF BAX GLOBAL; TBR N724CK]
B727-223 (F)	N6821	KITTY HAWK AIR CARGO		19496	669	12/17/68	JT8D-9A (HK3)		N706CA
B727-223 (F)	N6827	KITTY HAWK AIR CARGO (ACFT LSG)		20180	698	03/21/69	JT8D-9 (HK3)		
B727-223 (F)	N6831	KITTY HAWK AIR CARGO		20184	707	04/15/69	JT8D-9		[LST/OPF BAX GLOBAL]

A/C TYPE	CURRENT REG. NO.	LAST KNOWN OPERATOR (OWNER)	STATUS	ORIGINAL MSN	LINE NO.	DEL. DATE	ENG. TYPE	FLEET NO.	PREV. REG. [COMMENTS]
B727-223 (F)	N6833	KITTY HAWK AIR CARGO (ACFT LSG)		20186	721	05/21/69	JT8D-9 (HK3)		
B727-223 (F)	N6834	KITTY HAWK AIR CARGO		20187	722	05/26/69	JT8D-9 (HK3)		
B727-223 (F)	N6838	KITTY HAWK AIR CARGO		20191	739	07/28/69	JT8D-9 (HK3)		N723CK
B727-224 (A) (F)	N69735	KITTY HAWK AIR CARGO (PEGA)		20664	1079	10/25/74	JT8D-9A (HK3)		
B727-224 (A) (F)	N69739	KITTY HAWK AIR CARGO (ACFT LSG)		20667	1153	10/07/75	JT8D-9A (HK3)		
B727-224 (A) (F)	N69740	KITTY HAWK AIR CARGO (ACFT LSG)		20668	1154	10/14/75	JT8D-9A (HK3)		
B727-214 (A) (F)	N750US	KITTY HAWK AIR CARGO (ACFT LSG)		21512	1343	05/16/78	JT8D-7B (HK3)		N555PS
B727-214 (A) (F)	N751US	KITTY HAWK AIR CARGO (ACFT LSG)		21513	1365	07/18/78	JT8D-7B (HK3)		N556PS
B727-232 (A) (F)	N77780	KITTY HAWK AIR CARGO (PACA)		20635	918	01/26/73	JT8D-15 (HK3)		N453DA, N512PE, N13780
B727-224 (A) (F)	N79748	KITTY HAWK AIR CARGO (PACA)		22450	1760	06/22/81	JT8D-15		
B727-223 (A) (F)	N854AA	KITTY HAWK AIR CARGO (ACFT LSG)		20995	1192	06/22/76	JT8D-9A (HK3)		
B727-223 (A) (F)	N855AA	KITTY HAWK AIR CARGO (ACFT LSG)		20996	1193	06/22/76	JT8D-9A (HK3)		
B727-223 (A) (F)	N856AA	KITTY HAWK AIR CARGO		20997	1195	06/22/76	JT8D-9A (HK3)		
B727-223 (A) (F)	N858AA	KITTY HAWK AIR CARGO		21085	1200	04/27/76	JT8D-9A (HK3)		[LST/OPF BAX GLOBAL]
B727-259 (A) (F)	N901RF	KITTY HAWK AIR CARGO (REPUBLIC FIN.)		22476	1747	06/23/81	JT8D-17R (HK3)		N205AV, PP-ITV [PARKED IGM]
B727-225 (A) (F)	N902RF	KITTY HAWK AIR CARGO (REPUBLIC FIN.)		22549	1737	04/20/81	JT8D-15 (HK3)		N812EA, PP-ITR [PARKED IGM]
B727-222 (F)	N90AX	KITTY HAWK AIR CARGO		20040	729	06/17/69	JT8D-7B (HK3)		N7646U
B727-287 (A) (F)	N916PG	KITTY HAWK AIR CARGO (PACA)		21690	1469	04/18/79	JT8D-17 (HK3)		LV-MIO, CC-CSK, OB-1697
B727-225 (A) (F)	N936PG	KITTY HAWK AIR CARGO (PEGA)		22441	1695	12/15/80	JT8D-15A (HK3)		N810EA, HI-629CA, F-GKDZ
B727-022 (RE)	N400RG	MBI AVIATION INC.		19149	481	10/31/67	JT8D-217C/7B		N7085U
B727-225 (A)	N802MA	MIAMI AIR		22433	1668	10/08/81	JT8D-15/-15A		N802EA
B727-225 (A)	N803MA	MIAMI AIR		22434	1671	11/03/80	JT8D-15 (HK3)		N803EA
B727-225 (A)	N804MA	MIAMI AIR		22435	1674	11/07/80	JT8D-15 (HK3)		N804EA
B727-225 (A)	N887MA	MIAMI AIR (ACG ACQ.)		21857	1539	11/05/79	JT8D-15 (HK3)		N8888Z
B727-225 (A)	N889MA	MIAMI AIR		21854	1532	10/17/79	JT8D-15 (HK3)		N8885Z
B727-221 (A) (RE)	N727M	NOMADS		22541	1797	05/26/82	JT8D-217C/-17		N369PA
B727-046 (F)	N190AJ	NORTHERN AIR CARGO		18878	236	03/02/66	JT8D-7B (HK3)		JA8311, G-BAJW, 9N-ABW
B727-023 (F)	N930FT	NORTHERN AIR CARGO		19387	329	10/27/66	JT8D-7B (HK3)		N1929
B727-023 (F)	N992AJ	NORTHERN AIR CARGO		19428	358	01/20/67	JT8D-7B (HK3)		N1933, N941FT, N515FE
B727-251 (A)	N201US	NORTHWEST AIRLINES		22154	1645	07/25/80	JT8D-7B (HK3)	2201	
B727-251 (A)	N202US	NORTHWEST AIRLINES		22155	1648	08/04/80	JT8D-15 (HK3)	2202	
B727-251 (A)	N203US	NORTHWEST AIRLINES		22543	1700	01/07/81	JT8D-15 (HK3)	2203	
B727-251 (A)	N204US	NORTHWEST AIRLINES		22544	1703	01/13/81	JT8D-15 (HK3)	2204	
B727-251 (A)	N275US	NORTHWEST AIRLINES		21154	1168	10/20/75	JT8D-15 (HK3)	2275	
B727-251 (A)	N284US	NORTHWEST AIRLINES		21323	1284	08/09/77	JT8D-15 (HK3)	2284	
B727-251 (A)	N285US	NORTHWEST AIRLINES		21324	1286	08/22/77	JT8D-15 (HK3)	2285	

A/C TYPE	CURRENT REG. NO.	LAST KNOWN OPERATOR (OWNER)	STATUS	ORIGINAL MSN	LINE NO.	DEL. DATE	ENG. TYPE	FLEET NO.	PREV. REG. [COMMENTS]
B727-251 (A)	N286US	NORTHWEST AIRLINES		21325	1288	08/30/77	JT8D-7B (HK3)	2286	
B727-251 (A)	N287US	NORTHWEST AIRLINES		21375	1290	09/08/77	JT8D-15 (HK3)	2287	
B727-251 (A)	N288US	NORTHWEST AIRLINES		21376	1293	09/21/77	JT8D-15 (HK3)	2288	
B727-251 (A)	N289US	NORTHWEST AIRLINES		21377	1295	11/17/77	JT8D-15 (HK3)	2289	
B727-251 (A)	N290US	NORTHWEST AIRLINES		21378	1297	10/05/77	JT8D-15 (HK3)	2290	
B727-251 (A)	N291US	NORTHWEST AIRLINES		21379	1299	10/19/77	JT8D-15 (HK3)	2291	
B727-251 (A)	N292US	NORTHWEST AIRLINES		21503	1317	02/13/78	JT8D-15 (HK3)	2292	
B727-251 (A)	N293US	NORTHWEST AIRLINES		21504	1319	02/17/78	JT8D-15 (HK3)	2293	
B727-251 (A)	N295US	NORTHWEST AIRLINES		21506	1392	09/28/78	JT8D-15 (HK3)	2295	
B727-251 (A)	N296US	NORTHWEST AIRLINES		21788	1495	06/15/79	JT8D-15 (HK3)	2296	
B727-251 (A)	N297US	NORTHWEST AIRLINES		21789	1496	06/20/79	JT8D-15 (HK3)	2297	
B727-251 (A)	N298US	NORTHWEST AIRLINES		22152	1599	04/01/80	JT8D-15 (HK3)	2298	
B727-251 (A)	N299US	NORTHWEST AIRLINES		22153	1601	04/11/80	JT8D-15 (HK3)	2299	
B727-225 (A)	N8877Z	NORTHWEST AIRLINES (FSBU)		21450	1308	12/07/77	JT8D-15 (HK3)	2702	
B727-225 (A)	N816EA	NORTHWEST AIRLINES (FSBU)		22553	1775	10/02/81	JT8D-15 (HK3)	2707	
B727-225 (A)	N817EA	NORTHWEST AIRLINES (GECA)		22554	1781	11/02/81	JT8D-15 (HK3)	2708	
B727-225 (A)	N818EA	NORTHWEST AIRLINES (FSBU)		22555	1783	12/01/81	JT8D-15 (HK3)	2709	
B727-225 (A)	N820EA	NORTHWEST AIRLINES (FSBU)		22557	1795	04/07/82	JT8D-15 (HK3)	2710	
B727-2S7 (A)	N716RC	NORTHWEST AIRLINES		22021	1617	06/02/80	JT8D-17 (HK3)	2713	[LST CCP AS N686CA]
B727-2S7 (A)	N718RC	NORTHWEST AIRLINES		22344	1654	09/02/80	JT8D-17 (HK3)	2714	
B727-2S7 (A)	N719RC	NORTHWEST AIRLINES		22490	1721	02/26/81	JT8D-17 (HK3)	2715	[LST CCP 12/21/99 AS N683CA]
B727-2S7 (A)	N720RC	NORTHWEST AIRLINES		22491	1726	03/17/81	JT8D-17 (HK3)	2716	[LST CCP 12/21/99 AS N684CA]
B727-2S7 (A)	N721RC	NORTHWEST AIRLINES		22492	1729	03/26/81	JT8D-17 (HK3)	2717	[LST CCP 12/13/99 AS N685CA]
B727-2M7 (A)	N722RW	NORTHWEST AIRLINES		21201	1220	11/01/76	JT8D-17R (HK3)	2762	
B727-2M7 (A)	N727RW	NORTHWEST AIRLINES		21656	1455	03/12/79	JT8D-17R (HK3)	2767	
B727-2M7 (A)	N728RW	NORTHWEST AIRLINES		21741	1491	07/06/79	JT8D-17R (HK3)	2768	
B727-2M7 (A)	N729RW	NORTHWEST AIRLINES		21742	1514	08/10/79	JT8D-17R (HK3)	2769	
B727-076(RE) (WL)	N682G	OCCIDENTAL PETROLEUM		19254	298	08/09/66	JT8D-217C/-7B		VH-TJD, N8043B, N10XY
B727-232 (A)	N7270B	ORCA BAY AVIATION		20641	936	05/11/73	JT8D-15 (HK3)		N459DA, N518PE, N18786 [OPF VANCOUVER CANUCKS AND GRIZZLIES]
B727-225 (A) (WL)	N361PA	PAN AM (GUILFORD)		20623	939	05/01/73	JT8D-15 (HK3)		N8861E
B727-2J0 (A)	N362PA	PAN AM (GUILFORD)		21106	1160	10/10/75	JT8D-15 (HK3)		6Y-JMB, VR-CMB, 6Y-JMN
B727-221 (A) (WL)	N363PA	PAN AM (GUILFORD)		22535	1764	04/22/82	JT8D-17R (HK3)		[OPF SJI]
B727-2J0 (A) (WL)	N364PA	PAN AM (GUILFORD)		21107	1172	11/12/75	JT8D-15 (HK3)		6Y-JMC, VR-CMC, 6Y-JMO
B727-225 (A) (WL)	N365PA	PAN AM (GUILFORD)		20628	948	06/06/73	JT8D-15 (HK3)		N8866E
B727-221 (A)	N367PA	PAN AM (ARON)		22539	1794	04/22/82	JT8D-17R (HK3)		
B727-282 (A)	N369PA	PAN AM (GUILFORD)		21950	1579	03/03/80	JT8D-17 (HK3)		N57008, CS-TBX, N609KW [STD PSM; USED FOR PARTS]

A/C TYPE	CURRENT REG. NO.	LAST KNOWN OPERATOR (OWNER)	STATUS	ORIGINAL MSN	LINE NO.	DEL. DATE	ENG. TYPE	FLEET NO.	PREV. REG. [COMMENTS]
B727-023	N1910	PLANET AIRWAYS		19385	311	09/09/66	JT8D-7B (HK3)		
B727-224 (A)	N69741	PLANET AIRWAYS		22250	1684	11/18/80	JT8D-15		
B727-224 (A)	N69742	PLANET AIRWAYS		22251	1687	12/09/80	JT8D-15		
B727-224 (A)	N79745	PLANET AIRWAYS		22448	1740	05/21/81	JT8D-15		
B727-225 (A)	N806MA	QUEST CARGO INTL.		22437	1682	11/17/80	JT8D-15 (HK3)		N806EA
B727-231 (A) (F)	N808MA	QUEST CARGO INTL.		21988	1586	03/20/80	JT8D-15A (HK3)		N84356, TC-AFG, F-WKPZ [CVTD TO FRTR AT MIA]
B727-225 (A) (F)	N886MA	QUEST CARGO INTL.		21855	1535	10/23/79	JT8D-15 (HK3)		N8886Z [CVTD TO FRTR]
B727-191	N502MG	R.D. AVIATION LLC		19391	309	09/08/66	JT8D-7B (HK3)		N7270F, N297BN, N502RA [STD OSC]
B727-191	N503MG	R.D. AVIATION LLC		19392	317	10/04/66	JT8D-7B (HK3)		N7271F, N298BN, N503RA [LST ROUSH MGMT 11/27/00]
B727-191	N504MG	R.D. AVIATION LLC		19395	431	07/08/67	JT8D-7B (HK3)		N7274F, N301BN, N504RA, N801SC
B727-021 (F)	N329QS	RYAN INTL. AIRWAYS (EWW)	L	19038	285	06/29/66	JT8D-7B (HK3)		N329PA [OPF EWW/EWW C/S]
B727-021 (F)	N355QS	RYAN INTL. AIRWAYS (EWW)	L	19257	385	03/17/67	JT8D-7B (HK3)		N355PA [OPF EWW/EWW C/S]
B727-021 (F)	N356QS	RYAN INTL. AIRWAYS (EWW)	L	19258	397	04/13/67	JT8D-7B (HK3)		N356PA [OPF EWW/EWW C/S]
B727-021 (F)	N357QS	RYAN INTL. AIRWAYS (EWW)	L	19259	408	05/10/67	JT8D-7B (HK3)		N357PA [OPF EWW/EWW C/S]
B727-021 (F)	N359QS	RYAN INTL. AIRWAYS (EWW)	L	19007	269	05/18/66	JT8D-7B (HK3)		N325PA, HK-2846X [OPF EWW/EWW C/S]
B727-051C	N413EX	RYAN INTL. AIRWAYS (EWW)	L	19206	294	08/24/66	JT8D-7B (HK3)		N495US [OPF USPS/USPS C/S]
B727-051C	N416EX	RYAN INTL. AIRWAYS (EWW)	L	19287	383	03/12/67	JT8D-7B (HK3)		N496US [OPF USPS/USPS C/S]
B727-051C	N417EX	RYAN INTL. AIRWAYS (EWW)	L	19290	417	05/27/67	JT8D-7B (HK3)		N499US [OPF USPS/USPS C/S]
B727-022C	N421EX	RYAN INTL. AIRWAYS (EWW)	L	19099	322	10/27/66	JT8D-7B (HK3)		N7411U, HK-2474 [OPF USPS/USPS C/S]
B727-134C	N424EX	RYAN INTL. AIRWAYS (EWW)	L	20042	626	09/05/68	JT8D-7B (HK3)		SE-DDC [OPF USPS/USPS C/S]
B727-022C	N426EX	RYAN INTL. AIRWAYS (EWW)	L	19089	250	05/14/66	JT8D-7B (HK3)		N7401U [OPF USPS/USPS C/S]
B727-022C	N427EX	RYAN INTL. AIRWAYS (EWW)	L	19090	277	06/29/66	JT8D-7B (HK3)		N7402U [OPF USPS/USPS C/S]
B727-022C	N428EX	RYAN INTL. AIRWAYS (EWW)	L	19097	307	09/01/66	JT8D-7B (HK3)		N7409U [OPF USPS/USPS C/S]
B727-022C	N429EX	RYAN INTL. AIRWAYS (EWW)	L	19100	324	10/31/66	JT8D-7B (HK3)		N7412U [OPF USPS/USPS C/S]
B727-151C	N432EX	RYAN INTL. AIRWAYS (EWW)	L	19867	514	01/11/68	JT8D-7B (HK3)		N488US [OPF USPS/USPS C/S]
B727-151C	N433EX	RYAN INTL. AIRWAYS (EWW)	L	19868	529	01/29/68	JT8D-7B (HK3)		N489US [OPF USPS/USPS C/S]
B727-051C	N435EX	RYAN INTL. AIRWAYS (EWW)	L	19288	389	03/28/67	JT8D-7B (HK3)		N497US [OPF USPS/USPS C/S]
B727-051C	N436EX	RYAN INTL. AIRWAYS (EWW)	L	19289	403	04/22/67	JT8D-7B (HK3)		N498US [OPF USPS/USPS C/S]
B727-077C	N526PC	RYAN INTL. AIRWAYS (EWW)	L	20370	821	07/08/70	JT8D-7B (HK3)		VH-RMT, C2-RN4, N555BN [OPF USPS/USPS C/S]
B727-172C	N527PC	RYAN INTL. AIRWAYS (EWW)	L	19665	476	10/23/67	JT8D-7B (HK3)		N725AL, CS-TBQ, N444GM, N45498 [OPF USPS/USPS C/S]
B727-082C	N528PC	RYAN INTL. AIRWAYS (EWW)	L	19597	524	02/08/68	JT8D-7B (HK3)		CS-TBN, N4564U [OPF USPS/USPS C/S]
B727-076 (F)	N721JE	RYAN INTL. AIRWAYS (EWW)	L	18843	170	08/20/65	JT8D-7B (HK3)		VH-TJC, AN-BSQ, YN-BSQ, N4602D [OPF USPS/USPS C/S]

A/C TYPE	CURRENT REG. NO.	LAST KNOWN OPERATOR (OWNER)	STATUS	ORIGINAL MSN	LINE NO.	DEL. DATE	ENG. TYPE	FLEET NO.	PREV. REG. [COMMENTS]
B727-232 (A) (F)	N17789	RYAN INTL. AIRWAYS (FINO)		20643	951	06/23/73	JT8D-15		N461DA, N520PE [STD MZJ]
B727-243 (A)	N521DB	RYAN INTL. AIRWAYS (SPORTHAWK)	L	21266	1227	10/18/76	JT8D-9A (HK3)		N40115, I-DIRO, N573PE, N17403 [LST/OPB RYN]
B727-222 (F)	N7635U	RYAN INTL. AIRWAYS (EWW)	L	19908	653	12/05/68	JT8D-7B (HK3)		
B727-222 (F)	N7638U	RYAN INTL. AIRWAYS (EWW)	L	19911	668	12/27/68	JT8D-7B (HK3)		
B727-222 (F)	N7639U	RYAN INTL. AIRWAYS (EWW)	L	19912	670	01/06/69	JT8D-7B (HK3)		
B727-222 (F)	N7640U	RYAN INTL. AIRWAYS (EWW)	L	19913	672	02/10/69	JT8D-7B (HK3)		
B727-222 (F)	N7642U	RYAN INTL. AIRWAYS (EWW)	L	19915	681	03/03/69	JT8D-7B (HK3)		
B727-222 (F)	N7643U	RYAN INTL. AIRWAYS (EWW)	L	20037	701	03/19/69	JT8D-7B (HK3)		
B727-222 (F)	N7644U	RYAN INTL. AIRWAYS (EWW)	L	20038	716	05/14/69	JT8D-7B (HK3)		
B727-222 (F)	N7645U	RYAN INTL. AIRWAYS (EWW)	L	20039	720	05/26/69	JT8D-7B (HK3)		
B727-225 (A) (F)	N801EA	RYAN INTL. AIRWAYS (EWW)	L	22432	1658	10/06/80	JT8D-15/-15A		
B727-225 (A) (F)	N815EA	RYAN INTL. AIRWAYS (EWW)	L	22552	1773	10/02/81	JT8D-15/-15A		
B727-225 (A) (F)	N8878Z	RYAN INTL. AIRWAYS (EWW)	L	21451	1310	01/20/78	JT8D-15/-15A		
B727-2J4 (A)	N211DB	SUN COUNTRY AIRLINES (RIVERHORSE)		20766	993	12/03/73	JT8D-17A		OY-SAT, N729BE, N223FE, C-GRYP
B727-227 (A)	N275AF	SUN COUNTRY AIRLINES (FINO)		22092	1718	11/20/81	JT8D-17R (HK3)		N484BN
B727-282 (A)	N281SC	SUN COUNTRY AIRLINES (MACH A/C LSG)		21949	1494	06/28/79	JT8D-17 (HK3)		CS-TBW
B727-225 (A)	N282SC	SUN COUNTRY AIRLINES (GEMANCO)		22558	1798	05/03/82	JT8D-17R (HK3)		N821EA
B727-225 (A)	N283SC	SUN COUNTRY AIRLINES (GEMANCO)		22559	1800	05/03/82	JT8D-17R (HK3)		N822EA
B727-2J4 (A) (RE)	N284SC	SUN COUNTRY AIRLINES (ILFC)		21438	1301	10/27/77	JT8D-217C/-17A		OY-SBC, G-BHNF
B727-2J4 (A) (RE)	N285SC	SUN COUNTRY AIRLINES (ILFC)		21766	1417	11/30/78	JT8D-217C/-17A		OY-SBD, G-BHNE
B727-2J4 (A) (RE)	N288SC	SUN COUNTRY AIRLINES (PACA)		20765	984	11/03/73	JT8D-217C/-17A		OY-SAS, N728BE, N222FE, N727VA, CS-TKA
B727-259 (A)	N289SC	SUN COUNTRY AIRLINES (MACH A/C LSG)		22475	1690	12/04/80	JT8D-17R		N204AV
B727-2J4 (A) (RE)	N290SC	SUN COUNTRY AIRLINES (FINO)		20764	960	11/15/73	JT8D-217C/-17A		N1779B, N727BE, CS-TKB, OY-SAU
B727-2K3 (A) (RE)	N291SC	SUN COUNTRY AIRLINES (RIVERHORSE)		22770	1807	03/15/83	JT8D-217C/-17A		N776AL, OY-SBO, N891DB
B727-2M7 (A)	N294SC	SUN COUNTRY AIRLINES (PEGA)		21202	1221	12/01/76	JT8D-17 (HK3)		N723RW, OY-SEZ
B727-224 (A)	N296SC	SUN COUNTRY AIRLINES (PEGA)		22449	1756	06/11/81	JT8D-15		N79746
B727-225 (A) (RE)	G-OPMN	SUN COUNTRY AIRLINES (SBE)	L	21578	1409	11/10/78	JT8D-217C/-15		N8881Z
B727-227 (A)	N13759	SUN PACIFIC INTL.		21044	1132	05/14/75	JT8D-9A		N437BN, N562PE [STD MIA; ENGINES OFF; INCOMPLETE C-CHECK]
B727-227 (A)	N79771	SUN PACIFIC INTL.		20840	1036	05/09/74	JT8D-9A (HK3)		N433BN, N558PE [PARKED AT LORAIR AT TUS, LESS ENGINES]
B727-251 (A) (WL)	N281US	SUNWORLD INTL. AIRLINES		21160	1180	12/19/75	JT8D-17 (HK3)		
B727-251 (A) (WL)	N282US	SUNWORLD INTL. AIRLINES		21161	1181	12/22/75	JT8D-15A (HK3)		
B727-2B6 (A)	N119GA	TC AVIATION INC.		21068	1107	02/28/75	JT8D-15 (HK3)		CN-CCW, N610AG [OPF SEATTLE SUPERSONICS; TBR N119GD]

A/C TYPE	CURRENT REG. NO.	LAST KNOWN OPERATOR (OWNER)	STATUS	ORIGINAL MSN	LINE NO.	DEL. DATE	ENG. TYPE	FLEET NO.	PREV. REG. [COMMENTS]
B727-031(RE) (WL)	N908JE	THE LIMITED (JEGE INC.)		20115	735	07/07/69	JT8D-217C/-7B		N7893, N505T, N505C, N500LS, N505LS [VIP CONF]
B727-095	N727GG	TRANS-GULF CORP.		19252	327	10/22/66	JT8D-7A (HK3)		N1636, N835N, C2-RN5, N740EV, HZ-WBT, HZ-WBT2
B727-231 (A) (RE)	N54344	TRANSMERIDIAN AIRLINES (PEGA)		21631	1460	03/28/79	JT8D-217C/-9A		
B727-281 (A)	N906PG	TRANSMERIDIAN AIRLINES (PEGA)		20728	969	09/07/73	JT8D-17 (HK3)		JA8349, HL7353, N531MD, OB-1573
B727-287 (A)	N910PG	TRANSMERIDIAN AIRLINES (PEGA)		22606	1812	12/23/82	JT8D-17 (HK3)		LV-OLR, OB-1647
B727-231 (A)	N64339	TRANS WORLD AIRLINES		20844	1065	09/05/74	JT8D-9A	4339	[LRF 09/30/00; STD VCV 11/16/00]
B727-231 (A)	N54340	TRANS WORLD AIRLINES		20845	1066	09/10/74	JT8D-9A	4340	[LRF 09/06/00; STD VCV 11/14/00]
B727-212 (A) (RE) (WL)	N31TR	TRIANGLE AIRCRAFT SERVICES (280 HOLDINGS LLC)		21948	1510	08/01/79	JT8D-217C/-17 9		V-SGJ, N310AS, VR-COJ
B727-222 (A)	N7251U	UNITED AIRLINES		21398	1296	10/21/77	JT8D-15 (HK3)	7151	[WFU SFO]
B727-222 (A)	N7252U	UNITED AIRLINES		21399	1303	11/08/77	JT8D-15 (HK3)	7152	
B727-222 (A)	N7253U	UNITED AIRLINES		21400	1309	01/16/78	JT8D-15 (HK3)	7153	
B727-222 (A)	N7254U	UNITED AIRLINES		21401	1311	01/24/78	JT8D-15 (HK3)	7154	
B727-222 (A)	N7255U	UNITED AIRLINES		21402	1313	01/21/78	JT8D-15 (HK3)	7155	
B727-222 (A)	N7256U	UNITED AIRLINES		21403	1315	01/25/78	JT8D-15 (HK3)	7156	
B727-222 (A)	N7257U	UNITED AIRLINES		21404	1321	03/01/78	JT8D-15 (HK3)	7157	
B727-222 (A)	N7258U	UNITED AIRLINES		21405	1323	03/07/78	JT8D-15 (HK3)	7158	[LRF 03/04/01]
B727-222 (A)	N7259U	UNITED AIRLINES		21406	1325	03/14/78	JT8D-15 (HK3)	7159	
B727-222 (A)	N7260U	UNITED AIRLINES		21407	1332	04/04/78	JT8D-15 (HK3)	7160	
B727-222 (A)	N7261U	UNITED AIRLINES		21408	1334	04/12/78	JT8D-15 (HK3)	7161	
B727-222 (A)	N7262U	UNITED AIRLINES		21409	1336	04/20/78	JT8D-15 (HK3)	7162	
B727-222 (A)	N7263U	UNITED AIRLINES		21410	1344	05/16/78	JT8D-15 (HK3)	7163	
B727-222 (A)	N7264U	UNITED AIRLINES		21411	1346	05/23/78	JT8D-15 (HK3)	7164	
B727-222 (A)	N7265U	UNITED AIRLINES		21412	1348	05/30/78	JT8D-15 (HK3)	7165	
B727-222 (A)	N7266U	UNITED AIRLINES		21413	1351	06/05/78	JT8D-15 (HK3)	7166	
B727-222 (A)	N7267U	UNITED AIRLINES		21414	1354	06/14/78	JT8D-15 (HK3)	7167	
B727-222 (A)	N7268U	UNITED AIRLINES		21415	1356	06/20/78	JT8D-15 (HK3)	7168	
B727-222 (A)	N7269U	UNITED AIRLINES		21416	1366	07/20/78	JT8D-15 (HK3)	7169	
B727-222 (A)	N7270U	UNITED AIRLINES		21417	1368	07/27/78	JT8D-15 (HK3)	7170	
B727-222 (A)	N7271U	UNITED AIRLINES		21418	1370	08/04/78	JT8D-15 (HK3)	7171	
B727-222 (A)	N7272U	UNITED AIRLINES		21419	1375	08/16/78	JT8D-15 (HK3)	7172	
B727-222 (A)	N7273U	UNITED AIRLINES		21420	1377	08/21/78	JT8D-15 (HK3)	7173	
B727-222 (A)	N7274U	UNITED AIRLINES		21421	1383	09/06/78	JT8D-15 (HK3)	7174	
B727-222 (A)	N7275U	UNITED AIRLINES		21422	1385	09/12/78	JT8D-15 (HK3)	7175	
B727-222 (A)	N7276U	UNITED AIRLINES		21423	1387	09/18/78	JT8D-15 (HK3)	7176	
B727-222 (A)	N7277U	UNITED AIRLINES		21424	1393	10/02/78	JT8D-15 (HK3)	7177	
B727-222 (A)	N7278U	UNITED AIRLINES		21425	1395	10/05/78	JT8D-15 (HK3)	7178	

A/C TYPE	CURRENT REG. NO.	LAST KNOWN OPERATOR (OWNER)	STATUS	ORIGINAL MSN	LINE NO.	DEL. DATE	ENG. TYPE	FLEET NO.	PREV. REG. [COMMENTS]
B727-222 (A)	N7279U	UNITED AIRLINES		21557	1397	10/12/78	JT8D-15 (HK3)	7179	
B727-222 (A)	N7280U	UNITED AIRLINES		21558	1399	10/17/78	JT8D-15 (HK3)	7180	
B727-222 (A)	N7281U	UNITED AIRLINES		21559	1401	10/31/78	JT8D-15 (HK3)	7181	
B727-222 (A)	N7282U	UNITED AIRLINES		21560	1405	11/02/78	JT8D-15 (HK3)	7182	
B727-222 (A)	N7283U	UNITED AIRLINES		21561	1408	11/08/78	JT8D-15 (HK3)	7183	
B727-222 (A)	N7284U	UNITED AIRLINES		21562	1410	11/13/78	JT8D-15 (HK3)	7184	
B727-222 (A)	N7285U	UNITED AIRLINES		21563	1418	12/11/78	JT8D-15 (HK3)	7185	[WFU DEN 03/01/01]
B727-222 (A)	N7286U	UNITED AIRLINES		21564	1420	12/06/78	JT8D-15 (HK3)	7186	
B727-222 (A)	N7287U	UNITED AIRLINES		21565	1424	12/14/78	JT8D-15 (HK3)	7187	
B727-222 (A)	N7288U	UNITED AIRLINES		21566	1428	01/08/79	JT8D-15 (HK3)	7188	
B727-222 (A)	N7289U	UNITED AIRLINES		21567	1430	01/20/79	JT8D-15 (HK3)	7189	
B727-222 (A)	N7290U	UNITED AIRLINES		21568	1432	01/25/79	JT8D-15 (HK3)	7190	[PARKED VCV 03/21/01]
B727-222 (A)	N7291U	UNITED AIRLINES		21569	1441	02/06/79	JT8D-15 (HK3)	7191	
B727-222 (A)	N7292U	UNITED AIRLINES		21570	1443	02/13/79	JT8D-15 (HK3)	7192	
B727-222 (A)	N7293U	UNITED AIRLINES		21571	1445	02/19/79	JT8D-15 (HK3)	7193	
B727-222 (A)	N7294U	UNITED AIRLINES		21572	1447	02/22/79	JT8D-15 (HK3)	7194	
B727-222 (A)	N7295U	UNITED AIRLINES		21573	1449	03/01/79	JT8D-15 (HK3)	7195	[PARKED VCV 03/22/01]
B727-222 (A)	N7297U	UNITED AIRLINES		21892	1500	07/02/79	JT8D-15 (HK3)	7297	
B727-222 (A)	N7298U	UNITED AIRLINES		21893	1503	07/11/79	JT8D-15 (HK3)	7298	
B727-222 (A)	N7299U	UNITED AIRLINES		21894	1505	07/20/79	JT8D-15 (HK3)	7299	
B727-222 (A)	N7441U	UNITED AIRLINES		21895	1507	07/25/79	JT8D-15 (HK3)	7241	
B727-222 (A)	N7442U	UNITED AIRLINES		21896	1511	08/01/79	JT8D-15 (HK3)	7242	
B727-222 (A)	N7443U	UNITED AIRLINES		21897	1513	08/07/79	JT8D-15 (HK3)	7243	
B727-222 (A)	N7444U	UNITED AIRLINES		21898	1515	08/10/79	JT8D-15 (HK3)	7244	
B727-222 (A)	N7445U	UNITED AIRLINES		21899	1517	08/28/79	JT8D-15 (HK3)	7245	
B727-222 (A)	N7446U	UNITED AIRLINES		21900	1519	09/04/79	JT8D-15 (HK3)	7246	
B727-222 (A)	N7447U	UNITED AIRLINES		21901	1521	09/11/79	JT8D-15 (HK3)	7247	
B727-222 (A)	N7448U	UNITED AIRLINES		21902	1524	09/21/79	JT8D-15 (HK3)	7248	
B727-222 (A)	N7449U	UNITED AIRLINES		21903	1526	09/24/79	JT8D-15 (HK3)	7249	
B727-222 (A)	N7450U	UNITED AIRLINES		21904	1528	10/01/79	JT8D-15 (HK3)	7250	
B727-222 (A)	N7451U	UNITED AIRLINES		21905	1530	10/04/79	JT8D-15 (HK3)	7251	
B727-222 (A)	N7452U	UNITED AIRLINES		21906	1548	11/19/79	JT8D-15 (HK3)	7252	
B727-222 (A)	N7453U	UNITED AIRLINES		21907	1558	12/13/79	JT8D-15 (HK3)	7253	
B727-222 (A)	N7454U	UNITED AIRLINES		21908	1560	12/17/79	JT8D-15 (HK3)	7254	
B727-222 (A)	N7455U	UNITED AIRLINES		21909	1562	12/21/79	JT8D-15 (HK3)	7255	
B727-222 (A)	N7456U	UNITED AIRLINES		21910	1570	02/07/80	JT8D-15 (HK3)	7256	
B727-222 (A)	N7457U	UNITED AIRLINES		21911	1572	03/03/80	JT8D-15 (HK3)	7257	
B727-222 (A)	N7458U	UNITED AIRLINES		21912	1575	03/05/80	JT8D-15 (HK3)	7258	
B727-222 (A)	N7459U	UNITED AIRLINES		21913	1593	03/19/80	JT8D-15 (HK3)	7259	
B727-222 (A)	N7460U	UNITED AIRLINES		21914	1597	03/31/80	JT8D-15 (HK3)	7260	
B727-222 (A)	N7461U	UNITED AIRLINES		21915	1609	04/28/80	JT8D-15 (HK3)	7261	

A/C TYPE	CURRENT REG. NO.	LAST KNOWN OPERATOR (OWNER)	STATUS	ORIGINAL MSN	LINE NO.	DEL. DATE	ENG. TYPE	FLEET NO.	PREV. REG. [COMMENTS]
B727-222 (A)	N7462U	UNITED AIRLINES		21916	1611	04/30/80	JT8D-15 (HK3)	7262	
B727-222 (A)	N7463U	UNITED AIRLINES		21917	1616	05/12/80	JT8D-15 (HK3)	7263	
B727-222 (A)	N7464U	UNITED AIRLINES		21918	1625	06/11/80	JT8D-15 (HK3)	7264	
B727-222 (A)	N7465U	UNITED AIRLINES		21919	1632	06/27/80	JT8D-15 (HK3)	7265	
B727-222 (A)	N7466U	UNITED AIRLINES		21920	1634	06/30/80	JT8D-15 (HK3)	7266	
B727-222 (A)	N7467U	UNITED AIRLINES		21921	1639	07/25/80	JT8D-15 (HK3)	7267	
B727-051C (QF)	N902UP	UNITED PARCEL SERVICE		18898	244	04/13/66	TAY 651-54		N490US, N434EX
B727-051C (QF)	N903UP	UNITED PARCEL SERVICE		18945	263	05/12/66	TAY 651-54		N492US, N415EX
B727-051C (QF)	N904UP	UNITED PARCEL SERVICE		18946	274	05/27/66	TAY 651-54		N493US, N418EX
B727-051C (QF)	N905UP	UNITED PARCEL SERVICE		18947	286	08/13/66	TAY 651-54		N494US, N419EX
B727-030C (QF)	N906UP	UNITED PARCEL SERVICE		19314	437	07/28/67	TAY 651-54		D-ABIJ, EP-AMV, D-AFGK, CX-BNT, N423EX
B727-027C (QF)	N907UP	UNITED PARCEL SERVICE		19118	379	03/01/67	TAY 651-54		N7279
B727-027C (QF)	N908UP	UNITED PARCEL SERVICE		19114	312	09/21/66	TAY 651-54		N7275
B727-027C (QF)	N909UP	UNITED PARCEL SERVICE		19115	328	09/29/66	TAY 651-54		N7276, OB-R-1115
B727-027C (QF)	N910UP	UNITED PARCEL SERVICE		19117	376	02/28/67	TAY 651-54		N7278
B727-027C (QF)	N911UP	UNITED PARCEL SERVICE		19119	393	04/07/67	TAY 651-54		N7280
B727-062C (QF)	N912UP	UNITED PARCEL SERVICE		19244	338	11/24/66	TAY 651-54		N7284
B727-062C (QF)	N913UP	UNITED PARCEL SERVICE		19245	342	12/12/66	TAY 651-54		N7286
B727-027C (QF)	N914UP	UNITED PARCEL SERVICE		19246	423	06/08/67	TAY 651-54		N7287
B727-027C (QF)	N915UP	UNITED PARCEL SERVICE		19533	475	10/20/67	TAY 651-54		N7296
B727-172C (QF/QC)	N916UP	UNITED PARCEL SERVICE		19808	615	08/09/68	TAY 651-54		N732AL, N309BN
B727-030C (QF)	N917UP	UNITED PARCEL SERVICE		19310	395	04/18/67	TAY 651-54		D-ABII, N701EV, PP-SRY
B727-030C (QF)	N918UP	UNITED PARCEL SERVICE		19008	364	02/22/67	TAY 651-54		D-ABIW, N310BN
B727-030C (QF)	N919UP	UNITED PARCEL SERVICE		19012	391	04/10/67	TAY 651-54		D-ABIE, N311BN
B727-180C (QF)	N920UP	UNITED PARCEL SERVICE		19873	604	07/23/68	TAY 651-54		N9516T
B727-031C (QF)	N922UP	UNITED PARCEL SERVICE		19231	404	05/08/67	TAY 651-54		N892TW
B727-031C (QF)	N924UP	UNITED PARCEL SERVICE		19234	463	09/26/67	TAY 651-54		N895TW
B727-031C (QF)	N925UP	UNITED PARCEL SERVICE		19230	402	05/03/67	TAY 651-54		N891TW
B727-022C (QF)	N928UP	UNITED PARCEL SERVICE		19091	280	07/01/66	TAY 651-54		N7403U, N490W
B727-022C (QF)	N929UP	UNITED PARCEL SERVICE		19092	291	07/20/66	TAY 651-54		N7404U, N495WC
B727-022C (QF)	N930UP	UNITED PARCEL SERVICE		19096	305	09/14/66	TAY 651-54		N7408U, N497WC
B727-025C (QF)	N931UP	UNITED PARCEL SERVICE		19858	645	10/18/68	TAY 651-54		N8175G
B727-025C (QF)	N932UP	UNITED PARCEL SERVICE		19856	635	10/03/68	TAY 651-54		N8173G
B727-025C (QF)	N933UP	UNITED PARCEL SERVICE		19857	641	10/15/68	TAY 651-54		N8174G
B727-021C (QF)	N934UP	UNITED PARCEL SERVICE		19135	301	09/02/66	TAY 651-54		N340PA, J2-KAD, N47142, N724PL
B727-1A7C (QF)	N935UP	UNITED PARCEL SERVICE		20143	619	08/16/68	TAY 651-54		N8789R, N2915
B727-108C (QF)	N936UP	UNITED PARCEL SERVICE		19503	420	06/22/67	TAY 651-54		TF-FIE, TF-FLH, N727TG
B727-025C (QF)	N937UP	UNITED PARCEL SERVICE		19302	354	02/02/67	TAY 651-54		N8155G, TG-ALA
B727-173C (QF)	N938UP	UNITED PARCEL SERVICE		19506	447	08/20/67	TAY 651-54		N692WA, OB-R-1135, PJ-BOA, TG-AYA
B727-027C (QF)	N939UP	UNITED PARCEL SERVICE		19532	469	10/05/67	TAY 651-54		N7295, CC-CGD

A/C TYPE	CURRENT REG. NO.	LAST KNOWN OPERATOR (OWNER)	STATUS	ORIGINAL MSN	LINE NO.	DEL. DATE	ENG. TYPE	FLEET NO.	PREV. REG. [COMMENTS]
B727-185C (QF)	N940UP	UNITED PARCEL SERVICE		19826	546	04/01/68	TAY 651-54		N12826, TF-FIA, TF-FLG
B727-022C (QF)	N941UP	UNITED PARCEL SERVICE		19196	407	05/16/67	TAY 651-54		N7421U, FAC 901, CC-CLB
B727-022C (QF)	N942UP	UNITED PARCEL SERVICE		19101	333	11/21/66	TAY 651-54		N7413U, N430EX
B727-025C (QF/QC)	N946UP	UNITED PARCEL SERVICE		19721	490	11/14/67	TAY 651-54		N8165G, N130FE [PAX CONF]
B727-025C (QF/QC)	N947UP	UNITED PARCEL SERVICE		19722	493	11/20/67	TAY 651-54		N8166G, N131FE
B727-025C (QF/QC)	N948UP	UNITED PARCEL SERVICE		19357	360	02/06/67	TAY 651-54		N8157G, N121FE
B727-025C (QF/QC)	N949UP	UNITED PARCEL SERVICE		19717	468	09/30/67	TAY 651-54		N8161G, N125FE
B727-025C (QF/QC)	N950UP	UNITED PARCEL SERVICE		19718	474	10/15/67	TAY 651-54		N8162G, N126FE
B727-025C (QF/QC)	N951UP	UNITED PARCEL SERVICE		19850	497	12/02/67	TAY 651-54		N8167G, N132FE [PAX CONF]
B727-185C (QF)	N954UP	UNITED PARCEL SERVICE		19827	527	02/20/68	TAY 651-54		N12827, N308BN, PT-TYI, N744EV
B727-031C (QF)	OY-UPA	UNITED PARCEL SERVICE		19233	458	09/16/67	TAY 651-54		N894TW, N926UP [LST/OPB SRR]
B727-022C (QF)	OY-UPD	UNITED PARCEL SERVICE		19103	341	12/17/66	TAY 651-54		N7415U, N431EX, N944UP [LST/OPB SRR]
B727-022C (QF)	OY-UPJ	UNITED PARCEL SERVICE		19102	336	12/07/66	TAY 651-54		N7414U, HK-2476, N420EX, N943UP [LST/OPB SRR]
B727-031C (QF)	OY-UPM	UNITED PARCEL SERVICE		19229	390	04/16/67	TAY 651-54		N890TW, N923UP [LST/OPB SRR]
B727-031C (QF)	OY-UPS	UNITED PARCEL SERVICE		19232	425	06/30/67	TAY 651-54		N893TW, N927UP [LST/OPB SRR]
B727-022C (QF)	OY-UPT	UNITED PARCEL SERVICE		19094	295	09/23/66	TAY 651-54		N7406U, HK-2475, N422EX, N945UP [LST/OPB SRR]
B727-247 (A) (F)	N207UP	UNITED PARCEL SERVICE		21699	1485	05/22/79	JT8D-15 (HK3)		N287WA
B727-247 (A) (F)	N208UP	UNITED PARCEL SERVICE		21701	1493	06/19/79	JT8D-15 (HK3)		N289WA
B727-247 (A) (F)	N209UP	UNITED PARCEL SERVICE		21698	1474	05/01/79	JT8D-15 (HK3)		N286WA
B727-247 (A) (F)	N210UP	UNITED PARCEL SERVICE		21697	1471	04/24/79	JT8D-15 (HK3)		N284WA
B727-247 (A) (F)	N211UP	UNITED PARCEL SERVICE		21700	1489	06/07/79	JT8D-15 (HK3)		N288WA
B727-2A1 (A) (F)	N212UP	UNITED PARCEL SERVICE		21392	1305	12/15/77	JT8D-15 (HK3)		N2827W
B727-2A1 (A) (F)	N213UP	UNITED PARCEL SERVICE		21341	1253	04/19/77	JT8D-17 (HK3)		PP-SNE
B727-2A1 (A) (F)	N214UP	UNITED PARCEL SERVICE		21342	1256	04/29/77	JT8D-17 (HK3)		PP-SNF
B727-254	N912TS	US AIRWAYS SHUTTLE		20438	799	04/09/70	JT8D-7B		N536PS, N536EA [RTD MHV]
B727-254	N913TS	US AIRWAYS SHUTTLE		20250	781	12/12/69	JT8D-7B		N547PS, N547EA [RTD MHV]
B727-254	N914TS	US AIRWAYS SHUTTLE		20251	782	12/29/69	JT8D-7B		N548PS, N548EA [STD MHV 10/21/99]
B727-254	N916TS	US AIRWAYS SHUTTLE		20437	798	03/17/70	JT8D-7B		N384PS, N584EA [STD MHV]
B727-225	N918TS	US AIRWAYS SHUTTLE		20445	840	11/18/70	JT8D-7B (HK3)		N8847E [RTD MHV 10/09/00 FOR PARTS]
B727-225	N919TS	US AIRWAYS SHUTTLE		20447	843	11/20/70	JT8D-7B (HK3)		N8849E [RTD MHV 10/24/00 FOR PARTS]
B727-225	N922TS	US AIRWAYS SHUTTLE		20415	833	09/01/70	JT8D-7B		N8841E [RTD MHV]
B727-225	N923TS	US AIRWAYS SHUTTLE		20441	835	09/04/70	JT8D-7B		N8843E [STD MHV]
B727-227 (A)	N924TS	US AIRWAYS SHUTTLE		21041	1104	02/04/75	JT8D-9A (HK3)		N434BN, N559PE [RTD MHV 10/21/00]
B727-227 (A)	N925TS	US AIRWAYS SHUTTLE		21244	1201	04/29/76	JT8D-9A (HK3)		N443BN, N568PE [RTD MHV 09/26/00 FOR PARTS]
B727-227 (A)	N927TS	US AIRWAYS SHUTTLE		20837	1016	02/27/74	JT8D-9A		N430BN, N555PE [RTD MHV 01/22/00 FOR PARTS]]
B727-2X8 (A) (RE) (WL)	N721MF	WEDGE AVIATION		22687	1784	11/06/81	JT8D-217C/-17		N4523N

A/C TYPE	CURRENT REG. NO.	LAST KNOWN OPERATOR (OWNER)	STATUS	ORIGINAL MSN	LINE NO.	DEL. DATE	ENG. TYPE	FLEET NO.	PREV. REG. [COMMENTS]
OB-PERU									
B727-022	OB-1546	AERO CONTINENTE (PEGA)		19150	485	12/08/67	JT8D-7B		N7086U, N283AT
B727-022	OB-1548	AERO CONTINENTE (MILLENNIUM)		19152	507	12/20/67	JT8D-7B		N7088U, N285AT, OB-1548, N932PG
B727-022	OB-1570	AERO CONTINENTE (IAIL)		19153	508	12/20/67	JT8D-7B/9A		N7089U, N286AT
B727-051	OB-1601	AERO CONTINENTE (IAIL)		18943	203	12/02/65	JT8D-7B		N473US, N3606, N156FN, N288AT
B727-023	OB-1731	AERO CONTINENTE (CSAV)		18432	43	05/14/64	JT8D-7B		N1976, OB-1692, P4-BAC [LST VND]
B727-023	OB-1738	AERO CONTINENTE (INTL. PAC.)		19432	381	03/10/67	JT8D-9A		N1956, XA-SYA, N6293N, P4-BAB
B727-264 (A)	OB-1541	AERO CONTINENTE (INGL)		21072	1145	06/23/75	JT8D-17		XA-FIE [STD LIM]
B727-230 (A)	N22134	AERO PERU (AZTEC CAP.)		20903	1089	05/02/75	JT8D-15		N8293V, N87790, D-ABKE, OB-1560
B727-023	OB-1731	AVIANDINA (ACQ)	L	18432	43	05/14/64	JT8D-7B		N1976, OB-1692, P4-BAC
OO-BELGIUM									
B727-031 (F)	OO-DHM	EUROPEAN AIR TRANSPORT		20114	712	05/21/69	JT8D-7B (HK3)		N7892 [DHL C/S]
B727-031 (F)	OO-DHN	EUROPEAN AIR TRANSPORT		20113	711	05/07/69	JT8D-7B (HK3)		N97891, N260NE [DHL C/S]
B727-031 (F)	OO-DHO	EUROPEAN AIR TRANSPORT		20112	700	05/01/69	JT8D-7B (HK3)		N7890, N250NE [DHL C/S]
B727-035 (F)	OO-DHQ	EUROPEAN AIR TRANSPORT		19167	325	09/18/66	JT8D-7B (HK3)		N4622, N152FN [LST VEC AS YV-846C IN DHL C/S]
B727-035 (F)	OO-DHR	EUROPEAN AIR TRANSPORT		19834	489	11/14/67	JT8D-7B (HK3)		N1958, N932FT [DHL C/S]
B727-277 (A) (F)	OO-DHK	EUROPEAN AIR TRANSPORT		22643	1762	07/03/81	JT8D-15 (HK3)		VH-ANE, N70415 [DHL C/S]
B727-223 (F)	OO-DHS	EUROPEAN AIR TRANSPORT		20189	733	06/26/69	JT8D-9A (HK3)		N6836 [DHL C/S]
B727-223 (F)	OO-DHT	EUROPEAN AIR TRANSPORT		19489	593	06/28/68	JT8D-9A (HK3)		N6814, N317NE [DHL C/S; PARKED SEN]
B727-223 (A) (F)	OO-DHU	EUROPEAN AIR TRANSPORT		20992	1187	05/26/76	JT8D-9A (HK3)		N851AA [DHL C/S]
B727-223 (A) (F)	OO-DHV	EUROPEAN AIR TRANSPORT		21084	1199	04/27/75	JT8D-9A (HK3)		N857AA [LST SWT AS EC-HAH AND OPF DHL IN DHL C/S]
B727-223 (A) (F)	OO-DHW	EUROPEAN AIR TRANSPORT		20993	1189	05/26/76	JT8D-9A (HK3)		N852AA [DHL C/S]
B727-223 (A) (F)	OO-DHX	EUROPEAN AIR TRANSPORT		20994	1190	05/26/76	JT8D-9A (HK3)		N853AA [DHL C/S]
B727-230 (A) (F)	OO-DHY	EUROPEAN AIR TRANSPORT		20905	1091	02/07/75	JT8D-15 (HK3)		D-ABKG, N860SY, YV-855C, TC-AFV, N626DH [DHL C/S]
B727-2Q4 (A) (F)	OO-DHZ	EUROPEAN AIR TRANSPORT		22424	1683	12/05/80	JT8D-17R (HK3)		XA-MEQ, XA-SIV, N7563Q [DHL C/S]
B727-277 (A) (F)	OO-DLB	EUROPEAN AIR TRANSPORT		22642	1759	08/30/81	JT8D-15 (HK3)		N57002, VH-ANB, N86330 [DHL C/S]
B727-2J4 (A) (F)	VH-DHE	EUROPEAN AIR TRANSPORT		22080	1598	03/26/80	JT8D-17 (HK3)		N7278V, OY-SBF, N729DH [LST AXF]
OY-DENMARK									
B727-232 (A) (F)	OY-SER	TNT AIRWAYS (PACA)		20639	927	04/04/73	JT8D-7B (HK3)		N457DA, N516PE, N16784 [LST/OPF SNB]
B727-251 (F)	OY-SES	TNT AIRWAYS (PEGA)		19977	690	02/14/69	JT8D-7B (HK3)		N258US [LST/OPB SNB]
B727-227 (A) (F)	OY-SET	TNT AIRWAYS (WREN)		21245	1202	05/04/76	JT8D-7B (HK3)		N444BN, N569PE, N16762, EI-PAK, N1245K [LST TO KHA NTU; LST SNB 05/00]
B727-281 (F)	OY-SEV	TNT AIRWAYS (PACA)		20571	884	04/28/72	JT8D-7B (HK3)		JA8341, N7367, N530MD, N905PG, EI-SKY [LST/OPB SNB]

A/C TYPE	CURRENT REG. NO.	LAST KNOWN OPERATOR (OWNER)	STATUS	ORIGINAL MSN	LINE NO.	DEL. DATE	ENG. TYPE	FLEET NO.	PREV. REG. [COMMENTS]
B727-287 (A) (F)	OY-SEW	TNT AIRWAYS (PACA)		21688	1415	12/01/78	JT8D-7B (HK3)		LV-MIM, N920PG [LST/OPB SNB 09/97]
B727-224 (A) (F)	OY-SEY	TNT AIRWAYS (NAABI)		20659	979	10/15/73	JT8D-7B (HK3)		N29730 [LST/OPB SNB]
B727-031C (QF)	OY-UPA	STAR AIR (UPS)	L	19233	458	09/16/67	TAY 651-54		N894TW, N926UP [OPF UPS]
B727-022C (QF)	OY-UPD	STAR AIR (UPS)	L	19103	341	12/17/66	TAY 651-54		N7415U, N431EX, N944UP [OPF UPS]
B727-022C (QF)	OY-UPJ	STAR AIR (UPS)	L	19102	336	12/07/66	TAY 651-54		N7414U, HK-2476, N420EX, N943UP [OPF UPS]
B727-031C (QF)	OY-UPM	STAR AIR (UPS)	L	19229	390	04/16/67	TAY 651-54		N890TW, N923UP [OPF UPS]
B727-031C (QF)	OY-UPS	STAR AIR (UPS)	L	19232	425	06/30/67	TAY 651-54		N893TW, N927UP [OPF UPS]
B727-022C (QF)	OY-UPT	STAR AIR (UPS)	L	19094	295	09/23/66	TAY 651-54		N7406U, HK-2475, N422EX, N945UP [OPF UPS]
B727-232 (A) (F)	OY-SER	STERLING EUROPEAN AIRWAYS (TAY)	L	20639	927	04/04/73	JT8D-7B (HK3)		N457DA, N516PE, N16784 [OPF TAY]
B727-251 (F)	OY-SES	STERLING EUROPEAN AIRWAYS (TAY)	L	19977	690	02/14/69	JT8D-7B (HK3)		N258US [OPF TAY]
B727-227 (A) (F)	OY-SET	STERLING EUROPEAN AIRWAYS (TAY)	L	21245	1202	05/04/76	JT8D-7B (HK3)		N444BN, N569PE, N16762, EI-PAK, N1245K
B727-281 (F)	OY-SEV	STERLING EUROPEAN AIRWAYS (TAY)	L	20571	884	04/28/72	JT8D-7B (HK3)		JA8341, N7367, N530MD, N905PG, EI-SKY [OPF TAY; SKY PAK INTL. C/S]
B727-287 (A) (F)	OY-SEW	STERLING EUROPEAN AIRWAYS (TAY)	L	21688	1415	12/01/78	JT8D-7B (HK3)		LV-MIM, N920PG [OPF TAY]
B727-224 (A) (F)	OY-SEY	STERLING EUROPEAN AIRWAYS (TAY)	L	20659	979	10/15/73	JT8D-7B (HK3)		N29730 [OPF TAY]

PK-INDONESIA

A/C TYPE	CURRENT REG. NO.	LAST KNOWN OPERATOR (OWNER)	STATUS	ORIGINAL MSN	LINE NO.	DEL. DATE	ENG. TYPE	FLEET NO.	PREV. REG. [COMMENTS]
B727-025	PK-VBA	PENAS		18970	229	02/10/66	JT8D-7B (HK3)		N8146N, C-GQBE, N682FM, N680FM, N680AM [OPF BAKRIE BROS.; FOR SALE]

PP/PT-BRAZIL

A/C TYPE	CURRENT REG. NO.	LAST KNOWN OPERATOR (OWNER)	STATUS	ORIGINAL MSN	LINE NO.	DEL. DATE	ENG. TYPE	FLEET NO.	PREV. REG. [COMMENTS]
B727-243 (A)	PP-BLR	FLY S.A. LINHAS AEREAS (AEROTURBINE)		21661	1394	10/05/78	JT8D-9A		I-DIRD, N578PE
B727-224 (A)	PP-BLS	FLY S.A. LINHAS AEREAS (CSB BRASIL)		20655	934	04/10/73	JT8D-9A		N32725
B727-227 (A)	PP-JUB	FLY S.A. LINHAS AEREAS (MARSH AV.)		21242	1196	04/22/76	JT8D-9A		N441BN, N566PE, N15774 [PARKED GRU]
B727-2B6 (A)	PP-LBF	FLY S.A. LINHAS AEREAS		20705	945	05/18/73	JT8D-15		CN-CCH, N609AG
B727-243 (A) (F)	PT-MTQ	TOTAL LINHAS AEREAS (PAC. COAST GP.)		22053	1620	05/23/80	JT8D-15		I-DIRN, N582PE, N59412, VT-LCB, N198PC
B727-243 (A) (F)	PT-MTT	TOTAL LINHAS AEREAS (PAC. COAST GP.)		22167	1752	06/01/81	JT8D-15		N8280V, I-DIRR, N585PE, N34415, VT-LCC, N270PC
B727-041 (F)	PP-VLD	VARIG LOG		20425	824	10/23/70	JT8D-9A		
B727-172C	PP-VLE	VARIG LOG		19666	480	10/30/67	JT8D-9A		N726AL
B727-041 (F)	PP-VLG	VARIG LOG		20423	810	10/10/70	JT8D-9A		
B727-173C	PP-VLS	VARIG LOG		19508	457	09/22/67	JT8D-9A		N694WA
B727-030C	PP-VLV	VARIG LOG		19009	374	03/06/67	JT8D-7B		D-ABIX, N705EV

A/C TYPE	CURRENT REG. NO.	LAST KNOWN OPERATOR (OWNER)	STATUS	ORIGINAL MSN	LINE NO.	DEL. DATE	ENG. TYPE	FLEET NO.	PREV. REG. [COMMENTS]
B727-2J7 (A) (F)	PP-VQU	VARIG LOG (PEGA)		20880	1037	11/07/74	JT8D-15		N129NA, PP-SFF
B727-243 (A) (F)	PP-VQV	VARIG LOG (PEGA)		22166	1725	03/17/81	JT8D-9A		I-DIRQ, N584PE, N58414, PP-SFE
B727-264 (A) (F)	PP-SFC	VASP		21071	1143	06/23/75	JT8D-17R		XA-FID, OB-1537, N171G
B727-2Q4 (A) (F)	PP-SFG	VASP		22425	1698	12/22/80	JT8D-17R		PT-TCF, XA-MER, N63063, A7-ABF [VASPEX C/S]
B727-2B6 (A)	PT-MLM	VIABRASIL (A/C INV. CORP.)		21299	1247	03/22/77	JT8D-15		CN-RMQ

P4-ARUBA

A/C TYPE	CURRENT REG. NO.	LAST KNOWN OPERATOR (OWNER)	STATUS	ORIGINAL MSN	LINE NO.	DEL. DATE	ENG. TYPE	FLEET NO.	PREV. REG. [COMMENTS]
B727-193	P4-JLD	TATARSTAN FLIGHTS AVV		19620	377	03/10/67	JT8D-7B		N898PC, XY-ADR, G-BEGZ, VR-CBG, HZ-AMH, VR-CBV, VR-CWC, VP-CWC
B727-030	P4-MMG	AMEL ARUBA		18368	117	02/25/65	JT8D-7B (HK3)		D-ABIM, N9234Z, N72700, N728JE, N841MM, VR-CMM, VP-CMM [OPB LARVELON]
B727-022	P4-ONE	JOSS AVV		19148	473	10/17/67	JT8D-7B (HK3)		N7084U, N341TC

SU-EGYPT

A/C TYPE	CURRENT REG. NO.	LAST KNOWN OPERATOR (OWNER)	STATUS	ORIGINAL MSN	LINE NO.	DEL. DATE	ENG. TYPE	FLEET NO.	PREV. REG. [COMMENTS]
B727-2F2 (A)	TC-IYC	AIR MEMPHIS (TOP)	L	21260	1222	10/08/76	JT8D-15 (HK3)		TC-JBM

SU-Y-PALESTINE

A/C TYPE	CURRENT REG. NO.	LAST KNOWN OPERATOR (OWNER)	STATUS	ORIGINAL MSN	LINE NO.	DEL. DATE	ENG. TYPE	FLEET NO.	PREV. REG. [COMMENTS]
B727-230 (A)	SU-YAK	PALESTINIAN AIRLINES (KINGDOM 5-KR-80)		21621	1425	12/20/78	JT8D-15		D-ABKR, TC-AFR

SX-GREECE

A/C TYPE	CURRENT REG. NO.	LAST KNOWN OPERATOR (OWNER)	STATUS	ORIGINAL MSN	LINE NO.	DEL. DATE	ENG. TYPE	FLEET NO.	PREV. REG. [COMMENTS]
B727-230 (A)	SX-CBG	MACEDONIAN AIRLINES		20918	1093	04/04/75	JT8D-15		D-ABKJ [WFU ATH; FOR SALE]
B727-230 (A)	SX-CBH	MACEDONIAN AIRLINES		20790	1021	03/19/74	JT8D-15		D-ABTI, N1787B, N852SY [FOR SALE]

S9-SAO TOME AND PRINCIPE

A/C TYPE	CURRENT REG. NO.	LAST KNOWN OPERATOR (OWNER)	STATUS	ORIGINAL MSN	LINE NO.	DEL. DATE	ENG. TYPE	FLEET NO.	PREV. REG. [COMMENTS]
B727-173C	S9-BAH	AIR GEMINI		19507	449	09/06/67	JT8D-7B		N693WA, PP-VLW, PP-ITM
B727-022C	S9-BAQ	AIR GEMINI		19093	293	08/19/66	JT8D-7B		N7405U, N498WC, N831RV [PARKED MIA PENDING DEL]
B727-023	D2-FOO	AIR GEMINI		18426	15	02/27/64	JT8D-7B		N1970, ZS-NMX
B727-022C	N832RV	AIR GEMINI		19098	318	10/10/66	JT8D-7B		N7410U, N496WC [PARKED ANC]
B727-031 (F)	S9-BAE	TRANSAFRIK (T.W.L. LTD.)		18903	147	06/16/65	JT8D-7B		N833TW, N210NE
B727-030C	S9-BAG	TRANSAFRIK		19313	411	05/20/67	JT8D-7B		D-ABIY, SE-DDD, N727M, N727MJ, PP-ITP
B727-023 (F)	S9-BOC	TRANSAFRIK		18447	127	04/03/65	JT8D-7B		N1991, ZS-NMY
B727-025 (F)	S9-BOD	TRANSAFRIK		18968	223	01/25/66	JT8D-7B		N8144N, PP-CJL, PP-ITA
B727-022C	S9-BOE	TRANSAFRIK		19192	388	04/10/67	JT8D-7B (HK3)		N7417U, C-GAGY, N726PL, N706DH
B727-090C	S9-BOG	TRANSAFRIK (T.W.L. LTD.)		19170	332	11/18/66	JT8D-7B (HK3)		N798AS, N270AX
B727-095 (F)	S9-CAA	TRANSAFRIK (CARGO A/C)		19836	494	12/05/67	JT8D-7B		N1962, N936FT, OB-1533, HR-AMR

A/C TYPE	CURRENT REG. NO.	LAST KNOWN OPERATOR (OWNER)	STATUS	ORIGINAL MSN	LINE NO.	DEL. DATE	ENG. TYPE	FLEET NO.	PREV. REG. [COMMENTS]
B727-023 (F)	S9-CAB	TRANSAFRIK (IALI)		19182	266	05/13/66	JT8D-7B		N1907, N933FT, HR-AMI
B727-022 (F)	S9-CAH	TRANSAFRIK (IALI)		18849	178	09/16/65	JT8D-7B		N7042U, N40487, N727CD, HR-AMH, ZS-NMW
B727-023 (F)	S9-TAO	TRANSAFRIK (IALI)		19390	350	01/06/67	JT8D-7B		N1932, N931FT
TC-TURKEY									
B727-2F2 (A)	TC-JBF	KIBRIS TURKISH AIRLINES		20980	1085	11/27/74	JT8D-15		
B727-2F2 (A)	TC-JBG	KIBRIS TURKISH AIRLINES		20981	1086	11/21/74	JT8D-15		
B727-2F2 (A)	TC-JBJ	KIBRIS TURKISH AIRLINES		20983	1088	11/26/74	JT8D-15		
B727-228 (A)	TC-JEC	KIBRIS TURKISH AIRLINES		22287	1710	01/28/81	JT8D-15		F-GCDF
B727-2F2 (A)	TC-IYA	TOP AIR		22999	1811	09/03/82	JT8D-15		TC-JCE
B727-243 (A)	TC-IYB	TOP AIR		21664	1448	02/27/79	JT8D-15		I-DIRL, TC-JCK
B727-2F2 (A)	TC-IYC	TOP AIR		21260	1222	10/08/76	JT8D-15 (HK3)		TC-JBM [LST MHS]
B727-2F2 (A) (F)	TC-JCA	TURKISH AIRLINES		22992	1804	06/16/82	JT8D-15		
TC-CAMEROON									
B727-2R1 (A)	TJ-AAM	CAMEROON GOVERNMENT		21636	1414	11/22/78	JT8D-15		
TN-CONGO BRAZZAVILLE									
B727-035	TN-AFY	TRANS AIR CONGO		19833	486	11/07/67	JT8D-9A		N1957, D2-FLY [LST TRANS AIR BENIN]
B727-123	TN-AFZ	TRANS AIR CONGO		19839	542	03/08/68	JT8D-7B		N1965, D2-FLZ
TR-GABON									
B727-228 (A)	TR-LEV	AIR GABON		22083	1605	04/17/80	JT8D-15		F-GCDC, F-OHOA
TS-TUNISIA									
B727-2H9 (A)	YU-AKK	SOSOLISO AIRLINES (JAT)	L	22665	1786	12/30/81	JT8D-9A		N1780B, TS-JEA
B727-2H3 (A)	TS-JHR	TUNISAIR		21179	1171	11/06/75	JT8D-9A		
B727-2H3 (A)	TS-JHT	TUNISAIR		21235	1210	06/23/76	JT8D-9A		
B727-2H3 (A)	TS-JHU	TUNISAIR		21318	1252	03/17/77	JT8D-9A		
B727-2H3 (A)	TS-JHW	TUNISAIR		21320	1271	06/17/77	JT8D-9A		
TY-BENIN									
B727-035	TN-AFY	TRANS AIR BENIN (TSG)	L	19833	486	11/07/67	JT8D-9A		N1957, D2-FLY
VH-AUSTRALIA									
B727-077C	VH-TBS	AIR CARGO AUSTRALIA (ROTHSCHILD)		20278	768	10/31/69	JT8D-7A (HK3)		VH-RMS, C2-RN7 [LST/OPF XME]
B727-277 (A) (F)	VH-AUP	AIR CARGO AUSTRALIA		21695	1481	05/17/79	JT8D-15 (HK3)		VH-RMN [LST/OPF XME]

A/C TYPE	CURRENT REG. NO.	LAST KNOWN OPERATOR (OWNER)	STATUS	ORIGINAL MSN	LINE NO.	DEL. DATE	ENG. TYPE	FLEET NO.	PREV. REG. [COMMENTS]
B727-281 (A) (F)	VH-PAE	ANSETT AUSTRALIA (TRANSASIAN AIR EXPRESS)	L	21455	1316	02/01/78	JT8D-17		JA8353, HL7354, N528JS, H4-PAE, N214F
B727-2J4 (A) (F)	VH-DHE	ASIAN EXPRESS AIRLINES (BCS)	L	22080	1598	03/26/80	JT8D-17 (HK3)		N7278V, OY-SBF, N729DH
B727-077C	VH-TBS	AUSTRALIAN AIR EXPRESS (AIR CARGO AUSTRALIA)	L	20278	768	10/31/69	JT8D-7A (HK3)		VH-RMS, C2-RN7 [OPF AIR CARGO AUSTRALIA]
B727-277 (A) (F)	VH-AUP	AUSTRALIAN AIR EXPRESS (AIR CARGO AUSTRALIA)	L	21695	1481	05/17/79	JT8D-15 (HK3)		VH-RMN [OPB AIR CARGO AUSTRALIA]
B727-277 (A) (F) (WL)	VH-RMX	IAF AIR FREIGHTERS (IPID)		20551	1054	07/18/74	JT8D-15 (HK3)		
B727-281 (A) (F)	VH-PAE	TRANSASIAN AIR EXPRESS (FINO)		21455	1316	02/01/78	JT8D-17		JA8353, HL7354, N528JS, H4-PAE, N214F [OPF AAA FROM 02/05/01]

VP-B-BERMUDA

A/C TYPE	CURRENT REG. NO.	LAST KNOWN OPERATOR (OWNER)	STATUS	ORIGINAL MSN	LINE NO.	DEL. DATE	ENG. TYPE	FLEET NO.	PREV. REG. [COMMENTS]
B727-023 (WL)	VP-BDJ	D.J. AEROSPACE-BERMUDA		20046	605	07/23/68	JT8D-7B		N2914, N927DS, N725DT, VR-BSA, VR-BDJ [OPB TRUMP GROUP]
B727-030	VP-BGW	SIGAIR LTD.-BERMUDA		18366	98	12/18/64	JT8D-7 (HK3)		D-ABIK, N9233Z, N44R, VR-BGW
B727-1H2(RE) (WL)	VP-BIF	NEW CENTURY AIR LTD.-BERMUDA		20533	869	11/03/71	JT8D-217C/-9A		N320HG, N228G, HZ-122, VR-BKC, VP-BKC, VP-BIL

VP-C-CAYMAN IS.

A/C TYPE	CURRENT REG. NO.	LAST KNOWN OPERATOR (OWNER)	STATUS	ORIGINAL MSN	LINE NO.	DEL. DATE	ENG. TYPE	FLEET NO.	PREV. REG. [COMMENTS]
B727-076(WL)	VP-CJN	STARLING AVIATION-CAYMAN IS.		20371	822	07/09/70	JT8D-7B (HK3)		VH-TJF, VR-BAT, N888VT, VR-BRR, 5X-AMM
B727-082	VP-CKA	SAMCO AVIATION-CAYMAN IS.		20489	856	03/04/71	JT8D-7B (HK3)		CS-TBP, N46793, N727KS, N727FH, VR-CKA [FERRIED TO QLA 12/01/00]
B727-046	VP-CMN	IDG (CAYMAN) LTD.		19282	495	12/05/67	JT8D-7B (HK3)		JA8325, D-AHLQ, N4245S, VR-CBE, VR-CLM, VR-CMN [STD SAT]
B727-2P1 (A) (RE) (WL)	VP-CZY	DUNVIEW CO LTD.-CAYMAN IS.		21595	1406	02/01/79	JT8D-217C/17		A7-AAB, N727MJ [OPB JET AV. BUS. JETS]
B727-044C	C-GVFA	CAYMAN AIRWAYS (FAB)	L	20475	854	02/09/71	JT8D-7B (HK3)		ZS-SBH, N26879

XA- MEXICO

A/C TYPE	CURRENT REG. NO.	LAST KNOWN OPERATOR (OWNER)	STATUS	ORIGINAL MSN	LINE NO.	DEL. DATE	ENG. TYPE	FLEET NO.	PREV. REG. [COMMENTS]
B727-014	10501	MEXICAN AIR FORCE		18912	169	08/10/65	JT8D-7B		N974PS, XA-SEK, XA-SEP [3501/XC-FAD?]
B727-014	10503	MEXICAN AIR FORCE		18908	133	04/05/65	JT8D-7B		N970PS, XA-SER
B727-014	10504	MEXICAN AIR FORCE		18909	150	05/22/65	JT8D-7B		N971PS, XA-SEU
B727-031	XA-RWG	AEROEXO		18572	46	05/21/64	JT8D-7B		N853TW [STD MTY]
B727-031	XA-RYI	AEROEXO		19228	351	12/29/66	JT8D-7B		N889TW [STD MTY]

A/C TYPE	CURRENT REG. NO.	LAST KNOWN OPERATOR (OWNER)	STATUS	ORIGINAL MSN	LINE NO.	DEL. DATE	ENG. TYPE	FLEET NO.	PREV. REG. [COMMENTS]
B727-225	XA-RXI	AEROEXO		20150	771	11/14/69	JT8D-7B		N8831E [STD CUN]
B727-225	XA-RXJ	AEROEXO		20154	780	12/16/69	JT8D-7B		N8835E [STD MTY]
B727-225	XA-RZI	AEROEXO		20151	773	11/21/69	JT8D-7B		N8832E [STD MTY]
B727-276 (A)	XA-SDR	AEROEXO		20555	1056	07/27/74	JT8D-15		VH-TBJ [STD MEX IN AVIACSA C/S]
B727-235	XA-SFG	AEROEXO		19474	607	07/25/68	JT8D-7B		N4754 [STD MTY]
B727-276 (A)	XA-SIE	AEROEXO		22069	1661	09/19/80	JT8D-15		VH-TBR [LST CHP]
B727-276 (A)	XA-SIJ	AEROEXO		22017	1564	01/14/80	JT8D-15		VH-TBQ [LST CHP]
B727-276 (A)	XA-SJE	AEROEXO		21479	1357	06/26/78	JT8D-15		VH-TBN [LST CHP]
B727-276 (A)	XA-SJU	AEROEXO		20552	906	12/07/72	JT8D-15		N1779B, VH-TBG [STD MTY]
B727-276 (A)	XA-SLG	AEROEXO		21171	1232	11/18/76	JT8D-15		VH-TBM [LST CHP]
B727-276 (A) (WL)	XA-SLM	AEROEXO		21696	1483	05/22/79	JT8D-15		VH-TBP [LST CHP]
B727-276 (A)	XA-SMB	AEROEXO		21646	1434	01/25/79	JT8D-15		VH-TBO [LST CHP]
B727-225 (A)	XA-SXC	AEROEXO		20619	902	10/19/72	JT8D-15A		N8857E [LST CHP]
B727-225 (A)	XA-SXE	AEROEXO		20615	898	09/29/72	JT8D-15A		N8852E, N401PA [LST CHP]
B727-023	XA-SKC	AEROLINEAS INTERNACIONALES		19181	265	06/24/66	JT8D-7B		N1906
B727-023	XA-SNW	AEROLINEAS INTERNACIONALES		18450	140	05/15/65	JT8D-7B		N1994
B727-223 (A)	XA-AAD	AEROLINEAS INTERNACIONALES		20991	1185	05/26/76	JT8D-9A (HK3)		N850AA
B727-223	XA-SPU	AEROLINEAS INTERNACIONALES		20181	699	03/24/69	JT8D-9		N6828
B727-223 (A)	XA-TPV	AEROLINEAS INTERNACIONALES		19493	657	11/19/68	JT8D-9A		N6818 [CVTD -223]
B727-223 (A)	XA-TQT	AEROLINEAS INTERNACIONALES		20188	730	06/20/69	JT8D-9A		N6835 [CVTD -223]
B727-2K5 (A) (F)	N909PG	AEROMEXPRESS (PEGA)		21852	1553	11/29/79	JT8D-17 (HK3)		D-AHLU, A6-EMC
B727-231 (A)	XA-AAQ	ALLEGRO AIR (PEGA)		21628	1454	03/13/79	JT8D-9A		N54341
B727-232 (A)	XA-ABL	ALLEGRO AIR (PEGA)		20640	935	05/02/73	JT8D-15		N458DA, N517PE, N33785
B727-260 (A)	XA-ABM	ALLEGRO AIR (PACA)		21978	1520	09/18/79	JT8D-17R (HK3)		ET-AHL, N978AL, SX-CAO, ZS-OAO, N901PG
B727-247	XA-SXO	ALLEGRO AIR (IALI)		20268	764	11/14/69	JT8D-15		N2806W, N326AS
B727-225 (A)	XA-TCX	ALLEGRO AIR (IALI)		22440	1692	12/08/80	JT8D-15		N809EA [PARKED TUS]
B727-287 (A)	XA-TGP	ALLEGRO AIR (PACA)		22604	1777	10/15/81	JT8D-17		YV-132C, LV-OLO, N919PG [FERRIED TO TUS 11/10/00 FOR MX]
B727-2B7 (A)	XA-TLZ	ALLEGRO AIR (PACA)		22163	1735	04/10/81	JT8D-17A (HK3)		N771AL, OY-SBN, N923PG [STD TUS]
B727-2B7 (A)	XA-TMA	ALLEGRO AIR (PEGA)		22164	1743	05/05/81	JT8D-17 (HK3)		OY-SBH, N907PG
B727-231 (A)	XA-TMY	ALLEGRO AIR (PEGA)		21987	1582	03/11/80	JT8D-15		N84355 [PARKED TUS]
B727-231 (A)	XA-TRR	ALLEGRO AIR (PEGA)		21629	1456	03/20/79	JT8D-9A		N54342
B727-2A1 (A) (RE)	N102RK	ALLEGRO AIR (PEGA)		21343	1320	10/12/78	JT8D-217C/17R		HK-2151, HK-2151X, N997AA
B727-2A1 (A)	N118DF	ALLEGRO AIR (WFBN)		21344	1322	11/02/78	JT8D-17R		HK-2152X, N998AA
B727-2K5 (A)	N369FA	ALLEGRO AIR (PEGA)		21851	1551	11/30/79	JT8D-17 (HK3)		D-AHLT, ET-AJU, N851AL, SX-CAR, EC-GKL, F-GTCB, ZS-OAZ, N851AL

A/C TYPE	CURRENT REG. NO.	LAST KNOWN OPERATOR (OWNER)	STATUS	ORIGINAL MSN	LINE NO.	DEL. DATE	ENG. TYPE	FLEET NO.	PREV. REG. [COMMENTS]
B727-231 (A)	N64347	ALLEGRO AIR (PEGA)		21634	1466	04/11/79	JT8D-9A		
B727-221 (A) (RE)	N727FV	ALLEGRO AIR (FINO)		22536	1774	12/29/81	JT8D-217C/17A		N364PA, OY-SCB, XA-TKO
B727-221 (A) (RE)	N728FV	ALLEGRO AIR (FINO)		22537	1779	12/29/81	JT8D-217C/17A		N365PA, N728VA, XA-TKV
B727-276 (A)	XA-SIE	AVIACSA (AJO)	L	22069	1661	09/19/80	JT8D-15		VH-TBR
B727-276 (A)	XA-SIJ	AVIACSA (AJO)	L	22017	1564	01/14/80	JT8D-15		VH-TBQ
B727-276 (A)	XA-SJE	AVIACSA (AJO)	L	21479	1357	06/26/78	JT8D-15		VH-TBN
B727-276 (A)	XA-SLG	AVIACSA (AJO)	L	21171	1232	11/18/76	JT8D-15		VH-TBM
B727-276 (A) (WL)	XA-SLM	AVIACSA (AJO)	L	21696	1483	05/22/79	JT8D-15		VH-TBP
B727-276 (A)	XA-SMB	AVIACSA (AJO)	L	21646	1434	01/25/79	JT8D-15		VH-TBO
B727-225 (A)	XA-SXC	AVIACSA (AJO)	L	20619	902	10/19/72	JT8D-15A		N8857E
B727-225 (A)	XA-SXE	AVIACSA (AJO)	L	20615	898	09/29/72	JT8D-15A		N8852E, N401PA
B727-264 (A)	XA-HOH	MEXICANA		21577	1379	08/18/78	JT8D-17R		
B727-264 (A)	XA-HON	MEXICANA		21617	1416	11/29/78	JT8D-17R (HK3)		
B727-264 (A)	XA-HOV	MEXICANA		21637	1429	01/10/79	JT8D-17R (HK3)		
B727-264 (A)	XA-HOX	MEXICANA		21638	1457	03/20/79	JT8D-17R		
B727-264 (A)	XA-IEU	MEXICANA		21836	1497	06/27/79	JT8D-17R (HK3)		
B727-264 (A)	XA-MEB	MEXICANA		21837	1545	11/13/79	JT8D-17R (HK3)		XA-IEV
B727-264 (A)	XA-MEC	MEXICANA		21838	1547	11/13/79	JT8D-17R (HK3)		XA-IEW
B727-264 (A)	XA-MED	MEXICANA		22156	1607	04/18/80	JT8D-17R (HK3)		
B727-264 (A)	XA-MEE	MEXICANA		22157	1619	05/16/80	JT8D-17R (HK3)		
B727-264 (A)	XA-MEF	MEXICANA		22158	1642	07/18/80	JT8D-17R (HK3)		N1786B
B727-264 (A)	XA-MEH	MEXICANA		22409	1676	10/27/80	JT8D-17R (HK3)		
B727-264 (A)	XA-MEI	MEXICANA		22410	1678	10/27/80	JT8D-17R (HK3)		
B727-264 (A)	XA-MEJ	MEXICANA		22411	1696	12/12/80	JT8D-17R (HK3)		
B727-264 (A)	XA-MEK	MEXICANA		22412	1720	02/27/81	JT8D-17R (HK3)		
B727-264 (A)	XA-MEL	MEXICANA		22413	1728	03/27/81	JT8D-17R (HK3)		
B727-264 (A)	XA-MEZ	MEXICANA		22676	1754	06/04/81	JT8D-17R (HK3)		
B727-264 (A)	XA-MXA	MEXICANA		22661	1757	06/11/81	JT8D-17R (HK3)		
B727-264 (A)	XA-MXB	MEXICANA		22662	1776	09/14/81	JT8D-17R (HK3)		
B727-264 (A)	XA-MXC	MEXICANA		22663	1778	10/20/81	JT8D-17R (HK3)		
B727-264 (A)	XA-MXD	MEXICANA		22664	1780	10/20/81	JT8D-17R (HK3)		N1779B
B727-2A1 (A)	XA-MXI	MEXICANA (AIRPLANES III)		21346	1675	10/21/80	JT8D-17		N8285V, PP-SNH, XA-MXF

XT-BURKINA FASO

A/C TYPE	CURRENT REG. NO.	LAST KNOWN OPERATOR (OWNER)	STATUS	ORIGINAL MSN	LINE NO.	DEL. DATE	ENG. TYPE	FLEET NO.	PREV. REG. [COMMENTS]
B727-014	XT-BBE	BURKINA FASO GOVERNMENT		18990	238	03/07/66	JT8D-7B		N975PS, D-AHLP, N2741A, N21UC

YA-AFGHANISTAN

A/C TYPE	CURRENT REG. NO.	LAST KNOWN OPERATOR (OWNER)	STATUS	ORIGINAL MSN	LINE NO.	DEL. DATE	ENG. TYPE	FLEET NO.	PREV. REG. [COMMENTS]
B727-113C	YA-FAU	ARIANA AFGHAN AIRLINES		20343	784	01/25/70	JT8D-9		[STD KANDAHAR]
B727-155C	YA-FAW	ARIANA AFGHAN AIRLINES		19619	470	10/27/67	JT8D-7		N531EJ, G-BIUR, TF-FLJ [STD KANDAHAR]
B727-228 (A)	YA-FAY	ARIANA AFGHAN AIRLINES		22289	1719	02/26/81	JT8D-15		F-GCDH

	A/C TYPE	CURRENT REG. NO.	LAST KNOWN OPERATOR (OWNER)	STATUS	ORIGINAL MSN	LINE NO.	DEL. DATE	ENG. TYPE	FLEET NO.	PREV. REG. [COMMENTS]
YI-IRAQ										
	B727-270 (A)	YI-AGK	IRAQI AIRWAYS		21197	1186	03/08/76	JT8D-17		[STD AMM]
	B727-270 (A)	YI-AGL	IRAQI AIRWAYS		21198	1191	03/24/76	JT8D-17		[STD AMM]
	B727-270 (A)	YI-AGM	IRAQI AIRWAYS		21199	1203	05/18/76	JT8D-17		[GROUNDED]
	B727-270 (A)	YI-AGQ	IRAQI AIRWAYS		22261	1647	05/12/81	JT8D-17		N8284V [STD AMM]
	B727-270 (A)	YI-AGR	IRAQI AIRWAYS		22262	1686	05/14/81	JT8D-17		N8286V [GROUNDED]
	B727-270 (A)	YI-AGS	IRAQI AIRWAYS		22263	1809	07/29/82	JT8D-17		N1780B [STD AMM]
YK-SYRIA										
	B727-294 (A)	YK-AGA	SYRIANAIR		21203	1188	03/27/76	JT8D-17		
	B727-294 (A)	YK-AGB	SYRIANAIR		21204	1194	03/31/76	JT8D-17		
	B727-294 (A)	YK-AGC	SYRIANAIR		21205	1198	05/27/76	JT8D-17		[LST/OPF LAA]
	B727-269 (A)	YK-AGD	SYRIANAIR		22360	1670	10/09/80	JT8D-17R		9K-AFB
	B727-269 (A)	YK-AGE	SYRIANAIR		22361	1716	02/26/81	JT8D-17R		9K-AFC
	B727-269 (A)	YK-AGF	SYRIANAIR		22763	1788	12/10/81	JT8D-17R		9K-AFD
YU-YUGOSLAVIA										
	B727-2L8 (A)	YU-AKD	AVIOGENEX		21040	1142	06/26/75	JT8D-15		OY-SBJ [LST NCH]
	B727-2L8 (A)	YU-AKH	AVIOGENEX		21080	1146	07/31/75	JT8D-15		OY-SBP [LST NCH]
	B727-243 (A)	YU-AKM	AVIOGENEX		22702	1814	12/20/82	JT8D-15		I-DIRT, HK-3618X [LST NCH]
	B727-2H9 (A)	YU-AKB	JAT YUGOSLAV AIRLINES		20931	1045	06/12/74	JT8D-9A		
	B727-2H9 (A)	YU-AKE	JAT YUGOSLAV AIRLINES		21037	1094	12/20/74	JT8D-9A		
	B727-2H9 (A)	YU-AKF	JAT YUGOSLAV AIRLINES		21038	1118	03/14/75	JT8D-9A		
	B727-2H9 (A)	YU-AKG	JAT YUGOSLAV AIRLINES		21039	1119	03/28/75	JT8D-9A		
	B727-2H9 (A)	YU-AKI	JAT YUGOSLAV AIRLINES		22393	1681	12/15/80	JT8D-9A		
	B727-2H9 (A)	YU-AKJ	JAT YUGOSLAV AIRLINES		22394	1691	12/15/80	JT8D-9A		N8281V
	B727-2H9 (A)	YU-AKK	JAT YUGOSLAV AIRLINES		22665	1786	12/30/81	JT8D-9A		N1780B, TS-JEA [LST SOSOLISO AIRLINES]
	B727-2H9 (A)	YU-AKL	JAT YUGOSLAV AIRLINES		22666	1790	12/30/81	JT8D-9A		TS-JEB [OPF SAVANNAH AIRLINES]
YV-VENEZUELA										
	B727-231 (A) (RE)	YV-40C	AEROPOSTAL (PEGA)		21632	1462	04/02/79	JT8D-217C/-9A		N54345 [PARKED TUS]
	B727-231 (A) (RE)	YV-	AEROPOSTAL (PEGA)		21968	1565	02/26/80	JT8D-217C/-9A		N54349
	B727-231 (A) (RE)	N54354	AEROPOSTAL (PEGA)		21986	1580	03/06/80	JT8D-217C/-15		[PARKED TUS]
	B727-224 (A)	N79749	AEROPOSTAL (FAO)	L	22451	1767	07/21/81	JT8D-15 (HK3)		
	B727-224 (A)	N79750	AEROPOSTAL (FAO)	L	22452	1772	09/01/81	JT8D-15 (HK3)		
	B727-022	YV-765C	AVENSA		18855	195	11/03/65	JT8D-7B		N7048U, YV-88C
	B727-035	YV-838C	AVENSA		19165	292	07/23/66	JT8D-7B		N4620, YV-91C, XA-RAN, HK-3933X
	B727-022	YV-89C	AVENSA		18851	181	09/22/65	JT8D-7B		N7044U
	B727-2D3 (A) (RE)	YV-823C	AVENSA		22269	1701	01/16/81	JT8D-217C/17		JY-AFU

A/C TYPE	CURRENT REG. NO.	LAST KNOWN OPERATOR (OWNER)	STATUS	ORIGINAL MSN	LINE NO.	DEL. DATE	ENG. TYPE	FLEET NO.	PREV. REG. [COMMENTS]
B727-281 (A)	YV-94C	AVENSA		20877	1029	04/16/74	JT8D-17		JA8351, N773BE
B727-2D3 (A)	YV-97C	AVENSA		20885	1055	07/30/74	JT8D-17		JY-ADR
B727-027	YV-845C	SERVIVENSA		19534	454	09/06/67	JT8D-7B		N7293, N293AS, N765AS, N100MU, N803SC, XA-TYT, HK-3845X
B727-227	YV-608C	SERVIVENSA		20394	816	06/30/70	JT8D-9A		N403BN, YV-76C
B727-2D3 (A)	YV-762C	SERVIVENSA		22268	1641	07/22/80	JT8D-17		JY-AFT [STD CCS; NO ENGINES]
B727-281 (A)	YV-92C	SERVIVENSA		20724	954	07/06/73	JT8D-17		JA8345, N771BE
B727-035 (F)	YV-846C	VENESCAR INTL. (BCS)	L	19167	325	09/18/66	JT8D-7B (HK3)		N4622, N152FN, OO-DHQ [OPF DHL VENEZ/DHL C/S]

ZK-NEW ZEALAND

A/C TYPE	CURRENT REG. NO.	LAST KNOWN OPERATOR (OWNER)	STATUS	ORIGINAL MSN	LINE NO.	DEL. DATE	ENG. TYPE	FLEET NO.	PREV. REG. [COMMENTS]
B727-022C	NZ7271	ROYAL NEW ZEALAND AIR FORCE		19892	640	10/14/68	JT8D-7		N7435U
B727-022C	NZ7272	ROYAL NEW ZEALAND AIR FORCE		19895	658	11/19/68	JT8D-7		N7438U

ZS-SOUTH AFRICA

A/C TYPE	CURRENT REG. NO.	LAST KNOWN OPERATOR (OWNER)	STATUS	ORIGINAL MSN	LINE NO.	DEL. DATE	ENG. TYPE	FLEET NO.	PREV. REG. [COMMENTS]
B727-023 (F)	ZS-NPX	AIRWORLD (SFR)	L	19131	218	01/18/66	JT8D-7B		N1902, N512FE
B727-230 (A) (F)	ZS-NWA	AIRWORLD (SFR)	L	20757	1002	01/11/74	JT8D-15		D-ABQI, 5N-CMB
B727-232 (A) (F)	ZS-OBN	AIRWORLD (SFR)	L	20637	920	02/08/73	JT8D-15 (HK3)		N455DA, N514PE, N68782
B727-230 (A)	ZS-NOU	COMAIR (SFR)	L	21113	1176	12/02/75	JT8D-15		D-ABKK, N853SY, TC-AFD, TC-TCA
B727-230 (A)	ZS-NOV	COMAIR (SFR)	L	21114	1178	12/12/75	JT8D-15		D-ABKL, N850SY, TC-AFE, TC-TCB
B727-230 (A)	ZS-NVR	COMAIR (SFR)	L	20673	922	02/16/73	JT8D-15		D-ABKI, 5N-NEC
B727-230 (A)	ZS-NZV	COMAIR (SFR)	L	20792	1023	03/25/74	JT8D-15		D-ABWI, N851SY, TC-TUR, TC-RAC
B727-230 (A)	ZS-OBO	COMAIR (SFR)	L	21623	1433	01/19/79	JT8D-15		D-ABKT, OK-JGY
B727-116C	ZS-IJH	INTER AIR (AV. CONSULT.)		19813	594	07/11/68	JT8D-9A		CC-CFD, N70708, 9N-ABN, D2-TJA, N77AZ
B727-023	ZS-IJF	MILLION AIR CHARTER		18444	114	02/24/65	JT8D-7B		N1988, OK-UGZ, N1988
B727-116 (F)	ZS-NYX	NATIONWIDE AIRLINES		19811	520	02/06/68	JT8D-7B (Q)		CC-CAG
B727-095	ZS-NYY	NATIONWIDE AIRLINES		19251	315	09/29/66	JT8D-7B (Q)		N1635, G-BFGN, N29895, VR-BHO, CC-CHC
B727-231 (A)	ZS-ODO	NATIONWIDE AIRLINES		20843	1063	08/31/74	JT8D-9A		N54338
B727-023 (F)	ZS-NPX	SAFAIR		19131	218	01/18/66	JT8D-7B		N1902, N512FE [LST SPZ]
B727-230 (A)	ZS-NOU	SAFAIR		21113	1176	12/02/75	JT8D-15		D-ABKK, N853SY, TC-AFD, TC-TCA [LST CAW 10/01/96]
B727-230 (A)	ZS-NOV	SAFAIR		21114	1178	12/12/75	JT8D-15		D-ABKL, N850SY, TC-AFE, TC-TCB [LST CAW 09/15/96]
B727-230 (A)	ZS-NVR	SAFAIR		20673	922	02/16/73	JT8D-15		D-ABKI, 5N-NEC [LST CAW]

A/C TYPE	CURRENT REG. NO.	LAST KNOWN OPERATOR (OWNER)	STATUS	ORIGINAL MSN	LINE NO.	DEL. DATE	ENG. TYPE	FLEET NO.	PREV. REG. [COMMENTS]
B727-230 (A) (F)	ZS-NWA	SAFAIR		20757	1002	01/11/74	JT8D-15		D-ABQI, 5N-CMB [LST SPZ]
B727-230 (A)	ZS-NZV	SAFAIR		20792	1023	03/25/74	JT8D-15		D-ABWI, N851SY, TC-TUR, TC-RAC [LST CAW]
B727-294 (A)	ZS-OBM	SAFAIR		22044	1561	12/14/79	JT8D-17		YV-75C, N221AL, A7-ABE
B727-232 (A) (F)	ZS-OBN	SAFAIR (AIRCORP)		20637	920	02/08/73	JT8D-15 (HK3)		N455DA, N514PE, N68782 [LST SPZ]
B727-230 (A)	ZS-OBO	SAFAIR		21623	1433	01/19/79	JT8D-15		D-ABKT, OK-JGY [LST CAW 05/29/98]

3D-SWAZILAND

A/C TYPE	CURRENT REG. NO.	LAST KNOWN OPERATOR (OWNER)	STATUS	ORIGINAL MSN	LINE NO.	DEL. DATE	ENG. TYPE	FLEET NO.	PREV. REG. [COMMENTS]
B727-224 (A)	3D-SGH	GULF FALCON		20666	1151	09/08/75	JT8D-9A		N93738

4K-AZERBAIJAN

A/C TYPE	CURRENT REG. NO.	LAST KNOWN OPERATOR (OWNER)	STATUS	ORIGINAL MSN	LINE NO.	DEL. DATE	ENG. TYPE	FLEET NO.	PREV. REG. [COMMENTS]
B727-235	4K-AZ1	AZERBAIJAN AIRLINES		19460	531	02/27/68	JT8D-7B (HK3)		N4740, 4K-4201
B727-230	4K-AZ8	AZERBAIJAN AIRLINES		20525	870	12/12/71	JT8D-15		N1779B, D-ABFI, XA-RJV, XA-SJK, OB-1572, N877UM, OM-AHK

5A-LIBYA

A/C TYPE	CURRENT REG. NO.	LAST KNOWN OPERATOR (OWNER)	STATUS	ORIGINAL MSN	LINE NO.	DEL. DATE	ENG. TYPE	FLEET NO.	PREV. REG. [COMMENTS]
B727-2L5 (A)	5A-DIB	LIBYAN ARAB AIRLINES		21051	1109	02/26/75	JT8D-15		
B727-2L5 (A)	5A-DIC	LIBYAN ARAB AIRLINES		21052	1110	03/06/75	JT8D-15		
B727-2L5 (A)	5A-DID	LIBYAN ARAB AIRLINES		21229	1213	07/19/76	JT8D-15		
B727-2L5 (A)	5A-DIE	LIBYAN ARAB AIRLINES		21230	1215	07/30/76	JT8D-15		
B727-2L5 (A)	5A-DIF	LIBYAN ARAB AIRLINES		21332	1257	04/21/77	JT8D-15		
B727-2L5 (A)	5A-DIH	LIBYAN ARAB AIRLINES		21539	1371	11/07/78	JT8D-15		N1253E
B727-2L5 (A)	5A-DII	LIBYAN ARAB AIRLINES		21540	1386	11/03/78	JT8D-15		N1261E
B727-228	C5-DSZ	LIBYAN ARAB AIRLINES (MZS)	L	20470	853	03/12/71	JT8D-7B		F-BPJQ, J2-KBG, TT-DSZ
B727-294 (A)	YK-AGC	LIBYAN ARAB AIRLINES (SYR)	L	21205	1198	05/27/76	JT8D-17		

5B-CYPRUS

A/C TYPE	CURRENT REG. NO.	LAST KNOWN OPERATOR (OWNER)	STATUS	ORIGINAL MSN	LINE NO.	DEL. DATE	ENG. TYPE	FLEET NO.	PREV. REG. [COMMENTS]
B727-030	5B-DBE	A.I.M.E.S. LTD.		18371	145	05/25/65	JT8D-7 (HK3)		D-ABIQ, N727CH, VR-BHP, VR-UHM, VS-UHM, V8-UHM, V8-BG1, V8-BG2, 9M-SAS

5N-NIGERIA

A/C TYPE	CURRENT REG. NO.	LAST KNOWN OPERATOR (OWNER)	STATUS	ORIGINAL MSN	LINE NO.	DEL. DATE	ENG. TYPE	FLEET NO.	PREV. REG. [COMMENTS]
B727-2N6 (A) (RE) (WL)	5N-FGN	NIGERIA GOVERNMENT		22825	1805	07/14/82	JT8D-217C/-15		5N-AGY
B727-231	5N-BBF	ADC AIRLINES		20049	693	02/27/69	JT8D-9A		N44316
B727-231	5N-BBH	ADC AIRLINES		20050	694	03/07/69	JT8D-9A		N74317 [WFU LOS]
B727-2M7 (A)	5N-BCF	CHANCHANGI AIRWAYS		21655	1452	03/07/79	JT8D-17R		N726RW, N5772T, TN-AEB, VR-CDL, VP-CDL, CP-2389, CC-CSW
B727-2L8 (A)	YU-AKD	CHANCHANGI AIRLINES (AGX)	L	21040	1142	06/26/75	JT8D-15		OY-SBJ
B727-2L8 (A)	YU-AKH	CHANCHANGI AIRLINES (AGX)	L	21080	1146	07/31/75	JT8D-15		OY-SBP
B727-243 (A)	YU-AKM	CHANCHANGI AIRLINES (AGX)	L	22702	1814	12/20/82	JT8D-15		I-DIRT, HK-3618X

A/C TYPE	CURRENT REG. NO.	LAST KNOWN OPERATOR (OWNER)	STATUS	ORIGINAL MSN	LINE NO.	DEL. DATE	ENG. TYPE	FLEET NO.	PREV. REG. [COMMENTS]
B727-235	5N-	FREEDOM AIR SERVICES (IALI)		19461	538	03/08/68	JT8D-7B		N4741, 4K-AZ2, N461RD
B727-224 (A)	5N-MMM	KABO AIR		20656	938	04/27/73	JT8D-9A		N66726 [PARKED CGK SINCE 01/01]
B727-224	5N-TTT	KABO AIR		20463	807	03/06/72	JT8D-9A		N1781B, N32721 [PARKED CGK SINCE 01/01]
B727-023 (F)	5N-SMA	SMA AIRLINES (NATU EXPORTS)		19388	340	12/02/66	JT8D-7B		N1930, N939FT, N513FE, HC-BRF [WFU LOS]
B727-022	5N-TKT	TRIAX AIRLINES		18330	156	07/02/65	JT8D-7B		N7038U, N40482, 5N-ORI
B727-264	5N-TTK	TRIAX AIRLINES		20432	827	10/17/70	JT8D-7B		N1780B, XA-TAA, HK-3421X [STD LIS 01/98]

5Y-KENYA

A/C TYPE	CURRENT REG. NO.	LAST KNOWN OPERATOR (OWNER)	STATUS	ORIGINAL MSN	LINE NO.	DEL. DATE	ENG. TYPE	FLEET NO.	PREV. REG. [COMMENTS]
B727-231	5Y-AXB	AFRICAN AIRLINES INTL.		19565	603	07/22/68	JT8D-7B		N12308, 5V-TPB [AFRICAN EXPRESS]

6V-SENEGAL

A/C TYPE	CURRENT REG. NO.	LAST KNOWN OPERATOR (OWNER)	STATUS	ORIGINAL MSN	LINE NO.	DEL. DATE	ENG. TYPE	FLEET NO.	PREV. REG. [COMMENTS]
B727-2M1 (A)	6V-AEF	SENEGAL GOVERNMENT		21091	1134	11/02/76	JT8D-17		N8284V, N40104

70-YEMEN

A/C TYPE	CURRENT REG. NO.	LAST KNOWN OPERATOR (OWNER)	STATUS	ORIGINAL MSN	LINE NO.	DEL. DATE	ENG. TYPE	FLEET NO.	PREV. REG. [COMMENTS]
B727-2N8 (A)	70-ACV	YEMENIA		21844	1518	08/22/79	JT8D-17R		4W-ACF
B727-2N8 (A)	70-ACW	YEMENIA		21845	1529	10/01/79	JT8D-17R		4W-ACG
B727-2N8 (A)	70-ACX	YEMENIA		21846	1549	11/29/79	JT8D-17R		4W-ACH
B727-2N8 (A)	70-ACY	YEMENIA		21847	1557	12/13/79	JT8D-17R		4W-ACI
B727-2N8 (A)	70-ADA	YEMENIA		21842	1512	09/05/79	JT8D-17R		4W-ACJ [OPF GOVT; VIP CONF]

7T-ALGERIA

A/C TYPE	CURRENT REG. NO.	LAST KNOWN OPERATOR (OWNER)	STATUS	ORIGINAL MSN	LINE NO.	DEL. DATE	ENG. TYPE	FLEET NO.	PREV. REG. [COMMENTS]
B727-2D6	7T-VEA	AIR ALGERIE		20472	850	02/12/71	JT8D-9		
B727-2D6	7T-VEB	AIR ALGERIE		20473	855	03/12/71	JT8D-9		
B727-2D6 (A)	7T-VEI	AIR ALGERIE		21053	1111	03/04/75	JT8D-15		
B727-2D6 (A)	7T-VEM	AIR ALGERIE		21210	1204	05/26/76	JT8D-15		
B727-2D6 (A)	7T-VEP	AIR ALGERIE		21284	1233	11/19/76	JT8D-15		
B727-2D6 (A)	7T-VET	AIR ALGERIE		22372	1662	09/18/80	JT8D-15		
B727-2D6 (A)	7T-VEU	AIR ALGERIE		22373	1664	09/22/80	JT8D-15		
B727-2D6 (A)	7T-VEV	AIR ALGERIE		22374	1711	03/09/81	JT8D-15		N8292V
B727-2D6 (A)	7T-VEW	AIR ALGERIE		22375	1723	03/11/81	JT8D-15		N8295V
B727-2D6 (A)	7T-VEX	AIR ALGERIE		22765	1801	05/05/82	JT8D-15		

9G-GHANA

A/C TYPE	CURRENT REG. NO.	LAST KNOWN OPERATOR (OWNER)	STATUS	ORIGINAL MSN	LINE NO.	DEL. DATE	ENG. TYPE	FLEET NO.	PREV. REG. [COMMENTS]
B727-230 (A)	N359PA	CONTINENTAL CARGO AIRLINES (GM AIRLINES)	L	20789	1015	02/25/74	JT8D-15		D-ABSI

9M-MALAYSIA

A/C TYPE	CURRENT REG. NO.	LAST KNOWN OPERATOR (OWNER)	STATUS	ORIGINAL MSN	LINE NO.	DEL. DATE	ENG. TYPE	FLEET NO.	PREV. REG. [COMMENTS]
B727-2F2 (A) (F)	9M-TGA	TRANSMILE AIR SERVICES		22993	1808	07/19/82	JT8D-15		TC-JCB [PARKED TUS]
B727-2F2 (A) (F)	9M-TGB	TRANSMILE AIR SERVICES		22998	1810	08/23/82	JT8D-15		TC-JCD

A/C TYPE	CURRENT REG. NO.	LAST KNOWN OPERATOR (OWNER)	STATUS	ORIGINAL MSN	LINE NO.	DEL. DATE	ENG. TYPE	FLEET NO.	PREV. REG. [COMMENTS]
CONGO KINSHASA									
B727-030	9Q-CDC	CONGO KINSHASA GOVERNMENT		18934	222	01/21/66	JT8D-7		D-ABIS, N62119, JY-HMH, JY-AHS, VR-CHS, 9Q-RDZ
B727-041	9Q-CDJ	CONGO KINSHASA GOVERNMENT		20424	817	10/16/70	JT8D-9A		PP-VLH [RE-REG TO EL-GPX FOR NEW OPERATOR?]
B727-081	9Q-CDM	BLUE AIRLINES		18919	163	07/26/65	JT8D-7A		JA8305, D-AHLM, HR-SHF [STD GOMA]
B727-030	9Q-CRG	HEWA BORA AIRWAYS		18361	28	03/18/64	JT8D-9		D-ABIC, N16765, N18477, 9Q-CSE
B727-214	9Q-CRS	HEWA BORA AIRWAYS		19687	573	05/10/68	JT8D-7B		N532PS, N532EA, N910TS, 5H-ARS
B727-227 (A)	9Q-CWA	HEWA BORA AIRWAYS		20775	998	01/04/74	JT8D-9A		N429BN, N554PE
B727-022 (F)	9Q-CPJ	MIBA AVIATION (AVNET)		19088	365	02/09/67	JT8D-7A		N7075U, PT-TCH, N743EV
B727-089	9Q-CBT	SCIBE-AIRLIFT CONGO		19138	246	03/29/66	JT8D-7		JA8314, D-AHLR
B727-025	9Q-CWT	WETRAFA AIRLINES		18291	204	12/10/65	JT8D-7B		N8140N, N904TS
MILITARY									
B727-035 (C22B)	83-4610	USAF	M	18811	85	10/23/64	JT8D-7B		N4610 [OPB AIR NATIONAL GUARD; SPOTTED I/S 05/98]
B727-035 (C22B)	83-4615	USAF	M	18816	112	02/10/65	JT8D-7B		N4615 [OPB AIR NATIONAL GUARD; SPOTTED I/S 05/98]
B727-035 (C22B)	83-4616	USAF	M	18817	118	02/26/65	JT8D-7B		N4616 [OPB AIR NATIONAL GUARD]
B727-212 (A) (C22C)	83-4618	USAF	M	21946	1504	07/17/79	JT8D-15		9V-SGH, 9V-WGA, N48054, N8596C
OUT OF SERVICE									
B727-025	5N-AWY	KABO AIR	O	18258	20	01/21/64	JT8D-7B		N8107N [STD KAN]
B727-025 (F)	N511FE	FEDERAL EXPRESS	O	18283	155	07/16/65	JT8D-7B (HK3)		N8132N [ST GOODRICH; RTD BFI; WILL BE BU]
B727-022 (WL)	N727CF	SOUTHWEST JET INC.	O	18323	136	04/22/65	JT8D-7A		N7031U, HL7337, N1187Z, CC-CIW, N863SY, VR-BMC [VIP CONF; FOR SALE]
B727-022	N39KA	KEY AIRLINES (WORLDCORP)	O	18324	139	04/28/65	JT8D-7B		N7032U, N841N, N103MU [STD GWO]
B727-022	N40481	CONTINENTAL AIRLINES	O	18329	154	06/24/65	JT8D-7B		N7037U [STD MHV]
B727-022	N40483	CONTINENTAL AIRLINES	O	18331	158	07/13/65	JT8D-7B		N7039U [STD MHV]
B727-022	9Q-CSF	CONGO AIRLINES	O	18332	164	08/04/65	JT8D-7B		N7040U, N40485
B727-030	N46	FEDERAL AVIATION ADMINISTRATION	O	18360	24	02/22/64	JT8D-7		N68649, D-ABIB, N77, N97 [STD ACY]
B727-030 (C22A)	84-0193	USAF	O	18362	33	04/01/64	JT8D-7		D-ABID, N90558, N78 [STD DMAFB 11/91; CU0002]
B727-030	N18478	CONTINENTAL AIRLINES	O	18364	37	04/09/64	JT8D-9		D-ABIG, N16766 [STD SHERMAN, GRAYSON, TX]
B727-030	9Q-CBG	SCIBE-AIRLIFT CONGO	O	18367	109	02/03/65	JT8D-7		D-ABIL, N2703J, N727UD
B727-023	N1974	(AIRCRAFT SUPPORT)	O	18430	31	04/14/64	JT8D-7B		[STD MIA WITH MANY PARTS MISSING]

A/C TYPE	CURRENT REG. NO.	LAST KNOWN OPERATOR (OWNER)	STATUS	ORIGINAL MSN	LINE NO.	DEL. DATE	ENG. TYPE	FLEET NO.	PREV. REG. [COMMENTS]
B727-023 (F)	N1975	EMERY WORLDWIDE AIRLINES	O	18431	32	03/31/64	JT8D-7B		[STD MXE]
B727-023 (F)	N1978	EMERY WORLDWIDE AIRLINES	O	18434	50	06/17/64	JT8D-7B		[STD MXE]
B727-023 (F)	N1982	EMERY WORLDWIDE AIRLINES	O	18438	65	08/21/64	JT8D-7B		[STD MXE]
B727-023 (F)	N1983	EMERY WORLDWIDE AIRLINES	O	18439	67	08/24/64	JT8D-7B		[STD MXE]
B727-023 (F)	N1990	EMERY WORLDWIDE AIRLINES	O	18446	123	03/19/65	JT8D-7B		[STD DAY]
B727-077	XA-SIR	QUASSAR (CORS)	O	18743	78	09/29/64	JT8D-7B		VH-RME, XA-MEG, PT-TCE, N8140V, TC-AJT, N143CA, HK-3651X, HH-PRI, HH-JEC, XA-SDH [STD OPF 10/94]
B727-031	XA-SQO	TAESA	O	18752	76	09/21/64	JT8D-7B		N847TW, N727PJ
B727-022	N40484	CONTINENTAL AIRLINES	O	18791	165	08/03/65	JT8D-7B		N7003U [STD MHV]
B727-078 (F)	N728EV	EVERGREEN INTL. AIRLINES	O	18794	99	12/21/64	JT8D-7B		9Y-TCO, N305BN, PT-TYR [STD MZJ]
B727-051	YA-GAA	BALKH AIRLINES	O	18798	93	11/14/64	JT8D-7B		N462US, N974PS, OK-TGX [STD IST]
B727-051	XA-ASS	TAESA	O	18800	116	02/11/65	JT8D-7B		N464US, N977PS, XA-MEP, YV-79C, XA-TAE, XA-PAL [STD MEX]
B727-051	N29KA	KEY AIRLINES (WORLDCORP)	O	18803	137	04/22/65	JT8D-7		N467US, N838N [STD GWO]
B727-051	N471US	NORTHWEST AIRLINES	O	18807	193	10/22/65	JT8D-7B		[STD SHERMAN, GRAYSON, TX]
B727-035 (C22B)	83-4612	USAF	O	18813	94	12/03/64	JT8D-7B		N4612 [WFU AND STD MXE]
B727-035	OB-1465	FAUCETT PERU (IALI)	O	18845	175	09/03/65	JT8D-7B		N4617, HK-3203X [STD 06/93]
B727-035	N153FN	AERO CONTINENTE	O	18846	183	09/24/65	JT8D-7B		N4618, HK-3212X, OB-1543 [STD]
B727-022	N40486	CONTINENTAL AIRLINES	O	18848	177	09/14/65	JT8D-7B		N7041U [STD MHV]
B727-022	N40488	CONTINENTAL AIRLINES	O	18852	186	10/05/65	JT8D-7B		N7041U [STD MHV]
B727-022	N40489	CONTINENTAL AIRLINES	O	18854	191	10/26/65	JT8D-7B		N7041U [STD MHV]
B727-022	N30KA	KEY AIRLINES (WORLDCORP)	O	18857	200	11/18/65	JT8D-7		N7050U [STD GWO]
B727-095	N37KA	KEY AIRLINES (WORLDCORP)	O	18858	207	12/17/65	JT8D-7B		N1632, N834N, HK-3168X, N101MU [STD GWO]
B727-022	N27KA	KEY AIRLINES (WORLDCORP)	O	18859	208	12/14/65	JT8D-7		N7052U [STD GWO]
B727-022	N40490	CONTINENTAL AIRLINES	O	18860	210	12/16/65	JT8D-7B		N7053U [STD MHV]
B727-046	EL-AKE	NEW ACS	O	18877	226	01/31/66	JT8D-7A		JA8310, G-BAFZ, HK-3201X, G-BAFZ, HK-3270X, EI-BUP, N7046A, HK-3458X, 9Q-CRA
B727-023	N1995	(A/C SUPPORT & PARTS)	O	18900	151	06/23/65	JT8D-7B		YL-BAE [PARKED MIA]
B727-014 (F)	XA-RRA	TAESA	O	18911	167	08/01/65	JT8D-7B		N973PS, XA-SEA, TP-10505 [BEING BU MEX]
B727-051	OB-1588	AERO CONTINENTE (IAIL)	O	18942	198	11/09/65	JT8D-7B/9A		N472US, N3605, N160FN, N289AT [RT INTL. AIRLINE INV 08/99; STD TUS, MINUS ENGINES]
B727-025	9Q-CAV	SHABAIR	O	18967	220	01/15/66	JT8D-7B		N8143N, N906TS
B727-021 (F)	HK-1717	AEROSUCRE COLOMBIA	O	18993	215	01/14/66	JT8D-7A		N315PA [WFU BOG, LESS ENGINES, FOLLOWING 06/25/97 ACCIDENT]
B727-027C	N725EV	EVERGREEN INTL. AIRLINES	O	19112	299	08/26/66	JT8D-7B		N7273, PT-TYT [STD MZJ]
B727-027C	N731EV	EVERGREEN INTL. AIRLINES	O	19113	310	09/14/66	JT8D-7B		N7274, PT-TYP, 9N-ABY [STD MZJ]
B727-027C	N729EV	EVERGREEN INTL. AIRLINES	O	19116	330	11/04/66	JT8D-7B		N7277, PT-TYO [STD MZJ]
B727-051	N479US	NORTHWEST AIRLINES	O	19125	361	01/25/67	JT8D-7B		[STD SHERMAN, GRAYSON, TX]
B727-089	N511DB	LAKER AIRWAYS (RIVERHORSE)	O	19139	255	04/19/66	JT8D-7B (HK3)		JA8315, D-AHLS, VR-CRB, VR-CDB [DEPARTED FROM LAS]

A/C TYPE	CURRENT REG. NO.	LAST KNOWN OPERATOR (OWNER)	STATUS	ORIGINAL MSN	LINE NO.	DEL. DATE	ENG. TYPE	FLEET NO.	PREV. REG. [COMMENTS]
B727-022	N742EV	EVERGREEN INTL. AIRLINES	O	19140	369	02/12/67	JT8D-7A		N7076U, PT-TCI [STD MZJ]
B727-022	N931PG	AERO CONTINENTE (PEGA)	O	19151	504	12/20/67	JT8D-7B		N7087U, N284AT, OB-1547 [PARKED TUS AS OB-1547]
B727-035 (F)	TG-DHP	DHL GUATEMALA	O	19166	303	08/31/66	JT8D-7B (HK3)		N4621, N150FN, OO-DHP [RTD 02/99; TO BE BU]
B727-023 (F)	D2-TJC	ANGOLA AIR CHARTER	O	19180	251	04/15/66	JT8D-7B		N1905, N935FT, 9Q-CSY
B727-011 (F)	HK-3770X	SATENA COLOMBIA	O	19242	260	04/25/66	JT8D-7B		CF-FUN, N4509, N302BN, PP-CJI [WFU BOG]
B727-095	PP-VLT	(MISTRAL AERO)	O	19250	313	09/16/66	JT8D-7B		N1634 [VIP CONF; FOR SALE]
B727-077	N720DC	(AMERICANA AVIATION)	O	19253	296	08/09/66	JT8D-7		VH-RMR, N110AC, N111EK, VR-CKL, N340DR, N440DR, N448DR
B727-021	N727PX	(MISTRAL AERO)	O	19261	422	06/17/67	JT8D-7 (HK3)		N359PA, N727DG, N727RF, N260GS [VIP CONF; FOR SALE]
B727-046	HK-3841X	INTERAMERICANA COLOMBIA	O	19281	378	02/25/67	JT8D-7A		JA8320, G-BCDA, HK-3612X, N281ZV
B727-046 (F)	N745EV	EVERGREEN INTL. AIRLINES	O	19283	502	12/11/67	JT8D-7A		JA8326 [ST CASTLE PRECISION 08/29/95; STD MZJ]
B727-023 (F)	N1928	EMERY WORLDWIDE AIRLINES	O	19386	321	10/08/66	JT8D-7B		[STD DAY]
B727-191	N727X	(JB AVIATION.COM)	O	19394	418	06/02/67	JT8D-7B (HK3)		N7273F, N300BN, N3946A [VIP CONF; FOR SALE]
B727-082	5N-TKE	TRIAX AIRLINES	O	19406	430	07/11/67	JT8D-7B		CS-TBM, C-GWGV [STD MIA LESS ENGINES; TO BE BU]
B727-064	XA-RRB	TAESA	O	19427	375	03/14/67	JT8D-7B		XA-SEM, XC-FAC, TP-10502
B727-235	XA-SFF	AEROEXO	O	19462	539	03/23/68	JT8D-7B		N4742 [STD MTY 03/94; NOW MISSING; BU?]
B727-235	N4749	BRANIFF (CISL)	O	19469	568	04/29/68	JT8D-7B		[STD TUS]
B727-235	N4750	BRANIFF (CISL)	O	19470	569	05/03/68	JT8D-7B		[STD TUS]
B727-223 (F)	N705CA	KITTY HAWK AIR CARGO (ACFT LSG)	O	19479	544	03/18/68	JT8D-9A		N6804
B727-027C	D2-FAT	AIR NACOIA (CORS)	O	19497	429	06/30/67	JT8D-9		N7288, PT-TYH, PT-SAV, XA-SPK, XA-SGY [ST GLOBAL GROUPE, SOUTH AFRICA 01/10/98; STD JNB]
B727-024C	XA-BBI	TAESA	O	19528	465	09/23/67	JT8D-7B		N2475
B727-231	OB-1698	AERO PERU (PEGA)	O	19561	574	05/18/68	JT8D-9A		YV-909C, N12304 [RT PEGA 03/99; PARKED TUS; BEING BU]
B727-231	N52309	CAPITOL AIR EXPRESS (C&S ACQ.)	O	19828	609	07/29/68	JT8D-9A		
B727-180C (QF)	N921UP	UNITED PARCEL SERVICE	O	19874	534	02/19/68	TAY 651-54		N9515T, OY-UPB [REG CX]
B727-222	N7627U	UNITED AIRLINES	O	19900	618	08/13/68	JT8D-7B		[STD ARD]
B727-251	C5-ADA	AIR DABIA	O	19970	648	10/19/68	JT8D-7B		N251US, HI-656CA, 5V-TPC [SEEN BANJUL 11/19/99]
B727-251	5N-EDE	OKADA AIR	O	19972	662	11/21/68	JT8D-7B		N253US
B727-251	N256US	NORTHWEST AIRLINES	O	19975	674	01/04/69	JT8D-7B		[STD MQY]
B727-251	N260US	LASER (PEGA)	O	19979	697	03/05/69	JT8D-7B		YV-910C [RT LESSOR 01/08/98; STD TUS]
B727-251 (F)	N263US	EXPRESS ONE INTL. (AIRCORP)	O	19982	737	07/15/69	JT8D-7B (HK)		HK-3875
B727-284	SX-CBA	OLYMPIC AIRWAYS	O	20003	671	12/19/68	JT8D-9A		[TO BE BU ATH]

A/C TYPE	CURRENT REG. NO.	LAST KNOWN OPERATOR (OWNER)	STATUS	ORIGINAL MSN	LINE NO.	DEL. DATE	ENG. TYPE	FLEET NO.	PREV. REG. [COMMENTS]
B727-284	SX-CBB	OLYMPIC AIRWAYS	0	20004	678	01/16/69	JT8D-9A		[TO BE BU ATH]
B727-284	N727SH	(AERO CONTROLS)	0	20005	687	02/07/69	JT8D-9A		SX-CBC
B727-284	N727SR	(AERO CONTROLS)	0	20006	688	02/07/69	JT8D-9A		SX-CBD [PARKED OPF]
B727-023(WL)	N727WF	BOMBARDIER CAPITAL INC.	0	20045	596	07/09/68	TAY651-54		N2913 [VIP CONF]
B727-231	N590CA	PRESTIGE AIRLINES (CSAV)	0	20098	731	06/25/69	JT8D-9A		N64323 [STD MQY]
B727-225	5N-SSS	KABO AIR	0	20147	767	10/31/69	JT8D-7B		N8828E
B727-284	SX-CBE	OLYMPIC AIRWAYS	0	20201	765	10/24/69	JT8D-9A		[TO BE BU ATH]
B727-224	5A-DAI	LIBYAN ARAB AIRLINES	0	20245	663	07/27/71	JT8D-9		N1783B [CANNIBALIZED FOR PARTS; DERELICT AT TIP]
B727-247	OB-1301	FAUCETT PERU (IALI)	0	20263	750	10/16/69	JT8D-15		N2801W [CEASED OPERATIONS; STD LIM]
B727-251	N267US	DISCOVERY AIRLINES (PEGA)	0	20289	746	08/12/69	JT8D-7B (HK3)		[RT PEGA 05/00; STD TUS]
B727-251	N268US	HELLENIC AIR (C&S ACQ.)	0	20290	747	08/15/69	JT8D-7B		[STD MQY MINUS ENGINES AND OTHER PARTS]
B727-251	N389PA	CAPITOL AIR EXPRESS (C&S ACQ.)	0	20293	757	09/26/69	JT8D-7B		[STD MQY]
B727-251	N272US	NORTHWEST AIRLINES	0	20294	759	10/03/69	JT8D-7B		[STD MQY MINUS ENGINES AND OTHER PARTS]
B727-2B6	CN-CCF	ROYAL AIR MAROC	0	20304	808	04/24/70	JT8D-7B		[GRND INSTR]
B727-225 (F)	N8840E	MEXICARGO (JODA LLC)	0	20383	831	08/20/70	JT8D-7B		[STD TUS; ALL WHITE; NO TITLES]
B727-227	YV-464C	ZULIANA DE AVIACION (GLOBAL)	0	20392	811	06/30/70	JT8D-7B		N401BN, N205US, N378PA [SUSPENDED OPS 1997]
B727-227	N385PA	CAPITOL AIR EXPRESS (C&S ACQ.)	0	20393	813	06/30/70	JT8D-7B		N402BN, N206US [STD MQY]
B727-041	OB-1661	AMERICANA DE AVIACION (LSG TRNG CORP)	0	20422	803	10/10/70	JT8D-7B		PP-VLF, HK-3870X [DERELICT AT LIM]
B727-225	5N-KBY	KABO AIR	0	20442	836	09/28/70	JT8D-7B		N8844E [WFU ADDIS ABABA
B727-225	5N-KBX	KABO AIR	0	20444	839	11/16/70	JT8D-7B		N8846E [STD KAN]
B727-231	N54334	TRANS WORLD AIRLINES	0	20461	860	04/06/71	JT8D-9A		[STD VCV 08/18/99; ST CAPITAL A/C 11/99 FOR PARTS]
B727-2B6	CN-CCG	ROYAL AIR MAROC	0	20471	848	02/01/71	JT8D-7B		[STD]
B727-247 (A)	N2807W	DELTA AIRLINES	0	20579	886	05/12/72	JT8D-9A		[ST AVBORNE ACCESSORY GROUP; STD VCV 01/00]
B727-247 (A)	N2809W	DELTA AIRLINES	0	20581	890	06/16/72	JT8D-9A		[ST AVBORNE ACCESSORY GROUP; STD VCV 01/00; BEING BU?]
B727-256 (A)	N905RF	IBERIA	0	20595	905	05/12/73	JT8D-9		N1788B, N1787B, EC-CBA [ST REPUBLIC FINANCIAL (USA); PARKED SNN]
B727-256 (A)	YV-125C	VIASA	0	20596	908	05/01/73	JT8D-9		N1788B, N1786B, EC-CBB [STD LIS]
B727-256 (A)	EC-GCI	IBERIA	0	20598	910	04/03/73	JT8D-9		N1788B, EC-CBD [RTD 12/99, STD MAD]
B727-256 (A)	EC-CBM	IBERIA	0	20607	943	05/21/73	JT8D-9		LV-VFM, EC-327 [RTD 05/98, TO BE BU MAD]
B727-227	F-GCGQ	BEL AIR	0	20609	892	07/11/72	JT8D-9A		N411BN [STD PGF]
B727-232 (A)	N15781	CONTINENTAL AIRLINES	0	20636	919	02/02/73	JT8D-15	781	N454DA, N513PE [RT LESSOR 10/00; STD MHV]
B727-232 (A)	N15790	CONTINENTAL AIRLINES	0	20644	959	07/27/73	JT8D-15	790	N462DA, N521PE [RT LESSOR 10/03/00; STD MHV]

A/C TYPE	CURRENT REG. NO.	LAST KNOWN OPERATOR (OWNER)	STATUS	ORIGINAL MSN	LINE NO.	DEL. DATE	ENG. TYPE	FLEET NO.	PREV. REG. [COMMENTS]
B727-232 (A)	N59792	(FSBU)	0	20646	967	08/16/73	JT8D-15		N464DA, N523PE [RT LESSOR; PARKED MIA; NO TITLES]
B727-224 (A)	5N-LLL	KABO AIR	0	20654	930	03/28/73	JT8D-9A		N32724 [WFU ADDIS ABABA]
B727-224 (A)	N25729	(MIAMI JET LSG)	0	20658	978	10/08/73	JT8D-9A		5N-QQQ [STD MIA IN KABO AIR COLORS]
B727-230 (A)	N358PA	SKY TREK INTL. AIRLINES (GM AVN SVCS)	0	20674	923	02/24/73	JT8D-15		D-ABLI [WFU BQK]
B727-230 (A)	N360PA	KIWI INTL. (ATAS)	0	20676	925	03/07/73	JT8D-15		D-ABNI [STD ROW 07/02/98]
B727-230 (A)	5N-GBA	OKADA AIR	0	20677	932	04/02/73	JT8D-15		D-ABPI
B727-214 (A)	5N-PAX	HARCO AIR SERVICES	0	20678	931	03/30/73	JT8D-7B		N550PS, N373PA, LV-WFC [SUSPENDED OPS IN 1998]
B727-214 (A)	5N-PAL	HARCO AIR SERVICES	0	20679	942	05/11/73	JT8D-7B		N551PS, N374PA [SUSPENDED OPS IN 1998]
B727-2J7 (A)	XA-TRB	AERO PERU (AZTEC CAP.)	0	20706	949	06/14/73	JT8D-15		N552PS, OY-SBA, N552NA [STD LIM]
B727-281 (F)	N914PG	TNT AIRWAYS (PACA)	0	20725	958	07/16/73	JT8D-7B (HK3)		JA8346, HL7366, N526MD, N902PG, EI-TNT, OY-TNT [PARKED TUS AS OY-TNT]
B727-232 (A)	N466DA	DELTA AIRLINES	0	20743	971	09/06/73	JT8D-15		[ST AVBORNE ACCESSORY GROUP 11/99; STD VCV]
B727-232 (A)	N467DA	DELTA AIRLINES	0	20744	972	09/14/73	JT8D-15		[PARKED VCV 11/98; NO TITLES; WILL BE BU]
B727-232 (A)	N468DA	DELTA AIRLINES	0	20745	980	10/07/73	JT8D-15		[ST AVBORNE ACCESSORY GROUP 10/12/99; BEING BU VCV?]
B727-232 (A)	N469DA	DELTA AIRLINES	0	20746	981	10/18/73	JT8D-15		[STD VCV; ST AVBORNE ACCESSORY GROUP 10/12/99]
B727-232 (A)	N470DA	DELTA AIRLINES	0	20747	987	11/01/73	JT8D-15		[STD VCV; ST AVBORNE ACCESSORY GROUP 10/12/99]
B727-232 (A)	N471DA	DELTA AIRLINES	0	20748	988	11/15/73	JT8D-15 (HK)		[STD VCV; ST AVBORNE ACCESSORY GROUP 10/12/99]
B727-232 (A)	N472DA	DELTA AIRLINES	0	20749	990	11/22/73	JT8D-15 (HK)		[STD VCV; ST AVBORNE ACCESSORY GROUP 10/12/99]
B727-232 (A)	N474DA	DELTA AIRLINES	0	20751	1000	01/04/74	JT8D-15 (HK)		[BEING BU VCV?]
B727-232 (A)	N475DA	DELTA AIRLINES	0	20752	1001	01/09/74	JT8D-15		[STD VCV; ST AVBORNE ACCESSORY GROUP 10/12/99]
B727-232 (A)	N476DA	DELTA AIRLINES	0	20753	1012	04/29/74	JT8D-15		[STD VCV; ST MILLENNIUM AERO PARTS; TO BE BU]
B727-232 (A)	N477DA	DELTA AIRLINES	0	20754	1013	02/08/74	JT8D-15		[STD VCV; ST AVBORNE ACCESSORY GROUP 10/12/99]
B727-232 (A)	N478DA	DELTA AIRLINES	0	20755	1014	02/28/74	JT8D-15		[STD VCV; ST AVBORNE ACCESSORY GROUP 10/12/99]
B727-232 (A)	N479DA	DELTA AIRLINES	0	20756	1028	04/12/74	JT8D-15 (HK)		[STD VCV; ST AVBORNE ACCESSORY GROUP 10/12/99]
B727-256 (A)	EC-CFC	IBERIA	0	20813	1005	01/29/74	JT8D-9		[STD MAD; FOR SALE]
B727-256 (A)	EC-CFH	IBERIA	0	20818	1010	03/20/74	JT8D-9		[RTD 01/00; STD MAD]
B727-256 (A)	EC-CFK	IBERIA	0	20821	1035	05/09/74	JT8D-9		[WFU MAD 03/00]

A/C TYPE	CURRENT REG. NO.	LAST KNOWN OPERATOR (OWNER)	STATUS	ORIGINAL MSN	LINE NO.	DEL. DATE	ENG. TYPE	FLEET NO.	PREV. REG. [COMMENTS]
B727-2H3 (A)	F-GGGR	BEL AIR	O	20822	996	12/13/73	JT8D-9A		TS-JHP, N191CB, PH-AHD [STD PGF]
B727-225 (A)	N8867E	SUNBIRD AIRWAYS (SANWA)	O	20823	994	12/13/73	JT8D-15		[STD MYR]
B727-225 (A)	N8869E	SUNBIRD AIRWAYS (SANWA)	O	20824	995	12/07/73	JT8D-15		[STD HGR]
B727-232 (A)	N480DA	DELTA AIRLINES	O	20860	1038	05/16/74	JT8D-15 (HK3)		[STD VCV; ST AVBORNE ACCESSORY GROUP; TO BE BU]
B727-232 (A)	N481DA	DELTA AIRLINES	O	20861	1041	05/30/74	JT8D-15		[ST MILLENNIUM AERO PARTS; BEING BU VCV?]
B727-232 (A)	N483DA	DELTA AIRLINES	O	20863	1053	07/12/74	JT8D-15		[ST AVBORNE ACCESSORY GROUP 11/99; STD VCV]
B727-232 (A)	N484DA	DELTA AIRLINES	O	20864	1060	08/21/74	JT8D-15		[ST AVBORNE ACCESSORY GROUP 11/99; STD VCV]
B727-232 (A)	N485DA	DELTA AIRLINES	O	20865	1062	08/28/74	JT8D-15		[ST MILLENNIUM AERO PARTS; STD VCV]
B727-247 (A)	N2813W	DELTA AIRLINES	O	20869	1025	04/02/74	JT8D-15 (HK3)	563	[ST UNITED TECHNOLOGIES FOR PARTS]
B727-247 (A)	N2814W	DELTA AIRLINES	O	20870	1032	04/26/74	JT8D-15	564	[ST AVBORNE ACCESSORY GROUP 02/23/01]
B727-247 (A)	N2818W	FLY S.A. LINHAS AEREAS (IALI)	O	20874	1057	07/25/74	JT8D-15		PP-AIV [STD MIA; ALL WHITE; NO TITLES; RT LESSOR]
B727-230 (A)	N390PA	PAN AM (ATAS)	O	20899	1046	06/17/74	JT8D-7B		D-ABKA [STD HGR]
B727-230 (A)	N391PA	PAN AM (ATAS)	O	20900	1050	06/28/74	JT8D-7B		D-ABKB [STD MYR]
B727-230 (A)	N392PA	PAN AM (ATAS)	O	20901	1058	07/26/74	JT8D-7B		D-ABKC [STD MYR]
B727-230 (A)	N393PA	PAN AM (ATAS)	O	20902	1059	08/02/74	JT8D-7B		D-ABKD [STD MYR]
B727-230 (A)	TC-RUT	TUR EUROPEAN AIRWAYS	O	20904	1090	01/06/75	JT8D-15		D-ABKF
B727-2H3 (A) (F)	N722SK	KALITTA EQUIPMENT LLC	O	20948	1084	11/13/74	JT8D-9A		TS-JHQ [PARKED MIA; CVTD TO FRTR]
B727-2D6 (A)	7T-VEH	AIR ALGERIE	O	20955	1075	10/27/74	JT8D-15		
B727-282 (A)	HC-BRG	SAETA	O	20973	1099	02/06/75	JT8D-17		CS-TBS [RT LESSOR]
B727-223 (A)	N847AA	AMERICAN AIRLINES	O	20988	1141	06/13/75	JT8D-9A (HK3)	847	[LRF 06/03/00, ST AV SALES 06/13/00, PERMANENTLY RTD ARD 06/13/00]
B727-232 (A)	N490DA	DELTA AIRLINES	O	21020	1102	04/17/75	JT8D-15 (HK3)	490	[ST AVBORNE ACCESSORY GROUP 01/31/01; STD VCV]
B727-2J1 (A)	HI-242CT	DOMINICANA DE AVIACION	O	21036	1129	05/07/75	JT8D-9A		HI-242 [STD SJO]
B727-232 (A)	N491DA	DELTA AIRLINES	O	21060	1115	04/04/75	JT8D-9A (HK3)	491	[STD VCV 10/12/00; ST AVBORNE 10/27/00; TO BE BU]
B727-232 (A)	N492DA	DELTA AIRLINES	O	21061	1116	03/26/75	JT8D-15		[ST REPUBLIC ADVANCED FREIGHTER; STD VCV; TO BE BU]
B727-232 (A)	N494DA	DELTA AIRLINES	O	21074	1138	06/23/75	JT8D-15 (HK3)		[ST REPUBLIC ADVANCED FREIGHTER 12/03/99; STD VCV; TO BE BU]
B727-232 (A)	N495DA	DELTA AIRLINES	O	21075	1139	06/25/75	JT8D-15 (HK3)	495	[ST AVBORNE ACCESSORY GROUP 01/31/01]
B727-232 (A)	N496DA	DELTA AIRLINES	O	21076	1140	06/11/75	JT8D-15 (HK3)	496	[ST AVBORNE ACCESSORY GROUP 01/31/01; STD OPF]
B727-232 (A)	N403DA	DELTA AIRLINES	O	21147	1162	10/09/75	JT8D-15 (HK3)	403	[ST AVBORNE ACCESSORY GROUP 12/18/00; STD VCV]

A/C TYPE	CURRENT REG. NO.	LAST KNOWN OPERATOR (OWNER)	STATUS	ORIGINAL MSN	LINE NO.	DEL. DATE	ENG. TYPE	FLEET NO.	PREV. REG. [COMMENTS]
B727-232 (A)	N404DA	DELTA AIRLINES	0	21148	1163	11/05/75	JT8D-15 (HK3)	404	[ST AVBORNE ACCESSORY GROUP 01/31/01; STD OPF; TO BE BU]
B727-232 (A)	N405DA	DELTA AIRLINES	0	21149	1164	11/12/75	JT8D-15 (HK3)	405	[ST AVBORNE ACCESSORY GROUP 01/31/01; STD OPF]
B727-232 (A)	N406DA	DELTA AIRLINES	0	21150	1165	12/03/75	JT8D-15 (HK3)	406	[ST AVBORNE ACCESSORY GROUP 01/31/01]
B727-232 (A)	N409DA	DELTA AIRLINES	0	21153	1183	01/28/76	JT8D-15 (HK3)	409	[ST AVBORNE ACCESSORY GROUP 01/31/01]
B727-232 (A)	N411DA	DELTA AIRLINES	0	21223	1207	10/21/76	JT8D-15	411	[ST AVBORNE ACCESSORY GROUP 01/31/01; STD GYR]
B727-232 (A)	N412DA	DELTA AIRLINES	0	21232	1208	08/19/76	JT8D-9A (HK3)	412	[ST AVBORNE ACCESSORY GROUP; TO BE BU]
B727-232 (A)	N413DA	DELTA AIRLINES	0	21233	1211	08/25/76	JT8D-9A (HK3)	413	[ST AVBORNE ACCESSORY GROUP; STD VCV]
B727-227 (A) (RE)	N14GA	(B.F. GOODRICH/ROHR INC.)	0	21246	1216	07/30/76	JT8D-217C/-15A		N445BN, N570PE, HS-PTA [PARKED TNN FOR MX]
B727-227 (A)	N73751	(FINO)	0	21247	1217	07/27/76	JT8D-9A		N446BN [RT LESSOR; PARKED TUS]
B727-227 (A)	N76752	(FINO)	0	21248	1218	10/29/76	JT8D-9A		N447BN [RT LESSOR; PARKED TUS]
B727-227 (A) (F)	N76753	(FINO)	0	21249	1219	10/28/76	JT8D-9A		N448BN [RT LESSOR; CVTD TO FRTR TUS; STD MZJ]
B727-232 (A)	N415DA	DELTA AIRLINES	0	21257	1214	10/28/76	JT8D-9A (HK3)	415	[ST AVGROUP ACCESSORY GROUP; TO BE BU VCV]
B727-232 (A)	N416DA	DELTA AIRLINES	0	21258	1223	12/01/76	JT8D-15 (HK3)	416	[ST REPUBLIC ADVANCED FREIGHTER 10/31/00]
B727-243 (A)	N575PE	CONTINENTAL AIRLINES (USTC)	0	21268	1229	12/20/76	JT8D-9A		I-DIRB [STD MHV]
B727-243 (A)	N17407	CONTINENTAL AIRLINES	0	21270	1231	11/19/76	JT8D-9A		N1235E, I-DIRJ, N577PE [RT FSBU 11/99; STD MZJ]
B727-232 (A)	N418DA	DELTA AIRLINES	0	21271	1242	01/27/77	JT8D-15 (HK3)	418	[ST REPUBLIC ADVANCED FREIGHTER 10/31/00; STD VCV]
B727-232 (A)	N420DA	DELTA AIRLINES	0	21273	1244	02/02/77	JT8D-15	420	[ST AVBORNE ACCESSORY GROUP 01/31/01]
B727-232 (A)	N421DA	DELTA AIRLINES	0	21274	1245	02/09/77	JT8D-15 (HK3)		[ST REPUBLIC ADVANCED FREIGHTER 04/27/00; STD VCV]
B727-2B6 (A) (F)	N721SK	CUSTOM AIR TRANSPORT (KALITTA LSG)	0	21298	1246	03/16/77	JT8D-15		CN-RMP [ALL WHITE; NO TITLES; STD OPF]
B727-2L5 (A)	5A-DIG	LIBYAN ARAB AIRLINES	0	21333	1259	04/25/77	JT8D-15		
B727-227 (A) (F)	N79754	(FINO)	0	21363	1258	04/20/77	JT8D-9A		N449BN [RT LESSOR; CVTD TO FRTR TUS]
B727-227 (A)	N86426	(FINO)	0	21364	1261	05/19/77	JT8D-17R		N450BN, N322AS [RT LESSOR 12/99; STD TUS]
B727-230 (A)	N302FV	(FINO)	0	21442	1326	03/17/78	JT8D-15 (HK)		D-ABKM, TC-AFP
B727-281 (A)	N252RL	PACIFIC AIR EXPRESS	0	21456	1318	02/10/78	JT8D-17		JA8354, HL7356, H4-PAE [STD SBD LESS ONE ENGINE]
B727-2M7 (A)	N79751	SERVIVENSA (FSBU)	0	21457	1302	11/01/77	JT8D-17R		N724RW, LV-MCD, YV-77C, XA-MXE, YV-768C [RT LESSOR; STD TUS]
B727-212 (A)	N86425	(FINO)	0	21459	1329	03/31/78	JT8D-17		9V-SGE, N296AS [RT LESSOR; PARKED TUS]
B727-225 (A) (RE)	N8883Z	SABRE AIRWAYS	0	21580	1435	01/25/79	JT8D-217C/-15		
B727-2A1 (A)	N216AP	MEXICANA (AIRPLANES III)	0	21600	1679	11/03/80	JT8D-17		PP-SNI, XA-MXG, XA-MXJ [RT AEROUSA; STD GYR]

A/C TYPE	CURRENT REG. NO.	LAST KNOWN OPERATOR (OWNER)	STATUS	ORIGINAL MSN	LINE NO.	DEL. DATE	ENG. TYPE	FLEET NO.	PREV. REG. [COMMENTS]
B727-256 (A)	N903RF	IBERIA	0	21609	1369	07/28/78	JT8D-9		EC-DCC [ST REPUBLIC FINANCIAL 01/01; PARKED IGM]
B727-256 (A)	EC-DCD	IBERIA	0	21610	1380	08/30/78	JT8D-9		[ST REPUBLIC FINANCIAL 01/01]
B727-230 (A)	N303FV	(FINO)	0	21619	1407	11/03/78	JT8D-15 (HK)		D-ABKP, TC-AFN [TO TUS 01/30/99 FOR FRTR CONV]
B727-231 (A)	N64346	TRANS WORLD AIRLINES	0	21633	1464	04/05/79	JT8D-9A		[LRF 09/11/00, RTD; RT PEGA 09/29/00; STD TUS]
B727-287 (A)	N915PG	ECUATORIANA (PACA)	0	21689	1427	12/21/78	JT8D-17		LV-MIN, HC-BXU [RT PEGA; PARKED TUS 10/24 AS HC-BXU]
B727-256 (A)	EC-DDV	IBERIA	0	21778	1490	06/12/79	JT8D-9		[RTD 08/98, BEING BU MAD]
B727-256 (A)	EC-DDY	IBERIA	0	21780	1499	07/03/79	JT8D-9		[RTD 06/98, BEING BU MAD]
B727-256 (A)	N904RF	IBERIA	0	21781	1501	07/09/79	JT8D-9		EC-DDZ [ST REPUBLIC FINANCIAL; PARKED IGM]
B727-231 (A)	N54348	TRANS WORLD AIRLINES (PEGA)	0	21967	1563	03/18/80	JT8D-9A	4348	[RT PEGA 10/27/00; STD TUS 10/30/00]
B727-231 (A)	N54350	TRANS WORLD AIRLINES (PEGA)	0	21969	1567	02/29/80	JT8D-9A	4350	[RT PEGA 11/06/00; STD TUS 11/07/00]
B727-231 (A)	N54351	TRANS WORLD AIRLINES (PEGA)	0	21983	1569	02/13/80	JT8D-9A	4351	[LRF 09/30/00; RT PEGA 12/22/00; STD TUS 12/22/00]
B727-231 (A)	N54352	TRANS WORLD AIRLINES (PEGA)	0	21984	1574	02/20/80	JT8D-9A	4352	[RT PEGA; STD TUS 12/31/00]
B727-231 (A)	N54353	TRANS WORLD AIRLINES (PEGA)	0	21985	1576	02/21/80	JT8D-15	4353	[LRF 07/31/00; RT PEGA 09/05/00; STD TUS]
B727-223 (A)	N897AA	(PEGA)	0	22013	1659	09/15/80	JT8D-15 (HK3)	897	[LRF 12/02/00; PARKED TUS]
B727-2J4 (A)	PP-SFQ	VASP	0	22079	1588	03/11/80	JT8D-17		[PARKED CGH; NOT CVTD TO FRTR; BEING BU]
B727-243 (A)	N570C	(FSBU)	0	22165	1635	07/02/80	JT8D-9A		I-DIRP, N583PE, N17413, TV-TPA, 5V-SBB, 5V-TPA, 5Y-AXD
B727-2D3 (A) (RE)	YV-844C	SERVIVENSA	0	22270	1709	06/23/81	JT8D-217C/17		N57001, JY-AFV [DERELICT CCS]
B727-228 (A)	N191RD	(DODSON AVIATION)	0	22290	1724	03/10/81	JT8D-15		F-GCDI, YA-FAX [PARKED OLATHE, KANSAS]
B727-269 (A)	N169KT	(WTCI)	0	22359	1652	09/05/80	JT8D-17R		N8291V, 9K-AFA
B727-2B6 (A)	PP-LBO	FLY S.A. LINHAS AEREAS	0	22377	1633	06/30/80	JT8D-15		CN-RMR, N614AG [DERELICT GRU; NO ENGINES]
B727-223 (A) (RE)	N703AA	(B.F. GOODRICH/ROHR INC.)	0	22461	1750	05/26/81	JT8D-217C/-15A		[PARKED COMMODORE AVIATION, MIA]
B727-223 (A) (RE)	N705AA	(B.F. GOODRICH/ROHR INC.)	0	22462	1751	06/02/81	JT8D-217C/-15A		[PARKED PAE; RE-ENGINED]
B727-223 (A)	N710AA	AMERICAN AIRLINES	0	22467	1765	07/15/81	JT8D-15 (HK3)	710	[LRF 01/28/01; RT LESSOR 03/01/01; FERRIED TO TUS 03/01/01]
B727-221 (A)	N366PA	(FSBU)	0	22538	1782	04/22/82	JT8D-17R		CP-2365 [RT FSBU 01/06/00; PARKED MIA]
B727-221 (A)	N370PA	(WFBN)	0	22542	1799	05/26/82	JT8D-17R (HK3)		CP-2385 [EXPORTED TO BOLIVIA]

A/C TYPE	CURRENT REG. NO.	LAST KNOWN OPERATOR (OWNER)	STATUS	ORIGINAL MSN	LINE NO.	DEL. DATE	ENG. TYPE	FLEET NO.	PREV. REG. [COMMENTS]
PRESERVED									
B727-025	HK-2541	(MEDELLIN METROPARQUE)	P	18281	143	05/11/65	JT8D-7B		N8130N [DONATED TO METROPARQUE FOR DISPLAY 08/93]
B727-022	N7001U	(MUSEUM OF FLIGHT FOUND.)	P	18293	1	10/06/64	JT8D-7		[WFU AND PRESERVED 04/14/91]
B727-022	N7002U	(SFO COMMUNITY COLLEGE)	P	18294	3	06/24/64	JT8D-7		
B727-022	N7004U	(NATIONAL AIR & SPACE MUSEUM)	P	18296	5	10/29/63	JT8D-7B		[1ST 727 IN SERVICE, 03/64]
B727-022	N7015U	(SAN JOSE STATE UNIVERSITY)	P	18307	38	04/16/64	JT8D-7B		
B727-022	N7017U	(CHICAGO MUS. OF SCIENCE & INDUSTRY)	P	18309	47	05/27/64	JT8D-7B		[LS 11/14/91; TO CHI. MUS. OF SCI. & IND. (CGX)]
B727-022	N7020U	UNITED AIRLINES	P	18312	60	07/16/64	JT8D-7B		[TO PURDUE IND 04/01/93; ARR LAF 04/02/93]
B727-022	XA-JJA	TAESA	P	18326	142	05/21/65	JT8D-7B		N7034U, YV-80C, XA-RLM [FOR DISPLAY AND USE AS TICKET OFFICE, MEX]
B727-051	N461US	(EAST COAST AERO TECH)	P	18797	90	11/12/64	JT8D-7B		N973PS, XA-MEN [PRESERVED BED]
B727-014	N460US	(THIEF RIVER TECH SCHOOL)	P	18910	159	06/27/65	JT8D-7B		N972PS, XA-IUP
B727-051	N474US	(ALEXANDRIA TECHNICAL COLLEGE)	P	18944	209	12/17/65	JT8D-7B		[TO ALEXANDRIA TECH COLLEGE, MN 05/28/92]
B727-081	N3211M	(METRO TECH VOCATIONAL	P	18951	237	03/04/66	JT8D-7		JA8316, HP-620, N500JJ, N55AJ, D-AJAA, OO-JAA, G-BMUE, TC-AJU [STD IN OKLAHOMA CITY] DISTRICT 22)
B727-193	OB-1256	AERO PERU	P	19305	300	08/05/66	JT8D-7B		N2979G, PP-CJH, OB-R-1256 [DISPLAYED MX BASE, LIM]
B727-109	2722	TAIWANESE AIR FORCE	P	19520	466	09/27/67	JT8D-7		B-1820 [PRESERVED IN AIDC CORPORATION IN TAICHUNG, TAIWAN]
B727-228	F-BOJA	AIR FRANCE	P	19543	541	03/24/68	JT8D-7		[PRESERVED AT MERVILLE]
B727-214	N218TT	(TULSA COUNTY VOCATIONAL COLLEGE)	P	19684	503	01/12/68	JT8D-7		N529PS, F-BPJV [GROUND INSTRUCTION 12/92]
B727-109C	2723	TAIWANESE AIR FORCE	P	20111	695	02/28/69	JT8D-7		B-1822 [PRESERVED IN CHINA AVIATION SCHOOL OF CHINA INSTITUTE OF TECHNOLOGY, TAIPEI, TAIWA
B727-228	F-BPJK	AIR FRANCE	P	20202	774	11/26/69	JT8D-7		[AT ANNECY AIRPORT]
SCRAPPED									
B727-025	XA-GBP	AEROEXO	S	18252	8	02/28/64	JT8D-7B		N8101N, HK-2717X, XB-GBP [WFU 10/95 FOR PARTS]
B727-025	N727RL	(CHARLOTTE AIRCRAFT)	S	18253	11	11/15/63	JT8D-7B		N8102N, EL-GOL [SCR 02/89]
B727-025	5N-AWV	KABO AIR	S	18254	13	12/12/63	JT8D-7B		N8103N [SCR 02/90]
B727-025	N8105N	NEW WORLD AVIATION	S	18256	16	03/13/64	JT8D-7B		5N-AWX [SCR 04/90]
B727-025	N901TS	US AIR SHUTTLE	S	18257	17	01/30/64	JT8D-7B		N8106N [ST TRACOR 01/18/96, BU MHV]
B727-025	N8108N	(AVIATION SALES)	S	18259	25	03/12/64	JT8D-7B		[SCR 04/82]
B727-025	N8109N	(AVIATION SALES)	S	18260	29	03/27/64	JT8D-7B		[SCR 06/82]

A/C TYPE	CURRENT REG. NO.	LAST KNOWN OPERATOR (OWNER)	STATUS	ORIGINAL MSN	LINE NO.	DEL. DATE	ENG. TYPE	FLEET NO.	PREV. REG. [COMMENTS]
B727-025	N8110N	(CHARLOTTE AIRCRAFT)	S	18261	30	03/26/64	JT8D-7B		[SCR 07/81]
B727-025	N8111N	(AVIATION SALES)	S	18262	41	04/30/64	JT8D-7B		[SCR 09/82]
B727-025	N8112N	(AVIATION SALES)	S	18263	45	05/29/64	JT8D-7B		[SCR 05/82]
B727-025	N8113N	(AVIATION SALES)	S	18264	53	06/23/64	JT8D-7B		[SCR 04/82]
B727-025	N8114N	(AVIATION SALES)	S	18265	54	06/26/64	JT8D-7B		[SCR 06/82]
B727-025	N8115N	(AVIATION SALES)	S	18266	61	07/28/64	JT8D-7B		[SCR 06/82]
B727-025	N902TS	US AIR SHUTTLE	S	18267	62	08/07/64	JT8D-7B		N8116N [BU OKC, AAR ALLEN, WFU 04/92]
B727-025	N8117N	TRUMP SHUTTLE	S	18268	71	09/02/64	JT8D-7B		[SCR 11/89]
B727-025	OB-R1081	AERO PERU	S	18269	74	09/14/64	JT8D-7B		N8118N [SCR 09/83]
B727-025	N903TS	US AIR SHUTTLE	S	18272	89	11/12/64	JT8D-7B		N8121N [ST TRACOR 01/18/96, BU]
B727-025	N8139N	(AVIATION SALES)	S	18290	201	11/30/65	JT8D-7B		[SCR 02/82]
B727-022	N7005U	(AERO CONTROLS)	S	18297	6	11/27/63	JT8D-7B		N68644 [TO BE BU]
B727-022	N7006U	(AERO CONTROLS)	S	18298	7	11/23/63	JT8D-7B		[BU 2/92, SHELTON, REG CX 05/96; AERO CONTROLS]
B727-022	N7007U	(AERO CONTROLS)	S	18299	9	12/18/63	JT8D-7B		[SCR SHELTON 10/94]
B727-022	N7008U	(AERO CONTROLS)	S	18300	10	01/22/64	JT8D-7B		[SCR SHELTON 94]
B727-022	N7009U	(AERO CONTROLS)	S	18301	12	03/11/64	JT8D-7B		[SCR SHELTON 10/94]
B727-022	N7010U	(AERO CONTROLS)	S	18302	19	01/20/64	JT8D-7B		[BU 6/92 SHELTON, WA, REG CX 05/96]
B727-022	N7011U	(AERO CONTROLS)	S	18303	22	02/06/64	JT8D-7B		[ST AERO CONTROLS 04/07/92, TO BE BU]
B727-022	N7012U	(AERO CONTROLS)	S	18304	23	02/14/64	JT8D-7B		[ST AERO CONTROLS 02/28/92, TO BE BU]
B727-022	N7013U	(AERO CONTROLS)	S	18305	27	03/20/64	JT8D-7B		[BU SHELTON, WA, REG CX 05/96]
B727-022	N7014U	UNITED AIRLINES	S	18306	34	04/07/64	JT8D-7B		[SCR SHELTON 93]
B727-022	N7016U	UNITED AIRLINES	S	18308	40	05/01/64	JT8D-7B		[SCR SHELTON 93]
B727-022	N7018U	UNITED AIRLINES	S	18310	48	06/08/64	JT8D-7B		[ST AERO CONTROLS 02/27/92, TO BE BU]
B727-022	N7019U	UNITED AIRLINES	S	18311	55	06/29/64	JT8D-7B		[ST AERO CONTROLS 02/28/92, TO BE BU]
B727-022	N7021U	UNITED AIRLINES	S	18313	66	08/07/64	JT8D-7B		[ST AERO CONTROLS 02/28/92, TO BE BU]
B727-022 (F)	N157FE	FEDERAL EXPRESS	S	18314	73	09/16/64	JT8D-7B		N7022U [DERELICT DHN 06/95]
B727-022 (F)	N158FE	FEDERAL EXPRESS	S	18315	77	09/24/64	JT8D-7B		N7023U [ST AERO CONTROLS FOR PARTS]
B727-022 (F)	N159FE	FEDERAL EXPRESS	S	18316	80	10/07/64	JT8D-7B		N7024U [SCR GWO 05/94]
B727-022 (F)	N160FE	FEDERAL EXPRESS	S	18317	88	11/02/64	JT8D-7B		N7025U [SCR GWO 05/94]
B727-022 (F)	N162FE	FEDERAL EXPRESS	S	18318	95	12/03/64	JT8D-7B		N7026U [SCR GWO 05/94]
B727-022 (F)	N163FE	FEDERAL EXPRESS	S	18319	110	01/27/65	JT8D-7B		N7027U [SCR GWO 05/94]
B727-022	N28KA	KEY AIRLINES (WORLDCORP)	S	18320	119	05/05/65	JT8D-7		N7028U [BU GWO BY WORLDCUP LEASING]
B727-022	YV-839C	AVENSA	S	18325	141	05/12/65	JT8D-7B		N7033U, YV-82C, XA-LEX [BU CCS]
B727-022	YV-763C	AVENSA	S	18327	144	05/24/65	JT8D-7B		N7035U, YV-81C [SOLD AS SCRAP 05/98]
B727-023	N1971	AMERICAN AIRLINES (CALDWELL)	S	18427	18	01/25/64	JT8D-7		[BU MXE 03/98]
B727-023	CP-2322	AEROSUR (IASG)	S	18428	21	02/21/64	JT8D-7B		N1972, CC-CLJ, N1972 [BU OPF 1999]
B727-023	OB-1728	AVIANDINA (AIR VENTURES)	S	18433	44	05/26/64	JT8D-7B		N1977, ZS-IJG, P4-BAA [BU OPF]
B727-023	XA-SXZ	TAESA	S	18436	58	07/17/64	JT8D-7B		N1980 [BEING BU MIA]
B727-023	N1981	(RAM AIR SALES)	S	18437	59	07/24/64	JT8D-7B		CP-2278 [BU MIA BY BMI 1998]

A/C TYPE	CURRENT REG. NO.	LAST KNOWN OPERATOR (OWNER)	STATUS	ORIGINAL MSN	LINE NO.	DEL. DATE	ENG. TYPE	FLEET NO.	PREV. REG. [COMMENTS]
B727-023	N1984	(A/C SUPPORT & PARTS)	S	18440	69	08/28/64	JT8D-7B		YL-BAF [BU MIA]
B727-023	N1985	AV ATLANTIC (CSAV)	S	18441	97	12/18/64	JT8D-7B		[BEING DISMANTLED JNB]
B727-023	N1986	AMERICANA DE AVIACION (ALGI)	S	18442	105	01/22/65	JT8D-7B		[TO BE BU BY AMERICAN INTL.]
B727-023	CP-2320	AIR TRANSPORT INC.	S	18445	115	02/24/65	JT8D-7B		N1989, CC-CLZ, N81871 [BU OPF]
B727-023	N1992	AMERICAN AIRLINES	S	18448	131	04/12/65	JT8D-7		[BU MDW (AERO CONTROLS, BF AMR)]
B727-023	CP-2370	AEROSUR (MIAMI JET LEASE)	S	18449	132	04/27/65	JT8D-7B		N1993, N801MJ [BEING BU MIA]
B727-022	N72700	BOEING	S	18464	2	03/12/63	JT8D-7		N1784B [PROTOTYPE; DERELICT AT PAE, THEN SCR]
B727-031	N850TW	EXPRESS ONE	S	18569	36	04/29/64	JT8D-7		[SCR; DAL 03/94]
B727-031	N851TW	TRANS WORLD AIRLINES	S	18570	39	04/25/64	JT8D-7		[BU MCI 02/03/00]
B727-031	N854TW	TRANS WORLD AIRLINES	S	18573	49	06/05/64	JT8D-7B		[BU KANSAS CITY; AIRFRAME ST UAM/GAT]
B727-031	N855TW	TRANS WORLD AIRLINES	S	18574	56	07/10/64	JT8D-7B		[BU KANSAS CITY; AIRFRAME ST UAM/GAT]
B727-031	N856TW	TRANS WORLD AIRLINES	S	18575	57	07/14/64	JT8D-7B		[ST PINNACLE A/C; BU MCI 01/26/00]
B727-031	N857TW	TRANS WORLD AIRLINES	S	18576	63	08/11/64	JT8D-7B		[ST PINNACLE A/C; BU MCI 01/25/00]
B727-031	N858TW	TRANS WORLD AIRLINES	S	18577	64	07/31/64	JT8D-7		[SCR MXE 10/86]
B727-031	N859TW	TRANS WORLD AIRLINES	S	18578	68	08/18/64	JT8D-7		[SCR GWO 05/94]
B727-076	N18480	CONTINENTAL AIRLINES	S	18741	72	09/28/64	JT8D-7B		VH-TJA, N91891, N40AF [BU MHV]
B727-076	XA-SHT	QUASSAR (CORS)	S	18742	81	10/28/64	JT8D-7B		VH-TJB, YN-BWX, PT-TCF, HK-3442X, TC-ATU, N66510, HH-PRI, TG-ANP, HP-1179TLN [BU OPF 09/95]
B727-077	N134CA	AMERICANA DE AVIACION (AVEG)	S	18744	86	11/01/64	JT8D-7B		VH-RMF, PT-TCD, N8140P, TC-AJS [STRIPPED OF ALL USEFUL PARTS; HULK EXTANT, LIMA 04/95]
B727-031	N849TW	TRANS WORLD AIRLINES	S	18750	70	09/03/64	JT8D-7		[SCR 09/89]
B727-031	N848TW	TRANS WORLD AIRLINES	S	18751	75	08/18/64	JT8D-7B		[ST PINNACLE A/C; BU MCI 01/26/00]
B727-031	HC-BPL	SAETA	S	18753	83	10/26/64	JT8D-7		N846TW [BU GYE]
B727-031	N845TW	TRANS WORLD AIRLINES	S	18754	84	10/28/64	JT8D-7		[SCR 03/89]
B727-031	N844TW	TRANS WORLD AIRLINES	S	18755	87	11/09/64	JT8D-7B		[ST PINNACLE A/C; BU MCI 01/25/00]
B727-078	N4367J	LADECO AIRLINES (ILFC)	S	18796	108	01/28/65	JT8D-7B		9Y-TCQ, N307BN, CC-CFG [BU DMAFB; FUSELAGE TO DROSS METALS]
B727-051	N463US	NORTHWEST AIRLINES	S	18799	102	12/23/64	JT8D-7B		N976PS [ST IASG]
B727-051	S9-TBA	TRANSAFRIK (IASG)	S	18801	120	03/02/65	JT8D-7B		N465US, N978PS, 5N-MAM [BU LUANDA LATE 1996]
B727-051	TC-AJZ	TOROSAIR	S	18802	128	03/31/65	JT8D-7B		N466US, N837N, G-BMYT, N802SC [BU ISTANBUL 01/92]
B727-051	N287AT	AMERICAN TRANS AIR	S	18805	179	09/10/65	JT8D-7B		N469US, N5608, N151FN [SCR TOTAL AEROSPACE SERVICES 05/94]
B727-051	N5609	DESTINATION "ATLANTIS"	S	18806	188	10/07/65	JT8D-7B		N470US [SUNK IN BISCAYNE BAY, FL AS ARTIFICIAL REEF 09/93]

A/C TYPE	CURRENT REG. NO.	LAST KNOWN OPERATOR (OWNER)	STATUS	ORIGINAL MSN	LINE NO.	DEL. DATE	ENG. TYPE	FLEET NO.	PREV. REG. [COMMENTS]
B727-035	N290AT	AMERICAN TRANS AIR	S	18812	92	11/19/64	JT8D-7		N4611, N158FN [SCR GWO 05/94]
B727-035	N149FN	AERO CONTINENTE (CARGO A/C)	S	18814	100	12/16/64	JT8D-7B		N4613, HK-3229X [USED FOR SPARES]
B727-035	C-GOFA	FIRST AIR	S	18815	106	01/18/65	JT8D-7B		N4614, N154FN [SPARES USE; AFT FUSELAGE AS CABIN EGRESS SIMULATOR AT YOW]
B727-081	HR-SHE	SAHSA	S	18823	135	04/21/65	JT8D-7A		JA8303, D-AHLL [BU FT LAUDERDALE 1991]
B727-077	N133CA	AMERICANA DE AVIACION (AVEG)	S	18844	171	08/20/65	JT8D-7B		VH-RMD, PT-TCC [REMAINS AS HULK AT LIM]
B727-035 (F)	N728CK	KALITTA AMERICAN INTL. AIRWAYS	S	18847	187	11/11/65	JT8D-7B		N4619, N937FT [SCR OSCODA]
B727-095	N36KA	KEY AIRLINES (WORLDCORP)	S	18850	180	10/07/65	JT8D-7B		N1631, N836N [PARTED OUT MOBILE, AL; ULL EXTANT]
B727-022	YV-837C	AVENSA	S	18853	189	10/14/65	JT8D-7B		N7046U, C-GVCH, YV-87C, XA-BTO [BU CCS]
B727-022 (F)	N7054U	FEDERAL EXPRESS	S	18861	212	12/28/65	JT8D-7B		[SCR SHELTON BY 03/94]
B727-022 (F)	N7055U	FEDERAL EXPRESS	S	18862	216	01/12/66	JT8D-7B		[SOLD TO AERO CONTROLS FOR PARTS]
B727-022 (F)	N7062U	FEDERAL EXPRESS	S	18869	253	04/15/66	JT8D-7B		[SOLD TO AERO CONTROLS FOR PARTS]
B727-046	N11412	AIR TAXI INTL.	S	18874	166	07/15/65	JT8D-7A		JA8307, HL-7308, HK-2420X, N91392 [SCR]
B727-044	N61944	PANAMANIAN AIR FORCE	S	18894	168	08/10/65	JT8D-7		ZS-DYO, ZS-SBC, N727CR, FAP-400, FAP500A, HP-500A [BU OPF 05/98]
B727-044	HK-3133X	AVIANCA (NAAS)	S	18895	173	08/23/65	JT8D-7B		ZS-DYP, ZS-SBD, EL-AIZ, N95GS [BU COSTA RICA, ATASCO]
B727-044 (F)	N723JE	CUSTOM AIR TRANSPORT	S	18896	184	09/30/65	JT8D-7B		ZS-DYR, ZS-SBE, HK-2957X, N5458E, 5Y-CGO [BU MIA BY CHARTER AMERICA HOLDINGS]
B727-031	N831TW	TRANS WORLD AIRLINES	S	18902	138	05/20/65	JT8D-7B		[BU KANSAS CITY; AIRFRAME ST UAM/GAT]
B727-031	N839TW	TRANS WORLD AIRLINES	S	18904	152	06/24/65	JT8D-7B		[BU KANSAS CITY; AIRFRAME ST UAM/GAT]
B727-031 (F)	N240NE	(DODSON INTL.)	S	18906	176	09/09/65	JT8D-7B (HK3)		N841TW [PERMANENTLY RTD ALEXANDRIA, LA; BU BY UNIVERSAL ASSET MGMT]
B727-031	N230NE	EXPRESS ONE	S	18907	224	01/29/66	JT8D-7B		N842TW [BU SHERMAN, TX 03/95]
B727-081	N63584	PANAMA AIR	S	18920	174	08/22/65	JT8D-7B		JA8306, HP-619API [BU OPF 05/98]
B727-081 (F)	N110NE	EXPRESS ONE	S	18952	306	08/30/66	JT8D-7B		JA8317, D-AHLN [BU FOR PARTS]
B727-025	N905TS	US AIR SHUTTLE	S	18966	214	12/21/65	JT8D-7B		N8142N [ST DALFORT FOR SCRAP]
B727-025	HK-3798X	ISLENA COLOMBIA	S	18969	225	01/29/66	JT8D-7B		N8145N, PP-CJK [BU BOGOTA 02/97, EX-ISLENA]
B727-025	N907TS	TRUMP SHUTTLE	S	18973	245	03/25/66	JT8D-7B		N8149N [BU OKC]
B727-025 (F)	N300NE	(DODSON INTL.)	S	18974	252	04/15/66	JT8D-7B (HK3)		N8150N, C-FACW [RTD ALEXANDRIA, LA; BU BY UNIVERSAL ASSET MGMT]
B727-021	N314AS	ALASKA AIRLINES	S	18992	206	12/18/65	JT8D-7B		N314PA [SCR SHELTON 1994; HULK STILL EXTANT 12/95]
B727-021	N91392	(AIR TAXI INTL.)	S	18997	235	02/28/66	JT8D-7A		N319PA, N721PC, HK-3396X [BU SHELTON]
B727-051	N11415	AIR TAXI INTL.	S	19122	319	09/28/66	JT8D-7B		N476US, N105RK, N727TA, HK-3151X, HK-3803X [SCR]

A/C TYPE	CCURRENT REG. NO.	LAST KNOWN OPERATOR (OWNER)	STATUS	ORIGINAL MSN	LINE NO.	DEL. DATE	ENG. TYPE	FLEET NO.	PREV. REG. [COMMENTS]
B727-051	N480US	NORTHWEST AIRLINES	S	19126	363	01/30/67	JT8D-7B		[BU]
B727-023	N1997	AERO UNION	S	19128	196	11/24/65	JT8D-7B		[BU MHV 12/95 (AIRCRAFT LEASING)]
B727-023	EL-GPX	AIR GEMINI (GLIDER LTD)	S	19129	197	11/19/65	JT8D-7B		N1998, ZS-NMZ [BU ST. PIETERSBURG, SOUTH AFRICA]
B727-023	ZS-NSA	MILLIONAIR CHARTER	S	19130	213	12/21/65	JT8D-7B		N1901 [BU JNB]
B727-023	CP-2274	(FSBU)	S	19132	228	02/16/66	JT8D-7B		N1903, N8277Z [BU MIA]
B727-021C	N705A	EXPRESS.NET AIRLINES (CLARK)	S	19134	289	07/21/66	JT8D-7B (HK3)		N339PA, N1186Z [BU IGM]
B727-022 (F)	N7082U	FEDERAL EXPRESS	S	19146	452	09/05/67	JT8D-7B		[USED FOR SPARES]
B727-090C	C-FRST	FIRST AIR	S	19169	320	10/27/66	JT8D-7B		N797AS [RTD 06/10/00; BEING BU SPARES YOW]
B727-023 (F)	N1908	KITTY HAWK AIR CARGO	S	19183	267	05/19/66	JT8D-7B		[BU ROSWELL; HULK ONLY]
B727-023 (F)	N1909	EMERY WORLDWIDE AIRLINES	S	19184	282	06/24/66	JT8D-7B		[BU DAYTON 05/95]
B727-162	N65910	AMERICANA DE AVIACION (AVEG)	S	19243	273	05/20/66	JT8D-7B		N7282, PT-TYN, N113CA [REMAINS AS HULK AT LIM]
B727-095	N727ZV	KEY AIRLINES (WORLDCORP)	S	19249	304	08/25/66	JT8D-7B		N1633, G-BFGM, HK-2960X, 4X-BAE, EI-BUI [BU GWO]
B727-046	HK-3246X	ACES COLOMBIA (ARON)	S	19280	373	02/17/67	JT8D-7B		JA8319, HP-661 [BU BOGOTA 01/96]
B727-059	FAC-1145	SATENA COLOMBIA	S	19303	357	01/16/67	JT8D-7		HK-1337 [BU BOGOTA]
B727-030C	N726EV	EVERGREEN INTL. AIRLINES	S	19311	399	04/28/67	JT8D-7B		D-ABIO, N703EV, PP-SRZ, T3-ATB, N4936S [BEING BU MZJ]
B727-030C	OB-1141	AERO PERU	S	19312	409	05/18/67	JT8D-7B		D-ABIU, OB-R-1141 [BU LIMA 06/94]
B727-044C	PT-MDG	DIGEX AERO CARGO (BANCO NACIONAL)	S	19319	441	08/18/67	JT8D-7B		ZS-EKX, ZS-SBG, N26877, 9Q-CBS, N750UA, PT-TDG [BEING BU OPF 10/97]
B727-191 (F)	YV-813C	AEROLATIN (GEN AVN TECH)	S	19393	401	04/19/67	JT8D-9A		N7272F, N299BN, PT-TYJ, N8140G, TC-AJR, N135CA, PT-SAW, TG-LKA, HH-JJD, HP-1178TLN, HC-BSP [BU OPF]
B727-109	2721	TAIWANESE AIR FORCE	S	19399	380	03/03/67	JT8D-7		B-1818 [BU]
B727-029	OB-1277	AERO PERU	S	19400	400	04/25/67	JT8D-7B		OO-STA, PP-CJJ, OB-R-1277 [BU LIM 05/95]
B727-023	N1934	(FSBU)	S	19429	362	01/31/67	JT8D-7B		CP-2277 [BU OPF]
B727-295	N701US	US AIR	S	19444	445	01/29/68	JT8D-15		N1639 [BU AT AMA BY AEROCAR]
B727-295	N702US	US AIR	S	19445	455	12/18/67	JT8D-15		N1640 [BU AT AMA BY POLA (HULK EXTANT 06/97)]
B727-295	N703US	US AIR	S	19446	471	12/11/67	JT8D-15		N1641 [BU AT AMA BY AEROCAR]
B727-295	N705US	US AIR	S	19447	477	12/15/67	JT8D-15		N1642 [BU AT AMA BY POLA; HULK EXTANT 06/97]
B727-295	N707US	US AIR	S	19448	496	01/08/68	JT8D-15		N1643 [BU AT AMA BY AEROCAR]
B727-295	N708US	US AIR	S	19449	500	01/01/68	JT8D-15		N1644 [BU AMA 02/98]
B727-235	N4730	PAN AM	S	19450	464	12/12/67	JT8D-7B		[TO AMARILLO FIRE SERVICE]
B727-235	N4731	PAN AM	S	19451	483	12/19/67	JT8D-7B		[BU]

A/C TYPE	CURRENT REG. NO.	LAST KNOWN OPERATOR (OWNER)	STATUS	ORIGINAL MSN	LINE NO.	DEL. DATE	ENG. TYPE	FLEET NO.	PREV. REG. [COMMENTS]
B727-235	N4732	DELTA AIRLINES (GECC)	S	19452	492	12/26/67	JT8D-7B		[SOLD TO UAM, THEN TO NORTEK REPAIR CENTER FOR PARTS]
B727-235	N4733	PAN AM	S	19453	506	01/19/68	JT8D-7B		[BU MIA 03/93]
B727-235	N4734	PAN AM	S	19454	509	01/23/68	JT8D-7B		[BU AMA 07/95]
B727-235 (F)	N4735	KALITTA AMERICAN INTL. AIRWAYS	S	19455	513	01/25/68	JT8D-7B		[BU OSCODA]
B727-235	N4736	DELTA AIRLINES (GECC)	S	19456	515	01/30/68	JT8D-7B		[SOLD TO UAM, THEN TO NORTEK REPAIR CENTER FOR PARTS]
B727-235	N4738	DELTA AIRLINES	S	19458	525	02/16/68	JT8D-7B		[BU AMA]
B727-235	N4739	PAN AM (POLA)	S	19459	530	02/23/68	JT8D-7B		[BU MIA 03/93]
B727-235	N4743	PAN AM (POLA)	S	19463	552	03/29/68	JT8D-7B		[BU MIA 03/93]
B727-235	N4745	PAN AM	S	19465	554	04/03/68	JT8D-7B		[BU]
B727-235	N4746	AEROEJECUTIVO (POLA)	S	19466	561	04/18/68	JT8D-7B		[BU MIA 03/93]
B727-235	N4747	PAN AM	S	19467	566	04/26/68	JT8D-7B		[BU AMA 05/93]
B727-235	N4748	PAN AM	S	19468	567	04/30/68	JT8D-7B		[BU]
B727-235	N4751	PAN AM (POLA)	S	19471	590	06/18/68	JT8D-7B		[BU MIA 03/93]
B727-235	N4752	PAN AM (POLA)	S	19472	591	06/20/68	JT8D-7B		[BU MIA 03/93]
B727-235	N4753	PAN AM (POLA)	S	19473	606	07/23/68	JT8D-7B		[BU MIA 03/93]
B727-223 (A)	N6801	AMERICAN AIRLINES	S	19476	523	02/19/68	JT8D-9		[SCR 04/94]
B727-223 (A)	N6802	AMERICAN AIRLINES	S	19477	533	02/29/68	JT8D-9		[SCR 04/94]
B727-223 (A)	N6803	AMERICAN AIRLINES	S	19478	535	03/05/68	JT8D-9		[SCR 04/94]
B727-027	OB-1512	AMERICANA DE AVIACION	S	19499	444	08/10/67	JT8D-9A		N7289, PT-TYK, HK-3483X [USED FOR SPARES]
B727-027	N65894	AMERICANA DE AVIACION (AVEG)	S	19501	453	08/31/67	JT8D-7B		N7292, PT-TYL, N129CA [HULK ONLY; TO BE BU LIM]
B727-173C	HI-312CT	DOMINICANA DE AVIACION	S	19505	432	07/15/67	JT8D-7B		N691WA, HI-312 [BU MIA BY BMI 10/94]
B727-224	N88701	CONTINENTAL AIRLINES	S	19510	577	05/21/68	JT8D-9A		[SCR GWO 05/01/94, USED AS HOME, BENOIT, MS]
B727-224	N88702	CONTINENTAL AIRLINES	S	19511	581	05/28/68	JT8D-9A		[BU ATHV]
B727-224	N88703	CONTINENTAL AIRLINES	S	19512	582	05/29/68	JT8D-9A		[SCR IGM 1994 (AIRMOTIVE)]
B727-224	N88704	CONTINENTAL AIRLINES	S	19513	595	06/26/68	JT8D-9A		[BU TUS 09/95; AIR OPS INTL.]
B727-284	SX-CBF	OLYMPIC AIRWAYS	S	19536	433	10/22/70	JT8D-9A		N7270L, N3182B, SX-CBF [BUILT AS PROTOTYPE -200, CVTD TO -2C8, THEN TO -284; BEING BU ATH]
B727-222	N7620U	UNITED AIRLINES	S	19537	563	05/03/68	JT8D-7B		[LRF 09/23/93; FERRIED LAS ADM 03/29/94; SCR]
B727-222	N7621U	UNITED AIRLINES	S	19538	580	05/31/68	JT8D-7B		[BU]
B727-222	N7622U	UNITED AIRLINES	S	19539	583	06/09/68	JT8D-7B		[SCR ARDMORE 05/94]
B727-222	N7623U	UNITED AIRLINES	S	19540	584	06/12/68	JT8D-7B		[BU ADM (FOR PARTS)]
B727-222	N7624U	UNITED AIRLINES	S	19541	585	06/15/68	JT8D-7B		[FERRIED LAS ADM 04/27/94; SCR]
B727-222	N7625U	UNITED AIRLINES	S	19542	586	06/19/68	JT8D-7B		[SCR ARDMORE 05/94]
B727-228	F-BOJD	AIR FRANCE	S	19546	572	05/21/68	JT8D-7		[BU PARIS]
B727-231	9Q-CHS	AIR TRANSPORT OFFICE	S	19558	528	03/06/68	JT8D-9A		N12301 [BU OKC 05/21/97 BY ATO]
B727-231	N12302	TRANS WORLD AIRLINES	S	19559	550	04/02/68	JT8D-9A		[BU SPRINGFIELD 95 (GATS/NARA)]

A/C TYPE	CURRENT REG. NO.	LAST KNOWN OPERATOR (OWNER)	STATUS	ORIGINAL MSN	LINE NO.	DEL. DATE	ENG. TYPE	FLEET NO.	PREV. REG. [COMMENTS]
B727-231	N12303	TRANS WORLD AIRLINES	S	19560	565	05/02/68	JT8D-9A		[SCR OPF 1995]
B727-231	N12306	TRANS WORLD AIRLINES (AIRCORP)	S	19563	587	06/17/68	JT8D-9A		[SCR SAT 06/94]
B727-231	N12307	TRANS WORLD AIRLINES	S	19564	601	07/19/68	JT8D-9A		[SCR FT. LAUDERDALE 06/94]
B727-059	HK-1400	SAM COLOMBIA	S	19662	484	11/03/67	JT8D-7		[USED AS FLIGHT ATTENDANT TRAINER AT BOG]
B727-059	HK-1401	AVIANCA	S	19663	491	11/15/67	JT8D-7		[WFU; BU BOG 01/93]
B727-214	F-BPJU	AIR CHARTER	S	19683	488	12/18/67	JT8D-7		N528PS [USED AS FIRE DUMP AT ORY; BU 02/01]
B727-214	N908TS	US AIR SHUTTLE	S	19685	556	04/02/68	JT8D-7B		N530PS, N530EA [ST TRACOR 01/18/96; BU MHV]
B727-214	N909TS	US AIR SHUTTLE	S	19686	570	05/03/68	JT8D-7B		N531PS, N531EA [BU MIA BY BMI 05/94]
B727-214	N911TS	US AIR SHUTTLE	S	19689	610	07/20/68	JT8D-7B		N534PS, N534EA [ST TRACOR 01/18/96; BU]
B727-223 (A)	N6822	AMERICAN AIRLINES	S	19700	673	01/02/69	JT8D-9A		[CVTD -223; ST AV. SALES CO.; BEING BU ARD]
B727-223 (A)	N6823	AMERICAN AIRLINES	S	19701	677	01/14/69	JT8D-9A		[CVTD -223; ST AV. SALES CO.; BEING BU ARD]
B727-224	N88706	CONTINENTAL AIRLINES	S	19797	598	07/03/68	JT8D-9A		[BU TUCSON AIR OPS INTL.]
B727-224	N88708	CONTINENTAL AIRLINES	S	19799	612	08/02/68	JT8D-9A		[SCR MHV 1993 (TRACOR)]
B727-224	N88709	CONTINENTAL AIRLINES	S	19800	616	08/02/68	JT8D-9A		[SCR GWO 1994 (MEMPHIS)]
B727-224	N88710	CONTINENTAL AIRLINES	S	19801	617	08/07/68	JT8D-9A		[BU TUCSON AIR OPS INTL.]
B727-224	N88711	CONTINENTAL AIRLINES	S	19802	621	08/14/68	JT8D-9A		[SCR KINGMAN 1993 (AIRMOTIVE)]
B727-224	N88712	CONTINENTAL AIRLINES	S	19803	623	08/20/68	JT8D-9A		[SCR MOJAVE 1993 (TRACOR)]
B727-224	N88713	CONTINENTAL AIRLINES	S	19804	624	08/28/68	JT8D-9A		[BU TUCSON AIR OPS INTL.]
B727-114	YV-840C	AVENSA	S	19815	443	08/03/68	JT8D-7B		N977PS, XA-TUY, HK-2637X, HP-1001, FAP-501, N726JE, YV-90C, XA-NAD [BU]
B727-121C	2724	TAIWANESE AIR FORCE	S	19818	462	09/25/67	JT8D-7		N388PA, XV-NJB, B-188 [BU]
B727-231	N52310	TRANS WORLD AIRLINES	S	19829	629	09/17/68	JT8D-9A		[ST MAX POWER AEROSPACE, INC., SMYRNA, TN, FOR HOME CONVERSION]
B727-231	N52311	TRANS WORLD AIRLINES	S	19830	633	09/20/68	JT8D-9A		[ST MAX POWER AEROSPACE, INC., SMYRNA, TN, FOR HOME CONVERSION]
B727-231	N52312	TRANS WORLD AIRLINES	S	19831	636	09/27/68	JT8D-9A		[ST MAX POWER AEROSPACE, INC., SMYRNA, TN, FOR HOME CONVERSION]
B727-231	N52313	TRANS WORLD AIRLINES	S	19832	642	10/11/68	JT8D-9A		[ST MAX POWER AEROSPACE, INC., SMYRNA, TN, FOR HOME CONVERSION]
B727-123	HK-3973X	AIR COLOMBIA	S	19838	551	03/29/68	JT8D-7B		N1964 [BU 03/00]
B727-063	N32720	BOEING	S	19846	555	04/09/68	JT8D-7		OB-R-902 [BU 1990]
B727-228	TC-AFC	ISTANBUL AIRLINES	S	19863	691	02/19/69	JT8D-7B		F-BOJG, N874UM [BU ISTANBUL 01/98]
B727-228	TC-AFB	ISTANBUL AIRLINES	S	19864	696	02/28/69	JT8D-7B		F-BPJH [BU ISTANBUL 01/98]
B727-228	N601AR	KEY AIRLINES (AARL)	S	19865	703	03/27/69	JT8D-7		F-BPJI [BU 1993, OKC; REG CX 05/96]
B727-022QC	NZ7273	ROYAL NEW ZEALAND AF	S	19893	643	10/15/68	JT8D-7		N7436U [SCR WOODBURNE 1984]
B727-222	N7626U	UNITED AIRLINES	S	19899	614	08/16/68	JT8D-7B		[LS 11/05/92; SCR SHELTON 1993]
B727-222	N7628U	UNITED AIRLINES	S	19901	620	08/06/68	JT8D-7B		[LS 11/25/92, SCR SHELTON BY 03/94]
B727-222	N7629U	UNITED AIRLINES	S	19902	622	10/02/68	JT8D-7B		[ST AERO CONTROLS, SCR SHELTON 1994]
B727-222	N7630U	UNITED AIRLINES	S	19903	627	10/04/68	JT8D-7B		[RTD LAS; WILLIS AERONAUTICAL SERVICES]
B727-222	N7631U	UNITED AIRLINES	S	19904	637	11/04/68	JT8D-7B		[ST AERO CONTROLS 01/19/93, SCR SHELTON 07/94]

A/C TYPE	CURRENT REG. NO.	LAST KNOWN OPERATOR (OWNER)	STATUS	ORIGINAL MSN	LINE NO.	DEL. DATE	ENG. TYPE	FLEET NO.	PREV. REG. [COMMENTS]
B727-222	N7632U	UNITED AIRLINES	S	19905	639	11/08/68	JT8D-7B		[SCR ARD 05/94 (AERO CONTROLS)]
B727-222	N7633U	OMNI AIR EXPRESS	S	19906	644	11/15/68	JT8D-7B		[BU FOR PARTS]
B727-222	N7634U	UNITED AIRLINES	S	19907	651	11/21/68	JT8D-7B		[ST AERO CONTROLS 06/06/94, SCR SHELTON 1994]
B727-222	N7636U	OMNI AIR EXPRESS	S	19909	656	12/12/68	JT8D-7B		[BF UAL FOR SCRAP 08/01/94]
B727-222	N7637U	UNITED AIRLINES	S	19910	659	12/27/68	JT8D-7B		[ST AERO CONTROLS 07/14/94; SCR SHELTON 1994]
B727-222	N7641U	UNITED AIRLINES	S	19914	676	01/15/69	JT8D-7B		[ST AERO CONTROLS 04/24/95; SCR SHELTON 1995]
B727-251	N388PA	PAN AM	S	19976	683	01/24/69	JT8D-7B		N257US [BU TUS 08/96 (PEGASUS CAPITAL)]
B727-251	N259US	DISCOVERY AIRLINES (PACA)	S	19978	692	02/21/69	JT8D-7B		[BEING BU TUS]
B727-251	N261US	NORTHWEST AIRLINES	S	19980	706	03/28/69	JT8D-7B		[BU MZJ 05/97 (CL AIRCRAFT)]
B727-251	N262US	NORTHWEST AIRLINES	S	19981	736	07/11/69	JT8D-7B		[BU FT LAUDERDALE 12/92]
B727-251	N265US	NORTHWEST AIRLINES	S	19984	744	08/05/69	JT8D-7B		[BU SHERMAN GRAYSON 10/93]
B727-291	YV-465C	ZULIANA DE AVIACION	S	19992	526	02/18/68	JT8D-7B		N7277F, N407BN, N377PA [BU MIA BY BMI 1998]
B727-291	TC-AJY	TOROSAIR	S	19993	549	03/23/68	JT8D-7B		N7278F, N408BN [WFU AND BU OPF 11/93]
B727-291	N715US	US AIR	S	19994	654	01/30/69	JT8D-15		N7279F, N1648 [BU AMA 02/98]
B727-291	N717US	US AIR	S	19995	666	01/31/69	JT8D-15		N7275N, N1649 [SCR AMA 09/94]
B727-231	N94314	(AERO CONTROLS)	S	20047	675	02/03/69	JT8D-9A		[BU OPF 11/03/99]
B727-231	N64315	TRANS WORLD AIRLINES	S	20048	679	02/11/69	JT8D-9A		[BU OPF]
B727-231	N64319	(SPINNAKER CAPITAL)	S	20052	709	04/18/69	JT8D-9A (HK3)		[UNCOMPLETED HULL AND STRINGER REPAIR; BEING BU TUS]
B727-228	N602AR	KEY AIRLINES (AARL)	S	20075	704	03/28/69	JT8D-7		F-BPJJ [BU 1993 OKC; REG CX 05/96]
B727-231	N64324	TRANS WORLD AIRLINES	S	20099	734	07/02/69	JT8D-9A		[USED FOR SPARES]
B727-295	N709US	US AIR	S	20139	613	10/09/68	JT8D-15		N1645 [SCR AMA 09/94]
B727-295	N713US	US AIR	S	20140	638	10/28/68	JT8D-15		N1646 [SCR AMA 09/94]
B727-295	N716US	US AIR	S	20141	649	11/15/68	JT8D-15		N1647 [BU AMA 02/98]
B727-225	N8825E	AMERIJET INTL.	S	20144	742	08/22/69	JT8D-7B		[DEREGISTERED 01/29/96 AS SCR MHV]
B727-225	N8826E	EASTERN AIRLINES	S	20145	749	08/29/69	JT8D-7B		[BU 02/96 (TRACOR) MHV]
B727-225	N8827E	AMERIJET INTL.	S	20146	751	09/10/69	JT8D-7B		[DEREGISTERED 01/29/96 AS SCR MHV]
B727-225	N8829E	EASTERN AIRLINES	S	20148	769	11/07/69	JT8D-7B		[BU MOJAVE 1996 (RAM AIR SALES, BF IALI]
B727-225	N917TS	SUN PACIFIC	S	20149	770	11/12/69	JT8D-7B		N8830E [BU TUS]
B727-214	N718US	DALLAS AEROSPACE	S	20161	714	04/17/69	JT8D-7B		N535PS, N858N [BU DALLAS AEROSPACE; BU AMA 11/97]
B727-214	N719US	DALLAS AEROSPACE	S	20163	723	05/19/69	JT8D-7B		N537PS, N855N [BU SOLAIR]
B727-214	N720US	DALLAS AEROSPACE	S	20164	724	05/23/69	JT8D-7B		N538PS, N856N [BU SOLAIR]
B727-214	N721US	DALLAS AEROSPACE	S	20165	725	05/27/69	JT8D-7B		N539PS, N857N [BU DALLAS]
B727-214	N722US	DALLAS AEROSPACE	S	20166	727	06/04/69	JT8D-7B		N540PS, N860N [BU SOLAIR]
B727-214	N723US	DALLAS AEROSPACE	S	20167	728	06/04/69	JT8D-7B		N541PS, N861N [BU SOLAIR]

A/C TYPE	CURRENT REG. NO.	LAST KNOWN OPERATOR (OWNER)	STATUS	ORIGINAL MSN	LINE NO.	DEL. DATE	ENG. TYPE	FLEET NO.	PREV. REG. [COMMENTS]
B727-214	N728US	DALLAS AEROSPACE	S	20168	740	07/17/69	JT8D-7B		N542PS, N895N [BU SOLAIR]
B727-214	LV-WDS	AERO SUR	S	20169	743	07/31/69	JT8D-7B		N545PS, N376PA [RT LESSOR 05/94; BU EZE]
B727-223 (A)	N6829	AMERICAN AIRLINES	S	20182	702	03/31/69	JT8D-9		[BU AMA; HULK EXTANT 06/97]
B727-228	F-BPJL	AIR FRANCE	S	20203	776	12/06/69	JT8D-7		[BU OKC 1992]
B727-116	N7829A	ALASKA AIRLINES	S	20217	625	05/28/69	JT8D-7B		N304BN, XA-SEW, HK-2605X [ST AERO CONTROLS 06/93]
B727-231	N54325	TRANS WORLD AIRLINES	S	20232	785	02/03/70	JT8D-9A		[BU OPF]
B727-231	N54326	TRANS WORLD AIRLINES	S	20233	786	02/05/70	JT8D-9A		[ST AERO TURBINE; BU OPF]
B727-231	N54327	TRANS WORLD AIRLINES	S	20234	790	02/17/70	JT8D-9A		[BU OPF]
B727-224	N88714	CONTINENTAL AIRLINES	S	20243	646	04/24/69	JT8D-9A		[BU TUCSON; AIR OPS INTL.]
B727-295	YV-463C	ZULIANA DE AVIACION (CISA)	S	20248	761	10/10/69	JT8D-7A		N1650, N371PA [BU MIA 06/94]
B727-295	N372PA	BRANIFF (CISL)	S	20249	763	10/17/69	JT8D-7A		N11651 [BU TUCSON 08/96 (PEGASUS CAPITAL)]
B727-254	N915TS	US AIR SHUTTLE	S	20252	783	01/06/70	JT8D-7B		N549PS, N549EA [BU MHV 05/97 (TRACOR); NOSE SECTION AT LAX]
B727-247	XA-SYI	ALLEGRO AIR (IALI)	S	20264	756	10/16/69	JT8D-15		N2802W, N324AS [RT IALI 08/30/99; PARKED AT MIA MINUS ENGINES AND MANY PARTS; BU?]
B727-247	HI-637CA	DOMINICANA DE AVIACION (IALI)	S	20267	762	11/14/69	JT8D-9		N2805W, N325AS, N606CA [SCR MIA 09/94]
B727-281	N743US	US AIR	S	20285	868	08/17/71	JT8D-9A		JA8335, N870N [BU MARANA 10/95; EVERGREEN FOR RAM AIR SALES]
B727-251	N269US	NORTHWEST AIRLINES (CISL)	S	20291	753	09/12/69	JT8D-7B		[BU TUS 09/96]
B727-251	N270US	NORTHWEST AIRLINES (CISL)	S	20292	754	09/22/69	JT8D-7B		[BU 11/97 TUCSON (AERO CONTROLS)]
B727-251	N273US	NORTHWEST AIRLINES (CISA)	S	20295	772	11/18/69	JT8D-7B		[STD TUS; BEING SCR]
B727-2B7	HI-612CA	DOMINICANA DE AVIACION (FSBU)	S	20302	789	05/28/70	JT8D-7B		N750VJ, N404BN, N207US, N379PA [BU TUS 09/93]
B727-231	N54329	TRANS WORLD AIRLINES	S	20307	792	03/10/70	JT8D-9A		[BU OPF]
B727-231	N54330	TRANS WORLD AIRLINES	S	20308	795	04/02/70	JT8D-9A		[LRF 03/15/98; ST AERO TURBINE; BU OPF]
B727-231	N54331	TRANS WORLD AIRLINES	S	20309	796	04/07/70	JT8D-9A		[BU OPF]
B727-231	N54332	TRANS WORLD AIRLINES	S	20310	802	05/04/70	JT8D-9A		[BU OPF]
B727-214	N729US	DALLAS AEROSPACE	S	20366	828	11/24/70	JT8D-7B		N546PS, N859N [SCR AMA 12/91]
B727-214	N730US	DALLAS AEROSPACE	S	20367	832	05/27/71	JT8D-7B		N544PS, N896N [SCR AMA 08/94]
B727-225	N8836E	EASTERN AIRLINES	S	20379	818	06/17/70	JT8D-7B		[SCR MOJAVE 02/96 (AGES)]
B727-225	N8837E	AMERIJET INTL.	S	20380	820	06/30/70	JT8D-7B		[DEREGISTERED 01/29/96 AS SCR; MHV]
B727-224	N88715	CONTINENTAL AIRLINES	S	20384	794	02/12/70	JT8D-9A		[BU TUCSON 09/95]
B727-224	N32716	CONTINENTAL AIRLINES	S	20385	800	03/16/70	JT8D-9A		[BU KINGMAN 1997; FUSELAGE PIECES STILL EXTANT]
B727-224	N32717	CONTINENTAL AIRLINES	S	20386	801	03/27/70	JT8D-9A		[SCR; MHV 1993 (TRACOR)]
B727-224	N32718	CONTINENTAL AIRLINES	S	20387	804	04/08/70	JT8D-9A		[BU TUCSON; AIR OPS INTL.]
B727-228	F-BPJO	AIR FRANCE	S	20410	846	12/11/70	JT8D-7		[BU OKLAHOMA CITY 1992]
B727-225	N8842E	AMERIJET INTL.	S	20416	834	09/01/70	JT8D-7B		[DEREGISTERED 01/29/96 AS SCR MHV]
B727-0C3	HK-3739X	(KELLSTROM AVIATION)	S	20418	812	01/29/71	JT8D-9A		PP-CJE [BEING BU TUS 02/28/98]

A/C TYPE	CURRENT REG. NO.	LAST KNOWN OPERATOR (OWNER)	STATUS	ORIGINAL MSN	LINE NO.	DEL. DATE	ENG. TYPE	FLEET NO.	PREV. REG. [COMMENTS]
B727-0C3	9Q-DDD	KABO AIR	S	20419	815	01/29/71	JT8D-9A		PP-CJF [BU 1992]
B727-1F8	9N-ABD	ROYAL NEPAL AIRLINES	S	20421	826	08/16/72	JT8D-9A		N1781B [SCR HAM 10/22/93]
B727-1J1	HI-212CT	DOMINICANA DE AVIACION	S	20426	829	10/18/72	JT8D-9A		N1781B, HI-212 [DERELICT SDO]
B727-230	N876UM	AIR ALFA (ATAS)	S	20430	830	01/27/71	JT8D-15		N1785B, D-ABCI, TC-ALF, TC-JUC, TC-IHO, TC-ALK [BU BY AGES]
B727-230	TC-ALM	AIR ALFA (ATAS)	S	20431	851	03/11/71	JT8D-15		D-ABDI, N878UM, TC-ALB, TC-JUH, TC-IKO [FOR USE BY FIRE SERVICE AT EAST MIDLANDS]
B727-264	N433ZV	FLORIDA WEST	S	20433	838	10/26/70	JT8D-17R		XA-TAB, TC-JFB, HK-3606X [SCR MIA 05/94]
B727-264	N434ZV	AVIANCA (ARON)	S	20434	842	11/09/70	JT8D-17R		XA-TAC, TC-JFA, HK-3605X [BU MOBILE, AL 1995]
B727-281	JU-1054	MIAT-MONGOLIAN AIRLINES	S	20435	787	02/22/71	JT8D-9A		JA8328, HL7348, MT-1054 [BU ULAANBAATAR]
B727-225	N8848E	EASTERN AIRLINES	S	20446	841	11/19/70	JT8D-7B		[SCR MHV 1995 (AGES)]
B727-225	N30GA	B.F. GOODRICH/ROHR INC.	S	20448	844	11/23/70	JT8D-7B		N8850E, N920TS, HS-PTB [SCR]
B727-231	N54333	TRANS WORLD AIRLINES	S	20460	859	03/31/71	JT8D-9A		[LRF 04/12/99, BU MIA]
B727-231	N54335	TRANS WORLD AIRLINES	S	20462	862	05/01/71	JT8D-9A		[LRF 07/23/99; ST UNIVERSAL ASSET MGMT; BU OPF]
B727-224	N32722	SUN PACIFIC	S	20464	809	03/03/72	JT8D-9A		N1781B [BU TUS]
B727-281	N740US	US AIR	S	20467	866	06/25/71	JT8D-9A		JA8333, N869N [BU MARANA 10/95 (RAM AIR SALES)]
B727-281	N904PG	KOREAN AIR	S	20468	849	06/25/71	JT8D-9A		JA8330, HL7349, N528MD [BU TUS (HAMILTON AVN.)]
B727-231	N54336	TRANS WORLD AIRLINES	S	20490	863	05/11/71	JT8D-9A		[ST AV SYS; BEING BU OPF]
B727-231	N54337	TRANS WORLD AIRLINES	S	20491	864	05/26/71	JT8D-9A		[BU OPF]
B727-281	N741US	US AIR	S	20509	867	07/15/71	JT8D-9A		JA8334, N867N [WFU MZJ JET FINANCING INC.]
B727-281	N745US	US AIR	S	20510	876	05/24/72	JT8D-9A		JA8337, N863N [BU MARANA 10/95 (TOTAL AEROSPACE SERVICES)]
B727-017	N327JL	SAN	S	20513	861	04/23/71	JT8D-9A		CF-CUS, N117TA, XA-GUV, HC-BIB [BU MIA BY BMI 07/98]
B727-230	OM-CHD	AIR SLOVAKIA	S	20526	871	02/25/72	JT8D-15		D-ABGI, N879UM [BU QLA 04/18/00]
B727-228	F-BPJR	AIR FRANCE	S	20538	872	02/11/72	JT8D-7		[BU ORY 05/93; COCKPIT USED FOR INSTRUCTION AT AFR TRAINING SCHOOL "VILGENIS"]
B727-228	F-BPJS	AIR FRANCE	S	20539	873	01/18/72	JT8D-7		N1790B [BU OKC 1993]
B727-228	F-BPJT	AIR FRANCE	S	20540	874	03/13/72	JT8D-7		N1781B, N1788B [BU OKC 1992]
B727-276 (A)	VH-TBH	AUSTRALIAN AIRLINES	S	20553	991	11/20/73	JT8D-15		N1787B [BU GWO 06/92]
B727-276 (A)	N3459D	AUSTRALIAN AIRLINES	S	20554	1027	04/04/74	JT8D-15		VH-TBI [SCR GWO 05/94]
B727-281	N746US	US AIR	S	20568	878	04/17/72	JT8D-9A		N1788B, JA8338, N862N [BU]
B727-281	N747US	US AIR	S	20569	879	03/24/72	JT8D-9A		JA8339, N866N [BU NORTEK]
B727-281	N748US	US AIR	S	20570	880	03/10/72	JT8D-9A		JA8340, N865N [BU NORTEK]
B727-256 (A)	EC-CAI	IBERIA	S	20592	882	04/29/72	JT8D-9		N1791B [TRADED IN TO BOEING; BU MADRID 01/96]

A/C TYPE	CURRENT REG. NO.	LAST KNOWN OPERATOR (OWNER)	STATUS	ORIGINAL MSN	LINE NO.	DEL. DATE	ENG. TYPE	FLEET NO.	PREV. REG. [COMMENTS]
B727-256 (A)	EC-CAJ	IBERIA	S	20593	883	04/20/72	JT8D-9		LV-VFJ, EC-328 [TRADED IN TO BOEING; BU MAD 01/96]
B727-256 (A)	EC-GSX	IBERIA	S	20594	885	05/06/72	JT8D-9		EC-CAK, YV-126C [BEING SCR OPF]
B727-256 (A)	EC-GSY	IBERIA	S	20597	909	04/14/73	JT8D-9		N1788B, EC-CBC, YV-127C [BEING BU OPF]
B727-256 (A)	EC-GSZ	IBERIA	S	20599	911	03/23/73	JT8D-9		N1788B, EC-CBE, YV-129C [BEING BU OPF]
B727-256 (A)	EC-GTA	IBERIA	S	20605	921	02/14/73	JT8D-9		EC-CBK, YV-128C [BEING SCR OPF]
B727-225 (A)	YV-856C	J D VALENCIANA	S	20614	897	09/27/72	JT8D-15		N8851E, N351PA [BU BY TURBO AIR HOLDINGS]
B727-225 (A)	N8855E	FLORIDA WEST AIRLINES	S	20617	900	10/11/72	JT8D-15		[BU MIA 07/98 BY A/C SUPPORT AND PARTS FOR AVATAR ALLIANCE]
B727-225 (A)	N8856E	FLORIDA WEST AIRLINES	S	20618	901	10/16/72	JT8D-15		[BU MIA 07/98 BY A/C SUPPORT AND PARTS FOR AVATAR ALLIANCE]
B727-225 (A)	N8859E	FLORIDA WEST (AERO)	S	20621	904	11/03/72	JT8D-15		[DMGD MIA 08/24/92 IN HURRICANE; BU MIA 03/04/96 BY BMI]
B727-225 (A)	N355PA	TAESA (CITG)	S	20625	941	05/08/73	JT8D-15		N8863E, XA-THU [ST QWEST AIR PARTS; BEING BU GYR]
B727-232 (A)	N27783	CONTINENTAL AIRLINES	S	20638	926	04/12/73	JT8D-15		N456DA, N515PE [ST WORLD AIR LEASE; BU MIA]
B727-232 (A)	N14788	(JET CAPITAL)	S	20642	944	06/01/73	JT8D-15		N460DA, N519PE [BU MHV]
B727-232 (A)	N10791	CONTINENTAL AIRLINES (PACA)	S	20645	961	07/27/73	JT8D-15		N463DA, N522PE [BU TUS 02/01]
B727-232 (A)	N45793	(PEGA)	S	20647	968	08/31/73	JT8D-15		N465DA, N524PE [RT LESSOR; PARKED TUS; BEING BU]
B727-247 (A)	N2810W	DELTA AIRLINES	S	20648	895	08/04/72	JT8D-9A		[ST AVBORNE ACCESSORY GROUP; BEING BU]
B727-247 (A)	N2811W	DELTA AIRLINES	S	20649	896	08/16/72	JT8D-9A		[ST AVBORNE ACCESSORY GROUP; BEING BU]
B727-224 (A)	N24728	GEMINI AIRCRAFT CORP.	S	20657	970	09/07/73	JT8D-9A		[BU]
B727-224 (A)	N66734	CONTINENTAL AIRLINES (FSBU)	S	20663	1073	10/02/74	JT8D-9A		[RT WORLD AIR LEASE; BU MIA FOLLOWING #2 ENGINE FAILURE]
B727-281 (A)	YV-96C	AVENSA	S	20727	966	08/23/73	JT8D-9A		JA8348, N775BE [AT PUERTO ORDAZ; BU 11/25/98]
B727-264 (A)	XA-DAT	SARO (GPAG)	S	20787	999	12/14/73	JT8D-17R		[BU MEX 06/03/97 (GECAS)]
B727-232 (A)	N482DA	DELTA AIRLINES	S	20862	1042	06/17/74	JT8D-15		[ST AVBORNE ACCESSORY GROUP 11/99; BEING BU VCV]
B727-281 (A)	YV-843C	SERVIVENSA	S	20876	1026	04/04/74	JT8D-17R		JA8350, N772BE, YV-93C, XA-MXH, XA-TGU [BU]
B727-281 (A)	YV-95C	AVENSA	S	20878	1034	05/02/74	JT8D-9A		JA8352N774BE [BU CCS]
B727-230 (A)	N727SA	COMTRAN	S	20906	1092	03/07/75	JT8D-15		D-ABKH, 5N-MML [BU MIA BY BMI 08/05/98]
B727-232 (A)	N489DA	DELTA AIRLINES	S	21019	1097	03/20/75	JT8D-15		[ST AVBORNE ACC. GROUP 06/05/00; BU VCV]
B727-232 (A)	N493DA	DELTA AIRLINES	S	21062	1127	05/01/75	JT8D-15		[ST AVBORNE ACC. GROUP 06/05/00; BU VCV]
B727-232 (A)	N497DA	DELTA AIRLINES	S	21077	1147	06/18/75	JT8D-15 (HK3)	497	[BU BY AVBORNE ACCESSORY GROUP]
B727-232 (A)	N498DA	DELTA AIRLINES	S	21142	1155	08/28/75	JT8D-15 (HK3)		[BU BY AVBORNE ACCESSORY GROUP]
B727-232 (A)	N499DA	DELTA AIRLINES	S	21143	1156	09/04/75	JT8D-15 (HK3)	499	[ST AVBORNE ACCESSORY GROUP; BU OPF 03/01]
B727-232 (A)	N400DA	DELTA AIRLINES	S	21144	1157	09/12/75	JT8D-15 (HK3)		[BU BY AVBORNE ACCESSORY GROUP]
B727-232 (A)	N401DA	DELTA AIRLINES	S	21145	1159	09/17/75	JT8D-15 (HK3)	401	[BU BY AVBORNE ACCESSORY GROUP]
B727-232 (A)	N402DA	DELTA AIRLINES	S	21146	1161	10/02/75	JT8D-15 (HK3)	402	[BU BY AVBORNE ACCESSORY GROUP]

A/C TYPE	CURRENT REG. NO.	LAST KNOWN OPERATOR (OWNER)	STATUS	ORIGINAL MSN	LINE NO.	DEL. DATE	ENG. TYPE	FLEET NO.	PREV. REG. [COMMENTS]
B727-232 (A)	N407DA	DELTA AIRLINES	S	21151	1166	12/10/75	JT8D-15 (HK3)	407	[BU BY AVBORNE ACCESSORY GROUP]
B727-232 (A)	N408DA	DELTA AIRLINES	S	21152	1182	01/25/76	JT8D-15 (HK3)	408	[BU BY AVBORNE ACCESSORY GROUP]
B727-251 (A)	N280US	TRANSMERIDIAN (AFGR)	S	21159	1179	12/17/75	JT8D-15/-15A		[ST UNIVERSAL ASSET MGMT 05/25/00; BEING BU BY ALEXANDRIA, LA]
B727-232 (A)	N414DA	DELTA AIRLINES	S	21256	1212	10/27/76	JT8D-15 (HK3)	414	[BU BY AVBORNE ACCESSORY GROUP]
B727-232 (A)	N417DA	DELTA AIRLINES	S	21259	1224	12/08/76	JT8D-9A (HK3)	417	[BU BY AVBORNE ACCESSORY GROUP AT OPF 01/0
B727-232 (A)	N419DA	DELTA AIRLINES	S	21272	1243	01/28/77	JT8D-15 (HK3)	419	[BU BY AVBORNE ACCESSORY GROUP AT OPF 01/0
B727-2H3 (A)	TS-JHV	TUNIS AIR	S	21319	1269	06/10/77	JT8D-9A		[WFU AND USED FOR SPARES, TUNIS 12/92]
B727-222 (A)	N7296U	UNITED AIRLINES	S	21574	1451	03/05/79	JT8D-15		[BU OAK]

WRITTEN OFF

A/C TYPE	CURRENT REG. NO.	LAST KNOWN OPERATOR (OWNER)	STATUS	ORIGINAL MSN	LINE NO.	DEL. DATE	ENG. TYPE	FLEET NO.	PREV. REG. [COMMENTS]
B727-025 (F)	5Y-BMW	AERO ZAMBIA (TANA & MARA)	W	18255	14	02/28/64	JT8D-7B		N8104N [WO 06/05/98; ASMARA, ERITREA; ON DISPLAY AT EXPO SITE, LESS WINGS AND ENGINES]
B727-025	YN-BXW	AERONICA	W	18284	161	07/28/65	JT8D-7B		N8133N [WO 11/10/91 MANAGUA]
B727-022	N68650	PIEDMONT AIRLINES	W	18295	4	04/07/65	JT8D-7		[WO 07/19/67 HENDERSONVILLE, NC]
B727-022	N7030U	UNITED AIRLINES	W	18322	130	04/07/65	JT8D-7		[WO 11/11/65 SALT LAKE CITY]
B727-022	N7036U	UNITED AIRLINES	W	18328	146	06/03/65	JT8D-7		[WO 08/16/65 CHICAGO]
B727-030	9Q-CSG	CONGO AIRLINES	W	18369	125	03/19/65	JT8D-7		D-ABIN, A40-CF [WO 10/10/98 KINDU, CONGO]
B727-023	ZS-IJE	MILLIONAIR CHARTER	W	18443	111	02/10/65	JT8D-7B		N1987, OK-UGA [WO 04/27/99 LANSERIA, SOUTH AFRICA]
B727-031	N852TW	TRANS WORLD AIRLINES	W	18571	42	05/02/64	JT8D-7		[WO 08/27/88 CHICAGO]
B727-081	N124AS	ALASKA AIRLINES	W	18821	124	03/18/65	JT8D-7		JA8301, N124, XA-SEB [WO 04/05/76 KETCHIKAN, AK]
B727-081	JA8302	ALL NIPPON AIRWAYS	W	18822	126	03/27/65	JT8D-7		[WO 02/04/66 TOKYO BAY]
B727-022	TI-LRC	LACSA	W	18856	199	12/21/65	JT8D-7		N7049U, N31KA, YV-90C, N300AA [WO 05/23/88 SAN JOSE, COSTA RICA]
B727-046	HK-2421X	SAM COLOMBIA (NAAS)	W	18875	202	11/19/65	JT8D-7A		JA8308, HL-7307 [WO 08/04/93 BOGOTA]
B727-046	HK-2422X	SAM COLOMBIA (NAAS)	W	18876	217	01/07/66	JT8D-7A		JA8309, HL-7309 [WO 05/19/93 MEDELLIN]
B727-044 (F)	S9-TAN	TRANSAFRIK (IASG)	W	18893	157	07/08/65	JT8D-7B		ZS-DYN, ZS-SBB, N722GS, N93GS, TF-VLS, N188CL [WO 04/27/94 M'BANZA CONGO, ANGOLA]
B727-051C	N414EX	RYAN INTL. (EWW)	W	18899	256	05/09/66	JT8D-7B		N491US [OPF EWW/USPS C/S; WO 10/01/97 DENVER]
B727-023	N1996	AMERICAN AIRLINES	W	18901	153	06/28/65	JT8D-7		[WO 11/08/65 CINCINNATI]
B727-021	HK2559	AEROTAL	W	18994	219	01/15/66	JT8D-7		N316PA, N316AS [WO 08/04/82 SIMON BOLIVAR, COLOMBIA]
B727-021	N317PA	PAN AMERICAN	W	18995	221	01/20/66	JT8D-7		[WO 11/15/66 E. GERMANY]
B727-021	HK-2560X	AEROTAL	W	18996	233	02/19/66	JT8D-7		N318PA, N318AS [WO 11/29/82]
B727-021	HK1716	AVIANCA	W	18999	240	03/16/66	JT8D-7		N321PA [WO 03/17/88 CUCUTA, COLOMBIA]
B727-021 (F)	D2-TJB	SEAGREEN AIR TRANSPORT	W	19005	257	04/28/66	JT8D-7B		N323PA, HK-2845X, N358QS [WO 01/31/95 HUAMBO, ANGOLA]

A/C TYPE	CURRENT REG. NO.	LAST KNOWN OPERATOR (OWNER)	STATUS	ORIGINAL MSN	LINE NO.	DEL. DATE	ENG. TYPE	FLEET NO.	PREV. REG. [COMMENTS]
B727-021	HK1803	AVIANCA	W	19035	272	05/28/66	JT8D-7		N326PA [WO 11/27/89 BOGOTA, COLOMBIA]
B727-021	N327PA	PAN AMERICAN	W	19036	278	06/24/66	JT8D-7		[WO 09/03/80 SAN JOSE, COSTA RICA]
B727-021	HK-1804	SAM COLOMBIA	W	19037	284	06/22/66	JT8D-7		N328PA [WO 10/05/83 SAN ANDRES ISLAS, COLOMBIA; FUSELAGE SUNK AS ARTIFICIAL REEF]
B727-022C	N425EX	EMERY WORLDWIDE AIRLINES	W	19095	302	09/09/66	JT8D-7B		N7407U [WO 05/03/91 HARTFORD]
B727-027C	PT-TYS	TRANS BRAZIL	W	19111	297	08/14/66	JT8D-7		N7272 [WO 04/12/80 FLORIANOPOLIS, BRAZIL]
B727-086	EP-IRA	IRANAIR	W	19171	276	06/17/66	JT8D-7B		[WO 01/07/83 TEHRAN]
B727-092C	N18479	AIR MICRONESIA (COA)	W	19174	326	10/11/66	JT8D-9		N5092, CF-PXB [WO 11/21/80 YAP, CAROLINE IS.]
B727-092C	B-1018	CIVIL AIR TRANSPORT	W	19175	339	12/10/66	JT8D-9		N5093 [WO 02/16/68 TPE]
B727-022C	N7425U	UNITED AIRLINES	W	19200	416	06/19/67	JT8D-7		[WO 03/21/68 CHICAGO, IL]
B727-022C	N106FE	FEDERAL EXPRESS	W	19201	421	06/27/67	JT8D-7B (HK3)		N7426U [REG CX 05/26/99; STORM DMGD DBER; BEING USED BY EVERETT COMM. COLLEGE]
		(RFC N106FE/8)							
B727-064	XA-SEJ	MEXICANA	W	19255	331	11/08/66	JT8D-7B		[WO 09/21/69 MEX]
B727-064	XA-SEL	MEXICANA	W	19256	355	01/17/67	JT8D-7B		[WO 06/04/69 MONTERREY, MEXICO]
B727-046	G-BDAN	DAN AIR	W	19279	288	07/14/66	JT8D-7		JA8318 [WO 04/25/80 TENERIFE, CANARY IS.]
B727-193	N2969G	ALASKA AIRLINES	W	19304	287	11/01/67	JT8D-7B		[WO 09/04/71 JUNEAU, AK]
B727-014	XA-SEN	MEXICANA	W	19398	345	12/16/66	JT8D-7		N976PS [WO 10/20/73 MAZATLAN, MEXICO]
B727-082	S9-NAZ	TRANSAFRIK (EQUATORIAL)	W	19404	384	03/12/67	JT8D-7B		CS-TBK, C-GWGP, C-GWGP [WO 02/12/00 LUANDA]
B727-235	N4737	PAN AMERICAN	W	19457	518	01/31/68	JT8D-7B		[WO 07/09/82 NEW ORLEANS, LA]
B727-235	N4744	NATIONAL AIRLINES	W	19464	553	03/27/68	JT8D-7B		[WO 05/08/78 PENSACOLA, FL]
B727-224	N88705	TAN-SAHSA	W	19514	597	07/01/68	JT8D-9A		[WO 10/21/89 TEGUCIGALPA, HONDURAS]
B727-024C	HK1272	AVIANCA	W	19525	439	07/27/67	JT8D-7		N2472, N5472, N1781B [WO 09/30/75 BARRANQUILLA]
B727-214	N533PS	PACIFIC SOUTHWEST AIRLINES	W	19688	589	06/11/68	JT8D-7B		[WO 09/25/78 SAN DIEGO, CA]
B727-113C	YA-FAR	ARIANA AFGHAN	W	19690	540	03/25/68	JT8D-9		[WO 01/05/69 LONDON, ENGLAND]
B727-090QC	N766AS	ALASKA AIRLINES	W	19728	536	03/07/68	JT8D-7A		[WO 06/09/87 ANCHORAGE, AK]
B727-224	N88777	CONTINENTAL AIRLINES	W	19798	608	07/25/68	JT8D-9A		N88707 [WO 08/07/75 DENVER]
B727-116	CC-CAQ	LAN CHILE	W	19812	532	02/07/68	JT8D-7B		[WO 04/28/69 SANTIAGO, CHILE]
B727-086	EP-IRD	IRANAIR	W	19817	537	03/09/68	JT8D-7B		[WO 01/21/80 TEHRAN]
B727-121C	XV-NJC	AIR VIETNAM	W	19819	516	01/16/68	JT8D-7		N389PA [WO 09/15/74 PHAN RANG, VIETNAM]
B727-095	N1963	AMERICAN AIRLINES	W	19837	499	12/19/67	JT8D-7		[WO 04/26/76 ST THOMAS]
B727-228 (F)	N722DH	DHL AIRWAYS	W	19861	682	01/28/69	JT8D-7		F-BOJE [WO 08/31/98 KENNEDY AIRPORT, NY]
B727-022QC	N7434U	UNITED AIRLINES	W	19891	631	09/20/68	JT8D-7		[WO 01/18/69 LOS ANGELES, CA]
B727-231	5N-BBG	ADC AIRLINES	W	20054	718	05/15/69	JT8D-9A		N64321 [WO 11/07/96 LOS]
B727-046 (F)	S9-BAI	AIR GEMINI	W	20078	686	01/31/69	JT8D-9A		JA8327, N746EV, PP-ITL [WO 01/05/01 DUNDO, ANGOLA]
B727-2A7	N8790R	TRANS CARIBBEAN AIRLINES	W	20240	717	04/30/69	JT8D-		[WO 12/28/70 ST. THOMAS]
B727-224	5A-DAH	LIBYAN ARAB AIRLINES	W	20244	650	12/28/70	JT8D-		N1782B [WO 02/21/73 SINAI DESERT, LIBYA]
B727-247	TC-AJV	TOROSAIR	W	20265	758	10/16/69	JT8D-15		N2803W [WO 08/25/89 ANKARA, TURKEY]
B727-247	OB-1303	FAUCETT PERU	W	20266	760	11/14/69	JT8D-9		N2804W, OB-R-1303 [WO 09/11/90 NEWFOUNDLAND]
B727-251	N274US	NORTHWEST AIRLINES	W	20296	777	12/10/69	JT8D-7B		[WO 12/01/74 BEAR MOUNTAIN, NY]
B727-231	N54328	TRANS WORLD AIRLINES	W	20306	791	03/03/70	JT8D-9A		[WO 12/01/74 UPPERVILLE, VA]

A/C TYPE	CURRENT REG. NO.	LAST KNOWN OPERATOR (OWNER)	STATUS	ORIGINAL MSN	LINE NO.	DEL. DATE	ENG. TYPE	FLEET NO.	PREV. REG. [COMMENTS]
B727-281	JA8329	ALL NIPPON AIRWAYS	W	20436	788	03/12/71	JT8D-9A		[WO 07/30/71 MORIOKO, JAPAN]
B727-225	N8845E	EASTERN AIRLINES	W	20443	837	11/10/70	JT8D-7B		[WO 06/24/75 KENNEDY AIRPORT, NY]
B727-281	HL7350	KOREAN AIR	W	20469	852	05/10/71	JT8D-9A		JA8331 [WO 08/26/91 TAEGU, S. KOREA]
B727-281 (A)	HI-617CA	DOMINICANA DE	W	20726	962	08/09/73	JT8D-9A		JA8347, N504AV, HI-616CA [WO 09/05/93] AVIACION (IALI)
B727-232 (A)	N473DA	DELTA AIRLINES	W	20750	992	11/30/73	JT8D-15		[WO 08/31/88 DALLAS, TX]
B727-230 (A)	SX-CBI	OLYMPIC AIRWAYS	W	20791	1022	03/22/74	JT8D-15		D-ABVI, N854SY [WO 08/12/97 THESSALONIKI, GREECE]
B727-256 (A)	EC-CFJ	IBERIA	W	20820	1019	04/16/74	JT8D-9		[WO 12/07/83 MADRID, SPAIN]
B727-2D3 (A)	JY-ADU	ALIA-ROYAL JORDANIAN	W	20886	1061	08/14/74	JT8D-		[WO 04/14/79 DOHA, QATAR]
B727-2H9 (A)	TC-AKD	TALIA AIRWAYS	W	20930	1044	06/07/74	JT8D-9A		YU-AKA [WO 02/27/88 ERDZAN, CYPRUS]
B727-282 (A)	CS-TBR	TAP-AIR PORTUGAL	W	20972	1096	01/22/75	JT8D-		[WO 11/19/77 FUNCHAL, MADEIRA]
B727-2F2 (A)	TC-JBH	TURK HAVA YOLLARI	W	20982	1087	11/21/74	JT8D-		[WO 09/19/76 MT KARATEPE, TURKEY]
B727-223 (A)	N845AA	AMERICAN AIRLINES	W	20986	1125	05/15/75	JT8D-9A		[WO 02/09/98 CHICAGO, IL]
B727-2L5 (A)	5A-DIA	LIBYAN ARAB AIRLINES	W	21050	1108	02/19/75	JT8D-15		[WO 12/22/92 TRIPOLI]
B727-286 (A)	EP-IRU	IRAN AIR	W	21079	1131	07/10/75	JT8D-15		[WO 06/09/96 RASHT, IRAN]
B727-243 (A)	N571PE	CONTINENTAL AIRLINES	W	21264	1225	10/06/76	JT8D-9A		I-DIRA [WO 06/07/97 NEWARK; STRUCK TERMINAL BLDG]

A/C TYPE	CURRENT REG. NO.	LAST KNOWN OPERATOR (OWNER)	STATUS	ORIGINAL MSN	LINE NO.	DEL. DATE	ENG. TYPE	FLEET NO.	PREV. REG. [COMMENTS]
B727-2B6 (A)	PP-LBY	FLY LINEAS AEREAS (A/C INV. CORP)	W	21297	1236	12/09/76	JT8D-15		N1246E, CN-RMO, N612AG [WO 05/01/96 UIO, ECUADOR]
B727-251 (A)	N2132M	SAETA (FORTIS)	W	21322	1265	05/24/77	JT8D-15/-15A		N283US, HC-BVU [WO 08/22/97 GALAPAGOS IS.]
B727-212 (A)	PP-SRK	VASP	W	21347	1282	08/30/77	JT8D-17		9V-SGA [WO 06/08/82 FONTALEZA, BRAZIL]
B727-2F2 (A)	TC-JBR	TURKISH AIRLINES	W	21603	1389	12/19/78	JT8D-		[WO 01/16/83 ANKARA, TURKEY]
B727-230 (A)	HC-BSU	TAME	W	21622	1431	01/12/79	JT8D-15		D-ABKS, FAE622 [WO 04/20/98 BOGOTA, COLOMBIA]
B727-256 (A)	EC-DDU	IBERIA	W	21777	1487	02/13/79	JT8D-		[WO 02/19/85 DURANGO, SPAIN]
B727-232 (A)	N530DA	DELTA AIRLINES	W	21813	1552	11/30/79	JT8D-15		[WO 10/14/89 SALT LAKE CITY, UT]
B727-243 (A) (F)	VT-LCI	LUFTHANSA CARGO INDIA (LAL A/C LSG)	W	22168	1770	09/03/81	JT8D-15		I-DIRS, N586PE, N14416 [WO 07/07/99 KATHMANDU, NEPAL]
B727-2D3 (A)	JY-AFW	ALIA-ROYAL JORDANIAN	W	22271	1713	02/10/81	JT8D-		N8286V [WO 06/12/85 BEIRUT, LEBANON]
B727-228 (A)	YA-FAZ	ARIANA AFGHAN AIRLINES	W	22288	1712	02/06/81	JT8D-15		N8288V, F-GCDG [WO 03/19/98 KABUL, AFGHANISTAN]
B727-264 (A)	XA-MEM	MEXICANA	W	22414	1748	05/18/81	JT8D-17R		[WO 03/31/86 MORELIA, MEXICO]
B727-225 (A)	N819EA	EASTERN AIRLINES	W	22556	1793	04/07/82	JT8D-17AR		[WO 01/01/85 LA PAZ, BOLIVIA]

Chapter 5

Model 737

The 737 has already been built in greater numbers than any other jetliner. That success, however, did not come easily, as the third all-new Boeing jetliner entered rather late in an already crowded short-range twinjet market. In the West, the French Sud Caravelle had entered service in May 1959 and had been followed by the BAC One-Eleven in April 1965 and by the Douglas DC-9 in December 1965. On the other side of the Iron Curtain, the Tupolev Tu-104 had been placed in scheduled service in September 1956 with Tu-124 following in October 1962.

By the time the 737-100 entered service with Lufthansa in February 1968, its main rival was the DC-9, of which 83 had already been delivered to 16 airlines. Moreover, the Douglas' order book then included 502 DC-9s, while Boeing had notched orders for only 191 Model 737s. The sale of 110 Model 737-300s to United Airlines in November 1985 finally put the Boeing twinjet over the combined total of Douglas DC-9s and McDonnell Douglas MD-80s. Nineteen months later, the 737 reached another benchmark to become the best-selling Boeing jetliner when its sales went over the 1,831 total for the 727 trijet. By then, however, a new rival had entered the fray as Airbus Industrie had launched its A320 in March 1984 and flown its first single-aisle twin in February 1987. Once again Boeing was forced to play catch-up in the twinjet market, launching the Next-Generation 737 in 1993. Since then, more than 1,800 Next-Generation 737s have been sold.

For The Boeing Company and its stockholders, persistence has paid off, as nearly 5,000 737s had been sold at time of writing. In competition against Douglas and four European manufacturers of twinjets, Boeing has seen its 737 take a 45 percent share of the market.

Development of a Winner

After launching the 727 trijet in 1959, Boeing hoped not to have to come up with another jetliner for a number of years. For a while, that strategy appeared to be working, as an early inroad into the U.S. market by the French Caravelle twinjet had been blocked by the 727. Sales of British One-Eleven to Braniff Airways, in October 1961, and Mohawk Airlines, in July 1962, also appeared not to present much of a threat. In May 1963, however, Delta Air Lines chose to order DC-9s in preference to 727-100s. Two months later, American Airlines, a 727 customer since August the 1961, ordered 15 One-Elevens. After these two major trunk carriers had ordered rival twinjets, Boeing had to offer a competing design.

To reduce development costs and avoid having to come up with all-new tooling, Boeing elected to use as many existing features as possible. Thus, it chose to retain the upper-fuselage cross-section, nose, and three-crewmember cockpit design of its 707, 720, and 727 virtually unchanged. Wings for the new twinjet were to be scaled down from those of the trijet, with sweep at the quarter chord reduced from 32 to 25 degrees. Consideration was also given to retaining the rear-mounted engine installation of the 727. With the twinjet being initially planned to have eight fewer rows of seats than the trijet, this would have resulted in too many passengers sitting alongside the fuselage-mounted engines. Consequently, Boeing returned to an engine location it had first contemplated in early 1950 for a twin-engined concept study (the Model 473-47, one of many 707 forebears). In that design, the engines were to have been mounted in underwing nacelles similar to those used for the outboard engines of the company's B-47 jet bomber (and not unlike the installation of Jumo 004 turbojets in the wartime German Messerschmitt Me 262 jet fighter).

Conceived specifically to achieve low direct operating costs (DOC) over short routes, the Model 737 was first proposed with seating for 60 to 85 passengers to avoid encroaching on the market of the 727. Airlines, however, expressed preference for a larger aircraft. To meet this requirement, Boeing chose a fuselage some 10.5 feet (3.20 meters) shorter than that of the 727-100 and suitable for accommodating up to 103 passengers in a six-abreast high-density seating configuration. This revised configuration appealed to Lufthansa German Airlines, which became the launch customer on February 15, 1965, when it ordered 21 Model 737-100s. The next customer for the Boeing twinjet, United Airlines, demanded an aircraft with even greater seating, thus leading to the more successful 737-200 first ordered in April 1965.

Final assembly of the first 271 aircraft was undertaken in a new building at Boeing Field in Seattle. Starting with l/n 272 (a 737-2A8 that was delivered to Indian Airlines on December 11, 1970), however, all other 737s have been completed in the Renton plant. Production of 1,144 JT8D-powered Initial-Model 737-100s and -200s ended in 1988, with peak delivery of 114 aircraft in 1969. A total of 1,988 Classic 737-300s, -400s, and -500s powered by CFM56s were then delivered from the Renton plant between 1984 and 2000, with peak production being reached in 1992 with the delivery of 218 aircraft. Production of Next-Generation 737s was initiated at the Renton plant after Southwest Airlines became the first customer for the 737-700 in November 1993. By the end of July, 2001, when this was written, 895 Next-Generation 737s had been delivered from Renton, with an all-time delivery record of 320 aircraft being set in 1999.

737-100

Having reached project status in November 1964, the Boeing "Baby Jet" was announced publicly three months later on the strength of the initial order from Lufthansa. Powered by a pair of JT8D-7 engines rated at 14,000 pounds (62.3 kilonewtons) of static thrust housed in short

nacelles and fitted with clamshell thrust reversers, N73700 (l/n 1, s/n 19437) was Boeing-owned. It first flew on April 4, 1967, and was joined in the pre-certification program by three of the 737-130s for Lufthansa.

While the 737-100 was still under development, the competing Douglas DC-9 had been certificated for two-pilot operations. Accordingly, Boeing offered a two-pilot cockpit for the 737, and most customers chose that option. Some customers, however, were forced by their pilot union to take delivery of their 737s with provision for a third crew member. The FAA issued ATC A16WE for two-pilot operations of the 737 on December 15, 1967. Lufthansa accepted its first two 737-130s 12 days later and placed its new Boeing twinjet in revenue service on February 10, 1968.

The only other customers for new-built Series 100 aircraft were Avianca (two 737-159s) and Malaysia-Singapore Airlines (five 737-112s), which ordered aircraft powered by JT8D-9s rated at 14,500 pounds (64.5 kilonewtons) of static thrust for "hot-and-high" operations. The 30th and last of the smallest 737s (l/n 217, s/n 19772) was delivered to Malaysia-Singapore Airlines on October 31, 1969. In addition, the Boeing-owned prototype ended up being sold in 1973 to the National Aeronautics and Space Administration (NASA) for use at its Langley Research Center.

Beside the NASA aircraft, the only Series 737-100 still flying in the spring of 2001 was ex-Lufthansa l/n 3, s/n 19014, operated in Peru as OB1745 by Aero Continente.

737-200

To get its second 737 customer, Boeing was locked in a fierce competition. With Douglas marketing slightly stretched DC-9-30s for early delivery, the Seattle manufacturer countered by offering to United the lease of 727s until 737s were available. Moreover, it undertook to redesign the 737 to meet the seating and range demanded by United. The resulting 737-200 had a cabin lengthened by 6 feet 4 inches (1.93 meters) to provide for three more rows of seats (with single-class seating increasing to a maximum of 130, thus besting the DC-9-30 by 15 seats). Other modifications included a 6-foot (1.83-meter) wingspan expansion, with a resulting increase in wing area from 922 to 930 square feet (85.7 to 91.0 m^2). Standard fuel load was increased from 2,850 to 4,230 U.S. gallons (10,788 to 16,012 liters), while basic MTOW went up from 93,500 to 115,000 pounds (42,411 to 52,390 kilograms). That offer was accepted by United, which ordered a first batch of 40 737-222s on April 5, 1965. For Boeing, this willingness to cater to United's requirements eventually led to total orders from the largest U.S. carrier for 233 Series 200, 300, and 500 aircraft. More importantly, it established the 737-200 as a winning design.

The first Series 200 (l/n 6, s/n 19039) flew on August 31, 1967. Deliveries started on December 29, 1967, and United put the 737-200 into revenue service on April 28, 1968. Production of Series 200 aircraft continued for 20 years, with the last (l/n 1585, s/n 24236) being delivered to Xiamen Airlines in August 1988.

Over the years, Boeing has steadily improved the 737-200. The first significant change was made in March 1969 when the first aircraft with revised engine nacelles was delivered. Extended 45 inches (1.14 meters) rearward and fitted with target-type thrust reversers, the revised nacelles reduced significantly the risk of ingesting foreign objects when using the reversers. Moreover, some aircraft were fitted out for operation from unpaved runways with a gravel deflector on the nose gear and pipes extending forward of the engine intakes to blow away stones and other debris.

The first Advanced 737-200s with revised leading-edge flaps and slats and wider nacelle struts were delivered in April 1971, and "wide-look"

cabin fittings came online in December 1971. Along with these changes, MTOW grew in steps from 115,000 to 128,100 pounds (52,390 to 05, 58,105 kilograms), while more-powerful JT8D engines were installed.

Initial-production 737-200s were powered by JT8D-7 engines rated at 14,000 pounds (62.3 kilonewtons) of static thrust, but later -200s were built with JT8D-9s or -9As rated at 14,500 pounds (64.5 kilonewtons), JT8D-15/15As rated at 15,500 pounds (68.9 kilonewtons), JT8D-17s rated at 16,000 pounds (71.2 kilonewtons), and JT8D-17Rs rated at 17,400 pounds (77.4 kilonewtons). Hushkits have been certificated since 1992 to enable JT8D-powered 737s to comply with U.S. FAR 36 Stage 3 and ICAO Annex 16 Chapter 3 noise level requirements

Included in the total of 1,114 Series 200s were 19 T-43As supplied to the USAF as navigation trainers, a small number of aircraft fitted out as executive/VIP jets for private and government customers, and three 737-2X9s for the Indonesian Air Force with Motorola side-looking multi-mission radar for maritime surveillance. One hundred and four had an upward-hinged main-deck cargo-loading door and reinforced main-deck flooring.

Most of these cargo-carrying aircraft were delivered as 737-200C passenger cargo/convertible aircraft, but two were stripped of passenger accommodation as 737-230Fs for Lufthansa. Others were fitted out as 737-200QCs with palletized seats and galleys for fast conversion. In addition, beginning in the mid-1990s, Pemco World Air Services converted a small number of passenger-configured 737-200s to a combi configuration.

Including USAF T-43A/CT-43As, more than 860 of the 1,114 JT8D-powered 737-200s remained in service in the spring of 2001.

737-300

By the end of 1979, nearly 12 years after the 737 had entered service, orders for the Boeing twinjet were still trailing behind those for the Douglas twin (748 JT8D-powered 737s versus 968 DC-9-10/50s).

Moreover, McDonnell Douglas had already notched 64 firm orders for its DC-9-80 (latterly MD-80) with this stretched and refanned model promising greater seating capacity (172 seats in high-density configuration versus 130 for the Boeing jetliner) and lower noise than the 737-200. Boeing had to develop a 737 derivative with increased capacity and lower noise emission to gain the upper hand in the twinjet contest.

Boeing initially disregarded an approach by CFM International to use CFM56s to power the 737 derivative due to the large diameter of its fan. Favored engines for stretched 737s were the Pratt & Whitney JT8D-200, as selected by McDonnell Douglas for the DC-9-80, and a paper design by Rolls-Royce and Japanese Aero Engines, the RJ500. Acting swiftly, CFM International developed a -3 derivative of its CFM56-2 to fit in flattened nacelles mounted ahead and beneath the wing of the 737 without necessitating a major redesign of the main undercarriage.

Although the CFM56-3 installation was promising, prospective customers feared that it might prove to be the "world's most expensive runway vacuum cleaners" because the intakes of these large-diameter engines would be so close to the ground. Good salesmanship and believable engineering guarantees turned customers around, so Boeing stepped up efforts to sell the CFM56-powered 737-300. Accommodation in single-class configuration was increased to 149 passengers through the addition of a 44-inch (1.12-meter) plug forward of the wing and a 5-foot (1.52-meter) plug aft of the wing. The wings were strengthened, their span was increased from 93 feet (28.35 meters) to 94 feet 9 inches (28.88 meters), and their area was boosted up some 16 percent to 1,135 square feet (105.4 m^2). Other modifications included the addition of a dorsal fin; extended horizontal stabilizers; strengthened wheels, tires, and brakes; and a repositioning of the nose wheel. MTOW (def. pg. 33) started at 124,500 pounds (56,472 kilograms) but was raised to 138,500 pounds (62,823 kilograms) for some late-production 737-300s.

US Air placed the first order for this re-engined Boeing twinjet by signing for 10 737-3B7s on March 5, 1981. Unfortunately, other customers did not rush to order CFM56-powered 737s, and by the end of that year, Boeing only had firm orders for 20 –300s. Thereafter, orders continued trickling slowly until 1985 when orders for 737-300s and -500s increased by 253 to bring the total for CFM56-powered variants to 407. These orders, along with orders for 30 JT8D-powered 737-200s during that year, finally pushed sales of all 737 models over those of DC-9/MD-80s.

Characterized by a cabin with six more rows of seats, the first 737-300 (l/n 1001, s/n 22950, N73700 during test and N350AU on delivery to US Air) flew on February 24, 1984. This first CFM56-powered variant was certificated in November of that year. US Air and Southwest Airlines placed the type into scheduled service in December 1984. Initial production 737-300s were powered by CFM56-3B1 engines rated at 22,000 pounds (97.9 kilonewtons) of static thrust, but some later production aircraft were fitted with other CFM56-3 variants with thrust of up to 23,500 pounds (104.5 kilonewtons). The last aircraft in this series, a 737-319 (l/n 3130, s/n 25609) went to Air New Zealand in December 1999.

All 1,113 CFM-56-powered 737-300s were built as passenger aircraft and were delivered mostly to airlines and leasing companies, but Pemco World Air Services completed the first 737-300 freighter conversion for Polaris Aircraft Leasing in April 1994. Since then, Pemco has completed similar freighter and quick change conversions for several other customers. All Pemco conversions were fitted with an 11-foot 8-in by 7.5-foot (3.55- by 2.28-meter) main-deck cargo door and have stronger floor beams.

In the spring of 2001, a large majority of CFM56-powered 737-300s remained in service: only 10 have been written off and 9 others withdrawn from service.

737-400

Because the CFM56 developed 50 percent more thrust than the JT8D, Boeing was quickly able to offer a new version of the 737 with greater MTOW and seating capacity than the 737-300. The resulting 737-400, which had a 5.5-foot (1.68-meter) plug ahead of the wing and a 4-foot (1.22-meter) plug aft, was first ordered by Piedmont Airlines (a contract for 19 737-401s being signed on June 4, 1986). Standard single-class seating was increased to 159 with up to 168 passengers being accommodated in an inclusive-tour layout with reduced seat pitch. Takeoff weight started at 138,500 pounds (62,823 kilograms) but was later increased to 150,000 pounds (68,039 kilograms) to meet the need of some customers for greater range with maximum payload. In other respects, 737-400s were nearly identical to the -300s and were powered by CFM56-3B2 engines rated at 22,000 pounds (97.9 kilonewtons) of static thrust.

The first Series 400 (l/n 1528, s/n 23876) flew on April 19, 1988, and was given its certification the following September. Production of the Series 400 lasted until February 25, 2000, when l/n 3132, s/n 28478, was delivered to Czech Airlines in the Czech Republic to bring to an end the production history of the CFM56-powered Classic 737 family. It was the 389th 737-400 produced.

737-500

The third variant in the CFM56-powered Classic 737 family was launched in May 1987 with an initial order for 38 aircraft from Southwest Airlines. Whereas the 737-400 took advantage of the high thrust of the CFM56 to carry more passengers, the 737-500 was developed to capitalize on the lower noise emission of these engines. It carried the same payload as the JT8D-powered 737-200 in a 10-inch- (0.30-meter-) longer fuselage while generating less noise.

The first of these aircraft (l/n 1718, s/n 24178) flew on June 30, 1989, and certification was obtained a few months later. Accommodating up to 132 passengers in single-class high-density configuration, 737-500s were powered by CFM56-3B1s or -3C1s with thrust between 22,000 and 23,500 pounds st (97.9 and 104.5 kilonewtons). Structurally similar to the 737-300s except for their shorter fuselage, the -500s were certificated at a higher gross weight (133,500 pounds [60,555 kilograms]) in order to increase range with full payload.

The 737-500 remained in production for 10 years with the 389th and last (l/n 3116, s/n 29795) being delivered to Air Nippon in July 1999.

Next-Generation 737

During the 12-year period between 1970 and 1981, sales of Boeing jetliners had averaged 200 aircraft annually, reaching a peak of 459 in 1979. Sales then plummeted to 105 aircraft in 1982 and only rose back to 146 jetliners in 1983, the year in which Airbus Industrie announced a new 737 rival. Production of the 727 had just ended, 737 sales still trailed behind those of DC-9s, and Boeing was feeling compelled to give development priority to an "advanced series 300" of the 747. The magnitude of that project, which led to the extensively redesigned 747-400 launched in 1985, drained the company financial resources at a time when the airline industry was in a downturn.

After Boeing's long-time prime customer, Pan American, bolted to Airbus in September 1984 by ordering A320s to replace 727s on internal German and other European services, Boeing had to initiate development of a new twinjet on its own. To counter the A320 and fill the seating gap between its 737-400 and 757-200, Boeing sought for some seven years to initiate the development of a new 7-7 twinjet in cooperation with Japan Aircraft Development Consortium. Another approach called for the proposed 7J7 to be powered by UDF engines (also known as propfans or ultra-high-bypass [UHB] engines) then under development by General Electric and Allison.

Finally, having failed to reach an agreement with the Japanese and concluding that UDF engines would not live up to expectations, Boeing canvassed airlines to ascertain the merit of developing a 737X derivative of its twinjet. By 1991, the Seattle manufacturer could again afford to proceed on its own because sales of its other jetliners were again booming (a new peak of 593 combined sales of 737, 747, 757, and 767 Models having been reached). Nevertheless, it took another two years before the 737X, now renamed Next-Generation 737, could be launched on the strength of a 63-aircraft order from Southwest.

Although most people have difficulties recognizing a Next-Generation 737 from an earlier CFM56-powered 737 Classic, under the skin the Next-Generation is a much redesigned aircraft fully capable of matching and in some regards besting its Airbus competitor. The principal airframe changes were in the wing design, which incorporates an advanced-technology airfoil to increase fuel capacity, improve efficiency, and boost cruising speed. The chord was increased by about 20 inches (50 cm) and span was extended to 112 feet 7 inches (34.32 meters), for a net increase in wing area of just over 18 percent to 1,341.2 square feet (124.6 m^2).

Structurally, the Next-Generation was designed to take advantage of new alloys and composite material to reduce structural weight and manufacturing costs while also easing maintenance. Further improvements were obtained by replacing the CFM56-3s of Classic 737s with CFM56-7s that are not only more powerful but are also quieter and have lower fuel burn and lower maintenance costs.

To enable airlines to achieve maximum commonality with other aircraft in their fleets, Boeing elected to give carriers a choice between an advanced cockpit design for commonality with 777s and late-model 767s and a cockpit similar to that in their earlier 737s. Similarly, airlines were given a choice between an improved 737 cabin interior and an interior incorporating new ceiling panels and overhead bins similar to those of the 777. Flexibility of operations was further extended as Boeing quickly came up with four variants of its Next-Generation 737 offering various capacities of 132 to 189 seats.

The first of the Next-Generation 737s to be committed to production was the 149-seat Series 700 that was launched in November 1993. It was followed less than 10 months later by the 189-seat 737-800 and in March 1995 by the 132-seat 737-600. Finally, the 189-seat 737-900 was added to the product line in November 1997 on the strength of an order from Alaska Airlines.

Boeing's willingness to accommodate airline requirements with four new variants and choices of cockpits and interiors proved a strong selling point, and the company was soon able to claim that its Next-Generation 737 was the fastest selling new commercial jetliner in history. That was indeed a remarkable achievement as the basic 737 design goes back nearly 40 years.

737-600

The third and smallest version of the Next-Generation 737, the Series 600 was intended as a replacement for JT8D-powered 737-200s and CFM56-powered 737-500s. It was initially ordered by Scandinavian Airlines System.

With an overall length of 102.5 feet (31.24 meters), this version can accommodate up to 132 passengers and is available with MTOW of 140,000 to 143,500 pounds (63,503 to 65,091 kilograms). Compared with the 737-700, the "base" Next-Generation 737, the -600 has an overall length 7 feet 10 inches (2.39 meters) shorter and has room for three fewer rows of seats. Engine options include CFM56-7B variants with thrust between 19,500 and 22,700 pounds (86.7 and 101 kilonewtons).

The first 737-600 (l/n 21, s/n 28296) first flew at Renton on January 22, 1998. FAA type certification was obtained on August 14, 1998, and Scandinavian Airlines System initiated scheduled service shortly afterward.

737-700

The 737-700 is the "base" version of the Next-Generation 737s. It has a length of 110 feet 4 inches (33.63 meters), placing it in capacity between the Classic 737-300 (with which it shares maximum seating accommodation for 149) and the 168-seat 737-400. According to customers' requirements, MTOW ranges between 149,000 and 154,500 pounds (67,585 and 70,080 kilograms), with power being provided by CFM56-7B variants with static thrust of 22,000 to 24,200 pounds (91.6 to 107.6 kilonewtons).

Because Boeing considered the Next-Generation 737 a new aircraft, the l/n sequence was again started at 1, with s/n 27841 being rolled out on December 8, 1996, and first flying as N737X on February 9, 1997. The FAA granted its ATC to the 737-700 on November 7, 1997, and Europe's JAA validated that certification on February 19, 1998. The launch customer for the Next-Generation 737 took delivery of its first 737-7H4 on December 17, 1997, and started Next-Generation 737 service shortly afterward.

Since then, Boeing has come with a BBJ business jet version and a cargo/passenger military transport variant ordered by the U.S. Navy and the USAF as the C-40 Clipper. Jetliner and BBJ variants are now available with winglets developed in association with Aviation Partners to enable modified 737-700s to fly higher, faster, and further.

737-800

Third in numerical sequence but the second Next-Generation 737 version to fly, the 737-800 was first ordered by Hapag-Lloyd in Germany on September 4, 1994. This version is 19 feet 2 inches (5.84 meters) longer than the 737-700 to accommodate a maximum of 189 passengers in high-density, single-class configuration. Its MTOW varies between 168,500 and 174,200 pounds (76,430 and 79,016 kilograms) with power provided by CFM56-7B engines with static thrust ranging between 26,300 and 27,300 pounds (117 to 121.4 kilonewtons). Like the 737-700, the -800 is also available with winglets. Air Berlin and Hapag-Lloyd were the first airlines to specify winglets.

The 737-800 with standard wings first flew on July 31, 1997 (l/n 7, s/n 27981). It received FAA certification on March 13, 1998. Following validation of FAA certification by Europe's JAA, the 737-800 was put in service by Hapag-Lloyd in April 1998.

737-900

The most recent 737 version was announced in November 1997 when Alaska Airlines ordered 10 aircraft and placed options on 10 more. First flown on August 3, 2000 (l/n 596, s/n 30017), the 737-900 earned its FAA certification on April 17, 2001. Europe's JAA validation of that certification followed two days later.

Although the 737-900 has a fuselage 8 feet 8 inches (2.64 meters) longer than that of the -800, maximum seating accommodation in single-class configuration remains at 189 due to emergency-exit restrictions. However, the longer cabin length enables typical two-class accommodation to be increased from 162 to 177. Its MTOW remains at 174,200 pounds (79,016 kilograms) and 737-900s, ordered so far by four airlines, was offered with CFM56-7B models rated at between 26,300 and 27,300 pounds (117 to 121.4 kilonewtons).

Boeing 737 Principal Characteristics and Performance

	737-100	737-200	737-300	737-400	737-500
Span, ft in (m)	87' (26.52)	93' (28.35)	94' 9" (28.88)	94' 9" (28.88)	94' 9" (28.88)
Length, ft in (m)	95' 9" (29.18)	100' 2" (30.53)	109' 7" (33.40)	119' 7" (36.45)	101' 9" (31.01)
Height, ft in (m)	37' 1" (11.30)	36' 10" (11.23)	36' 6" (11.13)	36' 6" (11.13)	36' 6" (11.13)
Wing area, sq ft (m^2)	922 (85.7)	980 (91.0)	1,135 (105.4)	1,135 (105.4)	1,135 (105.4)
High-density seating	103/119	130	149	168	132
Two-class seating	85	95	128	146	110
Underfloor cargo, cu ft (m^3)	650 (18.4)	875 (24.8)	1,068 (30.2)	1,373 (38.9)	822 (23.3)
TO thrust per engine, lb st (kN)	14,000/14,500 (62.3/64.5)	14,500/16,000 (64.5/71.2)	18,500/23,500 (82.3/104.5)	22,000 (97.9)	18,500/23,500 (82.3/104.5)
Fuel capacity, U.S. gal (liters)	2,850/4,720 (10,788/17,867)	4,230/5,970 (16,012/22,598)	5,311 (20,104)	5,311 (20,104)	5,311 (20,104)
MTOW, lb (kg)	93,500/110,000 (42,411/49,895)	115,500/128,100 (52,390/58,105)	124,500/138,500 (56,472/62,823)	138,500/150,000 (62,823/68,039)	133,500 (60,555)
Typical cruise speed, Mach	N/A	N/A	0.745	0.745	0.745
Typical range, nm (km)	1,875 (3,475)	2,000/2,650 (3,705/4,910)	2,255 (4,175)	2,060 (3,815)	2,370 (4,390)

	737-600	737-700	737-800	737-900
Span, ft in (m)	112'7" (34.32)	112' 7" (34.32)	112' 7"/117' 5" (34.32/35.79)	112' 7"/117' 5" (34.32/35.79)
Length, ft in (m)	102' 6" (31.24)	110' 4" (33.63)	129' 6" (39.47)	138' 2" (42.11)
Height, ft in (m)	41' 3" (12.57)	41' 2" (12.55)	41' 2" (12.55)	41' 2" (12.55)
Wing area, sq ft (m2)	1,341.2 (124.6)	1,341.2 (124.6)	1,341.2 (124.6)	1,341.2 (124.6)
High-density seating	132	149	189	189
Two-class seating	110	126	162	177
Underfloor cargo, cu ft (m3)	720 (20.4)	966 (27.4)	1,555 (44.0)	1,835 (52.0)
TO thrust per engine, lb st (kN)	19,500/22,700 (86.7/101.0)	20,600/24,200 (91.6/107.6)	26,300/27,300 (117.0/121.4)	24,200/27,300 (107.6/121.4)
Fuel capacity, U.S. gal (liters)	6,875 (26,024)	6,875 (26,024)	6,875 (26,024)	6,875 (26,024)
MTOW, lb (kg)	140,000/143,500 (63,503/65,091)	149,000/154,500 (67,585/70,080)	168,500/174,200 (76,430/79,016)	174,200 (79,016)
Typical cruise speed, Mach	0.785	0.785	0.785	0.785
Typical range, nm (km)	3,050 (5,650)	3,260 (6,040)	2,940 (5,445)	2,745 (5,085)

Boeing 737-100 and 737-200 Commercial Jet Aircraft Census

The aircraft in the following tables are listed in order of the following: 1) ICAO country prefixes; 2) operator; 3) aircraft type; and 4) registration.

The total built was 1,144 (30 B737-100, 19 T-43 (-200), and 1,095 B737-200) from 1967 to 1988.

A/C TYPE	CURRENT REG. NO.	LAST KNOWN OPERATOR (OWNER)	STATUS	ORIGINAL MSN	LINE NO.	DEL. DATE	ENG. TYPE	FLEET NO.	PREV. REG. [COMMENTS]
B-CHINA (PEOPLE'S REPUBLIC)									
B737-2T4 (A)	B-2506	AIR GREAT WALL		23272	1093	03/25/85	JT8D-17A		
B737-2T4 (A)	B-2507	AIR GREAT WALL		23273	1097	04/02/85	JT8D-17A		N5375S
B737-2T4 (A)	B-2508	AIR GREAT WALL		23274	1099	04/09/85	JT8D-17A		N6067U
B737-2T4 (A)	B-2516	XIAMEN AIRLINES		23447	1167	11/19/85	JT8D-17A		N5573B
B737-25C (A)	B-2524	XIAMEN AIRLINES		24236	1585	08/02/88	JT8D-17A		N5573B
C-CANADA									
B737-2L9 (A)	C-FACP	AIR CANADA		22072	623	12/14/79	JT8D-17 (HK3)	728	OY-APO, C-GQBA, C2-RN9
B737-2T7 (A)	C-FCPM	AIR CANADA		22761	850	03/16/82	JT8D-17 (HK3)	730	G-DWHH, C-FPWD
B737-2T7 (A)	C-FCPN	AIR CANADA		22762	856	03/26/82	JT8D-17 (HK3)	731	G-DGDP, C-FPWE
B737-2T5 (A)	C-FHCP	AIR CANADA		22024	641	02/27/80	JT8D-17 (HK3)	729	G-BGTV, EI-BPV
B737-275 (A)	C-GAPW	AIR CANADA		20922	370	08/29/74	JT8D-9A (HK3)	739	N127AW
B737-275 (A)	C-GBPW	AIR CANADA		20958	391	01/13/75	JT8D-9A (HK3)	740	N128AW
B737-217 (A)	C-GCPM	AIR CANADA		21716	560	05/22/79	JT8D-17 (HK3)	708	N1262E
B737-217 (A)	C-GCPN	AIR CANADA		21717	581	06/20/79	JT8D-17 (HK3)	709	
B737-217 (A)	C-GCPO	AIR CANADA		21718	584	07/03/79	JT8D-17 (HK3)	710	
B737-217 (A)	C-GCPP	AIR CANADA		22255	666	05/28/80	JT8D-17 (HK3)	711	
B737-217 (A)	C-GCPQ	AIR CANADA		22256	672	06/18/80	JT8D-17 (HK3)	712	
B737-217 (A)	C-GCPS	AIR CANADA		22257	756	04/20/80	JT8D-17 (HK3)	714	
B737-217 (A)	C-GCPT	AIR CANADA (ARKIA LSG)		22258	770	06/10/81	JT8D-17 (HK3)	715	
B737-217 (A)	C-GCPU	AIR CANADA (TRIT)		22259	771	06/12/81	JT8D-17 (HK3)	716	
B737-217 (A)	C-GCPV	AIR CANADA (TRIT)		22260	784	07/29/81	JT8D-17 (HK3)	717	
B737-275 (A)	C-GCPW	AIR CANADA		20959	395	02/24/75	JT8D-9A (HK3)	741	N126AW
B737-217 (A)	C-GCPX	AIR CANADA (TRIT)		22341	786	08/06/81	JT8D-17 (HK3)	718	
B737-217 (A)	C-GCPY	AIR CANADA (TRIT)		22342	810	10/31/81	JT8D-17 (HK3)	719	
B737-217 (A)	C-GCPZ	AIR CANADA		22658	861	04/13/82	JT8D-17 (HK3)	720	
B737-2T2C (A)	C-GDPA	AIR CANADA	L	22056	655	04/22/80	JT8D-17	784	[OPF CANADIAN NORTH]
B737-275 (A)	C-GEPW	AIR CANADA		21115	425	12/12/75	JT8D-9A (HK3)	743	N129AW
B737-217 (A)	C-GFCP	AIR CANADA		22659	874	05/20/82	JT8D-17 (HK3)	721	
B737-275C (A)	C-GFPW	AIR CANADA		21294	481	12/23/76	JT8D-9A (HK3)	752	
B737-275 (A)	C-GGPW	AIR CANADA		21639	539	11/10/78	JT8D-9A (HK3)	744	
B737-275 (A)	C-GIPW	AIR CANADA		21712	556	02/28/79	JT8D-9A (HK3)	745	
B737-217 (A)	C-GJCP	AIR CANADA		22728	911	10/01/82	JT8D-17A (HK3)	722	N178EE
B737-275 (A)	C-GJPW	AIR CANADA (TRIT)		21713	598	09/05/79	JT8D-9A (HK3)	746	
B737-217 (A)	C-GKCP	AIR CANADA (ARKIA LSG)		22729	915	11/01/82	JT8D-17A (HK3)	723	

A/C TYPE	CURRENT REG. NO.	LAST KNOWN OPERATOR (OWNER)	STATUS	ORIGINAL MSN	LINE NO.	DEL. DATE	ENG. TYPE	FLEET NO.	PREV. REG. [COMMENTS]
B737-275 (A)	C-GKPW	AIR CANADA		21819	627	01/09/80	JT8D-9A (HK3)	748	
B737-217 (A)	C-GMCP	AIR CANADA (ARKIA LSG)		22864	945	03/01/83	JT8D-17A (HK3)	724	
B737-242C (A)	C-GNDC	AIR CANADA		21728	580	06/15/79	JT8D-9A (HK3)	761	
B737-242C (A)	C-GNDU	AIR CANADA		22877	880	06/06/82	JT8D-9A (HK3)	762	
B737-275 (A)	C-GNPW	AIR CANADA (TRIT)		22159	684	07/28/80	JT8D-9A (HK3)	751	
B737-275C (A)	C-GOPW	AIR CANADA (AIR CANADA NORTH)	L	22160	688	09/30/80	JT8D-17A	782	N8288V [OPF CANADIAN NORTH]
B737-275 (A)	C-GPPW	AIR CANADA		22264	753	04/10/81	JT8D-9A (HK3)	753	
B737-296 (A)	C-GQBB	AIR CANADA		22276	665	05/21/80	JT8D-9A (HK3)	732	N8280V, N387PA [FIRST A/C IN COMBINED ACA/CDN C/S]
B737-296 (A)	C-GQBH	AIR CANADA		22516	759	04/24/81	JT8D-9A (HK3)	734	G-BJZW, N389PA
B737-217 (A)	C-GQCP	AIR CANADA		22865	960	04/22/83	JT8D-17A (HK3)	725	
B737-275 (A)	C-GRPW	AIR CANADA (TRIT)		22266	765	05/28/81	JT8D-9A (HK3)	755	
B737-275C (A)	C-GSPW	AIR CANADA (ARKIA LSG)		22618	813	11/10/81	JT8D-17	783	
B737-275 (A)	C-GTPW	AIR CANADA (TRIT)		22807	824	12/18/81	JT8D-9A (HK3)	756	
B737-275 (A)	C-GUPW	AIR CANADA (GECA)		22873	898	07/23/82	JT8D-9A (HK3)	758	
B737-275 (A)	C-GVPW	AIR CANADA		22874	904	08/27/82	JT8D-9A (HK3)	759	
B737-275 (A)	C-GWPW	AIR CANADA		23283	1109	05/01/85	JT8D-17A (HK3)	760	
B737-2T2C (A)	C-GDPA	CANADIAN NORTH (ARKIA LSG)		22056	655	04/22/80	JT8D-17	784	[OPB CDN]
B737-275C (A)	C-GOPW	CANADIAN NORTH (ARKIA LSG)		22160	688	09/30/80	JT8D-17A	782	N8288V [OPB CDN]
B737-2Q9 (A)	C-FECJ	CAN JET (USA)	L	21975	612	11/07/79	JT8D-9A	230	N774N, N230AU
B737-201 (A)	C-FGCJ	CAN JET (USA)	L	22352	728	12/23/80	JT8D-9A (HK3)	236	N782N, N236US
B737-201 (A)	C-FHCJ	CAN JET (USA)	L	21666	547	12/21/78	JT8D-9A (HK3)	224	N762N, N224US
B737-201 (A)	C-FJCJ	CAN JET (USA)	L	21667	548	01/10/79	JT8D-9A (HK3)	225	N763N, N225US
B737-296 (A)	C-FMCJ	CAN JET (USA)	L	22398	733	02/25/81	JT8D-9A (HK3)	238	N789N, N238US
B737-201 (A)	C-FUCJ	CAN JET (USA)	L	22353	731	01/23/81	JT8D-9A (HK3)	237	N783N, N237US
B737-248C (A)	C-FNVT	FIRST AIR		21011	411	05/02/75	JT8D-9A (HK3)		EI-ASL, F-GKTK
B737-210C (A)	C-GNWI	FIRST AIR		21066	413	05/14/75	JT8D-9A		N4951W
B737-210C (A)	C-GNWN	FIRST AIR		21067	414	05/20/75	JT8D-9A		N4952W
B737-210C	C-GJLN	NORANDA AVIATION DEPARTMENT		19594	102	12/05/68	JT8D-9A		N4907, C-GQBD, N728JE, TF-ABJ
B737-2A9C	C-FJLT	ROYAL AVIATION (INTEGRATED)		20206	249	04/14/70	JT8D-9A		C-FTAN, N803AL
B737-201 (A)	C-FNAJ	ROYAL AVIATION (USA)	L	22354	736	02/10/81	JT8D-9A (HK3)		N784N, N239US
B737-242C	C-FNAP	ROYAL AVIATION (POLA)		20496	268	06/16/71	JT8D-9A (HK3)		N1788B
B737-242C	C-FNAQ	ROYAL AVIATION (POLA)		20455	254	05/13/70	JT8D-9A (HK3)		EI-BOC
B737-201 (A)	C-FNAX	ROYAL AVIATION (USA)	L	21815	589	07/27/79	JT8D-9A (HK3)		N768N, N226US
B737-2H4 (A)	C-FRYG	ROYAL AVIATION		21721	553	02/08/79	JT8D-9A		N56SW

A/C TYPE	CURRENT REG. NO.	LAST KNOWN OPERATOR (OWNER)	Status	ORIGINAL MSN	LINE NO.	DEL. DATE	ENG. TYPE	FLEET NO.	PREV. REG. [COMMENTS]
B737-201 (A)	C-FRYH	ROYAL AVIATION (USA)	L	21816	592	08/07/79	JT8D-9A (HK3)		N769N, N227AU
B737-2H4 (A)	C-FRYL	ROYAL AVIATION		21970	613	11/05/79	JT8D-9A (HK3)		N61SW
B737-2E1 (A) (F)	C-GCDG	ROYAL AVIATION (POLA)		20776	328	10/29/73	JT8D-9A		C-FEPU, N212PL
B737-2E1 (A) (F)	C-GDCC	ROYAL AVIATION (POLA)		20681	319	03/19/73	JT8D-9A		CF-EPP, N211PL [DMGD YYT 04/04/01; SKIDDED INTO SNOWBANK ON LDG; WO?]
B737-201 (A)	C-GEIM	ROYAL AVIATION (USA)	L	22355	741	02/27/81	JT8D-9A (HK3)		N785N, N240AU
B737-201 (A)	C-GNAU	ROYAL AVIATION (USA)	L	21817	602	09/26/79	JT8D-9A (HK3)		N772N, N228US
B737-201 (A)	C-GRYY	ROYAL AVIATION (USA)	L	22275	687	10/27/80	JT8D-9A (HK3)		N781N, N235US
B737-281 (A)	C-FAWJ	WESTJET AIRLINES		21770	588	07/27/79	JT8D-17	752	JA8456
B737-2E3 (A)	C-FCWJ	WESTJET AIRLINES		22703	811	10/29/81	JT8D-15 (HK3)	748	CC-CIN, EI-BRZ, EC-DYZ, G-BNZT, G-IBTY, VT-EWB, 9M-VMB
B737-217	C-FGWJ	WESTJET AIRLINES		20196	143	03/24/69	JT8D-9A (HK3)	706	CF-CPV, N197JQ, F-WGTP, F-GGTP, TC-RAF, F-GTCA
B737-2M8 (A)	C-FIWJ	WESTJET AIRLINES		21955	659	04/24/80	JT8D-15 (HK3)	749	G-BHCL, OO-TEN, N141AW
B737-2H4 (A)	C-FKWJ	WESTJET AIRLINES (PEGA)		21811	609	10/23/79	JT8D-9A (HK3)	753	N59SW
B737-2Q8 (A)	C-FLWJ	WESTJET AIRLINES		23148	1059	10/25/84	JT8D-15 (HK3)	750	N137AW, CC-CYV
B737-281 (A)	C-FTWJ	WESTJET AIRLINES		21767	585	07/09/79	JT8D-17	751	JA8453
B737-297 (A)	C-GCWJ	WESTJET AIRLINES		21739	561	03/23/79	JT8D-9A	723	N70723
B737-2T4 (A)	C-GEWJ	WESTJET AIRLINES (CITG)		22055	633	01/28/80	JT8D-15 (HK3)	745	N54AF, G-BJXM, N705ML, XA-SLC, N467AT
B737-284 (A)	C-GGWJ	WESTJET AIRLINES (POLA)		21500	491	09/15/77	JT8D-9A (HK3)	738	N70721, N195AW, N311VA
B737-281 (A)	C-GMWJ	WESTJET AIRLINES		21771	594	09/18/79	JT8D-17 (HK3)	739	JA8457
B737-281 (A)	C-GQWJ	WESTJET AIRLINES		21769	587	07/24/79	JT8D-17 (HK3)	740	JA8455
B737-2H4 (A)	C-GSWJ	WESTJET AIRLINES		21593	544	12/08/78	JT8D-9A (HK3)	755	N55SW
B737-204 (A)	C-GUWJ	WESTJET AIRLINES (FSBU)		20807	341	02/15/74	JT8D-15 (HK3)	743	G-BAZH, G-SBEB, N107TR
B737-281 (A)	C-GVWJ	WESTJET AIRLINES		21768	586	07/12/79	JT8D-17 (HK3)	746	JA8454
B737-275 (A)	C-GWJE	WESTJET AIRLINES		20588	300	04/27/72	JT8D-9A	735	CF-PWP, N381PA, N861SY, HP-1216CMP, XA-SJI, N861SY
B737-275 (A)	C-GWJG	WESTJET AIRLINES		20670	315	12/20/72	JT8D-9A	736	CF-PWW, N380PA, HP-1218CMF, N862SY
B737-269 (A)	C-GWJK	WESTJET AIRLINES (AERO TURBINE)		21206	448	02/17/76	JT8D-17	756	9K-ACV, VR-BOX, PP-SNP, EI-CHB, PT-WBB, OB-1538, N500AL
B737-2A3	C-GWJO	WESTJET AIRLINES		20299	158	12/31/69	JT8D-9A (HK3)	730	N1787B, N1797B, CX-BHM, HR-TNR, HR-SHO
B737-2H4 (A)	C-GWJT	WESTJET AIRLINES		21262	470	09/08/76	JT8D-9A	731	N27SW
B737-2H4 (A)	C-GWJU	WESTJET AIRLINES		21117	423	07/01/75	JT8D-9A (HK3)	733	N26SW
B737-204 (A)	C-GWWJ	WESTJET AIRLINES (TRIT)		21694	542	11/28/78	JT8D-15A (HK3)	741	G-BFVB, C-GNDW, G-SBEA, N109TR
B737-281 (A)	C-GXWJ	WESTJET AIRLINES		21766	583	06/29/79	JT8D-17 (HK3)	742	JA8452

CC-CHILE

A/C TYPE	CURRENT REG. NO.	LAST KNOWN OPERATOR (OWNER)	Status	ORIGINAL MSN	LINE NO.	DEL. DATE	ENG. TYPE	FLEET NO.	PREV. REG. [COMMENTS]
B737-201	CC-CJM	AERO CONTINENTE CHILE		20212	159	04/23/69	JT8D-9A		N743N, N212US
B737-222	CC-CJO	AERO CONTINENTE CHILE (INTL. PAC)		19059	50	07/31/68	JT8D-7B		N9021U, N69AF, TG-ANP, OB-1561, XA-SYX, OB-1672, P4-OYX, OB-1733

A/C TYPE	CURRENT REG. NO.	LAST KNOWN OPERATOR (OWNER)	STATUS	ORIGINAL MSN	LINE NO.	DEL. DATE	ENG. TYPE	FLEET NO.	PREV. REG. [COMMENTS]
B737-247	OB-1742	AERO CONTINENTE CHILE (JET A/C LSG)		19616	126	01/29/69	JT8D-9A/-15		N4519W, CC-CRI, OB-1619, P4-ARB, CC-CJO
B737-204	CC-CSD	AVANT AIRLINES (GLENDALE)		20417	255	05/12/70	JT8D-9A		G-AXNC, TF-ABD
B737-222	CC-CSF	AVANT AIRLINES (FORTITUDE)		19945	185	07/08/69	JT8D-9A		N9064U, CF-NAI, N7390F, N14237, N737KD, CC-CAS [WFU ATSCL]
B737-204 (A)	CC-CSH	AVANT AIRLINES (GLENDALE)		20632	316	01/10/73	JT8D-15		G-BADP
B737-204 (A)	CC-CSI	AVANT AIRLINES (GLENDALE)		20633	318	03/12/73	JT8D-15		G-BADR
B737-248	CC-CSL	AVANT AIRLINES (EUROJET LSG)		20223	252	04/25/70	JT8D-9A		EI-ASH, CF-TAR, C-GTAR, N7361F, N80AF, HR-TNS
B737-248C	CC-CEI	LADECO AIRLINES (EUROJET LSG)		20219	208	10/24/69	JT8D-9A		EI-ASD
B737-2T5 (A)	CC-CJW	LADECO AIRLINES (GECA)		22397	737	03/30/81	JT8D-15		N5701E, G-BHVI
B737-219 (A)	CC-CYC	LADECO AIRLINES		21131	428	11/20/75	JT8D-15		ZK-NAQ, EI-BCC, PH-TVM, N7362F, OO-TEJ, G-BGNW
B737-205 (A)	CC-CYD	LADECO AIRLINES (AIG LSG)		21219	460	05/14/76	JT8D-9A		LN-SUH, N7031A
B737-205 (A)	CC-CYK	LADECO AIRLINES (INTEGRATED)		21445	506	12/19/77	JT8D-9A		LN-SUM, N7031F
B737-2M8 (A)	CC-CYN	LADECO AIRLINES (ILFC)		21231	462	06/15/76	JT8D-15		OO-TEH, C-GQBS, 9M-MBN
B737-2E1 (A)	CC-CYT	LADECO AIRLINES (ACG ACQUISITION)		21112	424	10/10/75	JT8D-9A		C-GEPB, N4039W, N70720, EI-BEA, EI-BDY, C-GNDD, CN-RML, G-BNYT
B737-2M6 (A)	CC-CYW	LADECO AIRLINES (ACG ACQUISITION)		20913	399	04/24/75	JT8D-15		VR-UEB, 4R-ALD, V8-UEB, CC-CJZ, ZK-NAZ
B737-236 (A)	CC-CZK	LADECO AIRLINES (GECA)		21804	686	08/13/80	JT8D-15A		N8280P, G-BGDP
B737-236 (A)	CC-CZM	LADECO AIRLINES (GECA)		22027	654	04/17/80	JT8D-15A		G-BGJF
B737-236 (A)	CC-CZO	LADECO AIRLINES (GECA)		22030	693	10/01/80	JT8D-15A		G-BGJI
B737-291 (A)	CC-CDE	LAN CHILE (PLMI)		22744	923	12/10/82	JT8D-17A		N7358F, EI-BWY, VT-EQH, 9J-AFM
B737-2L9 (A)	CC-CEE	LAN CHILE (GECA)		22407	698	10/06/80	JT8D-17		OY-APR, TS-IEB, EC-DXV
B737-230 (A)	CC-CRP	LAN CHILE (JETZ)		22134	777	07/16/81	JT8D-15		D-ABHF
B737-230 (A)	CC-CRQ	LAN CHILE (JETZ)		22135	781	07/30/81	JT8D-15		D-ABHH
B737-230 (A)	CC-CRR	LAN CHILE (JETZ)		22114	657	05/28/81	JT8D-15		N1782B, D-ABFA
B737-230 (A)	CC-CRS	LAN CHILE (JETZ)		22139	791	09/03/81	JT8D-15		D-ABHN
B737-204 (A)	CC-CSP	LAN CHILE		20808	342	03/18/74	JT8D-15		G-BAZI, G-BOSA, XA-STE, 9Q-COW
B737-229 (A)	CC-CVC	LAN CHILE		21596	529	08/25/78	JT8D-15		OO-SBQ
B737-229 (A)	CC-CVD	LAN CHILE		21840	617	11/20/79	JT8D-15		OO-SBT
B737-236 (A)	CC-CZL	LAN CHILE (GECA)		21808	712	11/13/80	JT8D-15A		G-BGDU
B737-236 (A)	CC-CZN	LAN CHILE (GECA)		22029	662	05/13/80	JT8D-15A		G-BGJH
B737-236 (A)	CC-CZP	LAN CHILE (GECA)		22031	722	12/18/80	JT8D-15A		N8293V, G-BGJJ
B737-291 (A)	VP-BBL	LAN CHILE (AERGO CAP)		22743	909	10/28/82	JT8D-17A		N7357F, EI-BXW, CC-CEA
B737-291 (A)	VP-BBM	LAN CHILE (GECA)		23024	965	05/09/83	JT8D-17A		N7399F, EI-BWC, VT-EQJ, CS-TMC, CS-TIS, CC-CDG

CN-MOROCCO

A/C TYPE	CURRENT REG. NO.	LAST KNOWN OPERATOR (OWNER)	STATUS	ORIGINAL MSN	LINE NO.	DEL. DATE	ENG. TYPE	FLEET NO.	PREV. REG. [COMMENTS]
B737-2B6 (A)	CN-RMI	ROYAL AIR MAROC		21214	449	02/25/76	JT8D-15 (HK3)		
B737-2B6 (A)	CN-RMJ	ROYAL AIR MAROC		21215	452	03/22/76	JT8D-15 (HK3)		
B737-2B6 (A)	CN-RML	ROYAL AIR MAROC		22767	851	03/19/82	JT8D-15 (HK3)		

A/C TYPE	CURRENT REG. NO.	LAST KNOWN OPERATOR (OWNER)	STATUS	ORIGINAL MSN	LINE NO.	DEL. DATE	ENG. TYPE	FLEET NO.	PREV. REG. [COMMENTS]
B737-2B6C (A)	CN-RMM	ROYAL AIR MAROC		23049	951	03/25/83	JT8D-15A (HK3)		
B737-2B6C (A)	CN-RMN	ROYAL AIR MAROC		23050	975	06/28/83	JT8D-15A (HK3)		
CX-URUGUAY									
B737-2A3 (A)	CX-BON	PLUNA		22737	830	01/18/82	JT8D-9A		PH-TSI
B737-2A3 (A)	CX-BOO	PLUNA		22738	834	01/25/82	JT8D-9A		PH-TSA, G-BONM
B737-2A3 (A)	CX-BOP	PLUNA		22739	844	02/25/82	JT8D-9A		N8295V, PH-TSB
B737-2Q8 (A)	CX-FAT	PLUNA (VRG)	L	21518	522	06/22/78	JT8D-17		N977MP, B-2611, C-GNDS, VR-CNN, ZP-CAC, PP-VPD
B737-219 (A)	CX-VVT	PLUNA (VRG)	L	21130	426	09/04/75	JT8D-17		ZK-NAP, HC-BTI, ZP-CAB, PP-VPE
C6-BAHAMAS									
B737-275 (A)	C6-BGK	BAHAMASAIR		22086	667	05/23/80	JT8D-9A		C-GLPW
B737-275 (A)	C6-BGL	BAHAMASAIR		22087	673	06/20/80	JT8D-9A (HK3)		N8282V, C-GMPW
C9-MOZAMBIQUE									
B737-2B1	C9-BAA	LAM-MOZAMBIQUE		20280	224	12/10/69	JT8D-9		CR-BAA
B737-2B1C (A)	C9-BAC	LAM-MOZAMBIQUE		20536	289	10/28/71	JT8D-9		CR-BAC
D2-ANGOLA									
B737-214	D2-TBI	ANGOLA AIR CHARTER (AV. CONSULT.)		19681	68	09/20/68	JT8D-9A		N378PS, N7380F
B737-2M2C (A)	D2-TBC	TAAG ANGOLA AIRLINES		21173	447	03/09/76	JT8D-17		D2-TAB
B737-2M2 (A)	D2-TBD	TAAG ANGOLA AIRLINES		21723	567	04/27/79	JT8D-17		D2-TAH [LST GCB]
B737-2M2 (A)	D2-TBO	TAAG ANGOLA AIRLINES		22776	891	11/01/82	JT8D-17		N1782B
B737-2M2 (A)	D2-TBP	TAAG ANGOLA AIRLINES		23220	1084	02/15/85	JT8D-17A		
B737-2M2 (A)	D2-TBX	TAAG ANGOLA AIRLINES		23351	1117	06/14/85	JT8D-17A		
D6-COMOROS									
B737-2A9C	F-GFYL	KAMARIA AIRLINES		20205	242	03/13/70	JT8D-9A (HK3)		CF-TAO, N383PA [PARKED LBG; ALL WHITE; NO TITLES]
EI-IRELAND									
B737-204 (A)	EI-CJC	RYANAIR		22640	867	04/30/82	JT8D-15 (HK3)		G-BJCV, CS-TMA
B737-204 (A)	EI-CJD	RYANAIR		22966	946	02/25/83	JT8D-15A		G-BKHE
B737-204 (A)	EI-CJE	RYANAIR		22639	863	04/20/82	JT8D-15		G-BJCU, EC-DVE
B737-204 (A)	EI-CJF	RYANAIR		22967	953	03/21/83	JT8D-15		G-BKHF, G-BTZF
B737-204 (A)	EI-CJG	RYANAIR		22058	629	01/14/80	JT8D-15		G-BGYK, PP-SRW
B737-204 (A)	EI-CJH	RYANAIR		22057	621	01/07/80	JT8D-15A		N8278V, G-BGYJ
B737-2E7 (A)	EI-CJI	RYANAIR		22875	917	03/02/83	JT8D-15		N45708, 4X-BAB, G-BMDF
B737-2K2 (A)	EI-CKP	RYANAIR		22296	668	06/05/80	JT8D-15 (HK3)		PH-TVS, EC-DVN, LV-RAO, LV-RBH, PP-SRV
B737-2K2 (A)	EI-CKQ	RYANAIR		22906	888	06/21/82	JT8D-15		PH-TVU, C-FCAV, G-BPLA

A/C TYPE	CURRENT REG. NO.	LAST KNOWN OPERATOR (OWNER)	STATUS	ORIGINAL MSN	LINE NO.	DEL. DATE	ENG. TYPE	FLEET NO.	PREV. REG. [COMMENTS]
B737-2K2 (A)	EI-CKR	RYANAIR		22025	647	03/26/80	JT8D-15A		C-FICP, PH-TVR
B737-2T5 (A)	EI-CKS	RYANAIR		22023	636	02/11/80	JT8D-15		G-BGTW, OE-ILE, PH-TVX
B737-230 (A)	EI-CNT	RYANAIR		22115	694	12/19/80	JT8D-15 (HK3)		N1786B, D-ABFC
B737-230 (A)	EI-CNV	RYANAIR		22128	752	04/23/81	JT8D-15 (HK3)		D-ABFX
B737-230 (A)	EI-CNW	RYANAIR		22133	772	07/01/81	JT8D-15 (HK3)		D-ABHC
B737-230 (A)	EI-CNX	RYANAIR		22127	745	04/16/81	JT8D-15		D-ABFW
B737-230 (A)	EI-CNY	RYANAIR		22113	649	04/15/83	JT8D-15 (HK3)		N5573K, D-ABFB
B737-230 (A)	EI-CNZ	RYANAIR		22126	735	04/09/81	JT8D-15 (HK3)		D-ABFU
B737-230 (A)	EI-COA	RYANAIR (INGO)		22637	848	03/17/82	JT8D-17A		D-ABHX, CS-TES
B737-230 (A)	EI-COB	RYANAIR		22124	727	03/14/81	JT8D-15 (HK3)		D-ABFR
B737-2T5 (A)	EI-CON	RYANAIR		22396	730	02/23/81	JT8D-15 (HK3)		G-BHVH, G-GVRE, A40-BM, VT-EMF, PK-RIW
B737-230 (A)	EI-COX	RYANAIR		22123	726	03/15/81	JT8D-15 (HK3)		D-ABFP

EP-IRAN

A/C TYPE	CURRENT REG. NO.	LAST KNOWN OPERATOR (OWNER)	STATUS	ORIGINAL MSN	LINE NO.	DEL. DATE	ENG. TYPE	FLEET NO.	PREV. REG. [COMMENTS]
B737-286 (A)	EP-AGA	IRAN GOVERNMENT		21317	483	03/10/77	JT8D-15		
B737-270C (A)	EP-IGA	IRAN AIR		20892	368	08/07/74	JT8D-15		YI-AGH
B737-286 (A)	EP-IRF	IRAN AIR		20498	283	07/02/71	JT8D-15		
B737-286C (A)	EP-IRH	IRAN AIR		20500	286	09/02/71	JT8D-15		
B737-286C (A)	EP-IRI	IRAN AIR		20740	321	05/01/73	JT8D-15		

ET-ETHIOPIA

A/C TYPE	CURRENT REG. NO.	LAST KNOWN OPERATOR (OWNER)	STATUS	ORIGINAL MSN	LINE NO.	DEL. DATE	ENG. TYPE	FLEET NO.	PREV. REG. [COMMENTS]
B737-260 (A)	ET-AJB	ETHIOPIAN AIRLINES		23915	1583	07/21/88	JT8D-17A		
B737-2T4 (A)	ET-ALE	ETHIOPIAN AIRLINES (AERFI)		23446	1165	11/04/85	JT8D-17A		N1792B, B-2515

F-FRANCE

A/C TYPE	CURRENT REG. NO.	LAST KNOWN OPERATOR (OWNER)	STATUS	ORIGINAL MSN	LINE NO.	DEL. DATE	ENG. TYPE	FLEET NO.	PREV. REG. [COMMENTS]
B737-219 (A)	F-GLXF	AIGLE AZUR (ALTER BAIL)		22657	846	03/05/82	JT8D-15		N6066Z, N851L, G-BJXJ
B737-2K5 (A)	F-GMJD	AIGLE AZUR (BNP BAIL)		22599	814	11/24/81	JT8D-17		D-AHLG, CS-TMD [OPF AFR]
B737-229 (A)	F-GVAC	AIGLE AZUR (WEST AERO)		20907	351	04/26/74	JT8D-15 (HK3)		LX-LGN, OO-SDA [LSF/OPF WESTAIR]
B737-228 (A)	F-GBYB	AIR FRANCE (TASFUND IRELAND)		23001	936	01/21/83	JT8D-15A		
B737-228 (A)	F-GBYF	AIR FRANCE (TASL IRELAND)		23005	943	02/18/83	JT8D-15A		
B737-228 (A)	F-GBYL	AIR FRANCE (TASL IRELAND)		23011	971	06/13/83	JT8D-15A		
B737-228 (A)	F-GBYP	AIR FRANCE (TASFUND IRELAND)		23792	1397	06/13/87	JT8D-15A		
B737-2K5 (A)	F-GFLV	AIR FRANCE (TASFUND IRELAND)		22597	773	06/19/81	JT8D-15A		D-AHLE, EC-DTR
B737-2K5 (A)	F-GFLX	AIR FRANCE (TASFUND IRELAND)		22598	792	09/03/81	JT8D-15A		N5573B, D-AHLF, EC-DUB
B737-222	F-GCJL	AIR MEDITERRANEE		19067	71	09/24/68	JT8D-9A (HK3)		N9029U
B737-222	F-GCSL	AIR MEDITERRANEE		19066	69	09/23/68	JT8D-7B (HK3)		N9028U
B737-2K2C (A)	F-GGVP	AIR MEDITERRANEE (ARP)	L	20943	405	03/31/75	JT8D-15 (HK3)		PH-TVD, G-BKBT, VT-EKC
B737-2K2C (A)	F-GGVQ	AIR MEDITERRANEE (ARP)	L	20944	408	04/16/75	JT8D-15 (HK3)		PH-TVE, VT-EKD

A/C TYPE	CURRENT REG. NO.	LAST KNOWN OPERATOR (OWNER)	STATUS	ORIGINAL MSN	LINE NO.	DEL. DATE	ENG. TYPE	FLEET NO.	PREV. REG. [COMMENTS]
B737-2K2C (A)	F-GIXA	AIR MEDITERRANEE (ARP)	L	20836	354	05/17/74	JT8D-15A (HK3)		PH-TVC
B737-222	F-GYAL	AIR MEDITERRANEE		19074	95	11/23/68	JT8D-9A		N9036U, G-AZNZ, N144AW, N468AT
B737-229C (A)	F-	AXIS AIRLINES (EURO AV)		21738	576	05/25/79	JT8D-15/15A		OO-SDR, G-BYYF
B737-230C	F-GFVI	L'AEROPOSTALE		20256	238	02/11/70	JT8D-9A (HK3)		D-ABFE, N304XV
B737-2K2C (A)	F-GGVP	L'AEROPOSTALE		20943	405	03/31/75	JT8D-15 (HK3)		PH-TVD, G-BKBT, VT-EKC [LST BIE 11/12/00]
B737-2K2C (A)	F-GGVQ	L'AEROPOSTALE		20944	408	04/16/75	JT8D-15 (HK3)		PH-TVE, VT-EKD [LST BIE 11/12/00]
B737-2K2C (A)	F-GIXA	L'AEROPOSTALE		20836	354	05/17/74	JT8D-15A (HK3)		PH-TVC ["EUROPE AIR POST"; LST BIE]
B737-229 (A)	F-GVAC	WESTAIR (AAF)	L	20907	351	04/26/74	JT8D-15 (HK3)		LX-LGN, OO-SDA

G-UNITED KINGDOM

A/C TYPE	CURRENT REG. NO.	LAST KNOWN OPERATOR (OWNER)	STATUS	ORIGINAL MSN	LINE NO.	DEL. DATE	ENG. TYPE	FLEET NO.	PREV. REG. [COMMENTS]
B737-236 (A)	G-BGDR	BRITISH AIRWAYS (AEROCAR)		21805	697	09/18/80	JT8D-15A		[LRF 02/09/01; PARKED LGW; TO BE ST SFR]
B737-236 (A)	G-BKYH	BRITISH AIRWAYS		23166	1067	12/13/84	JT8D-15A		[LRF 01/17/01; OO TO AAR?]
B737-229C (A)	G-BYYK	EUROPEAN AIRCHARTER (EURO AV)		20916	403	03/19/75	JT8D-15/15A		OO-SDK
B737-229C (A)	G-BZKP	EUROPEAN AIRCHARTER (EURO AV)		20915	401	03/07/75	JT8D-15/15A		OO-SDJ [PARKED LBG; ALL WHITE, NO TITLES]
B737-229 (A)	G-CEAC	EUROPEAN AIRCHARTER (EURO AV)		20911	360	06/18/74	JT8D-15A (HK3)		C-GNDX, OO-SDE
B737-229 (A)	G-CEAD	EUROPEAN AIRCHARTER (EURO AV)		21137	421	07/01/75	JT8D-15A (HK3)		OO-SDM [OPF GBL FROM 03/26/00]
B737-229 (A)	G-CEAE	EUROPEAN AIRCHARTER (EURO AV)		20912	365	07/19/74	JT8D-15 (HK3)		OO-SDF [LST SIC 04/01]
B737-229 (A)	G-CEAF	EUROPEAN AIRCHARTER (EURO AV)		20910	358	06/06/74	JT8D-15 (HK3)		EC-EEG, OO-SDD, G-BYRI [LST SIC FOR SUMMER 2001]
B737-229 (A)	G-CEAG	EUROPEAN AIRCHARTER		21136	420	06/25/75	JT8D-15/15A		OO-SDL [LST SIC]
B737-229 (A)	G-CEAH	EUROPEAN AIRCHARTER (EURO AV)		21135	418	06/12/75	JT8D-15/15A		OO-SDG [PARKED LBG; TO BE LST PALMAIR]
B737-229 (A)	G-CEAI	EUROPEAN AIRCHARTER		21176	431	12/03/75	JT8D-15/15A		N8277V, 9M-MBP, OO-SDN [STD BRU AS OO-SDN]
B737-229 (A)	G-CEAJ	EUROPEAN AIRCHARTER (EURO AV)		21177	433	12/09/75	JT8D-15/15A		OO-SDO

HK-COLOMBIA

A/C TYPE	CURRENT REG. NO.	LAST KNOWN OPERATOR (OWNER)	STATUS	ORIGINAL MSN	LINE NO.	DEL. DATE	ENG. TYPE	FLEET NO.	PREV. REG. [COMMENTS]
B737-230C	HK-4216X	AEROSUCRE COLOMBIA (FSBU)		20253	223	12/15/69	JT8D-9		D-ABBE, N301XV, HP-1134CMP, HP-1408PVI

HP-PANAMA

A/C TYPE	CURRENT REG. NO.	LAST KNOWN OPERATOR (OWNER)	STATUS	ORIGINAL MSN	LINE NO.	DEL. DATE	ENG. TYPE	FLEET NO.	PREV. REG. [COMMENTS]
B737-204 (A)	HP-1163CMP	COPA PANAMA (FSBU)		21693	541	11/20/78	JT8D-15		G-BFVA
B737-204 (A)	HP-1195CMP	COPA PANAMA (FSBU)		20806	338	01/31/74	JT8D-15		G-BAZG
B737-2S3 (A)	HP-1234CMP	COPA PANAMA (INTERLEASE)		22660	849	03/17/82	JT8D-15		G-BRJP, VR-HYK
B737-2P6 (A)	HP-1255CMP	COPA PANAMA (POLA)		21359	500	09/13/77	JT8D-15		A40-BG, G-BGFS, OO-ABB, OO-TYB, HR-SHQ
B737-219 (A)	HP-1288CMP	COPA PANAMA (IAI PACIFIC)		22088	676	07/01/80	JT8D-15		ZK-NAS, N318CM
B737-219 (A)	HP-1297CMP	COPA PANAMA (INTL. A/C INV)		21645	535	10/12/78	JT8D-15		ZK-NAR, N237TA
B737-2P5 (A)	HP-1322CMP	COPA PANAMA (FSBU)		22667	794	09/29/81	JT8D-15		N5573X, HS-TBD, AP-BEV
B737-2P5 (A)	HP-1324CMP	COPA PANAMA (FSBU)		23113	1010	02/22/84	JT8D-15		HS-TBE, AP-BEW

A/C TYPE	CURRENT REG. NO.	LAST KNOWN OPERATOR (OWNER)	STATUS	ORIGINAL MSN	LINE NO.	DEL. DATE	ENG. TYPE	FLEET NO.	PREV. REG. [COMMENTS]
B737-2P6 (A)	HP-1339CMP	COPA PANAMA (GECA)		21677	538	11/02/78	JT8D-15		A40-BI, EI-CKW
B737-2P6 (A)	HP-1340CMP	COPA PANAMA (GECA)		21612	528	08/09/78	JT8D-15		A40-BH, EI-CKK
HS-THAILAND									
B737-2Z6 (A)	22-222	ROYAL THAI AIR FORCE		23059	980	12/15/83	JT8D-15		N45733 [STD BKK]
B737-281 (A)	HS-	PHUKET AIRLINES		20506	280	05/20/71	JT8D-9A		JA8412, PK-JHC
B737-281 (A)	HS-	PHUKET AIRLINES		20507	282	06/04/71	JT8D-9A		JA8413, PK-JHG
HZ-SAUDI ARABIA									
B737-2K5 (A)	HZ-MIS	H.E. SHEIKH MUSTAFA M.A. EDREES		22600	816	01/08/82	JT8D-17 (HK3)		D-AHLH, CS-TME
B737-268C (A)	HZ-AGA	SAUDI ARABIAN AIRLINES		20574	294	03/14/72	JT8D-15		
B737-268C (A)	HZ-AGB	SAUDI ARABIAN AIRLINES		20575	295	04/07/72	JT8D-15		
B737-268 (A)	HZ-AGC	SAUDI ARABIAN AIRLINES		20576	297	05/05/72	JT8D-15		
B737-268 (A)	HZ-AGD	SAUDI ARABIAN AIRLINES		20577	298	05/19/72	JT8D-15		
B737-268 (A)	HZ-AGE	SAUDI ARABIAN AIRLINES		20578	299	05/26/72	JT8D-15		
B737-268 (A)	HZ-AGF	SAUDI ARABIAN AIRLINES		20882	356	05/31/74	JT8D-15		
B737-268 (A)	HZ-AGG	SAUDI ARABIAN AIRLINES		20883	366	07/26/74	JT8D-15		
B737-268 (A)	HZ-AGH	SAUDI ARABIAN AIRLINES		21275	467	07/30/76	JT8D-15		
B737-268 (A)	HZ-AGI	SAUDI ARABIAN AIRLINES		21276	468	08/20/76	JT8D-15		
B737-268 (A)	HZ-AGJ	SAUDI ARABIAN AIRLINES		21277	469	08/26/76	JT8D-15		
B737-268 (A)	HZ-AGK	SAUDI ARABIAN AIRLINES		21280	471	11/01/76	JT8D-15		
B737-268 (A)	HZ-AGL	SAUDI ARABIAN AIRLINES		21281	472	10/01/76	JT8D-15		
B737-268 (A)	HZ-AGN	SAUDI ARABIAN AIRLINES		21283	477	12/01/76	JT8D-15		N1243E
B737-268 (A)	HZ-AGO	SAUDI ARABIAN AIRLINES		21360	485	03/18/77	JT8D-15		
B737-268 (A)	HZ-AGP	SAUDI ARABIAN AIRLINES		21361	488	04/29/77	JT8D-15		
B737-268 (A)	HZ-AGQ	SAUDI ARABIAN AIRLINES		21362	511	03/08/78	JT8D-15		
B737-268 (A)	HZ-AGR	SAUDI ARABIAN AIRLINES		21653	531	09/14/78	JT8D-15		
B737-268 (A)	HZ-AGS	SAUDI ARABIAN AIRLINES		21654	532	09/26/78	JT8D-15		
B737-268 (A)	HZ-HM4	SAUDI ARABIAN VIP AIRCRAFT		22050	622	12/14/79	JT8D-15 (HK3)		HZ-AGT
B737-2S2C (A)	N715A	SAUDI ARAMCO AVIATION		21928	603	09/28/79	JT8D-17		N204FE
B737-2X2 (A)	N719A	SAUDI ARAMCO AVIATION		22679	807	10/31/81	JT8D-17		DQ-FDM
B737-2S2C (A)	N720A	SAUDI ARAMCO AVIATION		21926	597	08/29/79	JT8D-17		N201FE
I-ITALY									
B737-229 (A)	I-JETA	AIR ONE		21839	593	08/14/79	JT8D-15A		OO-SBS, LX-OOO
B737-230 (A)	I-JETC	AIR ONE		23153	1075	01/17/85	JT8D-15 (HK3)		D-ABMA
B737-230 (A)	I-JETD	AIR ONE (SARDALEASING)		23158	1089	03/07/85	JT8D-15 (HK3)		D-ABMF

A/C TYPE	CURRENT REG. NO.	LAST KNOWN OPERATOR (OWNER)	STATUS	ORIGINAL MSN	LINE NO.	DEL. DATE	ENG. TYPE	FLEET NO.	PREV. REG. [COMMENTS]
B737-228 (A)	EI-CRN	AIR SICILIA (RANCEMONT)		23008	952	03/24/83	JT8D-15A		F-GBYI
B737-228 (A)	EI-CTX	AIR SICILIA (RANCEMONT)		23006	944	02/23/83	JT8D-15A		F-GBYG
B737-229 (A)	G-CEAE	AIR SICILIA (EAF)	L	20912	365	07/19/74	JT8D-15 (HK3)		OO-SDF
B737-229 (A)	G-CEAF	AIR SICILIA (EAF)	L	20910	358	06/06/74	JT8D-15 (HK3)		EC-EEG, OO-SDD, G-BYRI
B737-229 (A)	G-CEAG	AIR SICILIA (EAF)	L	21136	420	06/25/75	JT8D-15/15A		OO-SDL

JA-JAPAN

A/C TYPE	CURRENT REG. NO.	LAST KNOWN OPERATOR (OWNER)	STATUS	ORIGINAL MSN	LINE NO.	DEL. DATE	ENG. TYPE	FLEET NO.	PREV. REG. [COMMENTS]
B737-2Q3 (A)	JA8250	JAPAN TRANSOCEAN AIR		23481	1241	06/17/86	JT8D-17		
B737-205 (A)	JA8366	JAPAN TRANSOCEAN AIR (RYUICHI)		23469	1266	08/26/86	JT8D-17		LN-SUV
B737-2Q3 (A)	JA8492	JAPAN TRANSOCEAN AIR		23117	1033	06/19/84	JT8D-17		
B737-205 (A)	JA8528	JAPAN TRANSOCEAN AIR (AIR HAWK)		23464	1223	04/29/86	JT8D-17		LN-SUA, PP-SPA

LV-ARGENTINA

A/C TYPE	CURRENT REG. NO.	LAST KNOWN OPERATOR (OWNER)	STATUS	ORIGINAL MSN	LINE NO.	DEL. DATE	ENG. TYPE	FLEET NO.	PREV. REG. [COMMENTS]
B737-287	LV-JMW	AEROLINEAS ARGENTINAS		20403	236	02/27/70	JT8D-9A		[WFU 12/00]
B737-287	LV-JMX	AEROLINEAS ARGENTINAS		20404	243	03/25/70	JT8D-9A		
B737-287	LV-JMY	AEROLINEAS ARGENTINAS		20405	248	04/09/70	JT8D-9A		
B737-287	LV-JMZ	AEROLINEAS ARGENTINAS		20406	261	07/31/70	JT8D-9A		[RTD 11/99; TO BE BU AEP]
B737-287C	LV-JND	AEROLINEAS ARGENTINAS		20407	263	09/04/70	JT8D-9A		
B737-287 (A)	LV-JTD	AEROLINEAS ARGENTINAS		20523	285	10/08/71	JT8D-9A		LV-PRQ
B737-287 (A)	LV-JTO	AEROLINEAS ARGENTINAS		20537	291	12/23/71	JT8D-9A		
B737-287 (A)	LV-LEB	AEROLINEAS ARGENTINAS		20768	331	11/14/73	JT8D-9A		
B737-287 (A)	LV-LIV	AEROLINEAS ARGENTINAS		20965	381	12/12/74	JT8D-9A		
B737-212	LV-WRO	AEROLINEAS ARGENTINAS (PACA)		20521	288	11/18/71	JT8D-9A		9M-AQC, CF-NAW, EI-BNS, N130AW, C-GXPW, N161FN
B737-2A8 (A)	LV-WSU	AEROLINEAS ARGENTINAS (PACA)		21496	503	11/10/77	JT8D-17		VT-EFK, N912PG
B737-281 (A)	LV-WSY	AEROLINEAS ARGENTINAS		20562	293	04/03/72	JT8D-9A		JA8416
B737-2A8 (A)	LV-WTG	AEROLINEAS ARGENTINAS (PACA)		21498	505	12/08/77	JT8D-17		VT-EFM, K2370, N913PG
B737-281 (A)	LV-WTX	AEROLINEAS ARGENTINAS		20561	292	04/13/72	JT8D-9A		N1788B, JA8415, LV-PMI
B737-2P6 (A)	LV-YEB	AEROLINEAS ARGENTINAS (GECA)		21733	564	04/10/79	JT8D-15 (HK3)		A40-BJ, EI-CLK
B737-2P6 (A)	LV-YIB	AEROLINEAS ARGENTINAS (GECA)		21356	496	07/15/77	JT8D-15 (HK3)		A40-BD, EI-CKL
B737-236 (A)	LV-ZEC	AEROLINEAS ARGENTINAS (PEGA)		21796	648	04/07/80	JT8D-9A		G-BGDG, N921PG
B737-236 (A)	LV-ZIE	AEROLINEAS ARGENTINAS (PEGA)		21798	658	04/30/80	JT8D-15A		G-BGDI, N922PG
B737-266 (A)	LV-ZRD	AEROLINEAS ARGENTINAS (GECA)		21192	451	03/19/76	JT8D-17		SU-AYI, 4R-ULO, N192GP, TF-ABG, EI-CNP
B737-236 (A)	LV-ZRE	AEROLINEAS ARGENTINAS (PEGA)		23168	1077	01/28/85	JT8D-15A		G-BKYJ, N927PG
B737-236 (A)	LV-ZRO	AEROLINEAS ARGENTINAS (PEGA)		23164	1060	11/19/84	JT8D-15A		G-BKYF, OB-1712, N925PG
B737-236 (A)	LV-ZSD	AEROLINEAS ARGENTINAS (PEGA)		23171	1088	03/01/85	JT8D-15A		G-BKYM, N930PG [LV-OOO?]
B737-236 (A)	LV-ZSW	AEROLINEAS ARGENTINAS (PEGA)		23170	1086	02/22/85	JT8D-15A		G-BKYL, N937PG
B737-236 (A)	LV-ZTD	AEROLINEAS ARGENTINAS (PEGA)		23225	1102	04/12/85	JT8D-15A		G-BKYO, N939PG
B737-236 (A)	LV-ZTG	AEROLINEAS ARGENTINAS (PEGA)		23169	1081	02/01/85	JT8D-15A		G-BKYK, N938PG
B737-236 (A)	LV-ZTJ	AEROLINEAS ARGENTINAS (PEGA)		23172	1091	03/21/85	JT8D-15A		G-BKYN, N948PG
B737-236 (A)	LV-ZTT	AEROLINEAS ARGENTINAS (PEGA)		21806	699	09/26/80	JT8D-15A		G-BGDS, N947PG

A/C TYPE	CURRENT REG. NO.	LAST KNOWN OPERATOR (OWNER)	STATUS	ORIGINAL MSN	LINE NO.	DEL. DATE	ENG. TYPE	FLEET NO.	PREV. REG. [COMMENTS]
B737-236 (A)	LV-ZTY	AEROLINEAS ARGENTINAS (PEGA)		23159	1047	09/14/84	JT8D-15A		G-BKYA, N949PG
B737-236 (A)	LV-ZXC	AEROLINEAS ARGENTINAS (PEGA)		23160	1053	09/27/84	JT8D-15A		G-BKYB, N950PG
B737-236 (A)	LV-	AEROLINEAS ARGENTINAS (BOUL)		21794	643	03/12/80	JT8D-15A		G-BGDE
B737-236 (A)	LV-	AEROLINEAS ARGENTINAS (BOUL)		21795	645	03/20/80	JT8D-15A		G-BGDF
B737-236 (A)	N952PG	AEROLINEAS ARGENTINAS (PEGA)		23226	1105	04/24/85	JT8D-15A		G-BKYP
B737-236 (A)	LV-	AEROLINEAS ARGENTINAS (BOUL)		21799	660	05/07/80	JT8D-15A		G-BGDJ
B737-2P6 (A)	LV-WGX	AMERICAN FALCON (CAP A/C)		21358	498	08/09/77	JT8D-15		A40-BF, N930CA [O/S FOR MX]
B737-228 (A)	LV-ZTE	AUSTRAL (TRIT)		23349	1135	07/23/85	JT8D-15A		F-GBYM, N238TR
B737-228 (A)	LV-ZTI	AUSTRAL		23002	937	01/26/83	JT8D-15A		F-GBYC, N239TR
B737-228 (A)	LV-ZTX	AUSTRAL (FSBU)		23504	1267	08/28/86	JT8D-15A		F-GBYO, N240TR
B737-228 (A)	LV-ZXB	AUSTRAL (TRIT)		23009	958	04/27/83	JT8D-15A		F-GBYJ, N242TR
B737-228 (A)	LV-ZXH	AUSTRAL (TRIT)		23503	1256	08/03/86	JT8D-15A		F-GBYN, N243TR
B737-228 (A)	LV-ZXP	AUSTRAL (TRIT)		23003	939	02/04/83	JT8D-15A		F-GBYD, N244TR
B737-201	N288CD	CARDINAL AIRLINES		20211	141	03/03/69	JT8D-9A		N741N, N211US, C6-BFJ [O/S FOR MX]
B737-2M6 (A)	LV-VGF	LAPA (AFIN)		21138	422	07/31/75	JT8D-15		N1787B, VR-UEC, VS-UEC, V8-UEC, 9M-MBQ, ZK-NAL
B737-204C	LV-WSH	LAPA (ARDENNES)		20282	245	03/17/70	JT8D-9A		G-AXNA, PH-TVF, F-GGPC
B737-266 (A)	LV-YBS	LAPA (GECA)		21193	453	03/30/76	JT8D-17A		SU-AYJ, PH-TVN, SU-BBX, 5Y-BHV, N193GP, LV-PNI
B737-2S3 (A)	LV-YGB	LAPA (GECA)		22633	746	03/19/81	JT8D-15		G-DDDV, A40-BL, VT-EWD, N633GP
B737-204 (A)	LV-YXB	LAPA (TRIT)		21335	487	04/13/77	JT8D-15		G-BECG, N102TR, LV-PNO
B737-204 (A)	LV-YZA	LAPA (TRIT)		21336	489	05/06/77	JT8D-15		G-BECH, N103TR, LV-PNS
B737-2T4 (A)	LY-BSD	LITHUANIAN AIRLINES		22701	886	12/30/82	JT8D-17		N4569N
B737-2T2 (A)	LY-BSG	LITHUANIAN AIRLINES		22793	892	12/30/82	JT8D-17		N1779B, N4571M

N-UNITED STATES OF AMERICA

A/C TYPE	CURRENT REG. NO.	LAST KNOWN OPERATOR (OWNER)	STATUS	ORIGINAL MSN	LINE NO.	DEL. DATE	ENG. TYPE	FLEET NO.	PREV. REG. [COMMENTS]
B737-205 (A)	N370BC	BASIC CAPITAL MGMT INC.		23468	1262	08/12/86	JT8D-17A		LN-SUJ, N891FS, HZ-TBA
B737-247	N737BG	THE BOEING COMPANY		19612	93	11/16/68	JT8D-9A (HK3)		N4515W, N903LC [BOEING JSF AVIONICS FLYING LABORATORY]
B737-230 (A)	N621AC	ACCESS AIR		23156	1082	02/07/85	JT8D-15 (HK3)		D-ABMD [PARKED TUS]
B737-230 (A)	N623AC	ACCESS AIR		23157	1085	02/21/85	JT8D-15 (HK3)		D-ABME
B737-282 (A)	N233TM	AIR LAUGHLIN (CXP)	L	23043	972	06/30/83	JT8D-17A (HK3)		CS-TEM
B737-214	N457TM	AIR LAUGHLIN (CXP)	L	20156	181	06/19/69	JT8D-15 (HK3)		N983PS, ZK-NAK, N323XV, TF-ISA

A/C TYPE	CURRENT REG. NO.	LAST KNOWN OPERATOR (OWNER)	STATUS	ORIGINAL MSN	LINE NO.	DEL. DATE	ENG. TYPE	FLEET NO.	PREV. REG. [COMMENTS]
B737-2L9 (A)	N464AT	AIRTRAN AIRWAYS		21278	479	12/10/76	JT8D-17 (HK3)		N1787B, N8277V, OY-APG, 4R-ALC, F-GCGR, D2-TBT, EI-BMY, G-BKRO, C6-BFC, XA-TCP, N358
B737-2L9 (A)	N465AT	AIRTRAN AIRWAYS		21528	517	04/28/78	JT8D-17 (HK3)		OY-API, G-BICV, C6-BEX, XA-TCQ, N359AS
B737-284 (A)	N470AT	AIRTRAN AIRWAYS (POLA)		21501	492	08/31/77	JT8D-9A (HK3)		N70722, N196AW, N310VA
B737-2L9 (A)	N737Q	AIRTRAN AIRWAYS		21279	480	12/22/76	JT8D-17 (HK3)		N1787B, OY-APH, EI-BII, F-GCGS, D2-TBU, C6-BEQ [TO BE REG N466AT]
B737-290C (A)	N730AS	ALASKA AIRLINES		22577	760	05/24/81	JT8D-17 (HK3)		
B737-290C (A)	N740AS	ALASKA AIRLINES		22578	767	06/02/81	JT8D-17 (HK3)		
B737-2Q8C (A)	N741AS	ALASKA AIRLINES		21959	610	10/26/79	JT8D-17 (HK3)		N206FE
B737-290C (A)	N742AS	ALASKA AIRLINES		23136	1032	06/15/84	JT8D-17 (HK3)		
B737-210C (A)	N743AS	ALASKA AIRLINES		21821	590	07/27/79	JT8D-17 (HK3)		N492WC
B737-210C (A)	N744AS	ALASKA AIRLINES		21822	605	10/23/79	JT8D-17 (HK3)		N493WC
B737-298C (A)	N745AS	ALASKA AIRLINES		20794	346	04/30/74	JT8D-17 (HK3)		9Q-CNJ, N87WA
B737-2X6C (A)	N746AS	ALASKA AIRLINES		23123	1042	08/14/84	JT8D-17A (HK3)		N672MA
B737-2X6C (A)	N747AS	ALASKA AIRLINES		23124	1046	08/28/84	JT8D-17A		N673MA, 9M-PMU
B737-2S5C (A)	N802AL	ALOHA AIRLINES (ACG AQUISITION)		22148	663	05/20/80	JT8D-9A		C-GENL
B737-2Q9 (A)	N804AL	ALOHA AIRLINES (ACG AQUISITION)		21719	551	01/26/79	JT8D-9A		C-GNDG, OO-TEK, C-GQBT, N385PA
B737-2M6C (A)	N805AL	ALOHA AIRLINES (POLA)		21809	637	03/05/80	JT8D-15		VR-UED, VS-UED, V8-UED
B737-2S2C (A)	N806AL	ALOHA AIRLINES		21927	600	09/19/79	JT8D-9A		N203FE, CC-CHU
B737-2T4 (A)	N807AL	ALOHA AIRLINES (COMPASS CAP.)		23443	1151	10/05/85	JT8D-9A		N1785B, B-2511
B737-2T4 (A)	N808AL	ALOHA AIRLINES (COMPASS CAP.)		23445	1155	10/18/85	JT8D-9A		N1791B, B-2514
B737-2Q9 (A)	N809AL	ALOHA AIRLINES (FSBU)		21720	552	01/30/79	JT8D-15		N37AF, N458AC
B737-2Y5 (A)	N810AL	ALOHA AIRLINES (FSBU)		24031	1523	03/17/88	JT8D-9A		9H-ABG
B737-2X6C (A)	N816AL	ALOHA AIRLINES (AJET)		23122	1036	07/17/84	JT8D-9A		N671MA, TF-ABE
B737-2X6C (A)	N817AL	ALOHA AIRLINES (BJET)		23292	1113	07/05/85	JT8D-9A		N674MA
B737-230 (A)	N818AL	ALOHA AIRLINES (JETZ)		22117	703	01/27/81	JT8D-9A		N1786B, D-ABFF, VT-MGD
B737-25A (A)	N819AL	ALOHA AIRLINES (BCCI)		23791	1486	12/17/87	JT8D-9A		N725ML, N685MA
B737-230 (A)	N820AL	ALOHA AIRLINES (JETZ)		22138	790	08/27/81	JT8D-9A		N1800B, D-ABHM
B737-230 (A)	N821AL	ALOHA AIRLINES (BANCORP LSG)		23155	1079	01/31/85	JT8D-9A (HK3)		D-ABMC
B737-230 (A)	N823AL	ALOHA AIRLINES (JETZ)		23154	1078	01/24/85	JT8D-9A (HK3)		D-ABMB
B737-282 (A)	N824AL	ALOHA AIRLINES (FSBU)		23045	978	07/22/83	JT8D-9A		N1786B, CS-TEO
B737-282C (A)	N826AL	ALOHA AIRLINES (FSBU)		23051	1002	12/29/83	JT8D-9A		CS-TEQ
B737-209 (A)	N827AL	ALOHA AIRLINES (FSBU)		23913	1579	07/15/88	JT8D-9A		B-1876, 9M-PMY, PK-RIO
B737-2E3 (A)	N138AW	AMERICA WEST AIRLINES (CITG)		22792	887	06/29/82	JT8D-15 (HK3)		CC-CIY
B737-2U9 (A)	N149AW	AMERICA WEST AIRLINES		22575	749	03/31/81	JT8D-15 (HK3)		5W-PAL, ZK-POL, ZK-NEF
B737-277 (A)	N178AW	AMERICA WEST AIRLINES (IBM)		22645	768	06/15/81	JT8D-15 (HK3)		VH-CZM
B737-277 (A)	N179AW	AMERICA WEST AIRLINES		22646	778	07/15/81	JT8D-15 (HK3)		VH-CZN
B737-277 (A)	N180AW	AMERICA WEST AIRLINES (PAC'CORP)		22647	785	08/11/81	JT8D-15 (HK3)		VH-CZO

A/C TYPE	CURRENT REG. NO.	LAST KNOWN OPERATOR (OWNER)	STATUS	ORIGINAL MSN	LINE NO.	DEL. DATE	ENG. TYPE	FLEET NO.	PREV. REG. [COMMENTS]
B737-277 (A)	N181AW	AMERICA WEST AIRLINES (PAC'CORP)		22648	789	08/26/81	JT8D-15 (HK3)		N56807, VH-CZP
B737-277 (A)	N182AW	AMERICA WEST AIRLINES (PAC'CORP)		22649	801	10/13/81	JT8D-15 (HK3)		VH-CZQ
B737-277 (A)	N183AW	AMERICA WEST AIRLINES		22650	806	10/20/81	JT8D-15 (HK3)		VH-CZR
B737-277 (A)	N184AW	AMERICA WEST AIRLINES		22651	819	12/09/81	JT8D-15 (HK3)		VH-CZS
B737-277 (A)	N185AW	AMERICA WEST AIRLINES (PAC'CORP)		22652	831	01/26/82	JT8D-15 (HK3)		VH-CZT
B737-277 (A)	N186AW	AMERICA WEST AIRLINES (EDS LEASE)		22653	832	02/17/82	JT8D-15 (HK3)		N8293V, VH-CZU
B737-277 (A)	N187AW	AMERICA WEST AIRLINES (EDS LEASE)		22654	862	04/21/82	JT8D-15 (HK3)		VH-CZV
B737-277 (A)	N188AW	AMERICA WEST AIRLINES (IBM)		22655	872	05/17/82	JT8D-15 (HK3)		VH-CZW
B737-277 (A)	N189AW	AMERICA WEST AIRLINES (CITG)		22656	876	06/02/82	JT8D-15 (HK3)		VH-CZX
B737-230C	N737TW	AMERISTAR AIR CARGO (SIERRA AM.)		20257	274	01/19/71	JT8D-15 (HK3)		D-ABGE, TF-ABX
B737-230C	N767TW	AMERISTAR AIR CARGO (SIERRA AM.)		20258	276	02/18/71	JT8D-15 (HK3)		D-ABHE, TF-ABF
B737-205 (A)	N733AR	ARCO FLIGHT OPERATIONS (SANWA)		23466	1236	06/04/86	JT8D-17A (HK3)		PP-SPC, LN-SUZ
B737-205 (A)	N736BP	BP EXPLORATION ALASKA (SANWA)		23465	1226	05/06/86	JT8D-17A (HK3)		PP-SPB, LN-SUU
B737-282 (A)	N233TM	CASINO EXPRESS		23043	972	06/30/83	JT8D-17A (HK3)		CS-TEM [LST AIR LAUGHLIN]
B737-282 (A)	N344TM	CASINO EXPRESS		23044	973	06/30/83	JT8D-17A (HK3)		CS-TEN
B737-214	N457TM	CASINO EXPRESS		20156	181	06/19/69	JT8D-15 (HK3)		N983PS, ZK-NAK, N323XV, TF-ISA [LST AIR LAUGHLIN]
B737-282 (A)	N789TM	CASINO EXPRESS		23046	981	08/12/83	JT8D-17A		CS-TEP [OPF NATIONAL AIRLINES]
B737-2J8 (A)	N235WA	DELTA AIRLINES		22859	890	05/01/84	JT8D-15 (HK3)	359	N4562N
B737-247 (A)	N236WA	DELTA AIRLINES (FINO)		23184	1061	11/19/84	JT8D-15 (HK3)	360	["EXPRESS"]
B737-247 (A)	N237WA	DELTA AIRLINES (FINO)		23185	1065	11/28/84	JT8D-15 (HK3)	361	["EXPRESS"]
B737-247 (A)	N238WA	DELTA AIRLINES (FINO)		23186	1066	11/28/84	JT8D-15 (HK3)	362	["EXPRESS"]
B737-247 (A)	N239WA	DELTA AIRLINES (FINO)		23187	1070	12/13/84	JT8D-15 (HK3)	363	["EXPRESS"]
B737-247 (A)	N242WA	DELTA AIRLINES		23516	1257	08/04/86	JT8D-15A (HK3)	364	["EXPRESS"]
B737-247 (A)	N243WA	DELTA AIRLINES		23517	1261	08/13/86	JT8D-15A (HK3)	365	["EXPRESS"]
B737-247 (A)	N244WA	DELTA AIRLINES		23518	1265	08/22/86	JT8D-15A (HK3)	366	
B737-247 (A)	N245WA	DELTA AIRLINES		23519	1299	12/05/86	JT8D-15A (HK3)	372	
B737-232 (A)	N301DL	DELTA AIRLINES		23073	991	10/25/83	JT8D-15A (HK3)	301	["EXPRESS"]
B737-232 (A)	N302DL	DELTA AIRLINES		23074	993	11/10/83	JT8D-15A (HK3)	302	["EXPRESS"]
B737-232 (A)	N303DL	DELTA AIRLINES		23075	994	11/22/83	JT8D-15A (HK3)	303	["EXPRESS"]
B737-232 (A)	N304DL	DELTA AIRLINES		23076	995	12/02/83	JT8D-15A (HK3)	304	["EXPRESS"]
B737-232 (A)	N305DL	DELTA AIRLINES		23077	996	12/07/83	JT8D-15A (HK3)	305	["EXPRESS"]
B737-232 (A)	N306DL	DELTA AIRLINES		23078	1000	12/22/83	JT8D-15A (HK3)	306	["EXPRESS"]
B737-232 (A)	N307DL	DELTA AIRLINES		23079	1003	05/09/84	JT8D-15A (HK3)	307	["EXPRESS"]
B737-232 (A)	N308DL	DELTA AIRLINES		23080	1004	01/30/84	JT8D-15A (HK3)	308	["EXPRESS"]
B737-232 (A)	N309DL	DELTA AIRLINES		23081	1005	02/01/84	JT8D-15A (HK3)	309	["EXPRESS"]

A/C TYPE	CURRENT REG. NO.	LAST KNOWN OPERATOR (OWNER)	STATUS	ORIGINAL MSN	LINE NO.	DEL. DATE	ENG. TYPE	FLEET NO.	PREV. REG. [COMMENTS]
B737-232 (A)	N310DA	DELTA AIRLINES		23082	1006	02/08/84	JT8D-15A (HK3)	310	["EXPRESS"]
B737-232 (A)	N311DL	DELTA AIRLINES		23083	1008	02/14/84	JT8D-15A (HK3)	311	["EXPRESS"]
B737-232 (A)	N312DL	DELTA AIRLINES		23084	1009	03/01/84	JT8D-15A (HK3)	312	["EXPRESS"]
B737-232 (A)	N313DL	DELTA AIRLINES		23085	1011	03/14/84	JT8D-15A (HK3)	313	["EXPRESS"]
B737-232 (A)	N314DA	DELTA AIRLINES		23086	1012	03/21/84	JT8D-15A (HK3)	314	["EXPRESS"]
B737-232 (A)	N315DL	DELTA AIRLINES		23087	1013	04/03/84	JT8D-15A (HK3)	315	["EXPRESS"]
B737-232 (A)	N316DL	DELTA AIRLINES		23088	1018	04/11/84	JT8D-15A (HK3)	316	["EXPRESS"]
B737-232 (A)	N317DL	DELTA AIRLINES		23089	1019	05/09/84	JT8D-15A (HK3)	317	["EXPRESS"]
B737-232 (A)	N318DL	DELTA AIRLINES		23090	1020	05/16/84	JT8D-15A (HK3)	318	["EXPRESS"]
B737-232 (A)	N319DL	DELTA AIRLINES		23091	1021	11/14/84	JT8D-15A (HK3)	319	["EXPRESS"]
B737-232 (A)	N320DL	DELTA AIRLINES		23092	1023	06/01/84	JT8D-15A (HK3)	320	["EXPRESS"]
B737-232 (A)	N321DL	DELTA AIRLINES		23093	1024	09/05/84	JT8D-15A (HK3)	321	["EXPRESS"]
B737-232 (A)	N322DL	DELTA AIRLINES		23094	1026	08/10/84	JT8D-15A (HK3)	322	["EXPRESS"]
B737-232 (A)	N323DL	DELTA AIRLINES		23095	1027	06/06/84	JT8D-15A (HK3)	323	["EXPRESS"]
B737-232 (A)	N324DL	DELTA AIRLINES		23096	1028	07/03/84	JT8D-15A (HK3)	324	["EXPRESS"]
B737-232 (A)	N325DL	DELTA AIRLINES		23097	1029	07/10/84	JT8D-15A (HK3)	325	["EXPRESS"]
B737-232 (A)	N326DL	DELTA AIRLINES		23098	1031	10/10/84	JT8D-15A (HK3)	326	["EXPRESS"]
B737-232 (A)	N327DL	DELTA AIRLINES		23099	1035	08/02/84	JT8D-15A (HK3)	327	["EXPRESS"]
B737-232 (A)	N328DL	DELTA AIRLINES		23100	1038	09/12/84	JT8D-15A (HK3)	328	["EXPRESS"]
B737-232 (A)	N329DL	DELTA AIRLINES (GECA)		23101	1041	11/01/84	JT8D-15A (HK3)	329	["EXPRESS"]
B737-232 (A)	N330DL	DELTA AIRLINES		23102	1045	10/03/84	JT8D-15A (HK3)	330	["EXPRESS"]
B737-232 (A)	N331DL	DELTA AIRLINES		23103	1051	11/13/84	JT8D-15A (HK3)	331	["EXPRESS"]
B737-232 (A)	N332DL	DELTA AIRLINES		23104	1062	12/04/84	JT8D-15A (HK3)	332	["EXPRESS"]
B737-232 (A)	N334DL	DELTA AIRLINES		23105	1068	12/13/84	JT8D-15A (HK3)	333	["EXPRESS"]
B737-2S3 (A)	N367DL	DELTA AIRLINES (GECA)		21774	563	04/05/79	JT8D-15 (HK3)	367	G-BMHG, OO-TYD, EI-BPY [TO BE WFU 09/01]
B737-2S3 (A)	N369DL	DELTA AIRLINES (GECA)		21776	577	05/31/79	JT8D-15 (HK3)	369	G-BMEC, EI-BPW, N368DL [TO BE WFU 09/01]
B737-247 (A)	N373DL	DELTA AIRLINES		23520	1329	02/03/87	JT8D-15A (HK3)	373	
B737-247 (A)	N374DL	DELTA AIRLINES		23521	1342	02/18/87	JT8D-15A (HK3)	374	
B737-247 (A)	N375DL	DELTA AIRLINES		23602	1347	02/27/87	JT8D-15A (HK3)	375	
B737-247 (A)	N376DL	DELTA AIRLINES		23603	1361	03/26/87	JT8D-15A (HK3)	376	
B737-247 (A)	N377DL	DELTA AIRLINES		23604	1369	04/15/87	JT8D-15A (HK3)	377	
B737-247 (A)	N378DL	DELTA AIRLINES		23605	1371	04/17/87	JT8D-15A (HK3)	378	
B737-247 (A)	N379DL	DELTA AIRLINES		23606	1379	05/06/87	JT8D-15A (HK3)	379	
B737-247 (A)	N380DL	DELTA AIRLINES		23607	1387	05/22/87	JT8D-15A (HK3)	380	
B737-247 (A)	N381DL	DELTA AIRLINES		23608	1399	06/18/87	JT8D-15A (HK3)	381	
B737-247 (A)	N382DL	DELTA AIRLINES		23609	1403	06/29/87	JT8D-15A (HK3)	382	["EXPRESS"]
B737-275 (A)	N4529W	EG & G SPECIAL PROJECTS (USAF)		20785	335	12/19/73	JT8D-9A (HK3)		C-FPWB
CT43A (B737-200A)	N5175U	EG & G SPECIAL PROJECTS (USAF)	L	20689	334	12/20/73	JT8D-9A (HK3)		72-0282

A/C TYPE	CURRENT REG. NO.	LAST KNOWN OPERATOR (OWNER)	STATUS	ORIGINAL MSN	LINE NO.	DEL. DATE	ENG. TYPE	FLEET NO.	PREV. REG. [COMMENTS]
CT43A (B737-200A)	N5176Y	EG & G SPECIAL PROJECTS (USAF)	L	20692	339	02/19/74	JT8D-9A (HK3)		72-0285
CT43A (B737-200A) PROJECTS (USAF)	N5177C	EG & G SPECIAL	L	20693	340	02/27/74	JT8D-9A (HK3)		72-0286, N99890, N57JE
CT43A (B737-200A)	N5294E	EG & G SPECIAL PROJECTS (USAF)	L	20691	337	01/31/74	JT8D-9A (HK3)		72-0284
CT43A (B737-200A)	N5294M	EG & G SPECIAL PROJECTS (USAF)	L	20694	343	03/15/74	JT8D-9A (HK3)		72-0287
B737-2Y5 (A)	N118RW	FRONTIER AIRLINES (FIRSTAR)		23040	955	03/30/83	JT8D-15A (HK3)	276	9H-ABC, ZK-NAD, 5B-DBF
B737-2P6 (A)	N1PC	FRONTIER AIRLINES (INTL.)		21613	530	11/06/78	JT8D-15 (HK3)	272	A6-AAA
B737-228 (A)	N234TR	FRONTIER AIRLINES (TRIT)		23004	941	02/10/83	JT8D-15A (HK3)	273	F-GBYE
B737-228 (A)	N237TR	FRONTIER AIRLINES (TRIT)		23007	948	03/10/83	JT8D-15A (HK3)	274	F-GBYH
B737-2L9 (A)	N270FL	FRONTIER AIRLINES (POLA)		22733	812	11/06/81	JT8D-17 (HK3)	270	OY-MBZ, VR-HYN, N170PL
B737-2L9 (A)	N271FL	FRONTIER AIRLINES (POLA)		22734	818	11/25/81	JT8D-17 (HK3)	271	OY-MBW, VR-HYM, N171PL
B737-2Y5 (A)	N921WA	FRONTIER AIRLINES (FIRSTAR)		23039	954	03/31/83	JT8D-15A (HK3)	275	9H-ABB, ZK-NAH, PK-IJL
B737-291 (A)	N583CC	GUND SPORTS MARKETING LLC		21069	415	05/27/75	JT8D-9A		N7385F, N15255 [OP IN CLEVELAND CAVALIERS C/S]
T-43A (B737-253)	N146JS	JETT RACING AND SALES INC.		20688	330	11/29/73	JT8D-9A		71-1406
B737-247	N204AU	LORAIR (SIGNATURE)		19603	51	07/31/68	JT8D-9A		N4506W, N758N
B737-247	N165W	NORTHRUP GRUMMAN		19605	57	08/20/68	JT8D-9A		N4508W
B737-242 (A)	N159PL	PACE AIRLINES (COMPASS CAP.)		21186	438	11/12/75	JT8D-9A (HK3)		C-GNDL, N73AF, N132AW [TRASHERS/ATLANTA HAWKS C/S]
B737-247	N487GS	PACE AIRLINES (G.S. SPORTS)		19600	44	07/13/68	JT8D-9A		N4503W, N307VA [OPF CHARLOTTE HORNETS]
B737-222	N737AP	PACE AIRLINES (WS A/C LLC)		19956	211	10/10/69	JT8D-7B (HK3)		N9075U [OPF WASHINGTON WIZARDS/CAPITALS]
B737-2H4 (A)	N29SW	RYAN INTL. AIRLINES (RYAN LSG)		21340	499	09/01/77	JT8D-9A (HK3)		
B737-2H4 (A)	N54SW	RYAN INTL. AIRLINES (CL A/C)		21535	543	12/01/78	JT8D-9A		
B737-2T4 (A)	N703S	SIERRA PACIFIC AIRLINES		22529	750	03/27/81	JT8D-17 (HK3)		N51AF, EI-BRN, N703ML
B737-222	N135TA	SKY KING INC.		19940	171	05/27/69	JT8D-9A (HK3)		N9059U, PH-TVI, N135AW [OPF SACRAMENTO KINGS]
B737-297 (A)	N147AW	SKY KING INC.		22630	860	05/26/82	JT8D-9A		N729AL
B737-2H4 (A)	N102SW	SOUTHWEST AIRLINES		23108	1014	03/15/84	JT8D-9A (HK3)		
B737-2H4 (A)	N103SW	SOUTHWEST AIRLINES		23109	1016	03/23/84	JT8D-9A (HK3)		
B737-2H4 (A)	N104SW	SOUTHWEST AIRLINES		23110	1017	03/26/84	JT8D-9A (HK3)		
B737-2H4 (A)	N105SW	SOUTHWEST AIRLINES		23249	1095	03/15/85	JT8D-9A (HK3)		

A/C TYPE	CURRENT REG. NO.	LAST KNOWN OPERATOR (OWNER)	STATUS	ORIGINAL MSN	LINE NO.	DEL. DATE	ENG. TYPE	FLEET NO.	PREV. REG. [COMMENTS]
B737-2K6 (A)	N129SW	SOUTHWEST AIRLINES (CITI)		22340	678	07/11/80	JT8D-9A (HK3)		CC-CIM, N148AW
B737-2T4 (A)	N130SW	SOUTHWEST AIRLINES		22699	855	05/13/82	JT8D-9A (HK3)		N83AF
B737-2H4 (A)	N60SW	SOUTHWEST AIRLINES		21812	611	11/05/79	JT8D-9A		
B737-2H4 (A)	N62SW	SOUTHWEST AIRLINES		22060	638	03/27/80	JT8D-9A (HK3)		
B737-2H4 (A)	N63SW	SOUTHWEST AIRLINES		22061	639	03/27/80	JT8D-9A (HK3)		
B737-2H4 (A)	N64SW	SOUTHWEST AIRLINES		22062	640	03/27/80	JT8D-9A (HK3)		
B737-2H4 (A)	N67SW	SOUTHWEST AIRLINES		22356	719	12/03/80	JT8D-9A (HK3)		
B737-2H4 (A)	N68SW	SOUTHWEST AIRLINES		22357	725	12/17/80	JT8D-9A (HK3)		
B737-2T4 (A)	N702ML	SOUTHWEST AIRLINES		22054	624	12/17/79	JT8D-15 (HK3)		N53AF, G-BJXL, C-GNDG
B737-2H4 (A)	N71SW	SOUTHWEST AIRLINES		22358	732	01/23/81	JT8D-9A (HK3)		
B737-2T4 (A)	N721WN	SOUTHWEST AIRLINES		22697	817	11/25/81	JT8D-15 (HK3)		N81AF, N721ML
B737-2T4 (A)	N722WN	SOUTHWEST AIRLINES		22698	823	12/18/81	JT8D-15 (HK3)		N82AF, N722ML
B737-2H4 (A)	N73SW	SOUTHWEST AIRLINES		22673	826	12/18/81	JT8D-9A (HK3)		
B737-2H4 (A)	N74SW	SOUTHWEST AIRLINES		22674	827	12/23/81	JT8D-9A (HK3)		
B737-2H4 (A)	N80SW	SOUTHWEST AIRLINES		22675	839	02/12/82	JT8D-9A (HK3)		
B737-2H4 (A)	N81SW	SOUTHWEST AIRLINES		22730	841	02/17/82	JT8D-9A (HK3)		
B737-2H4 (A)	N82SW	SOUTHWEST AIRLINES		22731	864	04/23/82	JT8D-9A (HK3)		
B737-2H4 (A)	N83SW	SOUTHWEST AIRLINES		22732	877	05/28/82	JT8D-9A (HK3)		
B737-2H4 (A)	N85SW	SOUTHWEST AIRLINES		22826	878	06/03/82	JT8D-9A (HK3)		
B737-2H4 (A)	N86SW	SOUTHWEST AIRLINES		22827	882	06/04/82	JT8D-9A (HK3)		
B737-2H4 (A)	N89SW	SOUTHWEST AIRLINES		22904	913	09/30/82	JT8D-9A (HK3)		
B737-2H4 (A)	N90SW	SOUTHWEST AIRLINES		22905	918	10/18/82	JT8D-9A		
B737-2H4 (A)	N91SW	SOUTHWEST AIRLINES		22963	929	12/13/82	JT8D-9A		
B737-2H4 (A)	N92SW	SOUTHWEST AIRLINES		22964	933	01/04/83	JT8D-9A		
B737-2H4 (A)	N93SW	SOUTHWEST AIRLINES		22965	942	04/07/83	JT8D-9A		
B737-2H4 (A)	N94SW	SOUTHWEST AIRLINES		23053	968	05/25/83	JT8D-9A		
B737-2H4 (A)	N95SW	SOUTHWEST AIRLINES		23054	969	05/25/83	JT8D-9A		
B737-2H4 (A)	N96SW	SOUTHWEST AIRLINES		23055	970	06/30/83	JT8D-9A		
B737-236 (A)	N705S	SUNWEST INTL. (PACE)		21800	661	05/16/80	JT8D-15A (HK3)		N5700N, G-BGDK, N4361R, N923WA [OPB PACE AIRLINES]
B737-236 (A)	N920WA	SUNWEST INTL. (BOUL)		21791	626	02/14/80	JT8D-15A (HK3)		N8289V, G-BGDB [OPB PACE AIRLINES]
B737-2A1 (A)	N974UA	UNITED AIRLINES		21597	510	03/30/78	JT8D-17 (HK3)	1974	N7340F
B737-2A1 (A)	N976UA	UNITED AIRLINES		21598	512	04/12/78	JT8D-17 (HK3)	1976	N7341F
B737-291 (A)	N977UA	UNITED AIRLINES		21508	518	05/12/78	JT8D-9A (HK3)	1877	N7391F
B737-291 (A)	N978UA	UNITED AIRLINES		21509	521	06/09/78	JT8D-9A (HK3)	1878	N7392F
B737-291 (A)	N979UA	UNITED AIRLINES		21544	523	06/23/78	JT8D-9A (HK3)	1879	N7393F
B737-291 (A)	N980UA	UNITED AIRLINES		21545	525	07/19/78	JT8D-9A (HK3)	1880	N7394F
B737-291 (A)	N981UA	UNITED AIRLINES		21546	527	08/05/78	JT8D-9A (HK3)	1881	N7395F
B737-291 (A)	N982UA	UNITED AIRLINES		21640	536	10/19/78	JT8D-9A (HK3)	1882	N7396F

A/C TYPE	CURRENT REG. NO.	LAST KNOWN OPERATOR (OWNER)	STATUS	ORIGINAL MSN	LINE NO.	DEL. DATE	ENG. TYPE	FLEET NO.	PREV. REG. [COMMENTS]
B737-291 (A)	N983UA	UNITED AIRLINES		21641	537	10/26/78	JT8D-9A (HK3)	1883	N7397F
B737-291 (A)	N984UA	UNITED AIRLINES		21642	540	11/15/78	JT8D-17 (HK3)	1984	N7398F
B737-291 (A)	N985UA	UNITED AIRLINES		21747	555	02/20/79	JT8D-17 (HK3)	1985	N7342F
B737-291 (A)	N986UA	UNITED AIRLINES		21748	558	03/07/79	JT8D-17 (HK3)	1986	N7343F
B737-291 (A)	N987UA	UNITED AIRLINES		21749	569	04/30/79	JT8D-17 (HK3)	1987	N7344F
B737-291 (A)	N988UA	UNITED AIRLINES		21750	574	05/21/79	JT8D-17 (HK3)	1988	N7345F
B737-291 (A)	N989UA	UNITED AIRLINES		21751	575	05/24/79	JT8D-17 (HK3)	1989	N7346F
B737-291 (A)	N990UA	UNITED AIRLINES		21980	596	09/21/79	JT8D-17 (HK3)	1990	N7347F
B737-291 (A)	N991UA	UNITED AIRLINES		21981	601	10/02/79	JT8D-17 (HK3)	1991	N7348F
B737-291 (A)	N992UA	UNITED AIRLINES		22089	632	02/15/80	JT8D-17 (HK3)	1992	N7349F
B737-291 (A)	N993UA	UNITED AIRLINES		22383	713	11/06/80	JT8D-17 (HK3)	1993	N7350F
B737-291 (A)	N994UA	UNITED AIRLINES		22384	718	11/26/80	JT8D-17 (HK3)	1994	N7351F
B737-291 (A)	N995UA	UNITED AIRLINES		22399	723	12/15/80	JT8D-17 (HK3)	1995	N7352F
B737-291 (A)	N996UA	UNITED AIRLINES		22456	740	02/25/81	JT8D-17 (HK3)	1996	N7353F
B737-291 (A)	N997UA	UNITED AIRLINES		22457	757	04/22/81	JT8D-17 (HK3)	1997	N7354F
B737-291 (A)	N998UA	UNITED AIRLINES		22741	871	05/12/82	JT8D-17 (HK3)	1998	N7355F
B737-2B7 (A)	N125NJ	US AIRWAYS		22882	934	12/22/82	JT8D-15A (HK3)		N314AU, N270AU
B737-201 (A)	N223US	US AIRWAYS		21665	534	10/11/78	JT8D-9A (HK3)		N761N [LST CJA NTU]
B737-201 (A)	N224US	US AIRWAYS		21666	547	12/21/78	JT8D-9A (HK3)		N762N [LST CJA 09/15/00 AS C-FHCJ]
B737-201 (A)	N225US	US AIRWAYS		21667	548	01/10/79	JT8D-9A (HK3)		N763N [LST CJA 10/15/00 AS C-FJCJ]
B737-201 (A)	N226US	US AIRWAYS		21815	589	07/27/79	JT8D-9A (HK3)		N768N [LST ROY AS C-FNAX]
B737-201 (A)	N227AU	US AIRWAYS		21816	592	08/07/79	JT8D-9A (HK3)		N769N [LST ROY AS C-FRYH]
B737-201 (A)	N228US	US AIRWAYS		21817	602	09/26/79	JT8D-9A (HK3)		N772N [LST ROY 01/30/01 AS C-GNAU]
B737-201 (A)	N229US	US AIRWAYS		21818	606	10/16/79	JT8D-9A (HK3)		N773N
B737-2Q9 (A)	N230AU	US AIRWAYS		21975	612	11/07/79	JT8D-9A		N774N [LST CJA 07/20/00 AS C-FECJ]
B737-2Q9 (A)	N231US	US AIRWAYS		21976	625	12/20/79	JT8D-15 (HK3)		N775N [METROJET]
B737-201 (A)	N232US	US AIRWAYS		22018	651	04/01/80	JT8D-9A (HK3)		N778N [METROJET]
B737-201 (A)	N233US	US AIRWAYS		22273	680	07/17/80	JT8D-9A (HK3)		N779N [LST CJA NTU]
B737-201 (A)	N234US	US AIRWAYS		22274	682	07/22/80	JT8D-9A (HK3)		N780N
B737-201 (A)	N235US	US AIRWAYS		22275	687	10/27/80	JT8D-9A (HK3)		N781N [LST ROY AS C-GRYY]
B737-201 (A)	N236US	US AIRWAYS		22352	728	12/23/80	JT8D-9A (HK3)		N782N [LST CJA 07/27/00 AS C-FGCJ]
B737-201 (A)	N237US	US AIRWAYS		22353	731	01/23/81	JT8D-9A (HK3)		N783N [LST CJA 11/15/00 AS C-FVCJ]
B737-296 (A)	N238US	US AIRWAYS		22398	733	02/25/81	JT8D-9A (HK3)		N789N [LST CJA 09/25/00 AS C-FMCJ]
B737-201 (A)	N239US	US AIRWAYS		22354	736	02/10/81	JT8D-9A (HK3)		N784N [LST ROY AS C-FNAJ]
B737-201 (A)	N240AU	US AIRWAYS		22355	741	02/27/81	JT8D-9A (HK3)		N785N [LST ROY AS C-GEIM]
B737-201 (A)	N241US	US AIRWAYS		22443	782	07/29/81	JT8D-15 (HK3)		N786N [METROJET]
B737-201 (A)	N242US	US AIRWAYS		22444	800	10/01/81	JT8D-15 (HK3)		N787N [METROJET]
B737-201 (A)	N243US	US AIRWAYS		22445	837	01/22/82	JT8D-15 (HK3)		N788N [METROJET]
B737-201 (A)	N244US	US AIRWAYS		22752	845	03/02/82	JT8D-15 (HK3)		N791N [METROJET]
B737-201 (A)	N245US	US AIRWAYS		22751	857	04/02/82	JT8D-15 (HK3)		N798N [METROJET]

A/C TYPE	CURRENT REG. NO.	LAST KNOWN OPERATOR (OWNER)	STATUS	ORIGINAL MSN	LINE NO.	DEL. DATE	ENG. TYPE	FLEET NO.	PREV. REG. [COMMENTS]
B737-201 (A)	N246US	US AIRWAYS		22753	865	04/26/82	JT8D-15 (HK3)		N792N
B737-201 (A)	N247US	US AIRWAYS		22754	870	05/11/82	JT8D-15 (HK3)		N793N [METROJET]
B737-201 (A)	N248US	US AIRWAYS		22755	873	05/17/82	JT8D-15 (HK3)		N794N [METROJET]
B737-201 (A)	N249US	US AIRWAYS		22756	879	06/08/82	JT8D-15 (HK3)		N795N [METROJET]
B737-201 (A)	N251AU	US AIRWAYS		22757	883	06/15/82	JT8D-15 (HK3)		N796N [METROJET]
B737-201 (A)	N252AU	US AIRWAYS		22758	889	07/02/82	JT8D-15 (HK3)		N797N [METROJET]
B737-201 (A)	N253AU	US AIRWAYS		22795	912	09/27/82	JT8D-15 (HK3)		N799N [METROJET]
B737-201 (A)	N254AU	US AIRWAYS		22796	914	10/01/82	JT8D-15 (HK3)		N802N [METROJET]
B737-201 (A)	N255AU	US AIRWAYS		22797	916	10/15/82	JT8D-15 (HK3)		N803N [METROJET]
B737-201 (A)	N256AU	US AIRWAYS		22798	924	01/06/83	JT8D-15 (HK3)		N804N [METROJET]
B737-201 (A)	N257AU	US AIRWAYS		22799	932	02/01/83	JT8D-15 (HK3)		N805N [METROJET]
B737-201 (A)	N259AU	US AIRWAYS		22806	938	02/28/83	JT8D-15 (HK3)		N806N [METROJET]
B737-201 (A)	N260AU	US AIRWAYS		22866	940	04/01/83	JT8D-15 (HK3)		N807N [METROJET]
B737-201 (A)	N261AU	US AIRWAYS		22867	961	04/27/83	JT8D-15 (HK3)		N809N [METROJET]
B737-201 (A)	N262AU	US AIRWAYS		22868	963	05/02/83	JT8D-15 (HK3)		N810N [METROJET]
B737-201 (A)	N263AU	US AIRWAYS		22869	964	06/10/83	JT8D-15		N811N [METROJET; OO TO VGD 1QTR00]
B737-201 (A)	N264AU	US AIRWAYS		22961	984	08/30/83	JT8D-15 (HK3)		N813N [METROJET]
B737-201 (A)	N265AU	US AIRWAYS		22962	987	09/22/83	JT8D-15 (HK3)		N814N [METROJET]
B737-2B7 (A)	N266AU	US AIRWAYS		22878	921	11/15/82	JT8D-15A (HK3)		N310AU [METROJET]
B737-2B7 (A)	N267AU	US AIRWAYS		22879	926	11/22/82	JT8D-15A (HK3)		N311AU
B737-2B7 (A)	N268AU	US AIRWAYS		22880	927	12/01/82	JT8D-15A (HK3)		N312AU [METROJET]
B737-2B7 (A)	N269AU	US AIRWAYS		22881	931	12/16/82	JT8D-15A (HK3)		N313AU
B737-2B7 (A)	N271AU	US AIRWAYS		22883	935	12/22/82	JT8D-15A (HK3)		N315AU [METROJET]
B737-2B7 (A)	N273AU	US AIRWAYS		22885	966	05/13/83	JT8D-15A (HK3)		N317AU [METROJET]
B737-2B7 (A)	N275AU	US AIRWAYS (AMERIQUEST)		22887	976	07/11/83	JT8D-15A		N319AU
B737-2B7 (A)	N276AU	US AIRWAYS		22888	979	08/11/83	JT8D-15A (HK3)		N320AU
B737-2B7 (A)	N277AU	US AIRWAYS (AMERIQUEST)		22889	983	09/15/83	JT8D-15A (HK3)		N321AU [METROJET]
B737-2B7 (A)	N278AU	US AIRWAYS (BANC OF AMERICA)		22890	986	09/20/83	JT8D-15A (HK3)		N322AU [METROJET]
B737-2B7 (A)	N279AU	US AIRWAYS (BANC OF AMERICA)		22891	988	10/20/83	JT8D-15A (HK3)		N323AU [METROJET]
B737-2B7 (A)	N281AU	US AIRWAYS		23114	997	12/08/83	JT8D-15A (HK3)		N325AU [METROJET]
B737-2B7 (A)	N282AU	US AIRWAYS		23115	998	12/12/83	JT8D-15A (HK3)		N326AU [METROJET]
B737-2B7 (A)	N283AU	US AIRWAYS		23116	999	12/19/83	JT8D-15A (HK3)		N327AU
B737-2B7 (A)	N284AU	US AIRWAYS		23131	1039	07/24/84	JT8D-15A (HK3)		N328AU [METROJET]
B737-2B7 (A)	N285AU	US AIRWAYS		23132	1044	08/30/84	JT8D-15A (HK3)		N329AU [METROJET]
B737-2B7 (A)	N286AU	US AIRWAYS		23133	1049	09/25/84	JT8D-15A (HK3)		N330AU [METROJET]
B737-2B7 (A)	N287AU	US AIRWAYS		23134	1050	10/23/84	JT8D-15A (HK3)		N331AU [METROJET]
B737-2B7 (A)	N288AU	US AIRWAYS		23135	1054	11/20/84	JT8D-15A (HK3)		N332AU [METROJET]
B737-2T5 (A)	N120NJ	VANGUARD AIRLINES (AEROUSA)		22979	950	03/14/83	JT8D-15 (HK3)		G-BKHO, HA-LEC
B737-2Q8 (A)	N121NJ	VANGUARD AIRLINES (AEROUSA)		21735	582	06/20/79	JT8D-15 (HK3)		OO-TEM, N133AW, EI-BTR, HA-LEA
B737-230 (A)	N122NJ	VANGUARD AIRLINES (UNICAPITAL)		22120	715	02/06/81	JT8D-15 (HK3)		N8296B, VT-MGA, D-ABFL, N120SR

A/C TYPE	CURRENT REG. NO.	LAST KNOWN OPERATOR (OWNER)	STATUS	ORIGINAL MSN	LINE NO.	DEL. DATE	ENG. TYPE	FLEET NO.	PREV. REG. [COMMENTS]
B737-230 (A)	N123NJ	VANGUARD AIRLINES (UNICAPITAL)		22121	720	02/13/81	JT8D-15 (HK3)		VT-MGB, D-ABFM, N121SR
B737-230 (A)	N124NJ	VANGUARD AIRLINES (UNICAPITAL)		22122	721	02/19/81	JT8D-15 (HK3)		VT-MGC, D-ABFN
B737-2B7 (A)	N126NJ	VANGUARD AIRLINES (USAL)		22884	956	04/04/83	JT8D-15A		N316AU, N272AU
B737-2B7 (A)	N127NJ	VANGUARD AIRLINES (USAL)		22886	974	06/14/83	JT8D-15A		N318AU, N274US
B737-2B7 (A)	N128NJ	VANGUARD AIRLINES (USAL)		22892	990	12/01/83	JT8D-15A (HK3)		N324AU, N280AU
B737-297 (A)	N5WM	VANGUARD AIRLINES (INTL.)		22629	842	02/23/82	JT8D-15 (HK3)		N728AL
B737-247	N912MP	VANGUARD AIRLINES (INTL.)		19607	70	09/19/68	JT8D-9A (HK3)		N4510W
B737-2V6 (A)	N787WH	VICTORY AVIATION		22431	803	10/23/81	JT8D-17 (HK3)		N57008, HB-IEH, N737WH

OB-PERU

A/C TYPE	CURRENT REG. NO.	LAST KNOWN OPERATOR (OWNER)	STATUS	ORIGINAL MSN	LINE NO.	DEL. DATE	ENG. TYPE	FLEET NO.	PREV. REG. [COMMENTS]
B737-2N7 (A)	N119SW	PERUVIAN AIR FORCE (BBC A/C)		21226	458	05/28/76	JT8D-17		SU-AYN, SU-GAN
B737-130	OB-1745	AERO CONTINENTE (INTL. PAC)		19014	3	12/27/67	JT8D-7B		N2286C, D-ABEB, B-2621, XA-LBM, OB-1658, P4-ASA
B737-212 (A)	OB-1476	AERO CONTINENTE		20492	281	06/03/71	JT8D-9A		9V-BCR, N7382F, EI-BXV, VT-EQG, HR-SHJ
B737-2A9 (A)	OB-1544	AERO CONTINENTE (INGL)		20956	386	11/27/74	JT8D-9A		C-GTAQ, C6-BEK, N131AW, C-GVRD, YU-ANZ, HR-SHI, VT-EWA
B737-247	OB-1620	AERO CONTINENTE (INTL. A/L INV.)		19615	125	01/28/69	JT8D-9A		N4518W [REPAIRED AFTER 03/24/98 ACCIDENT]
B737-204	OB-1723	AERO CONTINENTE (MILLENNIUM LSG)		19712	162	04/28/69	JT8D-9A		G-AVRO, B-2605, N313XV, N199AW, OB-1493, P4-ARC, CC-CJP
B737-247	OB-1729	AERO CONTINENTE		20128	145	03/17/69	JT8D-9A		N4524W, N73718, C6-BEI, OO-PLH, N501AV, HR-SHU, OB-1670, XA-STB
B737-201	OB-1730	AERO CONTINENTE (SKYWAYS)		19422	61	08/29/68	JT8D-9A		N738N, N206AU, P4-CAD
B737-281	OB-1746	AERO CONTINENTE (INTL. PAC)		20277	235	01/30/70	JT8D-9A		JA8405, N1450Z, B-1874, N505AV, OB-1511, P4-ARA
B737-281	OB-1747	AERO CONTINENTE		20414	244	03/10/70	JT8D-9A		JA8407, N776N, N219US
B737-222	OB-1748	AERO CONTINENTE		19547	107	12/30/68	JT8D-9A		N9041U, N749N, N208AU
B737-205	OB-1751	AERO CONTINENTE (GMT)	L	19409	128	01/31/69	JT8D-9A		LN-SUP, SE-DLP, XA-SYT, XA-MAD
B737-205 (A)	OB-1752	AERO CONTINENTE (IALI)		20711	320	04/10/73	JT8D-9A		LN-SUD, N197SS, SE-DLD, XA-SWL
B737-201	OB-1753	AERO CONTINENTE		20214	172	05/29/69	JT8D-9A		N745N, N214AU, CC-CJN
B737-201	OB-1754	AERO CONTINENTE		20215	207	09/19/69	JT8D-9A		N746N, N217US, CC-CJQ
B737-222	OB-1755	AERO CONTINENTE (INTL.)		19955	210	10/07/69	JT8D-9A (HK3)		N9074U, PH-TVH, N841L, N603DJ
B737-205	N412CE	AERO PERU (AZTEC CAP.)		20412	225	08/03/71	JT8D-15 (HK3)		N1787B, LN-SUG, SE-DKH, TC-JUR, PK-IJC [STD LIM; ST IALI 02/14/01]
B737-2Q3 (A)	VP-BBO	LAN PERU (FSBU)		22367	706	11/13/80	JT8D-17		JA8467, N763AA [RTS]
B737-2Q3 (A)	VP-BBP	LAN PERU (FSBU)		22736	896	10/08/82	JT8D-17		JA8475, N763BA, PP-SFS [RTS]
B737-230 (A)	N271LR	TACA PERU (LRC)	L	22636	808	10/30/81	JT8D-17A		D-ABHT, CS-TER

	A/C TYPE	CURRENT REG. NO.	LAST KNOWN OPERATOR (OWNER)	STATUS	ORIGINAL MSN	LINE NO.	DEL. DATE	ENG. TYPE	FLEET NO.	PREV. REG. [COMMENTS]
	B737-244	OB-1713	TANS		19707	82	10/29/68	JT8D-9A	350	ZS-EUY, ZS-SBL, N754UA, XA-SFR
	B737-248	OB-1718	TANS (IALI)		19424	147	03/28/69	JT8D-9A		EI-ASA, 9J-ADZ, F-GHML, OO-PHE, N2117X, TC-VAA, TC-ALC, N424GB, CC-CVA
	B737-248	OB-1719	TANS (IALI)		20221	227	01/14/70	JT8D-9A		EI-ASF, CF-ASF, C6-BFB, N6658Y, TC-VAB, TC-ALT, CC-CVB
	B737-282 (A)	OB-1724	TANS		23042	967	06/03/83	JT8D-17A	352	CS-TEL, VT-PDC, FAP350
OM-SLOVAKIA										
	B737-2H4 (A)	OM-ERA	AIR SLOVAKIA (EQUIS)		21722	568	04/25/79	JT8D-9A		N57SW
PK-INDONESIA										
	B737-2X9 (A)	AI-7301	INDONESIAN AIR FORCE		22777	868	05/20/82	JT8D-17		N1779B
	B737-2X9 (A)	AI-7302	INDONESIAN AIR FORCE		22778	947	06/30/83	JT8D-17		N8288V
	B737-2X9 (A)	AI-7303	INDONESIAN AIR FORCE		22779	985	10/03/83	JT8D-17		N1786B
	B737-230C	PK-OCI	AIRFAST INDONESIA		20255	234	01/27/70	JT8D-9A		D-ABDE, N303XV, N800WA [OPF FREEPORT INDONESIA]
	B737-27A (A)	PK-OCP	AIRFAST INDONESIA		23794	1424	08/14/87	JT8D-9A		B-2625 [OPF FREEPORT INDONESIA]
	B737-2Q8 (A)	PK-OCQ	AIRFAST INDONESIA		21687	554	02/13/79	JT8D-9A		N821L, B-2615 [OPF FREEPORT INDONESIA]
	B737-209 (A)	PK-BYA	BAYU AIR INDONESIA (TSE)	L	23796	1420	07/30/87	JT8D-9A		B-182, PK-RIV, 9M-PMZ
	B737-2K2 (A)	PK-IJH	BOURAQ INDONESIA		21397	507	01/18/78	JT8D-15A		PH-TVP, G-BLEA, C-GRCP
	B737-230 (A)	PK-IJI	BOURAQ INDONESIA (PT PANN MULTI)		22125	734	04/02/81	JT8D-15		D-ABFS
	B737-230 (A)	PK-IJJ	BOURAQ INDONESIA (PT PANN MULTI)		22130	762	05/21/81	JT8D-15		D-ABFZ
	B737-230 (A)	PK-IJK	BOURAQ INDONESIA (PT PANN MULTI)		22143	838	02/16/82	JT8D-15		D-ABHU
	B737-230 (A)	PK-IJM	BOURAQ INDONESIA (PT PANN MULTI)		22131	764	06/04/81	JT8D-15		D-ABHA, PK-JHH
	B737-230 (A)	PK-IJN	BOURAQ INDONESIA (PT PANN MULTI)		22132	769	06/18/81	JT8D-15		N8298V, D-ABHB, PK-JHI
	B737-2H6 (A)	PK-IJO	BOURAQ INDONESIA (INGO)		21732	559	03/19/79	JT8D-15		9M-MBJ, PK-IJF, ZK-JJD, 3B-LXM
	B737-266 (A)	PK-KJK	BOURAQ INDONESIA (MSR)	L	21195	457	04/29/76	JT8D-17		SU-AYL
	B737-222	PK-JGS	JATAYU AIR (NAT AV USA)		19949	197	08/12/69	JT8D-7B		N9068U, RP-C2026
	B737-2P5 (A)	PK-LIA	LION AIRLINES (NAT AV)		21440	502	10/01/77	JT8D-15		HS-TBA, RDPL-34133, HS-TFS, SX-BFX, N440GB
	B737-2P6 (A)	PK-RIA	MANDALA AIRLINES (POLA)		21357	497	08/03/77	JT8D-15		A40-BE, LV-WFX
	B737-2S3 (A)	PK-RIC	MANDALA AIRLINES (GECA)		22278	646	03/18/80	JT8D-15		G-BJFH, EI-BXY, TF-ABN, AP-BEP, LV-PHT, LV-WJS, N803SR
	B737-2T4 (A)	PK-RID	MANDALA AIRLINES (GECA)		22803	906	02/22/83	JT8D-17A		N6018N, B-2502, B-614L, HA-LEI, N803SR
	B737-2T4 (A)	PK-RIE	MANDALA AIRLINES (GECA)		22804	908	03/01/83	JT8D-17A		N6038E, B-2503, B-615L, HA-LEM

A/C TYPE	CURRENT REG. NO.	LAST KNOWN OPERATOR (OWNER)	STATUS	ORIGINAL MSN	LINE NO.	DEL. DATE	ENG. TYPE	FLEET NO.	PREV. REG. [COMMENTS]
B737-2L9 (A)	PK-RIF	MANDALA AIRLINES (GECA)		21685	549	01/17/79	JT8D-17		OY-APJ, 9M-MBZ, G-BKAP, PP-SNO, PT-WBA, EI-CGZ, UR-BFA
B737-2E7 (A)	PK-RII	MANDALA AIRLINES		22876	922	03/15/83	JT8D-17A		N4571A, 4X-BAC, G-BLDE
B737-210 (A)	PK-RIJ	MANDALA AIRLINES		21820	578	06/11/79	JT8D-17		N491WC, 4X-BAA, G-BKNH
B737-2V5 (A)	PK-RIK	MANDALA AIRLINES (POLA)		22531	724	01/09/81	JT8D-15A		C6-BEH, N167PL
B737-230 (A)	PK-RIL	MANDALA AIRLINES (PT PANN MULTI)		22137	788	08/20/81	JT8D-15		N8297V, D-ABHL, TF-ABV
B737-230 (A)	PK-RIM	MANDALA AIRLINES (PT PANN MULTI)		22136	783	08/11/81	JT8D-15		D-ABHK, TF-ABY
B737-2H4 (A)	PK-RIP	MANDALA AIRLINES		22903	905	09/16/82	JT8D-9A (HK3)		N87SW
B737-291 (A)	PK-RIQ	MANDALA AIRLINES (ELASIS)		23023	957	04/27/83	JT8D-17A		N7359F, EI-BMZ, VT-EQI, CS-TMB, TF-ABI
B737-2L9 (A)	PK-RIR	MANDALA AIRLINES (POLA)		22735	825	12/23/81	JT8D-17A		OY-MBV, N164PL, B-2529
B737-230 (A)	PK-MBC	MERPATI (PT PANN MULTI)		22129	754	05/14/81	JT8D-15		D-ABFY
B737-230 (A)	PK-MBD	MERPATI (PT PANN MULTI)		22141	795	09/24/81	JT8D-15		D-ABHR
B737-230 (A)	PK-MBE	MERPATI (PT PANN MULTI)		22142	797	10/01/81	JT8D-15		D-ABHS
B737-2T4 (A)	PK-MBF	MERPATI (AERFI)		22368	707	10/23/80	JT8D-15 (HK3)		N52AF, G-BPAA, EI-BOM, LV-WNA, N368AP
B737-2T4 (A)	PK-MBG	MERPATI (GECA)		22369	708	10/23/80	JT8D-15		N56AF, EI-BON, EC-DUL, LV-WNB, N369AP
B737-2S3 (A)	N279AD	MERPATI (AERGO CAP.)		22279	650	03/27/80	JT8D-15		G-BMSM, EI-BRB, N368DE, VT-EWJ
B737-2U4 (A)	N576DF	MERPATI (AERGO CAP.)		22576	761	05/08/81	JT8D-15A		G-OSLA, N134AW, EI-BTZ, G-IBTZ, VT-EWC

PP/PR/PT-BRAZIL

A/C TYPE	CURRENT REG. NO.	LAST KNOWN OPERATOR (OWNER)	STATUS	ORIGINAL MSN	LINE NO.	DEL. DATE	ENG. TYPE	FLEET NO.	PREV. REG. [COMMENTS]
B737-2N3 (A)	FAB2115	BRAZILIAN AIR FORCE		21165	441	03/31/76	JT8D-17		
B737-2N3 (A)	FAB2116	BRAZILIAN AIR FORCE		21166	445	04/13/76	JT8D-17		
B737-2K9 (A)	PR-NAC	NACIONAL TRANSPORTES AEREOS		23405	1178	12/05/85	JT8D-15A		N701ML, N714A
B737-2K9 (A)	PR-NCT	NACIONAL TRANSPORTES AEREOS (BIAL)		23404	1176	12/03/85	JT8D-15A		N700ML, TC-JUU, VR-BMX, HA-LEK
B737-248C	PT-MTA	TAF LINHAS AEREAS (TSE)	L	20220	215	11/26/69	JT8D-9A		EI-ASE, 9M-PMP
B737-2C3 (A)	PP-CJN	VARIG BRASIL (PLMI)		21012	392	01/31/75	JT8D-17A		
B737-2C3 (A)	PP-CJR	VARIG BRASIL		21015	404	03/25/75	JT8D-17A		
B737-2C3 (A)	PP-CJT	VARIG BRASIL (PLMI)		21017	410	05/01/75	JT8D-17A		
B737-241 (A)	PP-VME	VARIG BRASIL (PLMI)		21000	378	10/21/74	JT8D-17A		
B737-241 (A)	PP-VMF	VARIG BRASIL		21001	384	11/19/74	JT8D-17A		
B737-241 (A)	PP-VMG	VARIG BRASIL (PLMI)		21002	385	11/26/74	JT8D-17A		
B737-241 (A)	PP-VMH	VARIG BRASIL (PLMI)		21003	389	12/19/74	JT8D-17A		
B737-241 (A)	PP-VMJ	VARIG BRASIL (PLMI)		21005	394	01/27/75	JT8D-17A		[PARKED POA]
B737-241 (A)	PP-VML	VARIG BRASIL (PLMI)		21007	400	03/12/75	JT8D-17A		
B737-241 (A)	PP-VMM	VARIG BRASIL (PLMI)		21008	402	03/12/75	JT8D-17A		
B737-241 (A)	PP-VMN	VARIG BRASIL (PLMI)		21009	417	06/10/75	JT8D-17A		
B737-2K9 (A)	PP-VNF	VARIG BRASIL (PLMI)		22504	804	05/17/82	JT8D-17A		N4529W

A/C TYPE	CURRENT REG. NO.	LAST KNOWN OPERATOR (OWNER)	STATUS	ORIGINAL MSN	LINE NO.	DEL. DATE	ENG. TYPE	FLEET NO.	PREV. REG. [COMMENTS]
B737-2Q8 (A)	PP-VPD	VARIG BRASIL (INGO)		21518	522	06/22/78	JT8D-17		N977MP, B-2611, C-GNDS, VR-CNN, ZP-CAC [LST PUA 02/98 AS CX-FAT]
B737-219 (A)	PP-VPE	VARIG BRASIL (INGO)		21130	426	09/04/75	JT8D-17		ZK-NAP, HC-BTI, ZP-CAB, PP-VPE [LST PUA 06/99 AS CX-VVT]
B737-2Q3 (A)	PP-SFI	VASP		21478	591	08/02/79	JT8D-17		JA8445
B737-2A1	PP-SMA	VASP		20092	161	07/18/69	JT8D-17		
B737-2A1 (F)	PP-SMB	VASP		20093	169	07/18/69	JT8D-17		[VASPEX C/S]
B737-2A1	PP-SMC	VASP		20094	182	07/18/69	JT8D-17		[RTS FOLLOWING DECOMPRESSION INCIDENT]
B737-2A1 (A)	PP-SMF	VASP		20589	301	07/14/72	JT8D-17		
B737-2A1 (A)	PP-SMG	VASP		20777	324	07/10/73	JT8D-17		[DMGD DURING HIJACKING 08/16/00]
B737-2A1 (A)	PP-SMH	VASP		20778	325	08/17/73	JT8D-17		
B737-2A1 (A)	PP-SMP	VASP		20779	327	09/21/73	JT8D-17		
B737-214	PP-SMQ	VASP (RURAL LEASE)		20155	180	06/18/69	JT8D-17		N382PS
B737-214	PP-SMR	VASP		20157	189	07/17/69	JT8D-17		N984PS
B737-214	PP-SMS	VASP		20159	193	07/29/69	JT8D-17		N986PS
B737-214	PP-SMT	VASP		20160	195	08/06/69	JT8D-17		N987PS
B737-2A1 (A)	PP-SMU	VASP		20967	364	09/04/74	JT8D-17		N1799B
B737-2H4C	PP-SMW	VASP		20346	258	09/29/71	JT8D-17		N23SW [VASPEX C/S]
B737-2A1 (A)	PP-SMZ	VASP		20971	382	11/07/74	JT8D-17		
B737-2A1 (A)	PP-SNA	VASP		21094	412	08/20/75	JT8D-17		
B737-2A1 (A)	PP-SNB	VASP		21095	432	10/02/75	JT8D-17		
B737-2L7C (A)	PP-SPF	VASP		21073	419	06/25/75	JT8D-17		C2-RN3
B737-2L7 (A)	PP-SPG	VASP		21616	533	09/29/78	JT8D-17		C2-RN6
B737-2L9 (A)	PP-SPH	VASP		22070	614	11/09/79	JT8D-17		OY-APL, D-AOUP, C-GQBQ, C2-RN8
B737-2Q3 (A)	PP-SPI	VASP		21476	519	05/26/78	JT8D-17		JA8443
B737-2M9 (A)	PP-SPJ	VASP		21236	461	06/07/76	JT8D-17		9J-AEG

RA-RUSSIA

A/C TYPE	CURRENT REG. NO.	LAST KNOWN OPERATOR (OWNER)	STATUS	ORIGINAL MSN	LINE NO.	DEL. DATE	ENG. TYPE	FLEET NO.	PREV. REG. [COMMENTS]
B737-247	RA-73003	SAT AIRLINES-SAKHALINSKIE (WHIRLPOOL)		19611	92	11/07/68	JT8D-9A		N4514W, N470TA
B737-236 (A)	RA-73000	TRANSAERO AIRLINES (FINAVION)		22032	742	03/10/81	JT8D-15A		G-BGJK, YL-BAB [RTS]
B737-236 (A)	RA-73001	TRANSAERO AIRLINES (FINAVION)		22028	656	04/29/80	JT8D-15A		G-BGJG, RA-71430, YL-BAA
B737-236 (A)	RA-73002	TRANSAERO AIRLINES (FINAVION)		22034	751	04/08/81	JT8D-15A		G-BGJM, YL-BAC
B737-2C9 (A)	VP-BTA	TRANSAERO AIRLINES (IASG)		21443	501	12/02/77	JT8D-15		N8277V, LX-LGH, RA-73000, EI-CLN
B737-2C9 (A)	VP-BTB	TRANSAERO AIRLINES (IASG)		21444	516	04/30/78	JT8D-15		LX-LGI, RA-73001, EI-CLO

RP-PHILIPPINES

A/C TYPE	CURRENT REG. NO.	LAST KNOWN OPERATOR (OWNER)	STATUS	ORIGINAL MSN	LINE NO.	DEL. DATE	ENG. TYPE	FLEET NO.	PREV. REG. [COMMENTS]
B737-222	RP-C1938	AIR PHILIPPINES		19553	122	02/10/69	JT8D-7B		N9047U, N63AF, VT-ERN, TF-ABH, RDPL-34126, 9M-PMR
B737-222	RP-C2020	AIR PHILIPPINES		19943	179	06/19/69	JT8D-7B		N9062U

A/C TYPE	CURRENT REG. NO.	LAST KNOWN OPERATOR (OWNER)	STATUS	ORIGINAL MSN	LINE NO.	DEL. DATE	ENG. TYPE	FLEET NO.	PREV. REG. [COMMENTS]
B737-222	RP-C2021	AIR PHILIPPINES		19039	6	09/09/67	JT8D-7B		N9001U
B737-222	RP-C2022	AIR PHILIPPINES		19942	175	06/10/69	JT8D-7B		N9061U
B737-222	RP-C2023	AIR PHILIPPINES		19947	187	07/15/69	JT8D-7B		N9066U, EI-ASK
B737-222	RP-C2024	AIR PHILIPPINES		19056	42	07/13/68	JT8D-7B		N9018U
B737-222	RP-C2025	AIR PHILIPPINES		19077	103	12/06/68	JT8D-7B		N9039U
B737-2H4 (A)	RP-C3011	AIR PHILIPPINES (AARL)		21533	524	07/11/78	JT8D-9A		N52SW
B737-2H4 (A)	RP-C3012	AIR PHILIPPINES (AARL)		21448	509	02/10/78	JT8D-9A		N51SW
B737-2H4 (A)	RP-C3015	AIR PHILIPPINES (AARL)		21534	526	07/21/78	JT8D-9A		N53SW
B737-222	N9052U	AIR PHILIPPINES (SILVER/GREEN)		19933	135	03/07/69	JT8D-7B		
B737-204	RP-C8890	GRANDAIR (ASKAR)		19711	155	04/08/69	JT8D-9		G-AVRN, PH-TVG, N172PL, N313VA [STD TPE]
B737-204	RP-C8891	GRANDAIR (ASKAR)		20236	166	05/12/69	JT8D-9		G-AWSY, N312VA, N173PL
B737-201	RP-C	PHIL AIR		19423	67	09/14/68	JT8D-9A		N740N, N207AU

ST-SUDAN

A/C TYPE	CURRENT REG. NO.	LAST KNOWN OPERATOR (OWNER)	STATUS	ORIGINAL MSN	LINE NO.	DEL. DATE	ENG. TYPE	FLEET NO.	PREV. REG. [COMMENTS]
B737-2J8C (A)	ST-AFK	SUDAN AIRWAYS		21169	429	09/15/75	JT8D-7		

SU-EGYPT

A/C TYPE	CURRENT REG. NO.	LAST KNOWN OPERATOR (OWNER)	STATUS	ORIGINAL MSN	LINE NO.	DEL. DATE	ENG. TYPE	FLEET NO.	PREV. REG. [COMMENTS]
B737-266 (A)	SU-AYK	AMC AVIATION		21194	455	04/21/76	JT8D-17		
B737-266 (A)	SU-AYL	EGYPT AIR		21195	457	04/29/76	JT8D-17		[LST BOU]
B737-222	SU-PMA	PHARAOH AIRLINES		19064	63	09/05/68	JT8D-7B		N9026U, F-GCLL

SX-GREECE

A/C TYPE	CURRENT REG. NO.	LAST KNOWN OPERATOR (OWNER)	STATUS	ORIGINAL MSN	LINE NO.	DEL. DATE	ENG. TYPE	FLEET NO.	PREV. REG. [COMMENTS]
B737-284 (A)	SX-BCA	OLYMPIC AIRWAYS		21224	463	06/23/76	JT8D-9A		
B737-284 (A)	SX-BCB	OLYMPIC AIRWAYS		21225	464	06/30/76	JT8D-9A		
B737-284 (A)	SX-BCC	OLYMPIC AIRWAYS		21301	474	10/13/76	JT8D-9A		
B737-284 (A)	SX-BCD	OLYMPIC AIRWAYS		21302	475	10/19/76	JT8D-9A		N40112
B737-284 (A)	SX-BCE	OLYMPIC AIRWAYS		22300	674	06/25/80	JT8D-9A		
B737-284 (A)	SX-BCF	OLYMPIC AIRWAYS		22301	683	07/24/80	JT8D-9A		
B737-284 (A)	SX-BCG	OLYMPIC AIRWAYS		22338	691	08/21/80	JT8D-9A		N8292V
B737-284 (A)	SX-BCH	OLYMPIC AIRWAYS		22339	692	08/26/80	JT8D-9A		
B737-284 (A)	SX-BCI	OLYMPIC AIRWAYS		22343	695	09/11/80	JT8D-9A		
B737-284 (A)	SX-BCK	OLYMPIC AIRWAYS		22400	766	06/10/81	JT8D-9A		
B737-284 (A)	SX-BCL	OLYMPIC AIRWAYS		22401	780	07/16/81	JT8D-9A		

A/C TYPE	CURRENT REG. NO.	LAST KNOWN OPERATOR (OWNER)	STATUS	ORIGINAL MSN	LINE NO.	DEL. DATE	ENG. TYPE	FLEET NO.	PREV. REG. [COMMENTS]
TC-TURKEY									
B737-236 (A)	TC-ESC	EURO SUN (PEGA)		23165	1064	11/19/84	JT8D-15A		G-BKYG, OB-1715, N625AC, N926PG
TF-ICELAND									
B737-210C	TF-ELL	ISLANDSFLUG (BUS. NAT. PARCELS)		20138	173	05/29/69	JT8D-9A (HK3)		N4906, F-GGFI [OPF DHL]
B737-2M8 (A)	TF-ELM	ISLANDSFLUG (LOCALEASE)		21736	557	03/01/79	JT8D-15 (HK3)		OO-TEL, 4X-ABL, PH-RAL, G-BTEB, G-IBTX, F-GLXG [EXPORTED TO FRANCE]
TG-GUATEMALA									
B737-2H6 (A)	N121GU	AVIATECA GUATEMALA (WFBN)		20583	303	08/07/72	JT8D-15 (HK3)		9M-AQM, 9M-MBB, TG-ALA
B737-2H6 (A)	N122GU	AVIATECA GUATEMALA (WFBN)		20586	307	09/01/72	JT8D-15		9M-AQP, 9M-MBE, TG-ALA
B737-2H6 (A)	N123GU	AVIATECA GUATEMALA (WFBN)		20587	308	09/13/72	JT8D-15 (HK3)		9M-AQQ, 9M-MBF, TG-AYA
B737-2H6 (A)	N126GU	AVIATECA GUATEMALA (WFBN)		20582	302	10/06/72	JT8D-15		9M-AQL, 9M-MBA, V2-LDT, HR-SHP, TG-ADA
B737-242 (A)	N127GU	AVIATECA GUATEMALA (WFBN)		22074	619	11/30/79	JT8D-9A		C-GNDM, VR-CYB, F-OHKA
TI-COSTA RICA									
B737-242 (A)	N238TA	LACSA COSTA RICA (TAI)	L	22075	630	01/31/80	JT8D-17A (HK3)		C-GNDR, N8536Z
B737-25A (A)	N239TA	LACSA COSTA RICA (TAI)	L	23789	1392	06/08/87	JT8D-17A (HK3)		N723ML, N222AW
B737-2L9 (A)	N251LF	LACSA COSTA RICA (FSBU)		22408	705	11/10/80	JT8D-17 (HK3)		OY-APS, Z-NAL, VR-HYL
B737-230 (A)	N261LR	LACSA COSTA RICA (FSBU)		22402	744	03/19/81	JT8D-17 (HK3)		D-ABFT, CS-TEV
B737-230 (A)	N271LR	LACSA COSTA RICA (FSBU)		22636	808	10/30/81	JT8D-17A		D-ABHT, CS-TER [LST TPU 09/99-03/21/02]
B737-2L9 (A)	N281LF	LACSA COSTA RICA (TAI)	L	22071	620	12/04/79	JT8D-17 (HK3)		OY-APN, SU-BCJ, G-BJSO, EI-BOJ, G-GPAB, VR-HKP
B737-2T5 (A)	N501NG	LACSA COSTA RICA (NIS)	L	22395	729	01/12/81	JT8D-15 (HK3)		G-BHVG, C-GEPM, 9M-MBO, H4-SAL [OPF NIS]
TJ-CAMEROON									
B737-229C (A)	TJ-AIO	CAMEROON AIRLINES		21139	437	11/03/75	JT8D-15/15A		OO-SDP, G-BYZN
TN-CONGO BRAZZAVILLE									
B737-2M2 (A)	D2-TBD	LINA CONGO (DTA)	L	21723	567	04/27/79	JT8D-17		D2-TAH
B737-217	TN-AGR	LINA CONGO (TYLER JET)		20197	149	03/28/69	JT8D-9A		CF-CPZ, SE-DLR, TC-JUT, N3160M, XA-SOM, XB-GRP, N780TJ, 5N-BBJ
TR-GABON									
B737-2Q2C (A)	TR-LXL	AIR GABON		21467	515	07/31/78	JT8D-17		
TS-TUNISIA									
B737-2H3C (A)	TS-IOD	MEDITERRANEAN AIR SERVICE (TAR)	L	21974	615	11/14/79	JT8D-9A		

A/C TYPE	CURRENT REG. NO.	LAST KNOWN OPERATOR (OWNER)	STATUS	ORIGINAL MSN	LINE NO.	DEL. DATE	ENG. TYPE	FLEET NO.	PREV. REG. [COMMENTS]
B737-2H6 (A)	TS-IEA	TUNINTER (INGO)		23320	1120	06/07/85	JT8D-15A		9M-MBL, PK-IJG
B737-2H3 (A)	TS-IOC	TUNISAIR		21973	607	10/22/79	JT8D-9A		[LST DEI]
B737-2H3C (A)	TS-IOD	TUNISAIR		21974	615	11/14/79	JT8D-9A		[OCC LST MEDITERRANEAN AIR SERVICE]
B737-2H3 (A)	TS-IOE	TUNISAIR		22624	758	04/27/81	JT8D-17		
B737-2H3 (A)	TS-IOF	TUNISAIR		22625	776	06/30/81	JT8D-17		

UN-KAZAKSTAN

A/C TYPE	CURRENT REG. NO.	LAST KNOWN OPERATOR (OWNER)	STATUS	ORIGINAL MSN	LINE NO.	DEL. DATE	ENG. TYPE	FLEET NO.	PREV. REG. [COMMENTS]
B737-291	UN-B3701	AIR KAZAKSTAN (TRIPLE J)		20364	219	11/14/69	JT8D-9A		N7376F, N730TJ, P4-RMB [PARKED BUD]
B737-2T4 (A)	UN-B3703	AIR KAZAKSTAN (GECA)		23444	1154	10/12/85	JT8D-17A		N1790B, B-2512, N234GE
B737-2Q3 (A)	UN-B3704	AIR KAZAKSTAN (AERGO)		24103	1565	06/15/88	JT8D-17		JA8282, N241AG
B737-2Q8 (A)	UN-B3705	AIR KAZAKSTAN (AEW)	L	22453	748	03/20/81	JT8D-15		OO-RVM, TF-VLK, G-BKMS, N143AW, VR-HYZ, TC-JUS, HA-LEH, LY-GPA, UR-BVZ
B737-2M8 (A)	UN-B3706	AIR KAZAKSTAN (GECA)		22090	664	05/19/80	JT8D-15		OO-TEO, 4X-ABM, TC-AJK, HA-LEB

UR-UKRAINE

A/C TYPE	CURRENT REG. NO.	LAST KNOWN OPERATOR (OWNER)	STATUS	ORIGINAL MSN	LINE NO.	DEL. DATE	ENG. TYPE	FLEET NO.	PREV. REG. [COMMENTS]
B737-2Q8 (A)	UR-BVY	AEROSVIT AIRLINES		22760	852	04/06/82	JT8D-17		N861L, F-GEXJ, VP-BYC
B737-2Q8 (A)	UR-BVZ	AEROSVIT AIRLINES (GECA)		22453	748	03/20/81	JT8D-15		OO-RVM, TF-VLK, G-BKMS, N143AW, VR-HYZ, TC-JUS, HA-LEH, LY-GPA [LST KZK AS UN-B3705]
B737-247 (A)	UR-GAC	UKRAINE INTL. AIRLINES (AIRGO IRELAND)		23188	1071	12/28/84	JT8D-17A		N240WA, B-2509
B737-2T4 (A)	UR-GAD	UKRAINE INTL. AIRLINES (GECA)		22802	901	02/22/83	JT8D-17A		N4561K, N6009F, B-2501, B-610L

VP-C-CAYMAN IS.

A/C TYPE	CURRENT REG. NO.	LAST KNOWN OPERATOR (OWNER)	STATUS	ORIGINAL MSN	LINE NO.	DEL. DATE	ENG. TYPE	FLEET NO.	PREV. REG. [COMMENTS]
B737-2S9 (A)	VP-CHK	HARRY A. AKANDE		21957	618	12/11/79	JT8D-17 (HK3)		N57008, VR-BEG, VR-BKO, N80CC, PK-HHS, N39BL
B737-2W8 (A)	VP-CSA	SKY AVIATION		22628	820	12/15/81	JT8D-17		N180RN, A6-ESH, A6-ESJ [PARKED QLA]
B737-205 (A)	VP-CAL	CAYMAN AIRWAYS (C.I. GOVT)		22022	616	11/21/79	JT8D-17A (HK3)		LN-SUT, ZK-NAQ, N8032M, VR-CAL
B737-236 (A)	VP-CKX	CAYMAN AIRWAYS (BOUL)		23162	1056	10/25/84	JT8D-15A (HK3)		G-BKYD, VR-CEF, VR-CKX
B737-2S2C (A)	VP-CYB	CAYMAN AIRWAYS (FSBU)		21929	608	10/17/79	JT8D-17		N205FE, N716A

VT-INDIA

A/C TYPE	CURRENT REG. NO.	LAST KNOWN OPERATOR (OWNER)	STATUS	ORIGINAL MSN	LINE NO.	DEL. DATE	ENG. TYPE	FLEET NO.	PREV. REG. [COMMENTS]
B737-2A8 (A)	K2412	INDIAN AIR FORCE		23036	977	07/20/83	JT8D-17		VT-EHW
B737-2A8 (A)	K2413	INDIAN AIR FORCE		23037	982	08/17/83	JT8D-17		VT-EHX
B737-2A8	K3186	INDIAN AIR FORCE		20484	275	02/08/71	JT8D-9A		VT-EAK
B737-2A8	K3187	INDIAN AIR FORCE		20483	273	01/05/71	JT8D-9A		VT-EAJ
B737-2A8 (A)	VT-EGE	ALLIANCE AIR		22281	679	07/16/80	JT8D-17A		N8291V
B737-2A8 (A)	VT-EGF	ALLIANCE AIR		22282	681	07/23/80	JT8D-17A		N8292V
B737-2A8 (A)	VT-EGG	ALLIANCE AIR		22283	689	08/13/80	JT8D-17A		

A/C TYPE	CURRENT REG. NO.	LAST KNOWN OPERATOR (OWNER)	STATUS	ORIGINAL MSN	LINE NO.	DEL. DATE	ENG. TYPE	FLEET NO.	PREV. REG. [COMMENTS]
B737-2A8 (A)	VT-EGH	ALLIANCE AIR		22284	739	02/18/81	JT8D-17A		
B737-2A8 (A)	VT-EGI	ALLIANCE AIR		22285	798	09/23/81	JT8D-17A		
B737-2A8 (A)	VT-EGJ	ALLIANCE AIR		22286	799	09/30/81	JT8D-17A		
B737-2A8C (A)	VT-EGM	ALLIANCE AIR		22473	747	03/18/81	JT8D-17A		
B737-2A8 (A)	VT-EHE	ALLIANCE AIR		22860	899	08/04/82	JT8D-17A		
B737-2A8 (A)	VT-EHF	ALLIANCE AIR		22861	902	08/11/82	JT8D-17A		
B737-2A8 (A)	VT-EHG	ALLIANCE AIR		22862	903	08/18/82	JT8D-17A		
B737-2A8 (A)	VT-EHH	ALLIANCE AIR		22863	907	09/08/82	JT8D-17A		
B737-2A8 (A) (F)	VT-EDR	BLUE DART AVIATION (ICICI LTD)		21163	434	10/08/75	JT8D-9A		
B737-2A8 (A) (F)	VT-EDS	BLUE DART AVIATION (ICICI LTD)		21164	435	10/15/75	JT8D-9A		
B737-2K9 (A)	VT-SIE	BLUE DART AVIATION		22415	702	09/30/80	JT8D-17		G-DFUB, CS-TET, C-GQCA, VT-PDA
B737-2K9 (A)	VT-SIF	SAHARA AIRLINES		22416	709	10/31/80	JT8D-17		N1786B, G-BMON, C-GPWC, CS-TEU, VT-PDB

V5-NAMIBIA

A/C TYPE	CURRENT REG. NO.	LAST KNOWN OPERATOR (OWNER)	STATUS	ORIGINAL MSN	LINE NO.	DEL. DATE	ENG. TYPE	FLEET NO.	PREV. REG. [COMMENTS]
B737-25A (A)	V5-ANA	AIR NAMIBIA (SFR)	L	23790	1422	08/03/87	JT8D-15A		N724ML
B737-2L9 (A)	V5-ANB	AIR NAMIBIA (SFR)	L	21686	550	01/22/79	JT8D-17		OY-APK, 9M-MBY, PP-SNK, PT-WBC, EI-CHC, TF-ABU, ZS-NLN
B737-2R8C (A)	5H-MRK	AIR NAMIBIA (ATC)	L	21711	573	05/16/79	JT8D-17		

XA-MEXICO

A/C TYPE	CURRENT REG. NO.	LAST KNOWN OPERATOR (OWNER)	STATUS	ORIGINAL MSN	LINE NO.	DEL. DATE	ENG. TYPE	FLEET NO.	PREV. REG. [COMMENTS]
B737-112	TP-03	MEXICAN AIR FORCE		19772	217	10/31/69	JT8D-7		9M-AOW, 9V-BFF, N48AF, TP-04, XB-IBV
B737-205 (A)	XA-ABC	AVIACSA		23467	1245	06/27/86	JT8D-17		LN-SUQ, N890FS, JA8577, N713A
B737-219 (A)	XA-NAF	AVIACSA		23470	1186	01/16/86	JT8D-15A (HK3)		ZK-NAT
B737-219 (A)	XA-NAK	AVIACSA		23474	1199	02/18/86	JT8D-15A (HK3)		ZK-NAX
B737-219 (A)	XA-NAV	AVIACSA (ARFI)		23472	1194	02/10/86	JT8D-15A (HK3)		ZK-NAV
B737-2T4 (A)	XA-SIW	AVIACSA (GECA)		22370	716	11/22/80	JT8D-15		N57AF, N139AW
B737-2T4 (A)	XA-SIX	AVIACSA (GECA)		22371	717	11/20/80	JT8D-15		N58AF, N140AW
B737-210C (A)	XA-ABX	ESTAFETA CARGA AEREA (FSBU)		20917	344	04/08/74	JT8D-17 (HK3)		N4905W
B737-2T4C (A)	XA-ACP	ESTAFETA CARGA AEREA (AVLEASE)		23065	989	10/14/83	JT8D-17 (HK3)		B-2504, EI-BXM, N675MA, LV-WPA, N230GE
B737-2T4C (A)	XA-ADV	ESTAFETA CARGA AEREA (AVLEASE)		23066	992	12/08/83	JT8D-17A (HK3)		N676MA, B-2505, N306GE
B737-275C	XA-TRW	FACTS AIR		19743	139	03/12/69	JT8D-9A		CF-PWE, EI-BJP, N331XV, C-GNWD, C-GWJK
B737-2C3 (A)	XA-MAB	MAGNICHARTERS (AARL)		21016	406	04/09/75	JT8D-17A		PP-CJS, XA-NBM
B737-2C3 (A)	XA-MAC	MAGNICHARTERS		21014	397	02/13/75	JT8D-17A		PP-CJP, N302AR
B737-205	XA-MAD	MAGNICHARTERS (NYCKELN)		19409	128	01/31/69	JT8D-9A		LN-SUP, SE-DLP, XA-SYT [LST ACQ 01/01 AS OB-1751]

A/C TYPE	CURRENT REG. NO.	LAST KNOWN OPERATOR (OWNER)	STATUS	ORIGINAL MSN	LINE NO.	DEL. DATE	ENG. TYPE	FLEET NO.	PREV. REG. [COMMENTS]
B737-2K9 (A)	XA-MAF	MAGNICHARTERS (AT A/C ONE)		22505	815	05/17/82	JT8D-17A		N1786B, N1800B, N4530W, PP-VNG, N303AR
B737-205 (A)	XA-MAG	MAGNICHARTERS (AARL)		21184	440	11/26/75	JT8D-9A		LN-SUI, N197QQ, TF-AIC, TF-ABF, N197QQ, CC-CYS, N1999L

XU-CAMBODIA

B737-248C	XU-711	ROYAL AIR CAMBODGE (EURO. CAP.)		20218	199	09/09/69	JT8D-9A		EI-ASC, PP-SNY, EC-DZB, F-GGFJ, N218TA, P4-RAC

YN-NICARAGUA

B737-2T5 (A)	N501NG	NICA (CITG)		22395	729	01/12/81	JT8D-15 (HK3)		G-BHVG, C-GEPM, 9M-MBO, H4-SAL [LST/OPB LRC]
B737-2K5 (A)	N231TA	TACA INTL. AIRLINES (FSBU)		22596	763	05/29/81	JT8D-17 (HK3)		N8279V, D-AHLD, N2941W, YU-AOF, PP-VPF
B737-296 (A)	N232TA	TACA INTL. AIRLINES (FSBU)		22277	675	06/24/80	JT8D-17A (HK3)		N57001, C-GQBJ, N388PA, LN-BRL
B737-2K5 (A)	N233TA	TACA INTL. AIRLINES (FSBU)		22601	833	01/29/82	JT8D-17 (HK3)		N1800B, D-AHLI, YU-AOG, HZ-SIR
B737-205 (A)	N235TA	TACA INTL. AIRLINES (FSBU)		21765	595	08/21/79	JT8D-17A (HK3)		LN-SUB, N73FS
B737-242 (A)	N238TA	TACA INTL. AIRLINES (FSBU)		22075	630	01/31/80	JT8D-17A (HK3)		C-GNDR, N8536Z [LST LRC]
B737-25A (A)	N239TA	TACA INTL. AIRLINES (FSBU)		23789	1392	06/08/87	JT8D-17A (HK3)		N723ML, N222AW [LST LRC]
B737-205 (A)	N240TA	TACA INTL. AIRLINES (FSBU)		21729	572	05/11/79	JT8D-17A (HK3)		LN-SUK, N73TH
B737-2L9 (A)	N281LF	TACA INTL. AIRLINES (FSBU)		22071	620	12/04/79	JT8D-17 (HK3)		OY-APN, SU-BCJ, G-BJSO, EI-BOJ, G-GPAB, VR-HKP [LST LRC]

YU-YUGOSLAVIA

B737-2K3 (A)	YU-ANP	AVIOGENEX		23912	1401	06/19/87	JT8D-15 (HK3)		[OPF NCH]

YV-VENEZUELA

B737-2N1 (A)	FAV0001	VENEZUELAN AIR FORCE		21167	442	01/30/76	JT8D-17		
B737-236 (A)	YV-52C	AVENSA (PEGA)		23161	1055	10/08/84	JT8D-15A		G-BKYC, OB-1711, N624AC
B737-229 (A)	YV-74C	AVENSA		20909	353	05/10/74	JT8D-15A (HK3)		OO-SDC, G-BTED
B737-229 (A)	YV-79C	SERVIVENSA		20908	352	05/04/74	JT8D-15A (HK3)		OO-SDB, G-BTEC

Z-ZIMBABWE

B737-2N0 (A)	Z-WPA	AIR ZIMBABWE		23677	1313	12/15/86	JT8D-17A		
B737-2N0 (A)	Z-WPB	AIR ZIMBABWE		23678	1405	06/23/87	JT8D-17A		
B737-2N0 (A)	Z-WPC	AIR ZIMBABWE		23679	1415	07/20/87	JT8D-17A		

ZK-NEW ZEALAND

B737-204 (A)	ZK-NAA	AIR NEW ZEALAND (KB FLYGPLANET)		22638	858	04/06/82	JT8D-15A (HK3)		N1780B, G-BJCT, EC-DXK
B737-204 (A)	ZK-NAB	AIR NEW ZEALAND (INTL. A/C INV)		22364	696	09/09/80	JT8D-15A (HK3)		G-BHWE
B737-204 (A)	ZK-NAI	AIR NEW ZEALAND (KB FLYGPLANET)		22365	700	12/01/80	JT8D-15A (HK3)		N57001, G-BHWF

A/C TYPE	CURRENT REG. NO.	LAST KNOWN OPERATOR (OWNER)	STATUS	ORIGINAL MSN	LINE NO.	DEL. DATE	ENG. TYPE	FLEET NO.	PREV. REG. [COMMENTS]
B737-219 (A)	ZK-NAU	AIR NEW ZEALAND		23471	1189	01/21/86	JT8D-15A (HK3)		[SALE TO FOM NTU]
B737-219 (A)	ZK-NAW	AIR NEW ZEALAND		23473	1197	02/13/86	JT8D-15A (HK3)		[RTS; SALE TO CHP ON HOLD]
B737-219 (A)	ZK-NAY	AIR NEW ZEALAND		23475	1203	03/05/86	JT8D-15A (HK3)		[SALE TO CHP ON HOLD]
B737-219C (A)	ZK-NQC	AIR POST NZ (AIRWORK)		22994	928	12/02/82	JT8D-15A (HK3)		[LST FOM 05/01/01]
B737-219C (A)	ZK-NQC	FREEDOM AIR (ANZ)	L	22994	928	12/02/82	JT8D-15A (HK3)		

ZS-SOUTH AFRICA

A/C TYPE	CURRENT REG. NO.	LAST KNOWN OPERATOR (OWNER)	STATUS	ORIGINAL MSN	LINE NO.	DEL. DATE	ENG. TYPE	FLEET NO.	PREV. REG. [COMMENTS]
B737-236 (A)	ZS-NNG	COMAIR (BOUL)		21793	635	02/23/80	JT8D-15A		G-BGDD, PH-TSE
B737-236 (A)	ZS-NNH	COMAIR		21797	653	04/14/80	JT8D-15A		G-BGDH, PH-TSD
B737-236 (A)	ZS-OKD	COMAIR		21803	677	07/25/80	JT8D-15A		G-BGDO
B737-236 (A)	ZS-OKE	COMAIR (LAROC)		21807	710	11/04/80	JT8D-15A		G-BGDT
B737-236 (A)	ZS-OLA	COMAIR		23163	1058	11/01/84	JT8D-15A		G-BKYE
B737-236 (A)	ZS-OLB	COMAIR (PEGA)		23167	1074	01/07/85	JT8D-15A		G-BKYI
B737-230 (A)	ZS-OLC	COMAIR (SFR)	L	22119	714	02/02/81	JT8D-15		N8298B, D-ABFK, RC-CTA, 9A-CTA, N219AS
B737-244	ZS-SBN	COMAIR		20229	214	10/22/69	JT8D-9		
B737-244	ZS-SBO	COMAIR		20329	250	04/15/70	JT8D-9		
B737-244	ZS-SBR	COMAIR		20331	260	06/29/70	JT8D-9		
B737-2H7C (A)	ZS-IJJ	INTER AIR		20591	309	09/28/72	JT8D-15		TJ-CBB, N24AZ
B737-2H7C (A)	ZS-	INTER AIR		20590	304	07/14/72	JT8D-15		TJ-CBA, N11AZ [3C-ZZM?]
B737-230 (A)	ZS-OEZ	NATIONWIDE AIRLINES (FINO)		22118	704	01/30/81	JT8D-15		N1786B, D-ABFH, RC-CTC, 9A-CTC
B737-230 (A)	ZS-OIV	NATIONWIDE AIRLINES (AEROTRANS)		22634	840	02/19/82	JT8D-15		D-ABHW, 9A-CTE
B737-230 (A)	ZS-OMG	NATIONWIDE AIRLINES (FINO)		22140	793	08/27/81	JT8D-15		D-ABHP, 9A-CTD
B737-258 (A)	ZS-OOC	NATIONWIDE AIRLINES		22856	910	09/30/82	JT8D-17A		CC-CJK, 4X-ABN
B737-258 (A)	ZS-OOD	NATIONWIDE AIRLINES		22857	919	11/09/82	JT8D-17A		CC-CJM, 4X-ABO
B737-2L9 (A)	ZS-NLN	SAFAIR		21686	550	01/22/79	JT8D-17		OY-APK, 9M-MBY, PP-SNK, PT-WBC, EI-CHC, TF-ABU [LST NMB AS V5-ANB]
B737-230 (A)	ZS-OLC	SAFAIR		22119	714	02/02/81	JT8D-15		N8298B, D-ABFK, RC-CTA, 9A-CTA, N219AS [BF/LST CAW 05/15/00]
B737-244 (A)	ZS-SIA	SAFAIR		22580	787	08/14/81	JT8D-17A		PP-SNW [LST SAA]
B737-244 (A)	ZS-SIB	SAFAIR		22581	796	09/18/81	JT8D-17A		D6-CAJ [LST SAA]
B737-244 (A)	ZS-SIC	SAFAIR		22582	805	10/19/81	JT8D-17A		[LST SAA]
B737-244 (A) (F)	ZS-SID	SAFAIR		22583	809	11/02/81	JT8D-17A		[LST SAA]
B737-244 (A)	ZS-SIE	SAFAIR		22584	821	12/14/81	JT8D-17A		[LST SAA]
B737-244 (A) (F)	ZS-SIF	SAFAIR		22585	828	01/14/82	JT8D-17A		[LST SAA]
B737-244 (A)	ZS-SIG	SAFAIR		22586	829	01/28/82	JT8D-17A		[LST SAA]
B737-244 (A)	ZS-SIH	SAFAIR		22587	835	05/14/82	JT8D-17A		[LST SAA]

A/C TYPE	CURRENT REG. NO.	LAST KNOWN OPERATOR (OWNER)	STATUS	ORIGINAL MSN	LINE NO.	DEL. DATE	ENG. TYPE	FLEET NO.	PREV. REG. [COMMENTS]
B737-244 (A)	ZS-SII	SAFAIR		22588	836	02/17/82	JT8D-17A		[LST SAA]
B737-244 (A)	ZS-SIJ	SAFAIR		22589	843	03/03/82	JT8D-17A		N8285V, CC-CHK [LST SAA]
B737-244 (A)	ZS-SIK	SAFAIR		22590	854	04/01/82	JT8D-17A		[LST SAA]
B737-244 (A)	ZS-SIL	SAFAIR		22591	859	04/15/82	JT8D-17A		[LST SAA]
B737-244 (A)	ZS-SIM	SAFAIR		22828	881	06/17/82	JT8D-17A		[LST SAA]
B737-236 (A)	ZS-SIN	SAFAIR (ICON/21802)		21802	670	06/11/80	JT8D-15A		G-BGDN, CC-CHS [LST SAA]
B737-236 (A)	ZS-SIO	SAFAIR		21792	628	02/07/80	JT8D-15A		G-BGDC, CC-CHR [LST SAA]
B737-230 (A)	ZS-SIP	SAFAIR		22116	701	01/16/81	JT8D-15		D-ABFD, RC-CTB, 9A-CTB, OM-BWJ, N392AS [LST SAA]
B737-236 (A)	ZS-SIS	SAFAIR		21801	669	06/09/80	JT8D-15A		G-BGDL [TO BE LST SAA]
B737-236 (A)	ZS-SIU	SAFAIR		22026	644	03/21/80	JT8D-15A		G-BGJE [LST SAA]
B737-25A (A)	ZS-	SAFAIR		23790	1422	08/03/87	JT8D-15A		N724ML [LST NMB AS V5-ANA]
B737-236 (A)	ZS-	SAFAIR		21790	599	12/04/81	JT8D-15A		N1285E, G-BGDA
B737-244 (A)	ZS-SIA	SOUTH AFRICAN AIRWAYS (SFR)	L	22580	787	08/14/81	JT8D-17A		PP-SNW
B737-244 (A)	ZS-SIB	SOUTH AFRICAN AIRWAYS (SFR)	L	22581	796	09/18/81	JT8D-17A		D6-CAJ
B737-244 (A)	ZS-SIC	SOUTH AFRICAN AIRWAYS (SFR)	L	22582	805	10/19/81	JT8D-17A		
B737-244 (A) (F)	ZS-SID	SOUTH AFRICAN AIRWAYS (SFR)	L	22583	809	11/02/81	JT8D-17A		
B737-244 (A)	ZS-SIE	SOUTH AFRICAN AIRWAYS (SFR)	L	22584	821	12/14/81	JT8D-17A		
B737-244 (A) (F)	ZS-SIF	SOUTH AFRICAN AIRWAYS (SFR)	L	22585	828	01/14/82	JT8D-17A		
B737-244 (A)	ZS-SIG	SOUTH AFRICAN AIRWAYS (SFR)	L	22586	829	01/28/82	JT8D-17A		
B737-244 (A)	ZS-SIH	SOUTH AFRICAN AIRWAYS (SFR)	L	22587	835	05/14/82	JT8D-17A		
B737-244 (A)	ZS-SII	SOUTH AFRICAN AIRWAYS (SFR)	L	22588	836	02/17/82	JT8D-17A		
B737-244 (A)	ZS-SIJ	SOUTH AFRICAN AIRWAYS (SFR)	L	22589	843	03/03/82	JT8D-17A		N8285V, CC-CHK
B737-244 (A)	ZS-SIK	SOUTH AFRICAN AIRWAYS (SFR)	L	22590	854	04/01/82	JT8D-17A		
B737-244 (A)	ZS-SIL	SOUTH AFRICAN AIRWAYS (SFR)	L	22591	859	04/15/82	JT8D-17A		
B737-244 (A)	ZS-SIM	SOUTH AFRICAN AIRWAYS (SFR)	L	22828	881	06/17/82	JT8D-17A		
B737-236 (A)	ZS-SIN	SOUTH AFRICAN AIRWAYS (SFR)	L	21802	670	06/11/80	JT8D-15A		G-BGDN, CC-CHS
B737-236 (A)	ZS-SIO	SOUTH AFRICAN AIRWAYS (SFR)	L	21792	628	02/07/80	JT8D-15A		G-BGDC, CC-CHR
B737-230 (A)	ZS-SIP	SOUTH AFRICAN AIRWAYS (SFR)	L	22116	701	01/16/81	JT8D-15		D-ABFD, RC-CTB, 9A-CTB, OM-BWJ, N392AS
B737-236 (A)	ZS-SIU	SOUTH AFRICAN AIRWAYS (SFR)	L	22026	644	03/21/80	JT8D-15A		G-BGJE

3X-GUINEA

A/C TYPE	CURRENT REG. NO.	LAST KNOWN OPERATOR (OWNER)	STATUS	ORIGINAL MSN	LINE NO.	DEL. DATE	ENG. TYPE	FLEET NO.	PREV. REG. [COMMENTS]
B737-2R6C (A)	3X-GCB	AIR GUINEE		22627	779	08/11/81	JT8D-17		

4X-ISRAEL

A/C TYPE	CURRENT REG. NO.	LAST KNOWN OPERATOR (OWNER)	STATUS	ORIGINAL MSN	LINE NO.	DEL. DATE	ENG. TYPE	FLEET NO.	PREV. REG. [COMMENTS]
B737-297 (A)	4X-AOT	ELTA ELECTRONICS		21740	562	03/29/79	JT8D-9A		N70724 [RADAR TESTBED]

5H-TANZANIA

A/C TYPE	CURRENT REG. NO.	LAST KNOWN OPERATOR (OWNER)	STATUS	ORIGINAL MSN	LINE NO.	DEL. DATE	ENG. TYPE	FLEET NO.	PREV. REG. [COMMENTS]
B737-2R8C (A)	5H-ATC	AIR TANZANIA		21710	546	12/15/78	JT8D-17		N57001
B737-2R8C (A)	5H-MRK	AIR TANZANIA		21711	573	05/16/79	JT8D-17		[LST NMB]

A/C TYPE	CURRENT REG. NO.	LAST KNOWN OPERATOR (OWNER)	STATUS	ORIGINAL MSN	LINE NO.	DEL. DATE	ENG. TYPE	FLEET NO.	PREV. REG. [COMMENTS]
5N-NIGERIA									
B737-2K3 (A)	YU-ANP	CHANCHANGI AIRLINES (AGX)	L	23912	1401	06/19/87	JT8D-15 (HK3)		
B737-2F9 (A)	5N-ANC	NIGERIA AIRWAYS		20671	312	01/16/73	JT8D-15/15A		[WFU LOS]
B737-2F9 (A)	5N-AND	NIGERIA AIRWAYS		20672	313	01/16/73	JT8D-15/15A		[WFU LOS]
B737-2F9 (A)	5N-ANW	NIGERIA AIRWAYS		22771	866	10/11/82	JT8D-15/15A		
B737-2F9 (A)	5N-AUB	NIGERIA AIRWAYS		22986	925	02/08/83	JT8D-15/15A		
5R-MADAGASCAR									
B737-2B2	5R-MFA	AIR MADAGASCAR		20231	204	09/19/69	JT8D-9		
B737-2B2 (A)	5R-MFB	AIR MADAGASCAR		20680	314	12/14/72	JT8D-15		
5U-NIGER									
B737-2N9C (A)	5U-BAG	NIGER GOVERNMENT		21499	513	04/28/78	JT8D-17		[STD BAMAKO]
5Y-KENYA									
B737-248 (A)	5Y-KQJ	KENYA AIRWAYS (EURO CAP)		21714	565	04/10/79	JT8D-9A		EI-BEB, VT-EWH, N1714T
B737-248 (A)	5Y-KQK	KENYA AIRWAYS (EURO CAP)		21715	579	06/08/79	JT8D-9A		TF-VLM, EI-BEC, VT-EWI, N1715Z
6V-SENEGAL									
B737-2B6 (A)	6V-AHK	AIR SENEGAL		21216	456	04/15/76	JT8D-15 (HK3)		CN-RMK
70-YEMEN									
B737-2R4C (A)	70-ACQ	YEMENIA		23129	1034	06/21/84	JT8D-17A		[ALL WHITE C/S; NO TITLES]
B737-2R4C (A)	70-ACR	YEMENIA		23130	1040	07/18/84	JT8D-17A		
B737-2N8 (A)	70-ACU	YEMENIA		21296	478	12/16/76	JT8D-15		N1238E, 4W-ABZ
7T-ALGERIA									
B737-2D6 (A)	7T-VEF	AIR ALGERIE		20759	332	11/21/73	JT8D-15		
B737-2D6 (A)	7T-VEG	AIR ALGERIE		20884	361	06/29/74	JT8D-15		
B737-2D6 (A)	7T-VEJ	AIR ALGERIE		21063	407	04/10/75	JT8D-15		
B737-2D6 (A)	7T-VEK	AIR ALGERIE		21064	409	04/22/75	JT8D-15		
B737-2D6 (A)	7T-VEL	AIR ALGERIE		21065	416	06/04/75	JT8D-15		
B737-2D6 (A)	7T-VEN	AIR ALGERIE		21211	454	04/12/76	JT8D-15		
B737-2D6 (A)	7T-VEO	AIR ALGERIE		21212	459	05/19/76	JT8D-15		
B737-2D6 (A)	7T-VEQ	AIR ALGERIE		21285	473	10/13/76	JT8D-15		
B737-2D6 (A)	7T-VER	AIR ALGERIE		21286	482	01/31/77	JT8D-15		
B737-2D6C (A)	7T-VES	AIR ALGERIE		21287	486	04/01/77	JT8D-15		
B737-2D6 (A)	7T-VEY	AIR ALGERIE		22766	853	03/25/82	JT8D-15		
B737-2T4 (A)	7T-VEZ	AIR ALGERIE		22700	885	12/08/83	JT8D-17A		N4563H
B737-2T4 (A)	7T-VJB	AIR ALGERIE		22801	900	12/14/83	JT8D-17A		N4558L

A/C TYPE	CURRENT REG. NO.	LAST KNOWN OPERATOR (OWNER)	STATUS	ORIGINAL MSN	LINE NO.	DEL. DATE	ENG. TYPE	FLEET NO.	PREV. REG. [COMMENTS]
B737-210C	7T-VVA	ANTINEA AIRLINES		20440	256	05/15/70	JT8D-9A (HK3)		N4902W, N200NE, F-GJDL [TO BE RT LESSOR]
B737-2H3 (A)	TS-IOC	ECOAIR INTL. (TUN)	L	21973	607	10/22/79	JT8D-9A		

9H-MALTA

A/C TYPE	CURRENT REG. NO.	LAST KNOWN OPERATOR (OWNER)	STATUS	ORIGINAL MSN	LINE NO.	DEL. DATE	ENG. TYPE	FLEET NO.	PREV. REG. [COMMENTS]
B737-2Y5 (A)	9H-ABE	AIR MALTA		23847	1414	07/21/87	JT8D-15A (HK3)		
B737-2Y5 (A)	9H-ABF	AIR MALTA		23848	1418	07/27/87	JT8D-15A (HK3)		

9J-ZAMBIA

A/C TYPE	CURRENT REG. NO.	LAST KNOWN OPERATOR (OWNER)	STATUS	ORIGINAL MSN	LINE NO.	DEL. DATE	ENG. TYPE	FLEET NO.	PREV. REG. [COMMENTS]
B737-202C	9J-AFW	AERO ZAMBIA (AV. CONSULT.)		19426	72	10/30/68	JT8D-9A		N2711R, C-GQBC, N801AL
B737-222	3C-AAJ	AERO ZAMBIA (AV. CONSULT.)		19075	97	11/24/68	JT8D-9A		N9037U, N7383F, 9J-AFU

9M-MALAYSIA

A/C TYPE	CURRENT REG. NO.	LAST KNOWN OPERATOR (OWNER)	STATUS	ORIGINAL MSN	LINE NO.	DEL. DATE	ENG. TYPE	FLEET NO.	PREV. REG. [COMMENTS]
B737-275C (A)	9M-PML	TRANSMILE AIR SERVICES		21116	427	10/10/75	JT8D-9A		C-GDPW
B737-205C	9M-PMM	TRANSMILE AIR SERVICES		20458	278	03/17/71	JT8D-9A		LN-SUA, TF-VLT, TF-ABT, RP-C2906
B737-248C	9M-PMP	TRANSMILE AIR SERVICES		20220	215	11/26/69	JT8D-9A		EI-ASE [LST TAF LINHAS AEREAS 09/00 AS PT-MTA]
B737-230C	9M-PMQ	TRANSMILE AIR SERVICES		20254	230	01/12/70	JT8D-9A		D-ABCE, N302XV, F-GFVJ [OPF POSLAJU KURIER NATIONAL]
B737-209 (A)	9M-PMW	TRANSMILE AIR SERVICES		24197	1581	07/21/88	JT8D-9A		B-1878
B737-209 (A)	9M-PMZ	TRANSMILE AIR SERVICES		23796	1420	07/30/87	JT8D-9A		B-182, PK-RIV [LST BAYU AIR INDONESIA AS PK-BYA]

9Q-CONGO KINSHASA

A/C TYPE	CURRENT REG. NO.	LAST KNOWN OPERATOR (OWNER)	STATUS	ORIGINAL MSN	LINE NO.	DEL. DATE	ENG. TYPE	FLEET NO.	PREV. REG. [COMMENTS]
B737-293	9Q-CKZ	HEWA BORA AIRWAYS (FLIGHTSTAR)		19309	47	07/31/68	JT8D-7A		N464GB, N464AC, N777EC [HEAVILY DMGD DURING FIRE 04/14/00 AT KINSHASA AIRPORT]

MILITARY

A/C TYPE	CURRENT REG. NO.	LAST KNOWN OPERATOR (OWNER)	STATUS	ORIGINAL MSN	LINE NO.	DEL. DATE	ENG. TYPE	FLEET NO.	PREV. REG. [COMMENTS]
T-43A (B737-253)	71-1403	USAF	M	20685	317	07/31/73	JT8D-9A		
T-43A (B737-253)	71-1404	USAF	M	20686	326	09/27/73	JT8D-9A		
T-43A (B737-253)	71-1405	USAF	M	20687	329	11/04/73	JT8D-9A		
CT-43A (B737-253)	72-0282	USAF	M	20689	334	12/20/73	JT8D-9A (HK)		[CVTD T-43A; LST EG&G AS N5175U]
T-43A (B737-253)	72-0283	USAF	M	20690	336	01/28/74	JT8D-9A		
CT-43A (B737-253)	72-0284	USAF	M	20691	337	01/31/74	JT8D-9A (HK)		[CVTD T-43A; LST EG&G AS N5294E]
CT-43A (B737-253)	72-0285	USAF	M	20692	339	02/19/74	JT8D-9A (HK)		[CVTD T-43A; LST EG&G AS N5176Y]
CT-43A (B737-253)	72-0286	USAF	M	20693	340	02/27/74	JT8D-9A (HK)		N99890, N57JE [CVTD T-43A; LST EG&G AS N5177C]
CT-43A (B737-253)	72-0287	USAF	M	20694	343	03/15/74	JT8D-9A (HK)		[CVTD T-43A; LST EG&G AS N5294M]
T-43A (B737-253)	72-0288	USAF	M	20695	345	03/31/74	JT8D-9A		
T-43A (B737-253)	73-1150	USAF	M	20697	349	04/25/74	JT8D-9A		
T-43A (B737-253)	73-1151	USAF	M	20698	350	05/03/74	JT8D-9A		

A/C TYPE	CURRENT REG. NO.	LAST KNOWN OPERATOR (OWNER)	STATUS	ORIGINAL MSN	LINE NO.	DEL. DATE	ENG. TYPE	FLEET NO.	PREV. REG. [COMMENTS]
T-43A (B737-253)	73-1152	USAF	M	20699	355	05/31/74	JT8D-9A		
T-43A (B737-253)	73-1153	USAF	M	20700	357	06/14/74	JT8D-9A		
CT-43A (B737-253)	73-1154	USAF	M	20701	359	06/26/74	JT8D-9A		[CVTD T-43A]
NT-43A (B737-253)	73-1155	USAF	M	20702	362	07/12/74	JT8D-9A		[CVTD T-43A]
T-43A (B737-253)	73-1156	USAF	M	20703	363	07/19/74	JT8D-9A		

OUT OF SERVICE

A/C TYPE	CURRENT REG. NO.	LAST KNOWN OPERATOR (OWNER)	STATUS	ORIGINAL MSN	LINE NO.	DEL. DATE	ENG. TYPE	FLEET NO.	PREV. REG. [COMMENTS]
B737-130	OB-1736	AERO CONTINENTE (AIR SWEDEN)	O	19017	7	02/28/68	JT8D-7B		D-ABEF, B-2623, XA-GBM, OB-1657, P4-ASB [RT LESSOR; STD TUS]
B737-222	N9016U	UNITED AIRLINES	O	19054	36	06/23/68	JT8D-7B		[LRF 02/23/98; STD LAS]
B737-222	N68AF	PAN AMERICAN (HELEASCO)	O	19058	49	08/08/68	JT8D-7B		N9020U [WFU AND STD MZJ 06/90]
B737-222	N9024U	UNITED AIRLINES	O	19062	59	08/26/68	JT8D-7B		[DONATED TO LEWIS UNIV., ROMEOVILLE, IL 07/21/99 AS GROUND TRAINER]
B737-293	N463GB	AMERICAN AIRLINES	O	19308	40	07/10/68	JT8D-7A		[RT INTEGRATED 04/02/92]
B737-205	N408CE	(JTI ENGINES & A/C LSG)	O	19408	110	12/31/68	JT8D-15 (HK)		LN-SUS, SE-DKG, TC-JUP, PK-IJA, OB-1615, RA-73005 [STD MIA; ALL WHITE; NO TITLES]
B737-201	N205AU	FRONTIER AIRLINES (FSBU)	O	19421	53	08/08/68	JT8D-9A		N737N [RT CSAV 09/15/99; TO BOEING FOR TESTS]
B737-222	N209US	VANGUARD AIRLINES (FSBU)	O	19548	114	12/31/68	JT8D-9A (HK3)		N9042U, N751N [ST AVIATION SYS FOR BU]
B737-222	N9044U	UNITED AIRLINES	O	19550	116	01/22/69	JT8D-7B		[ST IASG 06/25/92]
B737-222	OB-1635	FAUCETT PERU (IALI)	O	19554	123	02/17/69	JT8D-9A		N9048U, N67AF, 5N-MCI [STD LIM]
B737-247	N903RC	LORAIR (9 LIVES HOLDINGS)	O	19598	33	06/11/68	JT8D-9		N4501W, N314VA, C-GVJC [BEING BU TUS]
B737-247	PK-OCF	AIRFAST INDONESIA	O	19601	45	07/17/68	JT8D-9		N4504W, N466AC [ST AGES 04/17/00; PARKED KUL]
B737-247	N306VA	VISCOUNT AIR SERVICE (POLA)	O	19609	81	10/16/68	JT8D-9A		N4512W [RT GECAS 05/15/96]
B737-247	N902WC	LORAIR (9 LIVES HOLDINGS)	O	19613	104	12/09/68	JT8D-9A (HK3)		N4516W, N308VA [PARKED MZJ; CORROSION DAMAGE]
B737-247	N309VA	EASTWIND AIRLINES (CISA)	O	19614	105	12/09/68	JT8D-9A (HK3)		N4517W, N473AC [RT LESSOR]
B737-244	N620PC	VANGUARD AIRLINES (INTL.)	O	19708	87	10/29/68	JT8D-9A (HK3)		ZS-EUZ, ZS-SBM, 3D-ADA, N136AW, N236TA [RT INTL. 04/01/01]
B737-112	OB-1288	FAUCETT PERU	O	19769	194	07/31/69	JT8D-9A		9V-BBC, N40AF [STD LIM]
B737-112	N333RN	PRESIDENTIAL AIR	O	19770	203	09/03/69	JT8D-9A		9M-AOV, 9V-BFE, N42AF, N709AW, ZK-NED, N73GQ, N709SP [SUSPENDED OPS 04/96]
B737-242C	F-GOAF	AIR MEDITERRANEE (TAT SA)	O	19847	84	11/28/68	JT8D-9A (HK3)		N6241, C-FNAB, F-GGPA, N847TA [STD PGF; NO TITLES]
B737-214	HR-SHG	SAHSA (GPAG)	O	19921	111	12/17/68	JT8D-7B		N381PS, CF-PWM, C6-BES, N382PA [WFU AND STD 08/90]
B737-222	B-2601	FAR EASTERN AIR TRANSPORT	O	19936	146	04/02/69	JT8D-7A		N9055U [ST DALLAS AEROSPACE 02/18/97]
B737-247	RP-C8886	GRANDAIR (EASCO)	O	20130	156	04/15/69	JT8D-9A		N4526W, B-2617 [ST AGES A/C SALES AND LSG FOR SPARES]
B737-247	RP-C8887	GRANDAIR (EASCO)	O	20132	167	05/20/69	JT8D-9A		N4528W, B-2607 [STD TPE]
B737-293	PK-OCG	AIRFAST INDONESIA	O	20335	237	05/25/71	JT8D-7A		N469AC [ST AGES 04/17/00; STD KUL]

A/C TYPE	CURRENT REG. NO.	LAST KNOWN OPERATOR (OWNER)	STATUS	ORIGINAL MSN	LINE NO.	DEL. DATE	ENG. TYPE	FLEET NO.	PREV. REG. [COMMENTS]
B737-219	N10248	CONTINENTAL AIRLINES	O	20344	229	07/18/71	JT8D-9A		N73714, ZK-NAJ, N7310F [CVTD -297; ST RFC 737/23; RTD ARD]
B737-291	N17252	CONTINENTAL AIRLINES	O	20362	216	10/27/69	JT8D-9A		N7374F [ST RFC 737/23 INC 09/03/98]
B737-281	PK-JHA	SEMPATI AIR (ASIA MARKET)	O	20450	262	07/27/70	JT8D-9A		JA8409 [STD CGK; ST PHOENIX AV., SHARJAH]
B737-281	PK-JHD	SEMPATI AIR (ASIA MARKET)	O	20451	266	09/22/70	JT8D-9A		JA8410 [STD CGK]
B737-281	PK-JHE	SEMPATI AIR (ASIA MARKET)	O	20452	270	11/17/70	JT8D-9A		JA8411 [STD CGK]
B737-2H5	N220US	EASTWIND AIRLINES (PLMI)	O	20453	246	09/03/71	JT8D-9A		N1790B, LN-MTC, N753N [CVTD -201; PARKED GSO; ST AV. SYS. FOR PART OUT]
B737-2H5	N221US	EASTWIND AIRLINES (PLMI)	O	20454	247	10/27/71	JT8D-9A (HK3)		N1791B, LN-MTD, N754N [CVTD -201; PARKED GSO; ST AV. SYS. FOR PART OUT]
B737-2A8	VT-EAI	INDIAN AIRLINES	O	20482	272	12/23/70	JT8D-9A		[STD DEL; FOR SALE]
B737-2D6 (A)	F-GLXH	AERIS (LOCAL LEASE)	O	20544	290	12/17/71	JT8D-9A		7T-VEC, TZ-ADL, G-BMMZ [STD TLS; LST BLV?]
B737-2H6 (A)	XA-PBA	TAESA (AIRLEASE)	O	20631	310	10/16/72	JT8D-15		9M-ARG, 9M-MBG, PK-IJD, XA-APB [TO BOH FOR SPARES BY EUROPEAN AV.]
B737-298C (A)	9Q-CNK	LIGNES AERIENNES CONGOLAISES	O	20795	348	05/01/74	JT8D-15		[DMGD 01/99 KILIMANJARO; FERRIED TO HARARE FOR D-CHECK]
B737-270C (A)	EP-IGD	IRAN GOVERNMENT	O	20893	371	09/06/74	JT8D-15		J2-KAF, YI-AGI
B737-2H6 (A)	XA-TLJ	TAESA (AIRLEASE)	O	20926	372	09/09/74	JT8D-15		9M-ASR, 9M-MBH, PK-IJE
B737-2A8 (A)	VT-ECP	SKYLINE NEPC	O	20960	374	09/26/74	JT8D-9A		[SEEN AT MUMBAI 12/07/98; I/S?]
B737-2E1 (A)	N461AT	AIR TRAN AIRWAYS (POLA)	O	20976	388	12/06/74	JT8D-9A (HK3)		C-GEPA, N461AC [RT POLA 11/99; STD MZJ; ST CSAV]
B737-2H6C (A)	HP-1311CMP	COPA PANAMA (CITG)	O	21109	436	10/30/75	JT8D-15		9M-MBI, N124GU [RT CITG 06/13/00]
B737-266 (A)	LV-WYI	LAPA (GECA)	O	21196	465	07/13/76	JT8D-17A		SU-AYM, PH-TVO, SU-BBW, 5Y-BHW, N196AU, LV-PMW [RT GECA 11/00; PARKED GYR]
B737-266 (A)	N132SW	(BBC AIRCRAFT)	O	21227	466	07/20/76	JT8D-17		SU-AYO [STD MIA]
B737-2H4 (A)	N20SW	SOUTHWEST AIRLINES	O	21337	490	05/16/77	JT8D-9A		[ST FLIGHT DIRECTOR INC 04/20/99; BEING BU EL MIRAGE]
B737-2H4 (A)	N23SW	SOUTHWEST AIRLINES	O	21338	494	06/27/77	JT8D-9A		[ST FLIGHT DIRECTOR INC 05/05/99; BEING BU SBD]
B737-2H4 (A)	N74PW	(FSBU)	O	21339	495	07/11/77	JT8D-9A		N28SW, 9Y-TJC [STD VCV]
B737-2Q5C (A)	TN-AEE	LINA CONGO	O	21538	520	06/22/78	JT8D-15		EL-AIL, F-GFVR [PARKED SNN]
B737-2A1 (A)	F-GHXK	AERIS (ALTER BAIL)	O	21599	514	07/31/78	JT8D-17		N1247E, YS-08C, N171AW [STD TLS; LST BLV?]
B737-2S3 (A)	F-GHXL	ECOAIR INTL. (ALTER BAIL)	O	21775	570	05/02/79	JT8D-17		G-BMOR, EI-BPR [NTU; PARKED ORY; ALL WHITE; NO TITLES; LST BLV?]
B737-2Q8 (A)	N71PW	(FSBU)	O	21960	642	03/21/80	JT8D-15A (HK3)		G-BGTY, EI-BTW, G-IBTW, CC-CLD, 9Y-TJG [STD VCV]
B737-2U4 (A)	N161DF	(FSBU)	O	22161	652	04/17/80	JT8D-15		G-BOSL, G-ILFC, G-WGEL, VT-SIB
B737-2L9 (A)	F-GEXI	AERIS (ALTER BAIL)	O	22406	690	09/22/80	JT8D-17		N8295V, OY-APP, G-BNGK [STD TLS; ALL WHITE; NO TITLES; NO ENGINES]
B737-2H6 (A)	N626AC	(GARY AVIATION)	O	22620	822	12/18/81	JT8D-15		9M-MBK, HP-1245CMP, N22620 [TO RECEIVE VIP INTERIOR]

199

A/C TYPE	CURRENT REG. NO.	LAST KNOWN OPERATOR (OWNER)	STATUS	ORIGINAL MSN	LINE NO.	DEL. DATE	ENG. TYPE	FLEET NO.	PREV. REG. [COMMENTS]
B737-2T5 (A)	N75PW	(FSBU)	O	22632	847	03/22/82	JT8D-15		G-BJBJ, CN-RMH, CC-CYP, 9Y-TJH [STD VCV]
B737-2F9 (A)	5N-ANX	NIGERIA AIRWAYS	O	22772	884	10/11/82	JT8D-15		[WFU LOS]
B737-2F9 (A)	5N-ANY	NIGERIA AIRWAYS	O	22773	893	02/08/83	JT8D-15/-15A		[WFU LOS]
B737-2T4 (A)	7T-VJA	AIR ALGERIE	O	22800	897	12/12/83	JT8D-17A		N4556L
B737-228 (A)	N246TR	AIR FRANCE (TASFUND IRELAND)	O	23010	959	05/02/83	JT8D-15A		F-GBYK [RT TRIT 03/01/01; FERRIED TO DAL 02/25/01]
B737-2Y5 (A)	N712S	(FSBU)	O	23038	949	03/11/83	JT8D-15A		9H-ABA, ZK-NAF [RT INGO 03/01; PARKED TUS; OO TO SPA]
B737-228 (A)	N245TR	(FSBU)	O	23793	1426	08/13/87	JT8D-15A		N235TR, F-GBYQ [RT TASL IRELAND 02/01; ST FSBU]

PRESERVED

A/C TYPE	CURRENT REG. NO.	LAST KNOWN OPERATOR (OWNER)	STATUS	ORIGINAL MSN	LINE NO.	DEL. DATE	ENG. TYPE	FLEET NO.	PREV. REG. [COMMENTS]
B737-222	N9009U	UNITED AIRLINES	P	19047	24	05/10/68	JT8D-7B		[LRF 11/30/98, WFU SFO; DONATED TO SOUTHERN ILLINOIS UNIVERSITY 03/99]
B737-130	N515NA	MUSEUM OF FLIGHT	P	19437	1	07/26/73	JT8D-7A		N73700, N715NA [DONATED BY NASA 09/20/97; STD MOSES LAKE, WA]
B737-222	N60436	PURDUE UNIVERSITY	P	19932	133	03/10/69	JT8D-7B		N9051U [LST BOEING FOR 737 FLIGHT CONTROLS SYSTEMS TESTS 11/99 - 03/00]
B737-201	N213US	US AIR	P	20213	160	04/29/69	JT8D-9A		N744N [DONATED TO MUSEUM OF FLIGHT BFI]

SCRAPPED

A/C TYPE	CURRENT REG. NO.	LAST KNOWN OPERATOR (OWNER)	STATUS	ORIGINAL MSN	LINE NO.	DEL. DATE	ENG. TYPE	FLEET NO.	PREV. REG. [COMMENTS]
B737-130	N701PJ	ANSETT NEW ZEALAND	S	19013	2	04/24/68	JT8D-7A		N2282C, D-ABEA, N701AW, ZK-NEA [BU MZJ 10/95]
B737-130	N702PJ	ANSETT NEW ZEALAND	S	19015	4	12/27/67	JT8D-7A		N2289C, D-ABEC, N702AW, ZK-NEB [BU MZJ 10/95]
B737-130	N703PJ	ANSETT NEW ZEALAND	S	19016	5	02/02/68	JT8D-7A		D-ABED, YV-406C, N703AW, ZK-NEC [BU MZJ 10/95 (SPECTRUM AEROSPACE)]
B737-130	N16201	CONTINENTAL AIRLINES	S	19018	9	03/13/68	JT8D-7A		D-ABEG, N401PE [ST RFC 737/23 INC 10/07/98; BEING BU ARD]
B737-130	N33202	CONTINENTAL AIRLINES	S	19019	10	04/25/68	JT8D-7A		D-ABEH, N402PE [ST RFC; BEING BU ARD]
B737-130	N16203	CONTINENTAL AIRLINES	S	19020	11	04/14/68	JT8D-7A		D-ABEI, N403PE [ST REPUBLIC FINANCIAL FOR SCRAP; BU OKC]
B737-130	N77204	CONTINENTAL AIRLINES	S	19021	15	04/04/68	JT8D-7A		D-ABEK, N404PE [BEING BU ARD]
B737-130	N20205	CONTINENTAL AIRLINES	S	19022	17	04/05/68	JT8D-7A		D-ABEL, N405PE [ST OK AIRLINE SUPPORT (SCRAP)]
B737-130	N14206	CONTINENTAL AIRLINES	S	19023	23	04/29/68	JT8D-7A		D-ABEM, N406PE [ST RFC 737/23 01/14/99; BEING BU ARD]
B737-130	N59207	CONTINENTAL AIRLINES	S	19024	26	05/19/68	JT8D-7A		D-ABEN, N407PE [PERMANENTLY RTD; ARD]
B737-130	N14208	CONTINENTAL AIRLINES	S	19025	32	06/10/68	JT8D-7A		D-ABEO, N408PE [ST RFC 737/23 09/18/98; BEING BU ARD]
B737-130	N14209	CONTINENTAL AIRLINES	S	19026	35	06/25/68	JT8D-7A		D-ABEP, N409PE [BEING BU ARD]
B737-130	XA-RSY	SARO (ARLINGTON LSG)	S	19027	52	08/01/68	JT8D-7A		D-ABEQ, N410PE [BU]
B737-130	N14211	CONTINENTAL AIRLINES	S	19028	98	11/29/68	JT8D-7A		D-ABER, N411PE [ST REPUBLIC FINANCIAL FOR SCRAP; BU ARD]

A/C TYPE	CURRENT REG. NO.	LAST KNOWN OPERATOR (OWNER)	STATUS	ORIGINAL MSN	LINE NO.	DEL. DATE	ENG. TYPE	FLEET NO.	PREV. REG. [COMMENTS]
B737-130	N14212	CONTINENTAL AIRLINES	S	19029	108	12/15/68	JT8D-7A		D-ABES, N412PE [BU ARD; AVIATION SALES]
B737-130	N24213	CONTINENTAL AIRLINES	S	19030	113	12/31/68	JT8D-7A		D-ABET, N413PE [BEING BU ARD]
B737-130	N44214	CONTINENTAL AIRLINES	S	19031	118	01/09/69	JT8D-7A		D-ABEU, N414PE [BU ARD; AVIATION SALES]
B737-130	N77215	CONTINENTAL AIRLINES	S	19032	119	01/14/69	JT8D-7A		D-ABEV, N415PE [PERMANENTLY RTD ARD]
B737-130	XA-RSZ	SARO (ARLINGTON LSG)	S	19033	120	01/24/69	JT8D-7A		D-ABEW, N416PE [BU]
B737-222	N9002U	UNITED AIRLINES	S	19040	8	12/29/67	JT8D-7B		[LRF 03/15/98, WFU LAS; BU GWO]
B737-222	N9003U	UNITED AIRLINES	S	19041	12	02/23/68	JT8D-7B		[WFU 10/97; MAINTENANCE TRAINER; IND]
B737-222	N9004U	UNITED AIRLINES	S	19042	14	03/02/68	JT8D-7B		[ST MEMPHIS GROUP FOR PARTS 10/28/98; STILL AT MZJ; PERMANENTLY RTD]
B737-222	N9006U	UNITED AIRLINES	S	19044	19	03/25/68	JT8D-7B		[WFU 04/98; BU GWO 03/00]
B737-222	N9007U	UNITED AIRLINES	S	19045	21	04/29/68	JT8D-7B		[LRF 01/20/98, WFU LAS; ST MEMPHIS GROUP GWO; BEING SCR GWO]
B737-222	N9008U	UNITED AIRLINES	S	19046	22	05/03/68	JT8D-7B		[BU GWO BY 10/99]
B737-222	N9010U	UNITED AIRLINES	S	19048	25	05/15/68	JT8D-7B		[BU GWO BY 10/99]
B737-222	N9011U	UNITED AIRLINES	S	19049	27	05/24/68	JT8D-7B		[BU GWO BY 10/99; ONLY COCKPIT SECTION REMAINS]
B737-222	N9012U	UNITED AIRLINES	S	19050	28	05/26/68	JT8D-7B		[TO BE BU MZJ]
B737-222	N9013U	UNITED AIRLINES	S	19051	30	05/27/68	JT8D-7B		[WFU 04/98; BU GWO]
B737-222	N9014U	UNITED AIRLINES	S	19052	31	06/26/68	JT8D-7B		[ST IASG FOR SCRAP]
B737-222	N9015U	UNITED AIRLINES	S	19053	34	06/10/68	JT8D-7B		[LRF 03/25/98; WFU LAS; BU GWO 03/00]
B737-222	N9017U	UNITED AIRLINES	S	19055	37	06/28/68	JT8D-7B		[BU GWO BY 10/99]
B737-222	N9019U	UNITED AIRLINES	S	19057	48	07/27/68	JT8D-7B		[BU GWO BY 10/99]
B737-222	N9022U	UNITED AIRLINES	S	19060	55	08/16/68	JT8D-7B		[WFU SFO 04/98; TO BE BU GWO]
B737-222	N9023U	UNITED AIRLINES	S	19061	58	08/27/68	JT8D-7B		[BEING SCR MZJ]
B737-222	N9025U	UNITED AIRLINES	S	19063	62	09/04/68	JT8D-7B		[BU GWO BY 10/99]
B737-222	N9027U	UNITED AIRLINES	S	19065	65	09/14/68	JT8D-7B		[ST RAM AIR SALES; BEING BU MIA]
B737-222	N9030U	UNITED AIRLINES	S	19068	74	10/04/68	JT8D-7B		[BU GWO BY 10/99]
B737-222	N9032U	UNITED AIRLINES	S	19070	76	10/08/68	JT8D-7B		[TO BE BU GWO]
B737-222	N9033U	UNITED AIRLINES	S	19071	85	10/23/68	JT8D-7B		[ST IASG 06/24/92]
B737-222	N9038U	UNITED AIRLINES	S	19076	99	11/27/68	JT8D-7B		[ST RAM AIR SALES; BEING BU MIA]
B737-222	N9040U	UNITED AIRLINES	S	19078	106	12/13/68	JT8D-7B		[ST MEMPHIS GROUP 10/15/98 FOR PARTS; STILL MZJ; PERMANENTLY RTD]
B737-293	N461GB	AMERICAN AIRLINES	S	19306	13	05/03/68	JT8D-7A		[BU PHX 10/95, HULK DONATED FOR FIRE TRAINING]
B737-293	N462AC	AMERICAN AIRLINES	S	19307	20	09/18/68	JT8D-7A		N462GB [SCR IGM 1994]
B737-201	N200AU	US AIR	S	19418	29	05/30/68	JT8D-9A		N734N [BU MZJ 06/96 BY WESTJET]
B737-201	N202AU	CARNIVAL AIR (PLMI)	S	19419	41	07/03/68	JT8D-9A		N735N [SCR AERO CONTROLS 09/94]
B737-201	N203AU	EASTWIND AIRLINES	S	19420	43	07/15/68	JT8D-9A		N736N [BU MZJ 06/96]
B737-222	5N-DIO	BARNAX AIR (IALI)	S	19549	115	01/13/69	JT8D-7B		N9043U, N64AF [SCR 04/94 (ILFC)]
B737-222	N9045U	UNITED AIRLINES	S	19551	117	01/23/69	JT8D-7B		[STD LAS; TO BE BU GWO]
B737-222	N73714	ALOHA AIRLINES	S	19552	121	03/03/69	JT8D-9A		N9046U, N61AF [BU IGM]
B737-247	N4502W	BRANIFF (POLA)	S	19599	39	07/01/68	JT8D-		[RT POLARIS 02/90; BU MHV 01/94]

A/C TYPE	CURRENT REG. NO.	LAST KNOWN OPERATOR (OWNER)	STATUS	ORIGINAL MSN	LINE NO.	DEL. DATE	ENG. TYPE	FLEET NO.	PREV. REG. [COMMENTS]
B737-247	N4505W	BRANIFF (POLA)	S	19602	46	07/22/68	JT8D-		[RT POLARIS 02/90; BU MHV]
B737-247	N4507W	BRANIFF (POLA)	S	19604	56	08/16/68	JT8D-		[RT POLARIS 02/90; BU MHV 01/94]
B737-247	N305VA	NATIONS AIR (POLA)	S	19606	64	09/09/68	JT8D-9A		N4509W [BU BY SPECTRUM AERO (BF GECAS/POLA 04/97)]
B737-247	N4511W	PAN AFRICAN EXPRESS (POLA)	S	19608	73	09/30/68	JT8D-9		[BU SNN 08/93]
B737-247	OB-1317	FAUCETT PERU (IALI)	S	19610	83	10/18/68	JT8D-9A		N4513W [BU 01/04/98]
B737-247	N304VA	VISCOUNT AIR SERVICE (POLA)	S	19617	132	02/15/69	JT8D-9A		N4520W [BU BY BANNER AERO (EX-POLA)]
B737-159	N472GB	GATX CAPITAL LEASING	S	19679	89	11/15/68	JT8D-		HK-1403, D-ABWA, N1780B, N73715 [BU]
B737-159	N471GB	AAR FINANCIAL SERVICES	S	19680	94	11/20/68	JT8D-		HK-1404, D-ABWB, N1781B, N73717 [BU]
B737-214	N10238	PRESIDENTIAL AIR	S	19682	78	10/05/68	JT8D-9A		N379PS, N7387F, N333RN [BU 07/25/95 (AERO CONTROLS)]
B737-204	N197AW	AMERICA WEST AIRLINES (ASC)	S	19709	38	07/07/68	JT8D-9A		G-AVRL, N311XV [SCR MHV BY 05/94]
B737-293	N465AC	AMERICAN AIRLINES	S	19713	80	10/14/68	JT8D-7A		N465GB [SCR IGM 1994]
B737-293	OB-1572	AMERICANA DE AVIACION	S	19714	88	10/31/68	JT8D-7A		N467GB [PERMANENTLY GROUNDED LIM]
B737-275	4R-ULH	AIR LANKA	S	19742	96	11/26/68	JT8D-9A		CF-PWD, EI-BJE [BU 10/20/93]
B737-222	N12235	CONTINENTAL AIRLINES	S	19758	16	07/01/70	JT8D-9A		N737Q, N1359B, ZK-NAM, N7302F [RTD ARD]
B737-112	N708AW	AMERICA WEST AIRLINES (WILLIS)	S	19771	212	10/10/69	JT8D-9A		9V-BBE, N47AF, YV-405C, HP-1038 [BU OPF]
B737-130	XA-RSW	SARO (ARLINGTON LSG)	S	19794	127	02/06/69	JT8D-7A		D-ABEY, N417PE [SCR]
B737-217	N12230	CONTINENTAL AIRLINES	S	19884	79	10/21/68	JT8D-9A		CF-CPB, N431PE [ST RFC 737/23 INC 08/11/98; RTD ARD]
B737-217	N12231	CONTINENTAL AIRLINES	S	19885	91	11/09/68	JT8D-9A		CF-CPC, N432PE [ST RFC 737/23 INC 08/26/98; RTD ARD]
B737-217	N16232	CONTINENTAL AIRLINES	S	19886	101	12/01/68	JT8D-9A		CF-CPD, N433PE [ST RFC 737/23 INC 07/17/98; RTD ARD]
B737-217	N14233	CONTINENTAL AIRLINES	S	19887	109	12/20/68	JT8D-9A		CF-CPE, N434PE [ST RFC 737/23 INC; PERMANENTLY RTD ARD]
B737-217	N13234	CONTINENTAL AIRLINES	S	19888	112	12/27/68	JT8D-9A		CF-CPU, N435PE [ST REPUBLIC FINANCIAL FOR SCRAP 10/21/97; BU ARD]
B737-214	N14239	CONTINENTAL AIRLINES	S	19920	100	11/25/68	JT8D-9A		N380PS, N7388F [ST RFC 737/23 INC 11/12/98 FOR PARTS; RTD ARD]
B737-219	N321XV	OLYMPIC AIRWAYS (ASCO)	S	19929	60	08/29/68	JT8D-9A		ZK-NAC [SCR MHV 08/92 (AGES)]
B737-219	N322XV	OLYMPIC AIRWAYS (ASCO)	S	19930	66	09/11/68	JT8D-9A		ZK-NAD [BU MXE 03/15/91]
B737-219	N453AC	WEST JET	S	19931	77	10/05/68	JT8D-7A		ZK-NAE [BU ROW BY WEST JET]
B737-222	VP-BEE	EUROPEAN AIRCHARTER	S	19934	137	03/11/69	JT8D-7B		N9053U [BU BOH-HURN 07/98]
B737-222	N9054U	AIR PHILIPPINES (SILVER/GREEN)	S	19935	138	03/31/69	JT8D-7B		[BEING BU]
B737-222	N10236	CONTINENTAL AIRLINES	S	19937	148	04/09/69	JT8D-9A		N9056U, N7389F [ST RFC 737/23 INC 11/16/98; RTD ARD]
B737-222	N9057U	UNITED AIRLINES	S	19938	150	05/07/69	JT8D-7B		[FUSELAGE USED BY SINGAPORE-CHANGI FIRE SERVICE]

A/C TYPE	CURRENT REG. NO.	LAST KNOWN OPERATOR (OWNER)	STATUS	ORIGINAL MSN	LINE NO.	DEL. DATE	ENG. TYPE	FLEET NO.	PREV. REG. [COMMENTS]
B737-222	N9060U	UNITED AIRLINES	S	19941	174	05/29/69	JT8D-7B		[BU MIA]
B737-222	N9063U	UNITED AIRLINES	S	19944	183	06/30/69	JT8D-7B		[ST RAM AIR SALES 04/07/99; BEING BU MIA]
B737-222	N9065U	UNITED AIRLINES	S	19946	186	07/09/69	JT8D-7B		CF-NAP [LRF 06/05/98, DONATED TO CENTRAL ARIZONA COLLEGE 04/00; BEING DISMANTLED]
B737-222	N9067U	AIR PHILIPPINES (SILVER/GREEN)	S	19948	191	07/28/69	JT8D-7B		[BU AEX]
B737-222	N9069U	UNITED AIRLINES	S	19950	198	08/20/69	JT8D-7B		[ST RAM AIR SALES; BEING BU MIA]
B737-222	N9070U	AIR PHILIPPINES (SILVER/GREEN)	S	19951	200	08/28/69	JT8D-7B		[SCR 08/28/00]
B737-222	N9071U	UNITED AIRLINES	S	19952	201	09/02/69	JT8D-7B		[LRF 01/12/98; BEING BU MIA]
B737-222	VP-BEP	EUROPEAN AIRCHARTER	S	19953	202	09/12/69	JT8D-7B		N9072U [BU BOH-HURN 06/98]
B737-222	N216US	EASTWIND AIRLINES	S	19954	206	09/22/69	JT8D-9A		N9073U, N759N [BU MZJ 06/96; FUSELAGE VAN NUYS]
B737-2C0	N14241	CONTINENTAL AIRLINES	S	20070	124	01/31/69	JT8D-9A		N570GB, N7378F [ST RFC737/23; RTD ARD]
B737-2C0	N10242	CONTINENTAL AIRLINES	S	20071	131	02/11/69	JT8D-9A		N571GB, N7379F [SCR FOR PARTS BY RFC737/23 ARD]
B737-2C0	N73243	CONTINENTAL AIRLINES (USLI)	S	20072	136	03/04/69	JT8D-9A		N572GB, N7372F [ST RFC 737/23 INC FOR PARTS; RTD ARD]
B737-2C0	N14245	CONTINENTAL AIRLINES	S	20074	170	05/26/69	JT8D-9A		N574GB, N7371F [BEING BU ARD]
B737-2A1	N215US	US AIR	S	20095	188	07/18/69	JT8D-9A		PP-SMD, N25SW, N767N [BU MZJ BY AAR ALLEN GROUP; FUSELAGE DAL]
B737-247	N303VA	VISCOUNT AIR SERVICE (POLA)	S	20125	134	02/18/69	JT8D-9A		N4521W, N221AW [BU BY BANNER AERO (EX-POLA); FUSELAGE ROW]
B737-247	N302VA	VISCOUNT AIR SERVICE (POLA)	S	20126	140	03/04/69	JT8D-9A		N4522W, N470AC [BU ROSWELL 05/97 (AAR CORP)]
B737-247	N14246	CONTINENTAL AIRLINES	S	20129	154	04/14/69	JT8D-9A		N4525W, N7384F [TO BE BU; REG CX ARD]
B737-247	N14247	CONTINENTAL AIRLINES	S	20133	176	06/09/69	JT8D-9A		N4529W, N7363F [SCR AERO CONTROLS 07/93]
B737-247	PP-BMS	VICA (EASCO)	S	20134	177	06/16/69	JT8D-9A		N4530W, B-2613 [PARKED TPE; BEING BU; CVTD TO RESTAURANT?]
B737-214	N460AT	(CELCIUS AMTEC)	S	20158	192	07/24/69	JT8D-9A		N985PS, ZK-NAL, N4264Y, T3-VAL, N460AC [BU OPF]
B737-2A6	N145AW	AMERICA WEST AIRLINES (WILLIS)	S	20194	196	08/25/69	JT8D-9A		N520L, VR-BEH, N8527S, N3333M [BU OPF]
B737-297	N73712	ALOHA AIRLINES	S	20210	163	05/07/69	JT8D-		[SCR FOR SPARES 07/88]
B737-201	N218US	(AERO CONTROLS)	S	20216	213	10/15/69	JT8D-9A		N747N [BEING BU FLL]
B737-248	EI-ASG	AER LINGUS	S	20222	240	02/20/70	JT8D-9A		HR-SHD [BU DUB 01/95]
B737-281	N503AV	COPA PANAMA (AV SALES)	S	20227	178	06/17/69	JT8D-		JA8402, N1444Z, B-1872, YU-ANX [BU 08/92]
B737-297	N73713	ALOHA AIRLINES	S	20242	222	11/24/69	JT8D-		[SCR FOR SPARES 07/88]
B737-281	4X-BAG	ARKIA ISRAELI AIRLINES	S	20276	231	01/15/70	JT8D-9A (HK3)		JA8403, 9Q-CNL, EI-BCR, N20727 [BU BY IAI TLV]
B737-2E1	N197AL	ORIENT EXPRESS AIR	S	20300	164	07/17/70	JT8D-9A		N1788B, N1733B, CF-EPO [BU MHV]
B737-244	LV-WBO	LAPA	S	20330	257	05/27/70	JT8D-9		ZS-SBP [BU EZE]
B737-2H4	N456TM	CASINO EXPRESS	S	20336	239	06/15/71	JT8D-15 (HK3)		N22SW, EI-BFC, EC-DZH, N332XV, N709ML [BU BY A/C DISSASSEMBLY SPECIALISTS]

A/C TYPE	CURRENT REG. NO.	LAST KNOWN OPERATOR (OWNER)	STATUS	ORIGINAL MSN	LINE NO.	DEL. DATE	ENG. TYPE	FLEET NO.	PREV. REG. [COMMENTS]
B737-2H4	N73717	ALOHA AIRLINES (MARKETAIR)	S	20345	233	06/10/71	JT8D-9A		N21SW [SCR 12/27/91]
B737-291	N10251	CONTINENTAL AIRLINES	S	20361	209	10/07/69	JT8D-9A		N7373F [ST RFC 737/23; BEING BU ARD 03/99]
B737-291	N7375F	NATIONS AIR (IALI)	S	20363	218	11/07/69	JT8D-9A (HK3)		N14253, RDPL-34125, SE-DTV [BU OPF]
B737-214	N7386F	CONTINENTAL AIRLINES	S	20368	264	03/01/71	JT8D-9A		N988PS [BU MXE 1995]
B737-2H4	N7381F	CONTINENTAL AIRLINES	S	20369	267	06/02/71	JT8D-9A		N20SW [BU MHV 1993 (TRACOR)]
B737-2E1	C-FEPL	CANADIAN AIRLINES (POLA)	S	20396	221	11/25/69	JT8D-9		N1785B [BU TUS (HAVECO AVN)]
B737-2E1	C-FEPR	CANADIAN AIRLINES (POLA)	S	20397	226	12/11/69	JT8D-9		N1786B [BU TUS (HAVECO AVN)]
B737-281	4X-BAF	ARKIA ISRAELI AIRLINES	S	20413	241	02/20/70	JT8D-9A (HK3)		JA8406, C6-BEC, EI-BEE [BU BY IAI TLV]
B737-281	N722S	SIERRA PACIFIC (GECC)	S	20449	259	06/22/70	JT8D-9A		JA8408, EI-BEF, OB-R1263, N142AW [SCR AMA 09/94]
B737-2A8	VT-EAG	INDIAN AIRLINES	S	20480	269	11/09/70	JT8D-9A		[BU BOMBAY 05/95]
B737-281 (A)	C-GGOF	WESTJET AIRLINES	S	20563	296	03/17/72	JT8D-17 (HK3)		JA8417 [PARTIALLY BU YYC (TAIL AND WINGS OFF), BEING USED AS CABIN CREW TRAINER]
B737-287 (A)	LV-LIW	AEROLINEAS ARGENTINAS	S	20966	387	12/11/74	JT8D-9A		[RTD 11/99; BEING BU AEP]
B737-241 (A)	PP-VMI	VARIG	S	21004	390	01/06/75	JT8D-17A		[BU GIG; FUSELAGE FOR CREW TRAINING]
B737-297 (A)	N725S	(AMERICAN AIRCARRIERS SUPPORT)	S	22051	634	01/29/80	JT8D-9A		N725AL [RT GECAS 08/24/98; BU GYR]
B737-297 (A)	N726AL	ALOHA AIRLINES	S	22426	738	02/18/81	JT8D-9A		[BEING BU]
B737-297 (A)	N462AT	AIR TRAN AIRWAYS (UAMI)	S	22631	894	07/21/82	JT8D-9A (HK3)		N730AL [RT CITG 11/99; BU OPF 12/99]
B737-2F9 (A)	5N-ANZ	NIGERIA AIRWAYS	S	22774	895	02/08/83	JT8D-15/-15A		[BU LOS]

WRITTEN OFF

A/C TYPE	CURRENT REG. NO.	LAST KNOWN OPERATOR (OWNER)	STATUS	ORIGINAL MSN	LINE NO.	DEL. DATE	ENG. TYPE	FLEET NO.	PREV. REG. [COMMENTS]
B737-222	N9005U	UNITED AIRLINES	W	19043	18	03/16/68	JT8D-7B		[WO 07/19/70 PHILADELPHIA, PA]
B737-222	N9031U	UNITED AIRLINES	W	19069	75	09/30/68	JT8D-7B		[WO 12/08/72 CHICAGO, IL]
B737-222	OB-1451	FAUCETT PERU (IALI)	W	19072	86	10/28/68	JT8D-9A		N9034U, N73714, N459AC [WO 02/29/96 AREQUIPA, PERU]
B737-222	N752N	PIEDMONT AIRLINES	W	19073	90	11/04/68	JT8D-7B		N9035U [WO 10/25/86 CHARLOTTE, NC]
B737-248	OB-1314	FAUCETT PERU	W	19425	153	04/15/69	JT8D-		EI-ASB, SU-AYX, PP-SRX, OB-R-1314 [WO 04/03/89 IQUITOS, PERU]
B737-222	N210US	US AIR	W	19555	129	02/14/69	JT8D-9A		N9049U [WO 07/22/90 KINSTON, NC]
B737-222	N62AF	AIR FLORIDA	W	19556	130	02/15/69	JT8D-		N9050U [WO 01/13/82 WASHINGTON, DC]
B737-204	N198AW	AMERICA WEST AIRLINES (ASC)	W	19710	54	08/09/68	JT8D-9A		G-AVRM, N312XV [WO 12/30/89 TUCSON]
B737-112	HP-873CMP	COPA PANAMA	W	19768	184	07/16/69	JT8D-9A		N17117, 9M-AOU, 9V-BFD, N46AF [WO 11/19/93 PANAMA CITY, PANAMA]
B737-242C	TU-TAV	AIR AFRIQUE (POLA)	W	19848	157	04/18/69	JT8D-9A		CF-NAH, F-GFVK [WO 08/03/97 DOUALA, CAMEROON]
B737-222	B-2603	FAR EASTERN AIR TRANSPORT	W	19939	151	05/05/69	JT8D-		N9058U [WO 08/22/81 TPE]
B737-2C0	N11244	CONTINENTAL AIRLINES	W	20073	142	03/13/69	JT8D-9A		N573GB, N7370F [WO 11/26/94 HOUSTON]
B737-2A1	PP-SME	VASP	W	20096	190	07/25/69	JT8D-		[WO 01/28/86 GUARULHOS, BRAZIL]
B737-247	XC-IJI	MEXICAN AIR FORCE	W	20127	144	03/17/69	JT8D-9		N4523W, TP-03, B-12001 [WO 05/10/99 LOMA BONITA, MEXICO]

A/C TYPE	CURRENT REG. NO.	LAST KNOWN OPERATOR (OWNER)	STATUS	ORIGINAL MSN	LINE NO.	DEL. DATE	ENG. TYPE	FLEET NO.	PREV. REG. [COMMENTS]
B737-247	N4527W	WESTERN AIRLINES	W	20131	165	05/12/69	JT8D-		[WO 03/31/75 CASPER, WY]
B737-275	CF-PWC	PACIFIC WESTERN AIRLINES	W	20142	253	05/01/70	JT8D-		[WO 02/11/78 CRANBROOK, BRITISH COLUMBIA]
B737-2A6	CC-CYR	LADECO AIRLINES (CORS)	W	20195	205	09/16/69	JT8D-9A		N1288, N146AW, ZK-NEE, 4R-ULL, N909LH [WO 05/17/99 SANTIAGO DE CHILE]
B737-297	N73711	ALOHA AIRLINES	W	20209	152	04/09/69	JT8D-		[WO 03/29/88 KAHULUI, HAWAII]
B737-281	B-1870	CHINA AIRLINES	W	20226	168	05/22/69	JT8D-		JA8401, N1451Z [WO 02/16/86 MAKUNG, TAIWAN]
B737-2B1	C9-BAB	LAM-MOZAMBIQUE	W	20281	228	12/19/69	JT8D-9		CR-BAB [WO 03/28/83 QUELIMANE, MOZAMBIQUE]
B737-293	N468AC	AIR CALIFORNIA	W	20334	232	09/15/70	JT8D-		[WO 02/17/81 SANTA ANA, CA]
B737-291	N737RD	(RAM AIR SALES)	W	20365	220	12/05/69	JT8D-9A		N7377F, N16254, C-GVJB [WO 02/02/98 DBER IN TORNADO MIA]
B737-204C	LV-WRZ	LAPA	W	20389	251	04/17/70	JT8D-9A		G-AXNB, F-GGPB [WO 08/31/99 AEP]
B737-287C	LV-JNE	AEROLINEAS ARGENTINAS	W	20408	265	10/03/70	JT8D-9A		[WO 11/20/92 SAN LUIS]
B737-2A8	VT-EAH	INDIAN AIRLINES	W	20481	271	12/03/70	JT8D-		[WO 10/19/88 AHMADABAD, INDIA]
B737-2A8	VT-EAL	INDIAN AIRLINES	W	20485	277	03/09/71	JT8D-9A		[WO 12/17/78 HYDERABAD, INDIA]
B737-2A8	VT-EAM	INDIAN AIRLINES	W	20486	279	04/10/71	JT8D-9A		[WO 03/31/73 DELHI, INDIA]
B737-286 (A)	EP-IRG	IRAN AIR	W	20499	284	07/17/71	JT8D-		[WO 10/15/86 SHIRAZ, IRAN]
B737-281 (A)	PK-JHF	SEMPATI AIR (ASEAN LEASE)	W	20508	287	10/04/71	JT8D-9A		JA8414 [WO 01/16/95 JOGJAKARTA]
B737-2H6 (A)	N401SH	SAHSA (ILFC)	W	20584	305	07/31/72	JT8D-15		9M-AQN, 9M-MBC [WO 07/18/93 MANAGUA, NICARAGUA]
B737-2H6 (A)	9M-MBD	MALAYSIA AIRLINES (ILFC)	W	20585	306	09/21/72	JT8D-		9M-AQO [WO 12/04/77 SINGAPORE, MALAYSIA]
B737-2D6C (A)	7T-VED	AIR ALGERIE	W	20650	311	11/14/72	JT8D-9		[WO 08/02/96 TIEMCEN, ALGERIA]
CT-43A (B737-253)	73-1149	USAF	W	20696	347	04/11/74	JT8D-9A		[CVTD T-43A; WO 04/03/96 DUBROVNIK, CROATIA]
B737-2D6C (A)	7T-VEE	AIR ALGERIE	W	20758	322	05/25/73	JT8D-9		[WO 12/21/94 COVENTRY, UK]
B737-2B1 (A)	C9-BAD	LAM-MOZAMBIQUE	W	20786	323	10/31/73	JT8D-		CR-BAD [WO 02/09/89 LICHINGA, MOZAMBIQUE]
B737-298C (A)	9Q-CNI	AIR ZAIRE	W	20793	333	11/19/73	JT8D-15		[WO 01/02/95 KINSHASA; RAN OFF R/W; GEAR FAILED]
B737-229C (A)	OO-SDH	SABENA	W	20914	396	02/26/75	JT8D-15A		[WO 04/04/78 CHARLEROI, BELGIUM]
B737-2H4 (A)	P4-NEN	ORIENT EAGLE AIRWAYS (PALM BCH AERO)	W	20925	373	09/18/74	JT8D-9A		N24SW [WO 04/12/98 ALMATY, KAZAKSTAN]
B737-2K6 (A)	EI-CBL	SAHSA (GPAG)	W	20957	377	10/01/74	JT8D-15		HR-SHA [WO 11/17/91 SAN JOSE, COSTA RICA]
B737-2A8 (A)	VT-ECQ	INDIAN AIRLINES	W	20961	375	09/26/74	JT8D-9A		[WO 04/26/93 AURANGABAD, INDIA]
B737-2A8 (A)	VT-ECR	INDIAN AIRLINES	W	20962	380	10/28/74	JT8D-9A		[WO 04/26/79 MADRAS, INDIA]
B737-2A8 (A)	VT-ECS	INDIAN AIRLINES	W	20963	383	11/13/74	JT8D-9A		[WO 12/02/95 DELHI; OVERRAN INTO SOFT GROUND]
B737-287 (A)	LV-LIU	AEROLINEAS ARGENTINAS	W	20964	379	12/10/74	JT8D-		[WO 09/26/88 USHUAIA, ARGENTINA]
B737-2A1 (A)	PP-SMV	VASP	W	20968	367	08/09/74	JT8D-17		[WO 02/02/95 GRU]
B737-2A1 (A)	PP-SMX	VASP	W	20969	369	08/28/74	JT8D-7		[WO 04/03/78 CONGOHAS, BRAZIL]
B737-2A1 (A)	PP-SMY	VASP	W	20970	376	10/04/74	JT8D-7		[WO 05/24/82 BRASILIA, BRAZIL]
B737-241 (A)	PP-VMK	VARIG	W	21006	398	03/05/75	JT8D-		N87569 [WO 09/03/89 S. JOSE DO XINGU, BRAZIL]
B737-2C3 (A)	PP-CJO	VARIG	W	21013	393	01/31/75	JT8D-17A		[WO 02/14/97 CARAJAS, BRAZIL]
B737-2J8C (A)	ST-AFL	SUDAN AIRWAYS	W	21170	430	09/18/75	JT8D-7		[WO KHARTOUM, SUDAN 07/19/98]
B737-2M2C (A)	D2-TAA	TAAG ANGOLA AIRLINES	W	21172	439	11/19/75	JT8D-		[WO 11/05/80 BENGUALA, ANGOLA]
B737-270C (A)	YI-AGJ	IRAQI AIRWAYS	W	21183	446	01/26/76	JT8D-		[WO 12/25/86 ARAR, SAUDI ARABIA]

A/C TYPE	CURRENT REG. NO.	LAST KNOWN OPERATOR (OWNER)	STATUS	ORIGINAL MSN	LINE NO.	DEL. DATE	ENG. TYPE	FLEET NO.	PREV. REG. [COMMENTS]
B737-2A1C (A)	PP-SNC	VASP	W	21187	443	01/29/76	JT8D-		[WO 02/22/83 MANAUS, BRAZIL]
B737-2A1C (A)	PP-SND	VASP	W	21188	444	01/29/76	JT8D-17		[WO 06/22/92 CRUZIERO DO SUL, BRAZIL]
B737-266 (A)	SU-AYH	EGYPT AIR	W	21191	450	03/04/76	JT8D-		[WO 11/24/85 LUQA, MALTA]
B737-268 (A)	HZ-AGM	SAUDI ARABIAN AIRLINES	W	21282	476	11/04/76	JT8D-15		[WO 09/06/97 NAJRAN, SAUDI ARABIA]
B737-2H7C (A)	TJ-CBD	CAMEROON AIRLINES	W	21295	484	03/02/77	JT8D-		[WO 08/30/84 DOUALA, CAMEROON]
B737-2P6 (A)	EI-CJW	AIR TRAN AIRWAYS (GECA)	W	21355	493	06/28/77	JT8D-15 (HK)		A40-BC [WO 11/01/98 ATLANTA]
B737-2H4 (A)	RP-C3010	AIR PHILIPPINES	W	21447	508	02/02/78	JT8D-9A		N50SW [WO 04/19/00 DAVAO, PHILIPPINES]
B737-2Q3 (A)	JA8444	SOUTHWEST AIRLINES-JAPAN	W	21477	545	01/18/79	JT8D-		[WO 08/26/82 ISHIGAKI, JAPAN]
B737-2A8 (A)	VT-EFL	INDIAN AIRLINES	W	21497	504	11/28/77	JT8D-17		K2371 [WO 08/16/91 IMPHAL, INDIA]
B737-2P6 (A)	A40-BK	GULF AIR	W	21734	566	04/18/79	JT8D-15		[WO 09/23/83 MINO JEBEL ALI, UAE]
B737-2R4C (A)	VT-SIA	SAHARA INDIA AIRLINES	W	21763	571	12/12/79	JT8D-17		N1269E, LN-NPB, N801WA, N401MG, N673MA [WO 03/08/94 DELHI, INDIA]
B737-2P5 (A)	HS-TBB	THAI AIRWAYS	W	21810	604	10/10/79	JT8D-15		[WO 04/15/85 PHUKET, THAILAND]
B737-236 (A)	G-BGJL	BRITISH AIR TOURS	W	22033	743	04/02/81	JT8D-15A		[WO 08/22/85 MANCHESTER, ENGLAND]
B737-204 (A)	HP-1205CMP	COPA PANAMA (BRITANNIA)	W	22059	631	02/18/80	JT8D-15		N8985V, G-BGYL [WO 06/07/92 LA PALMA, PANAMA]
B737-275 (A)	C-GQPW	PACIFIC WESTERN AIRLINES	W	22265	755	04/15/81	JT8D-9A		N56807 [WO 03/22/84 CALGARY, ALBERTA]
B737-2P5 (A)	HS-TBC	THAI AIRWAYS	W	22267	685	08/18/80	JT8D-		[WO 08/31/87 PHUKET, THAILAND]
B737-2A8 (A)	VT-EGD	ALLIANCE AIR	W	22280	671	06/18/80	JT8D-17A		[WO 07/17/00 PATNA, INDIA]
B737-2A1 (A)	CC-CHJ	LAN CHILE	W	22602	711	12/22/80	JT8D-		N8286V [WO 08/04/87 SANTIAGO, CHILE]
B737-2V2 (A)	HC-BIG	TAME	W	22607	775	10/05/81	JT8D-		N8283V [WO 07/11/83 CUENCA, ECUADOR]
B737-2M2 (A)	D2-TBV	TAAG ANGOLA AIRLINES	W	22626	802	10/14/81	JT8D-		[WO 02/09/84 HUAMBO, ANGOLA]
B737-230 (A)	D-ABHD	CONDOR	W	22635	774	06/25/81	JT8D-		N8279V [WO 01/02/88 IZMIR, TURKEY]
B737-291 (A)	N999UA	UNITED AIRLINES	W	22742	875	05/24/82	JT8D-17		N7356F [WO 03/04/91 COLORADO SPRINGS, CO]
B737-2M2 (A)	D2-TBN	TAAG ANGOLA AIRLINES	W	22775	869	05/06/82	JT8D-17		[WO 11/09/83 LU BANGO, ANGOLA]
B737-2F9 (A)	5N-AUA	NIGERIA AIRWAYS	W	22985	920	02/08/83	JT8D-15		[WO 11/13/95 KADUNA]
B737-228 (A)	F-GBYA	AIR FRANCE	W	23000	930	12/15/82	JT8D-15A		N1787B [WO 03/04/99 BIARRITZ]
B737-282 (A)	FAP-351	PERUVIAN AIR FORCE	W	23041	962	06/03/83	JT8D-17A		CS-TEK, VT-PDD [WO 05/05/98 ANDOAS, PERU]
B737-2X6C (A)	N670MA	MARKAIR	W	23121	1025	05/11/84	JT8D-17A		[WO 06/02/90 UNALAKLEET, ALASKA]
B737-247 (A)	B-2510	XIAMEN AIRWAYS	W	23189	1072	12/28/84	JT8D-17A		N241WA [WO 10/02/90 CANTON, CHINA]
B737-2K9 (A)	TJ-CBE	CAMEROON AIRLINES	W	23386	1143	08/30/85	JT8D-15A		[WO 12/03/95 DOUALA]
B737-209 (A)	B-180	CHINA AIRLINES	W	23795	1319	12/19/86	JT8D-9A		[WO 10/26/89 HUALIEN, TAIWAN]
B737-2H6 (A)	N125GU	AVIATECA (ILFC)	W	23849	1453	10/08/87	JT8D-15A		9M-MBM [WO 08/09/95 SAN SALVADOR]
B737-260 (A)	ET-AJA	ETHIOPIAN AIRLINES	W	23914	1456	10/29/87	JT8D-17A		[WO 09/16/88 BAHAR DAR, ETHIOPIA]
B737-2K3 (A)	YU-ANU	CHANCHANGI AIRLINES (AGX)	W	24139	1530	03/31/88	JT8D-15		[WO 02/26/98 LOS]

Boeing 737-300 through 737-500 Commercial Jet Aircraft Census

The aircraft in the following tables are listed in order of the following: 1) ICAO country prefixes; 2) operator; 3) aircraft type; and 4) registration.

The total built was 1,988 (1,113 B737-300, 486 B737-400, and 389 B737-500) from 1984 to 2000.

A/C TYPE	CURRENT REG. NO.	LAST KNOWN OPERATOR (OWNER)	STATUS	ORIGINAL MSN	LINE NO.	DEL. DATE	ENG. TYPE	FLEET NO.	PREV. REG. [COMMENTS]
AP-PAKISTAN									
B737-340	AP-BCA	PAKISTAN INTL. AIRLINES		23294	1114	05/31/85	CFM56-3B2		
B737-340	AP-BCB	PAKISTAN INTL. AIRLINES		23295	1116	06/03/85	CFM56-3B2		
B737-340	AP-BCC	PAKISTAN INTL. AIRLINES		23296	1121	06/18/85	CFM56-3B2		
B737-340	AP-BCD	PAKISTAN INTL. AIRLINES		23297	1122	06/21/85	CFM56-3B2		
B737-340	AP-BCF	PAKISTAN INTL. AIRLINES		23299	1235	06/20/86	CFM56-3B2		
B737-33A	AP-BEH	PAKISTAN INTL. AIRLINES		25504	2341	09/08/92	CFM56-3B2		
B737-340	AP-BFT	PAKISTAN INTL. AIRLINES		23298	1123	06/25/85	CFM56-3B2		AP-BCE
A40-OMAN									
B737-4Q8	TC-APP	OMAN AIR (PGT)	L	28202	3009	03/31/98	CFM56-3C1		
B-CHINA (PEOPLE'S REPUBLIC)									
B737-3J6	B-2531	AIR CHINA		23302	1224	05/15/86	CFM56-3B1		N1792B
B737-3J6	B-2532	AIR CHINA		23303	1237	06/19/86	CFM56-3B1		N5573B
B737-3J6	B-2535	AIR CHINA		25078	2002	03/13/91	CFM56-3B1		
B737-3J6	B-2536	AIR CHINA		25079	2016	03/22/91	CFM56-3B1		
B737-3J6	B-2580	AIR CHINA		25080	2254	04/22/92	CFM56-3B1		
B737-3J6	B-2581	AIR CHINA		25081	2263	04/16/92	CFM56-3B1		
B737-3J6	B-2584	AIR CHINA		25891	2385	12/21/92	CFM56-3B1		
B737-3J6	B-2585	AIR CHINA		27045	2384	12/21/92	CFM56-3B1		
B737-3J6	B-2587	AIR CHINA		25892	2396	01/29/93	CFM56-3B1		
B737-3J6	B-2588	AIR CHINA		25893	2489	06/25/93	CFM56-3B1		
B737-3J6	B-2598	AIR CHINA		27128	2493	06/25/93	CFM56-3B1		
B737-33A	B-2905	AIR CHINA		25506	2360	12/10/92	CFM56-3B2		N403WA
B737-33A	B-2906	AIR CHINA		25507	2373	12/10/92	CFM56-3B2		N404WA
B737-33A	B-2907	AIR CHINA		25508	2414	06/25/93	CFM56-3B2		N405WA
B737-33A	B-2947	AIR CHINA		25511	2599	04/14/94	CFM56-3B2		
B737-3J6	B-2948	AIR CHINA		27361	2631	07/15/94	CFM56-3B1		
B737-3J6	B-2949	AIR CHINA		27372	2650	10/05/94	CFM56-3B1		
B737-3J6	B-2953	AIR CHINA		27523	2710	04/27/95	CFM56-3B1		
B737-3J6	B-2954	AIR CHINA		27518	2768	01/29/96	CFM56-3B1		
B737-31B	B-2582	AIR GUIZHOU (CSN)	L	25895	2499	08/02/93	CFM56-3B1		

A/C TYPE	CURRENT REG. NO.	LAST KNOWN OPERATOR (OWNER)	STATUS	ORIGINAL MSN	LINE NO.	DEL. DATE	ENG. TYPE	FLEET NO.	PREV. REG. [COMMENTS]
B737-3T0	B-4008	CAAC SPECIAL SERVICES DIVISION		23839	1507	03/02/88	CFM56-3B1		N19357
B737-3T0	B-4009	CAAC SPECIAL SERVICES DIVISION		23840	1516	03/10/88	CFM56-3B1		N27358
B737-34N	B-4020	CAAC SPECIAL SERVICES DIVISION		28081	2746	09/01/95	CFM56-3B1		
B737-34N	B-4021	CAAC SPECIAL SERVICES DIVISION		28082	2747	09/01/95	CFM56-3B1		
B737-39P	B-2571	CHINA EASTERN AIRLINES		29410	3053	07/28/98	CFM56-3C1		
B737-39P	B-2572	CHINA EASTERN AIRLINES		29411	3071	09/25/98	CFM56-3C1		
B737-39P	B-2573	CHINA EASTERN AIRLINES		29412	3080	11/03/98	CFM56-3C1		N1786B
B737-3L9	B-2653	CHINA EASTERN AIRLINES (SALE)		24570	1800	01/17/90	CFM56-3B2		OY-MME, 9V-TRC, G-OABD, N2332Q
B737-36N	B-2977	CHINA EASTERN AIRLINES (GECA)		28560	2888	05/29/97	CFM56-3B1		
B737-36N	B-2978	CHINA EASTERN AIRLINES (GECA)		28561	2896	06/23/97	CFM56-3B1		
B737-36N	B-2979	CHINA EASTERN AIRLINES (GECA)		28562	2908	07/25/97	CFM56-3B1		N1786B
B737-5Y0	B-2541	CHINA SOUTHERN AIRLINES (CITI)		24696	1960	01/14/91	CFM56-3B1		
B737-5Y0	B-2542	CHINA SOUTHERN AIRLINES (GECA)		24897	2003	02/27/91	CFM56-3B1		
B737-5Y0	B-2543	CHINA SOUTHERN AIRLINES (BBAM)		24898	2079	07/03/91	CFM56-3B1		
B737-5Y0	B-2544	CHINA SOUTHERN AIRLINES (GECA)		24899	2093	08/02/91	CFM56-3B1		
B737-5Y0	B-2545	CHINA SOUTHERN AIRLINES (GECA)		24900	2095	08/07/91	CFM56-3B1		
B737-5Y0	B-2546	CHINA SOUTHERN AIRLINES (GECA)		25175	2150	10/29/91	CFM56-3B1		
B737-5Y0	B-2547	CHINA SOUTHERN AIRLINES (GECA)		25176	2155	11/01/91	CFM56-3B1		
B737-5Y0	B-2548	CHINA SOUTHERN AIRLINES (GECA)		25182	2211	02/03/92	CFM56-3B1		
B737-5Y0	B-2549	CHINA SOUTHERN AIRLINES (GECA)		25183	2218	02/14/92	CFM56-3B1		
B737-5Y0	B-2550	CHINA SOUTHERN AIRLINES (GECA)		25188	2238	03/12/92	CFM56-3B1		
B737-5Y0	B-2912	CHINA SOUTHERN AIRLINES (GECA)		26100	2538	03/21/94	CFM56-3B1		N35108
B737-5Y0	B-2915	CHINA SOUTHERN AIRLINES (GECA)		26101	2544	03/21/94	CFM56-3B1		
B737-3Y0	B-2526	CHINA SOUTHERN AIRLINES (GECA)		25172	2089	07/19/91	CFM56-3B1		
B737-3Y0	B-2527	CHINA SOUTHERN AIRLINES (GECA)		25173	2097	08/09/91	CFM56-3B1		
B737-3Y0	B-2528	CHINA SOUTHERN AIRLINES (GECA)		25174	2168	11/21/91	CFM56-3B1		
B737-3Y0	B-2539	CHINA SOUTHERN AIRLINES (BBAM)		26068	2306	06/15/92	CFM56-3C1		
B737-31B	B-2582	CHINA SOUTHERN AIRLINES		25895	2499	08/02/93	CFM56-3B1		[LST CGH]
B737-31B	B-2583	CHINA SOUTHERN AIRLINES		25897	2554	12/03/93	CFM56-3B1		
B737-31B	B-2596	CHINA SOUTHERN AIRLINES		27151	2437	03/01/93	CFM56-3B1		
B737-3Y0	B-2909	CHINA SOUTHERN AIRLINES (GECA)		26082	2456	04/16/93	CFM56-3B1		
B737-3Y0	B-2910	CHINA SOUTHERN AIRLINES (GECA)		26083	2459	04/16/93	CFM56-3B1		
B737-3Y0	B-2911	CHINA SOUTHERN AIRLINES (GECA)		26084	2460	04/20/93	CFM56-3B1		
B737-3Q8	B-2920	CHINA SOUTHERN AIRLINES		27271	2523	09/14/93	CFM56-3B1		
B737-3Q8	B-2921	CHINA SOUTHERN AIRLINES		27286	2528	09/24/93	CFM56-3B1		
B737-31B	B-2922	CHINA SOUTHERN AIRLINES		27272	2555	12/06/93	CFM56-3B1		
B737-31B	B-2923	CHINA SOUTHERN AIRLINES		27275	2565	01/11/94	CFM56-3B1		
B737-31B	B-2924	CHINA SOUTHERN AIRLINES		27287	2575	02/22/94	CFM56-3B1		

A/C TYPE	CURRENT REG. NO.	LAST KNOWN OPERATOR (OWNER)	STATUS	ORIGINAL MSN	LINE NO.	DEL. DATE	ENG. TYPE	FLEET NO.	PREV. REG. [COMMENTS]
B737-31B	B-2926	CHINA SOUTHERN AIRLINES		27289	2593	03/31/94	CFM56-3B1		
B737-31B	B-2927	CHINA SOUTHERN AIRLINES		27290	2595	03/31/94	CFM56-3B1		
B737-31B	B-2929	CHINA SOUTHERN AIRLINES		27343	2619	06/09/94	CFM56-3B1		
B737-31B	B-2941	CHINA SOUTHERN AIRLINES		27344	2622	06/16/94	CFM56-3B1		
B737-31B	B-2952	CHINA SOUTHERN AIRLINES		27519	2678	12/09/94	CFM56-3B1		
B737-31B	B-2959	CHINA SOUTHERN AIRLINES		27520	2775	03/07/96	CFM56-3B1		
B737-3Y9	N999CZ	CHINA SOUTHERN AIRLINES (ITOH)		25604	2405	01/26/93	CFM56-3C1		N1784B
B737-3Z0	B-2519	CHINA SOUTHWEST AIRLINES		23448	1168	12/17/85	CFM56-3B1		N5573P
B737-3Z0	B-2520	CHINA SOUTHWEST AIRLINES		23449	1184	01/25/86	CFM56-3B1		N1789B
B737-3Z0	B-2521	CHINA SOUTHWEST AIRLINES		23450	1196	02/26/86	CFM56-3B1		N1790B
B737-3Z0	B-2522	CHINA SOUTHWEST AIRLINES		23451	1240	07/10/86	CFM56-3B1		N5573K
B737-3Z0	B-2530	CHINA SOUTHWEST AIRLINES		27046	2252	04/16/92	CFM56-3B1		
B737-3Z0	B-2533	CHINA SOUTHWEST AIRLINES		27138	2436	03/01/93	CFM56-3B1		
B737-3Z0	B-2537	CHINA SOUTHWEST AIRLINES		25089	2027	04/12/91	CFM56-3B1		
B737-3Z0	B-2586	CHINA SOUTHWEST AIRLINES		27047	2357	09/11/92	CFM56-3B1		
B737-3Z0	B-2590	CHINA SOUTHWEST AIRLINES		27126	2370	09/29/92	CFM56-3B1		
B737-3Z0	B-2597	CHINA SOUTHWEST AIRLINES		27176	2495	06/30/93	CFM56-3B1		
B737-3Z0	B-2599	CHINA SOUTHWEST AIRLINES		25896	2558	12/14/93	CFM56-3B1		
B737-3Z0	B-2950	CHINA SOUTHWEST AIRLINES		27374	2647	09/12/94	CFM56-3B1		
B737-3Z0	B-2951	CHINA SOUTHWEST AIRLINES		27373	2658	11/01/94	CFM56-3B1		
B737-3Z0	B-2957	CHINA SOUTHWEST AIRLINES		27521	2738	07/18/95	CFM56-3B1		
B737-33A	B-4018	CHINA UNITED AIRLINES		25502	2310	06/23/92	CFM56-3B1		
B737-33A	B-4019	CHINA UNITED AIRLINES		25503	2313	06/24/92	CFM56-3B1		
B737-3Q8	B-4052	CHINA UNITED AIRLINES (ILFC)		24701	1957	11/30/90	CFM56-3B1		PK-GWI
B737-3Q8	B-4053	CHINA UNITED AIRLINES (ILFC)		24702	1994	02/11/91	CFM56-3B1		PK-GWJ
B737-341	B-2908	CHINA XINHUA AIRLINES		26854	2303	04/15/93	CFM56-3B2		PP-VPC [NTU]
B737-39K	B-2934	CHINA XINHUA AIRLINES		27274	2559	12/21/93	CFM56-3B1		
B737-332	B-2942	CHINA XINHUA AIRLINES		25997	2506	08/02/93	CFM56-3B1		N304DE
B737-332	B-2943	CHINA XINHUA AIRLINES		25998	2510	08/06/93	CFM56-3B1		N305DE
B737-39K	B-2945	CHINA XINHUA AIRLINES		27362	2639	08/16/94	CFM56-3B1		
B737-36Q	B-2982	CHINA XINHUA AIRLINES (BOUL)		28657	2859	03/14/97	CFM56-3C1		
B737-46Q	B-2987	CHINA XINHUA AIRLINES (BOUL)		28663	2922	08/27/97	CFM56-3C1		
B737-46Q	B-2989	CHINA XINHUA AIRLINES (BOUL)		28758	2939	10/16/97	CFM56-3C1		
B737-46Q	B-2993	CHINA XINHUA AIRLINES (SALE)		28759	2981	01/21/98	CFM56-3C1		N1786B
B737-31L	B-2930	CHINA XINJIANG AIRLINES		27273	2556	12/09/93	CFM56-3B1		
B737-31L	B-2931	CHINA XINJIANG AIRLINES		27276	2567	01/31/94	CFM56-3B1		
B737-31L	B-2939	CHINA XINJIANG AIRLINES		27345	2625	07/11/94	CFM56-3B1		[LST CSZ]

A/C TYPE	CURRENT REG. NO.	LAST KNOWN OPERATOR (OWNER)	STATUS	ORIGINAL MSN	LINE NO.	DEL. DATE	ENG. TYPE	FLEET NO.	PREV. REG. [COMMENTS]
B737-31L	B-2940	CHINA XINJIANG AIRLINES		27346	2636	07/27/94	CFM56-3B1		[LST CSZ]
B737-3W0	B-2517	CHINA YUNNAN AIRLINES		23396	1166	12/12/85	CFM56-3B1		N5573K
B737-3W0	B-2518	CHINA YUNNAN AIRLINES		23397	1193	03/08/86	CFM56-3B1		N1791B
B737-3W0	B-2538	CHINA YUNNAN AIRLINES		25090	2040	05/08/91	CFM56-3B1		
B737-3W0	B-2589	CHINA YUNNAN AIRLINES		27127	2377	11/03/92	CFM56-3C1		
B737-341	B-2594	CHINA YUNNAN AIRLINES		26853	2275	08/17/92	CFM56-3C1		
B737-33A	B-2955	CHINA YUNNAN AIRLINES (AWAS)		27453	2687	02/15/95	CFM56-3C1		
B737-33A	B-2956	CHINA YUNNAN AIRLINES (AWAS)		27907	2690	02/23/95	CFM56-3C1		
B737-3W0	B-2958	CHINA YUNNAN AIRLINES		27522	2727	06/06/95	CFM56-3C1		
B737-33A	B-2966	CHINA YUNNAN AIRLINES (AWAS)		27462	2765	01/25/96	CFM56-3C1		
B737-3W0	B-2981	CHINA YUNNAN AIRLINES		28972	2919	08/21/97	CFM56-3C1		
B737-3W0	B-2983	CHINA YUNNAN AIRLINES		28973	2941	10/23/97	CFM56-3C1		
B737-3W0	B-2985	CHINA YUNNAN AIRLINES		29068	2945	11/12/97	CFM56-3C1		
B737-3W0	B-2986	CHINA YUNNAN AIRLINES		29069	2951	12/02/97	CFM56-3C1		
B737-505	B-2529	FUJIAN AIRLINES (CXA)	L	26297	2578	02/21/94	CFM56-3C1		LN-BUA [OPW CXA]
B737-505	B-2591	FUJIAN AIRLINES (CXA)	L	25792	2353	09/24/92	CFM56-3C1		LN-BRW [OPW CXA]
B737-33A	B-2578	HAINAN AIRLINES		25603	2333	04/14/93	CFM56-3B2		N401AW
B737-33A	B-2579	HAINAN AIRLINES		25505	2342	04/24/93	CFM56-3B2		N402AW
B737-3Q8	B-2937	HAINAN AIRLINES (ILFC)		26295	2557	12/10/93	CFM56-3B2		
B737-3Q8	B-2938	HAINAN AIRLINES (ILFC)		26296	2581	02/23/94	CFM56-3B2		
B737-3Q8	B-2963	HAINAN AIRLINES (ILFC)		26325	2772	02/19/96	CFM56-3B2		
B737-44P	B-2501	HAINAN AIRLINES		29914	3067	09/03/98	CFM56-3C1		N1786B
B737-44P	B-2576	HAINAN AIRLINES		29915	3106	04/13/99	CFM56-3C1		N1786B
B737-4Q8	B-2960	HAINAN AIRLINES (ILFC)		24332	1866	05/30/90	CFM56-3C1		G-BPNZ, N191LF
B737-4Q8	B-2965	HAINAN AIRLINES (ILFC)		26334	2782	04/02/96	CFM56-3C1		
B737-4Q8	B-2967	HAINAN AIRLINES (ILFC)		26335	2793	05/17/96	CFM56-3C1		
B737-4Q8	B-2970	HAINAN AIRLINES (ILFC)		26337	2811	08/21/96	CFM56-3C1		
B737-48E	B-2990	HAINAN AIRLINES (SUNR)		25766	2543	01/10/94	CFM56-3C1		HL7231
B737-3Y0	B-2534	SHANDONG AIRLINES (GECA)		26070	2349	09/03/92	CFM56-3B1		
B737-3Y0	B-2595	SHANDONG AIRLINES (GECA)		26072	2369	10/07/92	CFM56-3B1		
B737-35N	B-2961	SHANDONG AIRLINES		28156	2774	03/06/96	CFM56-3B1		
B737-35N	B-2962	SHANDONG AIRLINES		28157	2778	03/26/96	CFM56-3B1		
B737-35N	B-2968	SHANDONG AIRLINES		28158	2818	10/08/96	CFM56-3B1		
B737-35N	B-2995	SHANDONG AIRLINES		29315	3054	07/30/98	CFM56-3C1		N1786B
B737-35N	B-2996	SHANDONG AIRLINES		29316	3065	09/04/98	CFM56-3C1		N1786B
B737-3K9	B-2932	SHENZHEN AIRLINES (BIAL)		25787	2302	06/09/92	CFM56-3B2		N41069
B737-3K9	B-2933	SHENZHEN AIRLINES (BIAL)		25788	2331	08/14/93	CFM56-3B2		N4113D

A/C TYPE	CURRENT REG. NO.	LAST KNOWN OPERATOR (OWNER)	STATUS	ORIGINAL MSN	LINE NO.	DEL. DATE	ENG. TYPE	FLEET NO.	PREV. REG. [COMMENTS]
B737-31L	B-2939	SHENZHEN AIRLINES (CXJ)	L	27345	2625	07/11/94	CFM56-3B1		
B737-31L	B-2940	SHENZHEN AIRLINES (CXJ)	L	27346	2636	07/27/94	CFM56-3B1		
B737-3Q8	B-2971	SHENZHEN AIRLINES (ILFC)		25373	2290	05/21/92	CFM56-3B2		CC-CYJ
B737-33A	B-2972	SHENZHEN AIRLINES (AWAS)		27463	2831	11/22/96	CFM56-3C1		
B737-37K	B-2935	SICHUAN AIRLINES (CYN)	L	27283	2547	02/01/94	CFM56-3C1		
B737-3Q8	B-2918	WUHAN AIRLINES (ILFC)		24986	2192	01/08/92	CFM56-3B2		CS-TII, N551LF
B737-3Q8	B-2919	WUHAN AIRLINES (ILFC)		24987	2268	04/23/92	CFM56-3B2		CS-TIJ, N561LF
B737-3Q8	B-2928	WUHAN AIRLINES (ILFC)		26294	2550	12/03/93	CFM56-3B2		N261LF
B737-36R	B-2969	WUHAN AIRLINES		30102	3108	05/04/99	CFM56-3C1		N1787B
B737-3S3	B-2976	WUHAN AIRLINES (SUNR)		29244	3059	08/13/98	CFM56-3C1		N1786B, N244SR
B737-36R	B-2988	WUHAN AIRLINES		29087	2970	12/23/97	CFM56-3C1		
B737-505	B-2529	XIAMEN AIRLINES (BRA)	L	26297	2578	02/21/94	CFM56-3C1		LN-BUA [LST/OPW CFJ]
B737-505	B-2591	XIAMEN AIRLINES (BRA)	L	25792	2353	09/24/92	CFM56-3C1		LN-BRW [LST/OPW CFJ]
B737-505	B-2592	XIAMEN AIRLINES (BRA)	L	27153	2516	09/01/93	CFM56-3C1		LN-BRZ
B737-505	B-2593	XIAMEN AIRLINES (BRA)	L	27155	2449	03/23/93	CFM56-3C1		LN-BRY
B737-505	B-2973	XIAMEN AIRLINES (ILFC)		26336	2805	07/18/96	CFM56-3B1		
B737-505	B-2975	XIAMEN AIRLINES (ILFC)		26338	2822	10/16/96	CFM56-3B1		
B737-3Q8	B-2655	XIAMEN AIRLINES (ILFC)		26288	2480	06/01/93	CFM56-3B2		N471LF, B-2904
B737-3Q8	B-2661	XIAMEN AIRLINES (ILFC)		26284	2418	02/08/93	CFM56-3B2		N571LF, B-2901
B737-3Q8	B-2662	XIAMEN AIRLINES (ILFC)		24988	2466	04/30/93	CFM56-3B2		N481LF, B-2902
B737-3Q8	B-2903	XIAMEN AIRLINES (ILFC)		26292	2519	09/17/93	CFM56-3B2		
B737-37K	B-2574	ZHONGYUAN AIRLINES		29407	3100	03/31/99	CFM56-3C1		N1786B
B737-37K	B-2575	ZHONGYUAN AIRLINES		29408	3104	04/09/99	CFM56-3C1		N1786B, N1800B
B737-37K	B-2935	ZHONGYUAN AIRLINES		27283	2547	02/01/94	CFM56-3C1		[LST CSC 05/09/00]
B737-37K	B-2936	ZHONGYUAN AIRLINES		27335	2609	11/22/94	CFM56-3C1		
B737-37K	B-2946	ZHONGYUAN AIRLINES		27375	2655	11/22/94	CFM56-3C1		

CC-CHILE

A/C TYPE	CURRENT REG. NO.	LAST KNOWN OPERATOR (OWNER)	STATUS	ORIGINAL MSN	LINE NO.	DEL. DATE	ENG. TYPE	FLEET NO.	PREV. REG. [COMMENTS]
B737-58N	FAC921	CHILEAN AIR FORCE		28866	2929	09/18/97	CFM56-3C1		N1786B, PT996

CN-MOROCCO

A/C TYPE	CURRENT REG. NO.	LAST KNOWN OPERATOR (OWNER)	STATUS	ORIGINAL MSN	LINE NO.	DEL. DATE	ENG. TYPE	FLEET NO.	PREV. REG. [COMMENTS]
B737-5B6	CN-RMV	ROYAL AIR MAROC		25317	2157	11/12/91	CFM56-3C1		
B737-5B6	CN-RMW	ROYAL AIR MAROC (RAM2 LEASE)		25364	2166	11/21/91	CFM56-3C1		
B737-5B6	CN-RMY	ROYAL AIR MAROC		26525	2209	03/13/92	CFM56-3C1		
B737-5B6	CN-RNB	ROYAL AIR MAROC		26527	2472	05/14/93	CFM56-3C1		
B737-5B6	CN-RNG	ROYAL AIR MAROC		27679	2734	07/15/95	CFM56-3C1		
B737-5B6	CN-RNH	ROYAL AIR MAROC		27680	2855	02/28/97	CFM56-3C1		

A/C TYPE	CURRENT REG. NO.	LAST KNOWN OPERATOR (OWNER)	STATUS	ORIGINAL MSN	LINE NO.	DEL. DATE	ENG. TYPE	FLEET NO.	PREV. REG. [COMMENTS]
B737-4B6	CN-RMF	ROYAL AIR MAROC (CLS GARNET)		24807	1880	07/03/90	CFM56-3C1		
B737-4B6	CN-RMG	ROYAL AIR MAROC (CLS GARNET)		24808	1888	07/16/90	CFM56-3C1		
B737-4B6	CN-RMX	ROYAL AIR MAROC		26526	2219	03/13/92	CFM56-3C1		
B737-4B6	CN-RNA	ROYAL AIR MAROC (RAM3 LEASE)		26531	2453	04/08/93	CFM56-3C1		
B737-4B6	CN-RNC	ROYAL AIR MAROC		26529	2584	05/03/94	CFM56-3C1		
B737-4B6	CN-RND	ROYAL AIR MAROC		26530	2588	05/03/94	CFM56-3C1		
B737-4B6	CN-RNF	ROYAL AIR MAROC		27678	2733	07/15/95	CFM56-3C1		

CP-BOLIVIA

A/C TYPE	CURRENT REG. NO.	LAST KNOWN OPERATOR (OWNER)	STATUS	ORIGINAL MSN	LINE NO.	DEL. DATE	ENG. TYPE	FLEET NO.	PREV. REG. [COMMENTS]
B737-3A1	CP-2313	LAB AIRLINES		28389	2836	12/20/96	CFM56-3C1		
B737-382	CP-2391	LAB AIRLINES (PEGA)		24366	1699	04/06/89	CFM56-3B2		CS-TIC, N934PG

CS-PORTUGAL

A/C TYPE	CURRENT REG. NO.	LAST KNOWN OPERATOR (OWNER)	STATUS	ORIGINAL MSN	LINE NO.	DEL. DATE	ENG. TYPE	FLEET NO.	PREV. REG. [COMMENTS]
B737-3Q8	CS-TGP	SATA INTL. (POLA)		24131	1541	04/28/88	CFM56-3B2		EC-EII, EC-592, EC-FFC, OO-LTX
B737-36N	CS-TGQ	SATA INTL. (GECA)		28570	3010	03/30/98	CFM56-3C1		
B737-3Y0	CS-TGR	SATA INTL. (GECA)		24902	1973	01/07/91	CFM56-3B2		9V-TRB [OO FOR LST MAH 05/01 FROM GECA AS HA-LEX]
B737-4Y0	CS-	SATA INTL. (GECA)		23981	1678	02/25/89	CFM56-3C1		EC-251, EC-EMY, SU-BLL, F-GNFS, EI-CEW, TC-AFZ

C2-NAURU

A/C TYPE	CURRENT REG. NO.	LAST KNOWN OPERATOR (OWNER)	STATUS	ORIGINAL MSN	LINE NO.	DEL. DATE	ENG. TYPE	FLEET NO.	PREV. REG. [COMMENTS]
B737-4L7	VH-RON	AIR NAURU (NORDSTRESS)		26960	2483	06/09/93	CFM56-3C1		C2-RN10 [OCC LST/OPF NORFOLK JET EXPRESS]

C6-BAHAMAS

A/C TYPE	CURRENT REG. NO.	LAST KNOWN OPERATOR (OWNER)	STATUS	ORIGINAL MSN	LINE NO.	DEL. DATE	ENG. TYPE	FLEET NO.	PREV. REG. [COMMENTS]
B737-3Q8	TF-SUN	BAHAMASAIR (ICB)	L	23535	1301	11/10/86	CFM56-3B2		EC-EAK, N102GU, SP-LMB, TJ-CBF, N535GE [OPB IC

D-GERMANY

A/C TYPE	CURRENT REG. NO.	LAST KNOWN OPERATOR (OWNER)	STATUS	ORIGINAL MSN	LINE NO.	DEL. DATE	ENG. TYPE	FLEET NO.	PREV. REG. [COMMENTS]
B737-3M8	EC-GHD	AIR-BERLIN (AEA)	L	25071	2039	05/29/91	CFM56-3B2		HB-IIC, OO-LTN, N682MA, EC-262
B737-4K5	D-ABAB	AIR-BERLIN (KG A/C LSG)		24769	1839	04/05/90	CFM56-3C1		N11AB [TO BE RTD IN 05/01]
B737-46J	D-ABAH	AIR-BERLIN (EUCONUS)		27826	2694	02/08/95	CFM56-3C1		
B737-46J	D-ABAI	AIR-BERLIN		28038	2794	05/21/96	CFM56-3C1		
B737-46J	D-ABAK	AIR-BERLIN (J. HUNOLD)		28271	2801	06/25/96	CFM56-3C1		
B737-46J	D-ABAL	AIR-BERLIN (J. HUNOLD)		28334	2802	06/28/96	CFM56-3C1		
B737-46J	D-ABAM	AIR-BERLIN (AB DRITTE FLUGZEUG.)		28867	2879	04/28/97	CFM56-3C1		
B737-46B	D-ABCC	AIR-BERLIN (BOUL)		25262	2088	07/17/91	CFM56-3C1		OO-ILJ
B737-31S	D-ADBK	DEUTSCHE BA (DSFL)		29055	2923	08/29/97	CFM56-3C1		
B737-31S	D-ADBL	DEUTSCHE BA (DSFL)		29056	2928	09/06/97	CFM56-3C1		
B737-31S	D-ADBM	DEUTSCHE BA (DSFL)		29057	2942	10/24/97	CFM56-3C1		
B737-31S	D-ADBN	DEUTSCHE BA (DSFL)		29058	2946	11/04/97	CFM56-3C1		
B737-31S	D-ADBO	DEUTSCHE BA (DSFL)		29059	2967	12/18/97	CFM56-3C1		[LST/OPF ISS 06/01/00]
B737-31S	D-ADBP	DEUTSCHE BA (DSFL)		29060	2979	12/30/97	CFM56-3C1		N1786B

A/C TYPE	CURRENT REG. NO.	LAST KNOWN OPERATOR (OWNER)	STATUS	ORIGINAL MSN	LINE NO.	DEL. DATE	ENG. TYPE	FLEET NO.	PREV. REG. [COMMENTS]
B737-31S	D-ADBQ	DEUTSCHE BA (DSFL)		29099	2982	01/15/98	CFM56-3C1		
B737-31S	D-ADBR	DEUTSCHE BA (DSFL)		29100	2984	01/23/98	CFM56-3C1		
B737-31S	D-ADBS	DEUTSCHE BA (DSFL)		29116	3005	03/10/98	CFM56-3C1		
B737-31S	D-ADBT	DEUTSCHE BA (DSFL)		29264	3070	09/17/98	CFM56-3C1		N1795B
B737-31S	D-ADBU	DEUTSCHE BA (DSFL)		29265	3073	09/30/98	CFM56-3C1		N1787B
B737-31S	D-ADBV	DEUTSCHE BA (GECA)		29266	3092	02/01/99	CFM56-3C1		N1786B
B737-31S	D-ADBW	DEUTSCHE BA (GECA)		29267	3093	02/04/99	CFM56-3C1		N60436
B737-36Q	D-ADIA	DEUTSCHE BA (BOUL)		30333	3117	08/09/99	CFM56-3C1		N1786B
B737-36Q	D-ADIB	DEUTSCHE BA (BOUL)		30334	3120	09/03/99	CFM56-3C1		N1786B
B737-36Q	D-ADIC	DEUTSCHE BA (BOUL)		30335	3129	12/04/99	CFM56-3C1		N1786B
B737-4K5	D-AHLJ	HAPAG LLOYD (DEFAG)		24125	1687	03/29/89	CFM56-3C1		["HAPAG-LLOYD NETHERLANDS" TITLES]
B737-4K5	D-AHLO	HAPAG LLOYD (DEFAG)		24128	1715	05/11/89	CFM56-3C1		
B737-4K5	D-AHLT	HAPAG LLOYD (DEFAG)		27830	2670	11/14/94	CFM56-3C1		N934NU ["HAPAG-LLOYD NETHERLANDS" TITLES]
B737-530	D-ABIA	LUFTHANSA (CIT FSC)		24815	1933	12/20/90	CFM56-3B1		N3521N
B737-530	D-ABIB	LUFTHANSA (CIT FSC)		24816	1958	12/18/90	CFM56-3B1		
B737-530	D-ABIC	LUFTHANSA (CIT FSC)		24817	1967	12/20/90	CFM56-3B1		
B737-530	D-ABID	LUFTHANSA		24818	1974	01/09/91	CFM56-3B1		
B737-530	D-ABIE	LUFTHANSA		24819	1979	01/17/91	CFM56-3B1		
B737-530	D-ABIF	LUFTHANSA		24820	1985	01/29/91	CFM56-3B1		
B737-530	D-ABIH	LUFTHANSA		24821	1993	02/12/91	CFM56-3B1		
B737-530	D-ABII	LUFTHANSA		24822	1997	02/25/91	CFM56-3B1		
B737-530	D-ABIK	LUFTHANSA		24823	2000	02/25/91	CFM56-3B1		
B737-530	D-ABIL	LUFTHANSA		24824	2006	03/07/91	CFM56-3B1		
B737-530	D-ABIM	LUFTHANSA		24937	2011	03/14/91	CFM56-3B1		
B737-530	D-ABIN	LUFTHANSA		24938	2023	04/04/91	CFM56-3B1		
B737-530	D-ABIO	LUFTHANSA		24939	2031	04/18/91	CFM56-3B1		
B737-530	D-ABIP	LUFTHANSA		24940	2034	04/30/91	CFM56-3B1		
B737-530	D-ABIR	LUFTHANSA		24941	2042	05/03/91	CFM56-3B1		
B737-530	D-ABIS	LUFTHANSA		24942	2048	05/16/91	CFM56-3B1		
B737-530	D-ABIT	LUFTHANSA		24943	2049	05/23/91	CFM56-3B1		
B737-530	D-ABIU	LUFTHANSA		24944	2051	05/23/91	CFM56-3B1		
B737-530	D-ABIW	LUFTHANSA		24945	2063	06/13/91	CFM56-3B1		
B737-530	D-ABIX	LUFTHANSA		24946	2070	06/27/91	CFM56-3B1		
B737-530	D-ABIY	LUFTHANSA		25243	2086	07/18/91	CFM56-3B1		
B737-530	D-ABIZ	LUFTHANSA		25244	2098	08/08/91	CFM56-3B1		
B737-530	D-ABJA	LUFTHANSA		25270	2116	09/06/91	CFM56-3B1		
B737-530	D-ABJB	LUFTHANSA		25271	2117	09/12/91	CFM56-3B1		
B737-530	D-ABJC	LUFTHANSA		25272	2118	09/19/91	CFM56-3B1		
B737-530	D-ABJD	LUFTHANSA		25309	2122	09/23/91	CFM56-3B1		

A/C TYPE	CURRENT REG. NO.	LAST KNOWN OPERATOR (OWNER)	STATUS	ORIGINAL MSN	LINE NO.	DEL. DATE	ENG. TYPE	FLEET NO.	PREV. REG. [COMMENTS]
B737-530	D-ABJE	LUFTHANSA		25310	2126	09/27/91	CFM56-3B1		
B737-530	D-ABJF	LUFTHANSA		25311	2128	10/04/91	CFM56-3B1		
B737-530	D-ABJH	LUFTHANSA		25357	2141	10/17/91	CFM56-3B1		
B737-530	D-ABJI	LUFTHANSA		25358	2151	10/31/91	CFM56-3B1		
B737-330	D-ABEA	LUFTHANSA		24565	1818	02/20/90	CFM56-3B1		
B737-330	D-ABEB	LUFTHANSA		25148	2077	07/03/91	CFM56-3B1		
B737-330	D-ABEC	LUFTHANSA		25149	2081	07/09/91	CFM56-3B1		
B737-330	D-ABED	LUFTHANSA		25215	2082	07/12/91	CFM56-3B1		
B737-330	D-ABEE	LUFTHANSA		25216	2084	07/18/91	CFM56-3B1		
B737-330	D-ABEF	LUFTHANSA		25217	2094	07/31/91	CFM56-3B1		
B737-330	D-ABEH	LUFTHANSA		25242	2102	08/15/91	CFM56-3B1		
B737-330	D-ABEI	LUFTHANSA		25359	2158	11/07/91	CFM56-3B1		
B737-330	D-ABEK	LUFTHANSA		25414	2164	11/21/91	CFM56-3B1		
B737-330	D-ABEL	LUFTHANSA		25415	2175	12/05/91	CFM56-3B1		
B737-330	D-ABEM	LUFTHANSA		25416	2182	12/12/91	CFM56-3B1		
B737-330	D-ABEN	LUFTHANSA		26428	2196	01/16/92	CFM56-3B1		
B737-330	D-ABEO	LUFTHANSA		26429	2207	02/07/92	CFM56-3B1		
B737-330	D-ABEP	LUFTHANSA		26430	2216	02/13/92	CFM56-3B1		
B737-330	D-ABER	LUFTHANSA		26431	2242	03/20/92	CFM56-3B1		
B737-330	D-ABES	LUFTHANSA		26432	2247	03/25/92	CFM56-3B1		
B737-330	D-ABET	LUFTHANSA		27903	2682	01/12/95	CFM56-3B1		
B737-330	D-ABEU	LUFTHANSA		27904	2691	02/02/95	CFM56-3B1		
B737-330	D-ABEW	LUFTHANSA		27905	2705	03/23/95	CFM56-3B1		
B737-330(QC)	D-ABWC	LUFTHANSA		23835	1465	11/05/87	CFM56-3B2		[CVTD -330; ST AUTOMATIC, FL]
B737-330(QC)	D-ABWD	LUFTHANSA		23836	1508	02/18/88	CFM56-3B2		[CVTD -330; ST AUTOMATIC, FL]
B737-330(QC)	D-ABWE	LUFTHANSA		23837	1514	03/07/88	CFM56-3B2		[CVTD -330; ST AUTOMATIC, FL]
B737-330(QC)	D-ABWF	LUFTHANSA		24283	1677	02/23/89	CFM56-3B2		[CVTD -330; ST AUTOMATIC, FL]
B737-330	D-ABWH	LUFTHANSA		24284	1685	03/09/89	CFM56-3B2		
B737-330(QC)	D-ABXC	LUFTHANSA		23524	1272	09/18/86	CFM56-3B1		[CVTD -330; ST AUTOMATIC, FL]
B737-330	D-ABXD	LUFTHANSA		23525	1278	10/02/86	CFM56-3B1		TF-ABL
B737-330	D-ABXE	LUFTHANSA		23526	1282	10/09/86	CFM56-3B1		
B737-330	D-ABXF	LUFTHANSA		23527	1285	10/16/86	CFM56-3B1		
B737-330	D-ABXH	LUFTHANSA		23528	1290	11/06/86	CFM56-3B1		
B737-330	D-ABXI	LUFTHANSA		23529	1293	11/13/86	CFM56-3B1		
B737-330	D-ABXK	LUFTHANSA		23530	1297	11/20/86	CFM56-3B1		
B737-330	D-ABXL	LUFTHANSA		23531	1307	12/05/86	CFM56-3B1		
B737-330	D-ABXM	LUFTHANSA		23871	1433	08/27/87	CFM56-3B1		
B737-330	D-ABXN	LUFTHANSA		23872	1447	10/01/87	CFM56-3B1		
B737-330	D-ABXO	LUFTHANSA		23873	1489	01/07/88	CFM56-3B1		
B737-330	D-ABXP	LUFTHANSA		23874	1495	01/21/88	CFM56-3B1		
B737-330	D-ABXR	LUFTHANSA (GOAL)		23875	1500	02/04/88	CFM56-3B1		

A/C TYPE	CURRENT REG. NO.	LAST KNOWN OPERATOR (OWNER)	STATUS	ORIGINAL MSN	LINE NO.	DEL. DATE	ENG. TYPE	FLEET NO.	PREV. REG. [COMMENTS]
B737-330	D-ABXS	LUFTHANSA		24280	1656	01/12/89	CFM56-3B1		
B737-330	D-ABXT	LUFTHANSA		24281	1664	01/26/89	CFM56-3B1		
B737-330	D-ABXU	LUFTHANSA		24282	1671	02/09/89	CFM56-3B1		
B737-330	D-ABXW	LUFTHANSA		24561	1785	10/24/89	CFM56-3B1		
B737-330	D-ABXX	LUFTHANSA		24562	1787	10/24/89	CFM56-3B1		
B737-330	D-ABXY	LUFTHANSA		24563	1801	01/11/90	CFM56-3B1		
B737-330	D-ABXZ	LUFTHANSA		24564	1807	01/25/90	CFM56-3B1		

EC-SPAIN

A/C TYPE	CURRENT REG. NO.	LAST KNOWN OPERATOR (OWNER)	STATUS	ORIGINAL MSN	LINE NO.	DEL. DATE	ENG. TYPE	FLEET NO.	PREV. REG. [COMMENTS]
B737-3Y0	EC-GEQ	AIR EUROPA (CITG)		23750	1431	08/25/87	CFM56-3B1		PT-TED, EC-135
B737-375	EC-GEU	AIR EUROPA (INTEC)		23808	1434	09/02/87	CFM56-3B1		PT-TEE, EC-136
B737-3M8	EC-GGO	AIR EUROPA (ITOH)		24376	1717	05/12/89	CFM56-3B2		OO-LTD, N681MA, EC-238
B737-3M8	EC-GHD	AIR EUROPA (AV CAP)		25071	2039	05/29/91	CFM56-3B2		HB-IIC, OO-LTN, N682MA, EC-262 [LST BER 05/21/00]
B737-36Q	EC-GMY	AIR EUROPA (GEONET)		28658	2865	04/04/97	CFM56-3C1		
B737-4Q8	EC-FXP	AIR EUROPA (TRIT)		24706	1996	02/15/91	CFM56-3C1		9M-MJD, EC-644
B737-4Q8	EC-FXQ	AIR EUROPA (ILFC)		24707	2057	06/05/91	CFM56-3C1		9M-MJE, EC-645
B737-4Y0	EC-FZZ	AIR EUROPA (AL-RAHJI)		24686	1861	05/18/90	CFM56-3C1		9M-MJH, EC-772
B737-4Y0	EC-GAZ	AIR EUROPA (GECA)		24906	2009	03/12/91	CFM56-3C1		9M-MJO, EC-850 [LST/OPF IBE]
B737-4Y0	EC-GBN	AIR EUROPA (GECA)		24912	2064	06/14/91	CFM56-3C1		9M-MJQ, EC-851 [LST/OPF IBE]
B737-46Q	EC-GPI	AIR EUROPA (BOUL)		28661	2910	07/28/97	CFM56-3C1		[LST/OPF IBE]
B737-4Q8	EC-GUO	AIR EUROPA (ILFC)		26285	2416	01/14/93	CFM56-3C1		N402KW
B737-4Q8	EC-HNB	AIR EUROPA (TOMB)		26280	2239	03/13/92	CFM56-3C1		G-OBMO
B737-36Q	EC-GNU	AIR EUROPA CANARIAS (BOUL)		28660	2883	05/13/97	CFM56-3C1		
B737-4Y0	EC-GNZ	FUTURA INTL. AIRWAYS (GECA)		25178	2199	01/21/92	CFM56-3C1		N601TR, D-ABAD
B737-46B	EC-GRX	FUTURA INTL. AIRWAYS (CITG)		24123	1663	04/24/89	CFM56-3C1		G-BOPJ, G-OBMN
B737-4S3	EC-GUG	FUTURA INTL. AIRWAYS (KM ASS.)		25116	2061	06/11/91	CFM56-3C1		N4249R, 9M-MLF, OO-LTR, EC-997, EC-GFE, EC-GOA, EI-CNE, EC-GOA
B737-4Y0	EC-GUI	FUTURA INTL. AIRWAYS (GECA)		24690	1885	07/10/90	CFM56-3C1		TC-AFL, EC-603, EC-FBP, PT-TDA, EC-308, SE-DRR, EI-COU, EC-GHK [LST NACIONAL T/A AS PP-NAC]
B737-4Y0	EC-GVB	FUTURA INTL. AIRWAYS (GECA)		24689	1883	07/03/90	CFM56-3C1		EC-403, PT-TDD, EC-EXY
B737-4Y0	EC-HBZ	FUTURA INTL. AIRWAYS (GECA)		25180	2201	01/21/92	CFM56-3C1		EC-936, EC-FLD, D-ABAJ, EC-348, EI-CNF, EC-GHT, EC-GOB, PT-TDG
B737-4Y0	EC-GAZ	IBERIA (AEA)	L	24906	2009	03/12/91	CFM56-3C1		9M-MJO, EC-850
B737-4Y0	EC-GBN	IBERIA (AEA)	L	24912	2064	06/14/91	CFM56-3C1		9M-MJQ, EC-851
B737-46Q	EC-GPI	IBERIA (AEA)	L	28661	2910	07/28/97	CFM56-3C1		

A/C TYPE	CURRENT REG. NO.	LAST KNOWN OPERATOR (OWNER)	STATUS	ORIGINAL MSN	LINE NO.	DEL. DATE	ENG. TYPE	FLEET NO.	PREV. REG. [COMMENTS]
EI-IRELAND									
B737-548	EI-CDA	AER LINGUS		24878	1939	10/30/90	CFM56-3B1		EI-BXE [LST ROT 06/22/99 AS YR-BGZ]
B737-548	EI-CDB	AER LINGUS		24919	1970	12/19/90	CFM56-3B1		EI-BXF
B737-548	EI-CDC	AER LINGUS		24968	1975	01/10/91	CFM56-3B1		EI-BXG
B737-548	EI-CDD	AER LINGUS		24989	1989	02/04/91	CFM56-3B1		EI-BXH
B737-548	EI-CDE	AER LINGUS		25115	2050	05/21/91	CFM56-3B1		PT-SLM
B737-548	EI-CDF	AER LINGUS		25737	2232	03/27/92	CFM56-3B1		
B737-548	EI-CDG	AER LINGUS		25738	2261	04/27/92	CFM56-3B1		[TO BE LST RYN 05/01]
B737-548	EI-CDH	AER LINGUS		25739	2271	04/14/92	CFM56-3B1		
B737-448	EI-BXB	AER LINGUS		24521	1788	10/27/89	CFM56-3B2		
B737-448	EI-BXC	AER LINGUS		24773	1850	04/26/90	CFM56-3B2		
B737-448	EI-BXD	AER LINGUS		24866	1867	06/01/90	CFM56-3B2		
B737-448	EI-BXI	AER LINGUS		25052	2036	04/29/91	CFM56-3B2		[LST RYN 11/02/00-05/01/01 FOR APPLE VACATIONS]
B737-448	EI-BXK	AER LINGUS		25736	2269	04/23/92	CFM56-3B2		[LST RYN 12/12-05/01/01]
B737-43Q	EI-TVA	VIRGIN EXPRESS IRELAND (GECA)		28489	2827	11/22/96	CFM56-3C1		B-18671 [LST VOZ 05/30/00 AS VH-VGA]
B737-43Q	EI-TVB	VIRGIN EXPRESS IRELAND (BOUL)		28493	2838	12/19/96	CFM56-3C1		B-18676 [LST VOZ 02/16/01 AS VH-VGE]
ES-ESTONIA									
B737-5Q8	ES-ABC	ESTONIAN AIR (ILFC)		26324	2735	06/28/95	CFM56-3C1		
B737-5Q8	ES-ABD	ESTONIAN AIR (ILFC)		26323	2770	02/09/96	CFM56-3C1		
B737-5L9	ES-ABE	ESTONIAN AIR (ILFC)		28083	2784	04/08/96	CFM56-3C1		[LST DAN AS OY-APA]
EZ-TURKMENISTAN									
B737-341	EZ-A001	TURKMENISTAN AIRLINES		26855	2305	11/12/92	CFM56-3B2		EK-A001
B737-332	EZ-A002	TURKMENISTAN AIRLINES		25994	2439	03/20/93	CFM56-3C1		N301DE
B737-332	EZ-A003	TURKMENISTAN AIRLINES		25995	2455	04/07/93	CFM56-3C1		N302DE
F-FRANCE									
B737-36E	F-GNFC	AERIS (BBAM)		26315	2706	03/27/95	CFM56-3C1		EC-796, EC-GAP
B737-36E	F-GNFD	AERIS (ILFC)		26317	2719	05/10/95	CFM56-3C1		EC-797, EC-GBU
B737-382	F-GNFH	AERIS (TRIT)		25162	2241	03/13/92	CFM56-3B2		CS-TIL, OY-SEF
B737-3Y0	F-GNFT	AERIS (BBAM)		23921	1513	02/26/88	CFM56-3B2		EI-BTT, F-GLTT, 5B-CIO, PH-OZB
B737-3Y0	F-GNFU	AERIS (BBAM)		24256	1629	11/04/88	CFM56-3B1		G-MONM, EC-542, EC-FVJ, EC-204, EC-GFU
B737-53A	F-ODZJ	AIR AUSTRAL		24877	1943	11/06/90	CFM56-3C1		F-GHXN
B737-33A	F-ODZY	AIR AUSTRAL		27452	2679	12/13/94	CFM56-3C1		
B737-39M(QC)	F-ODZZ	AIR AUSTRAL (SNC AUSTRAL INVEST.)		28898	2906	07/31/97	CFM56-3C1		N1786B [CVTD -39M]

A/C TYPE	CURRENT REG. NO.	LAST KNOWN OPERATOR (OWNER)	STATUS	ORIGINAL MSN	LINE NO.	DEL. DATE	ENG. TYPE	FLEET NO.	PREV. REG. [COMMENTS]
B737-33A	F-ODGX	AIRCALIN		24094	1729	06/12/89	CFM56-3B2		
B737-53A	F-GHXM	AIR FRANCE (LAURE BAIL)		24788	1921	09/26/90	CFM56-3C1		
B737-528	F-GJNA	AIR FRANCE (GECA)		25206	2099	08/30/91	CFM56-3C1		
B737-528	F-GJNB	AIR FRANCE (GECA)		25227	2108	08/28/91	CFM56-3C1		
B737-528	F-GJNC	AIR FRANCE (SANDHILL)		25228	2170	11/26/91	CFM56-3C1		
B737-528	F-GJND	AIR FRANCE (PIEDMONT)		25229	2180	12/12/91	CFM56-3C1		
B737-528	F-GJNE	AIR FRANCE (GECA)		25230	2191	01/09/92	CFM56-3C1		
B737-528	F-GJNF	AIR FRANCE (GECA)		25231	2208	01/31/92	CFM56-3C1		
B737-528	F-GJNG	AIR FRANCE (GOLF 737 BAIL 1)		25232	2231	03/06/92	CFM56-3C1		
B737-528	F-GJNH	AIR FRANCE (GOLF 737 BAIL 1)		25233	2251	03/30/92	CFM56-3C1		
B737-528	F-GJNI	AIR FRANCE (GECA)		25234	2411	01/07/93	CFM56-3C1		
B737-528	F-GJNJ	AIR FRANCE (GECA)		25235	2428	02/11/93	CFM56-3C1		
B737-528	F-GJNK	AIR FRANCE (ST ORCHID)		25236	2443	03/12/93	CFM56-3C1		
B737-5H6	F-GJNL	AIR FRANCE (GECA)		26448	2484	07/11/93	CFM56-3C1		9M-MFC
B737-528	F-GJNM	AIR FRANCE (SCL BRONZE)		25237	2464	04/27/93	CFM56-3C1		
B737-528	F-GJNN	AIR FRANCE (FC UNCLE)		27304	2572	02/04/94	CFM56-3C1		
B737-528	F-GJNO	AIR FRANCE (FC VOICE)		27305	2574	02/10/94	CFM56-3C1		
B737-5H6	F-GJNP	AIR FRANCE (GECA)		27356	2654	10/03/94	CFM56-3C1		9M-MFI
B737-5H6	F-GJNQ	AIR FRANCE (GECA)		26445	2327	07/13/92	CFM56-3C1		9M-MFA
B737-5H6	F-GJNR	AIR FRANCE (GECA)		26446	2358	09/14/92	CFM56-3C1		9M-MFB
B737-53S	F-GJNS	AIR FRANCE (PEMB)		29073	3083	11/30/98	CFM56-3C1		N1786B
B737-53S	F-GJNT	AIR FRANCE (SUBSONIC)		29074	3086	12/07/98	CFM56-3C1		N1786B
B737-53S	F-GJNU	AIR FRANCE (NBB AVIGNON)		29075	3101	03/08/99	CFM56-3C1		N1786B
B737-548	F-GJNV	AIR FRANCE (TRIT)		26287	2427	02/09/93	CFM56-3B1		EI-CDS
B737-5H6	F-GJNX	AIR FRANCE (GECA)		26454	2511	08/13/93	CFM56-3C1		9M-MFE
B737-5H6	F-GJNY	AIR FRANCE (GECA)		26456	2527	09/29/93	CFM56-3C1		VT-JAY, 9M-MFF
B737-548	F-GJUA	AIR FRANCE (MSA I)		25165	2463	04/23/93	CFM56-3B1		PT-MNC, EI-CDT, SE-DUT, LN-TUX
B737-5H6	F-	AIR FRANCE (GECA)		26450	2503	06/28/93	CFM56-3C1		9M-MFD
B737-33A	F-GFUA	AIR FRANCE (AWAS)		23635	1436	02/09/88	CFM56-3B1		G-OUTA
B737-33A	F-GFUD	AIR FRANCE (AWAS)		24027	1597	09/14/88	CFM56-3B1		
B737-33A	F-GFUJ	AIR FRANCE (AWAS)		25118	2065	06/14/91	CFM56-3B1		
B737-33A	F-GHVM	AIR FRANCE (AWAS)		24026	1595	08/23/88	CFM56-3B1		F-GFUC, G-MONT
B737-33A	F-GHVN	AIR FRANCE (AWAS)		25138	2153	10/31/91	CFM56-3B1		F-OGRT
B737-33A	F-GHVO	AIR FRANCE (NORD)		24025	1556	06/01/88	CFM56-3B1		G-MONU
B737-36N	F-GRFA	AIR FRANCE (GECA)		28672	2976	01/18/98	CFM56-3C1		N1786B
B737-36N	F-GRFB	AIR FRANCE (GECA)		28673	2995	02/17/98	CFM56-3C1		
B737-36N	F-GRFC	AIR FRANCE (GECA)		28569	2996	02/19/98	CFM56-3C1		
B737-43Q	F-GLTG	CITY BIRD FRANCE (CTB)	L	28491	2832	11/22/96	CFM56-3C1		B-18673, TC-IAG, OO-CTG

A/C TYPE	CURRENT REG. NO.	LAST KNOWN OPERATOR (OWNER)	STATUS	ORIGINAL MSN	LINE NO.	DEL. DATE	ENG. TYPE	FLEET NO.	PREV. REG. [COMMENTS]
B737-3M8	F-GFUI	CORSAIR (GECA)		24023	1675	03/13/89	CFM56-3B2		HB-IIA, PH-TSR
B737-4B3	F-GFUG	CORSAIR (NOUVELLES)		24750	1916	09/21/90	CFM56-3C1		
B737-4B3	F-GFUH	CORSAIR (NOUVELLES)		24751	2107	08/28/91	CFM56-3C1		
B737-53C	F-GHOL	EURALAIR INTL. (BNP LEASE)		24825	1894	07/27/90	CFM56-3C1		[LST LOT]
B737-53C	F-GINL	EURALAIR INTL. (BNP LEASE)		24827	2243	03/18/92	CFM56-3C1		[LST LOT]
B737-430	F-GRNZ	EURALAIR INTL. (FLIT)		27003	2328	07/23/92	CFM56-3C1		EI-COK, D-ABKD, 9H-ADO
B737-3B3 (QC)	F-GFUE	L'AEROPOSTALE (SFA-STE FIN.)		24387	1693	04/01/89	CFM56-3B1		[OPF AFR]
B737-3B3 (QC)	F-GFUF	L'AEROPOSTALE (SFA-STE FIN.)		24388	1725	06/02/89	CFM56-3B1		[OP IN AFR C/S]
B737-33A (QC)	F-GIXB	L'AEROPOSTALE (CL JET LTD)		24789	1953	12/14/90	CFM56-3C1		F-GFUI, F-OGSD ["AIRPORT EUROPE"]
B737-38B (QC)	F-GIXC	L'AEROPOSTALE (CHAMPS ELYSEES)		25124	2047	05/20/91	CFM56-3C1		N4320B, F-GIXC, F-OGSS
B737-33A (QC)	F-GIXD	L'AEROPOSTALE (CIT FSC)		25744	2198	01/23/92	CFM56-3C1		N3213T
B737-3B3 (QC)	F-GIXE	L'AEROPOSTALE (CIT FSC)		26850	2235	03/09/92	CFM56-3C1		N854WT ["EUROPE AIR POST"]
B737-3B3 (QC)	F-GIXF	L'AEROPOSTALE (CIT FSC)		26851	2267	04/22/92	CFM56-3C1		N4361V ["EUROPE AIR POST"]
B737-382(QC)	F-GIXG	L'AEROPOSTALE (SPC A/C)		24364	1657	01/12/89	CFM56-3B1		CS-TIA, F-OGSX
B737-3S3(QC)	F-GIXH	L'AEROPOSTALE (ILFC)		23788	1393	05/29/87	CFM56-3B2		N851LF, G-BOYN, G-NAFH, 5W-FAX, N271LF ["EUROPE AIR POST"]
B737-348(QC)	F-GIXI	L'AEROPOSTALE (NBB BUCKINGHAM)		23809	1458	10/28/87	CFM56-3B1		N1786B, EC-FQP, EI-BUD, F-OGSY
B737-3Y0(QC)	F-GIXJ	L'AEROPOSTALE (ACG ACQUISITION)		23685	1357	03/19/87	CFM56-3B1		G-MONH [OP IN AFR C/S]
B737-33A (QC)	F-GIXK	L'AEROPOSTALE (TRANSCONTINENTAL)		24028	1599	10/14/88	CFM56-3B1		G-MONP [OP IN AFR C/S]
B737-348(QC)	F-GIXL	L'AEROPOSTALE (NBB KENSINGTON)		23810	1474	11/25/87	CFM56-3B1		N1787B, EC-FSC, EI-BUE, F-OHCS ["EUROPE AIR POST"]
B737-3Q8(QC)	F-GIXO	L'AEROPOSTALE (ACG ACQ.)		24132	1555	05/24/88	CFM56-3B2		EC-EIR, EC-593, EC-FET, N241LF
B737-3M8(QC)	F-GIXP	L'AEROPOSTALE (GUSTAV)		24021	1630	11/07/88	CFM56-3B2		OO-LTB, N40495, 9V-SQZ
B737-3H6 (F)	F-GIXR	L'AEROPOSTALE (AVIACARGO)		27125	2415	01/15/93	CFM56-3C1		9M-MZA
B737-3H6 (F)	F-GIXS	L'AEROPOSTALE (AVIACARGO)		27347	2615	05/27/94	CFM56-3C1		9M-MZB

G-UNITED KINGDOM

A/C TYPE	CURRENT REG. NO.	LAST KNOWN OPERATOR (OWNER)	STATUS	ORIGINAL MSN	LINE NO.	DEL. DATE	ENG. TYPE	FLEET NO.	PREV. REG. [COMMENTS]
B737-59D	G-GFFA	BRITISH AIRWAYS (BBAM)		25038	1969	12/21/90	CFM56-3B1		SE-DND, G-BVZF
B737-505	G-GFFB	BRITISH AIRWAYS (INGO)		25789	2229	02/27/92	CFM56-3C1		LN-BRT
B737-505	G-GFFC	BRITISH AIRWAYS (BBAM)		24272	1923	09/28/90	CFM56-3C1		LN-BRG
B737-59D	G-GFFD	BRITISH AIRWAYS (CHARLESTON PART.)		26419	2186	12/19/91	CFM56-3C1		SE-DNI, G-OBMY, OY-SEG, LY-BFV
B737-528	G-GFFE	BRITISH AIRWAYS (ITOH)		27424	2720	08/18/95	CFM56-3C1		LX-LGR
B737-53A	G-GFFF	BRITISH AIRWAYS (ITOH)		24754	1868	06/07/90	CFM56-3C1		SE-DNC, G-OBMZ
B737-505	G-GFFG	BRITISH AIRWAYS (BBAM)		24650	1792	03/07/90	CFM56-3C1		N5573K, LN-BRC
B737-5H6	G-GFFH	BRITISH AIRWAYS (GECA)		27354	2637	08/01/94	CFM56-3C1		9M-MFG, VT-JAW
B737-528	G-GFFI	BRITISH AIRWAYS (ITOH)		27425	2730	09/01/95	CFM56-3C1		LX-LGS
B737-5H6	G-GFFJ	BRITISH AIRWAYS (GECA)		27355	2646	09/09/94	CFM56-3C1		9M-MFH, VT-JAZ
B737-3Y0	G-LGTE	BRITISH AIRWAYS (GECA)		24908	2015	03/19/91	CFM56-3C1		TC-SUP

A/C TYPE	CURRENT REG. NO.	LAST KNOWN OPERATOR (OWNER)	STATUS	ORIGINAL MSN	LINE NO.	DEL. DATE	ENG. TYPE	FLEET NO.	PREV. REG. [COMMENTS]
B737-382	G-LGTF	BRITISH AIRWAYS (ORIX)		24450	1873	06/13/90	CFM56-3B2		CS-TIE, TC-IAC, N115GB [TO BE I/S 03/21/01]
B737-3Q8	G-LGTG	BRITISH AIRWAYS (AARL)		24470	1765	08/28/89	CFM56-3B1		PK-GWD, N470KB, SX-BFT, N696BJ [FERRIED TO LGW 04/05/01]
B737-3Y0	G-LGTH	BRITISH AIRWAYS (BBAM)		23924	1542	04/26/88	CFM56-3B2		G-BNGL, XA-SEM, G-BNGL, OO-LTV
B737-3Y0	G-LGTI	BRITISH AIRWAYS (BBAM)		23925	1544	05/03/88	CFM56-3B2		G-BNGM, XA-SEO, G-BNGM, OO-LTY
B737-37Q	G-OAMS	BRITISH AIRWAYS (NOVEL)		28548	2961	12/10/97	CFM56-3B2		[OPB REGIONAL]
B737-36Q	G-ODUS	BRITISH AIRWAYS (BOUL)		28659	2880	05/08/97	CFM56-3B2		D-ADBX [OPB REGIONAL]
B737-36Q	G-OFRA	BRITISH AIRWAYS (BOUL)		29327	3023	05/05/98	CFM56-3B2		[OPB REGIONAL]
B737-36Q	G-OHAJ	BRITISH AIRWAYS (BOUL)		29141	3035	06/02/98	CFM56-3B2		[OPB REGIONAL]
B737-36Q	G-OMUC	BRITISH AIRWAYS (BOUL)		29405	3047	06/30/98	CFM56-3B2		[OPB REGIONAL]
B737-36N	G-XBHX	BRITISH AIRWAYS (GECA)		28572	3031	05/21/98	CFM56-3B2		
B737-36N	G-XMAN	BRITISH AIRWAYS (GECA)		28573	3041	06/18/98	CFM56-3B2		[OPB EURO LGW]
B737-4Q8	G-BSNV	BRITISH AIRWAYS (ILFC)		25168	2210	02/05/92	CFM56-3C1		[OPB EURO LGW]
B737-4Q8	G-BSNW	BRITISH AIRWAYS (ILFC)		25169	2237	03/12/92	CFM56-3C1		[OPB EURO LGW]
B737-4Q8	G-BUHJ	BRITISH AIRWAYS (ILFC)		25164	2447	03/19/93	CFM56-3C1		[OPB EURO LGW]
B737-4Q8	G-BUHK	BRITISH AIRWAYS (ILFC)		26289	2486	06/14/93	CFM56-3C1		[OPB EURO LGW]
B737-4S3	G-BVNM	BRITISH AIRWAYS (LANIE)		24163	1700	04/14/89	CFM56-3C1		G-BPKA [OPB EURO LGW]
B737-4S3	G-BVNN	BRITISH AIRWAYS		24164	1702	04/14/89	CFM56-3C1		G-BPKB [OPB EURO LGW]
B737-4S3	G-BVNO	BRITISH AIRWAYS (LANIE)		24167	1736	06/30/89	CFM56-3C1		G-BPKE [OPB EURO LGW]
B737-436	G-DOCA	BRITISH AIRWAYS		25267	2131	10/21/91	CFM56-3C1		[OPB EURO LGW]
B737-436	G-DOCB	BRITISH AIRWAYS		25304	2144	10/16/91	CFM56-3C1		[OPB EURO LGW]
B737-436	G-DOCC	BRITISH AIRWAYS		25305	2147	10/25/91	CFM56-3C1		[OPB EURO LGW]
B737-436	G-DOCD	BRITISH AIRWAYS		25349	2156	11/06/91	CFM56-3C1		
B737-436	G-DOCE	BRITISH AIRWAYS		25350	2167	11/20/91	CFM56-3C1		
B737-436	G-DOCF	BRITISH AIRWAYS		25407	2178	12/10/91	CFM56-3C1		[OPB EURO LGW]
B737-436	G-DOCG	BRITISH AIRWAYS		25408	2183	12/19/91	CFM56-3C1		
B737-436	G-DOCH	BRITISH AIRWAYS		25428	2185	12/19/91	CFM56-3C1		[OPB EURO LGW]
B737-436	G-DOCI	BRITISH AIRWAYS		25839	2188	01/08/92	CFM56-3C1		
B737-436	G-DOCJ	BRITISH AIRWAYS		25840	2197	01/16/92	CFM56-3C1		
B737-436	G-DOCK	BRITISH AIRWAYS		25841	2222	02/25/92	CFM56-3C1		
B737-436	G-DOCL	BRITISH AIRWAYS		25842	2228	03/02/92	CFM56-3C1		[OPB EURO LGW]
B737-436	G-DOCM	BRITISH AIRWAYS		25843	2244	03/19/92	CFM56-3C1		[OPB EURO LGW]
B737-436	G-DOCN	BRITISH AIRWAYS		25848	2379	10/21/92	CFM56-3C1		[OPB EURO LGW]
B737-436	G-DOCO	BRITISH AIRWAYS		25849	2381	10/26/92	CFM56-3C1		[OPB EURO LGW]
B737-436	G-DOCP	BRITISH AIRWAYS		25850	2386	11/02/92	CFM56-3C1		[OPB EURO LGW]
B737-436	G-DOCR	BRITISH AIRWAYS		25851	2387	11/06/92	CFM56-3C1		[OPB EURO LGW]
B737-436	G-DOCS	BRITISH AIRWAYS		25852	2390	12/01/92	CFM56-3C1		[OPB EURO LGW]
B737-436	G-DOCT	BRITISH AIRWAYS		25853	2409	12/22/92	CFM56-3C1		
B737-436	G-DOCU	BRITISH AIRWAYS		25854	2417	01/18/93	CFM56-3C1		
B737-436	G-DOCV	BRITISH AIRWAYS		25855	2420	01/25/93	CFM56-3C1		
B737-436	G-DOCW	BRITISH AIRWAYS		25856	2422	02/02/93	CFM56-3C1		

A/C TYPE	CURRENT REG. NO.	LAST KNOWN OPERATOR (OWNER)	STATUS	ORIGINAL MSN	LINE NO.	DEL. DATE	ENG. TYPE	FLEET NO.	PREV. REG. [COMMENTS]
B737-436	G-DOCX	BRITISH AIRWAYS		25857	2451	03/29/93	CFM56-3C1		
B737-436	G-DOCY	BRITISH AIRWAYS		25844	2514	09/02/93	CFM56-3C1		G-BVBY, OO-LTQ
B737-436	G-DOCZ	BRITISH AIRWAYS		25858	2522	10/01/93	CFM56-3C1		G-BVBZ, EC-657, EC-FXJ [OPB EURO LGW]
B737-436	G-GBTA	BRITISH AIRWAYS		25859	2532	11/01/93	CFM56-3C1		G-BVHA [OPB EURO LGW]
B737-436	G-GBTB	BRITISH AIRWAYS		25860	2545	12/02/93	CFM56-3C1		OO-LTS [OPB EURO LGW]
B737-59D	G-BVKA	BMI-BRITISH MIDLAND (BBAM)		24694	1834	04/10/90	CFM56-3B1		SE-DNA
B737-59D	G-BVKB	BMI-BRITISH MIDLAND		27268	2592	03/24/94	CFM56-3B1		SE-DNM
B737-59D	G-BVKC	BMI-BRITISH MIDLAND (BBAM)		24695	1872	06/14/90	CFM56-3B1		SE-DNB
B737-59D	G-BVKD	BMI-BRITISH MIDLAND		26421	2279	05/11/92	CFM56-3B1		SE-DNK
B737-59D	G-BVZE	BMI-BRITISH MIDLAND		26422	2412	01/08/93	CFM56-3B1		SE-DNL
B737-5Q8	G-BVZG	BMI-BRITISH MIDLAND (BBAM)		25160	2114	09/11/91	CFM56-3B1		SE-DNF
B737-5Q8	G-BVZH	BMI-BRITISH MIDLAND (BBAM)		25166	2129	09/30/91	CFM56-3B1		SE-DNG
B737-5Q8	G-BVZI	BMI-BRITISH MIDLAND (BBAM)		25167	2173	12/02/91	CFM56-3B1		SE-DNH
B737-3Q8	G-BYZJ	BMI-BRITISH MIDLAND (GECA)		24962	2139	10/31/91	CFM56-3C1		PP-VOX, G-COLE
B737-36N	G-ECAS	BMI-BRITISH MIDLAND (GECA)		28554	2835	12/16/96	CFM56-3B2		
B737-3Q8	G-OBMP	BMI-BRITISH MIDLAND (TOMB)		24963	2193	01/10/92	CFM56-3B1		
B737-37Q	G-ODSK	BMI-BRITISH MIDLAND (GECA)		28537	2904	07/22/97	CFM56-3C1		N1786B
B737-36N	G-OJTW	BMI-BRITISH MIDLAND (GECA)		28558	2876	04/26/97	CFM56-3B2		
B737-36N	G-SMDB	BMI-BRITISH MIDLAND (GECA)		28557	2862	03/15/97	CFM56-3B2		
B737-4Y0	G-OBMM	BMI-BRITISH MIDLAND (GECA)		25177	2176	12/06/91	CFM56-3C1		
B737-46N	G-SFBH	BMI-BRITISH MIDLAND (FNBC)		28723	2886	05/28/97	CFM56-3C1		
B737-3Y0	G-OBWX	BRITISH WORLD AIRLINES (BBAM)		24255	1625	10/24/88	CFM56-3B2		OO-IID, XA-RJP, G-MONL, EI-CFQ, HB-IID, SE-DUS
B737-3S3	G-OBWY	BRITISH WORLD AIRWAYS (KG A/C)		24059	1517	03/07/88	CFM56-3B2		EC-771, G-BNPB, N309AC, EC-FGG, RP-C4006, G-DEBZ, N202KG
B737-3Q8	G-OBWZ	BRITISH WORLD AIRLINES (WTCI)		24699	1886	07/11/90	CFM56-3B1		PK-GWG, N699PU
B737-3L9	G-BZZA	BUZZ (UKA)	L	26441	2250	03/30/92	CFM56-3B2		D-ADBA, OY-MAL
B737-3L9	G-BZZB	BUZZ (UKA)	L	25125	2059	06/07/91	CFM56-3B2		PP-SOR, D-ADBG, OY-MMW
B737-330(QC)	TF-ELP	CHANNEL EXPRESS (ICB)	L	23522	1246	08/16/86	CFM56-3B1		D-ABXA [CVTD -330]
B737-3M8	G-EZYB	EASYJET AIRLINE (BBAM)		24020	1614	10/03/88	CFM56-3B2		OO-LTA, I-TEAA, N797BB
B737-3Y0	G-EZYC	EASYJET AIRLINE		24462	1691	04/28/89	CFM56-3B2		N5573K, EC-244, EC-ENS, EI-BZQ, G-TEAA, EC-897, EC-FJR, G-BWJA
B737-3M8	G-EZYD	EASYJET AIRLINE (BBAM)		24022	1662	01/19/89	CFM56-3B2		OO-LTC, I-TEAE, N798BB
B737-375	G-EZYF	EASYJET AIRLINE (BBAM)		23708	1395	06/12/87	CFM56-3B1		PT-TEC, 4L-AAA, D-AGEX
B737-33V	G-EZYG	EASYJET AIRLINE		29331	3062	08/19/98	CFM56-3C1		N1786B
B737-33V	G-EZYH	EASYJET AIRLINE		29332	3072	09/18/98	CFM56-3C1		N1787B
B737-33V	G-EZYI	EASYJET AIRLINE		29333	3084	11/23/98	CFM56-3C1		

A/C TYPE	CURRENT REG. NO.	LAST KNOWN OPERATOR (OWNER)	STATUS	ORIGINAL MSN	LINE NO.	DEL. DATE	ENG. TYPE	FLEET NO.	PREV. REG. [COMMENTS]
B737-33V	G-EZYJ	EASYJET AIRLINE		29334	3089	12/18/98	CFM56-3C1		N1786B
B737-33V	G-EZYK	EASYJET AIRLINE		29335	3094	01/30/99	CFM56-3C1		N1786B
B737-33V	G-EZYL	EASYJET AIRLINE		29336	3102	03/12/99	CFM56-3C1		N1787B
B737-33V	G-EZYM	EASYJET AIRLINE		29337	3113	06/23/99	CFM56-3C1		HB-IIK
B737-33V	G-EZYN	EASYJET AIRLINE		29338	3114	07/08/99	CFM56-3C1		[LST EZS AS HB-III]
B737-33V	G-EZYO	EASYJET AIRLINE		29339	3119	08/23/99	CFM56-3C1		N1786B
B737-33V	G-EZYP	EASYJET AIRLINE		29340	3121	09/17/99	CFM56-3C1		
B737-33V	G-EZYR	EASYJET AIRLINE		29341	3125	10/20/99	CFM56-3C1		N1787B
B737-33V	G-EZYS	EASYJET AIRLINE		29342	3127	11/09/99	CFM56-3C1		N1787B [LST EZS 12/14/99 AS HB-IIJ]
B737-3Q8	G-EZYT	EASYJET AIRLINE		26307	2664	11/01/94	CFM56-3C1		N721LF, HB-IIE
B737-34S	G-OGBB	GB AIRWAYS		29108	2983	01/27/98	CFM56-3C3		
B737-34S	G-OGBC	GB AIRWAYS		29109	3001	02/26/98	CFM56-3C3		N1787B
B737-3L9	G-OGBD	GB AIRWAYS (ORIX)		27833	2688	02/06/95	CFM56-3C1		D-ADBJ, OY-MAR [OP IN BA COLORS]
B737-3L9	G-OGBE	GB AIRWAYS (SANWA)		27834	2692	02/21/95	CFM56-3C1		OY-MAS [OP IN BA COLORS]
B737-4S3	G-BUHL	GB AIRWAYS (ILFC)		25134	2083	08/20/91	CFM56-3C1		9M-MLH [OP IN BA COLORS]
B737-4S3	G-OGBA	GB AIRWAYS (ILFC)		25596	2255	04/06/92	CFM56-3C1		G-OBMK [OP IN BA COLORS]
B737-4S3	G-TREN	GB AIRWAYS (ILFC)		24796	1887	07/12/90	CFM56-3C1		G-BRKG
B737-3Y0	G-IGOA	GO FLY (ORIX)		24678	1853	05/04/90	CFM56-3B1		EI-BZK
B737-3Y0	G-IGOC	GO FLY (ORIX)		24546	1811	01/30/90	CFM56-3B1		EI-BZH
B737-3Y0	G-IGOE	GO FLY (ORIX)		24547	1813	02/07/90	CFM56-3B1		EI-BZI
B737-3Q8	G-IGOF	GO FLY (OASI)		24698	1846	04/18/90	CFM56-3B1		PK-GWF
B737-3Y0	G-IGOG	GO FLY (BBAM)		23927	1580	07/19/88	CFM56-3B1		PT-TEK, F-GLLE
B737-3Y0	G-IGOH	GO FLY (BBAM)		23926	1562	07/01/88	CFM56-3B1		PT-TEJ, F-GLLD
B737-33A	G-IGOI	GO FLY (BBAM)		24092	1669	02/10/89	CFM56-3B1		G-OBMD
B737-36N	G-IGOJ	GO FLY (GECA)		28872	3082	11/11/98	CFM56-3C1		N1795B
B737-36N	G-IGOK	GO FLY (GECA)		28594	3107	04/23/99	CFM56-3C1		N1786B
B737-36N	G-IGOL	GO FLY (GECA)		28596	3112	06/26/99	CFM56-3C1		N1015X
B737-36N	G-IGOM	GO FLY (GECA)		28599	3115	07/13/99	CFM56-3C1		N1796B
B737-36N	G-IGOP	GO FLY (GECA)		28602	3118	08/12/99	CFM56-3C1		N1787B
B737-36N	G-IGOR	GO FLY (GECA)		28606	3124	10/22/99	CFM56-3C1		N1786B
B737-3L9	G-IGOS	GO FLY (HELLER)		27336	2587	03/11/94	CFM56-3C1		OY-MAO, D-ADBH
B737-3L9	G-IGOT	GO FLY (HELLER)		27337	2594	03/25/94	CFM56-3C1		OY-MAP, D-ADBI
B737-3L9	G-BZZA	KLM UK (PEMB)		26441	2250	03/30/92	CFM56-3B2		D-ADBA, OY-MAL [LST/OPF BUZZ]
B737-3L9	G-BZZB	KLM UK (PEMB)		25125	2059	06/07/91	CFM56-3B2		PP-SOR, D-ADBG, OY-MMW [LST/OPF BUZZ]
B737-5L9	G-MSKA	MAERSK AIR-U.K.		24859	1919	09/20/90	CFM56-3B1		OY-MAC [OP IN BA COLORS]
B737-5L9	G-MSKB	MAERSK AIR-U.K.		24928	1961	12/07/90	CFM56-3B1		OY-MAD [OP IN BA COLORS]
B737-5L9	G-MSKC	MAERSK AIR-U.K. (DAN)	L	25066	2038	05/17/91	CFM56-3B1		OY-MAE [OP IN BA COLORS]

A/C TYPE	CURRENT REG. NO.	LAST KNOWN OPERATOR (OWNER)	STATUS	ORIGINAL MSN	LINE NO.	DEL. DATE	ENG. TYPE	FLEET NO.	PREV. REG. [COMMENTS]
B737-5L9	G-MSKE	MAERSK AIR-U.K. (DAN)	L	28084	2788	04/26/96	CFM56-3C1		OY-APB [OP IN BA COLORS]
B737-33A	G-ZAPM	TITAN AIRWAYS (AWAS)		27285	2608	05/17/94	CFM56-3C1		CS-TKG, N102AN, DQ-FJD

HA-HUNGARY

A/C TYPE	CURRENT REG. NO.	LAST KNOWN OPERATOR (OWNER)	STATUS	ORIGINAL MSN	LINE NO.	DEL. DATE	ENG. TYPE	FLEET NO.	PREV. REG. [COMMENTS]
B737-5K5	HA-LEP	MALEV HUNGARIAN AIRLINES (DEFAG)		24776	1848	05/04/90	CFM56-3C1		D-AHLE
B737-5K5	HA-LER	MALEV HUNGARIAN AIRLINES (DEFAG)		24926	1966	12/15/90	CFM56-3C1		D-AHLD
B737-3Y0	HA-LED	MALEV HUNGARIAN AIRLINES (GECA)		24909	2021	04/01/91	CFM56-3C1		
B737-3Y0	HA-LEF	MALEV HUNGARIAN AIRLINES (BBAM)		24914	2054	05/24/91	CFM56-3C1		
B737-3Y0	HA-LEG	MALEV HUNGARIAN AIRLINES (GECA)		24916	2066	06/14/91	CFM56-3C1		
B737-3Q8	HA-LEJ	MALEV HUNGARIAN AIRLINES (ILFC)		26303	2635	07/22/94	CFM56-3C1		
B737-3Y0	HA-LES	MALEV HUNGARIAN AIRLINES (GECA)		24676	1829	03/13/90	CFM56-3B2		TC-SUN
B737-3Y0	HA-LET	MALEV HUNGARIAN AIRLINES (GECA)		24910	2030	04/18/91	CFM56-3C1		TC-SUR
B737-4Y0	HA-LEN	MALEV HUNGARIAN AIRLINES (GECA)		26069	2352	11/02/92	CFM56-3C1		N3509J, UR-GAA
B737-4Y0	HA-LEO	MALEV HUNGARIAN AIRLINES (GECA)		26071	2361	11/13/92	CFM56-3C1		N35108, UR-GAB
B737-4Y0	HA-LEU	MALEV HUNGARIAN AIRLINES (GECA)		25190	2256	04/08/92	CFM56-3C1		EC-991, EC-FMJ, OY-MBL, TC-SUT
B737-4Y0	HA-LEV	MALEV HUNGARIAN AIRLINES (DEBI)		24904	1988	02/07/91	CFM56-3C1		TC-JDE
B737-4Q8	HA-LEZ	MALEV HUNGARIAN AIRLINES (TRIT)		26290	2482	06/03/93	CFM56-3C1		TC-JEE, TC-APB
B737-4Y0	HA-LKA	TRAVEL SERVIS HUNGARY (GECA)		24911	2033	04/25/91	CFM56-3C1		PP-SOJ, PT-WBJ, OY-MBK, EI-CIX, SE-DTB, OK-TVS

HB-SWITZERLAND

A/C TYPE	CURRENT REG. NO.	LAST KNOWN OPERATOR (OWNER)	STATUS	ORIGINAL MSN	LINE NO.	DEL. DATE	ENG. TYPE	FLEET NO.	PREV. REG. [COMMENTS]
B737-3M8	HB-IIB	EASYJET SWITZERLAND (GECA)		24024	1689	03/23/89	CFM56-3B2		
B737-33V	HB-III	EASYJET SWITZERLAND (EZY)	L	29338	3114	07/08/99	CFM56-3C1		G-EZYN
B737-33V	HB-IIJ	EASYJET SWITZERLAND (EZY)	L	29342	3127	11/09/99	CFM56-3C1		N1787B, G-EZYS
B737-36M	HB-IIL	EASYJET SWITZERLAND		28333	2810	08/16/96	CFM56-3C1		EI-TVO, OO-VEB

HL-KOREA

A/C TYPE	CURRENT REG. NO.	LAST KNOWN OPERATOR (OWNER)	STATUS	ORIGINAL MSN	LINE NO.	DEL. DATE	ENG. TYPE	FLEET NO.	PREV. REG. [COMMENTS]
B737-3Z8	85101	REPUBLIC OF KOREA AIR FORCE		23152	1073	01/30/85	CFM56-3B1		
B737-58E	HL7232	ASIANA AIRLINES (CITG)		25767	2614	05/25/94	CFM56-3C1		
B737-58E	HL7233	ASIANA AIRLINES (INGO)		25768	2724	05/19/95	CFM56-3C1		
B737-58E	HL7250	ASIANA AIRLINES		25769	2737	07/13/95	CFM56-3C1		
B737-48E	HL7227	ASIANA AIRLINES		25764	2314	07/02/92	CFM56-3C1		
B737-48E	HL7228	ASIANA AIRLINES		25765	2335	07/24/92	CFM56-3C1		
B737-4Q8	HL7235	ASIANA AIRLINES (ILFC)		26308	2665	10/31/94	CFM56-3C1		
B737-4Y0	HL7251	ASIANA AIRLINES (BBAM)		23869	1639	12/05/88	CFM56-3C1		
B737-4Y0	HL7253	ASIANA AIRLINES (GECA)		23977	1655	01/05/89	CFM56-3C1		
B737-4Y0	HL7254	ASIANA AIRLINES (GECA)		23978	1659	01/12/89	CFM56-3C1		
B737-4Y0	HL7257	ASIANA AIRLINES (GECA)		24469	1749	07/25/89	CFM56-3C1		
B737-4Y0	HL7258	ASIANA AIRLINES (GECA)		24493	1751	07/28/89	CFM56-3C1		
B737-4Y0	HL7259	ASIANA AIRLINES (GECA)		24494	1757	08/09/89	CFM56-3C1		

A/C TYPE	CURRENT REG. NO.	LAST KNOWN OPERATOR (OWNER)	STATUS	ORIGINAL MSN	LINE NO.	DEL. DATE	ENG. TYPE	FLEET NO.	PREV. REG. [COMMENTS]
B737-4Y0	HL7260	ASIANA AIRLINES (GECA)		24520	1803	01/16/90	CFM56-3C1		
B737-48E	HL7508	ASIANA AIRLINES (OZ ALPHA)		25772	2791	05/08/96	CFM56-3C1		
B737-48E	HL7509	ASIANA AIRLINES (ILFC)		28198	2806	07/23/96	CFM56-3C1		
B737-48E	HL7510	ASIANA AIRLINES		25771	2816	09/20/96	CFM56-3C1		
B737-48E	HL7511	ASIANA AIRLINES (AV CAP)		27630	2848	01/31/97	CFM56-3C1		
B737-48E	HL7512	ASIANA AIRLINES (ILFC)		27632	2857	02/25/97	CFM56-3C1		N1786B
B737-48E	HL7513	ASIANA AIRLINES (OZ GAMMA)		25776	2860	03/17/97	CFM56-3C1		
B737-48E	HL7517	ASIANA AIRLINES		25774	2909	07/25/97	CFM56-3C1		
B737-48E	HL7518	ASIANA AIRLINES (ILFC)		28053	2954	11/18/97	CFM56-3C1		
B737-4Q8	HL7527	ASIANA AIRLINES (ILFC)		26299	2602	04/19/94	CFM56-3C1		TC-JEK
B737-4Q8	HL7591	ASIANA AIRLINES (ILFC)		26291	2513	08/09/93	CFM56-3C1		TC-JEF
B737-4Q8	HL7592	ASIANA AIRLINES (ILFC)		26320	2563	01/11/94	CFM56-3C1		TC-JEH
B737-43Q	HL7593	ASIANA AIRLINES (BOUL)		28492	2837	12/20/96	CFM56-3C1		B-18675, B-10001

HS-THAILAND

A/C TYPE	CURRENT REG. NO.	LAST KNOWN OPERATOR (OWNER)	STATUS	ORIGINAL MSN	LINE NO.	DEL. DATE	ENG. TYPE	FLEET NO.	PREV. REG. [COMMENTS]
B737-4Z6	55-555	THAILAND GOVERNMENT		27906	2698	02/28/95	CFM56-3C1		HS-RTA
B737-4H6	9M-MME	ANGEL AIRLINES (MAS)	L	26465	2362	09/22/92	CFM56-3C1		
B737-4H6	9M-MML	ANGEL AIRLINES (MAS)	L	27085	2407	12/22/92	CFM56-3C1		
B737-4D7	HS-TDA	THAI AIRWAYS INTL.		24830	1899	08/09/90	CFM56-3C1		
B737-4D7	HS-TDB	THAI AIRWAYS INTL.		24831	1922	09/27/90	CFM56-3C1		
B737-4D7	HS-TDD	THAI AIRWAYS INTL.		26611	2318	07/10/92	CFM56-3C1		
B737-4D7	HS-TDE	THAI AIRWAYS INTL.		26612	2330	07/22/92	CFM56-3C1		
B737-4D7	HS-TDF	THAI AIRWAYS INTL.		26613	2338	06/05/92	CFM56-3C1		
B737-4D7	HS-TDG	THAI AIRWAYS INTL.		26614	2481	05/27/93	CFM56-3C1		
B737-4D7	HS-TDH	THAI AIRWAYS INTL.		28703	2962	12/09/97	CFM56-3C1		
B737-4D7	HS-TDJ	THAI AIRWAYS INTL.		28704	2968	12/16/97	CFM56-3C1		
B737-4D7	HS-TDK	THAI AIRWAYS INTL.		28701	2977	01/06/98	CFM56-3C1		
B737-4D7	HS-TDL	THAI AIRWAYS INTL.		28702	2978	01/15/98	CFM56-3C1		

I-ITALY

A/C TYPE	CURRENT REG. NO.	LAST KNOWN OPERATOR (OWNER)	STATUS	ORIGINAL MSN	LINE NO.	DEL. DATE	ENG. TYPE	FLEET NO.	PREV. REG. [COMMENTS]
B737-3Y0	EI-CLW	AIR ONE (GECA)		25187	2248	03/26/92	CFM56-3C1		XA-SAB
B737-3Y0	EI-CLZ	AIR ONE (GECA)		25179	2205	02/12/92	CFM56-3C1		N3521N, XA-RJR
B737-36E	EI-CRZ	AIR ONE (ILFC)		26322	2769	02/12/96	CFM56-3C1		EC-798, EC-GGE
B737-36E	EI-CSU	AIR ONE (ILFC)		27626	2792	05/14/96	CFM56-3C1		EC-799, EC-GGZ
B737-3M8	F-GKTA	AIR ONE (ALTER BAIL)		24413	1884	07/06/90	CFM56-3B2		
B737-3M8	F-GKTB	AIR ONE (ALTER BAIL)		24414	1895	07/27/90	CFM56-3B2		
B737-430	EI-COI	AIR ONE (GOAL)		27002	2323	07/16/92	CFM56-3C1		D-ABKC
B737-430	EI-COJ	AIR ONE (GOAL)		27005	2359	09/17/92	CFM56-3C1		D-ABKK
B737-42C	EI-CWE	AIR ONE (PEGA)		24232	2060	06/07/91	CFM56-3C1		G-UKLD, PH-BPE, N941PG

A/C TYPE	CURRENT REG. NO.	LAST KNOWN OPERATOR (OWNER)	STATUS	ORIGINAL MSN	LINE NO.	DEL. DATE	ENG. TYPE	FLEET NO.	PREV. REG. [COMMENTS]
B737-42C	EI-CWF	AIR ONE		24814	2270	04/23/92	CFM56-3C1		G-UKLG, PH-BPG
B737-4K5	EI-CUA	BLUE PANORAMA AIRLINES (INGO)		24901	1854	05/04/90	CFM56-3C1		D-AHLR
B737-4Q8	EI-CUD	BLUE PANORAMA AIRLINES (ILFC)		26298	2564	03/01/94	CFM56-3C1		TC-JEI
B737-4K5	EI-CUN	BLUE PANORAMA AIRLINES (DEBI)		27074	2281	05/08/92	CFM56-3C1		D-AHLS [OPF LAA]
B737-4K5	EI-	BLUE PANORAMA AIRLINES		27831	2677	12/08/94	CFM56-3C1		D-AHLU
B737-31S	D-ADBO	MERIDIANA (BAG)	L	29059	2967	12/18/97	CFM56-3C1		[LST/OPF ISS 06/01/00]
B737-4Q8	G-BNNK	NATIONAL JETS ITALIA (ILFC)		24069	1635	11/30/88	CFM56-3C1		[OO FOR 04/01 DEL]
B737-4Q8	G-BNNL	NATIONAL JETS ITALIA (ILFC)		24070	1665	01/26/89	CFM56-3C1		[OO FOR 04/01 DEL]

JA-JAPAN

A/C TYPE	CURRENT REG. NO.	LAST KNOWN OPERATOR (OWNER)	STATUS	ORIGINAL MSN	LINE NO.	DEL. DATE	ENG. TYPE	FLEET NO.	PREV. REG. [COMMENTS]
B737-54K	JA300K	AIR NIPPON		27434	2872	05/19/97	CFM56-3C1		
B737-54K	JA301K	AIR NIPPON		27435	2875	05/20/97	CFM56-3C1		
B737-54K	JA302K	AIR NIPPON		28990	3002	03/09/98	CFM56-3C1		N1787B
B737-54K	JA303K	AIR NIPPON (SKY DOLPHIN)		28991	3017	04/13/98	CFM56-3C1		
B737-54K	JA304K	AIR NIPPON (MNE LEASE)		28992	3030	05/19/98	CFM56-3C1		N1786B
B737-54K	JA305K	AIR NIPPON (STAR DOLPHIN)		28993	3075	10/15/98	CFM56-3C1		N1786B, N1781B
B737-54K	JA306K	AIR NIPPON		29794	3109	05/17/99	CFM56-3C1		N1786B
B737-54K	JA307K	AIR NIPPON		29795	3116	07/21/99	CFM56-3C1		N1786B, N60436 [LAST B737-500 DELIVERED]
B737-5Y0	JA351K	AIR NIPPON (AGEHA)		25189	2240	03/13/92	CFM56-3B1		XA-RKQ, PT-SLV, N189NK
B737-5Y0	JA352K	AIR NIPPON (ANA)	L	26097	2534	10/14/93	CFM56-3B1		PT-SLP, N97NK
B737-5Y0	JA353K	AIR NIPPON (FSBU)		26104	2552	12/15/93	CFM56-3B1		PT-SLS, N104NK
B737-5Y0	JA354K	AIR NIPPON (GECA)		26105	2553	01/14/94	CFM56-3B1		PT-SLT, N105NK
B737-5L9	JA355K	AIR NIPPON (FSBU)		28129	2823	10/17/96	CFM56-3C1		OY-APC, N8129L
B737-54K	JA8195	AIR NIPPON (AIR DOLPHIN)		27433	2815	09/13/96	CFM56-3C1		
B737-54K	JA8196	AIR NIPPON		27966	2824	10/23/96	CFM56-3C1		
B737-54K	JA8404	AIR NIPPON		27381	2708	04/12/95	CFM56-3C1		N35108
B737-54K	JA8419	AIR NIPPON (MITSUI LEASE JIGYO)		27430	2723	07/28/95	CFM56-3C1		
B737-54K	JA8500	AIR NIPPON (SUMIGEN LEASE)		27431	2751	09/19/95	CFM56-3C1		
B737-54K	JA8504	AIR NIPPON		27432	2783	05/17/96	CFM56-3C1		
B737-54K	JA8595	AIR NIPPON		28461	2850	02/19/97	CFM56-3C1		
B737-54K	JA8596	AIR NIPPON (JL HAWK LEASE)		28462	2853	02/24/97	CFM56-3C1		
B737-4Y0	JA391K	AIR NIPPON (AGEHA)		24545	1805	02/02/90	CFM56-3C1		EC-401, EC-ETB, PT-TDE, EC-HBT, N545NK
B737-46M	JA	AIR NIPPON (TOMB)		28550	2847	01/27/97	CFM56-3C1		C-GBIX, OO-VED, N8550F [RT TOMB; OO]
B737-5Y0	JA352K	ALL NIPPON AIRWAYS (GECA)		26097	2534	10/14/93	CFM56-3B1		PT-SLP, N97NK [LST ANK 08/09/00]
B737-446	JA8991	JAL EXPRESS		27916	2718	05/31/95	CFM56-3C1		
B737-446	JA8992	JAL EXPRESS		27917	2729	06/28/95	CFM56-3C1		N1792B
B737-446	JA8993	JAL EXPRESS (JAL)	L	28087	2812	08/27/96	CFM56-3C1		

A/C TYPE	CURRENT REG. NO.	LAST KNOWN OPERATOR (OWNER)	STATUS	ORIGINAL MSN	LINE NO.	DEL. DATE	ENG. TYPE	FLEET NO.	PREV. REG. [COMMENTS]
B737-446	JA8999	JAL EXPRESS (JAL)	L	29864	3111	06/08/99	CFM56-3C1		N1786B
B737-446	JA8993	JAPAN AIRLINES (MARUBENI)		28087	2812	08/27/96	CFM56-3C1		[LST JEX]
B737-446	JA8994	JAPAN AIRLINES (ZONET)		28097	2907	07/22/97	CFM56-3C1		N1786B
B737-446	JA8995	JAPAN AIRLINES (ZONET)		28831	2911	07/29/97	CFM56-3C1		
B737-446	JA8996	JAPAN AIRLINES (ZONET)		28832	2953	11/14/97	CFM56-3C1		N1786B
B737-446	JA8998	JAPAN AIRLINES		28994	3044	06/25/98	CFM56-3C1		
B737-446	JA8999	JAPAN AIRLINES (LIVE LSG)		29864	3111	06/08/99	CFM56-3C1		N1786B [LST JEX]
B737-4Q3	JA8523	JAPAN TRANSOCEAN AIR (N.I. A/C)		26603	2618	06/13/94	CFM56-3C1		
B737-4Q3	JA8524	JAPAN TRANSOCEAN AIR (NIKKO LEASE)		26604	2684	02/01/95	CFM56-3C1		
B737-4Q3	JA8525	JAPAN TRANSOCEAN AIR (MARUBENI)		26605	2752	09/18/95	CFM56-3C1		
B737-4Q3	JA8526	JAPAN TRANSOCEAN AIR (NIKKO LEASE)		26606	2898	06/26/97	CFM56-3C1		
B737-4Q3	JA8597	JAPAN TRANSOCEAN AIR		27660	3043	06/18/98	CFM56-3C1		
B737-4K5	JA8930	JAPAN TRANSOCEAN AIR (TLC BEGONIA)		27102	2394	03/19/93	CFM56-3C1		D-AHLM
B737-4Q3	JA8938	JAPAN TRANSOCEAN AIR (NIKKO LEASE)		29485	3085	11/24/98	CFM56-3C1		
B737-4Q3	JA8939	JAPAN TRANSOCEAN AIR (SA SOUTHERN WIND)		29486	3088	01/21/99	CFM56-3C1		N1786B, N1800B
B737-4Q3	JA8940	JAPAN TRANSOCEAN AIR (SKL RUBELIGHT)		29487	3122	09/20/99	CFM56-3C1		
B737-4K5	JA8953	JAPAN TRANSOCEAN AIR (NIKKO LEASE)		24129	1783	10/18/89	CFM56-3C1		D-AHLP
B737-4K5	JA8954	JAPAN TRANSOCEAN AIR (CENTRAL LEASE)		24130	1827	03/09/90	CFM56-3C1		D-AHLQ
B737-429	JA	JAPAN TRANSOCEAN AIR		25247	2106	08/26/91	CFM56-3C1		OO-SYD, N931NU
B737-429	JA	JAPAN TRANSOCEAN AIR		25248	2120	09/13/91	CFM56-3C1		OO-SYF, N932NU

LN-NORWAY

A/C TYPE	CURRENT REG. NO.	LAST KNOWN OPERATOR (OWNER)	STATUS	ORIGINAL MSN	LINE NO.	DEL. DATE	ENG. TYPE	FLEET NO.	PREV. REG. [COMMENTS]
B737-505	LN-BRD	BRAATHENS (GUSTAV LSG)		24651	1842	04/19/90	CFM56-3C1		
B737-505	LN-BRF	BRAATHENS (CITG)		24652	1917	09/18/90	CFM56-3C1		D-ACBA
B737-505	LN-BRH	BRAATHENS (CITG)		24828	1925	10/08/90	CFM56-3C1		D-ACBB
B737-505	LN-BRJ	BRAATHENS (GRAND CAYMAN LTD)		24273	2018	03/28/91	CFM56-3C1		D-ACBC
B737-505	LN-BRK	BRAATHENS (ORIX)		24274	2035	04/26/91	CFM56-3C1		
B737-505	LN-BRM	BRAATHENS (ENGALY)		24645	2072	06/26/91	CFM56-3C1		
B737-505	LN-BRN	BRAATHENS (NBB NORDLAND)		24646	2138	10/10/91	CFM56-3C1		
B737-505	LN-BRO	BRAATHENS (ENGALY)		24647	2143	10/17/91	CFM56-3C1		
B737-505	LN-BRR	BRAATHENS (ENGALY)		24648	2213	02/07/92	CFM56-3C1		
B737-505	LN-BRS	BRAATHENS (ENGALY)		24649	2225	02/21/92	CFM56-3C1		
B737-505	LN-BRU	BRAATHENS		25790	2245	03/20/92	CFM56-3C1		
B737-505	LN-BRV	BRAATHENS (GECA)		25791	2351	09/01/92	CFM56-3C1		
B737-505	LN-BRW	BRAATHENS (BRA CAYMAN)		25792	2353	09/24/92	CFM56-3C1		[LST CXA AS B-2591]
B737-505	LN-BRX	BRAATHENS (ENGALY)		25797	2434	02/22/93	CFM56-3C1		
B737-505	LN-BRY	BRAATHENS		27155	2449	03/23/93	CFM56-3C1		[LST CXA AS B-2593]

A/C TYPE	CURRENT REG. NO.	LAST KNOWN OPERATOR (OWNER)	STATUS	ORIGINAL MSN	LINE NO.	DEL. DATE	ENG. TYPE	FLEET NO.	PREV. REG. [COMMENTS]
B737-505	LN-BRZ	BRAATHENS (BRA CAYMAN)		27153	2516	09/01/93	CFM56-3C1		[LST CXA AS B-2592]
B737-505	LN-BUA	BRAATHENS (ILFC)		26297	2578	02/21/94	CFM56-3C1		[LST CXA AS B-2529]
B737-505	LN-BUC	BRAATHENS (ILFC)		26304	2649	09/15/94	CFM56-3C1		
B737-505	LN-BUD	BRAATHENS (ENGALY)		25794	2803	07/29/96	CFM56-3C1		
B737-505	LN-BUE	BRAATHENS (ILFC)		27627	2800	06/17/96	CFM56-3C1		
B737-505	LN-BUG	BRAATHENS (ILFC)		27631	2866	03/25/97	CFM56-3C1		
B737-405	LN-BRE	BRAATHENS (BBAM)		24643	1860	05/18/90	CFM56-3C1		
B737-405	LN-BRI	BRAATHENS (K R PARTNERS)		24644	1938	10/24/90	CFM56-3C1		9M-MLL
B737-405	LN-BRP	BRAATHENS (PEGA)		25303	2137	10/09/91	CFM56-3C1		9M-MLK
B737-405	LN-BRQ	BRAATHENS (ENGALY)		25348	2148	10/24/91	CFM56-3C1		
B737-405	LN-BUF	BRAATHENS (CITG)		25795	2867	04/15/97	CFM56-3C1		

LX-LUXEMBOURG

A/C TYPE	CURRENT REG. NO.	LAST KNOWN OPERATOR (OWNER)	STATUS	ORIGINAL MSN	LINE NO.	DEL. DATE	ENG. TYPE	FLEET NO.	PREV. REG. [COMMENTS]
B737-5C9	LX-LGO	LUXAIR		26438	2413	01/08/93	CFM56-3C1		
B737-5C9	LX-LGP	LUXAIR		26439	2444	03/17/93	CFM56-3C1		
B737-59D	LX-LGN	LUXAIR (BBAM)		25065	2028	04/15/91	CFM56-3C1		SE-DNE, G-OBMX
B737-4C9	LX-LGF	LUXAIR (LUX SPRING)		25429	2215	02/21/92	CFM56-3C1		
B737-4C9	LX-LGG	LUXAIR (LUX EAST)		26437	2249	03/27/92	CFM56-3C1		

LY-LITHUANIA

A/C TYPE	CURRENT REG. NO.	LAST KNOWN OPERATOR (OWNER)	STATUS	ORIGINAL MSN	LINE NO.	DEL. DATE	ENG. TYPE	FLEET NO.	PREV. REG. [COMMENTS]
B737-382	LY-BAG	LITHUANIAN AIRLINES (INGO)		24449	1857	04/25/90	CFM56-3B2		CS-TID

N-UNITED STATES OF AMERICA

A/C TYPE	CURRENT REG. NO.	LAST KNOWN OPERATOR (OWNER)	STATUS	ORIGINAL MSN	LINE NO.	DEL. DATE	ENG. TYPE	FLEET NO.	PREV. REG. [COMMENTS]
B737-42C	N60669	BOEING (ICON CASH FLOW PARTNERS)		24231	1871	06/15/90	CFM56-3C1		G-UKLC, PH-BPD [FOR TEST OF "CONNEXION" INF INTERNET AND ENTERTAINMENT SERVICES]
B737-33A	N368CE	CLUB EXCELLENCE INC. (FINO)		27456	2749	09/11/95	CFM56-3C1		9M-LKY, 9M-CHG [OPB PREMIER]
B737-3L9	N	FLIGHT SERVICES GROUP-USA		27924	2760	10/14/95	CFM56-3C1		OY-MAT, HB-IIN
B737-408	N737DX	SPORTS JET LLC (BANKBOSTON)		24804	1851	04/25/90	CFM56-3C1		TF-FIC
B737-490	N703AS	ALASKA AIRLINES		28893	3039	06/11/98	CFM56-3C1		
B737-490	N705AS	ALASKA AIRLINES		29318	3042	06/16/98	CFM56-3C1		
B737-490	N706AS	ALASKA AIRLINES		28894	3050	07/10/98	CFM56-3C1		N1796B
B737-490	N708AS	ALASKA AIRLINES		28895	3098	02/23/99	CFM56-3C1		N1786B
B737-490	N709AS	ALASKA AIRLINES		28896	3099	03/06/99	CFM56-3C1		N1787B
B737-490	N713AS	ALASKA AIRLINES		30161	3110	05/24/99	CFM56-3C1		N1787B
B737-4Q8	N754AS	ALASKA AIRLINES		25095	2266	04/17/92	CFM56-3C1		
B737-4Q8	N755AS	ALASKA AIRLINES (ILFC)		25096	2278	05/05/92	CFM56-3C1		
B737-4Q8	N756AS	ALASKA AIRLINES		25097	2299	06/05/92	CFM56-3C1		
B737-4Q8	N760AS	ALASKA AIRLINES		25098	2320	07/10/92	CFM56-3C1		
B737-4Q8	N762AS	ALASKA AIRLINES		25099	2334	07/27/92	CFM56-3C1		

A/C TYPE	CURRENT REG. NO.	LAST KNOWN OPERATOR (OWNER)	STATUS	ORIGINAL MSN	LINE NO.	DEL. DATE	ENG. TYPE	FLEET NO.	PREV. REG. [COMMENTS]
B737-4Q8	N763AS	ALASKA AIRLINES		25100	2346	08/20/92	CFM56-3C1		
B737-4Q8	N764AS	ALASKA AIRLINES		25101	2348	09/21/92	CFM56-3C1		
B737-4Q8	N765AS	ALASKA AIRLINES		25102	2350	10/28/92	CFM56-3C1		
B737-490	N767AS	ALASKA AIRLINES		27081	2354	09/10/92	CFM56-3C1		
B737-490	N768AS	ALASKA AIRLINES		27082	2356	09/22/92	CFM56-3C1		
B737-4Q8	N769AS	ALASKA AIRLINES		25103	2452	03/31/93	CFM56-3C1		
B737-4Q8	N771AS	ALASKA AIRLINES (ILFC)		25104	2476	05/21/93	CFM56-3C1		
B737-4Q8	N772AS	ALASKA AIRLINES (ILFC)		25105	2505	07/27/93	CFM56-3C1		
B737-4Q8	N773AS	ALASKA AIRLINES (ILFC)		25106	2518	09/02/93	CFM56-3C1		
B737-4Q8	N774AS	ALASKA AIRLINES (ILFC)		25107	2526	10/01/93	CFM56-3C1		
B737-4Q8	N775AS	ALASKA AIRLINES (ILFC)		25108	2551	12/03/93	CFM56-3C1		
B737-4Q8	N776AS	ALASKA AIRLINES (MDFC)		25109	2561	01/10/94	CFM56-3C1		
B737-4Q8	N778AS	ALASKA AIRLINES (ILFC)		25110	2586	03/14/94	CFM56-3C1		
B737-4Q8	N779AS	ALASKA AIRLINES (ILFC)		25111	2605	04/29/94	CFM56-3C1		
B737-4Q8	N780AS	ALASKA AIRLINES (ILFC)		25112	2638	08/02/94	CFM56-3C1		
B737-4Q8	N782AS	ALASKA AIRLINES (ILFC)		25113	2656	10/14/94	CFM56-3C1		
B737-4Q8	N783AS	ALASKA AIRLINES		25114	2666	12/01/94	CFM56-3C1		
B737-4Q8	N784AS	ALASKA AIRLINES (ILFC)		28199	2826	11/19/96	CFM56-3C1		
B737-4Q8	N785AS	ALASKA AIRLINES (ILFC)		27628	2858	02/28/97	CFM56-3C1		
B737-4S3	N786AS	ALASKA AIRLINES		24795	1870	06/11/90	CFM56-3C1		G-BRKF, G-IEAE, N686MA, TF-FIE
B737-490	N788AS	ALASKA AIRLINES		28885	2891	06/09/97	CFM56-3C1		
B737-490	N791AS	ALASKA AIRLINES		28886	2902	07/10/97	CFM56-3C1		
B737-490	N792AS	ALASKA AIRLINES		28887	2903	07/14/97	CFM56-3C1		
B737-490	N793AS	ALASKA AIRLINES		28888	2990	02/05/98	CFM56-3C1		
B737-490	N794AS	ALASKA AIRLINES		28889	3000	02/27/98	CFM56-3C1		
B737-490	N795AS	ALASKA AIRLINES		28890	3006	03/12/98	CFM56-3C1		
B737-490	N796AS	ALASKA AIRLINES		28891	3027	05/12/98	CFM56-3C1		
B737-490	N797AS	ALASKA AIRLINES		28892	3036	06/09/98	CFM56-3C1		
B737-490	N799AS	ALASKA AIRLINES		29270	3038	06/06/98	CFM56-3C1		
B737-3A4	N680AA	AMERICAN AIRLINES (GECA)		23505	1318	12/19/86	CFM56-3B2		N310AC [LST SWA]
B737-3G7	N150AW	AMERICA WEST AIRLINES (EAST TRUST)		23218	1076	02/20/85	CFM56-3B2		
B737-3G7	N151AW	AMERICA WEST AIRLINES (EAST TRUST)		23219	1090	03/13/85	CFM56-3B2		
B737-3G7	N154AW	AMERICA WEST AIRLINES (FSBU)		23776	1417	07/23/87	CFM56-3B1		
B737-3G7	N155AW	AMERICA WEST AIRLINES (FSBU)		23777	1419	07/24/87	CFM56-3B1		
B737-3G7	N156AW	AMERICA WEST AIRLINES (FSBU)		23778	1455	10/15/87	CFM56-3B1		
B737-3G7	N157AW	AMERICA WEST AIRLINES (FSBU)		23779	1457	10/20/87	CFM56-3B1		
B737-3G7	N158AW	AMERICA WEST AIRLINES (FSBU)		23780	1459	10/23/87	CFM56-3B1		
B737-3G7	N160AW	AMERICA WEST AIRLINES		23782	1496	01/21/88	CFM56-3B2		
B737-33A	N164AW	AMERICA WEST AIRLINES (AWMS I)		23625	1283	10/02/86	CFM56-3B1		N3281V

A/C TYPE	CURRENT REG. NO.	LAST KNOWN OPERATOR (OWNER)	STATUS	ORIGINAL MSN	LINE NO.	DEL. DATE	ENG. TYPE	FLEET NO.	PREV. REG. [COMMENTS]
B737-33A	N165AW	AMERICA WEST AIRLINES (AWMS I)		23626	1284	10/03/86	CFM56-3B1		N3281W
B737-33A	N166AW	AMERICA WEST AIRLINES (AWMS I)		23627	1302	11/10/86	CFM56-3B1		
B737-33A	N167AW	AMERICA WEST AIRLINES (AWMS I)		23628	1304	11/13/86	CFM56-3B1		
B737-33A	N168AW	AMERICA WEST AIRLINES (AWMS I)		23629	1311	12/01/86	CFM56-3B1		
B737-33A	N169AW	AMERICA WEST AIRLINES (AWMS I)		23630	1312	12/03/86	CFM56-3B1		
B737-33A	N172AW	AMERICA WEST AIRLINES (AWMS I)		23631	1337	02/04/87	CFM56-3B1		
B737-33A	N173AW	AMERICA WEST AIRLINES (AWMS I)		23632	1344	02/19/87	CFM56-3B1		
B737-33A	N174AW	AMERICA WEST AIRLINES (AWAS)		23633	1421	08/27/87	CFM56-3B1		
B737-33A	N175AW	AMERICA WEST AIRLINES (AWAS)		23634	1423	08/28/87	CFM56-3B1		
B737-3G7	N302AW	AMERICA WEST AIRLINES		24009	1578	07/15/88	CFM56-3B1		
B737-3G7	N303AW	AMERICA WEST AIRLINES (MARCAP)		24010	1606	09/13/88	CFM56-3B1		
B737-3G7	N304AW	AMERICA WEST AIRLINES (CIT LEASE)		24011	1608	10/06/88	CFM56-3B1		
B737-3G7	N305AW	AMERICA WEST AIRLINES (BNYT)		24012	1612	10/11/88	CFM56-3B1		
B737-3G7	N306AW	AMERICA WEST AIRLINES		24633	1809	01/26/90	CFM56-3B2		
B737-3G7	N307AW	AMERICA WEST AIRLINES		24634	1823	02/27/90	CFM56-3B2		
B737-3G7	N308AW	AMERICA WEST AIRLINES		24710	1825	03/02/90	CFM56-3B2		
B737-3G7	N309AW	AMERICA WEST AIRLINES		24711	1843	03/27/90	CFM56-3B2		
B737-3G7	N311AW	AMERICA WEST AIRLINES		24712	1869	06/07/90	CFM56-3B2		
B737-3S3	N312AW	AMERICA WEST AIRLINES (KG A/C)		24060	1519	03/09/88	CFM56-3B2		RP-C4005, N200KG
B737-3S3	N313AW	AMERICA WEST AIRLINES (BOUL)		23712	1336	02/10/87	CFM56-3B2		EC-EBZ
B737-3S3	N314AW	AMERICA WEST AIRLINES (BOUL)		23733	1345	02/27/87	CFM56-3B2		G-BMTG
B737-3S3	N315AW	AMERICA WEST AIRLINES (BOUL)		23734	1359	03/25/87	CFM56-3B2		G-BMTH [PARKED MZJ]
B737-3S3	N316AW	AMERICA WEST AIRLINES (BOUL)		23713	1341	02/12/87	CFM56-3B2		G-BMTF
B737-3G7	N322AW	AMERICA WEST AIRLINES (GECA)		25400	2112	09/19/91	CFM56-3B1		
B737-3Y0	N323AW	AMERICA WEST AIRLINES (GECA)		23684	1353	03/11/87	CFM56-3B2		EI-BTF, TC-AFK, F-GLTF, EC-255, EC-FQB
B737-301	N324AW	AMERICA WEST AIRLINES (GECA)		23261	1157	10/11/85	CFM56-3B2		N312P, N583US
B737-301	N325AW	AMERICA WEST AIRLINES (GECA)		23260	1146	09/05/85	CFM56-3B2		N309P, N582US
B737-301	N326AW	AMERICA WEST AIRLINES (GECA)		23258	1126	06/25/85	CFM56-3B2		N306P, N579US
B737-3Q8	N327AW	AMERICA WEST AIRLINES (GECA)		23507	1252	07/18/86	CFM56-3B2		N348AU, N398US
B737-3B7	N328AW	AMERICA WEST AIRLINES (EAST TRUST)		23377	1320	12/18/86	CFM56-3B2		N371AU, N502AU
B737-3Y0 (QC)	N329AW	AMERICA WEST AIRLINES (GECA)		23500	1243	06/25/86	CFM56-3B1		PT-TEB, N304AL [WFU]
B737-3Y0 (QC)	N330AW	AMERICA WEST AIRLINES (GECA)		23499	1242	06/23/86	CFM56-3B1		PT-TEA, N303AL [WFU]
B737-3Y0	N331AW	AMERICA WEST AIRLINES (GECA)		23747	1363	04/01/87	CFM56-3B2		EC-EBX, SE-DLN, PP-SOA, PT-WBH, EI-CHA, EC-377, EC-FRZ, XA-SIY, EC-667, EC-FYE, EI-CKV
B737-3B7	N332AW	AMERICA WEST AIRLINES (GECA)		23384	1427	08/14/87	CFM56-3B2		N378AU, N509AU, N953WP
B737-3Y0	N334AW	AMERICA WEST AIRLINES (ACGA)		23748	1381	05/08/87	CFM56-3B2		EC-EBY, EI-BZT, SE-DLO, PP-SOB, EC-356, EC-FRP, XA-SIZ, SE-DLO, N962WP
B737-3U3	N335AW	AMERICA WEST AIRLINES (GECA)		28740	3003	06/30/98	CFM56-3C1		N1787B, N1790B
B737-375	N336AW	AMERICA WEST AIRLINES		23707	1388	05/27/87	CFM56-3B2		EC-ECS, EC-782, EC-FKI

A/C TYPE	CURRENT REG. NO.	LAST KNOWN OPERATOR (OWNER)	STATUS	ORIGINAL MSN	LINE NO.	DEL. DATE	ENG. TYPE	FLEET NO.	PREV. REG. [COMMENTS]
		(CASTLE HARBOR)							
B737-33A	N509DC	AMERICA WEST AIRLINES (AWAS)		23636	1438	03/01/88	CFM56-3B2		EC-EHJ
B737-524	N14601	CONTINENTAL AIRLINES		27314	2566	02/11/94	CFM56-3C1	601	
B737-524	N69602	CONTINENTAL AIRLINES		27315	2571	02/07/94	CFM56-3C1	602	
B737-524	N69603	CONTINENTAL AIRLINES		27316	2573	02/11/94	CFM56-3C1	603	
B737-524	N14604	CONTINENTAL AIRLINES		27317	2576	02/15/94	CFM56-3C1	604	
B737-524	N14605	CONTINENTAL AIRLINES		27318	2582	03/02/94	CFM56-3C1	605	
B737-524	N58606	CONTINENTAL AIRLINES		27319	2590	03/21/94	CFM56-3C1	606	
B737-524	N16607	CONTINENTAL AIRLINES		27320	2596	04/06/94	CFM56-3C1	607	
B737-524	N33608	CONTINENTAL AIRLINES		27321	2597	04/05/94	CFM56-3C1	608	
B737-524	N14609	CONTINENTAL AIRLINES		27322	2607	05/05/94	CFM56-3C1	609	
B737-524	N27610	CONTINENTAL AIRLINES		27323	2616	05/31/94	CFM56-3C1	610	
B737-524	N18611	CONTINENTAL AIRLINES		27324	2621	06/14/94	CFM56-3C1	611	
B737-524	N11612	CONTINENTAL AIRLINES		27325	2630	07/19/94	CFM56-3C1	612	
B737-524	N14613	CONTINENTAL AIRLINES		27326	2633	07/25/94	CFM56-3C1	613	
B737-524	N17614	CONTINENTAL AIRLINES (CASTLE HBR)		27327	2634	08/30/94	CFM56-3C1	614	
B737-524	N37615	CONTINENTAL AIRLINES		27328	2640	08/09/94	CFM56-3C1	615	
B737-524	N52616	CONTINENTAL AIRLINES		27329	2641	08/10/94	CFM56-3C1	616	
B737-524	N16617	CONTINENTAL AIRLINES (CASTLE HBR)		27330	2648	09/16/94	CFM56-3C1	617	
B737-524	N16618	CONTINENTAL AIRLINES		27331	2652	09/26/94	CFM56-3C1	618	
B737-524	N17619	CONTINENTAL AIRLINES		27332	2659	10/28/94	CFM56-3C1	619	
B737-524	N17620	CONTINENTAL AIRLINES (GECA)		27333	2660	02/21/95	CFM56-3C1	620	N1790B
B737-524	N19621	CONTINENTAL AIRLINES		27334	2661	12/05/94	CFM56-3C1	621	
B737-524	N18622	CONTINENTAL AIRLINES		27526	2669	12/08/94	CFM56-3C1	622	
B737-524	N19623	CONTINENTAL AIRLINES (GECA)		27527	2672	01/26/95	CFM56-3C1	623	
B737-524	N13624	CONTINENTAL AIRLINES (GECA)		27528	2675	02/07/95	CFM56-3C1	624	
B737-524	N46625	CONTINENTAL AIRLINES (GECA)		27529	2683	01/27/95	CFM56-3C1	625	
B737-524	N32626	CONTINENTAL AIRLINES (GECA)		27530	2686	04/13/95	CFM56-3C1	626	
B737-524	N17627	CONTINENTAL AIRLINES (GECA)		27531	2700	04/14/95	CFM56-3C1	627	
B737-524	N14628	CONTINENTAL AIRLINES		27532	2712	04/19/95	CFM56-3C1	628	
B737-524	N14629	CONTINENTAL AIRLINES		27533	2725	05/26/95	CFM56-3C1	629	
B737-524	N59630	CONTINENTAL AIRLINES		27534	2726	05/30/95	CFM56-3C1	630	
B737-524	N62631	CONTINENTAL AIRLINES (GECA)		27535	2728	06/12/95	CFM56-3C1	631	
B737-524	N16632	CONTINENTAL AIRLINES (GECA)		27900	2736	07/11/95	CFM56-3C1	632	
B737-524	N24633	CONTINENTAL AIRLINES (GECA)		27901	2743	08/04/95	CFM56-3C1	633	
B737-524	N19634	CONTINENTAL AIRLINES (ILFC)		26319	2748	08/31/95	CFM56-3C1	634	
B737-524	N33635	CONTINENTAL AIRLINES (ILFC)		26339	2771	02/14/96	CFM56-3C1	635	
B737-524	N19636	CONTINENTAL AIRLINES (ILFC)		26340	2777	04/03/96	CFM56-3C1	636	
B737-524	N33637	CONTINENTAL AIRLINES		27540	2776	04/02/96	CFM56-3C1	637	
B737-524	N19638	CONTINENTAL AIRLINES	28899		2912	07/31/97	CFM56-3C1	638	

A/C TYPE	CURRENT REG. NO.	LAST KNOWN OPERATOR (OWNER)	STATUS	ORIGINAL MSN	LINE NO.	DEL. DATE	ENG. TYPE	FLEET NO.	PREV. REG. [COMMENTS]
B737-524	N14639	CONTINENTAL AIRLINES		28900	2913	07/31/97	CFM56-3C1	639	
B737-524	N17640	CONTINENTAL AIRLINES		28901	2924	08/26/97	CFM56-3C1	640	
B737-524	N11641	CONTINENTAL AIRLINES (WFBN)		28902	2926	08/29/97	CFM56-3C1	641	
B737-524	N16642	CONTINENTAL AIRLINES		28903	2927	09/17/97	CFM56-3C1	642	
B737-524	N17644	CONTINENTAL AIRLINES		28905	2934	09/29/97	CFM56-3C1	644	
B737-524	N14645	CONTINENTAL AIRLINES		28906	2935	09/30/97	CFM56-3C1	645	
B737-524	N16646	CONTINENTAL AIRLINES (FSBU)		28907	2956	12/01/97	CFM56-3C1	646	
B737-524	N16647	CONTINENTAL AIRLINES		28908	2958	11/14/97	CFM56-3C1	647	
B737-524	N16648	CONTINENTAL AIRLINES (FSBU)		28909	2960	12/05/97	CFM56-3C1	648	
B737-524	N16649	CONTINENTAL AIRLINES (FSBU)		28910	2972	12/19/97	CFM56-3C1	649	
B737-524	N16650	CONTINENTAL AIRLINES (FSBU)		28911	2973	12/23/97	CFM56-3C1	650	
B737-524	N11651	CONTINENTAL AIRLINES (WFBN)		28912	2980	12/31/97	CFM56-3C1	651	
B737-524	N14652	CONTINENTAL AIRLINES (FSBU)		28913	2985	01/23/98	CFM56-3C1	652	
B737-524	N14653	CONTINENTAL AIRLINES (FSBU)		28914	2986	01/27/98	CFM56-3C1	653	
B737-524	N14654	CONTINENTAL AIRLINES		28915	2993	02/11/98	CFM56-3C1	654	
B737-524	N14655	CONTINENTAL AIRLINES		28916	2994	02/12/98	CFM56-3C1	655	
B737-524	N11656	CONTINENTAL AIRLINES		28917	3019	04/17/98	CFM56-3C1	656	
B737-524	N23657	CONTINENTAL AIRLINES		28918	3026	05/08/98	CFM56-3C1	657	N1787B
B737-524	N18658	CONTINENTAL AIRLINES		28919	3045	06/25/98	CFM56-3C1	658	N1786B
B737-524	N15659	CONTINENTAL AIRLINES		28920	3048	06/30/98	CFM56-3C1	659	N1786B
B737-524	N14660	CONTINENTAL AIRLINES		28921	3052	07/15/98	CFM56-3C1	660	
B737-524	N23661	CONTINENTAL AIRLINES		28922	3055	07/21/98	CFM56-3C1	661	N1786B
B737-524	N14662	CONTINENTAL AIRLINES		28923	3060	08/03/98	CFM56-3C1	662	N1786B
B737-524	N17663	CONTINENTAL AIRLINES		28924	3063	08/11/98	CFM56-3C1	663	N1786B
B737-524	N14664	CONTINENTAL AIRLINES		28925	3066	08/20/98	CFM56-3C1	664	
B737-524	N13665	CONTINENTAL AIRLINES		28926	3069	08/31/98	CFM56-3C1	665	N1786B
B737-524	N14667	CONTINENTAL AIRLINES		28927	3074	09/30/98	CFM56-3C1	666	N1786B
B737-524	N14668	CONTINENTAL AIRLINES		28928	3077	10/19/98	CFM56-3C1	667	N1786B
B737-3T0	N16301	CONTINENTAL AIRLINES (SSBT)		23352	1119	06/17/85	CFM56-3B1	301	
B737-3T0	N59302	CONTINENTAL AIRLINES (SSBT)		23353	1129	07/19/85	CFM56-3B1	302	
B737-3T0	N77303	CONTINENTAL AIRLINES (SSBT)		23354	1130	07/24/85	CFM56-3B1	303	
B737-3T0	N61304	CONTINENTAL AIRLINES (SSBT)		23355	1131	07/30/85	CFM56-3B1	304	
B737-3T0	N63305	CONTINENTAL AIRLINES		23356	1133	08/13/85	CFM56-3B1	305	
B737-3T0	N17306	CONTINENTAL AIRLINES		23357	1141	08/28/85	CFM56-3B1	306	
B737-3T0	N14307	CONTINENTAL AIRLINES		23358	1142	08/27/85	CFM56-3B1	307	
B737-3T0	N14308	CONTINENTAL AIRLINES		23359	1144	09/05/85	CFM56-3B1	308	
B737-3T0	N17309	CONTINENTAL AIRLINES		23360	1147	09/13/85	CFM56-3B1	309	
B737-3T0	N16310	CONTINENTAL AIRLINES		23361	1150	09/24/85	CFM56-3B1	310	
B737-3T0	N69311	CONTINENTAL AIRLINES		23362	1152	09/30/85	CFM56-3B1	311	
B737-3T0	N60312	CONTINENTAL AIRLINES		23363	1153	10/03/85	CFM56-3B1	312	
B737-3T0	N12313	CONTINENTAL AIRLINES		23364	1158	10/16/85	CFM56-3B1	313	

A/C TYPE	CURRENT REG. NO.	LAST KNOWN OPERATOR (OWNER)	STATUS	ORIGINAL MSN	LINE NO.	DEL. DATE	ENG. TYPE	FLEET NO.	PREV. REG. [COMMENTS]
B737-3T0	N71314	CONTINENTAL AIRLINES		23365	1159	10/24/85	CFM56-3B1	314	
B737-3T0	N34315	CONTINENTAL AIRLINES		23366	1174	11/27/85	CFM56-3B1	315	
B737-3T0	N17316	CONTINENTAL AIRLINES		23367	1180	12/18/85	CFM56-3B1	316	
B737-3T0	N17317	CONTINENTAL AIRLINES		23368	1181	12/19/85	CFM56-3B1	317	
B737-3T0	N12318	CONTINENTAL AIRLINES (CITG)		23369	1188	01/15/86	CFM56-3B1	318	
B737-3T0	N12319	CONTINENTAL AIRLINES (CITG)		23370	1190	01/22/86	CFM56-3B1	319	
B737-3T0	N14320	CONTINENTAL AIRLINES (SSBT)		23371	1191	01/30/86	CFM56-3B1	320	
B737-3T0	N17321	CONTINENTAL AIRLINES (SSBT)		23372	1192	02/05/86	CFM56-3B1	321	
B737-3T0	N12322	CONTINENTAL AIRLINES		23373	1202	02/27/86	CFM56-3B1	322	
B737-3T0	N10323	CONTINENTAL AIRLINES		23374	1204	03/10/86	CFM56-3B1	323	
B737-3T0	N14324	CONTINENTAL AIRLINES		23375	1207	03/17/86	CFM56-3B1	324	
B737-3T0	N14325	CONTINENTAL AIRLINES (SSBT)		23455	1228	05/19/86	CFM56-3B1	325	
B737-3T0	N17326	CONTINENTAL AIRLINES (SSBT)		23456	1230	05/20/86	CFM56-3B1	326	
B737-3T0	N12327	CONTINENTAL AIRLINES (SSBT)		23457	1238	06/12/86	CFM56-3B1	327	
B737-3T0	N17328	CONTINENTAL AIRLINES (GECA)		23458	1244	07/10/86	CFM56-3B1	328	
B737-3T0	N17329	CONTINENTAL AIRLINES		23459	1247	07/15/86	CFM56-3B1	329	
B737-3T0	N70330	CONTINENTAL AIRLINES		23460	1253	07/25/86	CFM56-3B1	330	
B737-3T0	N13331	CONTINENTAL AIRLINES		23569	1258	08/11/86	CFM56-3B1	331	
B737-3T0	N47332	CONTINENTAL AIRLINES		23570	1263	08/21/86	CFM56-3B1	332	
B737-3T0	N69333	CONTINENTAL AIRLINES		23571	1276	10/03/86	CFM56-3B1	333	
B737-3T0	N14334	CONTINENTAL AIRLINES		23572	1296	10/30/86	CFM56-3B1	334	
B737-3T0	N14335	CONTINENTAL AIRLINES		23573	1298	11/17/86	CFM56-3B1	335	
B737-3T0	N14336	CONTINENTAL AIRLINES (FSBU)		23574	1328	01/16/87	CFM56-3B1	336	
B737-3T0	N14337	CONTINENTAL AIRLINES (FSBU)		23575	1333	01/30/87	CFM56-3B1	337	
B737-3T0	N59338	CONTINENTAL AIRLINES (FSBU)		23576	1338	02/12/87	CFM56-3B1	338	
B737-3T0	N16339	CONTINENTAL AIRLINES (GECA)		23577	1340	02/12/87	CFM56-3B1	339	
B737-3T0	N39340	CONTINENTAL AIRLINES (GECA)		23578	1358	03/23/87	CFM56-3B1	340	
B737-3T0	N14341	CONTINENTAL AIRLINES (FSBU)		23579	1368	04/13/87	CFM56-3B1	341	
B737-3T0	N14342	CONTINENTAL AIRLINES (FSBU)		23580	1373	04/22/87	CFM56-3B1	342	
B737-3T0	N39343	CONTINENTAL AIRLINES (FSBU)		23581	1376	04/30/87	CFM56-3B1	343	
B737-3T0	N17344	CONTINENTAL AIRLINES (FSBU)		23582	1383	05/13/87	CFM56-3B1	344	
B737-3T0	N17345	CONTINENTAL AIRLINES (FSBU)		23583	1385	05/18/87	CFM56-3B1	345	
B737-3T0	N14346	CONTINENTAL AIRLINES		23584	1396	06/15/87	CFM56-3B1	346	
B737-3T0	N14347	CONTINENTAL AIRLINES		23585	1404	06/29/87	CFM56-3B1	347	
B737-3T0	N69348	CONTINENTAL AIRLINES		23586	1411	07/15/87	CFM56-3B1	348	
B737-3T0	N12349	CONTINENTAL AIRLINES		23587	1413	07/17/87	CFM56-3B1	349	
B737-3T0	N18350	CONTINENTAL AIRLINES (BONY)		23588	1448	09/30/87	CFM56-3B1	350	
B737-3T0	N69351	CONTINENTAL AIRLINES		23589	1466	11/09/87	CFM56-3B1	351	
B737-3T0	N70352	CONTINENTAL AIRLINES		23590	1468	11/09/87	CFM56-3B1	352	
B737-3T0	N70353	CONTINENTAL AIRLINES		23591	1472	11/19/87	CFM56-3B1	353	
B737-3T0	N76354	CONTINENTAL AIRLINES (FIRST UNION)		23592	1476	12/16/87	CFM56-3B1	354	

A/C TYPE	CURRENT REG. NO.	LAST KNOWN OPERATOR (OWNER)	STATUS	ORIGINAL MSN	LINE NO.	DEL. DATE	ENG. TYPE	FLEET NO.	PREV. REG. [COMMENTS]
B737-3T0	N76355	CONTINENTAL AIRLINES		23593	1478	12/16/87	CFM56-3B1	355	
B737-3T0	N17356	CONTINENTAL AIRLINES (ICX CORP)		23942	1522	03/31/88	CFM56-3B1	356	G-BOLM, N310AC, N320AW
B737-3T0	N19357	CONTINENTAL AIRLINES (FSBU)		23841	1518	03/15/88	CFM56-3B1	357	N301AC, N18359, N301AL
B737-3T0	N14358	CONTINENTAL AIRLINES (FSBU)		23943	1558	06/03/88	CFM56-3B1	358	N76362, N302AL
B737-3Q8	N73380	CONTINENTAL AIRLINES (ILFC)		26309	2674	12/05/94	CFM56-3B1	380	
B737-3Q8	N14381	CONTINENTAL AIRLINES (ILFC)		26310	2680	01/06/95	CFM56-3B1	381	
B737-3Q8	N19382	CONTINENTAL AIRLINES (ILFC)		26311	2681	01/09/95	CFM56-3B1	382	
B737-3Q8	N14383	CONTINENTAL AIRLINES (ILFC)		26312	2693	02/09/95	CFM56-3B1	383	
B737-3Q8	N14384	CONTINENTAL AIRLINES (ILFC)		26313	2704	03/20/95	CFM56-3B1	384	
B737-3Q8	N73385	CONTINENTAL AIRLINES (ILFC)		26314	2707	03/28/95	CFM56-3B1	385	
B737-3Q8	N17386	CONTINENTAL AIRLINES (ILFC)		26321	2764	12/18/95	CFM56-3B1	386	
B737-35B	N221DL	DELTA AIRLINES (CITG)		23970	1467	11/20/87	CFM56-3B2	221	D-AGEA
B737-35B	N222DZ	DELTA AIRLINES (CITG)		23971	1482	12/14/87	CFM56-3B2	222	D-AGEB
B737-35B	N223DZ	DELTA AIRLINES (PEMB)		23972	1537	04/14/88	CFM56-3B2	223	D-AGEC
B737-35B	N224DA	DELTA AIRLINES (PEMB)		24269	1628	10/31/88	CFM56-3B2	224	D-AGED
B737-35B	N225DL	DELTA AIRLINES (PEMB)		25069	2053	05/24/91	CFM56-3B2	225	D-AGEF
B737-3L9	N231DN	DELTA AIRLINES (PEMB)		23717	1365	04/06/87	CFM56-3B2	231	G-EURR, D-AGEH
B737-3L9	N232DZ	DELTA AIRLINES (PEMB)		24220	1602	09/29/88	CFM56-3B2	232	G-CMMP, OY-MMP, D-AGEI
B737-330	N241DL	DELTA AIRLINES (PEMB)		23833	1439	09/17/87	CFM56-3B2	241	D-ABWA
B737-330	N242DL	DELTA AIRLINES (PEMB)		23834	1454	10/22/87	CFM56-3B2	242	D-ABWB
B737-347	N3301	DELTA AIRLINES (BTM CAPITAL)		23181	1087	03/29/85	CFM56-3B1	201	
B737-347	N302WA	DELTA AIRLINES (BTM CAPITAL)		23182	1106	04/26/85	CFM56-3B1	202	
B737-347	N303WA	DELTA AIRLINES (BTM CAPITAL)		23183	1108	05/07/85	CFM56-3B1	203	
B737-347	N304WA	DELTA AIRLINES		23345	1170	11/19/87	CFM56-3B1	204	
B737-347	N305WA	DELTA AIRLINES (SSBT)		23346	1172	12/03/85	CFM56-3B1	205	
B737-347	N306WA	DELTA AIRLINES (SSBT)		23347	1173	12/06/85	CFM56-3B1	206	
B737-347	N307WA	DELTA AIRLINES		23440	1218	04/16/86	CFM56-3B1	207	
B737-347	N308WA	DELTA AIRLINES		23441	1220	04/22/86	CFM56-3B1	208	
B737-347	N309WA	DELTA AIRLINES		23442	1239	06/13/86	CFM56-3B1	209	
B737-347	N2310	DELTA AIRLINES		23596	1269	08/29/86	CFM56-3B1	210	
B737-347	N311WA	DELTA AIRLINES		23597	1287	10/16/86	CFM56-3B1	211	
B737-347	N312WA	DELTA AIRLINES		23598	1289	10/29/86	CFM56-3B1	212	
B737-347	N313WA	DELTA AIRLINES (SSBT)		23599	1324	12/23/86	CFM56-3B1	213	
B737-3B7	N947WP	DELTA AIRLINES (FSBU)		23376	1308	11/19/86	CFM56-3B2	253	N370AU, N501AU
B737-301	N948WP	DELTA AIRLINES (FSBU)		23259	1132	07/15/85	CFM56-3B2	252	N307P, N581US
B737-3B7	N951WP	DELTA AIRLINES (FSBU)		22951	1007	11/27/85	CFM56-3B1	251	N351AU, N372US
B737-3B7	N952WP	DELTA AIRLINES (FSBU)		23378	1339	02/09/87	CFM56-3B2	254	N372AU, N503AU
B737-3M8	N303FL	FRONTIER AIRLINES (SANWA)		25039	2007	03/15/91	CFM56-3B2	303	OO-LTJ

A/C TYPE	CURRENT REG. NO.	LAST KNOWN OPERATOR (OWNER)	STATUS	ORIGINAL MSN	LINE NO.	DEL. DATE	ENG. TYPE	FLEET NO.	PREV. REG. [COMMENTS]
B737-3Q8	N304FL	FRONTIER AIRLINES (ILFC)		27633	2878	05/01/97	CFM56-3C1	304	
B737-36Q	N305FA	FRONTIER AIRLINES (BOUL)		28662	2914	08/11/97	CFM56-3C1	305	
B737-36N	N306FL	FRONTIER AIRLINES (GECA)		28563	2921	08/26/97	CFM56-3C1	306	
B737-36Q	N307FL	FRONTIER AIRLINES (BOUL)		28760	2989	02/06/98	CFM56-3C1	307	
B737-3U3	N308FL	FRONTIER AIRLINES (FSBU)		28738	2988	11/23/98	CFM56-3C1	308	N6069R
B737-3L9	N310FL	FRONTIER AIRLINES (INGO)		26440	2234	03/06/92	CFM56-3B2	310	D-ADBB
B737-3S1	N311FL	FRONTIER AIRLINES (FSBU)		24856	1911	09/25/90	CFM56-3B2	311	N372TA
B737-3L9	N312FL	FRONTIER AIRLINES (CITG)		24569	1775	09/18/89	CFM56-3B2	312	OY-MMD, EC-FMS, D-ADBE
B737-3L9	N313FL	FRONTIER AIRLINES (INGO)		26442	2277	05/07/92	CFM56-3B2	313	OY-MAM, D-ADBC
B737-36E	N314FL	FRONTIER AIRLINES (AV FIN)		25256	2123	09/20/91	CFM56-3B2	314	EC-704, EC-FHR
B737-36E	N315FL	FRONTIER AIRLINES (AV FIN)		25159	2068	06/27/91	CFM56-3B2	315	EC-703, EC-FFN
B737-36E	N316FL	FRONTIER AIRLINES (AV FIN)		25264	2194	01/15/92	CFM56-3B2	316	EC-706, EC-FLG
B737-36E	N317FL	FRONTIER AIRLINES (AV FIN)		25263	2187	01/14/92	CFM56-3B2	317	EC-705, EC-FLF
B737-3Q8	N318FL	FRONTIER AIRLINES (ILFC)		26293	2541	10/22/93	CFM56-3C1	318	N351LF, EC-520, EC-FUT, N361PR
B737-3Q8	N319FL	FRONTIER AIRLINES (ILFC)		26301	2623	06/17/94	CFM56-3C1	319	EC-547, EC-FYF, N362PR
B737-301	N578US	FRONTIER AIRLINES (GECA)		23257	1124	06/20/85	CFM56-3B1	301	N305P
B737-317	EI-CHH	FRONTIER AIRLINES (GECA)		23177	1216	04/09/86	CFM56-3B1	302	C-FCPL, PP-SNU, EI-CGX, PT-WBG
B737-39A	N253DV	MAGIC CARPET AVIATION (AV. INC.)		23800	1409	07/29/87	CFM56-3B2		VR-CCD, N117DF [OPF ORLANDO MAGIC]
B737-4Y0	N37NY	PACE AIRLINES (MSG A/C LSG)		23976	1651	12/21/88	CFM56-3C1		HL7252, N773RA [OPF NY KNICKS AND RANGERS]
B737-448	EI-BXI	RYAN INTL. AIRLINES (EIN)	L	25052	2036	04/29/91	CFM56-3B2		
B737-448	EI-BXK	RYAN INTL. AIRLINES (EIN)	L	25736	2269	04/23/92	CFM56-3B2		
B737-5H4	N501SW	SOUTHWEST AIRLINES		24178	1718	09/07/90	CFM56-3B1		N73700
B737-5H4	N502SW	SOUTHWEST AIRLINES (SSBT)		24179	1744	05/07/90	CFM56-3B1		
B737-5H4	N503SW	SOUTHWEST AIRLINES		24180	1766	02/28/90	CFM56-3B1		
B737-5H4	N504SW	SOUTHWEST AIRLINES		24181	1804	03/05/90	CFM56-3B1		
B737-5H4	N505SW	SOUTHWEST AIRLINES		24182	1826	04/03/90	CFM56-3B1		
B737-5H4	N506SW	SOUTHWEST AIRLINES		24183	1852	05/02/90	CFM56-3B1		
B737-5H4	N507SW	SOUTHWEST AIRLINES (SSBT)		24184	1864	05/30/90	CFM56-3B1		
B737-5H4	N508SW	SOUTHWEST AIRLINES (SSBT)		24185	1932	10/17/90	CFM56-3B1		
B737-5H4	N509SW	SOUTHWEST AIRLINES (SSBT)		24186	1934	10/16/90	CFM56-3B1		
B737-5H4	N510SW	SOUTHWEST AIRLINES (SSBT)		24187	1940	10/30/90	CFM56-3B1		
B737-5H4	N511SW	SOUTHWEST AIRLINES (SSBT)		24188	2029	04/12/91	CFM56-3B1		
B737-5H4	N512SW	SOUTHWEST AIRLINES		24189	2056	05/31/91	CFM56-3B1		
B737-5H4	N513SW	SOUTHWEST AIRLINES		24190	2058	06/05/91	CFM56-3B1		
B737-5H4	N514SW	SOUTHWEST AIRLINES (SSBT)		25153	2078	07/02/91	CFM56-3B1		
B737-5H4	N515SW	SOUTHWEST AIRLINES (SSBT)		25154	2080	07/05/91	CFM56-3B1		
B737-5H4	N519SW	SOUTHWEST AIRLINES		25318	2121	09/17/91	CFM56-3B1		

233

A/C TYPE	CURRENT REG. NO.	LAST KNOWN OPERATOR (OWNER)	STATUS	ORIGINAL MSN	LINE NO.	DEL. DATE	ENG. TYPE	FLEET NO.	PREV. REG. [COMMENTS]
B737-5H4	N520SW	SOUTHWEST AIRLINES		25319	2134	10/07/91	CFM56-3B1		
B737-5H4	N521SW	SOUTHWEST AIRLINES		25320	2136	10/04/91	CFM56-3B1		
B737-5H4	N522SW	SOUTHWEST AIRLINES		26564	2202	01/21/92	CFM56-3B1		
B737-5H4	N523SW	SOUTHWEST AIRLINES		26565	2204	01/23/92	CFM56-3B1		
B737-5H4	N524SW	SOUTHWEST AIRLINES		26566	2224	02/27/92	CFM56-3B1		
B737-5H4	N525SW	SOUTHWEST AIRLINES		26567	2283	05/26/92	CFM56-3B1		
B737-5H4	N526SW	SOUTHWEST AIRLINES		26568	2285	05/22/92	CFM56-3B1		
B737-5H4	N527SW	SOUTHWEST AIRLINES		26569	2287	05/28/92	CFM56-3B1		
B737-5H4	N528SW	SOUTHWEST AIRLINES		26570	2292	05/29/92	CFM56-3B1		
B737-3H4	N300SW	SOUTHWEST AIRLINES		22940	1037	11/30/84	CFM56-3B1		
B737-3H4	N301SW	SOUTHWEST AIRLINES		22941	1048	12/20/84	CFM56-3B1		
B737-3H4	N302SW	SOUTHWEST AIRLINES		22942	1052	12/20/84	CFM56-3B1		
B737-3H4	N303SW	SOUTHWEST AIRLINES		22943	1101	04/15/85	CFM56-3B1		
B737-3H4	N304SW	SOUTHWEST AIRLINES		22944	1138	08/22/85	CFM56-3B1		
B737-3H4	N305SW	SOUTHWEST AIRLINES		22945	1139	08/28/85	CFM56-3B1		
B737-3H4	N306SW	SOUTHWEST AIRLINES		22946	1148	09/30/85	CFM56-3B1		
B737-3H4	N307SW	SOUTHWEST AIRLINES (SSBT)		22947	1156	10/30/85	CFM56-3B1		
B737-3Y0	N308SA	SOUTHWEST AIRLINES (GECA)		23498	1233	05/28/86	CFM56-3B1		C-GPWG, G-MONG, G-EZYA
B737-3H4	N309SW	SOUTHWEST AIRLINES (SSBT)		22948	1160	10/30/85	CFM56-3B1		
B737-3H4	N310SW	SOUTHWEST AIRLINES		22949	1161	12/20/85	CFM56-3B1		
B737-3H4	N311SW	SOUTHWEST AIRLINES		23333	1183	03/13/86	CFM56-3B1		
B737-3H4	N312SW	SOUTHWEST AIRLINES		23334	1185	03/14/86	CFM56-3B1		
B737-3H4	N313SW	SOUTHWEST AIRLINES		23335	1201	03/17/86	CFM56-3B1		
B737-3H4	N314SW	SOUTHWEST AIRLINES		23336	1229	05/19/86	CFM56-3B1		
B737-3H4	N315SW	SOUTHWEST AIRLINES		23337	1231	05/30/86	CFM56-3B1		
B737-3H4	N316SW	SOUTHWEST AIRLINES		23338	1232	05/30/86	CFM56-3B1		
B737-3Q8	N317WN	SOUTHWEST AIRLINES		24068	1506	02/11/88	CFM56-3B2		G-BNNJ, G-OCHA, SE-DTA, G-EZYE
B737-3H4	N318SW	SOUTHWEST AIRLINES (BTM CAP)		23339	1255	08/11/86	CFM56-3B1		
B737-3H4	N319SW	SOUTHWEST AIRLINES (SSBT)		23340	1348	03/04/87	CFM56-3B1		
B737-3H4	N320SW	SOUTHWEST AIRLINES (SSBT)		23341	1350	03/06/87	CFM56-3B1		
B737-3H4	N321SW	SOUTHWEST AIRLINES (SSBT)		23342	1351	03/06/87	CFM56-3B1		
B737-3H4	N322SW	SOUTHWEST AIRLINES (WTCI)		23343	1377	05/13/87	CFM56-3B1		
B737-3H4	N323SW	SOUTHWEST AIRLINES		23344	1378	05/13/87	CFM56-3B1		
B737-3H4	N324SW	SOUTHWEST AIRLINES (SSBT)		23414	1384	05/27/87	CFM56-3B1		
B737-3H4	N325SW	SOUTHWEST AIRLINES (SSBT)		23689	1398	06/25/87	CFM56-3B1		
B737-3H4	N326SW	SOUTHWEST AIRLINES		23690	1400	06/29/87	CFM56-3B1		
B737-3H4	N327SW	SOUTHWEST AIRLINES		23691	1407	06/29/87	CFM56-3B1		
B737-3H4	N328SW	SOUTHWEST AIRLINES		23692	1521	03/24/88	CFM56-3B1		
B737-3H4	N329SW	SOUTHWEST AIRLINES		23693	1525	03/28/88	CFM56-3B1		
B737-3H4	N330SW	SOUTHWEST AIRLINES		23694	1529	03/29/88	CFM56-3B1		
B737-3H4	N331SW	SOUTHWEST AIRLINES (WTCI)		23695	1536	04/25/88	CFM56-3B1		

A/C TYPE	CURRENT REG. NO.	LAST KNOWN OPERATOR (OWNER)	STATUS	ORIGINAL MSN	LINE NO.	DEL. DATE	ENG. TYPE	FLEET NO.	PREV. REG. [COMMENTS]
B737-3H4	N332SW	SOUTHWEST AIRLINES		23696	1545	05/09/88	CFM56-3B1		
B737-3H4	N333SW	SOUTHWEST AIRLINES		23697	1547	05/12/88	CFM56-3B1		
B737-3H4	N334SW	SOUTHWEST AIRLINES		23938	1549	05/22/88	CFM56-3B1		
B737-3H4	N335SW	SOUTHWEST AIRLINES		23939	1553	05/27/88	CFM56-3B1		
B737-3H4	N336SW	SOUTHWEST AIRLINES		23940	1557	05/31/88	CFM56-3B1		
B737-3H4	N337SW	SOUTHWEST AIRLINES		23959	1567	06/30/88	CFM56-3B1		
B737-3H4	N338SW	SOUTHWEST AIRLINES		23960	1571	06/30/88	CFM56-3B1		
B737-3H4	N339SW	SOUTHWEST AIRLINES		24090	1591	08/24/88	CFM56-3B1		
B737-3K2	N340LV	SOUTHWEST AIRLINES		23738	1360	03/26/87	CFM56-3B2		PH-HVJ
B737-3H4	N341SW	SOUTHWEST AIRLINES		24091	1593	08/24/88	CFM56-3B1		
B737-3H4	N342SW	SOUTHWEST AIRLINES		24133	1682	03/31/89	CFM56-3B1		
B737-3H4	N343SW	SOUTHWEST AIRLINES		24151	1686	03/23/89	CFM56-3B1		
B737-3H4	N344SW	SOUTHWEST AIRLINES		24152	1688	03/23/89	CFM56-3B1		
B737-3K2	N345SA	SOUTHWEST AIRLINES		23786	1386	05/13/87	CFM56-3B2		SU-BLC, SU-BLR, XA-SIH, XA-SVQ, PH-HVK
B737-3H4	N346SW	SOUTHWEST AIRLINES		24153	1690	03/27/89	CFM56-3B1		
B737-3H4	N347SW	SOUTHWEST AIRLINES		24374	1708	05/10/89	CFM56-3B1		
B737-3H4	N348SW	SOUTHWEST AIRLINES		24375	1710	05/12/89	CFM56-3B1		
B737-3H4	N349SW	SOUTHWEST AIRLINES		24408	1734	06/23/89	CFM56-3B1		
B737-3H4	N350SW	SOUTHWEST AIRLINES		24409	1748	08/10/89	CFM56-3B1		
B737-3H4	N351SW	SOUTHWEST AIRLINES		24572	1790	11/09/89	CFM56-3B1		
B737-3H4	N352SW	SOUTHWEST AIRLINES		24888	1942	11/06/90	CFM56-3B1		
B737-3H4	N353SW	SOUTHWEST AIRLINES		24889	1947	11/09/90	CFM56-3B1		
B737-3H4	N354SW	SOUTHWEST AIRLINES		25219	2092	07/23/91	CFM56-3B1		
B737-3H4	N355SW	SOUTHWEST AIRLINES		25250	2103	08/06/91	CFM56-3B1		
B737-3H4	N356SW	SOUTHWEST AIRLINES		25251	2105	08/09/91	CFM56-3B1		
B737-3H4	N357SW	SOUTHWEST AIRLINES		26594	2294	05/27/92	CFM56-3B1		
B737-3H4	N358SW	SOUTHWEST AIRLINES		26595	2295	06/01/92	CFM56-3B1		
B737-3H4	N359SW	SOUTHWEST AIRLINES (SSBT)		26596	2297	06/03/92	CFM56-3B1		
B737-3H4	N360SW	SOUTHWEST AIRLINES (SSBT)		26571	2307	06/15/92	CFM56-3B1		
B737-3H4	N361SW	SOUTHWEST AIRLINES (SSBT)		26572	2309	06/18/92	CFM56-3B1		
B737-3H4	N362SW	SOUTHWEST AIRLINES (SSBT)		26573	2322	07/09/92	CFM56-3B1		
B737-3H4	N363SW	SOUTHWEST AIRLINES (SSBT)		26574	2429	02/10/93	CFM56-3B1		
B737-3H4	N364SW	SOUTHWEST AIRLINES (SSBT)		26575	2430	02/12/93	CFM56-3B1		
B737-3H4	N365SW	SOUTHWEST AIRLINES (SSBT)		26576	2433	02/17/93	CFM56-3B1		
B737-3H4	N366SW	SOUTHWEST AIRLINES		26577	2469	05/05/93	CFM56-3B1		
B737-3H4	N367SW	SOUTHWEST AIRLINES		26578	2470	05/07/93	CFM56-3B1		
B737-3H4	N368SW	SOUTHWEST AIRLINES		26579	2473	05/13/93	CFM56-3B1		
B737-3H4	N369SW	SOUTHWEST AIRLINES		26580	2477	05/21/93	CFM56-3B1		
B737-3H4	N370SW	SOUTHWEST AIRLINES		26597	2497	07/02/93	CFM56-3B1		
B737-3H4	N371SW	SOUTHWEST AIRLINES		26598	2500	07/13/93	CFM56-3B1		
B737-3H4	N372SW	SOUTHWEST AIRLINES		26599	2504	07/21/93	CFM56-3B1		

A/C TYPE	CURRENT REG. NO.	LAST KNOWN OPERATOR (OWNER)	STATUS	ORIGINAL MSN	LINE NO.	DEL. DATE	ENG. TYPE	FLEET NO.	PREV. REG. [COMMENTS]
B737-3H4	N373SW	SOUTHWEST AIRLINES		26581	2509	08/02/93	CFM56-3B1		
B737-3H4	N374SW	SOUTHWEST AIRLINES		26582	2515	08/12/93	CFM56-3B1		
B737-3H4	N375SW	SOUTHWEST AIRLINES		26583	2520	09/07/93	CFM56-3B1		
B737-3H4	N376SW	SOUTHWEST AIRLINES		26584	2570	01/21/94	CFM56-3B1		
B737-3H4	N378SW	SOUTHWEST AIRLINES		26585	2579	02/18/94	CFM56-3B1		
B737-3H4	N379SW	SOUTHWEST AIRLINES		26586	2580	02/22/94	CFM56-3B1		
B737-3H4	N380SW	SOUTHWEST AIRLINES (SSBT)		26587	2610	05/12/94	CFM56-3B1		
B737-3H4	N382SW	SOUTHWEST AIRLINES (SSBT)		26588	2611	05/13/94	CFM56-3B1		
B737-3H4	N383SW	SOUTHWEST AIRLINES (SSBT)		26589	2612	05/16/94	CFM56-3B1		
B737-3H4	N384SW	SOUTHWEST AIRLINES (SSBT)		26590	2613	05/19/94	CFM56-3B1		
B737-3H4	N385SW	SOUTHWEST AIRLINES (SSBT)		26600	2617	05/31/94	CFM56-3B1		
B737-3H4	N386SW	SOUTHWEST AIRLINES (SSBT)		26601	2626	06/27/94	CFM56-3B1		
B737-3H4	N387SW	SOUTHWEST AIRLINES (SSBT)		26602	2627	06/29/94	CFM56-3B1		
B737-3H4	N388SW	SOUTHWEST AIRLINES (SSBT)		26591	2628	07/01/94	CFM56-3B1		
B737-3H4	N389SW	SOUTHWEST AIRLINES (SSBT)		26592	2629	07/06/94	CFM56-3B1		
B737-3H4	N390SW	SOUTHWEST AIRLINES (SSBT)		26593	2642	08/25/94	CFM56-3B1		
B737-3H4	N391SW	SOUTHWEST AIRLINES		27378	2643	09/02/94	CFM56-3B1		
B737-3H4	N392SW	SOUTHWEST AIRLINES		27379	2644	09/08/94	CFM56-3B1		
B737-3H4	N394SW	SOUTHWEST AIRLINES		27380	2645	09/12/94	CFM56-3B1		
B737-3H4	N395SW	SOUTHWEST AIRLINES		27689	2667	11/04/94	CFM56-3B1		
B737-3H4	N396SW	SOUTHWEST AIRLINES (SSBT)		27690	2668	11/08/94	CFM56-3B1		
B737-3H4	N397SW	SOUTHWEST AIRLINES (SSBT)		27691	2695	02/15/95	CFM56-3B1		
B737-3H4	N398SW	SOUTHWEST AIRLINES (SSBT)		27692	2696	02/17/95	CFM56-3B1		
B737-3H4	N399WN	SOUTHWEST AIRLINES (SSBT)		27693	2697	02/23/95	CFM56-3B1		
B737-3H4	N600WN	SOUTHWEST AIRLINES (SSBT)		27694	2699	02/28/95	CFM56-3B1		
B737-3H4	N601WN	SOUTHWEST AIRLINES (SSBT)		27695	2702	03/10/95	CFM56-3B1		
B737-3H4	N602SW	SOUTHWEST AIRLINES (SSBT)		27953	2713	04/19/95	CFM56-3B1		
B737-3H4	N603SW	SOUTHWEST AIRLINES (SSBT)		27954	2714	04/21/95	CFM56-3B1		
B737-3H4	N604SW	SOUTHWEST AIRLINES (SSBT)		27955	2715	04/25/95	CFM56-3B1		
B737-3H4	N605SW	SOUTHWEST AIRLINES (SSBT)		27956	2716	04/27/95	CFM56-3B1		
B737-3H4	N606SW	SOUTHWEST AIRLINES		27926	2740	07/24/95	CFM56-3B1		
B737-3H4	N607SW	SOUTHWEST AIRLINES		27927	2741	07/26/95	CFM56-3B1		
B737-3H4	N608SW	SOUTHWEST AIRLINES		27928	2742	07/31/95	CFM56-3B1		
B737-3H4	N609SW	SOUTHWEST AIRLINES		27929	2744	08/04/95	CFM56-3B1		
B737-3H4	N610WN	SOUTHWEST AIRLINES		27696	2745	08/24/95	CFM56-3B1		
B737-3H4	N611SW	SOUTHWEST AIRLINES		27697	2750	09/12/95	CFM56-3B1		
B737-3H4	N612SW	SOUTHWEST AIRLINES		27930	2753	09/23/95	CFM56-3B1		
B737-3H4	N613SW	SOUTHWEST AIRLINES		27931	2754	09/26/95	CFM56-3B1		
B737-3H4	N614SW	SOUTHWEST AIRLINES		28033	2755	09/29/95	CFM56-3B1		
B737-3H4	N615SW	SOUTHWEST AIRLINES		27698	2757	10/06/95	CFM56-3B1		
B737-3H4	N616SW	SOUTHWEST AIRLINES		27699	2758	10/10/95	CFM56-3B1		

A/C TYPE	CURRENT REG. NO.	LAST KNOWN OPERATOR (OWNER)	STATUS	ORIGINAL MSN	LINE NO.	DEL. DATE	ENG. TYPE	FLEET NO.	PREV. REG. [COMMENTS]
B737-3H4	N617SW	SOUTHWEST AIRLINES		27700	2759	10/30/95	CFM56-3B1		N1786B
B737-3H4	N618WN	SOUTHWEST AIRLINES		28034	2761	11/02/95	CFM56-3B1		
B737-3H4	N619SW	SOUTHWEST AIRLINES		28035	2762	11/09/95	CFM56-3B1		
B737-3H4	N620SW	SOUTHWEST AIRLINES		28036	2766	01/12/96	CFM56-3B1		
B737-3H4	N621SW	SOUTHWEST AIRLINES		28037	2767	01/19/96	CFM56-3B1		
B737-3H4	N622SW	SOUTHWEST AIRLINES		27932	2779	03/20/96	CFM56-3B1		
B737-3H4	N623SW	SOUTHWEST AIRLINES		27933	2780	03/25/96	CFM56-3B1		
B737-3H4	N624SW	SOUTHWEST AIRLINES		27934	2781	03/27/96	CFM56-3B1		
B737-3H4	N625SW	SOUTHWEST AIRLINES		27701	2787	04/23/96	CFM56-3B1		
B737-3H4	N626SW	SOUTHWEST AIRLINES		27702	2789	05/01/96	CFM56-3B1		
B737-3H4	N627SW	SOUTHWEST AIRLINES		27935	2790	05/06/96	CFM56-3B1		
B737-3H4	N628SW	SOUTHWEST AIRLINES		27703	2795	05/30/96	CFM56-3B1		
B737-3H4	N629SW	SOUTHWEST AIRLINES		27704	2796	06/06/96	CFM56-3B1		
B737-3H4	N630WN	SOUTHWEST AIRLINES		27705	2797	06/05/96	CFM56-3B1		
B737-3H4	N631SW	SOUTHWEST AIRLINES		27706	2798	06/19/96	CFM56-3B1		
B737-3H4	N632SW	SOUTHWEST AIRLINES		27707	2799	06/13/96	CFM56-3B1		
B737-3H4	N633SW	SOUTHWEST AIRLINES		27936	2807	07/29/96	CFM56-3B1		
B737-3H4	N634SW	SOUTHWEST AIRLINES		27937	2808	08/05/96	CFM56-3B1		
B737-3H4	N635SW	SOUTHWEST AIRLINES		27708	2813	09/03/96	CFM56-3B1		
B737-3H4	N636WN	SOUTHWEST AIRLINES		27709	2814	09/09/96	CFM56-3B1		
B737-3H4	N637SW	SOUTHWEST AIRLINES		27710	2819	10/03/96	CFM56-3B1		
B737-3H4	N638SW	SOUTHWEST AIRLINES		27711	2820	10/04/96	CFM56-3B1		
B737-3H4	N639SW	SOUTHWEST AIRLINES		27712	2821	10/07/96	CFM56-3B1		
B737-3H4	N640SW	SOUTHWEST AIRLINES		27713	2840	12/19/96	CFM56-3B1		
B737-3H4	N641SW	SOUTHWEST AIRLINES		27714	2841	12/20/96	CFM56-3B1		
B737-3H4	N642WN	SOUTHWEST AIRLINES		27715	2842	01/08/97	CFM56-3B1		
B737-3H4	N643SW	SOUTHWEST AIRLINES		27716	2843	01/13/97	CFM56-3B1		
B737-3H4	N644SW	SOUTHWEST AIRLINES		28329	2869	03/31/97	CFM56-3B1		
B737-3H4	N645SW	SOUTHWEST AIRLINES		28330	2870	04/02/97	CFM56-3B1		
B737-3H4	N646SW	SOUTHWEST AIRLINES		28331	2871	04/04/97	CFM56-3B1		
B737-3H4	N647SW	SOUTHWEST AIRLINES		27717	2892	06/09/97	CFM56-3B1		
B737-3H4	N648SW	SOUTHWEST AIRLINES		27718	2893	06/20/97	CFM56-3B1		
B737-3H4	N649SW	SOUTHWEST AIRLINES		27719	2894	06/09/97	CFM56-3B1		
B737-3H4	N650SW	SOUTHWEST AIRLINES		27720	2901	06/30/97	CFM56-3B1		
B737-3H4	N651SW	SOUTHWEST AIRLINES		27721	2915	08/06/97	CFM56-3B1		
B737-3H4	N652SW	SOUTHWEST AIRLINES		27722	2916	08/08/97	CFM56-3B1		
B737-3H4	N653SW	SOUTHWEST AIRLINES		28398	2917	08/11/97	CFM56-3B1		
B737-3H4	N654SW	SOUTHWEST AIRLINES		28399	2918	08/13/97	CFM56-3B1		
B737-3H4	N655SW	SOUTHWEST AIRLINES		28400	2931	09/10/97	CFM56-3B1		
B737-3H4	N656SW	SOUTHWEST AIRLINES		28401	2932	09/26/97	CFM56-3B1		N1786B
B737-3L9	N657SW	SOUTHWEST AIRLINES		23331	1111	05/24/85	CFM56-3B2		OY-MMK, EC-129, EC-EHA, EC-783, EC-FKS, N960WP

A/C TYPE	CURRENT REG. NO.	LAST KNOWN OPERATOR (OWNER)	STATUS	ORIGINAL MSN	LINE NO.	DEL. DATE	ENG. TYPE	FLEET NO.	PREV. REG. [COMMENTS]
B737-3L9	N658SW	SOUTHWEST AIRLINES		23332	1118	06/10/85	CFM56-3B2		OY-MML, EC-356, EC-EST, EC-784 ,EC-FKC, N961W
B737-301	N659SW	SOUTHWEST AIRLINES		23229	1112	05/20/85	CFM56-3B1		N303P, N301AU, N950WP
B737-301	N660SW	SOUTHWEST AIRLINES (AIRCORP)		23230	1115	05/23/85	CFM56-3B1		N304P, N302AU, N949WP
B737-317	N661SW	SOUTHWEST AIRLINES (BBAM)		23173	1098	04/12/85	CFM56-3B1		C-FCPG, PP-SNQ, PT-WBD, EI-CHQ, N946WP
B737-3Q8	N662SW	SOUTHWEST AIRLINES (MSA V)		23255	1125	06/26/85	CFM56-3B1		N399P, N327US
B737-3Q8	N663SW	SOUTHWEST AIRLINES (MSA V)		23256	1128	07/11/85	CFM56-3B1		N397P, N329US
B737-3Y0	N664WN	SOUTHWEST AIRLINES (GECA)		23495	1206	03/13/86	CFM56-3B1		C-FPWD, G-DHSW, EC-635, EC-FVT
B737-3Y0	N665WN	SOUTHWEST AIRLINES (GECA)		23497	1227	05/13/86	CFM56-3B1		C-FPWE, G-MONF
B737-3T5	N667SW	SOUTHWEST AIRLINES (NAT. CITY)		23063	1092	03/25/85	CFM56-3B1		G-BLKE, N752MA
B737-3A4	N669SW	SOUTHWEST AIRLINES (ACGA)		23752	1484	12/22/87	CFM56-3B2		EC-FFB, EC-591, N736S, N758MA
B737-3G7	N670SW	SOUTHWEST AIRLINES (GECC)		23784	1533	04/07/88	CFM56-3B1		N162AW, SE-DPO, N779MA
B737-3G7	N671SW	SOUTHWEST AIRLINES (GATX)		23785	1535	04/12/88	CFM56-3B1		N163AW, N778MA
B737-3Q8	N672SW	SOUTHWEST AIRLINES (ACG ACQ.)		23406	1215	04/08/86	CFM56-3B2		N153AW, N732S, N755MA
B737-3A4	N673AA	SOUTHWEST AIRLINES (PEGA)		23251	1063	02/01/85	CFM56-3B2		N307AC
B737-3A4	N674AA	SOUTHWEST AIRLINES (AIRLEASE)		23252	1094	04/01/85	CFM56-3B2		N674AA, N308AC, SU-BLN, N776MA
B737-3A4	N675AA	SOUTHWEST AIRLINES (PEGA)		23253	1096	03/27/85	CFM56-3B2		N309AC
B737-3A4	N676SW	SOUTHWEST AIRLINES		23288	1100	05/15/85	CFM56-3B2		N301AC, N676AA, N742MA
B737-3A4	N677AA	SOUTHWEST AIRLINES (OAK GROVE TRAINCARS)		23289	1182	12/19/85	CFM56-3B2		N303AC, N735MA
B737-3A4	N678AA	SOUTHWEST AIRLINES (GATX)		23290	1205	03/13/86	CFM56-3B2		N304AC
B737-3A4	N679AA	SOUTHWEST AIRLINES		23291	1211	04/02/86	CFM56-3B2		N306AC
B737-3A4	N680AA	SOUTHWEST AIRLINES (AAL)	L	23505	1318	12/19/86	CFM56-3B2		N310AC
B737-3Y0	N682SW	SOUTHWEST AIRLINES (ANAU)		23496	1217	04/11/86	CFM56-3B1		N67AB
B737-3G7	N683SW	SOUTHWEST AIRLINES (IMPLICIT)		24008	1576	07/11/88	CFM56-3B1		N301AW
B737-3T0	N684WN	SOUTHWEST AIRLINES (ANAU)		23941	1520	03/21/88	CFM56-3B1		EC-138, N304AC, EC-EID
B737-3Q8	N685SW	SOUTHWEST AIRLINES (ILFC)		23401	1209	03/17/86	CFM56-3B1		OO-ILF, G-BOWR
B737-317	N686SW	SOUTHWEST AIRLINES (ARFI)		23175	1110	05/07/85	CFM56-3B1		C-FCPJ, PP-SNS, EI-CHU
B737-3Q8	N687SW	SOUTHWEST AIRLINES		23388	1187	01/28/86	CFM56-3B1		N317AW, SE-DLG, TG-AMA, N103GU
B737-3Q8	N688SW	SOUTHWEST AIRLINES (ILFC)		23254	1107	05/02/85	CFM56-3B1		G-SCUH, N780MA
B737-3Q8	N689SW	SOUTHWEST AIRLINES		23387	1163	11/13/85	CFM56-3B1		N152AW, VR-CCW, N734MA
B737-3G7	N690SW	SOUTHWEST AIRLINES (GATX)		23783	1531	04/04/88	CFM56-3B1		N161AW, TC-JTC, N785MA
B737-3G7	N691WN	SOUTHWEST AIRLINES (GECC)		23781	1494	01/20/88	CFM56-3B2		N159AW, TC-JTB, N784MA
B737-3T5	N692SW	SOUTHWEST AIRLINES		23062	1083	03/18/85	CFM56-3B1		G-BLKD, N733MA
B737-317	N693SW	SOUTHWEST AIRLINES (GECA)		23174	1104	04/26/85	CFM56-3B1		C-FCPI, PP-SNR, N500MH, N775MA
B737-3T5	N694SW	SOUTHWEST AIRLINES		23061	1080	03/11/85	CFM56-3B1		G-BLKC, N744MA
B737-3Q8	N695SW	SOUTHWEST AIRLINES (WACHOVIA)		23506	1249	07/02/86	CFM56-3B2		N881LF, N318AW, N730S, N730MA
B737-3T5	N696SW	SOUTHWEST AIRLINES (AT&T CREDIT)		23064	1527	03/28/88	CFM56-3B1		EC-ELV, G-BNRT, N748MA
B737-3T0	N697SW	SOUTHWEST AIRLINES (CIRR)		23838	1505	03/02/88	CFM56-3B1		N75356, N319AW, N764MA
B737-317	N698SW	SOUTHWEST AIRLINES (GECA)		23176	1213	04/02/86	CFM56-3B1		C-FCPK, PP-SNT, PT-WBF, EI-CHD
B737-3Y0	N699SW	SOUTHWEST AIRLINES (GECA)		23826	1372	04/21/87	CFM56-3B1		EI-BTM, PP-SNV, EC-376, EC-FRZ, EC-FSA, EI-CHE
B737-522	N901UA	UNITED AIRLINES		25001	1948	11/27/90	CFM56-3C1	1601	

A/C TYPE	CURRENT REG. NO.	LAST KNOWN OPERATOR (OWNER)	STATUS	ORIGINAL MSN	LINE NO.	DEL. DATE	ENG. TYPE	FLEET NO.	PREV. REG. [COMMENTS]
B737-522	N902UA	UNITED AIRLINES		25002	1950	11/16/90	CFM56-3C1	1602	
B737-522	N903UA	UNITED AIRLINES		25003	1952	11/20/90	CFM56-3C1	1603	
B737-522	N904UA	UNITED AIRLINES		25004	1965	12/14/90	CFM56-3C1	1604	
B737-522	N905UA	UNITED AIRLINES		25005	1976	01/15/91	CFM56-3C1	1605	
B737-522	N906UA	UNITED AIRLINES		25006	1981	01/22/91	CFM56-3C1	1606	
B737-522	N907UA	UNITED AIRLINES		25007	1983	01/23/91	CFM56-3C1	1607	
B737-522	N908UA	UNITED AIRLINES		25008	1987	02/11/91	CFM56-3C1	1608	
B737-522	N909UA	UNITED AIRLINES		25009	1999	02/21/91	CFM56-3C1	1609	
B737-522	N910UA	UNITED AIRLINES		25254	2073	06/26/91	CFM56-3C1	9710	["SHUTTLE BY UNITED"]
B737-522	N911UA	UNITED AIRLINES		25255	2075	06/28/91	CFM56-3C1	9711	["SHUTTLE BY UNITED"]
B737-522	N912UA	UNITED AIRLINES		25290	2096	07/31/91	CFM56-3C1	9712	["SHUTTLE BY UNITED"]
B737-522	N913UA	UNITED AIRLINES		25291	2101	08/06/91	CFM56-3C1	9713	["SHUTTLE BY UNITED"]
B737-522	N914UA	UNITED AIRLINES		25381	2110	09/03/91	CFM56-3C1	9714	["SHUTTLE BY UNITED"]
B737-522	N915UA	UNITED AIRLINES		25382	2119	09/16/91	CFM56-3C1	9715	["SHUTTLE BY UNITED"]
B737-522	N916UA	UNITED AIRLINES		25383	2146	10/23/91	CFM56-3C1	9716	["SHUTTLE BY UNITED"]
B737-522	N917UA	UNITED AIRLINES		25384	2149	10/29/91	CFM56-3C1	9717	["SHUTTLE BY UNITED"]
B737-522	N918UA	UNITED AIRLINES		25385	2152	10/31/91	CFM56-3C1	9718	["SHUTTLE BY UNITED"]
B737-522	N919UA	UNITED AIRLINES		25386	2154	11/01/91	CFM56-3C1	9719	["SHUTTLE BY UNITED"]
B737-522	N920UA	UNITED AIRLINES		25387	2179	12/06/91	CFM56-3C1	9720	["SHUTTLE BY UNITED"]
B737-522	N921UA	UNITED AIRLINES		25388	2181	12/20/91	CFM56-3C1	9721	["SHUTTLE BY UNITED"]
B737-522	N922UA	UNITED AIRLINES		26642	2189	01/06/92	CFM56-3C1	9722	["SHUTTLE BY UNITED"]
B737-522	N923UA	UNITED AIRLINES		26643	2190	01/06/92	CFM56-3C1	9723	["SHUTTLE BY UNITED"]
B737-522	N924UA	UNITED AIRLINES		26645	2212	02/07/92	CFM56-3C1	9724	["SHUTTLE BY UNITED"]
B737-522	N925UA	UNITED AIRLINES		26646	2214	02/06/92	CFM56-3C1	9725	["SHUTTLE BY UNITED"]
B737-522	N926UA	UNITED AIRLINES		26648	2230	03/02/92	CFM56-3C1	9726	["SHUTTLE BY UNITED"]
B737-522	N927UA	UNITED AIRLINES		26649	2246	03/23/92	CFM56-3C1	9727	["SHUTTLE BY UNITED"]
B737-522	N928UA	UNITED AIRLINES		26651	2257	04/08/92	CFM56-3C1	9728	["SHUTTLE BY UNITED"]
B737-522	N929UA	UNITED AIRLINES		26652	2259	04/10/92	CFM56-3C1	9729	["SHUTTLE BY UNITED"]
B737-522	N930UA	UNITED AIRLINES		26655	2274	04/28/92	CFM56-3C1	9730	["SHUTTLE BY UNITED"]
B737-522	N931UA	UNITED AIRLINES		26656	2289	05/21/92	CFM56-3C1	9731	["SHUTTLE BY UNITED"]
B737-522	N932UA	UNITED AIRLINES		26658	2291	05/26/92	CFM56-3C1	9732	["SHUTTLE BY UNITED"]
B737-522	N933UA	UNITED AIRLINES		26659	2293	05/27/92	CFM56-3C1	9733	["SHUTTLE BY UNITED"]
B737-522	N934UA	UNITED AIRLINES		26662	2312	06/26/92	CFM56-3C1	9734	["SHUTTLE BY UNITED"]
B737-522	N935UA	UNITED AIRLINES		26663	2315	06/26/92	CFM56-3C1	1635	
B737-522	N936UA	UNITED AIRLINES		26667	2325	07/15/92	CFM56-3C1	1636	
B737-522	N937UA	UNITED AIRLINES		26668	2329	07/20/92	CFM56-3C1	1637	
B737-522	N938UA	UNITED AIRLINES		26671	2336	07/30/92	CFM56-3C1	1638	
B737-522	N939UA	UNITED AIRLINES		26672	2343	08/07/92	CFM56-3C1	1639	
B737-522	N940UA	UNITED AIRLINES		26675	2345	09/10/92	CFM56-3C1	1640	
B737-522	N941UA	UNITED AIRLINES		26676	2364	10/06/92	CFM56-3C1	1641	
B737-522	N942UA	UNITED AIRLINES		26679	2365	10/28/92	CFM56-3C1	1642	

A/C TYPE	CURRENT REG. NO.	LAST KNOWN OPERATOR (OWNER)	STATUS	ORIGINAL MSN	LINE NO.	DEL. DATE	ENG. TYPE	FLEET NO.	PREV. REG. [COMMENTS]
B737-522	N943UA	UNITED AIRLINES		26680	2366	11/02/92	CFM56-3C1	1643	
B737-522	N944UA	UNITED AIRLINES		26683	2368	11/03/92	CFM56-3C1	1644	
B737-522	N945UA	UNITED AIRLINES		26684	2388	12/01/92	CFM56-3C1	1645	
B737-522	N946UA	UNITED AIRLINES		26687	2402	12/16/92	CFM56-3C1	1646	
B737-522	N947UA	UNITED AIRLINES		26688	2404	12/11/92	CFM56-3C1	1647	
B737-522	N948UA	UNITED AIRLINES		26691	2408	12/21/92	CFM56-3C1	1648	
B737-522	N949UA	UNITED AIRLINES		26692	2421	02/01/93	CFM56-3C1	1649	
B737-522	N950UA	UNITED AIRLINES		26695	2423	02/01/93	CFM56-3C1	1650	
B737-522	N951UA	UNITED AIRLINES		26696	2440	03/08/93	CFM56-3C1	1651	
B737-522	N952UA	UNITED AIRLINES		26699	2485	06/14/93	CFM56-3C1	1652	
B737-522	N953UA	UNITED AIRLINES		26700	2490	06/23/93	CFM56-3C1	1653	
B737-522	N954UA	UNITED AIRLINES		26739	2494	07/02/93	CFM56-3C1	1654	
B737-522	N955UA	UNITED AIRLINES		26703	2498	07/12/93	CFM56-3C1	1655	
B737-522	N956UA	UNITED AIRLINES		26704	2508	08/02/93	CFM56-3C1	1656	
B737-522	N957UA	UNITED AIRLINES		26707	2512	08/12/93	CFM56-3C1	1657	
B737-322	N202UA	UNITED AIRLINES (SSBT)		24717	1930	10/12/90	CFM56-3C1	9002	
B737-322	N203UA	UNITED AIRLINES (SSBT)		24718	1937	10/25/90	CFM56-3C1	9003	
B737-322	N301UA	UNITED AIRLINES		23642	1300	11/12/86	CFM56-3C1	9901	
B737-322	N302UA	UNITED AIRLINES		23643	1315	12/11/86	CFM56-3C1	9902	
B737-322	N303UA	UNITED AIRLINES		23644	1322	12/23/86	CFM56-3C1	9903	
B737-322	N304UA	UNITED AIRLINES		23665	1330	01/23/87	CFM56-3C1	9904	
B737-322	N305UA	UNITED AIRLINES		23666	1332	01/27/87	CFM56-3C1	9905	
B737-322	N306UA	UNITED AIRLINES		23667	1334	01/30/87	CFM56-3C1	9906	
B737-322	N307UA	UNITED AIRLINES		23668	1346	02/26/87	CFM56-3C1	9907	
B737-322	N308UA	UNITED AIRLINES		23669	1354	03/16/87	CFM56-3C1	9908	
B737-322	N309UA	UNITED AIRLINES		23670	1364	04/11/87	CFM56-3C1	9909	
B737-322	N310UA	UNITED AIRLINES		23671	1370	04/16/87	CFM56-3C1	9910	
B737-322	N311UA	UNITED AIRLINES		23672	1470	11/18/87	CFM56-3C1	9911	
B737-322	N312UA	UNITED AIRLINES		23673	1479	12/07/87	CFM56-3C1	9912	
B737-322	N313UA	UNITED AIRLINES		23674	1481	12/08/87	CFM56-3C1	9913	
B737-322	N314UA	UNITED AIRLINES		23675	1483	12/16/87	CFM56-3C1	9914	
B737-322	N315UA	UNITED AIRLINES		23947	1485	12/23/87	CFM56-3C1	9915	
B737-322	N316UA	UNITED AIRLINES		23948	1491	01/15/88	CFM56-3C1	9916	
B737-322	N317UA	UNITED AIRLINES		23949	1493	01/19/88	CFM56-3C1	9917	
B737-322	N318UA	UNITED AIRLINES		23950	1504	02/09/88	CFM56-3C1	9918	
B737-322	N319UA	UNITED AIRLINES		23951	1532	04/12/88	CFM56-3C1	9919	
B737-322	N320UA	UNITED AIRLINES		23952	1534	04/18/88	CFM56-3C1	9920	
B737-322	N321UA	UNITED AIRLINES		23953	1546	05/06/88	CFM56-3C1	9921	
B737-322	N322UA	UNITED AIRLINES		23954	1548	05/11/88	CFM56-3C1	9922	
B737-322	N323UA	UNITED AIRLINES		23955	1550	05/17/88	CFM56-3C1	9923	
B737-322	N324UA	UNITED AIRLINES		23956	1564	06/16/88	CFM56-3C1	9924	

A/C TYPE	CURRENT REG. NO.	LAST KNOWN OPERATOR (OWNER)	STATUS	ORIGINAL MSN	LINE NO.	DEL. DATE	ENG. TYPE	FLEET NO.	PREV. REG. [COMMENTS]
B737-322	N325UA	UNITED AIRLINES		23957	1566	06/21/88	CFM56-3C1	9925	
B737-322	N326UA	UNITED AIRLINES		23958	1568	06/23/88	CFM56-3C1	9926	
B737-322	N327UA	UNITED AIRLINES		24147	1570	07/05/88	CFM56-3C1	9927	
B737-322	N328UA	UNITED AIRLINES		24148	1572	07/05/88	CFM56-3C1	9928	
B737-322	N329UA	UNITED AIRLINES		24149	1574	07/11/88	CFM56-3C1	9929	
B737-322	N330UA	UNITED AIRLINES		24191	1588	08/08/88	CFM56-3C1	9930	
B737-322	N331UA	UNITED AIRLINES		24192	1590	08/10/88	CFM56-3C1	9931	
B737-322	N332UA	UNITED AIRLINES		24193	1592	08/15/88	CFM56-3C1	9932	
B737-322	N333UA	UNITED AIRLINES		24228	1594	08/18/88	CFM56-3C1	9933	
B737-322	N334UA	UNITED AIRLINES		24229	1605	09/12/88	CFM56-3C1	9934	
B737-322	N335UA	UNITED AIRLINES		24230	1607	09/14/88	CFM56-3C1	9935	
B737-322	N336UA	UNITED AIRLINES		24240	1609	09/20/88	CFM56-3C1	9936	
B737-322	N337UA	UNITED AIRLINES		24241	1611	09/21/88	CFM56-3C1	9937	
B737-322	N338UA	UNITED AIRLINES		24242	1613	09/28/88	CFM56-3C1	9938	
B737-322	N339UA	UNITED AIRLINES		24243	1615	10/03/88	CFM56-3C1	9939	
B737-322	N340UA	UNITED AIRLINES		24244	1617	10/11/88	CFM56-3C1	9940	
B737-322	N341UA	UNITED AIRLINES		24245	1619	10/11/88	CFM56-3C1	9941	
B737-322	N342UA	UNITED AIRLINES		24246	1632	11/08/88	CFM56-3C1	9942	
B737-322	N343UA	UNITED AIRLINES		24247	1634	11/14/88	CFM56-3C1	9943	
B737-322	N344UA	UNITED AIRLINES		24248	1636	11/16/88	CFM56-3C1	9944	
B737-322	N345UA	UNITED AIRLINES		24249	1638	11/21/88	CFM56-3C1	9945	
B737-322	N346UA	UNITED AIRLINES		24250	1644	12/08/88	CFM56-3C1	9946	
B737-322	N347UA	UNITED AIRLINES		24251	1646	12/12/88	CFM56-3C1	9947	
B737-322	N348UA	UNITED AIRLINES		24252	1648	12/14/88	CFM56-3C1	9948	
B737-322	N349UA	UNITED AIRLINES		24253	1650	12/20/88	CFM56-3C1	9949	
B737-322	N350UA	UNITED AIRLINES		24301	1652	01/31/89	CFM56-3C1	9950	
B737-322	N351UA	UNITED AIRLINES		24319	1668	02/09/89	CFM56-3C1	9951	
B737-322	N352UA	UNITED AIRLINES		24320	1670	02/09/89	CFM56-3C1	9952	
B737-322	N353UA	UNITED AIRLINES		24321	1672	02/14/89	CFM56-3C1	9953	
B737-322	N354UA	UNITED AIRLINES		24360	1692	04/03/89	CFM56-3C1	9954	
B737-322	N355UA	UNITED AIRLINES		24361	1694	04/05/89	CFM56-3C1	9955	
B737-322	N356UA	UNITED AIRLINES		24362	1696	04/05/89	CFM56-3C1	9956	
B737-322	N357UA	UNITED AIRLINES		24378	1704	05/01/89	CFM56-3C1	9957	
B737-322	N358UA	UNITED AIRLINES		24379	1724	05/31/89	CFM56-3C1	1358	["SHUTTLE BY UNITED"]
B737-322	N359UA	UNITED AIRLINES		24452	1728	06/09/89	CFM56-3C1	9959	
B737-322	N360UA	UNITED AIRLINES		24453	1730	06/20/89	CFM56-3C1	9960	
B737-322	N361UA	UNITED AIRLINES		24454	1750	07/28/89	CFM56-3C1	9961	
B737-322	N362UA	UNITED AIRLINES		24455	1752	07/31/89	CFM56-3C1	9962	
B737-322	N363UA	UNITED AIRLINES		24532	1754	08/29/89	CFM56-3C1	9963	
B737-322	N364UA	UNITED AIRLINES		24533	1756	08/10/89	CFM56-3C1	9964	
B737-322	N365UA	UNITED AIRLINES		24534	1758	08/14/89	CFM56-3C1	9965	

A/C TYPE	CURRENT REG. NO.	LAST KNOWN OPERATOR (OWNER)	STATUS	ORIGINAL MSN	LINE NO.	DEL. DATE	ENG. TYPE	FLEET NO.	PREV. REG. [COMMENTS]
B737-322	N366UA	UNITED AIRLINES		24535	1760	09/01/89	CFM56-3C1	1366	["SHUTTLE BY UNITED"]
B737-322	N367UA	UNITED AIRLINES		24536	1762	09/01/89	CFM56-3C1	1367	["SHUTTLE BY UNITED"]
B737-322	N368UA	UNITED AIRLINES		24537	1774	09/20/89	CFM56-3C1	9968	
B737-322	N369UA	UNITED AIRLINES		24538	1776	10/03/89	CFM56-3C1	1369	
B737-322	N370UA	UNITED AIRLINES		24539	1778	10/02/89	CFM56-3C1	1370	["SHUTTLE BY UNITED"]
B737-322	N371UA	UNITED AIRLINES		24540	1780	10/03/89	CFM56-3C1	1371	["SHUTTLE BY UNITED"]
B737-322	N372UA	UNITED AIRLINES		24637	1782	10/27/89	CFM56-3C1	1372	["SHUTTLE BY UNITED"]
B737-322	N373UA	UNITED AIRLINES		24638	1784	11/10/89	CFM56-3C1	1373	["SHUTTLE BY UNITED"]
B737-322	N374UA	UNITED AIRLINES		24639	1786	11/30/89	CFM56-3C1	1374	["SHUTTLE BY UNITED"]
B737-322	N375UA	UNITED AIRLINES		24640	1798	12/18/89	CFM56-3C1	1375	["SHUTTLE BY UNITED"]
B737-322	N376UA	UNITED AIRLINES		24641	1802	01/17/90	CFM56-3C1	1376	["SHUTTLE BY UNITED"]
B737-322	N377UA	UNITED AIRLINES		24642	1806	01/24/90	CFM56-3C1	1377	["SHUTTLE BY UNITED"]
B737-322	N378UA	UNITED AIRLINES		24653	1810	01/30/90	CFM56-3C1	1378	["SHUTTLE BY UNITED"]
B737-322	N379UA	UNITED AIRLINES		24654	1812	02/05/90	CFM56-3C1	1379	["SHUTTLE BY UNITED"]
B737-322	N380UA	UNITED AIRLINES		24655	1814	02/09/90	CFM56-3C1	1380	["SHUTTLE BY UNITED"]
B737-322	N381UA	UNITED AIRLINES		24656	1822	02/27/90	CFM56-3C1	1381	["SHUTTLE BY UNITED"]
B737-322	N382UA	UNITED AIRLINES		24657	1830	03/19/90	CFM56-3C1	1382	["SHUTTLE BY UNITED"]
B737-322	N383UA	UNITED AIRLINES		24658	1832	03/20/90	CFM56-3C1	1383	["SHUTTLE BY UNITED"]
B737-322	N384UA	UNITED AIRLINES		24659	1836	03/28/90	CFM56-3C1	1384	["SHUTTLE BY UNITED"]
B737-322	N385UA	UNITED AIRLINES		24660	1838	04/02/90	CFM56-3C1	1385	["SHUTTLE BY UNITED"]
B737-322	N386UA	UNITED AIRLINES		24661	1840	04/05/90	CFM56-3C1	1386	["SHUTTLE BY UNITED"]
B737-322	N387UA	UNITED AIRLINES		24662	1862	05/22/90	CFM56-3C1	1387	["SHUTTLE BY UNITED"]
B737-322	N388UA	UNITED AIRLINES		24663	1875	06/25/90	CFM56-3C1	1388	["SHUTTLE BY UNITED"]
B737-322	N389UA	UNITED AIRLINES		24664	1877	06/26/90	CFM56-3C1	1389	["SHUTTLE BY UNITED"]
B737-322	N390UA	UNITED AIRLINES		24665	1889	07/17/90	CFM56-3C1	1390	["SHUTTLE BY UNITED"]
B737-322	N391UA	UNITED AIRLINES		24666	1891	07/23/90	CFM56-3C1	1391	["SHUTTLE BY UNITED"]
B737-322	N392UA	UNITED AIRLINES		24667	1893	07/26/90	CFM56-3C1	1392	["SHUTTLE BY UNITED"]
B737-322	N393UA	UNITED AIRLINES		24668	1905	08/14/90	CFM56-3C1	1393	["SHUTTLE BY UNITED"]
B737-322	N394UA	UNITED AIRLINES		24669	1907	08/20/90	CFM56-3C1	1394	["SHUTTLE BY UNITED"]
B737-322	N395UA	UNITED AIRLINES		24670	1909	08/21/90	CFM56-3C1	1395	["SHUTTLE BY UNITED"]
B737-322	N396UA	UNITED AIRLINES		24671	1913	09/12/90	CFM56-3C1	1396	["SHUTTLE BY UNITED"]
B737-322	N397UA	UNITED AIRLINES		24672	1915	09/14/90	CFM56-3C1	1397	["SHUTTLE BY UNITED"]
B737-322	N398UA	UNITED AIRLINES (SSBT)		24673	1920	09/24/90	CFM56-3C1	1398	["SHUTTLE BY UNITED"]
B737-322	N399UA	UNITED AIRLINES (SSBT)		24674	1928	10/09/90	CFM56-3C1	1399	["SHUTTLE BY UNITED"]
B737-301	N300AU	US AIRWAYS (CMTC)		23228	1103	04/19/85	CFM56-3B1		N301P
B737-301	N334US	US AIRWAYS (FIRST UNION)		23231	1164	12/04/85	CFM56-3B1		N313P
B737-301	N335US	US AIRWAYS (FIRST UNION)		23232	1169	12/12/85	CFM56-3B1		N314P
B737-301	N336US	US AIRWAYS		23233	1200	03/04/86	CFM56-3B1		N315P
B737-301	N337US	US AIRWAYS		23235	1214	04/03/86	CFM56-3B1		N317P
B737-301	N338US	US AIRWAYS		23234	1208	03/14/86	CFM56-3B1		N316P

A/C TYPE	CURRENT REG. NO.	LAST KNOWN OPERATOR (OWNER)	STATUS	ORIGINAL MSN	LINE NO.	DEL. DATE	ENG. TYPE	FLEET NO.	PREV. REG. [COMMENTS]
B737-301	N339US	US AIRWAYS (FIRST UNION)		23236	1219	05/01/86	CFM56-3B1		N319P
B737-301	N340US	US AIRWAYS (FIRST UNION)		23237	1222	05/01/86	CFM56-3B1		N320P
B737-301	N341US	US AIRWAYS (FIRST UNION)		23510	1248	07/09/86	CFM56-3B1		N321P [LAST 737-300 IN SHUTTLE SERVICE; RETURNED TO MAINLINE 11/00]
B737-301	N342US	US AIRWAYS (FIRST UNION)		23511	1268	09/03/86	CFM56-3B1		N322P
B737-301	N346US	US AIRWAYS (FIRST UNION)		23515	1355	03/13/87	CFM56-3B1		N326P
B737-301	N349US	US AIRWAYS (FIRST UNION)		23552	1382	05/11/87	CFM56-3B1		N334P
B737-301	N350US	US AIRWAYS		23553	1406	06/30/87	CFM56-3B1		N335P
B737-301	N351US	US AIRWAYS (FIRST UNION)		23554	1408	06/30/87	CFM56-3B1		N336P
B737-301	N352US	US AIRWAYS (FIRST UNION)		23555	1428	08/14/87	CFM56-3B1		N337P
B737-301	N353US	US AIRWAYS (FIRST UNION)		23556	1435	08/28/87	CFM56-3B1		N340P
B737-301	N354US	US AIRWAYS (FIRST UNION)		23557	1437	09/04/87	CFM56-3B1		N341P
B737-301	N355US	US AIRWAYS (FIRST UNION)		23558	1449	09/30/87	CFM56-3B1		N342P
B737-301	N356US	US AIRWAYS (FIRST UNION)		23559	1451	09/30/87	CFM56-3B1		N348P
B737-3B7	N371US	US AIRWAYS (CMTC)		22950	1001	04/30/85	CFM56-3B1		N350AU
B737-3B7	N373US	US AIRWAYS (CMTC)		22952	1015	04/11/85	CFM56-3B1		N352AU
B737-3B7	N374US	US AIRWAYS (CMTC)		22953	1022	11/28/84	CFM56-3B1		N353AU
B737-3B7	N375US	US AIRWAYS (CMTC)		22954	1030	12/05/84	CFM56-3B1		N354AU
B737-3B7	N376US	US AIRWAYS (CMTC)		22955	1043	12/11/84	CFM56-3B1		N355AU
B737-3B7	N383US	US AIRWAYS (CMTC)		22956	1057	12/19/84	CFM56-3B1		N356AU
B737-3B7	N384US	US AIRWAYS (CMTC)		22957	1127	06/28/85	CFM56-3B1		N357AU
B737-3B7	N385US	US AIRWAYS		22958	1137	07/31/85	CFM56-3B1		N358AU
B737-3B7	N387US	US AIRWAYS		22959	1140	08/23/85	CFM56-3B1		N359AU
B737-3B7	N389US	US AIRWAYS		23311	1149	09/18/85	CFM56-3B1		N361AU
B737-3B7	N390US	US AIRWAYS		23312	1162	11/08/85	CFM56-3B1		N362AU
B737-3B7	N391US	US AIRWAYS (CMTC)		23313	1177	12/20/85	CFM56-3B1		N363AU
B737-3B7	N392US	US AIRWAYS (CMTC)		23314	1179	12/20/85	CFM56-3B1		N364AU
B737-3B7	N393US	US AIRWAYS (CMTC)		23315	1210	03/24/86	CFM56-3B1		N365AU
B737-3B7	N394US	US AIRWAYS (CMTC)		23316	1212	03/31/86	CFM56-3B1		N366AU
B737-3B7	N395US	US AIRWAYS (CMTC)		23317	1221	04/23/86	CFM56-3B1		N367AU
B737-3B7	N396US	US AIRWAYS (CMTC)		23318	1234	05/30/86	CFM56-3B1		N368AU
B737-3B7	N397US	US AIRWAYS (CMTC)		23319	1250	07/17/86	CFM56-3B1		N369AU
B737-3B7	N504AU	US AIRWAYS (FIRST UNION)		23379	1362	03/26/87	CFM56-3B2		N373AU
B737-3B7	N505AU	US AIRWAYS (FIRST UNION)		23380	1366	04/07/87	CFM56-3B2		N374AU
B737-3B7	N506AU	US AIRWAYS (FIRST UNION)		23381	1394	06/08/87	CFM56-3B2		N375AU
B737-3B7	N507AU	US AIRWAYS (FIRST UNION)		23382	1410	07/10/87	CFM56-3B2		N376AU
B737-3B7	N508AU	US AIRWAYS (FIRST UNION)		23383	1425	08/11/87	CFM56-3B2		N377AU
B737-3B7	N510AU	US AIRWAYS (FIRST UNION)		23385	1440	09/14/87	CFM56-3B2		N379AU
B737-3B7	N511AU	US AIRWAYS		23594	1442	09/17/87	CFM56-3B2		N380AU
B737-3B7	N512AU	US AIRWAYS		23595	1450	10/05/87	CFM56-3B2		N381AU
B737-3B7	N514AU	US AIRWAYS		23700	1461	10/27/87	CFM56-3B2		N383AU

A/C TYPE	CURRENT REG. NO.	LAST KNOWN OPERATOR (OWNER)	STATUS	ORIGINAL MSN	LINE NO.	DEL. DATE	ENG. TYPE	FLEET NO.	PREV. REG. [COMMENTS]
B737-3B7	N515AU	US AIRWAYS		23701	1464	11/03/87	CFM56-3B2		N384AU
B737-3B7	N516AU	US AIRWAYS		23702	1475	11/25/87	CFM56-3B2		N385AU
B737-3B7	N517AU	US AIRWAYS		23703	1480	12/14/87	CFM56-3B2		N386AU
B737-3B7	N518AU	US AIRWAYS		23704	1488	12/23/87	CFM56-3B2		N387AU
B737-3B7	N519AU	US AIRWAYS		23705	1497	01/27/88	CFM56-3B2		N388AU
B737-3B7	N520AU	US AIRWAYS		23706	1499	02/01/88	CFM56-3B2		N389AU
B737-3B7	N521AU	US AIRWAYS		23856	1501	02/10/88	CFM56-3B2		N390AU
B737-3B7	N522AU	US AIRWAYS		23857	1503	03/14/88	CFM56-3B2		N391AU
B737-3B7	N523AU	US AIRWAYS (FIRST UNION)		23858	1509	04/13/88	CFM56-3B2		N392AU
B737-3B7	N524AU	US AIRWAYS (FIRST UNION)		23859	1551	05/16/88	CFM56-3B2		N393AU
B737-3B7	N525AU	US AIRWAYS		23860	1560	06/06/88	CFM56-3B2		N394AU
B737-3B7	N526AU	US AIRWAYS		23861	1584	07/27/88	CFM56-3B2		N395AU
B737-3B7	N527AU	US AIRWAYS		23862	1586	08/02/88	CFM56-3B2		N396AU
B737-3B7	N528AU	US AIRWAYS		24410	1703	04/17/89	CFM56-3B2		
B737-3B7	N529AU	US AIRWAYS		24411	1713	05/09/89	CFM56-3B2		
B737-3B7	N530AU	US AIRWAYS		24412	1735	06/26/89	CFM56-3B2		
B737-3B7	N531AU	US AIRWAYS		24478	1743	07/11/89	CFM56-3B2		
B737-3B7	N532AU	US AIRWAYS		24479	1745	07/17/89	CFM56-3B2		
B737-3B7	N533AU	US AIRWAYS		24515	1767	09/01/89	CFM56-3B2		
B737-3B7	N534AU	US AIRWAYS		24516	1769	09/01/89	CFM56-3B2		
B737-301	N558AU	US AIRWAYS (FIRST UNION)		23512	1291	10/16/86	CFM56-3B2		N323P, N343US
B737-301	N559AU	US AIRWAYS (FIRST UNION)		23513	1327	01/13/87	CFM56-3B2		N324P, N344US
B737-301	N560AU	US AIRWAYS		23514	1331	01/22/87	CFM56-3B2		N325P, N345US
B737-301	N562AU	US AIRWAYS (FIRST UNION)		23550	1367	04/08/87	CFM56-3B2		N327P, N347US
B737-301	N563AU	US AIRWAYS (FIRST UNION)		23551	1380	05/06/87	CFM56-3B2		N328P, N348US
B737-301	N573US	US AIRWAYS		23560	1463	10/30/87	CFM56-3B2		N349P, N357US
B737-301	N574US	US AIRWAYS		23739	1469	11/16/87	CFM56-3B2		N350P, N358US
B737-301	N575US	US AIRWAYS (FIRST UNION)		23740	1477	12/02/87	CFM56-3B2		N352P, N359US
B737-301	N576US	US AIRWAYS		23741	1498	01/26/88	CFM56-3B2		N353P, N360US
B737-301	N577US	US AIRWAYS		23742	1502	02/02/88	CFM56-3B2		N354P, N361US
B737-301	N584US	US AIRWAYS		23743	1510	02/19/88	CFM56-3B2		N355P
B737-301	N585US	US AIRWAYS (FIRST UNION)		23930	1539	04/20/88	CFM56-3B2		N357P
B737-301	N586US	US AIRWAYS (FIRST UNION)		23931	1552	05/18/88	CFM56-3B2		N358P
B737-301	N587US	US AIRWAYS (FIRST UNION)		23932	1554	05/24/88	CFM56-3B2		N359P
B737-301	N588US	US AIRWAYS		23933	1559	06/02/88	CFM56-3B2		
B737-301	N589US	US AIRWAYS		23934	1563	06/10/88	CFM56-3B2		
B737-301	N590US	US AIRWAYS		23935	1569	07/01/88	CFM56-3B2		
B737-301	N591US	US AIRWAYS		23936	1575	07/07/88	CFM56-3B2		
B737-301	N592US	US AIRWAYS		23937	1587	08/02/88	CFM56-3B2		
B737-401	N404US	US AIRWAYS		23886	1487	03/02/89	CFM56-3B2		N73700
B737-401	N405US	US AIRWAYS		23885	1512	02/28/89	CFM56-3B2		

A/C TYPE	CURRENT REG. NO.	LAST KNOWN OPERATOR (OWNER)	STATUS	ORIGINAL MSN	LINE NO.	DEL. DATE	ENG. TYPE	FLEET NO.	PREV. REG. [COMMENTS]
B737-401	N406US	US AIRWAYS		23876	1528	09/15/88	CFM56-3B2		
B737-401	N407US	US AIRWAYS		23877	1543	09/21/88	CFM56-3B2		
B737-401	N408US	US AIRWAYS		23878	1561	09/27/88	CFM56-3B2		
B737-401	N409US	US AIRWAYS		23879	1573	09/28/88	CFM56-3B2		
B737-401	N411US	US AIRWAYS		23880	1596	10/19/88	CFM56-3B2		
B737-401	N412US	US AIRWAYS		23881	1610	10/31/88	CFM56-3B2		
B737-401	N413US	US AIRWAYS		23882	1621	11/14/88	CFM56-3B2		
B737-401	N415US	US AIRWAYS		23883	1631	11/22/88	CFM56-3B2		
B737-401	N417US	US AIRWAYS		23984	1674	02/15/89	CFM56-3B2		
B737-401	N418US	US AIRWAYS		23985	1676	02/17/89	CFM56-3B2		
B737-401	N419US	US AIRWAYS		23986	1684	03/07/89	CFM56-3B2		
B737-401	N420US	US AIRWAYS		23987	1698	04/05/89	CFM56-3B2		
B737-401	N421US	US AIRWAYS		23988	1714	05/11/89	CFM56-3B2		
B737-401	N422US	US AIRWAYS		23989	1716	05/12/89	CFM56-3B2		
B737-401	N423US	US AIRWAYS		23990	1732	06/19/89	CFM56-3B2		
B737-401	N424US	US AIRWAYS		23991	1746	07/18/89	CFM56-3B2		
B737-401	N425US	US AIRWAYS		23992	1764	08/25/89	CFM56-3B2		
B737-4B7	N426US	US AIRWAYS		24548	1789	10/20/89	CFM56-3B2		
B737-4B7	N427US	US AIRWAYS		24549	1791	11/14/89	CFM56-3B2		
B737-4B7	N428US	US AIRWAYS		24550	1793	12/07/89	CFM56-3B2		
B737-4B7	N429US	US AIRWAYS		24551	1795	12/08/89	CFM56-3B2		
B737-4B7	N430US	US AIRWAYS		24552	1797	12/14/89	CFM56-3B2		
B737-4B7	N431US	US AIRWAYS		24553	1799	12/22/89	CFM56-3B2		
B737-4B7	N432US	US AIRWAYS		24554	1817	02/14/90	CFM56-3B2		
B737-4B7	N433US	US AIRWAYS		24555	1819	02/20/90	CFM56-3B2		
B737-4B7	N434US	US AIRWAYS		24556	1821	02/23/90	CFM56-3B2		
B737-4B7	N435US	US AIRWAYS		24557	1835	03/26/90	CFM56-3B2		
B737-4B7	N436US	US AIRWAYS		24558	1845	04/16/90	CFM56-3B2		
B737-4B7	N437US	US AIRWAYS		24559	1847	04/19/90	CFM56-3B2		
B737-4B7	N438US	US AIRWAYS		24560	1849	04/24/90	CFM56-3B2		
B737-4B7	N439US	US AIRWAYS		24781	1874	06/18/90	CFM56-3B2		
B737-4B7	N440US	US AIRWAYS		24811	1890	07/18/90	CFM56-3B2		
B737-4B7	N441US	US AIRWAYS		24812	1892	07/23/90	CFM56-3B2		
B737-4B7	N442US	US AIRWAYS		24841	1906	08/15/90	CFM56-3B2		
B737-4B7	N443US	US AIRWAYS		24842	1908	08/20/90	CFM56-3B2		
B737-4B7	N444US	US AIRWAYS		24862	1910	08/24/90	CFM56-3B2		
B737-4B7	N445US	US AIRWAYS		24863	1914	09/13/90	CFM56-3B2		
B737-4B7	N446US	US AIRWAYS		24873	1931	10/12/90	CFM56-3B2		
B737-4B7	N447US	US AIRWAYS		24874	1936	10/23/90	CFM56-3B2		
B737-4B7	N448US	US AIRWAYS		24892	1944	11/06/90	CFM56-3B2		
B737-4B7	N449US	US AIRWAYS		24893	1946	11/09/90	CFM56-3B2		

A/C TYPE	CURRENT REG. NO.	LAST KNOWN OPERATOR (OWNER)	STATUS	ORIGINAL MSN	LINE NO.	DEL. DATE	ENG. TYPE	FLEET NO.	PREV. REG. [COMMENTS]
B737-4B7	N775AU	US AIRWAYS		24933	1954	11/29/90	CFM56-3B2		
B737-4B7	N776AU	US AIRWAYS		24934	1956	11/29/90	CFM56-3B2		
B737-4B7	N777AU	US AIRWAYS		24979	1980	01/18/91	CFM56-3B2		
B737-4B7	N778AU	US AIRWAYS		24980	1982	01/22/91	CFM56-3B2		
B737-4B7	N779AU	US AIRWAYS		24996	1986	01/28/91	CFM56-3B2		
B737-4B7	N780AU	US AIRWAYS		24997	1990	02/07/91	CFM56-3B2		
B737-4B7	N781AU	US AIRWAYS		25020	1992	02/04/91	CFM56-3B2		
B737-4B7	N782AU	US AIRWAYS		25021	1995	02/14/91	CFM56-3B2		
B737-4B7	N783AU	US AIRWAYS		25022	2010	03/27/91	CFM56-3B2		
B737-4B7	N784AU	US AIRWAYS		25023	2020	04/03/91	CFM56-3B2		
B737-4B7	N785AU	US AIRWAYS		25024	2026	04/09/91	CFM56-3B2		

OB-PERU

A/C TYPE	CURRENT REG. NO.	LAST KNOWN OPERATOR (OWNER)	STATUS	ORIGINAL MSN	LINE NO.	DEL. DATE	ENG. TYPE	FLEET NO.	PREV. REG. [COMMENTS]
B737-528	FAP 356	FUERZA AEREA DEL PERU		27426	2739	09/01/95	CFM56-3C1		PRP-001 [VIP FOR PRESIDENT OF PERU]

OE-AUSTRIA

A/C TYPE	CURRENT REG. NO.	LAST KNOWN OPERATOR (OWNER)	STATUS	ORIGINAL MSN	LINE NO.	DEL. DATE	ENG. TYPE	FLEET NO.	PREV. REG. [COMMENTS]
B737-3Z9	OE-ILF	LAUDA AIR		23601	1254	07/28/86	CFM56-3B1		
B737-3Z9	OE-ILG	LAUDA AIR		24081	1515	03/02/88	CFM56-3B1		
B737-4Z9	OE-LNH	LAUDA AIR		25147	2043	05/07/91	CFM56-3C1		
B737-4Z9	OE-LNI	LAUDA AIR		27094	2432	02/23/93	CFM56-3C1		

OK-CZECH REPUBLIC

A/C TYPE	CURRENT REG. NO.	LAST KNOWN OPERATOR (OWNER)	STATUS	ORIGINAL MSN	LINE NO.	DEL. DATE	ENG. TYPE	FLEET NO.	PREV. REG. [COMMENTS]
B737-55S	OK-CGH	CSA CZECH AIRLINES		28469	2849	03/12/97	CFM56-3C1		
B737-55S	OK-CGJ	CSA CZECH AIRLINES		28470	2861	03/12/97	CFM56-3C1		
B737-55S	OK-CGK	CSA CZECH AIRLINES		28471	2885	05/23/97	CFM56-3C1		
B737-55S	OK-DGL	CSA CZECH AIRLINES		28472	3004	03/18/98	CFM56-3C1		N1786B
B737-55S	OK-EGO	CSA CZECH AIRLINES		28475	3096	02/17/99	CFM56-3C1		N1786B
B737-55S	OK-XGA	CSA CZECH AIRLINES		26539	2300	06/15/92	CFM56-3C1		N1790B
B737-55S	OK-XGB	CSA CZECH AIRLINES		26540	2317	07/06/92	CFM56-3C1		
B737-55S	OK-XGC	CSA CZECH AIRLINES		26541	2319	07/03/92	CFM56-3C1		
B737-55S	OK-XGD	CSA CZECH AIRLINES		26542	2337	07/03/92	CFM56-3C1		
B737-55S	OK-XGE	CSA CZECH AIRLINES		26543	2339	08/07/92	CFM56-3C1		
B737-43Q	OK-BGQ	CSA CZECH AIRLINES (BOUL)		28494	2839	12/20/96	CFM56-3C1		B-18677, N462PR
B737-49R	OK-CGI	CSA CZECH AIRLINES (KG LSG)		28882	2845	06/09/97	CFM56-3C1		N1786B, N3505D, N461PR
B737-45S	OK-DGM	CSA CZECH AIRLINES		28473	3014	04/07/98	CFM56-3C1		
B737-45S	OK-DGN	CSA CZECH AIRLINES		28474	3028	05/18/98	CFM56-3C1		
B737-45S	OK-EGP	CSA CZECH AIRLINES		28476	3103	03/19/99	CFM56-3C1		N1786B
B737-45S	OK-FGR	CSA CZECH AIRLINES		28477	3131	02/25/00	CFM56-3C1		
B737-45S	OK-FGS	CSA CZECH AIRLINES		28478	3132	02/25/00	CFM56-3C1		[LAST B737-400 AND "CLASSIC"]
B737-4Y0	OK-WGF	CSA CZECH AIRLINES (GECA)		24903	1978	01/17/91	CFM56-3C1		9M-MJN
B737-33A	OK-FAN	FISCHER AIR		27469	2864	03/26/97	CFM56-3C1		

A/C TYPE	CURRENT REG. NO.	LAST KNOWN OPERATOR (OWNER)	STATUS	ORIGINAL MSN	LINE NO.	DEL. DATE	ENG. TYPE	FLEET NO.	PREV. REG. [COMMENTS]
B737-36N	OK-FIT	FISCHER AIR (GECA)		28590	3097	03/15/99	CFM56-3C1		N1787B
B737-33A	OK-FUN	FISCHER AIR		27910	2873	04/18/97	CFM56-3C1		
B737-4Q8	OK-TVP	TRAVEL SERVICE AIRLINES (ILFC)		24234	1627	10/28/88	CFM56-3C1		OO-ILH, N521LF, N403KW, XA-TKM, N242GD, A6-NGA
B737-4Y0	OK-TVR	TRAVEL SERVICE AIRLINES (GECA)		23870	1647	03/31/89	CFM56-3C1		N1791B, G-OBMG

OO-BELGIUM

A/C TYPE	CURRENT REG. NO.	LAST KNOWN OPERATOR (OWNER)	STATUS	ORIGINAL MSN	LINE NO.	DEL. DATE	ENG. TYPE	FLEET NO.	PREV. REG. [COMMENTS]
B737-43Q	OO-CTG	CITY BIRD (GECA)		28491	2832	11/22/96	CFM56-3C1		B-18673, TC-IAG [XFRD TO CITY BIRD FRANCE AS F-GLTG]
B737-46Q	OO-CTV	CITY BIRD (BOUL)		29000	3033	06/01/98	CFM56-3C1		TC-IAA, N283CD
B737-46Q	OO-CTW	CITY BIRD (BOUL)		29001	3040	06/12/98	CFM56-3C1		TC-IAB, N284CD
B737-3L9	OO-CTX	CITY BIRD (CITG)		23718	1402	06/26/87	CFM56-3B2		OY-MMN, G-BOZA, 9H-ADP, PH-OZA, N2371
B737-405	OO-VEK	CITY BIRD (VEX)	L	24270	1726	06/07/89	CFM56-3C1		LN-BRA
B737-529	OO-SYE	SABENA (S.N.C.I.)		25218	2111	09/04/91	CFM56-3C1		
B737-529	OO-SYG	SABENA		25249	2145	10/31/91	CFM56-3C1		
B737-529	OO-SYH	SABENA (CITG)		25418	2163	11/27/91	CFM56-3C1		
B737-529	OO-SYI	SABENA (CITG)		25419	2165	11/27/91	CFM56-3C1		
B737-529	OO-SYJ	SABENA		26537	2296	06/01/92	CFM56-3C1		
B737-529	OO-SYK	SABENA		26538	2298	06/05/92	CFM56-3C1		
B737-329	OO-SDV	SABENA (CITG)		23771	1430	08/25/87	CFM56-3B2		
B737-329	OO-SDW	SABENA (CITG)		23772	1432	08/26/87	CFM56-3B2		
B737-329	OO-SDX	SABENA		23773	1441	09/15/87	CFM56-3B2		
B737-329	OO-SDY	SABENA		23774	1443	09/18/87	CFM56-3B2		
B737-329	OO-SYA	SABENA (SL SAB)		24355	1709	04/28/89	CFM56-3B2		
B737-329	OO-SYB	SABENA (SL SAB)		24356	1711	05/02/89	CFM56-3B2		
B737-429	OO-SYC	SABENA (WTCI)		25226	2104	08/13/91	CFM56-3C1		N933NU [LST SLR]
B737-3M8	OO-SBX	SOBELAIR (BBAM)		25040	2017	03/22/91	CFM56-3B2		OO-LTK, VR-CRC, TC-BIR
B737-329	OO-SBZ	SOBELAIR		23775	1412	07/17/87	CFM56-3B2		
B737-408	OO-RMV	SOBELAIR (SUNR)		24352	1705	04/28/89	CFM56-3C1		TF-FIA, OO-BXA
B737-46B	OO-SBJ	SOBELAIR (LLOYDS)		24573	1844	04/12/90	CFM56-3C1		G-BROC
B737-429	OO-SBM	SOBELAIR (EUROLEASE)		25729	2217	02/14/92	CFM56-3C1		
B737-429	OO-SYC	SOBELAIR (SAB)	L	25226	2104	08/13/91	CFM56-3C1		N933NU
B737-405	OO-VEJ	SOBELAIR (VEX)	L	24271	1738	06/29/89	CFM56-3C1		LN-BRB
B737-3M8	OO-LTL	VIRGIN EXPRESS (BALTIC)		25041	2024	04/05/91	CFM56-3B2		EI-TVP
B737-3M8	OO-LTM	VIRGIN EXPRESS (LOCABEL)		25070	2037	05/21/91	CFM56-3B2		F-GLTM, F-GMTM
B737-33A	OO-LTP	VIRGIN EXPRESS (AWAS)		25032	2014	04/10/91	CFM56-3C1		PP-SOG
B737-33A	OO-LTU	VIRGIN EXPRESS (AWAS)		27455	2709	04/04/95	CFM56-3C1		

A/C TYPE	CURRENT REG. NO.	LAST KNOWN OPERATOR (OWNER)	STATUS	ORIGINAL MSN	LINE NO.	DEL. DATE	ENG. TYPE	FLEET NO.	PREV. REG. [COMMENTS]
B737-33A	OO-LTW	VIRGIN EXPRESS (AWAS)		25010	2008	03/07/91	CFM56-3C1		PP-SOE, N226AW, VH-OAM
B737-36N	OO-VEG	VIRGIN EXPRESS (GECA)		28568	2987	02/04/98	CFM56-3C1		EI-TVQ
B737-36N	OO-VEH	VIRGIN EXPRESS (GECA)		28571	3022	04/28/98	CFM56-3C1		EI-TVR
B737-36N	OO-VEN	VIRGIN EXPRESS		28586	3090	01/19/99	CFM56-3C1		N1786B, EI-TVN
B737-36N	OO-VEX	VIRGIN EXPRESS (GECA)		28670	2948	11/18/97	CFM56-3C1		EI-TVS
B737-4Y0	OO-VBR	VIRGIN EXPRESS (ANTWERP)		24314	1680	02/28/89	CFM56-3C1		HL7256, F-GMBR
B737-46M	OO-VEC	VIRGIN EXPRESS (BBAM)		28549	2844	01/17/97	CFM56-3C1		C-GBIW [LST VIRGIN BLUE 11/00 AS VH-VGC]
B737-430	OO-VEF	VIRGIN EXPRESS (OASI)		27000	2311	07/02/92	CFM56-3C1		D-ABKA
B737-405	OO-VEJ	VIRGIN EXPRESS (INGO)		24271	1738	06/29/89	CFM56-3C1		LN-BRB [LST SLR]
B737-405	OO-VEK	VIRGIN EXPRESS (INGO)		24270	1726	06/07/89	CFM56-3C1		LN-BRA [LST CTB 11/01/00]
B737-4Y0	OO-VJO	VIRGIN EXPRESS (CITG)		23980	1667	01/28/89	CFM56-3C1		HL7255, F-GMJO [LST VIRGIN BLUE 11/00 AS VH-VGD]

OY-DENMARK

A/C TYPE	CURRENT REG. NO.	LAST KNOWN OPERATOR (OWNER)	STATUS	ORIGINAL MSN	LINE NO.	DEL. DATE	ENG. TYPE	FLEET NO.	PREV. REG. [COMMENTS]
B737-5L9	OY-APA	MAERSK AIR (ELL)	L	28083	2784	04/08/96	CFM56-3C1		ES-ABE [LST ROT 05/06/00 AS YR-BGT; OO TO ANA 09/01 AS N356K]
B737-5L9	OY-APB	MAERSK AIR		28084	2788	04/26/96	CFM56-3C1		[LST MSK AS G-MSKE]
B737-5L9	OY-APD	MAERSK AIR		28130	2825	10/24/96	CFM56-3C1		[OO TO ANA 04/02 AS JA358K]
B737-5L9	OY-APG	MAERSK AIR		28131	2828	11/12/96	CFM56-3C1		[OO TO ANA 01/02 AS JA357K]
B737-5L9	OY-APH	MAERSK AIR		28721	2856	02/24/97	CFM56-3C1		
B737-5L9	OY-API	MAERSK AIR		28722	2868	03/25/97	CFM56-3C1		
B737-5L9	OY-APK	MAERSK AIR		28995	2947	10/31/97	CFM56-3C1		
B737-5L9	OY-APL	MAERSK AIR		28996	2998	02/18/98	CFM56-3C1		[LST LOT AS SP-LKK]
B737-5L9	OY-APN	MAERSK AIR		28997	3008	03/23/98	CFM56-3C1		
B737-5L9	OY-APP	MAERSK AIR		29234	3068	08/31/98	CFM56-3C1		N1786B
B737-5L9	OY-APR	MAERSK AIR		29235	3076	10/21/98	CFM56-3C1		N1786B
B737-5L9	OY-MAA	MAERSK AIR		24778	1816	04/06/90	CFM56-3B1		G-MSKD [LST AMC 04/01/01]
B737-5L9	OY-MAE	MAERSK AIR		25066	2038	05/17/91	CFM56-3B1		[LST MSK 11/96 AS G-MSKC]
B737-5L9	OY-MAF	MAERSK AIR (F. SALLING)		28128	2817	09/23/96	CFM56-3C1		[OO TO ANA 04/02 AS JA359K]

PH-NETHERLANDS

A/C TYPE	CURRENT REG. NO.	LAST KNOWN OPERATOR (OWNER)	STATUS	ORIGINAL MSN	LINE NO.	DEL. DATE	ENG. TYPE	FLEET NO.	PREV. REG. [COMMENTS]
B737-306	PH-BDA	KLM (GECA)		23537	1275	09/30/86	CFM56-3B1		
B737-306	PH-BDB	KLM (GECA)		23538	1288	10/14/86	CFM56-3B1		
B737-306	PH-BDC	KLM (GECA)		23539	1295	10/29/86	CFM56-3B1		
B737-306	PH-BDD	KLM (GECA)		23540	1303	11/13/86	CFM56-3B1		
B737-306	PH-BDE	KLM (GECA)		23541	1309	11/29/86	CFM56-3B1		
B737-306	PH-BDG	KLM (GECA)		23542	1317	12/17/86	CFM56-3B1		
B737-306	PH-BDK	KLM (GECA)		23545	1343	02/04/87	CFM56-3B1		
B737-306	PH-BDN	KLM (LABORA)		24261	1640	11/30/88	CFM56-3B1		
B737-306	PH-BDO	KLM (BORA)		24262	1642	12/02/88	CFM56-3B1		
B737-306	PH-BDP	KLM (ORIX)		24404	1681	03/07/89	CFM56-3B1		

A/C TYPE	CURRENT REG. NO.	LAST KNOWN OPERATOR (OWNER)	STATUS	ORIGINAL MSN	LINE NO.	DEL. DATE	ENG. TYPE	FLEET NO.	PREV. REG. [COMMENTS]
B737-306	PH-BTD	KLM (DIA LTD)		27420	2406	12/18/92	CFM56-3B1		
B737-306	PH-BTE	KLM (DIA LTD)		27421	2438	03/06/93	CFM56-3B1		
B737-306	PH-BTH	KLM		28719	2930	10/08/97	CFM56-3B1		
B737-306	PH-BTI	KLM		28720	2957	12/17/97	CFM56-3B1		
B737-406	PH-BDR	KLM (KNIGHT)		24514	1768	09/06/89	CFM56-3B2		
B737-406	PH-BDS	KLM (CASTLE)		24529	1770	09/23/89	CFM56-3B2		
B737-406	PH-BDT	KLM (BISHOP)		24530	1772	09/28/89	CFM56-3B2		
B737-406	PH-BDU	KLM (LIBRA)		24857	1902	08/14/90	CFM56-3B2		
B737-406	PH-BDW	KLM (LIBRA)		24858	1903	08/21/90	CFM56-3B2		
B737-406	PH-BDY	KLM (MOLEN)		24959	1949	11/17/90	CFM56-3B2		
B737-406	PH-BDZ	KLM		25355	2132	10/10/91	CFM56-3B2		
B737-4Y0	PH-BPB	KLM (GECA)		24344	1723	05/25/89	CFM56-3C1		9M-MJL, 9M-MLI, G-UKLB
B737-4Y0	PH-BPC	KLM (GECA)		24468	1747	07/19/89	CFM56-3C1		G-UKLE
B737-406	PH-BTA	KLM (BLUE WING)		25412	2161	11/16/91	CFM56-3B2		
B737-406	PH-BTB	KLM (CF TOPAZ)		25423	2184	01/15/92	CFM56-3B2		
B737-406	PH-BTC	KLM (SF CANAL)		25424	2200	02/06/92	CFM56-3B2		
B737-406	PH-BTF	KLM (WOOD)		27232	2591	03/25/94	CFM56-3B2		
B737-406	PH-BTG	KLM (FRESH)		27233	2601	04/20/94	CFM56-3B2		
B737-3K2	PH-HVM	TRANSAVIA AIRLINES (CMK AIRCRAFT)		24326	1683	03/08/89	CFM56-3B2		[LST VSP NTU]
B737-3K2	PH-HVN	TRANSAVIA AIRLINES (CMK AIRCRAFT)		24327	1712	05/04/89	CFM56-3B2		[OPF AFR]
B737-3K2	PH-HVT	TRANSAVIA AIRLINES (CMK AIRCRAFT)		24328	1856	05/03/90	CFM56-3C1		
B737-3K2	PH-HVV	TRANSAVIA AIRLINES (CMK AIRCRAFT)		24329	1858	05/11/90	CFM56-3C1		
B737-3L9	PH-TSW	TRANSAVIA AIRLINES (CITG)		24219	1600	09/14/88	CFM56-3B2		G-BOZB, OY-MMO
B737-3K2	PH-TSY	TRANSAVIA AIRLINES (ILFC)		28085	2722	05/30/95	CFM56-3C1		[OO FOR LST ANZ 12/00 AS ZK-NGM]
B737-3K2	PH-TSZ	TRANSAVIA AIRLINES (ILFC)		27635	2721	05/17/95	CFM56-3C1		[OO FOR LST ANZ 04/01 AS ZK-NGO]

PK-INDONESIA

A/C TYPE	CURRENT REG. NO.	LAST KNOWN OPERATOR (OWNER)	STATUS	ORIGINAL MSN	LINE NO.	DEL. DATE	ENG. TYPE	FLEET NO.	PREV. REG. [COMMENTS]
B737-5U3	PK-GGA	GARUDA INDONESIA		28726	2920	12/26/97	CFM56-3C1		
B737-5U3	PK-GGC	GARUDA INDONESIA		28727	2937	12/26/97	CFM56-3C1		
B737-5U3	PK-GGD	GARUDA INDONESIA		28728	2938	12/27/97	CFM56-3C1		
B737-5U3	PK-GGE	GARUDA INDONESIA		28729	2950	12/31/98	CFM56-3C1		N3509J, N60436
B737-5U3	PK-GGF	GARUDA INDONESIA		28730	2952	12/27/97	CFM56-3C1		
B737-3U3	PK-GGG	GARUDA INDONESIA		28731	2949	12/31/97	CFM56-3C1		
B737-3U3	PK-GGN	GARUDA INDONESIA		28735	3029	12/29/98	CFM56-3C1		N6069E, N5002KN, N5573K
B737-3U3	PK-GGO	GARUDA INDONESIA		28736	3032	12/29/98	CFM56-3C1		N3134C
B737-3U3	PK-GGP	GARUDA INDONESIA		28737	3037	12/29/98	CFM56-3C1		N1799B, N1020L
B737-3U3	PK-GGQ	GARUDA INDONESIA		28739	3064	12/29/98	CFM56-3C1		N1799B, N6069D, N1024A
B737-3U3	PK-GGR	GARUDA INDONESIA		28741	3079	12/29/98	CFM56-3C1		N1799B, N1026G
B737-3Q8	PK-GWA	GARUDA INDONESIA (ILFC)		24403	1706	04/24/89	CFM56-3B1		
B737-4U3	PK-GWK	GARUDA INDONESIA		25713	2531	10/15/93	CFM56-3C1		

A/C TYPE	CURRENT REG. NO.	LAST KNOWN OPERATOR (OWNER)	STATUS	ORIGINAL MSN	LINE NO.	DEL. DATE	ENG. TYPE	FLEET NO.	PREV. REG. [COMMENTS]
B737-4U3	PK-GWL	GARUDA INDONESIA		25714	2535	12/23/93	CFM56-3C1		N6067B
B737-4U3	PK-GWM	GARUDA INDONESIA		25715	2537	10/25/93	CFM56-3C1		
B737-4U3	PK-GWN	GARUDA INDONESIA		25716	2540	11/01/93	CFM56-3C1		
B737-4U3	PK-GWO	GARUDA INDONESIA		25717	2546	11/09/93	CFM56-3C1		
B737-4U3	PK-GWP	GARUDA INDONESIA		25718	2548	12/23/93	CFM56-3C1		
B737-4U3	PK-GWQ	GARUDA INDONESIA		25719	2549	12/23/93	CFM56-3C1		
B737-4K5	PK-GWT	GARUDA INDONESIA (ILFC)		26316	2711	04/05/95	CFM56-3C1		D-AHLG
B737-4Q8	PK-GWU	GARUDA INDONESIA (ILFC)		24708	2076	07/02/91	CFM56-3C1		9M-MJF, OO-LTT, N631LF, VT-SIC, N708KS
B737-4Y0	PK-GWV	GARUDA INDONESIA (GECA)		24512	1777	09/21/89	CFM56-3C1		VR-CAL, TC-AGA, N512GE
B737-4Y0	PK-GWW	GARUDA INDONESIA (GECA)		24683	1901	08/07/90	CFM56-3C1		PP-SOH, HR-SHL, 9M-MJR, TC-AYA, N683GE
B737-4Y0	PK-GWX	GARUDA INDONESIA (ELASIS)		24691	1904	08/09/90	CFM56-3C1		PP-SOI, HR-SHK, 9M-MJS, TC-AZA, N691GE
B737-43Q	PK-GWY	GARUDA INDONESIA (GECA)		28490	2830	11/22/96	CFM56-3C1		B-18672, TC-IAF, N490GE
B737-49R	PK-GWZ	GARUDA INDONESIA (GECA)		28881	2833	06/27/97	CFM56-3C1		N1790B, N460PR
B737-4Q8	PK-	GARUDA INDONESIA (ILFC)		24705	1971	12/21/90	CFM56-3C1		9M-MJC, TC-AFY, N621LF, VT-SID

PP/PR/PT-BRAZIL

A/C TYPE	CURRENT REG. NO.	LAST KNOWN OPERATOR (OWNER)	STATUS	ORIGINAL MSN	LINE NO.	DEL. DATE	ENG. TYPE	FLEET NO.	PREV. REG. [COMMENTS]
B737-33A	PR-BRA	BRASIL RODO AEREO (NORWAY BANK)		23830	1462	01/21/88	CFM56-3B2		G-BRXJ, LN-NOS, CS-TKC, 9H-ACT, CS-TIO [RT EURO ATLANTIC 04/01/01?]
B737-4Y0	PP-NAC	NACIONAL TRANSPORTES AEREOS (FUA)	L	24690	1885	07/10/90	CFM56-3C1		TC-AFL, EC-603, EC-FBP, PT-TDA, EC-308, SE-DRR, EI-COU, EC-GHK, EC-GUI [TO BE RT FUA 12/01]
B737-53A	PT-MND	NORDESTE (AWAS)		24786	1898	08/02/90	CFM56-3C1		HL7261
B737-53A	PT-MNE	NORDESTE (AWAS)		24787	1900	08/07/90	CFM56-3C1		HL7262
B737-5Y0	PT-MNH	NORDESTE (AER FI)		26067	2304	06/11/92	CFM56-3C1		DQ-FJB
B737-53A	PT-MNI	NORDESTE (AWAS)		25425	2177	12/06/91	CFM56-3C1		LZ-BOC, N425AN
B737-5Y0	PT-SLN	RIO-SUL (GECA)		26075	2374	10/23/92	CFM56-3B1		
B737-5Y0	PT-SLU	RIO-SUL (GECA)		25186	2236	03/11/92	CFM56-3B1		XA-RKP
B737-53A	PT-SLW	RIO-SUL (AWAS)		24922	1964	12/15/90	CFM56-3B1		CN-RMU
B737-5Y0	PT-SSA	RIO-SUL (GECA)		25192	2262	04/14/92	CFM56-3B1		XA-SAC
B737-5Q8	PT-SSB	RIO-SUL (ILFC)		27629	2834	12/05/96	CFM56-3C1		
B737-5Q8	PT-SSC	RIO-SUL (ILFC)		27634	2889	05/30/97	CFM56-3C1		
B737-56N	PT-SSD	RIO-SUL (GECA)		28565	2944	11/11/97	CFM56-3C1		
B737-5Q8	PT-SSE	RIO-SUL (ILFC)		28052	2965	12/11/97	CFM56-3C1		
B737-5Q8	PT-SSF	RIO-SUL (ILFC)		28201	2999	02/20/98	CFM56-3C1		
B737-5Q8	PT-SSG	RIO-SUL (ILFC)		28055	3024	04/30/98	CFM56-3C1		
B737-58E	PT-SSH	RIO-SUL (SUNR)		29122	2991	06/05/98	CFM56-3C1		N6063S, N291SR
B737-53A	PT-SSI	RIO-SUL (AWAS)		24785	1882	07/13/90	CFM56-3B1		N35135, F-GGML, 5X-USM

A/C TYPE	CURRENT REG. NO.	LAST KNOWN OPERATOR (OWNER)	STATUS	ORIGINAL MSN	LINE NO.	DEL. DATE	ENG. TYPE	FLEET NO.	PREV. REG. [COMMENTS]
B737-5Y0	PT-SSL	RIO-SUL (A/P FIN.)		25185	2220	02/18/92	CFM56-3B1		XA-RJS, G-OBMR
B737-5Y0	PT-SSM	RIO-SUL (GECA)		25191	2260	04/10/92	CFM56-3B1		XA-SAS, N191G, VT-JAL, N191AP
B737-53A	PT-SSN	RIO-SUL (AWAS)		24881	1945	11/07/90	CFM56-3C1		LZ-BOA
B737-53A	PT-SSO	RIO-SUL (AWAS)		24921	1962	12/12/90	CFM56-3C1		LZ-BOB
B737-33A	PT-SSJ	RIO-SUL (AWAS)		24791	1984	02/07/91	CFM56-3C1		PP-SOD, N222AW, VT-JAB, TC-GHB, N791AW
B737-3Y0	PT-SSK	RIO-SUL (EAST)		23922	1538	04/20/88	CFM56-3B2		EC-151, EC-EHZ, EI-BZO, PP-VOM, N922AB, TF-ABK, OO-VEE
B737-3Q4	PT-TEG	TRANSBRASIL (FSBU)		24209	1492	01/12/88	CFM56-3B2		
B737-3Y0	PT-TEI	TRANSBRASIL (CITL)		23812	1511	02/25/88	CFM56-3B1		
B737-33A	PT-TEQ	TRANSBRASIL (AWAS)		25057	2046	06/20/91	CFM56-3C1		PP-SOK, N224AW
B737-33A	PT-TER	TRANSBRASIL (AWAS)		25119	2069	06/20/91	CFM56-3C1		PP-SOL, N225AW
B737-3M8	PT-TET	TRANSBRASIL (SAT FLUG)		25015	1991	02/07/91	CFM56-3B2		OO-LTF, I-TEAI, N799BB, D-AGEK
B737-3K9	PT-TEU	TRANSBRASIL (BIAL)		23797	1416	09/04/87	CFM56-3B2		PP-VNU
B737-3K9	PT-TEV	TRANSBRASIL (BIAL)		23798	1429	09/04/87	CFM56-3B2		PP-VNV
B737-3L9	PT-TEW	TRANSBRASIL (SAT FLUG)		24221	1604	10/21/88	CFM56-3B2		G-CMMR, OY-MMR, OO-SLR, D-AGEJ
B737-33A	PT-TEX	TRANSBRASIL (AWAS)		23827	1444	10/09/87	CFM56-3B2		G-BNXW, LN-NOR, CS-TKD, 9H-ACS, CS-TIN
B737-33A	PP-VNT	VARIG BRASIL (AWAS)		23828	1446	11/10/87	CFM56-3B2		
B737-33A	PP-VNX	VARIG BRASIL (AWAS)		23829	1460	11/10/87	CFM56-3B2		
B737-3K9	PP-VNY	VARIG BRASIL (BIAL)		24864	1918	09/20/90	CFM56-3B2		
B737-3K9	PP-VNZ	VARIG BRASIL (BIAL)		24869	1926	10/02/90	CFM56-3B2		
B737-341	PP-VOD	VARIG BRASIL (GECA)		24275	1637	11/29/88	CFM56-3B2		
B737-341	PP-VOE	VARIG BRASIL (GECA)		24276	1645	12/07/88	CFM56-3B2		
B737-341	PP-VOF	VARIG BRASIL (GECA)		24277	1658	01/12/89	CFM56-3B2		
B737-341	PP-VOG	VARIG BRASIL (GECA)		24278	1660	01/17/89	CFM56-3B2		
B737-341	PP-VOH	VARIG BRASIL (GECA)		24279	1673	02/13/89	CFM56-3B2		
B737-341	PP-VON	VARIG BRASIL (MITSUI)		24935	1935	11/01/90	CFM56-3B2		
B737-341	PP-VOO	VARIG BRASIL (MITSUI)		24936	1951	11/19/90	CFM56-3B2		
B737-33A	PP-VOR	VARIG BRASIL (AWAS)		24093	1727	06/08/89	CFM56-3B2		G-PATE
B737-341	PP-VOS	VARIG BRASIL (ORIX)		25048	2085	07/23/91	CFM56-3B2		
B737-341	PP-VOT	VARIG BRASIL (SL VRG)		25049	2091	07/23/91	CFM56-3B2		
B737-341	PP-VOU	VARIG BRASIL (WTCI)		25050	2125	12/11/91	CFM56-3B2		
B737-341	PP-VOV	VARIG BRASIL (WTCI)		25051	2127	12/11/91	CFM56-3B2		
B737-3Q8	PP-VOW	VARIG BRASIL (ILFC)		24961	2133	10/04/91	CFM56-3B2		
B737-3K9	PP-VOY	VARIG BRASIL (BIAL)		25210	2090	07/19/91	CFM56-3B2		
B737-3K9	PP-VOZ	VARIG BRASIL (BIAL)		25239	2100	08/06/91	CFM56-3B2		
B737-341	PP-VPA	VARIG BRASIL (CITG)		26852	2273	05/20/92	CFM56-3B2		
B737-341	PP-VPB	VARIG BRASIL (BIAL)		26856	2321	07/07/92	CFM56-3B2		
B737-341	PP-VPC	VARIG BRASIL (BIAL)		26857	2326	07/24/92	CFM56-3B2		
B737-3S1	PP-VPF	VARIG BRASIL (TAI)	L	24834	1896	07/31/90	CFM56-3B2		N371TA

A/C TYPE	CURRENT REG. NO.	LAST KNOWN OPERATOR (OWNER)	STATUS	ORIGINAL MSN	LINE NO.	DEL. DATE	ENG. TYPE	FLEET NO.	PREV. REG. [COMMENTS]
B737-36Q	PP-VPQ	VARIG BRASIL (BOUL)		28664	2940	10/22/97	CFM56-3C1		N1786B
B737-36Q	PP-VPR	VARIG BRASIL (BOUL)		28761	3011	03/24/98	CFM56-3C1		
B737-36N	PP-VPS	VARIG BRASIL (GECA)		28671	2955	11/21/97	CFM56-3C1		
B737-36N	PP-VPT	VARIG BRASIL (GECA)		28566	2964	12/09/97	CFM56-3C1		
B737-36N	PP-VPU	VARIG BRASIL (GECA)		28567	2971	12/18/97	CFM56-3C1		
B737-33R	PP-VPX	VARIG BRASIL (GATX)		28870	2899	06/27/97	CFM56-3C1		N965WP
B737-33R	PP-VPY	VARIG BRASIL (SUNR)		28871	2900	07/02/97	CFM56-3C1		N966WP
B737-3S3	PP-VPZ	VARIG BRASIL (SUNR)		29245	3061	09/17/98	CFM56-3C1		N1786B
B737-33A	PP-VQN	VARIG BRASIL (INGL)		24098	1763	09/18/89	CFM56-3B2		G-IEAA, PH-HVI, XA-SLY, N98NG
B737-3M8	PP-VQO	VARIG BRASIL (INGL)		24377	1719	05/18/89	CFM56-3B2		OO-LTE, D-AASL, XA-SNC, N77NG
B737-36N	PP-VQP	VARIG BRASIL (GECA)		28564	2936	11/14/97	CFM56-3C1		PT-TEP
B737-3S3	PP-VQW	VARIG BRASIL (ACG ACQ)		23787	1374	04/24/87	CFM56-3B2		G-BNXP, CC-CYE, N954WP, N375TA, PP-SFL [PT-TEY NTU]
B737-4Y0	PP-VQQ	VARIG BRASIL (GECA)		24467	1733	06/23/89	CFM56-3C1		PT-TEL
B737-4Y0	PP-VQR	VARIG BRASIL (GECA)		24511	1759	08/14/89	CFM56-3C1		PT-TEM
B737-4Y0	PP-VQS	VARIG BRASIL (GECA)		24513	1779	10/10/89	CFM56-3C1		PT-TEN
B737-4Y0	PP-VQT	VARIG BRASIL (GECA)		24692	1963	12/18/90	CFM56-3C1		EI-CBT, PT-TEO
B737-3K9	PP-SFJ	VASP (BIAL)		24212	1633	11/14/88	CFM56-3B2		CS-TIF, N945WP
B737-3L9	PP-SFN	VASP (VITORIA REGIA)		27925	2763	11/18/95	CFM56-3C1		OY-MAU
B737-3L9	PP-SOT	VASP (VITORIA REGIA)		25150	2074	06/27/91	CFM56-3B2		OY-MMY
B737-3L9	PP-SOU	VASP (VITORIA REGIA)		25360	2140	10/16/91	CFM56-3B2		OY-MMZ

P4-ARUBA

A/C TYPE	CURRENT REG. NO.	LAST KNOWN OPERATOR (OWNER)	STATUS	ORIGINAL MSN	LINE NO.	DEL. DATE	ENG. TYPE	FLEET NO.	PREV. REG. [COMMENTS]
B737-53A	P4-FZT	AMCUR INVESTMENTS		24970	1977	06/26/92	CFM56-3C1		N1789B, N778YY, VR-BOC, VP-BOC

RA-RUSSIA

A/C TYPE	CURRENT REG. NO.	LAST KNOWN OPERATOR (OWNER)	STATUS	ORIGINAL MSN	LINE NO.	DEL. DATE	ENG. TYPE	FLEET NO.	PREV. REG. [COMMENTS]
B737-4M0	VP-BAH	AEROFLOT (SAILPLANE)		29201	3018	05/01/98	CFM56-3C1		
B737-4M0	VP-BAI	AEROFLOT (SAILPLANE)		29202	3025	05/12/98	CFM56-3C1		
B737-4M0	VP-BAJ	AEROFLOT (SAILPLANE)		29203	3049	07/16/98	CFM56-3C1		N1787B
B737-4M0	VP-BAL	AEROFLOT (SAILPLANE)		29204	3051	07/17/98	CFM56-3C1		
B737-4M0	VP-BAM	AEROFLOT (SAILPLANE)		29205	3056	07/28/98	CFM56-3C1		
B737-4M0	VP-BAN	AEROFLOT (SAILPLANE)		29206	3058	08/10/98	CFM56-3C1		
B737-4M0	VP-BAO	AEROFLOT (SAILPLANE)		29207	3078	11/03/98	CFM56-3C1		N1786B
B737-4M0	VP-BAP	AEROFLOT (SAILPLANE)		29208	3081	12/29/98	CFM56-3C1		N1786B, N1003W
B737-4M0	VP-BAQ	AEROFLOT (SAILPLANE)		29209	3087	12/29/98	CFM56-3C1		
B737-4M0	VP-BAR	AEROFLOT (SAILPLANE)		29210	3091	04/27/99	CFM56-3C1		N1786B, N1015B

RP-PHILIPPINES

A/C TYPE	CURRENT REG. NO.	LAST KNOWN OPERATOR (OWNER)	STATUS	ORIGINAL MSN	LINE NO.	DEL. DATE	ENG. TYPE	FLEET NO.	PREV. REG. [COMMENTS]
B737-3Y0	EI-BZM	AIR PHILIPPINES (GECA)		24681	1929	10/15/90	CFM56-3B1		
B737-3Y0	EI-BZN	AIR PHILIPPINES (GECA)		24770	1941	10/30/90	CFM56-3B1		
B737-332	RP-C4007	PHILIPPINE AIRLINES		25996	2488	06/16/93	CFM56-3C1		N303DE, RP-C2000
B737-33A	RP-C4008	PHILIPPINE AIRLINES (CITG)		25033	2025	04/05/91	CFM56-3B1		G-MONV, OY-MBN, TC-IAD, N5033
B737-3Y0	EI-BZE	PHILIPPINE AIRLINES (BBAM)		24464	1753	08/02/89	CFM56-3B1		
B737-3Y0	EI-BZF	PHILIPPINE AIRLINES (GECA)		24465	1755	08/07/89	CFM56-3B1		
B737-3Y0	EI-BZJ	PHILIPPINE AIRLINES (GECA)		24677	1837	03/29/90	CFM56-3B1		
B737-3Y0	EI-BZL	PHILIPPINE AIRLINES (GECA)		24680	1927	10/04/90	CFM56-3B1		
B737-36N	EI-CUL	PHILIPPINE AIRLINES (GECA)		28559	2882	05/12/97	CFM56-3C1		PH-OZC
B737-4Y0	EI-CVN	PHILIPPINE AIRLINES (GECA)		24684	1841	04/09/90	CFM56-3C1		TC-AFK [FERRIED TO ATH 12/15/00]
B737-4S3	EI-CVO	PHILIPPINE AIRLINES (GECA)		25594	2223	02/18/92	CFM56-3C1		9M-MLJ, TC-AVA, N2423N, SP-LLH
B737-4Y0	EI-CVP	PHILIPPINE AIRLINES (GECA)		26081	2442	03/10/93	CFM56-3C1		D-ABAF, TC-AFU

SE-SWEDEN

A/C TYPE	CURRENT REG. NO.	LAST KNOWN OPERATOR (OWNER)	STATUS	ORIGINAL MSN	LINE NO.	DEL. DATE	ENG. TYPE	FLEET NO.	PREV. REG. [COMMENTS]
B737-33A (QC)	SE-DPA	FALCON AIR (AWAS)		25401	2067	06/18/91	CFM56-3C1		
B737-33A (QC)	SE-DPB	FALCON AIR (AWAS)		25402	2159	11/12/91	CFM56-3C1		N33AW
B737-33A (QC)	SE-DPC	FALCON AIR (AWAS)		25426	2172	12/04/91	CFM56-3C1		N34AW

SP-POLAND

A/C TYPE	CURRENT REG. NO.	LAST KNOWN OPERATOR (OWNER)	STATUS	ORIGINAL MSN	LINE NO.	DEL. DATE	ENG. TYPE	FLEET NO.	PREV. REG. [COMMENTS]
B737-55D	SP-LKA	LOT (MARTA)		27416	2389	12/22/92	CFM56-3C1		
B737-55D	SP-LKB	LOT (MARTA)		27417	2392	12/22/92	CFM56-3C1		
B737-55D	SP-LKC	LOT (MARTA)		27418	2397	12/22/92	CFM56-3C1		
B737-55D	SP-LKD	LOT (MARTA)		27419	2401	12/22/92	CFM56-3C1		
B737-55D	SP-LKE	LOT (MARTA)		27130	2448	03/23/93	CFM56-3C1		
B737-55D	SP-LKF	LOT (MARTA)		27368	2603	05/05/94	CFM56-3C1		
B737-53C	SP-LKG	LOT (EUL)	L	24825	1894	07/27/90	CFM56-3C1		F-GHOL
B737-53C	SP-LKH	LOT (BNP LEASE)		24826	2041	05/03/91	CFM56-3C1		F-GHUL
B737-53C	SP-LKI	LOT (EUL)	L	24827	2243	03/18/92	CFM56-3C1		F-GINL
B737-5L9	SP-LKK	LOT (DAN)	L	28996	2998	02/18/98	CFM56-3C1		OY-APL
B737-36N	SP-LMC	LOT (GECA)		28668	2890	06/12/97	CFM56-3C1		
B737-36N	SP-LMD	LOT (GECA)		28669	2897	06/24/97	CFM56-3C1		
B737-45D	SP-LLA	LOT (MARTA)		27131	2458	04/13/93	CFM56-3C1		
B737-45D	SP-LLB	LOT (MARTA)		27156	2492	06/25/93	CFM56-3C1		
B737-45D	SP-LLC	LOT (MARTA)		27157	2502	07/20/93	CFM56-3C1		
B737-45D	SP-LLD	LOT (MARTA)		27256	2589	03/18/94	CFM56-3C1		
B737-45D	SP-LLE	LOT (MARTA)		27914	2804	07/12/96	CFM56-3C1		N1786B
B737-45D	SP-LLF	LOT (FSBU)		28752	2874	04/23/97	CFM56-3C1		
B737-45D	SP-LLG	LOT (FSBU)		28753	2895	06/19/97	CFM56-3C1		
B737-4K5	SP-KEK	WHITE EAGLE AVIATION (DEFAG)		24127	1707	04/26/89	CFM56-3C1		D-AHLL

	A/C TYPE	CURRENT REG. NO.	LAST KNOWN OPERATOR (OWNER)	STATUS	ORIGINAL MSN	LINE NO.	DEL. DATE	ENG. TYPE	FLEET NO.	PREV. REG. [COMMENTS]
	B737-4K5	SP-KEI	WHITE EAGLE AVIATION (DEFAG)		24126	1697	04/07/89	CFM56-3C1		D-AHLK
SU-EGYPT	B737-566	SU-GBK	AIR SINAI (MSR)	L	26052	2276	05/01/92	CFM56-3C1		
	B737-566	SU-GBH	EGYPT AIR		25084	2019	04/10/91	CFM56-3C1		
	B737-566	SU-GBI	EGYPT AIR		25307	2135	10/11/91	CFM56-3C1		
	B737-566	SU-GBJ	EGYPT AIR		25352	2169	11/25/91	CFM56-3C1		
	B737-566	SU-GBK	EGYPT AIR		26052	2276	05/01/92	CFM56-3C1		[OCC LST ASD]
	B737-566	SU-GBL	EGYPT AIR		26051	2282	05/08/92	CFM56-3C1		
	B737-3Q8	SU-ZCD	HELIOPOLIS AIRLINE (ILFC)		26286	2424	02/01/93	CFM56-3C1		N374TA, G-COLC, N171LF
	B737-448	SU-HMD	LUXOR AIR (UNICAPITAL)		24474	1742	07/12/89	CFM56-3B2		EI-BXA [OPF DEI]
	B737-4Y0	N868AC	LUXOR AIR (AERCO USA)		23868	1616	11/04/88	CFM56-3C1		G-OBMF, TC-ANI
	B737-3Q8	SU-MBA	MEDITERRANEAN AIRLINES (ILFC)		26283	2383	10/22/92	CFM56-3C1		N373TA, G-COLB, N161LF, SU-ZCE, N221LF
SX-GREECE	B737-33A	SX-BBT	AEGEAN AIRLINES (CUS)	L	25011	2012	04/10/91	CFM56-3C1		PP-SOF, VH-OAN, OO-LTO, F-GRSA [LST AEGEAN AIRLINES]
	B737-42C	SX-BLM	AXON AIRLINES		24813	2062	06/11/91	CFM56-3C1		G-UKLF, PH-BPF
	B737-4Y0	SX-BLN	AXON AIRLINES		24688	1876	06/22/90	CFM56-3C1		9M-MJI, EC-738, EC-FZT, G-OABF, EC-GYK, EI-TVC
	B737-33A	SX-BBT	CRONUS AIRLINES (AWAS)		25011	2012	04/10/91	CFM56-3C1		PP-SOF, VH-OAN, OO-LTO, F-GRSA [LST AEGEAN AIRLINES]
	B737-33A	SX-BBU	CRONUS AIRLINES (AWAS)		25743	2206	03/19/92	CFM56-3C1		EC-970, EC-FMP
	B737-3L9	SX-BGI	CRONUS AIRLINES (TOMB)		27061	2347	09/25/92	CFM56-3B2		OY-MAN, D-ADBD
	B737-3Y0	SX-BGK	CRONUS AIRLINES (SALE)		24679	1897	07/30/90	CFM56-3B2		9V-TRA
	B737-4Y0	SX-BGH	CRONUS AIRLINES (BOUL)		23866	1589	10/25/88	CFM56-3C1		TC-ADA, VT-EWL, EI-CMO, B2969, N4360W
	B737-4S3	SX-BGJ	CRONUS AIRLINES (BOUL)		25595	2233	03/05/92	CFM56-3C1		9M-MLG, TC-APA, N280CD
	B737-5K5	SX-BFP	GALAXY AIRWAYS (DEFAG)		25062	2044	05/09/91	CFM56-3C1		D-AHLN
	B737-3M8	SX-	HELLENIC STAR AIRLINES (GECA)		25017	2005	09/17/91	CFM56-3B2		N760BE, 9V-TRD, LZ-BOF, N250GE
	B737-46J	SX-BMA	MACEDONIAN AIRLINES (PEMB)		27171	2465	04/18/93	CFM56-3C1		D-ABAE [OPF OAL]
	B737-46J	SX-BMB	MACEDONIAN AIRLINES (PEMB)		27213	2585	03/07/94	CFM56-3C1		D-ABAG [OPF OAL]
	B737-42J	SX-BMC	MACEDONIAN AIRLINES (OASI)		27143	2457	04/16/93	CFM56-3C1		TC-JEA, N734AB
	B737-33R	SX-BLA	OLYMPIC AIRWAYS (BOUL)		28869	2887	06/27/97	CFM56-3C1		N964WP

A/C TYPE	CURRENT REG. NO.	LAST KNOWN OPERATOR (OWNER)	STATUS	ORIGINAL MSN	LINE NO.	DEL. DATE	ENG. TYPE	FLEET NO.	PREV. REG. [COMMENTS]
B737-484	SX-BKA	OLYMPIC AIRWAYS		25313	2109	09/12/91	CFM56-3C1		
B737-484	SX-BKB	OLYMPIC AIRWAYS		25314	2124	09/20/91	CFM56-3C1		
B737-484	SX-BKC	OLYMPIC AIRWAYS		25361	2130	09/30/91	CFM56-3C1		
B737-484	SX-BKD	OLYMPIC AIRWAYS		25362	2142	10/17/91	CFM56-3C1		
B737-484	SX-BKE	OLYMPIC AIRWAYS		25417	2160	11/14/91	CFM56-3C1		
B737-484	SX-BKF	OLYMPIC AIRWAYS		25430	2174	12/12/91	CFM56-3C1		
B737-484	SX-BKG	OLYMPIC AIRWAYS		27149	2471	06/03/93	CFM56-3C1		
B737-4Q8	SX-BKH	OLYMPIC AIRWAYS (ILFC)		24703	1828	03/10/90	CFM56-3C1		9M-MJA, LN-BUB, N407KW
B737-4Y0	SX-BKI	OLYMPIC AIRWAYS (GECA)		24915	2055	05/30/91	CFM56-3C1		9M-MJP, OO-VDO, 9M-MJT
B737-4Q8	SX-BKK	OLYMPIC AIRWAYS (ILFC)		25371	2195	01/13/92	CFM56-3C1		VR-CAA, N404KW
B737-4Q8	SX-BKL	OLYMPIC AIRWAYS (ILFC)		24704	1855	04/25/90	CFM56-3C1		9M-MJB, N405KW
B737-4Q8	SX-BKM	OLYMPIC AIRWAYS (AV CAP)		24709	2115	09/12/91	CFM56-3C1		9M-MJG, N406KW
B737-4Q8	SX-BKN	OLYMPIC AIRWAYS (ILFC)		26281	2380	10/20/92	CFM56-3C1		N401KW

TC-TURKEY

A/C TYPE	CURRENT REG. NO.	LAST KNOWN OPERATOR (OWNER)	STATUS	ORIGINAL MSN	LINE NO.	DEL. DATE	ENG. TYPE	FLEET NO.	PREV. REG. [COMMENTS]
B737-4Q8	TC-ANH	ANATOLIA (ILFC)		25375	2598	04/07/94	CFM56-3C1		TC-JEJ
B737-4Q8	TC-ANL	ANATOLIA (ILFC)		25374	2562	01/07/94	CFM56-3C1		TC-JEG
B737-3K2	TC-ESA	EURO SUN (PEGA)		23411	1195	02/28/86	CFM56-3B2		CS-TIR, XA-STM, PH-HVF, N943PG
B737-3K2	TC-ESB	EURO SUN (PEGA)		23412	1198	03/17/86	CFM56-3B2		XA-SLK, XA-STN, PH-HVG, N945PG
B737-4Q8	TC-AFA	PEGASUS AIRLINES (ILFC)		26306	2653	10/03/94	CFM56-3C1		[OPF OMA]
B737-4Y0	TC-AFJ	PEGASUS AIRLINES (GECA)		23979	1661	01/18/89	CFM56-3C1		EC-239, EC-EMI, XA-SCA, OO-SBN [LST DAH 09/99]
B737-4Q8	TC-AFM	PEGASUS AIRLINES (ILFC)		26279	2221	02/19/92	CFM56-3C1		
B737-4Y0	TC-APC	PEGASUS AIRLINES (GECA)		24345	1731	06/23/89	CFM56-3C1		EC-308, EC-EPN, SU-BLM, VT-JAG, EI-CEU [LST DAH 07/15/00]
B737-42R	TC-APD	PEGASUS AIRLINES		29107	2997	03/27/98	CFM56-3C1		
B737-4Q8	TC-APP	PEGASUS AIRLINES (ILFC)		28202	3009	03/31/98	CFM56-3C1		[OPF OMA FROM 11/20/99]
B737-4Y0	TC-APR	PEGASUS AIRLINES (GECA)		24685	1859	05/15/90	CFM56-3C1		EC-402, PT-TDB, EC-EVE, EC-GXR [LST DAH]
B737-4Y0	TC-APT	PEGASUS AIRLINES (GECA)		24687	1865	05/25/90	CFM56-3C1		TC-ATA, N25AB, D-ABAC, VT-JAK [OPF KHALIFA AIRWAYS 11/00]
B737-4Y0	TC-SKA	SKY AIRLINES (ICON CAP.)		23865	1582	10/14/88	CFM56-3C1		9M-MLC, EL-CAR, RA-87351, VT-MGE, G-UKLA, PH-BPA
B737-430	TC-SKB	SKY AIRLINES (FLIT)		27004	2344	08/13/92	CFM56-3C1		D-ABKF, SX-BFV, EI-CPU
B737-5Y0	TC-JDU	TURKISH AIRLINES (GECA)		25288	2286	06/16/92	CFM56-3C1		
B737-5Y0	TC-JDV	TURKISH AIRLINES (GECA)		25289	2288	06/12/92	CFM56-3C1		N6069D
B737-4Y0	TC-JDF	TURKISH AIRLINES (GECA)		24917	2071	06/24/91	CFM56-3C1		
B737-4Y0	TC-JDG	TURKISH AIRLINES (GECA)		25181	2203	02/03/92	CFM56-3C1		

A/C TYPE	CURRENT REG. NO.	LAST KNOWN OPERATOR (OWNER)	STATUS	ORIGINAL MSN	LINE NO.	DEL. DATE	ENG. TYPE	FLEET NO.	PREV. REG. [COMMENTS]
B737-4Y0	TC-JDH	TURKISH AIRLINES (GECA)		25184	2227	03/02/92	CFM56-3C1		
B737-4Q8	TC-JDI	TURKISH AIRLINES (ILFC)		25372	2280	05/08/92	CFM56-3C1		
B737-4Y0	TC-JDT	TURKISH AIRLINES (GECA)		25261	2258	04/09/92	CFM56-3C1		N600SK
B737-4Y0	TC-JDY	TURKISH AIRLINES (GECA)		26065	2284	06/18/92	CFM56-3C1		
B737-4Y0	TC-JDZ	TURKISH AIRLINES (GECA)		26066	2301	06/19/92	CFM56-3C1		
B737-4Q8	TC-JEN	TURKISH AIRLINES (ILFC)		25376	2689	02/01/95	CFM56-3C1		
B737-4Q8	TC-JEO	TURKISH AIRLINES (ILFC)		25377	2717	05/02/95	CFM56-3C1		
B737-4Y0	TC-JER	TURKISH AIRLINES (GECA)		26073	2375	04/09/93	CFM56-3C1		
B737-4Y0	TC-JET	TURKISH AIRLINES (GECA)		26077	2425	04/09/93	CFM56-3C1		
B737-4Y0	TC-JEU	TURKISH AIRLINES (GECA)		26078	2431	04/16/93	CFM56-3C1		
B737-4Y0	TC-JEV	TURKISH AIRLINES (GECA)		26085	2468	05/06/93	CFM56-3C1		
B737-4Y0	TC-JEY	TURKISH AIRLINES (GECA)		26086	2475	05/18/93	CFM56-3C1		
B737-4Y0	TC-JEZ	TURKISH AIRLINES (GECA)		26088	2487	06/16/93	CFM56-3C1		
B737-4Q8	TC-JKA	TURKISH AIRLINES (ILFC)		26300	2604	05/02/94	CFM56-3C1		TC-JEL, SX-BFA

TF-ICELAND

A/C TYPE	CURRENT REG. NO.	LAST KNOWN OPERATOR (OWNER)	STATUS	ORIGINAL MSN	LINE NO.	DEL. DATE	ENG. TYPE	FLEET NO.	PREV. REG. [COMMENTS]
B737-3Y0 (F)	TF-BBD	BLUEBIRD CARGO		24463	1701	04/28/89	CFM56-3B2		N1779B, EC-245, EC-ENT, EI-BZR, YV-99C, N955WP, OY-SEE
B737-3S3 (QC)	TF-FIE	ICELANDAIR (ILFC)		23811	1445	10/01/87	CFM56-3B2		N852LF, G-BNPA, G-DIAR, 5W-FAY, N841LF, D-ABWS, N761LF [OPF NTR]
B737-408	TF-FID	ICELANDAIR (BOUL)		25063	2032	04/19/91	CFM56-3C1		
B737-3Q8 (QC)	TF-ELN	ISLANDSFLUG (INTL. A/C INVEST.)		23766	1375	04/24/87	CFM56-3B2		G-BNCT, N315SC, EC-153, EC-EHM, N101GU, VH-NJE, OO-ILK [OPF DHL]
B737-330 (QC)	TF-ELP	ISLANDSFLUG		23522	1246	08/16/86	CFM56-3B1		D-ABXA [CVTD -330; OPF EXS]
B737-330 (QC)	TF-ELR	ISLANDSFLUG		23523	1271	09/11/86	CFM56-3B1		D-ABXB [CVTD -330]
B737-3Q8	TF-FDA	ISLANDSFLUG (PLMI)		24700	1924	09/28/90	CFM56-3B1		PK-GWH, N300AR [OPF SUNBIRD]
B737-3Q8	TF-SUN	ISLANDSFLUG (GECA)		23535	1301	11/10/86	CFM56-3B2		EC-EAK, N102GU, SP-LMB, TJ-CBF, N535GE [LST BHS 11/30/00]

TJ-CAMEROON

A/C TYPE	CURRENT REG. NO.	LAST KNOWN OPERATOR (OWNER)	STATUS	ORIGINAL MSN	LINE NO.	DEL. DATE	ENG. TYPE	FLEET NO.	PREV. REG. [COMMENTS]
B737-33A	TJ-CBG	CAMEROON AIRLINES (AWAS)		27458	2959	11/26/97	CFM56-3C1		
B737-33A	TJ-CBH	CAMEROON AIRLINES (AWAS)		27457	2756	10/03/95	CFM56-3B2		9V-TRE

TR-GABON

A/C TYPE	CURRENT REG. NO.	LAST KNOWN OPERATOR (OWNER)	STATUS	ORIGINAL MSN	LINE NO.	DEL. DATE	ENG. TYPE	FLEET NO.	PREV. REG. [COMMENTS]
B737-408	TR-LFU	AIR GABON (CITG)		24353	1721	05/23/89	CFM56-3C1		TF-FIB

TS-TUNISIA

A/C TYPE	CURRENT REG. NO.	LAST KNOWN OPERATOR (OWNER)	STATUS	ORIGINAL MSN	LINE NO.	DEL. DATE	ENG. TYPE	FLEET NO.	PREV. REG. [COMMENTS]
B737-3Y0	TS-IEB	TUNINTER (GECA)		24905	2001	02/26/91	CFM56-3C1		EI-CBP, CS-TKE, PH-TSU
B737-5H3	TS-IOG	TUNISAIR		26639	2253	04/10/92	CFM56-3C1		
B737-5H3	TS-IOH	TUNISAIR		26640	2474	05/21/93	CFM56-3C1		
B737-5H3	TS-IOI	TUNISAIR		27257	2583	03/01/94	CFM56-3C1		
B737-5H3	TS-IOJ	TUNISAIR		27912	2701	03/09/95	CFM56-3C1		

TU-IVORY COAST

A/C TYPE	CURRENT REG. NO.	LAST KNOWN OPERATOR (OWNER)	STATUS	ORIGINAL MSN	LINE NO.	DEL. DATE	ENG. TYPE	FLEET NO.	PREV. REG. [COMMENTS]
B737-3Q8	TU-TAJ	AIR AFRIQUE (ILFC)		26333	2786	04/17/96	CFM56-3C1		N661LF, HB-IIF
B737-3Q8	TU-TAK	AIR AFRIQUE (ILFC)		28200	2854	02/14/97	CFM56-3C1		HB-IIG

UR-UKRAINE

A/C TYPE	CURRENT REG. NO.	LAST KNOWN OPERATOR (OWNER)	STATUS	ORIGINAL MSN	LINE NO.	DEL. DATE	ENG. TYPE	FLEET NO.	PREV. REG. [COMMENTS]
B737-35B	UR-GAG	AEROSVIT AIRLINES (AUI)	L	24238	1626	10/27/88	CFM56-3B2		D-AGEE
B737-3Q8	UR-VVA	AEROSVIT AIRLINES (TRIT)		24492	1808	01/24/90	CFM56-3B1		PK-GWE, N492KR, XA-TMB, N492GD
B737-35B	UR-GAF	UKRAINE INTL. AIRLINES		24237	1624	10/21/88	CFM56-3B2		G-EURP, D-AGEG
B737-35B	UR-GAG	UKRAINE INTL. AIRLINES		24238	1626	10/27/88	CFM56-3B2		D-AGEE [LST AEW 04/27/00]
B737-32Q	UR-GAH	UKRAINE INTL. AIRLINES		29130	3105	04/24/99	CFM56-3C1		N1787B, N1779B

VH-AUSTRALIA

A/C TYPE	CURRENT REG. NO.	LAST KNOWN OPERATOR (OWNER)	STATUS	ORIGINAL MSN	LINE NO.	DEL. DATE	ENG. TYPE	FLEET NO.	PREV. REG. [COMMENTS]
B737-377	VH-CZA	ANSETT AUSTRALIA		23653	1260	08/22/86	CFM56-3B1		
B737-377	VH-CZB	ANSETT AUSTRALIA		23654	1273	09/16/86	CFM56-3B1		N5573B
B737-377	VH-CZC	ANSETT AUSTRALIA		23655	1274	09/25/86	CFM56-3B1		
B737-377	VH-CZD	ANSETT AUSTRALIA		23656	1279	10/09/86	CFM56-3B1		
B737-377	VH-CZE	ANSETT AUSTRALIA		23657	1280	10/15/86	CFM56-3B1		
B737-377	VH-CZF	ANSETT AUSTRALIA		23658	1281	10/23/86	CFM56-3B1		
B737-377	VH-CZG	ANSETT AUSTRALIA		23659	1292	11/20/86	CFM56-3B1		
B737-377	VH-CZH	ANSETT AUSTRALIA		23660	1294	11/25/86	CFM56-3B1		
B737-377	VH-CZI	ANSETT AUSTRALIA		23661	1314	12/11/86	CFM56-3B1		
B737-377	VH-CZJ	ANSETT AUSTRALIA		23662	1316	12/16/86	CFM56-3B1		
B737-377	VH-CZK	ANSETT AUSTRALIA		23663	1323	01/08/87	CFM56-3B1		
B737-377	VH-CZL	ANSETT AUSTRALIA		23664	1326	01/15/87	CFM56-3B1		
B737-377	VH-CZM	ANSETT AUSTRALIA		24302	1618	10/11/88	CFM56-3B1		N113AW
B737-377	VH-CZN	ANSETT AUSTRALIA		24303	1620	10/12/88	CFM56-3B1		
B737-377	VH-CZO	ANSETT AUSTRALIA		24304	1622	10/18/88	CFM56-3B1		N114AW
B737-377	VH-CZP	ANSETT AUSTRALIA		24305	1641	11/28/88	CFM56-3B1		N115AW
B737-33A	VH-CZQ	ANSETT AUSTRALIA (CITG)		24461	1833	03/22/90	CFM56-3B1		G-OBMJ
B737-33A	VH-CZR	ANSETT AUSTRALIA (AWAS)		24460	1831	03/19/90	CFM56-3B2		G-OBMH
B737-33A	VH-CZS	ANSETT AUSTRALIA (AWAS)		24030	1654	01/09/89	CFM56-3B1		G-OBMC, XA-SGJ
B737-33A	VH-CZT	ANSETT AUSTRALIA (AWAS)		27454	2703	04/03/95	CFM56-3B1		
B737-33A	VH-CZU	ANSETT AUSTRALIA (AWAS)		27267	2600	04/19/94	CFM56-3B1		

A/C TYPE	CURRENT REG. NO.	LAST KNOWN OPERATOR (OWNER)	STATUS	ORIGINAL MSN	LINE NO.	DEL. DATE	ENG. TYPE	FLEET NO.	PREV. REG. [COMMENTS]
B737-33A	VH-CZV	ANSETT AUSTRALIA (AWAS)		23831	1471	11/18/87	CFM56-3B1		G-OBMA
B737-33A	VH-CZW	ANSETT AUSTRALIA (AWAS)		23832	1473	12/09/87	CFM56-3B1		G-OBMB
B737-33A	VH-CZX	ANSETT AUSTRALIA		24029	1601	10/04/88	CFM56-3B1		G-MONN
B737-4L7	VH-RON	NORFOLK JET EXPRESS (RON)	L	26960	2483	06/09/93	CFM56-3C1		C2-RN10 [OPB RON]
B737-476	VH-TJI	NORFOLK JET EXPRESS (QFA)	L	24434	1912	09/18/90	CFM56-3C1		9M-MLD
B737-376	VH-TAF	QANTAS		23477	1225	10/03/86	CFM56-3C1		N3281U
B737-376	VH-TAG	QANTAS		23478	1251	07/25/86	CFM56-3C1		
B737-376	VH-TAH	QANTAS		23479	1259	08/11/86	CFM56-3C1		
B737-376	VH-TAI	QANTAS		23483	1264	08/22/86	CFM56-3C1		
B737-376	VH-TAJ	QANTAS		23484	1270	09/05/86	CFM56-3C1		
B737-376	VH-TAK	QANTAS		23485	1277	11/03/86	CFM56-3C1		
B737-376	VH-TAU	QANTAS		23486	1286	12/01/86	CFM56-3C1		
B737-376	VH-TAV	QANTAS		23487	1306	12/12/86	CFM56-3C1		
B737-376	VH-TAW	QANTAS		23488	1352	04/06/87	CFM56-3C1		
B737-376	VH-TAX	QANTAS		23489	1356	04/06/87	CFM56-3C1		
B737-376	VH-TAY	QANTAS		23490	1390	06/22/87	CFM56-3C1		
B737-376	VH-TAZ	QANTAS		23491	1391	06/22/87	CFM56-3C1		
B737-376	VH-TJA	QANTAS		24295	1649	12/15/88	CFM56-3C1		
B737-376	VH-TJB	QANTAS		24296	1653	12/21/88	CFM56-3C1		
B737-376	VH-TJC	QANTAS		24297	1740	07/12/89	CFM56-3C1		
B737-376	VH-TJD	QANTAS		24298	1761	08/29/89	CFM56-3C1		
B737-476	VH-TJE	QANTAS		24430	1820	02/27/90	CFM56-3C1		
B737-476	VH-TJF	QANTAS		24431	1863	06/04/90	CFM56-3C1		
B737-476	VH-TJG	QANTAS		24432	1879	07/03/90	CFM56-3C1		9M-MLE
B737-476	VH-TJH	QANTAS		24433	1881	07/10/90	CFM56-3C1		
B737-476	VH-TJI	QANTAS		24434	1912	09/18/90	CFM56-3C1		9M-MLD [LST NORFOLK JET EXPRESS 11/18/00]
B737-476	VH-TJJ	QANTAS		24435	1959	12/11/90	CFM56-3C1		
B737-476	VH-TJK	QANTAS		24436	1998	02/26/91	CFM56-3C1		
B737-476	VH-TJL	QANTAS		24437	2162	11/12/91	CFM56-3C1		
B737-476	VH-TJM	QANTAS		24438	2171	11/26/91	CFM56-3C1		
B737-476	VH-TJN	QANTAS		24439	2265	04/22/92	CFM56-3C1		
B737-476	VH-TJO	QANTAS		24440	2324	07/13/92	CFM56-3C1		
B737-476	VH-TJP	QANTAS		24441	2363	09/21/92	CFM56-3C1		
B737-476	VH-TJQ	QANTAS		24442	2371	09/29/92	CFM56-3C1		
B737-476	VH-TJR	QANTAS		24443	2398	11/25/92	CFM56-3C1		
B737-476	VH-TJS	QANTAS		24444	2454	04/05/93	CFM56-3C1		
B737-476	VH-TJT	QANTAS		24445	2539	10/18/93	CFM56-3C1		
B737-476	VH-TJU	QANTAS		24446	2569	02/03/94	CFM56-3C1		
B737-4Q8	VH-TJV	QANTAS (ILFC)		25163	2264	04/17/92	CFM56-3C1		H4-SOL

A/C TYPE	CURRENT REG. NO.	LAST KNOWN OPERATOR (OWNER)	STATUS	ORIGINAL MSN	LINE NO.	DEL. DATE	ENG. TYPE	FLEET NO.	PREV. REG. [COMMENTS]
B737-4L7	VH-TJW	QANTAS		26961	2517	08/27/93	CFM56-3C1		C2-RN11
B737-476	VH-TJX	QANTAS		28150	2773	02/23/96	CFM56-3C1		
B737-476	VH-TJY	QANTAS		28151	2785	04/12/96	CFM56-3C1		
B737-476	VH-TJZ	QANTAS		28152	2829	11/08/96	CFM56-3C1		
B737-43Q	VH-VGA	VIRGIN BLUE (VEI)	L	28489	2827	11/22/96	CFM56-3C1		B-18671, EI-TVA
B737-4Q8	VH-VGB	VIRGIN BLUE (ILFC)		25740	2461	04/21/93	CFM56-3C1		TC-JED, EC-HAN, SU-PTA, N257BR
B737-46M	VH-VGC	VIRGIN BLUE (VEX)	L	28549	2844	01/17/97	CFM56-3C1		C-GBIW, OO-VEC
B737-4Y0	VH-VGD	VIRGIN BLUE (VEX)	L	23980	1667	01/28/89	CFM56-3C1		HL7255, F-GMJO, OO-VJO
B737-43Q	VH-VGE	VIRGIN BLUE (VEX)	L	28493	2838	12/19/96	CFM56-3C1		B-18676, EI-TVB
B737-4Q8	VH-VOZ	VIRGIN BLUE (ILFC)		26302	2620	06/09/94	CFM56-3C1		TC-JEM

VT-INDIA

A/C TYPE	CURRENT REG. NO.	LAST KNOWN OPERATOR (OWNER)	STATUS	ORIGINAL MSN	LINE NO.	DEL. DATE	ENG. TYPE	FLEET NO.	PREV. REG. [COMMENTS]
B737-4H6	VT-JAE	JET AIRWAYS (ANZ GRINDLAYS)		27086	2426	02/09/93	CFM56-3C1		9M-MMO
B737-4H6	VT-JAF	JET AIRWAYS (ANZ GRINDLAYS)		27168	2435	03/01/93	CFM56-3C1		9M-MMP
B737-48E	VT-JAM	JET AIRWAYS (SUNR)		25773	2905	08/08/97	CFM56-3C1		N773SR
B737-48E	VT-JAN	JET AIRWAYS (SUNR)		25775	2925	08/28/97	CFM56-3C1		N775SR
B737-497	VT-JAP	JET AIRWAYS (A/C FIN & TRADING)		25664	2393	11/13/92	CFM56-3C1		N402AL, F-GRSC
B737-497	VT-JAQ	JET AIRWAYS (A/C FIN & TRADING)		25663	2382	11/02/92	CFM56-3C1		N401AL, F-GRSB
B737-45R	VT-JAR	JET AIRWAYS		29032	2943	11/12/97	CFM56-3C1		
B737-45R	VT-JAS	JET AIRWAYS		29033	2963	12/16/97	CFM56-3C1		
B737-45R	VT-JAT	JET AIRWAYS		29034	3015	03/27/98	CFM56-3C1		
B737-45R	VT-JAU	JET AIRWAYS		29035	3046	06/30/98	CFM56-3C1		
B737-4Y0	VT-	ROYAL AIRWAYS (BBAM)		24519	1781	10/02/89	CFM56-3C1		VR-CAB, TC-ACA, N519AP
B737-4S3	VT-SIH	SAHARA AIRLINES (HANWAY)		24165	1720	05/23/89	CFM56-3C1		G-BPKC, N690MA, VT-JAI
B737-4S3	VT-SII	SAHARA AIRLINES (HANWAY)		24166	1722	05/26/89	CFM56-3C1		G-BPKD, N691MA, VT-JAJ

XA-MEXICO

A/C TYPE	CURRENT REG. NO.	LAST KNOWN OPERATOR (OWNER)	STATUS	ORIGINAL MSN	LINE NO.	DEL. DATE	ENG. TYPE	FLEET NO.	PREV. REG. [COMMENTS]
B737-33A	TP-02	MEXICAN AIR FORCE		24095	1737	06/29/89	CFM56-3B1		N731XL
B737-3K9	XA-AAU	LINEAS AEREAS AZTECA (BIAL)		24211	1623	10/28/88	CFM56-3B2		EC-188, EC-ELY, EC-HLM
B737-3K9	XA-AAV	LINEAS AEREAS AZTECA (BIAL)		24214	1796	12/12/89	CFM56-3B2		CS-TIH, EC-HNO

XU-CAMBODIA

A/C TYPE	CURRENT REG. NO.	LAST KNOWN OPERATOR (OWNER)	STATUS	ORIGINAL MSN	LINE NO.	DEL. DATE	ENG. TYPE	FLEET NO.	PREV. REG. [COMMENTS]
B737-4H6	9M-MMC	ROYAL AIR CAMBODGE (MAS)	L	26453	2332	07/20/92	CFM56-3C1		

XY-MYANMAR

A/C TYPE	CURRENT REG. NO.	LAST KNOWN OPERATOR (OWNER)	STATUS	ORIGINAL MSN	LINE NO.	DEL. DATE	ENG. TYPE	FLEET NO.	PREV. REG. [COMMENTS]
B737-4H6	9M-MMH	MYANMAR AIRWAYS INTL. (MAS)	L	27084	2391	11/12/92	CFM56-3C1		
B737-4H6	9M-MMY	MYANMAR AIRWAYS INTL. (MAS)	L	26455	2507	08/12/93	CFM56-3C1		
YJ-VANUATU									
B737-3Q8	YJ-AV18	AIR VANUATU (ILFC)		28054	3016	04/21/98	CFM56-3C1		
YR-ROMANIA									
B737-5L9	YR-BGT	TAROM (DAN)	L	28083	2784	04/08/96	CFM56-3C1		ES-ABE, OY-APA
B737-548	YR-BGZ	TAROM (EIN)	L	24878	1939	10/30/90	CFM56-3B1		EI-BXE, EI-CDA [TO RT EIN 05/01]
B737-38J	YR-BGA	TAROM		27179	2524	10/18/93	CFM56-3C1		
B737-38J	YR-BGB	TAROM		27180	2529	10/18/93	CFM56-3C1		
B737-38J	YR-BGC	TAROM		27181	2662	11/07/94	CFM56-3C1		
B737-38J	YR-BGD	TAROM		27182	2663	11/07/94	CFM56-3C1		
B737-38J	YR-BGE	TAROM		27395	2671	11/18/94	CFM56-3C1		
B737-33A	YR-BGU	TAROM (AWAS)		27284	2606	05/16/94	CFM56-3B2		CS-TKF, XA-SWO, N284AN
B737-36Q	YR-BGX	TAROM (BOUL)		29326	3020	04/25/98	CFM56-3C1		
B737-36M	YR-BGY	TAROM (BOUL)		28332	2809	08/16/96	CFM56-3C1		OO-VEA
YS-EL SALVADOR									
B737-3S1	N371TA	TACA INTL. AIRLINES (FSBU)		24834	1896	07/31/90	CFM56-3B2		[LST VRG 08/29/97 AS PP-VPF]
YU-YUGOSLAVIA									
B737-3H9	YU-AND	JAT YUGOSLAV AIRLINES		23329	1134	07/31/85	CFM56-3B1		
B737-3H9	YU-ANF	JAT YUGOSLAV AIRLINES		23330	1136	08/15/85	CFM56-3B1		
B737-3H9	YU-ANH	JAT YUGOSLAV AIRLINES		23415	1171	12/10/85	CFM56-3B1		PP-SNY, TC-CYO
B737-3H9	YU-ANI	JAT YUGOSLAV AIRLINES		23416	1175	12/17/85	CFM56-3B1		[LST MAK AS Z3-AAA]
B737-3H9	YU-ANJ	JAT YUGOSLAV AIRLINES		23714	1305	11/17/86	CFM56-3B1		TC-MIO [STD IST IN BHS C/S AS YU-ANJ]
B737-3H9	YU-ANK	JAT YUGOSLAV AIRLINES		23715	1310	11/26/86	CFM56-3B1		
B737-3H9	YU-ANL	JAT YUGOSLAV AIRLINES		23716	1321	12/19/86	CFM56-3B1		TS-IEC [LST MAK AS Z3-ARF]
B737-3H9	YU-ANV	JAT YUGOSLAV AIRLINES		24140	1524	03/21/88	CFM56-3B1		
B737-3H9	YU-ANW	JAT YUGOSLAV AIRLINES		24141	1526	03/25/88	CFM56-3B1		TS-IED
ZK-NEW ZEALAND									
B737-3U3	ZK-FRE	AIR NEW ZEALAND (HELLER FIN.)		28742	2992	11/19/98	CFM56-3C1		N1786B, N60436, N360PR
B737-33R	ZK-NGA	AIR NEW ZEALAND (GECA)		28873	2975	01/09/98	CFM56-3C1		N1787B
B737-36Q	ZK-NGB	AIR NEW ZEALAND (BOUL)		29140	3013	03/31/98	CFM56-3C1		
B737-36Q	ZK-NGC	AIR NEW ZEALAND (BOUL)		29189	3057	08/04/98	CFM56-3C1		N1786B
B737-3U3	ZK-NGD	AIR NEW ZEALAND		28732	2966	11/24/98	CFM56-3C1		N1786B, N1792B, (PK-GGH), N930WA
B737-3U3	ZK-NGE	AIR NEW ZEALAND (INGO)		28733	2969	12/14/98	CFM56-3C1		N6066Z, (PK-GGI), N931WA

A/C TYPE	CCURRENT REG. NO.	LAST KNOWN OPERATOR (OWNER)	STATUS	ORIGINAL MSN	LINE NO.	DEL. DATE	ENG. TYPE	FLEET NO.	PREV. REG. [COMMENTS]
B737-3U3	ZK-NGF	AIR NEW ZEALAND (INGO)		28734	2974	11/24/98	CFM56-3C1		N6067E, N309FL
B737-319	ZK-NGG	AIR NEW ZEALAND		25606	3123	10/14/99	CFM56-3C1		N1795B
B737-319	ZK-NGH	AIR NEW ZEALAND		25607	3126	10/27/99	CFM56-3C1		N1786B
B737-319	ZK-NGI	AIR NEW ZEALAND		25608	3128	11/20/99	CFM56-3C1		N1786B
B737-319	ZK-NGJ	AIR NEW ZEALAND		25609	3130	12/17/99	CFM56-3C1		N1787B [LAST B737-300 DEL]
B737-3K2	ZK-NGK	AIR NEW ZEALAND (ILFC)		26318	2731	06/28/95	CFM56-3C1		PH-TSX
B737-33S	ZK-NGN	AIR NEW ZEALAND (PEMB)		29072	3012	03/30/98	CFM56-3C1		OO-SLK
B737-3M8	ZK-FDM	FREEDOM AIR INTL. (KHASSAN)		25016	2004	02/28/91	CFM56-3B2		OO-XTG, OO-LTG, HB-IIC
B737-33R	ZK-SJB	FREEDOM AIR INTL. (ORIX)		28868	2881	05/14/97	CFM56-3C1		N35135, N963WP, PP-SFK

Z3-MACEDONIA

A/C TYPE	CCURRENT REG. NO.	LAST KNOWN OPERATOR (OWNER)	STATUS	ORIGINAL MSN	LINE NO.	DEL. DATE	ENG. TYPE	FLEET NO.	PREV. REG. [COMMENTS]
B737-3H9	Z3-AAA	MAT-MACEDONIAN AIRLINES (JAT)	L	23416	1175	12/17/85	CFM56-3B1		YU-ANI
B737-3H9	Z3-ARF	MAT-MACEDONIAN AIRLINES (JAT)	L	23716	1321	12/19/86	CFM56-3B1		TS-IEC, YU-ANL

4L-GEORGIA

A/C TYPE	CCURRENT REG. NO.	LAST KNOWN OPERATOR (OWNER)	STATUS	ORIGINAL MSN	LINE NO.	DEL. DATE	ENG. TYPE	FLEET NO.	PREV. REG. [COMMENTS]
B737-5K5	D-AHLF	AIRZENA GEORGIAN AIRLINES (DEFAG)		24927	1968	12/18/90	CFM56-3C1		
B737-5K5	D-AHLI	AIRZENA GEORGIAN AIRLINES (DEFAG)		25037	2022	04/03/91	CFM56-3C1		

5B-CYPRUS

A/C TYPE	CCURRENT REG. NO.	LAST KNOWN OPERATOR (OWNER)	STATUS	ORIGINAL MSN	LINE NO.	DEL. DATE	ENG. TYPE	FLEET NO.	PREV. REG. [COMMENTS]
B737-4Y0	5B-DBG	HELIOS AIRWAYS (GECA)		24682	1824	03/05/90	CFM56-3C1		9M-MJK, EC-737, EC-FZX, VT-JAH, N682GE, PT-TDF, EC-HCN [OO TO MAH FROM GECA 05/01 AS HA-LEY]

5H-TANZANIA

A/C TYPE	CCURRENT REG. NO.	LAST KNOWN OPERATOR (OWNER)	STATUS	ORIGINAL MSN	LINE NO.	DEL. DATE	ENG. TYPE	FLEET NO.	PREV. REG. [COMMENTS]
B737-33A	5H-TCA	AIR TANZANIA (AWAS)		24790	1955	02/11/91	CFM56-3C1		N1792B, PP-SOC, N223AW, VT-JAA

5R-MADAGASCAR

A/C TYPE	CCURRENT REG. NO.	LAST KNOWN OPERATOR (OWNER)	STATUS	ORIGINAL MSN	LINE NO.	DEL. DATE	ENG. TYPE	FLEET NO.	PREV. REG. [COMMENTS]
B737-3Q8	5R-MFH	AIR MADAGASCAR (TRIT)		26305	2651	09/12/94	CFM56-3C1		

5W-SAMOA

A/C TYPE	CCURRENT REG. NO.	LAST KNOWN OPERATOR (OWNER)	STATUS	ORIGINAL MSN	LINE NO.	DEL. DATE	ENG. TYPE	FLEET NO.	PREV. REG. [COMMENTS]
B737-3Q8	5W-ILF	POLYNESIAN AIRLINE OF SAMOA		26282	2355	09/08/92	CFM56-3B2		[SALE/LST SOLOMONS NTU]

5Y-KENYA

A/C TYPE	CCURRENT REG. NO.	LAST KNOWN OPERATOR (OWNER)	STATUS	ORIGINAL MSN	LINE NO.	DEL. DATE	ENG. TYPE	FLEET NO.	PREV. REG. [COMMENTS]
B737-33A	5Y-RAA	AIR KENYA/REGIONAL AIR (AWAS)		24097	1741	07/06/89	CFM56-3B2		PP-SNZ, G-BUSM, VT-JAD, G-OABA, XA-TQJ, N497AN
B737-33A	5Y-RAB	AIR KENYA/REGIONAL AIR (AWAS)		24096	1739	07/03/89	CFM56-3B2		PP-SNW, G-BUSL, VT-JAC, G-OABL, XA-TQI, N496AN
B737-3U8	5Y-KQA	KENYA AIRWAYS (SIMBA)		28746	2863	03/27/97	CFM56-3C1		
B737-3U8	5Y-KQB	KENYA AIRWAYS (SIMBA)		28747	2884	05/20/97	CFM56-3C1		
B737-3U8	5Y-KQC	KENYA AIRWAYS (SIMBA)		29088	3034	05/29/98	CFM56-3C1		

A/C TYPE	CURRENT REG. NO.	LAST KNOWN OPERATOR (OWNER)	STATUS	ORIGINAL MSN	LINE NO.	DEL. DATE	ENG. TYPE	FLEET NO.	PREV. REG. [COMMENTS]
B737-3U8	5Y-KQD	KENYA AIRWAYS		29750	3095	03/01/99	CFM56-3C1		N1795B, N5573L
7Q-MALAWI									
B737-33A	7Q-YKP	AIR MALAWI		25056	2045	05/20/91	CFM56-3C1		
7T-ALGERIA									
B737-4Y0	TC-AFJ	AIR ALGERIE (PGT)	L	23979	1661	01/18/89	CFM56-3C1		EC-239, EC-EMI, XA-SCA, OO-SBN
B737-4Y0	TC-APC	AIR ALGERIE (PGT)	L	24345	1731	06/23/89	CFM56-3C1		EC-308, EC-EPN, SU-BLM, VT-JAG, EI-CEU
B737-4Y0	TC-APR	AIR ALGERIE (PGT)	L	24685	1859	05/15/90	CFM56-3C1		EC-402, PT-TDB, EC-EVE, EC-GXR
B737-4Y0	TC-APT	KHALIFA AIRWAYS (PGT)	L	24687	1865	05/25/90	CFM56-3C1		TC-ATA, N25AB, D-ABAC, VT-JAK
9H-MALTA									
B737-5L9	OY-MAA	AIR MALTA (DAN)	L	24778	1816	04/06/90	CFM56-3B1		HL7230, G-MSKD
B737-3Y5	9H-ABR	AIR MALTA		25613	2446	03/26/93	CFM56-3C1		
B737-3Y5	9H-ABS	AIR MALTA		25614	2467	04/30/93	CFM56-3C1		
B737-3Y5	9H-ABT	AIR MALTA		25615	2478	05/25/93	CFM56-3C1		
B737-33A	9H-ADH	AIR MALTA (AWAS)		27459	3007	03/12/98	CFM56-3C1		N1787B
B737-33A	9H-ADI	AIR MALTA (AWAS)		27460	3021	04/22/98	CFM56-3C1		N1787B
B737-382	9H-ADM	AIR MALTA (ILFC)		24365	1695	03/30/89	CFM56-3B2		CS-TIB
B737-382	9H-ADN	AIR MALTA (ILFC)		25161	2226	02/25/92	CFM56-3B2		CS-TIK
9M-MALAYSIA									
B737-3Y0	9M-AAA	AIR ASIA (GECA)		24907	2013	03/15/91	CFM56-3C1		UR-GAE, EI-CBQ
B737-36N	9M-AAB	AIR ASIA (GECA)		28555	2846	01/27/97	CFM56-3C1		
B737-4H6	9M-MMA	MALAYSIA AIRLINES		26443	2272	04/30/92	CFM56-3C1		
B737-4H6	9M-MMB	MALAYSIA AIRLINES		26444	2308	06/12/92	CFM56-3C1		
B737-4H6	9M-MMC	MALAYSIA AIRLINES		26453	2332	07/20/92	CFM56-3C1		[LST ROYAL AIR CAMBODGE]
B737-4H6	9M-MMD	MALAYSIA AIRLINES		26464	2340	08/04/92	CFM56-3C1		
B737-4H6	9M-MME	MALAYSIA AIRLINES		26465	2362	09/22/92	CFM56-3C1		[LST NGE]
B737-4H6	9M-MMF	MALAYSIA AIRLINES		26466	2372	10/05/92	CFM56-3C1		
B737-4H6	9M-MMG	MALAYSIA AIRLINES		26467	2378	10/16/92	CFM56-3C1		
B737-4H6	9M-MMH	MALAYSIA AIRLINES		27084	2391	11/12/92	CFM56-3C1		[LST UBA]
B737-4H6	9M-MMI	MALAYSIA AIRLINES		27096	2395	11/23/92	CFM56-3C1		
B737-4H6	9M-MMJ	MALAYSIA AIRLINES		27097	2399	12/04/92	CFM56-3C1		
B737-4H6	9M-MMK	MALAYSIA AIRLINES		27083	2403	12/14/92	CFM56-3C1		
B737-4H6	9M-MML	MALAYSIA AIRLINES		27085	2407	12/22/92	CFM56-3C1		[OPF ANGEL AIRLINES]
B737-4H6	9M-MMM	MALAYSIA AIRLINES		27166	2410	01/08/93	CFM56-3C1		
B737-4H6	9M-MMN	MALAYSIA AIRLINES		27167	2419	01/26/93	CFM56-3C1		
B737-4H6	9M-MMQ	MALAYSIA AIRLINES		27087	2441	03/30/93	CFM56-3C1		

A/C TYPE	CURRENT REG. NO.	LAST KNOWN OPERATOR (OWNER)	STATUS	ORIGINAL MSN	LINE NO.	DEL. DATE	ENG. TYPE	FLEET NO.	PREV. REG. [COMMENTS]
B737-4H6	9M-MMR	MALAYSIA AIRLINES		26468	2445	03/19/93	CFM56-3C1		
B737-4H6	9M-MMS	MALAYSIA AIRLINES		27169	2450	04/01/93	CFM56-3C1		
B737-4H6	9M-MMT	MALAYSIA AIRLINES		27170	2462	04/27/93	CFM56-3C1		
B737-4H6	9M-MMU	MALAYSIA AIRLINES		26447	2479	05/28/93	CFM56-3C1		VT-JAV
B737-4H6	9M-MMV	MALAYSIA AIRLINES		26449	2491	06/24/93	CFM56-3C1		
B737-4H6	9M-MMW	MALAYSIA AIRLINES		26451	2496	07/26/93	CFM56-3C1		
B737-4H6	9M-MMX	MALAYSIA AIRLINES		26452	2501	07/20/93	CFM56-3C1		
B737-4H6	9M-MMY	MALAYSIA AIRLINES		26455	2507	08/12/93	CFM56-3C1		[LST UBA]
B737-4H6	9M-MMZ	MALAYSIA AIRLINES		26457	2521	09/30/93	CFM56-3C1		
B737-4H6	9M-MQA	MALAYSIA AIRLINES		26458	2525	10/29/93	CFM56-3C1		
B737-4H6	9M-MQB	MALAYSIA AIRLINES		26459	2530	10/29/93	CFM56-3C1		
B737-4H6	9M-MQC	MALAYSIA AIRLINES		26460	2533	10/29/93	CFM56-3C1		
B737-4H6	9M-MQD	MALAYSIA AIRLINES		26461	2536	11/09/93	CFM56-3C1		
B737-4H6	9M-MQE	MALAYSIA AIRLINES		26462	2542	12/02/93	CFM56-3C1		
B737-4H6	9M-MQF	MALAYSIA AIRLINES		26463	2560	01/10/94	CFM56-3C1		
B737-4H6	9M-MQG	MALAYSIA AIRLINES		27190	2568	02/01/94	CFM56-3C1		
B737-4H6	9M-MQH	MALAYSIA AIRLINES (GECA)		27352	2624	06/23/94	CFM56-3C1		
B737-4H6	9M-MQI	MALAYSIA AIRLINES		27353	2632	07/18/94	CFM56-3C1		
B737-4H6	9M-MQJ	MALAYSIA AIRLINES (TOMB)		27383	2657	11/01/94	CFM56-3C1		
B737-4H6	9M-MQK	MALAYSIA AIRLINES		27384	2673	12/07/94	CFM56-3C1		
B737-4H6	9M-MQL	MALAYSIA AIRLINES (GECA)		27191	2676	01/10/95	CFM56-3C1		
B737-4H6	9M-MQM	MALAYSIA AIRLINES (TOMB)		27306	2685	02/01/95	CFM56-3C1		
B737-4H6	9M-MQN	MALAYSIA AIRLINES		27673	2852	03/03/97	CFM56-3C1		N1786B, 9H-ADK
B737-4H6	9M-MQO	MALAYSIA AIRLINES		27674	2877	04/29/97	CFM56-3C1		9H-ADL

OUT OF SERVICE

A/C TYPE	CURRENT REG. NO.	LAST KNOWN OPERATOR (OWNER)	STATUS	ORIGINAL MSN	LINE NO.	DEL. DATE	ENG. TYPE	FLEET NO.	PREV. REG. [COMMENTS]
B737-306	PH-BDH	KLM (GECA)	O	23543	1325	01/15/87	CFM56-3B1		[RT GECA; TO BE ST DEI]
B737-306	PH-BDI	KLM (GECA)	O	23544	1335	02/04/87	CFM56-3B1		[RT GECA]
B737-306	PH-BDL	KLM (GECA)	O	23546	1349	02/25/87	CFM56-3B1		[RT GECA; TO BE SOLD IN FRANCE]
B737-3Y0	N749AP	(AERO USA)	O	23749	1389	05/22/87	CFM56-3B2		EC-ECR, EC-781, EC-FKJ, LZ-BOD [FERRIED TO ARUBA]
B737-3Y0	N923AP	(AERO USA)	O	23923	1540	04/22/88	CFM56-3B2		EC-152, EC-EIA, LN-AEQ, EI-BZP, G-TEAB, EI-CEE, EC-898, EC-FJZ, LZ-BOE
B737-46B	PT-TDH	TRANSBRASIL	O	24124	1679	03/21/89	CFM56-3C1		G-BOPK, N689MA, EC-655, EC-FYG, SU-SAA, EC-309, SU-SAB, EC-GHF, EI-CRC, EC-GNC, EC-HCP, EC-HME [RT LESSOR]
B737-3Q4	N181LF	TRANSBRASIL (FSBU)	O	24208	1490	01/12/88	CFM56-3B2		PT-TEF [PARKED GRU; NO TITLES]
B737-3Q4	PT-TEH	TRANSBRASIL (ACG INST. INV.)	O	24210	1577	07/12/88	CFM56-3B2		[RT ACG ACQ; STD POA]
B737-3K9	CS-TIG	TAP AIR PORTUGAL (BIAL)	O	24213	1794	12/07/89	CFM56-3B2		[RT BIAL 03/26/01]
B737-3Q8	N611LF	(MSA 1)	O	24299	1598	11/01/88	CFM56-3B2		EC-ELJ, EC-594, EC-FER, N956WP, PP-SFM

A/C TYPE	CURRENT REG. NO.	LAST KNOWN OPERATOR (OWNER)	STATUS	ORIGINAL MSN	LINE NO.	DEL. DATE	ENG. TYPE	FLEET NO.	PREV. REG. [COMMENTS]
B737-3Q8	N737FA	TAESA (IAI II)	O	24300	1666	01/31/89	CFM56-3B1		SE-DLA, G-OBML, B-2980, XA-AMH [RT IAI II 03/00; PARKED TUS; TO BE LST PANAIR, ITALY]
B737-3L9	N2393W	(TOMB)	O	24571	1815	02/13/90	CFM56-3B2		OY-MMF, D-ADBF, TC-IAE [FERRIED TO STN 04/01/0█
B737-4Y0	OK-WGG	CSA CZECH AIRLINES (GECA)	O	24693	1972	01/08/91	CFM56-3C1		9M-MJM [RT LESSOR]
B737-430	EI-COH	AIR ONE (GATX)	O	27001	2316	07/09/92	CFM56-3C1		D-ABKB
B737-430	D-AGMR	AIR MALTA (GOAL)	O	27007	2367	10/01/92	CFM56-3C1		D-ABKL, TC-SUS

WRITTEN OFF

A/C TYPE	CURRENT REG. NO.	LAST KNOWN OPERATOR (OWNER)	STATUS	ORIGINAL MSN	LINE NO.	DEL. DATE	ENG. TYPE	FLEET NO.	PREV. REG. [COMMENTS]
B737-3T5	N668SW	SOUTHWEST AIRLINES	W	23060	1069	01/29/85	CFM56-3B1		G-BLKB, N753MA [WO BUR 03/05/00; OVERSHOT R/W ON LDG]
B737-3B7	N388US	US AIR	W	23310	1145	09/13/85	CFM56-3B2		[WO 02/01/91 LOS ANGELES]
B737-3B7	N513AU	US AIR	W	23699	1452	10/08/87	CFM56-3B2		[WO 09/08/94 PITTSBURGH]
B737-4Y0	G-OBME	BRITISH MIDLAND (GPAG)	W	23867	1603	10/25/88	CFM56-3C1		[WO 01/08/89 LEICESTER, ENGLAND]
B737-401	N416US	US AIR	W	23884	1643	12/23/88	CFM56-3B2		[WO 09/21/89 LAGUARDIA AIRPORT]
B737-3Y0	EI-BZG	PHILIPPINE AIRLINES (GPAG)	W	24466	1771	10/02/89	CFM56-3B1		[WO 11/05/90 MANILA]
B737-3Z6	33-333	ROYAL THAI AIR FORCE	W	24480	1773	09/15/89	CFM56-3B1		[WO 03/30/93 BANGKOK]
B737-5L9	HL7229	ASIANA (DMA)	W	24805	1878	06/26/90	CFM56-3B1		OY-MAB [WO 07/26/93 MOKPO, KOREA]
B737-3Y0	B-2523	CHINA SOUTHERN AIRLINES (GPAG)	W	24913	2052	05/23/91	CFM56-3B1		[WO 11/24/92 GUILIN, CHINA]
B737-3Y0	B-2525	CHINA SOUTHERN AIRLINES (GECA)	W	24918	2087	07/17/91	CFM56-3B1		[OPB SHANTOU AIRLINES; WO 06/09/99 ZHANJIANG, CHINA]
B737-4D7	HS-TDC	THAI AIRWAYS INTL.	W	25321	2113	09/10/91	CFM56-3C1		[WO 03/03/01 BANGKOK, THAILAND]
B737-4Q8	TC-JEP	TURKISH AIRLINES (ILFC)	W	25378	2732	06/21/95	CFM56-3C1		[WO 04/06/99 CEYHAN, TURKEY]
B737-4Y0	TC-JES	TURKISH AIRLINES (GPAG)	W	26074	2376	04/21/93	CFM56-3C1		[WO 12/29/94 VAN, TURKEY]
B737-3W0	B-2540	YUNNAN PROVINCIAL	W	27139	2400	01/11/93	CFM56-3C1		[WO 07/29/94 KUNMING, CHINA]
B737-31B	B-2925	CHINA SOUTHERN AIRLINES	W	27288	2577	02/25/94	CFM56-3B1		[WO 05/08/97 SHENZHEN, CHINA]
B737-36N	9V-TRF	SILKAIR (GECA)	W	28556	2851	02/14/97	CFM56-3B2		[WO 12/19/97 PALEMBANG, INDONESIA]
B737-524	N20643	CONTINENTAL AIRLINES	W	28904	2933	09/24/97	CFM56-3C1		[WO 09/16/98 GUADALAHARA, MEXICO; FUSELAGE AT MHV 12/99]

Boeing 737-600 through 737-900 Commercial Jet Aircraft Census
The aircraft in the following tables are listed in order of the following: 1) ICAO country prefixes; 2) operator; 3) aircraft type; and 4) registration.
The total built was 822+ (39+ B737-600, 339+ B737-700, 443+ B737-800, and 1+ B737-900) from 1997 to present (still in production).

A/C TYPE	CURRENT REG. NO.	LAST KNOWN OPERATOR (OWNER)	STATUS	ORIGINAL MSN	LINE NO.	DEL. DATE	ENG. TYPE	FLEET NO.	PREV. REG. [COMMENTS]
A6-UNITED ARAB EMIRATES									
B737-7Z5 (BBJ)	A6-AIN	ABU DHABI AMIRI FLIGHT		29268	280	05/26/99	CFM56-7B26		N1786B
B737-7Z5 (BBJ)	A6-DAS	ABU DHABI AMIRI FLIGHT		29858	530	05/08/00	CFM56-7B26		
B737-7Z5 (BBJ)	A6-LIW	ABU DHABI AMIRI FLIGHT		29857	445	12/16/99	CFM56-7B26		N1795B
B737-7Z5 (BBJ)	A6-SIR	UNITED ARAB EMIRATES GOVERNMENT		29269	432	12/08/99	CFM56-7B26		N1786B
B737-7E0 (BBJ)	A6-HRS	DUBAI AIR WING		29251	150	12/08/98	CFM56-7B26		
B737-8EC (BBJ2)	A6-MRM	DUBAI AIR WING		32450	787	03/07/01	CFM56-7B26		
B-CHINA (PEOPLE'S REPUBLIC)									
B737-89L	B-2641	AIR CHINA		29876	337	08/17/99	CFM56-7B26		
B737-89L	B-2642	AIR CHINA		29877	359	09/07/99	CFM56-7B26		
B737-89L	B-2643	AIR CHINA		29878	379	09/27/99	CFM56-7B26		N1786B
B737-89L	B-2645	AIR CHINA		29879	427	11/29/99	CFM56-7B26		N1786B
B737-89L	B-2648	AIR CHINA		29880	511	04/15/00	CFM56-7B26		N1786B
B737-89L	B-2649	AIR CHINA		30159	572	06/05/00	CFM56-7B26		N1786B, N1784B
B737-89L	B-2650	AIR CHINA		30160	594	06/29/00	CFM56-7B26		N1786B
B737-8Z0	B-2509	CHINA SOUTHWEST AIRLINES		30072	466	01/21/00	CFM56-7B26		N1787B
B737-8Z0	B-2510	CHINA SOUTHWEST AIRLINES		30071	381	10/29/99	CFM56-7B26		N1786B
B737-8Z0	B-2511	CHINA SOUTHWEST AIRLINES		30073	487	03/28/00	CFM56-7B26		N1786B
B737-7W0	B-2502	CHINA YUNNAN AIRLINES		30075	311	07/07/99	CFM56-7B24		
B737-7W0	B-2503	CHINA YUNNAN AIRLINES		30074	292	06/14/99	CFM56-7B24		N1786B
B737-7W0	B-2639	CHINA YUNNAN AIRLINES		29912	140	12/08/98	CFM56-7B24		N1787B
B737-7W0	B-2640	CHINA YUNNAN AIRLINES		29913	148	12/16/98	CFM56-7B24		N1800B
B737-75C	B-2998	FUJIAN AIRLINES (CXA)	L	29042	73	08/21/98	CFM56-7B24		N1786B
B737-86N	B-2636	HAINAN AIRLINES (GECA)		28574	67	07/29/98	CFM56-7B26		N574GE
B737-86N	B-2637	HAINAN AIRLINES (GECA)		28576	103	09/30/98	CFM56-7B26		N576GE, N1786B
B737-8Q8	B-2638	HAINAN AIRLINES (ILFC)		28220	212	02/26/99	CFM56-7B26		N1786B, N361LF
B737-8Q8	B-2646	HAINAN AIRLINES (ILFC)		28056	273	05/17/99	CFM56-7B26		N1787B, N371LF
B737-84P	B-2647	HAINAN AIRLINES		29947	345	08/23/99	CFM56-7B26		N1787B
B737-84P	B-2651	HAINAN AIRLINES		30474	607	07/21/00	CFM56-7B26		N1786B, N1787B
B737-84P	B-2652	HAINAN AIRLINES		30475	731	12/19/00	CFM56-7B26		N1786B

A/C TYPE	CURRENT REG. NO.	LAST KNOWN OPERATOR (OWNER)	STATUS	ORIGINAL MSN	LINE NO.	DEL. DATE	ENG. TYPE	FLEET NO.	PREV. REG. [COMMENTS]
B737-76D	B-2577	SHANGHAI AIRLINES		30168	600	07/10/00	CFM56-7B24		
B737-7Q8	B-2631	SHANGHAI AIRLINES (ILFC)		28212	35	04/05/98	CFM56-7B24		N301LF
B737-7Q8	B-2632	SHANGHAI AIRLINES (ILFC)		28216	122	10/09/98	CFM56-7B24		N1795B
B737-7AD	B-2663	SHANGHAI AIRLINES (PEGA)		28437	72	07/28/98	CFM56-7B24		N701EW
B737-76D	B-2913	SHANGHAI AIRLINES		30167	550	05/25/00	CFM56-7B24		N1786B
B737-7Q8	B-2997	SHANGHAI AIRLINES (ILFC)		28223	272	05/18/99	CFM56-7B24		
B737-79K	B-2633	SHENZHEN AIRLINES		29190	110	09/30/98	CFM56-7B24		N1786B
B737-79K	B-2635	SHENZHEN AIRLINES		29191	127	10/20/98	CFM56-7B24		N1786B
B737-78S	B-2666	SHENZHEN AIRLINES		30169	631	08/25/00	CFM56-7B26		N1786B
B737-78S	B-2667	SHENZHEN AIRLINES		30170	654	09/15/00	CFM56-7B26		
B737-78S	B-2668	SHENZHEN AIRLINES		30171	681	12/20/00	CFM56-7B26		N1786B
B737-86R	B-2660	WUHAN AIRLINES (CITG)		30494	786	03/19/01	CFM56-7B26		
B737-75C	B-2658	XIAMEN AIRLINES		30512	637	08/24/00	CFM56-7B24		N1786B
B737-75C	B-2659	XIAMEN AIRLINES		30513	676	10/10/00	CFM56-7B24		
B737-75C	B-2991	XIAMEN AIRLINES		29085	90	09/03/98	CFM56-7B24		
B737-75C	B-2992	XIAMEN AIRLINES		29086	108	09/29/98	CFM56-7B24		N1786B
B737-75C	B-2998	XIAMEN AIRLINES		29042	73	08/21/98	CFM56-7B24		N1786B [LST/OPW CFJ]
B737-75C	B-2999	XIAMEN AIRLINES		29084	86	08/27/98	CFM56-7B24		N1796B

B-CHINA (TAIWAN)

A/C TYPE	CURRENT REG. NO.	LAST KNOWN OPERATOR (OWNER)	STATUS	ORIGINAL MSN	LINE NO.	DEL. DATE	ENG. TYPE	FLEET NO.	PREV. REG. [COMMENTS]
B737-809	B-18601	CHINA AIRLINES		28402	113	10/26/98	CFM56-7B26		N1787B [LST MDA]
B737-809	B-18605	CHINA AIRLINES		28404	130	11/13/98	CFM56-7B26		N1786B, N1784B
B737-809	B-18606	CHINA AIRLINES		28405	132	11/30/98	CFM56-7B26		N1786B
B737-809	B-18607	CHINA AIRLINES		29104	139	12/01/98	CFM56-7B26		
B737-809	B-18608	CHINA AIRLINES		28406	141	12/02/98	CFM56-7B26		N1786B
B737-809	B-18609	CHINA AIRLINES		28407	161	12/18/98	CFM56-7B26		N1786B
B737-809	B-18610	CHINA AIRLINES		29105	295	06/23/99	CFM56-7B26		N1786B
B737-809	B-18611	CHINA AIRLINES		29106	302	06/25/99	CFM56-7B26		N1787B
B737-809	B-18612	CHINA AIRLINES		30173	695	10/30/00	CFM56-7B26		N1785B
B737-809	B-18601	MANDARIN AIRLINES (CAL)	L	28402	113	10/26/98	CFM56-7B26		N1787B
B737-809	B-16802	MANDARIN AIRLINES (ILFC)		28236	739	01/16/01	CFM56-7B26		N1786B
B737-809	B-16803	MANDARIN AIRLINES (ILFC)		30664	743	01/12/01	CFM56-7B26		N1787B
B737-809	B-16805	MANDARIN AIRLINES (ILFC)		30636	768	02/24/01	CFM56-7B26		N1786B

C-CANADA

A/C TYPE	CURRENT REG. NO.	LAST KNOWN OPERATOR (OWNER)	STATUS	ORIGINAL MSN	LINE NO.	DEL. DATE	ENG. TYPE	FLEET NO.	PREV. REG. [COMMENTS]
B737-76N	C-FIWS	WESTJET AIRLINES (GECAS)	N	32404	851		CFM56-7B26		
CN-MOROCCO									
B737-7B6	CN-RNL	ROYAL AIR MAROC		28982	236	04/16/99	CFM56-7B24		N1786B
B737-7B6	CN-RNM	ROYAL AIR MAROC		28984	294	06/17/99	CFM56-7B24		N1786B
B737-7B6	CN-RNQ	ROYAL AIR MAROC		28985	501	04/11/00	CFM56-7B24		N1786B
B737-7B6	CN-RNR	ROYAL AIR MAROC		28986	519	04/22/00	CFM56-7B24		N1787B
B737-8B6	CN-RNJ	ROYAL AIR MAROC (RAM 7 LSG)		28980	55	07/10/98	CFM56-7B26		
B737-8B6	CN-RNK	ROYAL AIR MAROC (RAM 7 LSG)		28981	60	07/15/98	CFM56-7B26		N1786B
B737-86N	CN-RNN	ROYAL AIR MAROC (GECA)		28592	258	05/01/99	CFM56-7B26		N1786B, N1779B
B737-86N	CN-RNO	ROYAL AIR MAROC (GECA)		28595	285	06/04/99	CFM56-7B26		N1795B, N1784B
B737-8B6	CN-RNP	ROYAL AIR MAROC		28983	492	04/11/00	CFM56-7B26		
C6-BAHAMAS									
B737-7AH (BBJ)	C6-TTB	WESTMOUNT INVESTMENTS LTD. (FSBU)		29749	456	01/10/00	CFM56-7B26		N1787B, N73711
D-GERMANY									
B737-8Q8	D-ABAA	AIR-BERLIN (SBE)	L	30637	800	03/26/01	CFM56-7B26		G-OKJW
B737-86J	D-ABAC	AIR-BERLIN		30501	619	07/28/00	CFM56-7B27		N1786B
B737-86J	D-ABAD	AIR-BERLIN		30876	759	02/03/01	CFM56-7B27		
B737-86J	D-ABAE	AIR-BERLIN		30877	782	03/04/01	CFM56-7B27		
B737-86J	D-ABAF	AIR-BERLIN	N	30878	844		CFM56-7B27		
B737-86J (WL)	D-ABAN	AIR-BERLIN (BOUL)		26068	36	05/07/98	CFM56-7B27		N35153
B737-86J (WL)	D-ABAO	AIR-BERLIN (J. HUNOLD)		28069	42	05/10/98	CFM56-7B27		N5573B
B737-86J	D-ABAP	AIR-BERLIN (J. HUNOLD)		28070	106	10/06/98	CFM56-7B27		
B737-86J	D-ABAQ	AIR-BERLIN (J. HUNOLD)		28071	133	10/24/98	CFM56-7B27		
B737-86J	D-ABAR	AIR-BERLIN (J. HUNOLD)		28072	147	11/24/98	CFM56-7B27		N1786B
B737-86J	D-ABAS	AIR-BERLIN (J. HUNOLD)		28073	200	02/11/99	CFM56-7B27		N1795B
B737-86J	D-ABAT	AIR-BERLIN (J. HUNOLD)		29120	202	02/16/99	CFM56-7B27		N1786B
B737-86J	D-ABAU	AIR-BERLIN (J. HUNOLD)		29121	239	04/08/99	CFM56-7B27		N1786B
B737-86J	D-ABAV	AIR-BERLIN		30498	450	12/22/99	CFM56-7B27		N1787B
B737-86J	D-ABAW	AIR-BERLIN		30062	485	02/28/00	CFM56-7B27		N1786B
B737-86J	D-ABAX	AIR-BERLIN		30063	517	04/25/00	CFM56-7B27		N1786B
B737-86J	D-ABAY	AIR-BERLIN		30499	567	05/28/00	CFM56-7B27		N1795B
B737-86J	D-ABAZ	AIR-BERLIN		30500	593	06/29/00	CFM56-7B27		N1787B
B737-85H	OY-SEH	AIR-BERLIN (SNB)	L	29444	178	01/21/99	CFM56-7B26		N1787B
B737-75B	D-AGEL	GERMANIA (SAT FLUG)		28110	5	12/14/98	CFM56-7B22		N1791B [LST LTU]
B737-75B	D-AGEN	GERMANIA (SAT FLUG)		28100	16	03/23/98	CFM56-7B22		N1789B
B737-75B	D-AGEP	GERMANIA (SAT FLUG)		28102	18	03/21/98	CFM56-7B22		N5573B

A/C TYPE	CURRENT REG. NO.	LAST KNOWN OPERATOR (OWNER)	STATUS	ORIGINAL MSN	LINE NO.	DEL. DATE	ENG. TYPE	FLEET NO.	PREV. REG. [COMMENTS]
B737-75B	D-AGEQ	GERMANIA (SAT FLUG)		28103	23	07/31/98	CFM56-7B22		N1787B
B737-75B	D-AGER	GERMANIA		28107	27	06/10/98	CFM56-7B22		N1002R [LST LTU]
B737-75B	D-AGES	GERMANIA (BISCHOFF)		28108	28	06/30/98	CFM56-7B22		N1786B [RTS]
B737-75B	D-AGET	GERMANIA (SAT FLUG)		28109	31	03/23/98	CFM56-7B22		
B737-75B	D-AGEU	GERMANIA (SAT FLUG)		28104	39	04/11/98	CFM56-7B22		
B737-73S	D-AGEY	GERMANIA		29076	98	12/15/98	CFM56-7B22		N1786B, N102UN [LST AZI FOR 3 YEARS]
B737-73S	D-AGEZ	GERMANIA (SAT FLUG)		29077	104	12/15/98	CFM56-7B22		N103UN [LST AZI FOR 3 YEARS]
B737-73S	D-AHIA	HAMBURG INTL. (PEMB)		29082	229	03/31/99	CFM56-7B22		N1787B, D-ASKH
B737-73S	D-AHIB	HAMBURG INTL. (PEMB)		29083	392	10/27/99	CFM56-7B22		D-AWOH
B737-7BK	D-AHIC	HAMBURG INTL. (CITG)		30617	812	04/11/01	CFM56-7B22		
B737-8K5	D-AHFA	HAPAG LLOYD (DEFAG)		27981	7	12/29/98	CFM56-7B27		N737BX [737-800 PROTOTYPE]
B737-8K5	D-AHFB	HAPAG LLOYD (DEFAG)		27982	8	12/15/98	CFM56-7B27		N35030
B737-8K5	D-AHFC	HAPAG LLOYD (DEFAG)		27977	9	04/22/98	CFM56-7B27		N5573P
B737-8K5	D-AHFD	HAPAG LLOYD (DEFAG)		27978	40	04/24/98	CFM56-7B27		N35161
B737-8K5	D-AHFE	HAPAG LLOYD (DEFAG)		27979	44	05/13/98	CFM56-7B27		N3502P
B737-8K5	D-AHFF	HAPAG LLOYD (DEFAG)		27980	45	05/16/98	CFM56-7B27		N3509J
B737-8K5	D-AHFG	HAPAG LLOYD (DEFAG)		27989	59	06/24/98	CFM56-7B27		N1786B
B737-8K5	D-AHFH	HAPAG LLOYD (DEFAG)		27983	218	03/09/99	CFM56-7B27		N1786B
B737-8K5	D-AHFI	HAPAG LLOYD (DEFAG)		27984	220	03/11/99	CFM56-7B27		N1787B
B737-8K5	D-AHFJ	HAPAG LLOYD (DEFAG)		27990	246	04/15/99	CFM56-7B27		
B737-8K5	D-AHFK	HAPAG LLOYD (DEFAG)		27991	248	04/15/99	CFM56-7B27		N1786B
B737-8K5	D-AHFL	HAPAG LLOYD (DEFAG)		27985	470	01/31/00	CFM56-7B27		N1786B
B737-8K5	D-AHFM	HAPAG LLOYD (DEFAG)		27986	474	04/03/00	CFM56-7B27		
B737-8K5	D-AHFN	HAPAG LLOYD (ILFC)		28228	484	02/20/00	CFM56-7B27		N1786B
B737-8K5	D-AHFO	HAPAG LLOYD (ILFC)		27987	499	04/03/00	CFM56-7B27		
B737-8K5	D-AHFP	HAPAG LLOYD (ILFC)		27988	508	04/03/00	CFM56-7B27		N1786B
B737-8K5	D-AHFQ	HAPAG LLOYD (ILFC)		27992	523	04/26/00	CFM56-7B27		N1786B
B737-8K5	D-AHFR	HAPAG LLOYD		30593	528	05/03/00	CFM56-7B27		N1787B
B737-8K5	D-AHFS	HAPAG LLOYD (DEFAG)		28623	556	05/21/00	CFM56-7B27		
B737-8K5 (WL)	D-AHFT	HAPAG LLOYD		30413	636	12/20/00	CFM56-7B27		N1786B, N1015B [DEL DELAYED FOR WINGLET TESTING AT BOEING]
B737-8K5	D-AHFU	HAPAG LLOYD		30414	703	11/11/00	CFM56-7B27		N1787B
B737-8K5	D-AHFV	HAPAG LLOYD		30415	719	12/05/00	CFM56-7B27		N1786B
B737-8K5	D-AHFW	HAPAG LLOYD		30882	760	01/31/01	CFM56-7B27		N1786B
B737-8K5	D-AHFX	HAPAG LLOYD		30416	778	02/24/01	CFM56-7B27		N1786B
B737-8K5	D-AHFY	HAPAG LLOYD		30417	781	02/26/01	CFM56-7B27		N1787B
B737-8K5	D-AHFZ	HAPAG LLOYD		30883	783	02/26/01	CFM56-7B27		
B737-8K5	D-AHLH	HAPAG LLOYD (TOMB)		30783	804	03/27/01	CFM56-7B27		
B737-75B	D-AGEL	LTU INTL. AIRWAYS (GMI)	L	28110	5	12/14/98	CFM56-7B22		N1791B

A/C TYPE	CURRENT REG. NO.	LAST KNOWN OPERATOR (OWNER)	STATUS	ORIGINAL MSN	LINE NO.	DEL. DATE	ENG. TYPE	FLEET NO.	PREV. REG. [COMMENTS]
B737-75B	D-AGER	LTU INTL. AIRWAYS (GMI)	L	28107	27	06/10/98	CFM56-7B22		N1002R
DQ-FIJI									
B737-7X2	DQ-FJF	AIR PACIFIC		28878	96	09/22/98	CFM56-7B24		N1786B
B737-8X2	DQ-FJG	AIR PACIFIC		29968	275	05/24/99	CFM56-7B26		N1786B
B737-8X2	DQ-FJH	AIR PACIFIC		29969	339	08/13/99	CFM56-7B26		N1786B
EC-SPAIN									
B737-85P	EC-HBL	AIR EUROPA (ITOH)		28381	250	05/01/99	CFM56-7B26		N1787B
B737-85P	EC-HBM	AIR EUROPA (ITOH)		28382	256	05/03/99	CFM56-7B26		N1787B
B737-85P	EC-HBN	AIR EUROPA (ITOH)		28383	266	05/08/99	CFM56-7B26		N1786B
B737-85P	EC-HGO	AIR EUROPA (ITOH)		28384	420	11/20/99	CFM56-7B26		N1786B
B737-85P	EC-HGP	AIR EUROPA (ITOH)		28385	421	11/22/99	CFM56-7B26		N1786B
B737-85P	EC-HGQ	AIR EUROPA (ITOH)		28386	426	11/24/99	CFM56-7B26		N1786B
B737-85P	EC-HJP	AIR EUROPA (ITOH)		28535	480	04/12/00	CFM56-7B26		N1786B, N1800B
B737-85P	EC-HJQ	AIR EUROPA (ITOH)		28387	522	04/28/00	CFM56-7B26		
B737-85P	EC-HKQ	AIR EUROPA (ITOH)		28388	533	05/09/00	CFM56-7B26		
B737-85P	EC-HKR	AIR EUROPA (ITOH)		28536	540	05/16/00	CFM56-7B26		N1787B
B737-86N	EC-HHG	FUTURA INTL. AIRWAYS (GECA)		28608	410	11/12/99	CFM56-7B27		N1786B
B737-86N	EC-HHH	FUTURA INTL. AIRWAYS (HALVANA)		28610	449	12/20/99	CFM56-7B27		N1786B
B737-86N	EC-HJJ	FUTURA INTL. AIRWAYS (GECA)		28617	504	04/07/00	CFM56-7B27		N1787B
B737-86N	EC-HLN	FUTURA INTL. AIRWAYS (GECA)		28619	534	05/19/00	CFM56-7B27		N1786B
B737-86N	EC-HMJ	FUTURA INTL. AIRWAYS (HALVANA)		28621	570	05/30/00	CFM56-7B27		N1786B
B737-86N	EC-HMK	FUTURA INTL. AIRWAYS (GECA)		28624	585	06/15/00	CFM56-7B27		N1786B
EI-IRELAND									
B737-8AS	EI-CSA	RYANAIR		29916	210	03/19/99	CFM56-7B24		N1786B, N5573L
B737-8AS	EI-CSB	RYANAIR		29917	298	06/16/99	CFM56-7B24		
B737-8AS	EI-CSC	RYANAIR		29918	307	06/28/99	CFM56-7B24		N1786B
B737-8AS	EI-CSD	RYANAIR		29919	341	08/09/99	CFM56-7B24		N1786B
B737-8AS	EI-CSE	RYANAIR		29920	362	09/03/99	CFM56-7B24		N1786B
B737-8AS	EI-CSF	RYANAIR		29921	560	05/24/00	CFM56-7B24		N1786B
B737-8AS	EI-CSG	RYANAIR		29922	571	05/31/00	CFM56-7B24		
B737-8AS	EI-CSH	RYANAIR		29923	576	06/09/00	CFM56-7B24		N1787B
B737-8AS	EI-CSI	RYANAIR		29924	578	06/13/00	CFM56-7B24		N1796B
B737-8AS	EI-CSJ	RYANAIR		29925	588	06/20/00	CFM56-7B24		N1786B
B737-8AS	EI-CSM	RYANAIR		29926	722	12/07/00	CFM56-7B24		N1786B
B737-8AS	EI-CSN	RYANAIR		29927	727	12/11/00	CFM56-7B24		N1786B, N1784B
B737-8AS	EI-CSO	RYANAIR		29928	735	01/12/01	CFM56-7B24		N1786B
B737-8AS	EI-CSP	RYANAIR		29929	753	01/25/01	CFM56-7B24		N1786B

A/C TYPE	CURRENT REG. NO.	LAST KNOWN OPERATOR (OWNER)	STATUS	ORIGINAL MSN	LINE NO.	DEL. DATE	ENG. TYPE	FLEET NO.	PREV. REG. [COMMENTS]
B737-8AS	EI-CSQ	RYANAIR		29930	757	01/26/01	CFM56-7B24		N1786B
F-FRANCE									
B737-85F	F-GRNA	EURALAIR INTL. (GATX)		28823	174	01/31/99	CFM56-7B26		N1784B, N1795B
B737-85F	F-GRNB	EURALAIR INTL. (GATX)		28824	180	02/02/99	CFM56-7B26		N1782B, N500GX
B737-85F	F-GRNC	EURALAIR INTL. (GATX)		28821	151	12/14/98	CFM56-7B26		N1786B
B737-85F	F-GRND	EURALAIR INTL. (GATX)		28827	467	01/29/00	CFM56-7B26		N1787B
B737-85F	F-GRNE	EURALAIR INTL. (GATX)		30568	793	03/15/01	CFM56-7B26		
G-UNITED KINGDOM									
B737-73V	G-EZJA	EASYJET AIRLINE (GECA)		30235	672	10/13/00	CFM56-7B24		N1787B
B737-73V	G-EZJB	EASYJET AIRLINE (GECA)		30236	715	11/22/00	CFM56-7B24		N1787B
B737-73V	G-EZJC	EASYJET AIRLINE		30237	730	12/15/00	CFM56-7B24		N1786B
B737-804	G-BYNB	BRITANNIA AIRWAYS (ILFC)		30466	505	04/08/00	CFM56-7B27		
B737-804	G-BYNC	BRITANNIA AIRWAYS (ILFC)		30465	502	04/06/00	CFM56-7B27		
B737-8Q8	G-OKJW	EXCEL AIRWAYS (ILFC)		30637	800	03/26/01	CFM56-7B26		[LST BER AS D-ABAA]
B737-8Q8	G-XLAA	EXCEL AIRWAYS (ILFC)		28218	160	12/11/98	CFM56-7B26		G-OJSW
B737-8Q8	G-XLAA	EXCEL AIRWAYS (ILFC)		28226	77	07/27/98	CFM56-7B26		G-OKDN
B737-81Q	G-XLAC	EXCEL AIRWAYS (TOMB)		29051	479	02/06/00	CFM56-7B26		N1786B, N8254G, G-LFJB
B737-81Q	G-XLAD	EXCEL AIRWAYS (TOMB)		29052	557	05/24/00	CFM56-7B26		N8254Q, N1786B, G-ODMW
B737-8K2	PH-HZK	EXCEL AIRWAYS (TRA)	L	30390	555	05/16/00	CFM56-7B27		N1786B
B737-7CP (BBJ)	VP-BFE	FORD AIR SERVICES LLC (FSBU)		30753	481	02/08/00	CFM56-7B26		N1787B, N329K
B737-7CP (BBJ)	VP-BFO	FORD AIR SERVICES LLC (FSBU)		30755	545	05/05/00	CFM56-7B26		N1786B, N330K
HB-SWITZERLAND									
B737-7AK (BBJ)	HB-IIO	PRIVATAIR (GOODWATER)		29865	241	04/07/99	CFM56-7B26		N1786B
B737-7AK (BBJ)	HB-IIP	PRIVATAIR (ROSEMEAD)		29866	408	11/02/99	CFM56-7B26		N1786B, N1779B
B737-7AK (BBJ)	HB-IIQ	PRIVATAIR (MATELA OFFSHORE)		30752	451	12/22/99	CFM56-7B26		N1786B, N1026G
HL-KOREA									
B737-86N	HL7555	KOREAN AIR (GECA)		30230	460	01/20/00	CFM56-7B26		N1786B
B737-86N	HL7556	KOREAN AIR (GECA)		28615	482	02/22/00	CFM56-7B26		N1787B
B737-86N	HL7557	KOREAN AIR (GECA)		28622	562	05/26/00	CFM56-7B26		N1786B
B737-86N	HL7558	KOREAN AIR (GECA)		28625	590	06/24/00	CFM56-7B26		N1786B
B737-8B5	HL7559	KOREAN AIR (GECA)		28626	611	07/20/00	CFM56-7B26		N1786B
B737-8B5	HL7560	KOREAN AIR		29981	622	08/15/00	CFM56-7B26		N1786B
B737-8B5	HL7561	KOREAN AIR		29982	663	09/22/00	CFM56-7B26		
B737-8B5	HL7562	KOREAN AIR		29983	678	10/11/00	CFM56-7B26		

A/C TYPE	CURRENT REG. NO.	LAST KNOWN OPERATOR (OWNER)	STATUS	ORIGINAL MSN	LINE NO.	DEL. DATE	ENG. TYPE	FLEET NO.	PREV. REG. [COMMENTS]
B737-86N	HL7563	KOREAN AIR (GECA)		28636	756	01/29/01	CFM56-7B26		N1786B
B737-86N	HL7564	KOREAN AIR (GECA)		28638	765	02/08/01	CFM56-7B26		N1786B
B737-8B5	HL7565	KOREAN AIR	N	29984	848		CFM56-7B26		
B737-8B5	HL7566	KOREAN AIR	N	29985	852		CFM56-7B26		

HP-PANAMA

A/C TYPE	CURRENT REG. NO.	LAST KNOWN OPERATOR (OWNER)	STATUS	ORIGINAL MSN	LINE NO.	DEL. DATE	ENG. TYPE	FLEET NO.	PREV. REG. [COMMENTS]
B737-71Q	HP-1369CMP	COPA PANAMA (TOMB)		29047	235	04/08/99	CFM56-7B24	669	N1786B, N8251R
B737-71Q	HP-1370CMP	COPA PANAMA (TOMB)		29048	288	06/08/99	CFM56-7B24	670	N82521
B737-7V3	HP-1371CMP	COPA PANAMA (GECA)		30049	388	10/14/99	CFM56-7B24	671	N1787B
B737-7V3	HP-1372CMP	COPA PANAMA (GECA)		28607	399	10/21/99	CFM56-7B24		N1786B
B737-7V3	HP-1373CMP	COPA PANAMA		30458	459	01/21/00	CFM56-7B24		N1787B
B737-7V3	HP-1374CMP	COPA PANAMA		30459	494	04/17/00	CFM56-7B24		N1787B
B737-7V3	HP-1375CMP	COPA PANAMA		30460	558	05/19/00	CFM56-7B24		N1787B
B737-7V3	HP-1376CMP	COPA PANAMA		30497	574	06/07/00	CFM56-7B24		N1786B

HZ-SAUDI ARABIA

A/C TYPE	CURRENT REG. NO.	LAST KNOWN OPERATOR (OWNER)	STATUS	ORIGINAL MSN	LINE NO.	DEL. DATE	ENG. TYPE	FLEET NO.	PREV. REG. [COMMENTS]
B737-7BQ (BBJ)	HZ-DG5	DALLAH ALBARAKA (FSBU)		30547	423	11/22/99	CFM56-7B26		N1786B, N1787B, N79711
B737-7P3 (BBJ)	HZ-TAA	HRH TALAL BIN ABDUL AZIZ		29188	217	03/05/99	CFM56-7B26		N1787B, N1779B
B737-7AX	N737A	SAUDI ARAMCO AVIATION		30181	648	09/15/00	CFM56-7B26		N1787B [NOT BBJ's!!!]
B737-7AX	N738A	SAUDI ARAMCO AVIATION		30182	690	10/23/00	CFM56-7B26		N1785B
B737-7AX	N739A	SAUDI ARAMCO AVIATION		30183	702	11/08/00	CFM56-7B26		N1786B

I-ITALY

A/C TYPE	CURRENT REG. NO.	LAST KNOWN OPERATOR (OWNER)	STATUS	ORIGINAL MSN	LINE NO.	DEL. DATE	ENG. TYPE	FLEET NO.	PREV. REG. [COMMENTS]
B737-73S	EI-CRP	AZZURAAIR (PEMB)		29078	187	04/15/99	CFM56-7B24		N1787B, N1014S, N60436
B737-73S	EI-CRQ	AZZURAAIR (PEMB)		29080	211	04/14/99	CFM56-7B24		N1786B, N1782B
B737-73S	D-AGEY	AZZURAAIR (GMI)	L	29076	98	12/15/98	CFM56-7B22		N1786B, N102UN
B737-73S	D-AGEZ	AZZURAAIR (GMI)	L	29077	104	12/15/98	CFM56-7B22		N103UN

LN-NORWAY

A/C TYPE	CURRENT REG. NO.	LAST KNOWN OPERATOR (OWNER)	STATUS	ORIGINAL MSN	LINE NO.	DEL. DATE	ENG. TYPE	FLEET NO.	PREV. REG. [COMMENTS]
B737-705	LN-TUA	BRAATHENS (ILFC)		28211	33	04/13/98	CFM56-7B24		
B737-705	LN-TUB	BRAATHENS		29089	83	08/25/98	CFM56-7B24		N1786B [TBR SE-RAR]
B737-705	LN-TUC	BRAATHENS		29090	109	09/25/98	CFM56-7B24		N1786B [TBR SE-RAS]
B737-705	LN-TUD	BRAATHENS (ILFC)		28217	142	11/11/98	CFM56-7B24		N1786B
B737-705	LN-TUE	BRAATHENS		29091	230	03/24/99	CFM56-7B24		N5573L
B737-705	LN-TUF	BRAATHENS (ILFC)		28222	245	04/15/99	CFM56-7B24		N1786B
B737-705	LN-TUG	BRAATHENS		29092	260	05/07/99	CFM56-7B24		
B737-705	LN-TUH	BRAATHENS		29093	471	01/30/00	CFM56-7B24		N1786B
B737-705	LN-TUI	BRAATHENS		29094	507	04/11/00	CFM56-7B24		N1787B
B737-705	LN-TUJ	BRAATHENS		29095	773	02/21/01	CFM56-7B24		

A/C TYPE	CURRENT REG. NO.	LAST KNOWN OPERATOR (OWNER)	STATUS	ORIGINAL MSN	LINE NO.	DEL. DATE	ENG. TYPE	FLEET NO.	PREV. REG. [COMMENTS]
B737-705	LN-TUK	BRAATHENS		29096	794	03/14/01	CFM56-7B24		
LV-ARGENTINA									
B737-7Q8	LV-YYC	LAPA (ILFC)		28210	22	06/24/98	CFM56-7B24		N5573P, N801LF
B737-76N	LV-ZHX	LAPA (GECA)		28577	124	10/30/98	CFM56-7B24		N1786B, N577GE, LV-PNZ
B737-7Q8	LV-ZON	LAPA (ILFC)		28219	183	01/29/99	CFM56-7B24		N1786B, N1782B, LV-POF, N331LF
B737-76N	LV-ZRC	LAPA (GECA)		29904	347	08/18/99	CFM56-7B24		N1795B, N1784B, N904LP
B737-7Q8	LV-ZRM	LAPA (ILFC)		28224	369	09/16/99	CFM56-7B24		N1786B, N1784B, N411LF, LV-PIG
B737-76N	LV-ZRP	LAPA (GECA)		29905	372	09/27/99	CFM56-7B24		N1786B, N905LP
B737-76N	LV-ZSN	LAPA (GECA)		30050	429	11/29/99	CFM56-7B24		N1786B, N350LP
B737-7Q8	LV-ZXG	LAPA (ILFC)		30635	713	11/29/00	CFM56-7B24		N461LF
N-UNITED STATES OF AMERICA									
B737-79U (BBJ)	N1011N	(AIRCRAFT HOLDINGS LLC)		29441	111	10/06/99	CFM56-7B26		N1787B, N1779B
B737-7AV (BBJ)	N889NC	NEWS AMERICA INC.		30070	244	04/13/99	CFM56-7B26		N1787B, N18NC
B737-7CU (BBJ)	N315TS	TUTOR-SALIBA CORP.		30772	554	06/07/00	CFM56-7B26		N1798B, N1784B
B737-7BH (BBJ)	N348BA	(FSBU)		29791	336	08/05/99	CFM56-7B26		N1786B
B737-74T (BBJ)	N21KR	NORTH PACIFIC AVIATION (FSBU)		29139	189	01/26/99	CFM56-7B26		N1786B, N5573L, N73721
B737-73Q (BBJ)	N737BZ	BOEING (MDFC)		29102	101	12/22/98	CFM56-7B26		
B737-73Q (BBJ)	N349BA	BOEING (MDFC)		30789	602	09/21/00	CFM56-7B26		N1786B [BBJ DEMONSTRATOR]
B737-74Q (BBJ)	N737CC	JARVIS & ASSOCIATES		29135	206	02/24/99	CFM56-7B26		N1786B, N60436
B737-7BC (BBJ)	N515GM	KEVINAIR LLC		30782	586	10/24/00	CFM56-7B26		N1786B, N1006F
B737-74Q (BBJ)	N737GG	MID EAST JET		29136	225	03/18/99	CFM56-7B26		N1787B, N1779B
B737-74V (BBJ)	N737SP	RAYTHEON CO.		29272	323	08/12/99	CFM56-7B26		N1786B
B737-73U (BBJ)	N742PB	CHARTWELL AIRCRAFT CO.		29200	234	03/30/99	CFM56-7B26		
B737-7CJ (BBJ)	N61MJ	BBJ ONE INC.		30754	516	04/26/00	CFM56-7B26		N1786B, N349BA, N79715
B737-7CG (BBJ)	N888GW	GKW AVIATION LLC		30751	401	10/21/99	CFM56-7B26		N1786B, N1784B, N800GK
B737-74U (BBJ)	N4AS	AIR SHAMROCK		29233	197	02/12/99	CFM56-7B26		N1786B

A/C TYPE	CURRENT REG. NO.	LAST KNOWN OPERATOR (OWNER)	STATUS	ORIGINAL MSN	LINE NO.	DEL. DATE	ENG. TYPE	FLEET NO.	PREV. REG. [COMMENTS]
B737-81Q	N732MA	AIRTRAN AIRWAYS (BSK)	L	30618	830	04/26/01	CFM56-7B26		
B737-790	N607AS	ALASKA AIRLINES		29751	313	07/28/99	CFM56-7B24		
B737-790	N609AS	ALASKA AIRLINES		29752	350	08/20/99	CFM56-7B24		N1786B
B737-790	N611AS	ALASKA AIRLINES		29753	385	10/06/99	CFM56-7B24		N1796B
B737-790	N612AS	ALASKA AIRLINES		30162	406	11/01/99	CFM56-7B24		N1787B
B737-790	N613AS	ALASKA AIRLINES		30163	430	11/30/99	CFM56-7B24		N1786B
B737-790	N614AS	ALASKA AIRLINES		30343	439	12/13/99	CFM56-7B24		N1786B
B737-790	N615AS	ALASKA AIRLINES		30344	472	02/01/00	CFM56-7B24		N1787B
B737-790	N617AS	ALASKA AIRLINES		30542	532	05/31/00	CFM56-7B24		N1786B
B737-790	N618AS	ALASKA AIRLINES		30543	536	05/26/00	CFM56-7B24		N1787B
B737-790	N619AS	ALASKA AIRLINES		30164	597	06/30/00	CFM56-7B24		N1786B
B737-790	N622AS	ALASKA AIRLINES		30165	661	09/19/00	CFM56-7B24		
B737-790	N623AS	ALASKA AIRLINES		30166	700	11/14/00	CFM56-7B24		N1786B
B737-790	N624AS	ALASKA AIRLINES		30778	724	12/12/00	CFM56-7B24		N1786B
B737-790	N625AS	ALASKA AIRLINES		30792	754	01/31/01	CFM56-7B24		N1795B
B737-790	N626AS	ALASKA AIRLINES		30793	763	02/08/01	CFM56-7B24		N1786B
B737-790	N627AS	ALASKA AIRLINES		30794	796	03/28/01	CFM56-7B24		
B737-990	N737X	ALASKA AIRLINES	N	30017	596		CFM56-7B24		N1786B [737-900 PROTOTYPE; TBR N302AS]
B737-990	N303AS	ALASKA AIRLINES	N	30016	683		CFM56-7B24		N1786B [N672AS NTU]
B737-990	N305AS	ALASKA AIRLINES		30013	774	05/16/01	CFM56-7B24		[N673AS NTU]
B737-990	N306AS	ALASKA AIRLINES	N	30014	802		CFM56-7B24		[N674AS NTU]
B737-990	N307AS	ALASKA AIRLINES	N	30015	838		CFM56-7B24		
B737-73A	N738AL	ALOHA AIRLINES (AWAS)		28499	390	10/18/99	CFM56-7B24		
B737-73A	N739AL	ALOHA AIRLINES (AWAS)		28500	414	11/12/99	CFM56-7B24		N1787B
B737-76N	N740AL	ALOHA AIRLINES (GECA)		28640	799	03/23/01	CFM56-7B24		
B737-76N	N741AL	ALOHA AIRLINES (GECA)		28641	809	03/29/01	CFM56-7B24		
B737-823	N901AN	AMERICAN AIRLINES		29503	184	02/07/99	CFM56-7B26	3AA	
B737-823	N902AN	AMERICAN AIRLINES		29504	190	02/10/99	CFM56-7B26	3AB	
B737-823	N903AN	AMERICAN AIRLINES		29505	196	02/16/99	CFM56-7B26	3AC	
B737-823	N904AN	AMERICAN AIRLINES		29506	207	03/08/99	CFM56-7B26	3AD	
B737-823	N905AN	AMERICAN AIRLINES		29507	231	03/31/99	CFM56-7B26	3AE	
B737-823	N906AN	AMERICAN AIRLINES		29508	240	04/16/99	CFM56-7B26	3AF	
B737-823	N907AN	AMERICAN AIRLINES		29509	254	04/29/99	CFM56-7B26	3AG	
B737-823	N908AN	AMERICAN AIRLINES		29510	263	05/13/99	CFM56-7B26	3AH	
B737-823	N909AM	AMERICAN AIRLINES		29511	267	05/19/99	CFM56-7B26	3AJ	
B737-823	N910AN	AMERICAN AIRLINES		29512	271	05/26/99	CFM56-7B26	3AK	
B737-823	N912AN	AMERICAN AIRLINES		29513	289	06/25/99	CFM56-7B26	3AL	

A/C TYPE	CURRENT REG. NO.	LAST KNOWN OPERATOR (OWNER)	STATUS	ORIGINAL MSN	LINE NO.	DEL. DATE	ENG. TYPE	FLEET NO.	PREV. REG. [COMMENTS]
B737-823	N913AN	AMERICAN AIRLINES		29514	293	06/18/99	CFM56-7B26	3AM	
B737-823	N914AN	AMERICAN AIRLINES		29515	316	07/19/99	CFM56-7B26	3AN	
B737-823	N915AN	AMERICAN AIRLINES		29516	322	07/28/99	CFM56-7B26	3AP	
B737-823	N916AN	AMERICAN AIRLINES		29517	332	08/06/99	CFM56-7B26	3AR	
B737-823	N917AN	AMERICAN AIRLINES		29518	344	08/27/99	CFM56-7B26	3AS	
B737-823	N918AN	AMERICAN AIRLINES		29519	353	09/10/99	CFM56-7B26	3AT	
B737-823	N919AN	AMERICAN AIRLINES		29520	363	09/15/99	CFM56-7B26	3AU	
B737-823	N920AN	AMERICAN AIRLINES		29521	378	10/05/99	CFM56-7B26	3AV	
B737-823	N921AN	AMERICAN AIRLINES		29522	383	10/12/99	CFM56-7B26	3AW	
B737-823	N922AN	AMERICAN AIRLINES		29523	398	10/29/99	CFM56-7B26	3AX	
B737-823	N923AN	AMERICAN AIRLINES		29524	405	11/18/99	CFM56-7B26	3AY	
B737-823	N924AN	AMERICAN AIRLINES		29525	434	12/14/99	CFM56-7B26	3BA	
B737-823	N925AN	AMERICAN AIRLINES		29526	440	12/17/99	CFM56-7B26	3BB	
B737-823	N926AN	AMERICAN AIRLINES		29527	453	01/13/00	CFM56-7B26	3BC	
B737-823	N927AN	AMERICAN AIRLINES		30077	462	01/25/00	CFM56-7B26	3BD	
B737-823	N928AN	AMERICAN AIRLINES		29528	473	02/07/00	CFM56-7B26	3BE	
B737-823	N929AN	AMERICAN AIRLINES		30078	488	03/25/00	CFM56-7B26	3BF	
B737-823	N930AN	AMERICAN AIRLINES		29529	503	04/07/00	CFM56-7B26	3BG	
B737-823	N931AN	AMERICAN AIRLINES		30079	509	04/20/00	CFM56-7B26	3BH	
B737-823	N932AN	AMERICAN AIRLINES		29530	527	04/28/00	CFM56-7B26	3BJ	
B737-823	N933AN	AMERICAN AIRLINES		30080	531	05/12/00	CFM56-7B26	3BK	N1786B
B737-823	N934AN	AMERICAN AIRLINES		29531	553	05/15/00	CFM56-7B26	3BL	
B737-823	N935AN	AMERICAN AIRLINES		30081	559	05/19/00	CFM56-7B26	3BM	N1786B
B737-823	N936AN	AMERICAN AIRLINES		29532	575	06/15/00	CFM56-7B26	3BN	
B737-823	N937AN	AMERICAN AIRLINES		30082	579	06/16/00	CFM56-7B26	3BP	
B737-823	N938AN	AMERICAN AIRLINES		29533	608	07/24/00	CFM56-7B26	3BR	
B737-823	N939AN	AMERICAN AIRLINES		30083	612	07/26/00	CFM56-7B26	3BS	
B737-823	N940AN	AMERICAN AIRLINES		30598	616	07/31/00	CFM56-7B26	3BT	
B737-823	N941AN	AMERICAN AIRLINES		29534	624	08/14/00	CFM56-7B26	3BU	
B737-823	N942AN	AMERICAN AIRLINES		30084	629	08/14/00	CFM56-7B26	3BV	N1786B
B737-823	N943AN	AMERICAN AIRLINES		30599	635	08/25/00	CFM56-7B26	3BW	N1786B
B737-823	N944AN	AMERICAN AIRLINES		29535	645	09/06/00	CFM56-7B26	3BX	
B737-823	N945AN	AMERICAN AIRLINES		30085	649	09/14/00	CFM56-7B26	3BY	
B737-823	N946AN	AMERICAN AIRLINES		30600	655	09/19/00	CFM56-7B26	3CA	
B737-823	N947AN	AMERICAN AIRLINES		29536	671	10/12/00	CFM56-7B26	3CB	
B737-823	N948AN	AMERICAN AIRLINES		30086	679	10/26/00	CFM56-7B26	3CC	
B737-823	N949AN	AMERICAN AIRLINES		29537	699	11/10/00	CFM56-7B26	3CD	
B737-823	N950AN	AMERICAN AIRLINES		30087	704	11/18/00	CFM56-7B26	3CE	
B737-823	N951AA	AMERICAN AIRLINES		29538	720	12/12/00	CFM56-7B26	3CF	["ASTROJET" C/S]
B737-823	N952AA	AMERICAN AIRLINES		30088	726	12/21/00	CFM56-7B26	3CG	
B737-823	N953AN	AMERICAN AIRLINES		29539	741	01/17/01	CFM56-7B26	3CH	

A/C TYPE	CURRENT REG. NO.	LAST KNOWN OPERATOR (OWNER)	STATUS	ORIGINAL MSN	LINE NO.	DEL. DATE	ENG. TYPE	FLEET NO.	PREV. REG. [COMMENTS]
B737-823	N954AN	AMERICAN AIRLINES		30089	745	01/19/01	CFM56-7B26	3CJ	
B737-823	N955AN	AMERICAN AIRLINES		29540	762	02/08/01	CFM56-7B26	3CK	
B737-823	N956AN	AMERICAN AIRLINES		30090	764	02/13/01	CFM56-7B26	3CL	
B737-823	N957AN	AMERICAN AIRLINES		29541	788	03/12/01	CFM56-7B26	3CM	
B737-823	N958AN	AMERICAN AIRLINES		30091	797	03/23/01	CFM56-7B26	3CN	
B737-823	N959AM	AMERICAN AIRLINES		30828	801	03/29/01	CFM56-7B26	3CP	
B737-823	N960AN	AMERICAN AIRLINES		29542	818	04/19/01	CFM56-7B26	3CR	
B737-823	N961AN	AMERICAN AIRLINES		30092	822	04/25/01	CFM56-7B26	3CS	
B737-823	N962AN	AMERICAN AIRLINES		30858	825	04/30/01	CFM56-7B26	3CT	
B737-823	N963AN	AMERICAN AIRLINES	N	29543	834		CFM56-7B26	3CU	
B737-823	N964AN	AMERICAN AIRLINES	N	30093	837		CFM56-7B26	3CV	
B737-83N	N301TZ	AMERICAN TRANS AIR (ILFC)	N	28239	847		CFM56-7B26		
B737-7BJ (BBJ)	N737MC	ATLAS AIR (FSBU)		30076	179	01/29/99	CFM56-7B26		N1786B, N1784B, N374MC, D-AXXL
B737-724	N16701	CONTINENTAL AIRLINES (FSBU)		28762	29	03/30/98	CFM56-7B24	701	N1786B
B737-724	N24702	CONTINENTAL AIRLINES (FSBU)		28763	32	03/31/98	CFM56-7B24	702	
B737-724	N16703	CONTINENTAL AIRLINES (FSBU)		28764	37	04/07/98	CFM56-7B24	703	
B737-724	N14704	CONTINENTAL AIRLINES (FSBU)		28765	43	04/27/98	CFM56-7B24	704	
B737-724	N25705	CONTINENTAL AIRLINES (FSBU)		28766	46	05/12/98	CFM56-7B24	705	
B737-724	N24706	CONTINENTAL AIRLINES (FSBU)		28767	47	05/26/98	CFM56-7B24	706	
B737-724	N23707	CONTINENTAL AIRLINES (FSBU)		28768	48	05/27/98	CFM56-7B24	707	N1787B
B737-724	N23708	CONTINENTAL AIRLINES (FSBU)		28769	52	06/01/98	CFM56-7B24	708	
B737-724	N16709	CONTINENTAL AIRLINES		28779	93	08/31/98	CFM56-7B24	709	N1786B
B737-724	N15710	CONTINENTAL AIRLINES		28780	94	08/31/98	CFM56-7B24	710	
B737-724	N54711	CONTINENTAL AIRLINES		28782	97	09/18/98	CFM56-7B24	711	N1786B
B737-724	N15712	CONTINENTAL AIRLINES		28783	105	09/24/98	CFM56-7B24	712	N1786B
B737-724	N16713	CONTINENTAL AIRLINES		28784	107	09/24/98	CFM56-7B24	713	N1786B
B737-724	N33714	CONTINENTAL AIRLINES		28785	119	09/28/98	CFM56-7B24	714	N1786B
B737-724	N24715	CONTINENTAL AIRLINES (FSBU)		28786	125	10/21/98	CFM56-7B24	715	N1786B, N1795B
B737-724	N13716	CONTINENTAL AIRLINES		28787	156	12/04/98	CFM56-7B24	716	N1795B, N1782B
B737-724	N29717	CONTINENTAL AIRLINES		28936	182	01/22/99	CFM56-7B24	717	N1786B
B737-724	N13718	CONTINENTAL AIRLINES		28937	185	01/22/99	CFM56-7B24	718	N1786B
B737-724	N17719	CONTINENTAL AIRLINES		28938	195	02/03/99	CFM56-7B24	719	N1786B
B737-724	N13720	CONTINENTAL AIRLINES		28939	214	02/26/99	CFM56-7B24	720	
B737-724	N23721	CONTINENTAL AIRLINES		28940	219	03/09/99	CFM56-7B24	721	
B737-724	N27722	CONTINENTAL AIRLINES		28789	247	04/15/99	CFM56-7B24	722	N1786B
B737-724	N21723	CONTINENTAL AIRLINES		28790	253	04/22/99	CFM56-7B24	723	
B737-724	N27724	CONTINENTAL AIRLINES (FSBU)		28791	283	05/27/99	CFM56-7B24	724	N1787B
B737-724	N39726	CONTINENTAL AIRLINES (FSBU)		28796	315	07/09/99	CFM56-7B24	726	N1787B

A/C TYPE	CURRENT REG. NO.	LAST KNOWN OPERATOR (OWNER)	STATUS	ORIGINAL MSN	LINE NO.	DEL. DATE	ENG. TYPE	FLEET NO.	PREV. REG. [COMMENTS]
B737-724	N38727	CONTINENTAL AIRLINES (FSBU)		28797	317	07/13/99	CFM56-7B24	727	N1786B
B737-724	N39728	CONTINENTAL AIRLINES		28944	321	07/16/99	CFM56-7B24	728	N1786B
B737-724	N24729	CONTINENTAL AIRLINES		28945	325	07/28/99	CFM56-7B24	729	N1787B, N1784B
B737-724	N17730	CONTINENTAL AIRLINES (FSBU)		28798	338	08/04/99	CFM56-7B24	730	N1786B
B737-724	N14731	CONTINENTAL AIRLINES (FSBU)		28799	346	08/17/99	CFM56-7B24	731	N1786B
B737-724	N16732	CONTINENTAL AIRLINES		28948	352	08/23/99	CFM56-7B24	732	N1787B, N60436
B737-724	N27733	CONTINENTAL AIRLINES (FSBU)		28800	364	09/07/99	CFM56-7B24	733	
B737-724	N27734	CONTINENTAL AIRLINES		28949	371	09/15/99	CFM56-7B24	734	N1786B
B737-724	N14735	CONTINENTAL AIRLINES		28950	376	09/22/99	CFM56-7B24	735	N1786B
B737-724	N24736	CONTINENTAL AIRLINES		28803	380	09/27/99	CFM56-7B24	736	N1786B
B737-724	N13750	CONTINENTAL AIRLINES (FSBU)		28941	286	06/04/99	CFM56-7B24	750	
B737-824	N25201	CONTINENTAL AIRLINES		28958	443	12/15/99	CFM56-7B26	201	N1786B [OPF CMI; ETOPS]
B737-824	N24202	CONTINENTAL AIRLINES (FSBU)		30429	581	06/12/00	CFM56-7B26	202	N1786B
B737-824	N33203	CONTINENTAL AIRLINES (FSBU)		30613	591	06/21/00	CFM56-7B26	203	N1786B
B737-824	N35204	CONTINENTAL AIRLINES (FSBU)		30576	606	07/14/00	CFM56-7B26	204	N1786B, N1795B
B737-824	N27205	CONTINENTAL AIRLINES (FSBU)		30577	615	07/24/00	CFM56-7B26	205	N1786B
B737-824	N11206	CONTINENTAL AIRLINES (WFBN)		30578	618	07/26/00	CFM56-7B26	206	N1786B
B737-824	N36207	CONTINENTAL AIRLINES (FSBU)		30579	627	08/07/00	CFM56-7B26	207	
B737-824	N26208	CONTINENTAL AIRLINES (FSBU)		30580	644	08/28/00	CFM56-7B26	208	
B737-824	N33209	CONTINENTAL AIRLINES		30581	647	08/31/00	CFM56-7B26	209	
B737-824	N26210	CONTINENTAL AIRLINES (FSBU)		28770	56	06/23/98	CFM56-7B26	210	
B737-824	N24211	CONTINENTAL AIRLINES (FSBU)		28771	58	06/30/98	CFM56-7B26	211	
B737-824	N24212	CONTINENTAL AIRLINES (FSBU)		28772	63	06/30/98	CFM56-7B26	212	N1786B
B737-824	N27213	CONTINENTAL AIRLINES (FSBU)		28773	65	07/14/98	CFM56-7B26	213	N1786B
B737-824	N14214	CONTINENTAL AIRLINES (FSBU)		28774	74	07/24/98	CFM56-7B26	214	
B737-824	N26215	CONTINENTAL AIRLINES		28775	76	08/04/98	CFM56-7B26	215	N1786B
B737-824	N12216	CONTINENTAL AIRLINES (WFBN)		28776	79	08/04/98	CFM56-7B26	216	N1786B
B737-824	N16217	CONTINENTAL AIRLINES		28777	81	07/31/98	CFM56-7B26	217	
B737-824	N12218	CONTINENTAL AIRLINES (WFBN)		28778	84	08/14/98	CFM56-7B26	218	
B737-824	N14219	CONTINENTAL AIRLINES		28781	88	08/27/98	CFM56-7B26	219	N1786B
B737-824	N18220	CONTINENTAL AIRLINES (FSBU)		28929	134	11/05/98	CFM56-7B26	220	N1786B, N60436
B737-824	N12221	CONTINENTAL AIRLINES (WFBN)		28930	153	12/01/98	CFM56-7B26	221	N1796B
B737-824	N34222	CONTINENTAL AIRLINES		28931	159	12/08/98	CFM56-7B26	222	
B737-824	N18223	CONTINENTAL AIRLINES		28932	162	12/17/98	CFM56-7B26	223	N1786B
B737-824	N24224	CONTINENTAL AIRLINES		28933	165	12/18/98	CFM56-7B26	224	N1786B, N1782B
B737-824	N12225	CONTINENTAL AIRLINES (WFBN)		28934	168	12/22/98	CFM56-7B26	225	N1786B, N1782B
B737-824	N26226	CONTINENTAL AIRLINES		28935	171	12/22/98	CFM56-7B26	226	N1787B
B737-824	N13227	CONTINENTAL AIRLINES		28788	262	05/03/99	CFM56-7B26	227	N1787B
B737-824	N14228	CONTINENTAL AIRLINES		28792	281	05/27/99	CFM56-7B26	228	
B737-824	N17229	CONTINENTAL AIRLINES (FSBU)		28793	287	06/04/99	CFM56-7B26	229	
B737-824	N14230	CONTINENTAL AIRLINES (FSBU)		28794	296	06/16/99	CFM56-7B26	230	N1787B

A/C TYPE	CURRENT REG. NO.	LAST KNOWN OPERATOR (OWNER)	STATUS	ORIGINAL MSN	LINE NO.	DEL. DATE	ENG. TYPE	FLEET NO.	PREV. REG. [COMMENTS]
B737-824	N14231	CONTINENTAL AIRLINES (FSBU)		28795	300	06/21/99	CFM56-7B26	231	
B737-824	N26232	CONTINENTAL AIRLINES		28942	304	06/24/99	CFM56-7B26	232	
B737-824	N17233	CONTINENTAL AIRLINES (FSBU)		28943	328	07/23/99	CFM56-7B26	233	N1787B
B737-824	N16234	CONTINENTAL AIRLINES (FSBU)		28946	334	08/04/99	CFM56-7B26	234	N1787B
B737-824	N14235	CONTINENTAL AIRLINES		28947	342	08/10/99	CFM56-7B26	235	
B737-824	N35236	CONTINENTAL AIRLINES		28801	367	09/10/99	CFM56-7B26	236	N1786B
B737-824	N14237	CONTINENTAL AIRLINES (FSBU)		28802	374	09/20/99	CFM56-7B26	237	
B737-824	N12238	CONTINENTAL AIRLINES (WFBN)		28804	386	10/08/99	CFM56-7B26	238	N1786B
B737-824	N27239	CONTINENTAL AIRLINES (FSBU)		28951	391	10/15/99	CFM56-7B26	239	N1787B
B737-824	N14240	CONTINENTAL AIRLINES		28952	394	10/18/99	CFM56-7B26	240	N1786B
B737-824	N54241	CONTINENTAL AIRLINES (FSBU)		28953	395	10/19/99	CFM56-7B26	241	N1787B
B737-824	N14242	CONTINENTAL AIRLINES (FSBU)		28805	402	10/25/99	CFM56-7B26	242	N1786B
B737-824	N18243	CONTINENTAL AIRLINES		28806	403	10/26/99	CFM56-7B26	243	N1786B
B737-824	N17244	CONTINENTAL AIRLINES (FSBU)		28954	409	11/02/99	CFM56-7B26	244	N1787B
B737-824	N17245	CONTINENTAL AIRLINES (FSBU)		28955	411	11/05/99	CFM56-7B26	245	N1786B
B737-824	N27246	CONTINENTAL AIRLINES		28956	413	11/09/99	CFM56-7B26	246	N1786B ["WHIDBEY 24" CREW RECOVERY AIRPLANE]
B737-824	N36247	CONTINENTAL AIRLINES (FSBU)		28807	431	12/02/99	CFM56-7B26	247	N1786B
B737-824	N13248	CONTINENTAL AIRLINES (FSBU)		28808	435	12/06/99	CFM56-7B26	248	N1786B
B737-824	N14249	CONTINENTAL AIRLINES		28809	438	12/10/99	CFM56-7B26	249	N1786B
B737-824	N14250	CONTINENTAL AIRLINES		28957	441	12/13/99	CFM56-7B26	250	N1786B
B737-824	N73251	CONTINENTAL AIRLINES (FSBU)		30582	650	09/01/00	CFM56-7B26	251	N1786B
B737-824	N37252	CONTINENTAL AIRLINES		30583	656	09/12/00	CFM56-7B26	252	N1787B
B737-824	N37253	CONTINENTAL AIRLINES		30584	660	09/18/00	CFM56-7B26	253	
B737-824	N76254	CONTINENTAL AIRLINES		30779	667	09/27/00	CFM56-7B26	254	N1786B
B737-824	N37255	CONTINENTAL AIRLINES (FSBU)		30610	686	10/23/00	CFM56-7B26	255	
B737-824	N73256	CONTINENTAL AIRLINES (FSBU)		30611	692	10/30/00	CFM56-7B26	256	N1787B
B737-824	N38257	CONTINENTAL AIRLINES (FSBU)		30612	706	11/14/00	CFM56-7B26	257	N1786B
B737-824	N77258	CONTINENTAL AIRLINES		30802	708	11/15/00	CFM56-7B26	258	N1786B
B737-924	N30401	CONTINENTAL AIRLINES	N	30118	820		CFM56-7B26		
B737-832	N371DA	DELTA AIRLINES		29619	115	10/22/98	CFM56-7B26	3701	N1787B
B737-832	N372DA	DELTA AIRLINES		29620	118	10/26/98	CFM56-7B26	3702	N1786B, N1782B
B737-832	N3730B	DELTA AIRLINES		30538	662	09/22/00	CFM56-7B26	3730	["SHUTTLE"]
B737-832	N3731T	DELTA AIRLINES		30775	665	09/29/00	CFM56-7B26	3731	["SHUTTLE"]
B737-832	N3732J	DELTA AIRLINES		30380	674	10/04/00	CFM56-7B26	3732	N1786B ["SHUTTLE"]
B737-832	N3733Z	DELTA AIRLINES		30539	685	10/27/00	CFM56-7B26	3733	N1786B ["SHUTTLE"]
B737-832	N3734B	DELTA AIRLINES		30776	689	10/28/00	CFM56-7B26	3734	["SHUTTLE"]
B737-832	N3735D	DELTA AIRLINES		30381	694	11/03/00	CFM56-7B26	3735	N1786B ["SHUTTLE"]
B737-832	N3736C	DELTA AIRLINES		30540	709	11/27/00	CFM56-7B26	3736	N1786B ["SHUTTLE"]
B737-832	N3737C	DELTA AIRLINES		30799	712	11/30/00	CFM56-7B26	3737	N1786B ["SHUTTLE"]
B737-832	N3738B	DELTA AIRLINES		30382	723	12/14/00	CFM56-7B26	3738	N1786B ["SHUTTLE"]

A/C TYPE	CURRENT REG. NO.	LAST KNOWN OPERATOR (OWNER)	STATUS	ORIGINAL MSN	LINE NO.	DEL. DATE	ENG. TYPE	FLEET NO.	PREV. REG. [COMMENTS]
B737-832	N3739P	DELTA AIRLINES		30541	729	12/14/00	CFM56-7B26	3739	N1786B ["SHUTTLE"]
B737-832	N373DA	DELTA AIRLINES		29621	123	10/27/98	CFM56-7B26	3703	N1786B, N1800B
B737-832	N3740C	DELTA AIRLINES		30800	732	12/19/00	CFM56-7B26	3740	N1786B ["SHUTTLE"]
B737-832	N3741S	DELTA AIRLINES		30487	750	01/27/01	CFM56-7B26	3741	N1786B
B737-832	N3742C	DELTA AIRLINES		30835	755	02/01/01	CFM56-7B26	3742	N1787B, N1781B
B737-832	N3743H	DELTA AIRLINES		30836	770	02/21/01	CFM56-7B26	3743	N1795B
B737-832	N3744F	DELTA AIRLINES	N	30837	805		CFM56-7B26	3744	
B737-832	N3745B	DELTA AIRLINES	N	32373	831		CFM56-7B26		
B737-832	N3746H	DELTA AIRLINES	N	30488	842		CFM56-7B26		
B737-832	N3747D	DELTA AIRLINES	N	32374	846		CFM56-7B26		
B737-832	N374DA	DELTA AIRLINES		29622	128	11/04/98	CFM56-7B26	3704	N1787B
B737-832	N375DA	DELTA AIRLINES		29623	145	11/30/98	CFM56-7B26	3705	
B737-832	N376DA	DELTA AIRLINES		29624	176	01/14/99	CFM56-7B26	3706	N1786B
B737-832	N377DA	DELTA AIRLINES		29625	264	05/10/99	CFM56-7B26	3707	N1786B
B737-832	N378DA	DELTA AIRLINES		30265	340	08/13/99	CFM56-7B26	3708	N1786B, N1782B
B737-832	N379DA	DELTA AIRLINES		30349	351	08/23/99	CFM56-7B26	3709	N1786B
B737-832	N380DA	DELTA AIRLINES		30266	361	09/20/99	CFM56-7B26	3710	
B737-832	N381DN	DELTA AIRLINES		30350	365	09/13/99	CFM56-7B26	3711	N1786B
B737-832	N382DA	DELTA AIRLINES		30345	389	10/12/99	CFM56-7B26	3712	N1786B
B737-832	N383DN	DELTA AIRLINES		30346	393	10/19/99	CFM56-7B26	3713	
B737-832	N384DA	DELTA AIRLINES		30347	412	11/22/99	CFM56-7B26	3714	N1786B
B737-832	N385DN	DELTA AIRLINES		30348	418	11/19/99	CFM56-7B26	3715	N1786B
B737-832	N386DA	DELTA AIRLINES		30373	446	12/20/99	CFM56-7B26	3716	N1786B, N1780B
B737-832	N387DA	DELTA AIRLINES		30374	457	01/14/00	CFM56-7B26	3717	N1795B
B737-832	N388DA	DELTA AIRLINES		30375	469	02/01/00	CFM56-7B26	3718	N1786B
B737-832	N389DA	DELTA AIRLINES		30376	513	04/15/00	CFM56-7B26	3719	N1787B
B737-832	N390DA	DELTA AIRLINES		30536	518	04/28/00	CFM56-7B26	3720	N1786B, N6063S
B737-832	N391DA	DELTA AIRLINES		30560	535	05/08/00	CFM56-7B26	3721	N1787B
B737-832	N392DA	DELTA AIRLINES		30561	564	05/30/00	CFM56-7B26	3722	N1786B
B737-832	N393DA	DELTA AIRLINES		30377	584	06/30/00	CFM56-7B26	3723	N1795B, N1782B
B737-832	N394DA	DELTA AIRLINES		30562	589	06/29/00	CFM56-7B26	3724	N1786B
B737-832	N395DN	DELTA AIRLINES		30773	604	07/17/00	CFM56-7B26	3725	N1786B ["SHUTTLE"]
B737-832	N396DA	DELTA AIRLINES		30378	632	08/18/00	CFM56-7B26	3726	N1795B ["SHUTTLE"]
B737-832	N397DA	DELTA AIRLINES		30537	638	08/24/00	CFM56-7B26	3727	N1786B ["SHUTTLE"]
B737-832	N398DA	DELTA AIRLINES		30774	641	08/24/00	CFM56-7B26	3728	N1786B ["SHUTTLE"]
B737-832	N399DA	DELTA AIRLINES		30379	657	09/19/00	CFM56-7B26	3729	N1786B ["SHUTTLE"]
B737-7BC (BBJ)	N127QS	EXECUTIVE JET AVIATION (WFBN)	N	30327	356		CFM56-7B26		N1786B [LST BOEING BY FSBU?]
B737-7BC (BBJ)	N128QS	EXECUTIVE JET		30328	377	12/19/00	CFM56-7B26		N1787B [LST BOEING BY FSBU?]

A/C TYPE	CURRENT REG. NO.	LAST KNOWN OPERATOR (OWNER)	STATUS	ORIGINAL MSN	LINE NO.	DEL. DATE	ENG. TYPE	FLEET NO.	PREV. REG. [COMMENTS]
		AVIATION (WFBN)							
B737-7BC (BBJ)	N129QS	EXECUTIVE JET AVIATION	N	30329	384		CFM56-7B26		N1787B [LST BOEING BY FSBU?]
B737-7BC (BBJ)	N1300S	EXECUTIVE JET AVIATION	N	30330	415		CFM56-7B26		N1786B
B737-7BC (BBJ)	N156QS	EXECUTIVE JET AVIATION	N	30756	569		CFM56-7B26		N1787B, N1003W [LST BOEING BY FSBU?]
B737-7BC (BBJ)	N171QS	EXECUTIVE JET AVIATION		30572	491	03/01/01	CFM56-7B26		N1786B, N1005S [LST BOEING BY FSBU?]
B737-7BC (BBJ)	N191QS	EXECUTIVE JET AVIATION	N	30791	623		CFM56-7B26		N1786B [TO BE OPB NET JETS]
B737-7BF (BBJ)	N180SM	FUN AIR CORP.		30496	301	06/18/99	CFM56-7B26		N224TA
B737-75V (BBJ)	N366G	GENERAL ELECTRIC COMPANY		28581	126	11/23/98	CFM56-7B26		N1787B
B737-75V (BBJ)	N367G	GENERAL ELECTRIC COMPANY		28579	312	07/08/99	CFM56-7B26		
B737-7DF (BBJ)	N10040	GENERAL ELECTRIC INTL. CAPITAL HOLDINGS		30790	613	02/26/01	CFM56-7B26		N1786B, N1787B
B737-7DT (BBJ)	N372BJ	GENERAL ELECTRIC INTL. CAPITAL HOLDINGS		30829	738	02/21/01	CFM56-7B26		N1787B
B737-73T (BBJ)	N500LS	HAYES PRODUCTIONS LLC		29054	143	12/11/98	CFM56-7B26		N1787B, N1780B, N6067E
B737-81Q	N732MA	MIAMI AIR (CITG)		30618	830	04/26/01	CFM56-7B26		[LST TRS]
B737-8Q8	G-OJSW	MIAMI AIR (SBE)	L	28218	160	12/11/98	CFM56-7B26		
B737-76N	N311ML	MIDWAY AIRLINES (GECA)		30051	436	12/14/99	CFM56-7B24		NA786B
B737-76N	N312ML	MIDWAY AIRLINES (GECA)		28613	463	01/19/00	CFM56-7B24		N1786B
B737-76N	N313ML	MIDWAY AIRLINES (AV. FIN.)		29893	710	11/21/00	CFM56-7B24		N1787B
B737-76Q	N314ML	MIDWAY AIRLINES (BELLEVUE)		30271	740	01/24/01	CFM56-7B24		N1787B
B737-7BX	N361ML	MIDWAY AIRLINES (FIRST UNION)		30736	658	09/29/00	CFM56-7B24		N1785B
B737-7BX	N362ML	MIDWAY AIRLINES (FIRST UNION)		30737	687	10/19/00	CFM56-7B24		N1786B
B737-7BX	N363ML	MIDWAY AIRLINES		30738	716	11/29/00	CFM56-7B24		
B737-7BX	N364ML	MIDWAY AIRLINES		30739	758	01/30/01	CFM56-7B24		N1786B
B737-7BX	N365ML	MIDWAY AIRLINES (FIRST UNION)		30740	776	02/21/01	CFM56-7B24		N1786B
B737-7BX	N366ML	MIDWAY AIRLINES		30741	823	04/19/01	CFM56-7B24		
B737-8Q8	N800NA	NORTH AMERICAN AIRLINES (ILFC)		28215	75	08/02/98	CFM56-7B26		N1786B
B737-86N	N802NA	NORTH AMERICAN AIRLINES (FSBU)		28587	192	02/09/99	CFM56-7B26		N1795B
B737-7H4	N400WN	SOUTHWEST AIRLINES		27891	806	03/28/01	CFM56-7B22		
B737-7H4	N401WN	SOUTHWEST AIRLINES		29813	810	03/29/01	CFM56-7B22		
B737-7H4	N402WN	SOUTHWEST AIRLINES		29814	811	03/30/01	CFM56-7B22		
B737-7H4	N403WN	SOUTHWEST AIRLINES		29815	821	04/16/01	CFM56-7B22		
B737-7H4	N700GS	SOUTHWEST AIRLINES		27835	4	12/17/97	CFM56-7B22		[FIRST 737-700 DEL]

A/C TYPE	CURRENT REG. NO.	LAST KNOWN OPERATOR (OWNER)	STATUS	ORIGINAL MSN	LINE NO.	DEL. DATE	ENG. TYPE	FLEET NO.	PREV. REG. [COMMENTS]
B737-7H4	N701GS	SOUTHWEST AIRLINES		27836	6	12/19/97	CFM56-7B22		N35108
B737-7H4	N703SW	SOUTHWEST AIRLINES		27837	12	12/31/97	CFM56-7B22		N1792B
B737-7H4	N704SW	SOUTHWEST AIRLINES		27838	15	01/09/98	CFM56-7B22		
B737-7H4	N705SW	SOUTHWEST AIRLINES		27839	20	03/30/98	CFM56-7B22		
B737-7H4	N706SW	SOUTHWEST AIRLINES		27840	24	05/31/98	CFM56-7B22		
B737-7H4	N707SA	SOUTHWEST AIRLINES		27841	1	10/30/98	CFM56-7B22		N737X, N1787B
B737-7H4	N708SW	SOUTHWEST AIRLINES		27842	2	12/15/98	CFM56-7B22		[FF 02/27/97]
B737-7H4	N709SW	SOUTHWEST AIRLINES		27843	3	10/26/98	CFM56-7B22		
B737-7H4	N710SW	SOUTHWEST AIRLINES		27844	34	03/28/98	CFM56-7B22		N1787B
B737-7H4	N711HK	SOUTHWEST AIRLINES		27845	38	04/10/98	CFM56-7B22		
B737-7H4	N712SW	SOUTHWEST AIRLINES		27846	53	05/31/98	CFM56-7B22		
B737-7H4	N713SW	SOUTHWEST AIRLINES		27847	54	06/08/98	CFM56-7B22		
B737-7H4	N714CB	SOUTHWEST AIRLINES		27848	61	06/19/98	CFM56-7B22		
B737-7H4	N715SW	SOUTHWEST AIRLINES		27849	62	06/30/98	CFM56-7B22		
B737-7H4	N716SW	SOUTHWEST AIRLINES		27850	64	06/30/98	CFM56-7B22		N1786B
B737-7H4	N717SA	SOUTHWEST AIRLINES		27851	70	07/23/98	CFM56-7B22		N1799B
B737-7H4	N718SW	SOUTHWEST AIRLINES		27852	71	07/31/98	CFM56-7B22		N3134C
B737-7H4	N719SW	SOUTHWEST AIRLINES		27853	82	08/05/98	CFM56-7B22		N1786B
B737-7H4	N720WN	SOUTHWEST AIRLINES		27854	121	09/30/98	CFM56-7B22		N1787B
B737-7H4	N723SW	SOUTHWEST AIRLINES		27855	199	02/11/99	CFM56-7B22		N1787B
B737-7H4	N724SW	SOUTHWEST AIRLINES		27856	201	02/15/99	CFM56-7B22		N1787B
B737-7H4	N725SW	SOUTHWEST AIRLINES		27857	208	02/22/99	CFM56-7B22		N1786B
B737-7H4	N726SW	SOUTHWEST AIRLINES		27858	213	02/25/99	CFM56-7B22		
B737-7H4	N727SW	SOUTHWEST AIRLINES		27859	274	05/20/99	CFM56-7B22		N1786B
B737-7H4	N728SW	SOUTHWEST AIRLINES		27860	276	05/19/99	CFM56-7B22		N1787B
B737-7H4	N729SW	SOUTHWEST AIRLINES		27861	278	05/24/99	CFM56-7B22		
B737-7H4	N730SW	SOUTHWEST AIRLINES		27862	284	05/28/99	CFM56-7B22		
B737-7H4	N731SA	SOUTHWEST AIRLINES		27863	318	07/12/99	CFM56-7B22		
B737-7H4	N732SW	SOUTHWEST AIRLINES		27864	319	07/14/99	CFM56-7B22		
B737-7H4	N733SA	SOUTHWEST AIRLINES		27865	320	07/19/99	CFM56-7B22		N1787B
B737-7H4	N734SA	SOUTHWEST AIRLINES		27866	324	07/22/99	CFM56-7B22		N1795B
B737-7H4	N735SA	SOUTHWEST AIRLINES		27867	354	08/24/99	CFM56-7B22		N1786B
B737-7H4	N736SA	SOUTHWEST AIRLINES		27868	357	08/27/99	CFM56-7B22		N1786B
B737-7H4	N737JW	SOUTHWEST AIRLINES		27869	358	08/31/99	CFM56-7B22		
B737-7H4	N738CB	SOUTHWEST AIRLINES		27870	360	09/01/99	CFM56-7B22		N1786B
B737-7H4	N739GB	SOUTHWEST AIRLINES		29275	144	11/12/98	CFM56-7B22		
B737-7H4	N740SW	SOUTHWEST AIRLINES		29276	155	11/30/98	CFM56-7B22		
B737-7H4	N741SA	SOUTHWEST AIRLINES		29277	157	11/30/98	CFM56-7B22		
B737-7H4	N742SW	SOUTHWEST AIRLINES		29278	172	12/23/98	CFM56-7B22		
B737-7H4	N743SW	SOUTHWEST AIRLINES		29279	175	12/29/98	CFM56-7B22		N1786B, N60436
B737-7H4	N744SW	SOUTHWEST AIRLINES		29490	232	03/26/99	CFM56-7B22		N1786B, N1781B

A/C TYPE	CURRENT REG. NO.	LAST KNOWN OPERATOR (OWNER)	STATUS	ORIGINAL MSN	LINE NO.	DEL. DATE	ENG. TYPE	FLEET NO.	PREV. REG. [COMMENTS]
B737-7H4	N745SW	SOUTHWEST AIRLINES		29491	237	03/31/99	CFM56-7B22		N1786B
B737-7H4	N746SW	SOUTHWEST AIRLINES		29798	299	06/18/99	CFM56-7B22		N1786B
B737-7H4	N747SA	SOUTHWEST AIRLINES		29799	306	06/29/99	CFM56-7B22		
B737-7H4	N748SW	SOUTHWEST AIRLINES		29800	331	08/02/99	CFM56-7B22		N1786B
B737-7H4	N749SW	SOUTHWEST AIRLINES		29801	343	08/13/99	CFM56-7B22		N1786B
B737-7H4	N750SA	SOUTHWEST AIRLINES		29802	366	09/09/99	CFM56-7B22		
B737-7H4	N751SW	SOUTHWEST AIRLINES		29803	373	09/17/99	CFM56-7B22		N1786B
B737-7H4	N752SW	SOUTHWEST AIRLINES		29804	387	10/06/99	CFM56-7B22		
B737-7H4	N753SW	SOUTHWEST AIRLINES		29848	400	10/21/99	CFM56-7B22		N1787B
B737-7H4	N754SW	SOUTHWEST AIRLINES		29849	416	11/10/99	CFM56-7B22		N1787B
B737-7H4	N755SA	SOUTHWEST AIRLINES		27871	419	11/12/99	CFM56-7B22		N1787B
B737-7H4	N756SA	SOUTHWEST AIRLINES		27872	422	11/19/99	CFM56-7B22		N1786B
B737-7H4	N757LV	SOUTHWEST AIRLINES		29850	425	11/30/99	CFM56-7B22		N1786B
B737-7H4	N758SW	SOUTHWEST AIRLINES		27873	437	12/07/99	CFM56-7B22		N1786B
B737-7H4	N759GS	SOUTHWEST AIRLINES		30544	448	12/21/99	CFM56-7B22		N1786B
B737-7H4	N760SW	SOUTHWEST AIRLINES		27874	468	01/24/00	CFM56-7B22		N1786B
B737-7H4	N761RR	SOUTHWEST AIRLINES		27875	495	03/27/00	CFM56-7B22		
B737-7H4	N762SW	SOUTHWEST AIRLINES		27876	512	04/12/00	CFM56-7B22		N1786B
B737-7H4	N763SW	SOUTHWEST AIRLINES		27877	520	04/20/00	CFM56-7B22		
B737-7H4	N764SW	SOUTHWEST AIRLINES		27878	521	04/20/00	CFM56-7B22		
B737-7H4	N765SW	SOUTHWEST AIRLINES		29805	525	04/24/00	CFM56-7B22		N1786B
B737-7H4	N766SW	SOUTHWEST AIRLINES		29806	537	05/02/00	CFM56-7B22		N1786B
B737-7H4	N767SW	SOUTHWEST AIRLINES		29807	541	05/05/00	CFM56-7B22		N1787B
B737-7H4	N768SW	SOUTHWEST AIRLINES		30587	580	06/09/00	CFM56-7B22		N1786B
B737-7H4	N769SW	SOUTHWEST AIRLINES		30588	592	06/23/00	CFM56-7B22		
B737-7H4	N770SA	SOUTHWEST AIRLINES		30589	595	06/28/00	CFM56-7B22		
B737-7H4	N771SA	SOUTHWEST AIRLINES		27879	599	06/30/00	CFM56-7B22		N1786B
B737-7H4	N772SW	SOUTHWEST AIRLINES		27880	601	07/07/00	CFM56-7B22		
B737-7H4	N773SA	SOUTHWEST AIRLINES		27881	603	07/06/00	CFM56-7B22		N1786B
B737-7H4	N774SW	SOUTHWEST AIRLINES		27882	609	07/18/00	CFM56-7B22		N1786B
B737-7H4	N775SW	SOUTHWEST AIRLINES		30590	617	07/25/00	CFM56-7B22		N1786B
B737-7H4	N776WN	SOUTHWEST AIRLINES		30591	620	07/28/00	CFM56-7B22		
B737-7H4	N777QC	SOUTHWEST AIRLINES		30592	621	07/31/00	CFM56-7B22		
B737-7H4	N778SW	SOUTHWEST AIRLINES		27883	626	08/03/00	CFM56-7B22		N1786B
B737-7H4	N779SW	SOUTHWEST AIRLINES		27884	628	08/07/00	CFM56-7B22		N1786B
B737-7H4	N780SW	SOUTHWEST AIRLINES		27885	643	08/28/00	CFM56-7B22		N1786B
B737-7H4	N781WN	SOUTHWEST AIRLINES		30601	646	08/30/00	CFM56-7B22		
B737-7H4	N782SA	SOUTHWEST AIRLINES		29808	670	09/29/00	CFM56-7B22		N1787B
B737-7H4	N783SW	SOUTHWEST AIRLINES		29809	675	10/04/00	CFM56-7B22		
B737-7H4	N784SW	SOUTHWEST AIRLINES		29810	677	10/09/00	CFM56-7B22		
B737-7H4	N785SW	SOUTHWEST AIRLINES		30602	693	11/02/00	CFM56-7B22		N1786B

A/C TYPE	CURRENT REG. NO.	LAST KNOWN OPERATOR (OWNER)	STATUS	ORIGINAL MSN	LINE NO.	DEL. DATE	ENG. TYPE	FLEET NO.	PREV. REG. [COMMENTS]
B737-7H4	N786SW	SOUTHWEST AIRLINES		29811	698	10/31/00	CFM56-7B22		
B737-7H4	N787SA	SOUTHWEST AIRLINES		29812	705	11/13/00	CFM56-7B22		N1786B
B737-7H4	N788SA	SOUTHWEST AIRLINES		30603	707	11/17/00	CFM56-7B22		N1786B
B737-7H4	N789SW	SOUTHWEST AIRLINES		29816	718	11/29/00	CFM56-7B22		N1786B
B737-7H4	N790SW	SOUTHWEST AIRLINES		30604	721	12/04/00	CFM56-7B22		N1786B
B737-7H4	N791SW	SOUTHWEST AIRLINES		27886	736	12/26/00	CFM56-7B22		N1786B
B737-7H4	N792SW	SOUTHWEST AIRLINES		27887	737	12/21/00	CFM56-7B22		
B737-7H4	N793SA	SOUTHWEST AIRLINES		27888	744	01/11/01	CFM56-7B22		N1786B
B737-7H4	N794SW	SOUTHWEST AIRLINES		30605	748	01/12/01	CFM56-7B22		N1786B, N1781B
B737-7H4	N795SW	SOUTHWEST AIRLINES		30606	780	02/23/01	CFM56-7B22		N1786B
B737-7H4	N796SW	SOUTHWEST AIRLINES		27889	784	03/06/01	CFM56-7B22		
B737-7H4	N797MX	SOUTHWEST AIRLINES		27890	803	03/23/01	CFM56-7B22		
B737-7AD	N798SW	SOUTHWEST AIRLINES		28436	41	05/13/98	CFM56-7B24		N700EW
B737-7Q8	N799SW	SOUTHWEST AIRLINES (ILFC)		28209	14	03/25/98	CFM56-7B24		N3521N, HB-IIH, 9Y-TJI
B737-8Q8	N800SY	SUN COUNTRY AIRLINES (ILFC)		30627	752	01/30/01	CFM56-7B24		N1786B
B737-8Q8	N801SY	SUN COUNTRY AIRLINES (ILFC)		30332	777	02/23/01	CFM56-7B24		N1787B
B737-8Q8	N802SY	SUN COUNTRY AIRLINES (ILFC)		30628	808	03/30/01	CFM56-7B24		
B737-8Q8	N803SY	SUN COUNTRY AIRLINES (ILFC)	N	28241	841		CFM56-7B24		
B737-72T(BBJ)	N50TC	TRACINDA CORPORATION		29024	131	11/23/98	CFM56-7B26		N1786B
B737-75T(BBJ)	N737WH	VICTORY AVIATION (FIRST UNION COMM.)		29142	167	12/29/98	CFM56-7B26		N1787B, N1782B, N700WH

OE-AUSTRIA

A/C TYPE	CURRENT REG. NO.	LAST KNOWN OPERATOR (OWNER)	STATUS	ORIGINAL MSN	LINE NO.	DEL. DATE	ENG. TYPE	FLEET NO.	PREV. REG. [COMMENTS]
B737-6Z9	OE-LNL	LAUDA AIR		30137	526	05/04/00	CFM56-7B20		N1786B
B737-6Z9	OE-LNM	LAUDA AIR		30138	546	05/10/00	CFM56-7B20		N1795B
B737-7Z9	OE-LNN	LAUDA AIR		30418	815	04/19/01	CFM56-7B20		
B737-8Z9	OE-LNJ	LAUDA AIR		28177	69	07/28/98	CFM56-7B26		
B737-8Z9	OE-LNK	LAUDA AIR		28178	222	03/16/99	CFM56-7B26		N1786B, N1784B

OK-CZECH REPUBLIC

A/C TYPE	CURRENT REG. NO.	LAST KNOWN OPERATOR (OWNER)	STATUS	ORIGINAL MSN	LINE NO.	DEL. DATE	ENG. TYPE	FLEET NO.	PREV. REG. [COMMENTS]
B737-86N	OK-TVQ	TRAVEL SERVICE AIRLINES (GECA)		28618	514	04/30/00	CFM56-7B26		N1786B

OO-BELGIUM

A/C TYPE	CURRENT REG. NO.	LAST KNOWN OPERATOR (OWNER)	STATUS	ORIGINAL MSN	LINE NO.	DEL. DATE	ENG. TYPE	FLEET NO.	PREV. REG. [COMMENTS]
B737-86Q	OO-CYI	CITY BIRD (BOUL)		30274	845	05/14/01	CFM56-7B26		
B737-86Q	OO-CYN	CITY BIRD (BOUL)		30272	824	04/26/01	CFM56-7B26		
B737-86N	OO-CYS	CITY BIRD (GECA)		28644	839	05/11/01	CFM56-7B26		

OY-DENMARK

A/C TYPE	CURRENT REG. NO.	LAST KNOWN OPERATOR (OWNER)	STATUS	ORIGINAL MSN	LINE NO.	DEL. DATE	ENG. TYPE	FLEET NO.	PREV. REG. [COMMENTS]
B737-7L9	OY-MRC	MAERSK AIR		28006	26	05/25/98	CFM56-7B22		N5573K [POSS. TO BE LST AMC 03û10/00]
B737-7L9	OY-MRD	MAERSK AIR		28007	136	11/10/98	CFM56-7B22		N1786B
B737-7L9	OY-MRE	MAERSK AIR		28008	203	02/16/99	CFM56-7B22		N1786B
B737-7L9	OY-MRF	MAERSK AIR		28009	221	03/17/99	CFM56-7B22		N1787B, N1780B
B737-7L9	OY-MRG	MAERSK AIR		28010	396	10/19/99	CFM56-7B22		N1786B
B737-7L9	OY-MRH	MAERSK AIR		28013	682	10/19/00	CFM56-7B22		N1786B
B737-7L9	OY-MRI	MAERSK AIR		28014	766	02/12/01	CFM56-7B22		N1786B
B737-7L9	OY-MRJ	MAERSK AIR		28015	785	03/08/01	CFM56-7B22		
B737-8Q8	OY-SEA	STERLING EUROPEAN AIRWAYS		28213	50	06/10/98	CFM56-7B26		N3521N
B737-8Q8	OY-SEB	STERLING EUROPEAN AIRWAYS (ILFC)		28214	78	07/30/98	CFM56-7B26		N1786B
B737-8Q8	OY-SEC	STERLING EUROPEAN AIRWAYS (ILFC)		28221	226	03/19/99	CFM56-7B26		
B737-8Q8	OY-SED	STERLING EUROPEAN AIRWAYS (ILFC)		28237	769	02/09/01	CFM56-7B26		N1786B
B737-85H	OY-SEH	STERLING EUROPEAN AIRWAYS (ITOH)		29444	178	01/21/99	CFM56-7B26		N1787B [LST BER FOR SUMMER 2001]
B737-85H	OY-SEI	STERLING EUROPEAN AIRWAYS (ITOH)		29445	186	01/28/99	CFM56-7B26		N1786B

PH-NETHERLANDS

A/C TYPE	CURRENT REG. NO.	LAST KNOWN OPERATOR (OWNER)	STATUS	ORIGINAL MSN	LINE NO.	DEL. DATE	ENG. TYPE	FLEET NO.	PREV. REG. [COMMENTS]
B737-8K2	PH-BXA	KLM		29131	198	02/25/99	CFM56-7B27		N1786B
B737-8K2	PH-BXB	KLM		29132	261	05/10/99	CFM56-7B27		N1786B
B737-8K2	PH-BXC	KLM		29133	305	06/30/99	CFM56-7B27		
B737-8K2	PH-BXD	KLM		29134	355	08/30/99	CFM56-7B27		N1786B, N1784B
B737-8K2	PH-BXE	KLM		29595	552	05/18/00	CFM56-7B27		
B737-8K2	PH-BXF	KLM		29596	583	06/15/00	CFM56-7B27		N1787B
B737-8K2	PH-BXG	KLM		30357	605	07/22/00	CFM56-7B27		N1787B
B737-8K2	PH-BXH	KLM		29597	630	08/15/00	CFM56-7B27		N1786B
B737-8K2	PH-BXI	KLM		30358	633	08/23/00	CFM56-7B27		N1786B, N1787B
B737-8K2	PH-BXK	KLM		29598	639	09/12/00	CFM56-7B27		N1787B, N1015G
B737-8K2	PH-BXL	KLM		30359	659	09/26/00	CFM56-7B27		
B737-8K2	PH-BXM	KLM		30355	714	11/27/00	CFM56-7B27		N1786B
B737-8K2	PH-BXN	KLM		30356	728	12/16/00	CFM56-7B27		N1787B
B737-8K2	PH-HZA	TRANSAVIA AIRLINES		28373	51	06/16/98	CFM56-7B27		
B737-8K2	PH-HZB	TRANSAVIA AIRLINES		28374	57	06/18/98	CFM56-7B27		
B737-8K2	PH-HZC	TRANSAVIA AIRLINES		28375	85	08/26/98	CFM56-7B27		
B737-8K2	PH-HZD	TRANSAVIA AIRLINES		28376	252	04/22/99	CFM56-7B27		
B737-8K2	PH-HZE	TRANSAVIA AIRLINES		28377	277	05/24/99	CFM56-7B27		
B737-8K2	PH-HZF	TRANSAVIA AIRLINES		28378	291	06/11/99	CFM56-7B27		
B737-8K2	PH-HZG	TRANSAVIA AIRLINES		28379	498	03/25/00	CFM56-7B27		N1786B
B737-8K2	PH-HZI	TRANSAVIA AIRLINES		28380	524	04/25/00	CFM56-7B27		
B737-8K2	PH-HZJ	TRANSAVIA AIRLINES		30389	549	05/11/00	CFM56-7B27		N1796B
B737-8K2	PH-HZK	TRANSAVIA AIRLINES		30390	555	05/16/00	CFM56-7B27		N1786B [LST SBE 12/14/00-04/23/01]

A/C TYPE	CURRENT REG. NO.	LAST KNOWN OPERATOR (OWNER)	STATUS	ORIGINAL MSN	LINE NO.	DEL. DATE	ENG. TYPE	FLEET NO.	PREV. REG. [COMMENTS]
B737-8K2	PH-HZL	TRANSAVIA AIRLINES		30391	814	04/06/01	CFM56-7B27		
B737-8K2	PH-HZM	TRANSAVIA AIRLINES		30392	833	04/26/01	CFM56-7B27		
B737-8BG	PH-HZZ	TRANSAVIA AIRLINES (SAA)	L	32356	819	04/17/01	CFM56-7B26		ZS-SJL

PP/PR-BRAZIL

A/C TYPE	CURRENT REG. NO.	LAST KNOWN OPERATOR (OWNER)	STATUS	ORIGINAL MSN	LINE NO.	DEL. DATE	ENG. TYPE	FLEET NO.	PREV. REG. [COMMENTS]
B737-7L9	PR-GOA	GOL TRANSPORTES AEREOS (GECA)		28005	11	03/06/98	CFM56-7B22		N35161, OY-MRB
B737-75B	PR-GOB	GOL TRANSPORTES AEREOS (BCCI)		28099	13	03/10/98	CFM56-7B22		N3502P, D-AGEM
B737-75B	PR-GOC	GOL TRANSPORTES AEREOS (BCCI)		28101	17	04/23/98	CFM56-7B22		N5573K, D-AGEO
B737-75B	PR-GOD	GOL TRANSPORTES AEREOS (BCCI)		28105	66	06/30/98	CFM56-7B22		D-AGEV
B737-75B	PR-GOE	GOL TRANSPORTES AEREOS (BCCI)		28106	68	07/10/98	CFM56-7B22		D-AGEW
B737-73Q	PR-GOF	GOL TRANSPORTES AEREOS (BOUL)	N	30273	843		CFM56-7B22		
B737-7L9	PR-GOL	GOL TRANSPORTES AEREOS (GECA)		28004	10	03/02/98	CFM56-7B22		N35153, OY-MRA
B737-76N	PP-VQA	VARIG BRASIL (GECA)		28580	135	11/25/98	CFM56-7B24		N1786B, N1003N
B737-76N	PP-VQB	VARIG BRASIL (GECA)		28582	154	12/08/98	CFM56-7B24		
B737-76N	PP-VQC	VARIG BRASIL (GECA)		28583	163	12/21/98	CFM56-7B24		N1786B
B737-76N	PP-VQD	VARIG BRASIL (GECA)		28584	170	12/29/98	CFM56-7B24		N1786B, N5573L
B737-76N	PP-VQE	VARIG BRASIL (GECA)		28585	173	01/21/99	CFM56-7B24		N1795B, N1780B

RA-RUSSIA

A/C TYPE	CURRENT REG. NO.	LAST KNOWN OPERATOR (OWNER)	STATUS	ORIGINAL MSN	LINE NO.	DEL. DATE	ENG. TYPE	FLEET NO.	PREV. REG. [COMMENTS]
B737-7K9	N100UN	TRANSAERO AIRLINES (WFBN)		28088	19	04/27/98	CFM56-7B24		
B737-7K9	N101UN	TRANSAERO AIRLINES (WFBN)		28089	25	06/12/98	CFM56-7B24		

SE-SWEDEN

A/C TYPE	CURRENT REG. NO.	LAST KNOWN OPERATOR (OWNER)	STATUS	ORIGINAL MSN	LINE NO.	DEL. DATE	ENG. TYPE	FLEET NO.	PREV. REG. [COMMENTS]
B737-804	SE-DZH	BRITANNIA AIRWAYS AB (ILFC)		28227	452	01/15/00	CFM56-7B26		N1786B
B737-804	SE-DZI	BRITANNIA AIRWAYS AB (ILFC)		28229	478	02/09/00	CFM56-7B26		
B737-804	SE-DZK	BRITANNIA AIRWAYS AB (ILFC)		28231	538	05/18/00	CFM56-7B27		N1786B [G-BYNA NTU]
B737-85F	SE-DVO	NOVAIR (GATX)		28822	166	01/20/99	CFM56-7B26		N1787B, N1780B
B737-85F	SE-DVR	NOVAIR (GATX)		28826	238	04/06/99	CFM56-7B26		N1787B
B737-85F	SE-DVU	NOVAIR (GATX)		28825	188	02/02/99	CFM56-7B26		N1787B, N1784B, N501GX
B737-683	SE-DNM	SCANDINAVIAN-SAS		28288	49	09/18/98	CFM56-7B20		N1003M [1ST 737-600 DEL]
B737-683	SE-DNP	SCANDINAVIAN-SAS		28295	149	11/25/98	CFM56-7B20		N1786B
B737-683	SE-DNR	SCANDINAVIAN-SAS		28296	21	01/07/99	CFM56-7B20		N7376 [737-600 PROTOTYPE]
B737-683	SE-DNS	SCANDINAVIAN-SAS		28297	30	01/21/99	CFM56-7B20		N1786B, N35135
B737-683	SE-DNT	SCANDINAVIAN-SAS		28302	243	04/21/99	CFM56-7B20		N1786B
B737-683	SE-DNU	SCANDINAVIAN-SAS		28303	257	04/30/99	CFM56-7B20		
B737-683	SE-DNX	SCANDINAVIAN-SAS		28304	270	05/13/99	CFM56-7B20		
B737-683	SE-DTF	SCANDINAVIAN-SAS		28309	368	09/15/99	CFM56-7B20		N1787B

A/C TYPE	CURRENT REG. NO.	LAST KNOWN OPERATOR (OWNER) STATUS	ORIGINAL MSN	LINE NO.	DEL. DATE	ENG. TYPE	FLEET NO.	PREV. REG. [COMMENTS]
B737-683	SE-DTH	SCANDINAVIAN-SAS	28313	447	12/21/99	CFM56-7B20		
B737-683	SE-DTU	SCANDINAVIAN-SAS	28311	382	10/05/99	CFM56-7B20		N1786B
B737-683	LN-RCT	SCANDINAVIAN-SAS (FL ARROW)	30189	303	06/25/99	CFM56-7B20		N1786B, OY-KKF
B737-683	LN-RCU	SCANDINAVIAN-SAS (LG OLIVE)	30190	335	08/09/99	CFM56-7B20		N1786B, SE-DNZ
B737-683	LN-RCW	SCANDINAVIAN-SAS (FG UNITY KUMIAI)	28308	333	08/03/99	CFM56-7B20		N1787B, SE-DNY
B737-683	LN-RPA	SCANDINAVIAN-SAS (GLENHAGEN)	28290	100	10/10/98	CFM56-7B20		N1786B, N5002K
B737-683	LN-RPB	SCANDINAVIAN-SAS (GLENHAGEN)	28294	137	11/15/98	CFM56-7B20		
B737-683	LN-RPC	SCANDINAVIAN-SAS (STRUKTUR)	28322	614	07/27/00	CFM56-7B20		N1786B, N1795B, SE-DTZ
B737-683	LN-RPE	SCANDINAVIAN-SAS	28306	329	07/28/99	CFM56-7B20		N1795B
B737-683	LN-RPF	SCANDINAVIAN-SAS (SBL CHISHIMA)	28307	330	07/29/99	CFM56-7B20		N1786B, N1784B
B737-683	LN-RPG	SCANDINAVIAN-SAS (PEMB)	28310	255	04/27/99	CFM56-7B20		
B737-683	LN-RPH	SCANDINAVIAN-SAS (GECA)	28605	375	09/24/99	CFM56-7B20		N1786B
B737-683	LN-RPS	SCANDINAVIAN-SAS (NBB NAMSOS)	28298	191	01/30/99	CFM56-7B20		N1786B, OY-KKC
B737-683	LN-RPT	SCANDINAVIAN-SAS (NBB MOLDE)	28299	193	02/04/99	CFM56-7B20		N1787B, OY-KKD
B737-683	LN-RPU	SCANDINAVIAN-SAS (SBL ATLANTIC)	28312	407	11/05/99	CFM56-7B20		N1786B, OY-KKP
B737-683	LN-RPW	SCANDINAVIAN-SAS (FYN CO.)	28289	92	09/30/98	CFM56-7B20		N5002K, OY-KKA
B737-683	LN-RPX	SCANDINAVIAN-SAS (GLENHAGEN)	28291	112	10/21/98	CFM56-7B20		N1787B, SE-DNN
B737-683	LN-RPY	SCANDINAVIAN-SAS (ODDA CO.)	28292	116	10/19/98	CFM56-7B20		N1786B, N1780B, SE-DNO
B737-683	LN-RPZ	SCANDINAVIAN-SAS (GLENHAGEN)	28293	120	11/05/98	CFM56-7B20		N1787B, OY-KKB
B737-683	OY-KKE	SCANDINAVIAN-SAS	28305	290	06/09/99	CFM56-7B20		N1787B
B737-683	OY-KKG	SCANDINAVIAN-SAS	28300	209	02/25/99	CFM56-7B20		N1786B
B737-683	OY-KKH	SCANDINAVIAN-SAS	28301	227	03/19/99	CFM56-7B20		
B737-783	SE-DTG	SCANDINAVIAN-SAS	30191	404	11/03/99	CFM56-7B22		N1786B
B737-783	SE-DTI	SCANDINAVIAN-SAS	28314	458	01/12/00	CFM56-7B22		N1786B
B737-783	LN-RPJ	SCANDINAVIAN-SAS	30192	486	02/25/00	CFM56-7B22		
B737-783	LN-RPK	SCANDINAVIAN-SAS	28317	500	03/31/00	CFM56-7B22		N1786B
B737-783	OY-KKI	SCANDINAVIAN-SAS	28315	464	01/20/00	CFM56-7B22		N1796B
B737-783	OY-KKR	SCANDINAVIAN-SAS	28316	476	02/05/00	CFM56-7B22		N1786B
B737-883	SE-DTS	SCANDINAVIAN-SAS	30197	798	03/23/01	CFM56-7B26		
B737-883	SE-DTT	SCANDINAVIAN-SAS	28324	767	02/14/01	CFM56-7B26		N1786B
B737-883	SE-DYH	SCANDINAVIAN-SAS	30196	733	12/20/00	CFM56-7B26		N1787B
B737-883	LN-RCN	SCANDINAVIAN-SAS	28318	529	05/03/00	CFM56-7B26		SE-DTK
B737-883	LN-RCO	SCANDINAVIAN-SAS	28319	548	05/09/00	CFM56-7B26		N1786B, SE-DTL
B737-883	LN-RCP	SCANDINAVIAN-SAS	28320	551	05/16/00	CFM56-7B26		N1795B, SE-DTM
B737-883	LN-RCR	SCANDINAVIAN-SAS	28321	577	06/08/00	CFM56-7B26		N1786B, SE-DTX
B737-883	LN-RCS	SCANDINAVIAN-SAS	30193	587	06/20/00	CFM56-7B26		N1787B, SE-DTY
B737-883	LN-RPD	SCANDINAVIAN-SAS (STRUKTUR)	28323	625	08/09/00	CFM56-7B26		N1786B, SE-DYA
B737-883	LN-RPL	SCANDINAVIAN-SAS (STRUKTUR)	30469	673	10/06/00	CFM56-7B26		N1786B [SE-DYC NTU]
B737-883	LN-RPM	SCANDINAVIAN-SAS (STRUKTUR)	30195	696	11/09/00	CFM56-7B26		[SE-DYD NTU]
B737-883	LN-RPN	SCANDINAVIAN-SAS	30470	717	11/30/00	CFM56-7B26		N1786B [SE-DYG NTU]
B737-883	LN-RPO	SCANDINAVIAN-SAS (STRUKTUR)	30467	634	08/18/00	CFM56-7B26		N1786B, SE-DTN

A/C TYPE	CURRENT REG. NO.	LAST KNOWN OPERATOR (OWNER)	STATUS	ORIGINAL MSN	LINE NO.	DEL. DATE	ENG. TYPE	FLEET NO.	PREV. REG. [COMMENTS]
B737-883	LN-RPP	SCANDINAVIAN-SAS (STRUKTUR)		30194	666	09/27/00	CFM56-7B26		N1787B, SE-DTO
B737-883	LN-RPR	SCANDINAVIAN-SAS (STRUKTUR)		30468	668	09/28/00	CFM56-7B26		N1787B, SE-DTP

SX-GREECE

A/C TYPE	CURRENT REG. NO.	LAST KNOWN OPERATOR (OWNER)	STATUS	ORIGINAL MSN	LINE NO.	DEL. DATE	ENG. TYPE	FLEET NO.	PREV. REG. [COMMENTS]
B737-7K9	SX-BLT	AXON AIRLINES (BIAL)		28090	205	02/26/99	CFM56-7B24		N1786B, N73712
B737-7K9	SX-BLU	AXON AIRLINES (BIAL)		28091	223	03/23/99	CFM56-7B24		N1786B, N73713

TC-TURKEY

A/C TYPE	CURRENT REG. NO.	LAST KNOWN OPERATOR (OWNER)	STATUS	ORIGINAL MSN	LINE NO.	DEL. DATE	ENG. TYPE	FLEET NO.	PREV. REG. [COMMENTS]
B737-86N	TC-MAO	KTHY (GECA)		28645	840	5/—/01	CFM56-7B26		
B737-8S3	TC-MSO	KTHY (SUNR)		29246	475	04/20/00	CFM56-7B26		N1787B
B737-8S3	TC-MZZ	KTHY (SUNR)		29247	493	04/21/00	CFM56-7B26		N1786B
B737-86N	TC-APF	PEGASUS AIRLINES (GECA)		28642	813	04/06/01	CFM56-7B26		
B737-82R	TC-APG	PEGASUS AIRLINES		29329	224	03/25/99	CFM56-7B26		N1786B [LST DAH]
B737-8S3	TC-APH	PEGASUS AIRLINES (SUNR)		29250	792	03/26/01	CFM56-7B26		
B737-86N	TC-APK	PEGASUS AIRLINES (GECA)		28643	828	04/26/01	CFM56-7B26		
B737-86N	TC-APL	PEGASUS AIRLINES (GECA)		30231	515	04/30/00	CFM56-7B26		N1787B
B737-809	TC-APM	PEGASUS AIRLINES (GECA)		28403	117	10/29/98	CFM56-7B26		N1786B, B-18602 [LST KZW]
B737-86N	TC-APN	PEGASUS AIRLINES (GECA)		28628	573	06/02/00	CFM56-7B26		N1786B, N5573L [LST DAH]
B737-82R	TC-APU	PEGASUS AIRLINES (ILFC)	N	29344	849		CFM56-7B26		
B737-86N	TC-APV	PEGASUS AIRLINES (GECA)		28639	772	02/19/01	CFM56-7B26		N1786B
B737-86N	TC-APY	PEGASUS AIRLINES (GECA)		28591	233	04/14/99	CFM56-7B26		N1786B, TC-IAH [LST KZW]
B737-809	TC-APZ	PEGASUS AIRLINES (GECA)		29103	129	11/12/98	CFM56-7B26		N1786B, N1784B, B-18603
B737-73S	TC-SUE	SUNEXPRESS (PEMB)		29079	194	02/23/99	CFM56-7B24		4X-ABJ, PH-AAP
B737-73S	TC-SUF	SUNEXPRESS (PEMB)		29081	215	04/29/99	CFM56-7B24		N1786B, 4X-ABR, PH-AAQ
B737-86N	TC-SUA	SUNEXPRESS (GECA)		28612	455	01/14/00	CFM56-7B26		N1786B
B737-86N	TC-SUB	SUNEXPRESS (GECA)		28614	477	02/04/00	CFM56-7B26		N1786B
B737-86N	TC-SUC	SUNEXPRESS (GECA)		28616	483	02/22/00	CFM56-7B26		N1786B
B737-86N	TC-SUD	SUNEXPRESS (GECA)		28620	542	05/12/00	CFM56-7B26		N1786B
B737-8F2	TC-JFC	TURKISH AIRLINES		29765	80	10/30/98	CFM56-7B26		N1786B
B737-8F2	TC-JFD	TURKISH AIRLINES		29766	87	10/30/98	CFM56-7B26		
B737-8F2	TC-JFE	TURKISH AIRLINES		29767	95	10/30/98	CFM56-7B26		N1786B
B737-8F2	TC-JFF	TURKISH AIRLINES		29768	99	10/30/98	CFM56-7B26		N1786B
B737-8F2	TC-JFG	TURKISH AIRLINES		29769	102	10/30/98	CFM56-7B26		N1787B
B737-8F2	TC-JFH	TURKISH AIRLINES		29770	114	10/30/98	CFM56-7B26		N1787B
B737-8F2	TC-JFI	TURKISH AIRLINES		29771	228	03/24/99	CFM56-7B26		N1795B
B737-8F2	TC-JFJ	TURKISH AIRLINES		29772	242	04/12/99	CFM56-7B26		N1786B
B737-8F2	TC-JFK	TURKISH AIRLINES		29773	259	04/29/99	CFM56-7B26		N1786B
B737-8F2	TC-JFL	TURKISH AIRLINES		29774	269	05/13/99	CFM56-7B26		N1786B

A/C TYPE	CURRENT REG. NO.	LAST KNOWN OPERATOR (OWNER)	STATUS	ORIGINAL MSN	LINE NO.	DEL. DATE	ENG. TYPE	FLEET NO.	PREV. REG. [COMMENTS]
B737-8F2	TC-JFM	TURKISH AIRLINES		29775	279	05/26/99	CFM56-7B26		
B737-8F2	TC-JFN	TURKISH AIRLINES		29776	308	06/29/99	CFM56-7B26		
B737-8F2	TC-JFO	TURKISH AIRLINES		29777	309	06/29/99	CFM56-7B26		
B737-8F2	TC-JFP	TURKISH AIRLINES		29778	349	08/19/99	CFM56-7B26		N1787B
B737-8F2	TC-JFR	TURKISH AIRLINES		29779	370	09/15/99	CFM56-7B26		N1786B
B737-8F2	TC-JFT	TURKISH AIRLINES		29780	454	01/26/00	CFM56-7B26		N1787B
B737-8F2	TC-JFU	TURKISH AIRLINES		29781	461	01/26/00	CFM56-7B26		N1795B
B737-8F2	TC-JFV	TURKISH AIRLINES		29782	490	03/31/00	CFM56-7B26		N1786B
B737-8F2	TC-JFY	TURKISH AIRLINES		29783	497	04/03/00	CFM56-7B26		N1786B
B737-8F2	TC-JFZ	TURKISH AIRLINES		29784	539	05/12/00	CFM56-7B26		
B737-8F2	TC-JGA	TURKISH AIRLINES		29785	544	05/17/00	CFM56-7B26		N1786B
B737-8F2	TC-JGB	TURKISH AIRLINES		29786	566	06/01/00	CFM56-7B26		N1786B
B737-8F2	TC-JGC	TURKISH AIRLINES		29787	771	02/21/01	CFM56-7B26		N1786B
B737-8F2	TC-JGD	TURKISH AIRLINES		29788	791	03/14/01	CFM56-7B26		

TS-TUNISIA

A/C TYPE	CURRENT REG. NO.	LAST KNOWN OPERATOR (OWNER)	STATUS	ORIGINAL MSN	LINE NO.	DEL. DATE	ENG. TYPE	FLEET NO.	PREV. REG. [COMMENTS]
B737-7H3 (BBJ)	TS-IOO	REPUBLIC OF TUNISIA		29149	348	08/20/99	CFM56-7B26		N1786B, N5573L [OPB TAR]
B737-6H3	TS-IOK	TUNISAIR		29496	268	05/25/99	CFM56-7B20		N1786B
B737-6H3	TS-IOL	TUNISAIR		29497	282	05/28/99	CFM56-7B20		N1786B
B737-6H3	TS-IOM	TUNISAIR		29498	310	07/09/99	CFM56-7B20		N1786B
B737-6H3	TS-ION	TUNISAIR		29499	510	04/21/00	CFM56-7B20		N1786B
B737-6H3	TS-IOP	TUNISAIR		29500	543	05/08/00	CFM56-7B20		
B737-6H3	TS-IOQ	TUNISAIR		29501	563	05/25/00	CFM56-7B20		N1787B
B737-6H3	TS-IOR	TUNISAIR		29502	816	04/13/01	CFM56-7B20		

VH-AUSTRALIA

A/C TYPE	CURRENT REG. NO.	LAST KNOWN OPERATOR (OWNER)	STATUS	ORIGINAL MSN	LINE NO.	DEL. DATE	ENG. TYPE	FLEET NO.	PREV. REG. [COMMENTS]
B737-7Q8	VH-VBA	VIRGIN BLUE (ILFC)		28238	817	04/24/01	CFM56-7B26		
B737-7Q8	VH-VBB	VIRGIN BLUE (ILFC)	N	28240	832		CFM56-7B26		

VP-B-BERMUDA

A/C TYPE	CURRENT REG. NO.	LAST KNOWN OPERATOR (OWNER)	STATUS	ORIGINAL MSN	LINE NO.	DEL. DATE	ENG. TYPE	FLEET NO.	PREV. REG. [COMMENTS]
B737-72U (BBJ)	VP-BBJ	PICTON II LTD.		29273	146	12/17/98	CFM56-7B26		N1787B, N1011N
B737-75U (BBJ)	VP-BRM	DOBRO LTD.		28976	158	12/16/98	CFM56-7B26		N1786B
B737-79T (BBJ)	VP-BWR	USAL INC.		29317	265	05/06/99	CFM56-7B26		N1787B
B737-7AN (BBJ)	N371BJ	SAUDI OGER		29971	684	10/19/00	CFM56-7B26		
B737-7AN (BBJ)	VP-BYA	SAUDI OGER		29972	642	08/22/00	CFM56-7B26		N1786B
B737-8AN (BBJ2)	VP-BHN	SAUDI OGER		32438	779	02/28/01	CFM56-7B26		N1786B [INCORRECTLY REGISTERED AS

A/C TYPE	CURRENT REG. NO.	LAST KNOWN OPERATOR (OWNER)	STATUS	ORIGINAL MSN	LINE NO.	DEL. DATE	ENG. TYPE	FLEET NO.	PREV. REG. [COMMENTS]
									VP-BNH ON DEL]
VP-C-CAYMAN IS.									
B737-7AW (BBJ)	VP-CEC	(PRIVATE)		30031	251	04/27/99	CFM56-7B26		N1786B, N73715 [VP-CBB NTU]
VT-INDIA									
B737-71Q	VT-JNE	JET AIRWAYS (TOMB)		29043	138	12/02/98	CFM56-7B24		N29879
B737-71Q	VT-JNF	JET AIRWAYS (TOMB)		29044	152	12/04/98	CFM56-7B24		N29887
B737-71Q	VT-JNG	JET AIRWAYS (TOMB)		29045	169	12/23/98	CFM56-7B24		N1786B, N29975
B737-71Q	VT-JNH	JET AIRWAYS (TOMB)		29046	181	01/27/99	CFM56-7B24		N29976
B737-76N	VT-JNP	JET AIRWAYS (GECA)		28630	664	09/29/00	CFM56-7B24		N630GE
B737-76N	VT-JNQ	JET AIRWAYS (FSBU)		28635	734	12/20/00	CFM56-7B24		N1786B, N635GE
B737-73A	VT-JNS	JET AIRWAYS (AWAS)		28498	775	02/20/01	CFM56-7B24		N1786B, N498AW
B737-76N	VT-JNT	JET AIRWAYS (FSBU)		28609	417	11/19/99	CFM56-7B24		N1786B, N609LP, LV-ZSJ [AT QLA 12/04/00]
B737-75R	VT-JNU	JET AIRWAYS		30404	835	05/18/01	CFM56-7B24		
B737-86N	VT-JNA	JET AIRWAYS (GECA)		28578	89	08/28/98	CFM56-7B26		N578GE
B737-86N	VT-JNB	JET AIRWAYS (GECA)		28575	91	09/10/98	CFM56-7B26		N1786B, N575GE
B737-85R	VT-JNC	JET AIRWAYS		29036	164	12/24/98	CFM56-7B26		N1787B
B737-85R	VT-JND	JET AIRWAYS		29037	177	01/14/99	CFM56-7B26		N1787B
B737-85R	VT-JNJ	JET AIRWAYS		29038	297	06/21/99	CFM56-7B26		N1786B
B737-85R	VT-JNL	JET AIRWAYS		29039	326	09/02/99	CFM56-7B26		N1786B
B737-85R	VT-JNM	JET AIRWAYS		29040	465	01/21/00	CFM56-7B26		N1786B
B737-85R	VT-JNN	JET AIRWAYS		29041	489	02/29/00	CFM56-7B26		N1786B
B737-85R	VT-JNR	JET AIRWAYS		30403	749	02/15/01	CFM56-7B26		N1786B, N1781B
B737-73A	VT-SIG	SAHARA AIRLINES (AWAS)		28497	216	03/22/99	CFM56-7B24		N1786B, N1781B, N60436, N700AZ
B737-81Q	VT-SIJ	SAHARA AIRLINES (FSBU)		29049	424	11/30/99	CFM56-7B26		N1786B, N8253J
B737-81Q	VT-SIK	SAHARA AIRLINES (FSBU)		29050	444	12/16/99	CFM56-7B26		N1786B, N8253V
YR-ROMANIA									
B737-78J	YR-BGF	TAROM		28440	795	03/27/01	CFM56-7B26		
B737-78J	YR-BGG	TAROM		28442	827	04/25/01	CFM56-7B26		
ZS-SOUTH AFRICA									
B737-85F	ZS-SJA	SOUTH AFRICAN AIRWAYS (GATX)		29248	561	06/29/00	CFM56-7B26		
B737-8S3	ZS-SJB	SOUTH AFRICAN AIRWAYS (GATX)		29249	653	09/08/00	CFM56-7B26		N1786B
B737-85F	ZS-SJC	SOUTH AFRICAN AIRWAYS (GATX)		28828	565	06/30/00	CFM56-7B26		N1786B
B737-85F	ZS-SJD	SOUTH AFRICAN AIRWAYS (GATX)		28829	582	06/30/00	CFM56-7B26		
B737-85F	ZS-SJE	SOUTH AFRICAN AIRWAYS (GATX)		28830	669	09/29/00	CFM56-7B26		N1786B
B737-85F	ZS-SJF	SOUTH AFRICAN AIRWAYS (GATX)		30006	688	10/25/00	CFM56-7B26		N1787B
B737-8BG	ZS-SJG	SOUTH AFRICAN AIRWAYS (GAFM)		32353	711	11/21/00	CFM56-7B26		N1786B

A/C TYPE	CURRENT REG. NO.	LAST KNOWN OPERATOR (OWNER)	STATUS	ORIGINAL MSN	LINE NO.	DEL. DATE	ENG. TYPE	FLEET NO.	PREV. REG. [COMMENTS]
B737-8BG	ZS-SJH	SOUTH AFRICAN AIRWAYS (FLIT)		32354	725	12/12/00	CFM56-7B26		N1787B
B737-85F	ZS-SJI	SOUTH AFRICAN AIRWAYS (GATX)		30007	746	01/17/01	CFM56-7B26		N1787B
B737-85F	ZS-SJJ	SOUTH AFRICAN AIRWAYS (GATX)		30567	761	01/31/01	CFM56-7B26		N1787B
B737-8BG	ZS-SJK	SOUTH AFRICAN AIRWAYS (FLIT)		32355	807	03/29/01	CFM56-7B26		
B737-8BG	ZS-SJL	SOUTH AFRICAN AIRWAYS (FLIT)		32356	819	04/17/01	CFM56-7B26		[LST TRA AS PH-HZZ]
B737-85F (WL)	ZS-SJM	SOUTH AFRICAN AIRWAYS (GATX)	N	30476	789		CFM56-7B26		N788BA, N1014X
B737-85F	ZS-SJN	SOUTH AFRICAN AIRWAYS (GATX)	N	30569	850		CFM56-7B26		

4X-ISRAEL

A/C TYPE	CURRENT REG. NO.	LAST KNOWN OPERATOR (OWNER)	STATUS	ORIGINAL MSN	LINE NO.	DEL. DATE	ENG. TYPE	FLEET NO.	PREV. REG. [COMMENTS]
B737-758	4X-EKD	EL AL ISRAELI AIRLINES		29960	327	08/11/99	CFM56-7B24	701	
B737-758	4X-EKE	EL AL ISRAELI AIRLINES		29961	442	12/14/99	CFM56-7B24	702	N1786B
B737-858	4X-EKA	EL AL ISRAELI AIRLINES		29957	204	02/24/99	CFM56-7B26	801	N1786B
B737-858	4X-EKB	EL AL ISRAELI AIRLINES		29958	249	04/21/99	CFM56-7B26	802	N1786B
B737-858	4X-EKC	EL AL ISRAELI AIRLINES		29959	314	07/31/99	CFM56-7B26	803	N1795B

5B-CYPRUS

A/C TYPE	CURRENT REG. NO.	LAST KNOWN OPERATOR (OWNER)	STATUS	ORIGINAL MSN	LINE NO.	DEL. DATE	ENG. TYPE	FLEET NO.	PREV. REG. [COMMENTS]
B737-86N	5B-DBH	HELIOS AIRWAYS (GECA)		30806	790	03/20/01	CFM56-7B26		
B737-86N	5B-DBI	HELIOS AIRWAYS (GECA)		30807	829	04/25/01	CFM56-7B26		

5W-SAMOA

A/C TYPE	CURRENT REG. NO.	LAST KNOWN OPERATOR (OWNER)	STATUS	ORIGINAL MSN	LINE NO.	DEL. DATE	ENG. TYPE	FLEET NO.	PREV. REG. [COMMENTS]
B737-8Q8	5W-SAM	POLYNESIAN AIRLINE OF SAMOA (ILFC)		30039	701	11/14/00	CFM56-7B26		N1786B

7T-ALGERIA

A/C TYPE	CURRENT REG. NO.	LAST KNOWN OPERATOR (OWNER)	STATUS	ORIGINAL MSN	LINE NO.	DEL. DATE	ENG. TYPE	FLEET NO.	PREV. REG. [COMMENTS]
B737-8D6	7T-VJJ	AIR ALGERIE		30202	610	07/31/00	CFM56-7B26		N1786B
B737-8D6	7T-VJK	AIR ALGERIE		30203	640	08/25/00	CFM56-7B26		N1786B, N1787B, N1781B
B737-8D6	7T-VJL	AIR ALGERIE		30204	652	09/13/00	CFM56-7B26		N1786B
B737-8D6	7T-VJM	AIR ALGERIE		30205	691	10/27/00	CFM56-7B26		N1786B
B737-8D6	7T-VJN	AIR ALGERIE		30206	751	01/29/01	CFM56-7B26		N1786B
B737-82R	TC-APG	AIR ALGERIE (PGT)	L	29329	224	03/24/99	CFM56-7B26		N1786B
B737-86N	TC-APN	AIR ALGERIE (PGT)	L	28628	573	06/02/00	CFM56-7B26		N1786B, N5573L
B737-809	TC-APM	KHALIFA AIRWAYS (PGT)	L	28403	117	10/29/98	CFM56-7B26		N1786B, B-18602
B737-86N	TC-APY	KHALIFA AIRWAYS (PGT)	L	28591	233	04/14/99	CFM56-7B26		N1786B, TC-IAH

9M-MALAYSIA

A/C TYPE	CURRENT REG. NO.	LAST KNOWN OPERATOR (OWNER)	STATUS	ORIGINAL MSN	LINE NO.	DEL. DATE	ENG. TYPE	FLEET NO.	PREV. REG. [COMMENTS]
B737-7H6 (BBJ)	9M-BBJ	MALAYSIA AIRLINES		29274	397	11/02/99	CFM56-7B26		N1787B, N1785B, N6055X ["MASTAR"]

9Y-TRINIDAD & TOBAGO

A/C TYPE	CURRENT REG. NO.	LAST KNOWN OPERATOR (OWNER)	STATUS	ORIGINAL MSN	LINE NO.	DEL. DATE	ENG. TYPE	FLEET NO.	PREV. REG. [COMMENTS]
B737-8Q8	9Y-ANU	BWIA INTL. (ILFC)		28235	697	11/30/00	CFM56-7B26		N1786B
B737-8Q8	9Y-BGI	BWIA INTL. (ILFC)		28232	547	05/11/00	CFM56-7B26		N1786B
B737-8Q8	9Y-GEO	BWIA INTL. (ILFC)		28225	433	12/23/99	CFM56-7B26		N1787B
B737-8Q8	9Y-KIN	BWIA INTL. (ILFC)		28234	680	11/03/00	CFM56-7B26		N1786B
B737-8Q8	9Y-POS	BWIA INTL. (ILFC)		28230	506	04/12/00	CFM56-7B26		
B737-8Q8	9Y-TAB	BWIA INTL. (ILFC)		28233	598	07/07/00	CFM56-7B26		N1786B

UNDELIVERED BBJ AIRCRAFT

A/C TYPE	CURRENT REG. NO.	LAST KNOWN OPERATOR (OWNER)	STATUS	ORIGINAL MSN	LINE NO.	DEL. DATE	ENG. TYPE	FLEET NO.	PREV. REG. [COMMENTS]
B737-7BC (BBJ)	N184QS	(BOEING BBJ)	N	30884	747		CFM56-7B26		N1786B
B737-7ED (BBJ)	N373BJ	(BOEING BBJ)	N	32627	826		CFM56-7B26		
B737-8DP (BBJ2)	HB-IIZ	(BOEING BBJ)	N	32451	836		CFM56-7B26		N374BJ

MILITARY

A/C TYPE	CURRENT REG. NO.	LAST KNOWN OPERATOR (OWNER)	STATUS	ORIGINAL MSN	LINE NO.	DEL. DATE	ENG. TYPE	FLEET NO.	PREV. REG. [COMMENTS]
B737-7AF (C-40A)	165829	U.S. NAVY	M	29979	496	12/23/00	CFM56-7B26		N1003N [CARGO DOOR]
B737-7AF (C-40A)	165830	U.S. NAVY	M	29980	568	09/29/00	CFM56-7B26		N1786B, N1003M
B737-8AR	3701	TAIWANESE AIR FORCE	M	30139	428	12/08/99	CFM56-7B26		N1786B, N1787B
B737-7AF (C-40A)	165831	U.S. NAVY	M	30200	651	11/02/00	CFM56-7B26		N1786B
B737-7AF (C-40A)	165832	U.S. NAVY	M	30781	742	03/05/01	CFM56-7B26		N1787B

Chapter 6

Model 747

As related in the introductory chapter, Boeing started design of the world's first wide-body jetliner—the Model 747—to take advantage of the high-bypass-ratio turbofans developed to power the military CX-HLS. Although the new engines would result in aircraft with significantly lower seat-mile costs, it was believed by many in the mid-1960s that the future of commercial air transport was not large-capacity jetliners but supersonic aircraft. Even Boeing felt that its wide-body aircraft would mostly be used to complement SSTs by providing economy-class service and transporting cargo at ton-mile costs significantly below those of first-generation jet freighters. Subsequent events were rather different. The failure of SST technology to live up to commercial expectations created a much larger market for passenger-carrying 747s than had been forecast. Thus, 35 years after Pan American ordered the first 25 wide-bodies, Boeing has sold 1,344 Model 747s and still hopes to develop its largest jetliners to keep them in production well into the second decade of the third millennium.

The long and highly profitable career of the 747 began on January 22, 1970, when Pan American initiated "Jumbo Jet" service between New York and London. Standard-sized versions of the 747 were delivered to the airlines in passenger, freighter, convertible, combi, and short-range/high-density 747-100, -200, and -300 configurations between 1969 and 1991. Many of these "classic" 747s were later modified to a variety of configurations for service with civil and military/government customers, with fewer than 490 still in service worldwide. Forty-five "special-performance" 747SPs were delivered between 1976 and 1987,

while the USAF got four E-4A/Bs beginning in 1974. Today, however, the most significant 747 variants are the passenger-carrying 747-400, the passenger/cargo 747-400M Combi, and the 747-400F freighter. The first of these advanced variants flew on April 29, 1988, and production is continuing at a monthly rate of two airframes.

747-100

Initially simply known as the 747, but redesignated 747-100 after the higher-gross-weight, better-performing 747-200 was added to the product line, the original variant of the Boeing wide-body was in production until 1976. The 167th and last of these aircraft (l/n 281, s/n 21213) was delivered to British Airways on April 8, 1976.

First flown on February 9, 1969, with Pratt & Whitney JT9D-1 engines rated at 42,000 pounds (186.8 kilonewtons) of static thrust, the 747 went into service with JT9D-3s rated at 43,000 pounds (191.3 kilonewtons). MTOW at entry into service was 710,000 pounds (322,051 kilograms) but was later raised, in two steps, to 755,000 (342,462 kilograms). Structure and undercarriage were beefed up accordingly. The heaviest gross weight version was designated 747-100A in service with Pan American. To cope with increased weights and correct deficiencies with early engines, 747-100s later were powered by JT9D-3As rated at 43,000 pounds (191.3 kilonewtons) of static thrust, JT9D-7AWs rated at 45,000 pounds (200.2 kilonewtons), JT9D-7s rated at 47,000 pounds (209.1 kilonewtons), and JT9D-7As or -7AHs rated at 47,670 pounds (212 kilonewtons).

Under ATC A20WE issued by the FAA on December 30, 1969, the 747-100 could carry a maximum of 490 passengers in 10-abreast seating with reduced seat pitch. At entry into service, however, 747s typically were fitted with accommodation for 57 first-class passengers and 306 economy-class passengers in eight-abreast seating, both sections having two aisles, a first in scheduled airline operation. Seating on the upper deck was provided for eight first-class passengers, but because these seats could not be occupied during takeoff and landing, that area was then used as a first-class lounge. Later, when emergency-evacuation provisions were revised, the ATC was amended to allow airlines to fit up to 19 saleable seats on the upper deck.

The 747-100B variant, with beefed-up structure and a strengthened undercarriage to cope with a MTOW of 750,000 pounds (340,194 kilograms), was introduced in August 1979 when Iran Air took delivery of a 747-186B (l/n 381, s/n 21759, EP-IAM). Three more of these aircraft powered by JT9D-7F engines rated at 50, 000 pounds (222.4 kilonewtons) of static thrust had been ordered, but the contract was cancelled following the takeover of the U.S. Embassy in Tehran on November 4, 1979. Eight 747-168Bs powered by Rolls-Royce RB211-524Cs rated at 51,500 pounds (229.1 kilonewtons) of static thrust were delivered to Saudia between April 1981 and April 1982—the only Series 100/100A/100B 747s to be powered by other than Pratt & Whitney engines.

Conversions to freighter and combi configurations are described under the heading "Freighters, Convertibles, and Combis." Similarly, short-range (SR) aircraft, which were developed for the Japanese market, are described separately.

747-200

Proposed growth versions of the 747 began appearing soon after Pan American ordered the world's first wide-bodied jetliner. Initially, these growth versions included rather significant airframe and engine changes. Nevertheless, the first of these growth versions, the 747-200B, went into production with only minimal changes. They were primarily intended to increase MTOW, and consequently, payload-range performance. In particular, airlines were asking that the 747 be made capable of operating

between Western European capitals and destinations on the West Coast of the United States, then the longest non-stop sectors, even when flying against unusually strong winter winds.

Insufficient thrusts from early JT9D models to cope up with increased operating weights (early 747s being especially deficient in terms of time-to-climb to cruise altitude when operating in the midst of faster climbing 707s and DC-8s) delayed development of the proposed 747B. Finally, higher gross weight 747-200B variants—starting at 775,000 pounds (351,534 kilograms) and ending at 800,000 pounds (362.874 kilograms) as airframe and undercarriage were strengthened—were launched in December 1966. The first to order was Alitalia, which ordered two aircraft powered by JT9D-3AW engines rated at 45,000 pounds (200.2 kilonewtons) of static thrust. The first Series 200B delivered was a 747-206B (l/n 96, s/n 19922, PH-BUA), which went to KLM on January 16, 1971.

Later Pratt & Whitney–powered 747-200s had JT9D-7s, -7As, -7Fs, -7Js, and -70As, with maximum thrust increasing to a maximum of 53,000 pounds (235.7 kilonewtons) static. Eventually, they were joined by aircraft powered by General Electric and Rolls-Royce turbofans. The first with CF6-80 engines were ordered by KLM in July 1974, and the first with RB211-524 engines were contracted by British Airways in June 1975. CF6 engine variants ranged in thrust rating from the 51,000 pounds (226.8 kilonewtons) static of the CF6-80D to the 56,700 pounds (252.2 kilonewtons) static of the CF6-50C2B1, while the RB211 engine variant ranged in thrust rating from 50,000 pounds static (222.4 kilonewtons) for the RB211-524 to 53,000 pounds static (235.7 kilonewtons) for the -524D4.

In addition to being certificated for operations at higher gross weights and with engines from different manufacturers, 747-200Bs were characterized by their more capacious hump aft of the cockpit.

The hump's external dimensions remained unchanged from those of 747-100's, but internal modifications made it possible to accommodate up to 16 passengers with adequate provision for safe emergency egress. The first aircraft with the modified upper deck (identified by additional windows) was l/n 147 (s/n 20009, VH-EBA), which was delivered to Qantas on July 30, 1971. During production, a more practical straight stair arrangement, as developed for the 747-300 with its stretched upper deck (SUD), replaced the original spiral staircase well. That SUD conversion, which provided seating for up to 32 passengers, was also retrofitted to a number of 747-200Bs, thus creating a spotter nightmare.

The 747-200B remained in production until 1989, the last being delivered to All Nippon Airways on August 10 of that year. Over the years, as mentioned under the 747-300 and Combi headings, there have been numerous conversions and upgrades.

747-300

Higher-capacity versions of the 747 were planned soon after the original model had been committed to production, but none of them made it to market because seating capacity of the 747 was already larger than needed for the airline market of the 1960s and 1970s. Consequently, Boeing had to wait more than 10 years after the 747's entry into service before announcing in June 1980 the go-ahead for a larger-capacity 747 version. Even then, this 747-300 version offered only a modest increase in seating capacity through the use of a stretched upper deck. Extended aft by 23 feet 4 inches (7.11 meters) and fitted with a proper emergency exit door on both sides, this SUD could be used to seat up to 69 economy passengers. Maximum certificated accommodation was provided for up to 580 passengers in single-class configuration, or 32 first-class passengers and 400 to 450 economy passengers (depending on seat pitch and galley/lavatory arrangements) in dual-class configuration. As was the case with Series 200B aircraft, the Series 300s were available with the three makes of engines. Forty-two were delivered with JT9D turbofans, 22 with RB211s, and 17 with CF6-80s.

The first order for Model 300s was placed by Swissair on June 11, 1980, for four 747-357s. Earlier dated orders reported by Boeing reflect amendments to previously placed 747-200 contracts by Korean Air Lines (two aircraft from an April 1979 contract for nine 747-100s and -200s) and Swissair (one aircraft from a September 1979 contract for a single 747-200). The first Model 300 (l/n 570, s/n 22704, HB-IGC in Combi configuration) flew on October 5, 1982, and deliveries began in March 1983. The last genuine Model 300 (of the 56 passenger-configured aircraft, four short-range 747-300SRs, and 21 747-300M Combis) was delivered in Combi configuration to Air India in November 1988.

Beside these 81 genuine Model 300s, all built as such, there were 14 look-alike aircraft obtained through conversion of existing airframes. These "faux" 747-300s—which are visually undistinguishable from production Model 300s and can be positively identified only by referring to their registration numbers—were obtained when 12 747-200Bs and two 747-100B (SR)s were returned to Boeing to be fitted with SUDs. They were properly designated 747-200B (SUD)s and 747-100B (SR/SUD)s to differentiate them from purpose-built 747-300s.

747-400

A cursory look at a 747-400 parked next to a 747-300 may lead one to conclude, erroneously, that the Series 400 is nothing but a minimum-change improvement of the Series 300, differing from earlier aircraft only in being fitted with winglets. In fact, beneath the skin, the Series 400 comes close to being an all-new design.

Building on the experience gained with a KC-135 that had been modified with winglets developed by Dr. Richard Whitcomb at NASA, Boeing adopted winglets to reduce drag and extend range of the 747-400. The winglets were built of graphite (carbon fiber) and epoxy honeycomb and added a nominal 5 feet 9 inches (1.75 meters) to the span, for an overall span of 213 feet (64.92 meters) for the fully fueled aircraft. Another change to the wings of Series 400s was the addition of an additional segment of leading-edge flap to cope with the greater growth weight. (The 747-400 was certificated in January 1989 at a MTOW of 800,000 pounds [362,874 kilograms], but MTOW rose to 875,000 pounds [396,893 kilograms] for some late-production Series 400s and will reach 910,000 pounds [412,769 kilograms] for the yet-to-fly Longer-Range 747-400.)

Further range increases were made possible by adding 3,300 U.S. gallons (12,492 liters) of fuel in the horizontal stabilizer, using lighter material (including advanced aluminum alloys) wherever possible, and reducing drag by redesigning the composite fairing between the fuselage and wings. Moreover, all three engine manufacturers came through with greatly improved versions of their engines, with fuel-consumption rates decreased by 5 to 10 percent, thus helping Boeing turn its 747-400 into a very-long-range aircraft.

Development timing for these engine variants was most fortunate because the countries of Asia and the Pacific Rim were going through a spurt of economic growth, thus prompting airlines to open more direct but longer Asian routes from and to Europe and the United States. Pratt & Whitney smartly gave entirely new designations (in the PW4000 series starting with the PW4056 engine rated at 56,750 pounds [252.4 kilonewtons] of static thrust) to its JT9D derivatives. General Electric and Rolls-Royce came up with engines with similar performance but opted to retain "alphabet soup" designations for their new versions of the CF6-80 (the CF6-80C2B1F rated at 58,000 pounds [258 kilonewtons] static thrust) and RB211 (the RB211-524H rated at 60,600 pounds [269.6 kilonewtons] static thrust).

Not visible to the public eye but of considerable technical significance were cockpit improvements including the use of six cathode-ray-tube (CRT) displays, a Collins maintenance computer, a Honeywell flight-management computer, and a Collins autopilot flight-director system. Consequently, normal operating crew was reduced from three (including a flight engineer/second officer) to two pilots, with provision for a relief crew for very long flights.

The longer range of the 747-400 made it desirable to provide rest facilities for the cockpit crew (two bunks being provided aft of the cockpit) and cabin crew (four bunks and four seats being provided in a compartment above the main deck in the rear fuselage). No such rest facilities were provided for passengers. Passenger comfort was significantly improved, however, through the use of a new APU, a greater choice of internal arrangement (primarily through the use of the first vacuum-type toilet facilities), and the use of redesigned paneling to provide a feeling of greater space.

Announced in the fall of 1985, 20 years after Boeing had started work on its original wide-body model, the first order for a 747-400 was placed by Northwest Airlines on October 22, 1985. (However, a July 1984 contract from Air New Zealand for a 747-200 was subsequently modified, thus resulting in Air New Zealand being listed, in some records, as the first 747-400 customer.) After many delays, the 747-400 first flew on April 29, 1988, and was certificated in January 1989. The type was placed in U.S. domestic service February 1989 by Northwest and on intended long-range routes by Singapore Airlines at the end of May 1989.

Today, Series 400 aircraft are in production as passenger-configured 747-400s and 747-400ERs, 747-400M Combis, and 747-400F freighters. In November 2000, Qantas became the first customer for the 747-400ER, which will feature an increase in MTOW to 910,000 pounds (412,769 kilograms). This requires some local strengthening of the fuselage, wings, and landing gear. With two auxiliary tanks in the lower lobe of the fuselage, fuel capacity is increased to 63,765 U.S. gallons (241,372 liters), and the range of the 747-400ER is extended by 435 nautical miles (805 kilometers). These 747-400ERs are offered with a choice of 68,000-pound-thrust-class (302.5-kilonewton-class) turbofans from Rolls-Royce or Engine Alliance (a joint venture of General Electric and Pratt & Whitney). Further development of the 747 is now uncertain because Boeing faces stiff competition from the all-new Airbus A380, while Boeing is itself exploring the possibility of launching a revolutionary family of jetliners flying faster, higher, and further.

The growth of passenger-configured 747s, not clearly apparent when Classic and -400 aircraft are seen side by side, is best summarized by the following table:

	747-100	747-400
Overall length	231 ft 4 in (70.51 m)	231 ft 10 in (70.66 m)
Span (fully fueled)	195 ft 8 in (59.64 m)	213 ft (64.92 m)
Wing area	5,500 sq ft (511 m^2)	5,650 sq ft (524.9 m^2)
Maximum single-class seating accommodation	490	550
Typical two-class accommodation	363	497
Typical three-class accommodation	N/A	400
MTOW	710,000 lb (322,051 kg)	875,000 lb (396,893 kg)
Typical engines	JT9D-3	PW4060
Takeoff thrust per engine	43,000 lb st (191.3 kN)	60,000 lb st (266.9 kN)
Fuel tank capacity	48,445 U.S. gal (183,380 liters)	57,286 U.S. gal (216,843 liters)
Typical fuel burn on a 3,450-nm (6,390-km flight)	409 lb (238 liters) per passenger	300 lb (175 liters) per passenger
Typical cruising speed	Mach 0.84	Mach 0.85
Maximum range	4,600 nm (8,520 km)	7,325 nm (13,565 km)

747 Freighters, Convertibles, and Combis

Expecting that the top end of the passenger business would be the domain of SSTs, Boeing optimized the fuselage of the 747 so that two eight-by-eight containers could be carried side by side. To ease the loading of these containers, Boeing placed the cockpit above the main deck and designed an upward-swinging nose loading door. The 747 was expected to be in service four years before the Anglo-French Concorde and some eight years before the U.S. SST, so the airlines also anticipated that the wide-body aircraft would soon be used mostly to carry cargo. In fact, initial orders reflected the optimism of airlines regarding the cargo-carrying capabilities of the 747.

The initial Pan American order has been reported as covering 25 aircraft, with almost everyone since assuming that these were all passenger-configured aircraft. True, these aircraft were all delivered as passenger-carrying 747s, as were those ordered in 1966–1967 by other airlines. Less well known is that an internal Boeing document—*Announced Turbine Transport Sales*, prepared by the Sales Planning & Control Section and dated December 31, 1967—reveals 37 orders for freighter (F) and convertible (C) aircraft placed between April 1966 and the end of 1967 (16 of which were either canceled or renegotiated). According to this report, the April 1966 order from Pan American, later amended, covered 23 passenger-carrying 747s and 2 747F freighters. It was followed by 747F orders placed by TWA (3 freighters ordered in September 1966), Alitalia (1 in December 1966), and United (5 in July 1967). Five carriers ordered 747C convertibles (Continental, 3 in October 1966; American, 10 in November 1966; Northwest, 3 in November 1966; World Airways, 3 in December 1966; and Alaska, 1 in August 1967).

These promising orders for freighter and convertible variants of the early, low-gross-weight 747s (retroactively designated 747-100s) did not result in the production of a single aircraft in either of those configurations. Three factors conspired to preclude Boeing from realizing its overly sanguine hope to produce half of the first 400 Model 747s in freighter or convertible configurations. First, its market-research staff had grossly overestimated the potential demand. Second, with belly holds of passenger-configured 747s having almost 80 percent of the volume of all-freight 707s, much of the actual cargo demand could be accommodated by these passenger liners without the need for the airlines to operate dedicated 747 freighters. Third, failure of early JT9D engine variants to offer adequate thrust reduced the payload-range of 747 freighters and convertibles below requirements.

All initial customers for 747Fs and 747Cs ended up amending their contracts to substitute passenger-configured 747s for cargo-carrying aircraft or to cancel their orders for freighters and convertibles. Years later, after more powerful JT9D engines were available and the certificated gross weight of 747-100s had been increased, a number of carriers had some of their early 747s converted by Boeing to 747-100SF (Special Freighter) standard. That work included fitting a 10- by 11-foot 2-inch (3.95- by 3.40-meter) cargo-loading door on the left side of the fuselage, aft of the wings, and reinforcing the main-deck flooring and fitting it with a track-and-roller system. Work on the first of the modified 747-100SFs was initiated in 1974. Still later, 14 747-100s and 4 747-200Bs were similarly modified for Pan American under the Civil Reserve Air Fleet (CRAF) program. Because the conversion of these later aircraft was funded by the Department of Defense, they were given the seldom-used military designation of C-19A. Currently, the last C-19As are operated by Evergreen International Airlines. In addition, a number of 747-100SRs were also modified as Special Freighters.

Early 747s converted as 747-100SF and C-19A freighters were preceded in cargo operations by 747-200Cs, 747-200Fs, and 747-200Ms. Development of these variants was made possible by the higher thrust of later JT9D, CF6-80, and RB211 engines and the resulting increase in 747 MTOW (thus finally resulting in adequate payload-range performance for cargo-carrying 747s).

The first cargo-configured 747 to come off the Everett assembly line was a 747-200F for Lufthansa (l/n 168, s/n 20373, D-ABYE). Fitted with the upward-opening nose door and reinforced main-deck flooring designed by Boeing for the unbuilt C and F variants of the original 747, this aircraft first flew on November 30, 1971, and was certificated on March 7, 1972. Lufthansa placed it into service in April 1972. Boeing went on to build 73 747-200Fs, all without main-deck cabin windows, the last of which being delivered to Nippon Cargo Airlines in November 1991.

A side door, as later fitted to Special Freighter conversions of 747-100s, was first fitted to an all-freight 747-245F (built without cabin windows or possibility of conversion to passenger configuration) when l/n 242 was delivered to Seaboard World in July 1974 with both nose and side doors for loading and unloading of the main deck.

The 747-200C was initially built for World Airways, an Oakland-based supplemental carrier, as a substitute for the inadequately powered 747Cs the company had originally ordered in December 1966. It was first flown on March 23, 1973, and was delivered to World Airways five weeks later. This convertible version of the 747 was fitted with the same upward-swinging nose door as the 747-200F but retained the cabin windows of passenger-carrying 747-200s. Boeing went on to build a total of 13 747-200Cs for several customers.

With the benefit of hindsight, it is now difficult to understand why Boeing and its airline customers did not come up earlier with the 747M Combi—a passenger/freight combination version of the 747. That concept smartly offset the excessive number of seats being provided on some "thin" routes when 707s and DC-8s were replaced by all-passenger 747s. The Combi was optimized to carry passengers in the forward sections of the main deck and cargo on the aft sections of that deck. To get this capability, 747s were either modified or built with the rear-fuselage main-deck cargo door developed for Special Freighters and with a reinforced aft main-deck floor. Preceded by two Sabena 747-149s modified to Combi configuration in 1974, the first production Combi, l/n 250, was delivered to Air Canada in March 1975. Conversion of early aircraft, and production of new Combis, resulted in 747-200M, 747-200M (SUD), 747-300M, and 747-400M variants, with the 747-400M proving to be a particularly good seller during the 1990s. The 747-400M first flew on June 30, 1989, and was placed into service by KLM two months later. By the spring of 2001, a total of 63 747-400M Combis had been ordered.

Others companies also undertook freighter conversion of 747-100s and -200s, including some Combis. Notably, such work was performed by Chrysler Airborne Technologies in Waco, Texas; HAECO in the then Crown Colony of Hong Kong; Israeli Aircraft Industry's Bedek Aviation Division in Israel; Mobile Aerospace in Alabama; and Pemco Aeroplex in Dothan, Alabama.

In addition to all-passenger 747-400 and 747-400M Combi versions, the latter with an aft cargo door and a reinforced rear main deck for carriage of cargo behind a crash-resistant bulkhead, production versions of the Series 400 include the 740-400F. This freighter version, currently the best-selling 747 variant, combines the 747-200F fuselage (with the nose cargo door, short upper deck with only three windows on each side, reinforced flooring with the cargo handling system, and no main-deck cabin windows) with the wings and powerplant installation of passenger-carrying 747-400s. The first of the 747-400Fs (l/n 968, c/m 25632) flew on May 4, 1993. Six months later, Cargolux became the first operator of the current 747 freighter variant.

The latest version to be committed to production, the Longer-Range 747-400F freighter is a development of the 747-400F, with MTOW increased to 910,000 pounds (412,769 kilograms), the same as that of the 747-400ER passenger model. To cope with that increased weight, this freighter version features strengthened parts for its wings, fuselage, and undercarriage. Compared with the standard 747-400F, this translates into either 22,000 pounds (9,979 kilograms) more payload or an additional 530 nautical miles (980 kilometers) of range. By the early spring of 2001, Boeing had received orders for 90 747-400Fs and Longer-Range 747-400Fs.

747 SR (Short Range)

To meet the needs of Japanese carriers for aircraft with high-density seating for operation on short domestic routes, Boeing developed SR (Short Range) versions of the Series 100, 300, and 400. Compared with corresponding long-range versions of these three series, the SRs had reduced operating weight (due mostly to a significant reduction in fuel weight), beefed-up undercarriage (to cope with the higher number of takeoffs and landings on very short sectors), and other minor structural modifications. Seating capacity was increased by deleting some of the galleys and lavatories (not needed on short flights) and reducing seat pitch.

Production versions included 747SR-100s and 747-100B (SR)s powered by JT9D-7 and JT9D-7As derated to 43,500 pounds (193.5 kilonewtons) of static thrust, 747SR-100Bs powered by CF6-45As with 46,500 pounds (206.8 kilonewtons) of static thrust, and 747-300 (SR)s powered by JT9D-7R4G2s with 54,000 pounds (240.2 kilonewtons) of static thrust. The 747-100B (SR/SUD) designation identifies 747-100B (SR)s retrofitted with the SUD developed for the 747-300. The two-letter SR suffix is not

used for the short-range domestic version of the Series 400, these aircraft being designated 747-400Ds. Powered by CF6-80C2B1F engines, the 747-400Ds do not have the extended wing and winglets of other Series 400 aircraft. With reduced fuel load (including deletion of tanks normally fitted in the horizontal stabilizers of Series 400s), the 747-400Ds have a MTOW normally limited to 600,000 pounds (272,155 kilograms).

The first 747-100SR (l/n 221, s/n 20781, JA8117) entered service with Japan Airlines in October 1973 and was initially fitted with 498 seats (that number later being increased to 528 in a two-class configuration). The 747-300 (SR) models were delivered with 563 seats, while 747-400D models have 568 seats in a two-class configuration.

747SP (Special Performance)

Aimed at blocking inroads into the 747 market by long-range versions of the McDonnell Douglas DC-10 and Lockheed TriStars, development of this SP version was initiated in 1973. To achieve the desired performance, the design team traded capacity for range. Fuselage length was shortened by 48 feet 4 inches (14.73 meters) to bring seating capacity in a typical two-class configuration down from 385 for the 747-200B to 281 for the SP (maximum approved seating for the two versions then being 500 and 360). Further weight reduction resulted from a major wing redesign to substitute variable-pivot flaps for the triple slotted flaps fitted to other 747s. Other changes included taller vertical surfaces, increased-span stabilizers, and recontoured aft-fuselage and wing-fuselage fillets.

Maximum gross weight was reduced to 700,000 pounds (317,515 kilograms). Powered by either JT9D-7As or RB211-524s, the 747SP had a total fuel tank capacity of 47,210 U.S. gallons (178,705 liters) versus up to 51,430 gallons (194,680 liters) for the 747-200B. Nevertheless, as the result of its much lower drag and lower weight, the 747SP had greater range. It also cruised higher (up to 41,000 feet [12,500 meters]) and faster (Mach 0.85 versus 0.84) than the -200B.

An initial order for 10 747SPs was placed by Pan American in September 1973. The first of these aircraft (l/n 265, s/n 21022, N530PA) flew on July 4, 1975. Certificated by the FAA on February 4, 1976, the 747SP went into service in April of that year. Greatly admired by aviation enthusiasts, the "big balloon" 747SP proved to be a marketing and commercial failure for Boeing with its $193-million development price tag (about $550 million in today's dollars) resulting in the sale of only 45 aircraft (versus an initial forecast of 183 SP sales). The last SP was delivered in March 1987 to the United Arab Emirates as a VIP aircraft.

Military and Government 747s

Over the past four decades, military variants of the 747 were studied and proposed to cover a variety of missions. Seven were ordered by the USAF, including four Series 200 aircraft built as E-4A and E-4B National Emergency Airborne Command Posts (NEACP), two Series 200 aircraft as VC-25As for the presidential fleet, and one 747-400F currently being modified as the AL-1A airborne laser platform. Advanced Tanker Cargo Aircraft (ATCA) and MC747 missile-carrying variants proposed to the USAF were not built. The only other customer for new military 747 variants was the Imperial Iranian Air Force, which supplemented its fleet of ex-airline 747-100s with four new 747-200Fs. Other variants were developed to meet government requirements of a non-military nature and resulted in the delivery or conversion of a few plushy-configured VIP aircraft (mostly 747SPs but also a 747-300 for Saudi Arabia, and two 747-400s for Japan and one for Brunei).

The first military/government 747s to proceed past the study phase were the NEACP E-4s. Initially powered by JT9Ds rated at 47,000 pounds (209.1 kilonewtons) of static thrust but later re-engined with F103-GE-100 turbofans (military CF6-50E2s) rated at 53,500 pounds (233.5 kilonewtons) of static thrust, the first E-4A flew on June 19, 1973. A VC-25A was first used as Air Force One on September 7, 1990.

Besides noting again the previously described C-19As (Pan American's 747-100A/200s modified by Boeing for the CRAF), mention must be made of 12 Series 100s (3 ex-Continental 747-124s, 4 ex-Eastern 747-125s, and 5 ex-TWA 747-131s) modified by Boeing in Wichita for the Imperial Iranian Air Force. In addition to being fitted with a cargo door on the left side of the aft fuselage and reinforced main-deck flooring, these aircraft were provided with an air-refueling receptacle forward of the cockpit (that installation being similar to that developed for USAF VC-25As and E-4A/Bs). Three were also fitted with a remotely controlled air-refueling boom.

Finally, mention must be made of the two aircraft (an ex-American Airlines 747-143 and an ex-Japan Airlines 747SR-46) modified for NASA to the Shuttle Carrier Aircraft (SCA) configuration. These two aircraft have been used at Edwards Air Force Base for Approach and Landing Tests (ALTs) with the unpowered space shuttle *Enterprise* (the first air launch was made on August 12, 1977) and to ferry space shuttles.

Boeing 747 Principal Characteristics and Performance

	747-100	747-200	747-300	747-400	747-400F	747SP
Span, ft in (m)	195' 8" (59.64)	195' 8" (59.64)	195' 8" (59.64)	211' 5" (64.44)	211' 5" (64.44)	195' 8" (59.64)
Length, ft in (m)	231' 10" (70.67)	231' 10" (70.67)	231' 10" (70.67)	231' 10" (70.66)	231' 10" (70.66)	184' 9" (56.31)
Height, ft in (m)	63' 5" (19.33)	63' 5" (19.33)	63' 5" (19.33)	63' 8" (19.41)	63' 8" (19.41)	55' (19.94)
Wing area, sq ft (m^2)	5,685 (528.2)	5,685 (528.2)	5,685 (528.2)	5,825 (528.2)	5,825 (541.2)	5,685 (541.2)
High-density seating	490	500	544	569	N/A	360
Two-class seating	452	452	496	524	N/A	281
Three-class seating	366	366	412	416	N/A	N/A
Underfloor cargo, cu ft (m^3)	6,250 (177.0)	6,250 (177.0)	6,250 (177.0)		3,900 (110.4)	
Maximum cargo load, lb (kg)	N/A	N/A	N/A	N/A	249,120 (113,000)	N/A
TO thrust per engine, lb st (kN)	46,500/50,100 (206.8/222.8)	52,500/54,750 (233.5/243.5)	53,000/55,640 (235.7/247.5)	59,500/63,300 (264.7/281.6)	59,500/63,300 (264.7/281.6)	47,670 (212)
Fuel capacity, U.S. gal (liters)	47,210/48,445 (138,060/183,380)	52,410 (198,389)	52,410 (198,389)	57,285 (216,843)	53,985 (204,351)	48,780/50,360 (184,649/190,629)
MTOW, lb (kg)	710,000/735,000 (322,051,333,390)	775,000/833,000 (351,534/377,842)	775,000/833,000 (351,534/377,842)	800,000/875,000 (362,874/396,893)	800,000/875,000 (362,874/396,893)	630,000/700,000 (285.763/317,515)
Typical cruise speed, Mach	0.84	0.84	0.85	0.85	0.85	0.85
Typical range, nm (km)	5,300 (9,815)	6,865 (12,715)	6,690 (12,390)	7,325 (13,565)	3,870 (7,165)	6,000 (11,110)

Boeing 747 Commercial Jet Aircraft Census

The aircraft in the following tables are listed in order of the following: 1) ICAO country prefixes; 2) operator; 3) aircraft type; and 4) registration.

The total built was 1,273+ (45 B747SP, 29 B747SR, 177 B747-100, 4 E-4B, 2 VC-25A, 387 B747-200, 81 B747-300, 547+ B747-400, and 1+ AL1) from 1969 to present (B747-400 still in production).

A/C TYPE	CURRENT REG. NO.	LAST KNOWN OPERATOR (OWNER)	STATUS	ORIGINAL MSN	LINE NO.	DEL. DATE	ENG. TYPE	FLEET NO.	PREV. REG. [COMMENTS]
AP-PAKISTAN									
B747-282B	AP-AYV	PAKISTAN INTL. AIRLINES		20928	239	06/07/74	JT9D-7A		CS-TJC
B747-282B	AP-AYW	PAKISTAN INTL. AIRLINES		21035	256	10/17/75	JT9D-7A		CS-TJD
B747-240B (M)	AP-BAK	PAKISTAN INTL. AIRLINES		21825	383	07/26/79	CF6-50E2		
B747-240B (M)	AP-BAT	PAKISTAN INTL. AIRLINES		22077	429	03/07/80	CF6-50E2		
B747-217B	AP-BCL	PAKISTAN INTL. AIRLINES		20929	247	12/02/74	JT9D-7A		C-FCRE
B747-217B	AP-BCM	PAKISTAN INTL. AIRLINES		20802	226	12/03/73	JT9D-7A		C-FCRB
B747-217B	AP-BCN	PAKISTAN INTL. AIRLINES		20801	225	11/15/73	JT9D-7A		N1794B, C-FCRA
B747-217B	AP-BCO	PAKISTAN INTL. AIRLINES		20927	244	11/05/74	JT9D-7A		N620BN, C-FCRD
B747-367	AP-BFU	PAKISTAN INTL. AIRLINES (CPA)	L	23392	634	02/14/86	RB211-524C2		N6005C, VR-HIJ, B-HIJ
B747-367	AP-BFV	PAKISTAN INTL. AIRLINES (CPA)	L	23534	659	10/10/86	RB211-524C2		N6038E, VR-HIK, B-HIK
B747-367	AP-BFW	PAKISTAN INTL. AIRLINES (CPA)	L	23221	615	06/13/85	RB211-524C2		N6018N, VR-HII, B-HII
B747-367	AP-BFX	PAKISTAN INTL. AIRLINES (CPA)	L	23709	671	02/12/87	RB211-524C2		N6018N, VR-HOL, B-HOL
B747-367	AP-BFY	PAKISTAN INTL. AIRLINES (CPA)	L	23920	690	11/18/87	RB211-524C2		N6038E, VR-HOM, B-HOM
A40-OMAN									
B747SP-27	A40-SO	OMAN ROYAL FLIGHT		21785	405	10/30/79	JT9D-7J		N603BN, N351AS
B747SP-27	A40-SP	OMAN ROYAL FLIGHT		21992	447	05/30/80	JT9D-7A		N606BN, N529PA, N150UA
A6-UNITED ARAB EMIRATES									
B747SP-Z5	A6-ZSN	ABU DHABI AMIRI FLIGHT		23610	676	12/09/89	RB211-524		N60659, N60697
B747-4F6	A6-YAS	ABU DHABI AMIRI FLIGHT		28961	1174	11/30/99	CF6-80C2B1F		N1794B [N758PR NTU; AT HAM FOR UPPER DECK VIP OUTFITTING]
B747SP-31	A6-SMM	DUBAI AIR WING		21963	441	05/08/80	JT9D-7AH		N57203, N602AA
B747SP-31	A6-SMR	DUBAI AIR WING		21961	415	03/21/80	JT9D-7A		N58201
B747-2B4B (SF)	A6-GDP	DUBAI AIR WING		21098	263	06/20/75	JT9D-7FW		OD-AGI, G-BLVF, N203AE, N712CK [CVTD -2B4B (M)]
A9C-BAHRAIN									
B747SP-21	A9C-HHH	BAHRAIN AMIRI FLIGHT		21649	373	05/11/79	JT9D-7A		N540PA, N149UA, V8-JBB, V8-JP1, V8-AC1
B-CHINA (PEOPLE'S REPUBLIC)									
B747-2J6B (SF)	B-2446	AIR CHINA		23071	591	12/20/83	JT9D-7R4G2		N1781B [CVTD -2J6B (M)]
B747-2J6B (SF)	B-2448	AIR CHINA		23461	628	12/10/85	JT9D-7R4G2		N60668 [CVTD -2J6B (M)]
B747-2J6B (M)	B-2450	AIR CHINA		23746	670	03/28/87	JT9D-7R4G2		N6018N

A/C TYPE	CURRENT REG. NO.	LAST KNOWN OPERATOR (OWNER)	STATUS	ORIGINAL MSN	LINE NO.	DEL. DATE	ENG. TYPE	FLEET NO.	PREV. REG. [COMMENTS]
B747-2J6F (SCD)	B-2462	AIR CHINA		24960	814	10/25/90	JT9D-7R4G2		
B747-4J6	B-2443	AIR CHINA		25881	957	02/24/93	PW4056		
B747-4J6	B-2445	AIR CHINA		25882	1021	02/25/94	PW4056		
B747-4J6	B-2447	AIR CHINA		25883	1054	02/23/95	PW4056		
B747-4J6 (M)	B-2456	AIR CHINA		24346	743	10/13/89	PW4056		
B747-4J6 (M)	B-2458	AIR CHINA		24347	775	02/27/90	PW4056		
B747-4J6 (M)	B-2460	AIR CHINA		24348	792	06/21/90	PW4056		
B747-4J6	B-2464	AIR CHINA		25879	904	03/20/92	PW4056		
B747-4J6	B-2466	AIR CHINA		25880	926	08/06/92	PW4056		
B747-4J6 (M)	B-2467	AIR CHINA		28754	1119	06/30/97	PW4056		
B747-4J6 (M)	B-2468	AIR CHINA		28755	1128	09/16/97	PW4056		
B747-4J6 (M)	B-2469	AIR CHINA		28756	1175	09/28/98	PW4056		
B747-4J6 (M)	B-2470	AIR CHINA		29070	1181	10/29/98	PW4056		
B747-4J6 (M)	B-2471	AIR CHINA		29071	1229	09/22/99	PW4056		
B747-4J6	B-2472	AIR CHINA		30158	1243	05/02/00	PW4056		
B747-47UF (SCD)	N412MC	CHINA SOUTHERN AIRLINES (GTI)	L	30559	1244	04/25/00	CF6-80C2B5F		

B-H-HONG KONG

A/C TYPE	CURRENT REG. NO.	LAST KNOWN OPERATOR (OWNER)	STATUS	ORIGINAL MSN	LINE NO.	DEL. DATE	ENG. TYPE	FLEET NO.	PREV. REG. [COMMENTS]
B747-2L5B (SF)	B-HMD	AIR HONG KONG (CPA)	L	22105	435	01/30/81	CF6-50E2		PP-VNA, VR-HMD [CVTD -2L5B]
B747-2L5B (SF)	B-HME	AIR HONG KONG (CPA)	L	22106	443	02/09/81	CF6-50E2		PP-VNB, VR-HME [CVTD -2L5B]
B747-2L5B (SF)	B-HMF	AIR HONG KONG (CPA)	L	22107	469	03/05/81	CF6-50E2		PP-VNC, VR-HMF [CVTD -2L5B]
B747-267B	B-HIA	CATHAY PACIFIC		21966	446	04/24/80	RB211-524C2		VR-HIA [LST ABD AS TF-ATD]
B747-267B	B-HIB	CATHAY PACIFIC		22149	466	07/16/80	RB211-524C2		VR-HIB [LST ABD AS TF-ATC]
B747-267B	B-HIC	CATHAY PACIFIC		22429	493	12/19/80	RB211-524C4		VR-HIC [LST ABD AS TF-ABP]
B747-267B	B-HID	CATHAY PACIFIC		22530	531	06/25/81	RB211-524C2		VR-HID [LST ABD AS TF-ABA]
B747-267B	B-HIE	CATHAY PACIFIC		22872	566	07/23/82	RB211-524D4		VR-HIE [LST VIR AS G-VCAT]
B747-267B	B-HIF	CATHAY PACIFIC		23048	582	05/23/83	RB211-524D4		N6066U, VR-HIF [LST VIR AS VRUM]
B747-267B (SF)	B-HIH	CATHAY PACIFIC		23120	596	04/27/84	RB211-524D4		N5573B, VR-HIH
B747-2L5B (SF)	B-HMD	CATHAY PACIFIC		22105	435	01/30/81	CF6-50E2		PP-VNA, VR-HMD [LST AHK 06/18/96]
B747-2L5B (SF)	B-HME	CATHAY PACIFIC		22106	443	02/09/81	CF6-50E2		PP-VNB, VR-HME [LST AHK]
B747-2L5B (SF)	B-HMF	CATHAY PACIFIC		22107	469	03/05/81	CF6-50E2		PP-VNC, VR-HMF [LST AHK]
B747-267F (SCD)	B-HVX	CATHAY PACIFIC		24568	776	02/28/90	RB211-524D4		VR-HVX
B747-236F (SCD)	B-HVY	CATHAY PACIFIC		22306	480	09/30/80	RB211-524D4		G-KILO, VR-HVY
B747-267F (SCD)	B-HVZ	CATHAY PACIFIC		23864	687	09/22/87	RB211-524D4		N6005C, VR-HVZ
B747-367	B-HII	CATHAY PACIFIC		23221	615	06/13/85	RB211-524C2		N6018N, VR-HII [LST PIA 06/14/99 AS AP-BFW]
B747-367	B-HIJ	CATHAY PACIFIC		23392	634	02/14/86	RB211-524C2		N6005C, VR-HIJ [LST PIA 04/99 AS AP-BFU]
B747-367	B-HIK	CATHAY PACIFIC		23534	659	10/10/86	RB211-524C2		N6038E, VR-HIK [LST PIA 04/99 AS AP-BFV]
B747-367	B-HOL	CATHAY PACIFIC		23709	671	02/12/87	RB211-524C2		N6018N, VR-HOL [LST PIA 04/99 AS AP-BFX]

A/C TYPE	CURRENT REG. NO.	LAST KNOWN OPERATOR (OWNER)	STATUS	ORIGINAL MSN	LINE NO.	DEL. DATE	ENG. TYPE	FLEET NO.	PREV. REG. [COMMENTS]
B747-367	B-HOM	CATHAY PACIFIC		23920	690	11/18/87	RB211-524C2		N6038E, VR-HOM [LST PIA 07/07/99 AS AP-BFY]
B747-367	B-HON	CATHAY PACIFIC		24215	709	07/20/88	RB211-524C2		N6038E, VR-HON [STD VCV]
B747-467	B-HOO	CATHAY PACIFIC		23814	705	09/26/88	RB211-524G/H		N1788B, VR-HOO
B747-467	B-HOP	CATHAY PACIFIC		23815	728	06/08/89	RB211-524G/H		VR-HOP
B747-467	B-HOR	CATHAY PACIFIC		24631	771	02/09/90	RB211-524G/H		VR-HOR
B747-467	B-HOS	CATHAY PACIFIC		24850	788	05/11/90	RB211-524G/H		N6009F, VR-HOS
B747-467	B-HOT	CATHAY PACIFIC		24851	813	09/28/90	RB211-524G/H		VR-HOT
B747-467	B-HOU	CATHAY PACIFIC		24925	834	01/18/91	RB211-524G/H		VR-HOU
B747-467	B-HOV	CATHAY PACIFIC (WHIRLPOOL)		25082	849	04/24/91	RB211-524G/H		VR-HOV
B747-467	B-HOW	CATHAY PACIFIC		25211	873	08/20/91	RB211-524G/H		VR-HOW
B747-467	B-HOX	CATHAY PACIFIC (ILFC)		24955	877	09/25/91	RB211-524G/H		N6018N, VR-HOX
B747-467	B-HOY	CATHAY PACIFIC		25351	887	11/22/91	RB211-524G/H		VR-HOY
B747-467	B-HOZ	CATHAY PACIFIC		25871	925	06/22/92	RB211-524G/H		VR-HOZ
B747-467	B-HUA	CATHAY PACIFIC		25872	930	07/30/92	RB211-524G/H		VR-HUA
B747-467	B-HUB	CATHAY PACIFIC		25873	937	10/09/92	RB211-524G/H		N90665, VR-HUB
B747-467	B-HUD	CATHAY PACIFIC		25874	949	12/10/92	RB211-524G/H		VR-HUD
B747-467	B-HUE	CATHAY PACIFIC		27117	970	05/07/93	RB211-524G/H		N60697, VR-HUE
B747-467	B-HUF	CATHAY PACIFIC		25869	993	08/20/93	RB211-524G/H		VR-HUF
B747-467	B-HUG	CATHAY PACIFIC		25870	1007	12/10/93	RB211-524G/H		VR-HUG
B747-467F (SCD)	B-HUH	CATHAY PACIFIC		27175	1020	06/01/94	RB211-524G/H		N6055X, VR-HUH
B747-467	B-HUI	CATHAY PACIFIC		27230	1033	06/10/94	RB211-524G/H		VR-HUI
B747-467	B-HUJ	CATHAY PACIFIC (ILFC)		27595	1061	05/23/95	RB211-524G/H		VR-HUJ
B747-467F (SCD)	B-HUK	CATHAY PACIFIC		27503	1065	07/12/95	RB211-524G/H		VR-HUK
B747-467F (SCD)	B-HUL	CATHAY PACIFIC		30804	1255	09/12/00	RB211-524G/H		
B747-467F (SCD)	B-HUO	CATHAY PACIFIC		32571	1271	04/18/01	RB211-524G/H		[B-HUM NTU]
B747-230B (SF)	N507MC	DRAGONAIR (GTI)	L	21380	320	03/16/78	CF6-50E2		D-ABYL [CVTD -230B (M)]
B747-312 (M)	B-	DRAGONAIR		23409	637	03/25/86	JT9D-7R4G2		N6065Y, 9V-SKM [TO BE CVTD TO FRTR AT XIAMEN FOR DEL 07/01; LSF SIA?]
B747-312 (M)	B-	DRAGONAIR		23769	666	03/20/87	JT9D-7R4G2		N6005C, 9V-SKP [TO BE CVTD TO FRTR AT XIAMEN FOR DEL 09/01; LSF SIA?]

B-CHINA (TAIWAN)

A/C TYPE	CURRENT REG. NO.	LAST KNOWN OPERATOR (OWNER)	STATUS	ORIGINAL MSN	LINE NO.	DEL. DATE	ENG. TYPE	FLEET NO.	PREV. REG. [COMMENTS]
B747-209B	B-18255	CHINA AIRLINES		21843	386	07/31/79	JT9D-7AW		B-1866
B747-209B (SF)	B-18751	CHINA AIRLINES		21454	322	04/20/78	JT9D-7AW		B-1864 [CVTD -209B (SCD)]
B747-209F (SCD)	B-18752	CHINA AIRLINES		22299	462	07/24/80	JT9D-7R4G2		B-1894
B747-209B (SF)	B-18753	CHINA AIRLINES		22446	519	04/17/81	JT9D-7Q		B-1886 [CVTD -209B]
B747-209B (SF)	B-18755	CHINA AIRLINES		22447	556	03/04/82	JT9D-7Q		B-1888 [CVTD -209B]
B747-209F (SCD)	B-18771	CHINA AIRLINES (CCAA)		24308	752	08/29/89	JT9D-7R4G2		B-160
B747-409	B-18201	CHINA AIRLINES		28709	1114	05/29/97	PW4056		
B747-409	B-18202	CHINA AIRLINES		28710	1132	10/22/97	PW4056		

A/C TYPE	CURRENT REG. NO.	LAST KNOWN OPERATOR (OWNER)	STATUS	ORIGINAL MSN	LINE NO.	DEL. DATE	ENG. TYPE	FLEET NO.	PREV. REG. [COMMENTS]
B747-409	B-18203	CHINA AIRLINES		28711	1136	12/05/97	PW4056		
B747-409	B-18205	CHINA AIRLINES		28712	1137	12/18/97	PW4056		
B747-409	B-18206	CHINA AIRLINES		29030	1145	02/25/98	PW4056		
B747-409	B-18207	CHINA AIRLINES		29219	1176	09/26/98	PW4056		
B747-409	B-18208	CHINA AIRLINES		29031	1186	11/20/98	PW4056		
B747-409	B-18209	CHINA AIRLINES		29906	1219	06/25/99	PW4056		
B747-409	B-18251	CHINA AIRLINES		27965	1063	06/14/95	PW4056		B-16801
B747-409	B-18271	CHINA AIRLINES (CCAA)		24309	766	02/08/90	PW4056		B-161
B747-409	B-18272	CHINA AIRLINES		24310	778	03/27/90	PW4056		B-162
B747-409	B-18273	CHINA AIRLINES		24311	869	08/14/91	PW4056		B-163
B747-409	B-18275	CHINA AIRLINES		24312	954	01/11/93	PW4056		B-164
B747-409F	B-18701	CHINA AIRLINES		30759	1249	07/06/00	CF6-80C2B1F		
B747-409F	B-18702	CHINA AIRLINES		30760	1252	07/28/00	CF6-80C2B1F		
B747-409F	B-18703	CHINA AIRLINES		30761	1254	08/29/00	PW4056		
B747-409F	B-18705	CHINA AIRLINES		30762	1263	02/09/01	PW4056		
B747-409F	B-18706	CHINA AIRLINES		30763	1267	03/02/01	CF6-80C2B1F		
B747-409F	B-18707	CHINA AIRLINES		30764	1269	04/11/01	PW4056		
B747-45E	B-16401	EVA AIR (CHAILEASE)		27062	942	11/02/92	CF6-80C2B1F		
B747-45E	B-16402	EVA AIR (CHAILEASE)		27063	947	11/10/92	CF6-80C2B1F		
B747-45E (M)	B-16406	EVA AIR (FSBU)		27898	1051	01/11/95	CF6-80C2B1F		N406EV
B747-45E (M)	B-16407	EVA AIR (FSBU)		27899	1053	02/22/95	CF6-80C2B1F		N6018N, N407EV
B747-45E (M)	B-16408	EVA AIR (FSBU)		28092	1076	04/17/96	CF6-80C2B1F		N408EV
B747-45E (M)	B-16409	EVA AIR (FSBU)		28093	1077	05/01/96	CF6-80C2B1F		N409EV
B747-45E	B-16410	EVA AIR		29061	1140	01/19/98	CF6-80C2B1F		
B747-45E	B-16411	EVA AIR (CHAILEASE)		29111	1151	04/27/98	CF6-80C2B1F		
B747-45E	B-16412	EVA AIR		29112	1159	05/28/98	CF6-80C2B1F		
B747-45E (M)	B-16461	EVA AIR (HHL LEASE)		27154	994	09/16/93	CF6-80C2B1F		
B747-45E (M)	B-16462	EVA AIR		27173	998	10/07/93	CF6-80C2B1F		
B747-45E (M)	B-16463	EVA AIR		27174	1004	11/03/93	CF6-80C2B1F		
B747-45E (M)	B-16465	EVA AIR (CHAILEASE)		26062	1016	01/27/94	CF6-80C2B1F		
B747-45EF (SCD)	B-16481	EVA AIR		30607	1251	07/20/00	CF6-80C2B1F		
B747-45E (M)	N403EV	EVA AIR (FSBU)		27141	976	05/10/93	CF6-80C2B1F		
B747-45E (M)	N405EV	EVA AIR (FSBU)		27142	982	06/15/93	CF6-80C2B1F		

C-CANADA

A/C TYPE	CURRENT REG. NO.	LAST KNOWN OPERATOR (OWNER)	STATUS	ORIGINAL MSN	LINE NO.	DEL. DATE	ENG. TYPE	FLEET NO.	PREV. REG. [COMMENTS]
B747-475	C-FBCA	AIR CANADA		25422	912	04/22/92	CF6-80C2B1F	884	
B747-475	C-FCRA	AIR CANADA		24895	837	02/15/91	CF6-80C2B1F	882	
B747-4F6	C-FGHZ	AIR CANADA (GECA)		27827	1038	04/03/95	CF6-80C2B1F	885	N6055X [FERRIED TO SIN FOR HEAVY MX]
B747-433 (M)	C-GAGL	AIR CANADA (GECA)		24998	840	06/04/91	PW4056	341	N6018N

A/C TYPE	CURRENT REG. NO.	LAST KNOWN OPERATOR (OWNER)	STATUS	ORIGINAL MSN	LINE NO.	DEL. DATE	ENG. TYPE	FLEET NO.	PREV. REG. [COMMENTS]
B747-433 (M)	C-GAGM	AIR CANADA		25074	862	07/16/91	PW4056	342	
B747-433 (M)	C-GAGN	AIR CANADA (GECA)		25075	868	08/30/91	PW4056	343	N6009F
B747-475	C-GMWW	AIR CANADA		24883	823	12/11/90	CF6-80C2B1F	881	N6018N

CN-MOROCCO

| B747-2B6B (M) | CN-RME | ROYAL AIR MAROC | | 21615 | 338 | 09/29/78 | JT9D-7F | | |
| B747-428 | CN-RGA | ROYAL AIR MAROC (TANGERINE) | | 25629 | 956 | 01/25/93 | CF6-80C2B1F | | F-OGTG |

C5-GAMBIA

| B747-212B | C5-OAA | MAHFOOZ AVIATION | | 21439 | 312 | 09/14/77 | JT9D-7J | | 9V-SQG, N747BK, N723PA, N6186, N624FF, SE-RBH [OPF NGA] |

D-GERMANY

B747-230B (M)	D-ABYM	LUFTHANSA		21588	342	10/20/78	CF6-50E2		
B747-230B	D-ABYP	LUFTHANSA		21590	348	03/07/79	CF6-50E2		N8291V
B747-230B	D-ABYQ	LUFTHANSA		21591	350	12/13/78	CF6-50E2		
B747-230B (M)	D-ABYR	LUFTHANSA		21643	352	01/11/79	CF6-50E2		
B747-230B (M)	D-ABYX	LUFTHANSA		22670	550	02/25/82	CF6-50E2		
B747-230B	D-ABZD	LUFTHANSA		23407	639	04/10/86	CF6-50E2		N6005C
B747-230B (M)	D-ABZE	LUFTHANSA		23509	663	01/16/87	CF6-50E2		N6038E
B747-230B	D-ABZH	LUFTHANSA		23622	665	02/17/87	CF6-50E2		N6046P
B747-430 (M)	D-ABTA	LUFTHANSA		24285	747	09/19/89	CF6-80C2B1F		
B747-430 (M)	D-ABTB	LUFTHANSA		24286	749	12/22/89	CF6-80C2B1F		
B747-430 (M)	D-ABTC	LUFTHANSA		24287	754	02/03/90	CF6-80C2B1F		
B747-430 (M)	D-ABTD	LUFTHANSA		24715	785	04/27/90	CF6-80C2B1F		
B747-430 (M)	D-ABTE	LUFTHANSA (AERO CRANE)		24966	846	04/13/91	CF6-80C2B1F		N6046P
B747-430 (M)	D-ABTF	LUFTHANSA (WARD FSC)		24967	848	04/23/91	CF6-80C2B1F		
B747-430 (M)	D-ABTH	LUFTHANSA (OVERSEAS LSG ONE)		25047	856	06/05/91	CF6-80C2B1F		
B747-430	D-ABVA	LUFTHANSA		23816	723	05/23/89	CF6-80C2B1F		N6055X
B747-430	D-ABVB	LUFTHANSA		23817	700	09/30/89	CF6-80C2B1F		N5573S
B747-430	D-ABVC	LUFTHANSA		24288	757	10/26/90	CF6-80C2B1F		
B747-430	D-ABVD	LUFTHANSA		24740	786	05/15/90	CF6-80C2B1F		N60668
B747-430	D-ABVE	LUFTHANSA		24741	787	05/04/90	CF6-80C2B1F		
B747-430	D-ABVF	LUFTHANSA		24761	796	07/06/90	CF6-80C2B1F		N6018N
B747-430	D-ABVH	LUFTHANSA (LUKE FSC CO)		25045	845	04/03/91	CF6-80C2B1F		
B747-430	D-ABVK	LUFTHANSA (TOWER FSC)		25046	847	04/19/91	CF6-80C2B1F		N6009F
B747-430	D-ABVL	LUFTHANSA (OVERSEAS LSG FOUR)		26425	898	02/20/92	CF6-80C2B1F		N60659
B747-430	D-ABVM	LUFTHANSA		29101	1143	02/07/98	CF6-80C2B1F		
B747-430	D-ABVN	LUFTHANSA (DB EXPORT LSG)		26427	915	05/08/92	CF6-80C2B1F		
B747-430	D-ABVO	LUFTHANSA (DLLG)		28086	1080	05/17/96	CF6-80C2B1F		
B747-430	D-ABVP	LUFTHANSA		28284	1103	02/25/97	CF6-80C2B1F		

A/C TYPE	CURRENT REG. NO.	LAST KNOWN OPERATOR (OWNER)	STATUS	ORIGINAL MSN	LINE NO.	DEL. DATE	ENG. TYPE	FLEET NO.	PREV. REG. [COMMENTS]
B747-430	D-ABVR	LUFTHANSA		28285	1106	03/13/97	CF6-80C2B1F		
B747-430	D-ABVS	LUFTHANSA		28286	1109	04/18/97	CF6-80C2B1F		
B747-430	D-ABVT	LUFTHANSA (DLLG)		28287	1110	04/28/97	CF6-80C2B1F		
B747-430	D-ABVU	LUFTHANSA		29492	1191	12/21/98	CF6-80C2B1F		
B747-430	D-ABVW	LUFTHANSA		29493	1205	03/13/99	CF6-80C2B1F		
B747-430	D-ABVX	LUFTHANSA		29868	1237	12/22/99	CF6-80C2B1F		
B747-430	D-ABVY	LUFTHANSA		29869	1261	12/11/00	CF6-80C2B1F		
B747-430	D-ABVZ	LUFTHANSA		29870	1264	02/01/01	CF6-80C2B1F		
B747-230F (SCD)	D-ABYO	LUFTHANSA CARGO AIRLINES (DLLG)		21592	347	11/22/78	CF6-50E2		
B747-230F (SCD)	D-ABYU	LUFTHANSA CARGO AIRLINES (DLLG)		22668	538	09/04/81	CF6-50E2		N1785B
B747-230B (SF)	D-ABYZ	LUFTHANSA CARGO AIRLINES (DLLG)		23286	614	06/24/85	CF6-50E2		N6055X, I-DEMX [CVTD -230B (M)]
B747-230B (SF)	D-ABZA	LUFTHANSA CARGO AIRLINES (DLLG)		23287	617	06/28/85	CF6-50E2		N6038E [CVTD -230B (M)]
B747-230F (SCD)	D-ABZB	LUFTHANSA CARGO AIRLINES		23348	625	10/25/85	CF6-50E2		N6005F, N747MC
B747-230B (SF)	D-ABZC	LUFTHANSA CARGO AIRLINES		23393	633	02/14/86	CF6-50E2		N6046P [CVTD -230B (M)]
B747-230F (SCD)	D-ABZF	LUFTHANSA CARGO AIRLINES		23621	660	10/24/86	CF6-50E2		N6046P
B747-230F (SCD)	D-ABZI	LUFTHANSA CARGO AIRLINES		24138	706	06/29/88	CF6-50E2		N6005C

DQ-FIJI

A/C TYPE	CURRENT REG. NO.	LAST KNOWN OPERATOR (OWNER)	STATUS	ORIGINAL MSN	LINE NO.	DEL. DATE	ENG. TYPE	FLEET NO.	PREV. REG. [COMMENTS]
B747-238B	DQ-FJE	AIR PACIFIC (QFA)	L	22614	464	09/30/80	RB211-524D4		N1728B, N8296V, VH-EBR

D2-ANGOLA

A/C TYPE	CURRENT REG. NO.	LAST KNOWN OPERATOR (OWNER)	STATUS	ORIGINAL MSN	LINE NO.	DEL. DATE	ENG. TYPE	FLEET NO.	PREV. REG. [COMMENTS]
B747-312 (M)	D2-TEA	TAAG ANGOLA AIRLINES (SONANGOL)		23410	653	08/27/86	JT9D-7R4G2		N6055X, 9V-SKN
B747-357 (M)	D2-TEB	TAAG ANGOLA AIRLINES (DARTMOOR)		23751	686	12/04/87	JT9D-7R4G2		N6055X, HB-IGG, N375TC

EC-SPAIN

A/C TYPE	CURRENT REG. NO.	LAST KNOWN OPERATOR (OWNER)	STATUS	ORIGINAL MSN	LINE NO.	DEL. DATE	ENG. TYPE	FLEET NO.	PREV. REG. [COMMENTS]
B747-256B	EC-DIA	IBERIA		22238	450	05/01/80	JT9D-7Q		
B747-256B	EC-DIB	IBERIA		22239	451	05/22/80	JT9D-7Q		
B747-256B (M)	EC-DLC	IBERIA (ABD)		22454	509	02/18/81	JT9D-7Q3		[LST ABD AS TF-ATL AND WET LEASED BACK]
B747-256B (M)	EC-DLD	IBERIA (ABD)		22455	515	03/24/81	JT9D-7Q3		[LST ABD AS TF-ATM AND WET LEASED BACK]
B747-256B	EC-DNP	IBERIA		22764	554	02/26/82	JT9D-7Q3		N8296V
B747-256B	EC-GAG	IBERIA (BOEING)		20137	173	01/04/72	JT9D-7A		F-GHPC, EC-287, EC-BRQ, EC-765
B747-246B	TF-ATF	IBERIA (ABD)	L	19825	137	05/14/71	JT9D-7AW		JA8106, N556SW
B747-341	TF-ATH	IBERIA (ABD)	L	24106	701	04/30/88	CF6-80C2B1		N6046P, PP-VOA, N830DS
B747-341	TF-ATI	IBERIA (ABD)	L	24107	702	05/13/88	CF6-80C2B1		N6018N, PP-VOB, N824DS
B747-341	TF-ATJ	IBERIA (ABD)	L	24108	703	05/27/88	CF6-80C2B1		N6005C, PP-VOC, N420DS

EP-IRAN

A/C TYPE	CURRENT REG. NO.	LAST KNOWN OPERATOR (OWNER)	STATUS	ORIGINAL MSN	LINE NO.	DEL. DATE	ENG. TYPE	FLEET NO.	PREV. REG. [COMMENTS]
B747SP-86	EP-IAA	IRAN AIR		20998	275	03/12/76	JT9D-7F		
B747SP-86	EP-IAB	IRAN AIR		20999	278	05/10/76	JT9D-7F		
B747SP-86	EP-IAC	IRAN AIR		21093	307	05/27/77	JT9D-7F		

A/C TYPE	CURRENT REG. NO.	LAST KNOWN OPERATOR (OWNER)	STATUS	ORIGINAL MSN	LINE NO.	DEL. DATE	ENG. TYPE	FLEET NO.	PREV. REG. [COMMENTS]
B747SP-86	EP-IAD	IRAN AIR		21758	371	07/12/79	JT9D-7F		N1800B
B747-286B (M)	EP-IAG	IRAN AIR		21217	291	10/05/76	JT9D-7F		
B747-286B (M)	EP-IAH	IRAN AIR		21218	300	03/14/77	JT9D-7F		
B747-186B	EP-IAM	IRAN AIR		21759	381	08/02/79	JT9D-7F		N5573B
B747-2J9F	EP-ICC	IRAN AIR		21514	343	10/23/78	JT9D-7F		N8293V, 5-8116
B747-2J9F	EP-SHA	SAHA AIRLINES		21507	340	09/28/78	JT9D-7F		N8277V, 5-8115
B747-2J9F	EP-SHB	SAHA AIRLINES		21486	315	12/22/77	JT9D-7F		5-8113
B747-131 (SF)	EP-SHD	SAHA AIRLINES		20081	85	11/02/70	JT9D-7A		N93114, 5-284, 5-8105
B747-2J9F	EP-SHH	SAHA AIRLINES		21487	319	02/27/78	JT9D-7F		5-8114, EP-NHQ, EP-ICA

F-FRANCE

A/C TYPE	CURRENT REG. NO.	LAST KNOWN OPERATOR (OWNER)	STATUS	ORIGINAL MSN	LINE NO.	DEL. DATE	ENG. TYPE	FLEET NO.	PREV. REG. [COMMENTS]
B747-228F (SCD)	F-BPVR	AIR FRANCE (AFPL)		21255	295	10/13/76	CF6-50E2		N1783B
B747-228B (M)	F-BPVS	AIR FRANCE (AFPL)		21326	303	04/04/77	CF6-50E2		
B747-228B (M)	F-BPVT	AIR FRANCE (AFPL)		21429	313	09/30/77	CF6-50E2		
B747-228B (M)	F-BPVU	AIR FRANCE		21537	333	08/07/78	CF6-50E2		N1252E [PARKED ORY; MANY PARTS AND PAINT REMOVED]
B747-228B (M)	F-BPVX	AIR FRANCE (BBAM)		21731	364	03/28/79	CF6-50E2		
B747-228B	F-BPVY	AIR FRANCE		21745	370	04/28/79	CF6-50E2		
B747-228F (SCD)	F-BPVZ	AIR FRANCE (AFPL)		21787	398	09/18/79	CF6-50E2		
B747-2B3F (SCD)	F-GBOX	AIR FRANCE (ARKIA)		21835	388	08/06/79	CF6-50E2		
B747-228B	F-GCBA	AIR FRANCE (AFPL)		21982	428	02/29/80	CF6-50E2		
B747-228B (M)	F-GCBB	AIR FRANCE (WTCI)		22272	463	07/03/80	CF6-50E2		N1289E
B747-228B (SF)	F-GCBD	AIR FRANCE		22428	503	03/25/81	CF6-50E2		N1305E
B747-228F (SCD)	F-GCBE	AIR FRANCE (TBNY)		22678	535	09/11/81	CF6-50E2		N4508E
B747-228B (M)	F-GCBF	AIR FRANCE		22794	558	03/26/82	CF6-50E2		N4506H
B747-228F (SCD)	F-GCBG	AIR FRANCE		22939	569	10/01/82	CF6-50E2		N4544F
B747-228B (SF)	F-GCBH	AIR FRANCE		23611	656	09/16/86	CF6-50E2		N6046P
B747-228B (M)	F-GCBI	AIR FRANCE		23676	661	10/29/86	CF6-50E2		N6009F
B747-228B (M)	F-GCBJ	AIR FRANCE		24067	698	03/11/88	CF6-50E2		N6018N
B747-228F (SCD)	F-GCBK	AIR FRANCE (AFPL)		24158	714	09/20/88	CF6-50E2		N6055X
B747-228F (SCD)	F-GCBL	AIR FRANCE (PBA FOREIGN SALES)		24735	772	02/23/90	CF6-50E2		
B747-228F (SCD)	F-GCBM	AIR FRANCE (USW FCS ONE)		24879	822	11/30/90	CF6-50E2		
B747-228F (SCD)	F-GPVV	AIR FRANCE (GTI)	L	21576	334	08/09/78	CF6-50E2		N536MC
B747-2B3B (M) (SUD)	F-BTDG	AIR FRANCE		22514	518	04/23/81	CF6-50E2		
B747-2B3B (M) (SUD)	F-BTDH	AIR FRANCE		22515	521	05/05/81	CF6-50E2		
B747-3B3 (M)	F-GETA	AIR FRANCE		23413	632	01/31/86	CF6-50E2		N6009F
B747-3B3 (M)	F-GETB	AIR FRANCE		23480	641	04/24/86	CF6-50E2		N6018N
B747-4B3	F-GEXA	AIR FRANCE (TLC ASSET)		24154	741	09/22/89	CF6-80C2B1F		

A/C TYPE	CURRENT REG. NO.	LAST KNOWN OPERATOR (OWNER)	STATUS	ORIGINAL MSN	LINE NO.	DEL. DATE	ENG. TYPE	FLEET NO.	PREV. REG. [COMMENTS]
B747-4B3 (M)	F-GEXB	AIR FRANCE		24155	864	07/26/91	CF6-80C2B1F		
B747-428 (M)	F-GISA	AIR FRANCE		25238	872	09/17/91	CF6-80C2B1F		
B747-428 (M)	F-GISB	AIR FRANCE		25302	884	11/08/91	CF6-80C2B1F		
B747-428 (M)	F-GISC	AIR FRANCE		25599	899	02/18/92	CF6-80C2B1F		
B747-428 (M)	F-GISD	AIR FRANCE		25628	934	09/04/92	CF6-80C2B1F		
B747-428 (M)	F-GISE	AIR FRANCE (WRIGHT BROS.)		25630	960	02/10/93	CF6-80C2B1F		
B747-428	F-GITA	AIR FRANCE (WINGTIP)		24969	836	02/28/91	CF6-80C2B1F		
B747-428	F-GITB	AIR FRANCE (USW FSC THREE)		24990	843	04/05/91	CF6-80C2B1F		N6009F
B747-428	F-GITC	AIR FRANCE		25344	889	12/09/91	CF6-80C2B1F		
B747-428	F-GITD	AIR FRANCE		25600	901	02/19/92	CF6-80C2B1F		
B747-428	F-GITE	AIR FRANCE		25601	906	03/18/92	CF6-80C2B1F		
B747-428	F-GITF	AIR FRANCE (CIT FSC TWELVE)		25602	909	04/07/92	CF6-80C2B1F		
B747SP-44	F-GTOM	CORSAIR (SARL CORSAIR)		21253	293	09/10/76	JT9D-7F		ZS-SPD, CN-RMS, LX-ACO
B747-121	F-GKLJ	CORSAIR		19660	50	05/31/70	JT9D-7A		N770PA, LX-GCV [STD CHR]
B747-206B	F-GLNA	CORSAIR (SARL CORSAIR)		20399	156	09/30/71	JT9D-7J		HS-VGG, PH-BUE
B747-206B	F-GPJM	CORSAIR (SARL CORSAIR)		20427	170	12/15/71	JT9D-7J		PH-BUG
B747-312	F-GSEA	CORSAIR		23032	603	10/30/84	JT9D-7R4G2		N121KG
B747-312	F-GSEX	CORSAIR		23028	584	06/30/83	JT9D-7R4G2		VH-INK, N117KC, F-WSEX
B747-312	F-GSUN	CORSAIR		23030	593	02/24/84	JT9D-7R4G2		N119KE

G-UNITED KINGDOM

A/C TYPE	CURRENT REG. NO.	LAST KNOWN OPERATOR (OWNER)	STATUS	ORIGINAL MSN	LINE NO.	DEL. DATE	ENG. TYPE	FLEET NO.	PREV. REG. [COMMENTS]
B747-245F (SCD)	G-GAFX	AIRFREIGHT EXPRESS (US BANCORP)		20827	266	04/30/76	JT9D-70A		N702SW, N812FT, N641FE, VP-BXP [OPF CLX]
B747-245F (SCD)	G-INTL.	AIRFREIGHT EXPRESS (US BANCORP)		20826	242	07/31/74	JT9D-70A		N701SW, N811FT, N640FE [OPF CLX]
B747-236B	G-BDXA	BRITISH AIRWAYS (ICCO)		21238	292	07/27/77	RB211-524D4		N1790B [LRF 01/23/01; STD MZJ 02/06/01]
B747-236B	G-BDXB	BRITISH AIRWAYS		21239	302	06/16/77	RB211-524D4		N8280V
B747-236B	G-BDXC	BRITISH AIRWAYS		21240	305	06/22/77	RB211-524D4		
B747-236B	G-BDXE	BRITISH AIRWAYS		21350	321	03/27/78	RB211-524D4		
B747-236B	G-BDXF	BRITISH AIRWAYS		21351	323	04/24/78	RB211-524D4		
B747-236B	G-BDXG	BRITISH AIRWAYS		21536	328	06/16/78	RB211-524D4		
B747-236B	G-BDXH	BRITISH AIRWAYS		21635	365	03/27/79	RB211-524D4		
B747-236B	G-BDXI	BRITISH AIRWAYS		21830	430	03/05/80	RB211-524D4		[TO BE WFU 06/01/01]
B747-236B	G-BDXJ	BRITISH AIRWAYS		21831	440	05/02/80	RB211-524D4		N1792B
B747-236B	G-BDXK	BRITISH AIRWAYS		22303	495	03/30/83	RB211-524D4		
B747-236B	G-BDXL	BRITISH AIRWAYS		22305	506	02/10/84	RB211-524D4		N8280V
B747-236B (M)	G-BDXM	BRITISH AIRWAYS		23711	672	02/25/87	RB211-524D4		N6055X [TO BE WFU 06/01/01]
B747-236B (M)	G-BDXN	BRITISH AIRWAYS		23735	674	03/17/87	RB211-524D4		N6046P
B747-236B	G-BDXO	BRITISH AIRWAYS		23799	677	04/23/87	RB211-524D4		N6055X
B747-236B (M)	G-BDXP	BRITISH AIRWAYS		24088	697	02/24/88	RB211-524D4		N6009F [LRF 02/04/01; FERRIED TO HKG FOR FRTR CONV 02/13/01]

A/C TYPE	CURRENT REG. NO.	LAST KNOWN OPERATOR (OWNER)	STATUS	ORIGINAL MSN	LINE NO.	DEL. DATE	ENG. TYPE	FLEET NO.	PREV. REG. [COMMENTS]
B747-436	G-BNLA	BRITISH AIRWAYS		23908	727	06/30/89	RB211-524H2		N60665
B747-436	G-BNLB	BRITISH AIRWAYS		23909	730	07/31/89	RB211-524H2		
B747-436	G-BNLC	BRITISH AIRWAYS		23910	734	10/23/89	RB211-524H2		
B747-436	G-BNLD	BRITISH AIRWAYS		23911	744	09/05/89	RB211-524H2		N6018N
B747-436	G-BNLE	BRITISH AIRWAYS		24047	753	11/15/89	RB211-524H2		
B747-436	G-BNLF	BRITISH AIRWAYS		24048	773	02/28/90	RB211-524H2		
B747-436	G-BNLG	BRITISH AIRWAYS		24049	774	02/27/90	RB211-524H2		
B747-436	G-BNLH	BRITISH AIRWAYS		24050	779	03/28/90	RB211-524H2		[LST QFA 11/16/00 AS VH-NLH]
B747-436	G-BNLI	BRITISH AIRWAYS		24051	784	04/21/90	RB211-524H2		
B747-436	G-BNLJ	BRITISH AIRWAYS		24052	789	05/23/90	RB211-524H2		N60668
B747-436	G-BNLK	BRITISH AIRWAYS		24053	790	05/25/90	RB211-524H2		N6009F
B747-436	G-BNLL	BRITISH AIRWAYS		24054	794	06/14/90	RB211-524H2		
B747-436	G-BNLM	BRITISH AIRWAYS		24055	795	06/28/90	RB211-524H2		N6009F
B747-436	G-BNLN	BRITISH AIRWAYS		24056	802	07/27/90	RB211-524H2		
B747-436	G-BNLO	BRITISH AIRWAYS		24057	817	10/25/90	RB211-524H2		
B747-436	G-BNLP	BRITISH AIRWAYS		24058	828	12/17/90	RB211-524H2		
B747-436	G-BNLR	BRITISH AIRWAYS		24447	829	01/15/91	RB211-524H2		N6005C
B747-436	G-BNLS	BRITISH AIRWAYS		24629	841	03/13/91	RB211-524H2		
B747-436	G-BNLT	BRITISH AIRWAYS		24630	842	03/19/91	RB211-524H2		
B747-436	G-BNLU	BRITISH AIRWAYS		25406	895	01/28/92	RB211-524H2		
B747-436	G-BNLV	BRITISH AIRWAYS		25427	900	02/20/92	RB211-524H2		
B747-436	G-BNLW	BRITISH AIRWAYS		25432	903	03/05/92	RB211-524H2		
B747-436	G-BNLX	BRITISH AIRWAYS		25435	908	04/03/92	RB211-524H2		
B747-436	G-BNLY	BRITISH AIRWAYS		27090	959	02/10/93	RB211-524H2		N60659
B747-436	G-BNLZ	BRITISH AIRWAYS		27091	964	03/04/93	RB211-524H2		
B747-436	G-BYGA	BRITISH AIRWAYS		28855	1190	12/14/98	RB211-524H2		
B747-436	G-BYGB	BRITISH AIRWAYS		28856	1194	01/17/99	RB211-524H2		
B747-436	G-BYGC	BRITISH AIRWAYS		25823	1195	01/19/99	RB211-524H2		
B747-436	G-BYGD	BRITISH AIRWAYS		28857	1196	01/26/99	RB211-524H2		
B747-436	G-BYGE	BRITISH AIRWAYS		28858	1198	02/05/99	RB211-524H2		
B747-436	G-BYGF	BRITISH AIRWAYS		25824	1200	02/17/99	RB211-524H2		
B747-436	G-BYGG	BRITISH AIRWAYS		28859	1212	04/29/99	RB211-524H2		
B747-436	G-CIVA	BRITISH AIRWAYS		27092	967	03/24/93	RB211-524H2		
B747-436	G-CIVB	BRITISH AIRWAYS		25811	1018	02/15/94	RB211-524H2		[BRITISH ASIA TITLES]
B747-436	G-CIVC	BRITISH AIRWAYS		25812	1022	02/26/94	RB211-524H2		
B747-436	G-CIVD	BRITISH AIRWAYS		27349	1048	12/14/94	RB211-524H2		
B747-436	G-CIVE	BRITISH AIRWAYS		27350	1050	12/20/94	RB211-524H2		
B747-436	G-CIVF	BRITISH AIRWAYS		25434	1058	03/29/95	RB211-524H2		
B747-436	G-CIVG	BRITISH AIRWAYS		25813	1059	04/20/95	RB211-524H2		N6009F
B747-436	G-CIVH	BRITISH AIRWAYS		25809	1078	04/23/96	RB211-524H2		
B747-436	G-CIVI	BRITISH AIRWAYS		25814	1079	05/02/96	RB211-524H2		

A/C TYPE	CURRENT REG. NO.	LAST KNOWN OPERATOR (OWNER)	STATUS	ORIGINAL MSN	LINE NO.	DEL. DATE	ENG. TYPE	FLEET NO.	PREV. REG. [COMMENTS]
B747-436	G-CIVJ	BRITISH AIRWAYS		25817	1102	02/11/97	RB211-524H2		
B747-436	G-CIVK	BRITISH AIRWAYS		25818	1104	02/28/97	RB211-524H2		
B747-436	G-CIVL	BRITISH AIRWAYS		27478	1108	03/28/97	RB211-524H2		
B747-436	G-CIVM	BRITISH AIRWAYS		28700	1116	06/05/97	RB211-524H2		
B747-436	G-CIVN	BRITISH AIRWAYS		28848	1129	09/29/97	RB211-524H2		
B747-436	G-CIVO	BRITISH AIRWAYS		28849	1135	12/05/97	RB211-524H2		N6046P
B747-436	G-CIVP	BRITISH AIRWAYS		28850	1144	02/17/98	RB211-524H2		
B747-436	G-CIVR	BRITISH AIRWAYS		25820	1146	03/02/98	RB211-524H2		
B747-436	G-CIVS	BRITISH AIRWAYS		28851	1148	03/13/98	RB211-524H2		
B747-436	G-CIVT	BRITISH AIRWAYS		25821	1149	03/20/98	RB211-524H2		
B747-436	G-CIVU	BRITISH AIRWAYS		25810	1154	04/24/98	RB211-524H2		
B747-436	G-CIVV	BRITISH AIRWAYS		25819	1156	05/22/98	RB211-524H2		N6009F
B747-436	G-CIVW	BRITISH AIRWAYS		25822	1157	05/15/98	RB211-524H2		
B747-436	G-CIVX	BRITISH AIRWAYS		28852	1172	09/03/98	RB211-524H2		
B747-436	G-CIVY	BRITISH AIRWAYS		28853	1178	09/29/98	RB211-524H2		
B747-436	G-CIVZ	BRITISH AIRWAYS		28854	1183	10/31/98	RB211-524H2		
B747-47UF (SCD)	G-GSSA	BRITISH AIRWAYS (GTI)		29256	1213	05/26/99	CF6-80C2B5F		N495MC [OPB GTI IN BA WORLD CARGO C/S]
B747-47UF (SCD)	G-GSSB	BRITISH AIRWAYS (GTI)		29255	1184	12/04/98	CF6-80C2B5F		N494MC [OPB GTI IN BA WORLD CARGO C/S]
B747-219B	G-VBEE	VIRGIN ATLANTIC AIRWAYS		22723	527	06/09/81	RB211-524D4		ZK-NZW
B747-267B	G-VCAT	VIRGIN ATLANTIC AIRWAYS (CPA)	L	22872	566	07/23/82	RB211-524D4		VR-HIE, B-HIE
B747-243B	G-VGIN	VIRGIN ATLANTIC AIRWAYS		19732	134	05/07/71	JT9D-7J		I-DEMU, N358AS, B-2440, N747BL
B747-219B	G-VIBE	VIRGIN ATLANTIC AIRWAYS		22791	568	08/25/82	RB211-524D4		N6018N, 9M-MHH, ZK-NZZ
B747-287B	G-VIRG	VIRGIN ATLANTIC AIRWAYS		21189	274	12/16/76	JT9D-7J		N1791B, LV-LZD, N354AS
B747-238B	G-VJFK	VIRGIN ATLANTIC AIRWAYS		20842	238	05/24/74	JT9D-7J		VH-EBH
B747-238B	G-VLAX	VIRGIN ATLANTIC AIRWAYS		20921	241	10/10/74	JT9D-7J		VH-EBI
B747-219B	G-VPUF	VIRGIN ATLANTIC AIRWAYS		22725	563	06/22/82	RB211-524D4		N6005C, ZK-NZY
B747-267B	G-VRUM	VIRGIN ATLANTIC AIRWAYS (CPA)	L	23048	582	05/23/83	RB211-524D4		N6066U, VR-HIF, B-HIF
B747-219B	G-VSSS	VIRGIN ATLANTIC AIRWAYS		22724	528	06/21/81	RB211-524D4		9M-MHG, ZK-NZX
B747-219B	G-VZZZ	VIRGIN ATLANTIC AIRWAYS		22722	523	05/22/81	RB211-524D4		ZK-NZV
B747-267B	TF-ABA	VIRGIN ATLANTIC AIRWAYS (ABD)	L	22530	531	06/25/81	RB211-524C2		VR-HID, B-HID
B747-41R	G-VAST	VIRGIN ATLANTIC AIRWAYS		28757	1117	06/17/97	CF6-80C2B1F		
B747-4Q8	G-VBIG	VIRGIN ATLANTIC AIRWAYS (ILFC)		26255	1081	06/10/96	CF6-80C2B1F		
B747-4Q8	G-VFAB	VIRGIN ATLANTIC AIRWAYS (ILFC)		24958	1028	04/28/94	CF6-80C2B1F		
B747-443	G-VGAL	VIRGIN ATLANTIC AIRWAYS (GECA)		32337	1272	04/26/01	CF6-80C2B1F		
B747-4Q8	G-VHOT	VIRGIN ATLANTIC AIRWAYS (ILFC)		26326	1043	10/12/94	CF6-80C2B1F		
B747-443	G-VLIP	VIRGIN ATLANTIC AIRWAYS (GECA)		32338	1274	05/15/01	CF6-80C2B1F		

A/C TYPE	CURRENT REG. NO.	LAST KNOWN OPERATOR (OWNER)	STATUS	ORIGINAL MSN	LINE NO.	DEL. DATE	ENG. TYPE	FLEET NO.	PREV. REG. [COMMENTS]
B747-443	G-VROM	VIRGIN ATLANTIC AIRWAYS (GECA)	N	32339	1275		CF6-80C2B1F		
B747-443	G-VROS	VIRGIN ATLANTIC AIRWAYS (GECA)		30885	1268	03/22/01	CF6-80C2B1F		
B747-4Q8	G-VTOP	VIRGIN ATLANTIC AIRWAYS (ILFC)		28194	1100	01/28/97	CF6-80C2B1F		
B747-41R	G-VXLG	VIRGIN ATLANTIC AIRWAYS		29406	1177	09/30/98	CF6-80C2B1F		

HL-KOREA

A/C TYPE	CURRENT REG. NO.	LAST KNOWN OPERATOR (OWNER)	STATUS	ORIGINAL MSN	LINE NO.	DEL. DATE	ENG. TYPE	FLEET NO.	PREV. REG. [COMMENTS]
B747-48E (M)	HL7413	ASIANA AIRLINES		25405	880	11/01/91	CF6-80C2B1F		
B747-48E (M)	HL7414	ASIANA AIRLINES		25452	892	01/07/92	CF6-80C2B1F		
B747-48E (M)	HL7415	ASIANA AIRLINES		25777	946	12/03/92	CF6-80C2B1F		
B747-48E (M)	HL7417	ASIANA AIRLINES		25779	1006	12/03/93	CF6-80C2B1F		
B747-48E	HL7418	ASIANA AIRLINES		25780	1035	09/22/94	CF6-80C2B1F		
B747-48EF (SCD)	HL7419	ASIANA AIRLINES (SEAGALT)		25781	1044	11/04/94	CF6-80C2B1F		
B747-48EF (SCD)	HL7420	ASIANA AIRLINES (EAGLE)		25783	1064	06/27/95	CF6-80C2B1F		
B747-48E (M)	HL7421	ASIANA AIRLINES		25784	1086	08/16/96	CF6-80C2B1F		
B747-48EF (SCD)	HL7422	ASIANA AIRLINES (SALE)		28367	1096	12/18/96	CF6-80C2B1F		
B747-48E (M)	HL7423	ASIANA AIRLINES (OZ DELTA)		25782	1115	05/30/97	CF6-80C2B1F		
B747-48EF (SCD)	HL7426	ASIANA AIRLINES (ILFC)		27603	1210	04/14/99	CF6-80C2B1F		
B747-48E	HL7428	ASIANA AIRLINES		28552	1160	06/18/99	CF6-80C2B1F		N6018N
B747-2B5F (SCD)	HL7405	KOREAN AIR (K.I. FREIGHT)		24195	718	10/28/88	JT9D-7R4G2		N6038E, HL7475
B747-2B5F (SCD)	HL7408	KOREAN AIR		24196	720	12/02/88	JT9D-7R4G2		N6038E, HL7476
B747-2S4F (SCD)	HL7424	KOREAN AIR (SCT AIR)		22169	472	10/03/80	JT9D-7Q		TU-TAP, LX-TAP, HL7474
B747-2B5B	HL7443	KOREAN AIR		21772	363	03/23/79	JT9D-7A		
B747-2B5F (SCD)	HL7452	KOREAN AIR		22481	454	06/25/80	JT9D-7Q		N5573F
B747-2B5B (SF)	HL7454	KOREAN AIR		22482	484	11/13/80	JT9D-7Q		
B747-2B5B (SF)	HL7458	KOREAN AIR		22485	513	04/13/81	JT9D-7Q		
B747-2B5F (SCD)	HL7459	KOREAN AIR		22486	520	05/08/81	JT9D-7Q		
B747-3B5	HL7469	KOREAN AIR		22489	611	04/15/85	JT9D-7R4G2		N6009F
B747-3B5 (M)	HL7470	KOREAN AIR		24194	713	08/30/88	JT9D-7R4G2		N6038E
B747-4B5	HL7402	KOREAN AIR		26407	1155	12/30/98	PW4056		N6038E [RTS]
B747-4B5F (SCD)	HL7403	KOREAN AIR		26408	1163	12/30/98	PW4056		N60659
B747-4B5	HL7404	KOREAN AIR		26409	1170	12/30/98	PW4056		N6009F
B747-4B5	HL7407	KOREAN AIR (K.I. FREIGHT)		24198	729	06/13/89	PW4056		HL7477
B747-4B5	HL7409	KOREAN AIR		24199	739	07/28/89	PW4056		HL7478
B747-4B5	HL7412	KOREAN AIR		24200	748	09/13/89	PW4056		HL7479
B747-4B5F(SCD)	HL7448	KOREAN AIR (GECA)		26416	1246	05/25/00	PW4056		
B747-4B5F (SCD)	HL7449	KOREAN AIR (GECA)		26411	1248	06/08/00	PW4056		
B747-4B5	HL7460	KOREAN AIR (KE APPOLLO LSG)		26404	1107	03/26/97	PW4056		
B747-4B5	HL7461	KOREAN AIR		26405	1118	06/24/97	PW4056		
B747-4B5F (SCD)	HL7462	KOREAN AIR		26406	1123	07/31/97	PW4056		

A/C TYPE	CURRENT REG. NO.	LAST KNOWN OPERATOR (OWNER)	STATUS	ORIGINAL MSN	LINE NO.	DEL. DATE	ENG. TYPE	FLEET NO.	PREV. REG. [COMMENTS]
B747-4B5	HL7472	KOREAN AIR		26403	1095	11/26/96	PW4056		
B747-4B5	HL7473	KOREAN AIR		28335	1098	12/23/96	PW4056		
B747-4B5 (M)	HL7480	KOREAN AIR		24619	793	06/27/90	PW4056		N6009F
B747-4B5	HL7481	KOREAN AIR		24621	830	01/31/91	PW4056		
B747-4B5	HL7482	KOREAN AIR		25205	853	05/22/91	PW4056		
B747-4B5	HL7483	KOREAN AIR		25275	874	09/11/91	PW4056		
B747-4B5	HL7484	KOREAN AIR (OLC LEASING)		26392	893	01/28/92	PW4056		
B747-4B5	HL7485	KOREAN AIR		26395	922	06/23/92	PW4056		
B747-4B5	HL7486	KOREAN AIR		26396	951	01/12/93	PW4056		
B747-4B5	HL7487	KOREAN AIR		26393	958	02/09/93	PW4056		
B747-4B5	HL7488	KOREAN AIR		26394	986	07/27/93	PW4056		
B747-4B5	HL7489	KOREAN AIR		27072	1013	01/18/94	PW4056		
B747-4B5	HL7490	KOREAN AIR		27177	1019	02/17/94	PW4056		
B747-4B5	HL7491	KOREAN AIR		27341	1037	07/28/94	PW4056		
B747-4B5	HL7492	KOREAN AIR		26397	1055	02/23/95	PW4056		
B747-4B5	HL7493	KOREAN AIR		26398	1057	03/22/95	PW4056		
B747-4B5	HL7494	KOREAN AIR		27662	1067	08/10/95	PW4056		
B747-4B5	HL7495	KOREAN AIR		28096	1073	12/28/95	PW4056		
B747-4B5F (SCD)	HL7497	KOREAN AIR		26401	1087	09/06/96	PW4056		
B747-4B5	HL7498	KOREAN AIR		26402	1092	10/31/96	PW4056		
B747-47UF (SCD)	N499MC	KOREAN AIR (GTI)	L	29260	1240	02/17/00	CF6-80C2B1F		

HS-THAILAND

A/C TYPE	CURRENT REG. NO.	LAST KNOWN OPERATOR (OWNER)	STATUS	ORIGINAL MSN	LINE NO.	DEL. DATE	ENG. TYPE	FLEET NO.	PREV. REG. [COMMENTS]
B747-3D7	HS-TGD	THAI AIRWAYS INTL.		23721	681	12/16/87	CF6-80C2B1		N6046P
B747-3D7	HS-TGE	THAI AIRWAYS INTL.		23722	688	12/03/87	CF6-80C2B1		N60668
B747-4D7	HS-TGA	THAI AIRWAYS INTL.	N	32369	1273		CF6-80C2B1F		
B747-4D7	HS-TGH	THAI AIRWAYS INTL.		24458	769	02/21/90	CF6-80C2B1F		
B747-4D7	HS-TGJ	THAI AIRWAYS INTL.		24459	777	03/22/90	CF6-80C2B1F		
B747-4D7	HS-TGK	THAI AIRWAYS INTL.		24993	833	01/31/91	CF6-80C2B1F		
B747-4D7	HS-TGL	THAI AIRWAYS INTL.		25366	890	12/12/91	CF6-80C2B1F		
B747-4D7	HS-TGM	THAI AIRWAYS INTL.		27093	945	11/04/92	CF6-80C2B1F		
B747-4D7	HS-TGN	THAI AIRWAYS INTL.		26615	950	12/08/92	CF6-80C2B1F		
B747-4D7	HS-TGO	THAI AIRWAYS INTL.		26609	1001	10/20/93	CF6-80C2B1F		
B747-4D7	HS-TGP	THAI AIRWAYS INTL.		26610	1047	11/22/94	CF6-80C2B1F		
B747-4D7	HS-TGR	THAI AIRWAYS INTL.		27723	1071	11/07/95	CF6-80C2B1F		
B747-4D7	HS-TGT	THAI AIRWAYS INTL.		26616	1097	12/20/96	CF6-80C2B1F		
B747-4D7	HS-TGW	THAI AIRWAYS INTL.		27724	1111	04/28/97	CF6-80C2B1F		
B747-4D7	HS-TGX	THAI AIRWAYS INTL.		27725	1134	11/12/97	CF6-80C2B1F		
B747-4D7	HS-TGY	THAI AIRWAYS INTL.		28705	1164	12/22/98	CF6-80C2B1F		N60697
B747-4D7	HS-TGZ	THAI AIRWAYS INTL.		28706	1214	05/11/99	CF6-80C2B1F		

A/C TYPE	CURRENT REG. NO.	LAST KNOWN OPERATOR (OWNER)	STATUS	ORIGINAL MSN	LINE NO.	DEL. DATE	ENG. TYPE	FLEET NO.	PREV. REG. [COMMENTS]
HZ-SAUDI ARABIA									
B747SP-68	HZ-AIF	SAUDI ARABIAN AIRLINES		22503	529	06/23/81	RB211-524C2		
B747-168B	HZ-AIA	SAUDI ARABIAN AIRLINES		22498	512	04/24/81	RB211-524C2		N8281V
B747-168B	HZ-AIB	SAUDI ARABIAN AIRLINES		22499	517	04/02/81	RB211-524C2		
B747-168B	HZ-AIC	SAUDI ARABIAN AIRLINES		22500	522	05/20/81	RB211-524C2		
B747-168B	HZ-AID	SAUDI ARABIAN AIRLINES		22501	525	05/21/81	RB211-524C2		
B747-168B	HZ-AIE	SAUDI ARABIAN AIRLINES		22502	530	07/31/81	RB211-524C2		N1782B, N8284V
B747-168B	HZ-AIG	SAUDI ARABIAN AIRLINES		22747	551	01/19/82	RB211-524C2		
B747-168B	HZ-AII	SAUDI ARABIAN AIRLINES		22749	557	04/02/82	RB211-524C2		
B747-268F (SCD)	HZ-AIU	SAUDI ARABIAN AIRLINES		24359	724	01/13/89	RB211-524D4		N6018N
B747-368	HZ-AIK	SAUDI ARABIAN AIRLINES		23262	616	07/12/85	RB211-524D4		N6005C
B747-368	HZ-AIL	SAUDI ARABIAN AIRLINES		23263	619	08/02/85	RB211-524D4		N6009F
B747-368	HZ-AIM	SAUDI ARABIAN AIRLINES		23264	620	08/21/85	RB211-524D4		N6046P
B747-368	HZ-AIN	SAUDI ARABIAN AIRLINES		23265	622	12/20/85	RB211-524D4		N6046P
B747-368	HZ-AIO	SAUDI ARABIAN AIRLINES		23266	624	10/24/85	RB211-524D4		N6005C
B747-368	HZ-AIP	SAUDI ARABIAN AIRLINES		23267	630	01/17/86	RB211-524D4		N6055X
B747-368	HZ-AIQ	SAUDI ARABIAN AIRLINES		23268	631	03/14/86	RB211-524D4		N6005C
B747-368	HZ-AIR	SAUDI ARABIAN AIRLINES		23269	643	07/24/86	RB211-524D4		N6038E
B747-368	HZ-AIS	SAUDI ARABIAN AIRLINES		23270	645	08/20/86	RB211-524D4		N6046P
B747-368	HZ-AIT	SAUDI ARABIAN AIRLINES		23271	652	11/10/86	RB211-524D4		N6038N
B747-468	HZ-AIV	SAUDI ARABIAN AIRLINES		28339	1122	12/24/97	CF6-80C2B5F		N6005C
B747-468	HZ-AIW	SAUDI ARABIAN AIRLINES		28340	1138	02/13/98	CF6-80C2B5F		
B747-468	HZ-AIX	SAUDI ARABIAN AIRLINES		28341	1182	11/18/98	CF6-80C2B5F		
B747-468	HZ-AIY	SAUDI ARABIAN AIRLINES		28342	1216	12/09/99	CF6-80C2B5F		N6009F
B747-468	HZ-AIZ	SAUDI ARABIAN AIRLINES		28343	1265	03/30/01	CF6-80C2B5F		
B747SP-68	HZ-HM1B	SAUDI ARABIAN VIP AIRCRAFT		21652	329	07/11/79	RB211-524C2		HZ-HM1
B747SP-68	HZ-HM1C	SAUDI ARABIAN VIP AIRCRAFT		22750	560	05/25/82	RB211-524C2		N6046P, HZ-AIJ
B747-3G1	HZ-HM1A	SAUDI ARABIAN VIP AIRCRAFT		23070	592	12/22/83	JT9D-7R4G2		N1784B
I-ITALY									
B747-243B (SF)	I-DEMC	ALITALIA (COFIRI)		22506	492	11/26/80	CF6-50E2		
B747-243B	I-DEMG	ALITALIA (ROMA LEASING)		22510	533	08/05/81	CF6-50E2		
B747-243B	I-DEML	ALITALIA		22511	536	09/16/81	CF6-50E2		
B747-243B	I-DEMN	ALITALIA		22512	542	11/05/81	CF6-50E2		
B747-243B	I-DEMP	ALITALIA		22513	546	12/03/81	CF6-50E2		
B747-243F (SCD)	I-DEMR	ALITALIA		22545	545	12/18/81	CF6-50E2		
B747-243B	I-DEMS	ALITALIA		22969	575	02/28/83	CF6-50E2		N8289V
B747-243B	I-DEMV	ALITALIA		23301	618	07/24/85	CF6-50E2		N6018N
B747-230B	I-DEMY	ALITALIA		21589	345	11/10/78	CF6-50E2		D-ABYN
B747-47UF (SCD)	N409MC	ALITALIA (GTI)	L	30558	1242	04/05/00	CF6-80C2B5F		

A/C TYPE	CURRENT REG. NO.	LAST KNOWN OPERATOR (OWNER)	STATUS	ORIGINAL MSN	LINE NO.	DEL. DATE	ENG. TYPE	FLEET NO.	PREV. REG. [COMMENTS]
JA-JAPAN									
B747SR-81	JA8138	ALL NIPPON AIRWAYS (SHOWA)		21924	420	01/16/80	CF6-45A2		
B747SR-81	JA8139	ALL NIPPON AIRWAYS (SHOWA)		21925	422	02/15/80	CF6-45A2		
B747SR-81	JA8145	ALL NIPPON AIRWAYS (SHOWA)		22291	453	05/16/80	CF6-45A2		
B747SR-81	JA8146	ALL NIPPON AIRWAYS		22292	456	06/16/80	CF6-45A2		
B747SR-81	JA8147	ALL NIPPON AIRWAYS		22293	477	11/25/80	CF6-45A2		N5973L
B747SR-81	JA8148	ALL NIPPON AIRWAYS		22294	481	11/25/80	CF6-45A2		
B747SR-81	JA8152	ALL NIPPON AIRWAYS		22594	511	02/27/81	CF6-45A2		
B747SR-81	JA8153	ALL NIPPON AIRWAYS		22595	516	05/28/81	CF6-45A2		
B747SR-81	JA8156	ALL NIPPON AIRWAYS		22709	541	12/17/81	CF6-45A2		N5573B
B747SR-81	JA8157	ALL NIPPON AIRWAYS		22710	544	12/17/81	CF6-45A2		
B747SR-81	JA8159	ALL NIPPON AIRWAYS		22712	572	11/12/82	CF6-45A2		
B747-281B	JA8174	ALL NIPPON AIRWAYS (ORIX)		23501	648	06/25/86	CF6-50E2		N6055X
B747-281B	JA8175	ALL NIPPON AIRWAYS (ORIX)		23502	649	07/02/86	CF6-50E2		N60659
B747-281B	JA8190	ALL NIPPON AIRWAYS		24399	750	08/10/89	CF6-50E2		
B747-481	JA401A	ALL NIPPON AIRWAYS		28282	1133	11/13/97	CF6-80C2B1F		
B747-481	JA402A	ALL NIPPON AIRWAYS		28283	1142	01/30/98	CF6-80C2B1F		
B747-481	JA403A	ALL NIPPON AIRWAYS (FALCON LSG, ET AL)		29262	1199	02/25/99	CF6-80C2B1F		
B747-481	JA404A	ALL NIPPON AIRWAYS		29263	1204	03/30/99	CF6-80C2B1F		
B747-481	JA405A	ALL NIPPON AIRWAYS		30322	1250	06/28/00	CF6-80C2B1F		
B747-481	JA8094	ALL NIPPON AIRWAYS		24801	805	08/28/90	CF6-80C2B1F		
B747-481	JA8095	ALL NIPPON AIRWAYS		24833	812	10/10/90	CF6-80C2B1F		
B747-481	JA8096	ALL NIPPON AIRWAYS		24920	832	02/05/91	CF6-80C2B1F		
B747-481	JA8097	ALL NIPPON AIRWAYS		25135	863	07/11/91	CF6-80C2B1F		
B747-481	JA8098	ALL NIPPON AIRWAYS		25207	870	08/21/91	CF6-80C2B1F		
B747-481 (D)	JA8099	ALL NIPPON AIRWAYS		25292	891	01/13/92	CF6-80C2B1F		
B747-481	JA8955	ALL NIPPON AIRWAYS		25639	914	05/12/92	CF6-80C2B1F		
B747-481 (D)	JA8956	ALL NIPPON AIRWAYS		25640	920	06/09/92	CF6-80C2B1F		
B747-481	JA8957	ALL NIPPON AIRWAYS		25642	927	07/15/92	CF6-80C2B1F		
B747-481	JA8958	ALL NIPPON AIRWAYS (AFUKO)		25641	928	08/11/92	CF6-80C2B1F		N6009F
B747-481 (D)	JA8959	ALL NIPPON AIRWAYS		25646	952	01/11/93	CF6-80C2B1F		
B747-481	JA8960	ALL NIPPON AIRWAYS (SUMISHO)		25643	972	05/11/93	CF6-80C2B1F		
B747-481 (D)	JA8961	ALL NIPPON AIRWAYS (MITSUI)		25644	975	05/13/93	CF6-80C2B1F		
B747-481	JA8962	ALL NIPPON AIRWAYS (BETA)		25645	979	06/03/93	CF6-80C2B1F		
B747-481 (D)	JA8963	ALL NIPPON AIRWAYS (FUYO SOGO)		25647	991	08/31/93	CF6-80C2B1F		N6055X
B747-481 (D)	JA8964	ALL NIPPON AIRWAYS (SAKURA)		27163	996	03/24/94	CF6-80C2B1F		N5573S
B747-481 (D)	JA8965	ALL NIPPON AIRWAYS (SUMIGEN)		27436	1060	04/24/95	CF6-80C2B1F		
B747-481 (D)	JA8966	ALL NIPPON AIRWAYS (FUYO SOGO)		27442	1066	12/11/95	CF6-80C2B1F		N6018N

A/C TYPE	CURRENT REG. NO.	LAST KNOWN OPERATOR (OWNER)	STATUS	ORIGINAL MSN	LINE NO.	DEL. DATE	ENG. TYPE	FLEET NO.	PREV. REG. [COMMENTS]
B747-246B	JA8111	JAL WAYS		20505	182	03/21/72	JT9D-7AW		[LST JAL]
B747-246B	JA8114	JAL WAYS		20530	196	11/03/72	JT9D-7AW		[LST JAL]
B747-146	JA8116	JAL WAYS		20532	199	12/08/72	JT9D-7A		
B747-246B	JA8127	JAL WAYS		21031	255	05/12/75	JT9D-7A		[LST JAL]
B747-146	JA8128	JAL WAYS (JAL)	L	21029	259	06/20/75	JT9D-7A		[RESO'CHA]
B747-246B	JA8149	JAL WAYS		22478	489	03/13/81	JT9D-7Q		[LST JAL]
B747-246B	JA8150	JAL WAYS		22479	496	03/19/81	JT9D-7Q		N1783B [OPB JAL; SUPER RESORT EXPRESS; RESO'CHA C/S]
B747-246B	JA8111	JAPAN AIRLINES (JAZ)	L	20505	182	03/21/72	JT9D-7AW		[RESO'CHA]
B747-246B	JA8114	JAPAN AIRLINES (JAZ)	L	20530	196	11/03/72	JT9D-7AW		[RESO'CHA]
B747-246F (SCD)	JA811J	JAPAN AIRLINES (NIKKO)		22989	571	12/14/82	JT9D-7Q		N211JL [SUPER LOGISTICS]
B747-246F (SCD)	JA8123	JAPAN AIRLINES (SUMISHO)		21034	243	09/17/74	JT9D-7AW		[SUPER LOGISTICS; TO BE ST GLN 01/02]
B747-246B	JA8127	JAPAN AIRLINES (JAZ)	L	21031	255	05/12/75	JT9D-7A		
B747-146	JA8128	JAPAN AIRLINES (JAA)	L	21029	259	06/20/75	JT9D-7A		[RESO'CHA; LST JAZ]
B747-246B	JA8130	JAPAN AIRLINES (ZONET)		21679	376	06/14/79	JT9D-7Q		
B747-246B	JA8131	JAPAN AIRLINES		21680	380	06/28/79	JT9D-7Q		
B747-246F	JA8132	JAPAN AIRLINES (SHOWA)		21681	382	07/27/79	JT9D-7Q		N1782B [SUPER LOGISTICS]
B747-246B	JA8140	JAPAN AIRLINES (ZONET)		22064	407	11/08/79	JT9D-7Q		
B747-246B	JA8141	JAPAN AIRLINES		22065	411	12/03/79	JT9D-7Q		
B747-246B	JA8149	JAPAN AIRLINES (JAZ)	L	22478	489	03/13/81	JT9D-7Q		
B747-246B	JA8150	JAPAN AIRLINES (JAZ)	L	22479	496	03/19/81	JT9D-7Q		N1783B [SUPER RESORT EXPRESS; RESO'CHA C/S]
B747-246B	JA8154	JAPAN AIRLINES (NIARUKO)		22745	547	11/17/81	JT9D-7Q		[LST JAA]
B747-221F (SCD)	JA8160	JAPAN AIRLINES (NIKKO)		21744	392	08/28/79	JT9D-7Q		N905PA [SUPER LOGISTICS]
B747-246B	JA8161	JAPAN AIRLINES		22990	579	06/16/83	JT9D-7R4G2		N6046B
B747-246B	JA8162	JAPAN AIRLINES		22991	581	06/06/83	JT9D-7R4G2		N5573K
B747SR-146B	JA8164	JAPAN AIRLINES		23150	601	12/04/84	JT9D-7A		N1781B
B747-221F (SCD)	JA8165	JAPAN AIRLINES (SUMISHO)		21743	384	07/25/79	JT9D-7Q		N904PA [SUPER LOGISTICS]
B747-246B (F)	JA8169	JAPAN AIRLINES		23389	635	03/19/86	JT9D-7R4G2		N6018B [CVTD TO FRTR AT XIAMEN]
B747SR-146B (SUD)	JA8170	JAPAN AIRLINES		23390	636	03/24/86	JT9D-7A		N6009F
B747-246F (SCD)	JA8171	JAPAN AIRLINES (SHOWA)		23391	654	08/25/86	JT9D-7R4G2		N6038B [SUPER LOGISTICS]
B747SR-146B (SUD)	JA8176	JAPAN AIRLINES		23637	655	08/29/86	JT9D-7A		N60668
B747-246F (SCD)	JA8180	JAPAN AIRLINES (SUMIGIN)		23641	684	08/11/87	JT9D-7R4G2		[SUPER LOGISTICS]
B747-212B (SF)	JA8193	JAPAN AIRLINES (NIKKO LEASE)		21940	457	06/27/80	JT9D-7Q		9V-SQO [CVTD -212B; SUPER LOGISTICS]
B747-246F (SCD)	JA8937	JAPAN AIRLINES (NIKKO LEASE)		22477	494	04/15/81	JT9D-7Q		N8284V, JA8151, N740SJ [SUPER LOGISTICS]
B747-346	JA812J	JAPAN AIRLINES		23067	588	11/29/83	JT9D-7R4G2		N212JL
B747-346	JA813J	JAPAN AIRLINES		23068	589	12/08/83	JT9D-7R4G2		N213JL
B747-346	JA8163	JAPAN AIRLINES		23149	599	12/06/84	JT9D-7R4G2		N5573B
B747-346	JA8166	JAPAN AIRLINES		23151	607	02/04/85	JT9D-7R4G2		N1786B
B747-346	JA8173	JAPAN AIRLINES		23482	640	04/15/86	JT9D-7R4G2		N6009F

A/C TYPE	CURRENT REG. NO.	LAST KNOWN OPERATOR (OWNER)	STATUS	ORIGINAL MSN	LINE NO.	DEL. DATE	ENG. TYPE	FLEET NO.	PREV. REG. [COMMENTS]
B747-346	JA8177	JAPAN AIRLINES		23638	658	10/02/86	JT9D-7R4G2		N6009F
B747-346	JA8178	JAPAN AIRLINES		23639	664	12/15/86	JT9D-7R4G2		N6009F
B747-346	JA8179	JAPAN AIRLINES		23640	668	02/05/87	JT9D-7R4G2		N6009F
B747-346	JA8183	JAPAN AIRLINES		23967	692	12/10/87	JT9D-7R4G2		N6005C [CVTD -346 (SR)]
B747-346	JA8184	JAPAN AIRLINES		23968	693	01/28/88	JT9D-7R4G2		N6055X [CVTD -346 (SR); RESO'CHA C/S]
B747-346	JA8185	JAPAN AIRLINES		23969	691	03/07/88	JT9D-7R4G2		N6005C
B747-346	JA8186	JAPAN AIRLINES		24018	694	02/09/88	JT9D-7R4G2		N6018N [CVTD -346 (SR); RESO'CHA C/S]
B747-346	JA8187	JAPAN AIRLINES		24019	695	02/19/88	JT9D-7R4G2		N6038E [CVTD -346 (SR); RESO'CHA C/S]
B747-446	JA8071	JAPAN AIRLINES		24423	758	01/25/90	CF6-80C2B1F		
B747-446	JA8072	JAPAN AIRLINES		24424	760	01/25/90	CF6-80C2B1F		
B747-446	JA8073	JAPAN AIRLINES (NIKKO)		24425	767	02/19/90	CF6-80C2B1F		
B747-446	JA8074	JAPAN AIRLINES		24426	768	02/26/90	CF6-80C2B1F		
B747-446	JA8075	JAPAN AIRLINES		24427	780	03/30/90	CF6-80C2B1F		
B747-446	JA8076	JAPAN AIRLINES (NIKKO)		24777	797	07/10/90	CF6-80C2B1F		N6046P
B747-446	JA8077	JAPAN AIRLINES (NIKKO)		24784	798	07/10/90	CF6-80C2B1F		
B747-446	JA8078	JAPAN AIRLINES (NIKKO)		24870	821	11/19/90	CF6-80C2B1F		N60697
B747-446	JA8079	JAPAN AIRLINES (NIKKO)		24885	824	12/05/90	CF6-80C2B1F		N6005C
B747-446	JA8080	JAPAN AIRLINES (NIKKO)		24886	825	12/12/90	CF6-80C2B1F		
B747-446	JA8081	JAPAN AIRLINES		25064	851	05/13/91	CF6-80C2B1F		
B747-446	JA8082	JAPAN AIRLINES		25212	871	08/27/91	CF6-80C2B1F		
B747-446 (D)	JA8083	JAPAN AIRLINES		25213	844	10/10/91	CF6-80C2B1F		N60668
B747-446 (D)	JA8084	JAPAN AIRLINES		25214	879	10/14/91	CF6-80C2B1F		
B747-446	JA8085	JAPAN AIRLINES (SUMIGIN)		25260	876	09/24/91	CF6-80C2B1F		
B747-446	JA8086	JAPAN AIRLINES		25308	885	11/11/91	CF6-80C2B1F		
B747-446	JA8087	JAPAN AIRLINES (N I ACFT LSG)		26346	897	02/18/92	CF6-80C2B1F		
B747-446	JA8088	JAPAN AIRLINES (KOGIN LEASE)		26341	902	02/24/92	CF6-80C2B1F		
B747-446	JA8089	JAPAN AIRLINES (N I ACFT LSG)		26342	905	03/11/92	CF6-80C2B1F		
B747-446 (D)	JA8090	JAPAN AIRLINES (N I ACFT LSG)		26347	907	03/26/92	CF6-80C2B1F		
B747-446	JA8901	JAPAN AIRLINES		26343	918	06/01/92	CF6-80C2B1F		
B747-446	JA8902	JAPAN AIRLINES		26344	929	08/19/92	CF6-80C2B1F		N6018N
B747-446 (D)	JA8903	JAPAN AIRLINES (KOGIN LEASE)		26345	935	09/15/92	CF6-80C2B1F		
B747-446 (D)	JA8904	JAPAN AIRLINES		26348	941	11/03/92	CF6-80C2B1F		
B747-446 (D)	JA8905	JAPAN AIRLINES		26349	948	12/01/92	CF6-80C2B1F		
B747-446	JA8906	JAPAN AIRLINES (CHARLOTTE)		26350	961	03/01/93	CF6-80C2B1F		
B747-446 (D)	JA8907	JAPAN AIRLINES (SUMIGIN)		26351	963	03/02/93	CF6-80C2B1F		
B747-446 (D)	JA8908	JAPAN AIRLINES (KOGIN LEASE)		26352	978	06/01/93	CF6-80C2B1F		["DREAM EXPRESS 21"]
B747-446	JA8909	JAPAN AIRLINES		26353	980	06/07/93	CF6-80C2B1F		
B747-446	JA8910	JAPAN AIRLINES		26355	1024	03/29/94	CF6-80C2B1F		
B747-446	JA8911	JAPAN AIRLINES		26356	1026	03/30/94	CF6-80C2B1F		
B747-446	JA8912	JAPAN AIRLINES (ILLINOIS A/C LSG)		27099	1031	05/31/94	CF6-80C2B1F		
B747-446	JA8913	JAPAN AIRLINES		26359	1153	04/30/98	CF6-80C2B1F		

A/C TYPE	CURRENT REG. NO.	LAST KNOWN OPERATOR (OWNER)	STATUS	ORIGINAL MSN	LINE NO.	DEL. DATE	ENG. TYPE	FLEET NO.	PREV. REG. [COMMENTS]
B747-446	JA8914	JAPAN AIRLINES		26360	1166	07/23/98	CF6-80C2B1F		
B747-446	JA8915	JAPAN AIRLINES		26361	1188	11/30/98	CF6-80C2B1F		
B747-446	JA8916	JAPAN AIRLINES (URANUS LSG)		26362	1202	03/18/99	CF6-80C2B1F		
B747-446	JA8917	JAPAN AIRLINES (TWO CRANE)		29899	1208	04/20/99	CF6-80C2B1F		N6009F
B747-446	JA8918	JAPAN AIRLINES (TWO CRANE)		27650	1234	11/21/99	CF6-80C2B1F		N6009F
B747-446	JA8919	JAPAN AIRLINES (TWO CRANE)		27100	1236	12/16/99	CF6-80C2B1F		N6009F
B747-446	JA8920	JAPAN AIRLINES (ATIRAN)		27648	1253	08/17/00	CF6-80C2B1F		
B747-446	JA8921	JAPAN AIRLINES		27645	1262	12/19/00	CF6-80C2B1F		
B747-146	JA8128	JAPAN ASIA AIRWAYS		21029	259	06/20/75	JT9D-7A		[LST JAL]
B747-246B	JA8129	JAPAN ASIA AIRWAYS		21678	361	03/06/79	JT9D-7AW		
B747-246B	JA8154	JAPAN ASIA AIRWAYS (JAL)	L	22745	547	11/17/81	JT9D-7Q		
B747-246B	JA8155	JAPAN ASIA AIRWAYS		22746	548	12/15/81	JT9D-7Q		
B747-346	JA8189	JAPAN ASIA AIRWAYS		24156	716	10/18/88	JT9D-7R4G2		N6046P
B747SR-81 (SF)	JA8158	NIPPON CARGO AIRLINES		22711	559	06/17/82	CF6-45A2		[CVTD -81]
B747-281F (SCD)	JA8167	NIPPON CARGO AIRLINES		23138	604	12/13/84	CF6-50E2		N6066Z
B747-281F (SCD)	JA8168	NIPPON CARGO AIRLINES		23139	608	02/28/85	CF6-50E2		N6046P
B747-281F (SCD)	JA8172	NIPPON CARGO AIRLINES (ZEN NIKKU)		23350	623	10/15/85	CF6-50E2		N6018N
B747-281B (SF)	JA8181	NIPPON CARGO AIRLINES		23698	667	12/22/86	CF6-50E2		N6055C [CVTD -281B]
B747-281B (SF)	JA8182	NIPPON CARGO AIRLINES		23813	683	07/13/87	CF6-50E2		N60659 [CVTD -281B]
B747-281F (SCD)	JA8188	NIPPON CARGO AIRLINES		23919	689	01/27/88	CF6-50E2		N6009F
B747-281F (SCD)	JA8191	NIPPON CARGO AIRLINES		24576	818	11/06/90	CF6-50E2		
B747-2D3B (SF)	JA8192	NIPPON CARGO AIRLINES		22579	514	03/26/81	CF6-50E2		JY-AFS, G-CITB [CVTD -2D3B]
B747-281F (SCD)	JA8194	NIPPON CARGO AIRLINES		25171	886	11/19/91	CF6-50E2		

LV-ARGENTINA

A/C TYPE	CURRENT REG. NO.	LAST KNOWN OPERATOR (OWNER)	STATUS	ORIGINAL MSN	LINE NO.	DEL. DATE	ENG. TYPE	FLEET NO.	PREV. REG. [COMMENTS]
B747-287B	LV-MLO	AEROLINEAS ARGENTINAS		21725	349	01/13/79	JT9D-7Q		
B747-287B	LV-MLP	AEROLINEAS ARGENTINAS		21726	403	10/11/79	JT9D-7Q		
B747-287B	LV-MLR	AEROLINEAS ARGENTINAS		21727	404	10/26/79	JT9D-7Q		
B747-287B	LV-OEP	AEROLINEAS ARGENTINAS		22297	487	11/18/80	JT9D-7Q		
B747-287B	LV-OOZ	AEROLINEAS ARGENTINAS		22592	532	08/26/81	JT9D-7Q		
B747-287B	LV-OPA	AEROLINEAS ARGENTINAS		22593	552	01/23/82	JT9D-7Q		
B747-212B	LV-YPC	AEROLINEAS ARGENTINAS (PACA)		21938	436	04/10/80	JT9D-7Q		9V-SQM, HL7453, N924PG

LX-LUXEMBOURG

A/C TYPE	CURRENT REG. NO.	LAST KNOWN OPERATOR (OWNER)	STATUS	ORIGINAL MSN	LINE NO.	DEL. DATE	ENG. TYPE	FLEET NO.	PREV. REG. [COMMENTS]
B747-4R7F (SCD)	LX-FCV	CARGOLUX (ELENA)		25866	1002	11/17/93	CF6-80C2B1F		N1785B
B747-4R7F (SCD)	LX-GCV	CARGOLUX (GERALDINE)		25867	1008	12/08/93	CF6-80C2B1F		
B747-428F (SCD)	LX-ICV	CARGOLUX		25632	968	09/13/95	CF6-80C2B1F		N6005C, F-GIUA
B747-4R7F (SCD)	LX-KCV	CARGOLUX		25868	1125	08/26/97	CF6-80C2B1F		
B747-4R7F (SCD)	LX-LCV	CARGOLUX		29053	1139	12/19/97	CF6-80C2B1F		

A/C TYPE	CURRENT REG. NO.	LAST KNOWN OPERATOR (OWNER)	STATUS	ORIGINAL MSN	LINE NO.	DEL. DATE	ENG. TYPE	FLEET NO.	PREV. REG. [COMMENTS]
B747-4R7F (SCD)	LX-MCV	CARGOLUX		29729	1189	12/08/98	RB211-524G/H-T		
B747-4R7F (SCD)	LX-NCV	CARGOLUX		29730	1203	03/03/99	RB211-524G/H-T		
B747-4R7F (SCD)	LX-OCV	CARGOLUX		29731	1222	07/12/99	RB211-524G/H-T		
B747-4R7F (SCD)	LX-PCV	CARGOLUX		29732	1231	09/29/99	RB211-524G/H-T		
B747-4R7F (SCD)	LX-RCV	CARGOLUX		30400	1235	11/23/99	RB211-524G/H-T		

N-UNITED STATES OF AMERICA

A/C TYPE	CURRENT REG. NO.	LAST KNOWN OPERATOR (OWNER)	STATUS	ORIGINAL MSN	LINE NO.	DEL. DATE	ENG. TYPE	FLEET NO.	PREV. REG. [COMMENTS]
B747-121	N7470	BOEING (MUSEUM OF FLIGHT FOUND.)		20235	1	02/09/69	JT9D-7A		N1352B [PROTOTYPE; ENGINE TESTBED]
B747-121	N747GE	GENERAL ELECTRIC CO. (WTCI)		19651	25	03/21/70	JT9D-7A		N744PA [GE90 TESTBED; BASED AT MHV]
B747-2D3B (SF)	N505MC	ATLAS AIR		21251	296	04/13/77	CF6-50E2		N1239E, JY-AFA, N506DC, F-GFUK [CVTD -2D3B (M)]
B747-2D3B (SF)	N506MC	ATLAS AIR (POTO)		21252	297	05/11/77	CF6-50E2		JY-AFB, G-HUGE, N512DC, LX-ZCV [CVTD -2D3B (M); OPF CAL]
B747-230B (SF)	N507MC	ATLAS AIR (FSBU)		21380	320	03/16/78	CF6-50E2		D-ABYL [CVTD -230B (M); OPF HDA]
B747-230B (SF)	N508MC	ATLAS AIR (SSBT)		21644	356	02/08/79	CF6-50E2		D-ABYS [CVTD -230B (M))]
B747-230B (SF)	N509MC	ATLAS AIR		21221	299	12/15/76	CF6-50E2		D-ABYK [CVTD -230B (M); OPF MAS]
B747-230B (SF)	N512MC	ATLAS AIR		21220	294	11/23/76	CF6-50E2		N1786B, D-ABYJ [CVTD -230B (M); OPF CCA]
B747-243B (SF)	N516MC	ATLAS AIR		22507	497	12/12/80	CF6-50E2		I-DEMD [CVTD -243B (M)]
B747-243B (SF)	N517MC	ATLAS AIR		23300	613	05/29/85	CF6-50E2		N6009F, I-DEMT, N517DC [CVTD -243B (M); OPF CAL]
B747-243B (SF)	N518MC	ATLAS AIR		23476	647	06/13/86	CF6-50E2		I-DEMW [CVTD -243B (M) OPF; CAL]
B747-2D7B (SF)	N522MC	ATLAS AIR		21783	417	12/15/79	CF6-50E2		HS-TGB [CVTD -2D7B; OPF CES]
B747-2D7B (SF)	N523MC	ATLAS AIR		21782	402	11/02/79	CF6-50E2		HS-TGA, N323MC, ZK-TGA [CVTD -2D7B; OPF CCA]
B747-2D7B (SF)	N524MC	ATLAS AIR		21784	424	02/23/80	CF6-50E2		HS-TGC [CVTD -2D7B; OPF MAS]
B747-2D7B (SF)	N526MC	ATLAS AIR		22337	479	09/24/80	CF6-50E2		HS-TGF [CVTD -2D7B]
B747-2D7B (SF)	N527MC	ATLAS AIR		22471	504	03/16/81	CF6-50E2		HS-TGG [CVTD -2D7B; OPF CAL]
B747-2D7B (SF)	N528MC	ATLAS AIR		22472	597	06/01/84	CF6-50E2		N6066U, HS-TGS [CVTD -2D7B]
B747-2F6B (SF)	N534MC	ATLAS AIR		21832	421	12/21/79	CF6-50E2		N741PR [CVTD -2F6B]
B747-2F6B (SF)	N535MC	ATLAS AIR		21833	423	02/22/80	CF6-50E2		N742PR [CVTD -2F6B]
B747-228F (SCD)	N536MC	ATLAS AIR		21576	334	08/09/78	CF6-50E2		F-BPVV [OPF AFR 07/07/99 AS F-BPVV/GPVV]
B747-271C (SCD)	N537MC	ATLAS AIR		22403	524	06/01/81	CF6-50E2		N743TV, LX-BCV
B747-243B (M)	N540MC	ATLAS AIR		22508	499	12/22/80	CF6-50E2		I-DEMF
B747-212B (SF)	N808MC	ATLAS AIR		21048	253	02/06/75	CF6-50E2		9V-SQD, N747BC, N726PA [RE-ENGINED FROM JT9D-7J]
B747-228F (SCD)	N809MC	ATLAS AIR		20887	245	10/04/74	CF6-50E2		N18815, F-BPVO, LX-DCV [RE-ENGINED FROM JT9D-7J]
B747-329 (SF)	N24837	ATLAS AIR (UNICAPITAL)		24837	810	09/25/90	CF6-50E2		OO-SGD [CVTD TO FRTR AT IAB 10/00]
B747-341 (SF)	N354MC	ATLAS AIR		23394	627	12/10/85	CF6-50E2		N6005C, PP-VNH [CVTD TO FRTR AT IAB]
B747-341 (SF)	N355MC	ATLAS AIR		23395	629	12/19/85	CF6-50E2		N6009F, PP-VNI [CVTD TO FRTR AT IAB]

A/C TYPE	CURRENT REG. NO.	LAST KNOWN OPERATOR (OWNER)	STATUS	ORIGINAL MSN	LINE NO.	DEL. DATE	ENG. TYPE	FLEET NO.	PREV. REG. [COMMENTS]
B747-47UF (SCD)	N408MC	ATLAS AIR		29261	1192	12/15/98	CF6-80C2B5F		[OPF UAE IN UAE COLORS]
B747-47UF (SCD)	N409MC	ATLAS AIR (FSBU)		30558	1242	04/05/00	CF6-80C2B5F		[LST AZA IN AZA C/S]
B747-47UF (SCD)	N412MC	ATLAS AIR (FSBU)		30559	1244	04/25/00	CF6-80C2B5F		[OPF CSN]
B747-47UF (SCD)	N491MC	ATLAS AIR (FSBU)		29252	1165	07/29/98	CF6-80C2B5F		[OPF MAS]
B747-47UF (SCD)	N492MC	ATLAS AIR (FSBU)		29253	1169	08/12/98	CF6-80C2B5F		
B747-47UF (SCD)	N493MC	ATLAS AIR (FSBU)		29254	1179	10/19/98	CF6-80C2B5F		[OPF KAL]
B747-47UF (SCD)	N494MC	ATLAS AIR		29255	1184	12/04/98	CF6-80C2B5F		[OPF BAW IN BA WORLD CARGO C/S AS G-GSSB]
B747-47UF (SCD)	N495MC	ATLAS AIR		29256	1213	05/26/99	CF6-80C2B5F		[OPF BAW IN BA WORLD CARGO C/S AS G-GSSA]
B747-47UF (SCD)	N496MC	ATLAS AIR (FSBU)		29257	1217	06/30/99	CF6-80C2B5F		[OPF KAL]
B747-47UF (SCD)	N497MC	ATLAS AIR (FSBU)		29258	1220	07/15/99	CF6-80C2B5F		[OPF CAL]
B747-47UF (SCD)	N498MC	ATLAS AIR (FSBU)		29259	1227	08/26/99	CF6-80C2B5F		[OPF CAL]
B747-47UF (SCD)	N499MC	ATLAS AIR (FSBU)		29260	1240	02/17/00	CF6-80C2B5F		[OPF KAL]
B747-128 (SF)	N3203Y	EVERGREEN INTL. AIRLINES (ARKIA LSG)		19751	39	05/12/70	JT9D-7A		F-BPVC
B747-273C	N470EV	EVERGREEN INTL. AIRLINES		20653	237	06/10/74	JT9D-7J		N749WA
B747-273C	N471EV	EVERGREEN INTL. AIRLINES		20651	209	04/27/73	JT9D-7J		N747WA, N535PA, N747WR
B747-131 (SF)	N472EV	EVERGREEN INTL. AIRLINES		20320	98	05/20/71	JT9D-7AH		N93115 [CVTD -131; STD MZJ]
B747-121 (SF)	N474EV	EVERGREEN INTL. AIRLINES		19637	4	07/11/70	JT9D-7A		9Q-ARW, N731PA [CVTD -121; STD MZJ]
B747SR-46 (SF)	N477EV	EVERGREEN INTL. AIRLINES		20784	231	02/20/74	JT9D-7A		JA8120, N688UP [CVTD -46]
B747SR-46 (SF)	N478EV	EVERGREEN INTL. AIRLINES		21033	254	04/02/75	JT9D-7A		JA8126, N689UP [CVTD -46]
B747-132 (SF)	N479EV	EVERGREEN INTL. AIRLINES		19898	94	11/18/70	JT9D-7A		N9898, B-1860, EI-BOS, N725PA [CVTD -132]
B747-121 (SF)	N480EV	EVERGREEN INTL. AIRLINES		20348	106	04/08/71	JT9D-7A		N653PA, N690UP [CVTD -121]
B747-132 (SF)	N481EV	EVERGREEN INTL. AIRLINES		19896	72	09/26/70	JT9D-7A		N9896, N40108, B-1868, N902PA [CVTD -132]
B747-212B (SF)	N482EV	EVERGREEN INTL. AIRLINES		20713	219	08/29/73	JT9D-7J		9V-SIB, N748TA, N748FT, N729PA [CVTD -212B]
B747-212B (SF)	N485EV	EVERGREEN INTL. AIRLINES		20712	218	07/31/73	JT9D-7J		9V-SIA, N747TA, N747FT, N728PA [CVTD -212B; LST TFS]
B747-146 (SF)	N702CK	KALITTA AIR		20332	161	10/28/71	JT9D-7A		JA8107 [CVTD -146A]
B747-269B (SF)	N707CK	KALITTA AIR		21541	332	07/28/78	JT9D-7J		9K-ADA [CVTD -269B (M)]
B747-132 (SF)	N709CK	KALITTA AIR		20247	159	11/11/71	JT9D-7A		N9900, N805FT, N625FE, VR-HKC, N625PL [CVTD -132]
B747-269B (SF)	N708CK	KITTY HAWK INTL.		21543	359	02/28/79	JT9D-7J		9K-ADC [CVTD -269B (M)]
B747-2B4B (SF)	N710CK	KITTY HAWK INTL.		21097	262	05/30/75	JT9D-7FW		G-BLVE, OD-AGH, N202AE [CVTD -2B4B (M); STD MHV]
B747-2B4B (SF)	N713CK	KITTY HAWK INTL.		21099	264	08/20/75	JT9D-7FW		OD-AGJ, N204AE [CVTD -2B4B (M); STD MHV]
B747SP-21	N145UA	NASA		21441	306	05/06/77	JT9D-7A		N536PA [SOFIA PROGRAM]
B747-123	N905NA	NASA		20107	86	10/29/70	JT9D-3A		N9668 [SHUTTLE CARRIER; BASED MZJ]

A/C TYPE	CURRENT REG. NO.	LAST KNOWN OPERATOR (OWNER)	STATUS	ORIGINAL MSN	LINE NO.	DEL. DATE	ENG. TYPE	FLEET NO.	PREV. REG. [COMMENTS]
B747SR-46	N911NA	NASA		20781	221	09/26/73	JT9D-7A		N1795B, JA8117, N747BL [SHUTTLE SUPPORT; BASED MZJ]
B747-251B	N612US	NORTHWEST AIRLINES		20357	135	05/15/71	JT9D-7F	6612	[RTS]
B747-251B	N613US	NORTHWEST AIRLINES		20358	141	06/22/71	JT9D-7F	6613	[RTS]
B747-251B	N614US	NORTHWEST AIRLINES		20359	163	10/22/71	JT9D-7F	6614	
B747-251B	N615US	NORTHWEST AIRLINES		20360	165	11/23/71	JT9D-7Q	6615	
B747-251F (SCD)	N616US	NORTHWEST AIRLINES		21120	258	07/03/75	JT9D-7F	6716	
B747-251F (SCD)	N617US	NORTHWEST AIRLINES		21121	261	07/09/75	JT9D-7F	6717	
B747-251F (SCD)	N618US	NORTHWEST AIRLINES		21122	269	08/29/75	JT9D-7F	6718	
B747-251F (SCD)	N619US	NORTHWEST AIRLINES		21321	308	06/27/77	JT9D-7F	6719	
B747-251B	N622US	NORTHWEST AIRLINES		21704	357	09/24/79	JT9D-7Q	6622	
B747-251B	N623US	NORTHWEST AIRLINES		21705	374	05/25/79	JT9D-7Q	6623	
B747-251B	N624US	NORTHWEST AIRLINES		21706	377	06/06/79	JT9D-7Q	6624	
B747-251B	N625US	NORTHWEST AIRLINES		21707	378	06/17/79	JT9D-7Q	6625	
B747-251B	N626US	NORTHWEST AIRLINES		21708	379	06/28/79	JT9D-7Q	6626	
B747-251B	N627US	NORTHWEST AIRLINES		21709	412	01/02/80	JT9D-7Q	6627	
B747-251B	N628US	NORTHWEST AIRLINES		22389	442	04/08/80	JT9D-7Q	6628	
B747-251F (SCD)	N629US	NORTHWEST AIRLINES		22388	444	04/18/80	JT9D-7F	6729	
B747-2J9F	N630US	NORTHWEST AIRLINES		21668	400	09/15/83	JT9D-7F	6730	N1288E
B747-251B	N631US	NORTHWEST AIRLINES		23111	594	04/02/84	JT9D-7R4G2	6631	
B747-251B	N632US	NORTHWEST AIRLINES		23112	595	05/01/84	JT9D-7R4G2	6632	
B747-227B	N633US	NORTHWEST AIRLINES		21991	437	04/19/84	JT9D-7Q	6633	N8284V
B747-227B	N634US	NORTHWEST AIRLINES		22234	465	05/29/84	JT9D-7Q	6634	N1607B, N8285V
B747-227B	N635US	NORTHWEST AIRLINES		21682	375	05/31/79	JT9D-7Q	6635	N602BN, N602PE
B747-251B	N636US	NORTHWEST AIRLINES		23547	642	05/06/86	JT9D-7R4G2	6636	
B747-251B	N637US	NORTHWEST AIRLINES		23548	644	05/19/86	JT9D-7R4G2	6637	
B747-251B	N638US	NORTHWEST AIRLINES		23549	651	07/18/86	JT9D-7R4G2	6638	
B747-251F (SCD)	N639US	NORTHWEST AIRLINES		23887	680	06/03/87	JT9D-7Q	6739	
B747-251F (SCD)	N640US	NORTHWEST AIRLINES		23888	682	07/01/87	JT9D-7Q	6740	
B747-212B	N641NW	NORTHWEST AIRLINES		21941	470	09/12/80	JT9D-7Q	6641	RP-C5745, 9V-SQP
B747-212B	N642NW	NORTHWEST AIRLINES		21942	471	09/25/80	JT9D-7Q	6642	9V-SQQ
B747-249F (SCD)	N643NW	NORTHWEST AIRLINES (NEWCOURT)		22245	458	07/03/80	JT9D-7Q	6743	N808FT, N632FE, 9V-SQV, HL7401, N744SJ, N9401 ["INVESTING IN PACIFIC TRADE"]
B747-212F (SCD)	N644NW	NORTHWEST AIRLINES (FINO)		24177	710	08/29/88	JT9D-7R4G2	6744	N6046P, 9V-SKQ, N750SJ, ZS-SBJ ["SELECT 3-SPEED SERVICE"]
B747-222B (SF)	N645NW	NORTHWEST AIRLINES		23736	673	03/19/87	JT9D-7R4G2	6745	N151UA [CVTD TO FRTR AT IAB]
B747-222B	N646NW	NORTHWEST AIRLINES		23737	675	04/02/87	JT9D-7R4G2	6746	N152UA [FERRIED TO IAB; BEING CVTD TO FRTR]
B747-451	N661US	NORTHWEST AIRLINES		23719	696	12/08/89	PW4056	6301	N401PW
B747-451	N662US	NORTHWEST AIRLINES		23720	708	03/13/89	PW4056	6302	
B747-451	N663US	NORTHWEST AIRLINES		23818	715	01/26/89	PW4056	6303	

320

A/C TYPE	CURRENT REG. NO.	LAST KNOWN OPERATOR (OWNER)	STATUS	ORIGINAL MSN	LINE NO.	DEL. DATE	ENG. TYPE	FLEET NO.	PREV. REG. [COMMENTS]
B747-451	N664US	NORTHWEST AIRLINES		23819	721	04/28/89	PW4056	6304	
B747-451	N665US	NORTHWEST AIRLINES		23820	726	09/01/89	PW4056	6305	
B747-451	N666US	NORTHWEST AIRLINES		23821	742	08/18/89	PW4056	6306	
B747-451	N667US	NORTHWEST AIRLINES		24222	799	07/20/90	PW4056	6307	
B747-451	N668US	NORTHWEST AIRLINES		24223	800	07/26/90	PW4056	6308	
B747-451	N669US	NORTHWEST AIRLINES		24224	803	08/20/90	PW4056	6309	
B747-451	N670US	NORTHWEST AIRLINES		24225	804	08/31/90	PW4056	6310	
B747-451	N671US	NORTHWEST AIRLINES (FSBU)		26477	1206	03/29/99	PW4056	6311	
B747-451	N672US	NORTHWEST AIRLINES (FSBU)		30267	1223	07/19/99	PW4056	6312	
B747-451	N673US	NORTHWEST AIRLINES (FSBU)		30268	1226	08/24/99	PW4056	6313	
B747-451	N674US	NORTHWEST AIRLINES (FSBU)		30269	1232	10/18/99	PW4056	6314	
B747-249F (SCD)	N806FT	POLAR AIR CARGO (UT CAP.)		21827	406	10/31/79	JT9D-7Q		N631FE, N742SJ, N880WF, N888KH
B747-121 (SF)	N830FT	POLAR AIR CARGO (POLA)		19642	10	01/09/70	JT9D-7A		VR-HKB, N735PA, N735SJ [CVTD -121; STD BFM MINUS ENGINES]
B747-121 (SF)	N831FT	POLAR AIR CARGO (POLA)		19648	17	02/28/70	JT9D-7A		N494GX, N741PA, N741SJ [CVTD -121; STD BFM MINUS ENGINES]
B747-121 (SF)	N832FT	POLAR AIR CARGO (POLA)		20347	103	04/25/71	JT9D-7A		N652PA, N652SJ [CVTD -121; STD TLV]
B747-122 (SF)	N850FT	POLAR AIR CARGO		19755	61	08/08/70	JT9D-7A		N4710U [CVTD -122]
B747-122 (SF)	N851FT	POLAR AIR CARGO		19756	66	08/28/70	JT9D-7A		N4711U [CVTD -122]
B747-122 (SF)	N852FT	POLAR AIR CARGO		19757	67	08/31/70	JT9D-7A		N4712U [CVTD -122]
B747-122 (SF)	N853FT	POLAR AIR CARGO		19753	52	06/30/70	JT9D-7A		N4703U [CVTD -122]
B747-122 (SF)	N854FT	POLAR AIR CARGO		19754	60	08/04/70	JT9D-7A		N4704U [CVTD -122]
B747-124 (SF)	N855FT	POLAR AIR CARGO (FSBU)		19733	42	05/18/70	JT9D-7A		N26861, 5-289,5-8110, N750WA, N809FT, HK-2900X, N822FT, N630FE, N630SJ [CVTD -124]
B747-132 (SF)	N856FT	POLAR AIR CARGO		19897	82	10/22/70	JT9D-7A		N9897, N803FT, N623FE, VR-HKN [CVTD -132]
B747-123 (SF)	N858FT	POLAR AIR CARGO (PS GROUP)		20109	90	12/29/70	JT9D-7A		N9670 [CVTD -123]
B747-123 (SF)	N859FT	POLAR AIR CARGO (PS GROUP)		20326	133	05/12/71	JT9D-7AH		N9674 [CVTD -123]
B747-249F (SCD)	N920FT	POLAR AIR CARGO (POLA)		22237	460	09/12/80	JT9D-7Q		N810FT, N633FE, VR-HKO
B747-283B (SF)	N921FT	POLAR AIR CARGO		21575	358	03/22/79	JT9D-70A		SE-DFZ, LX-OCV, EI-BWF, N9727N [CVTD -283B (M)]
B747-2U3B (SF)	N922FT	POLAR AIR CARGO (TRIT)		22768	561	05/05/82	JT9D-7Q		PK-GSE, N105TR [CVTD -2U3B]
B747-2U3B (SF)	N923FT	POLAR AIR CARGO (TRIT)		22769	562	05/18/82	JT9D-7Q		PK-GSF, N106TR [CVTD -2U3B]
B747-259B (SF)	N924FT	POLAR AIR CARGO (AERO USA)		21730	372	06/08/79	JT9D-7Q		HK-2300, HK-2980X, EI-CEO, N621FF [LST UPS 02/01/01 FOR 2 YEARS]
B747-245F (SCD)	N638FE	POLAR AIR CARGO (BCCI)		21841	396	09/26/79	JT9D-70A		N704SW, N814FT, G-INTL. [TBR N925FT]
B747-2R7F	N639FE	POLAR AIR CARGO (BCCI) (SCD) (WL)		21650	354	01/31/79	JT9D-70A		LX-DCV, EI-BTQ, N809FT [TBR N926FT]
B747-46NF (SCD)	N450PA	POLAR AIR CARGO (GECA)		30808	1257	10/16/00	CF6-80C2B1F		
B747-46NF (SCD)	N451PA	POLAR AIR CARGO (SILVERMINE)		30809	1259	11/13/00	CF6-80C2B1F		
B747-46NF (SCD)	N452PA	POLAR AIR CARGO (SILVERMINE)		30810	1260	11/16/00	CF6-80C2B1F		

A/C TYPE	CURRENT REG. NO.	LAST KNOWN OPERATOR (OWNER)	STATUS	ORIGINAL MSN	LINE NO.	DEL. DATE	ENG. TYPE	FLEET NO.	PREV. REG. [COMMENTS]
B747-230B (SF)	N742SA	SOUTHERN AIR (FSBU)		22669	549	12/23/81	CF6-50E2		D-ABYW [CVTD -230B (M)]
B747-230B (SF)	N743SA	SOUTHERN AIR (GECA)		22671	574	12/20/82	CF6-50E2		D-ABYY [CVTD -230B (M)]
B747-230B (SF)	N744SA	SOUTHERN AIR (FSBU)		22363	490	11/19/80	CF6-50E2		D-ABYT [CVTD -230B (M)]
B747-238B	N160UA	UNITED AIRLINES (ELEC)		21237	285	06/29/76	JT9D-7J	8260	VH-EBL [STD MZJ 10/31/00]
B747-238B	N161UA	UNITED AIRLINES (POTO)		21352	310	08/15/77	JT9D-7J	8261	N8295V, VH-EBM [LRF 10/26/00; STD MZJ 11/08/0
B747-238B	N163UA	UNITED AIRLINES (SNNL)		21353	316	12/20/77	JT9D-7J	8263	VH-EBN [LRF 11/05/00; STD MZJ]
B747-238B	N164UA	UNITED AIRLINES		21657	339	09/18/78	JT9D-7J	8264	[FERRIED TO MZJ 12/16/00]
B747-238B	N165UA	UNITED AIRLINES		21658	341	10/16/78	JT9D-7J	8265	VH-EBP [STD MZJ 11/02/00]
B747-422	N104UA	UNITED AIRLINES		26902	1141	01/22/98	PW4056	8004	
B747-451	N105UA	UNITED AIRLINES (WFBN)		26473	985	06/17/94	PW4056	8405	N671US, N60659
B747-451	N106UA	UNITED AIRLINES		26474	988	07/25/94	PW4056	8406	N60668
B747-422	N107UA	UNITED AIRLINES		26900	1168	08/20/98	PW4056	8007	
B747-422	N108UA	UNITED AIRLINES		26903	1171	08/28/98	PW4056	8408	
B747-422	N109UA	UNITED AIRLINES		26906	1185	11/16/98	PW4056	8409	
B747-422	N116UA	UNITED AIRLINES		26908	1193	12/29/98	PW4056	8416	
B747-422	N117UA	UNITED AIRLINES		28810	1197	01/29/99	PW4056	8417	
B747-422	N118UA	UNITED AIRLINES		28811	1201	02/24/99	PW4056	8418	
B747-422	N119UA	UNITED AIRLINES		28812	1207	03/29/99	PW4056	8419	
B747-422	N120UA	UNITED AIRLINES		29166	1209	04/12/99	PW4056	8420	
B747-422	N121UA	UNITED AIRLINES		29167	1211	04/22/99	PW4056	8421	
B747-422	N122UA	UNITED AIRLINES		29168	1218	06/14/99	PW4056	8422	
B747-422	N127UA	UNITED AIRLINES		28813	1221	08/02/99	PW4056	8427	
B747-422	N128UA	UNITED AIRLINES		30023	1245	05/12/00	PW4056	8428	
B747-422	N171UA	UNITED AIRLINES (SSBT)		24322	733	06/30/89	PW4056	8671	
B747-422	N172UA	UNITED AIRLINES		24363	740	08/21/89	PW4056	8672	
B747-422	N173UA	UNITED AIRLINES		24380	759	12/08/89	PW4056	8673	
B747-422	N174UA	UNITED AIRLINES		24381	762	01/20/90	PW4056	8674	
B747-422	N175UA	UNITED AIRLINES		24382	806	08/16/90	PW4056	8675	
B747-422	N176UA	UNITED AIRLINES		24383	811	09/19/90	PW4056	8676	
B747-422	N177UA	UNITED AIRLINES		24384	819	11/08/90	PW4056	8477	
B747-422	N178UA	UNITED AIRLINES		24385	820	11/08/90	PW4056	8478	
B747-422	N179UA	UNITED AIRLINES		25158	866	07/31/91	PW4056	8479	
B747-422	N180UA	UNITED AIRLINES		25224	867	07/30/91	PW4056	8480	
B747-422	N181UA	UNITED AIRLINES		25278	881	10/23/91	PW4056	8481	N6005C
B747-422	N182UA	UNITED AIRLINES		25279	882	10/24/91	PW4056	8482	
B747-422	N183UA	UNITED AIRLINES		25379	911	04/20/92	PW4056	8483	
B747-422	N184UA	UNITED AIRLINES		25380	913	05/01/92	PW4056	8484	
B747-422	N185UA	UNITED AIRLINES		25395	919	06/01/92	PW4056	8485	
B747-422	N186UA	UNITED AIRLINES		26875	931	08/24/92	PW4056	8486	
B747-422	N187UA	UNITED AIRLINES		26876	939	09/28/92	PW4056	8487	

A/C TYPE	CURRENT REG. NO.	LAST KNOWN OPERATOR (OWNER)	STATUS	ORIGINAL MSN	LINE NO.	DEL. DATE	ENG. TYPE	FLEET NO.	PREV. REG. [COMMENTS]
B747-422	N188UA	UNITED AIRLINES		26877	944	12/04/92	PW4056	8488	
B747-422	N189UA	UNITED AIRLINES		26878	966	03/23/93	PW4056	8489	
B747-422	N190UA	UNITED AIRLINES		26879	973	04/22/93	PW4056	8490	
B747-422	N191UA	UNITED AIRLINES		26880	984	06/24/93	PW4056	8491	
B747-422	N192UA	UNITED AIRLINES		26881	989	08/02/93	PW4056	8492	
B747-422	N193UA	UNITED AIRLINES		26890	1085	08/07/96	PW4056	8493	
B747-422	N194UA	UNITED AIRLINES		26892	1088	09/19/96	PW4056	8094	
B747-422	N195UA	UNITED AIRLINES		26899	1113	05/23/97	PW4056	8095	
B747-422	N196UA	UNITED AIRLINES		28715	1120	06/30/97	PW4056	8096	
B747-422	N197UA	UNITED AIRLINES		26901	1121	07/21/97	PW4056	8097	
B747-422	N198UA	UNITED AIRLINES		28716	1124	08/20/97	PW4056	8098	
B747-422	N199UA	UNITED AIRLINES		28717	1126	09/16/97	PW4056	8099	
B747-212B (SF)	N520UP	UNITED PARCEL SERVICE		21943	475	10/30/80	JT9D-7Q		RP-C5746, 9V-SQR [CVTD -212B]
B747-212B (SF)	N521UP	UNITED PARCEL SERVICE		21944	510	03/19/81	JT9D-7Q		9V-SQS [CVTD -212B]
B747-212B (SF)	N522UP	UNITED PARCEL SERVICE		21936	401	10/01/79	JT9D-7Q		9V-SQK, VT-ENQ [CVTD -212B]
B747-283B (SF)	N523UP	UNITED PARCEL SERVICE (BBAM)		22381	500	02/17/81	JT9D-7Q		N4501Q, EI-BTS, N155FW [CVTD -283B (M)]
B747-237B (SF)	N524UP	UNITED PARCEL SERVICE (FSBU)		21446	318	02/03/78	JT9D-7J		VT-EFJ, N104TR [CVTD -237B]
B747-212B (SF)	N525UP	UNITED PARCEL SERVICE (FINO)		21939	449	05/29/80	JT9D-7Q		9V-SQN, G-TKYO, N616FF
B747-212B	N526UP	UNITED PARCEL SERVICE (TRIT)		21937	419	02/01/80	JT9D-7Q		9V-SQL, G-VRGN, N618FF
B747-259B (SF)	N527UP	UNITED PARCEL SERVICE (PAC)	L	21730	372	06/08/79	JT9D-7Q		HK-2300, HK-2980X, EI-CEO, N621FF, N924FT
B747-256B (M)	N528UP	UNITED PARCEL SERVICE (TRIT)		24071	699	04/05/88	JT9D-7Q3		N6005C, EC-136, EC-EEK [BEING CVTD TO FRTR BY IAI AT TLV]
B747-123 (SF)	N671UP	UNITED PARCEL SERVICE		20323	115	02/26/71	JT9D-7A		N9671, N802FT [CVTD -123]
B747-123 (SF)	N672UP	UNITED PARCEL SERVICE		20324	119	04/16/71	JT9D-7A		N9672 [CVTD -123]
B747-123 (SF)	N673UP	UNITED PARCEL SERVICE		20325	125	04/20/71	JT9D-7A		N9673 [CVTD -123]
B747-123 (SF)	N674UP	UNITED PARCEL SERVICE		20100	46	06/18/70	JT9D-7A		N9661, N800FT, N903PA [CVTD -123]
B747-123 (SF)	N675UP	UNITED PARCEL SERVICE		20390	136	05/25/71	JT9D-7A		N9675, OD-AGM [CVTD -123]
B747-123 (SF)	N676UP	UNITED PARCEL SERVICE		20101	57	07/16/70	JT9D-7A		N9662, N801FT, N662AA, N9676 [CVTD -123]
B747-123 (SF)	N677UP	UNITED PARCEL SERVICE		20391	143	06/25/71	JT9D-7A		N9676, OD-AGC, N901PA, N820FT, N629FE [CVTD -123]
B747SR-46 (SF)	N680UP	UNITED PARCEL SERVICE		20923	234	03/28/74	JT9D-7A		JA8121 [CVTD -46]
B747-121 (SF)	N681UP	UNITED PARCEL SERVICE		19661	70	08/04/70	JT9D-7A		N771PA, N819FT, N628FE [CVTD -121]
B747-121 (SF)	N682UP	UNITED PARCEL SERVICE		20349	110	04/27/71	JT9D-7A		N654PA, N817FT, N626FE [CVTD -121]
B747-121 (SF)	N683UP	UNITED PARCEL SERVICE		20353	131	06/30/76	JT9D-7A		N658PA, N818FT, N627FE [CVTD -121]
B747-121 (SF)	N691UP	UNITED PARCEL SERVICE (GATX)		19641	7	12/19/69	JT9D-7A		N734PA, N491GX [CVTD -121]

PH-NETHERLANDS

A/C TYPE	CURRENT REG. NO.	LAST KNOWN OPERATOR (OWNER)	STATUS	ORIGINAL MSN	LINE NO.	DEL. DATE	ENG. TYPE	FLEET NO.	PREV. REG. [COMMENTS]
B747-206B (SF) (SUD)	PH-BUH	KLM		21110	271	10/19/75	CF6-50E2		[CVTD -206B (M)]
B747-206B (SF) (SUD)	PH-BUI	KLM		21111	276	12/16/75	CF6-50E2		N8297V [CVTD -206B (M)]

323

A/C TYPE	CURRENT REG. NO.	LAST KNOWN OPERATOR (OWNER)	STATUS	ORIGINAL MSN	LINE NO.	DEL. DATE	ENG. TYPE	FLEET NO.	PREV. REG. [COMMENTS]
B747-206B (M) (SUD)		PH-BUK	KLM (NCLB LEASE)	21549	336	09/01/78	CF6-50E2		[CVTD -206B (M); TO BE RTD 11/00]
B747-206B (M) (SUD)		PH-BUL	KLM	21550	344	11/03/78	CF6-50E2		[CVTD -206B (M); TO BE RTD 12/00]
B747-206B (M) (SUD)		PH-BUM	KLM	21659	369	05/15/79	CF6-50E2		N1792B [CVTD -206B (M)]
B747-206B (M) (SUD)		PH-BUN	KLM (WTCI)	21660	389	08/17/79	CF6-50E2		[CVTD -206B (M)]
B747-206B (SUD)	PH-BUO	KLM (WTCI)		21848	397	09/21/79	CF6-50E2		[CVTD -206B (M)]
B747-206B (SUD)	PH-BUP	KLM (ILFC)		22376	474	09/11/80	CF6-50E2		N1295E [CVTD -206B (M); RT LESSOR; STD MHV 05/01/01]
B747-206B (SUD)	PH-BUR	KLM (SPA INC)		22379	491	12/15/80	CF6-50E2		N1298E [CVTD -206B (M); STD MZJ 05/01/01]
B747-206B (M) (SUD)		PH-BUT	KLM (ILFC)	22380	539	09/29/80	CF6-50E2		N1785B, N1309E [CVTD -206B (M)]
B747-306 (M)	PH-BUU	KLM (ILFC)		23056	587	09/30/83	CF6-50E2		N4548M
B747-306 (M)	PH-BUV	KLM (WTCI)		23137	600	09/13/84	CF6-50E2		N4551N
B747-306 (M)	PH-BUW	KLM (ORIENT)		23508	657	10/03/86	CF6-50E2		N6055X
B747-406	PH-BFA	KLM (CROWN)		23999	725	05/18/89	CF6-80C2B1F		N6018N
B747-406	PH-BFB	KLM (WESTRIBA ONE)		24000	732	06/20/89	CF6-80C2B1F		
B747-406 (M)	PH-BFC	KLM (WESTRIBA TWO)		23982	735	09/01/89	CF6-80C2B1F		N6038E
B747-406 (M)	PH-BFD	KLM (BNE AIRFL.)		24001	737	09/29/89	CF6-80C2B1F		["KLM ASIA"]
B747-406 (M)	PH-BFE	KLM (ORIX)		24201	763	01/24/90	CF6-80C2B1F		N6046P
B747-406 (M)	PH-BFF	KLM (ORIX)		24202	770	02/23/90	CF6-80C2B1F		N6046P
B747-406	PH-BFG	KLM (BARNESBURY)		24517	782	04/11/90	CF6-80C2B1F		
B747-406 (M)	PH-BFH	KLM (WINDMILL)		24518	783	04/26/90	CF6-80C2B1F		N60668 ["KLM ASIA"]
B747-406 (M)	PH-BFI	KLM (WINDMILL)		25086	850	05/05/91	CF6-80C2B1F		
B747-406 (M)	PH-BFK	KLM (LG BEST)		25087	854	05/21/91	CF6-80C2B1F		
B747-406	PH-BFL	KLM		25356	888	12/05/91	CF6-80C2B1F		
B747-406 (M)	PH-BFM	KLM (CIT FSC)		26373	896	02/14/92	CF6-80C2B1F		["KLM ASIA"]
B747-406	PH-BFN	KLM (AMSTELVEEN)		26372	969	04/08/93	CF6-80C2B1F		
B747-406 (M)	PH-BFO	KLM (ROCHESTER)		25413	938	10/08/92	CF6-80C2B1F		
B747-406 (M)	PH-BFP	KLM (NIGHT WATCH)		26374	992	09/01/93	CF6-80C2B1F		["KLM ASIA"]
B747-406 (M)	PH-BFR	KLM (WTCI)		27202	1014	01/14/94	CF6-80C2B1F		
B747-406 (M)	PH-BFS	KLM (WTCI)		28195	1090	10/15/96	CF6-80C2B1F		
B747-406 (M)	PH-BFT	KLM (WTCI)		28459	1112	05/15/97	CF6-80C2B1F		
B747-406 (M)	PH-BFU	KLM		28196	1127	09/08/97	CF6-80C2B1F		
B747-406 (M)	PH-BFV	KLM		28460	1225	08/16/99	CF6-80C2B1F		
B747-406 (M)	PH-BFW	KLM		30454	1258	10/24/00	CF6-80C2B1F		
B747-21AC (M)	PH-MCE	MARTINAIR (MITSUI)		23652	669	02/23/87	CF6-50E2		N6038E
B747-21AC (M)	PH-MCF	MARTINAIR (MEGA CARRIER)		24134	712	09/26/88	CF6-50E2		N6009F
B747-228F (SCD)	PH-MCN	MARTINAIR (STELLAR LSG)		25266	878	10/11/91	CF6-50E2		F-GCBN

A/C TYPE	CURRENT REG. NO.	LAST KNOWN OPERATOR (OWNER)	STATUS	ORIGINAL MSN	LINE NO.	DEL. DATE	ENG. TYPE	FLEET NO.	PREV. REG. [COMMENTS]
PK-INDONESIA									
B747-2U3B	PK-GSA	GARUDA INDONESIA		22246	452	07/02/80	JT9D-7Q		
B747-2U3B	PK-GSB	GARUDA INDONESIA		22247	459	07/03/80	JT9D-7Q		
B747-2U3B	PK-GSC	GARUDA INDONESIA		22248	461	08/11/80	JT9D-7Q		
B747-2U3B	PK-GSD	GARUDA INDONESIA		22249	468	08/26/80	JT9D-7Q		
B747-4U3	PK-GSG	GARUDA INDONESIA		25704	1011	01/14/94	CF6-80C2B1F		
B747-4U3	PK-GSH	GARUDA INDONESIA		25705	1029	05/27/94	CF6-80C2B1F		N6038E
B747-441	PK-GSI	GARUDA INDONESIA (ILFC)		24956	917	06/01/92	CF6-80C2B1F		PP-VPG, N791LF
P4-ARUBA									
B747SP-31	P4-AFE	SHAMROCK AVV (AIR FINANCE)		21962	439	03/21/80	JT9D-7A		N57202, N601AA, UN-001, TF-ABN [STD LUX]
RP-PHILIPPINES									
B747-2F6B	RP-C8820	PHILIPPINE AIRLINES (MAJOR WIN)		21834	425	03/21/80	CF6-50E2		N743PR
B747-211B	RP-C8830	PHILIPPINE AIRLINES (AMBOY LLC)		21517	368	04/25/79	CF6-50E2		C-GXRD, G-NIGB, N208AE
B747-211B	RP-C8850	PHILIPPINE AIRLINES (AMBOY LLC)		21516	326	06/09/78	CF6-50E2		C-GXRA, G-GLYN, N207AE
B747-4F6	N751PR	PHILIPPINE AIRLINES (WTCI)		27261	1005	11/19/93	CF6-80C2B1F		
B747-4F6	N752PR	PHILIPPINE AIRLINES (WTCI)		27262	1012	12/21/93	CF6-80C2B1F		
B747-4F6	N753PR	PHILIPPINE AIRLINES (WTCI)		27828	1039	04/27/95	CF6-80C2B1F		N6038E
B747-469 (M)	N754PR	PHILIPPINE AIRLINES (WTCI)		27663	1068	03/29/96	CF6-80C2B1F		N6009F
SU-EGYPT									
B747-366 (M)	SU-GAL	EGYPT AIR		24161	704	06/22/88	JT9D-7R4G2		N6038E
B747-366 (M)	SU-GAM	EGYPT AIR		24162	707	06/30/88	JT9D-7R4G2		N6018N
SX-GREECE									
B747-284B	SX-OAB	OLYMPIC AIRWAYS		20825	223	12/07/73	JT9D-7J		[STD ATH 06/99]
B747-212B	SX-OAC	OLYMPIC AIRWAYS		21683	387	08/02/79	JT9D-7Q		9V-SQH [STD ATH 02/00]
B747-212B	SX-OAD	OLYMPIC AIRWAYS		21684	391	08/16/79	JT9D-7Q		9V-SQI
B747-212B	SX-OAE	OLYMPIC AIRWAYS		21935	399	09/25/79	JT9D-7Q		9V-SQJ [STD ATH 11/99]
TF-ICELAND									
B747-267B	TF-ABA	AIR ATLANTA ICELAND (CPA)	L	22530	531	06/25/81	RB211-524C2		VR-HID, B-HID [LST VIR 01/15/01]
B747-267B	TF-ABP	AIR ATLANTA ICELAND (CPA)	L	22429	493	12/19/80	RB211-524C4		VR-HIC, B-HIC [OPF GIA FOR HADJ]
B747-246B	TF-ABQ	AIR ATLANTA ICELAND (JUMBO JET)		20529	192	06/29/72	JT9D-7AW		JA8113, N554SW [OPF RKA, RAM, AFR, AOM, TUN, A&K; "ABERCROMBIE & KENT"]
B747-230B	TF-ATA	AIR ATLANTA ICELAND (JUMBO JET)		20527	179	02/25/72	JT9D-7F		D-ABYG, N611BN, G-BJXN, N78019 [STD MZJ]
B747-246B	TF-ATB	AIR ATLANTA ICELAND (JUMBO JET)		19824	122	03/01/71	JT9D-7AW		JA8105, N558SE [LST/OPF DAH]
B747-267B	TF-ATC	AIR ATLANTA ICELAND (CPA)	L	22149	466	07/16/80	RB211-524C2		VR-HIB, B-HIB [OPF SVA FOR HADJ]
B747-267B	TF-ATD	AIR ATLANTA ICELAND (CPA)	L	21966	446	04/24/80	RB211-524C2		VR-HIA, B-HIA
B747-146	TF-ATE	AIR ATLANTA ICELAND (JUMBO JET)		20531	197	10/04/72	JT9D-7A		JA8115, N557SW

A/C TYPE	CURRENT REG. NO.	LAST KNOWN OPERATOR (OWNER)	STATUS	ORIGINAL MSN	LINE NO.	DEL. DATE	ENG. TYPE	FLEET NO.	PREV. REG. [COMMENTS]
B747-246B	TF-ATF	AIR ATLANTA ICELAND (JUMBO JET)		19825	137	05/14/71	JT9D-7AW		JA8106, N556SW [OPF IBE FROM 12/00]
B747-256B (M)	TF-ATL	AIR ATLANTA ICELAND (IBE)	L	22454	509	02/18/81	JT9D-7Q3		EC-DLC [LSF IBE AND WET LEASED BACK TO IBE
B747-256B (M)	TF-ATM	AIR ATLANTA ICELAND (IBE)	L	22455	515	03/24/81	JT9D-7Q3		EC-DLD [LSF IBE AND WET LEASED BACK TO IBE
B747-341	TF-ATH	AIR ATLANTA ICELAND (MSA I)		24106	701	04/30/88	CF6-80C2B1		N6046P, PP-VOA, N830DS [LST IBE 12/00]
B747-341	TF-ATI	AIR ATLANTA ICELAND (ILFC)		24107	702	05/13/88	CF6-80C2B1		N6018N, PP-VOB, N824DS [LST IBE 12/00]
B747-341	TF-ATJ	AIR ATLANTA ICELAND (ILFC)		24108	703	05/27/88	CF6-80C2B1		N6005C, PP-VOC, N420DS [LST IBE 12/00]

TR-GABON

A/C TYPE	CURRENT REG. NO.	LAST KNOWN OPERATOR (OWNER)	STATUS	ORIGINAL MSN	LINE NO.	DEL. DATE	ENG. TYPE	FLEET NO.	PREV. REG. [COMMENTS]
B747-2Q2B (M)	F-ODJG	AIR GABON		21468	324	10/05/78	CF6-50E2		N1248E

VH-AUSTRALIA

A/C TYPE	CURRENT REG. NO.	LAST KNOWN OPERATOR (OWNER)	STATUS	ORIGINAL MSN	LINE NO.	DEL. DATE	ENG. TYPE	FLEET NO.	PREV. REG. [COMMENTS]
B747-412	VH-ANA	ANSETT AUSTRALIA (SIA)	L	24062	722	03/18/89	PW4056		N6005C, 9V-SMB
B747-412	VH-ANB	ANSETT AUSTRALIA (SIA)	L	24064	755	11/01/89	PW4056		9V-SMD
B747-412	9V-SMA	ANSETT AUSTRALIA (SIA)	L	24061	717	03/29/89	PW4056		N5573B
B747SP-27	VH-OZX	GLOBAL AIR AUSTRALIA		22302	473	12/29/82	JT9D-7J		N1301E, B-2454, N142SW
B747SP-38	VH-EAA	QANTAS		22495	505	01/19/81	RB211-524D4		
B747SP-38	VH-EAB	QANTAS		22672	537	08/31/81	RB211-524D4		
B747-238B	VH-EBQ	QANTAS		22145	410	12/11/79	RB211-524D4		DQ-FJI
B747-238B	VH-EBR	QANTAS		22614	464	09/30/80	RB211-524D4		N1728B, N8296V [LST FJI 08/03/96 AS DQ-FJE]
B747-238B	VH-EBS	QANTAS		22616	543	11/30/81	RB211-524D4		N6005C, N1785B, N5700T
B747-238B (M)	VH-ECB	QANTAS		21977	409	11/14/79	RB211-524D4		
B747-238B (M)	VH-ECC	QANTAS		22615	483	10/15/80	RB211-524D4		
B747-338	VH-EBT	QANTAS		23222	602	11/13/84	RB211-524D4		N1784B
B747-338	VH-EBU	QANTAS		23223	606	01/24/85	RB211-524D4		N5573P
B747-338	VH-EBV	QANTAS		23224	610	04/15/85	RB211-524D4		N6005C
B747-338	VH-EBW	QANTAS		23408	638	03/31/86	RB211-524D4		N6055X [DMGD ROM 04/22/00; MAIN LANDING GEAR COLLAPSE ON TAXIWAY]
B747-338	VH-EBX	QANTAS		23688	662	11/12/86	RB211-524D4		N6005C
B747-338	VH-EBY	QANTAS		23823	678	05/01/89	RB211-524D4		N6005C
B747-436	VH-NLH	QANTAS (BAW)	L	24050	779	03/28/90	RB211-524H2		G-BNLH
B747-48E	VH-OEB	QANTAS		25778	983	06/24/93	CF6-80C2B1F		HL7416
B747-4H6	VH-OEC	QANTAS		24836	808	09/27/90	CF6-80C2B1F		N6009F, 9M-MHN
B747-4H6	VH-OED	QANTAS		25126	858	06/10/91	CF6-80C2B1F		9M-MHO
B747-438	VH-OJA	QANTAS		24354	731	08/11/89	RB211-524G		N6046P
B747-438	VH-OJB	QANTAS		24373	746	09/15/89	RB211-524G		
B747-438	VH-OJC	QANTAS		24406	751	10/09/89	RB211-524G		
B747-438	VH-OJD	QANTAS		24481	764	01/16/90	RB211-524G		
B747-438	VH-OJE	QANTAS		24482	765	01/26/90	RB211-524G		
B747-438	VH-OJF	QANTAS		24483	781	04/06/90	RB211-524G		

A/C TYPE	CURRENT REG. NO.	LAST KNOWN OPERATOR (OWNER)	STATUS	ORIGINAL MSN	LINE NO.	DEL. DATE	ENG. TYPE	FLEET NO.	PREV. REG. [COMMENTS]
B747-438	VH-OJG	QANTAS		24779	801	08/15/90	RB211-524G		N6009F
B747-438	VH-OJH	QANTAS		24806	807	08/30/90	RB211-524G		
B747-438	VH-OJI	QANTAS		24887	826	12/21/90	RB211-524G		N6009F
B747-438	VH-OJJ	QANTAS		24974	835	02/19/91	RB211-524G		
B747-438	VH-OJK	QANTAS		25067	857	06/17/91	RB211-524G		
B747-438	VH-OJL	QANTAS		25151	865	07/23/91	RB211-524G		
B747-438	VH-OJM	QANTAS		25245	875	09/17/91	RB211-524G		
B747-438	VH-OJN	QANTAS		25315	883	11/07/91	RB211-524G		N6009F
B747-438	VH-OJO	QANTAS		25544	894	05/21/92	RB211-524G		N6055X, N6005C
B747-438	VH-OJP	QANTAS		25545	916	06/26/92	RB211-524G		
B747-438	VH-OJQ	QANTAS		25546	924	09/18/92	RB211-524G		N6005C
B747-438	VH-OJR	QANTAS		25547	936	10/15/92	RB211-524G		N6018N
B747-438	VH-OJS	QANTAS		25564	1230	09/30/99	RB211-524G/H-T		
B747-438	VH-OJT	QANTAS		25565	1233	10/26/99	RB211-524G/H-T		
B747-438	VH-OJU	QANTAS		25566	1239	01/24/00	RB211-524G/H-T		

VP-B-BERMUDA

A/C TYPE	CURRENT REG. NO.	LAST KNOWN OPERATOR (OWNER)	STATUS	ORIGINAL MSN	LINE NO.	DEL. DATE	ENG. TYPE	FLEET NO.	PREV. REG. [COMMENTS]
B747SP-21	VP-BAT	WORLDWIDE AIRCRAFT HOLDING CO.		21648	367	04/20/79	JT9D-7A		N539PA, N148UA, VR-BAT [PARKED BOH]

VT-INDIA

A/C TYPE	CURRENT REG. NO.	LAST KNOWN OPERATOR (OWNER)	STATUS	ORIGINAL MSN	LINE NO.	DEL. DATE	ENG. TYPE	FLEET NO.	PREV. REG. [COMMENTS]
B747-237B	VT-EDU	AIR-INDIA		21182	277	12/23/75	JT9D-7J		[ST MON AVIATION]
B747-237B	VT-EFU	AIR-INDIA		21829	390	08/14/79	JT9D-7Q		
B747-237B	VT-EGA	AIR-INDIA		21993	414	12/21/79	JT9D-7Q		
B747-237B	VT-EGB	AIR-INDIA		21994	431	02/20/80	JT9D-7Q		
B747-237B	VT-EGC	AIR-INDIA		21995	434	04/04/80	JT9D-7Q		
B747-337 (M)	VT-EPW	AIR-INDIA		24159	711	10/21/88	CF6-80C2B1		N6018N
B747-337 (M)	VT-EPX	AIR-INDIA (LINDEN CITY A/C)		24160	719	11/22/88	CF6-80C2B1		N6046P
B747-437	VT-ESM	AIR-INDIA		27078	987	08/04/93	PW4056		
B747-437	VT-ESN	AIR-INDIA		27164	1003	11/12/93	PW4056		
B747-437	VT-ESO	AIR-INDIA		27165	1009	12/10/93	PW4056		
B747-437	VT-ESP	AIR-INDIA		27214	1034	06/28/94	PW4056		
B747-437	VT-EVA	AIR-INDIA (VEENA)		28094	1089	10/31/96	PW4056		
B747-437	VT-EVB	AIR-INDIA (VEENA)		28095	1093	11/15/96	PW4056		

V5-NAMIBIA

A/C TYPE	CURRENT REG. NO.	LAST KNOWN OPERATOR (OWNER)	STATUS	ORIGINAL MSN	LINE NO.	DEL. DATE	ENG. TYPE	FLEET NO.	PREV. REG. [COMMENTS]
B747-48E (M)	V5-NMA	AIR NAMIBIA		28551	1131	10/21/99	CF6-80C2B1F		N6055X

	A/C TYPE	CURRENT REG. NO.	LAST KNOWN OPERATOR (OWNER)	STATUS	ORIGINAL MSN	LINE NO.	DEL. DATE	ENG. TYPE	FLEET NO.	PREV. REG. [COMMENTS]
V8-BRUNEI										
	B747-430	V8-ALI	SULTAN'S FLIGHT-BRUNEI		26426	910	04/17/92	CF6-80C2B1F		N6009F, D-ABVM [REGISTRATION IS V8-ALI, NOT -AL1]
XA-MEXICO										
	B747-2D7B (SF)	N524MC	MAS AIR CARGO (GTA)	L	21784	424	02/23/80	CF6-50E2		HS-TGC [CVTD -2D7B]
YI-IRAQ										
	B747SP-70	YI-ALM	IRAQI AIRWAYS		22858	567	08/30/82	JT9D-7FW		[GROUNDED; STD TOE]
	B747SP-09	3D-GFD	IRAQI AIRWAYS		22298	445	04/30/80	JT9D-7A		B-1880, B-18253, P4-GFD, 5Y-GFD, 3C-GFD [DONATED FROM GLN]
	B747-270C (M)	YI-AGN	IRAQI AIRWAYS		21180	287	06/24/76	JT9D-7FW		[GROUNDED]
	B747-270C (M)	YI-AGO	IRAQI AIRWAYS		21181	289	08/15/76	JT9D-7FW		[GROUNDED; STD THR]
	B747-270C (M)	YI-AGP	IRAQI AIRWAYS		22366	565	07/15/82	JT9D-7FW		[GROUNDED; STD TOE]
YK-SYRIA										
	B747SP-94	YK-AHA	SYRIANAIR		21174	284	05/21/76	JT9D-7A		
	B747SP-94	YK-AHB	SYRIANAIR		21175	290	07/16/76	JT9D-7A		
ZK-NEW ZEALAND										
	B747-419	ZK-NBS	AIR NEW ZEALAND		24386	756	12/14/89	RB211-524G		
	B747-419	ZK-NBT	AIR NEW ZEALAND		24855	815	10/31/90	RB211-524G		N6018N
	B747-419	ZK-NBU	AIR NEW ZEALAND		25605	933	09/15/92	RB211-524G		
	B747-419	ZK-NBV	AIR NEW ZEALAND		26910	1180	10/31/98	CF6-80C2B1F		
	B747-419	ZK-NBW	AIR NEW ZEALAND (ILFC)		29375	1228	09/08/99	CF6-80C2B1F		
	B747-475	ZK-SUH	AIR NEW ZEALAND (ILFC)		24896	855	05/31/91	CF6-80C2B1F		N6009F, PP-VPI, N891LF
	B747-441	ZK-SUI	AIR NEW ZEALAND (ILFC)		24957	971	04/20/93	CF6-80C2B1F		PP-VPH, N821LF
	B747-4F6	ZK-SUJ	AIR NEW ZEALAND (ILFC)		27602	1161	06/29/98	CF6-80C2B1F		N1788B, N756PR
ZS-SOUTH AFRICA										
	B747-258C	ZS-OOS	HYDRO AIR CARGO		21190	272	12/31/75	JT9D-7J		4X-AXD
	B747SP-44	ZS-SPA	SOUTH AFRICAN AIRWAYS		21132	280	03/19/76	JT9D-7FW		3B-NAJ
	B747SP-44	ZS-SPC	SOUTH AFRICAN AIRWAYS		21134	288	06/16/76	JT9D-7FW		N8297V, 3B-NAG
	B747SP-44	ZS-SPE	SOUTH AFRICAN AIRWAYS		21254	298	11/22/76	JT9D-7FW		3B-NAR, V5-SPE
	B747-244B	ZS-SAL	SOUTH AFRICAN AIRWAYS		20237	154	01/26/72	JT9D-7R4G2		N1795B
	B747-244B	ZS-SAM	SOUTH AFRICAN AIRWAYS		20238	158	12/13/71	JT9D-7R4G2		PP-VNW
	B747-244B	ZS-SAN	SOUTH AFRICAN AIRWAYS		20239	160	10/22/71	JT9D-7R4G2		
	B747-244B	ZS-SAO	SOUTH AFRICAN AIRWAYS		20556	194	08/07/72	JT9D-7R4G2		
	B747-244B	ZS-SAP	SOUTH AFRICAN AIRWAYS		20557	198	09/29/72	JT9D-7R4G2		
	B747-312	ZS-SAC	SOUTH AFRICAN AIRWAYS		23031	598	06/28/84	JT9D-7R4G2		N120KF

A/C TYPE	CURRENT REG. NO.	LAST KNOWN OPERATOR (OWNER)	STATUS	ORIGINAL MSN	LINE NO.	DEL. DATE	ENG. TYPE	FLEET NO.	PREV. REG. [COMMENTS]
B747-312	ZS-SAJ	SOUTH AFRICAN AIRWAYS		23027	583	06/21/83	JT9D-7R4G2		N116KB
B747-344	ZS-SAT	SOUTH AFRICAN AIRWAYS		22970	577	05/02/83	JT9D-7R4G2		N8279V
B747-344	ZS-SAU	SOUTH AFRICAN AIRWAYS		22971	578	04/14/83	JT9D-7R4G2		N8296V [OPF NGA]
B747-357	ZS-SKA	SOUTH AFRICAN AIRWAYS (GATX)		22996	586	11/30/83	JT9D-7R4G2		N221GF, HB-IGF
B747-357	ZS-SKB	SOUTH AFRICAN AIRWAYS (GATX)		22995	585	12/16/83	JT9D-7R4G2		N221GE, HB-IGE
B747-444	ZS-SAK	SOUTH AFRICAN AIRWAYS		28468	1162	06/30/98	RB211-524G/H-T		N60697
B747-444	ZS-SAV	SOUTH AFRICAN AIRWAYS		24976	827	01/19/91	RB211-524H		N6009F
B747-444	ZS-SAW	SOUTH AFRICAN AIRWAYS		25152	861	06/28/91	RB211-524H		N60668
B747-444	ZS-SAX	SOUTH AFRICAN AIRWAYS		26637	943	10/27/92	RB211-524H		
B747-444	ZS-SAY	SOUTH AFRICAN AIRWAYS		26638	995	10/05/93	RB211-524H		
B747-444	ZS-SAZ	SOUTH AFRICAN AIRWAYS		29119	1187	11/30/98	RB211-524G/H-T		
B747-4F6	ZS-SBK	SOUTH AFRICAN AIRWAYS		28959	1158	12/30/98	CF6-80C2B1F		N1785B, N755PR
B747-4F6	ZS-SBS	SOUTH AFRICAN AIRWAYS		28960	1167	12/30/98	CF6-80C2B1F		N60668, N757PR

3D-SWAZILAND

A/C TYPE	CURRENT REG. NO.	LAST KNOWN OPERATOR (OWNER)	STATUS	ORIGINAL MSN	LINE NO.	DEL. DATE	ENG. TYPE	FLEET NO.	PREV. REG. [COMMENTS]
B747SP-09	5Y-GFC	GULF FALCON		21300	304	04/06/77	JT9D-7A		B-1862, B-18252, P4-GFC, 3C-GFC
B747-136	3C-GFB	GULF FALCON		20953	248	03/14/75	JT9D-7A		G-BBPU, P4-GFB [WFU SHARJAH; "SPIRIT OF AFRICA"]
B747-230F	N79713	GULF FALCON		20373	168	03/09/72	JT9D-7A		N1794B, D-ABYE, HL7441 [STD MZJ]
B747-273C	N79712	GULF FALCON		20652	211	05/25/73	JT9D-7A		N748WA, HL7471 [STD MZJ; OO FOR 11/00]
B747-246B	ST-AQL	GULF FALCON		20504	181	03/13/72	JT9D-7AW		JA8110, P4-GFE, 3C-GFE, 5Y-GFE ["SPIRIT OF AFRICA"]
B747-246B	ST-AQN	GULF FALCON		20333	166	11/30/71	JT9D-7AW		JA8108, N559SW, P4-GFF, 3D-GFF, 3D-GFB ["SPIRIT OF AFRICA"]

4X-ISRAEL

A/C TYPE	CURRENT REG. NO.	LAST KNOWN OPERATOR (OWNER)	STATUS	ORIGINAL MSN	LINE NO.	DEL. DATE	ENG. TYPE	FLEET NO.	PREV. REG. [COMMENTS]
B747-271C (SCD)	4X-ICL	CARGO AIR LINES		21964	416	12/21/79	CF6-50E2		N741TV, LX-ACV, N538MC
B747-271C (SCD)	4X-ICM	CARGO AIR LINES		21965	438	03/26/80	CF6-50E2		N742TV, LX-ECV, N539MC
B747-258B	4X-AXC	EL AL ISRAELI AIRLINES		20704	212	04/18/73	JT9D-7J	403	N1799B [TO BE WFU AND BU]
B747-258C	4X-AXF	EL AL ISRAELI AIRLINES		21594	327	06/16/78	JT9D-7J	405	
B747-258B (M)	4X-AXH	EL AL ISRAELI AIRLINES		22254	418	12/21/79	JT9D-7J	407	
B747-245F (SCD)	4X-AXK	EL AL ISRAELI AIRLINES		22151	478	10/14/80	JT9D-7Q	410	N816FT, N635FE, 9V-SQU
B747-245F (SCD)	4X-AXL	EL AL ISRAELI AIRLINES		22150	476	10/03/80	JT9D-7Q	411	N815FT, N634FE, 9V-SQT ["CARGO" TITLES]
B747-238B	4X-AXQ	EL AL ISRAELI AIRLINES		20841	233	03/19/74	JT9D-7J	408	VH-EBG
B747-458	4X-ELA	EL AL ISRAELI AIRLINES		26055	1027	04/27/94	PW4056	201	
B747-458	4X-ELB	EL AL ISRAELI AIRLINES		26056	1032	05/27/94	PW4056	202	N60697
B747-458	4X-ELC	EL AL ISRAELI AIRLINES		27915	1062	05/31/95	PW4056	203	N6009F
B747-458	4X-ELD	EL AL ISRAELI AIRLINES		29328	1215	05/24/99	PW4056	204	

	A/C TYPE	CURRENT REG. NO.	LAST KNOWN OPERATOR (OWNER)	STATUS	ORIGINAL MSN	LINE NO.	DEL. DATE	ENG. TYPE	FLEET NO.	PREV. REG. [COMMENTS]
5N-NIGERIA										
	B747-148	5N-AAA	KABO AIR		19745	108	03/18/71	JT9D-7A		HS-VGF, G-BDPZ, EI-ASJ, TF-ABN
	B747-136	5N-JJJ	KABO AIR		19766	111	03/14/71	JT9D-7A		G-AWNF
	B747-136	5N-OOO	KABO AIR		20952	246	11/06/74	JT9D-7A		G-AWNP
	B747-136	5N-RRR	KABO AIR		19765	109	03/05/71	JT9D-7A		G-AWNE
	B747-148	5N-ZZZ	KABO AIR		19744	84	12/15/70	JT9D-3A		HS-VGB, EI-ASI [STD ROW]
	B747-344	ZS-SAU	NIGERIA AIRWAYS (SAA)	L	22971	578	04/14/83	JT9D-7R4G2		N8296V [OPB SAA]
5R-MADAGASCAR										
	B747-2B2B (M)	5R-MFT	AIR MADAGASCAR		21614	353	01/26/79	JT9D-70A		[RTD-STD CHR; FOR SALE]
5Y-KENYA										
	B747-212B (SF)	N485EV	FAST AIRWAYS (EIA)	L	20712	218	07/31/73	JT9D-7J		9V-SIA, N747TA, N747FT, N728PA
70-YEMEN										
	B747SP-27	70-YMN	PEOPLE'S REPUBLIC OF YEMEN		21786	413	04/23/80	JT9D-7J		N604BN, LV-OHV, 3B-NAQ, A7-ABM, A7-AHM [VIP CFG]
9G-GHANA										
	B747-246F (SCD)	9G-MKI	MK AIRLINES (FINO)		22063	432	03/17/80	JT9D-7Q		JA8144, N741SJ
	B747-244B (SF)	9G-MKJ	MK AIRLINES (FINO)		22170	486	11/06/80	JT9D-7Q		3B-NAS, ZS-SAR [CVTD -244B (M)]
	B747-212B (SF)	9G-MKL	MK AIRLINES		20888	240	07/29/74	JT9D-7J		9V-SQC, N749TA, N749FT, N730PA, N202PH, N745SJ
9K-KUWAIT										
	B747-269B (M)	9K-ADB	KUWAIT AIRWAYS		21542	335	08/17/78	JT9D-7J		[STD KWI; FOR SALE]
	B747-269B (M)	9K-ADD	KUWAIT AIRWAYS		22740	553	01/20/82	JT9D-7J		[LST GIA FOR HADJ]
	B747-469 (M)	9K-ADE	KUWAIT AIRWAYS		27338	1046	11/29/94	CF6-80C2B1F		[OPF GOVT]
9M-MALAYSIA										
	B747-236B (SF)	9M-MHI	MALAYSIA AIRLINES		22304	502	03/14/82	RB211-524D4		[MASKARGO DIVISION]
	B747-236B (SF)	9M-MHJ	MALAYSIA AIRLINES		22442	526	04/08/82	RB211-524D4		[MASKARGO DIVISION]
	B747-3H6 (SF)	9M-MHK	MALAYSIA AIRLINES		23600	650	07/17/86	JT9D-7R4G2		[CVTD -3H6 (M)]
	B747-4H6 (M)	9M-MHL	MALAYSIA AIRLINES		24315	738	11/17/89	CF6-80C2B1F		
	B747-4H6 (M)	9M-MHM	MALAYSIA AIRLINES		24405	745	10/06/89	CF6-80C2B1F		
	B747-4H6	9M-MPA	MALAYSIA AIRLINES		27042	932	08/27/92	PW4056		
	B747-4H6	9M-MPB	MALAYSIA AIRLINES		25699	965	04/01/93	PW4056		
	B747-4H6	9M-MPC	MALAYSIA AIRLINES		25700	974	05/10/93	PW4056		
	B747-4H6	9M-MPD	MALAYSIA AIRLINES		25701	997	10/05/93	PW4056		
	B747-4H6	9M-MPE	MALAYSIA AIRLINES		25702	999	11/09/93	PW4056		

A/C TYPE	CURRENT REG. NO.	LAST KNOWN OPERATOR (OWNER)	STATUS	ORIGINAL MSN	LINE NO.	DEL. DATE	ENG. TYPE	FLEET NO.	PREV. REG. [COMMENTS]
B747-4H6	9M-MPF	MALAYSIA AIRLINES		27043	1017	01/31/94	PW4056		
B747-4H6	9M-MPG	MALAYSIA AIRLINES		25703	1025	03/30/94	PW4056		
B747-4H6	9M-MPH	MALAYSIA AIRLINES		27044	1041	09/22/94	PW4056		N60668
B747-4H6	9M-MPI	MALAYSIA AIRLINES		27672	1091	10/25/96	PW4056		
B747-4H6	9M-MPJ	MALAYSIA AIRLINES		28426	1130	10/14/97	PW4056		
B747-4H6	9M-MPK	MALAYSIA AIRLINES (GECA)		28427	1147	03/20/98	PW4056		
B747-4H6	9M-MPL	MALAYSIA AIRLINES		28428	1150	03/30/98	PW4056		
B747-4H6	9M-MPM	MALAYSIA AIRLINES		28435	1152	04/14/98	PW4056		
B747-4H6	9M-MPN	MALAYSIA AIRLINES		28432	1247	05/31/00	PW4056		

9V-SINGAPORE

A/C TYPE	CURRENT REG. NO.	LAST KNOWN OPERATOR (OWNER)	STATUS	ORIGINAL MSN	LINE NO.	DEL. DATE	ENG. TYPE	FLEET NO.	PREV. REG. [COMMENTS]
B747-312	9V-SKJ	SINGAPORE AIRLINES		23243	612	04/30/85	JT9D-7R4G2		N123KJ [STD SIN 02/21/99]
B747-412F (SCD)	9V-SFA	SINGAPORE AIRLINES		26563	1036	08/05/94	PW4056		
B747-412F (SCD)	9V-SFB	SINGAPORE AIRLINES		26561	1042	09/29/94	PW4056		
B747-412F (SCD)	9V-SFC	SINGAPORE AIRLINES		26560	1052	02/14/95	PW4056		
B747-412F (SCD)	9V-SFD	SINGAPORE AIRLINES		26553	1069	08/29/95	PW4056		
B747-412F (SCD)	9V-SFE	SINGAPORE AIRLINES		28263	1094	11/26/96	PW4056		
B747-412F (SCD)	9V-SFF	SINGAPORE AIRLINES		28026	1105	03/13/97	PW4056		
B747-412F (SCD)	9V-SFG	SINGAPORE AIRLINES		26558	1173	09/03/98	PW4056		
B747-412F (SCD)	9V-SFH	SINGAPORE AIRLINES		28032	1224	08/05/99	PW4056		
B747-412F (SCD)	9V-SFI	SINGAPORE AIRLINES		28027	1256	09/28/00	PW4056		
B747-412	9V-SMA	SINGAPORE AIRLINES		24061	717	03/29/89	PW4056		N5573B [LST AAA]
B747-412	9V-SMB	SINGAPORE AIRLINES		24062	722	03/18/89	PW4056		N6005C [LST AAA AS VH-ANA 08/99]
B747-412	9V-SMC	SINGAPORE AIRLINES		24063	736	07/11/89	PW4056		3B-SMC
B747-412	9V-SMD	SINGAPORE AIRLINES		24064	755	11/01/89	PW4056		[LST AAA AS VH-ANB 09/99]
B747-412	9V-SME	SINGAPORE AIRLINES		24065	761	12/13/89	PW4056		
B747-412	9V-SMF	SINGAPORE AIRLINES		24066	791	06/19/90	PW4056		N60668
B747-412	9V-SMG	SINGAPORE AIRLINES		24226	809	09/27/90	PW4056		N6005C
B747-412	9V-SMH	SINGAPORE AIRLINES		24227	831	01/24/91	PW4056		N6009F
B747-412	9V-SMI	SINGAPORE AIRLINES		24975	838	02/25/91	PW4056		
B747-412	9V-SMJ	SINGAPORE AIRLINES		25068	852	05/21/91	PW4056		N6005C
B747-412	9V-SMK	SINGAPORE AIRLINES		25127	859	06/25/91	PW4056		
B747-412	9V-SML	SINGAPORE AIRLINES		25128	860	06/20/91	PW4056		
B747-412	9V-SMM	SINGAPORE AIRLINES		26547	921	06/11/92	PW4056		N6038E
B747-412	9V-SMN	SINGAPORE AIRLINES		26548	923	06/16/92	PW4056		
B747-412	9V-SMO	SINGAPORE AIRLINES		27066	940	10/13/92	PW4056		
B747-412	9V-SMP	SINGAPORE AIRLINES		27067	953	12/22/92	PW4056		
B747-412	9V-SMQ	SINGAPORE AIRLINES		27132	955	01/30/93	PW4056		
B747-412	9V-SMR	SINGAPORE AIRLINES		27133	962	02/26/93	PW4056		
B747-412	9V-SMS	SINGAPORE AIRLINES		27134	981	06/20/93	PW4056		
B747-412	9V-SMT	SINGAPORE AIRLINES		27137	990	08/19/93	PW4056		N60697

A/C TYPE	CURRENT REG. NO.	LAST KNOWN OPERATOR (OWNER)	STATUS	ORIGINAL MSN	LINE NO.	DEL. DATE	ENG. TYPE	FLEET NO.	PREV. REG. [COMMENTS]
B747-412	9V-SMU	SINGAPORE AIRLINES		27068	1000	10/13/93	PW4056		
B747-412	9V-SMV	SINGAPORE AIRLINES		27069	1010	12/22/93	PW4056		
B747-412	9V-SMW	SINGAPORE AIRLINES		27178	1015	01/28/94	PW4056		N6018N
B747-412	9V-SMY	SINGAPORE AIRLINES		27217	1023	03/17/94	PW4056		
B747-412	9V-SMZ	SINGAPORE AIRLINES		26549	1030	05/27/94	PW4056		N6018N
B747-412	9V-SPA	SINGAPORE AIRLINES		26550	1040	09/21/94	PW4056		
B747-412	9V-SPB	SINGAPORE AIRLINES		26551	1045	10/28/94	PW4056		
B747-412	9V-SPC	SINGAPORE AIRLINES		27070	1049	12/16/94	PW4056		
B747-412	9V-SPD	SINGAPORE AIRLINES		26552	1056	03/30/95	PW4056		N6009F
B747-412	9V-SPE	SINGAPORE AIRLINES		26554	1070	10/13/95	PW4056		
B747-412	9V-SPF	SINGAPORE AIRLINES		27071	1072	12/04/95	PW4056		
B747-412	9V-SPG	SINGAPORE AIRLINES		26562	1074	02/15/96	PW4056		
B747-412	9V-SPH	SINGAPORE AIRLINES		26555	1075	03/07/96	PW4056		
B747-412	9V-SPI	SINGAPORE AIRLINES		28022	1082	06/20/96	PW4056		
B747-412	9V-SPJ	SINGAPORE AIRLINES		26556	1084	07/17/96	PW4056		
B747-412	9V-SPL	SINGAPORE AIRLINES		26557	1101	01/30/97	PW4056		
B747-412	9V-SPM	SINGAPORE AIRLINES		29950	1241	03/30/00	PW4056		
B747-412	9V-SPN	SINGAPORE AIRLINES		28031	1266	02/08/01	PW4056		
B747-412	9V-SPO	SINGAPORE AIRLINES		28028	1270	03/29/01	PW4056		

MILITARY

A/C TYPE	CURRENT REG. NO.	LAST KNOWN OPERATOR (OWNER)	STATUS	ORIGINAL MSN	LINE NO.	DEL. DATE	ENG. TYPE	FLEET NO.	PREV. REG. [COMMENTS]
E-4B (B747-200B)	73-1676	USAF	M	20682	202	07/16/73	CF6-50E2		[COMMAND POST; CVTD FROM E-4A 1984]
E-4B (B747-200B)	73-1677	USAF	M	20683	204	10/03/73	CF6-50E2		[COMMAND POST; CVTD FROM E-4A 1984]
E-4B (B747-200B)	74-0787	USAF	M	20684	232	10/15/74	CF6-50E2		[COMMAND POST; CVTD FROM E-4A 1984]
E-4B (B747-200B)	75-0125	USAF	M	20949	257	08/04/75	CF6-50E2		[COMMAND POST]
VC-25A (B747-2G4B)	82-8000	USAF	M	23824	679	08/23/90	CF6-80C2B1		N1788B, N6005C [PRESIDENTIAL AIRCRAFT]
VC-25A (B747-2G4B)	92-9000	USAF	M	23825	685	12/20/90	CF6-80C2B1		N60659 [PRESIDENTIAL AIRCRAFT]
B747-47C	20-1101	JAPAN AIR SELF-DEFENCE FORCE	M	24730	816	09/17/91	CF6-80C2B1F		N6055X, JA8091
B747-47C	20-1102	JAPAN AIR SELF-DEFENCE FORCE	M	24731	839	11/18/91	CF6-80C2B1F		N6038E, JA8092
YAL-1A (B747-4G4F)	00-0001	USAF	M	30201	1238	01/21/00	CF6-80C2B1F		[DELIVERED AS B747-4G4F; BEING CVTD TO YAL-1A BY USAF]

OUT OF SERVICE

A/C TYPE	CURRENT REG. NO.	LAST KNOWN OPERATOR (OWNER)	STATUS	ORIGINAL MSN	LINE NO.	DEL. DATE	ENG. TYPE	FLEET NO.	PREV. REG. [COMMENTS]
B747-121 (F) (SCD)	N615FF	KALITTA AIR	O	19638	3	07/13/70	JT9D-7A		N732PA, N475EV [STD OSC; PURCHASED FOR PARTS]
B747-121A	5N-THG	TRANS-AIR SERVICES (ALG)	O	19640	6	12/12/69	JT9D-7A		N733PA
B747-121 (F) (SCD)	N613FF	TOWER AIR	O	19647	16	02/24/70	JT9D-7A		N740PA, N493GX [RTD FOR PARTS; STD JFK]
B747-121 (SF)	N617FF	(FINO)	O	19650	24	03/28/70	JT9D-7A		N743PA, N490GX [CVTD -121; STD MZJ 10/25/00]
B747-121	F-GIMJ	CORSAIR	O	19658	47	05/26/70	JT9D-7A		N754PA, LX-FCV [ST AGES 07/31/95; TO BE BU]

A/C TYPE	CURRENT REG. NO.	LAST KNOWN OPERATOR (OWNER)	STATUS	ORIGINAL MSN	LINE NO.	DEL. DATE	ENG. TYPE	FLEET NO.	PREV. REG. [COMMENTS]
B747-121	N604FF	TOWER AIR	O	19659	49	05/31/70	JT9D-7A		N755PA [PERMANENTLY WFU; SPARES USE JFK]
B747-131F (SCD)	EP-NHV	IRAN GOVERNMENT/IRIAF	O	19667	5	08/18/70	JT9D-7A		N93101, 5-280, 5-8101, EP-NHJ
B747-131F (SCD)	EP-NHD	IRAN GOVERNMENT/IRIAF	O	19668	8	12/31/69	JT9D-7A		N93102, 5-285, 5-8106
B747-131F (SCD)	EP-NHK	IRAN GOVERNMENT/IRIAF	O	19669	9	12/31/69	JT9D-7A		N93103, 5-287, 5-8108
B747-131	N608FF	TOWER AIR	O	19672	28	04/03/70	JT9D-7A		N93106 [STD VCV]
B747-131	N93107	TRANS WORLD AIRLINES	O	19673	35	04/29/70	JT9D-7A		[RTD MZJ; ST BPI AEROSPACE 03/00 FOR PARTS]
B747-131	N93108	TRANS WORLD AIRLINES	O	19674	38	05/07/70	JT9D-7A		[LRF 02/20/98; WFU MZJ 11/04/98; ST BPI AEROSPACE 03/00 FOR PARTS]
B747-131F (SCD)	EP-NHT	IRAN GOVERNMENT/IRIAF	O	19678	78	10/04/70	JT9D-7A		N53112, 5-281, 5-8102
B747-146 (SF)	N701CK	KITTY HAWK INTL.	O	19725	31	04/22/70	JT9D-7A		JA8101 [STD OSC]
B747-146	5N-EDO	OKADA AIR	O	19726	51	05/28/70	JT9D-7A		JA8102 [DERELICT AT LOS]
B747-146	N703CK	KITTY HAWK INTL.	O	19727	54	06/27/70	JT9D-7A		JA8103 [FOR SALE/SCRAP]
B747-124	N602FF	(TRANSCONTINENTAL ASSET MGMT)	O	19734	58	07/13/70	JT9D-7A		N26862, N747AV, HK-2000, N747BA
B747-130	N603FF	(TRANSCONTINENTAL ASSET MGMT)	O	19746	12	03/10/70	JT9D-7A		N1800B, D-ABYA, N610BN, N480GX, N780T
B747-136	G-AWNB	BRITISH AIRWAYS	O	19762	41	05/22/70	JT9D-7A		[ST AAR A/C LSG; TO ROW 09/28/98]
B747-136	3D-GFA	GULF FALCON	O	19763	48	06/29/70	JT9D-7A		G-AWNC, P4-GFA [FERRIED TO MZJ FOR SCRAPPING]
B747-151	N601US	NORTHWEST AIRLINES	O	19778	27	04/30/70	JT9D-7A		[LRF 09/25/00; FERRIED TO MXE; FOR SMITHSONIAN MUSEUM; NOSE SECTION PRESERVATION]
B747-151	N608US	NORTHWEST AIRLINES	O	19785	75	09/17/70	JT9D-7A		[AIRFRAME DONATED TO WESTERN MICHIGAN UNIVERSITY 02/04/00]
B747-246B	N570SW	JAPAN AIRLINES (JUMBO JET)	O	19823	116	02/11/71	JT9D-7AW		JA8104 [LRF 08/17/00; ST JUMBO JET LSG; STD MZJ 09/06/00]
B747-122	C5-FBS	AIR DABIA	O	19875	89	11/03/70	JT9D-7A		N4713U, N4724U [STD PLATTSBURG, NY; REPOSSESSED?]
B747-238B	N307TW	(FSBU)	O	20009	147	07/30/71	JT9D-7F		4R-ULF, VH-EBA, N614AR, LV-WYT [STD MZJ]
B747-238 (SF)	N706CK	KITTY HAWK INTL.	O	20010	149	08/14/71	JT9D-7F		4R-ULG, VH-EBB [ST STEWART INDUSTRIES; STD OSC; TO BE BU]
B747-238B	N608PE	CONTINENTAL AIRLINES	O	20012	171	12/08/71	JT9D-7F		VH-EBD, N747BN [RT LESSOR 10/05/91]
B747-131 (F) (SCD)	EP-SHC	SAHA AIRLINES	O	20080	80	10/22/70	JT9D-7A		N93113, 5-282, 5-8103, EP-NHS
B747-131F (SCD)	EP-NHP	IRAN GOVERNMENT/IRIAF	O	20082	151	09/02/71	JT9D-7A		N93118, 5-286, 5-8107
B747-123	N154UA	THE BOEING COMPANY (FSBU)	O	20103	65	08/27/70	JT9D-7A		N9664, LX-NCV [FERRIED TO GWO; TO BE BU]
B747-123	N156UA	UNITED AIRLINES	O	20105	77	10/02/70	JT9D-7A		N9666, N14936, LX-LCV [LRF 12/15/00; FERRIED TO MZJ; TO BE BU]
B747-123	N157UA	UNITED AIRLINES	O	20106	79	10/08/70	JT9D-7A		N9667, N14937, LX-MCV [FERRIED TO GWO; TO BE BU]

A/C TYPE	CURRENT REG. NO.	LAST KNOWN OPERATOR (OWNER)	STATUS	ORIGINAL MSN	LINE NO.	DEL. DATE	ENG. TYPE	FLEET NO.	PREV. REG. [COMMENTS]
B747-257B	N303TW	(FSBU)	O	20116	112	01/29/71	JT9D-7A		HB-IGA, LX-SAL, TF-ABK, LV-YSB [RT LESSOR; FERRIED TO MZJ]
B747-132 (SF)	N857FT	POLAR AIR CARGO (POLA)	O	20246	155	09/30/71	JT9D-7A		N9899, N804FT, N624FE, VR-HKM, N624PL [FERRIED TO GWO 03/30/00; BEING BU]
B747-136	G-AWNG	BRITISH AIRWAYS	O	20269	150	09/08/71	JT9D-7A		[WFU 12/01/98; STD ROW 12/14/98]
B747-136	G-AWNH	BRITISH AIRWAYS (AARL)	O	20270	169	11/23/71	JT9D-7A		[LRF 06/02/99; ST SANDIA NATIONAL LABS 06/14/99; WFU ROW]
B747-136	G-AWNJ	BRITISH AIRWAYS (AARL)	O	20272	183	03/21/72	JT9D-7A		[WFU 12/01/98; STD ROW 12/17/98]
B747-136	N606FF	TOWER AIR	O	20273	184	03/24/72	JT9D-7A		G-AWNK, N17126 [RT LESSOR 08/15/00; BEING DISMANTLED]
B747-258B	4X-AXB	EL AL	O	20274	164	11/22/71	JT9D-7J		[WFU AND TO BE USED FOR TRNG AT TLV]
B747-136	G-AWNL	BRITISH AIRWAYS (AARL)	O	20284	187	04/19/72	JT9D-7A		[TO ROW 11/30/98; FOR SALE]
B747-121	N609FF	TOWER AIR	O	20354	142	12/20/73	JT9D-7A		N659PA [LRF 01/11/98, STD MZJ 04/14/98]
B747-251B	N611US	(EVERGREEN A/C SALES & LSG)	O	20356	88	03/26/71	JT9D-7F		[LRF 11/27/98, STD MZJ LESS ENGINES; TO BE BU]
B747-206B	N306TW	TRANS WORLD AIRLINES (PACA)	O	20398	152	08/31/71	JT9D-7W		PH-BUD, N534AW [STD MZJ]
B747-237B	N459JS	AIR INDIA	O	20459	185	03/28/72	JT9D-7J		VT-EBN [ST AERO CONTROLS 06/00 (SCRAP); STD MHV]
B747-282B	N610FF	TOWER AIR	O	20501	178	02/16/72	JT9D-7A		CS-TJA, N301TW [STD VCV]
B747-282B	N611FF	TOWER AIR	O	20502	189	05/16/72	JT9D-7A		CS-TJB, N302TW [STD VCV]
B747-243B	N33021	CONTINENTAL AIRLINES	O	20520	190	05/26/72	JT9D-7A		I-DEMB, N45224, N359AS, N605PE [WFU; RTD MHV 10/01/98]
B747-146	N704CK	KITTY HAWK INTL.	O	20528	191	06/14/72	JT9D-7A		JA8112 [STD OSC; FOR SALE/SCRAP]
B747-238B	N14024	CONTINENTAL AIRLINES	O	20534	195	08/10/73	JT9D-7F		VH-EBE, N609PE, N10024, N614FF [STD MHV]
B747-238B	N17025	(FSBU)	O	20535	217	08/01/72	JT9D-7F		VH-EBF, N610PE [RT CALFINCO 06/15/99; STD MHV]
B747-136	G-AWNM	BRITISH AIRWAYS (AARL)	O	20708	210	05/03/73	JT9D-7A		[LRF 10/30/99, RTD ROW 12/17/99]
B747-133	C-FTOD	EVERGREEN INTL. AIRLINES	O	20767	214	05/14/73	JT9D-7		[ST EIA/P&W 10/28/98; RTD OPF 10/98]
B747-2B5B	HL7463	KOREAN AIR	O	20770	213	05/01/73	JT9D-7A		N1798B, HL7410, N747BA [ST BOEING]
B747-2B5B	N710BA	KOREAN AIR	O	20771	215	07/12/73	JT9D-7A		N1796B, HL7411, N747BC, HL7464 [ST BOEING; STD MZJ]
B747-128	F-BPVL	AIR FRANCE	O	20798	224	03/21/74	JT9D-7		N88931 [FERRIED TO VCV; TO BE BU FOR PARTS]
B747-128	F-BPVM	AIR FRANCE	O	20799	227	12/21/73	JT9D-7		N63305 [STD CHR 06/08/00]
B747-136	G-AWNN	BRITISH AIRWAYS (AARL)	O	20809	220	11/07/73	JT9D-7A		[LRF 05/01/99; WFU ROW]
B747-136	G-AWNO	BRITISH AIRWAYS (AARL)	O	20810	222	12/07/73	JT9D-7A		[LRF 10/31/99, RTD ROW 12/06/99]
B747-133	C-FTOE	EVERGREEN INTL. AIRLINES	O	20881	236	05/13/74	JT9D-7		[ST EIA/P&W; STD MZJ 10/98]
B747-233B (M)	C-GAGA	AIR CANADA	O	20977	250	03/07/75	JT9D-7J	306	N8287V [STD MZJ 01/14/99; FOR SALE]
B747-238B	N158UA	UNITED AIRLINES (POTO)	O	21054	260	05/30/75	JT9D-7J	8258	VH-EBJ [LRF 12/15/00; FERRIED TO SIN 06/11/01]
B747SP-44	N747KS	PANAIR INC.	O	21133	282	04/22/76	JT9D-7FW		7Q-YKL, LX-LGX, ZS-SPB [STD MZJ 09/99]

334

A/C TYPE	CURRENT REG. NO.	LAST KNOWN OPERATOR (OWNER)	STATUS	ORIGINAL MSN	LINE NO.	DEL. DATE	ENG. TYPE	FLEET NO.	PREV. REG. [COMMENTS]
B747-238B	N159UA	UNITED AIRLINES (CITG)	O	21140	267	11/07/75	JT9D-7J	8259	VH-EBK [FERRIED TO ROW 02/01/01; ST UNIVERSAL ASSET MGMT FOR BU]
B747-128	N129TW	TRANS WORLD AIRLINES (ALGI)	O	21141	279	02/27/76	JT9D-7		N40116, F-BPVQ, 5N-GAB, TF-ABZ, N174GM [STD MZJ]
B747-212B	N620FF	(FINO)	O	21162	283	03/30/76	JT9D-7J		9V-SQE, N747BH, N727PA, C-FNXP, N514DC, C-GCIH, N511P
B747-136	G-BDPV	BRITISH AIRWAYS (AARL)	O	21213	281	04/08/76	JT9D-7A		[LRF 06/01/99; WFU ROW]
B747-236B	G-BDXD	BRITISH AIRWAYS	O	21241	317	04/04/78	RB211-524D4		N8285V [LRF 12/05/99; FERRIED TO ROW FOR STORAGE 12/17/99]
B747-212B	N619FF	(FINO)	O	21316	309	06/27/77	JT9D-7J		9V-SQF, N747BJ, N724PA, C-FXCE, TF-ABZ, N504DC [FERRIED TO MZJ 12/05/00]
B747-238B (M)	C-GAGC	AIR CANADA	O	21354	314	10/27/77	JT9D-7J	308	VH-ECA [STD MZJ 01/29/99; FOR SALE]
B747SP-21	N146UA	FEDERAL AVIATION ADMINISTRATION	O	21547	325	06/09/78	JT9D-7A		N537PA [STD MZJ; FOR RESEARCH AND TESTING PROGRAMS]
B747SP-21	N147UA	UNITED AIRLINES	O	21548	331	07/12/78	JT9D-7A		N538PA [ST FAA FOR FUEL TANK INERTING TESTS; FERRIED TO ACY]
B747-233B (M)	C-GAGB	AIR CANADA	O	21627	355	01/31/79	JT9D-7J	307	[STD MZJ 01/21/99; FOR SALE]
B747-245F (SCD)	N636FE	FEDERAL EXPRESS (DLLG)	O	21764	394	09/06/79	JT9D-70A		N703SW, N813FT [STD MZJ]
B747SP-J6	N135SW	AIR CHINA	O	21932	433	02/29/80	JT9D-7J		B-2442 [ST UT FINANCE 12/23/99; STD MZJ]
B747SP-J6	N136SW	AIR CHINA	O	21933	455	06/26/80	JT9D-7J		B-2444, B-2438 [ST UT FINANCE 12/99; STD VCV]
B747SP-J6	N139SW	AIR CHINA	O	21934	467	09/23/80	JT9D-7J		N1304E, B-2452 [ST UT FINANCE 12/99; STD MZJ]
B747SR-146B	N552SW	KALITTA AIR	O	22066	426	01/31/80	JT9D-7A		JA8142 [STD OSC; FOR PARTS?]
B747SR-146B	N553SW	CARLIN AIRLINES (JUMBO JET)	O	22067	427	02/14/80	JT9D-7A		JA8143 [STD MZJ]
B747-2F6B	N623FF	TOWER AIR (GECA)	O	22382	498	12/12/80	CF6-50E2		N744PR [RT GECA 02/00; FERRIED TO TLV FOR CONV TO FRTR]
B747SP-B5	N709BA	KOREAN AIR	O	22483	501	01/22/81	JT9D-7A		HL7456 [ST BOEING A/C HOLDING; STD MZJ 12/98]
B747SP-B5	N708BA	(BCCI)	O	22484	507	03/18/81	JT9D-7A		HL7457 [STD MZJ]
B747SP-09	N4508H	(TAG AVIATION)	O	22547	534	09/30/81	JT9D-7A		[RT LESSOR 03/18/97; STD MZJ]
B747-357 (SCD)	N270BC	(GATX)	O	22704	570	03/19/83	JT9D-7R4G2		N6005C, N8277V, HB-IGC [STD MZJ]
B747-357 (M)	N705BC	SWISSAIR (GATX)	O	22705	576	03/05/83	JT9D-7R4G2		N1784B, HB-IGD [ST DARTMORE ASSOC. 08/25/99; STD MZJ]
B747SP-09	N4522V	MANDARIN AIRLINES (SANWA)	O	22805	564	06/29/82	JT9D-7A		[RT SANWA BUSINESS CREDIT 12/31/97; STD LAS 01/98]
B747-312	9V-SKA	SINGAPORE AIRLINES	O	23026	580	04/29/83	JT9D-7R4G2		N6006C, N8279V, VH-INH [ST BOEING HOLDINGS; STD SIN]
B747-312	N793BA	(BCCI)	O	23029	590	11/22/83	JT9D-7R4G2		N118KD, VH-INJ, 9V-SKD [STD SIN]
B747-312	9V-SKH	(WTCI)	O	23033	609	03/20/85	JT9D-7R4G2		N122KH [STD VCV; ST POTO]
B747-312	N680SW	AIR ATLANTA ICELAND (UTFC)	O	23244	621	09/24/85	JT9D-7R4G2		N124KK, ZS-OKK, 9V-SKK, TF-ATG [RT UTFC 04/01]
B747-312	N681SW	AIR ATLANTA ICELAND (UTFC)	O	23245	626	12/11/85	JT9D-7R4G2		N125KL, 9V-SKL, TF-ATS [RT UTFC 04/01]

A/C TYPE	CURRENT REG. NO.	LAST KNOWN OPERATOR (OWNER)	STATUS	ORIGINAL MSN	LINE NO.	DEL. DATE	ENG. TYPE	FLEET NO.	PREV. REG. [COMMENTS]
B747-329 (M)	N3439F	SABENA	O	23439	646	06/10/86	CF6-50E2		N6005C, OO-SGC [LRF 10/29/99; RT LESSOR; FERRIED TO TLV 12/01/00 FOR FRTR CONV]
PRESERVED									
B747-128	F-BPVJ	AIR FRANCE	P	20541	200	02/21/73	JT9D-7		N28903 [ON DISPLAY AT MUSEE DE L'AIR AT LBG]
SCR									
B747-121 (SCD)	N747PA	AEROPOSTA (GECC)	S	19639	2	10/03/70	JT9D-7A		N747QC [BU SBD; FUSELAGE SHIPPED TO SOUTH KOREA FOR USE AS RESTAURANT]
B747-121A	5N-HHS	TRANS-AIR SERVICES (ALG)	S	19644	13	01/21/70	JT9D-7A		N737PA [BU]
B747-121A	N742PA	PAN AMERICAN	S	19649	18	03/02/70	JT9D-7A		[ST RYDER 02/28/92; BU]
B747-121A	N748PA	PAN AMERICAN	S	19652	26	03/31/70	JT9D-7A		[BU MZJ 95]
B747-121A	N749PA	PAN AMERICAN	S	19653	30	04/10/70	JT9D-7A		[RT CITIBANK 12/05/91; BU FOR SPARES]
B747-121A	N750PA	PAN AMERICAN	S	19654	32	04/26/70	JT9D-7A		[RT CITIBANK 09/91; BU FOR SPARES]
B747-121A	N476EV	EVERGREEN INTNL AIRLINES	S	19655	33	04/24/70	JT9D-7A		N751PA [BU MZJ]
B747-121 (F) (SCD)	N473EV	EVERGREEN INTNL AIRLINES	S	19657	37	04/29/70	JT9D-7AH		N753PA [TO BE BU MZJ]
B747-131	N93104	TRANS WORLD AIRLINES	S	19670	20	02/20/70	JT9D-7A		[BU MZJ]
B747-131	N93105	TRANS WORLD AIRLINES	S	19671	21	03/09/70	JT9D-7A		[BU KANSAS CITY BY JET-AWAY 01/27/00]
B747-131	N93109	TRANS WORLD AIRLINES	S	19675	43	05/23/70	JT9D-7A		[LRF 1/13/97; WFU MZJ; BEING BU]
B747-131	N53110	TRANS WORLD AIRLINES	S	19676	63	08/10/70	JT9D-7A		[BEING BU MHV; TO BECOME A SUSHI BAR IN JAPAN]
B747-143	N128BP	TRANS WORLD AIRLINES (PEGA)	S	19729	36	05/13/70	JT9D-7A		I-DEMA, N355AS, N603PE, N17010, N128TW [BEING BU MZJ BY BPI]
B747-143	N17011	CONTINENTAL AIRLINES	S	19730	56	07/01/70	JT9D-7A		N1796B, I-DEME, N356AS, N606PE [MHV 06/96; STILL AWAITING SCRAPPING 12/31/00]
B747-243B	N78020	CONTINENTAL AIRLINES	S	19731	120	03/30/71	JT9D-7A		I-DEMO, N357AS, N604PE [HULK EXTANT MJZ 12/96]
B747-124 (F) (SCD)	4X-AXZ	EL AL	S	19735	64	08/12/70	JT9D-7J		N26863, 5-291, 5-8112, N8289V, HK-2400X [BU TLV 1999]
B747-130	EI-BED	AER LINGUS	S	19748	44	05/23/70	JT9D-7		D-ABYC [BU MZJ 96]
B747-128	N611AR	AIR FRANCE	S	19749	19	03/20/70	JT9D-7		F-BPVA [SCR OKC 03/94]
B747-128	F-BPVB	AIR FRANCE	S	19750	22	03/25/70	JT9D-7		[ST AVIATION SYSTEMS INTL. FOR SCRAP]
B747-128	N612AR	TOWER AIR	S	19752	53	07/14/70	JT9D-7		F-BPVD [SCR OKC 03/94]
B747-136	G-AWNA	BRITISH AIRWAYS (AARL)	S	19761	23	04/22/70	JT9D-7A		N1799B [BU BRUNTINGTHORPE]
B747-151	N602PR	NORTHWEST AIRLINES	S	19779	40	05/11/70	JT9D-7A		N602US [STD MXE 09/94]
B747-151	N603US	(CHARLOTTE AIRCRAFT)	S	19780	45	05/22/70	JT9D-7A		[BEING BU MXE]
B747-151	N604US	NORTHWEST AIRLINES	S	19781	55	06/24/70	JT9D-7A		[BU MHV 07/94]
B747-151	N605US	NORTHWEST AIRLINES	S	19782	62	07/24/70	JT9D-7A		[BU GWO 01/00]
B747-151	N606PB	NORTHWEST AIRLINES	S	19783	71	08/30/70	JT9D-7A		N606US [STD MXE]
B747-151	N607US	NORTHWEST AIRLINES	S	19784	74	09/09/70	JT9D-7A		[SCR GWO 09/98]

A/C TYPE	CURRENT REG. NO.	LAST KNOWN OPERATOR (OWNER)	STATUS	ORIGINAL MSN	LINE NO.	DEL. DATE	ENG. TYPE	FLEET NO.	PREV. REG. [COMMENTS]
B747-151	N609US	NORTHWEST AIRLINES	S	19786	83	10/28/70	JT9D-7A		[BU MHV 1995 (TRACOR)]
B747-151	N610US	NORTHWEST AIRLINES	S	19787	93	11/11/70	JT9D-7A		[BU GWO BY 10/99]
B747-122	N4714U	UNITED AIRLINES	S	19876	97	11/28/70	JT9D-7A		[ST AVN SALES; STD ARD FOR PARTS]
B747-122	N4716U	UNITED AIRLINES	S	19877	99	12/11/70	JT9D-7A		[ST AVN SALES; STD ARD LESS ENGINES AND SOME PARTS]
B747-122	N4717U	UNITED AIRLINES	S	19878	101	12/28/70	JT9D-7A		[ST AVN SALES; STD ARD LESS ENGINES AND SOME PARTS]
B747-122	N4718U	UNITED AIRLINES	S	19879	139	05/27/71	JT9D-7A		[ST AVN SALES; STD ARD LESS ENGINES AND SOME PARTS]
B747-122	N4719U	UNITED AIRLINES	S	19880	145	06/26/71	JT9D-7A		[ST WILLIS LEASE FINANCE 06/23/98; STD MZJ]
B747-122	N4720U	UNITED AIRLINES	S	19881	148	07/23/71	JT9D-7A		[ST WILLIS 05/22/98; RTD; TO BE BU; STD MZJ]
B747-122	N4723U	UNITED AIRLINES	S	19882	175	01/06/72	JT9D-7A		[ST WILLIS; RTD; TO BE BU; STD MZJ]
B747-122	N4727U	UNITED AIRLINES	S	19883	193	06/27/72	JT9D-7A		[ST AVN SALES; STD ARD LESS ENGINES AND SOME PARTS]
B747-135	N620US	NORTHWEST AIRLINES	S	19918	68	09/08/70	JT9D-7A		N77772 [BU GWO 03/00]
B747-135	N621US	NORTHWEST AIRLINES	S	19919	81	10/20/70	JT9D-7A		N77773 [SCR GWO 09/98]
B747-206B	N531AW	AMERICA WEST AIRLINES	S	19922	96	01/16/71	JT9D-7W		PH-BUA [BU IGM 02/96]
B747-206B	N532AW	AMERICA WEST AIRLINES	S	19923	118	03/04/71	JT9D-7W		PH-BUB [BU MHV 08/94]
B747-206B	N533AW	AMERICA WEST AIRLINES	S	19924	138	05/21/71	JT9D-7W		PH-BUC [SCR SAT 05/94]
B747-122	N4728U	UNITED AIRLINES	S	19925	205	04/27/73	JT9D-7A		[BEING BU FOR PARTS GWO]
B747-122	N4729U	UNITED AIRLINES	S	19926	206	04/24/73	JT9D-7A		[ST WILLIS 05/22/98; RTD; TO BE BU; STD MZJ]
B747-122	N4732U	UNITED AIRLINES	S	19927	207	03/19/73	JT9D-7A		[PERMANENTLY RTD FOR SPARES; STD MZJ]
B747-122	N4735U	UNITED AIRLINES	S	19928	208	05/30/73	JT9D-7A		[ST WILLIS; RTD; TO BE BU]
B747-156	N133TW	TRANS WORLD AIRLINES	S	19957	76	10/02/70	JT9D-7A		EC-BRO [BU MHV; TO BECOME A SUSHI BAR IN JAPAN]
B747-156	N134TW	TRANS WORLD AIRLINES	S	19958	91	11/10/70	JT9D-7A		EC-BRP [BU BY KELLSTROM INDUSTRIES MZJ, AFTER 04/99]
B747-237B	N960JS	AIR INDIA	S	19960	130	04/20/71	JT9D-7J		VT-EBE [ST AERO CONTROLS 06/00; BEING BU MHV]
B747-238B	N607FF	TOWER AIR (CITG)	S	20011	162	10/21/71	JT9D-7J		VH-EBC, N747BM, N607PE [RT CITG 04/00; BEING BU JFK]
B747-133	N890FT	FEDERAL EXPRESS (ANAU)	S	20013	104	02/11/71	JT9D-7A		C-FTOA, N749R, EI-BPH [BU MZJ 10/95]
B747-133	TF-ABR	AIR ATLANTA ICELAND (MIDO)	S	20014	121	03/18/71	JT9D-7AH		C-FTOB, EC-DXE, EI-BRR, N621FE, N874UM [TO BE BU MZJ]
B747-133	C-FTOC	EVERGREEN INTL. AIRLINES	S	20015	144	06/24/71	JT9D-7		[BU FOR PARTS MIA 1999]
B747-123	N153UA	UNITED AIRLINES	S	20102	59	07/30/70	JT9D-7A		N9663, N14943, LX-KCV [BEING SCR GWO]
B747-123	N155UA	UNITED AIRLINES	S	20104	69	09/18/70	JT9D-7A		HI-472, N9665 [ST WILLIS FINANCE; BEING BU TUS]
B747-123	G-VMIA	VIRGIN ATLANTIC AIRWAYS	S	20108	87	11/27/70	JT9D-7AH		N9669, N14939, G-HIHO, VH-EEI, EI-CAI [SCR KEMBLE]
B747-257B	N304TW	AIR ATLANTA	S	20117	126	03/25/71	JT9D-7A		HB-IGB, OH-KSA, SU-GAK, N304TW [BU ARD]

A/C TYPE	CURRENT REG. NO.	LAST KNOWN OPERATOR (OWNER)	STATUS	ORIGINAL MSN	LINE NO.	DEL. DATE	ENG. TYPE	FLEET NO.	PREV. REG. [COMMENTS]
B747-283B	F-GHBM	AIR OUTRE MER (AERONAT)	S	20120	114	02/22/71	JT9D-7		SE-DDL, LN-AET [SCR SAT 07/94]
B747-283B	G-VOYG	VIRGIN ATLANTIC AIRWAYS	S	20121	167	11/12/71	JT9D-7J		OY-KHA, LN-AEO, G-BMGS [BU RAF KEMBLE]
B747-258B	4X-AXA	EL AL	S	20135	140	05/26/71	JT9D-7J		[BU TLV 10/99]
B747-127 (SCD)	N601BN	TOWER AIR	S	20207	100	01/05/71	JT9D-7A		[SCR JFK 05/94; STD SINCE 03/21/92]
B747-1D1	TF-ABO	AIR ATLANTA ICELAND (MIDO)	S	20208	123	04/23/73	JT9D-7AH		C-FDJC, N502SR [CVTD -127; SCR MSE]
B747-1D1	TF-ABS	AIR ATLANTA ICELAND (FSBU)	S	20305	146	06/25/71	JT9D-7AH		N26864, C-FFUN, N875UM, N25WA [CVTD -124; BU BY WILLIS AERO SVCES MZJ]
B747-131	N53116	TRANS WORLD AIRLINES	S	20321	102	05/21/71	JT9D-7A		[LRF 12/28/97, TO BE BU MZJ]
B747-131	N93117	FAMILY AIRLINES (FSBU)	S	20322	113	05/24/71	JT9D-7A		[BU MHV]
B747-121A (SCD)	N492GX	PAN AMERICAN	S	20350	117	05/28/71	JT9D-7A		N655PA [BEING BU MZJ]
B747-121	N483EV	EVERGREEN INTNL AIRLINES	S	20351	127	06/18/71	JT9D-7A		N656PA [TO BE BU MZJ]
B747-121	N484EV	EVERGREEN INTNL AIRLINES	S	20352	129	06/19/71	JT9D-7A		N657PA [TO BE BU MZJ]
B747-128	F-BPVE	AIR FRANCE (ELEC)	S	20355	105	03/16/71	JT9D-7		[BU AFTER BOMB EXPLOSION TESTS BY DERA 05/17/97]
B747-230B	N488GX	KOREAN AIR (ITEL)	S	20372	132	05/05/71	JT9D-7A		D-ABYD, HL7440 [BU MHV (GATX CAPITAL)]
B747-128	TF-ABW	AIR ATLANTA ICELAND	S	20376	174	02/04/72	JT9D-7A		F-BPVF, C-GCIS [BU MSE]
B747-128	TF-ABG	AIR ATLANTA ICELAND (AGES)	S	20377	176	02/01/72	JT9D-7A		F-BPVG [RT AGES 09/99; BEING SCR MZJ]
B747-128	F-BPVH	AIR FRANCE (VEGA)	S	20378	177	03/01/72	JT9D-7		[BU OPF 12/96]
B747-129 (SCD)	OO-SGA	NATIONAIR CANADA	S	20401	92	11/19/70	JT9D-7A		[SCR BRU 12/94]
B747-129 (SCD)	N822AL	NATIONAIR CANADA (UASI)	S	20402	95	12/04/70	JT9D-7A		OO-SGB, C-GNXH [BU MHV (AAR ENG GRP)]
B747-230B	C-FNXA	NATIONAIR CANADA (GATX)	S	20493	128	04/02/71	JT9D-7A		D-ABYF, HL7447, N487GX [BU SHELTON (AERO CONTROLS)]
B747-128	N615AR	AIR ATLANTA (AAR TURBINE)	S	20543	203	02/21/73	JT9D-7		N28899, F-BPVK, TF-ABQ [BU 04/95 OKC BY AAR AVN TRADING]
B747-284B	N305TW	TRANS WORLD AIRLINES	S	20742	216	06/21/73	JT9D-7A		SX-OAA [LRF 5/31/97, TO BE BU MZJ]
B747SR-46	N747BN	BOEING EQUIPMENT HOLDING CO.	S	20782	229	12/21/73	JT9D-7AW		JA8118 [DESTROYED IN STRUCTURAL TESTING 07/88]
B747-128	N601AR	AIR FRANCE	S	20800	228	02/08/74	JT9D-7		N28366, F-BPVN [SCR OKC 06/94; FUSELAGE AT FAA TRAINING SCHOOL]
B747-246B	TF-ABI	AIR ATLANTA ICELAND (JUMBO JET)	S	20924	235	03/29/74	JT9D-7AW		JA8122, N550SW [BEING SCR MZJ]
B747-128	F-BPVP	AIR FRANCE	S	20954	252	03/13/75	JT9D-7		[RTD 05/24/99; BU FOR PARTS BY AFR AT CHR]
B747SP-21	N140UA	UNITED AIRLINES	S	21022	265	04/26/76	JT9D-7A		N747SP, N530PA [BU ARD 02/96]
B747SP-21	N141UA	UNITED AIRLINES	S	21023	268	05/17/76	JT9D-7A		N247SP, N531PA [BU ARD; PORTION OF FUSELAGE USED AS SOFIA MODEL]

338

A/C TYPE	CURRENT REG. NO.	LAST KNOWN OPERATOR (OWNER)	STATUS	ORIGINAL MSN	LINE NO.	DEL. DATE	ENG. TYPE	FLEET NO.	PREV. REG. [COMMENTS]
B747SP-21	N142UA	UNITED AIRLINES	S	21024	270	03/29/76	JT9D-7A		N347SP, N532PA [BU ARD 02/96]
B747SP-21	N143UA	UNITED AIRLINES	S	21025	273	03/05/76	JT9D-7A		N40135, N533PA [BU ARD]
B747SP-21	N144UA	UNITED AIRLINES	S	21026	286	05/28/78	JT9D-7A		N534PA [BU ARD]
B747-246B	TF-ABY	AIR ATLANTA ICELAND (FSBU)	S	21030	251	12/17/74	JT9D-7AW		JA8125 [RT UNICAPITAL; BEING SCR MZJ]
B747SR-46	N705CK	KALITTA AMERICAN INTL.	S	21032	249	11/22/74	JT9D-7A		JA8124 [BU 1995 OSC]
B747SR-81	A7-ABK	QATAR AIRWAYS	S	21604	346	12/21/78	CF6-45A2		N8286V, JA8133, N747BK [TO ROW FOR BU FOR PARTS 03/99]
B747SR-81	A7-ABL	QATAR AIRWAYS	S	21605	351	12/20/78	CF6-45A2		JA8134, N747BL [TO ROW FOR BU FOR PARTS 03/99]
B747SR-81	N8078M	ATLAS AIR	S	21606	360	02/28/79	CF6-45A2		JA8135 [BU FOR PARTS ARD]
B747-267B	B-HKG	CATHAY PACIFIC	S	21746	385	07/20/79	RB211-524C2		VR-HKG [BU VCV 06/17/99]
B747SR-81	N8078H	ATLAS AIR	S	21922	393	10/09/79	CF6-45A2		JA8136 [BU FOR PARTS IAB 06/99]
B747SR-81	N8078Q	ATLAS AIR	S	21923	395	09/05/79	CF6-45A2		JA8137 [BU FOR PARTS IAB 06/99]
B747-283B	N622FF	(AERCO)	S	22496	540	10/22/81	JT9D-7Q		N4502R, EI-BZA [BEING BU JFK]

WRITTEN OFF

A/C TYPE	CURRENT REG. NO.	LAST KNOWN OPERATOR (OWNER)	STATUS	ORIGINAL MSN	LINE NO.	DEL. DATE	ENG. TYPE	FLEET NO.	PREV. REG. [COMMENTS]
B747-121	N736PA	PAN AMERICAN	W	19643	11	01/20/70	JT9D-7A		[WO 03/27/77 TENERIFE]
B747-121	N738PA	PAN AMERICAN	W	19645	14	02/05/70	JT9D-7A		[WO 08/04/83 KHI]
B747-121A	N739PA	PAN AMERICAN	W	19646	15	02/15/70	JT9D-7A		[WO 12/21/88 LOCKERBIE]
B747-121	N752PA	PAN AMERICAN	W	19656	34	05/02/70	JT9D-7A		[WO 09/06/70 CAIRO]
B747-131F	5-8104	IMPERIAL IRANIAN AF	W	19677	73	09/26/70	JT9D-7A		N53111, 5-283 [WO 05/09/76 MADRID]
B747-130	D-ABYB	LUFTHANSA	W	19747	29	04/13/70	JT9D-7		[WO 11/20/74 NAIROBI]
B747-136	G-AWND	BRITISH AIRWAYS	W	19764	107	02/28/71	JT9D-7A		[WO 02/27/91 KUWAIT CITY]
B747-237B	VT-EBD	AIR INDIA	W	19959	124	03/22/71	JT9D-7J		[WO 01/01/78 BOMBAY]
B747-131	N93119	TRANS WORLD AIRLINES	W	20083	153	10/27/71	JT9D-7A		[WO 07/17/96 MORICHES, NY]
B747-136	N605FF	TOWER AIR	W	20271	172	01/07/72	JT9D-7A		G-AWNI, N17125 [WO 12/20/95 JFK, NY]
B747-206B	PH-BUF	KLM	W	20400	157	10/19/71	JT9D-7W		[WO 03/27/77 TENERIFE]
B747-246B	JA8109	JAPAN AIRLINES	W	20503	180	03/02/72	JT9D-7A		[WO 07/24/73 LIBYA]
B747-128	N28888	AIR FRANCE (WILMINGTON)	W	20542	201	03/20/73	JT9D-7		[WO 06/12/75 BOMBAY]
B747-237B	VT-EBO	AIR INDIA	W	20558	188	06/01/72	JT9D-7J		[WO 05/07/90 DELHI]
B747-230B	HL7442	KOREAN AIRLINES	W	20559	186	03/31/72	JT9D-7A		D-ABYH [WO 09/01/83 RUSSIA]
B747SR-46	JA8119	JAPAN AIRLINES	W	20783	230	02/19/74	JT9D-7AW		[WO 08/12/85 TOKYO]
B747SP-44	ZS-SPF	LAM-MOZAMBIQUE (SAA)	W	21263	301	01/31/77	JT9D-7FW		3B-NAO, LX-LGY, V5-SPF [WO 10/05/98 MAPUTO; SCR MAPUTO 03/00]

A/C TYPE	CURRENT REG. NO.	LAST KNOWN OPERATOR (OWNER)	STATUS	ORIGINAL MSN	LINE NO.	DEL. DATE	ENG. TYPE	FLEET NO.	PREV. REG. [COMMENTS]
B747-283B (SCD)	HK-2910X	AVIANCA	W	21381	311	10/27/77	JT9D-70A		LN-RNA [WO 11/27/83 MADRID]
B747-237B	VT-EFO	AIR INDIA	W	21473	330	06/30/78	JT9D-7J		[WO 06/23/85 IRELAND]
B747-2B3F (SCD)	F-GPAN	AIR FRANCE	W	21515	337	09/26/78	CF6-50E2		N1780B [WO 03/06/99 MADRAS, INDIA]
B747-258F (SCD)	4X-AXG	EL AL	W	21737	362	03/19/79	JT9D-7J		[WO 10/04/92 AMSTERDAM]
B747-2B5B	HL7445	KOREAN AIR	W	21773	366	04/11/79	JT9D-7Q		[WO 11/19/80 SEOUL]
B747-249F	N807FT	FLYING TIGERS	W	21828	408	12/11/79	JT9D-7Q		[WO 02/18/89 MALAYSIA]
B747-244B (SCD)	ZS-SAS	SOUTH AFRICAN AIRWAYS	W	22171	488	11/24/80	JT9D-7Q		[WO 11/28/87 MAURITIUS]
B747-2H7B (M)	TJ-CAB	CAMEROON AIRLINES	W	22378	508	02/26/81	JT9D-7Q		[WO 11/04/00 PARIS, FRANCE]
B747-2R7F (SCD)	B-198	CHINA AIRLINES (CAA/GOVT)	W	22390	482	10/10/80	JT9D-7R4G2		LX-ECV [WO 12/29/91 TPE]
B747-228B	F-GCBC	AIR FRANCE	W	22427	485	10/17/80	CF6-50E		[WO 12/02/85 RIO DE JANEIRO]
B747-2B5F (SCD)	HL7451	KOREAN AIR	W	22480	448	06/25/80	JT9D-7Q		[WO 12/22/99 LONDON-STANSTED]
B747-3B5	HL7468	KOREAN AIR	W	22487	605	12/12/84	JT9D-7R4G2		N6069D [WO 08/06/97 GUAM]
B747-168B	HZ-AIH	SAUDIA	W	22748	555	03/17/82	RB211-524C2		[WO 11/12/96 DADRI, INDIA]
B747-3B3	F-GDUA	UTA	W	22870	573	03/01/83	CF6-50E2		N6067B, N8278V [WO 03/16/85 PARIS]
B747-409	B-165	CHINA AIRLINES (CAA/GOVT)	W	24313	977	06/08/93	PW4056		[WO 11/04/93 HONG KONG]
B747-4B5	HL7496	KOREAN AIR	W	26400	1083	06/27/96	PW4056		[WO 08/05/98 SEOUL, KOREA; ST SOURCE ONE SPARES FOR PARTS]
B747-412	9V-SPK	SINGAPORE AIRLINES	W	28023	1099	01/21/97	PW4056		[WO 10/31/00 TPE]

Chapter 7

Model 757

After United Airlines chose in August 1975 not to order 727-300s—a proposed development of the Boeing trijet with revised wings, increased weights, and accommodation for up to 215 passengers in high-density configuration or 179 passengers in a typical two-class arrangement—Boeing began studying all-new 727 replacements. While some carriers favored a wide-body aircraft with twin aisles and a fuselage diameter sufficient to accommodate standard cargo containers, United indicated its preference for a single-aisle aircraft to minimize aircraft-mile cost. Design studies for that single-aisle aircraft continued in parallel with studies for twin-aisle models, but progress was slow because most airlines were then either losing money or making only a modest profit. Moreover, to minimize development costs for the new aircraft, Boeing was seeking risk-sharing partners but was not getting foreign manufacturers to commit. Finally, following a business upturn for the airlines, Boeing was able in 1978 to proceed on its own with the single-aisle 757.

As proposed in 1978, the 757 retained the cockpit (but with new avionics for two-pilot operations), fuselage, and T-tail of the 727. Later, the variable-incidence horizontal stabilizer was relocated to the rear fuselage and the vertical tail surfaces were redesigned. The wing design, which had less sweep than those of the 727 (25 degrees at the quarter-chord instead of 32 degrees), improved lift, and reduced drag for greater aerodynamic efficiency and lower fuel consumption. Power was to be provided by two high-bypass-ratio turbofans in the 35,000-pound-thrust (155-kilonewton) class that were to be mounted in underwing nacelles.

The 757 program appeared to have a good start when, in August 1978, orders and options were received from British Airways and Eastern Air Lines (respectively 19 orders and 18 options, and 21 orders and 24 options). No other contracts were announced during the next 26 months, however, but this worrisome lack of orders finally came to an end in November 1980 when Delta Air Lines became the third 757 customer with an order for 60 aircraft. Since then, sales have continued at a slow but steady pace, and the 1,000-aircraft mark was reached after 23 years (versus only 13 years for the 727 and 18 years for the 737).

The main production version is the 757-200, built mostly as a passenger transport with up to 239 seats but also available in combi and freighter variants. The other production version is the stretched-fuselage 757-300, with seating for up to 289. Plans for a 757-100 with a shortened fuselage have been discontinued as Next-Generation 737 models now adequately cover that market segment.

757-200

Manufacturing began on the strength of orders from British Airways and Eastern Air Lines and led to the roll out of the first 757-200 (s/n 22212, N757A) on January 13, 1982. Powered by four Rolls-Royce RB.211-535C engines rated at 37,400 pounds (166.4 kilonewtons) of static thrust, N757A first flew on February 19, 1982. Boeing retained N757A and has used it in recent years as an avionics test bed for the Lockheed Martin F-22 Raptor.

The FAA ATC A2NM for the 757-200 was awarded on December 31, 1982. Nine days earlier Eastern Air Lines had taken delivery of l/n 7, s/n 22196, N506EA. Eastern started revenue service on January 1, 1983. The majority of 757-200s have been delivered with either the original RB.211-535Cs or with more-powerful RB.211-535E4s (40,200 pounds [178.8 kilonewtons] static thrust) or RB.211-535E4Bs (43,500 pounds

[193.5 kilonewtons]). Others, starting with l/n 37, s/n 22808, N601DL, first flown on June 1, 1984, have been delivered with Pratt & Whitney turbofans, either the PW2037 of 36,600 pounds (162.8 kilonewtons) or the PW2040 of 40,100 pounds (178.4 kilonewtons).

In keeping with the new trend toward ETOPS (Extended-range Twin-engine OPerationS), 757-200ERs powered by Rolls-Royce turbofans were certificated for 120-minute ETOPS in December 1986 and for 180-minute ETOPS in July 1990. Those with Pratt & Whitney engines received 120-minute ETOPS certification in March 1990 and 180-minute certification in April 1992. For ETOPS, 757-200Ms are fitted with a backup hydraulic-motor generator and an auxiliary fan to cool the equipment in the electronics bay.

757 Combis and Freighters

When the U.S. airline industry was deregulated, UPS, the world's largest express and package carrier, chose to acquire its own aircraft. While most of its aircraft were previously owned, UPS also became the launch customer for the Package Freight (PF) version of the 757-200 by ordering a first batch of 20 757-200PFs in December 1985. That version differs from the passenger versions in lacking cabin windows and provision for galleys, lavatories, and other associated passenger amenities. Moreover, the -200PFs have a 134- by 86-inch (3.40- by 2.18–meter) upward-opening main-deck cargo door on the left side of the fuselage, forward of the wing. With other minor internal modifications, the 757-200PFs can carry 15 88- by 125-inch (2.24- by 3.18–meter) containers, for a maximum cargo load of 87,700 pounds (39,780 kilograms).

The first 757-200PF (l/n 139, s/n 23723, N401UP) flew on August 13, 1987. UPS accepted its first 757-24APF on September 17, 1987, and has gone on to place several repeat orders to acquire a fleet of 75 PFs.

The only other PF customer is Ansett Worldwide Aviation in Australia, which first ordered PF aircraft in November 1988 for leasing out.

The only other 757 built by Boeing with a main-deck cargo door was a 757-2F8(M) combi aircraft for Royal Nepal Airlines. In mixed configuration, that aircraft could typically carry 2 containers, 14 first-class passengers, and 174 Y-class passengers. Line number 182, s/n 23863, first flew on July 15, 1988, and was delivered as 9N-ACB in September of that year.

Pre-owned 757-200Ms, starting with ex-British Airways aircraft, are at the time of this writing being modified to 757-200SF Special Freighter configuration for DHL Worldwide Express and its associated organizations. After modifications by Boeing, including the fitting of a main-deck cargo door, the first aircraft (l/n 9, s/n 22172, ex G-BIKA) was rolled out in Wichita, Kansas, on March 2, 2001. It went to European Air Transport as OO-DLN on lease from DHL Holdings (UK). Forty-two airframes are to be modified by Boeing Airplane Services Global Modification and Engineering Work, with work being subcontracted to Israeli Aircraft Industries and Singapore Technologies Aerospace.

757-300

Mostly intended for all-inclusive tour operators in Europe, the 757-300 is a stretched version of the 757, with fuselage length increased from 155 feet 3 inches to 178 feet 7 inches (47.32 to 54.43 meters). Maximum seating capacity in all-economy configuration is 289 passengers, up from 259 passengers for the 757-200. In other respects, the 757-300 is fairly similar to the original model.

The initial order for 757-300s was placed in September 1986 when Condor Flugdienst ordered 12 aircraft. The first 757-300 (l/n 804, s/n 29016) flew on August 2, 1998. The FAA issued its certification in January 1999, and deliveries to Condor began on March 10, 1999.

Boeing 757 Principal Characteristics and Performance

	757-200	757-200PF	757-300
Span, ft in (m)	124′ 10″ (38.05)	124′ 10″ (38.05)	124′ 10″ (38.05)
Length, ft in (m)	155′ 3″ (47.32)	155′ 3″ (47.32)	178′ 7″ (54.43)
Height, ft in (m)	44′ 6″ (13.56)	44′ 6″ (13.56)	44′ 6″ (13.56)
Wing area, sq ft (m^2)	1,994 (185.2)	1,994 (185.2)	1,994 (185.2)
High-density seating	239	N/A	289
Two-class seating	192	N/A	239
Underfloor cargo, cu ft (m^3)	1,670 (47.3)	1,830 (51.8)	2,370 (67.1)
Maximum cargo load, lb (kg)	N/A	87,700 (39,780)	N/A
TO thrust per engine, lb st (kN)	36,600/43,500 (162.8/193.5)	40,100/43,500 (178.4/193.5)	42,600/43,500 (189.5/193.5)
Fuel capacity, U.S. gal (liters)	11,276 (42,683)	11,276 (42,683)	11,466 (43,403)
MTOW, lb (kg)	220,000/255,000 (99,790/115,666)	255,000 (115,666)	272,500 (123,604)
Typical cruise speed, Mach	0.80	0.80	0.80
Typical range, nm (km)	3,925 (7,270)	2,520 (4,665)	3,010 (5,575)

Boeing 757Commercial Jet Aircraft Census
The aircraft in the following tables are listed in order of the following: 1) ICAO country prefixes; 2) operator; 3) aircraft type; and 4) registration.
The total built was 961+ (945+ B757-200 and 16+ B757-300) from 1982 to present (still in production).

A/C TYPE	CURRENT REG. NO.	LAST KNOWN OPERATOR (OWNER)	Status	ORIGINAL MSN	LINE NO.	DEL. DATE	ENG. TYPE	FLEET NO.	PREV. REG. [COMMENTS]
B-CHINA (PEOPLE'S REPUBLIC)									
B757-21B	B-2801	CHINA SOUTHERN AIRLINES		24014	144	09/22/87	RB211-535E4		N1792B
B757-21B	B-2802	CHINA SOUTHERN AIRLINES		24015	148	10/27/87	RB211-535E4		N5573B
B757-21B	B-2803	CHINA SOUTHERN AIRLINES		24016	150	11/07/87	RB211-535E4		N5573K
B757-21B	B-2804	CHINA SOUTHERN AIRLINES (TOMB)		24330	200	11/22/88	RB211-535E4		
B757-21B	B-2805	CHINA SOUTHERN AIRLINES (TOMB)		24331	203	12/16/88	RB211-535E4		
B757-21B	B-2806	CHINA SOUTHERN AIRLINES (PEGA)		24401	232	08/28/89	RB211-535E4		N6067B
B757-21B	B-2807	CHINA SOUTHERN AIRLINES		24402	233	08/28/89	RB211-535E4		N6069D
B757-21B	B-2811	CHINA SOUTHERN AIRLINES		24714	262	02/15/90	RB211-535E4		
B757-21B	B-2815	CHINA SOUTHERN AIRLINES		24774	288	06/05/90	RB211-535E4		
B757-21B	B-2816	CHINA SOUTHERN AIRLINES		25083	359	04/14/91	RB211-535E4		
B757-21B	B-2817	CHINA SOUTHERN AIRLINES		25258	389	08/22/91	RB211-535E4		
B757-21B	B-2818	CHINA SOUTHERN AIRLINES		25259	392	09/03/91	RB211-535E4		
B757-21B	B-2822	CHINA SOUTHERN AIRLINES		25884	461	06/11/92	RB211-535E4		
B757-21B	B-2823	CHINA SOUTHERN AIRLINES		25888	575	09/17/93	RB211-535E4		
B757-21B	B-2824	CHINA SOUTHERN AIRLINES		25889	583	11/04/93	RB211-535E4		
B757-21B	B-2825	CHINA SOUTHERN AIRLINES		25890	585	11/12/93	RB211-535E4		
B757-236	B-2835	CHINA SOUTHERN AIRLINES		25598	445	06/03/93	RB211-535E4		N5573P
B757-2Z0	B-2838	CHINA SOUTHERN AIRLINES		27260	613	05/02/94	RB211-535E4		
B757-2Z0	B-2820	CHINA SOUTHWEST AIRLINES		25885	476	08/05/92	RB211-535E4		
B757-2Z0	B-2821	CHINA SOUTHWEST AIRLINES		25886	480	08/19/92	RB211-535E4		
B757-2Y0	B-2826	CHINA SOUTHWEST AIRLINES (GECA)		26155	495	10/29/92	RB211-535E4		
B757-2Z0	B-2832	CHINA SOUTHWEST AIRLINES		25887	554	06/04/93	RB211-535E4		
B757-2Z0	B-2836	CHINA SOUTHWEST AIRLINES		27258	595	02/25/94	RB211-535E4		
B757-2Z0	B-2837	CHINA SOUTHWEST AIRLINES		27259	609	08/11/94	RB211-535E4		
B757-2Z0	B-2839	CHINA SOUTHWEST AIRLINES		27269	615	08/12/94	RB211-535E4		
B757-2Z0	B-2840	CHINA SOUTHWEST AIRLINES		27270	622	08/12/94	RB211-535E4		
B757-2Z0	B-2841	CHINA SOUTHWEST AIRLINES		27367	624	08/15/94	RB211-535E4		
B757-2Z0	B-2844	CHINA SOUTHWEST AIRLINES		27511	669	05/04/95	RB211-535E4		[OPF NGE]
B757-2Z0	B-2845	CHINA SOUTHWEST AIRLINES		27512	674	06/01/96	RB211-535E4		
B757-2Z0	B-2855	CHINA SOUTHWEST AIRLINES		29792	822	09/28/98	RB211-535E4		[LST RNA]
B757-2Z0	B-2856	CHINA SOUTHWEST AIRLINES		29793	833	11/24/98	RB211-535E4		[LST RNA 03/99]
B757-28S	B-2812	CHINA XINJIANG AIRLINES		32341	961	04/19/01	RB211-535E4		
B757-28S	B-2813	CHINA XINJIANG AIRLINES	N	32342	966		RB211-535E4		

344

A/C TYPE	CURRENT REG. NO.	LAST KNOWN OPERATOR (OWNER)	Status	ORIGINAL MSN	LINE NO.	DEL. DATE	ENG. TYPE	FLEET NO.	PREV. REG. [COMMENTS]
B757-2Y0	B-2827	CHINA XINJIANG AIRLINES (GECA)		26156	503	11/25/92	RB211-535E4		
B757-2Y0	B-2831	CHINA XINJIANG AIRLINES (GECA)		26153	482	08/26/92	RB211-535E4		
B757-28S	B-2851	CHINA XINJIANG AIRLINES		29215	797	04/30/98	RB211-535E4		
B757-28A	B-2852	CHINA XINJIANG AIRLINES (ILFC)		28833	782	12/12/97	RB211-535E4		N711LF
B757-28S	B-2853	CHINA XINJIANG AIRLINES		29216	811	07/08/98	RB211-535E4		
B757-28S	B-2859	CHINA XINJIANG AIRLINES		29217	868	06/02/99	RB211-535E4		
B757-26D	B-2808	SHANGHAI AIRLINES		24471	231	08/04/89	PW2037		N1792B
B757-26D	B-2809	SHANGHAI AIRLINES		24472	235	08/29/89	PW2037		N5573B
B757-26D	B-2810	SHANGHAI AIRLINES (PEGA)		24473	301	08/03/90	PW2037		
B757-26D	B-2833	SHANGHAI AIRLINES		27152	560	06/29/93	PW2037		
B757-26D	B-2834	SHANGHAI AIRLINES		27183	576	09/24/93	PW2037		
B757-26D	B-2842	SHANGHAI AIRLINES		27342	626	08/24/94	PW2037		
B757-26D	B-2843	SHANGHAI AIRLINES		27681	684	07/26/95	PW2037		
B757-25C	B-2819	XIAMEN AIRLINES		25898	475	08/12/92	RB211-535E4		
B757-25C	B-2828	XIAMEN AIRLINES		25899	565	07/21/93	RB211-535E4		
B757-25C	B-2829	XIAMEN AIRLINES		25900	574	08/30/93	RB211-535E4		
B757-25C	B-2848	XIAMEN AIRLINES		27513	685	08/07/95	RB211-535E4		
B757-25C	B-2849	XIAMEN AIRLINES		27517	698	02/07/96	RB211-535E4		

B-CHINA (TAIWAN)

A/C TYPE	CURRENT REG. NO.	LAST KNOWN OPERATOR (OWNER)	Status	ORIGINAL MSN	LINE NO.	DEL. DATE	ENG. TYPE	FLEET NO.	PREV. REG. [COMMENTS]
B757-2Q8	B-27001	FAR EASTERN AIR TRANSPORT (ILFC)		25044	369	05/28/91	PW2037		CC-CYG, N341LF
B757-29J	B-27007	FAR EASTERN AIR TRANSPORT		27204	591	11/08/94	PW2037		SU-RAD
B757-27A	B-27011	FAR EASTERN AIR TRANSPORT		29607	832	12/08/98	PW2037		
B757-27A	B-27013	FAR EASTERN AIR TRANSPORT		29608	835	12/14/98	PW2037		
B757-27A	B-27015	FAR EASTERN AIR TRANSPORT		29609	876	07/08/99	PW2037		N1786B
B757-27A	B-27017	FAR EASTERN AIR TRANSPORT		29610	904	12/22/99	PW2037		
B757-27A	B-27021	FAR EASTERN AIR TRANSPORT		29611	910	01/27/00	PW2037		N1787B

C-CANADA

A/C TYPE	CURRENT REG. NO.	LAST KNOWN OPERATOR (OWNER)	Status	ORIGINAL MSN	LINE NO.	DEL. DATE	ENG. TYPE	FLEET NO.	PREV. REG. [COMMENTS]
B757-23A	C-GTSE	AIR TRANSAT (FINO)		25488	471	11/20/92	RB211-535E4	TSE	N1792B
B757-23A (ET)	C-GTSF	AIR TRANSAT (AWAS)		25491	511	12/10/92	RB211-535E4	TSF	
B757-236	C-GTSJ	AIR TRANSAT (ILFC)		24772	271	03/26/90	RB211-535E4	TSJ	G-BRJF, I-BRJF, C-GNXB
B757-28A	C-GTSN	AIR TRANSAT (ILFC)		24543	268	03/12/90	RB211-535E4	TSN	C-GTDL, N911AW, N871LF, C-GNXU
B757-28A	C-GTSV	AIR TRANSAT (ILFC)		25622	530	03/10/93	RB211-535E4	622	S7-AAX
B757-28A	C-FOOE	CANADA 3000 (AWAS)		24369	226	05/05/89	RB211-535E4		[LST JMC AS G-JMCF]
B757-23A (ET)	C-FOOH	CANADA 3000 (AWAS)		24293	220	04/06/89	RB211-535E4		G-OOOH, N989AN
B757-28A	C-FOON	CANADA 3000 (ILFC)		28161	723	09/23/96	RB211-535E4		
B757-28A	C-FXOF	CANADA 3000 (ILFC)		24544	280	04/30/90	RB211-535E4		

A/C TYPE	CURRENT REG. NO.	LAST KNOWN OPERATOR (OWNER)	Status	ORIGINAL MSN	LINE NO.	DEL. DATE	ENG. TYPE	FLEET NO.	PREV. REG. [COMMENTS]
B757-23A (ET)	C-FXOK	CANADA 3000 (AWAS)		24924	333	03/12/91	RB211-535E4		5Y-BHG
B757-2Q8	C-FXOO	CANADA 3000 (ILFC)		25621	457	05/18/92	RB211-535E4		
B757-236	C-GRYO	CANADA 3000 (BBAM)		24118	163	03/01/88	RB211-535E4		G-BNSD, EC-204, EC-EMA, PH-TKY, N769BE
B757-236	C-GRYZ	CANADA 3000 (BBAM)		24119	167	04/05/88	RB211-535E4		EC-157, EC-EHY, G-BPSN, PH-TKZ, N770BE
B757-236	C-GRYK	ROYAL AVIATION (BBAM)		25593	466	06/25/92	RB211-535E4		C-FNXY, G-BUDZ, SE-DSL, N593KA

CN-MOROCCO

B757-2B6	CN-RMT	ROYAL AIR MAROC (CHEMCO)		23686	103	07/11/86	PW2037		N32831
B757-2B6	CN-RMZ	ROYAL AIR MAROC (CHEMCO)		23687	106	08/07/86	PW2037		

D-GERMANY

B757-230	D-ABNB	CONDOR (DLLG)		24738	274	04/05/90	PW2040		[LST DUTCH BIRD AS PH-DBB]
B757-230	D-ABNC	CONDOR (DLLG)		24747	275	04/11/90	PW2040		[LST DUTCH BIRD AS PH-DBA]
B757-230	D-ABND	CONDOR (DLLG)		24748	285	05/24/90	PW2040		[LST DUTCH BIRD AS PH-DBH]
B757-230	D-ABNE	CONDOR (DLLG)		24749	295	07/12/90	PW2040		N35153
B757-230	D-ABNF	CONDOR (HAVEL)		25140	382	07/29/91	PW2040		
B757-230	D-ABNH	CONDOR		25436	419	01/24/92	PW2040		
B757-230	D-ABNI	CONDOR (SPRUCE)		25437	422	01/30/92	PW2040		
B757-230	D-ABNK	CONDOR (MOSEL&LAHN)		25438	428	02/20/92	PW2040		
B757-230	D-ABNL	CONDOR		25439	437	03/19/92	PW2040		
B757-230	D-ABNM	CONDOR (DIA LTD)		25440	443	04/09/92	PW2040		
B757-230	D-ABNN	CONDOR		25441	446	04/21/92	PW2040		
B757-230	D-ABNO	CONDOR		25901	464	06/27/92	PW2040		
B757-230	D-ABNP	CONDOR		26433	521	02/12/93	PW2040		
B757-230	D-ABNR	CONDOR		26434	532	03/16/93	PW2040		
B757-230	D-ABNS	CONDOR		26435	537	04/01/93	PW2040		
B757-230	D-ABNT	CONDOR (DLLG)		26436	587	03/10/94	PW2040		N3502P, N1790B
B757-330	D-ABOA	CONDOR		29016	804	06/25/99	RB211-535E4B		N757X [FIRST 757-300]
B757-330	D-ABOB	CONDOR		29017	810	05/20/99	RB211-535E4B		N6067B
B757-330	D-ABOC	CONDOR		29015	818	05/05/99	RB211-535E4B		N6069D
B757-330	D-ABOE	CONDOR		29012	839	03/10/99	RB211-535E4B		N1012N
B757-330	D-ABOF	CONDOR		29013	846	03/13/99	RB211-535E4B		
B757-330	D-ABOG	CONDOR		29014	849	03/19/99	RB211-535E4B		N1786B
B757-330	D-ABOH	CONDOR		30030	855	03/30/99	RB211-535E4B		N1787B
B757-330	D-ABOI	CONDOR		29018	909	03/22/00	RB211-535E4B		N1002R
B757-330	D-ABOJ	CONDOR		29019	915	03/13/00	RB211-535E4B		
B757-330	D-ABOK	CONDOR		29020	918	03/25/00	RB211-535E4B		N1795B
B757-330	D-ABOL	CONDOR		29021	923	04/29/00	RB211-535E4B		
B757-330	D-ABOM	CONDOR		29022	926	05/17/00	RB211-535E4B		
B757-330	D-ABON	CONDOR		29023	929	06/02/00	RB211-535E4B		N1003M

A/C TYPE	CURRENT REG. NO.	LAST KNOWN OPERATOR (OWNER)	Status	ORIGINAL MSN	LINE NO.	DEL. DATE	ENG. TYPE	FLEET NO.	PREV. REG. [COMMENTS]
B757-2G5	D-AMUG	LTU INTL. AIRWAYS (UNICAPITAL)		29488	830	10/31/98	RB211-535E4		
B757-2G5	D-AMUH	LTU INTL. AIRWAYS (UNICAPITAL)		29489	834	11/20/98	RB211-535E4		
B757-2G5	D-AMUI	LTU INTL. AIRWAYS (UNICAPITAL)		28112	708	04/15/96	RB211-535E4		
B757-225	D-AMUK	LTU INTL. AIRWAYS (UNICAPITAL)		22689	117	12/19/86	RB211-535E4		N525EA, EC-390, EC-ETZ [LST ATLAS INTL. TURKEY]
B757-2G5	D-AMUM	LTU INTL. AIRWAYS (UNICAPITAL)		24451	227	05/05/89	RB211-535E4		
B757-225	D-AMUU	LTU INTL. AIRWAYS (UNICAPITAL)		22688	115	12/19/86	RB211-535E4		N524EA, EC-FIY [LST ATLAS INTL. TURKEY]
B757-2G5	D-AMUV	LTU INTL. AIRWAYS (UNICAPITAL)		23928	146	10/01/87	RB211-535E4		
B757-2G5	D-AMUW	LTU INTL. AIRWAYS (UNICAPITAL)		23929	153	11/18/87	RB211-535E4		
B757-2G5	D-AMUX	LTU INTL. AIRWAYS (UNICAPITAL)		23983	161	03/08/88	RB211-535E4		
B757-2G5	D-AMUY	LTU INTL. AIRWAYS (UNICAPITAL)		24176	173	04/21/88	RB211-535E4		
B757-2G5	D-AMUZ	LTU INTL. AIRWAYS (UNICAPITAL)		24497	228	05/11/89	RB211-535E4		

D4-CAPE VERDE IS.

| B757-2Q8 | D4-CBG | TACV (ILFC) | | 27599 | 696 | 03/15/96 | PW2037 | | |

EC-SPAIN

B757-236	EC-FEE	AIR EUROPA (CITG)		25053	358	04/11/91	RB211-535E4		EC-667 [LST/OPF IBE]
B757-236	EC-FFK	AIR EUROPA (INGL)		24122	187	07/29/88	RB211-535E4		G-BNSF, EC-203, EC-ELS, EC-744 [LST/OPF IBE]
B757-256	EC-FYJ	AIR EUROPA (ITOH)		26242	593	07/27/94	RB211-535E4		N35030, EC-608 [LST IBE]
B757-256	EC-FYK	AIR EUROPA (ITOH)		26243	603	07/29/94	RB211-535E4		EC-609 [LST/OPF IBE]
B757-256	EC-FYN	AIR EUROPA (CITG)		26246	620	08/04/94	RB211-535E4		EC-612 [OPF IBE]
B757-236	EC-GBX	AIR EUROPA (GEONET)		25597	441	04/15/92	RB211-535E4		EC-957, EC-FLY, D-AMUL, EC-897 [LST/OPF IBE]
B757-236	EC-FEE	IBERIA (AEA)	L	25053	358	04/11/91	RB211-535E4		EC-667 [OPB AEA]
B757-236	EC-FFK	IBERIA (AEA)	L	24122	187	07/29/88	RB211-535E4		G-BNSF, EC-203, EC-ELS, EC-744 [OPB AEA]
B757-256	EC-FTR	IBERIA		26239	553	06/07/93	RB211-535E4		EC-420
B757-256	EC-FXV	IBERIA (CITI)		26241	572	08/17/93	RB211-535E4		EC-422, EC-FUB, EC-618
B757-256	EC-FYJ	IBERIA (AEA)	L	26242	593	07/27/94	RB211-535E4		N35030, EC-608
B757-256	EC-FYK	IBERIA (AEA)	L	26243	603	07/29/94	RB211-535E4		EC-609
B757-236	EC-GBX	IBERIA (AEA)	L	25597	441	04/15/92	RB211-535E4		EC-957, EC-FLY, D-AMUL, EC-897 [OPB AEA]
B757-256	EC-GZY	IBERIA		26247	860	04/30/99	RB211-535E4		N1795B
B757-256	EC-GZZ	IBERIA		26248	863	04/30/99	RB211-535E4		
B757-256	EC-HAA	IBERIA		26249	881	08/16/99	RB211-535E4		N1786B
B757-256	EC-HDM	IBERIA		26250	889	09/22/99	RB211-535E4		
B757-256	EC-HDR	IBERIA		26251	897	11/12/99	RB211-535E4		
B757-256	EC-HDS	IBERIA		26252	900	12/02/99	RB211-535E4		
B757-256	EC-HDU	IBERIA		26253	902	12/07/99	RB211-535E4		
B757-256	EC-HDV	IBERIA		26254	905	12/22/99	RB211-535E4		N1786B
B757-256	EC-HIP	IBERIA		29306	920	04/24/00	RB211-535E4		
B757-256	EC-HIQ	IBERIA		29307	924	05/12/00	RB211-535E4		
B757-256	EC-HIR	IBERIA		29308	935	07/20/00	RB211-535E4		N1795B

A/C TYPE	CURRENT REG. NO.	LAST KNOWN OPERATOR (OWNER)	Status	ORIGINAL MSN	LINE NO.	DEL. DATE	ENG. TYPE	FLEET NO.	PREV. REG. [COMMENTS]
B757-256	EC-HIS	IBERIA		29309	936	07/31/00	RB211-535E4		
B757-256	EC-HIT	IBERIA		29310	938	08/14/00	RB211-535E4		
B757-256	EC-HIU	IBERIA		29311	940	09/13/00	RB211-535E4		
B757-256	EC-HIV	IBERIA		29312	943	10/10/00	RB211-535E4		
B757-256	EC-HIX	IBERIA		30052	948	12/06/00	RB211-535E4		
B757-2G5	EC-HQV	LTE INTL. AIRWAYS (A/C 23118)		23118	36	05/25/84	RB211-535C		D-AMUR, D-AMUA, EC-EFX
B757-2G5	EC-HQX	LTE INTL. AIRWAYS (A/C 23651)		23651	116	12/08/86	RB211-535C		D-AMUT, EC-256, D-AMUC, EC-ENQ
B757-2G5	EC-HRB	LTE INTL. AIRWAYS		23119	51	02/11/85	RB211-535C		EC-116, D-AMUB, EC-EGH
B757-236(ER)	EC-EEC	SOUTH ATLANTIC AIRWAYS (AIZ)	L	24121	183	06/30/88	RB211-535E4		G-BNSE, EC-544, EC-EXH, G-BPEH, TC-AHA, 4X-BAZ

ET-ETHIOPIA

A/C TYPE	CURRENT REG. NO.	LAST KNOWN OPERATOR (OWNER)	Status	ORIGINAL MSN	LINE NO.	DEL. DATE	ENG. TYPE	FLEET NO.	PREV. REG. [COMMENTS]
B757-260PF	ET-AJS	ETHIOPIAN AIRLINES		24845	300	08/24/90	PW2040		N3519L, VH-AWE
B757-260	ET-AJX	ETHIOPIAN AIRLINES		25014	348	02/25/91	PW2040		
B757-260	ET-AKC	ETHIOPIAN AIRLINES		25353	408	11/18/91	PW2040		
B757-260	ET-AKE	ETHIOPIAN AIRLINES		26057	444	04/22/92	PW2040		
B757-260	ET-AKF	ETHIOPIAN AIRLINES		26058	496	10/29/92	PW2040		

EZ-TURKMENISTAN

A/C TYPE	CURRENT REG. NO.	LAST KNOWN OPERATOR (OWNER)	Status	ORIGINAL MSN	LINE NO.	DEL. DATE	ENG. TYPE	FLEET NO.	PREV. REG. [COMMENTS]
B757-23A	EZ-A010	TURKMENISTAN AIRLINES		25345	412	01/12/94	RB211-535E4		N58AW [VIP CONF; OPF GOVT]
B757-22K	EZ-A011	TURKMENISTAN AIRLINES		28336	725	08/29/96	RB211-535E4		VR-BTA
B757-22K	EZ-A012	TURKMENISTAN AIRLINES		28337	726	08/30/96	RB211-535E4		VR-BTB
B757-22K	EZ-A014	TURKMENISTAN AIRLINES		30863	952	01/30/01	RB211-535E4		

G-UNITED KINGDOM

A/C TYPE	CURRENT REG. NO.	LAST KNOWN OPERATOR (OWNER)	Status	ORIGINAL MSN	LINE NO.	DEL. DATE	ENG. TYPE	FLEET NO.	PREV. REG. [COMMENTS]
B757-225	G-JALC	AIRTOURS INTL. (ANFIELD)		22194	5	02/28/83	RB211-535E4		N504EA
B757-23A (ET)	G-LCRC	AIRTOURS INTL. (AWAS)		24636	259	02/01/90	RB211-535E4		G-IEAB
B757-225	G-MCEA	AIRTOURS INTL. (GOODISON)		22200	20	06/28/83	RB211-535E4		N510EA
B757-225	G-PIDS	AIRTOURS INTL. (ELLAND)		22195	6	05/20/83	RB211-535E4		N505EA
B757-225	G-RJGR	AIRTOURS INTL. (EWOOD)		22197	8	12/28/82	RB211-535E4		N507EA, N701MG
B757-21K	G-WJAN	AIRTOURS INTL. (ALCUDIA)		28674	746	03/20/97	RB211-535E4		
B757-26N	G-OOBA	AIR 2000 (GECA)		32446	950	02/05/01	RB211-535E4		N558NA, N446GE
B757-26N	G-OOBB	AIR 2000 (GECA)		32447	951	02/06/01	RB211-535E4		N559NA, N447GE
B757-28A	G-OOOA	AIR 2000 (ILFC)		23767	127	04/01/87	RB211-535E4		C-FOOA
B757-28A	G-OOOB	AIR 2000 (CEFL)		23822	130	04/27/87	RB211-535E4		C-FOOB, C-FRYH
B757-28A (ER)	G-OOOC	AIR 2000 (BBAM)		24017	162	03/10/88	RB211-535E4		C-FXOC, C-FRYL
B757-28A	G-OOOD	AIR 2000 (BBAM)		24235	180	05/27/88	RB211-535E4		C-FXOD, C-GRYU
B757-23A (ER)	G-OOOG	AIR 2000 (AWAS)		24292	219	03/29/89	RB211-535E4		C-FOOG [OPF "TCS EXPEDITIONS"]
B757-23A (ER)	G-OOOI	AIR 2000 (AWAS)		24289	209	02/15/89	RB211-535E4		EC-247, EC-EMV, N510SK

A/C TYPE	CURRENT REG. NO.	LAST KNOWN OPERATOR (OWNER)	Status	ORIGINAL MSN	LINE NO.	DEL. DATE	ENG. TYPE	FLEET NO.	PREV. REG. [COMMENTS]
B757-23A (ER)	G-OOOJ	AIR 2000 (AWAS)		24290	212	02/27/89	RB211-535E4		EC-248, EC-EMU, N510FP
B757-225	G-OOOM	AIR 2000 (CITG)		22612	114	11/11/86	RB211-535E4		N523EA, SE-DUN
B757-236 (ER)	G-OOOS	AIR 2000 (PHOENIX III INVEST.)		24397	221	04/13/89	RB211-535E4		G-BRJD, EC-349, EC-ESC
B757-2Y0 (ER)	G-OOOU	AIR 2000 (BUCKINGHAM PART.)		25240	388	08/30/91	RB211-535E4		[OPF "TCS EXPEDITIONS"]
B757-225	G-OOOV	AIR 2000 (GATX)		22211	74	12/06/85	RB211-535E4		N521EA
B757-225	G-OOOW	AIR 2000 (GATX)		22611	75	12/05/85	RB211-535E4		N522EA
B757-2Y0 (ER)	G-OOOX	AIR 2000 (ALPS-94-1)		26158	526	02/24/93	RB211-535E4		[LST RDN 12/26/00]
B757-28A (ER)	G-OOOY	AIR 2000 (ILFC)		28203	802	05/21/98	RB211-535E4		
B757-204 (ER)	G-BYAD	BRITANNIA AIRWAYS		26963	450	05/06/92	RB211-535E4		
B757-204 (ER)	G-BYAE	BRITANNIA AIRWAYS		26964	452	05/12/92	RB211-535E4		
B757-204 (ER)	G-BYAF	BRITANNIA AIRWAYS (ILFC)		26266	514	01/13/93	RB211-535E4		
B757-204	G-BYAH	BRITANNIA AIRWAYS (THOMSON)		26966	520	02/05/93	RB211-535E4		
B757-204	G-BYAI	BRITANNIA AIRWAYS (THOMSON)		26967	522	03/01/93	RB211-535E4		
B757-204 (ER)	G-BYAJ	BRITANNIA AIRWAYS (ILFC)		25623	528	03/04/93	RB211-535E4		
B757-204	G-BYAK	BRITANNIA AIRWAYS (ILFC)		26267	538	04/06/93	RB211-535E4		
B757-204	G-BYAL	BRITANNIA AIRWAYS (ILFC)		25626	549	05/13/93	RB211-535E4		
B757-204	G-BYAN	BRITANNIA AIRWAYS (ILFC)		27219	596	01/26/94	RB211-535E4		
B757-204	G-BYAO	BRITANNIA AIRWAYS (ITID LSG)		27235	598	02/03/94	RB211-535E4		
B757-204	G-BYAP	BRITANNIA AIRWAYS		27236	600	02/15/94	RB211-535E4		
B757-204	G-BYAR	BRITANNIA AIRWAYS		27237	602	03/01/94	RB211-535E4		
B757-204	G-BYAS	BRITANNIA AIRWAYS		27238	604	03/09/94	RB211-535E4		
B757-204	G-BYAT	BRITANNIA AIRWAYS (ILFC)		27208	606	03/21/94	RB211-535E4		
B757-204	G-BYAU	BRITANNIA AIRWAYS (ILFC)		27220	618	05/18/94	RB211-535E4		
B757-204	G-BYAW	BRITANNIA AIRWAYS		27234	663	04/03/95	RB211-535E4		
B757-204	G-BYAX	BRITANNIA AIRWAYS (ILFC)		28834	850	02/24/99	RB211-535E4		
B757-204	G-BYAY	BRITANNIA AIRWAYS (ILFC)		28836	861	04/13/99	RB211-535E4		N1786B
B757-236	G-BIKB	BRITISH AIRWAYS		22173	10	01/25/83	RB211-535C		[TO BE CVTD TO SF FOR BCS]
B757-236	G-BIKC	BRITISH AIRWAYS		22174	11	01/31/83	RB211-535C		[LRF 04/17/01; TO BE CVTD TO SF FOR BCS]
B757-236	G-BIKD	BRITISH AIRWAYS		22175	13	03/10/83	RB211-535C		[LRF 05/05/01; TO BE CVTD TO SF FOR BCS]
B757-236	G-BIKF	BRITISH AIRWAYS		22177	16	04/28/83	RB211-535C		[TO BE CVTD TO SF FOR BCS]
B757-236	G-BIKG	BRITISH AIRWAYS		22178	23	08/26/83	RB211-535C		[TO BE CVTD TO SF FOR BCS]
B757-236	G-BIKH	BRITISH AIRWAYS		22179	24	10/18/83	RB211-535C		[LRF 03/23/01; TO BE CVTD TO SF FOR BCS]
B757-236	G-BIKI	BRITISH AIRWAYS		22180	25	11/30/83	RB211-535C		[LRF 09/22/00; TO IAB; TO BE CVTD TO SF FOR BCS]
B757-236	G-BIKJ	BRITISH AIRWAYS		22181	29	01/09/84	RB211-535C		[LRF 07/01/00; TO BE CVTD TO SF FOR BCS/DHL; FERRIED TO MZJ 01/18/01]
B757-236	G-BIKK	BRITISH AIRWAYS		22182	30	02/01/84	RB211-535C		[TO BE CVTD TO SF FOR BCS]
B757-236	G-BIKL	BRITISH AIRWAYS		22183	32	02/29/84	RB211-535C		[TO BE CVTD TO SF FOR BCS]
B757-236	G-BIKM	BRITISH AIRWAYS		22184	33	03/21/84	RB211-535C		N8293V [TO BE CVTD TO SF FOR BCS]

A/C TYPE	CURRENT REG. NO.	LAST KNOWN OPERATOR (OWNER)	Status	ORIGINAL MSN	LINE NO.	DEL. DATE	ENG. TYPE	FLEET NO.	PREV. REG. [COMMENTS]
B757-236	G-BIKN	BRITISH AIRWAYS		22186	50	01/23/85	RB211-535C		[TO BE CVTD TO SF FOR BCS]
B757-236	G-BIKO	BRITISH AIRWAYS		22187	52	02/14/85	RB211-535C		[PARKED CHR; TO BE CVTD TO SF FOR BCS]
B757-236	G-BIKP	BRITISH AIRWAYS		22188	54	03/11/85	RB211-535C		[LRF 02/14/01; TO BE CVTD TO SF FOR BCS]
B757-236	G-BIKR	BRITISH AIRWAYS		22189	58	03/29/85	RB211-535C		[TO BE CVTD TO SF FOR BCS]
B757-236	G-BIKS	BRITISH AIRWAYS		22190	63	05/31/85	RB211-535C		[TO BE CVTD TO SF FOR BCS]
B757-236	G-BIKT	BRITISH AIRWAYS		23398	77	11/01/85	RB211-535C		[TO BE CVTD TO SF FOR BCS]
B757-236	G-BIKU	BRITISH AIRWAYS		23399	78	11/07/85	RB211-535C		[TO BE CVTD TO SF FOR BCS]
B757-236	G-BIKV	BRITISH AIRWAYS		23400	81	12/09/85	RB211-535C		[TO BE CVTD TO SF FOR BCS]
B757-236	G-BIKW	BRITISH AIRWAYS		23492	89	03/07/86	RB211-535C		[TO BE CVTD TO SF FOR BCS]
B757-236	G-BIKX	BRITISH AIRWAYS		23493	90	03/14/86	RB211-535C		[TO BE CVTD TO SF FOR BCS]
B757-236	G-BIKY	BRITISH AIRWAYS		23533	93	03/28/86	RB211-535C		[TO BE CVTD TO SF FOR BCS]
B757-236	G-BIKZ	BRITISH AIRWAYS		23532	98	05/15/86	RB211-535C		[TO BE CVTD TO SF FOR BCS]
B757-236	G-BMRA	BRITISH AIRWAYS		23710	123	03/02/87	RB211-535C		[TO BE CVTD TO SF FOR BCS]
B757-236	G-BMRB	BRITISH AIRWAYS		23975	145	09/25/87	RB211-535C		[TO BE CVTD TO SF FOR BCS]
B757-236	G-BMRC	BRITISH AIRWAYS		24072	160	01/22/88	RB211-535C		[TO BE CVTD TO SF FOR BCS]
B757-236	G-BMRD	BRITISH AIRWAYS		24073	166	02/29/88	RB211-535C		[TO BE CVTD TO SF FOR BCS]
B757-236	G-BMRE	BRITISH AIRWAYS		24074	168	03/23/88	RB211-535C		[TO BE CVTD TO SF FOR BCS]
B757-236	G-BMRF	BRITISH AIRWAYS		24101	175	05/13/88	RB211-535C		[TO BE CVTD TO SF FOR BCS]
B757-236	G-BMRG	BRITISH AIRWAYS		24102	179	05/31/88	RB211-535C		[TO BE CVTD TO SF FOR BCS]
B757-236	G-BMRH	BRITISH AIRWAYS		24266	210	02/21/89	RB211-535C		[TO BE CVTD TO SF FOR BCS]
B757-236	G-BMRI	BRITISH AIRWAYS		24267	211	02/17/89	RB211-535C		[TO BE CVTD TO SF FOR BCS]
B757-236	G-BMRJ	BRITISH AIRWAYS		24268	214	03/06/89	RB211-535C		[TO BE CVTD TO SF FOR BCS]
B757-236 (ET)	G-BPEB	BRITISH AIRWAYS (BBAM)		24371	225	04/27/89	RB211-535E4		[LRF 02/28/01; PARKED TUS 03/10/01]
B757-236 (ET)	G-BPEC	BRITISH AIRWAYS		24882	323	11/06/90	RB211-535E4		
B757-236 (ET)	G-BPED	BRITISH AIRWAYS		25059	363	04/30/91	RB211-535E4		
B757-236 (ET)	G-BPEE	BRITISH AIRWAYS		25060	364	05/03/91	RB211-535E4		
B757-236 (ET)	G-BPEF	BRITISH AIRWAYS (BBAM)		24120	174	05/04/88	RB211-535E4		G-BOHC, EC-202, EC-ELA
B757-236	G-BPEI	BRITISH AIRWAYS		25806	601	03/09/94	RB211-535E4		
B757-236	G-BPEJ	BRITISH AIRWAYS		25807	610	04/25/94	RB211-535E4		
B757-236	G-BPEK	BRITISH AIRWAYS		25808	665	03/17/95	RB211-535E4		
B757-236	G-CPEL	BRITISH AIRWAYS		24398	224	04/26/89	RB211-535E4		G-BRJE, EC-278, EC-597, EC-EOL, N602DF
B757-236	G-CPEM	BRITISH AIRWAYS		28665	747	03/28/97	RB211-535E4		
B757-236	G-CPEN	BRITISH AIRWAYS		28666	751	04/23/97	RB211-535E4		
B757-236	G-CPEO	BRITISH AIRWAYS		28667	762	07/12/97	RB211-535E4		
B757-2Y0	G-CPEP	BRITISH AIRWAYS		25268	400	10/19/91	RB211-535E4		XA-TAE, N400KL, EI-CLP, C-GTSU [LRF 07/12/00; TO BE CVTD TO FRTR FOR BCS; STD MZJ]
B757-236	G-CPER	BRITISH AIRWAYS		29113	784	12/02/97	RB211-535E4		
B757-236	G-CPES	BRITISH AIRWAYS		29114	793	03/17/98	RB211-535E4		
B757-236	G-CPET	BRITISH AIRWAYS		29115	798	05/12/98	RB211-535E4		
B757-236	G-CPEU	BRITISH AIRWAYS (CITG)		29941	864	05/01/99	RB211-535E4		
B757-236	G-CPEV	BRITISH AIRWAYS (CITG)		29943	871	06/11/99	RB211-535E4		N1795B

A/C TYPE	CURRENT REG. NO.	LAST KNOWN OPERATOR (OWNER)	Status	ORIGINAL MSN	LINE NO.	DEL. DATE	ENG. TYPE	FLEET NO.	PREV. REG. [COMMENTS]
B757-28A	G-FCLA	JMC AIR (ILFC)		27621	738	02/26/97	RB211-535E4		N1789B
B757-28A	G-FCLB	JMC AIR (ILFC)		28164	749	03/25/97	RB211-535E4		N751NA
B757-28A	G-FCLC	JMC AIR (ILFC)		28166	756	05/09/97	RB211-535E4		
B757-25F (ET)	G-FCLD	JMC AIR (GATX)		28718	752	04/25/97	RB211-535E4		
B757-28A	G-FCLE	JMC AIR (ILFC)		28171	805	05/24/98	RB211-535E4		
B757-28A	G-FCLF	JMC AIR (ILFC)		28835	858	03/23/99	RB211-535E4		
B757-28A	G-FCLG	JMC AIR (ILFC)		24367	208	02/01/89	RB211-535E4		C-GAWB, C-GNXI, C-GTSK, N240LA, N381LF, EI-CLM, N701LF
B757-28A	G-FCLH	JMC AIR (ILFC)		26274	676	06/06/95	RB211-535E4		N161LF, EI-CLU, N751LF
B757-28A	G-FCLI	JMC AIR (ILFC)		26275	672	05/01/95	RB211-535E4		N151LF, EI-CLV, N651LF
B757-2Y0	G-FCLJ	JMC AIR (GECA)		26160	555	04/01/94	RB211-535E4		N3519M, EI-CJX, N160GE
B757-2Y0	G-FCLK	JMC AIR (GECA)		26161	557	04/13/94	RB211-535E4		N3521N, EI-CJY, N161GE
B757-25F	G-JMCD	JMC AIR (GATX)		30757	928	05/26/00	RB211-535E4		N1795B
B757-25F	G-JMCE	JMC AIR (GATX)		30758	932	06/23/00	RB211-535E4		N1795B
B757-28A	G-JMCF	JMC AIR (CMM)	L	24369	226	05/05/89	RB211-535E4		C-FOOE
B757-2G5	G-JMCG	JMC AIR (ILFC)		26278	671	04/26/95	RB211-535E4		D-AMUQ
B757-3CQ	G-JMAA	JMC AIR		32241	960	04/24/01	RB211-535E4		N5002K
B757-3CQ	G-JMAB	JMC AIR	N	32242	963		RB211-535E4		
B757-2T7	G-DAJB	MONARCH AIRLINES		23770	125	03/16/87	RB211-535E4		
B757-2T7	G-MONB	MONARCH AIRLINES		22780	15	03/22/83	RB211-535E4		
B757-2T7	G-MONC	MONARCH AIRLINES		22781	18	04/25/83	RB211-535E4		D-ABNY, PH-AHO
B757-2T7	G-MOND	MONARCH AIRLINES		22960	19	05/16/83	RB211-535E4		D-ABNZ
B757-2T7	G-MONE	MONARCH AIRLINES		23293	56	03/13/85	RB211-535E4		
B757-2T7	G-MONJ	MONARCH AIRLINES		24104	170	04/22/88	RB211-535E4		
B757-2T7	G-MONK	MONARCH AIRLINES		24105	172	04/15/88	RB211-535E4		
HB-SWITZERLAND									
B757-2G5	HB-IHR	BALAIR/CTA LEISURE (ILFC)		29379	919	04/19/00	RB211-535E4		
B757-2G5	HB-IHS	BALAIR/CTA LEISURE (ILFC)		30394	922	04/28/00	RB211-535E4		
B757-23A	HB-IEE	PRIVATAIR (TIERRALTA HOLDINGS)		24527	249	10/02/89	RB211-535E4		HB-IHU
HK-COLOMBIA									
B757-2Y0	EI-CEY	AVIANCA (GECA)		26152	478	08/13/92	RB211-535E4		
B757-2Y0	EI-CEZ	AVIANCA (GECA)		26154	486	09/22/92	RB211-535E4		
B757-2Q8	N321LF	AVIANCA (ILFC)		26269	612	04/28/94	RB211-535E4		[RETROJET C/S]

A/C TYPE	CURRENT REG. NO.	LAST KNOWN OPERATOR (OWNER)	STATUS	ORIGINAL MSN	LINE NO.	DEL. DATE	ENG. TYPE	FLEET NO.	PREV. REG. [COMMENTS]
HS-THAILAND									
B757-2Z0	B-2844	ANGEL AIRLINES (CXN)	L	27511	669	05/04/95	RB211-535E4		
HZ-SAUDI ARABIA									
B757-24Q	N757MA	MID EAST JET (FSBU)		28463	739	01/27/97	PW2040		[VIP CONF]
B757-23A	HZ-HMED	SAUDI ARABIAN VIP AIRCRAFT		25495	599	06/03/94	RB211-535E4		N1786B, N1789B, N275AW (MOBILE HOSPITAL)
B757-23APF	VH-BRN	SNAS AVIATION (NORDSTRESS)		24868	314	09/24/90	RB211-535E4		N572CA [OPB NORDSTRESS]
LV-ARGENTINA									
B757-2Y0(ER)	G-OOOX	DINAR LINEAS AEREAS (AMM)	L	26158	526	02/24/93	RB211-535E4		
B757-2Q8	LV-WMH	LAPA (ILFC)		26332	688	09/15/95	PW2040		
B757-2Q8	LV-WTS	LAPA (ILFC)		25131	458	06/02/92	PW2040		CC-CYH
N-UNITED STATES OF AMERICA									
B757-200	N757A	BOEING LOGISTICS SPARES INC.		22212	1	02/18/82	PW2037		[PROTOTYPE; BOEING DEFENSE & SPACE GROUP]
B757-2J4	N770BB	THE YUCAIPA COMPANIES		25220	387	09/25/91	RB211-535E4		N3510B, OY-SHB, VR-CAU, VP-CAU
B757-223	N181AN	AMERICAN AIRLINES		29591	852	02/27/99	RB211-535E4B	5EN	N5573L
B757-223	N182AN	AMERICAN AIRLINES		29592	853	03/03/99	RB211-535E4B	5EP	
B757-223 (ET)	N183AN	AMERICAN AIRLINES		29593	862	04/22/99	RB211-535E4B	5ER	
B757-223 (ET)	N184AN	AMERICAN AIRLINES		29594	866	05/13/99	RB211-535E4B	5ES	N1787B
B757-223	N185AN	AMERICAN AIRLINES	N	32379	962		RB211-535E4B		
B757-223	N186AN	AMERICAN AIRLINES	N	32380	964		RB211-535E4B		
B757-223	N187AN	AMERICAN AIRLINES	N	32381	965		RB211-535E4B		
B757-223	N188AN	AMERICAN AIRLINES	N	32382	969		RB211-535E4B		
B757-223	N189AN	AMERICAN AIRLINES	N	32383	970		RB211-535E4B		
B757-223	N601AN	AMERICAN AIRLINES		27052	661	02/17/95	RB211-535E4B	5DU	
B757-223	N602AN	AMERICAN AIRLINES		27053	664	03/10/95	RB211-535E4B	5DV	
B757-223	N603AA	AMERICAN AIRLINES		27054	670	04/21/95	RB211-535E4B	5DW	
B757-223	N604AA	AMERICAN AIRLINES		27055	677	06/12/95	RB211-535E4B	5DX	
B757-223	N605AA	AMERICAN AIRLINES		27056	680	06/28/95	RB211-535E4B	5DY	
B757-223	N606AA	AMERICAN AIRLINES		27057	707	04/11/96	RB211-535E4B	5EA	
B757-223	N607AM	AMERICAN AIRLINES		27058	712	05/16/96	RB211-535E4B	5EB	
B757-223 (ET)	N608AA	AMERICAN AIRLINES		27446	720	07/16/96	RB211-535E4B	5EC	
B757-223 (ET)	N609AA	AMERICAN AIRLINES		27447	722	07/29/96	RB211-535E4B	5ED	
B757-223	N610AA	AMERICAN AIRLINES		24486	234	07/31/89	RB211-535E4B	610	
B757-223	N611AM	AMERICAN AIRLINES		24487	236	07/17/89	RB211-535E4B	611	

A/C TYPE	CURRENT REG. NO.	LAST KNOWN OPERATOR (OWNER)	STATUS	ORIGINAL MSN	LINE NO.	DEL. DATE	ENG. TYPE	FLEET NO.	PREV. REG. [COMMENTS]
B757-223	N612AA	AMERICAN AIRLINES		24488	240	08/04/89	RB211-535E4B	612	
B757-223	N613AA	AMERICAN AIRLINES		24489	242	08/11/89	RB211-535E4B	613	
B757-223	N614AA	AMERICAN AIRLINES (WTCI)		24490	243	08/18/89	RB211-535E4B	614	
B757-223	N615AM	AMERICAN AIRLINES (WTCI)		24491	245	09/12/89	RB211-535E4B	615	
B757-223	N616AA	AMERICAN AIRLINES (WTCI)		24524	248	09/28/89	RB211-535E4B	616	
B757-223	N617AM	AMERICAN AIRLINES		24525	253	11/17/89	RB211-535E4B	617	
B757-223	N618AA	AMERICAN AIRLINES (FIRST UNION)		24526	260	02/05/90	RB211-535E4B	618	
B757-223	N619AA	AMERICAN AIRLINES (FIRST UNION)		24577	269	03/19/90	RB211-535E4B	619	
B757-223	N620AA	AMERICAN AIRLINES (FIRST UNION)		24578	276	04/17/90	RB211-535E4B	620	
B757-223	N621AM	AMERICAN AIRLINES		24579	283	05/17/90	RB211-535E4B	621	
B757-223	N622AA	AMERICAN AIRLINES		24580	289	06/11/90	RB211-535E4B	622	
B757-223	N623AA	AMERICAN AIRLINES		24581	296	07/11/90	RB211-535E4B	623	
B757-223	N624AA	AMERICAN AIRLINES		24582	297	07/16/90	RB211-535E4B	624	
B757-223	N625AA	AMERICAN AIRLINES		24583	303	08/08/90	RB211-535E4B	625	
B757-223	N626AA	AMERICAN AIRLINES		24584	304	08/14/90	RB211-535E4B	626	
B757-223	N627AA	AMERICAN AIRLINES		24585	308	09/10/90	RB211-535E4B	627	
B757-223	N628AA	AMERICAN AIRLINES		24586	309	08/31/90	RB211-535E4B	628	
B757-223	N629AA	AMERICAN AIRLINES (FIRST UNION)		24587	315	09/28/90	RB211-535E4B	629	
B757-223	N630AA	AMERICAN AIRLINES (FIRST UNION)		24588	316	10/04/90	RB211-535E4B	630	
B757-223	N631AA	AMERICAN AIRLINES		24589	317	10/09/90	RB211-535E4B	631	
B757-223	N632AA	AMERICAN AIRLINES		24590	321	10/26/90	RB211-535E4B	632	
B757-223	N633AA	AMERICAN AIRLINES		24591	324	11/16/90	RB211-535E4B	633	
B757-223	N634AA	AMERICAN AIRLINES		24592	327	11/19/90	RB211-535E4B	634	
B757-223	N635AA	AMERICAN AIRLINES		24593	328	11/28/90	RB211-535E4B	635	
B757-223	N636AM	AMERICAN AIRLINES		24594	336	01/18/91	RB211-535E4B	636	
B757-223	N637AM	AMERICAN AIRLINES		24595	337	01/16/91	RB211-535E4B	637	
B757-223	N638AA	AMERICAN AIRLINES		24596	344	02/22/91	RB211-535E4B	638	
B757-223	N639AA	AMERICAN AIRLINES		24597	345	02/26/91	RB211-535E4B	639	
B757-223	N640A	AMERICAN AIRLINES		24598	350	03/15/91	RB211-535E4B	640	
B757-223	N641AA	AMERICAN AIRLINES		24599	351	03/25/91	RB211-535E4B	641	
B757-223	N642AA	AMERICAN AIRLINES		24600	357	04/05/91	RB211-535E4B	642	
B757-223	N643AA	AMERICAN AIRLINES		24601	360	04/19/91	RB211-535E4B	643	
B757-223	N644AA	AMERICAN AIRLINES		24602	365	05/08/91	RB211-535E4B	5BP	
B757-223	N645AA	AMERICAN AIRLINES		24603	370	05/30/91	RB211-535E4B	5BR	
B757-223	N646AA	AMERICAN AIRLINES		24604	375	06/21/91	RB211-535E4B	5BS	
B757-223	N647AM	AMERICAN AIRLINES		24605	378	07/02/91	RB211-535E4B	5BT	
B757-223	N648AA	AMERICAN AIRLINES		24606	379	07/10/91	RB211-535E4B	5BU	
B757-223	N649AA	AMERICAN AIRLINES		24607	383	07/25/91	RB211-535E4B	5BV	
B757-223	N650AA	AMERICAN AIRLINES (FIRST UNION)		24608	384	07/31/91	RB211-535E4B	5BW	
B757-223	N652AA	AMERICAN AIRLINES (FIRST UNION)		24610	391	08/28/91	RB211-535E4B	5BY	
B757-223	N653A	AMERICAN AIRLINES		24611	397	10/08/91	RB211-535E4B	5CA	

A/C TYPE	CURRENT REG. NO.	LAST KNOWN OPERATOR (OWNER)	Status	ORIGINAL MSN	LINE NO.	DEL. DATE	ENG. TYPE	FLEET NO.	PREV. REG. [COMMENTS]
B757-223	N654A	AMERICAN AIRLINES		24612	398	10/10/91	RB211-535E4B	5CB	
B757-223	N655AA	AMERICAN AIRLINES		24613	402	10/29/91	RB211-535E4B	5CC	
B757-223	N656AA	AMERICAN AIRLINES		24614	404	11/06/91	RB211-535E4B	5CD	
B757-223	N657AM	AMERICAN AIRLINES		24615	409	12/06/91	RB211-535E4B	5CE	
B757-223	N658AA	AMERICAN AIRLINES		24616	410	11/27/91	RB211-535E4B	5CF	
B757-223	N659AA	AMERICAN AIRLINES		24617	417	01/09/92	RB211-535E4B	5CG	["PRIDE OF AMERICAN"]
B757-223	N660AM	AMERICAN AIRLINES		25294	418	01/17/92	RB211-535E4B	5CH	
B757-223	N661AA	AMERICAN AIRLINES		25295	423	01/30/92	RB211-535E4B	5CJ	
B757-223	N662AA	AMERICAN AIRLINES		25296	425	02/07/92	RB211-535E4B	5CK	
B757-223	N663AM	AMERICAN AIRLINES		25297	432	03/05/92	RB211-535E4B	5CL	
B757-223	N664AA	AMERICAN AIRLINES		25298	433	03/02/92	RB211-535E4B	5CM	
B757-223	N665AA	AMERICAN AIRLINES		25299	436	03/17/92	RB211-535E4B	5CN	
B757-223	N666A	AMERICAN AIRLINES		25300	451	05/07/92	RB211-535E4B	5CP	
B757-223	N7667A	AMERICAN AIRLINES		25301	459	06/04/92	RB211-535E4B	5CR	
B757-223	N668AA	AMERICAN AIRLINES		25333	460	06/10/92	RB211-535E4B	5CS	
B757-223	N669AA	AMERICAN AIRLINES		25334	463	06/24/92	RB211-535E4B	5CT	
B757-223	N670AA	AMERICAN AIRLINES		25335	468	07/10/92	RB211-535E4B	5CU	
B757-223	N671AA	AMERICAN AIRLINES		25336	473	07/24/92	RB211-535E4B	5CV	
B757-223	N672AA	AMERICAN AIRLINES		25337	474	07/29/92	RB211-535E4B	5CW	
B757-223	N673AN	AMERICAN AIRLINES		29423	812	08/05/98	RB211-535E4B	5EE	
B757-223	N674AN	AMERICAN AIRLINES		29424	816	08/17/98	RB211-535E4B	5EF	
B757-223	N675AN	AMERICAN AIRLINES		29425	817	08/24/98	RB211-535E4B	5EG	
B757-223	N676AN	AMERICAN AIRLINES		29426	827	10/27/98	RB211-535E4B	5EH	N1798B
B757-223	N677AN	AMERICAN AIRLINES		29427	828	11/02/98	RB211-535E4B	5EJ	
B757-223	N678AN	AMERICAN AIRLINES		29428	837	12/11/98	RB211-535E4B	5EK	N1787B
B757-223	N679AN	AMERICAN AIRLINES		29589	842	01/15/99	RB211-535E4B	5EL	N1795B, N1800B [40TH JET ANNIVERSARY "ASTROJET" C/S TO BE REMOVED]
B757-223	N680AN	AMERICAN AIRLINES		29590	847	01/28/99	RB211-535E4B	5EM	N1787B
B757-223	N681AA	AMERICAN AIRLINES		25338	483	08/28/92	RB211-535E4B	5CX	
B757-223	N682AA	AMERICAN AIRLINES		25339	484	09/02/92	RB211-535E4B	5CY	
B757-223	N683A	AMERICAN AIRLINES		25340	491	10/14/92	RB211-535E4B	5DA	
B757-223	N684AA	AMERICAN AIRLINES		25341	504	12/02/92	RB211-535E4B	5DB	
B757-223	N685AA	AMERICAN AIRLINES		25342	507	12/09/92	RB211-535E4B	5DC	
B757-223	N686AA	AMERICAN AIRLINES		25343	509	12/16/92	RB211-535E4B	5DD	
B757-223 (ET)	N687AA	AMERICAN AIRLINES		25695	536	03/31/93	RB211-535E4B	5DE	
B757-223 (ET)	N688AA	AMERICAN AIRLINES		25730	548	05/12/93	RB211-535E4B	5DF	
B757-223 (ET)	N689AA	AMERICAN AIRLINES		25731	562	07/09/93	RB211-535E4B	5DG	
B757-223 (ET)	N690AA	AMERICAN AIRLINES		25696	566	07/26/93	RB211-535E4B	5DH	
B757-223 (ET)	N691AA	AMERICAN AIRLINES		25697	568	08/11/93	RB211-535E4B	5DJ	
B757-223 (ET)	N692AA	AMERICAN AIRLINES		26972	578	10/08/93	RB211-535E4B	5DK	
B757-223	N693AA	AMERICAN AIRLINES		26973	580	01/07/94	RB211-535E4B	5DL	

A/C TYPE	CURRENT REG. NO.	LAST KNOWN OPERATOR (OWNER)	Status	ORIGINAL MSN	LINE NO.	DEL. DATE	ENG. TYPE	FLEET NO.	PREV. REG. [COMMENTS]
B757-223	N694AN	AMERICAN AIRLINES		26974	582	01/26/94	RB211-535E4B	5DM	
B757-223	N695AN	AMERICAN AIRLINES		26975	621	06/13/94	RB211-535E4B	5DN	
B757-223	N696AN	AMERICAN AIRLINES		26976	627	07/15/94	RB211-535E4B	5DP	
B757-223	N697AN	AMERICAN AIRLINES		26977	633	08/17/94	RB211-535E4B	5DR	
B757-223	N698AN	AMERICAN AIRLINES		26980	635	08/30/94	RB211-535E4B	5DS	
B757-223	N699AN	AMERICAN AIRLINES		27051	660	02/10/95	RB211-535E4B	5DT	
B757-23N (ET)	N514AT	AMERICAN TRANS AIR (SSBT)		27971	690	09/26/95	RB211-535E4	514	
B757-23N (ET)	N515AT	AMERICAN TRANS AIR (ICX CORP)		27598	692	10/11/95	RB211-535E4	515	
B757-23N (ET)	N516AT	AMERICAN TRANS AIR (FINO)		27972	694	12/04/95	RB211-535E4	516	
B757-23N (ET)	N517AT	AMERICAN TRANS AIR (FINO)		27973	735	11/25/96	RB211-535E4	517	
B757-23N (ET)	N518AT	AMERICAN TRANS AIR (GECA)		27974	737	12/10/96	RB211-535E4	518	
B757-23N (ET)	N519AT	AMERICAN TRANS AIR (GECA)		27975	779	11/17/97	RB211-535E4	519	
B757-23N (ET)	N520AT	AMERICAN TRANS AIR (FANB LEASE)		27976	814	07/31/98	RB211-535E4	520	
B757-28A (ET)	N521AT	AMERICAN TRANS AIR (ACG ACQUISITION)		24368	213	03/03/89	RB211-535E4	521	G-MCKE
B757-23N (ET)	N522AT	AMERICAN TRANS AIR (DEBI)		29330	843	12/30/98	RB211-535E4	522	
B757-23N (ET)	N523AT	AMERICAN TRANS AIR (NATIONSCREDIT)		30232	888	09/21/99	RB211-535E4	523	
B757-23N (ET)	N524AT	AMERICAN TRANS AIR (NATIONSCREDIT)		30233	895	10/25/99	RB211-535E4	524	N1795B
B757-23N (ET)	N525AT	AMERICAN TRANS AIR (FSBU)		30548	930	06/16/00	RB211-535E4	525	N1795B
B757-23N (ET)	N526AT	AMERICAN TRANS AIR (FSBU)		30735	931	06/23/00	RB211-535E4	526	
B757-23N (ET)	N527AT	AMERICAN TRANS AIR (FSBU)		30886	945	11/01/00	RB211-535E4	527	
B757-23N (ET)	N528AT	AMERICAN TRANS AIR (FSBU)		30887	946	11/15/00	RB211-535E4	528	
B757-2S7	N901AW	AMERICA WEST AIRLINES (FIRST UNION)		23321	76	12/19/85	RB211-535E4		N601RC
B757-2S7	N902AW	AMERICA WEST AIRLINES (FIRST UNION)		23322	79	12/06/85	RB211-535E4		N602RC
B757-2S7	N903AW	AMERICA WEST AIRLINES		23323	80	12/30/85	RB211-535E4		N603RC
B757-2S7	N904AW	AMERICA WEST AIRLINES		23566	96	05/19/86	RB211-535E4		N604RC
B757-2S7	N905AW	AMERICA WEST AIRLINES		23567	97	05/19/86	RB211-535E4		N605RC
B757-2S7	N906AW	AMERICA WEST AIRLINES		23568	99	05/28/86	RB211-535E4		N606RC
B757-225	N907AW	AMERICA WEST AIRLINES (CITG)		22691	155	12/10/87	RB211-535E4		N527EA, XA-TCD
B757-2G7	N908AW	AMERICA WEST AIRLINES		24233	244	08/25/89	RB211-535E4		
B757-2G7	N909AW	AMERICA WEST AIRLINES (FSBU)		24522	252	11/07/89	RB211-535E4		
B757-2G7	N910AW	AMERICA WEST AIRLINES (PLC LSG)		24523	256	11/29/89	RB211-535E4		
B757-225	N913AW	AMERICA WEST AIRLINES (WTCI)		22207	35	10/29/84	RB211-535E4		N517EA
B757-225	N914AW	AMERICA WEST AIRLINES (WTCI)		22208	38	10/30/84	RB211-535E4		N518EA
B757-225	N915AW	AMERICA WEST AIRLINES (WTCI)		22209	40	11/21/84	RB211-535E4		N519EA, TC-GUL, N747BJ
B757-224	N58101	CONTINENTAL AIRLINES		27291	614	05/12/94	RB211-535E4B	101	
B757-224	N14102	CONTINENTAL AIRLINES		27292	619	06/03/94	RB211-535E4B	102	
B757-224	N33103	CONTINENTAL AIRLINES		27293	623	06/24/94	RB211-535E4B	103	
B757-224	N17104	CONTINENTAL AIRLINES (GECA)		27294	629	07/29/94	RB211-535E4B	104	

355

A/C TYPE	CURRENT REG. NO.	LAST KNOWN OPERATOR (OWNER)	Status	ORIGINAL MSN	LINE NO.	DEL. DATE	ENG. TYPE	FLEET NO.	PREV. REG. [COMMENTS]
B757-224	N17105	CONTINENTAL AIRLINES (GECA)		27295	632	08/18/94	RB211-535E4B	105	
B757-224	N14106	CONTINENTAL AIRLINES (GECA)		27296	637	09/22/94	RB211-535E4B	106	
B757-224	N14107	CONTINENTAL AIRLINES (GECA)		27297	641	10/14/94	RB211-535E4B	107	
B757-224	N21108	CONTINENTAL AIRLINES (GECA)		27298	645	11/07/94	RB211-535E4B	108	
B757-224	N12109	CONTINENTAL AIRLINES (WFBN)		27299	648	12/05/94	RB211-535E4B	109	
B757-224	N13110	CONTINENTAL AIRLINES (GECA)		27300	650	12/06/94	RB211-535E4B	110	
B757-224	N57111	CONTINENTAL AIRLINES		27301	652	12/11/94	RB211-535E4B	111	
B757-224	N18112	CONTINENTAL AIRLINES (GECA)		27302	653	02/02/95	RB211-535E4B	112	
B757-224	N13113	CONTINENTAL AIRLINES (GECA)		27555	668	04/11/95	RB211-535E4B	113	
B757-224	N12114	CONTINENTAL AIRLINES (WFBN)		27556	682	07/03/95	RB211-535E4B	114	
B757-224	N14115	CONTINENTAL AIRLINES		27557	686	08/14/95	RB211-535E4B	115	
B757-224	N12116	CONTINENTAL AIRLINES (WFBN)		27558	702	03/27/96	RB211-535E4B	116	
B757-224	N19117	CONTINENTAL AIRLINES		27559	706	04/24/96	RB211-535E4B	117	
B757-224	N14118	CONTINENTAL AIRLINES		27560	748	03/21/97	RB211-535E4B	118	
B757-224	N18119	CONTINENTAL AIRLINES		27561	753	05/12/97	RB211-535E4B	119	
B757-224	N14120	CONTINENTAL AIRLINES		27562	761	06/24/97	RB211-535E4B	120	
B757-224	N14121	CONTINENTAL AIRLINES		27563	766	07/29/97	RB211-535E4B	121	
B757-224	N17122	CONTINENTAL AIRLINES		27564	768	08/26/97	RB211-535E4B	122	
B757-224	N26123	CONTINENTAL AIRLINES (FSBU)		28966	781	12/12/97	RB211-535E4B	123	
B757-224	N29124	CONTINENTAL AIRLINES (FSBU)		27565	786	01/16/98	RB211-535E4B	124	
B757-224	N12125	CONTINENTAL AIRLINES (WFBN)		28967	788	02/02/98	RB211-535E4B	125	N1787B
B757-224 (ET)	N17126	CONTINENTAL AIRLINES		27566	790	02/20/98	RB211-535E4B	126	
B757-224 (ET)	N48127	CONTINENTAL AIRLINES		28968	791	02/25/98	RB211-535E4B	127	
B757-224 (ET)	N17128	CONTINENTAL AIRLINES		27567	795	03/20/98	RB211-535E4B	128	
B757-224 (ET)	N29129	CONTINENTAL AIRLINES		28969	796	03/27/98	RB211-535E4B	129	
B757-224 (ET)	N19130	CONTINENTAL AIRLINES		28970	799	05/08/98	RB211-535E4B	130	
B757-224	N34131	CONTINENTAL AIRLINES		28971	806	06/09/98	RB211-535E4B	131	
B757-224	N33132	CONTINENTAL AIRLINES		29281	809	06/30/98	RB211-535E4B	132	
B757-224	N17133	CONTINENTAL AIRLINES		29282	840	12/22/98	RB211-535E4B	133	N1795B
B757-224	N67134	CONTINENTAL AIRLINES		29283	848	02/02/99	RB211-535E4B	134	N1795B, N1800B
B757-224	N41135	CONTINENTAL AIRLINES		29284	851	02/19/99	RB211-535E4B	135	
B757-224	N19136	CONTINENTAL AIRLINES		29285	856	03/19/99	RB211-535E4B	136	
B757-224	N34137	CONTINENTAL AIRLINES		30229	899	11/29/99	RB211-535E4B	137	
B757-224	N13138	CONTINENTAL AIRLINES		30351	903	12/07/99	RB211-535E4B	138	N1795B
B757-224	N17139	CONTINENTAL AIRLINES		30352	911	02/03/00	RB211-535E4B	139	
B757-224	N41140	CONTINENTAL AIRLINES		30353	913	02/28/00	RB211-535E4B	140	
B757-224	N19141	CONTINENTAL AIRLINES		30354	933	06/30/00	RB211-535E4B	141	
B757-232	N601DL	DELTA AIRLINES		22808	37	02/28/85	PW2037	601	
B757-232	N602DL	DELTA AIRLINES		22809	39	11/05/84	PW2037	602	
B757-232	N603DL	DELTA AIRLINES		22810	41	11/07/84	PW2037	603	

A/C TYPE	CURRENT REG. NO.	LAST KNOWN OPERATOR (OWNER)	Status	ORIGINAL MSN	LINE NO.	DEL. DATE	ENG. TYPE	FLEET NO.	PREV. REG. [COMMENTS]
B757-232	N604DL	DELTA AIRLINES		22811	43	12/03/84	PW2037	604	
B757-232	N605DL	DELTA AIRLINES		22812	46	12/07/84	PW2037	605	
B757-232	N606DL	DELTA AIRLINES		22813	49	01/17/85	PW2037	606	
B757-232	N607DL	DELTA AIRLINES		22814	61	05/14/85	PW2037	607	
B757-232	N608DA	DELTA AIRLINES		22815	64	05/31/85	PW2037	608	
B757-232	N609DL	DELTA AIRLINES		22816	65	06/11/85	PW2037	609	
B757-232	N610DL	DELTA AIRLINES		22817	66	06/28/85	PW2037	610	
B757-232	N611DL	DELTA AIRLINES		22818	71	08/23/85	PW2037	611	
B757-232	N612DL	DELTA AIRLINES		22819	73	10/18/85	PW2037	612	
B757-232	N613DL	DELTA AIRLINES		22820	84	01/24/86	PW2037	613	
B757-232	N614DL	DELTA AIRLINES		22821	85	01/27/86	PW2037	614	
B757-232	N615DL	DELTA AIRLINES		22822	87	02/28/86	PW2037	615	
B757-232	N616DL	DELTA AIRLINES		22823	91	04/02/86	PW2037	616	
B757-232	N617DL	DELTA AIRLINES		22907	92	05/21/86	PW2037	617	
B757-232	N618DL	DELTA AIRLINES		22908	95	04/25/86	PW2037	618	
B757-232	N619DL	DELTA AIRLINES (BTM CAP.)		22909	101	06/11/86	PW2037	619	
B757-232	N620DL	DELTA AIRLINES		22910	111	11/05/86	PW2037	620	
B757-232	N621DL	DELTA AIRLINES		22911	112	11/14/86	PW2037	621	
B757-232	N622DL	DELTA AIRLINES		22912	113	12/03/86	PW2037	622	
B757-232	N623DL	DELTA AIRLINES		22913	118	01/08/87	PW2037	623	
B757-232	N624DL	DELTA AIRLINES		22914	120	01/23/87	PW2037	624	
B757-232	N625DL	DELTA AIRLINES		22915	126	04/01/87	PW2037	625	
B757-232	N626DL	DELTA AIRLINES		22916	128	05/22/87	PW2037	626	
B757-232	N627DL	DELTA AIRLINES		22917	129	04/24/87	PW2037	627	
B757-232	N628DL	DELTA AIRLINES		22918	133	06/03/87	PW2037	628	
B757-232	N629DL	DELTA AIRLINES		22919	134	10/14/87	PW2037	629	
B757-232	N630DL	DELTA AIRLINES		22920	135	11/25/87	PW2037	630	
B757-232	N631DL	DELTA AIRLINES		23612	138	12/03/87	PW2037	631	
B757-232	N632DL	DELTA AIRLINES		23613	154	12/09/87	PW2037	632	
B757-232	N633DL	DELTA AIRLINES		23614	157	12/23/87	PW2037	633	
B757-232	N634DL	DELTA AIRLINES		23615	158	01/13/88	PW2037	634	
B757-232	N635DL	DELTA AIRLINES		23762	159	02/03/88	PW2037	635	
B757-232	N636DL	DELTA AIRLINES		23763	164	03/03/88	PW2037	636	
B757-232	N637DL	DELTA AIRLINES		23760	171	04/13/88	PW2037	637	
B757-232	N638DL	DELTA AIRLINES		23761	177	05/25/88	PW2037	638	
B757-232	N639DL	DELTA AIRLINES		23993	198	11/09/88	PW2037	639	
B757-232	N640DL	DELTA AIRLINES		23994	201	11/30/88	PW2037	640	
B757-232	N641DL	DELTA AIRLINES		23995	202	12/07/88	PW2037	641	
B757-232	N642DL	DELTA AIRLINES		23996	205	12/22/88	PW2037	642	
B757-232	N643DL	DELTA AIRLINES		23997	206	01/13/89	PW2037	643	
B757-232	N644DL	DELTA AIRLINES		23998	207	01/18/89	PW2037	644	

A/C TYPE	CURRENT REG. NO.	LAST KNOWN OPERATOR (OWNER)	Status	ORIGINAL MSN	LINE NO.	DEL. DATE	ENG. TYPE	FLEET NO.	PREV. REG. [COMMENTS]
B757-232	N645DL	DELTA AIRLINES		24216	216	04/06/89	PW2037	645	
B757-232	N646DL	DELTA AIRLINES		24217	217	04/05/89	PW2037	646	
B757-232	N647DL	DELTA AIRLINES		24218	222	05/03/89	PW2037	647	
B757-232	N648DL	DELTA AIRLINES		24372	223	05/04/89	PW2037	648	
B757-232	N649DL	DELTA AIRLINES		24389	229	05/25/89	PW2037	649	
B757-232	N650DL	DELTA AIRLINES		24390	230	06/28/89	PW2037	650	
B757-232	N651DL	DELTA AIRLINES		24391	238	07/26/89	PW2037	651	
B757-232	N652DL	DELTA AIRLINES		24392	239	07/27/89	PW2037	652	
B757-232	N653DL	DELTA AIRLINES		24393	261	02/09/90	PW2037	653	
B757-232	N654DL	DELTA AIRLINES		24394	264	02/22/90	PW2037	654	
B757-232	N655DL	DELTA AIRLINES		24395	265	02/28/90	PW2037	655	
B757-232	N656DL	DELTA AIRLINES		24396	266	03/07/90	PW2037	656	
B757-232	N657DL	DELTA AIRLINES		24419	286	05/21/90	PW2037	657	
B757-232	N658DL	DELTA AIRLINES		24420	287	05/24/90	PW2037	658	
B757-232	N659DL	DELTA AIRLINES		24421	293	06/25/90	PW2037	659	
B757-232	N660DL	DELTA AIRLINES		24422	294	06/22/90	PW2037	660	
B757-232	N661DN	DELTA AIRLINES		24972	335	12/23/90	PW2037	661	
B757-232	N662DN	DELTA AIRLINES		24991	342	01/28/91	PW2037	662	
B757-232	N663DN	DELTA AIRLINES		24992	343	02/09/91	PW2037	663	
B757-232	N664DN	DELTA AIRLINES		25012	347	02/21/91	PW2037	664	
B757-232	N665DN	DELTA AIRLINES		25013	349	03/01/91	PW2037	665	
B757-232	N666DN	DELTA AIRLINES		25034	354	03/22/91	PW2037	666	
B757-232	N667DN	DELTA AIRLINES		25035	355	03/27/91	PW2037	667	
B757-232	N668DN	DELTA AIRLINES		25141	376	06/26/91	PW2037	668	
B757-232	N669DN	DELTA AIRLINES		25142	377	06/28/91	PW2037	669	
B757-232	N6700	DELTA AIRLINES		30337	890	09/24/99	PW2037	6700	N1787B
B757-232	N6701	DELTA AIRLINES		30187	892	10/07/99	PW2037	6701	N1786B [2002 OLYMPIC C/S]
B757-232	N6702	DELTA AIRLINES		30188	898	11/20/99	PW2037	6702	
B757-232	N6703D	DELTA AIRLINES		30234	908	01/21/00	PW2037	6703	N1795B
B757-232	N6704Z	DELTA AIRLINES		30396	914	04/04/00	PW2037	6704	N1795B
B757-232	N6705Y	DELTA AIRLINES		30397	917	04/07/00	PW2037	6705	N1786B
B757-232	N6706Q	DELTA AIRLINES		30422	921	05/03/00	PW2037	6706	
B757-232	N6707A	DELTA AIRLINES		30395	927	05/31/00	PW2037	6707	
B757-232	N6708D	DELTA AIRLINES		30480	934	07/20/00	PW2037	6708	
B757-232	N6709	DELTA AIRLINES		30481	937	08/10/00	PW2037	6709	
B757-232	N670DN	DELTA AIRLINES		25331	415	01/09/92	PW2037	670	
B757-232	N6710E	DELTA AIRLINES		30482	939	08/28/00	PW2037	6710	
B757-232	N6711M	DELTA AIRLINES		30483	941	09/28/00	PW2037	6711	
B757-232	N6712B	DELTA AIRLINES		30484	942	10/02/00	PW2037	6712	
B757-232	N6713Y	DELTA AIRLINES		30777	944	10/31/00	PW2037	6713	
B757-232	N6714Q	DELTA AIRLINES		30485	949	12/19/00	PW2037	6714	

A/C TYPE	CURRENT REG. NO.	LAST KNOWN OPERATOR (OWNER)	Status	ORIGINAL MSN	LINE NO.	DEL. DATE	ENG. TYPE	FLEET NO.	PREV. REG. [COMMENTS]
B757-232	N6715C	DELTA AIRLINES		30486	953	02/14/01	PW2037	6715	
B757-232	N6716C	DELTA AIRLINES		30838	955	03/09/01	PW2037	6716	
B757-232	N67171	DELTA AIRLINES		30839	959	04/12/01	PW2037	6717	
B757-232	N671DN	DELTA AIRLINES		25332	416	01/10/92	PW2037	671	
B757-232	N672DL	DELTA AIRLINES		25977	429	02/21/92	PW2037	672	
B757-232	N673DL	DELTA AIRLINES		25978	430	02/24/92	PW2037	673	
B757-232	N674DL	DELTA AIRLINES		25979	439	03/25/92	PW2037	674	
B757-232	N675DL	DELTA AIRLINES		25980	448	04/29/92	PW2037	675	
B757-232	N676DL	DELTA AIRLINES		25981	455	05/28/92	PW2037	676	
B757-232	N677DL	DELTA AIRLINES		25982	456	05/22/92	PW2037	677	
B757-232	N678DL	DELTA AIRLINES		25983	465	06/26/92	PW2037	678	
B757-232	N679DA	DELTA AIRLINES		26955	500	11/12/92	PW2037	679	
B757-232	N680DA	DELTA AIRLINES		26956	502	11/19/92	PW2037	680	
B757-232	N681DA	DELTA AIRLINES		26957	516	01/23/93	PW2037	681	
B757-232	N682DA	DELTA AIRLINES		26958	518	01/15/93	PW2037	682	
B757-232	N683DA	DELTA AIRLINES		27103	533	03/18/93	PW2037	683	
B757-232	N684DA	DELTA AIRLINES		27104	535	03/26/93	PW2037	684	
B757-232	N685DA	DELTA AIRLINES		27588	667	03/31/95	PW2037	685	
B757-232	N686DA	DELTA AIRLINES		27589	689	09/20/95	PW2037	686	
B757-232	N687DL	DELTA AIRLINES		27586	800	05/04/98	PW2037	687	
B757-232	N688DL	DELTA AIRLINES		27587	803	05/21/98	PW2037	688	
B757-232	N689DL	DELTA AIRLINES		27172	807	06/18/98	PW2037	689	
B757-232	N690DL	DELTA AIRLINES		27585	808	06/26/98	PW2037	690	
B757-232	N692DL	DELTA AIRLINES		29724	820	09/04/98	PW2037	692	N1799B
B757-232	N693DL	DELTA AIRLINES		29725	826	10/17/98	PW2037	693	N1799B
B757-232	N694DL	DELTA AIRLINES		29726	831	11/11/98	PW2037	694	
B757-232	N695DL	DELTA AIRLINES		29727	838	12/11/98	PW2037	695	N1795B
B757-232	N696DL	DELTA AIRLINES		29728	845	01/27/99	PW2037	696	N1795B
B757-232	N697DL	DELTA AIRLINES		30318	880	08/01/99	PW2037	697	
B757-232	N698DL	DELTA AIRLINES		29911	885	08/31/99	PW2037	698	
B757-232	N699DL	DELTA AIRLINES		29970	887	09/13/99	PW2037	699	N1795B
B757-212	N750AT	DELTA AIRLINES		23126	45	11/26/84	PW2037	6902	9V-SGL
B757-212	N751AT	DELTA AIRLINES		23125	44	11/12/84	PW2037	6901	9V-SGK
B757-212	N752AT	DELTA AIRLINES		23128	48	12/12/84	PW2037	6904	9V-SGN
B757-212	N757AT	DELTA AIRLINES		23127	47	12/11/84	PW2037	6903	9V-SGM
B757-26D	N900PC	DELTA AIRLINES		28446	740	01/21/97	PW2037	691	
B757-236	N757BJ	LUXURY AIR LLC (U.S. BANCORP)		22176	14	03/30/83	RB211-535C		EC-EGI, G-BKRM, C-GANX, N501MH, EC-451, EC-FTL, N261PW

A/C TYPE	CURRENT REG. NO.	LAST KNOWN OPERATOR (OWNER)	Status	ORIGINAL MSN	LINE NO.	DEL. DATE	ENG. TYPE	FLEET NO.	PREV. REG. [COMMENTS]
B757-225	N557NA	NASA		22191	2	08/18/83	RB211-535E4		N501EA [ATMOSPHERIC AND ENVIRONMENTAL STUDIES]
B757-236	N506NA	NATIONAL AIRLINES (CITG)		24771	272	03/27/90	RB211-535E4		G-BRJG, PH-AHN, P4-AAA, G-IEAD, TF-FIK, G-SRJG, TC-AJA
B757-256	N508NA	NATIONAL AIRLINES (FSBU)		26244	616	08/02/94	RB211-535E4		EC-610, EC-FYL
B757-204	N512NA	NATIONAL AIRLINES (FSBU)		26962	440	04/10/92	RB211-535E4		G-BYAC, TC-ARA
B757-2T7	N513NA	NATIONAL AIRLINES (NIMBUS)		23895	132	05/11/87	RB211-535E4		G-DRJC, G-BYAM
B757-28A	N517NA	NATIONAL AIRLINES (MSA1)		24260	204	12/20/88	RB211-535E4		C-FNBC, C-GNXC, C-GTSV, N757GA
B757-236	N521NA	NATIONAL AIRLINES (PEGA)		25592	453	05/13/92	RB211-535E4		G-BUDX, SE-DSK, N592KA
B757-236	N522NA	NATIONAL AIRLINES (PEGA)		25133	374	06/18/91	RB211-535E4		N1786B, I-AEJA, OO-TBI, N127MA, B-17501, SE-DSN, XA-TJC
B757-28A	N523NA	NATIONAL AIRLINES (ILFC)		30043	925	05/19/00	RB211-535E4		N1787B
B757-236	N526NA	NATIONAL AIRLINES (TOMB)		24794	278	04/20/90	RB211-535E4		G-BRJH, EC-669, EC-FEF, EC-HDG
B757-23A	N541NA	NATIONAL AIRLINES (AWAS)		24291	215	03/02/89	RB211-535E4		G-OAHK, N250LA, N916AW, PH-AHK, N291AN
B757-256	N542NA	NATIONAL AIRLINES (SUNR)		26245	617	08/03/94	RB211-535E4		EC-611, EC-FYM
B757-236	N544NA	NATIONAL AIRLINES (WTCI)		29942	867	05/21/99	RB211-535E4		N1795B
B757-236	N545NA	NATIONAL AIRLINES (WTCI)		29944	872	06/14/99	RB211-535E4		
B757-236	N546NA	NATIONAL AIRLINES (WTCI)		29945	873	06/21/99	RB211-535E4		
B757-236	N547NA	NATIONAL AIRLINES (WTCI)		29946	877	07/13/99	RB211-535E4		N1795B
B757-23A	N757NA	NATIONAL AIRLINES (AWAS)		24567	257	03/01/90	RB211-535E4		N1791B
B757-28A	N750NA	NORTH AMERICAN AIRLINES (ILFC)		26277	658	01/27/95	RB211-535E4		
B757-28A	N752NA	NORTH AMERICAN AIRLINES (ILFC)		28174	865	05/12/99	RB211-535E4		N1795B
B757-28A	N754NA	NORTH AMERICAN AIRLINES (ILFC)		29381	958	04/03/01	RB211-535E4		
B757-28A	N756NA	NORTH AMERICAN AIRLINES (GECA)	N	32448	967				
B757-251	N501US	NORTHWEST AIRLINES		23190	53	02/28/85	PW2037	5501	
B757-251	N502US	NORTHWEST AIRLINES		23191	55	03/11/85	PW2037	5502	
B757-251	N503US	NORTHWEST AIRLINES		23192	59	04/22/85	PW2037	5503	
B757-251	N504US	NORTHWEST AIRLINES		23193	60	04/25/85	PW2037	5504	
B757-251	N505US	NORTHWEST AIRLINES		23194	62	05/17/85	PW2037	5505	
B757-251	N506US	NORTHWEST AIRLINES		23195	67	07/08/85	PW2037	5506	
B757-251	N507US	NORTHWEST AIRLINES		23196	68	07/22/85	PW2037	5507	
B757-251	N508US	NORTHWEST AIRLINES		23197	69	08/23/85	PW2037	5508	
B757-251	N509US	NORTHWEST AIRLINES		23198	70	10/04/85	PW2037	5509	
B757-251	N511US	NORTHWEST AIRLINES		23199	72	10/22/85	PW2037	5511	
B757-251	N512US	NORTHWEST AIRLINES		23200	82	12/18/85	PW2037	5512	
B757-251	N513US	NORTHWEST AIRLINES		23201	83	02/11/86	PW2037	5513	
B757-251	N514US	NORTHWEST AIRLINES		23202	86	02/19/86	PW2037	5514	

A/C TYPE	CURRENT REG. NO.	LAST KNOWN OPERATOR (OWNER)	Status	ORIGINAL MSN	LINE NO.	DEL. DATE	ENG. TYPE	FLEET NO.	PREV. REG. [COMMENTS]
B757-251	N515US	NORTHWEST AIRLINES		23203	88	05/01/86	PW2037	5515	
B757-251	N516US	NORTHWEST AIRLINES (SSBT)		23204	104	07/08/86	PW2037	5516	
B757-251	N517US	NORTHWEST AIRLINES (SSBT)		23205	105	08/01/86	PW2037	5517	
B757-251	N518US	NORTHWEST AIRLINES		23206	107	08/22/85	PW2037	5518	
B757-251	N519US	NORTHWEST AIRLINES		23207	108	10/06/86	PW2037	5519	
B757-251	N520US	NORTHWEST AIRLINES		23208	109	10/27/86	PW2037	5520	
B757-251	N521US	NORTHWEST AIRLINES		23209	110	12/01/86	PW2037	5521	
B757-251	N522US	NORTHWEST AIRLINES		23616	119	01/14/87	PW2037	5522	
B757-251	N523US	NORTHWEST AIRLINES		23617	121	01/29/87	PW2037	5523	
B757-251	N524US	NORTHWEST AIRLINES		23618	122	02/14/87	PW2037	5524	
B757-251	N525US	NORTHWEST AIRLINES		23619	124	04/14/87	PW2037	5525	
B757-251	N526US	NORTHWEST AIRLINES		23620	131	05/13/87	PW2037	5526	
B757-251	N527US	NORTHWEST AIRLINES (BANKBOSTON)		23842	136	07/02/87	PW2037	5527	
B757-251	N528US	NORTHWEST AIRLINES		23843	137	09/21/87	PW2037	5528	
B757-251	N529US	NORTHWEST AIRLINES		23844	140	09/28/87	PW2037	5529	
B757-251	N530US	NORTHWEST AIRLINES		23845	188	08/10/88	PW2037	5530	
B757-251	N531US	NORTHWEST AIRLINES		23846	190	08/25/88	PW2037	5531	
B757-251	N532US	NORTHWEST AIRLINES		24263	192	09/27/88	PW2037	5532	
B757-251	N533US	NORTHWEST AIRLINES		24264	194	09/30/88	PW2037	5533	
B757-251	N534US	NORTHWEST AIRLINES		24265	196	10/21/88	PW2037	5534	
B757-251	N535US	NORTHWEST AIRLINES		26482	693	11/14/95	PW2037	5635	
B757-251	N536US	NORTHWEST AIRLINES		26483	695	12/11/95	PW2037	5636	
B757-251	N537US	NORTHWEST AIRLINES		26484	697	02/20/96	PW2037	5637	
B757-251	N538US	NORTHWEST AIRLINES		26485	699	03/01/96	PW2037	5638	
B757-251	N539US	NORTHWEST AIRLINES		26486	700	03/25/96	PW2037	5639	
B757-251	N540US	NORTHWEST AIRLINES		26487	701	04/15/96	PW2037	5640	
B757-251	N541US	NORTHWEST AIRLINES		26488	703	04/19/96	PW2037	5641	
B757-251	N542US	NORTHWEST AIRLINES		26489	705	05/10/96	PW2037	5642	
B757-251	N543US	NORTHWEST AIRLINES		26490	709	05/15/96	PW2037	5643	
B757-251	N544US	NORTHWEST AIRLINES		26491	710	05/20/96	PW2037	5644	
B757-251	N545US	NORTHWEST AIRLINES		26492	711	06/20/96	PW2037	5645	
B757-251	N546US	NORTHWEST AIRLINES		26493	713	07/19/96	PW2037	5646	
B757-251	N547US	NORTHWEST AIRLINES		26494	714	08/23/96	PW2037	5647	
B757-251	N548US	NORTHWEST AIRLINES		26495	715	08/30/96	PW2037	5648	
B757-251	N549US	NORTHWEST AIRLINES		26496	716	09/20/96	PW2037	5649	
B757-251	N550NW	NORTHWEST AIRLINES	N	26497	968		PW2037		
B757-256	N286CD	PACE AIRLINES (MLW AVIATION)		26240	561	08/12/93	RB211-535E4		EC-421, EC-FUA, EC-616, EC-FXU

A/C TYPE	CURRENT REG. NO.	LAST KNOWN OPERATOR (OWNER) Status	ORIGINAL MSN	LINE NO.	DEL. DATE	ENG. TYPE	FLEET NO.	PREV. REG. [COMMENTS]
B757-22L	N1018N	STARFLIGHT INTL. CORP.	29304	870	12/17/99	RB211-535E4		
B757-23A	N757AV	STARFLIGHT INTL. CORP. (ASNET)	25493	523	11/15/94	RB211-535E4		N59AW, N512AT, N312SF [A.K.A. "86006" FOR U.S. GOVT?]
B757-2Q8	N701TW	TRANS WORLD AIRLINES (ILFC)	28160	721	07/22/96	PW2037	7501	
B757-2Q8	N702TW	TRANS WORLD AIRLINES (ILFC)	28162	732	10/22/96	PW2037	7502	
B757-2Q8(ET)	N703TW	TRANS WORLD AIRLINES (ILFC)	27620	736	11/22/96	PW2037	7503	
B757-2Q8	N704X	TRANS WORLD AIRLINES (ILFC)	28163	741	01/30/97	PW2037	7504	
B757-231	N705TW	TRANS WORLD AIRLINES (PEGA)	28479	742	02/10/97	PW2037	7505	
B757-2Q8	N706TW	TRANS WORLD AIRLINES (ILFC)	28165	743	02/18/97	PW2037	7506	
B757-2Q8(ET)	N707TW	TRANS WORLD AIRLINES (ILFC)	27625	744	02/24/97	PW2037	7507	
B757-231	N708TW	TRANS WORLD AIRLINES (AFIN)	28480	750	04/07/97	PW2037	7508	
B757-2Q8	N709TW	TRANS WORLD AIRLINES (ILFC)	28168	754	05/14/97	PW2037	7509	["ST. LOUIS RAMS" C/S]
B757-2Q8	N710TW	TRANS WORLD AIRLINES (ILFC)	28169	757	05/29/97	PW2037	7510	
B757-231	N711ZX	TRANS WORLD AIRLINES (SSBT)	28481	758	06/03/97	PW2037	7511	
B757-2Q8(ET)	N712TW	TRANS WORLD AIRLINES (ILFC)	27624	760	06/18/97	PW2037	7512	
B757-2Q8	N713TW	TRANS WORLD AIRLINES (ILFC)	28173	764	07/16/97	PW2037	7513	
B757-231	N714P	TRANS WORLD AIRLINES (PEGA)	28482	770	08/28/97	PW2037	7514	
B757-231	N715TW	TRANS WORLD AIRLINES (PEGA)	28483	777	10/23/97	PW2037	7515	
B757-231	N716TW	TRANS WORLD AIRLINES (FSBU)	28484	825	10/15/98	PW2037	7516	N1799B
B757-231	N717TW	TRANS WORLD AIRLINES (PEGA)	28485	854	03/15/99	PW2037	7517	
B757-231	N718TW	TRANS WORLD AIRLINES (FSBU)	28486	869	05/26/99	PW2037	7518	
B757-231	N719TW	TRANS WORLD AIRLINES (AFIN)	28487	878	07/26/99	PW2037	7519	
B757-231	N720TW	TRANS WORLD AIRLINES (AFIN)	30319	883	08/16/99	PW2037	7520	N1795B
B757-231	N721TW	TRANS WORLD AIRLINES (ILFC)	29954	874	06/29/99	PW2037	7521	
B757-231	N722TW	TRANS WORLD AIRLINES (ILFC)	29385	893	10/25/99	PW2037	7522	N1795B
B757-231	N723TW	TRANS WORLD AIRLINES (ILFC)	29378	907	01/18/00	PW2037	7523	
B757-231	N724TW	TRANS WORLD AIRLINES (PEGA)	28488	884	09/08/99	PW2037	7524	N1787B [PARKED LAX, LESS ENGINES(?)]
B757-231	N725TW	TRANS WORLD AIRLINES (FSBU)	30338	891	10/12/99	PW2037	7525	N1787B
B757-231	N726TW	TRANS WORLD AIRLINES (FSBU)	30339	896	11/18/99	PW2037	7526	N1795B
B757-231	N727TW	TRANS WORLD AIRLINES (PEGA)	30340	901	12/02/99	PW2037	7527	
B757-222	N501UA	UNITED AIRLINES (CITG)	24622	241	08/24/89	PW2037	5401	
B757-222	N502UA	UNITED AIRLINES	24623	246	09/14/89	PW2037	5402	
B757-222	N503UA	UNITED AIRLINES	24624	247	09/20/89	PW2037	5403	
B757-222	N504UA	UNITED AIRLINES	24625	251	10/16/89	PW2037	5404	
B757-222	N505UA	UNITED AIRLINES	24626	254	11/13/89	PW2037	5405	
B757-222	N506UA	UNITED AIRLINES	24627	263	02/21/90	PW2037	5406	
B757-222	N507UA	UNITED AIRLINES	24743	270	03/20/90	PW2037	5407	
B757-222	N508UA	UNITED AIRLINES	24744	277	04/18/90	PW2037	5408	
B757-222	N509UA	UNITED AIRLINES (TOMB)	24763	284	05/21/90	PW2037	5409	

A/C TYPE	CURRENT REG. NO.	LAST KNOWN OPERATOR (OWNER)	Status	ORIGINAL MSN	LINE NO.	DEL. DATE	ENG. TYPE	FLEET NO.	PREV. REG. [COMMENTS]
B757-222	N510UA	UNITED AIRLINES		24780	290	06/13/90	PW2037	5410	
B757-222	N511UA	UNITED AIRLINES		24799	291	06/20/90	PW2037	5411	
B757-222	N512UA	UNITED AIRLINES		24809	298	07/20/90	PW2037	5412	
B757-222	N513UA	UNITED AIRLINES		24810	299	07/24/90	PW2037	5413	
B757-222	N514UA	UNITED AIRLINES		24839	305	08/17/90	PW2037	5414	
B757-222	N515UA	UNITED AIRLINES		24840	306	08/21/90	PW2037	5415	
B757-222	N516UA	UNITED AIRLINES		24860	307	08/24/90	PW2037	5416	
B757-222	N517UA	UNITED AIRLINES		24861	310	09/24/90	PW2037	5417	
B757-222	N518UA	UNITED AIRLINES		24871	311	09/14/90	PW2037	5418	
B757-222	N519UA	UNITED AIRLINES		24872	312	09/14/90	PW2037	5419	
B757-222	N520UA	UNITED AIRLINES		24890	313	09/21/90	PW2037	5420	
B757-222	N521UA	UNITED AIRLINES (CUMBERLAND)		24891	319	10/16/90	PW2037	5421	
B757-222	N522UA	UNITED AIRLINES		24931	320	10/19/90	PW2037	5422	
B757-222	N523UA	UNITED AIRLINES		24932	329	11/29/90	PW2037	5423	
B757-222	N524UA	UNITED AIRLINES		24977	331	12/10/90	PW2037	5424	
B757-222	N525UA	UNITED AIRLINES		24978	338	01/15/91	PW2037	5425	
B757-222	N526UA	UNITED AIRLINES		24994	339	01/22/91	PW2037	5426	
B757-222	N527UA	UNITED AIRLINES		24995	341	02/27/91	PW2037	5427	
B757-222	N528UA	UNITED AIRLINES		25018	346	02/19/91	PW2037	5428	
B757-222	N529UA	UNITED AIRLINES		25019	352	03/22/91	PW2037	5429	
B757-222	N530UA	UNITED AIRLINES		25043	353	03/20/91	PW2037	5430	
B757-222	N531UA	UNITED AIRLINES		25042	361	04/19/91	PW2037	5431	
B757-222	N532UA	UNITED AIRLINES		25072	366	05/15/91	PW2037	5432	
B757-222	N533UA	UNITED AIRLINES		25073	367	05/16/91	PW2037	5433	
B757-222	N534UA	UNITED AIRLINES		25129	372	06/07/91	PW2037	5434	
B757-222	N535UA	UNITED AIRLINES		25130	373	06/12/91	PW2037	5435	
B757-222	N536UA	UNITED AIRLINES		25156	380	07/31/91	PW2037	5436	
B757-222	N537UA	UNITED AIRLINES		25157	381	07/18/91	PW2037	5437	
B757-222	N538UA	UNITED AIRLINES		25222	385	08/02/91	PW2037	5438	
B757-222	N539UA	UNITED AIRLINES		25223	386	08/07/91	PW2037	5439	
B757-222	N540UA	UNITED AIRLINES		25252	393	09/23/91	PW2037	5440	
B757-222	N541UA	UNITED AIRLINES		25253	394	09/27/91	PW2037	5441	
B757-222	N542UA	UNITED AIRLINES		25276	396	10/04/91	PW2037	5442	
B757-222 (ET)	N543UA	UNITED AIRLINES		25698	401	10/29/91	PW2037	5543	
B757-222 (ET)	N544UA	UNITED AIRLINES		25322	405	11/10/91	PW2037	5544	
B757-222 (ET)	N545UA	UNITED AIRLINES		25323	406	11/13/91	PW2037	5545	
B757-222 (ET)	N546UA	UNITED AIRLINES		25367	413	12/13/91	PW2037	5546	
B757-222 (ET)	N547UA	UNITED AIRLINES		25368	414	12/20/91	PW2037	5547	
B757-222 (ET)	N548UA	UNITED AIRLINES		25396	420	01/30/92	PW2037	5548	
B757-222 (ET)	N549UA	UNITED AIRLINES		25397	421	01/21/92	PW2037	5549	
B757-222 (ET)	N550UA	UNITED AIRLINES		25398	426	02/11/92	PW2037	5550	

A/C TYPE	CURRENT REG. NO.	LAST KNOWN OPERATOR (OWNER)	Status	ORIGINAL MSN	LINE NO.	DEL. DATE	ENG. TYPE	FLEET NO.	PREV. REG. [COMMENTS]
B757-222 (ET)	N551UA	UNITED AIRLINES		25399	427	02/18/92	PW2037	5551	
B757-222 (ET)	N552UA	UNITED AIRLINES		26641	431	02/27/92	PW2037	5552	
B757-222	N553UA	UNITED AIRLINES		25277	434	03/10/92	PW2037	5453	
B757-222	N554UA	UNITED AIRLINES		26644	435	03/12/92	PW2037	5454	
B757-222	N555UA	UNITED AIRLINES (SSBT)		26647	442	04/16/92	PW2037	5455	
B757-222	N556UA	UNITED AIRLINES (SSBT)		26650	447	04/23/92	PW2037	5456	
B757-222	N557UA	UNITED AIRLINES (SSBT)		26653	454	05/19/92	PW2037	5457	
B757-222	N558UA	UNITED AIRLINES (SSBT)		26654	462	06/17/92	PW2037	5458	
B757-222	N559UA	UNITED AIRLINES (SSBT)		26657	467	07/06/92	PW2037	5459	
B757-222	N560UA	UNITED AIRLINES (SSBT)		26660	469	07/13/92	PW2037	5460	
B757-222	N561UA	UNITED AIRLINES (SSBT)		26661	479	08/17/92	PW2037	5461	
B757-222	N562UA	UNITED AIRLINES (SSBT)		26664	487	09/28/92	PW2037	5462	
B757-222	N563UA	UNITED AIRLINES (SSBT)		26665	488	09/29/92	PW2037	5463	
B757-222	N564UA	UNITED AIRLINES (SSBT)		26666	490	10/08/92	PW2037	5464	
B757-222	N565UA	UNITED AIRLINES (SSBT)		26669	492	10/15/92	PW2037	5465	
B757-222	N566UA	UNITED AIRLINES (SSBT)		26670	494	10/23/92	PW2037	5466	
B757-222	N567UA	UNITED AIRLINES (SSBT)		26673	497	11/02/92	PW2037	5467	
B757-222	N568UA	UNITED AIRLINES (SSBT)		26674	498	11/05/92	PW2037	5468	
B757-222	N569UA	UNITED AIRLINES (SSBT)		26677	499	11/10/92	PW2037	5469	
B757-222	N570UA	UNITED AIRLINES (SSBT)		26678	501	11/19/92	PW2037	5470	
B757-222	N571UA	UNITED AIRLINES (SSBT)		26681	506	12/07/92	PW2037	5471	
B757-222	N572UA	UNITED AIRLINES (SSBT)		26682	508	12/14/92	PW2037	5472	
B757-222	N573UA	UNITED AIRLINES		26685	512	12/22/92	PW2037	5473	
B757-222	N574UA	UNITED AIRLINES		26686	513	12/23/92	PW2037	5474	
B757-222	N575UA	UNITED AIRLINES		26689	515	02/02/92	PW2037	5475	
B757-222	N576UA	UNITED AIRLINES		26690	524	02/17/92	PW2037	5676	
B757-222	N577UA	UNITED AIRLINES		26693	527	03/01/93	PW2037	5677	
B757-222	N578UA	UNITED AIRLINES		26694	531	03/12/93	PW2037	5678	
B757-222	N579UA	UNITED AIRLINES		26697	539	04/09/93	PW2037	5679	
B757-222	N580UA	UNITED AIRLINES		26698	542	04/21/93	PW2037	5680	
B757-222	N581UA	UNITED AIRLINES		26701	543	05/03/93	PW2037	5681	
B757-222	N582UA	UNITED AIRLINES		26702	550	05/19/93	PW2037	5682	
B757-222	N583UA	UNITED AIRLINES		26705	556	06/14/93	PW2037	5683	
B757-222	N584UA	UNITED AIRLINES		26706	559	06/24/93	PW2037	5684	
B757-222	N585UA	UNITED AIRLINES		26709	563	07/13/93	PW2037	5685	
B757-222	N586UA	UNITED AIRLINES		26710	567	07/29/93	PW2037	5686	
B757-222	N587UA	UNITED AIRLINES		26713	570	08/11/93	PW2037	5687	
B757-222	N588UA	UNITED AIRLINES		26717	571	08/16/93	PW2037	5688	
B757-222 (ET)	N589UA	UNITED AIRLINES		28707	773	11/03/97	PW2040	5589	N3509J
B757-222 (ET)	N590UA	UNITED AIRLINES		28708	785	12/31/97	PW2040	5590	
B757-222	N591UA	UNITED AIRLINES		28142	718	06/28/96	PW2037	5491	

A/C TYPE	CURRENT REG. NO.	LAST KNOWN OPERATOR (OWNER)	Status	ORIGINAL MSN	LINE NO.	DEL. DATE	ENG. TYPE	FLEET NO.	PREV. REG. [COMMENTS]
B757-222	N592UA	UNITED AIRLINES		28143	719	07/10/96	PW2037	5492	
B757-222	N593UA	UNITED AIRLINES		28144	724	08/12/96	PW2037	5493	
B757-222	N594UA	UNITED AIRLINES		28145	727	09/11/96	PW2037	5494	
B757-222 (ET)	N595UA	UNITED AIRLINES		28748	789	02/04/98	PW2040	5595	
B757-222 (ET)	N596UA	UNITED AIRLINES		28749	794	03/17/98	PW2040	5596	
B757-222 (ET)	N597UA	UNITED AIRLINES		28750	841	01/11/99	PW2040	5597	
B757-222 (ET)	N598UA	UNITED AIRLINES		28751	844	01/22/99	PW2040	5598	N1787B
B757-24APF	N401UP	UNITED PARCEL SERVICE		23723	139	10/06/87	PW2040		
B757-24APF	N402UP	UNITED PARCEL SERVICE		23724	141	09/17/87	PW2040		
B757-24APF	N403UP	UNITED PARCEL SERVICE		23725	143	09/18/87	PW2040		
B757-24APF	N404UP	UNITED PARCEL SERVICE		23726	147	10/27/87	PW2040		
B757-24APF	N405UP	UNITED PARCEL SERVICE		23727	149	10/29/87	PW2040		
B757-24APF	N406UP	UNITED PARCEL SERVICE		23728	176	06/02/88	PW2040		
B757-24APF	N407UP	UNITED PARCEL SERVICE		23729	181	06/24/88	PW2040		
B757-24APF	N408UP	UNITED PARCEL SERVICE		23730	184	07/15/88	PW2040		
B757-24APF	N409UP	UNITED PARCEL SERVICE		23731	186	07/29/88	PW2040		
B757-24APF	N410UP	UNITED PARCEL SERVICE		23732	189	09/01/88	PW2040		
B757-24APF	N411UP	UNITED PARCEL SERVICE		23851	191	09/01/88	PW2040		
B757-24APF	N412UP	UNITED PARCEL SERVICE		23852	193	09/30/88	PW2040		
B757-24APF	N413UP	UNITED PARCEL SERVICE		23853	195	09/30/88	PW2040		
B757-24APF	N414UP	UNITED PARCEL SERVICE		23854	197	10/28/88	PW2040		
B757-24APF	N415UP	UNITED PARCEL SERVICE		23855	199	10/28/88	PW2040		
B757-24APF	N416UP	UNITED PARCEL SERVICE		23903	318	10/11/90	PW2040		
B757-24APF	N417UP	UNITED PARCEL SERVICE		23904	322	10/26/90	PW2040		
B757-24APF	N418UP	UNITED PARCEL SERVICE		23905	326	11/14/90	PW2040		
B757-24APF	N419UP	UNITED PARCEL SERVICE		23906	330	12/04/90	PW2040		
B757-24APF	N420UP	UNITED PARCEL SERVICE		23907	334	12/19/90	PW2040		
B757-24APF	N421UP	UNITED PARCEL SERVICE		25281	395	09/27/91	PW2040		
B757-24APF	N422UP	UNITED PARCEL SERVICE		25324	399	10/25/91	PW2040		
B757-24APF	N423UP	UNITED PARCEL SERVICE		25325	403	10/31/91	PW2040		
B757-24APF	N424UP	UNITED PARCEL SERVICE		25369	407	11/15/91	PW2040		
B757-24APF	N425UP	UNITED PARCEL SERVICE		25370	411	12/05/91	PW2040		
B757-24APF	N426UP	UNITED PARCEL SERVICE		25457	477	08/13/92	PW2040		[BASED CGN]
B757-24APF	N427UP	UNITED PARCEL SERVICE		25458	481	09/03/92	PW2040		[BASED CGN]
B757-24APF	N428UP	UNITED PARCEL SERVICE		25459	485	09/10/92	PW2040		
B757-24APF	N429UP	UNITED PARCEL SERVICE		25460	489	10/08/92	PW2040		
B757-24APF	N430UP	UNITED PARCEL SERVICE		25461	493	10/22/92	PW2040		
B757-24APF	N431UP	UNITED PARCEL SERVICE		25462	569	08/12/93	PW2040		
B757-24APF	N432UP	UNITED PARCEL SERVICE		25463	573	09/02/93	PW2040		
B757-24APF	N433UP	UNITED PARCEL SERVICE		25464	577	09/30/93	PW2040		

A/C TYPE	CURRENT REG. NO.	LAST KNOWN OPERATOR (OWNER)	Status	ORIGINAL MSN	LINE NO.	DEL. DATE	ENG. TYPE	FLEET NO.	PREV. REG. [COMMENTS]
B757-24APF	N434UP	UNITED PARCEL SERVICE		25465	579	10/14/93	PW2040		
B757-24APF	N435UP	UNITED PARCEL SERVICE		25466	581	10/21/93	PW2040		
B757-24APF	N436UP	UNITED PARCEL SERVICE		25467	625	07/07/94	RB211-535E4		
B757-24APF	N437UP	UNITED PARCEL SERVICE		25468	628	07/21/94	RB211-535E4		
B757-24APF	N438UP	UNITED PARCEL SERVICE		25469	631	08/11/94	RB211-535E4		
B757-24APF	N439UP	UNITED PARCEL SERVICE		25470	634	08/25/94	RB211-535E4		
B757-24APF	N440UP	UNITED PARCEL SERVICE		25471	636	09/26/94	RB211-535E4		
B757-24APF	N441UP	UNITED PARCEL SERVICE		27386	638	09/29/94	RB211-535E4		
B757-24APF	N442UP	UNITED PARCEL SERVICE		27387	640	10/13/94	RB211-535E4		
B757-24APF	N443UP	UNITED PARCEL SERVICE		27388	642	10/27/94	RB211-535E4		
B757-24APF	N444UP	UNITED PARCEL SERVICE		27389	644	11/03/94	RB211-535E4		
B757-24APF	N445UP	UNITED PARCEL SERVICE		27390	646	11/18/94	RB211-535E4		
B757-24APF	N446UP	UNITED PARCEL SERVICE		27735	649	12/02/94	RB211-535E4		
B757-24APF	N447UP	UNITED PARCEL SERVICE		27736	651	12/13/94	RB211-535E4		
B757-24APF	N448UP	UNITED PARCEL SERVICE		27737	654	01/13/95	RB211-535E4		
B757-24APF	N449UP	UNITED PARCEL SERVICE		27738	656	01/19/95	RB211-535E4		
B757-24APF	N450UP	UNITED PARCEL SERVICE		25472	659	02/09/95	RB211-535E4		
B757-24APF	N451UP	UNITED PARCEL SERVICE		27739	675	06/01/95	RB211-535E4		
B757-24APF	N452UP	UNITED PARCEL SERVICE		25473	679	07/06/95	RB211-535E4		
B757-24APF	N453UP	UNITED PARCEL SERVICE		25474	683	08/04/95	RB211-535E4		
B757-24APF	N454UP	UNITED PARCEL SERVICE		25475	687	09/08/95	RB211-535E4		
B757-24APF	N455UP	UNITED PARCEL SERVICE		25476	691	09/28/95	RB211-535E4		
B757-24APF	N456UP	UNITED PARCEL SERVICE		25477	728	09/13/96	RB211-535E4		
B757-24APF	N457UP	UNITED PARCEL SERVICE		25478	729	09/25/96	RB211-535E4		
B757-24APF	N458UP	UNITED PARCEL SERVICE		25479	730	10/03/96	RB211-535E4		
B757-24APF	N459UP	UNITED PARCEL SERVICE		25480	733	10/31/96	RB211-535E4		
B757-24APF	N460UP	UNITED PARCEL SERVICE		25481	734	11/14/96	RB211-535E4		
B757-24APF	N461UP	UNITED PARCEL SERVICE		28265	755	05/30/97	RB211-535E4		
B757-24APF	N462UP	UNITED PARCEL SERVICE		28266	759	06/19/97	RB211-535E4		
B757-24APF	N463UP	UNITED PARCEL SERVICE		28267	763	07/17/97	RB211-535E4		
B757-24APF	N464UP	UNITED PARCEL SERVICE		28268	765	09/09/97	RB211-535E4		
B757-24APF	N465UP	UNITED PARCEL SERVICE		28269	767	09/16/97	RB211-535E4		
B757-24APF	N466UP	UNITED PARCEL SERVICE		25482	769	09/30/97	RB211-535E4		
B757-24APF	N467UP	UNITED PARCEL SERVICE		25483	771	09/29/97	RB211-535E4		
B757-24APF	N468UP	UNITED PARCEL SERVICE		25484	774	10/14/97	RB211-535E4		
B757-24APF	N469UP	UNITED PARCEL SERVICE		25485	776	10/29/97	RB211-535E4		
B757-24APF	N470UP	UNITED PARCEL SERVICE		25486	778	11/21/97	RB211-535E4		
B757-24APF	N471UP	UNITED PARCEL SERVICE		28842	813	07/23/98	RB211-535E4		
B757-24APF	N472UP	UNITED PARCEL SERVICE		28843	815	08/12/98	RB211-535E4		
B757-24APF	N473UP	UNITED PARCEL SERVICE		28846	823	09/22/98	RB211-535E4		N5573L

A/C TYPE	CURRENT REG. NO.	LAST KNOWN OPERATOR (OWNER)	Status	ORIGINAL MSN	LINE NO.	DEL. DATE	ENG. TYPE	FLEET NO.	PREV. REG. [COMMENTS]
B757-24APF	N474UP	UNITED PARCEL SERVICE		28844	879	07/29/99	RB211-535E4		
B757-24APF	N475UP	UNITED PARCEL SERVICE		28845	882	08/12/99	RB211-535E4		
B757-225	N600AU	US AIRWAYS (GECA)		22192	3	09/28/83	RB211-535E4		N502EA
B757-225	N601AU	US AIRWAYS (GECA)		22193	4	05/25/83	RB211-535E4		N503EA
B757-225	N602AU	US AIRWAYS (GECA)		22196	7	12/22/82	RB211-535E4		N506EA
B757-225	N603AU	US AIRWAYS (GECA)		22198	12	02/18/83	RB211-535E4		N508EA
B757-225	N604AU	US AIRWAYS (GECA)		22199	17	04/15/83	RB211-535E4		N509EA
B757-225	N605AU	US AIRWAYS (GECA)		22201	21	07/28/83	RB211-535E4		N511EA
B757-225	N606AU	US AIRWAYS (GECA)		22202	22	08/19/83	RB211-535E4		N512EA
B757-225	N607AU	US AIRWAYS (GECA)		22203	26	11/09/83	RB211-535E4		N513EA
B757-225	N608AU	US AIRWAYS (GECA)		22204	27	11/14/83	RB211-535E4		N514EA
B757-225	N609AU	US AIRWAYS (GECA)		22205	28	12/14/83	RB211-535E4		N515EA
B757-2B7	N610AU	US AIRWAYS		27122	525	02/26/93	RB211-535E4		
B757-2B7	N611AU	US AIRWAYS		27123	534	03/22/93	RB211-535E4		
B757-2B7	N612AU	US AIRWAYS		27124	540	04/12/93	RB211-535E4		
B757-2B7	N613AU	US AIRWAYS		27144	544	04/27/93	RB211-535E4		
B757-2B7	N614AU	US AIRWAYS		27145	546	05/03/93	RB211-535E4		
B757-2B7	N615AU	US AIRWAYS		27146	551	05/19/93	RB211-535E4		
B757-2B7	N616AU	US AIRWAYS		27147	552	05/24/93	RB211-535E4		
B757-2B7	N617AU	US AIRWAYS		27148	564	07/15/93	RB211-535E4		
B757-225	N618AU	US AIRWAYS		22210	42	11/30/84	RB211-535E4		N520EA
B757-2B7	N619AU	US AIRWAYS		27198	584	11/05/93	RB211-535E4		
B757-2B7	N620AU	US AIRWAYS		27199	586	11/15/93	RB211-535E4		
B757-2B7	N621AU	US AIRWAYS		27200	589	12/06/93	RB211-535E4		
B757-2B7	N622AU	US AIRWAYS		27201	605	03/14/94	RB211-535E4		
B757-2B7	N623AU	US AIRWAYS		27244	607	03/24/94	RB211-535E4		
B757-2B7	N624AU	US AIRWAYS		27245	630	07/29/94	RB211-535E4		
B757-2B7	N625VJ	US AIRWAYS		27246	643	10/26/94	RB211-535E4		
B757-2B7	N626AU	US AIRWAYS		27303	647	11/08/94	RB211-535E4		
B757-2B7	N627AU	US AIRWAYS		27805	655	01/23/95	RB211-535E4		
B757-2B7	N628AU	US AIRWAYS		27806	657	01/27/95	RB211-535E4		
B757-2B7	N629AU	US AIRWAYS		27807	662	02/24/95	RB211-535E4		
B757-2B7	N630AU	US AIRWAYS		27808	666	03/24/95	RB211-535E4		
B757-2B7	N631AU	US AIRWAYS		27809	673	05/11/95	RB211-535E4		
B757-2B7	N632AU	US AIRWAYS		27810	678	06/13/95	RB211-535E4		
B757-2B7	N633AU	US AIRWAYS		27811	681	07/07/95	RB211-535E4		
B757-23A	N756AF	VULCAN NORTHWEST		24923	332	05/30/91	RB211-535E4		N5573B, N680EM, N680FM
B757-2J4	N757AF	VULCAN NORTHWEST (CITI)		25155	371	06/07/91	RB211-535E4		OY-SHA, XA-SPG, N115FS

A/C TYPE	CURRENT REG. NO.	LAST KNOWN OPERATOR (OWNER)	Status	ORIGINAL MSN	LINE NO.	DEL. DATE	ENG. TYPE	FLEET NO.	PREV. REG. [COMMENTS]
OH-FINLAND									
B757-2Q8	OH-LBO	FINNAIR (ILFC)		28172	772	10/07/97	PW2040		N1789B
B757-2Q8	OH-LBR	FINNAIR (ILFC)		28167	775	10/16/97	PW2040		
B757-2Q8	OH-LBS	FINNAIR (ILFC)		27623	792	03/09/98	PW2040		N5573K
B757-2Q8	OH-LBT	FINNAIR (ILFC)		28170	801	05/03/98	PW2040		
B757-2Q8	OH-LBU	FINNAIR (ILFC)		29377	857	04/10/99	PW2040		[OPF PGT?]
OO-BELGIUM									
B757-23APF	OO-DLJ	EUROPEAN AIR TRANSPORT		24971	340	08/29/91	RB211-535E4		N5002K, G-OBOZ, N573CA [IN DHL C/S]
B757-23APF	OO-DLK	EUROPEAN AIR TRANSPORT		24635	258	10/18/90	RB211-535E4		N3502P, 9J-AFO, VH-AWE [IN DHL C/S]
B757-236 (SF)	OO-DLN	EUROPEAN AIR TRANSPORT (DHL UK)		22172	9	03/28/83	RB211-535C		G-BIKA [CVTD TO SF AT IAB; TO BE OPF DHL]
OY-DENMARK									
B757-236	OY-GRL	GREENLANDAIR (FIH LSG)		25620	449	04/28/92	RB211-535E4		G-IEAC, G-CSVS, TF-GRL
PH-NETHERLANDS									
B757-27B	PH-AHE	AIR HOLLAND (FINO)		24135	165	03/09/88	RB211-535E4		OY-SHE [OPF DSB]
B757-27B	PH-AHF	AIR HOLLAND (INGL)		24136	169	03/23/88	RB211-535E4		PH-AHF, OY-SHF, G-OAHF, 4X-EBF
B757-230	PH-DBA	DUTCHBIRD (CFG)	L	24747	275	04/11/90	PW2040		D-ABNC
B757-230	PH-DBB	DUTCHBIRD (CFG)	L	24738	274	04/05/90	PW2040		D-ABNB
B757-230	PH-DBH	DUTCHBIRD (CFG)	L	24748	285	05/24/90	PW2040		D-ABND
B757-27B	PH-AHI	MARTINAIR (INGL)		24137	178	05/31/88	RB211-535E4		G-OAHI
B757-2K2	PH-TKA	TRANSAVIA AIRLINES (JL CANAL)		26633	519	02/22/93	RB211-535E4		
B757-2K2	PH-TKB	TRANSAVIA AIRLINES (JL DELFT)		26634	545	05/03/93	RB211-535E4		
B757-2K2	PH-TKC	TRANSAVIA AIRLINES (JL POLDER)		26635	608	04/12/94	RB211-535E4		
B757-2K2	PH-TKD	TRANSAVIA AIRLINES (ILFC)		26330	717	06/24/96	RB211-535E4		C-GTSR, XA-TMU
SE-SWEDEN									
B757-236	SE-DUK	BRITANNIA AIRWAYS AB (BBAM)		25054	362	12/04/91	RB211-535E4		EC-668, N5002K, N3502P, XA-MMX, EI-CMA, N100FS
B757-2Y0	SE-DUL	BRITANNIA AIRWAYS AB		26151	472	07/23/92	RB211-535E4		XA-SCB, XA-KWK, SX-BBY, SE-DUL [LST AIZ]
B757-236	SE-DUO	BRITANNIA AIRWAYS AB (BBAM)		24792	279	04/30/90	RB211-535E4		G-BRJI, EC-446, EC-EVC, EC-886, EC-FMQ, G-BRJI, SX-BBZ, G-BRYI
B757-236	SE-DUP	BRITANNIA AIRWAYS AB (ACG ACQ.)		24793	292	06/20/90	RB211-535E4		G-BRJJ, EC-490, G-OOOT
TC-TURKEY									
B757-225	D-AMUK	ATLAS INTL.-TURKEY (LTU)	L	22689	117	12/19/86	RB211-535E4		N525EA, EC-390, EC-ETZ
B757-225	D-AMUU	ATLAS INTL.-TURKEY (LTU)	L	22688	115	12/19/86	RB211-535E4		N524EA, EC-FIY

A/C TYPE	CURRENT REG. NO.	LAST KNOWN OPERATOR (OWNER)	Status	ORIGINAL MSN	LINE NO.	DEL. DATE	ENG. TYPE	FLEET NO.	PREV. REG. [COMMENTS]
TF-ICELAND									
B757-23APF	TF-FIG	ICELANDAIR (AWAS)		24456	237	07/26/89	RB211-535E4		N571CA
B757-208	TF-FIH	ICELANDAIR (BBAM)		24739	273	04/04/90	RB211-535E4		
B757-208	TF-FII	ICELANDAIR (CITG)		24760	281	05/03/90	RB211-535E4		
B757-208	TF-FIJ	ICELANDAIR		25085	368	05/23/91	RB211-535E4		G-BTEJ
B757-28A	TF-FIK	ICELANDAIR (ILFC)		26276	704	03/15/96	RB211-535E4		
B757-208	TF-FIN	ICELANDAIR		28989	780	01/21/98	RB211-535E4		N1790B
B757-208	TF-FIO	ICELANDAIR		29436	859	04/20/99	RB211-535E4		
B757-208	TF-FIP	ICELANDAIR (HEKLA)		30423	916	04/25/00	RB211-535E4		N1006K
B757-27B	TF-FIW	ICELANDAIR (AV. INV.)		24838	302	08/02/90	RB211-535E4		PH-AHL, D-ABNX ["ICELANDAIR HOLIDAYS"; TO BE LST SCY SUMMER 2001]
B757-208	TF-FIV	ICELANDAIR		30424	956	03/12/01	RB211-535E4		
UK-UZBEKISTAN									
B757-23P	UK-75700	UZBEKISTAN AIRWAYS		28338	731	10/19/96	PW2037		[VIP CONF; OPF GVMT]
B757-23P	VP-BUB	UZBEKISTAN AIRWAYS (UZBEC FIN)		30060	875	09/03/99	PW2037		UK-75701
B757-23P	VP-BUD	UZBEKISTAN AIRWAYS (UZBEC FIN)		30061	886	12/09/99	PW2037		N1787B, N1020L, N6066Z
UN-KAZAKSTAN									
B757-2M6(ER)	P4-NSN	ORIENT EAGLE AIRWAYS (AIR FIN EUROPE)		23454	102	07/29/86	RB211-535E4		N6067U, V8-HB1, V8-RBC, VR-CRK [OPF KAZAK GVMT]
V8-BRUNEI									
B757-2M6	V8-RBA	ROYAL BRUNEI AIRLINES		23452	94	05/06/86	RB211-535E4		
B757-2M6	V8-RBB	ROYAL BRUNEI AIRLINES		23453	100	06/13/86	RB211-535E4		
XA-MEXICO									
B757-225	TP-01	MEXICAN GOVERNMENT		22690	151	11/16/87	RB211-535E4		[PRESIDENTIAL A/C]
B757-29J	XA-TQU	AEROMEXICO		27203	588	11/18/94	PW2037		N1792B, SU-RAC, B-27005
B757-2Q8	N301AM	AEROMEXICO (ILFC)		30045	957	03/21/01	PW2037		
B757-23A	N490AM	AEROMEXICO (AWAS)		25490	510	12/18/92	PW2037		XA-SKQ, XA-SMD, N53AW
B757-2Q8	N801AM	AEROMEXICO (ACG ACQ)		25624	541	04/16/93	PW2037		XA-SIK
B757-2Q8	N802AM	AEROMEXICO (MDFC)		26270	558	06/18/93	PW2037		N26270, XA-SJD
B757-2Q8	N803AM	AEROMEXICO (ILFC)		26268	590	01/07/94	PW2037		XA-SMJ
B757-2Q8	N804AM	AEROMEXICO (ILFC)		26271	592	01/27/94	PW2037		XA-SMK
B757-2Q8	N805AM	AEROMEXICO (ILFC)		26272	594	03/01/94	PW2037		XA-SML
B757-2Q8	N806AM	AEROMEXICO (ILFC)		26273	597	04/01/94	PW2037		XA-SMM
B757-230	XA-TRA	MEXICANA (PEGA)		24737	267	03/19/90	PW2040		D-ABNA
B757-2Q8	N380RM	MEXICANA (ILFC)		29380	836	12/09/98	PW2040		N1799B, N1795B

A/C TYPE	CURRENT REG. NO.	LAST KNOWN OPERATOR (OWNER)	Status	ORIGINAL MSN	LINE NO.	DEL. DATE	ENG. TYPE	FLEET NO.	PREV. REG. [COMMENTS]
B757-2Q8	N755MX	MEXICANA (ILFC)		24964	424	02/05/92	PW2040		N754AT
B757-2Q8	N758MX	MEXICANA (MSA V)		24965	438	03/24/92	PW2040		N755AT
B757-2Q8	N762MX	MEXICANA (ILFC)		29442	819	09/11/98	PW2040		
B757-2Q8	N763MX	MEXICANA (ILFC)		29443	821	09/16/98	PW2040		
B757-2Q8	N764MX	MEXICANA (ILFC)		27351	639	10/04/94	PW2040		N756AT, N809AM
B757-2Q8	N765MX	MEXICANA (ILFC)		30044	954	02/23/01	PW2040		

4K-AZERBAIJAN

A/C TYPE	CURRENT REG. NO.	LAST KNOWN OPERATOR (OWNER)	Status	ORIGINAL MSN	LINE NO.	DEL. DATE	ENG. TYPE	FLEET NO.	PREV. REG. [COMMENTS]
B757-22L	VP-BBR	AZERBAIJAN AIRLINES		29305	894	09/27/00	RB211-535E4		N1024A, N6046P [4K-AZ12 NTU?]
B757-22L	VP-BBS	AZERBAIJAN AIRLINES		30834	947	12/19/00	RB211-535E4		

4X-ISRAEL

A/C TYPE	CURRENT REG. NO.	LAST KNOWN OPERATOR (OWNER)	Status	ORIGINAL MSN	LINE NO.	DEL. DATE	ENG. TYPE	FLEET NO.	PREV. REG. [COMMENTS]
B757-236(ER)	4X-BAZ	ARKIA ISRAELI AIRLINES		24121	183	06/30/88	RB211-535E4		G-BNSE, EC-544, EC-EXH, G-BPEH, TC-AHA [LST SOUTH ATLANTIC AIRWAYS AS EC-EEC?]
B757-2Y0	4X-	ARKIA ISRAELI AIRLINES (BLX)	L	26151	472	07/23/92	RB211-535E4		XA-SCB, XA-KWK, SX-BBY, SE-DUL
B757-3E7	4X-BAU	ARKIA ISRAELI AIRLINES		30178	906	01/31/00	RB211-535E4B		N1786B, N1003M
B757-3E7	4X-BAW	ARKIA ISRAELI AIRLINES		30179	912	02/23/00	RB211-535E4B		[LST ELY 04/01/01]
B757-258(ER)	4X-EBI	EL AL ISRAELI AIRLINES (ILFC)		27622	745	03/24/97	RB211-535E4		
B757-258	4X-EBM	EL AL ISRAELI AIRLINES		23918	156	12/17/87	RB211-535E4	502	[LST ISR 04/01 FOR SUMMER]
B757-258	4X-EBR	EL AL ISRAELI AIRLINES		24254	185	07/19/88	RB211-535E4	503	
B757-258(ER)	4X-EBS	EL AL ISRAELI AIRLINES		24884	325	11/13/90	RB211-535E4	504	
B757-258(ER)	4X-EBT	EL AL ISRAELI AIRLINES		25036	356	04/01/91	RB211-535E4	505	
B757-258(ER)	4X-EBU	EL AL ISRAELI AIRLINES		26053	529	03/08/93	RB211-535E4	506	
B757-258(ER)	4X-EBV	EL AL ISRAELI AIRLINES		26054	547	05/05/93	RB211-535E4	507	
B757-3E7	4X-BAW	EL AL ISRAELI AIRLINES (AIZ)	L	30179	912	02/23/00	RB211-535E4B		
B757-258	4X-EBM	ISRAIR (ELY)	L	23918	156	12/17/87	RB211-535E4	502	

6V-SENEGAL

A/C TYPE	CURRENT REG. NO.	LAST KNOWN OPERATOR (OWNER)	Status	ORIGINAL MSN	LINE NO.	DEL. DATE	ENG. TYPE	FLEET NO.	PREV. REG. [COMMENTS]
B757-27B	PH-AHE	AIR SENEGAL (AHR)	L	24135	165	03/09/88	RB211-535E4		OY-SHE

8R-GUYANA

A/C TYPE	CURRENT REG. NO.	LAST KNOWN OPERATOR (OWNER)	Status	ORIGINAL MSN	LINE NO.	DEL. DATE	ENG. TYPE	FLEET NO.	PREV. REG. [COMMENTS]
B757-23A(ER)	VH-NOF	GUYANA AIR 2000 (NORDSTRESS)		24566	255	12/06/89	RB211-535E4		5Y-BGI, N251LA, XA-RLM, N566AN

	A/C TYPE	CURRENT REG. NO.	LAST KNOWN OPERATOR (OWNER)	Status	ORIGINAL MSN	LINE NO.	DEL. DATE	ENG. TYPE	FLEET NO.	PREV. REG. [COMMENTS]
9N-NEPAL										
	B757-2F8	9N-ACA	ROYAL NEPAL AIRLINES		23850	142	09/07/88	RB211-535E4		
	B757-2F8C	9N-ACB	ROYAL NEPAL AIRLINES		23863	182	09/15/88	RB211-535E4		N5573K
	B757-2Z0	B-2855	ROYAL NEPAL AIRLINES (CXN)	L	29792	822	09/28/98	RB211-535E4		
	B757-2Z0	B-2856	ROYAL NEPAL AIRLINES (CXN)	L	29793	833	11/24/98	RB211-535E4		
MILITARY										
	B757-23A	T-01	ARGENTINIAN AIR FORCE	M	25487	470	07/22/92	RB211-535E4		
	B757-23A (ER)	25001	USAF	M	25494	611	04/22/94	RB211-535E4		N987AN
	B757-2G4 (VC-32A)	98-0001	USAF	M	29025	783	06/01/98	PW2040		N3519L
	B757-2G4 (VC-32A)	98-0002	USAF	M	29026	787	05/29/98	PW2040		N3519M
	B757-2G4 VC-32A)	99-0003	USAF	M	29027	824	11/20/98	PW2040		
	B757-2G4 (VC-32A)	99-0004	USAF	M	29028	829	11/25/98	PW2040		
OUT OF SERVICE										
	B757-236	N951PG	AIR EUROPA (FINO)	O	22185	34	03/27/84	RB211-535C		G-BPGW, EC-265, EC-EOK, YV-78C, EC-845, EC-GCA [RT LESSOR; PARKED TUS]
	B757-236	EC-GCB	AIR EUROPA (PEGA)	O	23227	57	03/26/85	RB211-535C		G-BLVH, YV-77C, EC-847 [RT LESSOR; STD TUS; ALL WHITE; NO TITLES]
	B757-258	N789BA	(BOEING AICRAFT HOLDING COMPANY)	O	23917	152	11/25/87	RB211-535E4		4X-EBL [PARKED MZJ]
	B757-236(ET)	N903PG	(PEGA)	O	24370	218	03/31/89	RB211-535E4		G-BPEA [LRF 09/30/00; RT LESSOR; PARKED TUS 03/15/01]
	B757-23A	PH-AHP	TRANSAVIA AIRLINES (TOMB)	O	24528	250	10/06/89	RB211-535E4		OO-ILI, SE-DSM, G-BXOL [RT TOMB 10/30/00; PARKED AMS; NO MARKINGS]
WRITTEN OFF										
	B757-225	TC-GEN	ALAS NACIONALES (BHY)	W	22206	31	02/26/85	RB211-535E4		N516EA, C-GNXN, N7079S, 8P-GUL [WO 02/07/96 PUERTA PLATA, DOMINICAN REPUBLIC]
	B757-223	N651AA	AMERICAN AIRLINES	W	24609	390	08/27/91	RB211-535E4B		[WO 12/20/95 CALI, COLOMBIA]
	B757-21B	B-2812	CHINA SOUTHERN AIRLINES	W	24758	282	05/16/90	RB211-535E4		[WO 10/02/90 CANTON, CHINA]
	B757-23A	N52AW	AERO PERU (AWAS)	W	25489	505	09/27/93	PW2037		N52AW, XA-SKR, XA-SME [WO 10/02/96 LIMA]
	B757-204	G-BYAG	BRITANNIA AIRWAYS	W	26965	517	01/22/93	RB211-535E4		[WO 09/14/99 GERONA, SPAIN]

Chapter 8

Model 767

Twelve years after the 727 had entered service, U.S. airlines were ready for a follow-on aircraft with new-generation engines to achieve reduced fuel burn and lower noise emission levels. As recounted in the 757 chapter, however, they were not in agreement regarding the cabin arrangement for the new jetliner. Some preferred a single-aisle, narrow-body configuration, while others insisted on a twin-aisle, wide-body aircraft. For those customers wanting a twin-aisle aircraft, Boeing initiated 7X7 design studies. At first these studies concentrated on trijet configurations with two-class accommodation for around 180 passengers. To meet the requirements of U.S. airlines and foreign carriers, variants were offered with range covering one-stop and non-stop U.S. transcontinental routes as well as medium-range transatlantic sectors. Over a period of three years the design remained in a state of constant flux because the airlines were not in agreement on size and range. Moreover, with the industry in a downturn, they were not yet ready to commit to all-new aircraft. In mid-1977, seeking to appeal to as many airlines as possible, Boeing first proposed a "semi-wide-body" twinjet 7S7 to supplement its twinjet narrow-body 7N7 an trijet wide-body 7X7 studies. Choosing and advanced wing design similar in concept to that of the 7N7 (the future Model 757) but featuring greater sweep (31.5 degrees at the quarter-cord), Boeing actively pursued risk-sharing foreign partners for its new jetliner project.

As the 7S7 called for the use of new baggage containers as its narrower fuselage cross-section prevented the use of containers such as carried by true wide-body aircraft, airlines did not show much interest in this 'semi-wide-body' project. However, as their initial seating requirements would have resulted in full wide-body aircraft with a short and dumpy fuselage generating too much drag, they finally came to see the merit of the Boeing proposal. Calling for a maximum width of 15.5 feet (4.72 meters), the 7S7 fuselage provided for standard economy accommodation in a seven-abreast arrangement with two aisles. Its use enabled Boeing to come up with an aircraft combining the passenger appeal and ease of loading and unloading of twin-aisle jetliners with the seat-mile cost of narrow-body aircraft. That argument convinced United Airlines, which ordered 30 twin-aisle 767-200s on July 14, 1978, instead of the single-aisle 7N7 that it had favored earlier. (United finally did order 757s but that contract was not signed until 10 years later.)

Having planned a family of 7S7 variants to cover a broad range of capacity and range, Boeing provided that design with wings of area greater than required for the original 767-200 production model. As a result of this choice, Boeing has been able to stretch the 767 twice, increasing maximum single-class accommodation first from 255 to 351 seats and then to 375 seats. It has also increased its range from the original 3,160 nautical miles (5,850 kilometers) of the low-gross-weight domestic version of the 767-200 as ordered by United to as much as 6,805 nautical miles (12,605 kilometers) for 767-200ERs with auxiliary fuel tanks.

Boeing's board of directors authorized production of the 767-200 on the strength of the July 1978 order from United Airlines. Unlike the 757, which was to be built in the Renton plant alongside other narrow-body Boeing jetliners, the 767 was to be assembled in a new building at the wide-body plant in Everett. Risk-sharing partners in Japan (Civil Transport Development Corp., a consortium of Japanese aircraft manufacturers and component suppliers) were to produce center- and rear-fuselage panels, wing fairings, passenger and cargo doors, and other smaller components. Other foreign risk-sharing partners included Aeritalia (now Alenia) in Italy and Canadair in Canada. The former took responsibility for advanced composite structures including wing control surfaces, flaps and slats, nose radome, elevators, and fin and rudder). The latter was to manufacture the rear fuselage. Northrop (now Northrop Grumman) and Vought (absorbed by Northrop Grumman in August 1994) became the principal U.S. subcontractors.

767-200 and -200ER

By the time the Boeing-owned prototype (s/n 22233, N767BA) was rolled out on August 4, 1981, orders stood at 173 aircraft for 17 airlines. The first 767 flew on September 26, 1981, powered by two Pratt & Whitney JT9D-7R4 turbofans rated at 48,000 pounds (213.5 kilonewtons) of static thrust. It was joined in the accelerated flight-test program by five similarly engined aircraft (all intended for United) and by an aircraft powered by General Electric CF6-80A engines rated at 48,000 pounds (213.5 kilonewtons), as specified by the second and third customers (American Airlines and Delta Air Lines). Later on, some 767-200s were powered by CF6-80A2s rated at 50,000 pounds (222.4 kilonewtons) static or CF6-80C2B2s rated at 52,500 pounds (233.5 kilonewtons) static.

During initial flight trials, all seven 767-200 development aircraft had a three-crew flight deck, with the two pilots being provided with two CRT displays directly in front of them and two more centrally located. Already, however, Boeing and the FAA were working to certify the 767 for two-crew operations. To that end, s/n 21866, N605UA—the seventh aircraft to fly with a three-crew flight deck—was modified and became the first to fly with a two-pilot cockpit on May 27, 1982. All customers went on to specify the two-pilot arrangement, and the ATC for the 767, A1NM, issued by the FAA on July 30, 1982, provided for standard two-crew operations. Moreover, due to extensive similarities between the cockpit of the 767 and that of the narrow-body 757, the FAA cleared the way for pilots to fly both of the new-generation Boeing twinjets after passing a type-rating test for either of the two. To date, the 757 and 767 are the only jetliners to share a common type rating.

United accepted its first 767 on August 19, 1982, and started commercial service 20 days later. As initially certificated, the 767-200 could carry a maximum of 255 passengers in single-class, seven-abreast accommodation (or 224 passengers in typical two-class U.S. service). Later, with the addition of another overwing emergency exit on both sides of the cabin, maximum accommodation was increased to 290 passengers in eight-abreast seating.

Following the announcement of the 767-200ER in January 1983 and that of the stretched 767-300 in September of that year, several airlines curtailed their 767-200 orders in favor of the newer variants. Cancelled aircraft included 20 767-222s for United, 5 767-232s for Delta, and 2 767-265s for Pacific Western Airlines. Boeing ultimately delivered 130 standard 767-200s, the last being l/n 535, s/n 27195, which went to Eva Air in Taiwan on April 1, 1994. Several aircraft delivered as standard 767-200s were later upgraded as 767-200ERs.

Announced barely four months after the 767-200 had entered service, the 767-200ER was an extended-range version initially aimed at foreign carriers. It differed from the standard -200 in having a higher gross weight (initially 345,000 pounds [156,489 kilograms] but eventually increased to 395,000 pounds [179,169 kilograms]) and an additional center-section tank to increase fuel capacity by 3,750 U.S. gallons (14,195 liters). Later, fuel capacity of the -200ER was increased by still another 3,530 U.S. gallons (13,362 liters). The main and nose undercarriages were strengthened, and the fuselage and lower wing surface were beefed up.

The first customer for the -200ER was Ethiopian Airlines, which ordered two in January 1983. This African carrier took delivery of its first aircraft on May 23, 1984 (l/n 90, s/n 23106).

Noteworthy is the first revenue flight by El Al, which started non-stop transatlantic service from Canada on March 27, 1984, one day after taking delivery of its first 767-258 (l/n 62, s/n 22972). To offer similar twinjet transatlantic service from or to the United States, other airlines needed FAA approval and hence had to await completion of the EROPS Extended Range OPerationS (EROPS) certification.

When turbofans proved remarkably reliable during the 1970s and early 1980s, many airlines started eyeing the possibility of replacing some of their fuel-thirsty four and three-engine aircraft operating on long overwater flights with more economical twinjets. Working with the three manufacturers of big turbofan engines (General Electric, Pratt & Whitney, and Rolls-Royce) and the FAA, Boeing took the lead in demonstrating that such EROPS (an acronym soon replaced by the more descriptive ETOPS, for Extended-range Twin-engine OPerationS) was safe and practical. On May 29, 1985, the 727-200ER powered by JT9D engines became the world's first jetliner to receive approval for 120-minute ETOPS flights (that is, remaining no more than 2 hours at single-engine speed from a suitable alternate airport). This version next received approval for 180-minute ETOPS flights in April 1990.

Boeing 767-200ERs powered by CF6-80As, PW4000s, and RB.211-524Hs were approved for 120- and 180-minute ETOPS, respectively, in August 1985 and April 1989 (the CF6-powered version becoming the world's first aircraft with 180-minute approval), April 1990 and July 1993, and March 1991 and March 1993. In all instances, ETOPS approval was conditional on the aircraft being provided with additional system redundancy and other safety items, and on the airline's maintenance procedures meeting stringent requirements.

While ETOPS 120 certification enabled airlines to operate their 767-200ERs non-stop in either direction over the North Atlantic during most of the year, more severe winds often necessitated a stop when flying eastbound during the winter months. That limitation disappeared when the 767-200ER received ETOPS 180 certification, enabling airlines to rely increasingly on this fuel-efficient twinjet. Consequently, the 767-200ER became in February 1994 the most widely used aircraft across the Atlantic.

Although superseded to a large extent by later passenger variants (767-300, -300ER, and -400ER), the 767-200ER remains in limited production. Powerplants for 767-200ERs include various models of the CF6-80, JT9D, PW4000, and RB.211-524 series with takeoff thrust between 50,000 and 63,300 pounds (222.4 and 281.6 kilonewtons).

767-300 and -300ER

The rapid increase in MTOW made possible by the generously sized wings of the 767 and by the availability of more-powerful turbofans also enabled Boeing to offer a stretched version of the aircraft, the 767-300. Announced in September 1983 when Japan Airlines placed an initial order for six aircraft, the 767-300 combined features of the 767-200ER (increased MTOW, local structural strengthening, and sturdier undercarriage) with a longer fuselage. By inserting a 10-foot 1-inch (3.07-meter) plug forward of the wings and an 11-foot (3.35-meter) plug aft, maximum seating in single-class configuration was increased to 351.

Powered by JT9Ds, the first 767-300 (l/n 132, s/n 23215, registered N767S during pre-certification testing but re-registered

JA8236 prior to delivery) flew on January 30, 1986. Deliveries of JT9D-powered aircraft commenced on September 9, 1986 (l/n 148, s/n 23216 for Japan Airlines); those of aircraft with CF6-80s on November 7, 1986 (l/n 152, s/n 23277 for Delta Air Lines); and those with PW4056s on July 22, 1994 (l/n 546, s/n 27309 for Shanghai Airlines). Six airlines have ordered 767-300s in standard passenger configuration, but this version has now effectively been supplanted by the extended-range variant.

First ordered by All Nippon Airways in December 1985, the 767-300ER has the stretched fuselage of the -300 and the maximum fuel capacity of the 767-200ER. The first 767-300ER was delivered to American Airlines on February 19, 1988 (l/n 202, s/n 24032), and the 767-300ER has become the most-built version of the 767. General Electric (various models of the CF6-80C series), Pratt & Whitney (various PW4000 series), and Rolls-Royce (RB.211-524H) engines with thrust of up to 63,300 pounds (281.5 kilonewtons) provide power for these aircraft.

767-300 Freighter

UPS, which in December 1985, had become the launch customer for the freighter version of the 757, became the first customer for the 767 freighter in January 1993 when it ordered 30 767-300 freighters and took options on 30 more. The variant ordered by UPS was based on the heaviest 767-300ER with MTOW of 412,000 pounds (186,680 kilograms) and fuel-tank capacity of 23,980 U.S. gallons (90,772 liters).

Optimized for the package-freighter business, the 767-300 freighters for UPS differs from passenger variants in lacking cabin windows and main-cabin air conditioning. In addition, they have reinforced main-deck flooring and a 8-foot 9-inch by 11-foot 1-inch (2.67- by 3.40-meter) main-deck cargo-loading door forward of the wing on the left side. Each is fitted with a powered handling system on the main deck and lower holds for highly automated cargo loading and unloading. Completed in the austere configuration chosen by UPS for its package business, the first 767-300 Freighter (l/n 580, s/n 27239) flew on June 1995, powered by General Electric CF6-80C2B7F turbofans rated at 60,800 pounds (270.5 kilonewtons) of static thrust. Deliveries to UPS commenced four months later.

For customers with more diversified operations, the 767-300 Freighter is available with air conditioning for transporting animals and perishables on the main deck or in the forward lower decks. The first of these aircraft went to Asiana Airlines (already an operator of passenger-configured 767-300/300ERs) in December 1996.

767-400ER

The next increase in 767 seating (to a maximum of 375 in single-class, high-density configuration) could not be accommodated just by a 21-foot (6.40-meter) fuselage stretch but also required an increase in wing area to cope with the 450,000-pound (204,117-kilogram) MTOW. Announced in April 1997, the resulting 767-400ER was fitted with redesigned wings with raked tips increasing span from 156 feet 1 inch to 170 feet 4 inches (47.57 to 51.92 meters) and significantly improving aerodynamic efficiency. Other important differences with earlier 767 versions included the use of an all-new main landing gear and of an updated cockpit arrangement similar to that of the 777 and featuring six large LCDs. Moreover, cabin interiors were revised to incorporate award-winning features developed for the 777 (and now available for installation in current production 767-300/300ERs).

The launch customer for the 767-400ER was Delta Air Lines, which ordered 21 aircraft in April 1997. Its first aircraft (l/n 758, s/n 29703) flew on October 9, 1999. The FAA and European JAA certifications for the 767-400ER powered by General Electric CF6-80C2B7F turbofans rated at 60,800 pounds (270.5 kilonewtons) of static thrust were issued in July 2000. Continental Airlines became the first to place the 767-400ER into service, doing so on September 15, 2000.

In September 2000, Boeing announced its commitment to produce a longer-range version of the 767-400ER, to be powered by Engine Alliance GP7100s or Rolls-Royce Trent 600s rated at 72,000 pounds (320.3 kilonewtons) of static thrust. With an additional 2,145 U.S. gallons (8,120 liters) of fuel in stabilizer tanks, the longer-range 767-400ER was expected to have a MTOW of 465,000 pounds (210,920 kilograms). At the time of this writing, however, it appeared that development and production of this version may be shelved in favor of the advanced-technology "sonic cruiser" Boeing announced in March 2001.

Boeing 767 Principal Characteristics and Performance

	767-200	767-200ER	767-300	767-300ER	767-300F Freighter	767-400
Span, ft in (m)	156' 1" (47.57)	156' 1" (47.57)	156' 1" (47.57)	156' 1" (47.57)	156' 1" (47.57)	170' 4" (51.92)
Length, ft in (m)	159' 2" (48.51)	159' 2" (48.51)	180' 3" (54.94)	180' 3" (54.94)	180' 3" (54.94)	201' 4 (61.37)
Height, ft in (m)	52 (15.85)	52 (15.85)	52 (15.85)	52 (15.85)	52 (15.85)	55' 4" (16.87)
Wing area, sq ft (m^2)	3,050 (283.4)	3,050 (283.4)	3,050 (283.4)	3,050 (283.4)	3,050 (283.4)	unavailable
High-density seating	255/290	255	351	351	N/A	375
Two-class seating	224	224	269	269	N/A	304
Three-class seating	181	181	218	218	N/A	245
Underfloor cargo, cu ft (m^3)	2,875 (81.4)	2,875 (81.4)	3,770 (106.8)	3,770 (106.8)	4,150 (117.5)	4,580 (129.7)
Maximum cargo load, lb (kg)	N/A	N/A	N/A	N/A	121,000 (54,885)	N/A
TO thrust per engine, lb st (kN)	48,000/52,500 (213.5/233.5)	50,000/63,300 (222.4/281.6)	48,000/60,600 (213.5/269.5)	51,950/63,300 (231.1/281.5)	51,950/63,300 (231.1/281.5)	63,300/63,500 (281.5/282.5)
Fuel capacity, U.S. gal (liters)	11,320/16,700 (42,850/63,215)	20,450/23,980 (77,410/90,772)	16,700 (63,215)	23,980 (90,772)	23,980 (90,772)	23,980 (90,772)
MTOW, lb (kg)	300,000/315,000 (136,078/142,882)	345,000/395,000 (156,489/179,169)	345,000/351,000 (156,489/159,211)	387,000/412,000 (175,540/186,880)	408,000/412,000 (185,066/186,880)	450,000 (204,117)
Typical cruise speed, Mach	0.80	0.80	0.80	0.80	0.80	0.80
Typical range, nm (km)	3,160/3,850 (5,850/7,130)	5,365/6,805 (9,935/12,605)	4,000 (7,410)	6,115 (11,325)	3,270 (6,055)	5,635 (10,435)A

Boeing 767Commercial Jet Aircraft Census
The aircraft in the following tables are listed in order of the following: 1) ICAO country prefixes; 2) operator; 3) aircraft type; and 4) registration.
The total built was 831+ (237+ B767-200, 574+ B757-300, AND 20+ B767-400) from 1981 to present (still in production).

A/C TYPE	CURRENT REG. NO.	LAST KNOWN OPERATOR (OWNER)	Status	ORIGINAL MSN	LINE NO.	DEL. DATE	ENG. TYPE	FLEET NO.	PREV. REG. [COMMENTS]
A40-OMAN									
B767-3P6 (ER)	A40-GI	GULF AIR		24485	264	05/03/89	CF6-80C2B4	604	
B767-3P6 (ER)	A40-GJ	GULF AIR		24495	267	06/13/89	CF6-80C2B4	605	
B767-3P6 (ER)	A40-GK	GULF AIR		24496	270	06/26/89	CF6-80C2B4	606	
B767-3P6 (ER)	A40-GS	GULF AIR		26236	436	06/05/92	CF6-80C2B4	613	
B767-3P6 (ER)	A40-GT	GULF AIR		26238	440	06/17/92	CF6-80C2B4	614	
B767-3P6 (ER)	A40-GU	GULF AIR		26233	501	06/17/93	CF6-80C2B4	615	
B767-3P6 (ER)	A40-GV	GULF AIR		26235	502	06/22/93	CF6-80C2B4	616	
B767-3P6 (ER)	A40-GY	GULF AIR		26234	538	05/25/94	CF6-80C2B4	619	
B767-3P6 (ER)	A40-GZ	GULF AIR		26237	544	06/23/94	CF6-80C2B4	620	
A6-UNITED ARAB EMIRATES									
B767-341 (ER)	A6-SUL	ABU DHABI AMIRI FLIGHT		30341	768	12/15/99	CF6-80C2B7F		N60659
B-CHINA (PEOPLE'S REPUBLIC)									
B767-2J6 (ER)	B-2551	AIR CHINA		23307	126	10/08/85	JT9D-7R4E4		N6065Y
B767-2J6 (ER)	B-2552	AIR CHINA		23308	127	10/29/85	JT9D-7R4E4		N60659
B767-2J6 (ER)	B-2553	AIR CHINA		23744	155	03/04/87	JT9D-7R4E4		N60659
B767-2J6 (ER)	B-2554	AIR CHINA		23745	156	03/12/87	JT9D-7R4E4		N6009F
B767-2J6 (ER)	B-2555	AIR CHINA		24007	204	06/27/88	PW4052		
B767-2J6 (ER)	B-2556	AIR CHINA		24157	253	02/21/89	PW4052		N6018N
B767-3J6	B-2557	AIR CHINA		25875	429	05/20/92	PW4056		
B767-3J6	B-2558	AIR CHINA		25876	478	03/24/93	PW4056		
B767-3J6	B-2559	AIR CHINA		25877	530	03/16/93	PW4056		
B767-3J6	B-2560	AIR CHINA		25878	569	03/17/95	PW4056		
B767-3W0 (ER)	B-2568	CHINA YUNNAN AIRLINES		28148	620	07/26/96	RB211-524H		
B767-3W0 (ER)	B-2569	CHINA YUNNAN AIRLINES		28149	627	09/11/96	RB211-524H		
B767-3W0 (ER)	B-5001	CHINA YUNNAN AIRLINES		28264	644	01/30/97	RB211-524H		
B767-36D	B-2563	SHANGHAI AIRLINES		27309	546	07/22/94	PW4056		
B767-36D	B-2567	SHANGHAI AIRLINES		27685	686	01/29/98	PW4056		
B767-36D	B-2570	SHANGHAI AIRLINES		27941	770	10/21/99	PW4056		

	A/C TYPE	CURRENT REG. NO.	LAST KNOWN OPERATOR (OWNER)	Status	ORIGINAL MSN	LINE NO.	DEL. DATE	ENG. TYPE	FLEET NO.	PREV. REG. [COMMENTS]
B-CHINA (TAIWAN)										
	B767-25E	B-16621	EVA AIR		27192	524	01/13/94	CF6-80C2B2F		
	B767-25E	B-16622	EVA AIR		27193	527	02/01/94	CF6-80C2B2F		
	B767-25E	B-16623	EVA AIR		27194	532	03/01/94	CF6-80C2B2F		
	B767-25E	B-16625	EVA AIR		27195	535	04/01/94	CF6-80C2B2F		
	B767-35E (ER)	B-16603	EVA AIR (HHL LEASE)		26063	434	06/12/92	CF6-80C2B6F		
	B767-35E (ER)	B-16605	EVA AIR (HHL LEASE)		26064	438	06/15/92	CF6-80C2B6F		
	B767-3T7 (ER)	N601EV	EVA AIR (SALE)		25076	366	05/30/91	CF6-80C2B6F		B-16601
	B767-3T7 (ER)	N602EV	EVA AIR (SALE)		25117	370	05/30/91	CF6-80C2B6F		B-16602
C-CANADA										
	B767-233 (ER)	C-FBEF	AIR CANADA		24323	250	12/30/88	JT9D-7R4D	617	N6009F
	B767-233 (ER)	C-FBEG	AIR CANADA		24324	252	02/04/89	JT9D-7R4D	618	N6009F
	B767-233 (ER)	C-FBEM	AIR CANADA		24325	254	03/17/89	JT9D-7R4D	619	N6038E
	B767-209 (ER)	C-FUCL	AIR CANADA (BOUL)		22682	60	06/27/83	JT9D-7R4D	622	N1781B, B-1838, N682SH, ZK-NBH
	B767-209 (ER)	C-FVNM	AIR CANADA (AFIN)		22681	18	12/20/82	JT9D-7R4D	621	B-1836, ZK-NBF, N681SH
	B767-233	C-GAUB	AIR CANADA		22517	16	10/30/82	JT9D-7R4D	601	
	B767-233	C-GAUE	AIR CANADA		22518	22	12/14/82	JT9D-7R4D	602	
	B767-233	C-GAUH	AIR CANADA		22519	40	02/11/83	JT9D-7R4D	603	
	B767-233	C-GAUN	AIR CANADA		22520	47	03/30/83	JT9D-7R4D	604	["GIMLI GLIDER"; STD YUL]
	B767-233	C-GAUP	AIR CANADA		22521	66	09/01/83	JT9D-7R4D	605	N1791B
	B767-233	C-GAUS	AIR CANADA		22522	75	12/01/83	JT9D-7R4D	606	N60659
	B767-233	C-GAUU	AIR CANADA		22523	87	04/12/84	JT9D-7R4D	607	N1784B
	B767-233	C-GAUW	AIR CANADA		22524	88	04/19/84	JT9D-7R4D	608	N6038E
	B767-233	C-GAUY	AIR CANADA		22525	91	05/31/84	JT9D-7R4D	609	N6055X
	B767-233	C-GAVA	AIR CANADA		22526	92	06/13/84	JT9D-7R4D	610	
	B767-233 (ER)	C-GAVC	AIR CANADA		22527	102	10/18/84	JT9D-7R4D	611	N1783B
	B767-233 (ER)	C-GAVF	AIR CANADA		22528	105	11/21/84	JT9D-7R4D	612	N6066U
	B767-233 (ER)	C-GDSP	AIR CANADA		24142	229	07/13/88	JT9D-7R4D	613	N6009F
	B767-233 (ER)	C-GDSS	AIR CANADA		24143	233	08/17/88	JT9D-7R4D	614	N6005C
	B767-233 (ER)	C-GDSU	AIR CANADA		24144	234	08/30/88	JT9D-7R4D	615	N6018N
	B767-233 (ER)	C-GDSY	AIR CANADA		24145	236	09/15/88	JT9D-7R4D	616	N6005C
	B767-275	C-GPWA	AIR CANADA		22683	36	03/04/83	JT9D-7R4D	671	[LRF 03/31/01; WFU TO YWG]
	B767-275	C-GPWB	AIR CANADA		22684	52	04/23/83	JT9D-7R4D	672	N1791B
	B767-375 (ER)	C-FCAB	AIR CANADA		24082	213	04/15/88	CF6-80C2B6	681	N6055X
	B767-375 (ER)	C-FCAE	AIR CANADA		24083	215	05/03/88	CF6-80C2B6	682	N6046P
	B767-375 (ER)	C-FCAF	AIR CANADA		24084	219	05/13/88	CF6-80C2B6	683	N6038E
	B767-375 (ER)	C-FCAG	AIR CANADA (GECA)		24085	220	05/19/88	CF6-80C2B6	684	N6009F
	B767-333 (ER)	C-FMWP	AIR CANADA		25583	508	08/10/93	PW4060	631	
	B767-333 (ER)	C-FMWQ	AIR CANADA		25584	596	10/28/95	PW4060	632	
	B767-333 (ER)	C-FMWU	AIR CANADA		25585	597	11/10/95	PW4060	633	

A/C TYPE	CURRENT REG. NO.	LAST KNOWN OPERATOR (OWNER)	Status	ORIGINAL MSN	LINE NO.	DEL. DATE	ENG. TYPE	FLEET NO.	PREV. REG. [COMMENTS]
B767-333 (ER)	C-FMWV	AIR CANADA		25586	599	12/08/95	PW4060	634	
B767-333 (ER)	C-FMWY	AIR CANADA		25587	604	02/23/96	PW4060	635	
B767-333 (ER)	C-FMXC	AIR CANADA		25588	606	03/13/96	PW4060	636	
B767-375 (ER)	C-FOCA	AIR CANADA		24575	311	06/12/90	CF6-80C2B6F	640	
B767-375 (ER)	C-FPCA	AIR CANADA		24306	258	04/18/89	CF6-80C2B6F	637	
B767-375 (ER)	C-FTCA	AIR CANADA		24307	259	04/25/89	CF6-80C2B6F	638	
B767-375 (ER)	C-FXCA	AIR CANADA (GECA)		24574	302	04/27/90	CF6-80C2B6F	639	
B767-38E (ER)	C-GBZR	AIR CANADA (ILFC)		25404	411	01/24/92	CF6-80C2B6F	645	HL7267
B767-38E (ER)	C-GDUZ	AIR CANADA (ILFC)		25347	399	11/07/92	CF6-80C2B6F	646	HL7266
B767-375 (ER)	C-GEOQ	AIR CANADA (ILFC)		30112	765	09/15/99	CF6-80C2B6F	647	
B767-375 (ER)	C-GEOU	AIR CANADA (GECA)		30108	771	11/18/99	CF6-80C2B6F	648	
B767-3S1 (ER)	C-GGBI	AIR CANADA (FSBU)		26608	559	11/22/94	CF6-80C2B4F		N769TA
B767-35H (ER)	C-GGBJ	AIR CANADA (CITG)		26389	459	10/23/92	CF6-80C2B6F		N60659, N800CZ, ZK-NCM [OO FOR LST ANZ]
B767-3S1 (ER)	C-GGBK	AIR CANADA (FSBU)		25221	384	08/26/91	CF6-80C2B6F		B-16688, N688EV, PH-AAM, G-BXOP , SE-DZF, N770TA
B767-3Y0 (ER)	C-GGFJ	AIR CANADA (WHIRLPOOL)		24952	357	03/19/91	PW4060		XA-RWW, EI-CAL, N249WP, SE-DKZ
B767-3Y0 (ER)	C-GGMX	AIR CANADA (AERCO USA)		24947	351	03/11/91	PW4060		CC-CDL, PT-TAD, CC-CEY, N947AC
B767-3Y0 (ER)	C-GGOH	AIR CANADA (GECA)		26200	450	09/01/92	PW4060		XA-RKI, N200GE
B767-35H (ER)	C-GHLA	AIR CANADA (ITOH)		26387	445	08/14/92	CF6-80C2B6F		S7-AAQ, EI-CJA, HB-IHT [OO FOR LST ANZ]
B767-35H (ER)	C-GHLK	AIR CANADA (ITOH)		26388	456	10/07/92	CF6-80C2B6F	657	S7-AAV, EI-CJB, HB-IHU [OO FOR LST ANZ]
B767-333 (ER)	C-GHLQ	AIR CANADA (GECA)	N	30846	832		CF6-80C2B6F	658	N6009F
B767-333 (ER)	C-GHLT	AIR CANADA (GECA)	N	30850	835		CF6-80C2B6F	659	N6018N
B767-333 (ER)	C-GHLU	AIR CANADA (GECA)	N	30851	836		CF6-80C2B6F	660	N6046P
B767-3Y0 (ER)	C-GHML	AIR CANADA (GECA)		24948	380	07/19/91	PW4060	655	N6005C, PT-TAE, N948GE
B767-375 (ER)	C-GLCA	AIR CANADA		25120	361	04/05/91	CF6-80C2B6F	641	
B767-375 (ER)	C-GSCA	AIR CANADA (CITG)		25121	372	06/04/91	CF6-80C2B6F	642	B-2564
CC-CHILE									
B767-219 (ER)	CC-CJP	AERO CONTINENTE CHILE (ACQ) L		24150	239	09/26/88	CF6-80A		N6038E, ZK-NBE, PT-TAG, N141LF
B767-316 (ER)	CC-CBJ	LAN CHILE (ILFC)		27613	652	03/24/97	CF6-80C2B6F		
B767-352 (ER)	CC-CDM	LAN CHILE (ILFC)		26261	575	05/03/95	PW4062		N181LF
B767-316 (ER)	CC-CDP	LAN CHILE (ILFC)		27597	602	05/03/95	CF6-80C2B6F		
B767-316 (ER)	CC-CEB	LAN CHILE (ILFC)		26327	621	07/17/96	CF6-80C2B6F		
B767-316 (ER)	CC-CEK	LAN CHILE (ILFC)		26329	641	12/19/96	CF6-80C2B6F		
B767-3Y0 (ER)	CC-CEL	LAN CHILE (AIRPLANES LTD)		26204	464	11/25/92	PW4060		XA-RKJ
B767-375 (ER)	CC-CRG	LAN CHILE (CITL)		25865	430	11/04/92	CF6-80C2B6F		EI-CFR, B-2561
B767-375 (ER)	CC-CRH	LAN CHILE (GECA)		25864	426	04/23/92	CF6-80C2B6F		HA-LHC, B-2562
B767-316 (ER)	CC-CRT	LAN CHILE (ILFC)		27615	681	12/10/97	CF6-80C2B7F		
B767-316 (ER)	CC-CZT	LAN CHILE (CONDOR LSG)		29228	699	04/29/98	CF6-80C2B7F		
B767-316 (ER)	CC-CZU	LAN CHILE (EAGLE LSG)		29229	729	12/09/98	CF6-80C2B7F		
B767-316 (ER)	CC-CZW	LAN CHILE (CONDOR LSG)		29227	698	04/30/98	CF6-80C2B7F		

A/C TYPE	CURRENT REG. NO.	LAST KNOWN OPERATOR (OWNER)	Status	ORIGINAL MSN	LINE NO.	DEL. DATE	ENG. TYPE	FLEET NO.	PREV. REG. [COMMENTS]
B767-316F (ER)	CC-CZX	LAN CHILE		29881	778	12/22/99	CF6-80C2B7F		
B767-316F (ER)	CC-CZY	LAN CHILE		30780	806	08/23/00	CF6-80C2B7F		
B767-316F (ER)	CC-CZZ	LAN CHILE (CONDOR LSG)		25756	712	09/23/98	CF6-80C2B7F		
C9-MOZAMBIQUE									
B767-2B1 (ER)	C9-BAF	LAM-MOZAMBIQUE		26471	511	08/24/93	PW4056		ZS-SRA
D-GERMANY									
B767-304 (ER)	D-AGYF	BRITANNIA AIRWAYS, GMBH (BAL)	L	28208	705	06/06/98	CF6-80C2B7F		G-OBYF
B767-304 (ER)	D-AGYH	BRITANNIA AIRWAYS, GMBH (BAL)	L	28883	737	02/04/99	CF6-80C2B7F		G-OBYH
B767-330 (ER)	D-ABUA	CONDOR (NBB FRANKFURT)		26991	455	10/02/92	PW4060		
B767-330 (ER)	D-ABUB	CONDOR (CG-KUMIAI)		26987	466	12/04/92	PW4060		
B767-330 (ER)	D-ABUC	CONDOR (NBB BONN)		26992	470	01/08/93	PW4060		
B767-330 (ER)	D-ABUD	CONDOR (NBB BONN)		26983	471	01/15/93	PW4060		
B767-330 (ER)	D-ABUE	CONDOR (DLLG)		26984	518	10/11/93	PW4060		
B767-330 (ER)	D-ABUF	CONDOR		26985	537	04/08/94	PW4060		
B767-330 (ER)	D-ABUH	CONDOR		26986	553	09/29/94	PW4060		
B767-330 (ER)	D-ABUI	CONDOR		26988	562	01/12/95	PW4060		
B767-330 (ER)	D-ABUZ	CONDOR		25209	382	07/30/91	PW4060		
B767-3G5 (ER)	D-AMUJ	LTU INTL. AIRWAYS		28111	612	04/28/96	PW4060		
B767-3G5 (ER)	D-AMUN	LTU INTL. AIRWAYS		24259	268	06/08/89	PW4060		
B767-3G5 (ER)	D-AMUO	LTU INTL. AIRWAYS		29435	720	09/24/98	PW4060		
B767-33A (ER)	D-AMUP	LTU INTL. AIRWAYS		25531	423	03/30/92	PW4060		
B767-3G5 (ER)	D-AMUR	LTU INTL. AIRWAYS		24257	251	02/02/89	PW4060		N6046P
B767-3G5 (ER)	D-AMUS	LTU INTL. AIRWAYS		24258	255	02/17/89	PW4060		
DQ-FIJI									
B767-3X2 (ER)	DQ-FJC	AIR PACIFIC (ILFC)		26260	552	09/16/94	CF6-80C2B6		
EC-SPAIN									
B767-204 (ER)	EC-GOJ	AIR EUROPA (HELLER)		23072	107	02/11/85	CF6-80A2		N6067E, G-BLKV, ZK-NBI
B767-3Q8 (ER)	EC-HKS	AIR EUROPA (ILFC)		27686	793	05/21/00	CF6-80C2B7F		
B767-3Q8 (ER)	EC-HPU	AIR EUROPA (ILFC)		30048	828	03/01/01	CF6-80C2B7F		
B767-3Q8 (ER)	EC-HSV	AIR EUROPA (ILFC)	N	29387	840		CF6-80C2B7F		
B767-3Y0 (ER)	EC-GSU	IBERIA		26206	487	05/03/93	CF6-80C2B6F		HL7269
B767-3Y0 (ER)	EC-GTI	IBERIA		26207	503	07/21/93	CF6-80C2B6F		HL7286

A/C TYPE	CURRENT REG. NO.	LAST KNOWN OPERATOR (OWNER)	Status	ORIGINAL MSN	LINE NO.	DEL. DATE	ENG. TYPE	FLEET NO.	PREV. REG. [COMMENTS]
B767-3Y0 (ER)	EC-FCU	SPANAIR (GECA)		24999	354	02/28/91	PW4060		EC-547
B767-3Y0 (ER)	EC-FHA	SPANAIR (BBAM)		25000	386	08/21/91	PW4060		EC-548
B767-3Z9 (ER)	OE-LAY	SPANAIR (LDA)	L	29867	731	12/29/98	PW4060		

ET-ETHIOPIA

A/C TYPE	CURRENT REG. NO.	LAST KNOWN OPERATOR (OWNER)	Status	ORIGINAL MSN	LINE NO.	DEL. DATE	ENG. TYPE	FLEET NO.	PREV. REG. [COMMENTS]
B767-260 (ER)	ET-AIE	ETHIOPIAN AIRLINES		23106	90	05/23/84	JT9D-7R4E		N1792B
B767-260 (ER)	ET-AIF	ETHIOPIAN AIRLINES		23107	93	06/06/84	JT9D-7R4E		N6065Y
B767-33A (ER)	ET-AKW	ETHIOPIAN AIRLINES (BBAM)		25346	403	12/13/91	PW4056		V8-RBE
B767-33A (ER)	ET-ALC	ETHIOPIAN AIRLINES (AWAS)		28043	734	01/19/99	PW4060		

F-FRANCE

A/C TYPE	CURRENT REG. NO.	LAST KNOWN OPERATOR (OWNER)	Status	ORIGINAL MSN	LINE NO.	DEL. DATE	ENG. TYPE	FLEET NO.	PREV. REG. [COMMENTS]
B767-3Q8 (ER)	F-GHGF	AIR FRANCE (ACG ACQ)		24745	355	03/21/91	PW4060		
B767-3Q8 (ER)	F-GHGG	AIR FRANCE (CHAMPAGNE)		24746	378	07/19/91	PW4060		
B767-37E (ER)	F-GHGH	AIR FRANCE (PEGA)		25077	385	08/22/91	PW4060		
B767-328 (ER)	F-GHGI	AIR FRANCE (FLORITA FIN.)		27135	493	05/14/93	CF6-80C2B6F		
B767-328 (ER)	F-GHGJ	AIR FRANCE (NBB PARIS)		27136	497	05/28/93	CF6-80C2B6F		

G-UNITED KINGDOM

A/C TYPE	CURRENT REG. NO.	LAST KNOWN OPERATOR (OWNER)	Status	ORIGINAL MSN	LINE NO.	DEL. DATE	ENG. TYPE	FLEET NO.	PREV. REG. [COMMENTS]
B767-31K (ER)	G-DAJC	AIRTOURS INTL. (BLUEBIRD)		27206	533	04/15/94	CF6-80C2B7F		
B767-31K (ER)	G-DIMB	AIRTOURS INTL.		28865	657	04/28/97	CF6-80C2B7F		
B767-31K (ER)	G-SJMC	AIRTOURS INTL. (CROWN GREEN)		27205	528	03/16/94	CF6-80C2B7F		N6038E
B767-38A (ER)	G-OOAL	AIR 2000 (GECA)		29617	741	03/30/99	CF6-80C2B7F		
B767-38A (ER)	G-OOAM	AIR 2000 (GECA)		29618	792	05/09/00	CF6-80C2B7F		
B767-39H (ER)	G-OOAN	AIR 2000 (ILFC)		26256	484	04/01/93	CF6-80C2B6F		G-UKLH
B767-39H (ER)	G-OOAO	AIR 2000 (ILFC)		26257	488	04/13/93	CF6-80C2B6F		G-UKLI [OPF BAL]
B767-204 (ER)	G-BRIF	BRITANNIA AIRWAYS		24736	296	03/10/90	CF6-80A2		
B767-204 (ER)	G-BRIG	BRITANNIA AIRWAYS		24757	299	04/10/90	CF6-80A2		
B767-204 (ER)	G-BYAA	BRITANNIA AIRWAYS		25058	362	04/23/91	CF6-80C2B4		N60697, PH-AHM
B767-204 (ER)	G-BYAB	BRITANNIA AIRWAYS		25139	373	06/11/91	CF6-80C2B4		
B767-304 (ER)	G-OBYA	BRITANNIA AIRWAYS (MCC LSG)		28039	610	05/15/96	CF6-80C2B7F		D-AGYA [OPF GIA FOR HADJ]
B767-304 (ER)	G-OBYB	BRITANNIA AIRWAYS		28040	613	05/17/96	CF6-80C2B7F		[OPF GIA FOR HADJ]
B767-304 (ER)	G-OBYC	BRITANNIA AIRWAYS (ITID LSG)		28041	614	05/21/96	CF6-80C2B7F		D-AGYC
B767-304 (ER)	G-OBYD	BRITANNIA AIRWAYS (ALE-FOUR)		28042	649	03/04/97	CF6-80C2B7F		
B767-304 (ER)	G-OBYE	BRITANNIA AIRWAYS		28979	691	02/25/98	CF6-80C2B7F		D-AGYE [OPF GIA FOR HADJ]
B767-304 (ER)	G-OBYF	BRITANNIA AIRWAYS (ILFC)		28208	705	06/06/98	CF6-80C2B7F		[LST DBY AS D-AGYF]
B767-304 (ER)	G-OBYG	BRITANNIA AIRWAYS (ILFC)		29137	733	01/13/99	CF6-80C2B7F		
B767-304 (ER)	G-OBYH	BRITANNIA AIRWAYS (ILFC)		28883	737	02/04/99	CF6-80C2B7F		[LST DBY AS D-AGYH]
B767-304 (ER)	G-OBYI	BRITANNIA AIRWAYS		29138	783	02/01/00	CF6-80C2B7F		[OPF GIA FOR HADJ]
B767-304 (ER)	G-OBYJ	BRITANNIA AIRWAYS (ILFC)		29384	784	02/19/00	CF6-80C2B7F		[OPF GIA FOR HADJ]

A/C TYPE	CURRENT REG. NO.	LAST KNOWN OPERATOR (OWNER)	Status	ORIGINAL MSN	LINE NO.	DEL. DATE	ENG. TYPE	FLEET NO.	PREV. REG. [COMMENTS]
B767-336 (ER)	G-BNWA	BRITISH AIRWAYS		24333	265	04/25/90	RB211-524H		N6009F
B767-336 (ER)	G-BNWB	BRITISH AIRWAYS		24334	281	02/08/90	RB211-524H		N6046P
B767-336 (ER)	G-BNWC	BRITISH AIRWAYS		24335	284	02/21/90	RB211-524H		
B767-336 (ER)	G-BNWD	BRITISH AIRWAYS		24336	286	02/27/90	RB211-524H		N6018N
B767-336 (ER)	G-BNWE	BRITISH AIRWAYS		24337	288	03/18/90	RB211-524H		[LST QFA AS VH-ZXA]
B767-336 (ER)	G-BNWF	BRITISH AIRWAYS		24338	293	06/23/90	RB211-524H		N1788B [LST QFA AS VH-ZXB 11/16/00]
B767-336 (ER)	G-BNWG	BRITISH AIRWAYS		24339	298	07/13/90	RB211-524H		[LST QFA AS VH-ZXC]
B767-336 (ER)	G-BNWH	BRITISH AIRWAYS		24340	335	10/31/90	RB211-524H		N6005C
B767-336 (ER)	G-BNWI	BRITISH AIRWAYS		24341	342	12/18/90	RB211-524H		
B767-336 (ER)	G-BNWJ	BRITISH AIRWAYS		24342	363	04/24/91	RB211-524H		[LST QFA AS VH-ZXD]
B767-336 (ER)	G-BNWK	BRITISH AIRWAYS		24343	364	04/18/91	RB211-524H		[LST QFA AS VH-ZXE 12/24/00]
B767-336 (ER)	G-BNWL	BRITISH AIRWAYS		25203	365	04/30/91	RB211-524H		[LST QFA AS VH-ZXF]
B767-336 (ER)	G-BNWM	BRITISH AIRWAYS		25204	376	06/25/91	RB211-524H		
B767-336 (ER)	G-BNWN	BRITISH AIRWAYS		25444	398	10/30/91	RB211-524H		
B767-336 (ER)	G-BNWO	BRITISH AIRWAYS		25442	418	03/03/92	RB211-524H		
B767-336 (ER)	G-BNWP	BRITISH AIRWAYS		25443	419	03/10/92	RB211-524H		[LRF 09/30/00; LST QFA AS VH-ZXG 11/10/00]
B767-336 (ER)	G-BNWR	BRITISH AIRWAYS		25732	421	03/20/92	RB211-524H		
B767-336 (ER)	G-BNWS	BRITISH AIRWAYS		25826	473	02/19/93	RB211-524H		N6018N
B767-336 (ER)	G-BNWT	BRITISH AIRWAYS		25828	476	02/08/93	RB211-524H		
B767-336 (ER)	G-BNWU	BRITISH AIRWAYS		25829	483	03/16/93	RB211-524H		
B767-336 (ER)	G-BNWV	BRITISH AIRWAYS		27140	490	04/29/93	RB211-524H		
B767-336 (ER)	G-BNWW	BRITISH AIRWAYS		25831	526	02/03/94	RB211-524H		
B767-336 (ER)	G-BNWX	BRITISH AIRWAYS		25832	529	03/01/94	RB211-524H		
B767-336 (ER)	G-BNWY	BRITISH AIRWAYS		25834	608	04/22/96	RB211-524H		N5005C
B767-336 (ER)	G-BNWZ	BRITISH AIRWAYS		25733	648	02/25/97	RB211-524H		
B767-336 (ER)	G-BZHA	BRITISH AIRWAYS		29230	702	05/22/98	RB211-524H3		N60668
B767-336 (ER)	G-BZHB	BRITISH AIRWAYS		29231	704	05/30/98	RB211-524H3		
B767-336 (ER)	G-BZHC	BRITISH AIRWAYS		29232	708	06/29/98	RB211-524H3		

HA-HUNGARY

A/C TYPE	CURRENT REG. NO.	LAST KNOWN OPERATOR (OWNER)	Status	ORIGINAL MSN	LINE NO.	DEL. DATE	ENG. TYPE	FLEET NO.	PREV. REG. [COMMENTS]
B767-27G (ER)	HA-LHA	MALEV HUNGARIAN AIRLINES		27048	475	04/30/93	CF6-80C2B4F		N6009F
B767-27G (ER)	HA-LHB	MALEV HUNGARIAN AIRLINES		27049	482	04/30/93	CF6-80C2B4F		N60668
B767-3P6 (ER)	HA-LHD	MALEV HUNGARIAN AIRLINES (SAMA)		24484	260	04/13/89	CF6-80C2B4		A40-GH

HB-SWITZERLAND

A/C TYPE	CURRENT REG. NO.	LAST KNOWN OPERATOR (OWNER)	Status	ORIGINAL MSN	LINE NO.	DEL. DATE	ENG. TYPE	FLEET NO.	PREV. REG. [COMMENTS]
B767-3BG (ER)	HB-IHV	BALAIR/CTA LEISURE (FLIT)		30564	798	08/11/00	PW4060		
B767-3BG (ER)	HB-IHW	BALAIR/CTA LEISURE (FLIT)		30565	802	09/26/00	PW4060		

A/C TYPE	CURRENT REG. NO.	LAST KNOWN OPERATOR (OWNER)	Status	ORIGINAL MSN	LINE NO.	DEL. DATE	ENG. TYPE	FLEET NO.	PREV. REG. [COMMENTS]
HK-COLOMBIA									
B767-2B1 (ER)	N421AV	AVIANCA (GECA)		25421	407	01/14/92	PW4056		EI-CEM, PT-TAK
B767-33A (ER)	N535AW	AVIANCA (AWMS III)		25535	491	05/26/93	PW4060		N6018N, N768TA, F-GKAU, OO-VAS, V5-NMB, VH-NOE
B767-259 (ER)	N985AN	AVIANCA (WTCI)		24618	292	02/26/90	PW4056		
B767-259 (ER)	N986AN	AVIANCA (WTCI)		24835	321	08/14/90	PW4056		
B767-284 (ER)	N988AN	AVIANCA (BAY 2 BAY LSG)		24742	303	06/08/90	PW4056		N6046P, V8-RBD, VH-RMA
B767-383 (ER)	N984AN	AVIANCA (PEGA)		24357	262	04/22/89	PW4060		LN-RCB, I-AEJC
HL-ASIANA									
B767-38E	HL7247	ASIANA AIRLINES		25757	523	01/31/94	CF6-80C2B2F		
B767-38E	HL7248	ASIANA AIRLINES		25758	582	07/12/95	CF6-80C2B2F		
B767-3Q8 (ER)	HL7249	ASIANA AIRLINES (ILFC)		26265	570	03/17/95	CF6-80C2B6F		
B767-38E	HL7263	ASIANA AIRLINES		24797	328	09/27/90	CF6-80C2B2F		
B767-38E	HL7264	ASIANA AIRLINES		24798	331	10/05/90	CF6-80C2B2F		
B767-38E (ER)	HL7268	ASIANA AIRLINES (GREENFLY)		25132	417	02/24/92	CF6-80C2B4F		HL7268, N132KR, EI-CPV
B767-38E	HL7506	ASIANA AIRLINES (OZ GAMMA LSG)		25760	639	12/19/96	CF6-80C2B2F		
B767-38EF (ER)	HL7507	ASIANA AIRLINES (OZ ALPHA LSG)		25761	616	08/23/96	CF6-80C2B7F		N6005C
B767-38E	HL7514	ASIANA AIRLINES (OZ EVEREST LSG)		25763	656	04/22/97	CF6-80C2B2F		
B767-38E	HL7515	ASIANA AIRLINES (OZ DELTA LSG)		25762	658	05/23/97	CF6-80C2B2F		N6055X
B767-38E	HL7516	ASIANA AIRLINES (OZ EVEREST LSG)		25759	668	07/17/97	CF6-80C2B2F		
B767-38E	HL7528	ASIANA AIRLINES		29129	693	09/30/99	CF6-80C2B2F		N6005C
B767-38E (ER)	HL7595	ASIANA AIRLINES (GECA)		30840	829	03/23/01	CF6-80C2B2F		
B767-328 (ER)	HL	ASIANA AIRLINES (SUNR)		27212	531	03/07/94	CF6-80C2B6F		F-GHGK, OO-STF [PARKED AUH AS OO-STF]
HZ-SAUDI ARABIA									
B767-3P6 (ER)	HZ-WBT3	KINGDOM HOLDING		27255	525	12/10/93	CF6-80C2B4		A40-GX, N255KD
B767-29N (ER)	N767KS	MID EAST JET (FSBU)		28270	629	10/04/96	CF6-80C2B4		N6038E
I-ITALY									
B767-330 (ER)	I-PEIY	AIR EUROPE		25208	381	07/30/91	PW4060		D-ABUY, EI-CIY, I-AEIY
B767-352 (ER)	I-PIMQ	AIR EUROPE (PEGA)		27993	619	06/28/96	PW4060		EI-CMQ, I-AIMQ
B767-3Q8 (ER)	EI-CNS	AIR EUROPE (ILFC)		27600	655	04/16/97	PW4060		N6005C
B767-33A (ER)	I-DEIB	ALITALIA (AWAS)		27376	560	01/21/95	CF6-80C2B6F		VH-ITA, G-OITA
B767-33A (ER)	I-DEIC	ALITALIA (AWAS)		27377	561	01/27/95	CF6-80C2B6F		VH-ITB, G-OITB
B767-33A (ER)	I-DEID	ALITALIA (AWAS)		27468	584	06/28/95	CF6-80C2B6F		G-OITC
B767-33A (ER)	I-DEIF	ALITALIA (SALE)		27908	578	08/04/95	CF6-80C2B6F		G-OITF
B767-33A (ER)	I-DEIG	ALITALIA (SALE)		27918	603	02/26/96	CF6-80C2B6F		G-OITG
B767-33A (ER)	I-DEIL	ALITALIA		28147	611	04/30/96	CF6-80C2B6F		G-OITL
B767-343 (ER)	EI-CRL	ALITALIA (GECA)		30008	743	03/22/99	CF6-80C2B6F		

A/C TYPE	CURRENT REG. NO.	LAST KNOWN OPERATOR (OWNER)	Status	ORIGINAL MSN	LINE NO.	DEL. DATE	ENG. TYPE	FLEET NO.	PREV. REG. [COMMENTS]
B767-343 (ER)	EI-CRM	ALITALIA (GECA)		30009	746	04/08/99	CF6-80C2B6F		
B767-3Q8 (ER)	EI-CRO	ALITALIA (ILFC)		29383	747	04/16/99	CF6-80C2B6F		
B767-31B (ER)	EI-CRD	EUROFLY (ILFC)		26259	534	03/18/94	CF6-80C2B6F		B-2565 [OP IN AZA C/S]
B767-31B (ER)	EI-CRF	EUROFLY (ILFC)		25170	542	05/27/94	CF6-80C2B6F		B-2566
B767-341 (ER)	EI-CTW	EUROFLY (GECA)		30342	774	12/08/99	CF6-80C2B6F		
B767-31A (ER)	OE-LAT	LAUDA AIR SPA (LDA)	L	25273	393	10/18/91	PW4060		N6046P, I-LAUD, PH-MCK
B767-3Z9 (ER)	OE-LAU	LAUDA AIR SPA (LDA)	L	23765	165	04/29/88	PW4056		N767PW, N6009F [LST RNA]
B767-3Z9 (ER)	OE-LAW	LAUDA AIR SPA (LDA)	L	26417	448	08/21/92	PW4060		
B767-3Z9 (ER)	OE-LAX	LAUDA AIR SPA (LDA)	L	27095	467	12/04/92	PW4060		

JA-JAPAN

A/C TYPE	CURRENT REG. NO.	LAST KNOWN OPERATOR (OWNER)	Status	ORIGINAL MSN	LINE NO.	DEL. DATE	ENG. TYPE	FLEET NO.	PREV. REG. [COMMENTS]
B767-381 (ER)	JA8286	AIR JAPAN (ANA)	L	24400	269	06/26/89	CF6-80C2B6		
B767-281	JA8239	ALL NIPPON AIRWAYS (KC FIVE)		23141	108	03/05/85	CF6-80A		N5573K
B767-281	JA8240	ALL NIPPON AIRWAYS (MARUBENI)		23142	110	04/04/85	CF6-80A		N6038E
B767-281	JA8241	ALL NIPPON AIRWAYS (KC FIVE)		23143	114	05/10/85	CF6-80A		N6018N
B767-281	JA8242	ALL NIPPON AIRWAYS (KC FIVE)		23144	115	06/10/85	CF6-80A		N6038E
B767-281	JA8243	ALL NIPPON AIRWAYS (MARUBENI)		23145	116	09/03/85	CF6-80A		N6005C
B767-281	JA8244	ALL NIPPON AIRWAYS (KC SIX)		23146	121	10/10/85	CF6-80A		N6055X
B767-281	JA8245	ALL NIPPON AIRWAYS (MARUBENI)		23147	123	11/19/85	CF6-80A		N6005C
B767-281	JA8251	ALL NIPPON AIRWAYS (KC SIX)		23431	143	06/18/86	CF6-80A		N6009F
B767-281	JA8252	ALL NIPPON AIRWAYS (MARUBENI)		23432	145	07/08/86	CF6-80A		N6005C
B767-281	JA8254	ALL NIPPON AIRWAYS		23433	167	04/01/87	CF6-80A		N6038E
B767-281	JA8255	ALL NIPPON AIRWAYS		23434	171	04/27/87	CF6-80A		N6046P
B767-381	JA601A	ALL NIPPON AIRWAYS (F.I. STRAWBERRY, ET AL)		27943	669	08/07/97	CF6-80C2B6		
B767-381	JA602A	ALL NIPPON AIRWAYS		27944	684	01/20/98	CF6-80C2B6		
B767-381	JA8256	ALL NIPPON AIRWAYS		23756	176	06/30/87	CF6-80C2B6		N6005C
B767-381	JA8257	ALL NIPPON AIRWAYS		23757	177	07/01/87	CF6-80C2B2		N6038E
B767-381	JA8258	ALL NIPPON AIRWAYS		23758	179	07/09/87	CF6-80C2B2		N6055X
B767-381	JA8259	ALL NIPPON AIRWAYS		23759	185	09/23/87	CF6-80C2B2		N6038E
B767-381	JA8271	ALL NIPPON AIRWAYS		24002	199	02/08/88	CF6-80C2B2		N60668
B767-381	JA8272	ALL NIPPON AIRWAYS		24003	212	04/18/88	CF6-80C2B2		N6038E
B767-381	JA8273	ALL NIPPON AIRWAYS		24004	218	05/12/88	CF6-80C2B2		N6055X
B767-381	JA8274	ALL NIPPON AIRWAYS		24005	222	06/06/88	CF6-80C2B2		N6046P
B767-381	JA8275	ALL NIPPON AIRWAYS		24006	223	06/09/88	CF6-80C2B2		N6018N
B767-381	JA8285	ALL NIPPON AIRWAYS		24350	245	04/06/89	CF6-80C2B2		N1789B
B767-381 (ER)	JA8286	ALL NIPPON AIRWAYS		24400	269	06/26/89	CF6-80C2B6		[LST AIR JAPAN]
B767-381	JA8287	ALL NIPPON AIRWAYS		24351	271	07/06/89	CF6-80C2B2		

A/C TYPE	CURRENT REG. NO.	LAST KNOWN OPERATOR (OWNER)	Status	ORIGINAL MSN	LINE NO.	DEL. DATE	ENG. TYPE	FLEET NO.	PREV. REG. [COMMENTS]
B767-381	JA8288	ALL NIPPON AIRWAYS		24415	276	08/14/89	CF6-80C2B2		
B767-381	JA8289	ALL NIPPON AIRWAYS		24416	280	09/18/89	CF6-80C2B2		
B767-381	JA8290	ALL NIPPON AIRWAYS		24417	290	01/23/90	CF6-80C2B2		
B767-381	JA8291	ALL NIPPON AIRWAYS		24755	295	02/28/90	CF6-80C2B2		
B767-381	JA8322	ALL NIPPON AIRWAYS (GLOBAL, ET AL)		25618	458	10/14/92	CF6-80C2B2		
B767-381 (ER)	JA8323	ALL NIPPON AIRWAYS (FUYO SOGO)		25654	463	11/19/92	CF6-80C2B6		[OP JTLY WITH ANA, ANK, AIR JAPAN]
B767-381	JA8324	ALL NIPPON AIRWAYS (MITSUI)		25655	465	11/23/92	CF6-80C2B2		
B767-381	JA8342	ALL NIPPON AIRWAYS (KOGIN)		27445	573	04/27/95	CF6-80C2B2		
B767-381 (ER)	JA8356	ALL NIPPON AIRWAYS		25136	379	07/16/91	CF6-80C2B2		[OP JTLY WITH ANA, ANK, AIR JAPAN]
B767-381	JA8357	ALL NIPPON AIRWAYS		25293	401	11/14/91	CF6-80C2B2		
B767-381 (ER)	JA8358	ALL NIPPON AIRWAYS		25616	432	05/14/92	CF6-80C2B2		[OP JTLY WITH AIR JAPAN]
B767-381	JA8359	ALL NIPPON AIRWAYS		25617	439	06/12/92	CF6-80C2B2		
B767-381	JA8360	ALL NIPPON AIRWAYS		25055	352	02/18/91	CF6-80C2B2		
B767-381 (ER)	JA8362	ALL NIPPON AIRWAYS		24632	285	10/26/89	CF6-80C2B6		[OP JTLY WITH ANA, ANK, AIR JAPAN]
B767-381	JA8363	ALL NIPPON AIRWAYS		24756	300	04/12/90	CF6-80C2B2		
B767-381	JA8368	ALL NIPPON AIRWAYS		24880	336	10/31/90	CF6-80C2B2		
B767-381	JA8567	ALL NIPPON AIRWAYS (MACH LSG, ET AL)		25656	510	08/16/93	CF6-80C2B2		
B767-381	JA8568	ALL NIPPON AIRWAYS (DIAMOND)		25657	515	09/15/93	CF6-80C2B2		
B767-381	JA8569	ALL NIPPON AIRWAYS (FUYO SOGO)		27050	516	12/01/93	CF6-80C2B2		
B767-381	JA8578	ALL NIPPON AIRWAYS (SUMISHO)		25658	519	11/01/93	CF6-80C2B2		
B767-381	JA8579	ALL NIPPON AIRWAYS (KOGIN)		25659	520	12/01/93	CF6-80C2B2		
B767-381 (ER)	JA8664	ALL NIPPON AIRWAYS (ORIX)		27339	556	10/19/94	CF6-80C2B6		[OP JTLY WITH ANA, ANK, AIR JAPAN]
B767-381	JA8669	ALL NIPPON AIRWAYS (SAKURA)		27444	567	03/01/95	CF6-80C2B2		
B767-381	JA8670	ALL NIPPON AIRWAYS		25660	539	05/09/94	CF6-80C2B2		
B767-381	JA8674	ALL NIPPON AIRWAYS (FUYO SOGO)		25661	543	06/15/94	CF6-80C2B2		
B767-381	JA8677	ALL NIPPON AIRWAYS (KOGIN)		25662	551	08/24/94	CF6-80C2B2		
B767-381 (ER)	JA8970	ALL NIPPON AIRWAYS (FI ORCHARD, ET AL)		25619	645	02/18/97	CF6-80C2B6		[OP JTLY WITH ANA, ANK, AIR JAPAN]
B767-381 (ER)	JA8971	ALL NIPPON AIRWAYS (FI ORCHARD)		27942	651	03/18/97	CF6-80C2B6		
B767-33A (ER)	JA01HD	HOKKAIDO INTL. AIRLINES (AWAS)		28159	689	02/20/98	CF6-80C2B6F		OO-CTQ
B767-33A (ER)	JA98AD	HOKKAIDO INTL. AIRLINES (NICK OX)		27476	687	02/13/98	CF6-80C2B7F		N767AN
B767-246	JA8231	JAPAN AIRLINES (NIKKO)		23212	117	07/22/85	JT9D-7R4D		N6046P
B767-246	JA8232	JAPAN AIRLINES		23213	118	08/15/85	JT9D-7R4D		N6038E
B767-246	JA8233	JAPAN AIRLINES		23214	122	11/12/85	JT9D-7R4D		N6038E
B767-346	JA8234	JAPAN AIRLINES (ZONET)		23216	148	09/25/86	JT9D-7R4D		N6005C
B767-346	JA8235	JAPAN AIRLINES (KOWA FUDOSAN)		23217	150	10/02/86	JT9D-7R4D		N60659
B767-346	JA8236	JAPAN AIRLINES (WORLD CORP)		23215	132	12/16/86	JT9D-7R4D		N767S
B767-346	JA8253	JAPAN AIRLINES (ZONET)		23645	174	06/11/87	JT9D-7R4D		N6038E
B767-346	JA8264	JAPAN AIRLINES		23965	186	09/21/87	JT9D-7R4D		N6018N
B767-346	JA8265	JAPAN AIRLINES (ZONET)		23961	192	11/12/87	JT9D-7R4D		N6005C

A/C TYPE	CURRENT REG. NO.	LAST KNOWN OPERATOR (OWNER)	Status	ORIGINAL MSN	LINE NO.	DEL. DATE	ENG. TYPE	FLEET NO.	PREV. REG. [COMMENTS]
B767-346	JA8267	JAPAN AIRLINES (ZONET)		23962	193	12/16/87	JT9D-7R4D		N6038E
B767-346	JA8268	JAPAN AIRLINES (ZONET)		23963	224	06/21/88	JT9D-7R4D		N6055X
B767-346	JA8269	JAPAN AIRLINES (ZONET)		23964	225	06/23/88	JT9D-7R4D		N6046P
B767-346	JA8299	JAPAN AIRLINES (KOGIN LEASE)		24498	277	08/24/89	JT9D-7R4D		N6055X
B767-346	JA8364	JAPAN AIRLINES (NIKKO LEASE)		24782	327	09/20/90	JT9D-7R4D		
B767-346	JA8365	JAPAN AIRLINES (NIKKO LEASE)		24783	329	09/25/90	JT9D-7R4D		
B767-346	JA8397	JAPAN AIRLINES		27311	547	08/01/94	CF6-80C2B2		
B767-346	JA8398	JAPAN AIRLINES (SAKURA, ET AL)		27312	548	08/02/94	CF6-80C2B2		
B767-346	JA8399	JAPAN AIRLINES (KOGIN LEASE, ET AL)		27313	554	10/03/94	CF6-80C2B2		
B767-346	JA8975	JAPAN AIRLINES		27658	581	06/11/95	CF6-80C2B2		
B767-346	JA8980	JAPAN AIRLINES		28837	673	09/15/97	CF6-80C2B2		
B767-346	JA8986	JAPAN AIRLINES		28838	680	12/09/97	CF6-80C2B2		
B767-346	JA8987	JAPAN AIRLINES		28553	688	02/16/98	CF6-80C2B2		[LST JAA 02/17/98]
B767-346	JA8988	JAPAN AIRLINES (TWIN CRANE)		29863	772	11/28/99	CF6-80C2B2		
B767-346	JA8266	JAPAN ASIA AIRLINES		23966	191	12/08/87	JT9D-7R4D		N6018N
B767-346	JA8976	JAPAN ASIA AIRLINES		27659	667	07/21/97	CF6-80C2B2		
B767-346	JA8987	JAPAN ASIA AIRLINES (JAL)	L	28553	688	02/16/98	CF6-80C2B2		
B767-3Q8 (ER)	JA767A	SKYMARK AIRLINES (ILFC)		27616	714	08/18/98	CF6-80C2B6F		
B767-3Q8 (ER)	JA767B	SKYMARK AIRLINES (ILFC)		27617	722	10/27/98	CF6-80C2B6F		

N-UNITED STATES OF AMERICA

A/C TYPE	CURRENT REG. NO.	LAST KNOWN OPERATOR (OWNER)	Status	ORIGINAL MSN	LINE NO.	DEL. DATE	ENG. TYPE	FLEET NO.	PREV. REG. [COMMENTS]
B767-200	N767BA	THE BOEING COMPANY		22233	1	09/26/81	JT9D-7R4D		[PROTOTYPE AIRBORNE SURVEILLANCE TESTE
B767-205 (ER)	N651TW	AIRBORNE EXPRESS		23058	101	09/28/84	JT9D-7R4D		N6018N, LN-SUW, N768BE, PP-VNM, ZK-NBD, DQ-FJA [IN MOD GSO; I/S 06/01]
B767-231 (ER) (PC)	N702AX	AIRBORNE EXPRESS		22566	29	01/13/83	JT9D-7R4D		N603TW [CVTD -231]
B767-231 (ER) (PC)	N707AX	AIRBORNE EXPRESS		22570	63	07/26/83	JT9D-7R4D		N607TW [CVTD -231]
B767-231 (ER) (PC)	N708AX	AIRBORNE EXPRESS		22571	64	09/28/83	JT9D-7R4D		N608TW [CVTD -231]
B767-231 (ER) (PC)	N709AX	AIRBORNE EXPRESS		22572	65	09/07/83	JT9D-7R4D		N609TW [CVTD -231]
B767-281 (PC)	N767AX	AIRBORNE EXPRESS		22785	51	04/25/83	CF6-80A		N1784B, JA8479 [CVTD -281]
B767-281 (PC)	N768AX	AIRBORNE EXPRESS		22786	54	05/17/83	CF6-80A		N6018N, JA8480 [CVTD -281]
B767-281 (PC)	N769AX	AIRBORNE EXPRESS		22787	58	06/14/83	CF6-80A		N60668, JA8481 [CVTD -281]
B767-281 (PC)	N773AX	AIRBORNE EXPRESS		22788	61	07/07/83	CF6-80A		N1784B, JA8482 [CVTD -281]
B767-281 (PC)	N774AX	AIRBORNE EXPRESS		22789	67	09/12/83	CF6-80A		N1792B, JA8483 [CVTD -281]
B767-281 (PC)	N775AX	AIRBORNE EXPRESS		22790	69	10/11/83	CF6-80A		N5573B, JA8484 [CVTD -281]
B767-281 (PC)	N783AX	AIRBORNE EXPRESS		23016	80	01/31/84	CF6-80A		N1788B, JA8485 [CVTD -281]
B767-281 (PC)	N784AX	AIRBORNE EXPRESS		23017	82	03/01/84	CF6-80A		N1789B, N56807, JA8486 [CVTD -281]
B767-281 (PC)	N785AX	AIRBORNE EXPRESS		23018	84	04/09/84	CF6-80A		N1781B, JA8487 [CVTD -281]
B767-281 (PC)	N786AX	AIRBORNE EXPRESS		23019	85	05/01/84	CF6-80A		N1791B, JA8488 [CVTD -281]

A/C TYPE	CURRENT REG. NO.	LAST KNOWN OPERATOR (OWNER)	Status	ORIGINAL MSN	LINE NO.	DEL. DATE	ENG. TYPE	FLEET NO.	PREV. REG. [COMMENTS]
B767-281 (PC)	N787AX	AIRBORNE EXPRESS		23020	96	07/03/84	CF6-80A		N1784B, JA8489 [CVTD -281]
B767-281 (PC)	N788AX	AIRBORNE EXPRESS		23021	103	10/22/84	CF6-80A		N1785B, JA8490 [CVTD -281]
B767-281 (PC)	N789AX	AIRBORNE EXPRESS		23022	104	11/15/84	CF6-80A		N1792B, JA8491 [CVTD -281]
B767-281 (PC)	N790AX	AIRBORNE EXPRESS		23140	106	02/07/85	CF6-80A		[MOD COMPLETED GSO 02/01; I/S]
B767-223	N301AA	AMERICAN AIRLINES		22307	8	11/04/82	CF6-80A	301	
B767-223	N302AA	AMERICAN AIRLINES		22308	19	11/18/82	CF6-80A	302	
B767-223	N303AA	AMERICAN AIRLINES		22309	23	12/09/82	CF6-80A	303	
B767-223	N304AA	AMERICAN AIRLINES		22310	25	03/30/83	CF6-80A	304	
B767-223	N305AA	AMERICAN AIRLINES		22311	34	05/27/83	CF6-80A	305	
B767-223	N306AA	AMERICAN AIRLINES		22312	44	04/14/83	CF6-80A	306	
B767-223	N307AA	AMERICAN AIRLINES		22313	72	11/07/83	CF6-80A	307	
B767-223	N308AA	AMERICAN AIRLINES		22314	73	11/10/83	CF6-80A	308	
B767-223 (ER)	N312AA	AMERICAN AIRLINES		22315	94	06/11/84	CF6-80A2	312	[CVTD -223]
B767-223 (ER)	N313AA	AMERICAN AIRLINES		22316	95	06/21/84	CF6-80A2	313	[CVTD -223]
B767-223 (ER)	N315AA	AMERICAN AIRLINES		22317	109	02/15/85	CF6-80A2	315	[CVTD -223]
B767-223 (ER)	N316AA	AMERICAN AIRLINES		22318	111	04/01/85	CF6-80A2	316	[CVTD -223]
B767-223 (ER)	N317AA	AMERICAN AIRLINES		22319	112	04/29/85	CF6-80A2	317	[CVTD -223]
B767-223 (ER)	N319AA	AMERICAN AIRLINES (SSBT)		22320	128	11/18/85	CF6-80A2	319	
B767-223 (ER)	N320AA	AMERICAN AIRLINES (SSBT)		22321	130	12/05/85	CF6-80A2	320	
B767-223 (ER)	N321AA	AMERICAN AIRLINES		22322	139	04/22/86	CF6-80A2	321	
B767-223 (ER)	N322AA	AMERICAN AIRLINES		22323	140	05/06/86	CF6-80A2	322	
B767-223 (ER)	N323AA	AMERICAN AIRLINES		22324	146	07/25/86	CF6-80A2	323	
B767-223 (ER)	N324AA	AMERICAN AIRLINES		22325	147	08/14/86	CF6-80A2	324	
B767-223 (ER)	N325AA	AMERICAN AIRLINES		22326	157	11/24/86	CF6-80A2	325	
B767-223 (ER)	N327AA	AMERICAN AIRLINES (FIRST UNION)		22327	159	12/12/86	CF6-80A2	327	
B767-223 (ER)	N328AA	AMERICAN AIRLINES (SSBT)		22328	160	12/23/86	CF6-80A2	328	
B767-223 (ER)	N329AA	AMERICAN AIRLINES (SSBT)		22329	164	02/24/87	CF6-80A2	329	
B767-223 (ER)	N330AA	AMERICAN AIRLINES		22330	166	03/13/87	CF6-80A2	330	
B767-223 (ER)	N332AA	AMERICAN AIRLINES		22331	168	03/27/87	CF6-80A2	332	
B767-223 (ER)	N334AA	AMERICAN AIRLINES (FIRST UNION)		22332	169	04/13/87	CF6-80A2	334	[ST BTM CAPITAL]
B767-223 (ER)	N335AA	AMERICAN AIRLINES		22333	194	11/25/87	CF6-80A2	335	
B767-223 (ER)	N336AA	AMERICAN AIRLINES		22334	195	12/08/87	CF6-80A2	336	
B767-223 (ER)	N338AA	AMERICAN AIRLINES		22335	196	12/16/87	CF6-80A2	338	
B767-223 (ER)	N339AA	AMERICAN AIRLINES		22336	198	01/11/88	CF6-80A2	339	
B767-323 (ER)	N351AA	AMERICAN AIRLINES		24032	202	02/19/88	CF6-80C2B6	351	
B767-323 (ER)	N352AA	AMERICAN AIRLINES		24033	205	03/10/88	CF6-80C2B6	352	
B767-323 (ER)	N353AA	AMERICAN AIRLINES		24034	206	03/17/88	CF6-80C2B6	353	
B767-323 (ER)	N354AA	AMERICAN AIRLINES		24035	211	04/15/88	CF6-80C2B6	354	
B767-323 (ER)	N355AA	AMERICAN AIRLINES		24036	221	05/25/88	CF6-80C2B6	355	
B767-323 (ER)	N39356	AMERICAN AIRLINES		24037	226	06/23/88	CF6-80C2B6	356	

A/C TYPE	CURRENT REG. NO.	LAST KNOWN OPERATOR (OWNER)	Status	ORIGINAL MSN	LINE NO.	DEL. DATE	ENG. TYPE	FLEET NO.	PREV. REG. [COMMENTS]
B767-323 (ER)	N357AA	AMERICAN AIRLINES		24038	227	06/29/88	CF6-80C2B6	357	
B767-323 (ER)	N358AA	AMERICAN AIRLINES		24039	228	07/06/88	CF6-80C2B6	358	
B767-323 (ER)	N359AA	AMERICAN AIRLINES		24040	230	07/25/88	CF6-80C2B6	359	
B767-323 (ER)	N360AA	AMERICAN AIRLINES		24041	232	07/19/88	CF6-80C2B6	360	
B767-323 (ER)	N361AA	AMERICAN AIRLINES		24042	235	08/29/88	CF6-80C2B6	361	
B767-323 (ER)	N362AA	AMERICAN AIRLINES		24043	237	09/09/88	CF6-80C2B6	362	
B767-323 (ER)	N363AA	AMERICAN AIRLINES		24044	238	09/16/88	CF6-80C2B6	363	
B767-323 (ER)	N39364	AMERICAN AIRLINES		24045	240	09/30/88	CF6-80C2B6	364	
B767-323 (ER)	N39365	AMERICAN AIRLINES		24046	241	10/12/88	CF6-80C2B6	365	
B767-323 (ER)	N366AA	AMERICAN AIRLINES (FIRST UNION)		25193	388	09/17/91	CF6-80C2B6	366	
B767-323 (ER)	N39367	AMERICAN AIRLINES (FIRST UNION)		25194	394	10/16/91	CF6-80C2B6	367	
B767-323 (ER)	N368AA	AMERICAN AIRLINES		25195	404	12/05/91	CF6-80C2B6	368	
B767-323 (ER)	N369AA	AMERICAN AIRLINES (CMTC)		25196	422	03/25/92	CF6-80C2B6	369	
B767-323 (ER)	N370AA	AMERICAN AIRLINES		25197	425	04/08/92	CF6-80C2B6	370	
B767-323 (ER)	N371AA	AMERICAN AIRLINES (FIRST UNION)		25198	431	05/28/92	CF6-80C2B6	371	
B767-323 (ER)	N372AA	AMERICAN AIRLINES		25199	433	05/22/92	CF6-80C2B6	372	
B767-323 (ER)	N373AA	AMERICAN AIRLINES		25200	435	06/08/92	CF6-80C2B6	373	
B767-323 (ER)	N374AA	AMERICAN AIRLINES		25201	437	06/17/92	CF6-80C2B6	374	
B767-323 (ER)	N7375A	AMERICAN AIRLINES		25202	441	07/09/92	CF6-80C2B6	375	
B767-323 (ER)	N376AN	AMERICAN AIRLINES		25445	447	08/11/92	CF6-80C2B6	376	
B767-323 (ER)	N377AN	AMERICAN AIRLINES		25446	453	09/16/92	CF6-80C2B6	377	
B767-323 (ER)	N378AN	AMERICAN AIRLINES		25447	469	12/18/92	CF6-80C2B6	378	
B767-323 (ER)	N379AA	AMERICAN AIRLINES		25448	481	03/05/93	CF6-80C2B6	379	
B767-323 (ER)	N380AN	AMERICAN AIRLINES		25449	489	04/19/93	CF6-80C2B6	380	
B767-323 (ER)	N381AN	AMERICAN AIRLINES		25450	495	05/27/93	CF6-80C2B6	381	
B767-323 (ER)	N382AN	AMERICAN AIRLINES		25451	498	05/28/93	CF6-80C2B6	382	
B767-323 (ER)	N383AN	AMERICAN AIRLINES		26995	500	06/21/93	CF6-80C2B6	383	
B767-323 (ER)	N384AA	AMERICAN AIRLINES		26996	512	08/27/93	CF6-80C2B6	384	
B767-323 (ER)	N385AM	AMERICAN AIRLINES		27059	536	03/30/94	CF6-80C2B6	385	
B767-323 (ER)	N386AA	AMERICAN AIRLINES		27060	540	05/13/94	CF6-80C2B6	386	
B767-323 (ER)	N387AM	AMERICAN AIRLINES		27184	541	05/19/94	CF6-80C2B6	387	
B767-323 (ER)	N388AA	AMERICAN AIRLINES		27448	563	01/13/95	CF6-80C2B6	388	
B767-323 (ER)	N389AA	AMERICAN AIRLINES		27449	564	01/13/95	CF6-80C2B6	389	
B767-323 (ER)	N390AA	AMERICAN AIRLINES		27450	565	01/13/95	CF6-80C2B6	390	
B767-323 (ER)	N391AA	AMERICAN AIRLINES		27451	566	02/16/95	CF6-80C2B6	391	
B767-323 (ER)	N392AN	AMERICAN AIRLINES		29429	700	04/30/98	CF6-80C2B6	392	
B767-323 (ER)	N393AN	AMERICAN AIRLINES		29430	701	05/18/98	CF6-80C2B6	393	
B767-323 (ER)	N394AN	AMERICAN AIRLINES		29431	703	06/13/98	CF6-80C2B6	394	
B767-323 (ER)	N395AN	AMERICAN AIRLINES		29432	709	07/10/98	CF6-80C2B6	395	
B767-323 (ER)	N396AN	AMERICAN AIRLINES		29603	739	02/25/99	CF6-80C2B6	396	
B767-323 (ER)	N397AN	AMERICAN AIRLINES		29604	744	04/01/99	CF6-80C2B6	397	

A/C TYPE	CURRENT REG. NO.	LAST KNOWN OPERATOR (OWNER)	Status	ORIGINAL MSN	LINE NO.	DEL. DATE	ENG. TYPE	FLEET NO.	PREV. REG. [COMMENTS]
B767-323 (ER)	N398AN	AMERICAN AIRLINES		29605	748	04/30/99	CF6-80C2B6	398	
B767-323 (ER)	N399AN	AMERICAN AIRLINES		29606	752	05/28/99	CF6-80C2B6	399	
B767-224 (ER)	N76151	CONTINENTAL AIRLINES		30430	811	11/09/00	CF6-80C2B4F	151	
B767-224 (ER)	N73152	CONTINENTAL AIRLINES		30431	815	11/21/00	CF6-80C2B4F	152	
B767-224 (ER)	N76153	CONTINENTAL AIRLINES		30432	819	12/13/00	CF6-80C2B4F	153	
B767-224 (ER)	N69154	CONTINENTAL AIRLINES		30433	823	01/19/01	CF6-80C2B4F	154	
B767-224 (ER)	N68155	CONTINENTAL AIRLINES		30434	825	02/07/01	CF6-80C2B4F	155	
B767-224 (ER)	N76156	CONTINENTAL AIRLINES		30435	827	02/15/01	CF6-80C2B4F	156	
B767-224 (ER)	N67157	CONTINENTAL AIRLINES (FSBU)		30436	833	04/11/01	CF6-80C2B4F	157	
B767-224 (ER)	N67158	CONTINENTAL AIRLINES	N	30437	839		CF6-80C2B4F		
B767-424 (ER)	N66051	CONTINENTAL AIRLINES		29446	799	08/30/00	CF6-80C2B7F	051	
B767-424 (ER)	N67052	CONTINENTAL AIRLINES		29447	805	09/22/00	CF6-80C2B7F	052	
B767-424 (ER)	N59053	CONTINENTAL AIRLINES		29448	809	10/06/00	CF6-80C2B7F		
B767-424 (ER)	N76054	CONTINENTAL AIRLINES (FSBU)		29449	816	12/04/00	CF6-80C2B7F		
B767-424 (ER)	N76055	CONTINENTAL AIRLINES (FSBU)		29450	826	02/21/01	CF6-80C2B7F		
B767-232	N101DA	DELTA AIRLINES		22213	6	03/25/83	CF6-80A	101	
B767-232	N102DA	DELTA AIRLINES		22214	12	10/25/82	CF6-80A	102	
B767-232	N103DA	DELTA AIRLINES		22215	17	10/29/82	CF6-80A	103	
B767-232	N104DA	DELTA AIRLINES		22216	26	12/20/82	CF6-80A	104	
B767-232	N105DA	DELTA AIRLINES		22217	27	01/19/83	CF6-80A	105	
B767-232	N106DA	DELTA AIRLINES		22218	31	12/08/82	CF6-80A	106	
B767-232	N107DL	DELTA AIRLINES		22219	37	01/22/83	CF6-80A	107	
B767-232	N108DL	DELTA AIRLINES		22220	38	01/28/83	CF6-80A	108	
B767-232	N109DL	DELTA AIRLINES		22221	53	05/10/83	CF6-80A	109	
B767-232	N110DL	DELTA AIRLINES		22222	56	06/04/83	CF6-80A	110	
B767-232	N111DN	DELTA AIRLINES		22223	74	11/14/83	CF6-80A	111	
B767-232	N112DL	DELTA AIRLINES		22224	76	12/08/83	CF6-80A	112	
B767-232	N113DA	DELTA AIRLINES		22225	77	12/14/83	CF6-80A	113	
B767-232	N114DL	DELTA AIRLINES		22226	78	01/25/84	CF6-80A2	114	
B767-232	N115DA	DELTA AIRLINES		22227	83	02/28/84	CF6-80A2	115	
B767-332	N116DL	DELTA AIRLINES		23275	136	11/15/86	CF6-80A2	116	
B767-332	N117DL	DELTA AIRLINES		23276	151	12/11/86	CF6-80A2	117	
B767-332	N118DL	DELTA AIRLINES		23277	152	11/07/86	CF6-80A2	118	
B767-332	N119DL	DELTA AIRLINES		23278	153	12/03/86	CF6-80A2	119	
B767-332	N120DL	DELTA AIRLINES		23279	154	12/08/86	CF6-80A2	120	
B767-332	N121DE	DELTA AIRLINES		23435	162	03/08/87	CF6-80A2	121	
B767-332	N122DL	DELTA AIRLINES		23436	163	03/07/87	CF6-80A2	122	
B767-332	N123DN	DELTA AIRLINES		23437	188	11/05/87	CF6-80A2	123	
B767-332	N124DE	DELTA AIRLINES		23438	189	11/06/87	CF6-80A2	124	

A/C TYPE	CURRENT REG. NO.	LAST KNOWN OPERATOR (OWNER)	Status	ORIGINAL MSN	LINE NO.	DEL. DATE	ENG. TYPE	FLEET NO.	PREV. REG. [COMMENTS]
B767-332	N125DL	DELTA AIRLINES		24075	200	02/05/88	CF6-80A2	125	
B767-332	N126DL	DELTA AIRLINES		24076	201	03/04/88	CF6-80A2	126	
B767-332	N127DL	DELTA AIRLINES		24077	203	04/01/88	CF6-80A2	127	
B767-332	N128DL	DELTA AIRLINES		24078	207	04/06/88	CF6-80A2	128	
B767-332	N129DL	DELTA AIRLINES		24079	209	05/16/88	CF6-80A2	129	
B767-332	N130DL	DELTA AIRLINES		24080	216	05/23/88	CF6-80A2	130	
B767-332	N131DN	DELTA AIRLINES		24852	320	08/03/90	CF6-80A2	131	
B767-332	N132DN	DELTA AIRLINES		24981	345	01/10/91	CF6-80A2	132	
B767-332	N133DN	DELTA AIRLINES		24982	348	01/24/91	CF6-80A2	133	
B767-332	N134DL	DELTA AIRLINES		25123	353	02/22/91	CF6-80A2	134	
B767-332	N135DL	DELTA AIRLINES		25145	356	03/08/91	CF6-80A2	135	
B767-332	N136DL	DELTA AIRLINES		25146	374	06/15/91	CF6-80A2	136	
B767-332	N137DL	DELTA AIRLINES		25306	392	09/25/91	CF6-80A2	137	
B767-332	N138DL	DELTA AIRLINES		25409	410	01/17/92	CF6-80A2	138	
B767-332	N139DL	DELTA AIRLINES		25984	427	05/08/92	CF6-80A2	139	
B767-332	N140LL	DELTA AIRLINES		25988	499	06/17/93	PW4060	1401	
B767-332	N1402A	DELTA AIRLINES		25989	506	07/20/93	PW4060	1402	
B767-332	N143DA	DELTA AIRLINES		25991	721	10/15/98	PW4060	1403	
B767-332	N144DA	DELTA AIRLINES		27584	751	05/13/99	PW4060	1404	
B767-3P6 (ER)	N1501P	DELTA AIRLINES		24983	334	11/29/90	CF6-80C2B4	1501	N6046P, A40-GL
B767-3P6 (ER)	N152DL	DELTA AIRLINES		24984	339	11/29/90	CF6-80C2B4	1502	A40-GM
B767-3P6 (ER)	N153DL	DELTA AIRLINES		24985	340	11/29/90	CF6-80C2B4	1503	A40-GN
B767-3P6 (ER)	N154DL	DELTA AIRLINES		25241	389	09/25/91	CF6-80C2B4	1504	A40-GO
B767-3P6 (ER)	N155DL	DELTA AIRLINES		25269	390	09/25/91	CF6-80C2B4	1505	A40-GP
B767-3P6 (ER)	N156DL	DELTA AIRLINES		25354	406	12/13/91	CF6-80C2B4	1506	A40-GR
B767-332 (ER)	N1602	DELTA AIRLINES		29694	735	01/22/99	CF6-80C2B6F	1602	
B767-332 (ER)	N1603	DELTA AIRLINES		29695	736	02/05/99	CF6-80C2B6F	1603	
B767-332 (ER)	N1604R	DELTA AIRLINES		30180	749	04/28/99	CF6-80C2B6F	1604	
B767-332 (ER)	N1605	DELTA AIRLINES		30198	753	05/27/99	CF6-80C2B6F	1605	
B767-332 (ER)	N16065	DELTA AIRLINES		30199	755	06/10/99	CF6-80C2B6F	1606	
B767-332 (ER)	N1607B	DELTA AIRLINES		30388	787	04/21/00	CF6-80C2B6F	1607	
B767-332 (ER)	N1608	DELTA AIRLINES		30573	788	04/21/00	CF6-80C2B6F	1608	
B767-332 (ER)	N1609	DELTA AIRLINES		30574	789	04/25/00	CF6-80C2B6F	1609	
B767-332 (ER)	N1610D	DELTA AIRLINES		30594	790	04/26/00	CF6-80C2B6F	1610	
B767-332 (ER)	N1611B	DELTA AIRLINES		30595	794	05/15/00	CF6-80C2B6F	1611	
B767-332 (ER)	N1612T	DELTA AIRLINES	N	30575	838	05/26/01	CF6-80C2B6F	1612	
B767-332 (ER)	N169DZ	DELTA AIRLINES		29689	706	06/18/98	CF6-80C2B6F	169	
B767-332 (ER)	N171DN	DELTA AIRLINES		24759	304	06/09/90	PW4060	171	
B767-332 (ER)	N171DZ	DELTA AIRLINES		29690	717	09/11/98	CF6-80C2B6F	1701	
B767-332 (ER)	N172DN	DELTA AIRLINES		24775	312	06/22/90	PW4060	172	
B767-332 (ER)	N172DZ	DELTA AIRLINES		29691	719	09/25/98	CF6-80C2B6F	1702	

A/C TYPE	CURRENT REG. NO.	LAST KNOWN OPERATOR (OWNER)	Status	ORIGINAL MSN	LINE NO.	DEL. DATE	ENG. TYPE	FLEET NO.	PREV. REG. [COMMENTS]
B767-332 (ER)	N173DN	DELTA AIRLINES		24800	313	06/29/90	PW4060	173	
B767-332 (ER)	N173DZ	DELTA AIRLINES		29692	723	11/02/98	CF6-80C2B6F	1703	
B767-332 (ER)	N174DN	DELTA AIRLINES		24802	317	07/20/90	PW4060	174	
B767-332 (ER)	N174DZ	DELTA AIRLINES		29693	725	11/05/98	CF6-80C2B6F	1704	
B767-332 (ER)	N175DN	DELTA AIRLINES		24803	318	07/26/90	PW4060	175	
B767-332 (ER)	N175DZ	DELTA AIRLINES		29696	740	03/04/99	CF6-80C2B6F	1705	
B767-332 (ER)	N176DN	DELTA AIRLINES		25061	341	12/15/90	PW4060	176	
B767-332 (ER)	N176DZ	DELTA AIRLINES		29697	745	04/22/99	CF6-80C2B6F	1706	
B767-332 (ER)	N177DN	DELTA AIRLINES		25122	346	01/19/91	PW4060	177	
B767-332 (ER)	N177DZ	DELTA AIRLINES		29698	750	05/06/99	CF6-80C2B6F	1707	
B767-332 (ER)	N178DN	DELTA AIRLINES		25143	349	04/05/91	PW4060	178	
B767-332 (ER)	N178DZ	DELTA AIRLINES		30596	795	05/23/00	CF6-80C2B6F	1708	
B767-332 (ER)	N179DN	DELTA AIRLINES		25144	350	04/17/91	PW4060	179	
B767-332 (ER)	N180DN	DELTA AIRLINES		25985	428	04/25/92	PW4060	180	
B767-332 (ER)	N181DN	DELTA AIRLINES		25986	446	08/07/92	PW4060	181	
B767-332 (ER)	N182DN	DELTA AIRLINES		25987	461	11/05/92	PW4060	182	
B767-332 (ER)	N183DN	DELTA AIRLINES		27110	492	04/29/93	PW4060	183	
B767-332 (ER)	N184DN	DELTA AIRLINES		27111	496	05/25/93	PW4060	184	
B767-332 (ER)	N185DN	DELTA AIRLINES		27961	576	05/03/95	PW4060	185	
B767-332 (ER)	N186DN	DELTA AIRLINES		27962	585	07/07/95	PW4060	186	
B767-332 (ER)	N187DN	DELTA AIRLINES		27582	617	06/19/96	PW4060	187	
B767-332 (ER)	N188DN	DELTA AIRLINES		27583	631	10/17/96	PW4060	188	
B767-332 (ER)	N189DN	DELTA AIRLINES		25990	646	02/13/97	PW4060	189	
B767-332 (ER)	N190DN	DELTA AIRLINES		28447	653	03/25/97	PW4060	190	
B767-332 (ER)	N191DN	DELTA AIRLINES		28448	654	04/09/97	PW4060	191	
B767-332 (ER)	N192DN	DELTA AIRLINES		28449	664	06/26/97	PW4060	192	
B767-332 (ER)	N193DN	DELTA AIRLINES		28450	671	08/21/97	PW4060	193	
B767-332 (ER)	N194DN	DELTA AIRLINES		28451	675	09/26/97	PW4060	194	
B767-332 (ER)	N195DN	DELTA AIRLINES		28452	676	09/30/97	PW4060	195	
B767-332 (ER)	N196DN	DELTA AIRLINES		28453	679	10/30/97	PW4060	196	
B767-332 (ER)	N197DN	DELTA AIRLINES		28454	683	12/23/97	PW4060	197	
B767-332 (ER)	N198DN	DELTA AIRLINES		28455	685	02/02/98	PW4060	198	
B767-332 (ER)	N199DN	DELTA AIRLINES		28456	690	03/02/98	PW4060	199	
B767-332 (ER)	N1200K	DELTA AIRLINES		28457	696	04/10/98	PW4060	1200	
B767-332 (ER)	N1201P	DELTA AIRLINES		28458	697	04/17/98	PW4060	1201	
B767-324 (ER)	N394DL	DELTA AIRLINES (GECA)		27394	572	11/10/95	CF6-80C2B7F	1521	N5573S, N68903, HL7505
B767-432 (ER)	N825MH	DELTA AIRLINES		29703	758	12/14/00	CF6-80C2B7F	1801	N76400, N6067U [PROTOTYPE 767-400; FF 10/09/99]
B767-432 (ER)	N826MH	DELTA AIRLINES		29713	769	11/30/00	CF6-80C2B7F	1802	
B767-432 (ER)	N827MH	DELTA AIRLINES		29705	773	02/24/01	CF6-80C2B7F	1803	N76400
B767-432 (ER)	N828MH	DELTA AIRLINES		29699	791	08/11/00	CF6-80C2B7F	1804	
B767-432 (ER)	N829MH	DELTA AIRLINES		29700	801	08/22/00	CF6-80C2B7F	1805	

A/C TYPE	CURRENT REG. NO.	LAST KNOWN OPERATOR (OWNER)	Status	ORIGINAL MSN	LINE NO.	DEL. DATE	ENG. TYPE	FLEET NO.	PREV. REG. [COMMENTS]
B767-432 (ER)	N830MH	DELTA AIRLINES		29701	803	09/13/00	CF6-80C2B7F	1806	
B767-432 (ER)	N831MH	DELTA AIRLINES		29702	804	09/20/00	CF6-80C2B7F	1807	
B767-432 (ER)	N832MH	DELTA AIRLINES		29704	807	09/26/00	CF6-80C2B7F	1808	
B767-432 (ER)	N833MH	DELTA AIRLINES		29706	810	10/13/00	CF6-80C2B7F	1809	
B767-432 (ER)	N834MH	DELTA AIRLINES		29707	813	11/06/00	CF6-80C2B7F	1810	
B767-432 (ER)	N835MH	DELTA AIRLINES		29708	814	11/04/00	CF6-80C2B7F	1811	
B767-432 (ER)	N836MH	DELTA AIRLINES		29709	818	12/13/00	CF6-80C2B7F	1812	
B767-432 (ER)	N837MH	DELTA AIRLINES		29710	820	12/20/00	CF6-80C2B7F	1813	
B767-432 (ER)	N838MH	DELTA AIRLINES		29711	821	01/10/01	CF6-80C2B7F		
B767-432 (ER)	N839MH	DELTA AIRLINES		29712	824	01/26/01	CF6-80C2B7F		
B767-432 (ER)	N840MH	DELTA AIRLINES	N	29718	830		CF6-80C2B7F		
B767-3P6 (ER)	VP-BKS	KALAIR USA CORPORATION		27254	522	11/04/93	CF6-80C2B4		A40-GW
B767-231 (ER)	N601TW	TRANS WORLD AIRLINES		22564	14	11/22/82	JT9D-7R4D	16001	[STD VCV 04/10/01]
B767-231 (ER)	N602TW	TRANS WORLD AIRLINES		22565	21	12/08/82	JT9D-7R4D	16002	[STD VCV 04/10/01]
B767-231 (ER)	N604TW	TRANS WORLD AIRLINES		22567	30	02/23/83	JT9D-7R4D	16004	[LRF 03/30/01; WFU MZJ]
B767-231 (ER)	N605TW	TRANS WORLD AIRLINES		22568	33	12/17/82	JT9D-7R4D	16005	[LRF 04/07/01; PARKED JFK]
B767-231 (ER)	N610TW	TRANS WORLD AIRLINES		22573	70	11/23/83	JT9D-7R4D	16010	[LRF 03/22/01; WFU JFK]
B767-3Y0 (ER)	N632TW	TRANS WORLD AIRLINES (GECA)		24953	405	12/12/91	PW4060	16102	XA-RWX, EI-CAM
B767-330 (ER)	N691LF	TRANS WORLD AIRLINES (ILFC)		25137	377	07/13/91	PW4060	16103	D-ABUX
B767-3Q8 (ER)	N634TW	TRANS WORLD AIRLINES (ILFC)		28132	692	03/10/98	PW4060	16104	
B767-3Q8 (ER)	N635TW	TRANS WORLD AIRLINES (ILFC)		28207	695	04/08/98	PW4060	16105	
B767-3Q8 (ER)	N636TW	TRANS WORLD AIRLINES (ILFC)		30301	762	08/24/99	PW4060	16106	
B767-33A (ER)	N637TW	TRANS WORLD AIRLINES (POLA)		25403	409	01/22/92	PW4060	16107	CC-CEU, 5R-MFC
B767-3Y0 (ER)	N638TW	TRANS WORLD AIRLINES (GECA)		26205	474	09/13/94	PW4060	16108	N6046P, EI-CKD
B767-3Y0 (ER)	N639TW	TRANS WORLD AIRLINES (GECA)		26208	505	09/15/94	PW4060	16109	N6009F, EI-CKE
B767-3Y0 (ER)	N640TW	TRANS WORLD AIRLINES (GECA)		25411	408	01/16/92	PW4060	16110	PT-TAF, XA-SKY, SE-DKY, XA-EDE, XA-TJD, EI-CL■
B767-222	N601UA	UNITED AIRLINES		21862	2	04/29/83	JT9D-7R4D	6201	
B767-222 (ET)	N602UA	UNITED AIRLINES		21863	3	01/24/83	JT9D-7R4D	6002	[CVTD -222]
B767-222	N603UA	UNITED AIRLINES		21864	4	04/13/83	JT9D-7R4D	6203	
B767-222	N604UA	UNITED AIRLINES		21865	5	01/12/83	JT9D-7R4D	6204	
B767-222 (ET)	N605UA	UNITED AIRLINES		21866	7	11/03/82	JT9D-7R4D	6005	[CVTD -222]
B767-222 (ET)	N606UA	UNITED AIRLINES		21867	9	08/19/82	JT9D-7R4D	6006	[CVTD -222]
B767-222 (ET)	N607UA	UNITED AIRLINES		21868	10	09/01/82	JT9D-7R4D	6007	[CVTD -222]
B767-222 (ET)	N608UA	UNITED AIRLINES		21869	11	09/16/82	JT9D-7R4D	6008	[CVTD -222]
B767-222 (ET)	N609UA	UNITED AIRLINES		21870	13	09/29/82	JT9D-7R4D	6009	[CVTD -222]
B767-222 (ET)	N610UA	UNITED AIRLINES		21871	15	09/27/82	JT9D-7R4D	6010	[CVTD -222]
B767-222 (ET)	N611UA	UNITED AIRLINES		21872	20	11/29/82	JT9D-7R4D	6011	[CVTD -222]
B767-222	N612UA	UNITED AIRLINES		21873	41	02/23/83	JT9D-7R4D	6212	

A/C TYPE	CURRENT REG. NO.	LAST KNOWN OPERATOR (OWNER)	Status	ORIGINAL MSN	LINE NO.	DEL. DATE	ENG. TYPE	FLEET NO.	PREV. REG. [COMMENTS]
B767-222	N613UA	UNITED AIRLINES		21874	42	02/25/83	JT9D-7R4D	6213	
B767-222	N614UA	UNITED AIRLINES		21875	43	03/02/83	JT9D-7R4D	6214	
B767-222	N615UA	UNITED AIRLINES		21876	45	03/14/83	JT9D-7R4D	6215	
B767-222	N617UA	UNITED AIRLINES		21877	46	03/24/83	JT9D-7R4D	6217	
B767-222	N618UA	UNITED AIRLINES		21878	48	04/18/83	JT9D-7R4D	6218	
B767-222	N619UA	UNITED AIRLINES		21879	49	04/20/83	JT9D-7R4D	6219	
B767-222	N620UA	UNITED AIRLINES		21880	50	04/25/83	JT9D-7R4D	6220	
B767-322 (ER)	N641UA	UNITED AIRLINES		25091	360	04/18/91	PW4060	6641	
B767-322 (ER)	N642UA	UNITED AIRLINES		25092	367	05/08/91	PW4060	6642	
B767-322 (ER)	N643UA	UNITED AIRLINES		25093	368	05/24/91	PW4060	6643	
B767-322 (ER)	N644UA	UNITED AIRLINES		25094	369	05/15/91	PW4060	6644	
B767-322 (ER)	N645UA	UNITED AIRLINES		25280	391	09/24/91	PW4060	6645	
B767-322 (ER)	N646UA	UNITED AIRLINES		25283	420	03/18/92	PW4060	6646	
B767-322 (ER)	N647UA	UNITED AIRLINES		25284	424	04/06/92	PW4060	6647	
B767-322 (ER)	N648UA	UNITED AIRLINES		25285	443	07/20/92	PW4060	6648	
B767-322 (ER)	N649UA	UNITED AIRLINES		25286	444	07/27/92	PW4060	6649	
B767-322 (ER)	N650UA	UNITED AIRLINES		25287	449	09/01/92	PW4060	6650	
B767-322 (ER)	N651UA	UNITED AIRLINES		25389	452	09/14/92	PW4060	6651	
B767-322 (ER)	N652UA	UNITED AIRLINES		25390	457	09/30/92	PW4060	6652	
B767-322 (ER)	N653UA	UNITED AIRLINES		25391	460	10/27/92	PW4060	6653	[STAR ALLIANCE C/S]
B767-322 (ER)	N654UA	UNITED AIRLINES		25392	462	11/10/92	PW4060	6654	
B767-322 (ER)	N655UA	UNITED AIRLINES		25393	468	12/11/92	PW4060	6655	
B767-322 (ER)	N656UA	UNITED AIRLINES		25394	472	01/20/93	PW4060	6656	
B767-322 (ER)	N657UA	UNITED AIRLINES (GECA)		27112	479	03/01/93	PW4060	6657	
B767-322 (ER)	N658UA	UNITED AIRLINES (GECA)		27113	480	03/04/93	PW4060	6658	
B767-322 (ER)	N659UA	UNITED AIRLINES (GECA)		27114	485	04/01/93	PW4060	6659	
B767-322 (ER)	N660UA	UNITED AIRLINES (GECA)		27115	494	05/17/93	PW4060	6660	
B767-322 (ER)	N661UA	UNITED AIRLINES		27158	507	07/29/93	PW4060	6661	
B767-322 (ER)	N662UA	UNITED AIRLINES		27159	513	08/30/93	PW4060	6662	
B767-322 (ER)	N663UA	UNITED AIRLINES		27160	514	08/30/93	PW4060	6663	
B767-322 (ER)	N664UA	UNITED AIRLINES		29236	707	06/29/98	PW4052	6764	
B767-322 (ER)	N665UA	UNITED AIRLINES		29237	711	07/27/98	PW4052	6765	
B767-322 (ER)	N666UA	UNITED AIRLINES		29238	715	08/25/98	PW4052	6766	
B767-322 (ER)	N667UA	UNITED AIRLINES		29239	716	08/31/98	PW4052	6767	
B767-322 (ER)	N668UA	UNITED AIRLINES		30024	742	03/15/99	PW4052	6768	
B767-322 (ER)	N669UA	UNITED AIRLINES		30025	757	06/28/99	PW4052	6769	
B767-322 (ER)	N670UA	UNITED AIRLINES		29240	763	08/31/99	PW4052	6770	
B767-322 (ER)	N671UA	UNITED AIRLINES		30026	766	10/01/99	PW4052	6771	
B767-322 (ER)	N672UA	UNITED AIRLINES		30027	777	12/22/99	PW4052	6772	
B767-322 (ER)	N673UA	UNITED AIRLINES		29241	779	01/11/00	PW4052	6773	
B767-322 (ER)	N674UA	UNITED AIRLINES		29242	782	04/05/00	PW4052	6774	

A/C TYPE	CURRENT REG. NO.	LAST KNOWN OPERATOR (OWNER)	Status	ORIGINAL MSN	LINE NO.	DEL. DATE	ENG. TYPE	FLEET NO.	PREV. REG. [COMMENTS]
B767-322 (ER)	N675UA	UNITED AIRLINES		29243	800	08/01/00	PW4052	6475	
B767-322 (ER)	N676UA	UNITED AIRLINES		30028	834	04/23/01	PW4052	6476	
B767-34AF (ER)	N301UP	UNITED PARCEL SERVICE		27239	580	10/27/95	CF6-80C2B7F		
B767-34AF (ER)	N302UP	UNITED PARCEL SERVICE		27240	590	10/12/95	CF6-80C2B7F		
B767-34AF (ER)	N303UP	UNITED PARCEL SERVICE		27241	594	11/07/95	CF6-80C2B7F		
B767-34AF (ER)	N304UP	UNITED PARCEL SERVICE		27242	598	11/21/95	CF6-80C2B7F		
B767-34AF (ER)	N305UP	UNITED PARCEL SERVICE		27243	600	12/08/95	CF6-80C2B7F		
B767-34AF (ER)	N306UP	UNITED PARCEL SERVICE		27759	622	07/30/96	CF6-80C2B7F		
B767-34AF (ER)	N307UP	UNITED PARCEL SERVICE		27760	624	08/20/96	CF6-80C2B7F		
B767-34AF (ER)	N308UP	UNITED PARCEL SERVICE		27761	626	09/05/96	CF6-80C2B7F		
B767-34AF (ER)	N309UP	UNITED PARCEL SERVICE		27740	628	09/24/96	CF6-80C2B7F		
B767-34AF (ER)	N310UP	UNITED PARCEL SERVICE		27762	630	10/10/96	CF6-80C2B7F		
B767-34AF (ER)	N311UP	UNITED PARCEL SERVICE		27741	632	10/24/96	CF6-80C2B7F		
B767-34AF (ER)	N312UP	UNITED PARCEL SERVICE		27763	634	11/07/96	CF6-80C2B7F		
B767-34AF (ER)	N313UP	UNITED PARCEL SERVICE		27764	636	11/21/96	CF6-80C2B7F		
B767-34AF (ER)	N314UP	UNITED PARCEL SERVICE		27742	638	12/06/96	CF6-80C2B7F		
B767-34AF (ER)	N315UP	UNITED PARCEL SERVICE		27743	640	12/13/96	CF6-80C2B7F		
B767-34AF (ER)	N316UP	UNITED PARCEL SERVICE		27744	660	05/30/97	CF6-80C2B7F		
B767-34AF (ER)	N317UP	UNITED PARCEL SERVICE		27745	666	07/10/97	CF6-80C2B7F		
B767-34AF (ER)	N318UP	UNITED PARCEL SERVICE		27746	670	09/18/97	CF6-80C2B7F		
B767-34AF (ER)	N319UP	UNITED PARCEL SERVICE		27758	672	09/10/97	CF6-80C2B7F		
B767-34AF (ER)	N320UP	UNITED PARCEL SERVICE		27747	674	09/26/97	CF6-80C2B7F		[SPECIAL OLYMPIC SPONSOR C/S]
B767-34AF (ER)	N322UP	UNITED PARCEL SERVICE		27748	678	12/03/97	CF6-80C2B7F		
B767-34AF (ER)	N323UP	UNITED PARCEL SERVICE		27749	682	12/15/97	CF6-80C2B7F		
B767-34AF (ER)	N324UP	UNITED PARCEL SERVICE		27750	724	10/30/98	CF6-80C2B7F		
B767-34AF (ER)	N325UP	UNITED PARCEL SERVICE (WTCI)		27751	726	11/13/98	CF6-80C2B7F		
B767-34AF (ER)	N326UP	UNITED PARCEL SERVICE		27752	728	11/25/98	CF6-80C2B7F		
B767-34AF (ER)	N327UP	UNITED PARCEL SERVICE (C.C. & E.)		27753	730	12/14/98	CF6-80C2B7F		
B767-34AF (ER)	N328UP	UNITED PARCEL SERVICE (C.C. & E.)		27754	732	12/17/98	CF6-80C2B7F		
B767-34AF (ER)	N329UP	UNITED PARCEL SERVICE		27755	756	06/24/99	CF6-80C2B7F		
B767-34AF (ER)	N330UP	UNITED PARCEL SERVICE (C.C. & E.)		27756	760	08/10/99	CF6-80C2B7F		
B767-34AF (ER)	N331UP	UNITED PARCEL SERVICE		27757	764	09/09/99	CF6-80C2B7F		
B767-201 (ER)	N645US	US AIRWAYS		23897	173	05/21/87	CF6-80C2B2		N603P
B767-201 (ER)	N646US	US AIRWAYS		23898	175	06/03/87	CF6-80C2B2		N604P
B767-201 (ER)	N647US	US AIRWAYS		23899	182	08/10/87	CF6-80C2B2		N607P
B767-201 (ER)	N648US	US AIRWAYS		23900	190	02/24/88	CF6-80C2B2		N608P
B767-201 (ER)	N649US	US AIRWAYS		23901	197	12/22/87	CF6-80C2B2		N614P
B767-201 (ER)	N650US	US AIRWAYS		23902	217	05/03/88	CF6-80C2B2		N617P
B767-2B7 (ER)	N651US	US AIRWAYS		24764	306	05/22/90	CF6-80C2B2		

A/C TYPE	CURRENT REG. NO.	LAST KNOWN OPERATOR (OWNER)	Status	ORIGINAL MSN	LINE NO.	DEL. DATE	ENG. TYPE	FLEET NO.	PREV. REG. [COMMENTS]
B767-2B7 (ER)	N652US	US AIRWAYS		24765	308	05/25/90	CF6-80C2B2		
B767-2B7 (ER)	N653US	US AIRWAYS		24894	338	11/15/90	CF6-80C2B2		
B767-2B7 (ER)	N654US	US AIRWAYS		25225	375	06/20/91	CF6-80C2B2		[DMGD BY FIRE DURING ENGINE MX 09/21/00; STD PHL; WO?]
B767-2B7 (ER)	N655US	US AIRWAYS		25257	383	07/30/91	CF6-80C2B2		
B767-2B7 (ER)	N656US	US AIRWAYS		26847	486	04/01/93	CF6-80C2B2		

OB-PERU

A/C TYPE	CURRENT REG. NO.	LAST KNOWN OPERATOR (OWNER)	Status	ORIGINAL MSN	LINE NO.	DEL. DATE	ENG. TYPE	FLEET NO.	PREV. REG. [COMMENTS]
B767-219 (ER)	N141LF	AERO CONTINENTE (ILFC)		24150	239	09/26/88	CF6-80A		N6038E, ZK-NBE, PT-TAG, N141LF [LST NTI AS CC-CJP]

OE-AUSTRIA

A/C TYPE	CURRENT REG. NO.	LAST KNOWN OPERATOR (OWNER)	Status	ORIGINAL MSN	LINE NO.	DEL. DATE	ENG. TYPE	FLEET NO.	PREV. REG. [COMMENTS]
B767-3Z9 (ER)	OE-LAE	LAUDA AIR		30383	812	11/15/00	PW4060		
B767-31A (ER)	OE-LAT	LAUDA AIR		25273	393	10/18/91	PW4060		N6046P, I-LAUD, PH-MCK [LST LDI]
B767-3Z9 (ER)	OE-LAU	LAUDA AIR		23765	165	04/29/88	PW4056		N767PW, N6009F [LST LDI]
B767-3Z9 (ER)	OE-LAW	LAUDA AIR		26417	448	08/21/92	PW4060		[LST LDI]
B767-3Z9 (ER)	OE-LAX	LAUDA AIR		27095	467	12/04/92	PW4060		[LST LDI]
B767-3Z9 (ER)	OE-LAY	LAUDA AIR		29867	731	12/29/98	PW4060		[LST JKK]
B767-3Z9 (ER)	OE-LAZ	LAUDA AIR		30331	759	08/09/99	PW4060		

OO-BELGIUM

A/C TYPE	CURRENT REG. NO.	LAST KNOWN OPERATOR (OWNER)	Status	ORIGINAL MSN	LINE NO.	DEL. DATE	ENG. TYPE	FLEET NO.	PREV. REG. [COMMENTS]
B767-33A (ER)	OO-CTA	CITY BIRD (AWAS)		27477	780	03/10/00	PW4060		N6005C
B767-33A (ER)	OO-CTR	CITY BIRD (AWAS)		28495	643	03/12/97	CF6-80C2B6F		VH-NOA [TO BE RT AWAS 07/01]
B767-3BG (ER)	OO-SLR	SOBELAIR (FLIT)		30563	786	04/04/00	PW4060		
B767-3BG (ER)	OO-SLS	SOBELAIR (FLIT)		30566	817	11/22/00	PW4060		

PH-NETHERLANDS

A/C TYPE	CURRENT REG. NO.	LAST KNOWN OPERATOR (OWNER)	Status	ORIGINAL MSN	LINE NO.	DEL. DATE	ENG. TYPE	FLEET NO.	PREV. REG. [COMMENTS]
B767-306 (ER)	PH-BZA	KLM (ILFC)		27957	587	07/28/95	CF6-80C2B6F		
B767-306 (ER)	PH-BZB	KLM (ILFC)		27958	589	08/18/95	CF6-80C2B6F		
B767-306 (ER)	PH-BZC	KLM (ILFC)		26263	592	10/02/95	CF6-80C2B6F		
B767-306 (ER)	PH-BZD	KLM (ILFC)		27610	605	03/02/96	CF6-80C2B6F		[8,000TH BOEING COMM. JET DEL]
B767-306 (ER)	PH-BZE	KLM (ILFC)		28098	607	05/10/96	CF6-80C2B6F		
B767-306 (ER)	PH-BZF	KLM (ILFC)		27959	609	06/25/96	CF6-80C2B6F		
B767-306 (ER)	PH-BZG	KLM (ILFC)		27960	625	08/29/96	CF6-80C2B6F		
B767-306 (ER)	PH-BZH	KLM (ILFC)		27611	633	10/31/96	CF6-80C2B6F		
B767-306 (ER)	PH-BZI	KLM (ILFC)		27612	647	02/21/97	CF6-80C2B6F		
B767-306 (ER)	PH-BZK	KLM (ILFC)		27614	661	05/28/97	CF6-80C2B6F		
B767-306 (ER)	PH-BZM	KLM (ILFC)		28884	738	02/25/99	CF6-80C2B6F		
B767-306 (ER)	PH-BZO	KLM (ILFC)		30393	781	02/01/00	CF6-80C2B6F		
B767-31A (ER)	PH-MCG	MARTINAIR (MEGA FLIGHT)		24428	279	09/21/89	PW4060		
B767-31A (ER)	PH-MCH	MARTINAIR (MEGA FLIGHT)		24429	294	02/28/90	PW4060		

A/C TYPE	CURRENT REG. NO.	LAST KNOWN OPERATOR (OWNER)	Status	ORIGINAL MSN	LINE NO.	DEL. DATE	ENG. TYPE	FLEET NO.	PREV. REG. [COMMENTS]
B767-31A (ER)	PH-MCI	MARTINAIR (RUBY)		25312	400	11/08/91	PW4060		
B767-31A (ER)	PH-MCL	MARTINAIR (JL ZODIAC)		26469	415	02/12/92	PW4060		
B767-31A (ER)	PH-MCM	MARTINAIR (APPLE A/C)		26470	416	02/25/92	PW4060		
B767-31A (ER)	PH-MCV	MARTINAIR (ILFC)		27619	595	11/06/95	PW4060		

PP/PT-BRAZIL

A/C TYPE	CURRENT REG. NO.	LAST KNOWN OPERATOR (OWNER)	Status	ORIGINAL MSN	LINE NO.	DEL. DATE	ENG. TYPE	FLEET NO.	PREV. REG. [COMMENTS]
B767-2Q4	PT-TAA	TRANSBRASIL		22921	55	06/23/83	CF6-80A		N6038E, N8277V, N4574M
B767-2Q4	PT-TAB	TRANSBRASIL		22922	57	07/11/83	CF6-80A		N6067B, N45742 [PARKED GIG]
B767-2Q4	PT-TAC	TRANSBRASIL		22923	59	07/11/83	CF6-80A		N6018N, N8286V, N4575L
B767-3P6 (ER)	PT-TAL	TRANSBRASIL (PEGA)		23764	158	06/14/88	CF6-80C2B4		N767GE, N6009F, A40-GF
B767-3P6 (ER)	PT-TAM	TRANSBRASIL (PEGA)		24349	244	11/28/88	CF6-80C2B4		A40-GG
B767-241 (ER)	PP-VNN	VARIG BRASIL (NBB BRIDGEPORT)		23803	161	07/02/87	CF6-80C2B2		N60668 [DMGD BY FIRE 06/07/00 GRU; REPAIRED; RTS 10/00]
B767-241 (ER)	PP-VNO	VARIG BRASIL (NBB NEW HAVEN)		23801	170	07/02/87	CF6-80C2B2		N6009F
B767-241 (ER)	PP-VNP	VARIG BRASIL (NBB HARTFORD)		23802	172	07/02/87	CF6-80C2B2		N6018N
B767-241 (ER)	PP-VNQ	VARIG BRASIL (GECA)		23804	178	07/24/87	CF6-80C2B2		N6009F
B767-241 (ER)	PP-VNR	VARIG BRASIL (GECA)		23805	180	07/13/87	CF6-80C2B2		N6005C
B767-241 (ER)	PP-VNS	VARIG BRASIL (GECA)		23806	181	08/05/87	CF6-80C2B2		N6018N
B767-341 (ER)	PP-VOI	VARIG BRASIL (NISSHO IWAI)		24752	289	12/12/89	CF6-80C2B6		
B767-341 (ER)	PP-VOJ	VARIG BRASIL (NISSHO IWAI)		24753	291	02/01/90	CF6-80C2B6		
B767-341 (ER)	PP-VOK	VARIG BRASIL (ITOH)		24843	314	06/27/90	CF6-80C2B6		
B767-341 (ER)	PP-VOL	VARIG BRASIL (ITOH)		24844	324	08/27/90	CF6-80C2B6		
B767-375 (ER)	PP-VPV	VARIG BRASIL (SUNR)		24086	248	03/29/89	CF6-80C2B6F		N6055X, C-FCAJ
B767-375 (ER)	PP-VPW	VARIG BRASIL (CITG)		24087	249	03/31/89	CF6-80C2B6F		N6038E, C-FCAU

RA-RUSSIA

A/C TYPE	CURRENT REG. NO.	LAST KNOWN OPERATOR (OWNER)	Status	ORIGINAL MSN	LINE NO.	DEL. DATE	ENG. TYPE	FLEET NO.	PREV. REG. [COMMENTS]
B767-36N (ER)	VP-BAV	AEROFLOT (GECA)		30107	761	08/20/99	CF6-80C2B7F		
B767-36N (ER)	VP-BAX	AEROFLOT (GECA)		30109	767	10/01/99	CF6-80C2B7F		
B767-36N (ER)	VP-BAY	AEROFLOT (GECA)		30110	775	12/15/99	CF6-80C2B7F		
B767-36N (ER)	VP-BAZ	AEROFLOT (GECA)		30111	776	12/16/99	CF6-80C2B7F		

SE-SWEDEN

A/C TYPE	CURRENT REG. NO.	LAST KNOWN OPERATOR (OWNER)	Status	ORIGINAL MSN	LINE NO.	DEL. DATE	ENG. TYPE	FLEET NO.	PREV. REG. [COMMENTS]
B767-383 (ER)	LN-RCD	SCANDINAVIAN-SAS		24847	315	07/09/90	PW4060		
B767-383 (ER)	LN-RCE	SCANDINAVIAN-SAS (ICON)		24846	309	06/28/90	PW4060		SE-DKR
B767-383 (ER)	LN-RCF	SCANDINAVIAN-SAS (AARL)		24849	330	09/28/90	PW4060		SE-DKT, OY-KDO
B767-383 (ER)	LN-RCG	SCANDINAVIAN-SAS (FSBU)		24475	273	08/14/89	PW4060		SE-DOA, OY-KDI
B767-383 (ER)	LN-RCH	SCANDINAVIAN-SAS (SUNR)		24318	257	03/29/89	PW4060		N6046P, SE-DKO
B767-383 (ER)	LN-RCI	SCANDINAVIAN-SAS (KUTA-TWO)		24476	274	08/21/89	PW4060		OY-KDK, SE-DOB
B767-383 (ER)	LN-RCK	SCANDINAVIAN-SAS (GILMAN FIN.)		24729	358	03/19/91	PW4060		SE-DKU
B767-383 (ER)	LN-RCL	SCANDINAVIAN-SAS (AV INV)		25365	395	10/25/91	PW4060		SE-DKX

A/C TYPE	CURRENT REG. NO.	LAST KNOWN OPERATOR (OWNER) Status	ORIGINAL MSN	LINE NO.	DEL. DATE	ENG. TYPE	FLEET NO.	PREV. REG. [COMMENTS]
B767-383 (ER)	LN-RCM	SCANDINAVIAN-SAS (NORDBANKEN)	26544	412	02/13/92	PW4060		N6055X, SE-DOC
B767-383 (ER)	OY-KDH	SCANDINAVIAN-SAS (AARHUS)	24358	263	05/04/89	PW4060		I-AEJB [STAR ALLIANCE C/S]
B767-383 (ER)	OY-KDL	SCANDINAVIAN-SAS (DIA COS.)	24477	337	11/19/90	PW4060		
B767-383 (ER)	OY-KDM	SCANDINAVIAN-SAS (MUZEN)	25088	359	03/26/91	PW4060		
B767-383 (ER)	OY-KDN	SCANDINAVIAN-SAS	24848	325	09/05/90	PW4060		SE-DKS

SP-POLAND

A/C TYPE	CURRENT REG. NO.	LAST KNOWN OPERATOR (OWNER)	ORIGINAL MSN	LINE NO.	DEL. DATE	ENG. TYPE	FLEET NO.	PREV. REG. [COMMENTS]
B767-25D (ER)	SP-LOA	LOT (AV CAP)	24733	261	04/21/89	CF6-80C2B4		N6046P
B767-25D (ER)	SP-LOB	LOT (AV CAP)	24734	266	05/19/89	CF6-80C2B4		
B767-35D (ER)	SP-LPA	LOT (BOUL)	24865	322	08/21/90	CF6-80C2B6		
B767-35D (ER)	SP-LPB	LOT (FSBU)	27902	577	05/12/95	CF6-80C2B6		
B767-35D (ER)	SP-LPC	LOT	28656	659	05/15/97	CF6-80C2B6		

SU-EGYPT

A/C TYPE	CURRENT REG. NO.	LAST KNOWN OPERATOR (OWNER)	ORIGINAL MSN	LINE NO.	DEL. DATE	ENG. TYPE	FLEET NO.	PREV. REG. [COMMENTS]
B767-366 (ER)	SU-GAO	EGYPT AIR	24541	275	08/15/89	PW4060		

S7-SEYCHELLES

A/C TYPE	CURRENT REG. NO.	LAST KNOWN OPERATOR (OWNER)	ORIGINAL MSN	LINE NO.	DEL. DATE	ENG. TYPE	FLEET NO.	PREV. REG. [COMMENTS]
B767-37D (ER)	S7-AHM	AIR SEYCHELLES (ILFC)	26328	637	12/03/96	CF6-80C2B6F		
B767-3Q8 (ER)	S7-ASY	AIR SEYCHELLES (ILFC)	29386	831	04/09/01	CF6-80C2B6F		

TF-ICELAND

A/C TYPE	CURRENT REG. NO.	LAST KNOWN OPERATOR (OWNER)	ORIGINAL MSN	LINE NO.	DEL. DATE	ENG. TYPE	FLEET NO.	PREV. REG. [COMMENTS]
B767-204 (ER)	TF-ATO	AIR ATLANTA ICELAND (SUMIMOTO)	24013	210	03/29/88	CF6-80A2		N6009F, G-BNYS [OPF SBE 05/01]
B767-204 (ER)	TF-ATP	AIR ATLANTA ICELAND (SUMIMOTO)	24239	243	11/01/88	CF6-80A2		N6009F, G-BOPB [TO BE LST SBE 05/01]
B767-204 (ER)	TF-ATR	AIR ATLANTA ICELAND (GECA)	24457	256	03/27/89	CF6-80A2		G-BPFV, EC-276, EC-GHM
B767-204 (ER)	TF-ATU	AIR ATLANTA ICELAND (AFIN)	23250	113	03/25/85	CF6-80A		G-BLKW, ZK-NBJ

TJ-CAMEROON

A/C TYPE	CURRENT REG. NO.	LAST KNOWN OPERATOR (OWNER)	ORIGINAL MSN	LINE NO.	DEL. DATE	ENG. TYPE	FLEET NO.	PREV. REG. [COMMENTS]
B767-334 (ER)	TJ-CAC	CAMEROON AIRLINES (AWAS)	28138	822	01/19/01	PW4060		

TR-GABON

A/C TYPE	CURRENT REG. NO.	LAST KNOWN OPERATOR (OWNER)	ORIGINAL MSN	LINE NO.	DEL. DATE	ENG. TYPE	FLEET NO.	PREV. REG. [COMMENTS]
B767-266 (ER)	TR-LFH	AIR GABON (LEOPARD LSG)	23178	97	07/20/84	JT9D-7R4E		N1785B, SU-GAH, N574SW, N767ER

UK-UZBEKISTAN

A/C TYPE	CURRENT REG. NO.	LAST KNOWN OPERATOR (OWNER)	ORIGINAL MSN	LINE NO.	DEL. DATE	ENG. TYPE	FLEET NO.	PREV. REG. [COMMENTS]
B767-33P (ER)	VP-BUA	UZBEKISTAN AIRWAYS (UZB FIN LTD)	28370	635	11/27/96	PW4062		N6005C, VR-BUA, VP-BUA [TBR UK-76701]
B767-33P (ER)	VP-BUZ	UZBEKISTAN AIRWAYS (UZB FIN LTD)	28392	650	03/07/97	PW4062		[TBR UK-76702]

VH-AUSTRALIA

A/C TYPE	CURRENT REG. NO.	LAST KNOWN OPERATOR (OWNER)	ORIGINAL MSN	LINE NO.	DEL. DATE	ENG. TYPE	FLEET NO.	PREV. REG. [COMMENTS]
B767-277	VH-RMD	ANSETT AUSTRALIA (GECA)	22692	24	06/06/83	CF6-80A		N8278V
B767-277	VH-RME	ANSETT AUSTRALIA (GECA)	22693	28	06/13/83	CF6-80A		N8292V
B767-277	VH-RMF	ANSETT AUSTRALIA (GECA)	22694	32	06/22/83	CF6-80A		N8287V
B767-277	VH-RMG	ANSETT AUSTRALIA (GECA)	22695	35	08/23/84	CF6-80A		N8289V

A/C TYPE	CURRENT REG. NO.	LAST KNOWN OPERATOR (OWNER)	Status	ORIGINAL MSN	LINE NO.	DEL. DATE	ENG. TYPE	FLEET NO.	PREV. REG. [COMMENTS]
B767-277	VH-RMH	ANSETT AUSTRALIA (GECA)		22696	100	09/20/84	CF6-80A		N1791B
B767-204	VH-RMK	ANSETT AUSTRALIA (GECA)		22981	79	02/06/84	CF6-80A		N1785B, G-BKVZ
B767-204	VH-RML	ANSETT AUSTRALIA (GECA)		22980	71	02/27/84	CF6-80A		N5573K, N8289V, G-BKPW
B767-216 (ER)	VH-RMM	ANSETT AUSTRALIA (GATX)		24973	347	01/25/91	CF6-80A2		CC-CEF, N483GX
B767-204	VH-RMO	ANSETT AUSTRALIA (ILFC)		23807	184	08/25/87	CF6-80A2		N6005C, G-BNCW [RTS 07/13/00]
B767-324 (ER)	VH-BZF	ANSETT AUSTRALIA (GECA)		27569	601	03/25/96	CF6-80C2B7F		N6055X
B767-238 (ER)	VH-EAJ	QANTAS		23304	119	07/03/85	JT9D-7R4E		N6055X
B767-238 (ER)	VH-EAK	QANTAS		23305	120	07/11/85	JT9D-7R4E		N6009F
B767-238 (ER)	VH-EAL	QANTAS		23306	125	09/30/85	JT9D-7R4E		N6009F
B767-238 (ER)	VH-EAM	QANTAS		23309	129	12/12/85	JT9D-7R4E		N6018N
B767-238 (ER)	VH-EAN	QANTAS		23402	133	02/05/86	JT9D-7R4E		N6018N
B767-238 (ER)	VH-EAO	QANTAS		23403	137	03/19/86	JT9D-7R4E		N6046P
B767-238 (ER)	VH-EAQ	QANTAS		23896	183	08/27/87	JT9D-7R4E		N6009F
B767-338 (ER)	VH-OGA	QANTAS		24146	231	08/30/88	CF6-80C2B6		N6055X
B767-338 (ER)	VH-OGB	QANTAS		24316	242	10/20/88	CF6-80C2B6		N6005C [OPF FJI]
B767-338 (ER)	VH-OGC	QANTAS		24317	246	11/23/88	CF6-80C2B6		N6005C
B767-338 (ER)	VH-OGD	QANTAS		24407	247	12/05/88	CF6-80C2B6		N6009F
B767-338 (ER)	VH-OGE	QANTAS		24531	278	09/05/89	CF6-80C2B6		
B767-338 (ER)	VH-OGF	QANTAS		24853	319	07/27/90	CF6-80C2B6		
B767-338 (ER)	VH-OGG	QANTAS		24929	343	12/12/90	CF6-80C2B6		
B767-338 (ER)	VH-OGH	QANTAS		24930	344	12/19/90	CF6-80C2B6		
B767-338 (ER)	VH-OGI	QANTAS		25246	387	08/29/91	CF6-80C2B6		
B767-338 (ER)	VH-OGJ	QANTAS		25274	396	10/16/91	CF6-80C2B6		
B767-338 (ER)	VH-OGK	QANTAS		25316	397	10/23/91	CF6-80C2B6		N6018N
B767-338 (ER)	VH-OGL	QANTAS		25363	402	11/21/91	CF6-80C2B6		N6018N
B767-338 (ER)	VH-OGM	QANTAS		25575	451	09/03/92	CF6-80C2B6		
B767-338 (ER)	VH-OGN	QANTAS		25576	549	08/23/94	CF6-80C2B6		
B767-338 (ER)	VH-OGO	QANTAS		25577	550	08/26/94	CF6-80C2B6		
B767-338 (ER)	VH-OGP	QANTAS		28153	615	05/30/96	CF6-80C2B6		
B767-338 (ER)	VH-OGQ	QANTAS		28154	623	08/14/96	CF6-80C2B6		
B767-338 (ER)	VH-OGR	QANTAS		28724	662	06/06/97	CF6-80C2B6		
B767-338 (ER)	VH-OGS	QANTAS		28725	665	06/26/97	CF6-80C2B6		
B767-338 (ER)	VH-OGT	QANTAS		29117	710	07/20/98	CF6-80C2B6		
B767-338 (ER)	VH-OGU	QANTAS		29118	713	08/02/98	CF6-80C2B6		
B767-338 (ER)	VH-OGV	QANTAS		30186	796	06/19/00	CF6-80C2B6		
B767-336 (ER)	VH-ZXA	QANTAS (BAW)	L	24337	288	03/18/90	RB211-524H		G-BNWE
B767-336 (ER)	VH-ZXB	QANTAS (BAW)	L	24338	293	06/23/90	RB211-524H		N1788B, G-BNWF
B767-336 (ER)	VH-ZXC	QANTAS (BAW)	L	24339	298	07/13/90	RB211-524H		G-BNWG
B767-336 (ER)	VH-ZXD	QANTAS (BAW)	L	24342	363	04/24/91	RB211-524H		G-BNWJ
B767-336 (ER)	VH-ZXE	QANTAS (BAW)	L	24343	364	04/18/91	RB211-524H		G-BNWK

A/C TYPE	CURRENT REG. NO.	LAST KNOWN OPERATOR (OWNER)	Status	ORIGINAL MSN	LINE NO.	DEL. DATE	ENG. TYPE	FLEET NO.	PREV. REG. [COMMENTS]
B767-336 (ER)	VH-ZXF	QANTAS (BAW)	L	25203	365	04/30/91	RB211-524H		G-BNWL
B767-336 (ER)	VH-ZXG	QANTAS (BAW)	L	25443	419	03/10/92	RB211-524H		G-BNWP

VN-VIETNAM

B767-324 (ER)	VN-A762	VIETNAM AIRLINES (GECA)		27392	568	01/25/96	CF6-80C2B7F		N1785B, EI-CMD, S7-RGV [LST/OPB RGA]
B767-324 (ER)	VN-A764	VIETNAM AIRLINES (GECA)		27393	571	02/13/96	CF6-80C2B7F		N1794B, EI-CME, S7-RGW [LST/OPB RGA]
B767-324 (ER)	VN-A765	VIETNAM AIRLINES (GECA)		27568	593	02/13/96	CF6-80C2B7F		EI-CMH, S7-RGU [LST/OPB RGA]
B767-33A (ER)	VN-A768	VIETNAM AIRLINES (AWAS)		27310	545	06/24/94	CF6-80C2B6F		OO-SBY
B767-352 (ER)	VN-A769	VIETNAM AIRLINES (ILFC)		26262	583	06/22/95	PW4062		N171LF, EI-CLS
B767-328 (ER)	S7-AAB	VIETNAM AIRLINES (RBA)	L	27427	579	04/04/96	CF6-80C2B6F		N6065S, 3B-NAZ, V8-RBN
B767-33A (ER)	V8-RBF	VIETNAM AIRLINES (RBA)	L	25530	414	02/11/92	PW4056		

V8-BRUNEI

B767-33A (ER)	V8-RBF	ROYAL BRUNEI AIRLINES		25530	414	02/11/92	PW4056		[LST/OPF HVN]
B767-33A (ER)	V8-RBG	ROYAL BRUNEI AIRLINES		25532	442	09/28/92	PW4056		N6055X
B767-33A (ER)	V8-RBH	ROYAL BRUNEI AIRLINES		25534	477	03/26/93	PW4056		N6055X
B767-33A (ER)	V8-RBJ	ROYAL BRUNEI AIRLINES		25533	454	12/03/92	PW4056		N6009F, N67AW
B767-33A (ER)	V8-RBK	ROYAL BRUNEI AIRLINES		25536	504	08/30/93	PW4056		N96AC
B767-33A (ER)	V8-RBL	ROYAL BRUNEI AIRLINES		27189	521	01/18/94	PW4056		N1794B
B767-328 (ER)	V8-RBM	ROYAL BRUNEI AIRLINES		27428	586	03/08/96	CF6-80C2B6F		N60668 [LST DAH AS S7-RGT]
B767-328 (ER)	V8-RBN	ROYAL BRUNEI AIRLINES		27427	579	04/04/96	CF6-80C2B6F		N60659, 3B-NAZ [LST HVN AS S7-AAB]
B767-27G (ER)	V8-MHB	SULTAN'S FLIGHT-BRUNEI		25537	517	09/28/93	CF6-80C2B4F		V8-MJB [OP IN RBA COLORS]

XA-MEXICO

B767-284 (ER)	XA-JBC	AEROMEXICO (AWAS)		24762	307	06/12/90	PW4056		CC-CEY, XA-RVY, CC-CDJ
B767-284 (ER)	XA-RVZ	AEROMEXICO (AWAS)		24716	297	05/01/90	PW4056		N6046P, CC-CEX, XA-RVZ, CC-CDH
B767-283 (ER)	XA-TNS	AEROMEXICO (PLMI)		24728	305	05/11/90	PW4056		LN-RCC, PT-TAJ, N301AR
B767-283 (ER)	XA-TOJ	AEROMEXICO (BCCI)		24727	301	06/01/90	PW4056		N6018N, SE-DKP, PT-TAI
B767-3Q8 (ER)	XA-APB	AEROMEXICO (ILFC)		27618	727	11/24/98	PW4062		

YS-EL SALVADOR

B767-216 (ER)	N762TA	TACA INTL. AIRLINES (FSBU)		23623	142	05/29/86	CF6-80A2		N4529T, CC-CJU [STD SAL; ALL WHITE; NO TITLES]

Z-ZIMBABWE

B767-2N0 (ER)	Z-WPE	AIR ZIMBABWE		24713	287	11/28/89	PW4056		
B767-2N0 (ER)	Z-WPF	AIR ZIMBABWE		24867	333	10/26/90	PW4056		

A/C TYPE	CURRENT REG. NO.	LAST KNOWN OPERATOR (OWNER)	Status	ORIGINAL MSN	LINE NO.	DEL. DATE	ENG. TYPE	FLEET NO.	PREV. REG. [COMMENTS]
ZK-NEW ZEALAND									
B767-219 (ER)	ZK-NBA	AIR NEW ZEALAND (GECA)		23326	124	09/03/85	CF6-80A		N6018N, VH-RMC, HB-IIX [OPF AAA FROM 04/13/01]
B767-219 (ER)	ZK-NBB	AIR NEW ZEALAND (GECA)		23327	134	03/04/86	CF6-80A		N6055X
B767-219 (ER)	ZK-NBC	AIR NEW ZEALAND (GECA)		23328	149	09/08/86	CF6-80A		N6009F
B767-319 (ER)	ZK-NCE	AIR NEW ZEALAND (ILFC)		24875	371	06/14/91	CF6-80C2B6		
B767-319 (ER)	ZK-NCF	AIR NEW ZEALAND (ILFC)		24876	413	02/14/92	CF6-80C2B6		
B767-319 (ER)	ZK-NCG	AIR NEW ZEALAND		26912	509	08/11/93	CF6-80C2B6		
B767-319 (ER)	ZK-NCH	AIR NEW ZEALAND (ILFC)		26264	555	10/10/94	CF6-80C2B6		
B767-319 (ER)	ZK-NCI	AIR NEW ZEALAND		26913	558	11/09/94	CF6-80C2B6		N6009F
B767-319 (ER)	ZK-NCJ	AIR NEW ZEALAND		26915	574	04/21/95	CF6-80C2B6		N6018N
B767-319 (ER)	ZK-NCK	AIR NEW ZEALAND		26971	663	06/23/97	CF6-80C2B6F		
B767-319 (ER)	ZK-NCL	AIR NEW ZEALAND		28745	677	10/28/97	CF6-80C2B6F		[LST AAA 04/03/01-05/03/01]
B767-319 (ER)	ZK-NCN	AIR NEW ZEALAND (ILFC)		29388	785	04/03/00	CF6-80C2B6F		
B767-319 (ER)	ZK-NCO	AIR NEW ZEALAND (ILFC)		30586	808	08/31/00	CF6-80C2B6F		
ZS-SOUTH AFRICA									
B767-266 (ER)	ZS-SRB	SOUTH AFRICAN AIRWAYS (UT FIN)		23179	98	08/13/84	JT9D-7R4E		N1788B, SU-GAI, N573SW
B767-266 (ER)	ZS-SRC	SOUTH AFRICAN AIRWAYS (UT FIN)		23180	99	08/31/84	JT9D-7R4E		N1789B, SU-GAJ, N575SW
3B-MAURITIUS									
B767-23B (ER)	3B-NAK	AIR MAURITIUS		23973	208	04/05/88	CF6-80C2B4	01	N6046P
B767-23B (ER)	3B-NAL	AIR MAURITIUS		23974	214	04/14/88	CF6-80C2B4	02	N6018N
4X-ISRAEL									
B767-258	4X-EAA	EL AL ISRAELI AIRLINES		22972	62	07/12/83	JT9D-7R4D	601	N6066Z
B767-258	4X-EAB	EL AL ISRAELI AIRLINES		22973	68	09/13/83	JT9D-7R4D	602	N6018N
B767-258 (ER)	4X-EAC	EL AL ISRAELI AIRLINES		22974	86	03/26/84	JT9D-7R4D	603	N6018N
B767-258 (ER)	4X-EAD	EL AL ISRAELI AIRLINES		22975	89	06/01/84	JT9D-7R4D	604	N6046P
B767-27E (ER)	4X-EAE	EL AL ISRAELI AIRLINES		24832	316	07/26/90	PW4060A	605	F-GHGD
B767-27E (ER)	4X-EAF	EL AL ISRAELI AIRLINES		24854	326	09/28/90	PW4060A	606	N6018E, F-GHGE
5R-MADAGASCAR									
B767-216 (ER)	5R-MFE	AIR MADAGASCAR (ILFC)		23624	144	06/30/86	CF6-80A2		N4528Y, CC-CJV, PT-TAH, N151LF
B767-36N (ER)	5R-MFD	AIR MADAGASCAR (GECA)		29898	754	06/21/99	PW4060		
5Y-KENYA									
B767-36N (ER)	5Y-KQZ	KENYA AIRWAYS (GECA)	N	30853	837				
B767-33A (ER)	VH-NOA	KENYA AIRWAYS (NORDSTRESS)		27909	591	08/22/95	PW4056		OE-LAS, N909SH

	A/C TYPE	CURRENT REG. NO.	LAST KNOWN OPERATOR (OWNER)	Status	ORIGINAL MSN	LINE NO.	DEL. DATE	ENG. TYPE	FLEET NO.	PREV. REG. [COMMENTS]
7T-ALGERIA										
	B767-3D6	7T-VJG	AIR ALGERIE		24766	310	06/28/90	CF6-80C2B2F		
	B767-3D6	7T-VJH	AIR ALGERIE		24767	323	08/17/90	CF6-80C2B2F		
	B767-3D6	7T-VJI	AIR ALGERIE		24768	332	10/12/90	CF6-80C2B2F		N6009F
	B767-328 (ER)	S7-RGT	AIR ALGERIE (RBA)	L	27428	586	03/08/96	CF6-80C2B6F		N60668, V8-RBM
9N-NEPAL										
	B767-3Z9 (ER)	OE-LAU	ROYAL NEPAL AIRLINES (LDA)	L	23765	165	04/29/88	PW4056		N767PW, N6009F
9V-SINGAPORE										
	B767-324 (ER)	S7-RGU	REGIONAIR (HVN)	L	27568	593	02/13/96	CF6-80C2B7F		EI-CMH [OPF HVN]
	B767-324 (ER)	S7-RGV	REGIONAIR (HVN)	L	27392	568	01/25/96	CF6-80C2B7F		N1785B, EI-CMD [OPF HVN]
	B767-324 (ER)	S7-RGW	REGIONAIR (HVN)	L	27393	571	02/13/96	CF6-80C2B7F		N1794B, EI-CME [OPF HVN]
MILITARY										
	B767-27C (ER)	64-3501	JAPANESE AIR FORCE	M	27385	557	06/28/96	CF6-80C2B6FA		N60697, N767JA [AWACS; FF 10/19/94; DD TO ITOUCHU 06/28/96]
	B767-27C (ER)	64-3502	JAPANESE AIR FORCE	M	27391	588	12/17/96	CF6-80C2B6FA		N60659, N767JB [AWACS; FF 07/18/95; DD TO ITOUCHU 12/17/96]
	B767-27C (ER)	74-3503	JAPANESE AIR FORCE	M	28016	618	06/12/97	CF6-80C2B6FA		N767JC [AWACS]
	B767-27C (ER)	74-3504	JAPANESE AIR FORCE	M	28017	642	01/15/98	CF6-80C2B6FA		N767JD [AWACS]
	B767-332 (ER)	B-	PEOPLE'S REPUBLIC OF CHINA AIR FORCE	M	30597	797	06/15/00	CF6-80C2B6F		N179DZ [OPB CUA; CHINESE PRESIDENTIAL A/C]
OUT OF SERVICE										
	B767-231 (ER)	N606TW	TRANS WORLD AIRLINES (767-231 HOLDINGS)	O	22569	39	04/13/83	JT9D-7R4D	16006	[LRF 01/15/01; RT LESSOR AND FERRIED TO VCV 01/31/01]
	B767-205 (ER)	N650TW	TRANS WORLD AIRLINES	O	23057	81	03/23/84	JT9D-7R4D	16050	N57008, LN-SUV, N767BE, PP-VNL, G-BNAX [RT ILFC 03/16/01; PARKED XNA 03/17/01]
	B767-269 (ER)	N6373P	(CS AVIATION OF NEW YORK)	O	23280	131	03/20/86	JT9D-7R4E4		N6038E, 9K-AIA, 5W-TEA, TC-ASK, HI-660CA, CC-CDX, TR-LEJ [STD GSO]
	B767-2Q8 (ER)	S7-AAS	AIR SEYCHELLES (ILFC)	O	24448	272	07/19/89	CF6-80C2B4		[RT ILFC; FERRIED TO OZR]
	B767-3Q8 (ER)	LV-ZPL	LAPA (ILFC)	O	28206	694	03/26/98	CF6-80C2B6F		N601LF [RT LESSOR 04/09/01]
UNASSIGNED										
			(UNASSIGNED)(NOT BUILT)	U		718				[CONSTRUCTION STARTED BUT NOT COMPLETED]
WRITTEN OFF										
	B767-269ER	9K-AIB	KUWAIT AIRWAYS	W	23281	135	04/02/86	JT9D-7R4E4		[WO 02/15/91; DESTROYED DURING PERSIAN GULF WAR]
	B767-269ER	9K-AIC	KUWAIT AIRWAYS	W	23282	138	04/15/86	JT9D-7R4E4		[WO 02/15/91; DESTROYED DURING PERSIAN GULF WAR]
	B767-2S1	N767TA	TACA INTL. AIRLINES (FSBU)	W	23494	141	05/22/86	CF6-80A		[WO 04/05/93; GUATEMALA CITY; OVERRAN ON LDG]
	B767-260 (ER)	ET-AIZ	ETHIOPIAN AIRLINES (E.A.C. LSG)	W	23916	187	10/22/87	JT9D-7R4E		N6009F [WO 11/23/96; MORONI, COMORES IS.]
	B767-366 (ER)	SU-GAP	EGYPT AIR	W	24542	282	09/26/89	PW4060		[WO 10/31/99 NANTUCKET, MA]
	B767-3Z9ER	OE-LAV	LAUDA AIR	W	24628	283	10/16/89	PW4060		[WO 05/26/91 BANGKOK; IN-FLIGHT THRUST REVERSAL]

Chapter 9

Model 777

The 777 designation was first used publicly in 1978 when 7X7 studies for a wide-body trijet with U.S. transcontinental range capability were appearing to reach fruition. However, after American Airlines chose instead to order 767-200s, Boeing redirected the 777 effort toward developing a fully intercontinental aircraft sized below the DC-10 and TriStar. Failing to gain customers for this proposal, Boeing shelved its 777 until the mid-1980s.

One year after having secured launch orders for its extensively upgraded 747-400, Boeing Commercial Airplanes turned its attention to plugging the gap in seating capacity between its largest twin, the 767-300, and its 747. Doing so would also counter moves in the very-long-range market by McDonnell Douglas and Airbus Industrie. The former had announced the development of its MD-11 at the 1985 Paris Air Show while the latter was known to be working on the large-capacity A330 twinjet and A340 four-engined jetliners.

In the fall of 1986, before Airbus announced the go-ahead for the A330/A340 family with initial seating in high-density configuration for up to 440 passengers, Boeing sought to minimize development costs by proposing a stretched version of the 767-300. It next looked at the feasibility of developing another 767 derivative with a novel rear fuselage design with passenger accommodation on two decks. Members of an airline advisory group did not find much merit in either proposal. Shortly thereafter, Boeing engineers concluded that to fill the gap between the 767-300 and the 747 with an aircraft having the range capability now demanded by international carriers operating to and from Asia would require new wings. Building on the 767 to save costs was no longer feasible. It was time to come up with an all-new design tailored to meet the recently implemented ETOPS certification requirements. The resulting Model 777 would become a trendsetter.

Making extensive use of computer-aided design/computer-aided manufacturing (CAD/CAM) and computer-aided three-dimensional interactive application (CATIA), Boeing ended up with a twin-engine aircraft of conventional appearance but incorporating a number of advanced features. Notably, the wings of the Model 777 were designed to combine an aerodynamically efficient airfoil, increased thickness, and long span to achieve higher cruising speeds and altitudes while providing ample space for fuel tanks. Although consideration was given to having the outer wing panels fold hydraulically upward to reduce space requirements at the gate, no customers opted for this feature. The circular-cross-section fuselage was given a diameter sufficient for seating of up to 10 passengers per row with twin aisles. Initially providing accommodation for up to 440 passengers in high-density configuration, the cabin was designed to provide maximum configuration flexibility, with galleys and lavatories easily repositioned. It also featured improved overhead stowage units. Other advanced features included a three-axis fly-by-wire flight-control system and a flight deck with six LCD screens and integrated Airplane Information Management System (AIMS).

For 777 production, Boeing chose to continue the practice initiated with 767 production and to have much of the airframe built outside the United States. Three Japanese risk-sharing partners were chosen to manufacture fuselage panels and doors, the wing center section, the wing-to-body fairing, and the wing in-spar ribs. Other foreign subcontractors were located in Australia, Brazil, Italy, Singapore, and the United Kingdom. Furthermore, major elements of the airframe were to be built in the United States by Northrop Grumman and by Rockwell (the latter since acquired by Boeing). Boeing would build the balance of the airframe, with final assembly in the Everett plant. Also noteworthy was the fact that the Model 777 was the first Boeing jetliner designed to make extensive use of new, lightweight structural materials, including an improved aluminum alloy, carbon fibers, and other composites.

In December 1989, three years into the development program, the Boeing Commercial Airplane Group was authorized to offer the 777 to the world's airlines. Unfortunately, airlines that had served on the advisory group did not rush to firm up orders, so the Boeing board of directors gave the go-ahead only on October 29, 1990. Thereafter, the program proceeded forward rapidly, with sales quickly reaching satisfactory levels. During the first years in production, the 777 has outsold all other Boeing jetliners, with the exception of the 727. Currently three 777 versions—the -200, -200ER, and -300—are in service. Two more, the -200LR and -300ER, are under development.

777-200 and -200ER

United Airlines became the first 777 customer on October 15, 1990, when it signed a firm contract for 34 777-200s and took an option on 34 others. That contract was later amended to provide for a majority of the aircraft to be delivered in the extended-range 777-200ER configuration.

The maiden flight took place at Payne Field (Everett, Washington) on June 12, 1994. The 10-month test program proceeded smoothly, and the 777-200 powered by Pratt & Whitney turbofans received FAA and JAA type certification on April 19, 1995. This was followed on May 15 by the delivery of the first aircraft for United, on May 30 by FAA approval for 180-minute ETOPS, and on June 7 by the first revenue flight. After taking delivery of 16 standard 777-222s (with 6 more delivered in 2000), United received the first of its 777-222ERs (l/n 57, s/n 26948, N782UA) on March 7, 1997.

By the spring of 2001, four other airlines had ordered 777-200s powered by Pratt & Whitney PW4000-series turbofans (either PW4074s rated at 74,000 pounds [329.2 kilonewtons] of static thrust or PW4077s rated at 77,200 pounds [343.4 kilonewtons] static). Starting with Thai Airways International in June 1991, three airlines ordered 777-200s with Rolls-Royce Trent turbofans (Trent 871, 875, 877, or 884 engines with takeoff thrust ranging between 72,000 and 86,500 pounds [320.3 and 324.8 kilonewtons]). Finally, beginning with an August 1991 order from British Airways, two carriers chose to have their 777s powered by variants of the General Electric GE90 (GE90-76B, -85B, or 90B with takeoff thrust ranging between 76,400 and 90,000 pounds [339.8 and 400.3 kilonewtons]).

Dimensionally identical to the 777-200, the 777-200ER (initially designated 777-200 [IGW] for Increased Gross Weight) is an extended-range version with MTOW increased some 20 percent to 656,000 pounds (297,555 kilograms). Fuel capacity is boosted to 45,220 U.S. gallons (171,173 liters) to increase range by 50 percent. Power is provided by variants of the same three engines as powering the 777-200, but takeoff thrust is increased by some 25 percent to a maximum of 93,700 pounds (416.8 kilonewtons) of static thrust in the case of General Electric GE90-94Bs. To date, engine variants chosen by customers include the General Electric GE90-85B, -90B, and -92B; the Pratt & Whitney PW4090; and the Rolls-Royce Trent 890, 892, and 895. Orders for 777-200ERs have been received from 26 airlines, including six that have also ordered 777-200s.

The first extended range 777, a 777-236ER (l/n 53, s/n 27485, G-VIIC) powered by GE90-85Bs, was delivered to British Airways on February 6, 1997.

777-300

This stretched model was launched when All Nippon Airways placed an order for Pratt & Whitney–powered -300s (along with 12 777-200s and -200ERs) in December 1990. Since then, however, sales of this model have proven disappointing, with only 50 more 777-300s ordered by the spring of 2001.

So far all Series 300 aircraft are powered by Pratt & Whitney turbofans (PW4090 or PW4098) or Rolls-Royce turbofans (Trent 890 or 892) with thrust ranging between 90,000 and 98,000 pounds (400.3 and 435.9 kilonewtons), but the 777-300 can also be powered by GE90 variants, if so specified by a customer. In all instances, the fuel-tank capacity is the same as that of the 777-200ER. Because it carries 66 more passengers in typical three-class accommodation (or 110 more passengers in single-class, high-density configuration) than the 777-200ER, the -300 has a 23 percent shorter range (but still 15 percent more than the standard -200). Maximum takeoff weight is increased to 660,000 pounds (299,730 kilograms).

The first 777-300, a 777-367 (l/n 136, s/n 27504, B-HNH) powered by Trent 890s, was delivered to Cathay Pacific Airways on May 22, 1998.

777-200LR and -300ER

With customers showing a marked preference for increased range, as evidenced by slow sales of 777-300s, Boeing decided to proceed with the development of longer-range variants of the 777-200ER and 777-300. Retaining the same fuselage as these two earlier versions, the 777-200LR and 777-300ER will be characterized by raked-tip wings of increased span and area. Additional fuel will be carried in the modified wings and in tanks fitted in the aft cargo compartment to bring total fuel capacity to 51,590 U.S. gallons (195,285 liters) in the case of the 777-200LR—a remarkable 66 percent increase over the fuel-tank capacity of the original 777-200.

Other modifications include local airframe strengthening, new main landing gear, revised struts and nacelles, and an electronically controlled tailskid commanding elevator movement to prevent inadvertent scraping of the tail on the runway. Both models will be powered by advanced versions of the General Electric GE90. The GE90-110B1s for the 777-200LR will be rated at 110,000 pounds (489.3 kilonewtons) static thrust on takeoff, while the GE90-115Bs for the 777-300ER will be rated at 115,000 pounds (511.5 kilonewtons) static, making them the world's most powerful engine to be placed in production.

Both of these longer-range models were launched in February 2000, with an initial order for eight 777-300ERs being placed by Japan Airlines. Five other customers have ordered 38 additional 777-300ERs, but by the spring of 2001, Eva Air was the only customer for the 777-200LR (three ordered in June 2000 along with four 777-300ERs).

On entry into service at the end of 2003, the 777-300ER will be the world's largest and heaviest twinjet. Moreover, it will carry more payload farther than any other twin. To put that remarkable aircraft into perspective within the Boeing jetliner family, it is worth comparing it with the first of these aircraft, the 1958-vintage 707-120. The latest 777 will have a MTOW more than three times that of the 707-120 and its two turbofans will generate 4.4 times the takeoff thrust of the four turbojets of the pioneer jetliner. In typical three-class configuration the 777-300ER will carry 2.7 times as many passengers as a 707-120 in two-class configuration and will take them 2.2 times farther.

In comparison with the 777-300ER even the 1976-vintage 747SP pales. The newest Boeing jetliner will carry 35 more passengers in a typical configuration. Its MTOW, takeoff thrust, and typical range will respectively be 10 percent, 15 percent, and 30 percent greater than those of the 747SP.

Boeing 777 Principal Characteristics and Performance

	777-200	777-200ER	777-200LR	777-300	777-300ER
Span, ft in (m)	199' 11" (60.93)	199' 11" (60.93)	212' 7" (64.80)	199' 11" (60.93)	212' 7" (64.80)
Length, ft in (m)	209' 1" (63.73)	209' 1" (63.73)	209' 1" (63.73)	242 4 (73.86)	242 4 (73.86)
Height, ft in (m)	60' 9" (18.52)	60' 9" (18.52)	60' 1" (18.31)	60' 8" (18.49)	60' 11" (18.57)
Wing area, sq ft (m^2)	4,605 (427.8)	4,605 (427.8)		4,605 (427.8)	
High-density seating	440	440	440	550	550
Two-class seating	400	400	400	479	479
Three-class seating	320	320	301	386	365
Underfloor cargo, cu ft (m^3)	5,656 (160.2)	5,656 (160.2)	5,302 (150.1)	7,552 (213.8)	7,080 (200.5)
TO thrust per engine, lb st (kN)	73,000/77,200 (324.7/343.4)	90,200/93,700 (401.2/416.8)	110,000 (489.3)	90,000/98,000 (400.3/435.9)	115,000 (511.5)
Fuel capacity, U.S. gal (liters)	31,000 (117,345)	45,220 (171,173)	51,590 (195,285)	45,220 (171,173)	47,890 (181,280)
MTOW, lb (kg)	545,000 (247,210)	656,000 (297,555)	752,000 (341,100)	660,000 (299,370)	752,000 (341,100)
Typical cruise speed, Mach	0.84	0.84	0.84	0.84	0.84
Typical range, nm (km)	5,150 (9,540)	7,695 (14,250)	8,860 (16,410)	5,960 (11,040)	7,200 (13,335)

Boeing 777 Commercial Jet Aircraft Census
The aircraft in the following tables are listed in order of the following: 1) ICAO country prefixes; 2) operator; 3) aircraft type; and 4) registration.
The total built was 336+ (78+ B777-200, 222+ B777-200 (ER), AND 36+ B777-300) from 1995 to present (still in production).

A/C TYPE	CURRENT REG. NO.	LAST KNOWN OPERATOR (OWNER)	Status	ORIGINAL MSN	LINE NO.	DEL. DATE	ENG. TYPE	FLEET NO.	PREV. REG. [COMMENTS]
A6-UNITED ARAB EMIRATES									
B777-21H	A6-EMD	EMIRATES		27247	30	06/05/96	TRENT871		
B777-21H	A6-EME	EMIRATES		27248	33	07/03/96	TRENT871		
B777-21H	A6-EMF	EMIRATES		27249	42	10/16/96	TRENT871		
B777-21H (ER)	A6-EMG	EMIRATES		27252	63	04/11/97	TRENT890		N5020K
B777-21H (ER)	A6-EMH	EMIRATES		27251	54	05/15/97	TRENT890		
B777-21H (ER)	A6-EMI	EMIRATES		27250	47	07/25/97	TRENT890		N5028V
B777-21H (ER)	A6-EMJ	EMIRATES		27253	91	09/30/97	TRENT890		
B777-21H (ER)	A6-EMK	EMIRATES		29324	171	10/30/98	TRENT892		
B777-21H (ER)	A6-EML	EMIRATES		29325	176	11/25/98	TRENT892		
B777-31H	A6-EMM	EMIRATES (SALE)		29062	256	11/12/99	TRENT892		
B777-31H	A6-EMN	EMIRATES (SALE)		29063	262	12/23/99	TRENT892		
B777-31H	A6-EMO	EMIRATES (ILFC)		28680	300	09/26/00	TRENT892		
B777-31H (ER)	A6-EMP	EMIRATES (ILFC)		29395	326	03/22/01	TRENT892		N50281
B-CHINA (PEOPLE'S REPUBLIC)									
B777-2J6	B-2059	AIR CHINA		29153	168	10/26/98	PW4077		
B777-2J6	B-2060	AIR CHINA		29154	173	10/30/98	PW4077		
B777-2J6	B-2061	AIR CHINA		29155	179	11/24/98	PW4077		
B777-2J6	B-2063	AIR CHINA		29156	214	04/30/99	PW4077		
B777-2J6	B-2064	AIR CHINA		29157	240	08/30/99	PW4077		
B777-2J6	B-2065	AIR CHINA		29744	280	05/23/00	PW4077		
B777-2J6	B-2066	AIR CHINA		29745	290	06/30/00	PW4077		
B777-2J6	B-2067	AIR CHINA	N	29746	338		PW4077		
B777-2J6	B-2068	AIR CHINA	N	29747	344		PW4077		
B777-21B	B-2051	CHINA SOUTHERN AIRLINES		27357	20	12/28/95	GE90-85B		
B777-21B	B-2052	CHINA SOUTHERN AIRLINES		27358	24	02/28/96	GE90-85B		N5017V
B777-21B	B-2053	CHINA SOUTHERN AIRLINES		27359	46	11/15/96	GE90-85B		
B777-21B	B-2054	CHINA SOUTHERN AIRLINES		27360	48	12/05/96	GE90-85B		
B777-21B (ER)	B-2055	CHINA SOUTHERN AIRLINES		27524	55	02/28/97	GE90-92B		
B777-21B (ER)	B-2056	CHINA SOUTHERN AIRLINES		27525	66	04/18/97	GE90-92B		
B777-21B (ER)	B-2057	CHINA SOUTHERN AIRLINES		27604	106	01/08/98	GE90-92B		N5022E
B777-21B (ER)	B-2058	CHINA SOUTHERN AIRLINES		27605	110	01/12/98	GE90-92B		N5028Y
B777-21B (ER)	N688CZ	CHINA SOUTHERN AIRLINES (ILFC)		27606	121	02/13/98	GE90-92B		B-2062

A/C TYPE	CURRENT REG. NO.	LAST KNOWN OPERATOR (OWNER)	Status	ORIGINAL MSN	LINE NO.	DEL. DATE	ENG. TYPE	FLEET NO.	PREV. REG. [COMMENTS]
B-H-HONG KONG									
B777-267	B-HNA	CATHAY PACIFIC		27265	14	08/23/96	TRENT877		N77772; VR-HNA
B777-267	B-HNB	CATHAY PACIFIC		27266	18	10/25/96	TRENT877		N77773; VR-HNB
B777-267	B-HNC	CATHAY PACIFIC		27263	28	05/09/96	TRENT877		VR-HNC
B777-267	B-HND	CATHAY PACIFIC		27264	31	06/13/96	TRENT877		VR-HND
B777-267	B-HNL	CATHAY PACIFIC		27116	1	12/06/00	TRENT884		N7771
B777-367	B-HNE	CATHAY PACIFIC		27507	94	10/27/98	TRENT890		N5014K
B777-367	B-HNF	CATHAY PACIFIC		27506	102	09/23/98	TRENT890		N5016R
B777-367	B-HNG	CATHAY PACIFIC		27505	118	06/25/98	TRENT890		N5017V
B777-367	B-HNH	CATHAY PACIFIC		27504	136	05/22/98	TRENT890		[1ST 777-300 DEL]
B777-367	B-HNI	CATHAY PACIFIC		27508	204	03/25/99	TRENT890		
B777-367	B-HNJ	CATHAY PACIFIC		27509	224	06/24/99	TRENT890		
B777-367	B-HNK	CATHAY PACIFIC		27510	248	09/29/99	TRENT890		
F-FRANCE									
B777-228 (ER)	F-GSPA	AIR FRANCE		29002	129	03/27/98	GE90-90B		
B777-228 (ER)	F-GSPB	AIR FRANCE		29003	133	04/21/98	GE90-90B		
B777-228 (ER)	F-GSPC	AIR FRANCE		29004	138	05/05/98	GE90-90B		
B777-228 (ER)	F-GSPD	AIR FRANCE		29005	187	01/12/99	GE90-90B		
B777-228 (ER)	F-GSPE	AIR FRANCE		29006	189	01/19/99	GE90-90B		
B777-228 (ER)	F-GSPF	AIR FRANCE		29007	201	03/11/99	GE90-90B		
B777-228 (ER)	F-GSPG	AIR FRANCE (ILFC)		27609	195	02/19/99	GE90-90B		
B777-228 (ER)	F-GSPH	AIR FRANCE (ILFC)		28675	210	05/21/99	GE90-90B		
B777-228 (ER)	F-GSPI	AIR FRANCE		29008	258	12/06/99	GE90-90B		
B777-228 (ER)	F-GSPJ	AIR FRANCE		29009	263	12/22/99	GE90-90B		
B777-228 (ER)	F-GSPK	AIR FRANCE (EUROLEASE)		29010	267	01/27/00	GE90-90B		
B777-228 (ER)	F-GSPL	AIR FRANCE (ILFC)		30457	284	12/09/00	GE90-94B		N50281
B777-228 (ER)	F-GSPM	AIR FRANCE (ILFC)		30456	307	11/14/00	GE90-94B		N50281
B777-228 (ER)	F-GSPN	AIR FRANCE (GIE HUGO BAIL)		29011	314	12/15/00	GE90-94B		
B777-228 (ER)	F-GSPO	AIR FRANCE		30614	320	02/03/01	GE90-94B		
B777-228 (ER)	F-GSPP	AIR FRANCE		30615	327	02/28/01	GE90-94B		
B777-228 (ER)	F-GSPQ	AIR FRANCE (ILFC)		28682	331	03/21/01	GE90-94B		
G-UNITED KINGDOM									
B777-236 (ER)	G-RAES	BRITISH AIRWAYS		27491	76	06/10/97	GE90-85B		
B777-236 (ER)	G-VIIA	BRITISH AIRWAYS		27483	41	07/03/97	GE90-85B		N5022E
B777-236 (ER)	G-VIIB	BRITISH AIRWAYS		27484	49	05/23/97	GE90-85B		N5023Q
B777-236 (ER)	G-VIIC	BRITISH AIRWAYS		27485	53	02/06/97	GE90-85B		N5016R
B777-236 (ER)	G-VIID	BRITISH AIRWAYS		27486	56	02/18/97	GE90-85B		
B777-236 (ER)	G-VIIE	BRITISH AIRWAYS		27487	58	02/25/97	GE90-85B		
B777-236 (ER)	G-VIIF	BRITISH AIRWAYS		27488	61	03/18/97	GE90-85B		

A/C TYPE	CURRENT REG. NO.	LAST KNOWN OPERATOR (OWNER)	Status	ORIGINAL MSN	LINE NO.	DEL. DATE	ENG. TYPE	FLEET NO.	PREV. REG. [COMMENTS]
B777-236 (ER)	G-VIIG	BRITISH AIRWAYS		27489	65	04/09/97	GE90-85B		
B777-236 (ER)	G-VIIH	BRITISH AIRWAYS		27490	70	05/07/97	GE90-85B		
B777-236 (ER)	G-VIIJ	BRITISH AIRWAYS		27492	111	12/29/97	GE90-85B		
B777-236 (ER)	G-VIIK	BRITISH AIRWAYS		28840	117	02/03/98	GE90-85B		
B777-236 (ER)	G-VIIL	BRITISH AIRWAYS		27493	127	03/13/98	GE90-85B		
B777-236 (ER)	G-VIIM	BRITISH AIRWAYS		28841	130	03/26/98	GE90-85B		
B777-236 (ER)	G-VIIN	BRITISH AIRWAYS		29319	157	08/21/98	GE90-85B		
B777-236 (ER)	G-VIIO	BRITISH AIRWAYS		29320	182	01/26/99	GE90-85B		
B777-236 (ER)	G-VIIP	BRITISH AIRWAYS		29321	193	02/09/99	GE90-90B		
B777-236 (ER)	G-VIIR	BRITISH AIRWAYS		29322	203	03/18/99	GE90-90B		
B777-236 (ER)	G-VIIS	BRITISH AIRWAYS		29323	206	04/01/99	GE90-90B		
B777-236 (ER)	G-VIIT	BRITISH AIRWAYS		29962	217	05/26/99	GE90-90B		
B777-236 (ER)	G-VIIU	BRITISH AIRWAYS		29963	221	05/28/99	GE90-90B		
B777-236 (ER)	G-VIIV	BRITISH AIRWAYS		29964	228	06/29/99	GE90-90B		
B777-236 (ER)	G-VIIW	BRITISH AIRWAYS		29965	233	07/30/99	GE90-90B		
B777-236 (ER)	G-VIIX	BRITISH AIRWAYS		29966	236	08/11/99	GE90-90B		
B777-236 (ER)	G-VIIY	BRITISH AIRWAYS		29967	251	10/22/99	GE90-90B		
B777-236 (ER)	G-YMMA	BRITISH AIRWAYS		30302	242	01/07/00	TRENT895		N5017Q
B777-236 (ER)	G-YMMB	BRITISH AIRWAYS		30303	265	01/18/00	TRENT895		
B777-236 (ER)	G-YMMC	BRITISH AIRWAYS		30304	268	02/04/00	TRENT895		
B777-236 (ER)	G-YMMD	BRITISH AIRWAYS		30305	269	02/18/00	TRENT895		
B777-236 (ER)	G-YMME	BRITISH AIRWAYS		30306	275	04/16/00	TRENT895		
B777-236 (ER)	G-YMMF	BRITISH AIRWAYS		30307	281	05/17/00	TRENT895		
B777-236 (ER)	G-YMMG	BRITISH AIRWAYS		30308	301	09/27/00	TRENT895		
B777-236 (ER)	G-YMMH	BRITISH AIRWAYS		30309	303	10/14/00	TRENT895		
B777-236 (ER)	G-YMMI	BRITISH AIRWAYS		30310	308	11/02/00	TRENT895		
B777-236 (ER)	G-YMMJ	BRITISH AIRWAYS		30311	311	12/08/00	TRENT895		
B777-236 (ER)	G-YMMK	BRITISH AIRWAYS		30312	312	12/08/00	TRENT895		
B777-236 (ER)	G-YMML	BRITISH AIRWAYS		30313	334	04/14/01	TRENT895		
B777-236 (ER)	G-YMMM	BRITISH AIRWAYS	N	30314	342		TRENT895		
B777-236	G-ZZZA	BRITISH AIRWAYS		27105	6	05/20/96	GE90-76B		N77779 [FF 02/02/95]
B777-236	G-ZZZB	BRITISH AIRWAYS		27106	10	03/28/97	GE90-76B		N77771
B777-236	G-ZZZC	BRITISH AIRWAYS		27107	15	11/11/95	GE90-76B		N5014K [1ST GE DEL]
B777-236	G-ZZZD	BRITISH AIRWAYS		27108	17	12/28/95	GE90-76B		
B777-236	G-ZZZE	BRITISH AIRWAYS		27109	19	01/12/96	GE90-76B		

HL-KOREA

A/C TYPE	CURRENT REG. NO.	LAST KNOWN OPERATOR (OWNER)	Status	ORIGINAL MSN	LINE NO.	DEL. DATE	ENG. TYPE	FLEET NO.	PREV. REG. [COMMENTS]
B777-28E (ER)	HL7596	ASIANA AIRLINES (ILFC)		28681	322	02/14/01	PW4090		
B777-2B5 (ER)	HL7526	KOREAN AIR		27947	148	12/29/98	PW4090		N50217
B777-2B5 (ER)	HL7530	KOREAN AIR (KE APPOLLO)		27945	59	03/21/97	PW4090		

A/C TYPE	CURRENT REG. NO.	LAST KNOWN OPERATOR (OWNER)	Status	ORIGINAL MSN	LINE NO.	DEL. DATE	ENG. TYPE	FLEET NO.	PREV. REG. [COMMENTS]
B777-2B5 (ER)	HL7531	KOREAN AIR (KE APPOLLO)		27946	62	03/28/97	PW4090		
B777-2B5 (ER)	HL7574	KOREAN AIR		28444	305	10/18/00	PW4090		
B777-2B5 (ER)	HL7575	KOREAN AIR		28445	309	11/09/00	PW4090		
B777-3B5	HL7532	KOREAN AIR		28371	162	08/12/99	PW4098		
B777-3B5	HL7533	KOREAN AIR		27948	178	08/12/99	PW4098		
B777-3B5	HL7534	KOREAN AIR		27950	120	12/28/99	PW4098		N5020K
B777-3B5	HL7573	KOREAN AIR		27952	288	06/27/00	PW4098		

HS-THAILAND

A/C TYPE	CURRENT REG. NO.	LAST KNOWN OPERATOR (OWNER)	Status	ORIGINAL MSN	LINE NO.	DEL. DATE	ENG. TYPE	FLEET NO.	PREV. REG. [COMMENTS]
B777-2D7	HS-TJA	THAI AIRWAYS INTL.		27726	25	03/31/96	TRENT875		[1ST RR DEL]
B777-2D7	HS-TJB	THAI AIRWAYS INTL.		27727	32	06/13/96	TRENT875		
B777-2D7	HS-TJC	THAI AIRWAYS INTL.		27728	44	10/25/96	TRENT875		
B777-2D7	HS-TJD	THAI AIRWAYS INTL.		27729	51	12/19/96	TRENT875		
B777-2D7	HS-TJE	THAI AIRWAYS INTL. (PALOMINO)		27730	89	08/15/97	TRENT875		
B777-2D7	HS-TJF	THAI AIRWAYS INTL. (MUSTANG)		27731	95	09/29/97	TRENT875		
B777-2D7	HS-TJG	THAI AIRWAYS INTL.		27732	100	10/31/97	TRENT875		
B777-2D7	HS-TJH	THAI AIRWAYS INTL.		27733	113	01/09/98	TRENT875		
B777-3D7	HS-TKA	THAI AIRWAYS INTL.		29150	156	12/23/98	TRENT892		N5028Y
B777-3D7	HS-TKB	THAI AIRWAYS INTL.		29151	170	12/30/98	TRENT892		
B777-3D7	HS-TKC	THAI AIRWAYS INTL.		29211	250	10/18/99	TRENT892		
B777-3D7	HS-TKD	THAI AIRWAYS INTL.		29212	260	12/08/99	TRENT892		
B777-3D7	HS-TKE	THAI AIRWAYS INTL.		29213	304	10/17/00	TRENT892		
B777-3D7	HS-TKF	THAI AIRWAYS INTL.		29214	310	12/09/00	TRENT892		

HZ-SAUDI ARABIA

A/C TYPE	CURRENT REG. NO.	LAST KNOWN OPERATOR (OWNER)	Status	ORIGINAL MSN	LINE NO.	DEL. DATE	ENG. TYPE	FLEET NO.	PREV. REG. [COMMENTS]
B777-24Q (ER)	N777AS	MID EAST JET		29271	174	11/24/98	GE90-92B		
B777-268 (ER)	HZ-AKA	SAUDI ARABIAN AIRLINES		28344	98	12/29/97	GE90-90B		N50217
B777-268 (ER)	HZ-AKB	SAUDI ARABIAN AIRLINES		28345	99	12/27/97	GE90-90B		N5023Q
B777-268 (ER)	HZ-AKC	SAUDI ARABIAN AIRLINES		28346	101	12/26/97	GE90-90B		
B777-268 (ER)	HZ-AKD	SAUDI ARABIAN AIRLINES		28347	103	12/30/97	GE90-90B		
B777-268 (ER)	HZ-AKE	SAUDI ARABIAN AIRLINES		28348	109	01/19/98	GE90-90B		
B777-268 (ER)	HZ-AKF	SAUDI ARABIAN AIRLINES		28349	114	02/15/98	GE90-90B		
B777-268 (ER)	HZ-AKG	SAUDI ARABIAN AIRLINES		28350	119	03/19/98	GE90-90B		
B777-268 (ER)	HZ-AKH	SAUDI ARABIAN AIRLINES		28351	124	04/17/98	GE90-90B		
B777-268 (ER)	HZ-AKI	SAUDI ARABIAN AIRLINES		28352	143	06/11/98	GE90-90B		
B777-268 (ER)	HZ-AKJ	SAUDI ARABIAN AIRLINES		28353	147	07/31/98	GE90-90B		
B777-268 (ER)	HZ-AKK	SAUDI ARABIAN AIRLINES		28354	154	09/17/98	GE90-90B		
B777-268 (ER)	HZ-AKL	SAUDI ARABIAN AIRLINES		28355	166	11/14/98	GE90-90B		
B777-268 (ER)	HZ-AKM	SAUDI ARABIAN AIRLINES		28356	175	12/14/98	GE90-90B		
B777-268 (ER)	HZ-AKN	SAUDI ARABIAN AIRLINES		28357	181	12/17/98	GE90-90B		

A/C TYPE	CURRENT REG. NO.	LAST KNOWN OPERATOR (OWNER)	Status	ORIGINAL MSN	LINE NO.	DEL. DATE	ENG. TYPE	FLEET NO.	PREV. REG. [COMMENTS]
B777-268 (ER)	HZ-AKO	SAUDI ARABIAN AIRLINES		28358	186	01/29/99	GE90-90B		
B777-268 (ER)	HZ-AKP	SAUDI ARABIAN AIRLINES		28359	194	03/25/99	GE90-90B		
B777-268 (ER)	HZ-AKQ	SAUDI ARABIAN AIRLINES		28360	219	12/09/99	GE90-90B		N5016R
B777-268 (ER)	HZ-AKR	SAUDI ARABIAN AIRLINES		28361	230	12/09/99	GE90-90B		N5017V
B777-268 (ER)	HZ-AKS	SAUDI ARABIAN AIRLINES		28362	255	12/09/99	GE90-90B		
B777-268 (ER)	HZ-AKT	SAUDI ARABIAN AIRLINES		28363	298	09/30/00	GE90-90B		
B777-268 (ER)	HZ-AKU	SAUDI ARABIAN AIRLINES		28364	306	11/17/00	GE90-90B		
B777-268 (ER)	HZ-AKV	SAUDI ARABIAN AIRLINES		28365	323	03/30/01	GE90-90B		

I-ITALY

A/C TYPE	CURRENT REG. NO.	LAST KNOWN OPERATOR (OWNER)	Status	ORIGINAL MSN	LINE NO.	DEL. DATE	ENG. TYPE	FLEET NO.	PREV. REG. [COMMENTS]
B777-2Q8 (ER)	EI-CRS	AIR EUROPE (ILFC)		29908	229	07/16/99	PW4090		
B777-2Q8 (ER)	EI-CRT	AIR EUROPE (ILFC)		28676	246	10/08/99	PW4090		

JA-JAPAN

A/C TYPE	CURRENT REG. NO.	LAST KNOWN OPERATOR (OWNER)	Status	ORIGINAL MSN	LINE NO.	DEL. DATE	ENG. TYPE	FLEET NO.	PREV. REG. [COMMENTS]
B777-281	JA701A	ALL NIPPON AIRWAYS (ALPINE ROSE)		27938	77	06/23/97	PW4074		
B777-281	JA702A	ALL NIPPON AIRWAYS		27033	75	06/30/97	PW4077		
B777-281	JA703A	ALL NIPPON AIRWAYS (SBL AQUA MARINE)		27034	81	08/21/97	PW4077		N50217
B777-281	JA704A	ALL NIPPON AIRWAYS (PHOENIX)		27035	131	03/26/98	PW4077		
B777-281	JA705A	ALL NIPPON AIRWAYS (SL SEAGULL)		29029	137	04/27/98	PW4074		
B777-281	JA706A	ALL NIPPON AIRWAYS		27036	141	05/20/98	PW4074		
B777-281 (ER)	JA707A	ALL NIPPON AIRWAYS		27037	247	10/06/99	PW4090		
B777-281 (ER)	JA708A	ALL NIPPON AIRWAYS (ARCADIA ET AL)		28277	278	05/10/00	PW4090		
B777-281 (ER)	JA709A	ALL NIPPON AIRWAYS		28278	286	06/15/00	PW4090		
B777-281 (ER)	JA710A	ALL NIPPON AIRWAYS		28279	302	10/03/00	PW4090		
B777-281	JA8197	ALL NIPPON AIRWAYS (SUMISHIN)		27027	16	10/04/95	PW4074		N5016R
B777-281	JA8198	ALL NIPPON AIRWAYS (SUMIGIN)		27028	21	12/21/95	PW4074		
B777-281	JA8199	ALL NIPPON AIRWAYS (SUMISHIN)		27029	29	05/23/96	PW4074		
B777-281	JA8967	ALL NIPPON AIRWAYS		27030	37	08/12/96	PW4074		
B777-281	JA8968	ALL NIPPON AIRWAYS (MACH)		27031	38	08/14/96	PW4074		
B777-281	JA8969	ALL NIPPON AIRWAYS (FI KIWI)		27032	50	12/16/96	PW4074		
B777-381	JA751A	ALL NIPPON AIRWAYS (ANACREON)		28272	142	06/30/98	PW4090		
B777-381	JA752A	ALL NIPPON AIRWAYS (FO SERENADE)		28274	160	08/27/98	PW4090		
B777-381	JA753A	ALL NIPPON AIRWAYS (ORIX SKYBLUE)		28273	132	07/29/98	PW4090		
B777-381	JA754A	ALL NIPPON AIRWAYS (ORIX SKYLARK)		27939	172	10/20/98	PW4090		
B777-381	JA755A	ALL NIPPON AIRWAYS		28275	104	04/06/99	PW4090		N5017Q
B777-246	JA8981	JAPAN AIRLINES		27364	23	02/15/96	PW4077		
B777-246	JA8982	JAPAN AIRLINES		27365	26	03/28/96	PW4077		
B777-246	JA8983	JAPAN AIRLINES		27366	39	09/12/96	PW4077		
B777-246	JA8984	JAPAN AIRLINES (SKYWALK, ET AL)		27651	68	04/21/97	PW4077		
B777-246	JA8985	JAPAN AIRLINES		27652	72	05/14/97	PW4077		

A/C TYPE	CURRENT REG. NO.	LAST KNOWN OPERATOR (OWNER)	Status	ORIGINAL MSN	LINE NO.	DEL. DATE	ENG. TYPE	FLEET NO.	PREV. REG. [COMMENTS]
B777-346	JA8941	JAPAN AIRLINES (CAMPER, ET AL)		28393	152	07/28/98	PW4090		
B777-346	JA8942	JAPAN AIRLINES (FO HARVEST, ET AL)		28394	158	08/26/98	PW4090		N5028Y
B777-346	JA8943	JAPAN AIRLINES (TOGA LSG, ET AL)		28395	196	02/17/99	PW4090		
B777-346	JA8944	JAPAN AIRLINES (PLUTO LSG, ET AL)		28396	212	04/22/99	PW4090		
B777-346	JA8945	JAPAN AIRLINES (SATURN, ETAL)		28397	238	08/17/99	PW4090		
B777-289	JA007D	JAPAN AIR SYSTEM		27639	134	04/27/98	PW4074		
B777-289	JA008D	JAPAN AIR SYSTEM		27640	146	06/23/98	PW4074		
B777-289	JA009D	JAPAN AIR SYSTEM (SONY, ET AL)		27641	159	09/02/98	PW4074		N5017V
B777-289	JA010D	JAPAN AIR SYSTEM (SONY, ET AL)		27642	213	05/13/99	PW4074		N371LF
B777-289	JA8977	JAPAN AIR SYSTEM (SUMIGIN)		27636	45	12/03/96	PW4074		
B777-289	JA8978	JAPAN AIR SYSTEM		27637	79	06/26/97	PW4074		
B777-289	JA8979	JAPAN AIR SYSTEM		27638	107	11/26/97	PW4074		

N-UNITED STATES OF AMERICA

A/C TYPE	CURRENT REG. NO.	LAST KNOWN OPERATOR (OWNER)	Status	ORIGINAL MSN	LINE NO.	DEL. DATE	ENG. TYPE	FLEET NO.	PREV. REG. [COMMENTS]
B777-223 (ER)	N750AN	AMERICAN AIRLINES		30259	332	03/27/01	TRENT892-17	7BJ	
B777-223 (ER)	N751AN	AMERICAN AIRLINES		30798	333	04/04/01	TRENT892-17	7BK	
B777-223 (ER)	N752AN	AMERICAN AIRLINES	N	30260	339		TRENT892-17	7BL	
B777-223 (ER)	N753AN	AMERICAN AIRLINES	N	30261	341		TRENT892-17	7BM	
B777-223 (ER)	N754AN	AMERICAN AIRLINES	N	30262	345		TRENT892-17	7BN	
B777-223 (ER)	N770AN	AMERICAN AIRLINES		29578	185	01/21/99	TRENT892-17	7AA	
B777-223 (ER)	N771AN	AMERICAN AIRLINES		29579	190	01/29/99	TRENT892-17	7AB	
B777-223 (ER)	N772AN	AMERICAN AIRLINES		29580	198	03/01/99	TRENT892-17	7AC	
B777-223 (ER)	N773AN	AMERICAN AIRLINES		29583	199	03/08/99	TRENT892-17	7AD	
B777-223 (ER)	N774AN	AMERICAN AIRLINES		29581	208	04/12/99	TRENT892-17	7AE	
B777-223 (ER)	N775AN	AMERICAN AIRLINES		29584	209	04/20/99	TRENT892-17	7AF	
B777-223 (ER)	N776AN	AMERICAN AIRLINES		29582	215	05/18/99	TRENT892-17	7AG	
B777-223 (ER)	N777AN	AMERICAN AIRLINES		29585	218	05/25/99	TRENT892-17	7AH	
B777-223 (ER)	N778AN	AMERICAN AIRLINES		29587	223	06/21/99	TRENT892-17	7AJ	
B777-223 (ER)	N779AN	AMERICAN AIRLINES		29955	225	06/27/99	TRENT892-17	7AK	
B777-223 (ER)	N780AN	AMERICAN AIRLINES		29956	241	09/10/99	TRENT892-17	7AL	
B777-223 (ER)	N781AN	AMERICAN AIRLINES		29586	266	01/27/00	TRENT892-17	7AM	
B777-223 (ER)	N782AN	AMERICAN AIRLINES		30003	270	02/29/00	TRENT892-17	7AN	
B777-223 (ER)	N783AN	AMERICAN AIRLINES		30004	271	03/01/00	TRENT892-17	7AP	
B777-223 (ER)	N784AN	AMERICAN AIRLINES		29588	272	03/29/00	TRENT892-17	7AR	
B777-223 (ER)	N785AN	AMERICAN AIRLINES		30005	274	04/12/00	TRENT892-17	7AS	
B777-223 (ER)	N786AN	AMERICAN AIRLINES		30250	276	04/21/00	TRENT892-17	7AT	
B777-223 (ER)	N787AL	AMERICAN AIRLINES		30010	277	04/28/00	TRENT892-17	7AU	
B777-223 (ER)	N788AN	AMERICAN AIRLINES		30011	283	05/31/00	TRENT892-17	7AV	
B777-223 (ER)	N789AN	AMERICAN AIRLINES		30252	285	06/05/00	TRENT892-17	7AW	
B777-223 (ER)	N790AN	AMERICAN AIRLINES		30251	287	06/22/00	TRENT892-17	7AX	

A/C TYPE	CURRENT REG. NO.	LAST KNOWN OPERATOR (OWNER)	Status	ORIGINAL MSN	LINE NO.	DEL. DATE	ENG. TYPE	FLEET NO.	PREV. REG. [COMMENTS]
B777-223 (ER)	N791AN	AMERICAN AIRLINES		30254	289	06/28/00	TRENT892-17	7AY	
B777-223 (ER)	N792AN	AMERICAN AIRLINES		30253	292	07/31/00	TRENT892-17	7BA	
B777-223 (ER)	N793AN	AMERICAN AIRLINES		30255	299	09/14/00	TRENT892-17	7BB	
B777-223 (ER)	N794AN	AMERICAN AIRLINES		30256	313	12/01/00	TRENT892-17	7BC	
B777-223 (ER)	N795AN	AMERICAN AIRLINES		30257	315	12/16/00	TRENT892-17	7BD	
B777-223 (ER)	N796AN	AMERICAN AIRLINES		30796	316	12/18/00	TRENT892-17	7BE	
B777-223 (ER)	N797AN	AMERICAN AIRLINES		30012	321	01/26/01	TRENT892-17	7BF	
B777-223 (ER)	N798AN	AMERICAN AIRLINES		30797	324	02/16/01	TRENT892-17	7BG	
B777-223 (ER)	N799AN	AMERICAN AIRLINES		30258	328	03/16/01	TRENT892-17	7BH	
B777-224 (ER)	N78001	CONTINENTAL AIRLINES (FSBU)		27577	161	09/28/98	GE90-92B	001	
B777-224 (ER)	N78002	CONTINENTAL AIRLINES (FSBU)		27578	165	09/29/98	GE90-92B	002	
B777-224 (ER)	N78003	CONTINENTAL AIRLINES (FSBU)		27579	167	11/10/98	GE90-92B	003	
B777-224 (ER)	N78004	CONTINENTAL AIRLINES (FSBU)		27580	169	11/19/98	GE90-92B	004	
B777-224 (ER)	N78005	CONTINENTAL AIRLINES		27581	177	12/07/98	GE90-92B	005	
B777-224 (ER)	N77006	CONTINENTAL AIRLINES		29476	183	12/08/98	GE90-92B	006	
B777-224 (ER)	N74007	CONTINENTAL AIRLINES (FSBU)		29477	197	02/18/99	GE90-92B	007	
B777-224 (ER)	N78008	CONTINENTAL AIRLINES (FSBU)		29478	200	03/01/99	GE90-92B	008	
B777-224 (ER)	N78009	CONTINENTAL AIRLINES		29479	211	04/21/99	GE90-92B	009	
B777-224 (ER)	N76010	CONTINENTAL AIRLINES (FSBU)		29480	220	05/27/99	GE90-92B	010	
B777-224 (ER)	N79011	CONTINENTAL AIRLINES		29859	227	06/29/99	GE90-92B	011	
B777-224 (ER)	N77012	CONTINENTAL AIRLINES (FSBU)		29860	234	08/04/99	GE90-92B	012	
B777-224 (ER)	N78013	CONTINENTAL AIRLINES		29861	243	09/14/99	GE90-92B	013	
B777-224 (ER)	N77014	CONTINENTAL AIRLINES (FSBU)		29862	253	10/21/99	GE90-92B	014	[PETER MAX "NYC 2000" C/S]
B777-224 (ER)	N27015	CONTINENTAL AIRLINES (ILFC)		28678	273	04/07/00	GE90-92B	015	
B777-224 (ER)	N57016	CONTINENTAL AIRLINES (ILFC)		28679	279	05/05/00	GE90-92B	016	
B777-232 (ER)	N860DA	DELTA AIRLINES		29951	202	03/23/99	TRENT 892	7001	
B777-232 (ER)	N861DA	DELTA AIRLINES		29952	207	03/29/99	TRENT 892	7002	
B777-232 (ER)	N862DA	DELTA AIRLINES		29734	235	12/13/99	TRENT 892	7003	N5022E
B777-232 (ER)	N863DA	DELTA AIRLINES		29735	245	12/21/99	TRENT 892	7004	N5014K
B777-232 (ER)	N864DA	DELTA AIRLINES		29736	249	12/17/99	TRENT 892	7005	N50217
B777-232 (ER)	N865DA	DELTA AIRLINES		29737	257	12/07/99	TRENT 892	7006	
B777-232 (ER)	N866DA	DELTA AIRLINES		29738	261	12/10/99	TRENT 892	7007	
B777-222 (ER)	N204UA	UNITED AIRLINES		28713	191	02/03/99	PW4090	2404	
B777-222 (ER)	N205UA	UNITED AIRLINES		28714	205	03/22/99	PW4090	2405	
B777-222 (ER)	N206UA	UNITED AIRLINES		30212	216	05/18/99	PW4090	2406	
B777-222 (ER)	N207UA	UNITED AIRLINES		30213	232	07/21/99	PW4090	2407	
B777-222 (ER)	N208UA	UNITED AIRLINES		30214	254	11/12/99	PW4090	2408	
B777-222 (ER)	N209UA	UNITED AIRLINES		30215	259	12/16/99	PW4090	2609	

A/C TYPE	CURRENT REG. NO.	LAST KNOWN OPERATOR (OWNER)	Status	ORIGINAL MSN	LINE NO.	DEL. DATE	ENG. TYPE	FLEET NO.	PREV. REG. [COMMENTS]
B777-222	N210UA	UNITED AIRLINES		30216	264	01/28/00	PW4077	2510	
B777-222	N211UA	UNITED AIRLINES		30217	282	05/18/00	PW4077	2511	
B777-222	N212UA	UNITED AIRLINES		30218	293	07/28/00	PW4077	2512	
B777-222	N213UA	UNITED AIRLINES		30219	295	08/15/00	PW4077	2513	
B777-222	N214UA	UNITED AIRLINES		30220	296	08/25/00	PW4077	2514	
B777-222	N215UA	UNITED AIRLINES		30221	297	08/30/00	PW4077	2515	
B777-222 (ER)	N216UA	UNITED AIRLINES		30549	291	07/21/00	PW4090	2616	
B777-222 (ER)	N217UA	UNITED AIRLINES		30550	294	08/14/00	PW4090	2617	
B777-222 (ER)	N218UA	UNITED AIRLINES		30222	317	01/10/01	PW4090	2618	
B777-222 (ER)	N219UA	UNITED AIRLINES		30551	318	01/23/01	PW4090	2619	
B777-222 (ER)	N220UA	UNITED AIRLINES	N	30223	340		PW4090	2620	
B777-222	N766UA	UNITED AIRLINES		26917	8	05/24/95	PW4077	2066	N77776
B777-222	N767UA	UNITED AIRLINES		26918	9	05/31/95	PW4077	2067	N77774
B777-222	N768UA	UNITED AIRLINES		26919	11	06/26/95	PW4077	2068	N77775
B777-222	N769UA	UNITED AIRLINES		26921	12	06/28/95	PW4077	2069	N77773
B777-222	N770UA	UNITED AIRLINES		26925	13	07/13/95	PW4077	2070	N77772
B777-222	N771UA	UNITED AIRLINES		26932	3	11/27/95	PW4077	2071	N7773
B777-222	N772UA	UNITED AIRLINES		26930	5	09/29/95	PW4077	2072	[FF 11/11/94]
B777-222	N773UA	UNITED AIRLINES		26929	4	01/31/96	PW4077	2073	N7774 [FF 10/28/94]
B777-222	N774UA	UNITED AIRLINES		26936	2	03/29/96	PW4077	2174	N7772
B777-222	N775UA	UNITED AIRLINES		26947	22	01/22/96	PW4077	2075	
B777-222	N776UA	UNITED AIRLINES		26937	27	04/11/96	PW4077	2076	
B777-222	N777UA	UNITED AIRLINES		26916	7	05/15/95	PW4077	2077	[1ST B777 DEL; FRF 06/07/95]
B777-222	N778UA	UNITED AIRLINES		26940	34	07/18/96	PW4077	2078	
B777-222	N779UA	UNITED AIRLINES		26941	35	07/26/96	PW4077	2079	
B777-222	N780UA	UNITED AIRLINES		26944	36	08/06/96	PW4077	2180	
B777-222	N781UA	UNITED AIRLINES		26945	40	09/12/96	PW4077	2081	
B777-222 (ER)	N782UA	UNITED AIRLINES		26948	57	03/07/97	PW4090	2482	
B777-222 (ER)	N783UA	UNITED AIRLINES		26950	60	03/11/97	PW4090	2483	
B777-222 (ER)	N784UA	UNITED AIRLINES		26951	69	04/29/97	PW4090	2484	
B777-222 (ER)	N785UA	UNITED AIRLINES		26954	73	05/21/97	PW4090	2485	
B777-222 (ER)	N786UA	UNITED AIRLINES		26938	52	04/04/97	PW4090	2486	
B777-222 (ER)	N787UA	UNITED AIRLINES		26939	43	06/05/97	PW4090	2487	
B777-222 (ER)	N788UA	UNITED AIRLINES		26942	82	07/15/97	PW4090	2488	
B777-222 (ER)	N789UA	UNITED AIRLINES		26935	88	08/11/97	PW4090	2489	
B777-222 (ER)	N790UA	UNITED AIRLINES		26943	92	09/01/97	PW4090	2490	
B777-222 (ER)	N791UA	UNITED AIRLINES		26933	93	08/28/97	PW4090	2491	
B777-222 (ER)	N792UA	UNITED AIRLINES		26934	96	09/25/97	PW4090	2492	
B777-222 (ER)	N793UA	UNITED AIRLINES		26946	97	10/07/97	PW4090	2493	
B777-222 (ER)	N794UA	UNITED AIRLINES		26953	105	11/18/97	PW4090	2494	
B777-222 (ER)	N795UA	UNITED AIRLINES		26927	108	12/09/97	PW4090	2495	

A/C TYPE	CURRENT REG. NO.	LAST KNOWN OPERATOR (OWNER)	Status	ORIGINAL MSN	LINE NO.	DEL. DATE	ENG. TYPE	FLEET NO.	PREV. REG. [COMMENTS]
B777-222 (ER)	N796UA	UNITED AIRLINES		26931	112	01/28/98	PW4090	2496	
B777-222 (ER)	N797UA	UNITED AIRLINES		26924	116	02/20/98	PW4090	2497	
B777-222 (ER)	N798UA	UNITED AIRLINES		26928	123	02/28/98	PW4090	2498	
B777-222 (ER)	N799UA	UNITED AIRLINES		26926	139	05/08/98	PW4090	2499	
OE-AUSTRIA									
B777-2Z9 (ER)	OE-LPA	LAUDA AIR		28698	87	09/24/97	GE90-92B		N5022E
B777-2Z9 (ER)	OE-LPB	LAUDA AIR		28699	163	09/28/98	GE90-92B		
RA-RUSSIA									
B777-2Q8 (ER)	VP-BAS	AEROFLOT (ILFC)		27607	135	06/17/98	GE90-92B		N5022E
B777-2Q8 (ER)	VP-BAU	AEROFLOT (ILFC)		27608	164	10/02/98	GE90-92B		
SU-EGYPT									
B777-266 (ER)	SU-GBP	EGYPT AIR		28423	71	05/23/97	PW4090		
B777-266 (ER)	SU-GBR	EGYPT AIR		28424	80	07/02/97	PW4090		
B777-266 (ER)	SU-GBS	EGYPT AIR		28425	85	08/07/97	PW4090		
VP-B-BERMUDA									
B777-2AN (ER)	VP-BRH	EASTERN SKYS LTD/SAUDI OGER		29953	252	10/22/99	GE90-92B		
4X-ISRAEL									
B777-258 (ER)	4X-ECA	EL AL ISRAELI AIRLINES		30831	319	01/29/01	TRENT 895		
B777-258 (ER)	4X-ECB	EL AL ISRAELI AIRLINES		30832	325	02/21/01	TRENT 895		
B777-258 (ER)	4X-ECC	EL AL ISRAELI AIRLINES		30833	335	04/11/01	TRENT 895		
9K-KUWAIT									
B777-269 (ER)	9K-AOA	KUWAIT AIRWAYS		28743	125	03/30/98	GE90-92B		
B777-269 (ER)	9K-AOB	KUWAIT AIRWAYS		28744	145	06/12/98	GE90-92B		
9M-MALAYSIA									
B777-2H6 (ER)	9M-MRA	MALAYSIA AIRLINES		28408	64	04/23/97	TRENT890		N5017V
B777-2H6 (ER)	9M-MRB	MALAYSIA AIRLINES (GECA)		28409	74	05/30/97	TRENT890		N50217
B777-2H6 (ER)	9M-MRC	MALAYSIA AIRLINES (CITI)		28410	78	06/24/97	TRENT890		

A/C TYPE	CURRENT REG. NO.	LAST KNOWN OPERATOR (OWNER)	Status	ORIGINAL MSN	LINE NO.	DEL. DATE	ENG. TYPE	FLEET NO.	PREV. REG. [COMMENTS]
B777-2H6 (ER)	9M-MRD	MALAYSIA AIRLINES (OASI)		28411	84	07/30/97	TRENT890		
B777-2H6 (ER)	9M-MRE	MALAYSIA AIRLINES		28412	115	01/13/98	TRENT890		
B777-2H6 (ER)	9M-MRF	MALAYSIA AIRLINES (GECA)		28413	128	03/18/98	TRENT890		
B777-2H6 (ER)	9M-MRG	MALAYSIA AIRLINES (SALE)		28414	140	05/15/98	TRENT890		
B777-2H6 (ER)	9M-MRH	MALAYSIA AIRLINES (OASI)		28415	151	07/20/98	TRENT890		
B777-2H6 (ER)	9M-MRI	MALAYSIA AIRLINES (GECA)		28416	155	10/20/98	TRENT890		
B777-2H6 (ER)	9M-MRJ	MALAYSIA AIRLINES		28417	222	06/22/99	TRENT890		
B777-2H6 (ER)	9M-MRK	MALAYSIA AIRLINES		28418	231	07/26/99	TRENT890		
B777-2H6 (ER)	9M-MRL	MALAYSIA AIRLINES (SALE)		29065	329	03/20/01	TRENT890		
B777-2H6 (ER)	9M-MRM	MALAYSIA AIRLINES (SALE)		29066	336	04/24/01	TRENT890		

9V-SINGAPORE

A/C TYPE	CURRENT REG. NO.	LAST KNOWN OPERATOR (OWNER)	Status	ORIGINAL MSN	LINE NO.	DEL. DATE	ENG. TYPE	FLEET NO.	PREV. REG. [COMMENTS]
B777-212 (ER)	9V-SQA	SINGAPORE AIRLINES		28507	67	05/05/97	TRENT884		
B777-212 (ER)	9V-SQB	SINGAPORE AIRLINES		28508	83	07/18/97	TRENT884		
B777-212 (ER)	9V-SQC	SINGAPORE AIRLINES		28509	86	08/06/97	TRENT884		
B777-212 (ER)	9V-SQD	SINGAPORE AIRLINES		28510	90	09/11/97	TRENT884		
B777-212 (ER)	9V-SQE	SINGAPORE AIRLINES		28511	122	02/12/98	TRENT884		
B777-212 (ER)	9V-SQF	SINGAPORE AIRLINES		28512	126	03/12/98	TRENT884		
B777-212 (ER)	9V-SQG	SINGAPORE AIRLINES		28518	226	06/24/99	TRENT884		
B777-212 (ER)	9V-SQH	SINGAPORE AIRLINES		28519	237	08/12/99	TRENT884		
B777-212 (ER)	9V-SRA	SINGAPORE AIRLINES		28513	144	06/18/98	TRENT892		
B777-212 (ER)	9V-SRB	SINGAPORE AIRLINES		28998	149	06/27/98	TRENT892		
B777-212 (ER)	9V-SRC	SINGAPORE AIRLINES		28999	150	07/09/98	TRENT892		
B777-212 (ER)	9V-SRD	SINGAPORE AIRLINES		28514	153	08/07/98	TRENT892		
B777-212 (ER)	9V-SRE	SINGAPORE AIRLINES		28523	239	08/26/99	TRENT892		
B777-212 (ER)	9V-SRF	SINGAPORE AIRLINES		28521	330	03/22/01	TRENT892		
B777-212 (ER)	9V-SRG	SINGAPORE AIRLINES	N	28522	337		TRENT892		
B777-212 (ER)	9V-SRH	SINGAPORE AIRLINES	N	30866	343		TRENT892		
B777-312	9V-SYA	SINGAPORE AIRLINES		28515	180	12/10/98	TRENT892		
B777-312	9V-SYB	SINGAPORE AIRLINES		28516	184	12/17/98	TRENT892		
B777-312	9V-SYC	SINGAPORE AIRLINES		28517	188	01/14/99	TRENT892		
B777-312	9V-SYD	SINGAPORE AIRLINES		28534	192	01/28/99	TRENT892		
B777-312	9V-SYE	SINGAPORE AIRLINES		28531	244	09/24/99	TRENT892		

Index